A GUIDE TO THE MAKERS OF AMERICAN WOODEN PLANES

Fifth Edition
THOMAS L. ELLIOTT

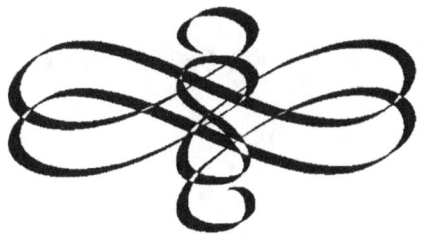

Astragal Press
www.astragalpress.com

Copyright © 2018 Thomas L. Elliott

All rights reserved. No part of this book may be reproduced or transmitted in any form or by any means, electrical or mechanical, including photo-copying, recording, or by any information or retrieval system, without the written permission of the Publisher, except where permitted by law.

ISBN 978-1-931626-38-5

Published by
Astragal Press
An Imprint of Finney Company
www.astragalpress.com

Dedicated to:

William L. Curtis, Jr.
(1941-2018)

And

To the many plane collectors and
dedicated researchers, who were kind
enough to share their knowledge with
us and thus make this book possible.

Publisher Note:

The publisher would like to recognize **Emil Pollak** (1925 - 1995) and **Martyl Pollak** (1927 - 2010) who together produced the first (1983), second (1987), and third (1994) editions of this title and we the founder's of Astragal Press (1983). They entrusted **Thomas Elliott** to work with them to complete the updating for the fourth (2001) edition and certainly would be pleased to know this book lives on, with Elliott completely revising and enhancing this fifth edition.

CONTENTS

INTRODUCTION
IX

HOW TO USE THIS GUIDE
XIV

WHAT'S A PLANE WORTH?
XV

A-XYZ: DIRECTORY OF PLANEMAKERS
1

GLOSSARY
426

BIBLIOGRAPHY
433

ACKNOWLEDGMENTS

This book was made possible through the efforts of many persons. Some of the material we have used has been previously published in a variety of sources; much has been generously contributed by individual collectors from their personal research. Our primary role has been that of organizer, interpreter, illustrator, and editor:

• We own a great debt to **Ken** and **Jane Roberts**, who pioneered in this field and whose research has stood the test of time. With the Roberts' kind permission, we made extensive use of *Wooden Planes in 19th Century America, Volumes I and II*, and *Planemakers in New York State*.

To **Herman Freedman**, who provided biographical articles on I. Day, Charles Dupee, Levi Little, L. Sampson, John and Moses Sleeper, Timothy Tileston, the Waltons, and T. Waterman.

• To **Elliot Sayward**, who created and edited *Plane Talk* during its first nine years as a quarterly clearing house of information, and who allowed us full use of this material.

• To **James I. Garvin**, Curator of the New Hampshire Historical Society, for the planemakers of New Hampshire.

• To **Austin Heicher**, who shared with us the work he had done on wedge outlines.

• To **Larry Brundage**, whose love for research helped solve many puzzles for us.

• To **Don** and **Anne Wing**, who shared both their collection and their store of information with us, who provided invaluable information in their series of articles on major New England planemakers that appeared in *Plane Talk*, and authored the catalog *The Mechanick's Workbench*.

• To **Ed Ingraham** for his generosity in making available to us his research on early New England planemakers.

• To **Bud Steere** for the review of his extensive collection in order to provide us with rubbings and descriptive material.

• To **Dick Hay**, whose excellent *Directory of Baltimore Plane & Edge Tool Makers* was of great help to us and who gave additional help on Baltimore area planes.

• To **Dom Micalizzi** for cheerfully tracking down New York City planemakers whenever asked.

• To **Paul Kebabian** for making his fine collection available to us and patiently answering our many questions.

• To **Jack Kebabian** for the use of his pioneering work on the Nicholsons, Cesar Chelor, and other important early makers.

• To **Bill Hilton** who provided us with information on the Boston and Eastern Massachusetts makers and dealers.

• To **Carl Bopp** for making available his original research on the **Whites** and other early Philadelphia planemakers.

• To **Alex Farnham**, who gave us access to information on the New Jersey planemakers included in his fine book *Early Tools of New Jersey and the Men Who Made Them*.

• To **Charles Ewing** for his extensive research on the planemakers of Kentucky, Indiana, Michigan, and Illinois.

• To **Gil** and **Mary Gandenberger** for information on the Cincinnati planemakers, provided by them in the monograph *Cincinnati Plane, Edgetool Makers, and Dealers 1819-1851*.

• To **Michael Humphery** for the generous use of the material appearing in his *The Catalog of American Wooden Planes*, a quarterly that he edited and published from 1991-98, continuing the work of *Plane Talk*.

• To **John Tannehill** and **William Warner** for making available their research on the Carpenter family, and providing a substantial portion of the biographical material shown.

• To **Chuck Prine** for his original research on the early Pittsburgh planemakers included in his book *Planemakers of Western Pennsylvania and Environs*.

• To **Sara Holmes** for her work on New Orleans hardware dealers.

• To **Bob Graham**, another pioneer whose work has stood the test of time.

• To **Ben Blumenberg** for his extensive research on new unidentified makers.

• To **Bob Jones** for the review of his extensive collection for new imprints, wedge profiles, and descriptive information.

• To **Milton** and **Sue Bacheller** for their in-depth biographical research on gage makers, many of whom were also important planemakers and included in his book *American Marking Gages Patented and Manufactured*.

• To **Bill Curtis** for the information on New York plane makers and permission to review his collection for new imprints and missing wedge profiles.

• To **Pat Lasswell** for the generous use of the material appearing in his *Sign of the Joiner*, a quarterly starting in 1999, that he edited and published, continuing the work of *Plane Talk* and *The Catalog of American Wooden Planes*.

• To **Randy Bell** for his encouragement and early enthusiasm for this project.

• To **Roger Smith** who gave freely of his information on patented and transitional wooden planes included in his outstanding books *Patented Transitional & Metallic Planes in America 1827-1927*, Vols. I and II.

We would also like to thank for their contributions:

- Donald Achenberg
- Bill Ackroyd
- Roger G. Alexander
- Hank Allen
- Charles Alley
- Robert L. Allinger
- Al Anderson
- Glenn Anderson
- Donald A. Armistead
- Mo Arnold
- Karl Ashline
- Bill Baader
- Wendell E. Badger
- James S. Baird
- Sett Balise
- Bob Bernard
- Willis Barschied, Jr.
- Jim Bassett
- Kendall Bassett
- Alan Bates
- Ray Beauduy
- Frank Beck
- Dale R. Beeks
- Merc Beitler
- Chris Bender
- Dave Benze
- Rick Benze
- Joel Bergeron
- Robert Bernard
- Jeff Biddle
- Russell Bigelow
- Bill Bilancio
- Jerold Billings
- Robert Bills
- Jack Birky
- Dan Blackburst
- Clarence Blanchard
- Jim Blower
- Jim Bode
- Bill Boltz
- B. J. Bond, Jr.
- Len Borkowski
- Jim Bovay
- Bruce Bradley
- George Braun
- Joe Brennan
- Ray Brody
- Bud Brown
- Douglas V. Brown
- James Brown
- Seth Burchard
- Jean M. Burks
- Kenneth Butler
- Dale Butterworth
- Richard Cammauf, Jr.
- Rich Cannant
- Thomas O. Carlsen
- Dale Carpenter
- Joe Casilli
- Herbert Candle
- Sherwood Chamberlain
- Richard Chapman
- Darrel Chapnick
- George Christie
- Mark Christisen
- Joe Clarkin
- Ken Clay
- Eric Clingen
- Jack Clouser
- Brian Coe
- Rodney Cole
- Victor Cole
- Gary Coleman
- Dan Comerford
- James A. Conrad
- James Cooley
- Bill Corsetti
- Fred Courser
- J. B. Cox
- John Crane
- Talbot Crane
- Dick Croteau
- Andy D'Elia
- Tim Daniels
- Charles W. Darling, Sr.
- John Davis
- Ron Davis
- Thomas J. Davis
- Richard De Avila
- Ed Delaney
- Andrew Delans
- Emmet De Lay
- John De Lay
- Gordon Deming
- John Dempsey
- Barry Deutchmann
- L. G. De Wolf
- Malcolm Dick
- Dick Dickerson
- George Dodge
- Philip Dodson
- Lee Donnelly
- Martin J. Donnelly
- Roger Draheim
- Ralph Drew
- Rick Ducey
- Michael Dunbar
- Stanley Duvall
- Joe Dzaidul
- Mark Eastlick
- Henrey Ebling
- Tony Eckert
- David Elliott
- Robert Elliot
- Bob Endellicate
- Dave Englund
- Jim Erdman
- David Estes
- Bill Eviston
- Charles & Cherie Fish
- Frank Flynn
- Norman Forgit
- Gregg Forrester
- Allan Foster
- W. R. Fowle
- Gene Fox
- Leonard France
- Chuck Frannick
- Charles L. Frank
- Jim Frederick
- John Freeman
- Rod Galstep
- Eric G. Gannicott
- Bob Garay
- Rev. Dan Gatti, S. J.
- James F. Gauntlett
- James H. Gettle
- John Gillis
- Edward M. Gipson
- Howard Godfrey
- Jerold Goolsby
- Robert Gordon
- John C. Goss
- Ronald Grabowski
- Chuck Granick
- Lee Greenwood
- Joe Grasso
- John Grossman
- Jack Grossman
- Bill Gustafson
- Peter Habicht
- Joe Haesche
- Robert Haffner
- John Halymeyer
- Dale Hanchett
- Edward Harbulak
- Peter Hathaway
- Joe Hauck
- Don Hawkins
- Jack S. Hays
- Dave Heckel
- Ted Heicher
- Don Henschel
- Oliver L. Herrick
- John W. Hess
- Carson Hicks
- John Higdon
- Ray and Jim Hill
- William B. Hilton
- Richard Holland
- Micky Holmes
- Ken Hopfel
- Doug Houser
- Dick Howe
- Jack Howe
- Charles Hummel
- David Hunkins
- Doug James
- Michael Jenkins
- Craig Jensen
- Eugene Johnson
- Forrest Johnson
- Frank D. Johnson
- Gene Johnson
- Jake Johnson
- Frank Jones IV
- John Kahn
- Trip Kahn
- Leon Kashishian
- Ray Kauffman
- Steve Kayser
- Herb & Steve Kean
- Patrick Kelly
- John Kesterson
- J. T. Kett
- Arthur Kevorkian
- Gene Kijowski
- Ted Kinsey
- Todd Kissam
- Gerald R. Kline
- Mike Knudson
- Andrew Knapp
- Tom Kohanski
- Frank Kosmerl
- Alan Lane
- Walt Lane
- Harvey Lauer
- James Lea
- Pat Leach
- Jim Leamy
- Robert M. Leary
- Glenn Leathersich
- Richard Lee
- Robert G. Leckie
- David Lefkowith
- John Letson
- Charles Leverone
- Michael H. Lewis
- R. Lewis
- Ted Lindquist
- Joe Link
- Bill Linstromberg
- George M. Little
- Jeff Lock
- Carol Lomax
- Mary Lou Lomax
- Phil Lothrop
- Dan Ludwig
- Harry Ludwig
- John Mansavage
- Ernie Martin
- Marty Martin
- Walter J. Marx
- Richard Mason
- Bill McCoy
- Ed MacCubbin
- James McCue
- Tom McGill

Malcolm McGregor
Barton McGuire
Larry McKEE
Michael B. McKee
Larry McManus
David Mello
John Meloney
William Melton
Charles Miecznikowski
Jason Miller
Terry Miller
Robert Mindek
Ed Mohler
Lloyd Monk
Frank Moody
Cort Moore
Robert W. Moore
Ross Morcomb
Joe Morton
Ron Mossing
Ronald E. Mower
Jim Mulder
Norman Muller
William Munsil
Tony Murland
Donald K. Myers
H. Nelke
Bob Nelson
Bill Neyer
Bob Nichols
Norm Nilsson
Bob Ochenas
Robert Oehman
Robert Olesen
E. A. Olsen
Eric C. Olson
Steve Orbine
Douglas Orr
Bill Overholt
Robert Palm
Charles S. Parsons
Don Paschall
Roy Paulson
Jeff Pearson
Ron Pearson
Rich Peiffer
Tony Pellecchia
David G. Perch
Arnold Peterson
Bill Petremont
Francis Pfrank
Melvin Phaff
Bill Philips
Myron Piper
Jeff Plante
John Porrit
Robert Pratt
Jim Preusser
Don Prowant
Hal Prucha
Bernard Prue
Jim Puckett
Steve Radisevich
Robert M. Reilly
Tom Relihan
Patrick Renehan
E. J. Renier
Morrill Reynolds
H. R. Richardson
Max Richardson
Lee Richmond
Floyd Ridley
Bill Rigler
J. D. Riley
Gary Roberts
Warren Roberts
Joe Robichau
Trevor Robinson
Randy Roeder
Dick Rosenblatt
John M. Ross
Luke Rubbens
Greg Sabasino
Daniel Sachse
Ray Sager
Robert Sand
George Sawyer
Erv Schaffer
Edna & Merrill Schmidt
Louis Schmidt
Richard Schusler
Jack Sciara
Art Scipione
David Scofield
Steve Scruggs
Gary Seekings
Dan Semel
Al Seymour
Bruce Shaughnessy
Barry Shaw
Mike Sheen
David Short
Tom Silberg
Eric Skopec
Rick Slaney
Frank Sleeper
Edward C. Smith
Edward Sorilla
Robert M. Soule
Richard Souza
Dave Spang
Roger Springate
Richard Spurgeon
Richard Stair
Richard Stair
Joe Stakes
David Stanley
John H. Stanley, Jr.
Philip & Andrea Stanley
Don Stark
Richard Starr
Nicholas Starr
Charles Staude
Max Stelton
Harold Stiffler
Von Stoffer
Neil R. Stoll
Christopher Storb
Bob St. Peter
Tom Strader
Tom Sturges
Edward Swift
Daniel P. Taber
Mike Taber
Tony Tafel
Chris Tahk
John Tallis
John Tannehill
Don Taylor
Terry Thackery
A. R. Thompson
David Thompson
Doug Thompson
Mark Thompson
Neil B. Todd
Laurent Torno, Jr.
Ray Townsend
Douglas Treadgold
Wayne Treadway
Paul Troutman
Dave Truesdale
John Turbeck
Richard Turpen
Bruce Van Sloun
William R. Velich
Kenneth Vliet
Darrell M. Vogt
Henry Voigt
Gene Walbridge
Philip Walker
John Walter
Ron Walter
Tom Ward
Vern Ward
James Wareham
William Warner
Bill Watkins
Berry Weaver
Merle Webb
Michael Weichbrod
Paul Weidenschilling
Dave Weinbaum
Dan Weinstock
Peter Welcker
Greg Welsh
Ron Wessels
Karl West
Bob Westley
Bob Wheeler
John Whelan
Philip Whitby
Paul Whitehouse
Bill Wilkins
Randy Wilfinson
Hampton Williams
Leslie Williams
Charles Williamson
James E. Wilson
John H. Wilson
David Wingot
Ray Wismieski
Dick Wood
Don Wood
Dan Woodford
Parker Worley
Charles R. Wright
Robin Wyllie
Cliff Yaun
Bob Zarich
Gale Zerkle
Jack Zimmerman
John Zimmers

INTRODUCTION

The purpose of *A Guide to the Makers of American Wooden Planes, 5th edition* is to bring together in a concise and convenient form the significant information now available about the makers of wood planes. We have made the book useful and accessible to both the beginner and the advanced collector, to historians and genealogists, and to all others with an interest in the subject. We have included an illustrated glossary explaining the types and parts of planes, common molding profiles, the terms used in this guide, and an extensive bibliography. Since value is an important element in collecting, included is a discussion on **What's A Plane Worth**.

The heart of the guide is the alphabetical directory of planemakers and dealers. The fifth edition contains over 4,590 biographical entries, 6,160 imprint illustrations, and 3,030 wedge outlines to help with identification.

The first thing that most collectors look for on a wooden plane is the name imprinted on the toe. From the imprint much can be learned, especially with the help of this guide book. Every plane bears additional information expressed in the details of the plane's style, such as wood type, length, type of chamfer, wedge profile, tote, boxing, etc. An observant and thoughtful collector has the opportunity to explore the significance of these details and the story they tell. That, in part, is the appeal of collecting wooden planes.

The first planes used in this country were brought from England and the Continent by immigrant artisans. We have documentation of this dating back to the early 17th century. These early examples were probably for the most part bench planes, grooving planes, and rabbets, used for preparing the wood surfaces and for joinery. Molding planes appeared in listings toward the end of the 17th century: hollows and rounds, beads and reeds, together with some ovolos and ogees. The earliest documented English planemakers were **Thomas Granford** and **Francis Purdew** who made planes in London, probably before 1700. **John Davenport** is believed to be a contemporary, as were possibly others still awaiting documentation. One of Granford's apprentices was **Robert Wooding**, who worked in London from 1710-28. His planes have been found in this country possibly their having been brought here by craftsman.

Prior to the early 1700's, imported English planes predominated, certainly in the major seaport cities of Boston, New York, and Philadelphia. Here mercantile connections, the tradition of superior workmanship, governmental control, and the economy of sea transportation favored the English makers. In addition to planes, plane irons were imported in large quantities from Sheffield and Birmingham. The appearance of the first professional planemakers coincided with the change in architectural and furniture style with the use of more ornamental moldings. The wood used in fine furniture evolved from oak to walnut and mahogany, which were more suited to the new ornamental styles. Shipping improved, trade expanded, and a whole new prosperous middle class developed, both in England and the colonies, anxious to acquire fine homes and furniture as symbols of their success.

The first documented American planemaker, **Francis Nicholson**, began his planemaking not long after Wooding. He was listed as a joiner in Rehoboth, MA in 1716 and worked in Wrentham, MA, from 1728-1753. Other early planemakers included Francis' son **John Nicholson** and Francis' slave **Cesar Chelor**, both of Wrentham; **Samuel Dean** of Dedham, MA, active from 1737-47; and **John Walton** in Reading, MA, north of Boston, who was active by the 1730's. By the 1750's **Samuel Doggett** was active in Dedham, **Jon Ballou** in Providence, RI, and **Henry Wetherel** in Norton, MA.

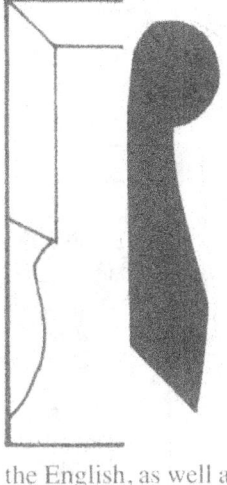

F. Nicholson Chamfer and wedge style

The chamfers on their planes were flat and mostly on the side of the planes, usually ending with a lamb's tongue detail that tipped down toward the center of the plane. Their wedges had small round finials, some with relief on the back and a shallow curved cutout under the finial. The planes made by these early New Englanders differed from those of the English, as well as those makers in the southern colonies, in several ways:

- They made their early planes out of yellow birch, rather than the beech used in other areas.
- Their plow planes, called Yankee plows, had a distinctive style. They were longer (10" vs. 7" to 8 1/2"), their fence arms were square, not rounded, and secured by thumbscrews or wedges, and the fences were the same length as the stock.
- The New Englanders also lagged behind the other areas in reducing the size of their molding planes to the final standard length of 9 1/2". Many of their planes still measured 9 7/8" to 10" right up to and through the Revolutionary War.

During the pre-Revolutionary War period, planemakers also began to appear in the Mid–Atlantic area. These were shadowy figures: **Thomas Grant** was in New York City by the 1750's and **James Stiles** from 1768 until the British occupation. **Samuel Caruthers** was making planes in Philadelphia, as early as 1740. **Benjamin Armitage** was an apprentice of Caruthers and was advertising on his own by 1764. Even with local skilled planemakers, Philadelphia and New York City still looked to England for most of their planes until after the Revolution.

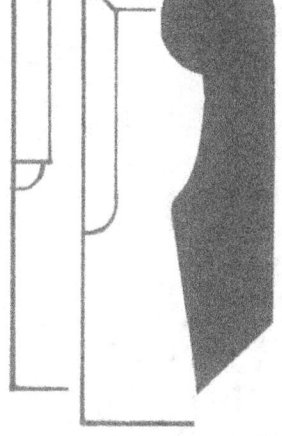

Tho. Grant chamfers and wedge style.

The chamfers of these Mid-Atlantic planemakers were flat, ending in a horizontal step and turn out or just a turn out. Their wedges were similar to the English wedges of this same period with a round finial. The Revolutionary War, and the economic distress that followed it, created a hiatus in the economy that lasted until the 1790's. American makers began to produce planes in quantity when the new nation recovered its prosperity, growth resumed, and expansion into the western territories began. Planes were gradually standardized to 9 1/2" long, made of beech, and with a standard wedge style. Flat chamfers became round, then shallow round stopped with a gouge cut. **Joseph Fuller** (b. 1746) is a good example of this transition. He was making joiner's tools in Providence, RI, by 1772. His early planes are pre-war in style. His most noted style, made between 1780-1800, has a heavily relieved wedge and a separate flute below the chamfer stop. The planes remained 10" in length and were made of birch. His planes made after 1810 are 9 1/2" and beech, with flat end and round top chamfers that end with a turnout, and have a non-relieved wedge.

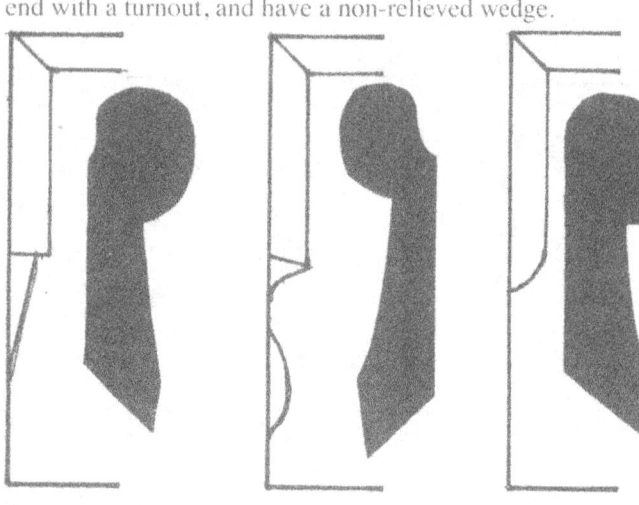

Before 1780   **1780-90**   **After 1810**
Jo. Fuller Chamfer and wedge styles.

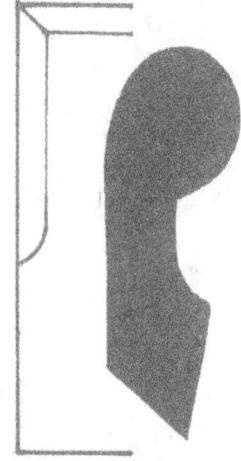

I. Sleeper chamfer and wedge style.

New Englanders of this period include **John Sleeper**, who was a planemaker in Newburyport, MA, as early as the 1770's and is best remembered for his unique wedge style. Other important New Englanders of the post-Revolutionary War period, 1790-1810, include:
John Lindenberger in Providence, RI, who learned Planemaking in Baltimore, MD; **Jeremiah Sampson** in Kingston, MA; **Joshua Wilbur** in Newport, RI; **Nicholas Taber** in New Bedford, MA; **William Raymond** in Beverly, MA; **Henry Wetherell**, the son of **Henry Wetherel**, in Chatham, CT; **Leonard Kennedy** in Hartford, CT, **Aaron Smith** of Rehoboth, MA, and **Levi Little** in Boston.

    Robert Eastburn was a planemaker in Brunswick, NJ. **Thomas Napier** and **William Martin** were both planemakers in Philadelphia before the Revolutionary War. Post-Revolutionary War Philadelphia planemakers included **William Brooks**, **Thomas Goldsmith**, **John Butler**, **Amos Wheaton**, and **John Stall**. Further to the west in Lancaster, PA, **Dietrich Heis** and his sons **John Heis** and **Jacob Heiss** were active planemakers. Further south in Maryland, **William Vance** and **John Keller** began the tradition of the Baltimore planemakers.
Joseph Brumley was an active planemaker in Georgetown, Washington, DC, by 1800.

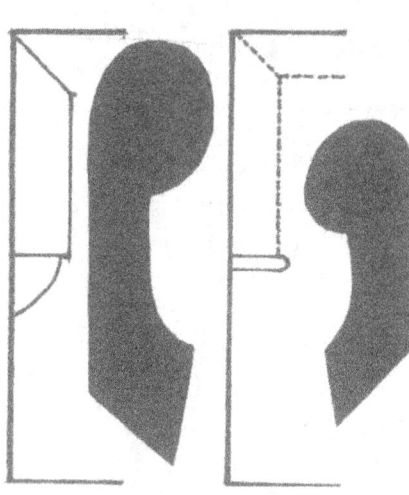

D. Heis chamfer (L) and wedge styles.

W. Vance chamfer (R) and wedge style.

Only New York City, among the major American cities, lacked a major documented maker during the 1790-1810 period. Perhaps this was because it was primarily a trading port where English imports remained competitive. New York, unlike Philadelphia and Baltimore, never established itself as a center of fine furniture and homes after the Revolutionary War.

During the early years of the 19th century, the country moved westward, first to Western PA and Pittsburgh, then into the OH territories, and beyond. Cincinnati, OH, became an important planemaking center, and later St. Louis, MO, gained that distinction. The number of planemakers proliferated. Their various business endeavors prospered and failed as the country was periodically racked with financial panics and war.

By the second quarter of the 19th century, the wooden plane had reached its zenith. The introduction of machines, the use of water and steam power, and the great improvements in transportation and communications led to the formation of large companies and the use by some of convict labor. Some of the largest of the plane factories were:

- **H. Chapin/ Union Factory** (1828-97) of New Hartford, CT.
- **Arrowmammett** (1836-57) of Middletown, CT.
- **The Greenfield Tool Co.** (1851-83) of Greenfield, MA.
- **The Auburn Tool Co.** (1864-93) of Auburn, NY.
- **The Ohio Tool Co.** (11851-1920) of Columbus, OH.
- **The Sandusky Tool Co.** (1869-1925) of Sandusky, OH.

The development of wholesale distribution systems, through catalogs and by hardware stores, allowed planes to be distributed far beyond the place of fabrication. This period also saw the beginnings of patented features on wooden Planes, transitional wood planes, and finally the all metal planes, which would supersede the wooden plane. By the 1880's the end was in sight. Though wooden planes continued to be offered in catalogs into the 20th century, the quality and pride in craftsmanship was gone.

A Guide to the Makers of American Wooden Planes, is a reference to an important period in our economic and cultural history. It provides an insight into a group of men and the tools they made; tools that helped build the houses, the furniture, the ships, the coaches & wagons, the barrels, and the many other items vital to everyday life. The tools were made with pride and craftsmanship and were beautiful in themselves. When you pick up these tools, they fit comfortably in your hands and often you can feel the slight worn indents caused by a thumb or fingers. The question that is brought to mind is whose hands polished these surfaces over years of use. To hold these tools, therefore, is to touch, feel and embrace history.

PRE-REVOLUTIONARY NEW ENGLAND COLONIES ca. 1760. In 1700 the total colonial population was about 250,000 persons. By 1760 the population had grown to over 1,500,000, located mostly along the sea coast or upon navigable rivers. Inland travel was slow and limited until Ben Franklin developed the postal system along the King's Highway, which became known as the Boston Post Road. The Lower, the Middle, and Upper roads were originally Indian trails. The area between Boston, Massachusetts and Providence, Rhode Island, served by this road system, became a fertile area for early planemaking.

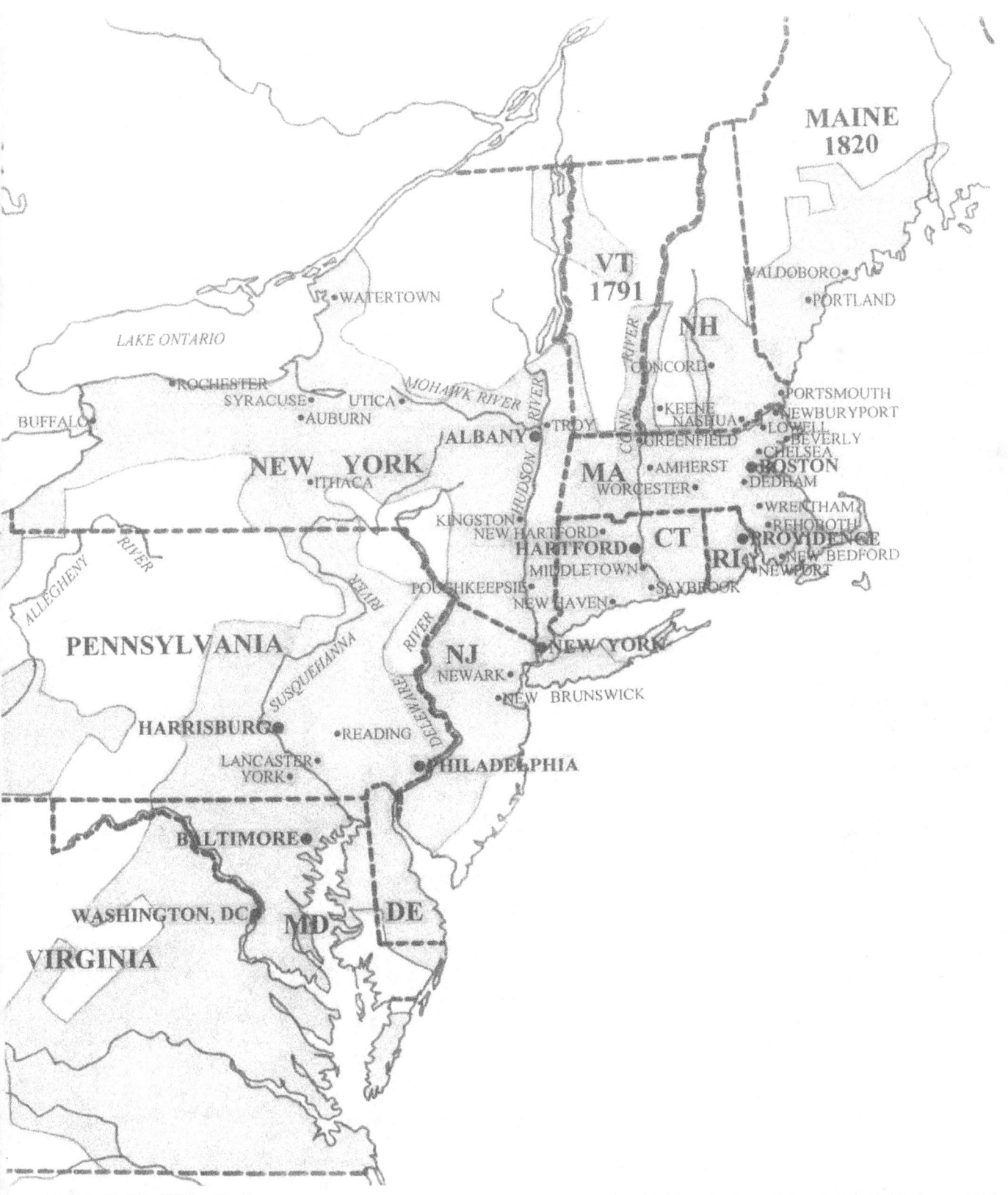

UNITED STATES - 1840

The first Federal census of 1790 indicated a population of 3,930,000 and by 1820 the population was over 9,640,000. Vermont was added to the Union in 1791, followed by Kentucky in 1792, and Ohio in 1803. The War of 1812, fought against the British, created only a blip in the western expansion. Indiana was added as a state in 1816, with Illinois following in 1819, and Maine in 1820. Pittsburgh became the major gateway to the west, with easy travel along the Ohio River to Cincinnati, Ohio, and St. Louis, Missouri.

From Albany, the Mohawk River Valley and the Erie Canal opened up western New York and the Great Lakes. By 1840, the population of the United States was over 17,000,000 and by 1860 over 31,400,000. With the development of the railroads and more reliable transportation, plane manufacturers no longer sold directly to local markets but sold wholesale, nationwide, through catalogs and large hardware stores.

HOW TO USE THIS GUIDE

The major portion of *A Guide to the Makers of American Wooden Planes* is an alphabetically arranged biographical directory of planemakers and dealers. The maker or dealer is listed as his name appears on his imprint. The imprint is almost always found near the top of the toe (front) of the plane. A few have double or multiple imprints in a decorative pattern, and may also include an early initial group or two or more different imprints for the same maker.

Dealer imprints are often found on the toe or heel of planes along with makers' imprints. Of even more interest is the multiple imprints of two or more known makers. These usually tell an interesting story.

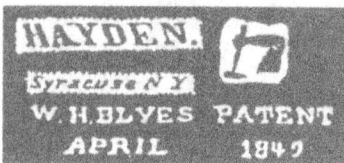

RARITY RATINGS

We have used a system of stars to indicate the relative rarity of a majority of the imprints that are illustrated. In determining rarity we have considered examples already known and those likely to be discovered. Single imprint examples or ones that have no known location or personage can not be rated.

*****   **Unique** denotes fewer than 10 examples.
****   **Extremely Rare** denotes between 10 to 50 examples.
***   **Very Rare** denotes between 50 to 100 examples.
**   **Rare** denotes between 100 to 250 examples.
*   **Uncommon** denotes between 250 to 500 examples.
FF   **Found Frequently** denotes over 500 examples.
UR   **Unrated** denoted imprints and makers that we presently have insufficient information to rate.

We wish to emphasize strongly that what we are offering is only an educated guess and a rough guide to relative rarity. We are not setting values. Our judgments are based on dealer's price lists, catalogs and listed auctions; on discussions with dealers and collectors, on seemingly endless visits to museums, antique shows, dealers' shops, tool society meetings, flea markets, and exposure to literally hundreds of plane collections. Still, what we offer is only our opinion and is subject to revision as new information becomes available.

Regarding the **FF** category, found frequently, we would like to point out that there are important qualifications that should be born in mind. For instance, while **Sandusky Tool Co.** was a prolific manufacturer, whose planes are common, most designated **FF**, one of the highest priced wooden planes sold at auction was a **Sandusky** center-wheel plow that sold for $20,000. Also, though some **Jo. Fuller** imprints are rated **FF**, they are eagerly sought after as classic examples of late 18th century, American wooden planemaking, and all sell for significant prices. On the other hand, many late 18th century planes, whose makers' imprints are quite rare, sell for less.

The **UR** category, unrated, denotes imprints, makers and dealers on which we presently have insufficient information to rate. As genealogical research continues and more examples surface and are reported, it will be possible to assign a rating.

All imprint reproductions are actual size. The imprints were taken from rubbings of actual planes. Some of these planes are over 250 years old. Many have been much used and abused. Wood has shrunk and expanded, cracked, checked, suffered from rot, insects and rodents. Planes were dropped, hammered on, or used as a hammer. Imprint dies were damaged, worn down, or modified. The imprints shown are only as authentic and accurate as what we had to work with. Wedge outlines are shown at 55 per cent of actual size and represent that portion of the wedge that appears above the body of the plane. In the text we have included a description of reported examples in order to assist in judging approximate age, duration of work, and origin. Where a location is known, it is also included to assist in future research and identification.

In the 18th and early 19th centuries, I was used for **J**, therefore **I. IONES** stands for **J. JONES**. The long f was used for **s**, therefore **T. Tilefton Bofton** stands for **T. Tileston Boston**.

Asa Hide the father became **Asa Hyde** the son. We would also like to point out that spelling in the 18th and 19th centuries was rather haphazard and was often changed in succeeding generations.

As for geographical locations, towns and villages have frequently been renamed or incorporated into nearby cities, boundary lines have been relocated, townships and counties divided, and territories made into states. We have included tool dealers and hardware dealers when their imprints appear on a plane. In some cases they made planes as well as distributed them. Not included are imprints from Canada, the United Kingdom, and continental Europe unless they worked in part in this country.

WHAT'S A PLANE WORTH?

Prices of wooden planes sold at auction:
- A prototype double beveling plane by **M. B. Tidey** in ebony and ivory - $27,000.
- A **Sandusky Tool Co.** handled boxwood center-wheel plow plane with ivory tips - $20,000.
- A **Francis Nicholson** crown molder - $12,000.
- A double beveling plane by **M. B. Tidey** in beech and boxwood - $11,500.

These of course are the exceptional prices. It is still possible to buy common but good, usable wood planes for as little as $10. However, rare 18th century planes, as well as choice 19th century ones, frequently sell for $1,000 and more, and it's seldom that an 18th century plane by a known maker, in good condition, will sell for less than $100. In a free market, price is set by supply and demand. The supply side of tools is, by definition, finite. Most planemakers, the early ones in particular, made planes over relatively short periods of time and supplied small market areas. Considering the daily wear and tear and the hazards the planes were exposed to over the past 150 to 250 years, it's remarkable that so many have survived.

Emil Pollak undertook a census of the planes of **Francis Nicholson**, **John Nicholson**, and **Cesar Chelor** in *The Chronicle*, June 1985 with 248 planes being reported: 106 by **Francis Nicholson**, 51 by **John Nicholson**, and 91 by **Cesar Chelor**. The census was updated by Ted Ingraham in *The Chronicle*, March 2001 resulting in a total of 562 reported examples: 211 by Francis Nicholson, 126 by John Nicholson and 193 by Cesar Chelor. The percentages of each maker remained similar. The new study also analyzes the type of planes unique to each maker. Alan Bates made a similar census of **Thomas Napier**, *Thomas Napier, The Scottish Connection*, 1986, another 18th century Philadelphia planemaker. Only 46 examples were reported. The middle to late 19th century witnessed a tremendous number of machine made planes produced. Nevertheless, certain types of planes and certain makers from this period are quite rare.

There is great demand, from collectors, for signed examples as these are among this country's oldest signed artifacts. These were the tools used to make the fine furniture now exhibited in museums and to decorate the historic buildings we so admire.

TYPE OF PLANES

A cornice plane will typically sell for many times, the price of a hollow or round by the same maker. Partly because of visual appeal but mostly by the numbers made. A study made by Anne and Donald Wing of the production records of the **Greenfield Tool Co.** for November 1854 illustrates the point. Of a total of 11,900 planes made in that month, 4,600 (38%) were bench planes, 4,300 (37%) were molding planes, 1,300 (11%) were match planes, 700 (6%) were rabbets, 262 (2%) were plow planes, and 700 (6%) were others. Of the 4,300 molding planes, 2,400 were hollows and rounds, 1,100 were beads, 795 were complex molding planes, and only 15 were wide, handled planes, which presumably included cornice planes. An ordinary, unhandled plow plane will sell for four or five times the price of a hollow or round. Plows represented only 2% of the total production for November 1854, compared to 20% for the hollows and rounds.

The following is a list of relative rarity based on the type of plane in ascending order from least to most rare:
- Hollows and rounds.
- Rabbets.
- Beads.
- Match planes, tongue and grooves.
- Ordinary moldings.
- Dadoes, filletsters, and sash planes.
- Complex molding planes.
- Unhandled plow planes.
- Handled plow planes.
- Panel raisers.
- Cornice planes/ crown molders.

Bench planes made after the first quarter of the 19th century are fairly common. Earlier ones, particularly with 18th century makers' imprints, are quite rare, perhaps because users at that time tended to make their own and save money; or perhaps it was because bench planes got harder use and, being easier to replace, were simply used up and discarded.

MATERIAL USED

In 1853, **Greenfield Tool Co.** produced 1843 plow planes, 1227 were made of beech, 356 of boxwood, 182 of rosewood, and 78 of ebony. Only 2 of the boxwood and 2 of the ebony planes were ivory tipped. The 1872 **Greenfield Tool Co.** catalog priced the following planes:
- Handled beech plows .... $ 7.00
- Rosewood or boxwood .... $ 9.00
- Ebony $12.00
- Rosewood trimmed with ivory. $13.50 to $18.20
- Ebony trimmed with ivory .... $16.50 to $20.20.

The following is a list of relative rarity based on the material used, in ascending order from least to most rare:
- Beech
- Boxwood
- Rosewood
- Ebony

Ivory trim or parts adds another magnitude of rarity to each category, as does exotica such as German silver trim. Lignum, rosewood and ebony were also used as boxing. Cherry and fruit woods, such as apple and pear, were also used occasionally by the 18th century makers. Bench planes, particularly jointers, are found made of apple, maple or mahogany, and were usually owner-made. Unusual woods, particularly when they enhance the appearance of a plane, adds significantly to its value.

REGIONAL PREFERENCES

There is a strong tendency to collect planemakers by region. For example, the planes made by a Massachusetts maker will most often be found in Massachusetts and thus will be more available to Massachusetts collectors. Research can more readily be done in one's own locality. While premium prices may be paid at a New Hampshire auction when two determined local collectors want a plane made by a New Hampshire maker, the same plane might arouse little interest in Pennsylvania.

CONDITION

And finally, one of the most important factors is condition, which includes original parts and finish.

I.A/ IN. NORTON
John Astin (Austin) was a private in the American Revolution. He enlisted on Dec. 20, 1776 and was discharged on Mar. 20, 1777. **John Bassett** purchased land from a certain **John Astin** of neighboring Easton, MA and **Henry Wetherel Sr.**'s land bordered on **John Astin**'s. **Henry Wetherel Jr.** married a **Phebe Austin**, possibly a relative. Examples: from 3 molding planes all 10" birch with flat chamfers and a relieved wedge; a 13 7/8" birch panel raiser with an offset tote and flat chamfers. The **IN. NORTON** imprint is the same as on **H. WETHEREL/ IN. NORTON** planes, ca. 1780. *****

BA/ B.ABBELL
Example: on a 9 1/2" beech hollow with flat chamfers, ca. 1800. **UR**

 A

 B

B. ABBOT
Example: on a 9 1/4" beech complex molder with flat chamfers, ca. 1805. **UR**

S. ABBOT
Possibly **Samuel W. Abbott** (b. Feb. 9, 1812 in MA, d. May 17, 1864 in Lowell, MA) who moved to Bedford, NH, ca. 1827 and learned cabinetmaking from **Ephraim Abbott**. **Samuel** advertised as a cabinetmaker in Nashua, NH in 1845. In 1849, he was in Montpelier, VT. In the 1850 census, he was listed as a cabinetmaker with four cabinetmakers in his household including **John D. Kimball**. Between 1849-55, **Samuel** was in partnership as **Abbott & Emery** with **John C. Emery**. In 1856, **Samuel** was listed as a cabinetmaker in Berlin, VT. Examples: on a 9 7/8"x 5/8" birch round; and a 10"x 1/2" beech skew round but could be of a latter date or a different person, ca. 1810. **UR**

MOSES ABBOTT
Moses Abbott (b. Feb. 14, 1698/99 in Andover, Essex Co., MA, d. Nov. 8, 1791 in Greenwich, MA) was the sixth of nine children, the Son of George and Elizabeth (Ballard) Abbott. The first record of **Moses** is in 1722 when he bought land in Brookfield, Worcester Co., MA. He served as a Private in Capt. Samuel Partridge's Co. from Sep. 10, to Nov. 4, 1722. **Moses** married Martha Barns on Feb. 5, 1724/25 in Brookfield. In 1749, he joined a petition to set off the northwest part of Brookfield, where he lived, to form New Braintree, MA. In 1780, He moved to Greenwich, near, Belchertown, Hampshire Co., MA, where he died on Nov. 8, 1791. Example: on a 10" birch thumbnail with shallow flat chamfers. *****

THOMAS H. ABBOTT
(see Taber Plane Co.)

S. ACHE
Samuel Ache (Achey) (b. 1764 in Lebanon Co., PA, d. Nov. 28, 1832 in Reistville, PA) who was a Pennsylvania "Dutch" German instrument maker from the Lancaster, PA area. A dulcimer instrument called a "Scheitholt" was inscribed on the side indicating that it was a gift of love from the maker, **Samuel Ache**, to his fiancée, dated 1788. Examples: on a 9 3/4" beech large round with heavy flat chamfers, found near Harrisburg, PA; and a 9 13/16" cherry quarter round with continental style details and a bead on the shoulder, ca. 1780-1800. *****

W.F. ACHENBACH
W. F. Achenbach of Reading, PA, was issued Patent No. 310,163 on Jan. 6, 1885, consisting of two 1/2" wide steel wear strips set into the sole of the plane, one in front of the mouth, the second toward the rear. Examples: on a 16" jack; and a 7 9/16" smoothing plane, both manufactured under the **Ogontz Tool Co.** name. *****

ACORN/ H. ACORN
Examples: the imprint A is on an 8 3/4" small round. The B imprint is on a 9 5/8" self-fenced rabbet, both have shallow round chamfers. The A imprint appears to be earlier and a first attempt, ca. 1805-20. **UR**

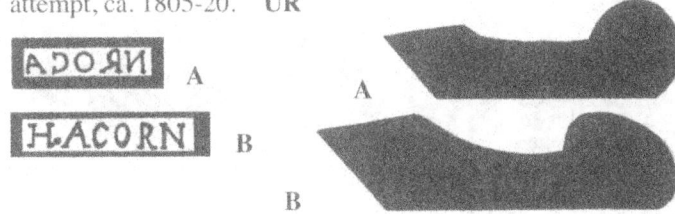

ACUSHNET
The town of Acushnet is near New Bedford, MA. **Acushnet** is possibly a trade name used by **Lamb & Brownell** or the **Taber Plane Co.**. Examples are from several bench planes, two smoothing planes have. carried the style numbers No. 21 & No. 93. A, A1 & B ***

A

A1, B

ACUSHNET WORKS

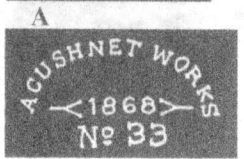

Presumably this is the same company as **Acushnet**, New Bedford. Examples: on a 21" beech bench plane; and a 16" jack plane. **A & B** ***

A, B

PETER ADAM
Peter Adam, at age 11, was apprenticed to **William Vance** to learn the trade of a planemaker, on Apr. 7, 1803.
No imprint has been reported.

A. ADAMS
Possibly **Amos Adams** (b. Dec. 25, 1762 in Roxbury, MA, d. Dec. 17, 1786 in Medfield, MA) was the older Brother of **Joseph Adams** and son of **Reverend Amos Adams** who was a Chaplin in the American Revolution and died of dysentery in 1775 at Dorchester Heights, leaving **Amos** fatherless at age 13. Examples: The A imprint is the earliest and is on a 7 1/4" birch smoother with round-top wedge and single iron marked **Weldon**, flat chamfers and flutes. The B imprint is on a crown molder with offset tote; a Yankee-style plow; a 14"x 4 13/16" (3 3/4" iron) jack and several 10" complex molders with relieved wedges all birch; a 25" fruitwood jointer, with offset tote, round-top wedge and iron, and strike button; all with flat chamfers, from southeastern New England, ca. 1780.
A & B ****

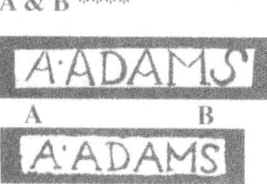

A, B

A. A. ADAMS
Example: on a 9 5/8" beech molder with shallow round chamfers, ca. 1830-40. **UR**

C. ADAMS/ T. ADAMS
Example: on a 9 1/2" birch single boxed complex molder with round chamfers, ca. 1820. **UR**

D. P. ADAMS
Example: on a 9 1/2" cherry round with flat chamfers, ca. 1810. **UR**

A. H. ADAMS
Example: on a 7 1/2" stair rail plane, ca. 1850. **UR**

H. ADAMS
H. Adams was listed in an 1856 directory as a Hopkinton, MA, planemaker. (see **William Adams**)
No imprint has been reported.

H. ADAMS & CO.
There is no record of a **H. Adams & Co.** in the New York City directories. There was, a **J. H. Adams & Co.** listed as a hardware dealer, active from 1841-70, and then **Joseph H. Adams & Son** until 1873. Examples: the Imprint A is on a cove molding plane, with **156** on heel, the style number for a cove in the **Auburn Tool Co.** 1869 price list; a boxwood handled screw-arm plow; and a size **3/4** match grooving plane. The Imprint B is preceded by an owner's imprint **A. Campbell**, which might help locate this firm. ***

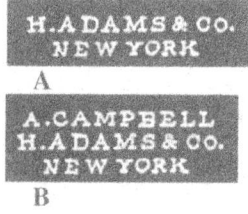

A, B

J. ADAMS
Joseph Adams (b. Jul. 11, 1767 in Roxbury, MA, d. Jul. 14, 1856 in Litchfield, CT) was listed as a cabinet and chairmaker on Center St., Boston in 1789. This may be the same **Joseph Adams** who was listed as a cabinetmaker in Litchfield, CT from 1790-1802. He was the younger Brother of **Amos Adams** and son of **Reverend Amos Adams** who was a Chaplin in the American Revolution who died of dysentery in 1775 at Dorchester Heights leaving **Joseph** fatherless at age 8. He advertised in the *Weekly Monitor* on Jun. 7, 1790 and Jan. 18, 1792 for four apprentices. On Nov. 20, 1799, he advertised "a runaway apprentice, **Hail Barns**, age 19". Examples: on a panel raiser; a 16 1/4" beech jack with a **James Cam** iron and with round chamfer; and a 28" beech jointer struck twice on the toe, both with flat chamfers, ca. 1800. ****

J. K. ADAMS
Joshua Knight Adams (b. Jan. 1, 1791, d. Feb. 7, 1876 at Hartford, PA) was the son of **James and Jerusha Knight Adams** of Canterbury, CT. In 1812, He settled in Hartford, Susquehanna Co., PA. He taught for 20 years at the Franklin Academy and the Hartford University as a cabinetmaker. He was a member of the Masonic Fraternity and served as sheriff for four years. Examples: on several 9 3/8" boxed side beads, with an ogee molded shoulder, and heavy round chamfers; and a smoother with shallow flat chamfers, ca. 1810-20. *****

M A/ M. ADAMS
Possibly **Moses Adams** (b. 1759 in Ipswich, MA, d. Oct. 7, 1796 in Beverly, MA) who was a cabinetmaker in Beverly, MA. Vital records indicate that he had a son, also **Moses Adams** (bapt. Dec. 28, 1794). Another **Moses Adams** (b. 1781) was listed in the censuses from 1810-50. In the 1850 census, he was listed as a carpenter in Holliston, MA. Examples: the A imprint and initials are on a 14" beech cornice plane with a 5 3/4" wide blade, offset-tote, pull-bar, and heavy round chamfers. The B imprint is on a 9 5/16" skew rabbet; and a complex molder, all are beech with heavy round chamfers, ca. 1820. **A & B** *****

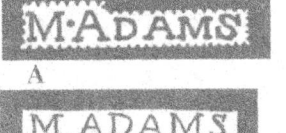
A
B

R. ADAMS
Example: on a 9 1/2" beech coping plane with round chamfers, ca. 1820. **UR**

W. ADAMS
Example: on a 9 7/16" beech altered narrow round with narrow flat chamfers, ca. 1800. **UR**

WILLIAM ADAMS
William Adams was listed in the 1856 directory as a Hopkinton, MA, planemaker. (see **H. Adams**)
No imprint has been reported.

ADAMS HARDWARE & PAINT CO.
Adams Hardware & Paint Co. was a Lowell, MA, hardware company. Example: on an 8" smoothing plane with a **Globe Mfg. Co.** of Middletown, CT, single-iron. ****

C. W. ADDIS
C. W. Addis was listed as a planemaker in the 1850 New Haven, CT, directory. (see **Beacher & Addis**)
No imprint has been reported.

WM. ADGER
William Adger (b. Sep. 4, 1816 in Charleston, SC, d. Dec. 14, 1853 in New York, NY, buried in Charleston) was a hardware dealer was listed in the 1850 census as a merchant living in Charleston, SC. He was on a business trip to NY when he rushed into a burning building and saved a trapped lady. **Adger** died several days later. ***

ADVERTISING RESULTS CO.
Example: on a 3 1/8" tiny bench plane, complete with wedge and iron. Marked in ink on the left side "Compliments of the **National Recording Safe Co.**, Heyworth Bldg., Chicago." Different companies used this advertising on a pencil sharpener used for square carpenter's pencils. ****

D. E. & A. A. AIKEN
D. E. & A. A. Aiken of Adrian, MI, had a May 5, 1868 patent. Example on a 23" long with a 19" cutted and wedge, at a low angle.
```
        D. E. & A. A. AIKEN
            SLAT CUTTER
         PAT. MAY 5, 1868
           ADRIAN, MICH.
```

T. AIKMAN
Thomas Aikman (b. ca. 1780 in Scotland, d. May 17, 1850 in Burlington, NJ) was listed, ca. 1800, as a cabinetmaker and planemaker who lived on Pearl St. in Burlington, NJ, just across the Delaware River from Philadelphia. Some planes are marked **PHILa**. Listings in his estate inventory read "lumber in shop" and "tools, saws, planes, etc." Examples: the A1 imprint is on a 22" beech fore plane with an offset-tote imprinted three times on the toe. **A** ***; **A1** ****

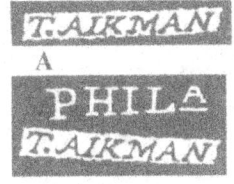
A
A1

AKERS/ JOHN AKERS
Possibly **John Akers** (d. Oct. 20, 1770). Examples: The full name, **JOHN AKERS**, is on a 10" beech rabbit; and a 15" panel raiser. The **AKERS** imprint is on a 10" molder. ca. 1770. **UR**

ALBANY TOOL CO.
Albany Tool Co. is thought to be a hardware dealer. Examples: on a boxwood, screw-arm handled plow with **M. Crannell** style nuts and fence profile; on a skew rabbet marked **181**, which was the **Auburn Tool Co.** style number for skew rabbets; and on a size **14** round marked number **180**, the **Auburn Tool Co.** style number for hollows and rounds, ca. 19c. ***

FRED ALBECHT
Fred Albecht was a cooper in Baltimore, MD. Example: on an 18 7/8" bench plane with a curved open-tote so it could be used as a miter or shoot board plane, ca. 19c. **UR**

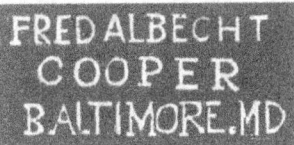

G. P. ALBERT
George P. Albert (b. Jan. 18, 1830 in Jefferson Co., KY, d. Jun. 25, 1921 in Louisville, Jefferson Co.) was listed as a planemaker in 1850 in Madison, IN. He was listed in the Louisville, KY 1850's as working for **Alexander McBride**. In 1870 & 80, George was listed as a carpenter in Louisville. In 1900 & 10, as a pattern maker working for a stove manufacturing co. in Louisville. Example: on a 6 5/8" beech coffin smoothing plane with a **Spear & Jackson** iron. ****

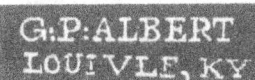

H. ALBERT & CO.
Henry Albert was listed as a planemaker in the 1808 & 18 in Philadelphia, PA directories. ***

P. ALBERT
Examples: on a 9 1/2" sash; and a 10 3/4" sash coping, both with full round chamfers; and an 11 3/4" wedge-locked fenced grooving plane with flat chamfers, all are beech, possibly from western PA or OH, ca. 1790-1820. UR

 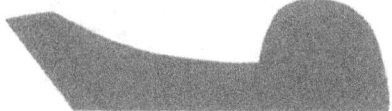

ALBERT & STEEL
Albert & Steel was listed as a plane making partnership or possibly a hardware dealer located in Philadelphia, PA, and is listed in the *Directory of American Toolmakers*.
No imprint has been reported.

ALBERTSON & CO./ A. ALBERTSON & CO.
Albertson & Co. and **Albertson Edge Tool Co.** were used interchangeably. **Samuel Albertson** (b. 1780, d. Mar. 2, 1852) operated as **Albertson Edge Tool Co.** at Hyde Park, NY, from ca. 1830-52. **Burrow Albertson** (b. 1820, d. 1867) was **Samuel's** son and worked with him in Hyde Park, before moving to Poughkeepsie, NY, as **Albertson & Co.**, from 1850-67. Examples: on two jack planes with the **A. Albertson & Co.** imprint. **No imprint is available.**

C. ALDEN
Believed to be **Caleb Alden** (b. Jan. 30, 1790, d. Sep. 1, 1863 in Bridgewater, MA) who was a carpenter from N. Middleboro, MA, or son **Caleb Alden** of Lyme, NH. Examples: on a 9 3/8" beech complex molder; and a hollow, both with round chamfers, ca. 1810-20. ****

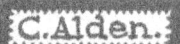 

C+ ALDRIDGE
Example: on a 10 1/16" beech hollow with narrow flat chamfers, ca. 1790. UR

ALEXANDER
Example: on a 9 5/16"x 3/16" beech side bead with flat chamfers, found in Southeastern PA, ca. early 19c.
No imprint is available.

S. ALEXANDER
Examples: two 9 1/2" beech rounds with shallow round chamfer, ca. 1830. UR

I: ALEXR
Possibly **John Alexander** (b. Jul. 1, 1764 in York Co., PA) who was listed as a cabinetmaker in Baltimore, MD, from 1800-03. Examples: on a 9 1/2"x 2/8" small quarter round molder; and a very narrow halving plane, both beech with flat chamfers, ca. 1790-1800. UR

ALFORD
Consider Alford (b. Dec. 12, 1778 in Devonshire, England) worked from 1812-17 and was one of the earliest New York City planemakers. An ad in the *Connecticut Courant* of June 29, 1819, offering a reward of $20 for a runaway apprentice, is signed **Consider Alford**, blind-maker, No. 15 Catherine St., New York. **Alford** married **Lucy Fitch Kennedy** on Dec. 28, 1800 in Windham, CT. **Lucy** was the sister of **Leonard Kennedy** and the aunt of **Samuel L. Kennedy**. By 1817, **Samuel L. Kennedy** was making planes at **Alford's** former address. A & A1 **

A. & A. ALFORD PLANE CO.
Alfred Alford (b. Sep. 15, 1812 in Litchfield, CT, d. Aug. 28, 1892 in Riverton, CT) and brother-in-law **Arba Alford Jr.** (b. Nov. 7, 1807 in Riverton, CT, d. Jan. 9, 1881 in Riverton, CT) were the principals in a partnership that made chairs from 1843-46 in **Lambert Hitchcock's** old chair factory in Riverton, CT (then called Hitchcockville). They also operated a general store in one wing of the factory. From 1849-53, they manufactured planes and were succeeded by the **Phoenix Co.** in 1853.
No imprint has been reported.

ALFORD & MARVIN
Example: on a single boxed beech 1/4" side bead with round chamfers, ca. 19c. UR

J. M. ALLARD
James Madison Allard (b. Apr. 9, 1819, in Eaton (now Madison), NH, d. Mar. 24, 1888 in North Conway, NH) was a carpenter. He married **Eleanor Howe Gile** on Jan. 2, 1839 in Conway, NH, where he owned a farm, was elected constable and selectman. Examples: on a 17" razee closed handle fore plane with a **Moulson Bros.** double-iron; and a 9 3/8" molding plane with round chamfers, ca. 1830-40. ***

ALLEN
Examples: on a 9 5/8" astragal; and a 9 1/4" side rabbet with a birch wedge, both beech with flat chamfers, ca. 1800. **UR**

A. D. ALLEN
Amos Denison Allen (b. Mar. 14, 1774, d. Aug. 19, 1855) was an active chairmaker and cabinetmaker from 1796-1813. He was apprenticed to **Ebenezer Tracy** (b. 1744, d.1803) of Lisbon, CT, from Feb. 1790 to his 21st. birthday, Mar. 14, 1795. **Amos** married **Tracy's** daughter, **Lydia**, in 1796, and opened a shop in Obwebetuck, Windham, CT. **Amos's** order book is in the Connecticut Historical Society and covers the period from 1796-1803. On May 10, 1804, **Amos Allen** received a patent for a plane used to shave wood strips for making baskets, hats, etc. He advertised in the *Windham Herald*, on April 15, 1813, as a cabinet & chairmaker and branded His furniture **A. D. ALLEN**. **No imprint is available**.

C. ALLEN
Caleb Allen (b. 1777, in Providence, RI, d. Feb. 18, 1854, in Lansingburgh, NY) came to Lansingburgh with his family in 1787, before Lansingburgh became part of Troy, NY, in 1791. He appeared on an 1814 jury list as "tool cutter" and was listed, in 1850, as a carpenter in Lansingburgh. Examples: all beech from 9 3/8"-9 3/4", the shorter later planes have rounded chamfers and the longer earlier planes have flat chamfers. One example has an iron made by **Green** (Sheffield 1774-1824). Both the wedge shape and the incuse imprint is very similar to those of **S. E. Jones**, also from Lansingburgh, who preceded Allen, and to whom Allen may have been apprenticed. **A1 **A ******

I. ALLEN
Possibly **Joseph Allen** (b. ca. 1755, d. Sept. 21, 1786) who was listed as a cabinetmaker in Salem, MA. Example: on a 24" beech jointer with a centered tote and flat chamfers, ca. 18c. **UR**

IRA. ALLEN
Example: on a 10 3/16"x 1 1/8" beech skew rabbet with a nicker and heavy flat chamfers, found in VT, ca. 1770-80. **UR**

J. ALLEN
Possibly **Jonathan Allen** (b. Oct. 27, 1776 in Enfield, CT, d. July. 15, 1826 in Vernon, OH) **Jonathan** was a wheelwright and a cabinetmaker. He was noted for his restless energy and industry. He was the father of **James Sullivan Allen**. He married first, **Mary Pease** (1774-1818) on Jan. 25, 1799. In 1815, the family moved to Ohio. He married twice more, to **Miriam Kibbe** (d. 1821) on Dec. 21, 1818, at age 42, and then to **Polly Thining** on Mar. 14, 1822, at age 44. Examples: on a 9 11/16" bead with flat chamfers; a 10" birch complex molder, and a double-boxed beech center bead. The last two with round chamfers. Possibily two persons, ca. 1790-1810. **A & B ******

J. S. ALLEN
James Sullivan Allen (b. Nov. 7, 1808 in Springfield, MA, d. Aug. 1873 in Vernon, OH) was listed in the 1850 Vernon, OH, census as a cabinet and toolmaker. He was the son of **Jonathan Allen** and came to OH, in 1815 age 7, with his family. He married Mary Ann Read on Mar. 13, 1834 in Vernon, OH. In the 1860 census, he was listed as a joiner. Example: on a plow plane. ********

O x ALLEN
Oliver Allen (b. 1750 in MA) served as a private during the American Revolution. Example: on a 16" birch jack with a decorative offset tote, a round top wedge and iron, found in CT, with **B. Dean** planes, ca. 1760-80. ********

T. C. G. ALLEN
Thomas C. G. Allen (b. Mar. 8, 1818 in Scotland, d. Feb. 12, 1900 in Peck, Sumner Co., KA) was listed in the 1850 census as a carpenter. He was listed in the Milwaukee, WI directories from 1851-57 as a planemaker. In 1880 & 85, he was a farmer in London, Sumner Co., KA. **No imprint has been reported**.

W. ALLEN
Examples: The A imprint is on on a 10" birch hollow; and a 10 1/8" sash molder with an ogee molded shoulder, both have flat chamfers. The larger B imprint is on a birch bench plane with a decorative off-set handle and round chamfers; and on a 10" applewood halving plane, with heavy round chamfers, ca. 1780-1820. **A & B: UR**

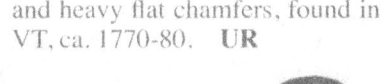

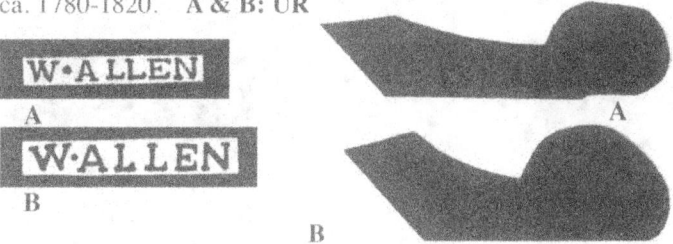

WILLIAM DAUK ALLEN
William Dauk Allen (b. 1801) was apprenticed, on Jan. 6, 1813, to **William Vance** a Baltimore, MD planemaker. **No imprint has been reported.**

ALLEN & CO.

Allen & Co. was a Providence, RI, hardware dealer. An advertisement in the Dec. 2, 1829, *Providence Daily Advertiser* listed a **Benjamin Allen & Co.**. Examples: on a beech boxed bead. Found with this plane were a matching single cope; and an adjustable sash made by **J. R. Gale**. Both overstruck by an **Allen & Co.** imprint. **Allen's** Broad St. location was one block from **Gale's** shop. Their imprints are similar in style. The A1 imprint is on a 9 1/4" beech double-boxed side bead. A & A1 ****

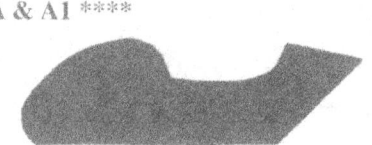

ALLEN, DORSEY & TENNEY

Allen, **Stephen W. Dorsey** and **L. H. Tenney** were in a plane making partnership in Sandusky, OH, active from 1868-69. They operated a general woodworking plant before making planes and tool handles in 1868. The name was changed to the **Sandusky Tool Co.** in 1869. **No imprint has been reported.**

ALLEN & ELDRIDGE

Squire S. Allen (b. 1816 in NY) and **James A. Eldridge** (b. 1821 in MA) were listed as **Allen & Eldridge** in the 1850 Products of Industry census, as planemakers and merchants in Williamstown, MA, employing nine hands and producing 14,000 planes worth $4,000. If these figures were correct, the output probably included unfinished parts for others, since examples are seldom found. Examples: the A imprint is on an 11 1/4" handled rabbet; a 9 1/2" beech ship's hollow. The A1 imprint is on a 9 1/2" beech molder. The A2 imprint is on a 21" foreplane also marked **T. S. CLARK/ N.Y.** with a double-iron marked **PROVIDENCE TOOL Co.** A & A1 **; A2 ****

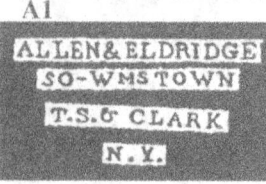

ALLEN & NOBLE

Allen & Noble was a Boston, MA hardware dealer in 1855. **

ALLEN & STORM

In the first Poughkeepsie City Directory of 1843, **Joseph E. Allen** had a hardware store at 346 Main Street. The **Allen** name then continued in the hardware business every year until 1884 with entries for: **Joseph E. Allen**, **James H. Allen**, **James H. Allen & Co.**, **Allen Brothers** and **Allen & Co.**. The **Storm** name also appears just about every year during the same period. In 1843, **Abraham G. Storm** had a hardware store at 279 Main Street, not far from **Joseph Allen**. After **Abraham** came **Edward**; in 1853-54 there was **Storm & Uhl**; and then **Storm & Wilkinson** from 1863-67. Oddly, there was no entry for **Allen & Storm**, although the mark was reported on the

toe of an **Edward Carter** reverse ogee, and on an **E. & C. Carter/ Troy, N.Y.**, astragal. ****

I. ALLYN

Possibly **Isaac Allyn** (b. 1787 in Groton, New London Co., CT, d. Jan. 30, 1839 in Riley, Huron, OH) was a cabinet and chairmaker, active until 1813 in Preston, CT. An advertisement in *Connecticut Gazette* of May 26, 1813 stated that the shop formerly occupied by **Isaac Allyn** has been taken over by **Allyn Chapman**. **Isaac Allyn** married **Permella Downing** (1795-1874) from Canterbury, CT. Their first child was born in 1814 in Riley, Huron, OH. Examples: on a 12 5/8" beech panel raiser with a birch wedge, flat chamfers and a pegged tote; and a 9" beech plow with screw and wedge-stopped arms, a wood depth stop and flat chamfers, ca. 1800. *****

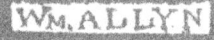
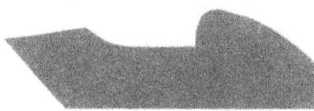

Wm. ALLYN

Possibly **William H. Allyn** (b. Apr. 4, 1817 at Barkhamsted, Litchfield Co. on the Farmington River, CT, d. Jan. 26, 1890 in Hardin, OH) who in 1822 moved to "New Connecticut" or "The Western Reserve" in OH. William was a carpenter, as were two brothers and one brother-in-law, all living in Hardin, OH. **William** married **Sarah Ann Slayton** (1819-1909) with one child born in 1857 in Union Co., OH. Examples: on a 9 1/2" beech hollow; and a 1" boxed bead, ca. 1840. ****

ALSASAM

Examples: on a 9 7/8" astragal; a 10" sash; a 10" cove & bead; a 5 1/2" smoother; and a 5 1/2" wide crown molder, all beech with heavy round chamfers. One example has interrupted lignum wear strips on the sole, probably from PA, ca. 1810-20. *****

S AMBLER

Squire Ambler (b ca. 1757, d. Feb. 3, 1829 in Danbury, CT) and **Silas Ambler** (b. ca. 1760 in Fairfield Co., CT, d. 1829) advertised on Nov. 10, 1791 that they "will carry all kinds of Joiner's tools at their shop on the main road from Danbury to New Milford, (CT) Cafh (cash), cattle, country produce, timber, boards, and shingles will be received in payment." They also wanted, "two journeymen, to whom good pay will be made and two fprightly (sprightly) lads 14-15 years of age, as apprentice". Examples: on a 9 1/2"x 1 1/2" beech skew rabbet with flat chamfers, with an A wedge; and on a 9 3/8" beech single boxed bead with heavy round chamfers with a B wedge, ca. 1800-30. A & B: ****

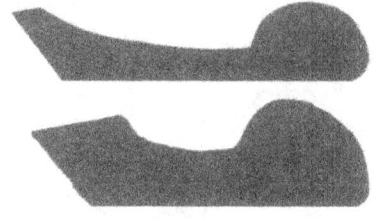

AMERICAN PLANE - CO
Probably a private brand used by a New York City hardware dealer. Examples: on a 9 3/8" skew rabbet; a bead; and a 26" jointer, ca. 1850. ***

J. AMES
Example: on a 9 1/2"x 1 3/4" beech skew rabbet, found in a tool chest with **Wm. Woodward** and **D. Presbrey** planes. The A imprint is on a fixed sash with a double-iron and round chamfers. The A1 imprint border was modified from the same die as the A imprint. The B imprint is on a 13 1/2" beech plank tongue plane with birch wedge and tote. flat chamfers, ca. 1850. **A & A1: UR**

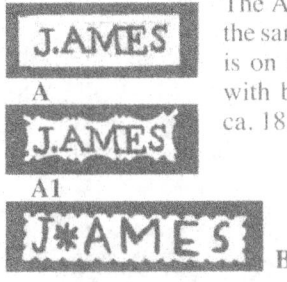

L. AMES
Possibly **Luther Ames** (b. Aug. 31, 1770, d. 1841 in Marlboro, VT) who was a cabinetmaker from Guilford, VT. He was listed in Marlboro, VT, from 1800-40. Example: on a 9 3/8" beech quarter round with small round chamfers with an owner's imprint, **W. I. AMES**. Also on the heel of a **T. Tileston** molder, ca. 1820. **A & A1 ******

M. AMES

Example: on a 15" gutter plane, found on ME coast. **UR**

AMHERST TOOL CO.
The **Amherst Tool Co.** was located in Amherst, MA. The location die was the same as used by **S. Hastings** and **J. Kellogg** and may be a J. Kellogg brand name. Examples: The A imprint is on a 7 7/8" coffin smoother. The B imprint is on a 16" jack, both with an **Auburn Tool Co. Thistle Brand** double-iron, ca. 1870. **A & B ******

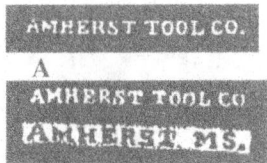

D. AMSDEN
Downing Amsden (b. ca. 1790) was a planemaker and joiner, who worked in Lebanon, NH, from 1807-28. Downing served in The War of 1812 as a Corporal in Field's 2 Regt., Vermont Militia. **Downing** Married Sarah Amsden (d. 1838 in Lebanon, NH). **Downing** was listed in 1840 census in Kingsville, Ashtabula, OH. Examples: on a 9 1/2" beech molders with round chamfers. The earlier A & A1 imprints are on molding planes with an **I. Sleeper** style wedge. **B & B1 ****; **A & A1 *****

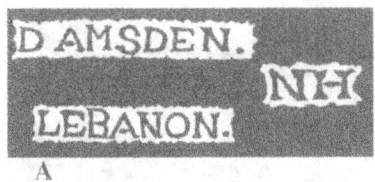
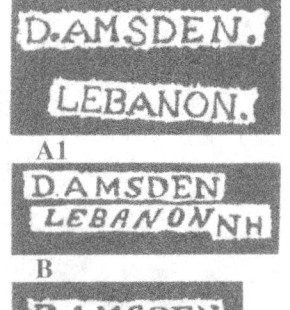
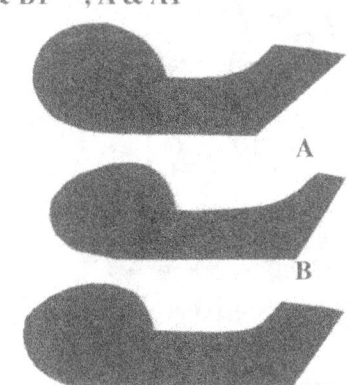

ANCHOR PLANE CO.
The **Anchor Plane Co.** is probably a brand name. Examples: on a 16" razee jack plane with a **Buck Bros.** double-iron; a 22" razee fore plane; and a coffin smoother, all beech with toe and iron bearing this imprint. ***

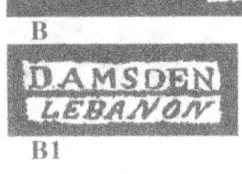

I. ANDERS
Example: on a 10 1/16" maple sash plane with flat chamfers, possibly from eastern PA. ca. 1800. **UR**

CHARLES ANDERSON
Example: on a fruitwood screw-arm plow with brass depth stop. ca. 1840. **UR**

JOHN ANDERSON
Longworth's *American Almanac, New York Register, and City Directory* of 1807 lists **John Anderson**, as a planemaker at 71 Chatham St., New York City. **No imprint has been reported.**

ANDERSON & LAING
James T. Anderson and **Alexander Laing** were partners in a hardware dealership at 13 Monroe St., Wheeling, VA (now WV), active from 1839-56. They sold wood planes made by the **Ohio Tool Co.** starting in 1851. From 1856-65 it became **Greer & Laing**. Examples: on a pair of screw-arm plank planes and a boxwood plow plane with ivory tips. **A & A1 *****

ANDERSON & TRUM
Anderson & Trum was a hardware dealer. Example: on a size 3/8 astragal made by **Cooper**. UR

G. ANDRE
Example: on a 14 1/4" birch grooving plane with an offset tote and shallow round chamfers, ca. 1810-20. UR

J. W. ANDREWS
Example: on the toe of a pair of size 3/4 match planes made by **Randall & Cook** and the date **1840**. *****

ANDRINE BROS
Andrine Brothers was a hardware dealer located at 204 Grove St., Jersey City, NJ. Examples: on the heel of a 9 1/2"x 3/16" beech center bead; and a boxwood screw-arm plow, both made by **Lamb & Brownell** of New Bedford, MA, ca 1870. ****

O. ANDRUS
Obed Andrus (b. Apr. 7, 1810 in Glastonbury, CT, d. Mar. 1, 1871 in Glastonbury) was a Glastonbury, CT, planemaker, active from 1840's-71. In the 1850 census, Andrus was listed as a planemaker, and in the 1860 census as a toolmaker.
D & E *; A, A1, B & C **

A

A1

B

C

D

E

ANDRUSS
David T. Andruss (b. 1803, d. 1832) and brother **George Washington Andruss** (b. Jul. 27, 1806, d. May, 1860 in Newark, NJ), were Sons of **Jonathan Andruss**, and manufactured planes from 1821-41. The firm advertised "wholesale and retail plane manufacturing" and "coach making tools of every description." Andruss was listed in the 1837-38 Newark, NJ directory as "Plane Factory" at 150 Washington St. This was the same address used by **Thomas Burns** from 1836-38. **George W. Andruss** was listed in the 1859 *Essex, Union & Hudson Counties New Jersey Directory* as a plane maker. Imprints were often carelessly applied and the name is sometimes inverted. **Andruss & King** was a firm listed in Newark, in 1847, possibly with **George W. Andruss** as one of the partners. It advertised as making "improved plough & fillister planes." (see **J. Andruss** and **Samuel E. Farrand**)
A, A1 & B *

A

A1

B

J. ANDRUSS
Jonathan Andruss (b. Dec. 17, 1766, d. Jan. 2, 1843), was the father of **David T. Andruss** and **George W. Andruss**. **Jonathan** married Charity Meeker (1775-1840) on May 23, 1802, in Newark, NJ. Jonathan Andruss appears on the 1812 Newark, NJ tax list. Jonathan was probably the earliest Newark, NJ, planemakers and was working before 1821 **

J. ANGERMYER
Possibly **Jacob Angermyer** (Angermire) who was a carpenter in Zelienople, PA, from 1825-36. He purchased a lot in the original plan for the town in 1826. Example: on a adjustable beech screw-arm sash plane. (see **J. J. Angermyer**) A & A1 ****

A

A1

J. J. ANGERMYER
J. J. Angermyer (Angermire) (b. 1795, d. 1852) was listed in the 1830 census for Connoquenssing Township, Butler Co., PA. Examples: on a 9 1/2" round with 3/8" round chamfers, with the A wedge, found in Columbiana Co., OH, on the PA border; and a screw-arm sash with the B wedge. ca. 1820.
(see **J. Angermyer**) *****

ANTARCTIC CO.
Antarctic Co. of New York, NY, was active in the 1880's. Example: on a round plane. ca. 1880. ********

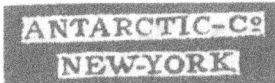

G. T. ANTHONY
George Tobey Anthony (b. June 9, 1824 in Mayfield, NY, d. Aug. 5, 1896 in KS.) In 1842, he moved to Union Springs, NY, as an apprentice to a tanner. In 1843, he moved to Ridgeway, NY. In the 1850 industrial census, he was listed as a hardware merchant and tin ware manufacturer in Ridgeway. An 1854 gazetteer describes Medina, NY as "a thriving post-office county, about 36 miles northeast of Buffalo on the Erie Canal and the Rochester, Lockport and Niagara Falls Railroad, population 3000-4000." He served as a Capt. in the Civil War from 1862-65. In 1865, he moved to Leavenworth, KS, and was active in the newspaper business. From 1877-79, he was the Governor of KS. Examples: on a beading plane; and on a plane also imprinted **Casey & Co.**, Auburn. (For a photo of **George Tobey Anthony** and additional biographical information, see *American Marking Gages*, by **Milton H. Bacheller, Jr.**) ********

JOHN APPLE
Example: on an 8 3/4" maple complex molder with round chamfers and a relieved wedge, ca. 1810-20. **UR**

JOHN APPLE. H. I
Possibly a variation of **John Apple**. Example: on a 10 3/4" fruitwood tongue plane with shallow round chamfers, ca. 1830. **UR**

THOS. L. APPLETON.
Thomas L. Appleton (b. Jul. 27, 1842 in MA) was a prolific Boston/ Chelsea (just north of Boston) plane manufacturer. On May 30, 1863, **Thomas L. Appleton** was Second Lieutenant in the Massachusetts 54th., an African American Civil War volunteer Regiment. By 1864, He was a Captain and by 1865 a Provost Marshal, Northern District, Department of the South. He started in the hardware and cutlery business in 1866 as **Tucker, Appleton & Whitney**; from 1868-72 as **Tucker & Appleton**; and from 1872-78 as **Gladwin & Appleton** plane manufacturers in Chelsea, MA. From 1878-79, he worked under his own name at Margin Street, Chelsea. In 1880, **Thomas L. Appleton** was listed in Chelsea Directory as a plane manufacturer. In 1892, the firm was reorganized as **Mass. Mfg. & Electrical Co.** with **Appleton** as Treasurer. The firm advertised electrical supplies, stair building, wood working & planes. Planes were dropped after 1895. It is not known when he was part of **Gardner & Appleton**.
A: FF; B *; A/C, C & D *********

JOHN: APS
Example: on a 9 5/8" birch skew rabbet with flat chamfers and flutes, ca. 1780. **No imprint is available**.

B. ARMITAGE
Benjamin Armitage Jr. (b. Feb. 1698 in Holmfirth, Yorkshire, England, d. Dec. 23, 1781 in Abington, Philadelphia, PA) was an early Philadelphia, planemaker, active from 1760-72. He was an apprentice to **Samuel Caruthers**, who was perhaps Philadelphia's earliest planemaker. In 1718, he married **Elizabeth Thomas** in Abington, PA. **Armitage** was a member of the Carpenter's Company of the City and County of Philadelphia, PA. An ad titled **Benjamin Armitage** appeared in *Penn. Gazette* on Feb. 16, 1764. In his will, written Oct. 25, 1773, He called himself a yeoman. Examples: on 9 5/8"-10" beech molders with flat chamfers.
A ********; B *******

W. H. ARMITAGE & CO.
Probably a hardware dealer. Example: on an 8" beech smoother, ca. 1850. **UR**

G. ARMS
Reported from the Berks County Historical Society. Example: on a 9 1/4" beech boxed complex molder with flat chamfers, ca. 1790. **UR**

J. ARMSBY
Example: on a 9 1/2" beech molder, ca. 1830. **UR**

WILLIAM ARMSTRONG
William Armstrong (b. 1810 in LA, d. 1872) was a hardware dealer in New Orleans and a native of St. Martinville, LA, who appears in the city directories from 1838-72. He was listed in the 1850 Federal census as a merchant, living in New Orleans. His firm was in business at several locations in the Vieux Carree, the French Quarter. **A ***; A1, B & C ******

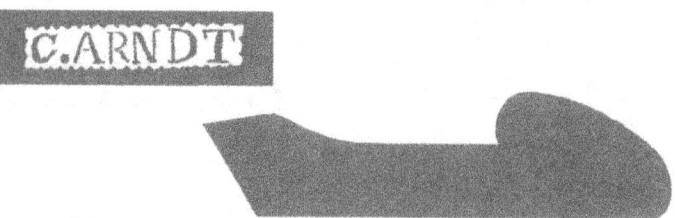

C. ARNDT
Examples: on a 13 1/2" beech fenced tongue plane with wedged locked arms, centered tote, and heavy round chamfers; and a 10" beech skew rabbit with flat chamfers, ca. 1830. **UR**

D. ARNDT
Example: on a 9 1/2" adjustable fillister with a wood tombstone depth stop, found in Maine, ca. 1800. **UR**

D. ARNEEL
David Arneel (b. 1775) appears in the 1810 and 1820 censuses and the earliest surviving tax records of 1819 thru 1831 for Zelienople, in Butler Co., 28 miles north of Pittsburgh, PA. He is listed as a carpenter owning property in Zelienople, which was laid out in 1804. There were probably fewer than 100 people living there in the 1810-20 period. The most interesting feature of the **Arneel** planes is the heart-shaped dot after the initial **D**, which may tie **Arneel** to planemakers **William Evans** and **William Wilson**, of Pittsburgh, PA, and users of the heart-shaped dot. Examples: on two panel raisers, one 13" that puts a bead on the thin edge of the panel; a 9 5/16" round; a complex molder; a plow; and a sash plane, all are beech with heavy round chamfers, ca. 1820. ********

T. ARNER
Example: on an 8 5/8" beech combination opposed tongue & groove plane with flat chamfers, ca. 1810. **UR**

ARNOLD
Example: on a 10" beech molder with flat chamfers and a relieved wedge, found in ME. The plane has the appearance of planes made by **Jo. Fuller** or **Arnold & Field**, ca. 1790. **No imprint is available.**

C. ARNOLD
Examples: on a 9 1/2" birch halving plane with shallow round chamfers; a 9 1/2" beech complex molder with flat chamfers; and a birch round with heavy round chamfers, ca. 1800-30. ********

E. W. ARNOLD
Edgar W. Arnold (b. 1815 in NY, d. Nov. 4, 1880 in Saybrook, CT) married **Lucy A. Gladwin** (1812-1897) on May 28, 1837 at Winthrop/ Saybrook. **Lucy** was related to **Porter A. Gladwin**. Arnold was listed in the 1848 Saybrook Vital Records as a Mechanic in Winthrop. **Edgar's** son, **Wilber F. Arnold** married **Clara P. Denison**, daughter of **John Denison**. The 1857 H. F. Walling Map of Connecticut lists **E. W. Arnold** as "Manufacturers of stops and plates for joiner's planes". The 1874 Beers Map of Winthrop Center lists **E. W. Arnold** as Plane Mfy., located next to **Lester Denison**. **Arnold** did not make completed planes, but supplied the two generations of **Denisons** with plane irons, brass and iron plates, machine screws and brass depth stops. Examples: on an overstrike over a **C & S Buckley**; on a 2 1/8" complex molding plane and an overstrike over a **J. & L. Denison**; a beech screw-arm plow plane. *********

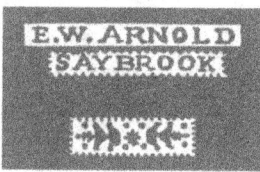

L ARNOLD
Possibly **Lemuel Arnold** (b. Sep.15, 1776 in Norton, MA, d. Feb. 13, 1861 Norton, MA). In 1798, Lemuel Arnold was listed as a cabinetmaker in Norton. On May 18, 1802, Lemuel Arnold married in Norton. Examples: on a 9 3/8" beech snipe bill, with a boxed edge and flat chamfers; and on a **H. Wetherell**/ Chatham, CT molder with an iron by **P. Law**, Sheffield, England, 1787-1833. *********

W. ARNOLD

William F. Arnold of Oakland, CA, active from 1905-09, was a carpenter. He was issued a Patent No. 840,418 on Jan. 1, 1907 for a 16" beech bench plane with a cast iron open tote, frog, lever cap and shoe. Two examples have been reported and are beech with round chamfers. **No imprint is available.**

ARNOLD & CROUCH

Arnold & Crouch were planemakers in Northampton, MA, ca. 1850-60. **Charles S. Crouch** (b. 1826 in MA) was listed in the 1850 census as a toolmaker in Williamsburg, MA, and living with **Ansell Strong**, a carpenter. In 1853, he was employed by the **Greenfield Tool Co.**. He was probably the **Crouch** of both **Arnold & Crouch** and **Peck & Crouch**. **Arnold** may have been **W. F. Arnold** who was a hardware dealer in Northampton at that time. The eagle imprint shown is also found on the planes of **H. Wells**, **Peck & Crouch** and **J. D. Kellogg**, all of Northampton. *

ARNOLD & FIELD

Arnold & Field was a Providence planemaking partnership of **Richard M. Field** (b. Jul. 8, 1775 in Providence, RI) and **Daniel Arnold** (b.1775 in Providence, RI, d. Mar. 15, 1875 in Bellingham, Norfolk Co., MA). Richard M. Field was apprenticed to **Joseph Fuller** and was listed in 1799, as a toolmaker; in 1817, as a merchant, and was the younger brother of **Joseph Fuller, Jr.**, born **Joseph Field**. **Daniel Arnold** was the older brother of **Anthony B. Arnold** who married **Abby Fuller**, the daughter of **Joseph Fuller, Jr.**. **Daniel** may have apprenticed to **Joseph Fuller**. **Arnold & Field** planes are similar in style to the **Fuller & Field** and the **Jo. Fuller** planes. Examples: on 10" birch and beech planes with relieved wedges, and flat chamfers, ca. 1790. ****

ARROWMAMMETT WORKS

Arrowmammett Works was the trade name used by the **Baldwin Tool Co.** for planes produced at their **Arrowmammett Works** in Middletown, CT. The **Baldwin Tool Co.** was established in Middletown in 1836 by **Austin Baldwin**, who made planes earlier in New York City as part of **A. & E. Baldwin**. A plank tongue plane and a molding plane have been reported with an **A. & E. Baldwin/ New York** imprint and an overstamp of **Arrowmammett Works/ Middletown**. The A1 imprint with the added **NEW YORK** was probably a marketing feature and is on a skewed rabbet plane. **Arrowmammett** offered an extensive line of planes, shown in its 1857 catalog, and produced a variety of plane irons under the **Baldwin Tool Co.** name. In 1850, **Arrowmammett Works** reported production of 40,000 planes worth $25,000. In 1857, Arrowmammett Works was sold to the **Globe Mfg. Co.** of Rhodestown, CT, a maker of plane irons.

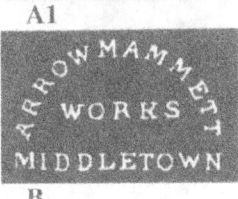

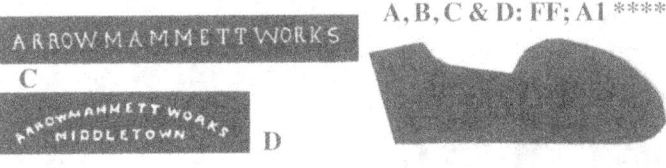

A, B, C & D: FF; A1 ****

P. J. ASH

Park J. Ash (b. Aug. 31, 1824 in PA, m. Nov. 9, 1849 in Jefferson Co., KY, d. Sep. 14, 1894 in Olathe, Montrose Co., CO) was listed in Louisville, KY in 1850-52 as planemaker at **A. M'Bride's**, boarding at **Thomas Houghton's**. In 1870, Ash was listed as a carpenter in Silver Creek, Clark Co., IN. In 1880, He was listed as a carpenter in Longmont, Boulder, CO. Examples: on a handled coffin smoother with the date **1867**; another dated **1871**; and a handled fruitwood screw-arm plow with boxwood wedge and nuts, and a brass depth stop. The B imprint is on a 13 1/2" beech cornice plane with a double-iron. **A (some dated) & A1 ***;**
B ***

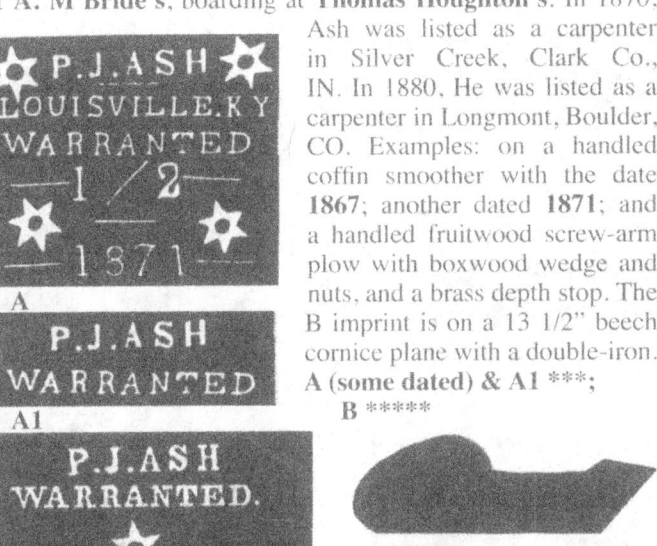

J. ASHCRAFT

Examples: on a wedge-lock plow with a depth stop secured by a wedge thru the body of the plane; and a 9" beech boxed complex molder, both with round chamfers, ca. 1830. ****

CHAS. ASHLEY

Charles Ashley, of Ogdensburg, NY, was a hardware dealer ca. 1855. Examples: on the heel of a **Benson & Crannell** complex molder, and on an **A. Miller/ New York** molder. **

G. ASHLEY

George Ashley was a Little Falls and Binghamton, NY, hardware dealer, active from 1845-70. Examples: the B imprint is on an astragal with **102** on its heel, the **Auburn Tool Co.** style number for an astragal. The A1 imprint is on a complex molder with **127**, the style number for a Grecian reverse ogee. A, A1 & B ***

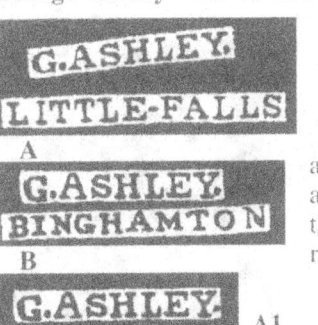

L. C. ASHLEY
Lewis C. Ashley (b. 1835 in NY, d. 1913) of Troy, NY, received Patent No. 14,436 on March 18, 1856, although the example reads **L. C. ASHLEY/ PATENTED, FEB 1856**. Ashley apparently jumped the gun in ordering his die stamp. The patent utilized a metallic throat piece to adjust the mouth of a bench plane as the sole wore down. ********

S. ASHLEY
Ashley is an area in N. Bedford. Example: on a 12 5/8" tropical wood skew ships rabbet with a closed integral-tote and two nickers, ca. 1850-60. **UR**

ASTEN & THROCKMORTON
Asten & Throckmorton was a New York City hardware dealer, active in 1876. Example: on a handled boxwood plow plane made by **Lamb & Brownell**. ********

ATKINSON
John Atkinson was a Baltimore, MD, planemaker and plane manufacturer, who was active from 1829-56. (see **Atkinson & Co.** and **Atkinson & Chapin**) A & A1 ******

G. ATKINSON
Example: on a 9 1/2" beech molder with flat chamfers, ca. 1800. **UR**

S. ATKINSON
Example: on a 19" foreplane. **UR**

T. ATKINSON
Thomas H. Atkinson (b. 1811 in England, d. 1867 in Louisville, KY) was a Corporal in 34er. KY Infantry from Oct. 3, 1861-Dec. 7, 1864. He was listed in the Louisville, KY, city directories in 1832-66 as a plane manufacturer or planemaker. In 1838-39, He was a partner in **Littell & Atkinson**. An imprint **THOS. ATKINSON** with **1862** has been reported on a beech smoothing plane, **but the imprint is not available.**
A, B & B1 ******

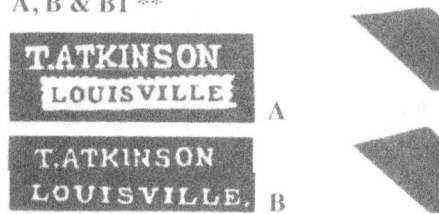

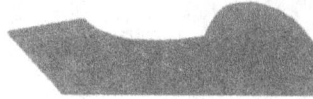

W. ATKINSON
Example: on a 9 1/2"x 5/8" beech bead with flat chamfers, found in NJ/ PA area, ca. 1810. **UR**

ATKINSON & CO.
John Atkinson (b. 1798 in MD, d. 1870 in Baltimore, MD) was listed as a Baltimore, MD, planemaker and plane manufacturer at corner of Light & Balderston Streets in 1837-38. (see **Atkinson** and **Atkinson & Chapin**) *******

ATKINSON & CHAPIN
John Atkinson and **Philip C. Chapin** were listed as planemakers at corner of Light & Balderston Streets in a 1836 Baltimore directory. (see **Atkinson & Co.**)
No imprint has been reported.

ATWATER & MALLET
Example: An ink stamp on the side of a full-boxed bead by **H. Chapin** reads: ********

ATWATER & MALLET
HARDWARE DEALERS
880 CHAPEL ST.
NEW HAVEN, CT.

A. AUBERY
Examples: the A imprint is on a narrow fixed panel raiser; a boxed bead; a 9 1/8" narrow dado; a 9 1/4" double bead; and a 9 3/16" wide molder, all planes are beech with shallow round chamfers. The dado has a **Butcher** iron and the wide molder a **Swinscow & Manuel** iron. The larger B imprint is on a 9 13/16" beech rabbet with flat chamfers, ca. 1800-20. A, B & C: ********

AUBURN TOOL CO.
The **Auburn Tool Co.** was a major manufacturer of wooden planes located in Auburn, NY., as a successor to **Casey, Clark & Co.**. It operated under the **Auburn Tool Co.** name with **George Casey** as president. **Auburn Tool Co.** was part of a collective effort between **H. Chapin**'s son, **Greenfield Tool Co.**, and **Sandusky Tool Co.** called the Plane Maker's Association, organized ca. 1858, to fix prices. From 1864-67, **Auburn Tool Co.** used prison labor. In 1867, it was out bid by

J. M. Easterly & Co. which later became A. Howland & Co.. In 1874, Auburn Tool Co. resumed the use of prison labor until 1877. On Nov. 14, 1893, Auburn Tool Co. merged with Ohio Tool Co. of Columbus, OH. While plane production continued in Auburn, it was under Ohio Tool Co.'s name. Auburn Tool Co. used a number of brand names: New York Tool Co., Owasco Tool Co., Genesee Tool Co., Ensenore, and Excelsior Works, Thistle Brand, and Star. The 1865 NY census reported that 50 men were employed using 35 tons of iron, 8 tons of steel and 30,000 board feet of lumber to producing 35,000 planes worth $35,000, 25,000 dozen plane irons worth $12,000 and 30,000 pairs of ice skates worth $45,000, with the utilization of steam power. The average monthly wage was $16 (prison labor rate). On a Jan. 24, 1867 statement, probably made between their convict-labor contracts of 1864-67 and 1874-77 read: "We have lately moved our plane manufacturing business from the State Prison to our new factory. All our work is done by good mechanics, we employ no convict labor, consequently are not obliged to receive work that is defective." An Oct. 21, 1881 hand bill reads: "Cash prices for white beech logs and plane woods. By the Auburn Tool Co. $20.00 per m. feet. Logs are to be green timber to be straight grained, and must have at least 3 inches in thickness of sap or white on all sides, and must be cut before the sap rises in the spring. Also offered $30.00 per m. feet for sound apple tree logs. Delivered to be at our factory, Aurelins Avenue and Clark Street." In 1884, the Company's annual plane production at 30,000, nearly half of which were toy planes for children. It made 16" and 22" planes, called the "Phelps Combination Plane," incorporating a level vial and rule. A **Frank Phelps** of Auburn had a Feb. 9, 1892 plane patent that might relate. (see the Bibliography for the reprint of the **Auburn Tool Co.** 1869 price list.) (see **Brown Tool Co.**, **Cayuga**, **Eagle Tool Co.**, **Easterly & Co.**, **Empire Tool Co.**, **Garard Tool Co.**, and **John Augustus Howland & Co.**) A & B: FF; A1 & B1 **

AUBURN TOOL MANUFACTORY
Probably a label used by the **T. J. M'Master & Co.** of Auburn in an add in *The Albany and Argus City Gazette* on Apr. 28, 1826. No imprint is available.

M. AUGUR
Examples: on two 9 1/2" beech, boxed complex molder with heavy round chamfers, ca. 1820. **UR**

J: AULENBACH
Example: on a 9 1/2" beech molder with heavy round chamfers. Probably from PA, ca. 1820. **UR**

A. AULT/ ADAM AULT
Johann Adam Ault (b. Feb. 17, 1768 in Springfield Twp., York, PA, d. Jul. 10, 1848 in Hanover, PA) was an early Hanover, PA, organ builder. **Jonhann Adam Ault** was the son of **Adam Ault** (1734-1774) and **Susanna Kirkman** (1730-1822). He Married **Mary Beard** (1772-1840) ca. 1736 in York, PA. **Adam Ault** was listed in 1790 in Shrewsbury Twp.; in 1800 & 10 in Heldelberg; 1820, 30 & 40 in Hanover, York Co., PA. **Adam Ault** was a machinist by trade and learned organ building in the factory of **David Tannelberger,** in 1825. He moved to Hanover, PA and built a two-story brick building at the corner of York and Middle streets. He built 25 pipe organs, the first for the Lutheran and Reform Congregational Church, known as the Stone Church in Codorus Twp. He also built parts for **David Tannelberger** in Lititz. In addition to organs, he built a threshing machine for grain harvesting, drilled and bored rifle barrels, made gun stocks, shoe lasts, and wooden planes. Examples: on a wedge-lock tongue & groove pair with open totes; and a gun stocking plane, both of beech. His planes have heavy round to shallow round chamfers indicating production over a period of time, ca. 1820-30.
A, B, C & D ***

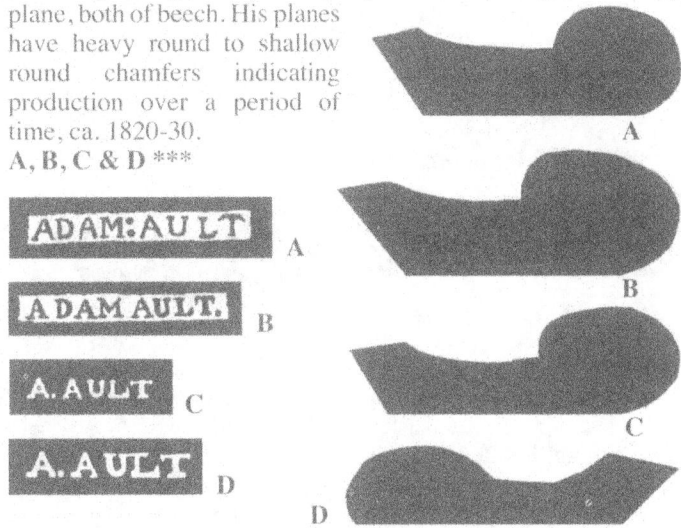

J. AULT
Example: on a 32" cherry jointer, possibly from PA, ca. 1840. **UR**

AUSTIN
Probably **Austin Baldwin** (b. Jun. 11, 1807 in Albany, NY, d. May 28, 1886). This imprint appears as an overstrike of an **A. & E. Baldwin**, N. York plane. In addition, the **Austin** wedge matches that of **A. & E. Baldwin**. The A of **A. & E. Baldwin** was **Austin Baldwin**. In 1841, **Austin** departed from his brother, in New York City and moved to CT to manufacture planes as **Arrowmammett Works**. A number of planes bear both **Arrowmammett Works** and **A. & E. Baldwin** imprints, indicating a continued relationship. In addition to his tool businesses, **Austin Baldwin** was Speaker of the Connecticut

House in 1855 at age 48, and was twice nominated for Governor. In 1872, **Baldwin** was head of the State Steamship Line. Examples: on a molder; and a single boxed bead, all 9 1/2" of beech, ca. 1850. ****

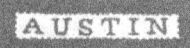 

M. AUSTIN
Example: on a 9 1/2" beech molder with an added wedge locked fence and shallow round chamfers, ca. 19c. **UR**

SAMUEL AUXER
Samuel Auxer (b. Sept. 17, 1834 near Elizabethtown, Lancaster Co., PA, d. Jan. 5, 1909) moved with his family to Lancaster, PA, ca. 1850, where his father, **Jacob Auxer**, was a flour merchant. **Samuel** became a Lancaster planemaker working from 1860-82. Some of his bench planes use the double-wedge patented by **E. W. Carpenter** and there is a self-adjusting screw-arm sash plane using the **E. W. Carpenter** improved arm patent. He was 21 years old when **E. W. Carpenter** died in 1863. The partnership of **Kieffer & Auxer** with **William Kieffer** took over from **Sarah Carpenter** and continued to 1869. On his trade card, He described himself as "formerly of **Kieffer & Auxer**, successor to **E. W. Carpenter**" and said that he made "planes, gauges, yardsticks & etc." From 1869-70, he was part of **Auxer & Remley**. After retiring from tool making, some time prior to 1880, he became active in the used book business with **Samuel H. Zahm** until 1907. **

AUXER & REMLEY
Samuel Auxer and **Reuben J. Remley** (b. 1837 in PA, d. 1898) were Lancaster, PA, planemakers in 1869-70 succeeding **Kieffer & Auxer**. From 1859-63, **Reuben** was a carpenter in Lancaster, PA and served in the Civil War for a short time in 1863 before he was injured. The 1870 census reported that **Auxer & Remley** made planes worth $900, employing two men plus themselves. From 1870-92, **Reuben Remley** was a part of **Remley & Zimmerman** who were stair builders and carpenters. ***

A. AVERY
Asahel Avery (b. May 6, 1765 at Coventry, CT, d. Feb. 1813 at Great Bend, Susquehanna Co., PA) was a cabinetmaker, carpenter and coffin maker in Groton, CT, active in 1799. He moved to Great Bend, NY where he was Justice of the Peace in 1812. His son also **Asahel Avery** (b. Oct. 15, 1793, d. Apr. 17, 1872 at Morris, NY) was a cabinetmaker. Example: on a 9" beech round with a birch wedge and heavy flat chamfers, ca. 1790, making the father the most likely maker. ****

J. AVERY
Possibly **Jedutham Avery** (b. Feb. 15, 1780 in Windham, d. Nov. 1, 1862 in Manchester, CT) who was a cabinetmaker in 1840-60 in Bolton, CT. **Jedutham** Married **Hannah Brown** (1785-1863) on Apr. 21, 1806 in Coventry, CT. Examples: on a dado plane made by **J. Kellogg/ Amherst, MA**; a combination tongue & groove plane by **Fox & Co.**; and a plow plane, all 9 1/2" beech; and a 9 3/8" beech single boxed bead by **Burnham, Fox & Co./ Amherst, MA**, ca. 1840. **A & B:** ****

JOSH. AVERY
Believed to be **Joshua Avery** (b. Mar. 10, 1777 at Groton, CT, d. Apr. 23, 1840 at Arlington, MA) who moved to Arlington, MA, prior to 1807. He was a carpenter and became a Arlington Selectman from 1826-36. Example: on a beech wedge-lock plow with flat chamfers. A large 1 3/4" wide tombstone depth stop is held in place by a wood thumbscrew, ca. 1800. **UR**

J. T. AVERY & Co.
Example: on a 9 3/8" beech panel raiser with solid boxing and slightly rounded chamfers, ca. 1830-40. ****

O. AVERY
Possibly **Oliver Avery** (b. May 8, 1797 in E. Charlemont, MA, d. Nov. 13, 1877 in Groton, NY) who was a cabinetmaker. Example: on a 22" beech joiner with a centered closed tote and heavy round chamfers, ca. 1820-30. **UR**

S: AVERY
Example: on a 10" beech tongue plane with flat chamfers, ca. 1800. **UR**

G. AXE
George Axe (b. 1796 in Sheffield, Yorkshire, England, d. 1884) made planes in Buffalo, NY, from 1855-80. Examples: the A imprint is on two sets of hollows & rounds. The B imprint was struck on the inside of both halves of a sash plane imprinted **M. Lang**, a Buffalo, NY hardware dealer. **A **; B ****

I. AYER
Example: on a 13 3/4" beech handled complex molder. ca. 1850. **UR**

N. AYER/ N. AYERS
Nathaniel (Nathan) Ayers of Boston, MA was listed from 1801-25 as a housewright and in the building trades at Frog Lane, Boston, MA. He was listed in the 1840 Boston City Directory as a housewright. Examples: the A imprint is on a 9 15/16" birch complex molder with wide flat chamfers with an **I. Sleeper** style wedge. The iron is made by **R. Hildik** and branded on the side is **N. SHATTUCK**, ca. 1790. The B imprint is on a fruitwood gunstock plane. ca. 1840. These planes possibly represent two generations or two completely different persons. **A & B:** ****

AYERS & CO.
Ayers & Co. with **B. Ayers** and **Francis Ayers** were hardware dealers in Jacksonville, IL, from 1831-60. In 1860, the name was changed to **Marshall P. Ayers & Co.** and then **Marshall & Agustus Ayers** with **Agustus E. Ayers**. Examples: on a double-coping plane with the **Ohio Tool Co.** style number **45** on the toe; and a single-boxed complex molder. ***

B & CO.
B & Co. probably was a hardware dealer. Example: on a dovetail plane made by **Edgerton**. **UR**

B. T. & CO.
B. T. & Co. probably was a hardware dealer. Example: on the heel of a 16" beech gutter plane. **UR**

J. M. BABBIT
James M. Babbit (b. Oct. 6, 1811 in OH, d. Feb. 21, 1867 in OH) was listed in the 1850 census as a tool cutter and later as a planemaker, working in Turtle Creek, Lebanon, Warren Co., OH. Turtle Creek was the same town in which **H. B. Miller** and **P. Probasco** had worked earlier. He produced 2,600 planes with 5 hands and power provided by one horse probably on a tread mill. He was also listed as a planemaker in an 1856 Mason, OH, directory. Mason is just north of Cincinnati and the Kentucky state line and close to Louisville, KY, where **James** apparently also operated. **

BABCOCK BROTHERS
Babcock Brothers consisted of three brothers, **Charles Babcock** (b. dec.10, 1812 in Utica, NY, d. Jul. 22, 1894 in Evansville, OH); **Elisha Spurr Babcock** (b. Aug 10, 1814 in Utica, NY, d. Apr. 2, 1890 in San Diego, CA; and **Henry Babcock** (b. Jul.20, 1822 in Troy, NY, d. Sep. 10, 1879 in Evansville, IN) who operated an Evansville, IN, hardware, grocery, saddlery, and crockery business from 1837-63. **Henry Babcock** served as a Lt. in the Civil War with the 10th. Indiana Cavalry Reg. from Jan. 8,1864 to Aug. 31, 1865. **Charles Babcock** and **Henry Babcock** appear as hardware dealers and woodworkers in the 1870-71 directory. Example: on a 9 1/2" double-boxed, screw-arm adjustable sash plane with shallow round chamfers. **

J. R. BACHELDER
J. R. Bachelder (b. Sept. 13, 1826 in Danville, VT) was a North Danville, VT, planemaker. **Bachelder** worked with his father **Daniel B. Bachelder** (1804-1874) a carpenter. In 1850, he operated a carriage and furniture shop in Peacham, VT. In 1863, he was recorded as selling a shop and sawmill with tools in North Danville, VT, and was employed by **E. & T. Fairbanks Co.** as an ornamental sign painter. In 1887, he was listed as retired. Example: on a 16" beech jack with closed tote. ***

L. BACHELDOR
Segago (ME). Examples: on an 8 1/2" beech smoother made by

J. Bradford/ Portland, ME.; and on a 9 7/8" fruitwood plow plane with a heart shaped depth stop iron. **UR**

I. BACHMAN
John Bachman II (b. Mar. 20, 1746 in Switzerland, d. Apr. 20, 1829) trained as an "Ebeniste" in Bern, Switzerland and came to America with his father, in 1766, and settled in Lancaster, Co., PA. He made clock cases for **Christian and Daniel Forrer** who were active from 1754-74, and **John Heintzelman** of Manhem, Lancaster, active from 1785-1803. **John Bachman II** was considered to be the maker of certain well-regarded furniture at Winterthur Museum, DE, and The Museum of Fine Arts, Boston, MA. There were four other cabinetmakers and clock-case makers in the family who worked in the PA area including: **John Bachman** (b. Jan. 20, 1775, d. Apr. 10, 1849) who made clock cases for **Joseph Bowman** of Strasburg, PA, active from 1820-50 and **Martin Shreiner** of Lancaster, active from 1790-1830: **Jacob Bachman** (b. Sept. 24, 1798, d. Nov. 6, 1869) who made clock cases for **Anthony Baldwin** of Lampeter Square, active from 1810-1840. Examples: on a 9" unhandled, wedge-locked plow; a 10" birch astragal; a 10" maple thumb plane; and a 9 15/16" beech complex molder, all planes have flat chamfers, probably from PA, ca. 1800. ****

AB, BACON
Abner Bacon (b. Aug.15, 1768 in Pomfret, Windham Co., CT, d. May 16, 1864 in Putney, Windham Co., VT) was admitted on April 19, 1790 as a member of the Providence Association of Mechanics and Manufacturers, and was listed as a Joiner Toolmaker. **Abner** was the son of **Nehemiah Bacon** (1736-1832). His older brother **Henry Bacon** (1757-1838) was a chairmaker and preceded **Abner** to Providence, RI. Examples: on a narrow nosing plane; a size 3/4 round; and a skewed rabbit with an integral fence, all 10" birch with a relieved wedge, flat chamfers, and fluting, found in the RI and CT area. Also reported is an overstamp on a **Jo, Fuller/ In/ Providence** molder. The comma after the initials is similar to that used by **Jo, Fuller**, from southeastern New England, ca.1780. *****

I. BACON
Examples: on a 9 3/8" table plane; and a large 9 1/2" hollow, both beech with flat chamfers, ca. 1800. **UR**

R. BACON
Rufus Bacon, Sr. (b. Nov. 12, 1758 in Spencer, MA, d. Sep. 23, 1820 in Suttin, MA) was the son of **Daniel Bacon**. Rufus was called a house joiner in 1787 & 91 land deeds and a mechanic in a May 5, 1813 deed. His probate inventory, dated Oct. 21, 1820 includes: "1 Chest of Carpenters tools, benches & shop tools - 15.00." **Rufus** had a son also named **Rufus Bacon, Jr.** (b. Mar. 24, 1794 in Sutton, Worcester Co., MA, d. Jan. 8, 1846 in Sutton). His probate inventory, dated Mar. 3, 1846, lists work benches, saws, planes, chisels, and every other imaginable shop tool. Two entries may relate to plane making: "1 lot old molding tools & sash clamps" and the other "Lumber for Plane woods Chisel handles". On Apr. 11, 1846, when his tools and lumber were sold at public auction, with the following: "Irons & Plane Woods - $3.30" and "20 Set of Moulding tools - $2.60".

Rufus Bacon Sr. lived in Spencer, Charlton, and Sutton, MA, a cluster of towns in Worcester Co. about 45 miles west of Boston and about 16 miles south of Rutland, MA where both **Jonathan Tower** and **Uriah Clapp** lived and worked. Examples: on 10" molding planes with a slight relief on the wedge; an 8" coffin smoother with a round-top iron and wedge; a 12 1/2" rabbet; and a 13 1/2" tongue plane with a pegged-offset open tote; and a 22 3/4"x 2 3/4" jointer plane with a 7/8" round strike and a forward sloping handle similar to jointer handles made by **Jonathan Tower** and **Uriah Clapp** (a unique feature to this group of planemakers). All birch (one beech) with heavy flat chamfers. ca. 1760. Two **R. Bacon** planes that were in a group of five found in VT have **E. Eddy** written in script on the toe. This is possibly **Edmund Eddy** (b. 1749 in Oxford, MA) who lived in Charlton, or his son also named **Edmund Eddy** (b. 1776 in Charlton) who moved to VT after 1800. In 1820, **Edmund Eddy Jr.** was listed as a carriage maker in Walden, VT. Also reported is a ca. 1820-30, 24" birch jointer with a centered tote and heavy round chamfers, in the collection of Old Sturbridge Village. This jointer has an owner's imprint **Stedman** on the toe. **William Stedman**, a carpenter, lived in Oxford, MA in the 1840's. Oxford borders on both Charlton and Sutton. ****

T. B/ T. BADGER
Example: on a 9 1/2" wide complex molder, ca. 1800. **UR**

J. BAGLEY
Examples: on several 9 1/2" molders of birch and beech with narrow flat chamfers, ca. 1795-1805. ****

J. BAILEY
There are two possibilities for this imprint: **Jonathan Bailey** (b. Aug. 4, 1791), a cabinetmaker from Haverhill, MA, who was in Cincinnati, OH, in 1817; and **John Bailey** (b. Sept. 9, 1741, d. 1826) a cabinetmaker in Rowley, MA. Examples: on a 12" maple halving plane; a 9 1/2" side bead; and a 13 1/2" round, all beech with open pegged totes and small flat chamfers, ca. 1800. ****

JOSEPH BAILEY
Joseph Bailey was listed in 1850, in Newark, NJ, as a carpenter tool manufacturer working for and living with **P. Quigley**. **No imprint has been reported**.

LEONARD BAILEY
Leonard Bailey (b. May 8, 1825 in Hollis, NH, d. Feb. 5, 1905 in New York City) of Boston, MA, was primarily a metal planemaker with working dates from 1858-64. In 1848, he was a cabinetmaker in Ipswich, MA, and from 1855-60 in Winchester, MA. He was at 73 Haverhill, Boston, MA, from 1861-67, as **Bailey L. & Co.**; and from 1868-69, as **Bailey, Chaney & Co.** with **Jacob Chaney**. Some of his earliest plane patent features were incorporated into the bodies of conventional wooden planes. **Bailey** was issued Patent No. 20,615 on June 22, 1858 and Patent No. 21,311 on Aug. 31, 1858 that made provision for a longitudinal cutter adjustment mechanism. **Bailey's** 2nd and 3rd patents are referred to in this imprint along with the **H. H. Cleveland** name. (see *Patented Transitional & Metallic Planes in America-Vol. II*, p. 21, by Roger K. Smith)

A, A1 & B ****

M. BAILEY
Examples: the A imprint is on a small bead; and a dado. The B imprint is on a handled grooving plane, all are 9 1/2" beech with round chamfers, ca. 1820. **UR**

R. C. BAILEY
Roswell C. Bailey (b. Apr. 27, 1814 in Shoreham, NY, d. Oct. 27, 1884 in Lockport, NY) was listed as a planemaker in Ogdensburg, NY, in the 1850 NY State business directory. The 1850 Federal census listed a **Roswell C. Bailey** as a millwright working in Oswegatchie, St. Lawrence Co., NY, the same county in which Ogdensburg is located. **Bailey's** imprint with **OGDENSBURGH** used the old spelling of the town. The **H** was dropped in 1868, when Ogdensburg became a city.

A, A1, A2 & B ****

T. BAILEY
Example: on a 9 3/8" beech square rabbet with small flat chamfers, ca. 1810. **UR**

BAILEY & RICHARDSON
Stephen A. Bailey (b. 1818 in NY) and **William Richardson** (b. 1846, d. Jun. 4, 1890 in St. Louis) were St. Louis, MO, hardware dealers from 1866-86. Planes with the **608 MARKET ST/ ST. LOUIS MO** address were probably imprinted during 1867-82, when they occupied that address. They moved to 844 Market St. in 1883 and were last listed in 1886. Examples: the B imprint is on a 1 1/2" **Ohio Tool Co.** skew rabbet. Also reported is an ink stamp on a number **47 Ohio Tool Co.** 7/8" dado.

BAILEY & RICHARDSON
DEALERS IN
HARDWARE
NO. 608 MARKET ST.
SAINT LOUIS, MO. (****)

A, B, B1 & B2 ***

D. BAIRD
Example: on a 9 1/4" tiger maple plow with wedge-lock arms, a brass depth stop, a screw attached skate, and shallow round chamfers, ca. 1830. **UR**

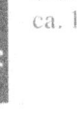

F BAKER
Example: on a 9 15/16" round with flat chamfers, ca. 1800. **UR**

J. N. BAKER
Jacob N. Baker (b. 1791 in PA, d. Jan. 1870 in N. Wales, Montgomery Co., PA) was listed in the 1850-60 census in Hatfield, Montgomery Co. PA. Example: on a 10" beech skew rabbet with two

intermittent boxing strips and round chamfers, ca. 1820. **UR**

BAKER & GAMWELL

Isaac Baker (b. 1821 in MA) & **Marcus Gamwell** (b. 1827 in MA) partnership in Pittsfield (MA) completes the triangle, since we already have **Webb & Baker** and **Webb & Gamwell**. The **BAKER** portion of the imprint is the same as the **BAKER** in **Webb & Baker**, who may have preceded **Baker & Gamwell**.

Examples: on a 7 1/2" smoother; and a boxed moving filletster with one nicker and a brass depth stop, both beech, ca. 1850. ***

A. A. BALCH

Example: on a 16 1/2" beech jack plane, with a closed centered tote and shallow round chamfers, ca. 1830-40. UR

A. & E. BALDWIN

New York City planemakers **Austin Baldwin** (b. June 11, 1807 in Albany, NY, d. May 28, 1886) and his half brother, **Elbridge Gerry Baldwin** (b. 1810 in Albany, NY, d. Sept. 1, 1870 in New York City) made planes under this name from 1830-1841. **Austin** had studied law from 1822-28, was a teacher and wrote a primary arithmetic text. The firm was the successor to **E. Baldwin**. **Enos Baldwin** was their father. In 1836, **Austin Baldwin** moved to Middletown, CT, where he purchased the land and business of the **Arrowmammett Manufacturing Co.** and founded the **Baldwin Tool Co. Austin** was active in the early opposition to the use of prison labor, a sore point for many years between those planemakers who used prison contract labor and those who did not. The 1850 industrial census listed **Austin Baldwin** as a plane manufacturer with 30 hands producing 40,000 planes worth $25,000. **Eldridge Baldwin** continued as a plane maker under the **A & E Baldwin** imprint until at least 1841 and had a tool store until 1852, when he was listed as a clerk in the Post Office. **Elbridge** was also a member of the NY legislature for two years. In 1855, Austin was speaker of the CT House of Representatives. The A & C imprints have been reported on some examples overprinted by an **Arrowmammett Works** imprint B.

A, B, C & D: FF; D1 & D2 **

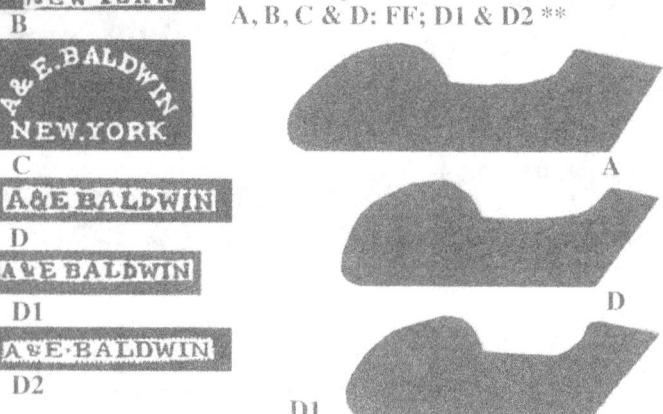

E. BALDWIN

Enos Baldwin (b. June 28, 1783 in Cavendish, VT, d. 1829 in New York City) was the father of **Austin Baldwin** and **Eldridge Gerry Baldwin**, to whom he taught plane making and who succeeded him as **A. & E. Baldwin** in 1830. **Enos** made planes starting in 1807 in Albany, NY; in Newburgh, NY, in 1815; and in New York City from 1817-29. An advertisement in *The Statesman*, published on Apr. 23, 1824 in New York City, illustrated a fore plane and a molder by "ENOS BALDWIN, Planemaker, No. 90 Elizabeth Street, New York" and offered a general assortment of carpenter's, joiner's, cooper's, cabinet and coachmaker's planes. **Enos Baldwin** apprenticed **Samuel Cumings** and **Jonas R. Gale**. **Elbridge Baldwin** continued under the name **E. Baldwin** 1842-50 after **A. & E. Baldwin** ceased operations in 1841, using the same E. BALDWIN stamp as his father.

A1 & B: FF; A2 *; A ***

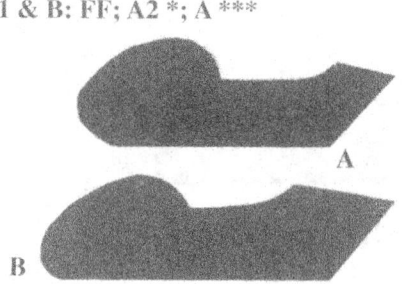

I. BALDWIN / IOHN BALDWIN

John Baldwin (b. 1803 in DE) was listed as a cabinetmaker in Brandywine Hundred, DE, in 1825. Example: the A imprint is on a 10" birch skew rabbet with flat chamfers. ca. 1790. The B imprint IOHN BALDWIN is on a 9 1/2" beech molder with a tall wedge, ca. 1840.

The B imprint is not available.

A: UR

J. BALDWIN J

The ending **J** could be for Junior. Example: on a complex molder and as an owner imprint on a **T. J. McMasters, Auburn, NY** complex molder. UR

BALDWIN PLANE WORKS

Example: on a handled plow of apple body, arms and nuts, with beech fence and wedge. On the heel it is marked **No. 190** which, along with the imprint, suggests a factory operation. There is no information as to how it fits into the other **Baldwin** operations. ****

BALDWIN TOOL CO.

The **Baldwin Tool Co.** was founded in Middletown, CT, in 1836 by **Austin Baldwin**, after leaving New York City. The company manufactured planes from 1836-59. The factory was located on the Arrowmammett River and was called the **Arrowmammett Works**. In 1850, the company employed 30 hands and produced 40,000 planes worth $25,000. **Austin Baldwin** resigned as president in 1857 and on June 28, 1859, he sold his interest to **Cox & Wright** and returned to New York City where he founded the **Baldwin European Express Co.** dealing in foreign exchange and express. The **Baldwin Tool Co.** became a joint stock corporation. The company was listed in 1860, as making 60,000 planes and 30,000 plane irons. The **Globe Manufacturing Co.** who continued to make plane irons only eventually bought it out. **No imprint has been reported.**

W+ BALFOUR
Example: on a 9 3/4" halving plane with flat chamfers, ca. 1790. **UR**

W. BALIS
Example: on a 9 1/4" beech small tongue plane with flat chamfers, ca. 1800. **UR**

GEORGE BALL
Longworth's New York City Directory for 1827, lists **George Ball** as a planemaker at 109 Mercer St., New York City. He was listed in the 1842-60 directories as a planemaker "colored". No imprint has been reported.

N. BALL
Example: on a 10 1/4" apple small round with narrow flat chamfers, ca. 1800. **UR**

BALL & SHARLAND
Examples: on a 9 1/4" beech size **2 & 4** hollows with small round chamfers. **UR**

L. BALLARD
Example: on a 9 1/8" beech stick & rebate sash plane with flat chamfers, ca. 1800. **UR**

FRANKLIN BALLARD
Franklin Ballard was listed as a planemaker in Buckland, MA, in 1848. In 1849, he was listed in the New England Mercantile Union Business Directory as a plane manufacturer. **No imprint has been reported**.

ION. BALLOU
Jonathan Ballou (b. Nov. 10, 1723 in Lincoln, RI, d. Oct. 2, 1770 in Providence, RI) was one of the earliest planemakers in Providence, RI, active from 1751-69. He married **Elizabeth West** on April 3, 1768, but had no children. He was admitted as a freeman in Providence, in 1751. In a 1752 land transfer, he was referred to as a shop joiner. In 1757, he signed a declaration to participate in the French and Indian War. **William Donnison**, a block maker, owned **Ballou's** shop near the west end of the great bridge over the Providence River. **Ballou** also sharpened scissors, shears and razors. He was 1/8 owner in a paper mill with **John Waterman** and **Jonathan Olney**. Ballou died in 1770, leaving a modest estate that included his interest in the paper mill and "a large number of tools of all kinds, new and old with some stock". His widow advertised for sale, a month after his death, "a parcel of carpenters' and joiners' tools and sundry other things". His planes are generally 10" birch with molded shoulders, an unrelieved wedge with a small round finial, and heavy flat chamfers. Example: on a birch panel raiser with an offset tote, round-top wedge & iron, imprinted **ROBERT MOORE**, and heavy flat chamfers. ****

S. BALLOU
Maturin Smith Ballou (b. Aug. 16, 1830 in Smithfield, Providence, RI, d. Aug. 23, 1913 in Smithfield) "learned the trade of toolmaker with **Ezekiel Smith** and worked at that occupation in Smithfield (RI) and vicinity." Examples: on a 13 1/2" skew jack plane, altered from a panel raiser, with a centered tote; and a filletster plane, ca. 1850.
A, B & C *****

A

B

C

BALTIMORE PLANE CO.
James A. Carlin and **David C. Fulton** were hardware dealers in Baltimore, MD, ca. 1890. Examples: the A imprint is on a 22" beech jointer with closed tote. The B imprint is on a jointer with number **21** on the toe, the **Ohio Tool Co.** style number for a fore plane.
A & B ****

A   B

I. BANCKER
Example: on a 9 1/2" beech dado with a dovetailed wood depth stop and flat chamfers, ca. 1800. **UR**

D. BANCROFT
Daniel Bancroft (will Probated Jul 7, 1818, at Salem, MA) was listed as housewright and was an assistant to **Samuel McIntire** Example: on a 9 3/8" beech complex molder with molded shoulder and heavy flat chamfers, ca. 1780. *****

G. P. BANCROFT
Gerard Pratt Bancroft (b. Oct. 26, 1792 in Granville, MA, d. Jan. 18, 1883 in Granville, OH) was the great grandson of the founder of Granville, MA. Migrants from Granville, MA, and Granby, CT founded Granville, Licking Co., OH (east of Columbus). In 1805, **G. P. Bancroft** was a planemaker, house builder, cabinetmaker, and a coffin maker. **Bancroft's** brother-in-law,

A

Knowles Linnel, was a clock maker for whom **Bancroft** made cases, ca. 1820. **A & B** ****

 B

I. BANCROFT
Example: on a single 9 1/4" beech round with heavy round chamfers, ca. 1820-30. **UR**

J. H. BANNISTER
Example: on a pair of 9 1/2" of size **4** hollow & round, ca. 19c. **UR**

J. H. BAPTIS
John H. Baptis was a New York City planemaker. From 1874-88, he was a gold pan manufacturer in San Francisco, CA. Examples: on a narrow size **4** round; a boxed complex molder; and a filletster, all 9 1/2" beech with round chamfers, ca. 1820-30. ****

JOHN BARBER
John Barber was a planemaker who worked for **E.W. Carpenter** in 1829-30. Example: on a 25 1/2" beech jointer. ****

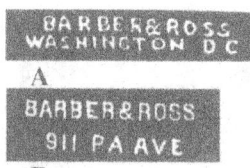

BARBER & ROSS

Barber & Ross with **Benjamin Barber** (b. 1818 in NJ) was a hardware dealer, located at 911 PA Ave., Washington, DC, who made or imprinted wooden planes, ca. 1875. Example: on a 9 1/2" skew rabbet. ****

EDWARD BARD
Edward Bard was listed as a Philadelphia, PA, planemaker active from 1850-59. The names **Conrad Bard & Son** and **Edwin M. Bard** were listed in relationship to **Edward's** name. **No imprint has been reported.**

G. S. BARDWELL (possibly **C. S. BARDWELL**)
Example: on an 8 7/8" beech plow with round-toped arms, wood thumbscrews, a wood depth stop, and heavy round chamfers, ca. 1810-20. **UR**

F+ BARINGER
Molding planes are typically 9 1/2" beech with shallow round chamfers. Examples: on molding planes; a crown molder; and a door check plane, probably from eastern PA, ca. 1810-30. **UR**

J. L. BARKER
Example: on a 9 1/2" beech square rabbet with a double-iron, ca. 1840-50. **UR**

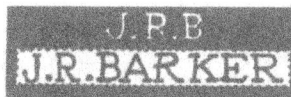

J. R. B/ J. R. BARKER
Example: on a 9 1/2" beech fixed sash with two irons & wedges and shallow round chamfers, ca. 1840-50. **UR**

BARKER & BALDWIN
Barker & Baldwin with **Lovewell H. Baldwin** (b. ca. 1830, in NY) were Auburn, NY, hardware merchants from 1850-57 and may have been the successors to **Watrous & Osborne**. ****

BARKER & ILLSLEY
Barker & Illsley was a hardware dealer at 273 & 275 State St. (possibly Chicago, IL) on a plow plane made by **Ohio Tool Co.** ****

BARKLEY/ JNO. M. BARKLEY
On May 21, 1805, **Jonathan M. Barkley** (b. 1792), at age 13, was apprenticed to **William Vance** "plain maker" of Baltimore, MD. When **Jonathan** was a journeyman, he took on two apprentices: **Richard Taylor**, age 14, on July 26, 1815 and **John Allen**, age 12, on Apr. 1, 1816. **Jonathan** was part of **Barkley & Hughes** with **William P. Hughes** from Feb. 14, 1815 until May 30, 1815. He may have been the **John Barclay** listed in the Pittsburgh City directory in 1815. **John M. Barkley** had returned to Baltimore where he was listed as a planemaker from 1816-24. In the 1827 directory he was listed as **Barclay**. Example: on an imprint with an overstamp **W. VANCE**.
B & C **; **A** ***

 A

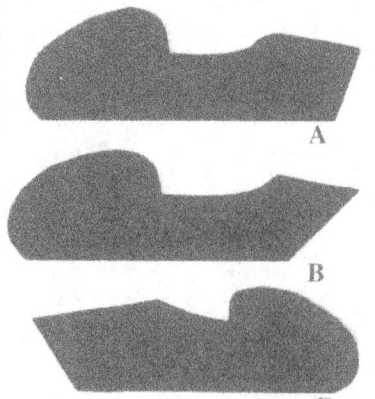

BARKLEY & HUGHES
Jonathan M. Barkley and **William P. Hughes** were planemakers who advertised on Feb. 14, 1815, that they were taking over the plane making business of **Owings & Roy** at 3 Light St., Baltimore, MD. 3 1/2 months after the first ad, on May 30, 1815, **Barkley & Hughes** announced their partnership was dissolved and that **John M. Barkley** would carry on at the 3 Light St. address. ***

ALVIN BARLOW
Alvin Barlow was listed, from 1822-29, as a planemaker & Stockmaker in Paris, Bourbon Co., KY. **No imprint has been reported.**

T. BARLOW
Example: on a 9 1/2" beech molder with a relieved wedge, ca. 1810. **No imprint is available.**

A. BARNARD
Examples: on three molders; a beech bead; a birch skew rabbet; and a birch hollow & round, all 9" with round chamfers. Also on a smoother; a 15 1/2" jack; and a 26 1/8" jointer with a closed tote, wood strike, a single iron and round chamfers imprinted with the date **1835**. The style, wedge and boxing are similar to that of **A. Hathaway**, ca. 1815-35.   A ***: B *****

E. BARNARD
Example: on a 9 1/4" beech hollow with narrow flat chamfers, found in northern VA, ca. 1800. **UR**

J. BARNARD
Julius Barnard (b. Jul. 18, 1769 in Northampton, MA, still living in 1821). From 1783-90, he was apprenticed to **Eliphant Chapin**. He then went to New York City for a short period of time. In 1792-1796, he was at Lickingwater (later South) St. then in the Tontine Building on Bridge St. Northampton, MA. On Dec. 5, 1792, he advertised in the Northampton, MA, *Hampshire Gazette* that "he made and had for sale, a variety of items including bench planes and molding tools". In 1796, he advertised for two apprentices. By June 1801, **Barnard** was working in Hanover, NH, in a shop near Dartmouth College. On Sep. 23, 1801, **Barnard** bought a tract of land with buildings near the courthouse common in Windsor, VT. From 1802-05, he advertised as a cabinetmaker in Windsor. In 1806, **Barnard** was among the founders of the Windsor Mechanics' Institute. In 1807, **Julius Barnard** was a part of **Barnard & Norton** with **Rufus Norton** (1781-1818). On Mar. 14, 1809, **Barnard** sold his shop and house in Windsor, dissolved his partnership with **Rufus Norton** and moved in Sep. to Montreal, Canada. As a result of the War of 1812 with Great Britain, he was forced from Canada and relocated to Pittsfield, MA. He opened a furniture shop near the Pittsfield Hotel in the center of town and remained in Pittsfield until 1821. Examples: on a 10" beech bead with round chamfers; and a 10" birch plow with square arms, thumbscrews, a relieved wedge and round chamfers, ca. 1790-1810. **UR**

A. BARNES
Amory Barnes (b. Feb. 8, 1806 in Cambridge, MA, d. Oct. 28, 1893) was the son of **Russell Barnes**, from whom he learned plane making. In 1840, He was listed as engaged in manufacturing in Orange, MA. In 1850, He was listed in Cumberland, Providence, RI.; from 1860-80 in Wrentham, MA engaged in Agriculture; in 1890, as a toolmaker in Wrentham. Example: on a 16 3/8"x 5 1/2" beech crown molder with two throats, irons and wedges and a centered tote. A, A1, B, B1 & C ****

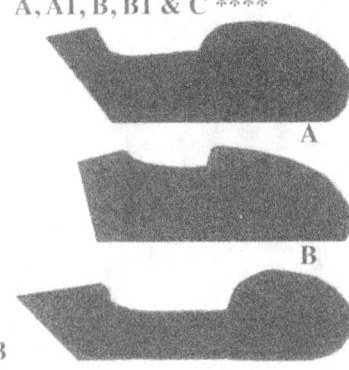

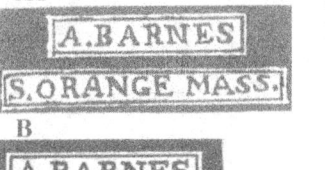

I. BARNES
Example: on a 9 3/8" beech halving plane with heavy round chamfers, ca. 1820. **UR**

J. BARNES
Example: on an 8 3/4" beech Yankee slide-arm plow with thumbscrew and shallow large round chamfers, ca. 1830. **UR**

L. BARNES
Example: on a 22" birch jointer with a centered tote, ca. 1840. **UR**

LL. BARNES
Example: on a 9 1/2" beech, full-boxed bead, ca. 1850. **UR**

P. BARNES
Examples: on a beech plow with birch fence and riveted skate; and a complex molder. **No imprint is available.**

R. BARNES
Russell Barnes (b. 1774 in Cambridge, MA, d. Aug. 11, 1853, age 79, in Orange, MA) was the father of **Amory Barnes**. He was listed as plainmaker in Orange town records and was listed in the 1840 census for Orange as being engaged in manufacturing. **Russell's** wife had the memorable name of Submit. An inventory of tools and shop equipment for **Russell Barnes,** dated Nov. 6, 1852 is as follows:

```
"1 wheel barrow  50/ 1 grind stone 1 00      1 50
 1 stove in shop  75/ 1 tool chest  1 50     2 25
 2 sets bench planes with irons              4.00
 2 jack planes  80/ 1 bench vice  2 00       2 80
 2 try squares  50/ 1 bitstock & bitts  1 25 1 75
 2 hand saws  1 25/ 2 fine saws  50          1 75
 2 steel squares  1 00/ 2 key hole saws  50  1 50
 4 aric (?)  1 50/ 1 hay hook  20            1 70
 1 adze  50/ 1 wood screw  75                1 25
 chisels, gouges, files, rasps in racks      2.25
 3 shaves                                      50
 1 set bench planes                          1 37
 27 bead planes                              2 40
 5 plows                                     4 33
 18 gages                                    1 33
 2 sets match planes                         2 00
 1 rabbit plane                                50
 1 set bench planes                          1 25
 lot of plane wood                             75
 1 clock in shop                             1 00
 2 short jointers/ 1 long do/ 2 jack planes/
 5 smooth planes woods                       2 50
 beech timber on hand                        1 50
 1 Note: Amory Barnes (Russell's Son)       19 96"
```

Comment: "It appears that there was work in progress and at least two sets of working tools". Some examples of his planes are dated: a smoother is dated **1823**; a 9 1/4" beech large cove is dated **1825**; and a 28" beech jointer is dated **1842**. An impressive example of his work is illustrated on p. 187 of **Sellen's Woodworking Planes**, a 15 3/4" cornice plane with two wedges & irons. There are at least two examples of a combination tongue & groove plane similar to those patented by **P. A. Gladwin** in 1857, four years after **Barnes'** death in 1853.
A1*; A, A2, B, B1 & B2 *****

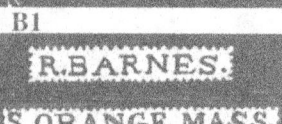

SHERMAN BARNES
Sherman Barnes was listed as a planemaker from New Haven, CT, active ca. 1840. Example: on a 9 1/2"x 7/8" boxed bead by **Kennedy & Co.** Hartford. ****

T. P. BARNES
T. P. Barnes probably was a hardware dealer located at 28 Dock Sq., Boston. Example: on an 8" smoother made by **W. G. Lamb**. No operating dates are known. ****

T. BARNET
Example: on a 9 7/16" beech complex molder with shallow round chamfers, ca. 1830. UR

BARNEY BROTHERS
Barney Brothers was a hardware dealer in Mobile, AL. Example: on a match plane made by **D. Colton** and **B. Sheneman** with the imprint: ****

```
       MADE FOR
    BARNY BROTHERS
     MOBILE ALA.
```

M. B/ M. BARNITZ
Example: on a 9 1/4" beech complex molder with flat chamfers, possibly from PA, ca. 1800.
A & B: UR

H. BARNS
H. Barnes was listed in the Goshen, MA, directory. Examples: on a 16" beech scrub plane with a closed centered tote and large round chamfers; and an 8 3/4" beech Yankee plow, ca. 1820. UR

L. BARNS
L. Barns of Portsmouth, NH was listed as a chairmaker, working 1810-20. Example: on a 22" birch jointer. No imprint is available.

R. H. BARNUM
R. H. Barnum was a Warren, OH, hardware dealer. Example: on a wide hollow with an **Ohio Tool Co.** style number on the toe. ****

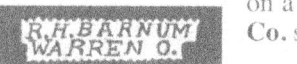

A. BARR
Example: on a 9 7/8"x 1" beech hollow with heavy flat chamfers, ca. 1800. UR

M. BARR & CO.
Matthew Barr was a Nashua, NH, hardware dealer whose
planes may have been supplied by

C. Warren of Nashua, NH. Examples:
on rosewood smoothing planes,
ca. 1865. ****

J. N. S. BARRELL
J. N. S. Barrell was listed in Norwell, Plymouth Co., MA, ca. 1820. Examples: on an 8 7/8" shipwright round; a 9 13/16" large round; a 10" ship rabbet; and a 10" circular compass ship rabbet, all beech with a double-iron and round chamfers. The last three with **J.N.S.** initials incised on the side, all in the tool collection at Old Sturbridge Village. **No imprint is available.**

J. BARRINGER
Example: on a 9" beech, narrow round with size **2** stamped
on the heel and with tight
round chamfers,
ca. 1810-20. **UR**

L. M. BARROWS
Example: on a 9" slightly compassed smoother. The location
VASS was Vasselborough, ME, on the

east bank of the Kennebec River, 14 miles
northeast of Augusta, with a population
of 3,000 in 1850. *****

H. BARRUS & CO.
H. Barrus & Co. was located in Goshen, MA, with working dates from 1854-59. It was comprised of **Hiram Barrus** (b. Jul 3, 1823 in Hampshire Co., MA, d. Mar. 21, 1883 in Goshen, MA), **Theron Levi Barrus** (b. Sep., 1, 1829 in Goshen, MA, d. Dec. 30, 1905 in Williamsburg, MA) and **Lorin Barrus**
(b. May 31, 1825 Goshen, MA,
d. Jan. 20, 1899 Goshen), who were
sons of **Levi Barrus** (b. 1795,
d. 1877). Hiram was a principal in the
Union Tool Co. from 1852-54.
A & A1.***; A2 *****

L. BARRUS
Nathan L. Barrus (b. Dec. 13, 1810 in Warren, RI, d. Nov. 24, 1879 in Warren, RI) was apprenticed to **E. Smith** in Rhoboth, MA, ca. 1828. On Nov. 1, 1836, **Nathan L. Barrus** entered partnership with **Leonard B. Bigelow** which lasted until Dec. 21, 1836, when a fire terminated the business. (see **Bigelow & Barrus**). Nathan was listed in Warren, RI, as a planemaker in 1845. In 1846, Nathan's sister married **Leonard B. Bigelow**, making him Nathan's brother-in-law. In 1850, Nathan was listed as a housewright; by 1870, a conductor; in 1876, a railroad agent; and in 1879, a street commissioner. ***
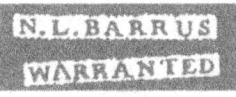

WILLIAM A. BARRUS
William A. Barrus was a Cummington, MA, planemaker working in 1877. He was the son of **Hiram Barrus**. In 1879, a **Willie Barrus** was employed by **Jacob Lovell**, his uncle who married **Hiram Barrus's** sister. (see **H. Barrus & Co.**)
No imprint has been reported.

S. S. BARRY
Samuel S. Barry was a planemaker in New York City from
1827-41, a hardware dealer with various

partners, **Kennedy, Barry & Way**;
Barry & Way; and **Barry, Way & Sherman** between 1841-47, and again a

planemaker from 1848-51. **A & B ***

T. BARRY
Example: on a 9 11/16"x 1/2" beech hollow with heavy flat chamfers, ca. 1800. **UR**

BARRY/ BARRY & CO.
Samuel Barry was listed as a planemaker in the 1817-18, 1830-31, and 1833 Philadelphia directories. The **BARRY** imprint B
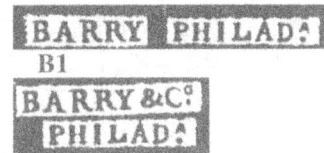
has a straight edge after the
Y, suggesting that it was cut
down from the
BARRY & CO. imprint A.
A, B & B1 ***

BARRY & WAY
A partnership composed of **Samuel S. Barry** and **William
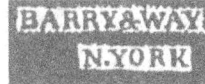
Way**, hardware dealers in New York City
from 1842-47. It was the successor to
Kennedy, Barry & Way and predecessor
to **Barry, Way & Sherman**. **FF**

BARRY, WAY & SHERMAN
A partnership composed of **Samuel S. Barry**, **William Way** and **Byron Sherman**, hardware dealers in New York City in 1847 and successor to **Barry & Way**.
No imprint has been reported.

I.B/ I. Barter
Example: on a 9 1/2"x 2 2/7" beech complex molder,
ca. 19c. **UR**
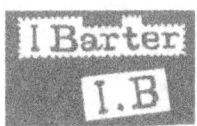

A. C. BARTLETT./ PRES'T
A. C. BARTLETT'S/ OHIO PLANES
These are imprints used by the **Sandusky Tool Co.** on planes

manufactured for **Hibbard, Spencer, Bartlett & Co.**, a
large Chicago hardware firm,

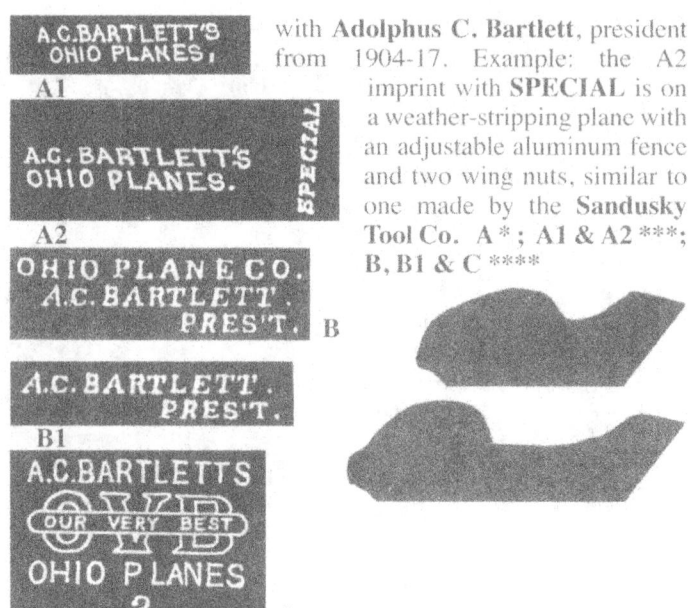

with **Adolphus C. Bartlett**, president from 1904-17. Example: the A2 imprint with **SPECIAL** is on a weather-stripping plane with an adjustable aluminum fence and two wing nuts, similar to one made by the **Sandusky Tool Co.** A *; A1 & A2 ***; B, B1 & C ****

C. BARTLETT
Examples: on a 9 1/2" dado; a 9 3/8" side bead; a jack; a 14 1/2" panel raiser; and a 22 1/2" jointer, all of beech with round chamfers. Of interest is a clapboard gauge with this imprint, beech with round chamfers, ca. 1810-20. ****

S. B. BARTLETT
Samuel B. Bartlett (b. 1828 in England) was listed in the 1850-70 census as a toolmaker in Watertown, NY. In 1880, he was listed as a pattern maker. Examples: on a combination hollow & round with two irons; a combination 5/16" tongue & groove plane; a 7 1/2" beech handled block plane; and a "T" rabbet. ****

Z. L. BARTLETT
This imprint with **MADE BY** has been reported from a rosewood smoother with a closed tote and a **Stanley** cutter & lever cap. **No imprint is available.**

JOHN BARTLEY
John Bartley was a Philadelphia, PA, planemaker, at 97 Duke St. in 1793. **No imprint has been reported.**

D. R. BARTON/ D. R. BARTON & CO.
D. R. Barton was a major Rochester, NY, edge tool and plane manufacturing company founded in 1832 by **David R. Barton** (b. July 4, 1805 in Hudson River valley, NY, d. April 26, 1875 in Rochester, NY). He first arrived in Rochester in 1826, to learn the trade of nail making from blacksmith **Thomas Morgan**. In the same shop as **Henry W. Stager**, making edge tools. **D. R. Barton** went thru a number of partnerships after Morgan died in Nov. 1828, first as **Barton & Stager**, in 1831-32, with **Henry W. Stager**; then **Barton & Babcock**, from 1833-34, with **John H. Babcock**; **Barton & Banker**, in 1836, with **Hiram Banker** at 3 Buffalo St.; then **Barton, Banker & Avery**, in 1836-37, with the addition of **Carlton Avery**; **Barton & Guild**, in 1837 with **C. Guild** that ended with a fire in Nov. 1837; followed by a short period, in 1837, on his own as **D. R. Barton** at a new address on Front St.; then **Barton & Smith**, in 1841-42 with **William P. Smith** or **Albert H. Smith**; and finally **Barton & Belden**, from 1844-47, at 3 Buffalo St. In 1848, **D. R. Barton** again went on his own and greatly expanded his operation. By 1849, he had a number of other planemakers working for him including **James S. Benton** (see Benton & Evans), **Samuel G. Crane**, **John Evans** (see E. & J. Evans and Benton & Evans), **John H. Babcock** as a blacksmith, and **Alonzo D. McMaster** (see **Young & McMaster**). By 1850, he was employing 50 hands. In 1854, **D. R. Barton** purchased plane blades from the **Providence Tool Co.**. On Oct. 31, 1855, the **Providence Tool Co.** made a cast steel die stamp **D. R. BARTON/ROCHESTER** which included 17 letters at 15 ct. ea. for a charge of $2.55. From 1855-61, **D. R. Barton** had a working relationship with **Joel P. Milliner** to use prison labor in Kingston, Ontario. On Aug. 17, 1858, the factory was again destroyed by fire. By 1860, the factory was rebuilt and the firm was employing 150 hands. In 1863 only, **Barton & Milliner** formed a partnership. In 1865, the main manufacturing buildings and retail sales store were completely destroyed by a flood. With the lack of adequate insurance, the company **D. R. Barton & Co.** was formed with the added partners of **Royal L. Mack** & **William W. Mack**. The plane and edge tool facilities moved to Mill Street and by 1870 were employing 193 hands. **D. R. Barton** and his two sons **Charles Barton** and **Edward Barton**, continued until 1874, when the business was taken over by **Royal L. Mack** and **William W. Mack**. The firm was renamed **Mack & Co.** after the death of **David R. Barton** in 1875. It retained the trade name of **D. R. Barton & Co.** and used it until the end in 1939. Examples exist of planes with a partially removed **Greenfield Tool Co.** imprint overstruck with imprint E. The firm made a wide variety of tools besides planes and plane irons, including cooper's tools, draw knives, axes, saws and chisels. The 1850 census reported 85 employees and in 1870, 193 employees. The **1832,** in the trademark, is the founding date of the firm. A, B, and C imprints were used before 1865. The imprint **EXTRA** has been reported on a B Imprint. Imprints D through G were used from 1865-1923 when the **Mack Brothers** came into the business. Imprint D being the earliest. Imprint E and F were used in 1874, but discontinued in 1875 and then revived by the **Mack Brothers** when they absorbed **D. R. Barton Tool Co.** into **D. R. Barton & Co.** in 1879. B, C, D, D1, E, E1, F, G & H: FF; A & I ***

D. R. BARTON TOOL CO.
D. R. Barton Tool Co. was formed in Rochester, NY, in 1874 by **David R. Barton** and his sons, **Charles Barton** and **Edward Barton**. It advertised planes, edge tools and axes. **David** died in 1875 and the company continued until 1879 when it went into receivership. It was then taken over by **Mack & Co.** For several years two Rochester firms were turning out products using the **D. R. Barton** trade name. Advertisements placed in the 1874 and 1875 Rochester City Directory by the **D. R. Barton Tool Co.** state: "Goods stamped **D. R. Barton & Co.** are not made by us. For **GENUINE D. R. Barton** edge tools, planes, axes &c be sure to address **D. R. Barton Tool Co.** and not **D. R. Barton & Co.**" No imprint of D. R. Barton Tool Co. are known.

W. H. BARTON
Example: on a 9 1/4" beech modified size **12** hollow, marked toe and heel, ca. 1840-50. **UR**

W. J. BARTON
W. J. Barton was listed in the 1837 & 1840 Philadelphia directories as a cabinetmaker. Examples: on a pair of screw-arm tongue & groove planes; a gutter plane; and two smoothing planes. ca. 1830-40. On one plane the **Barton** imprint overstamped another imprint that was rendered illegible except for the **WARRANTED**, suggesting that **Barton** may also have been a hardware dealer. ****

D. R. BARTON/ I. BELDEN
D. R. Barton and **I. Belden** was a Rochester, NY, partnership consisting of **David R. Barton** and **Ira Belden**, a hardware merchant. The partnership seems to have lasted only a short time, ca. 1840. The 1844 directory lists the firm as edge tool makers. Example: on a screw-arm plow made by **Z. J. M'Master/ Auburn**. (see **D. R. Barton & Co.**) ****

BARTON & MILLINER
Barton & Milliner was a partnership, formed in 1863, between **David R. Barton** and **Joel P. Milliner** in Rochester, NY. The partnership lasted only one year. **Milliner** was earlier in the edge tool business in Kingston, Ontario, Canada, using prison labor from 1855-61, as **J. P. Milliner & Co.** (see **D. R. Barton & Co.**) No example has been reported.

BARTON & SMITH
Barton & Smith was a Rochester, NY, partnership consisting of **David R. Barton** and **William P. Smith**, which operated in 1841. A ***; B ****

D. BASSETT
Probably from two generations, Father and Son. **Daniel Bassett Sr.** (b. Jul. 13, 1731 in Norton, MA, d. 1802 in Taunton, MA) was the son of **Jeremiah Bassett** (1678-1768) and brother of **John Bassett**; and **Daniel's** son **Daniel Bassett Jr.** (b. Oct. 14, 1761 in Norton, MA, d. Mar. 24, 1843 in Norton, MA). Early examples include a 14 7/8" birch complex molder with offset tote, round top wedge and iron by **I Marsh**; and a 9 1/2" beech hollow with flat chamfers. ca. 1780-1800. The later examples include a 15 1/8" jack; a 22 1/4" fore plane with a single **James Cam** iron; a plow; and a 10" fixed sash with two irons & wedges, all are beech with heavy round chamfers, ca. 1820. ****

E. BASSETT
Probably **Elijah Bassett** (b. May 12, 1754 in Norton, MA, d. Aug. 2, 1803 in Taunton, MA) who was the son of **Jeremiah Bassett Jr.** (1722-93) and nephew of **John Basset**. He served in the Revolutionary War. In 1786, **Elijah** was noted as a laborer in Taunton, MA; and in 1797, a yeoman. There is no written record that he was a planemaker. Examples: on 10" beech molding planes, some boxed, and with flat chamfers. The wedge style is similar to the B wedge of **John Basset**. One example on a 10" beech adjustable fenced rabbet with flat chamfers has the incuse imprint **J. G. BASSETT** which is a latter owner's imprint of **John G. Bassett** (b. 1830) and grandson of **John Bassett** and the iron is marked **J.P**, ca. 1780. ****

J. BASSETT
Examples: on a yellow birch molder with flat chamfers and fluting, with an incuse **1796**; and on a 10" beech complex molder with heavy flat chamfers and size **7/8** marked on the heel, probably from southeastern New England (see **John Basset**), ca. 1780. ****

25

IOHN BASSET/ JOHN BASSETT

Possibly **John Basset** (b. Jun. 6, 1725 in Norton, MA, d. in Weare, NH in 1810), who was the father of **Elijah Bassett**; and noted in 1757 as a joiner in Taunton, MA; in 1749 & 61, as a shop joiner in Norton, MA; from 1762-68, in Sharon, MA; in 1776, in Stoughtonham, MA; in 1783, in Goffstown, NH; in 1790, he was a miller in Dunbarton, NH. Examples: the A imprint is on two 9 7/8" birch molders; a plow; and two 9 7/8" beech molders, all with flat chamfers. The C imprint is on a 10" rabbet with flat chamfers. The C1 imprint is on a 9 15/16" chestnut large bead, ca. 1760. **B ****; A, C & C1 *****

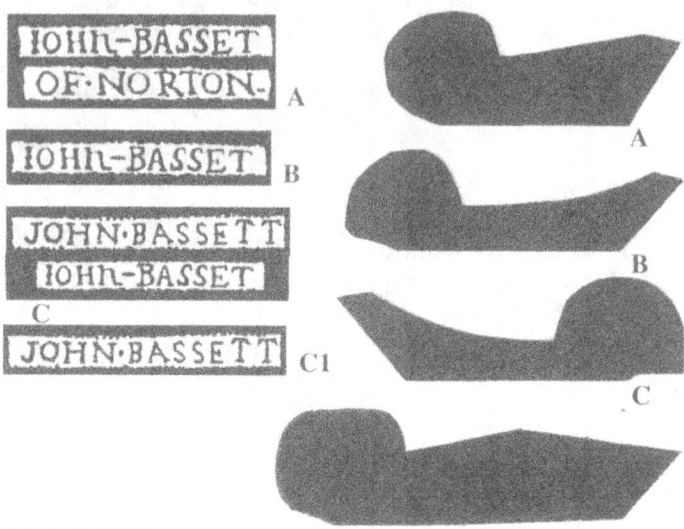

M. BASSET

Example: on a 10 5/8" birch skew rabbet with heavy flat chamfers and fluting, dated **1822**. ca. 1790   UR

J. E. BASSETT & CO./ JOHN E. BASSETT & CO.

J. E. Bassett & Co. was a New Haven, CT hardware firm founded in 1784 by Titus Street; in 1792, it became **Street & Hughes**; in 1821, **S. Hughes & Son**; in 1838, **E. B. M. Hughes**; and from 1855-1967, **J. E. Bassett & Co.** with **John E. Bassett**. On the top is a green and orange paper label. The image in the center is a yellow and green paper label that was affixed to the side of a hollow made by **W. H. Pond** and on two **Union Factory/ H. Chapin** hollows. 236 was changed to 754 Chapel St. in the 1800's. A green label is on a **H. L. Narramore** hollow. Below is a yellow label on a full-boxed center bead by **H. Chapin**.

> J. E. BASSETT & CO.
> HARDWARE
> CUTLERY
> MECHANIC'S TOOLS
> 236 CHAPEL ST.
> NEW HAVEN, CONN.

Imprint C is a copper disk on the side of a **W. H. Pond** jointer; and a 10" hollow.
B *; A & C ****
(paper lables ***)

I. BATCHELDER

I. Batchelder was listed as a planemaker in Sebago, ME, ca. 1800. **No example has been reported.**

G. BATEMAN

Example: on a 9 3/8"x 2/8 beech boxed complex molder with flat chamfers, ca. 1800.   UR

A. BATES

Examples: on a round; and a shiplap rabbet, both 10 1/8" birch with flat chamfers, ca. 1800.   ***

C. BATES

Example: on a massive 14 1/8"x 8 1/8" beech crown molder, with a slight offset tote and heavy round chamfers, ca. 1805-15.   UR

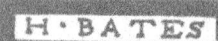

H. BATES

Examples: on a 14" birch crown molder; and a 10 1/4" beech complex molder, both with flat chamfers, ca. 1790.   UR

GEORGE BATES

George Bates with the location **SHAFTSBURY. VT**, located in Bennington Co., VT. Example: on a 9 1/2" beech skew rabbet with small flat chamfers, ca. 19c.   UR

J. BATES

Examples: on a 13"x 5" birch crown molder with an off-set tote, round toped iron & wedge and flat chamfers. ca. 1790. Also on a 9 1/2" square rabbet; and a 9" beech sash coping plane, both with relieved wedge, and small round chamfers, ca. 1810-20.   UR

M BATES
Example: on an 8" beech thumbnail plane dated **1850**, found in Norwich, OH. **UR**

W M BATES
W. M. Bates and Jos. Potter were hardware dealer in Lima, OH. Example: on a 3/8" tongue & groove combination plane made by H. L. James, marked on the heel. ****

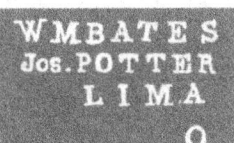

I. S. BATTEY
Isaac S. Battey (b. 1817 in RI, d. Aug. 29, 1904) was a Providence, RI, planemaker located at 112 Dyer St., active from 1841-55. He was listed from 1847-50 as a planemaker; from 1854-57 as a clerk; in 1880, he was listed as a retired planemaker. In 1840, he married Clarissa Ann Child (1823-1898), sister of J. E. Child. In 1850-53, Isaac was living in the same household with his brother-in-law J. Edward Child and his father-in-law John G. Child. Examples: on a reeding plane; a 30" jointer; a 15 1/4" handled pump plane; and a 9 3/8" beech side rabbet. **A & A1 ****

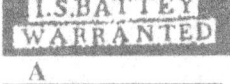
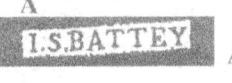

BATTEY & EDDY
Battey & Eddy were in a partnership founded on Apr. 1, 1841 between Isaac S. Battey and James A. Eddy. They were hardware merchants and plane manufacturers at 5 Broad St., Providence, RI. The partnership was short-lived and was dissolved in Sep. of that same year. Examples: on a 9 1/2"x 3" beech boxed complex molder; and a 4 5/8" wide (3 1/2" iron) crown molder. *****

J. F. BAUDER
Jacob Frederick Bauder (b. Aug. 5, 1817 in Philadelphia, PA, d. Dec. 15, 1893 in Palmyra, NJ across the Delaware River from Philadelphia) was baptized in Manheim, Lancaster Co., PA. Bauder is listed as a "plainmaker" in Lancaster City, in 1840-41. He made planes in Manheim, from 1841-47. Since planes exist with his Philadelphia address stamped over Manheim and with Manheim stamped over Philadelphia, it seems likely that he briefly tried the larger market. Bauder became the proprietor of a hat manufacturer in Manheim in 1847. Tax records list Bauder through 1852, but list him as NR (nonresident) in 1848. In the 1850s, he appears in Philadelphia as a provisioner or victualer in the Southwark area (S. Front St.), servicing ships. He does not appear in the PA 1860-70 census as he may have moved to NJ. His plane making style, particularly his wedges, bear a resemblance to that of E. W. Carpenter, for whom he may have apprenticed and worked for as a journeyman in 1840-41. Example: on an adjustable split sash plane with the A imprint

MANHEIM/ LANr Co. Pa. overstamped with the B imprint of St. John St./ PHILa. **A ***; B ****

W. BAUM & CO.
William Baum (b. Oct. 14, 1814 in PA, d. Nov. 14, 1881 in Batavia, OH) was a Cincinnati, OH, planemaker from 1850-52; in 1841, as a plane manufacturer in Louisville, KY; in 1853, as a foreman at Schaeffer & Cobb in Cincinnati, OH; in 1860, as a planemaker in Batavia, OH. One example with both the W. Baum & Co. and J. Harrison & Co. imprints has been reported. **A & A1 *** B ****

G. BAURMANN
G. Baurmann was a hardware dealer in Louisville, KY. Examples: The A imprint is on a Ohio Tool Co. pair of screw-arm plank planes; and an Ohio Tool Co. rabbet. The B imprint is on an 8 1/8" coffin smoother made by Sciote Works. **A & B ****

EZ, BAXTER
Possibly Ezekial Baxter (b. July 13, 1767 in Yarmouth, MA, d. Aug. 26, 1805 in Yarmouth, MA) the son of Shubal Baxter (1726-80) of Barnstable, MA. He married Catherine Bearse on Oct. 20, 1789, on Nantucket, MA. Their first child was born Oct. 29, 1792, at Yarmouth, MA. Examples: on a dozen 10" birch molders with relieved wedges and flat chamfers. One example is also marked WHITNEY D. BAXTER as an owner, ca. 1790. ****

BAY STATE WORKS
Possibly located in Northampton, MA, which has a "Bay State" section. Examples: The A imprint is on two smoothing planes; a plow; and two hollows. The B imprint is on an 8" beech smoother with a strike button on the heel, ca. 1850-75. **A & B ****

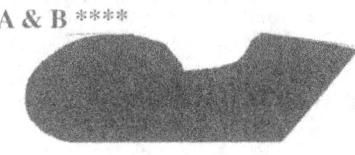

J. BAYLEY
The Bayley family were founders of Newbury, VT. Examples: on a 9 1/2" complex molder; and a 12 1/4" gutter plane with offset birch pegged tote, both beech with 1/4" flat chamfers, from New England, ca. 1800-10. ***

M. BAYLEY
Example: on a beech body, birch handled round with flat chamfers. ca. 1790. **No imprint is available.**

BEACHER & ADDIS
Baldwin Beacher (Beecher) (b. 1810 in CT) and **Charles W. Addis** (b. 1829 in CT, d. Mar. 24, 1853 in New Haven, CT) were planemakers in New Haven, CT, from 1850-53. **Baldwin Beacher** was listed as a joiner at 122 George & Temple St. in Patten's 1840 New Haven, CT directory; as a joiner in the 1850 census; and as a carpenter, in 1860; as a sash & blind maker, in 1870; and joiner & carpenter, in 1880. **Charles Addis** was listed as a planemaker in the 1850 & 53 census and living with **Nathan Fenn**, a joiner. ***

I. BEAL
Possibly **Jacob Beal Jr.** (b. Sep. 18, 1774 in Hingham, Ma, d. Oct. 28, 1805) was listed as a cabinetmaker and chair maker from 1790-1805. Or his father **Jacob Beal Sr.** (b. Jun. 14, 1742 in Hingham, MA, d. Sep. 3, 1819 in Hingham, MA). Examples: the A imprint is on a small birch astragal; a small birch boxed bead; and a 9 1/2" wide beech round, all 9 1/2" with wide flat chamfers. The B imprint is on a 9 1/2"x 1 5/8" birch skew rabbet with round chamfers, ca. 1800-20.
A & B ***

GEORGE E. BEALE
George E. Beale (b. Oct. 7, 1822 in PA, d. Aug. 27, 1885 in Gilman, Marshall Co., IA) had worked at **Woodruff & McBride's** plane factory with **Americus Huling** and **James Bogert** in the 1848-49 Louisville, KY directory. He was listed in 1851-52, as a planemaker at **McBride's**. **Woodruff** is listed as a hardware and cutlery dealer, in 1851-52; in 1860, **George E. Beale** was a master carpenter in Wauseon, Fulton Co., OH; in 1870, he was a lumber dealer in Wauseon; in 1880, he was a grain dealer in Gilman, Marshall Co., IA.
No imprint has been reported.

J. BEALS
Example: on a 10" beech hollow with flat chamfers, ca. 1800-10. **UR**

I: BEAM
Example: on a Yankee style 10 1/2" apple plow plane, with wedge-lock arms, a wood depth stop, and flat chamfers, ca. early 19c. **UR**

CHRISTIAN BEAR
Christian Bear (b. 1783 in PA, d. 1847 in Augusta, VA) was a wood worker and mill operator. Planes with this imprint have been reported and are shown (not to scale) in *The Chronicle* June 2005. **No imprint is available.**

J. BEAR
Example: the A imprint is on a 9 1/2" beech bead with intermittent boxing and round chamfers. The B imprint is branded on side of a 13 1/4"x 4" beech crown molder with an offset tote, round top iron & wedge and round chamfers, also with the A imprint. possibly from PA, ca. 1820.
A & B ****

A. BEARD
Example: on a 13 5/8" birch panel raiser with round top iron & wedge, and heavy flat chamfers, probably from New England, ca. 1790-1800. *****

CLARENCE A. BEARSE
Clarence A. Bearse (b. ca. 1842 in MA, d. 1921 in New Bedford, MA) was listed as a boat builder in Acushnet, Bristol Co., MA, in 1860. On Sep. 20, 1862, he enlisted as a private in the Civil War in Co. D, MA 47th. Infantry Reg. He was listed as a boat builder and mustered out on Sep. 1, 1863. **Clarence** was listed as a planemaker in the New Bedford, MA, from 1867-72; in 1870, as a tool maker. He worked in RI, as part of **Bodman & Bearse** and **Bodman, Bearse & Hussey** (see **J. M. Taber**). **No imprint has been reported.**

C. BEARY
Examples: on a 10" beech complex molder with flat chamfers and branded on the side with **J. BENNER**; and a 10" beech bead with heavy round chamfers, ca. 1800-10. **UR**

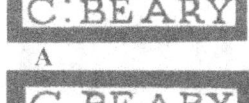

ISRAEL O. BEATTIE/ I. O. BEATTIE
Israel Oakley Beattie (b. Mar. 5, 1821 in Orange Co., NY, d. Feb. 24, 1882 in Salt Lake Co., UT, buried in Warwick, Orange Co., NY) advertised in the Goshen, Orange Co., NY *Independent Republican* on Jan. 27, 1854, as "a hardware dealer". He was active from 1854-72 in Middletown, Orange Co., NY. In 1880, he was listed as agent selling goods in Warwick. Example: on a wide complex molder with the B imprint obliterating an earlier imprint. **A** **; **B** ****

C. BECK
Example: on a 10" beech large round with a fence and large flat chamfers, ca. 1800   **UR**

BECK & LANG
Examples: on a fore plane; and a 9 1/2"x 1/2" skewed rabbet. The Buffalo location imprint may have been the same one used by **Lang & Co./ Buffalo**, a hardware store run by **Michael Lang**.   ****

THOMAS BECKMAN
Thomas Beckman (b. ca. 1818 in Philadelphia, PA, d. Nov. 18, 1881 in Philadelphia) was listed as a planemaker, in 1845 & 50, in North Liberties, Philadelphia directories.
No imprint has been reported.

SAMUEL M. BECKWITH
Samuel M. Beckwith was listed as a planemaker in Utica, NY, from 1829-34, boarding with **R. J. Collins**, in 1829; and working for **L. Kennedy**. **No imprint has been reported.**

BENJAMIN F. BEE
Benjamin F. Bee of Harwich, MA, was issued Patent No. 8503 on Nov. 11, 1851 for a set screw placed at the back of the iron, the head of the screw working in a slot near the top of the iron. It also provided for spring and cam operated arms to lock the iron in position. This patent is reported on a 22"x 3 3/8" jointer made by **A. Cumings/ Boston** (1848-51) which has **B. F. BEE PATENT NOV. 1851** stamped on a pewter disc attached to the side. **No imprint is available.**

BALDWIN BEECHER
Baldwin Beecher (b. ca. 1809 in Waterbury, CT, d. Mar. 6, 1889 in New Haven, CT) moved to New Haven, CT after 1830; from 1840–50, he was listed as a joiner; from 1850-53, his occupation was listed as a plane manufacturer at the Union Works. In 1851, **Baldwin Beecher** advertised in *Connecticut Business Directory* as "Manufacturer of planes for carpenters, coopers, cabinet and coach makers at the **Union Works**, Union St., New Haven, CT"; from 1854–56, **Beecher's** occupation was sash maker; from 1857-66, he was listed a foreman at **Lewis & Beecher's** sash and blind manufacturer and lumber dealers; from 1866–88, **Beecher's** occupation was listed as door maker, joiner and carpenter. **No imprint has been reported.**

H. BEEDEN
Example: on a 9 3/8" beech complex molder with heavy flat chamfers, possibly from PA, ca. 1800.   **UR**

N. N. BEERS
Example: on a 9 3/8" beech table hollow with tight round chamfers, ca. 1820.   **UR**

JONATHAN BEILEY
Jonathan Beiley was a Milwaukee, WI, sash and planemaker listed in the 1859 Milwaukee city directory.
No imprint has been reported.

W. B. BELCH
William B. Belch was a hardware dealer and planemaker in New York City, from 1831-64. Belch had moved to New York from VT, in 1831. He was listed in the 1843-44 New York City directory as a planemaker at 14 Norfolk St. The 1850 census listed Belch as a "plainmaker" employing seven men to make 7000 "plains" selling for $9000. Examples: on a 9 3/8" beech rabbet with a **Mottram** (Sheffield 1800-33) iron; and a 14" grooving plane, both with a C imprint made prior to 1831. The C1 imprint is on a 9 3/8" beech fixed sash plane. One example of the B imprint has an overstamp of **J. Hannan/ N. York**, A imprint. **A & B ****   A1, C & D *****

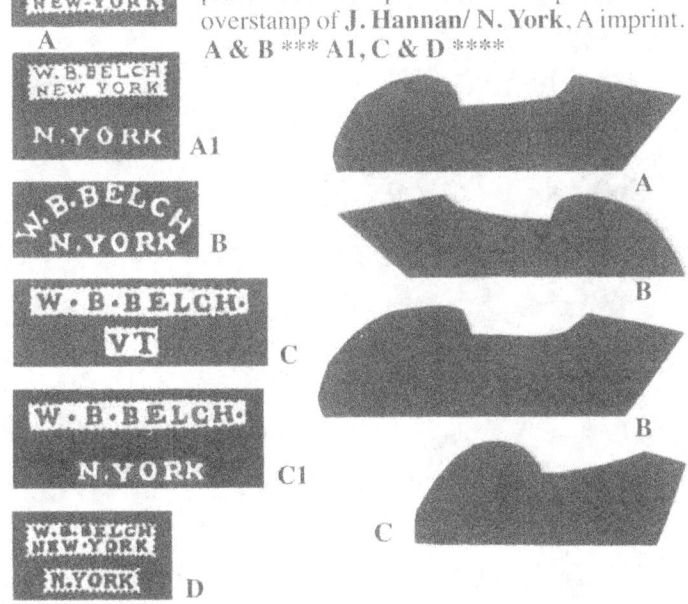

E. BELCHER
Edward Belcher has been listed as a Newport, RI, joiner and housewright, in 1770. Examples: on a 10 1/4" fruitwood astragal; and a 9 3/8" beech small round with small flat chamfers, ca. 1800.   **UR**

J.B/ J. BELCHER
Possibly **Joseph Belcher** a 1832-38 hardware dealer at 11 Broad St., Providence, RI, with **James A. Eddy** clerk. Example: on a 28" beech jointer with an offset tote. In addition to the full name imprinted in two sizes there is the 18c style initials **J.B**. **A & B:**   **UR**

BELCHER BROS.
Belcher Bros. was a hardware company located in Providence, RI. It was founded in 1826 by **Joseph Belcher** and was continued by his sons, **Joseph H. Belcher** and **Leander C. Belcher** as **Belcher Bros.** from 1857-84. When **Edward A. Loomis** became a partner, the name was changed to **Belcher and Loomis**. **

BELDING BROS. & CO.
Belding Bros. & Co. was a large silk manufacturer with factories in Rockville, CT and Northampton, MA; and a hardware dealer. Example: on a **Union Factory/ H. Chapin** hollow. ****

BELKNAP-H-&-M-CO
Belknap-H-&-M-CO with **BLUEGRASS** and **No. 706** is on a 15" Transitional plane, believed to be made by **Sargent**. UR

C. BELL
C. Bell was probably a hardware dealer in Jersey City, NJ, in the mid 1800's. Example: on a **Marley/ New York** plane. ****

JOHN BELL
John Bell (b. 1800 in PA, d. Jan. 2, 1890 in Philadelphia, PA) was a prolific Philadelphia, PA, planemaker whose working period was 1829-51. He was listed in the 1850 census as a planemaker and living with **Henry Bibighaus,** age 72, a Lutheran minister. Henry was the father of **Samuel H. Bibighaus** and **Elizabeth Bibighaus** whom **John Bell** married on Dec. 20, 1824. **Samuel H. Bibighaus** succeeded him in 1852. Example: on a **Spayd & Bell** imprint with the **JOHN BELL** A imprint overstruck, suggesting that John Bell may have succeeded that partnership.
A & C: FF ;B **; D ****

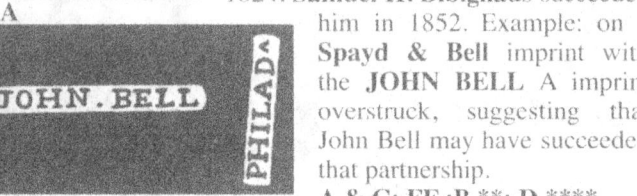

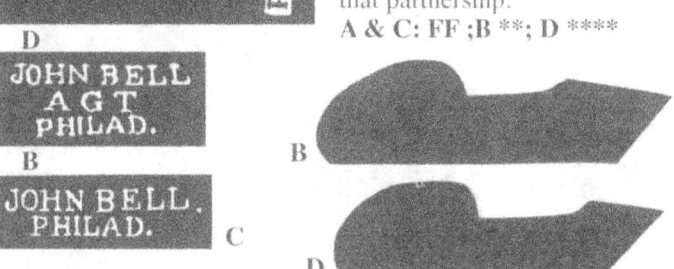

J. B. BELL
Examples: on a size **10** hollow; and a single-boxed side bead, both 9 1/2" beech with heavy round chamfers, ca. 1820. UR

W. BELL/ W. B
William. Bell (b. May 1, 1790 in KY. D. Mar. 1, 1865 in Louisville, KY) was listed in the Lexington, KY, 1818 city directory as a planemaker and in the 1837-38 city directory as a plane manufacturer on High St. at Main Cross & Spring St. He was also a homebuilder and owned 1 slave. Examples: on a smooth plane; a pair of screw-arm plank match planes; and an unusual plow with one slide-arm and one screw-arm threaded with a lock nuts.
A & A1 ****

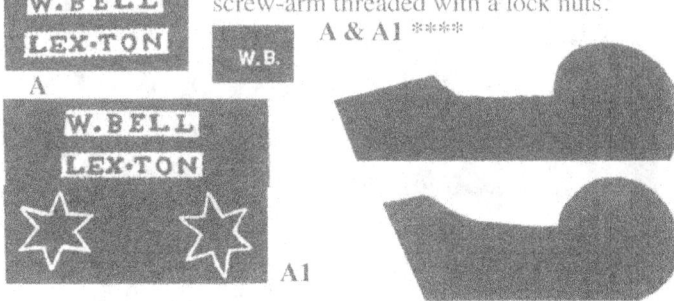

BELLVILLE/ STORE/ HARDWARE
Bellville Store was a hardware dealer. Example: on a 9 1/2" beech round with a **Hall Case & Co.** iron. ****

C:BELSTEI
Example: on a 9 3/16" beech astragal bead with heavy flat chamfers. ca. 1800-10. UR

T: P x BELT.
Examples: on a 9 1/4" bead; a wedge-arm match groove plane; and a panel raiser; all beech with heavy round chamfers, ca. 1810-20. UR

J+BELTZ
Example: on a 13 1/8" beech gutter plane with an open offset tote, single iron and shallow round chamfers, probably from southeast PA, ca. 1820-30. UR

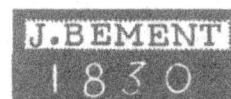

J. BEMENT
Example: on a 6" beech smoother with a double-iron and dated **1830**. UR

E. BENCRAFT
Examples: on a 9 7/8" complex molder; a 9 1/4" fixed sash; and a 9 1/2" hollow; all birch with flat chamfers, ca. 1795. ****

A. BENEDICT
Example: on a 10" beech large hollow with a birch wedge and round chamfers, ca. 1805-15. UR

BENEDICTUM

 **Benedictum** was possibly a hardware dealer. This imprint has been reported on a size **2** hollow made by **Cross Brothers/ Warranted**. UR

A. BENJAMIN

Asher Benjamin's (b. Jun. 15, 1773 in Hartland, CT, d. July 26, 1845 in Springfield, MA) father died when he was young leaving **Asher** poor and with little support. He was apprenticed to **Thomas Hayden** who worked in Windsor and Suffield, CT. From Oct. 25, 1794 to Feb. 26, 1795, **Asher Benjamin** was working under **Thomas Hayden** carving the Ionic capitals on the frontispiece of the Oliver Phelps's residence in Suffield, Ct. In 1797, he was in Greenfield, MA where he completed several residences. On August 31, 1797, the *Greenfield Gazette* announced that **Benjamin**'s *The Country Builder's Assistant* was available at **Thomas Dickman**'s book store. This was the first Anglo-American builder's guide. The selected house designs were less elaborate than the British examples and were better suited to the taste of the local carpenters, joiners, and builders of rural America. Also in 1797, he married **Achsah Hitchcock** (1773-1805) in Brookfield, MA. He designed Deerfield Academy's first building, a three story brick structure. In 1798, he had moved further up the Connecticut River Valley to Windsor, VT where he designed the Old South Congregational Church. By Sep. 1798, his first child was born in Boston, MA. Between 1797 and 1843, **Asher Benjamin** had published 7 builder's guides that went thru 23 editions and at least 44 known printings. From 1806 thru 1809, **Asher Benjamin** was listed in the Boston directory with the occupation of house wright, building trades. In 1823–24, he was an alderman of Boston. In 1825, **Asher** declared bankruptcy. He left Boston and returned after 1827. From 1828–39, his occupation was listed as architect, building trades. **Asher Benjamin** was instrumental in the development of the "Professional Architect". In 1837, he was one of the founders of the American Institute of Architects. Examples: on a fenced skew rabbet; a dado; an astragal, all 9 1/8"; and a coffin smoothing plane, beech with flat chamfers, ca. 1790. ****

SAMUEL BENJAMIN

Samuel Benjamin was apprenticed to **Joseph Metcalf** a Winthrop, ME planemaker, ca. 1790.
No imprint has been reported.

J. BENNER

Examples: on a 1/4" bead; and a wide hollow, both with flat chamfers; a complex molder found in NH; and a reed & follow, the latter two with heavy round chamfers, all 9 1/2" beech, ca. 1800-20. UR

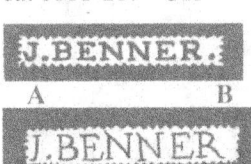

B. BENNET

Possibly **B. Bennet** (b. 1786 in New Market, NH, d. 1859) who was a cabinetmaker in Salem, MA, in 1808. He joined the **Salem Mech. Assoc.** in 1817 and was in Beverly that same year. Examples: on a 1/4" astragal bead with narrow flat chamfers; and a 9 3/8" beech skew rabbet with tight round chamfers, ca. 1800-20. ****

I. BENNET

Example: on a 9 1/2" beech skewed rabbet with flat chamfers, ca. 1800. UR

JAs BENNET

Example: on a 9 1/2" fruitwood skew rabbet with heavy flat chamfers, ca. 1800. UR

G. BENNETT

Examples: on 9 1/4"-9 1/8" beech complex molders with flat chamfers, ca. 1800. UR

D. BENSEN/ DAVID BENSEN

David Bensen (b. Nov. 1, 1802 in Schwnwctady, NY, d. Nov. 17, 1853 in Albany, NY) was an Albany, NY, planemaker who made planes under his name and that of five different partnerships between 1827-1850: **Randall & Bensen**, from 1827-29, with **Samuel Randall** (1799-1860); **Bensen & Mockridge**, from 1830-31, with **Abraham Mockridge** (1802-1872); **Bensen & Parry**, from 1838-39, with **John H. Parry**; **Benson & M'Call**, in 1842, with **Thomas L. McCall** (1806-1850); and **Bensen & Munsell**, from 1849-50, with **Joel Munsell** (1808-1880).
A: FF; B, C & D *

BENSEN & CRANNELL

One of the most frequently found imprints among Albany-made planes. **Bensen & Crannell** was a partnership of **Nicholas Bensen** (b. Jan. 17, 1810 in NY, d. Oct. 30, 1862 in Albany, NY), probably a relation of **David Bensen**, and **Matthew Crannell Jr.** (b. 1816 in NY, d. 1892). **Bensen & Crannell** made planes over the period 1843-62. From 1843-45, it was located at 116 State corner of Lodge; and from 1853-62, at 108 State; in 1850, they added a "Mechanics Tool Store" to their shop; in 1855, they employed 15 hands producing $10,000 worth of planes and tools. The 1860 census listed them as having 5 employees producing 6000 planes worth $4000.

A, B & C: FF

BENSEN & M'CALL
David Bensen and **Thomas J. McCall** (b. Apr. 10, 1806 in PA, d. Nov. 28, 1850 Albany, NY) was a plane making partnership in Albany, NY, in 1842. **

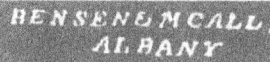

BENSEN & MOCKRIDGE
David Bensen and **Abraham Mockridge** was a plane making partnership in Albany, NY from 1830-31. (see **Benson & Mockridge**) No imprint is available.

BENSEN & MUNSELL
Bensen & Munsell was a partnership consisting of **David Bensen** and **Joel Munsell** (b. Apr, in Albany, NY, in 1849-50. Munsell was a printer and publisher and probably provided capital for the firm. **

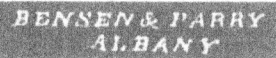

BENSEN & PARRY
Bensen & Parry was a plane making partnership of **David Bensen** and **John S. Parry**, in Albany, NY, in 1838-39. ***

J. BENSON
Examples: on molders 9 3/8"-9 1/2" beech with round chamfers, found in the Hudson River Valley of NY. Three are 10" and one, a tongue with an adjustable base fence, is dated **1818**.
A1 **; A ****

SAMUEL L. BENSON
Samuel L. Benson (b. 1805 in VT, d. Jan. 22, 1882 in Franklin, NH) was listed in the 1850 census as a carpenter in Lowell, MA. He employed 5 hands, making $5000 worth of sash, blinds and planes. In 1880, He was listed as a retired Millwright in Franklin, Merrimack, NH. **No imprint has been reported**.

BENSON & MOCKRIDGE
Benson & Mockridge was a partnership of **David Bensen** and **Abraham Mockridge** (b. Aug. 5, 1802 in Litchfield, CT, d. 1872 in Newark, NJ) who was successor to **Randall & Bensen** in Albany, NY, in 1830-31. This is the only instance where **Bensen** was spelled **Benson**. **Abraham Mockridge** moved to Newark, NJ, in 1833. **

DAVID BENTON
David Benton was a planemaker listed in Columbus, OH, in 1856-57. **No imprint has been reported**.

G. A. BENTON
George A. Benton (b. Apr. 1815 in Glastonbery, CT) made planes at Marginal St., Chelsea, MA, (but stamped them Boston), from 1855-72. In the 1840 census, he was listed in manufacturing or trade, in Glastonbury, CT; in the 1850 census, he was listed as a planemaker living at the same address as **A. Cummings**; in 1880, he was listed as a furniture grainer in Chelsea. He used **Leonard Bailey**'s adjustment patent. Example: on an 8 1/4" beech smoother with a double-iron.
A **; B, C & D ***

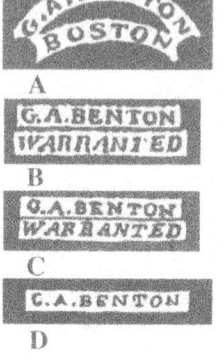

THOMAS BENTON
Thomas H. Benton (b. 1803 in Elizabeth City, NC, d. 1871 in Richmond, IN) came to Wayne Co., IN, by 1832. He farmed and engaged in freighting by team between Richmond and Cincinnati, OH. From 1846-57, he was in the hardware firm of **Fletcher & Benton** with **S. F. Fletcher** in Richmond, IN. From 1857-68, the firm was **T. Benton & Co.** and then **T. Benton & Son**, in 1868-71, with his son **George W. Benton** at 48 Main. ****

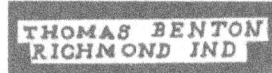

BENTON, EVANS & CO.
Benton, Evans & Co. was a Rochester, NY, plane making partnership of **James S. Benton** (b. 1805 in CT, d. 1867) and **Evan Evans** (b. 1811 in New York City) during the period from 1834-38. The business was announced by an ad placed in the *Rochester Daily Democrat* on Apr. 8, 1834, by **L. Kennedy Jr.**. **James S. Benton** was listed as a planemaker in 1832; and as agent for **Leonard Kennedy Jr.**, in Utica, NY, in 1833. Between 1838-1855, **Benton** worked mainly for **D. R. Barton**, in Rochester, NY. Benton was listed as a planemaker in the 1850 census. After 1855, he was in the canal mercantile trade. **Evans** was employed by Utica planemaker **John Reed**, in 1829; and was listed as a planemaker in Rochester, from 1834-41. He was a partner in **E. & J. Evans** with **James Evans** starting in 1841. **

W. BENTON
William S. Benton was listed as a planemaker in Utica, NY, in 1833, and is believed to have worked for **R. J. Collins**. Example: on a 9 1/2" beech astragal with flat chamfers and

 found in Rochester, NY. ****

J. E. BERNALD
Example: on a 17 3/4"x 2 5/16" birch round or gutter plane with a centered closed tote, diamond strike, and a round topped **James Cam** single-iron, ca. 1800. **UR**

ALFD BERRY
Example: on a 9 1/2" fully boxed reeding plane also marked **MAKER**, ca. 1850. **UR**

A. BERRY
Example: on a 9 3/8" skew rabbet with shallow round chamfers, ca. 1830. **UR**

A. G. BERRY
Example: on a 16 1/2" beech jack with an ornament at the front base of the open tote and a long tip extending back. **UR**

B. F. BERRY
Benjamin F. Berry (b. 1809 in MA) made planes under his own imprint in Watertown, NY, ca. 1840, with **Lorenzo Case** working as a journeyman planemaker. In 1834-35, **Berry** was listed as a planemaker in the Utica directory, but was probably a bench hand for **R. J. Collins. Berry** was listed in the 1850 census as a toolmaker in Pamelia across the Black River from Watertown, NY. **A1 **; A *****

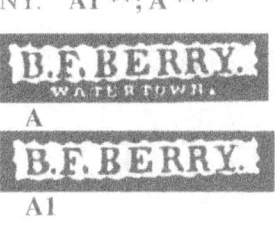

E. BERRY/ E. BERRY & CO.
Ebenezer Berry (b. Oct. 10, 1788, d. Sept. 19, 1839) of Beverley, MA, is the stepson of **William Raymond** from whom he probably learned plane making. The inventory of his estate lists a "Work Shop & Shed - $75; Stock, Tools & Furniture in Shop - $100." Examples: the C imprint appears to have been modified to the A imprint and was reported on a 9 3/4" beech fenced rabbet with flat chamfers, ca. 1820.
A **; B ***; C *****

F. BERRY
Example: on a 9 1/8" molder with heavy round chamfers, ca. 1820. **UR**

JOHN L. BERRY
John L. Berry was a Springfield, OH, cabinetmaker from 1825-52. He advertised, on Feb. 13, 1830, in *The Western Pioneer*: "The subscriber has now on hand and will keep constantly for sale at his cabinet shop on South Street, a general assortment of carpenter and cabinetmaker's tools, which will be disposed of at the Cincinnati prices. He will warrant them equal if not superior to any maker in the country, both for neatness and utility." **No imprint has been reported**.

L. BERRY
Example: on a pair of match planes. **UR**

BERRY & VANNAMER
Examples: on a 9 1/2" bead; and a 9 3/8" two iron complex molder with the irons set at different pitches (52 & 45) and different wedge profiles; both beech with round chamfers, ca. 1820. ****

BEVIL DEVIL
Kimball Mfg. Co. of Royal Oak, MI, offered a line of wooden planes for fiberboard work. They were sold under the name **BEVIL DEVIL**. A set of three planes was sold in either an oak or pasteboard box in the 1930's. **No imprint is available**.

BEWLEY
Bewley was a New York City planemaking firm that operated from 1822-32 and consisted of **Edward Bewley**, who is listed in the directories from 1822-30, and **Thomas Bewley** in 1831-32. There was apparently no connection with the English firm **Robert Bewley**, which made planes from 1798-1847 under the imprint **BEWLEY/ LEEDS**. Example: on a wedge-lock plow plane with the A imprint also with **G. Robinson/ N-York**. **A1, A2 & B **; A *****

W. BIBBER
Example: on a 9 1/2" beech straight rabbet with round chamfers, ca. 1820-30. **UR**

S. H. BIBIGHAUS/ SAMUEL H. BIBIGHAUS
Samuel H. Bibighaus (b. Mar. 29, 1813 in PA, D. Mar. 9, 1889) was the brother-in-law to both **John Bell** and **John E. Spayd**. He was a prolific planemaker and hardware dealer in Philadelphia, PA, as early as 1840. He became the successor to **John Bell,** in 1852. He was listed as a planemaker in the 1853, 56-57 & 60 directories; and as a hardware dealer in the 1840, 44 & 49 directories. In 1870, he was listed as retired. Example: the C1 imprint is on a 15"x 4 7/8" beech panel raiser.
A, A1 & D *; B, C, C1& E **

A

A1

B

C

D

C1

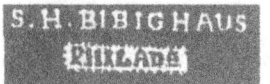
D

E

I BICKFORD
Example: on a 15 3/4" beech jack plane with a centered closed tote, diamond strike, and heavy flat chamfers, ca. 1800-10. **UR**

[L.BICKFORD imprint]

BIDDLE & CO.
Biddle & Co. was a hardware distributor and wholesaler in Philadelphia, PA, sometime after 1862, it succeeded **R. & W. C. Biddle & Co.**
A & A1 ***

[BIDDLE & Co. PHILADA imprint] A

[BIDDLE & Co PHILADA imprint] A1

R. & W. C. BIDDLE & CO.
Robert Biddle (b. 1818 in Philadelphia, PA) and **William C. Biddle** (b. 1817 in Philadelphia, PA, d. Dec. 22, 1887 in Philadelphia) were listed as a hardware merchants in Philadelphia, PA in 1840, 54 & 62, before the formation of **Biddle & Co.** **

A. F. BIDWELL
Alonzo Frank Bidwell (b. June 1, 1823 in Griegsville, NY, d. Nov. 17, 1869 in Kansas City, MO) was the brother of **G. L. Bidwell** and a cousin of **L. B. Bidwell**. He was listed in the 1850 census as a merchant in Coldwater, MI, probably a hardware dealer. He served as a Major in the Civil War in Company S, 1st. Michigan Infantry. Example: on a screw-arm match plane. ****

[A.F.BIDWELL / COLD WATER.MICH imprint]

G. L. BIDWELL
George L. Bidwell (b. Oct. 2, 1814 in Colebrook, Litchfield Co., CT, d. Jul. 12, 1899 in Adrian, MI) was the brother of **A. F. Bidwell** and a cousin of **L. B. Bidwell**. He was listed in the 1850 census as a hardware merchant in Adrian, MI. Example: on a pair of hollow and rounds with number **72** on the toe, the **Ohio Tool Co.** style number. A & A1 ****

[G.L.BIDWELL ADRIAN.MICH] A

[G.L.BIDWELL ADRIAN.MICH] A1

L. B. BIDWELL
Leonard Benton Bidwell (b. 1809 in Hartford Co., CT, d. Nov. 30, 1882 in Newark, Wirt Co., WV) was the cousin of both **A. F. Bidwell** and **G. L. Bidwell**. Leonard Bidwell advertised on Dec. 17, 1842 in *The New England Weekly Review* "The subscriber having purchased of **Melvin Copeland**'s business, at 110 State Street in Hartford, Connecticut, his stock in trade, has removed to the rear of the building where he is prepared to manufacture planes of the best quality, of every description, wholesale and retail." He was listed as a Hartford, CT, planemaker from 1842-48. He was listed as living in East Hartford in 1830 & 40. The 1840 census showed seven members of his household engaged in manufacturing and trade. He lived five houses away from **Peter Brooks**. He was a part of **Bidwell & Hale** in Newark, W. VA, from 1850-64. In 1850 & 60, he was listed as "plainmaker". In 1870, **Leonard Bidwell** was listed as farmer. Example: the A1 imprint is on a large round, ca. 1850. A & A1 ***

[L.B.BIDWELL HARTFORD] A

[L.B.BIDWELL] A1

BIDWELL & BICKFORD
Bidwell & Bickford was a hardware store founded on Apr. 2, 1854 in Valparaiso, IN, which became **H. Bickford & Co.** with **Henry Bidwell** on Dec. 18 1854. ****

BIDWELL & HALE
Bidwell & Hale was a partnership in Newark, Wirt County, WV (near the OH line), consisting of **Leonard Benton Bidwell** and **Joseph White Hale**. Leonard Bidwell and Joseph Hale both moved from CT, to Newark, WV, in 1848 to operate a sawmill. It is believed that **Hale** was not involved in the plane making, but a partner in the sawmill only. **Leonard** advertised, on Feb. 23, 1850, in the *Parkersburg Gazette & Western Virginia Courier*, "Planes- A full assortment of **Bidwell's** manufacture, for sale to the trade at whole sale," which were sold through agent **Edgar C. Phelps**. He continued to advertise thru 1855. A price broadside of the firm, ca. 1860, describes them as "Manufacturers of Planes and bench, hand, or clamp screws of all sizes" and lists a wide variety of plane types and offers a "liberal discount to wholesale purchasers." Planes continued to be sold until 1864 when **Bidwell & Hale** sold the saw mill. **No imprint has been reported.** (see **M. Hovey**)

J. BIGELOW
Examples: on a 16 1/8" beech panel raiser with offset tote; and a 9 1/2" double-boxed sash plane with two-irons and wedges, both beech and with round chamfers, ca. 1830-50. **UR**

L. B. BIGELOW
Leonard Bacon Bigelow (b. Aug. 1809 in East Hartford, CT, d. Nov. 4, 1865 in MA) was a Providence, RI, planemaker from 1831-53. He was a partner with **Nathan L. Barrus** in **Bigelow & Barrus**, in 1836. In 1841, he was listed as a planemaker in Providence. **Leonard** became **Nathan's** brother-in-law when he married **Nathan's** sister **Prudence**, in 1846. By 1854, Leonard was listed as a machinist employed by the **Providence Machine Co.**. Bigelow was also reported as the maker of a plane patented by **Charles Hall**.
A & A1 ***

S. G. BIGELOW
Example: on a 9 9/16" birch astragal with round chamfers, ca. 1810-30. **UR**

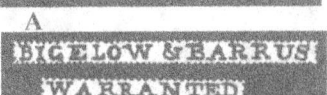

BIGELOW & BARRUS
Bigelow & Barrus was a partnership between **Nathan L. Barrus** and **Leonard B. Bigelow** which was announced in a newspaper notice dated Nov. 1, 1836, "**Barrus & Bigelow**, located at 77 Weybosset St., Providence, RI, recently vacated by **Jonas R. Gale**", this partnership lasted until Dec. 21, 1836 when a fire terminated the business.
A & A1 ***

J. BIGLOW
Possibly **John Bigelow** (b. Dec. 6, 1775 in Hartford Co., CT, d. Feb. 12, 1812) of Colchester, CT, a cabinetmaker active in 1812. Examples: on a 15" beech gutter plane with pegged offset tote, skew blade, nickers, and flat chamfers; a 10 1/4" molder; an 8 1/4" hollow, both birch with flat chamfers; and a 10" beech round with shallow round chamfers, ca. 1800-20. ********

L. BIGLOW
Possibly **Levi Biglow** (b. Sept. 6, 1794 in Fitzwilliam, NH, d. July 8, 1874 in Randolph, VT) who was listed as a mechanic at his death. Examples: 12 planes including a quarter round; a round; and a Grecian ovolo & ogee, all 10" beech, ca. 1800. ********

J. BILL
Possibly **John Bill** (b. Nov. 15, 1796 in Middletown, CT) who married Clarissa Gillman on Nov. 12, 1823 in Middletown, CT. Bill was listed in 1850 as a carpenter in Charlestown, Portage Co., OH. In 1860, he was listed as a joiner in Charlestown. Example: on a 21 1/2" beech jointer with a slight offset tote, round strike, and round chamfers on top and flat chamfers on toe and heel, ca. 1820. **UR**

BILLETER & STRAUCH
Billeter & Strauch was a hardware dealer in Allegheny, PA. Example: on a **D. R. Barton** toothing plane. ********

T. BILLINGS
Timothy Billings (b. Aug. 16, 1770 in Canton, Franklin Co., MA, d. Jul. 7, 1860 in Deerfield, Franklin Co.) was a housewright and furniture maker in Greenfield and Deerfield, MA. He moved to Deerfield, at age 16, and was apprenticed to **Capt. Hopkins King** of Northfield. In 1799, he advertised in the *Greenfield Gazette* as a joiner. In 1802, he was credited for building the West Springfield Meeting House. In 1850, he was listed as in agriculture in Deerfield, MA. The inventory of his estate listed $26 worth of bench tools and lumber. Examples: on a beech molder with relieved wedge and flat chamfers; a cooper's howel with two rams horn iron wing nuts, ca. 1800; and a 9 1/8" beech complex molder with a birch relieved wedge and round chamfers, ca. 1810-20. ********

J. BINGHAM
Example: on a 9 1/2" beech narrow skew rabbet with flat Chamfers, found in western NY, ca. 1812. **UR**

ROBERT BINGHAM
Robert Bingham was listed as a planemaker working for **D. R. Barton**, in 1849; for **L. & I. J. White**, from 1854-63, then for himself in Buffalo, NY, in 1864-65.
No imprint has been reported.

G. H. BIRD
Possibly **George H. Bird** (b. 1809 in England, d. Apr. 26, 1899 in Kings Co., NY), came to America on Aug. 28, 1832. He was listed as a cabinetmaker at 507 Grand St., New York City in 1843-44. Example: on the toe and heel of a fixed sash. **UR**

M. BIRD
Example: on a 9 15/16" birch fenced rabbet with flat chamfers, possibly from New England, ca. 1790. ********

B. PLANE/ THE BIRMINGHAM PLANE MFG. CO.
George E. Mosher of Birmingham, CT, was issued Patent No. 309,400, on Dec. 16, 1884 and Patent No. 413,300, on Oct. 22, 1889, for a wood-bottom 10 1/8" smoothing plane; and a 15" Jack, both with a single iron, and the same adjustment mechanism as used on this companies cast iron planes. The company name was changed to **Derby Plane Manufacturing Co.** when the Birmingham area became part of Derby, CT in 1891. In 1900, the Derby Plane Manufacturing Co. was purchased by the **Union Manufacturing Co.** of New Britain, CT. It continued listing only a few sizes of wood bottom planes along with its all-metallic bench planes. (see *Patented Transitional & Metallic Planes in America*, 1827-1927, p. 192, by Roger K. Smith) **UR**

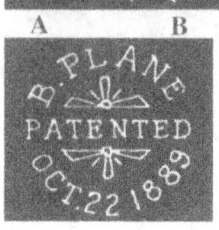

A   B

LEVI BISBEE
In 1794, **Levi Bisbee** (b. Mar. 22, 1776 in Plymouth Co. MA, d. Jul. 15, 1846 in Rochester, Plymouth Co.) was apprenticed to **Elisha Clark** of Middleboro, MA "to learn the art and mystery of cabinet maker or shop joiner". **Levi** became a Windsor chair maker. **No imprint has been reported.**

F. BISCHOFF
Example: on a 9 1/2" beech astragal with flat chamfers, possibly from rural PA, ca. 1800. **UR**

J. BISCOS
John Biscos (b. Apr. 20, 1738 in Watertown, MA, d. Mar. 15, 1808 in Spencer, Worcester Co., MA) was from Leicester, Worcester Co. of which Spencer was a part of until 1753. **John Biscos** was the representative to the MA General Court in 1777, 1780-81. He was appointed Justice of Peace, in 1781, by Gov. Hancock. This imprint appeared on a group of planes found together in western MA, including an **F. Nicholson**, five **Ce. Chelors** and two with the **J. BISCOS** imprint only. It appears that **J. Biscos** was a cabinetmaker contemporary to **Cesar Chelor** who made several additional planes for himself. Example: on a 9 7/8" birch complex molder with a relieved wedge, wide flat chamfers and chamfer stops similar to **Ce. Chelor**. *****

HOMER BISHOP & CO.
Homer Bishop & Co. was a hardware store at 112 & 114 Milk St., Boston, MA, in 1870. It was succeeded, in 1873, by **MaComber, Bigelow & Dowse**. Example: as an overstrike on a 11 7/8" handled moving filletster made by the **Taber Plane Co.**. (see *Patented Transitional & Metallic Planes in America, Vol. II*, p. 79, by Roger K. Smith) ***

I. BISHOP
Examples: on a 9 1/2" straight rabbet; and a 9 3/8" hollow also imprinted with **I. SYM** and branded on the side with an incuse **I ADAM**, both beech with flat chamfers, ca. 1790-1800. **UR**

L. BISHOP
Examples: on a skew rabbet with relieved wedge; an 1" ogee with bead, both are 10" beech with flat chamfers; and a 9 1/2" beech straight rabbet with 19c chamfers, ca. 1790-1830. **UR**

E. BITNER
Examples: on a 9 1/2" beech complex molder; and a 15 1/2"x 3 1/4" beech, center toted complex molder, ca. 19c. **UR**

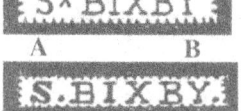

R. BIXBY
Example: on a 9 3/4" birch narrow hollow with shallow wide flat chamfers. ca. 1790. **UR**.

S. BIXBY
Soloman Bixby (b. ca. 1775 in MA, d. Dec. 4, 1864 in Vergennes, VT) was listed in 1850 as a cabinetmaker in Vergennes, VT. Examples: on a wide round; and a skew rabbet, both 10" beech with wide flat chamfers, ca. 1790. **UR**

A   B

E. BLABY
Examples: on a 10" beech rabbet with small flat chamfers; and a 9 1/4" beech hollow with round chamfers, ca. 1800-20. **UR**

J. B. BLACK
Example: on a square compassed rabbet, ca. 1850. **UR**

C. BLACKBURN
Examples: on a 1/2" single-boxed side bead; a wide ogee; a 9 5/8" dado with size **7/8** on the heel; and a 9 9/16" molder, all beech, ca. 1840. ****

BENJAMIN BLACKLIDGE
Benjamin Blacklidge was listed as a planemaker in New York City, in 1835. **No imprint has been reported.**

BLACKSTONE WORKS
A number of Boston planemakers **Cooley, Montgomery** and **Woodbridge** made planes on Blackstone Street. A little further south and west, running from Worcester, MA, to Providence, RI, is the Blackstone River, and at the RI border is Blackstone, MA. The **Blackstone Works** could have derived its name from any of these locations. Example: on a narrow coffin miter, ca. 1850. *****

D. BLAIR
Example: on a 9 1/2" yellow birch molder, ca. 19c. **UR**

BLAIR & CO./ W. BLAIR & CO./ WM. BLAIR & CO.
William Blair & Co. was a Chicago, IL, hardware company from 1844-88; from 1844, it was listed as **Wm. Blair, Stove & Tin Factory**; from 1845-46, as **C. B. Blair & Co.**; from 1846-48, as **Blair & Stinson Iron & Hardware**; and from 1853-88, it was **Wm. Blair & Co.**
A, B & C ***

E: BLAKE
Example: on a single 20" birch jointer with round chamfers, ca. 1820. **No imprint is available.**

E. BLANCHARD
Ephraim Blanchard (b. Mar. 1, 1778 in Billerica, Middlesex Co., MA, d. Jun. 27, 1841 in Amherst, Hampshire Co., MA) was a cabinetmaker active in Amherst, NH, from 1800-30. Examples: on 9 1/2" birch molders including a size **1/2** bead with flat chamfers, ca. 1800. **No imprint is available.**

I. BLANCHARD
Examples: on a beading plane; a table round; and a complex molder, all 9 1/2" beech with heavy flat chamfers. The front of the wedge slot is chamfered as are the upper edges of the wedge, possibly from rural New England, ca. 1800 ****

J. BLANCHD
Example: on a 21" birch fore plane with a decorative closed tote and flat chamfers, ca. 1780. **UR**

I+ BLANK
Examples: on a 9 3/4" side bead; a 9 13/16" round; and a 9 13/16" quarter round, all beech with heavy flat chamfers, ca. 1800. **UR**

BLASDELL/ C. BLASDELL
Examples: on a round; and two complex molders, one double-boxed, all 9 3/4" beech with heavy flat chamfers and an **I. Sleeper** style wedge. One example is also struck with an owner's mark **M. R. Ranlet**. There were several **Blasdell's** clockmakers in Chester, NH, and two clockmakers named **Ranlet** in Gilmanton, NH, confirming a NH origin, ca. 1800. An earlier appearing **BLASDELL** imprint with a straight border is on a 10 1/4" birch ogee molding with an ogee shoulder, a round finial and large shallow flat chamfers. ca. 1780, possibly more than one generation. No example of the early imprint is available. ***

J. E. BLISS
J. E. Bliss was listed as a Northampton, MA, planemaker. **No dates known. No imprint has been reported.**

L. BLISS
Lemuel Bliss (b. Aug. 15, 1791 in Rehoboth, MA, d. Jul. 19, 1859 in Jericho Corners, VT) settled in Calais, VT, and was listed there in 1820, engaged in manufacturing. In 1829-30, he advertised in the **Vermont Watchman & State Gazette** for a "journeyman cabinetmaker" in the adjacent town of Marshfield where he remained until after 1830. In 1840, he was listed in Jericho, VT, in "manufactures & trades", and in 1850, as a carpenter. Examples: on a 9 3/8" beech tongue & groove pair with round chamfers, ca. 1820. **UR**

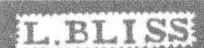

R. BLISS MFG. CO.
Rufus Bliss (b. Mar. 7, 1802 in Bristol. MA, d. 1879) remained on the family farm until he was 21 when he became a carpenter's apprentice for 2 years. In 1825, he removed to Pawtucket, Providence Co., RI. In 1832, at age 30, **Rufus Bliss** founded **R. Bliss Manufacturing, Co.** They produced wooden screws, clamps and bench vises for piano and cabinet makers. He invented a machine for cutting wood screws. In 1845, he sold a half interest to **Albert N. Bullock**, his nephew, and took the name **R. Bliss & Co**. In 1857, the firm was joined by **Edwin R. Clark** and **Alva C. Bullock**. From 1850-70, Rufus was listed as a wood turner. **Rufus** retired in 1863 due to poor health. In 1871, the company started to produce wooden toys. By 1917, **Bliss Manufacturing Co.** was primarily known for its wooden toys, "A, B, & C" wood blocks, and doll houses that were covered with lithographed color prints. Example: on a scraper shaped like a rabbet plane. *****

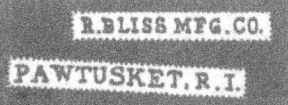

T. BLISS

T. Bliss worked in Buckston, ME, prior to 1807. (In 1807 Buckston's name was changed to Buncksport) Examples: the A1 imprint is on a 9 1/4" hollow. The A imprint is on a 9 1/4" nosing plane, both beech with small flat chamfers. The B imprint is on a beech bead; and birch skew rabbet, both 9 1/2" with round chamfers, ca. 1820. ****

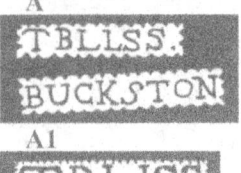

C. BLOOD

C. Blood was a cooper's tool and wooden plane maker. This name has been reported on a cooper's howel plane. **No imprint is available.**

D. BLOOM

Example: on a 23 3/4"x 2 1/2" beech skew ship's rabbet with a nicker, an open centered tote, and shallow round chamfers, ca. 1830-40. **UR**

C. BLOOMER

Possibly a modification of the **C. G. Boomer** imprint and use by the next generation. Example: on a 22"x 3 1/2" beech jointer with a centered closed tote, heavy flat chamfers on the toe and heel, and round chamfers on the top, ca. 1810. **UR**

C. G. BLOOMER

Example: on a 17 7/8" beech panel raiser with a closed tote and flat chamfers, ca. 1790. **UR**

R. BLOOMER

Example: on a 9 5/8" hickory single-boxed bead with shallow round chamfers, ca. 1830. **UR**

W. BLOSER

Examples: on a 10" beech complex molder with intermittent boxing; a 10 1/16" fruitwood astragal; and a panel raiser with offset tote and square wedge top, all with heavy flat chamfers, possibly from rural PA, ca. 1790. **UR**

I. B/ I. BLOSFOM

Probably a descendant of **Thomas Blossom** who was a 1629 immigrant to the Plymouth Colony from Holland. Examples: on a large hollow with size **8** on the toe; a large unboxed bead; a plow; and an astragal, all 9 1/2" beech with heavy flat chamfers. Two of these planes plus a third, an unsprung complex molder, are also marked with the 18c. style initial group **I.B**. ca. 1790-1820. ****

RD BLOSS

Example: on a 9 1/2" beech size **5** round with flat chamfers and a **Butcher** iron, ca. 19c. **UR**

W. H. BLY/ .W. H. BLYE/ W. H. BLYES PATENT

William H. Blye (b. Oct. 3, 1807 in DeRuyter, Madison Co., NY, d. Nov. 17, 1874 in Syracuse, Onondaga Co., NY) was listed in 1850-60, as a carpenter & joiner in DeRuyter, a town south of Cazenovia, NY. In 1864-65, he was listed as a carpenter in Syracuse; from 1867-72, he was listed as a pattern maker. **Blye** received Patent No. 6304, on April 10, 1849, for a hinged plane fence that was used for chamfering. Examples: the A imprint appears on a plane that was made by **Joseph Hayden** who was licensed by **Blye**. In 1850-51, Hayden made planes in Syracuse. The **Blye**-patented wooden fences have been reported on planes made by **M. B. Tidey** and **E. C. Ring**. A handled rabbet with the patented fence, has an adjustable tie rod attached. The B imprint is on a 9 1/2"x 3/4" beech boxed bead without the fence, a conventional plane. The C imprint is on an 11 3/4" closed handled grooving plane made by **Hayden/ Syracuse, NY**. A, B & C ****

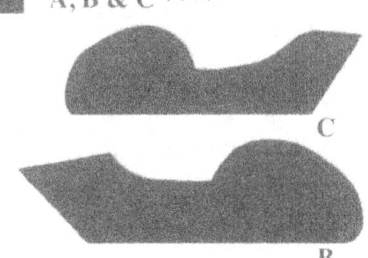

I BOCK

Examples: on a 13 1/2" sash; and a 13 7/16" beech tongue, both with offset open totes and heavy flat chamfers. The sash plane has the added decoration of a colonial eagle with shield in an embossed circle on the single iron, ca. 1800. **UR**

T. BODDY, JR. & CO.

T. Boddy, Jr. & Co. probably was a hardware dealer in Rochester, NY. Example: on a skew rabbet, ca. 1850. ********

BODMAN & BEARSE

Bodman & Bearse was a Pawtucket, RI, planemaking partnership of **Henry A. Bodman** and **Clarance A. Bearse** (b. 1843 in MA, d. Oct. 20, 1921). In 1860, Clarance, age 18, was listed in Acushnet, MA, in the household of **Ebrnezar Leonard**. In 1870, **Clarance** was listed in New Bedford, MA as a toolmaker. On Sep. 2, 1862, he called himself a boat builder and enlisted in the MA, 47th. Infantry, as a Private. From 1880-1910, **Clarance** was listed as a carpenter in New Bedford, MA. The firm of **Bodman & Bearse** was listed in the 1871 Pawtucket Directory as a plane manufacturer at 57 Pleasant St. Example: on a 16" razee bench plane with the additional location imprint of **PAWTUCKET**. ca. 1860-70. (see **Bodman Bearse & Hussey**, and **Bodman & Hussey**)
No imprint is available.

BODMAN, BEARSE & HUSSEY

Bodman, Bearse & Hussey was a 1871 Pawtucket, RI, planemaking partnership of **Henry A. Bodman, Clarence A. Bearse** and **John Hussey**. In the 1870 census, they were listed in New Bedford, MA, working for **J. M. Taber**. This firm lasted about six months and was listed in the 1871 Pawtucket Directory at 57 Pleasant St., stating "We sharpen our molding planes ready for use. Particular attention paid to repairing and sharpening planes, every plane warranted." They were succeeded by **Bodman & Hussey** in late 1871. Examples: on a size **10** hollow & round pair. *******

BODMAN & HUSSEY

A partnership of **Henry A. Bodman** and **John Hussey**, planemakers from Pawtucket, RI, who were successors, in 1871, to **Bodman, Bearse & Hussey**. The firm was listed in the 1872 Pawtucket, RI, directory as "Plane Manufs.", located at 57 Pleasant St. ******

C. BOEHLKE

Chadwick Boehlke is a contemporary plane maker located in North Platte, NE. Example: on an 8 11/16" smoother with the added date **04**, for the year 2004. Made of a maple core with walnut laminated sides and a Russian olive wedge. *******

JOHN BOERNHOEFT

John Boernhoeft was listed as a planemaker in New York City, for 1850 only. In the years preceding and following he was listed as a "piano maker". **No imprint has been reported.**

J. BOGERT

John B. Bogert was a New York City hardware dealer from 1842-70. He was listed for one year as an "Imp(orter)". Also listed as **J. Bogert, Welch, White, Vanglaw & Co.**. Examples: the A imprint is from a 9 1/2"x 3/4" beech beading plane. The B imprint is from a 13 1/2" boxed and toted complex molder with a 2 1/2" wide **James Cam** iron. **A, A1, B & B1 ******

M. BOGGS

Example on an 8 5/8"x 2/8" boxed bead, yellow birch with flat chamfers. ca. 1800. **No imprint is available.**

WILLIAM K. BOGGES/ WILLIAM K. BOGGUS

William K. Boggus was listed as a planemaker in Cincinnati, OH, in 1839-40. In 1850, **William K. Bogges** was listed as a planemaker in St. Louis, MO directories.
No imprint of either name has been reported.

BOGMAN & VINAL

Bogman & Vinal was a hardware partnership of **George E. Bogman** (b. 1843, d. Jan. 30, 1882 in Brookline, MA) and **James W. Vinal** (b. 1842 in Quincy, MA, d. Mar. 21, 1901 in Boston, Suffolk Co., MA) in Roxbury, MA. In 1851, **G. E. Bogman** was listed as a "hardware dealer", at 7 Dock Sq., Boston. **James W. Vinal** was listed 1860, age 18, as a "clerk".

Bogman & Vinal were dealers in "builder's hardware and carpenter's tools" at No. 7 Dock Square, Boston, MA, from 1867-82. Example: on a 9 1/2" beech double-iron ship hollow made by **J. R. Tolman**. *********

G. BOHN

Examples: on a 9 1/2" beech small molder with the B wedge; and a 9 1/4" fruitwood small complex molder with the A wedge, both with heavy round chamfers, possibly from eastern PA, ca. 1810-20. *******

HENRY BOKER

Example: on an 8 1/2" beech smoothing plane with a double-iron and rounded chamfers, ca. 19c. **UR**

N. BOMEN
Example: on a 9 7/8" birch, lignum vitae boxed style **NO. 4** bead with flat chamfers, ca. 1800. **UR**

J. BOND
Example: on a 10" beech complex molder possibly altered from a rabbet with heavy flat chamfers, ca. 1790. **UR**

N. BOND
Example: on a 9 1/2" beech round with heavy round chamfers. **UR**

BOND & SARGEANT
Bond & Sargeant advertised themselves as "General Dealers in Hardware" in the 1836 Buffalo, NY, city directory. ***

CHRISTOPHER BONNELL
Christopher Bonnell was listed in 1851, as a planemaker, on Zanes Island near Wheeling, VA, (now WV). Probably he worked for **W. Steele** as a bench hand.
No imprint has been reported.

BONNELL & WILLIAMS
James Bonnell & **Henry Williams** were Milwaukee, WI, hardware dealers who handled tools into the late 1840's.
No imprint has been reported.

I. BOON
Examples: on a pair of 9 3/8" beech side rabbets with round chamfers. The embossed imprint is on both toes and the incuse imprint on one heel. **UR**

BEBEE BOOTH
Bebee Booth (b. Jul. 7, 1793 in New Haven, CT, d. Mar. 8, 1888 in Putnam Co., IN) was listed as a merchant, in 1850, in Harrison, Vigo Co., IN. In 1860, he was listed as a merchant in Terre Haute, Vigo Co.; in 1880, as retired merchant in Terre Haute. ****
BOOTH
TERRE HAUTE

R. W. BOOTH
Ralph W. Booth (b. May 26, 1818, d. Feb. 14, 1884 in Brooklyn, Kings Co., NY) was a partner in **Clark & Booth**, in 1846, in Cincinnati, OH, as a wholesale hardware dealer. From 1849-52, it was **R. W. Booth**, wholesale hardware and cutlery, 93 Main, "will remove in the fall to s.w.c. Walnut and Pearl". From 1853-79, it was **R. W. Booth & Co.** importers and wholesale dealers in hardware, cutlery and guns, s.w.c. Pearl & Walnut. In 1861, the firm was with **R. W. Booth, John Young, Frank Alter**, and **A. D. Rogerg**. In 1866, the firm was with **R. W. Booth, C. B. Waldo,** and **Thos. Colville**. In 1878, the firm was with **R. W. Booth, R. W. Booth Jr.,** and **W. T. Minor**. Example: the D imprint is form a 21 3/4" fore plane.
A & C **; B, C1, D & D1 ***

JACOB BOPE
Jacob Bope (b. Nov. 17, 1798 in VT, d. Sep. 8, 1889 in Lancaster, OH) was listed in Lancaster, Fairfield Co., OH, as a house carpenter and cabinet-maker. In 1828, he had an apprentice in Pleasant Township, Fairfield Co., OH. In 1850-70, he was listed as a farmer. Example: on a smoother with the date **1847**. ****

E. BORDMAN
Examples: the A imprint is on an 11" beech thumbscrew-lock slide-arm fenced skewed rabbet with a **I. Sleeper** style wedge; a 9 1/8" birch straight rabbet with shallow flat chamfers; a 9 5/8" beech astragal with tight round chamfers; and a 9 1/2" beech dado with early 19c. chamfers. The B imprint is on a 9 1/2" beech molder; and a wide hollow, both with shallow round chamfers, found with a **L. Bordman** plane in Westminster, MA, ca. 1790-1820. ****

L. BORDMAN
Possibly **Langlet Bordman** (b. 1760 in MA, d. 1829) a cabinetmaker in Portsmouth, NH. He served an apprenticeship in NH, shortly after the close of the Revolutionary War. Two examples were found with **E. Bordman** planes in Westminster, MA: on a 9 1/4" rabbet; and a 9 5/8" dado, both birch with heavy flat chamfers, ca. 1790. ****

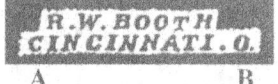

HENRY BORKINBINE
Henry Borkinbine was listed as a planemaker in 1846, boarding with **H. Taylor** in Cincinnati, OH.
No imprint has been reported.

M. BORLAND
Example: on the toe of a split sash also marked **C. Woodruff**, possibly a hardware dealer in New Albany, IA, ca. 19c. **UR**

RUDOLPH BORN
Rudolph Born (b. in Prussia, d. will probated Feb. 28, 1912 in Cook Co., IL) was a tools and hardware dealer at 99 W. Randolph Street, Chicago, IL, from 1876-89. ********

I. BORN/ J. BORN
Example: on an 8 13/16" beech side rabbet with tight flat chamfers, ca. 1810. **A & B: UR**

JOHN BORNHOEFT
Was listed as a planemaker in NY City in 1850.
No imprint has been reported.

F. H. BORRMANN
F. H. Borrmann was a contemporary plane maker in Eastham, MA. Example: dated **1977**. ********

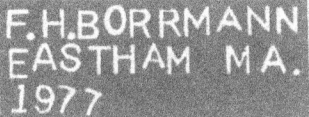

JOSEPH L. BOSS
Joseph L. Boss was a Boston, MA, hardware dealer. An incuse arched imprint with the location **BOSTON** is on the heel of a **Tileston** plane. **No imprint is available.**

P. BOSSART
Examples: on a 12 3/8" fruitwood tongue & groove match pair; and a 9 3/8" beech round with round chamfers on top and flat chamfers on toe and heel, ca. 1840. ********

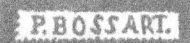 

BOSTON FACTORY
The **Boston Factory** was located on George St., in Cambridge, MA, from 1834-38. Examples: on a 9 3/8" filletster with a boxed edge; and a wide beech molding plane. ********

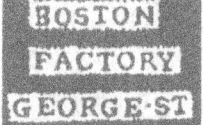 

E. R. BOSWORTH
Example: on a 9 1/2" beech molder, ca. 1860. **UR**

W. W. BOTTUM
Example: on a 9 3/8" beech boxed complex molder with shallow round chamfers, ca. 1820-30. **UR**

 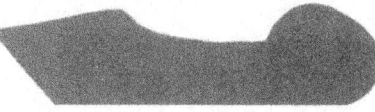

H. E. BOUCHER MFG. CO.
H. E. Boucher Mfg. Co. was located in New York City. Example: on a 3 3/4" miniature smoothing plane. **UR**

D B/ D. BOULTON/ DANIEL BOULTON
Example: the A imprint is branded on the side with the initials **DB** on the toe of a 7 3/4" beech complex molder with flat chamfers, ca. 1800. **A & B: UR**

ABNER BOURN
Example: on a 9 7/16" beech skew rabbet with flat chamfers, found with **T. Waterman** and **E. Clark/Middleboro** planes. *********

BOURNE
This imprint has been observed a few times in both England and America, found with early English makers and a group of mostly **Eastburn** and **Tho. Grant** planes. Example: on a 10 3/16" beech astragal with flat chamfers, ca. 1800. **UR**

BOUTON
Example: on a 9 1/2" small boxed bead with shallow round chamfers, ca. 1810 **UR**

T. J. BOWDEN & SON
Example: on a 11 1/2" low-angle steel-soled coffin-shaped smoother, with an **A. L. Whiting & Co./ Worcester, Mass.** iron, ca. 1850. **UR**

A. BOWEN
One of three 18c imprints on the toe of a 9 7/8" yellow birch skew rabbet with flat chamfers and a relieved wedge of **Jo. Fuller** style, ca. 1790. **UR**

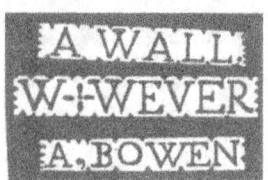

J. H. BOWER
Example: on a 9 1/2" beech double-boxed sash molder plan with screw arms tipped with brass end caps and with the added location of **OHIO** and dated **1846**. **UR**

J. E. BOWKER & CO.
J. E. Bowker & Co. was a Boston, MA, hardware dealer, with **John E. Bowker** (b. Oct. 1843 in MA), in 1872. In 1900, **John E. Bowker** was listed in Chicago, IL. *******

J. J. BOWLES
John Julius Bowles (b. Oct 22, 1811 in Hartford, CT, d. Sep. 16, 1897 in Huntington, Hampshire Co., MA) was an East Hartford, CT, planemaker from 1838-43. He advertised during this period, and a broadside exists offering 48 different types of planes. "Joiners' Tools, Manufactured by **John J. Bowles**, Main Street, Hartford, Conn. and every article warranted good." **John** was listed as a toolmaker in the 1860 census, in Huntington, MA. In 1865, he was listed as an armorer in Springfield, Hampden Co., MA. **Bowles** may have been part of **Brooks & Bowles**. *******

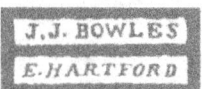

A. BOWMAN
Example: on a 9 1/4" beech large hollow with round chamfers. ca. 1820. **No imprint is available**.

C. E. BOWMAN
C. E. Bowman was a hardware dealer. This imprint with **WARRANTED** is from a skew bead made by **A. E. Baldwin**. **UR**

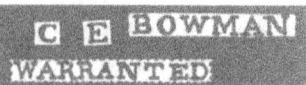

J. BOWMAN
Joseph Bowman (b. 1801) was a shop joiner in New Bedford, MA, in 1821 & 1849. In 1867, **Bowman** was listed as a ship carpenter. Example: on a 16"x 3 1/2" complex molder with slight offset tote and round chamfers. **UR**

I. BOWMAN
Example: on a 9 1/2"x 1/4" beech dado plane with round chamfers and a slotted screw steel and brass depth stop, found in PA, ca. 1820-30. **UR**

B: BOWN
Example: on a 9 3/8" beech side bead with round top chamfers and flat end chamfers, ca. early 19c. **UR**

JOSEPH B. BOYCE
Joseph B. Boyce of Lockport, NY, was issued Patent No. 199,956, on Feb. 5, 1878, for a wood smoothing plane equipped with a cast iron throat piece. The iron was held in place by a wooden wedge. This feature has been reported on an 8"x 2 5/8" beech smoothing plane with a double-iron made by the **Greenfield Tool Co. No imprint is available**. (see *Patented Transitional & Metallic Planes in America - Vol. II*, p. 103, by Roger K. Smith)

A. BOYD
Examples: on a 1 1/4" wide rabbet with the A wedge; and a friction-arm plow with the B wedge, both 9 5/8" beech with heavy flat chamfers, from PA, ca. 1800. **UR**

J. BOYD/ JOHN BOYD
John Quincy Adams Boyd (b. 1784 in Carlisle, Cumberland Co., PA, d. July 22, 1866 in W. Middletown, PA) was in the Hopewell Township, Washington Co., PA (southwest of Pittsburgh, PA) tax records, from 1808-40's. **John Boyd** served in the War of 1812. In 1820, **Boyd** was listed as a carpenter, innkeeper, constable, justice of the peace, and leader in the abolitionist movement. He was also referred to as a planemaker in local memoirs of West Middletown, Washington Co., PA. Examples: most planes are 9 1/2"-9 15/16", one 10 3/4"; most are beech, two are fruitwood, all with round chamfers and found in western PA. (see *Planemakers of Western Pennsylvania and Environs*, by Charles Paine, Jr.) The **J. Boyd** (no imprint available) was reported on a 21" beech foreplane with a steel strike pin and round chamfers, ca. 1820. ********

Jn BOYD
John Boyd with the embossed imprint and a incuse owner imprint of **J. W. BOYD** found in PA. Example: on a 9 3/8" beech dado with a friction wood depth stop, and flat chamfers, ca.1820-30. **UR**

42

N. J. BOYD
Nathaniel Boyd was listed in the New York City directory as a cabinetmaker, in 1821. In 1825, **N. J. Boyd** was listed as "hardware" at 504 Grand. In 1838, he was listed as **Nathaniel I. Boyd**; in 1839, at 518 Grand. There is no record in of the 522 Grand address. Example: on a molding plane made by **J. & W. Webb**. *

BOYD & TOMPSON
Boyd & Tompson was a hardware dealer. Example: on a beech jointer with round chamfers made by **R. M. Tilburn**. *****

A. BOYDEN
Examples: on a beech round with round chamfers; a 9 3/8" astragal; a 16 7/8" skew rabbet with a pegged tote and nicker, both beech with flat chamfers, ca. 1800-20. **UR**

A. BOYER
Examples: the A imprint is on a 10 1/2" beech large round with heavy flat chamfers. The B imprint is on a 14" beech complex molder with an offset tote and a round top iron, possibly from rural PA, ca. 1800. **A & B: UR**

A

B

D. BOYER
Example: on a 10" beech grooving plane with heavy flat chamfers, possibly from rural PA, ca. 1800. **UR**

W. W. & L. C. BOYINGTON
W. W. & L. C. Boyington probably was a hardware dealer. Example: on a fore plane made by **J. Kellogg**. **UR**

J. BRACELIN
James Bracelin (b. Sep. 1814 in NY, d. Jan. 8, 1865 in Dayton, OH) was listed in 1850-64 as an edge tool maker living in Dayton, OH. The **DAYTON. O** location imprint appears to be from the same die as used by **David N. Garrison**, also of Dayton, suggesting some kind of relationship. **A, B & C **

EDWIN L. BRACKETT
Edwin L. Brackett (b. 1835) was listed as a planemaker in Southampton, MA, in the 1860 census. **No imprint has been reported**.

N x BRAD
Example: on a 9 9/16" cherry halving plane with large shallow flat chamfers found in CT, ca. 1780. **UR**

JOHN BRADFORD
John Bradford was a Boston, MA, hardware dealer active ca. 1820-47. He was listed in the 1841 directory under "planes", located at 21 Dock Sq. **No imprint has been reported**.

J. BRADFORD
Joseph Bradford (b. June 1806 in Turner, ME, d. May 21, 1884) made cooper's, carpenter's, and ship joiner's tools in Portland, ME, from 1837-1884. In 1837, He was reported on Union St., the same location as **Abel Sampson**. The 1860 census reported **Bradford** had one employee, and produced $1000 worth of cooper's tools, $200 worth of joiner's tools and $100 in repairs. The 1870 census reported 600 tools made worth $2000. **B, B1 & C *; A, ****

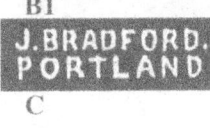

F. S. BRADLEY & CO.
F. S. Bradley & Co. was a New Haven, CT, hardware dealer, active from 1866-91. The B imprint, in ink, has the name **F. S. BRADLEY & Co.** in an arch with an anvil below and HARDWARE/ 243 STATE STREET/ NEW HAVEN, CONN. The B imprint is not available. ****

BRADLY (possibly BRADLEY)
Examples: on a 9 3/4" beech complex molder with flat chamfers; and two molders 9 3/16" & 9 1/8", both with flat chamfers and interrupted lignum boxing. **No imprint is available**.

JAMES BRADLEY
James Bradley was a New Haven, CT, planemaker who worked ca. 1800. Examples: the A imprint is on a 9 3/8" fixed sash with two irons and wedges. The B imprint is on a panel raiser; and a 9 1/2" steep pitch round, all beech with flat chamfers. A ****; B *****

A

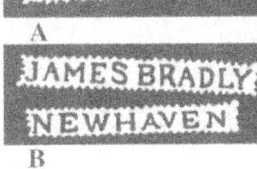
B

JOHN S. BRADLEY
A name die with **JOHN S. BRADLEY** and the location **NEW HAVEN, CONN** has been reported.
No plane with this imprint has been reported.

G: S. BRADWELL
Example: on a 9" beech plow with wood thumbscrews, a slopping wood depth stop, a riveted skate and heavy flat chamfers. ca. 1800-15. **No imprint is available.**

BRAGAW & BLAKE
Isaac Bragaw and **Howard P. Blake** were plane manufacturers and hardware dealers in Hartford, CT, from 1847-50. (see **Kennedy & Bragaw**) **No imprint has been reported.**

L. C. BRAGDON
Example: on a 9 1/2" beech skew rabbet, ca. 1850-60.   **UR**

J. G. BRAGG
Examples: three 9 3/8" birch molders with relieved wedges; and a beech smoother, imprinted twice, ca. 1800.   **UR**

S. BRANCH
Believed to be **Stephen Branch** (b. 1762, d. Nov. 28, 1828 in Lisbon, CT), of Lisbon, New London Co., CT. He appeared in the Federal Census in 1790 & 1800. He was a joiner with joiner's and turning tools, bench, vise and lathe in the inventory of his estate. Another **Samuel Branch** (b. 1701, d. 1756) from Preston, CT, was a cabinetmaker but is too early for these planes. Examples: on a Yankee plow; molders are 9 7/8"-10", one with a small pegged open tote; and one is 8", all birch with flat chamfers, ca. 1780.   ********

F. C. BRANDT
F. C. Brandt was a hardware dealer located at 55 Elder St., Cincinnati, OH, active from 1850-70. Example: on a **Scioto Works** 15 3/4" Jack plane with an **Ohio Tool Co.** iron.   *********

BRAUNSDORF & GERSTNER
Braunsdorf & Gerstner was a hardware firm. Example: on a **G. W. Denison** plane and account book.   *********

W. BRAZENER
Examples: on a pair of 9 1/2" beech side rabbet planes with flat chamfers, ca. 1800-10.   **UR**

BRAZER
Benjamin Brazer (b. Dec. 8, 1803, d. Apr. 3, 1857 in Boston, MA) was a partner in **Gardner & Brazer** in Boston, MA, in 1825, when he was also listed as a planemaker. He was listed in the Lowell, MA, directory of 1832, as a toolmaker; and in the 1833-35 directories, as a planemaker; He appears in the 1840-50 census, as a carpenter, in Boston, MA. The **Wentworth & Brazer** partnership preceding both **Brazer**'s Lowell and Boston periods of working by himself and with **Brazer/Lowell** preceding **Brazer/Boston**.
A & B *******

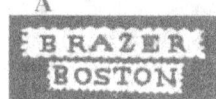
A

B

J. G. BREARLY & CO.
Example: on a single 9 1/2" x 7/8" beech boxed bead, ca. 1850.   **UR**

G. BREMERMAN
Gerd Bremermann was a St. Louis hardware merchant. He operated under **G. Bremerman**, from 1848-54; **Bremermann Raschoe & Co.**, from 1857-60; and **G. Bremermann & Co.**, from 1864-67. No imprints of **G. Bremermann & Co.** or **Bremermann Raschoe & Co.** have been reported.   ********

C. BRETT
Believed to be **Calvin Brett** (b. 1768, d. 1801), a blacksmith in Bridgewater, MA. Example: on a 9 3/4" birch stick and rebate sash with flat chamfers, ca. 1790.   **UR**

J. BRETT
This imprint is similar in appearance to that of **C. Bett** and is also from New England. Example: on a 9 1/2" Birch single-boxed bead with round chamfers, ca. 1820.   **UR**

H. BREWER
Example: on a 9 3/8" beech complex molding plane with flat chamfers, ca. 1800-10.   **UR**

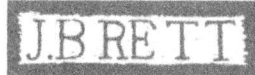

J. BREWER
J. Brewer was a hardware dealer in **RICHMOND** (VA). Example: on a pair of molding planes made by **SIMS**, London.   ********

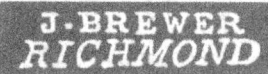

N. BREWER
Examples: on a 10 1/4" fruitwood complex molder; and a 9 3/4" birch hollow, both with heavy flat chamfers. One example was found in VT, ca. 1790.   UR

THOMAS J. BREWER
Thomas J. Brewer was listed in 1827, as a planemaker, located at 401 Broome St, New York City, the address of **David Hanley**. **No imprint has been reported**.

A. BREWSTER
Example: on a 14 1/2" scrub plane with a slight off set tote, ca. 1820-30.   UR

JOHN BRICE
John Brice of Sand Hill, NY, was issued Patent No. 357,454, on Feb. 8, 1887, for a beech jack plane. Example: imprinted with **Brown Tool Co.** on the toe and with an **Auburn Tool Co.** iron. **No imprint is available**.

BRIDGE/ J. B. BRIDGE
Joseph Bushnell Bridge (b. Aug. 22, 1803 in Liverpool, England, d. Oct. 3, 1864 in Washington, DC). In 1841, the Islington, Liverpool, England census listed **J. B. Bridge's** occupation as plane maker. He arrived in New York, on Apr. 27, 1852, from Liverpool, England and was listed as a toolmaker; from 1855-64, he was listed as a planemaker in Washington, DC; in 1867, he was a carpenter in DC. Examples: The B imprint is from a rosewood screw-arm plow; and a raze toted dado with a brass depth stop.
A & B ****

BRIDGE TOOL CO.
The Bridge Tool Co. was a brand used by **Shapleigh Hardware Co.**, St Louis, MO, for second quality iron and wood-bottomed planes, during the 20c. Examples: on a transitional style 26" fore plane with a lever cap; and an 8" coffin smoothing plane with **BRIDGE/REGISTERED** on the iron.   **

N. BRIDGES
Example: on a 9 3/4" birch bead with a fruitwood wedge, a small round finial, and wide shallow flat chamfers, ca. 1750.   UR

DAVID A BRIDGES
David Allen Bridge (b. Apr. 29, 1831 in Stamford, VT) was listed in the 1880 census, as a mechanist of Vineland, Cumborland Co., NJ. In 1881-82, he was listed as a cabinetmaker and pattern maker. **David A. Bridges** was issued Patent No. 271,569, on Jan. 30, 1883, assigning 3/4 interested to **John Gage, Sr.** The plane was produced by the **Gage Tool Co.** The design was a wood body razee bench plane with an adjustable metallic throat insert with the longitudinal adjustment of the cutter and cutter clamping device. In 1900, he was listed as a pattern maker in Holly Beach, Cape May, NJ. In 1862, **David A. Bridge** enlisted in the Civil War at Haniver, NY, and was mustered out on Jun. 13, 1865. **No imprint has been reported**.

BRIGGS
Example: imprinted on the toe and heel of a 9 1/2"x 1/8" beech dado plane, ca. 1850.   UR

C. BRIGGS
Possibly **Cornelius Briggs** (b. 1787 in Weymouth, MA, d. Feb. 2, 1847 in Roxbury, MA) who was believed to be apprenticed to **Abel White.** In 1817, **Briggs** was listed as a cabinetmaker in Boston, MA. Example on a 14 1/8"x 7" wide (6" iron) cherry crown molder with heavy flat chamfers, ca. 1810.   UR

E. BRIGGS
Probably **Elisha Briggs** (b. 1738 in Bristol Co., MA, d. Sep. 5, 1803 in Keene, NH) who was a joiner, millwright, and housebuilder. He married in Wrentham in 1758. He came to Keene, NH, in 1763. In 1775, **Elisha** excavated a canal to a grist and saw mill in Keene. Other possibilities include **Eliphalet Briggs** (b. 1713 in Wrentham, MA, d. Jun. 28, 1780 in Keene, NH), who was **Elisha's** father and who came to Keene in 1767, or earlier. A third possibility is **Capt. Eliphalet Briggs** (b. 1735 in Taunton, MA, d. Oct. 11, 1776 in Keene, NH of small pox), who came to Keene in 1768 or earlier and was selectman and a delegate to the Convention on Safety. A fourth possibility was his son **Eliphalet Briggs** (b. Jan. 26, 1765 in Norton, MA, d. Mar. 23, 1827 in Keene, NH). Finally **Eliphalet Briggs Jr.** (b 1788 in Keene, NH, d. Jun. 13, 1853 in Keen, NH) was a cabinetmaker, active in 1810. All came from Norton, MA, where **H. Wetherel** made planes, using a similar **IN NORTON** imprint. Examples: on a 10 3/16" birch molder (wedge profile shown); and a 9 7/8" birch tongue & groove pair with flat chamfers, ca. 1765.   *****

J. G. BRIGGS
Joseph G. Brigg (b. 1805, d. Nov. 12, 1876 in Keene, NH) who was listed as a carpenter, joiner and cabinetmaker and his brother **Lyman Briggs** (b. May 15, 1803 in VT, d. Apr. 11, 1868 in Detroit, MI) and was listed in 1850, as a cabinetmaker in Montpelier, VT. Both were sons of **Eliphalet Briggs** and were partners in **L. & J. G. Briggs** in Montpelier, VT, from 1826-29. In 1829, **J. G. Briggs** moved to Claremont, NH, where he was a cabinetmaker. Example: on a 9 1/2" beech round with round chamfers, found in VT, ca. 1820.   UR

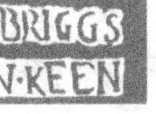

N. BRIGGS
Nathaniel Briggs (b. Aug. 23, 1744 in Norton, MA, d. Oct. 18, 1777 of wounds received at the Battle of Bennington, VT). He was the second cousin of **Elisha Briggs** and **Eliphalet Briggs, Jr.** Nathaniel's brother, **Rufus Briggs**, married Margaret Wetherel and stayed in MA. Nathaniel moved from Norton to Keene about 1773. On Aug. 16, 1777, a Hessian detachment, on a foraging mission, was struck by **John Stark's** Green Mountain militiamen at the Battle of Bennington, VT. The entire British force of 700 were killed, wounded or captured. Seventy American patriots were killed including **Nathaniel Briggs**. His estate included planes and other woodworking tools but there is no record as to his trade. His father and brothers were all woodworkers. Examples: on a 10 1/8" tongue & groove pair with relieved wedges; and a 9 7/8" round, all birch with flat chamfers, ca. 1775. *****

S. BRIGGS
Probably **Seth Briggs** (b. Nov. 8, 1748 in Milton, MA, d. Jun. 17, 1781 in Pembroke, MA) who was listed as a shipbuilder. Examples: on a 12 5/8" tongue & groove plank match pair with heavy flat chamfers; and a 14 1/8" skew rabbet with a relieved wedge and round chamfers, all birch with open totes; and a 7 5/8" birch smoothing plane with round chamfers, ca. 1790-1800. ****

T B/ THOMs. BRIGGS
Example: on a 9 1/4" beech straight rabbet with flat chamfers, ca. 1790. UR

W. BRIGGS
Possibly **William Briggs** who was listed as a cabinetmaker at Cranston St., Providence, RI, in 1832. Examples: on a 9 1/2" beech round with round chamfers; and a 9 1/2" fruitwood molder with a birch wedge, ca. 1820-30. UR

W. A. BRIGGS (see Pond & Briggs)

A. BRIGHT
A **Bright** was a Pittsburgh, PA planemaker who was in the partnership of **A. Bright & J. Chappell**, from 1836-39. Example: on a 1 3/4" wide skew rabbet. *****

A. BRIGHT/ J. CHAPPELL/ A. BRIGHT & J. CHAPPELL
A. Bright & J. Chappel (Chappell) were listed in the 1837 Pittsburgh, PA, business directory as planemakers. By 1839, Chappell was listed without Bright. Example: the B imprint with the date **1836**, is on a screw-arm beech plow with boxwood arms and nuts. (see **J. Chappell**)
A, & B ****

BRIGHT & CO.
Bright & Co. was a hardware dealer in Pottsville, PA, ca. mid to late 19c. UR

EARL M. BRINTON
Earl M. Brinton was listed as a planemaker in Severn, MD. No date given. **No example has been reported.**

E. P. BRINTNALL
Example: on a 30" fore plane with a **W. Butcher** iron, ca. 1850. UR

C. BRITTON
C. Britton with **HAWKINS/ 136 LEWIS ST.** has been reported. **No imprint is available.**

J. F. BROADHEAD
J. F. Broadhead was listed as a maker of cooper's tools and wooden planes. **No imprint has been reported.**

T. BROBIN
Example: on a 9 1/4" round with round chamfers, ca. 1820. UR

A. F. BROMBACHER & CO.
A. F. Brombacher & Co. was a New York City hardware dealer, that claimed to have been established in 1760, carried tools for coopers, and issued a catalog as late as 1922. The **A. F. Brombacher & Co.** line included howel and croze head floats, sun planes, and cooper's jointers made by both **D. R. Barton** and **L. & I. J. White**. The 1870 directory listed **Swan & Brombacher**, at 33 Fulton. ***

B. G. BROOKS
B. G. Brooks was listed as a planemaker in Nashua, NH. **No imprint has been reported.**

D. BROOKS
Example: on a gutter plane with an offset tote and the location imprint **PHILa**. **No imprint is available.**

J. BROOKS
Jonathan Brooks (b. 1745 in Woburn, MA, d. 1808 in New London, CT) married **Mercy Chapman**, daughter of **James Chapman** of New London, CT, in 1766, he was 21, probably just finishing his apprenticeship. He was a cabinetmaker active in New London, CT, from 1766-1801. **Jonathan** advertised on

Feb. 26, 1768 and Apr. 22, 1768 in the *New London Gazette* as a cabinetmaker. He also advertised on Nov. 13, 1778 and Nov. 26, 1780 in the *Connecticut Gazette* and the *Universal Intelligencer*: Furniture, real estate, building frames and shingles. On Sep. 6, 1781, a British force, led by **Gen. Benedict Arnold**, landed on the west bank of the Thames River and quickly subdued Fort Trumbull, a land battery facing towards the river. This left the town of New London defenseless. **Jonathan Brooks** took up arms and joined other citizen volunteers in the defense of the town. It was to little and to late and New London was sacked and burned. A second force of 800 British red coats attacked the 160 Patriots at Fort Griswold on the eastern side of the river. After several assaults, the British overwhelmed the defenders. Upon **Jonathan's** death in 1808, his cabinetmaking shop on Second St. was given to his middle son **Nathan**. Example: The A imprint has been reported on a birch jointer with an offset tote; a 10 1/8" birch molder with flat chamfers; and a third example in a museum in Canterbury, NH. ca. 1780-90; The B imprint is on a 10" birch Grecian ogee with flat chamfers with an iron marked **GILLAT**, (Sheffield, England. ca. 1790); The C imprint is on a beech 9 3/8" complex molder with flat chamfers, ca. 1800.
A, A1, B & C *****

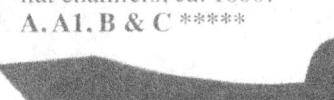

J. R. BROOKS
Example: on a 6 1/2" beech coffin smoother, ca. 1840. **UR**

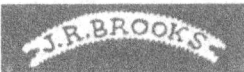

O. H. BROOKS
Examples: on a 10 1/2" molder; and a 15 1/2" panel raising plane, both beech with flat chamfers, ca. 1810. **UR**

P. BROOKS/ P. BROOKS & CO.
Peter Brooks (b. Jun. 23, 1803 in Upton, MA, d. Oct. 19, 1872 in Westfield, MA) made planes in Williamstown, So. Williamstown, Westfield, and Pittsfield, MA, and East Hartford, CT. The 1840 census showed **Peter Brooks** in East Hartford, CT, with five members of his household in manufacturing, living next door to **H. Crane**. In 1847, **T. Nutting**, invoiced **Brooks** for 450 jointer and 410 jack plane handles. In 1850, **Brooks** was a toolmaker in Westfield, MA. A combination tongue & groove plane has been reported with The D imprint. There is no record of a patent having been issued. He was part of **Brooks & Bowles**. He was also part of **Brooks & Kellogg** in Williamstown, MA, in 1849. In 1860-70, **Peter** was listed in Westfield as a whip maker. Examples: The A2 imprint has a location imprint **N. YORK**, although there is no record of his working in NY. One example of the C imprint has an over stamp by **E. Moses**.

C & C1: FF; B & B1 **;
A, A1, A2 & D *******

W. BROOKS
William Brooks was one of the important 18c Philadelphia, PA, planemakers who worked at 25 key's Alley from 1791 or earlier until 1807. A rabbet plane has the date **1808** on the toe. Listed in 1808-13, "**Brooks Widow** of **William**, plane maker, 25 Key's Alley" and could have continued to sell off stock. From 1814-18 **Rachael Brooks**, **Widow**, was listed as mangler. A mangler is a laundry apparatus used for pressing fabrics, located at 25 Key's Alley. Examples: on a massive 12 1/2" skew rabbet; and a 9 1/2" sash coping plane, both beech with flat chamfers. The B imprint is from a panel raiser with a **John Green** iron (Sheffield 1781-1800), an angled and dovetailed depth stop, chamfered wedge and copper wear plates on the depth stop & fence. **A1 & A2 **; A & B ******

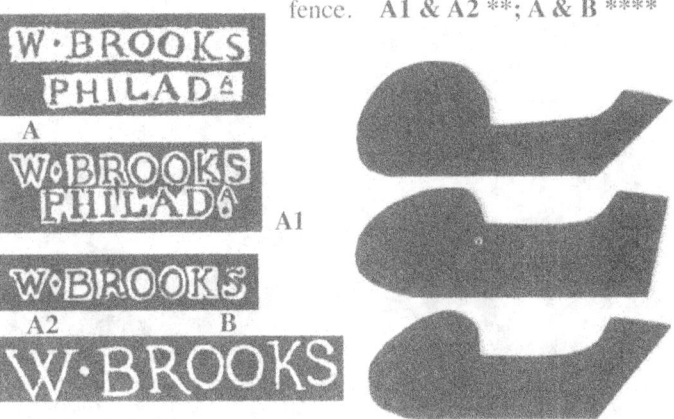

BROOKS & BOWLES
Brooks & Bowles was probably a partnership of **Peter Brooks** and **John J. Bowles**. Example: on a 28" razee jointer, ca. 1850. ********

I + BROUGH
Examples: on a 15" birch ogee molder with an offset tote, a round top iron and flat chamfers; a 9 7/8" molder; a 10" beech large hollow with an **I. Sleeper** style wedge and flat chamfers; and a 9 1/2" beech fixed sash with round chamfers, ca. 1790-1820. (This is not the John Brough from London, ca. 1777). **UR**

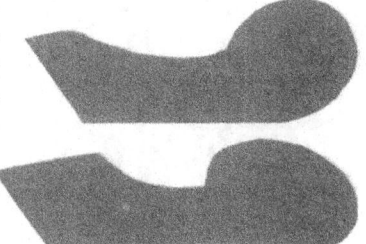

J: BROUSTER
Example: on a 9 3/8" beech complex molder with size **7/8** on the heel and flat chamfers, ca. 1800. **UR**

A. BROWN
One possibility is **Abraham Brown** (b. 1705, d. 1777 in Rowley) who was a housewright. His inventory specified 3 saws, an auger, 7 chisels, a square, a hammer and 3 plane irons. A second and more probable possibility is **Asher Brown** (d. 1815) who was a cabinetmaker in Lisbon, CT. His probate inventory shows **Asher Brown** owned joiners' tools, turning tools and lumber in shop. Examples: are possibly from two separate makers. The A imprint is on a 10 1/16" beech complex molder with an **I. Sleeper** style wedge; and a 10 1/2" beech rabbet with thumbscrew, birch fence, both with flat chamfers. The B imprint is on a 9 3/4" beech molder; and a 10" birch narrow dado, both with flat chamfers, ca. 1780-90, from New England. A & B: *****

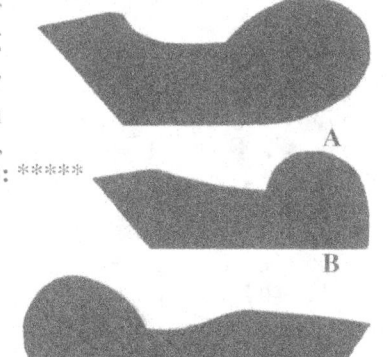

B: BROWN
Example: the A imprint is on a 9 3/8" side bead with round chamfers on the top and flat on the ends. The B imprint is on a match pair of 14"x 1/2" beech tongue & groove planes with round chamfers, ca 19c.
A & B: UR

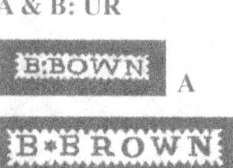
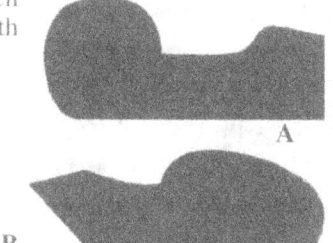

C: BROWN
Example: on a 16" beech panel raising plane with small flat chamfers and dated **1846**, found in the Midwest. **UR**

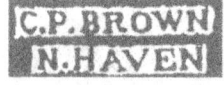

C. P. BROWN
Charles P. Brown was a New Haven, CT, planemaker, whose planes appear to have been made ca. 1840-50. There are two possibilities: **Charles P. Brown** (b. 1798 in CT, d. Nov. 1859 in Genesee Co., NY) and **Charles Brown** (b. Mar. 17, 1801, d. Jan. 13,1876 in New Haven, CT) who was listed in New Haven in the 1840 census as being in "manufacturing of trade" and in the 1850 census as a manufacturer. *****

F. BROWN
Example: on a size **8** round. **UR**

H. BROWN
Example: on a 9 1/2" birch Yankee plow with wedge-lock arms and flat chamfers, ca. 1790-1800. **UR**

H. H. BROWN
Example: on a 16 1/4" beech gutter plane with a centered tote and heavy round chamfers, ca 1820. **UR**

I. BROWN
Example: on a 13 1/2"x 2 1/8" panel raiser with round top wedge & iron and an off set tote; and a 10" thumbnail, both birch with flat chamfers, probably from New England, ca. 1790-1800. **UR**

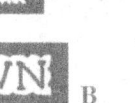

J + BROWN
The initial **J** and name **Brown** are common. There are two strong possibilities: **Jedediah Brown** (b. 1716, d. Oct. 31, 1797 in Stonington, New London CO., CT) who received a pension on Mar. 4, 1789 for service in Washington's 1st. Guards during the American Revolution. Jedediah was a New London, CT, cabinetmaker and farmer. **Brown's** inventory includes a number of woodworking tools including 32 planes. A second possibility is **John Brown**, a cabinetmaker who apprenticed to **O. Pomeroy**. He was active from 1795-1816 in Northampton, MA. Example: on a 13" beech match plank tongue & groove pair, with a birch offset open totes, wedge lock-arms and heavy flat chamfers, probably from New England, ca. 1790. **UR**

J. BROWN
Two possibilities: **Jacob Brown** (b. July, 15 1724, still living on Nov. 18, 1797) who was a cabinetmaker and joiner, and **John Brown** (b. Apr. 9, 1756, Inventory Jan. 18, 1780) a joiner, both from Chester Co., PA. Examples: on a 19 7/8" apple fixed sash with Birch wedge and heavy round chamfers; and a 10 3/8" beech rabbet with heavy flat chamfers, ca. 1790-1820.
A & B: UR

J: BROWN
Example: on a 9 7/16" beech round, found in PA. **UR**

JOn BROWN
Still another **J. Brown** possibly of Chester Co., PA for it was reported from PA. Example: on a 9 1/2" beech side bead with flat chamfers, ca. 1800. **UR**

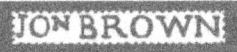

J. G. & F. H. BROWN
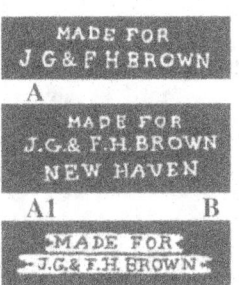

J. G. & F. H. Brown was a New Haven, CT, hardware dealer. Examples: the A imprint is on a **W. H. Pond** T-rabbet. The B imprint is on a **Winstead Plane Co.** molder and a 1/2" combination tongue & groove plane made by **C & S Bulkley** overstruck by **John Denison**. (see **Brown Brothers**)
A & A1 ****; B *****

JAMES R. & WILLIAM BROWN
James R. & William Brown of Boston, MA, were issued Patent No. 112,218, on Feb. 28, 1871, for a 12" beech plow with an integral handle, steel skate & frame and brass adjustment screws. (see *Patented Transitional & Metallic Planes in America, 1827-1927*, p. 78, by Roger K. Smith)
No imprint has been reported.

J. S. BROWN/ NEWBURGH

J. S. Brown was a hardware dealer from Newburgh, NY, in Hudson River Valley. Example: on a **De Forest** plane. ****

J. T. BROWN
J. T. Brown was a Baltimore, MD, planemaker, active in 1842. Example: on a size **7** hollow & round pair. *****

J. T. BROWN
John T. Brown was a planemaker, plane manufacturer, and edge tool maker on Lexington St. Baltimore, MD, active from 1824-43. Examples: the A1 imprint is on a unhandled beech screw-arm plow with boxwood arms and nuts. The B imprint is on an 8 3/4" birch combination tongue & grove plane with size **1/2** on the heel.
A *; A1 & B ****

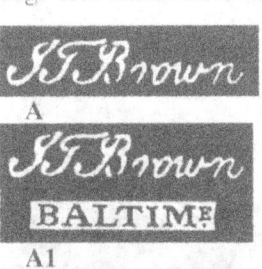

N. BROWN
Examples: on two crown molders; a 9 1/2" birch complex molder with flat chamfers and double crowns similar to **H. Wetherel**; and an 8 5/8" beech thumbnail molder with flat chamfers. Planes were found in the Hartford, CT area, ca. 1790-1800. ****

Sx BROWN
Example: on an 8" birch hollow smoother with heavy shallow flat chamfers and a round top iron by **Weldon**, ca. 1790-1800. **UR**

S: BROWN
Another common initial and name combination. There was a joiner and two cabinetmakers named **Samuel Brown** in Essex, Co., MA, in the late 18c. Also possible is **Silas Brown** (b. Dec. 23, 1780 in New London, CT, d. Oct. 21, 1852 in Lyme, CT) from Lyme, CT. In 1806, **Silas** advertised for an apprentice in the cabinetmaking business. Examples: on a nosing; a double-coping plane; a 1" wide round; a table hollow & round pair; a dado, all 9 7/8" birch with heavy flat chamfers; and a 25" jointer from southern New England, ca. 1790. **UR**

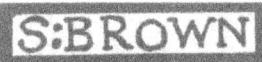

S. BROWN
This imprint has been reported. **UR**

S. B. Jr/ S. T. B./ S. T. BROWN
Example: on a 9 1/2" beech large round with flat chamfers, found in PA, and possibly imprinted by more than one generation, ca. 1800. **UR**

T+ BROWN
Example: on a 9 1/4" fruitwood medium round with a hickory wedge and flat chamfers, from New England, ca. 1790. **UR**

W. BROWN
William Brown (b. 1822 in England) was listed from 1844-49 as a planemaker in Pittsfield, MA. In 1844, he employed 10 hands. In 1849, he was listed in New England Mercantile Union Directory as a plane manufacturer in Pittsfield, MA. In 1870, **William Brown** was listed as a carpenter in Pittsfield, MA. Examples: on a 10 1/2" beech double in-line "V" iron, birch wedges and flat chamfers; and a beading plane, probably from New England, ca. 1810. **UR**

WM. P. BROWN.
William P. Brown (b. 1816 in NY, d. Apr. 6, 1896 in Bath, NY), in 1829, at age 13, William was boarding with and probably apprenticed to **Thomas Fugate**. In 1834, **Brown** was listed as a planemaker in Cincinnati, OH. In 1844, he advertised as a

cabinetmaker in Lawrenceburgh, IA (IN). He was listed in the 1850 census as a planemaker living in the house of **J. Burke** in Madison, IN. Example: on a 9 1/2" apple screw-adjustable split double-iron sash with four added thumbscrews in the shape of a heart to adjust the width, and shallow flat chamfers, found in western PA, ca. 1830. ****

BROWN BROTHERS
This incuse imprint is similar to the **MADE FOR/ J. G. & F. H. BROWN/ NEW HAVEN** imprint and probably refers to the same hardware firm in New Haven, CT. *****

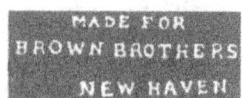

BROWN & PIKE
Brown & Pike probably was a Boston, MA, hardware dealer. Example: on a 16" open handled jack, ca. 19c. *****

BROWN TOOL CO.
Brown Tool Co. was possibly a hardware dealer or a brand name. The **Brown Tool Co.** of New York City made a plane patented by **John Brice** of Sandy Hill, NY, Patent No. 357,454, issued on Feb. 8, 1887. Examples: on both bench and molding planes with **Sandusky Tool Co.** and **Auburn Tool Co.** style numbers; a 16" jack has been reported with a **No. 12** on the toe, the **Auburn Tool Co.** style number for a 16" jack; and a jack with an **Auburn Tool Co./ Thistle Brand** iron. A & B **

BROWN & WOOD
Brown & Wood probably were hardware dealers in Worcester, MA, ca. 1865. Example: on the heel of a **J. F. & G. M. Lindsey** side rabbet. *****

H. BROWNING
Horace Browning (b. Dec. 31, 1808 in Windham, CT, d. Jun. 12, 1866 in Rowe, MA) moved with his family to Colerain, MA, in 1811, at age 2. He went to Rowe, MA, and worked with his brother **Anson Browning**, a wheelwright, who also operated a carriage manufacturer. **Horace** took over this operation in 1834. In 1848, **Horace** was listed as a plane manufacturer; and in the 1850 census as a manufacturer of joiners' tools, employing three hands and producing bench and molding planes worth $2000. In 1855, he was listed as a toolmaker, and in 1860 as a mechanic. **Horace Browning's** shop is still standing in Rowe, MA. (see *American Marking Gauges* by Milton H. Bacheller, Jr.) *

BRUFF BROTHERS & SEAVER
Bruff Brothers & Seaver were hardware dealers comprising **Charles Bruff** and **George A. Seaver**, listed in the New York City directories for 1857-60. ****

BRUMLEY
Joseph Brumley (b. 1749 in NJ, d. Aug. 12, 1823 in Washington, DC) on Dec. 26, 1777, in Trenton, NJ, **Brumley** placed a bond for his license to marry **Hannah Clark** (1758-1799). **Brumley's** name first appears as signing, in chalk, a walnut tall case clock in Mt. Holly, NJ, in 1785. In 1788, he was in Mt. Holly. In 1792, he served in the Trenton Township, NJ Militia. On Jan. 1, 1798, he advertised as a cabinetmaker in Trenton, NJ. By Sep. 16, 1799, he had moved to Georgetown, Washington, DC, where he advertised as a cabinetmaker, but also practiced ironmongery, and had available a large assortment of planes. He stated that "any kind of plane could be supplied on short notice and that orders for planes from merchants will be speedily executed." On Mar. 5, 1801, he married **Mary Smith** in Alexandria, DC. **Joseph Brumley's** household furnishings and tools were sold at public auction. A notice for the auction appeared in the *Daily National Intelligencer* (Washington, DC), on Aug. 19, 1823. Examples: on 9 3/8"-91/2" molders; and an 11 1/2" handled fenced groove with wedge-locked arms, all beech with flat chamfers. ****

H. J. BRUNNER
Henry Jacob Brunner (b. 1822 in Nazareth, PA, d. Oct. 10, 1897 in Bethlehem, PA) made wooden spill planes in Bethlehem, PA. Listed in 1860, Brunner was a carpenter in Nazareth, PA with **Joseph Shaffer**, age 19, a carpenter's apprentice living in his household. Brunner was listed in 1870, in Nazareth, PA, as a carpenter. At least three spill planes have been reported with the ink stamp: *****

MANUFACTURED BY
H. J. BRUNNER
BETHLEHEM, PA.

R. BRUNTON
Example: on a 9 1/2" beech complex molder, ca. 1810-20 UR

JOHN A. BRUSCUP, JR.
John A. Bruscup, Jr. was listed as a planemaker in Cincinnati, OH, in 1839-40. **No imprint has been reported**.

BRYAN
Example: on a 9 1/2" birch round with flat chamfers, found in Smithtown, Long Island, NY, ca. 1800 UR

G. BRYAN
Example: on a 26" birch jointer with an offset closed tote and shallow round chamfers, ca. 1820. **UR**

W. W. BRYAN
William W. Bryan (b. Nov. 13, 1811 in Shecomeco, Duchess Co., NY, d. Aug. 5, 1876 in Rochester, NY) was a Rochester, NY, hardware merchant active 1833-48, and an edge tool maker from 1847-54, succeeding **H. Haight & Co.**, at the same address. Some time after 1847, he was located adjacent to **D. R. Barton**. He was part of **Bush & Bryan** from 1833-36. He bought out the stock of **Schuyler & Sandborn** a Rochester edge tool maker in 1846-47. ********

A. BRYANT
Example: on a 9 5/8" beech complex molder with heavy flat chamfers, ca. 1800. **UR**

E. BRYANT
Example: on a 10" beech handled smoother with an apple wood wedge and an 8 5/8" rosewood smoother with a wood strike and found on the coast of ME, ca. 1850. **UR**

J. BRYANT.
Example: on a 10" beech wedge-lock moving filletster with small round chamfers, probably from rural PA, ca. 1820-30 **UR**

W. BRYCE & CO.
William Bryce (b. 1815 in NY) operated a hardware store in New York City, active from 1846-83. Example: the B imprint is on a jack plane. **A & B ******

BUCKEYE PLANE CO.
Examples: on two 16" beech jack planes. Their irons are stamped BUCKEYE PLANE CO./ OHIO. There is a **13** on each plane's toe. The **Ohio Tool Co.**, **Sandusky Tool Co.**, and **Greenfield Tool Co.**, all used style number **13** for jack planes. On a filletster with OHIO imprinted on the toe, and on a medium hollow with style number **379** on the heel, the **Greenfield Tool Co.'s** catalog number. Possible that this was a **Greenfield Tool Co.** brand name for marketing in the Midwest. Not to be confused with the brand name BUCKEYE used by the **Buckeye Manufacturing and Foundry Co.**, active 1904-23 for its iron bench planes. **A, A1 A2 & B *****

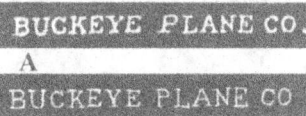

G. BUCKEL
George Buckel of Detroit, MI was issued Patent Number 81,335, on Aug. 25, 1868, for a removable sole for bench planes. In 1868 & 70, **George Buckel** was listed as a brush maker in Detroit, MI. Example: on a 15 7/8" jack plane with this feature. *********

J. BUDD
Possibly **John Budd** listed as a cabinetmaker in Manhattan active from 1817-40. Example: on a 9 1/2" beech tongue plane with round chamfers, ca. 1810-20. **UR**

F. A. BUELL
F. A. Buell was a Saint Paul, MN, hardware dealer. Examples: on a bead, and a molder with the **Sandusky Tool Co.** catalog number on the toe, ca. 1850. ********

I BUELL
Example: on a 10 3/8" beech plow with wood thumbscrews and flat chamfers and a riveted skate, ca. 1800. **UR**

BUFFALO TOOL CO.
The **Buffalo Tool Co.** location is unknown, though quite possibly a hardware dealer in Buffalo, NY, ca. 1865. Examples: on a size **3/4** boxed bead with style number **105** on its heel, the style number for a **Greenfield Tool Co.**'s 3/4 boxed bead in the 1854 price list, and a handled smooth plane with a **Sandusky** iron and a style number **5**, which corresponds to a handled smoother in the **Sandusky Tool Co.**'s 1877 illustrated price list. An **Auburn Tool Co.** closed tote adjustable plane stamped **92** corresponding to the inventory number in the **Auburn** catalog, dated 1869. The C imprint is on a smoother. **A, B & C ******

BUHL, DUCHARME & CO.
Buhl, Ducharme & Co. was a hardware firm in Detroit, MI, active from 1855-76. The partners were **Christian H. Buhl**, **Charles Ducharme** and **Alfred Ducharme**. They succeeded **A. H. Newbould** and were succeeded by **Buhl & Sons**. Example: on a 9 1/2" beech match groove with style number **70** on the heel. ********

C. & S. BULKLEY/ C. F. BULKLEY & CO.
Charles F. Bulkley (b. 1814 in Saybrook, CT, d. 1893 in Saybrook, CT) and **Samuel S. Bulkley** (b. 1817, d. 1860) were partners in the Saybrook, CT, plane making enterprise. In 1832, the **Denison** brothers negotiated the **J. & L. Denison** mill site from **Joel Bulkley**, father of **Charles**, age 18, and **Samuel**, age 15. The **Bulkleys** learned plane making in this mill from the Denisons and their apprenticeship may have been part of the land lease agreement. In 1836, the **Denisons** sold a 1/3 interest in their business to **Jeremiah Gladding** (see **P. A. Gladwin**). In 1847 and again in 1853, when **Charles** was married, his occupation was given as planemaker. In 1849, **Charles** built his house on land that he purchased from **William Denison**, **John Denison**'s and **Lester Denison**'s father. In 1850, **Charles Bulkley** and **Samuel Bulkley** as toolmakers. After the death of **Samuel** in 1860, **Charles F.** adopted the B imprint. In 1870, **Charles** was listed as a house carpenter. The Saybrook planemakers have the highest incidence of double maker's imprints overstamped on the same planes. The majority of the **C. & S. Bulkley** planes are overstamped on one of the **J. & L. Denison** or **John Denison** imprints, and one is overstamped by **P. A. Gladwin**, Wallingford. The decorative cartouche that appears on the C imprint was also used by **J. & L. Denison** and **John Denison**.
A & A1 *; A2 **; B ***

F. C. BULKLEY
Possibly an incorrect stamp used by **C. F. Bulkley** for a short period of time, or a separate person. Examples: the A imprint is on a 9 1/8" beech table hollow. The A1 imprint without the F. C. is placed high on the toe and possibly a temporary use of the incorrect die, and is on a 9 1/2" hollow, ca. 1850. **A & B:** ****

L. & C. H. BULL
Lorenzo Bull (b. Mar. 21, 1819 in Hartford, CT, Nov. 1, 1905 in Pike, IL) and **Charles H. Bull** (b. Dec. 16, 1822 in Hartford, CT, d. Nov. 27, 1908 in Quincy, IL) were Quincy, IL, hardware dealers active from 1845-61. In 1863, they were bankers. ****

O. T. BULL & CO.
Oliver T. Bull & Co. was a Louisville, KY, hardware firm, active from 1851-66, consisting of **Oliver T. Bull** (b. Aug. 1825 in MD, d. after 1909) and **George W. Bull**. ****

D: BULLARD
Possibly **Daniel Bullard** (b. May 15, 1778 in Barre, MA, d. Mar. 18, 1872 in Swanton, VT) who moved to Swanton, VT, ca. 1802, and was a cabinetmaker who advertised in 1810. In 1820, he was listed engaged in manufactures; and in 1850, a farmer; and in 1860, a gentleman in Swanton, VT. Example: on a 10 1/2" Yankee plow with beech body, arms and fence, a birch wedge, and flat chamfers, from New England, ca. 1780. **UR**

L. BUNDY
Lewis Bundy of Moores Forks, NY, was issued Patent No. 109,174, on Nov. 15, 1870 for a combination match and plow plane. The B imprint is from a brass medallion applied to the plane. Examples: on four planes which may have been prototypes. (see *Patented Transitional & Metallic Planes in America-Vol. II*, p. 72, by Roger K. Smith) **A & B** *****

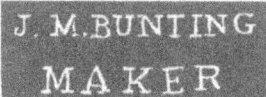

J. M. BUNTING
Example: on a 13" fruitwood raze skew rabbet without chamfers and marked **MAKER**, ca 19c. **UR**

BUNTING & MIDDLETON
Bunting & Middleton were probably hardware dealers in Philadelphia, PA. Example: on a fore plane made by **E. Nutting**, and on a smoother made by **N. Chapin & Co.** ****

G. BURCKHER
Example: on a 10 3/8" beech molder with an iron marked **SCHARFF** and heavy flat chamfers, possibly from PA, ca. 1800. **UR**

F. BURDICK
Examples: on a filletster; a sash; a single boxed ovolo; a tongue & groove pair; and a nosing plane, all 9 1/2" beech with heavy round chamfers, ca. 1810-20. ****

W. BURDOCK
Example: on a pair of birch 9 9/16" hollow and round with flat chamfers, probably from New England, ca. 1790. **A & A1: UR**

A

A1

W. BURGES

Example: on a 30" beech jointer with a centered closed tote and flat chamfers, ca. 1800-10. **UR**

J. BURKE
James Burke (b. 1817 in MD, d. 1853 in Madison, IN) who came to Madison, IN ca. 1844. **James Burke** was listed as a cabinetmaker in New York City in 1843-44. The 1845-46 Jefferson, IN City Directory lists **J. Burke,** Merchant, Spring St. He was listed in the 1850 Madison, IN census as a planemaker, using 10,000 board feet of beech per year at $250, producing planes worth $4,000 per year. He used hand power only in his shop, and employed five hands who were paid $40 per month. One of them may have been **William Brown**. Burke probably stopped making planes in the 1850's for he is listed in the 1859 Madison city directory as living in Madison, but is not described as a planemaker. Examples: on a 9 3/8 skew rabbet; a 9 7/16" bead; an adjustable sash; and a plow plane, all beech, ca. 1850. ********

J. J. BURLEIGH
Example: on a 9 1/2" birch fixed sash with two irons and wedges and heavy round chamfers, ca. 1820-30. **UR**

J. BURLEY
Example: on a 9" beech double-iron fixed door plane with round chamfers, ca. 1820. **A & B: UR**

A

B

JOHN BURLEY
Examples: on a coffin shaped smoother with a double iron by **Greaves & Son**, possibly from PA, ca. 1850. *********

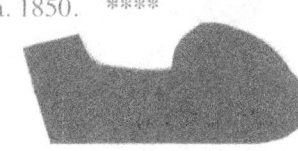

T x B/ T=BURLEY
Thomas Burley (b. Jul. 2, 1723, d. Jun. 1, 1805 in Epping, NH) was a joiner in Epping, NH. Examples: molding planes are 10"-9 1/2" beech with flat, and several with round, chamfers; bench planes include a 7 3/8" smoother; a panel raising plane with the A1 imprint; and a 12 1/2" crown molder with the A imprint, all beech with shallow flat chamfers. The A wedge is earlier and on flat-chamfered molders. The B wedge is later and on round chamfered molders. The initial group is on a 10" beech skew rabbet with flat chamfers and an appropriate wedge, ca. 1780-1800.
A, A1, B & C *********

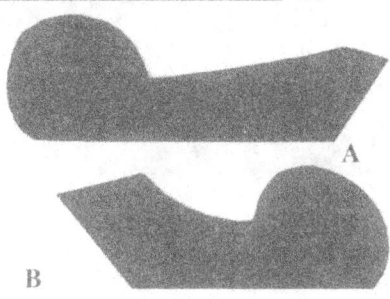

B

C

ISAAC BURNAM
Examples: on a 9 3/4" maple complex molder with a birch wedge; and an 11 1/8" birch molder, both with flat chamfers, ca. 1750-75. **UR**

JOSEPH BURNESTON
Joseph Burneston (b. Dec. 3, 1794), age 16, was apprenticed on July 20, 1811 to planemaker **William Vance**.
No imprint has been reported.

CHARLOTTE BURNET (see **Israel White**)

J. BURNET
Jacob Burnet was a planemaker in Madison, IN, with no active dates listed. **No imprint has been reported**.

GEO. BURNHAM, JR.
George Burnham, Jr. (b. Jan. 17, 1817 in Hartford, CT, d. 1893) was an Amherst, MA, planemaker. He apprenticed in New Hartford, Ct, probably with **H. Chapin** and arrived in Amherst on Apr. 10, 1841. He was a journeyman for **Luther Fox** in the bench plane business, and in about a year **George Burnham**, together with **Benoni Thayer**, **Hiram Fox**, and **Aaron Ferry** bought **Luther Fox** out and founded **Burnham, Fox, & Co.**, from 1842-44. In 1844, **George Burnham** bought out his partners and traded under this imprint, from 1844-53. He was listed in the 1849 New England Mercantile Union Directory as a plane manufacturer in East Amherst. He was listed in 1850 as a planemaker; and as an axe handle manufacturer in 1860. In the Products of Industry census of 1850, **George Burnham** was listed as a tool manufacturer using 20,000 feet of beech worth $800, 4 tons of boxwood worth $120, plane irons worth $2000, employing 14 male hands who were paid $364 total/month to make tools worth $12,000 annually. In 1880, **George Burnham** was living in Worcester, MA. **FF**

BURNHAM & BROTHERS
Burnham & Brothers was an East Hartford, CT, planemaker, ca. 1850. ****

BURNHAM, FOX & CO.
Burnham, Fox & Co. was a partnership of **George Burnham, Jr.**, **Benoni Thayer**, **Hiram Fox** and **Aaron Ferry**. They bought out **Luther Fox** and made planes from 1842-44 in Amherst, MA; they were in turn bought out by **Geo. Burnham Jr.** In 1850, **Benoni Thayer**, age 41, was listed as a mechanic in Amherst, MA. *

THOMAS BURNS
Thomas Burns was listed as a planemaker in Newark, NJ, directories from 1836-38 at 150 Washington St., the same address as **George W. Andruss**.
No imprint has been reported.

J: BURNSIDE
Example: on a 9 3/4" beech molder with heavy round chamfers, ca. 1820-30. **UR**

 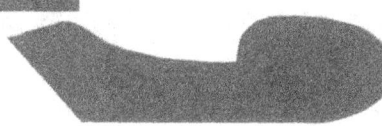

A. H. BURR
Archer H. Burr (b. Jul. 26, 1855 in Durham, Middlesex Co., CT, d. Oct. 1942 in Omaha, Douglas Co. NE) was a hardware dealer from 1901-12 in Omaha. On Oct. 5, 1898, **Archer H. Burr** was issued a patent for an incubator. Example: on a **Keen Kutter** jack. *****

H. M. BURR
Example: on a 9 1/4" beech molder with round chamfers on top and flat chamfers on the ends, ca. 1810. **UR**

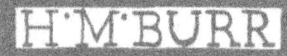 

T. BURREL
Example: on a 9 1/4" beech small hollow with flat chamfers, ca. 1800-20. **UR**

E. T. BURROWES CO.
Edward Thomas Burrowes (b. Jul. 25, 1852 in Portland, ME, d. Mar. 19, 1818 in Portland, Cumberland Co. ME) was Pres. of **E. T. Burrowes Co.**, at 68-70 Free, Portland, ME. **E. T. Burrowes** patented a sliding wire window and door screen in 1878. The firm was in business until 1928. The plane bearing the following message was part of the installation package. On a 12" level and a 3ft. inside rule marked **E. T. Burrowes** has also been reported and was part of the same installation kit. *

**USE THIS TOOL FOR FITTING BURROWE'S
PATENT SLIDING SCREENS
E. T. BURROWES CO., -MANUFAC-
TURERS- PORTLAND, MAINE.
IF SCREENS DO NOT RUN EASILY,
GROOVE OUT THE SHALLOW GROVE
A LITTLE WITH THIS PLANE.**

G. W. BURT
George W. Burt (b. ca. 1791) was listed, in 1830, as a cabinetmaker in Woodstock, VT. Example: on a 14" beech, closed toted, fixed sash with two irons & wedges and shallow round chamfers, ca. 1820. ****

J. BURT
John Burt (b. May 28, 1791 in Berkley, Bristol Co., MA, d. Mar. 1, 1858 in Millbury, Worcester Co., MA) was listed as a creditor to **Spencer M. Burt** of Berkley, MA. Molding planes are 9 1/4"-9 1/2" and beech. Examples: on two hollows; a round; a fixed sash; and a skew rabbet, all beech with round chamfers, probably from New England, ca. 1820. ****

S. M. BURT
Spencer M. Burt (d. Dec. 28, 1835 in Berkley, Bristol Co., MA,) was a turner and wheelwright who died intestate. The inventory of his estate included a turning mill, wheelwright shop, grindstone, iron vise and shop tools. Creditors included such names as **Betsy H. Woodward**, possibly wife to **William Woodward** of nearby Taunton; **Seth Presbrey** of Norton; **Charles P. Dean**, **Enos W. Dean**, **Benjamin F. Dean**, **Barney Dean**, **John Burt** and **George Briggs**, many prominent plane making names from southeastern MA. Examples: on two boxed beads; and a wide hollow, all 9 1/2" beech with shallow round chamfers found with planes by **William Woodward** of Taunton, **A. Smith** of Rehoboth, and **J. M. Taber** of New Bedford, ca. 1820-30. ****

T. BURT
 This imprint with **MAKER** has been reported. **UR**

A. BUSENGER
A. Busenger was listed as a planemaker in Mt. Solon, VA in 1871. **No imprint has been reported**.

BUSH
Examples: molders are beech with wide flat chamfers, found in eastern PA, ca. 1800. On an **AB. DEAN** imprint has appeared on a **Bush** plane, as has an owner imprint of **J. SHAUB**.

Possibly **John Bush** of London, England, active from 1794-99 as is reported in *British Planemakers, 3 rd edition*. This suggests that the planes found in the U.S. were imported or came over with emigrants, or perhaps **Bush** emigrated himself. More examples have been reported in the U. S. than in England. **

CHARLES V. BUSH
Charles V. Bush (b. Dec. 1819, d. 1907, Penn Yan, NY) was a carpenter who built two churches, one in 1839 and the other in 1849. Pen Yan was founded in 1835, and is located on Keuka Lake in the Finger Lakes Region of NY. They had a wood jail and when they put an arsonist in it, he burned it down. **Charles Bush** rebuilt the jail in 1857. He was listed in 1850, as a carpenter living in Milo, Yates Co., NY. In 1860, as an architect and a builder in Boston; in 1870, as a builder in Penn Yan; in 1880, as an architect in Oswego; and in 1900, as a real estate agent. Example: on a closed-toted match grooving plane, ca. 1850 *****

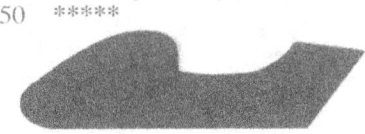

H. BUSH
Henry Bush was a hardware and tool dealer in Rochester, NY, starting in 1828. He was a part of **Bush & Butler**, with **George Butler**, from Aug. to Nov. of 1831. He was a part of **Bush & Bryan**, with **William W. Bryan**, from 1833-36. They were hardware, saddlery, and cutlery dealers. ****

BUSHNELL
Edward Wolcott Bushnell (b. Sept. 1, 1804 in Saybrook, CT, d. Feb. 23, 1876) may be the same as the **E. W. Bushnell** listed as a planemaker in Utica, NY, in 1829. **Edward W. Bushnell** was in Philadelphia, prior to 1837. He was listed in an 1839 directory, working as a machinist and living with **Edwin Bushnell**, planemaker (this is the only appearance of Edwin). **Edward W. Bushnell** was listed in 1843-54, 57-60 as a manufacturer of cabinetmakers and carpenters tools. In 1854, he was in partnership with **Edward Tull** as **Bushnell & Tull Machinists** until 1857, when **Tull** died. In 1860, **Edward Bushnell** became an innkeeper. Example: on a wide smoother; and on marking gauges, ca. 1850. (see *American Marking Gauges* by Milton H. Bacheller, Jr.) ****

N. T. BUSHNELL & CO.
This imprint appears on the toe of a double-iron nosing plane made by **H. Chapin/ Union Factory** and is probably a New Haven, CT. hardware dealer, ca. 1845. ****

BUTLER
John Butler is one of the early Philadelphia, PA, planemakers. His first directory listing was in 1785, as a house carpenter at 3rd. between Arch & Race streets; and in 1791, he was listed as a planemaker at 111 No. 3rd. St. It is believed that **Butler** worked as late as 1830. He was listed in the 1790 census as a carpenter ; and in the 1800 census as a planemaker. Example: on a 9 1/2" beech beading plane with flat chamfers with the A imprint and also the owner's brand **A. HAINS** (Adam Hains, an important Philadelphia cabinetmaker, active ca. 1790) is owned by Winterthur Museum, together with **Hains** furniture. Imprints B, C, C1, and D were used by both **John Butler** and **George Butler**, a Philadelphia PA, planemaker active 1819-35; he was listed with **John Butler** from 1819-30. **Andrew Butler** and **Frederick Butler**, were also listed as planemakers at the same address in 1825. **Andrew Butler** was listed as a planemaker, alone, in 1830. The E imprint is on a size **12** hollow with the imprint of **M. LONG**.   B, C & C1 *; D ***; A, E & F *****

N B/ N. BUTLER
The initial **NB** has the rear stroke of the N as the vertical stroke of the B. Example: on a 9 1/8" maple molder with flat chamfers. ca. 1790. **No imprint is available**.

BUTTLES & RUNYON
Joel Buttles (b. Feb. 1, 1787 in CT, d. Aug. 14, 1850 in Columbus, Franklin Co., OH) and **Clark Runyon** (b. Feb. 24, 1800 in Bloomfield, Essex Co., NJ, d, Nov. 26, 1886 in Chicago, Cook Co., IL, buried Bloomfield, NJ) operated as a partnership in Columbus, OH, in 1843-44, and may have been planemakers, or hardware dealers or both. **Clark Runyon** enlisted, age 64, on Sep. 23, 1864, and served in the Civil War, as quartermaster in Co. S, OH, 176th. Infantry Reg. He was mustered out on Feb. 18, 1865 ****

D. BUTTS
Example: on a 7 1/2" birch block smoother with a round top wedge and a **Weldon** iron (Sheffield 1774-1788) and flat chamfers, ca. 1775. **UR**

I. BYRNE
Example: on a 9 3/8"x 3/8" beech dado with a wood depth stop, separate nicker with wedge and heavy round chamfers, ca. 1820.   **UR**

W. H. BYRON
William H. Byron (b. Mar. 11, 1820 in Scotland, d. Jan. 11, 1883 in Milwaukee, WI) was a Milwaukee, WI, hardware dealer active in 1848-49.
A & B **; C *****

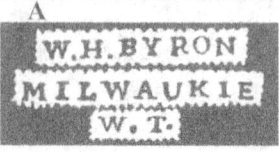

G. H. BUZZELL
Examples: on a 21 7/8" beech foreplane with shallow round chamfers found in New Boston, NH; and a 16" beech jack plane, ca. 1830-40.   **UR**

JOHN. C
Example: on a 12" beech fixed sash with a birch offset open tote and round chamfers, ca. 1800-20.   **UR**

C. A. S. & CO.
C. A. S. & Co. is believed to be a Detroit hardware dealer.
Example: on a **H. Chapin, No. 126** center bead plane with style number **No. 126**.   ****

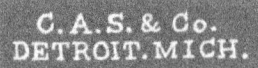

C & M. M. CO.
Example: on a 9 1/2" boxed beech bead. The iron is made by Humphreysville which may suggest a CT origin, ca. 1860.   **UR**

C. R. & W.
The meaning of these initials is not known. A hollow owned by the Farmers Museum at Cooperstown, NY, is also imprinted **NY. CO**. The museum dates the plane from 1878-83. There is an additional imprint on the plane **C. F. RAYMER**. This may be the **C. R.** of the **C. R. & W.** imprint. Examples: on a 9 1/2" beech molder with the A imprint; and a 9 9/16" beech size **14** hollow with the B imprint.   **A & B: UR**

C. S. C.
Example: on a tongue plane with an eagle logo, probably a **Chapin-Stephens & Co.** imprint. The company was founded in 1901. **No imprint is available**.

C. T. & CO.
C. T. & Co. is possibly an imprint for **Charles Tollner**. Examples: one with the location **N.Y.C.** and another with **NEW YORK**. **No imprint is available**.

M. CABI
Examples: on three panel raisers, one apple, one tiger maple, all with offset totes, adj. side board depth stops, adj. bottom board fences and flat chamfers; a molder; a 10" hollow & round table plane pair; and a 11 1/2" maple "hawk" plane with adj. fence and flat chamfers, possibly from Berks Co., PA, ca. 1790.   ****

F. CABOT
Examples: on a panel; a 9 1/2" size **10** round; a hollow; a molder; a bead with interrupted boxing; and a 9 5/8" complex molder, all beech with flat chamfers, possibly from northern New England, ca. 1800. ****

A. CADY
Example: on a 9 3/4" birch rabbit plane with flat chamfers that stop with a long tapered lamb's tongue. The finial is round with a slight point at the top, similar to several CT River Valley plane makers, probably from New England, ca. 1780-90. (See **Lavius Fillmore**) UR

I. F. CADY
Probably **Jonathan Cady** (b. June 14, 1746 in Killingly, Windham Co., CT, d. July 12, 1834 in Providence, RI). He married **Rebecca Cady** (His Cousin) on Nov. 20, 1766 in Killingly. **Jonathan Cady** is listed in the Providence directories of 1824 & 30 as a house carpenter at Richmond St. Example: on a 10 1/4" birch large hollow with a relieved wedge (similar to a **Jo. Fuller** wedge, ca. 1795) and heavy flat chamfers mostly on the side, probably from RI, ca. 1790-1800 *****

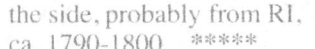

W. CAIGER
Example: on a 9 7/8" beech size **14** round with flat chamfers, ca. 1800. UR

JAMES CAIN
James Cain (Caine) (b. ca. 1828 in Ireland) was listed as a plane manufacturer at 19 Orange St. in the Cleveland, OH, directories, from 1851-53. Earlier from 1849-50, he was employed by **J. J. Vinall**, located at 15 Seneca St. In 1851, **J. J. Vinall** moved to 21 Orange St. indicating a continued relationship. In the 1863-67 directories, **James Cain** was listed as a toolmaker. **No imprint has been reported**.

T. C. CAIN
Thomas C. Cain (Caine) was listed as a planemaker in Utica, NY, in 1834, boarding with **R. J. Collins**. He is also listed as a contemporary of **F. K. Collins**, of Ravenna, OH, from 1838-50. ***

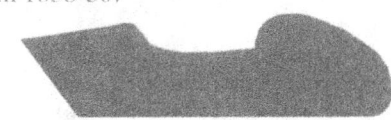

E. CALDWELL
Edward Caldwell was a Baltimore, MD, planemaker, active from 1840-57, at the following locations:
  1840-41 - Hume St. w. of Exeter.
  1842-43 - cor. Calvert & Mercer.
  1845   - S. Calvert St.
  1847-48 - 117 N. Pala St.
  1849-50 - S. Mercer St.
  1851-57 - 3 Mercer.

Example: on a 24" beech jointer that bears **E. W. Carpenter**'s B imprint. The plane has **E. W. Carpenter**'s double-wedge patent feature; however, the top wedge has rounded edges in the **E. Caldwell** style and the back wedge has the angled edges that **E. W. Carpenter** used. Probably **E. W. Carpenter** added his patent feature and imprint to an **E. Caldwell** plane. A **; B ****

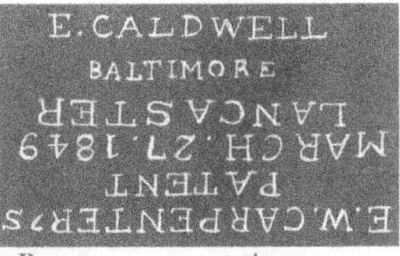

N. CALL
Examples: on a plow; a panel raiser; and 14 other molding planes, all 9 7/16" beech with flat chamfers. The irons are typically marked **DK**. A number of the planes are marked with **AW** and are from the **A. Webster** cabinet shop in Manchester, NH. A bead has been observed imprinted **I. LONG**. Probably **N. Call** worked in or around Hopkinton, NH, ca. 1800. ****

P. CALLEN
Peter T. Callen (b. May 31, 1942 in WI) is a contemporary planemaker from Milwaukee, WI. Example: on a 9 1/2" fancy moving filletster made of African mahogany with tiger maple fences, rosewood insets and round chamfers. ***

B. CALLENDER & CO.
Benjamin Callender (d. 1887) was a Boston, MA, hardware dealer who traded as **Benjamin Callender** from 1851-61, and as **Benjamin Callender & Co.** from 1862-87. Example: on a tongue & groove pair dated **1874**. He was listed as the Boston agent for the **American File Co.**, of RI. A & B ***

CALVERT
Garrald Calvert (b. Mar. 18, in Prince William, VA, d. Mar. 18, 1840 in Lewisburg, Mason Co., KY) was in Mason Co. by Mar. 14, 1798 when he married **Rosannah McIlvain** (1781-1858). He was listed as a master craftsman. Another possibility is **Garrald**'s son **Archibald M. Calvert** (b. 1807 in KY,

d. Sep. 6, 1860). In 1850, **Archibald** was living in Lewisburg, KY, as a cabinetmaker. Example: on a 12"x 4 1/2" D-router plane, ca. 1832-50. *****

CHARLES CAMBELL
Charles Cambell was listed as a Cincinnati, OH, planemaker active in 1829. **No imprint has been reported**.

JA. CAMPBELL
Believed to be **James Campbell** (d. Jan. 1, 1807 in Boston, MA), from 1791-1800. **Campbell** was listed as a cabinetmaker of Spring Lane, Boston, MA. In 1791, he was a partner in **Cambell & Ward** with **Moses Ward**. Examples: on a 10 1/2" bead; and a 10 1/4" complex molder, both birch with relieved wedges and flat chamfers, ca. 1790. *****

N. CAMPER
Napoleon Camper (b. 1824 in MD, d. Mar. 13, 1883 in Baltimore, MD) was a Baltimore, MD, planemaker, toolmaker, manufacturer and tool store owner. His wife ran a fancy store at the same address. **Camper** was listed in the 1850 census and believed active from 1850-80. Locations:

1851 – 170 N Exeter
1853-54 – 122 Lexington
1855-60 – 128 Lexington
1864-68 – 123 Lexington
1870-74 – over 21 Mercer
1875-80 – over 19 Mercer

Napoleon Camper served in the Civil War as a Confederate, Sergeant, Co. E, 1st. Infantry Reg. Maryland. He was a prisoner on Nov. 22, 1863 in Baltimore, MD. Example: on a 12 3/8" toted beech razee complex molder. **A, B, B1, C, D & D1** *

P. CANAVAN
This imprint is similar to **Glenn & Duke**. Example: on a 6 7/8" beech toothing plane, ca. 1850. **UR**

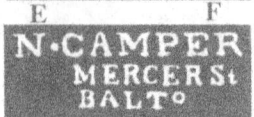

D. J. CANFIELD
D. J. Canfield was listed as a maker of coachmaker's tools and a planemaker from Newark, NJ, in 1849. **No imprint has been reported**.

E. CANFIELD
Example: on a 9 3/8" beech molder with round chamfers, ca. 1820. **UR**

WM. CANK
This curved imprint is on a 10 3/8" match plane with flat chamfers, ca. 1800. **UR**

I. CAPELL. I
An **I** was often used for **J** in the 18c. This imprint could be **J. CAPELL. J** with the last **J** possibly for "Junior". Example: on a birch astragal, ca. 1800-10. **UR**

J. F. CARD & CO.
J. F. Card & Co. probably was a hardware firm in Toledo, OH, ca. 1850. Example: on a round with number **72** on toe, an **Ohio Tool Co.** style number. ***

J. L. CARD
Example: on a 9" smoothing plane with a double-iron by **Charles Buck**, ca. 1850-70. **UR**

H. & W. T. CAREY
H. & W. T. Carey was probably a hardware dealer in Xenia, OH, a town close to Dayton. Also possibly located in Zanesville, OH, although no imprint has been reported. Example: on a screw stop dado with **Ohio Tool Co.** irons and with a stile number **48** on the toe, **Ohio Tool Co.**'s catalog number for a screw-stop dado. ****

T. G. CARLEY
This **T. G. Carley** imprint is similar to **J. Woods** and might help in locating this maker. Example: on a 14 1/2"x 2 1/2" wide beech gutter plane with round chamfers. **UR**

CARLIN & FULTON
Carlin & Fulton with **James F. Carlin (Carling)** and **David C. Fulton** (b. Sep. 19, 1827 in VA, d. Aug. 1, 1880 in Howard Co., MD, burial in Baltimore, MD) were hardware dealers and importers, at 130 Harlem Ave. Ellicott City, Baltimore, MD, active from 1864-1900. **James F. Carlin** served as a Private in the Civil War, Co. D, 207th. PA Infantry Reg. Example: on a bench plane with this imprint confirming a connection to the shadowy **Baltimore Plane Co.** *****

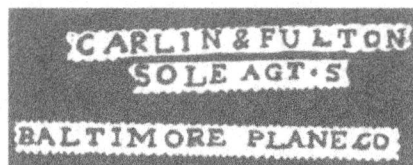

C. CARLSON
Example: on a 5 1/2" lignum smoothing plane, dated **1910**, found on the ME coast. **No imprint is available**.

I. C/ I. CARMONT
Example: on an 8 1/8" beech, wedge-locked slide-arm plow with an iron depth stop, iron thumbscrews, riveted skate and flat chamfers, ca. 1800. **UR**

CARNES + SON
I. Carnes had a hardware store, **Carnes & Son**, in N(ew) Richmond, OH in the early 19c., located about 16 miles east of Cincinnati on the Ohio River. Example: on a 22" beech jointer, ca. 19c. ********

E. CARPENTER
Example: on a 14" beech rabbet with shallow round chamfers, ca. 1840. **UR**

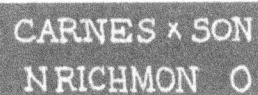

E. W. CARPENTER
Emanuel Weidler Carpenter (b. Aug. 22, 1791 in Earl Township, Lancaster, PA, d. Sept. 15, 1856 in Lancaster) was a fifth generation Pennsylvania Dutch. The original family name was **Zimmermann**, German for carpenter. Son of **Samuel Carpenter** who moved with **E. W. Carpenter**, at age 16, to Lancaster, PA, where **Samuel Carpenter** became an innkeeper and mayor. **E. W. Carpenter** was a cabinetmaker, toolmaker, planemaker and "practitioner of medicine". By 1813, he left Lancaster and married **Sarah Stevens Sangston** from Baltimore City, in 1818. The **BALTIMORE** imprint C is from ca. 1818-19. **Carpenter** returned to Lancaster by 1820, where he was listed as a joiner, from 1821-25. In 1826, he opened his plane making business at South Queen and German (Farnum) St. In 1828, **Joseph L. Hurst**, was apprenticed to **E. W. Carpenter** in the art, trade and mystery of making planes. Others who worked in **E. W. Carpenter's** shop included **John Barber**, listed as a planemaker, from 1824-30; **Samuel Gills**, from 1826-29; **Daniel Cox**, listed as a planemaker, in 1829; **Edward C. Duro**, listed as a planemaker, in 1829; and a harnessmaker, in 1830; **Benjamin Eatenburn** was listed as a planemaker, in 1835-36; **Joseph Stallings** was listed as a planemaker, in 1843; and **Carpenter's** son **Samuel Sangston Carpenter**; son **John Edwin Carpenter** (b. Sept. 15, 1831), listed as a planemaker 1850-67 & 1873-4, otherwise listed as a carpenter; and son **(Emanuel) Warner Carpenter**; son-in-law **William Kieffer**; nephew **Israel B. Carpenter**; **John Kilheffer**, a 16 year old planemaker who lived with **E. W. Carpenter** in 1850; probably **J. F. Bauder** until 1841; **Samuel Auxer**; possibly son **James A. S. Carpenter** (b. 1827) before becoming a medical doctor in 1848; possibly **Lawrence Charles Carpenter** (b. 1840); **Michael Carpenter**, **E. W. Carpenter's** brother; **Charles Gottfried Siewer**, **E. W Carpenter's** son-in-law and a Cincinnati planemaker, may have been trained by **E. W. Carpenter** in the 1830's. **Jacob Heiss** may have been **E. W. Carpenter's** first journeyman. **E. W. Carpenter** retailed planes at his shop and sold them through hardware stores including **Oglesby & Pool** (see Kelker), **John F. Steinman**, **George Mayer**, **John A. Duncan**, of Wilmington, DE, **Yarnall & McClure** and **W. M. McClure**. His first Patent No. 5807X, issued on Jan. 30, 1830, was for an adjustable bit-in-tongue plane, E imprint. The E2 Imprint is on a 13 1/2" boxed plank tongue with a screw-arm fence and a split adjustable iron. His second Patent No. 594, issued on Feb. 6, 1838, was for "Improved Arm" planes, imprint D. This involved cutting threads through the body of the plane and engineering arms "which regulate the fence with great ease and accuracy and give it an increased firmness". His third Patent, No. 6226 of March 27, 1849, was for a second wedge to adjust the throat opening on planes, and to regulate the cut by changing the pitch of the iron, imprint B. The appearance of his planes, including his distinctive wedges, are significantly larger or thicker than those of others, almost massive. **E. W. Carpenter** was listed in the 1850 Census of Manufacturing as a planemaker who made 150 bench screws worth $140 and 1000 planes worth $1500 from June 1849 to May 1850, employing five males possibly sons **John E. Carpenter**, **Warner Carpenter**, **William Kieffer**, **Kieffer and Auxer**. **Sarah Stevens Sangston Carpenter** (b. 1796, d. Oct. 17, 1878 in Cincinnati, OH), **E. W. Carpenter's** wife **Sarah**, took over the shop when he died in 1856 and continued production with the help of **William Kieffer** until about 1863 when she was age 67, the shop being sold in 1865. **Sarah S. Carpenter** was listed in the 1860 Census of Manufacturing as a "plainmaker", who produced 2000 "plains" worth $4000, employing three men likely **William Kieffer**, **Samuel Auxer** and son **John E. Carpenter**. **Sarah Carpenter** died in Cincinnati on a visit to her son **Samuel**. The successors to the planemaking business were **Kieffer & Auxer** from about 1863-69; **Auxer & Remley** from 1869-70; and finally **Samuel Auxer** from 1870-82. Attention should be given to the **COUNTERFIT** imprint found on many otherwise unmarked planes and even some with original imprints shaved including a Sandusky.
A: FF; A1 *; A2 ***;
B, D, D1, D2, D3, D4, E, E1 & E2 ****;
C & F *****
One example with **J. STAMM** as an owner.

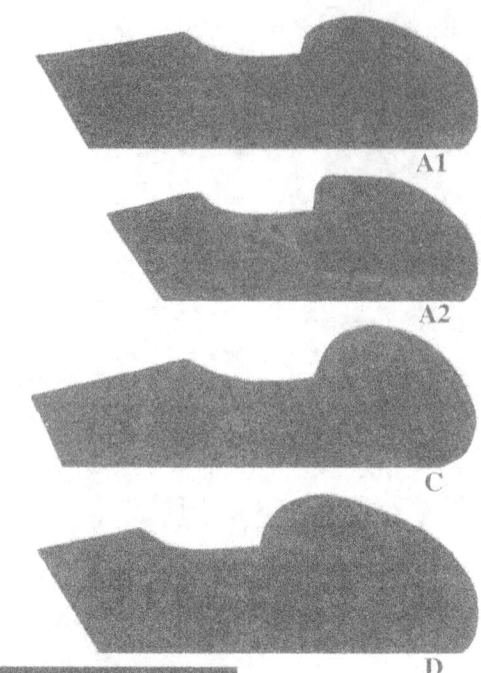

```
E.W.CARPENTER'S
IMPROVED AMS
PATENT
LANCASTER         D4

E.W.CARPENTER'S
PATENTBIT
LANCASTER.        E

E.W.CARPENTER'S
PATENT
LANCASTER         E1

E.W.CARPENTER'S
IMPROVED ARMS.
8 BIT
PATENT
LANCASTER.        E2

E.W.CARPENTER
LANCASTER.
PENNSYLVANIA      F

E.W. CARPENTER    COUNTERFIT
LANCASTER         IMPRINT
```

F. E. CARPENTER
F. E. Carpenter was possibly a hardware dealer with a location **153 ALLEN AVENUE/ PORTLAND, MAINE**, which appears stamped in ink on the side and toe of a 10 5/8" beech dado with the double-nicker iron screwed into the plane sole, and the depth stop a right-angle piece of steel, ca. 1870. ****

```
F. E. CARPENTER
153 ALLEN AVENUE
PORTLAND,   MAINE
```

G. CARPENTER
Example: on an 8 7/8" beech medium hollow with narrow flat chamfers. ca. 1800. This is different from **George Carpenter**, the British maker.   UR

```
G.CARPENTER
```

I. CARPENTER
Rev. Israel B. Carpenter (b. Oct. 17, 1824, d. Oct. 2, 1890 in Reading, PA), the nephew of **E. W. Carpenter**, was listed as a planemaker in Lancaster, PA, active 1847-48. He probably trained under **E. W. Carpenter**, then served as a journeyman for these two years. In 1850, **Israel** was converted and in 1852, he became a minister of the United Brethren in Christ. He served ten churches, mostly in Lancaster Co., Dauphin Co. and Berks Co. between 1852-79. **Israel** helped support himself with woodworking and was listed in 1876 as a carpenter in Reading, PA; where he lived from 1872-90, except for a one year appointment outside Lancaster. In 1885, **Israel** went blind and ran a grocery store from his home, until his death in 1890. **F. Smith** and **I. Carpenter** of Lancaster, PA, were issued Patent No. 81425, on Aug. 25, 1868, for a metal top for wooden bench planes intended to strengthen and lighten them and, with a double-wedge like that of **E. W. Carpenter's**, to adjust the mouth of the plane (see *Patented Transitional & Matalic Planes in America, 1827-1927*, p. 127, by Roger K. Smith). **Frederick Smith** was a hatter married to **Israel's sister**. **Smith's** shop address was given to write for further information on the patent. Examples: on a patent smoother; a jack; a fore plane; an all wood fore plane, an all wood astragal with **E. W. Carpenter** style wedge, and a yard stick.   ****

```
I.CARPENTER
READING
```

M. CARPENTER
Michael Carpenter was **E. W. Carpenter**'s younger brother, a turner, chairmaker, and joiner. He probably made some of the turnings for bench screws and plane arms, perhaps on a piece work basis during the 1830's. He was Mayor of Lancaster from 1843-52. This name with the added **MAKER** is from a 20 3/8" beech foreplane with a closed centered tote of birch and with round chamfers. ca. 1850. A large **M. CARPENTER** branded on the end grain of a spinning wheel. **No imprint is available.**

S. CARPENTER
Samuel Sangston Carpenter (b. Jan. 22, 1823, d. 1889), was the eldest son of **E. W. Carpenter**. He was listed in 1844 as a Lancaster, PA, planemaker. **Samuel Carpenter** also studied law, but did not practice until He moved, in Dec. 1844, to Cincinnati, OH, where his brother-in-law, **C. G. Siewers**, was living. He was appointed a U. S. Commissioner, but declined to enforce the Fugitive Slave Law, which cost him most of his business. A & B *****

```
S.CARPENTER
LANCASTER         A

S.CARPENTER       B
```

W. CARPENTER
Possibly (**Emanuel**) **Warner Carpenter** (b. Mar. 26, 1834), who used his middle name. **Warner** was the son of **E. W. Carpenter**. He was listed as a planemaker, age 17, living with his father, in the 1850 census. In 1856, when his father died, he was living in Hamilton Co., OH, perhaps working for his brother-in-law, **C. G. Siewers**, making tools while studying law with his older brother **Samuel Carpenter**. He became "a lawyer who removed South" and in 1864, he was in Capiah Co., MS. He may have received his own imprint stamp, when he reached age 21, in 1855, and used it briefly before leaving **E. W. Carpenter**'s shop. *****

CARPENTER & FLOWER
Carpenter & Flowers was listed as a dealer in hardware & cutlery in Willimantic, CT. Examples: in ink on the side of three **H. Chapin** hollows and rounds that reads: ****

CARPENTER & FOWLER
Wholesale & Retail
DEALERS IN
HARDWARE IRON & STEEL
CUTLERY, Etc.
WILLIMANTIC, CT.

C. CARR & SONS
C. Carr & Sons represents a hardware firm in Chicago, Cook Co., IL. It was reported stamped in ink on the side of a **Sandusky** side bead. **UR**

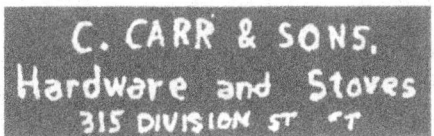

M. CARR
Examples: on a 9 7/16" round; a 9 1/2" complex molder; and a size 7/8" wide tongue & groove pair, all beech with heavy round to shallow round chamfers, ca. 1820-30. **A & B: UR**

R. CARRIER
Example: on a 9 3/8" beech large round with flat chamfers; also with double-crown imprints found with planes by **H. Wetherell**, ca. 1790. **UR**

M. A. CARRINGTON
Miles A. Carrington (b. ca. 1826, d. Mar. 30, 1857 in New Haven, CT) was listed as a New Haven, planemaker in 1856-57. Example: on a double-boxed bead. *****

P. CARROLL
Examples: on a 13" hollow; and a 9 9/16" rabbet, both beech with heavy round chamfers, ca. 1810-20. **UR**

C. CARTER
Charles Carter (b. Feb. 22, 1826 in England) arrived in NY on Jun. 25, 1847; and made planes in Troy, NY, from 1847-49. He was in partnership with his father **Richard Carter** as **R. & C. Carter** from 1847-48; and then from 1849-53, with his brother, **Edward A. Carter** as **E. & C. Carter**; then in Utica, NY, in 1855, working for others; for himself in Syracuse, NY, from 1856-59; and from 1860-63, as a carpenter and toolmaker at the Auburn, NY prison workshop. On October 6, 1858, while in Syracuse, NY, **Charles Carter** received Patent No. 82692, for a machine "for forming the throats of planes after the main part of the mouth has been roughed out". The machines were assigned to the **Ohio Tool Co.** and **H. Chapin's Son**. One machine was conveyed to **Chapin**, on Oct. 22, 1869, for $1000. In 1864, **Charles Carter** enlisted as a private in the 3rd. Artillery, from Auburn City. In 1875, he was listed as a pattern maker in Albany. In 1880, he was a stove pattern maker in Troy. ***

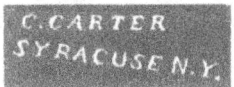

E. CARTER
Believed to be **Elias Carter** (b. May 30, 1781 in Ware, MA, d. Mar. 23, 1864 in Chicopee Falls, MA). **Elias Carter** was the son of **Timothy Carter**, an Architect, who planned and built meetinghouses with his Brother **Benjamin Carter** as **Carter & Carter**. **Timothy Carter** died on July 30, 1784, as the consequence of a fall during the building of the Leicester, MA meetinghouse. **Elias Carter**, became a master builder and noted Architect, settling in 1807, in Brimfield, MA, where he had already built the Church, in 1805. The town history relates how at the frame raising, "one whole side was raised at a time, the west side first with **Mr. Carter** going up with it, standing on the gallery girth." In 1817, **Elias** moved to Thompson, CT, where he had built the church in 1815. In 1818, he built the Killingly, CT church followed, in 1820, by the churches in Mendon and Milford. He moved to Worcester, MA, in 1828, where he built the Unitarian Church and a number of mansions in the classic revival style. In 1837, he finally moved to Chicopee Falls, MA, although he continued to do work in Worcester thru 1845. Found with the family papers was a small bound notebook containing a list of tools dated Apr. 1, 1834 (**Elias Carter** would have been 53) and listed among other tools:

Bench Planes:
one joiner-	new	2.75
one do-	old	1.50
one jack plane-	new	1.00
one smooth do-	new	1.25
one miter-	do	.90
		(7.40)
one screw handled plough with eight bits-		7.50
one philister-		3.00
one 2 inch dado -		2.50
one 1 1/2 inch do -		2.00
one 1 inch do -		.75
one 1 inch do with frame		1.25
one 1/4 inch with stop		1.35
one 1 5/8 in back rabbit		1.00
one pr. Side rabbits		1.25
one bead do		1.00
one pr. Quirk planes		1.75
one 1 3/4 in sash plane		3.25
		(26.65)

one 6/8 Grecian ovolo & Fillet	1.65
one 5/8 do do	1.45
one 4/8 do do	1.35
one 3/8 do do	1.25
one 2/8 Grecian ovolo & bead	1.25
one G. ogee & Fillet	1.00
one 3/8 astragal	.75
one 4/8 reeding plane	1.00
one 1/2 in stair cove	1.15
one stair rail plane	1.50
	(12.40)
one 1 1/4 in bead new	1.00
one 1 1/8 in do -	1.00
one 1 in do -	.75
one 6/8 do -	.67
one 5/8 do -	.67
one 4/8 do -	1.00
one 3/16 in do -	1.00
one 1/2 in center do -	.75
one 3/4 in Grecian base tool	4.75
	(11.59)
one pr 1 1/2 in match planes	3.00
one pr 7/8 in do do	1.50
one pr 3/8 in do do	1.75
	(6.25)

Beginning at the back of this same notebook (upside down) is a listing of lumber for a church (meetinghouse) with "steeple". Examples: on an 18 1/2" gutter plane (possibly modified from a jack plane); a 9 7/16" sash; a 9 1/2" round; a 9 7/8" side bead; a 10" bead; and a sash coping plane, all of birch with relieved wedges, flat chamfers and deep fluting. ca. 1790. Also reported is a 9 1/2" birch complex molder with a relieved wedge and heavy round chamfers, from southeastern New England. ca. 1810. Several examples are located at the Old Sturbridge Village Museum. ********

E. CARTER/ TROY/ EDWARD CARTER

Edward Carter (b. Nov. 40, 1825 in England, d. Mar. 18, 1903) was the son of **Richard Carter** and brother of **Charles Carter**. **Edward** worked with **Charles** as **E. & C. Carter**, from 1849-53, and with another brother **Cyrus**, from 1862-64. He made planes in Troy, NY, under his own imprint from 1854-61, at 171 then 255 River St.; and from 1865-97 at 244 then 179 River St.. An advertisement, in the 1866 Troy directory, indicates the diversity of his firm. It had both a plane factory and a tool store called **Carter's Tool Store** established in 1833, by his father, **Richard Carter**. They advertised manufacture of planes, mechanic's tools, wood moldings, and hand tendening machines. Sawing, planning, turning, boring and mortising was done to order. **Edward's** son, **Edward Carter Jr.**, took over management in 1898. In 1903, after the death of **Edward**, plane making was dropped. A *; B. B1 & C: FF

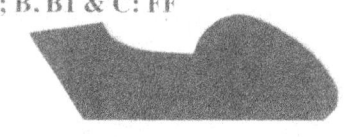

EPHRAIM CARTER

Ephraim Carter (b. Nov. 14, 1748 in Leominster, Worcester Co., MA, d. May 7, 1817 in Leominster) served (12 days) as a Corporal in Capt. Joshua Wood's Co. from Leominster, MA, during the Lexington Alarm on Apr. 19, 1775. Example: on a 9 3/8" beech bead and cove molding plane with heavy flat chamfers. The blade is marked **DK**, ca. 1780-1800. *********

E. & C. CARTER

E. & C. Carter was a partnership between brothers **Edward Carter**, **Charles Carter** and possibly **Richard Carter** that made planes at 11 Ferry St. then 171 River St. Troy, NY, between 1849-53. Later from 1862-64, **Edward Carter** was in partnership with stepbrother **Cyrus Carter** replacing **Charles Carter** and again possibly with **Richard Carter** at 249 River St. Apparently the same imprint was used for both partnerships. A & B: FF

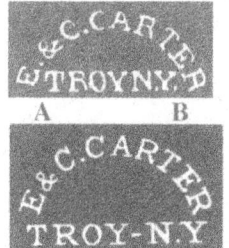

I. M. CARTER

Israel M. Carter (b. June 1829 at Hyde Park, NY) was reported in the *History of Duchess County*, by James Smith of 1882, as an edge tool manufacturer, active in 1847. He was a tax collector, a constable, and a trustee of the fire district. Example: on a bookbinder's plow plane with **HYDE PARK, N.Y.** **No imprint is available.**

J. E. CARTER

Example: on a 16"x 2 3/8" beech jack rabbet plane with small round chamfers, ca. 1810-20. **UR**

JOHN CARTER

John Carter was listed, in 1833, in Troy as a planemaker, boarding with **Richard Carter**, possibly his brother. The age of **John's** wife (b. 1812, d. 1847) would have made **John** about **Richard's** age. **No imprint has been reported.**

L. R. CARTER

Lewis R. Carter (b. 1811 in PA, d. Dec. 5, 1862 in Chillicothe, Livingston Co., MO) was a Cincinnati, OH, planemaker in 1834, at New Market between Race & Vine. Prior to that, a partner in **Carter, Donaldson & Fugate**, in 1831; and **Carter, Donaldson & Co.**, in 1832. In 1850, **Lewis Carter** was listed as a mill wright in Lawrence, Clearfield Co., PA. In 1860, he was a farmer in Chillicothe, MO. A & B ***

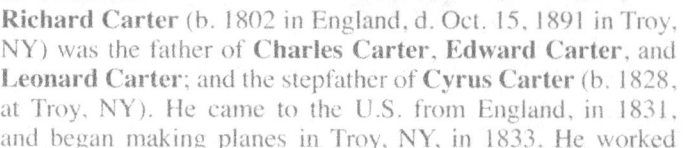

R. CARTER

Richard Carter (b. 1802 in England, d. Oct. 15, 1891 in Troy, NY) was the father of **Charles Carter**, **Edward Carter**, and **Leonard Carter**; and the stepfather of **Cyrus Carter** (b. 1828, at Troy, NY). He came to the U.S. from England, in 1831, and began making planes in Troy, NY, in 1833. He worked under his own imprint from 1833-41 and 1850-62. He was in partnership with brother **Leonard Carter** as **R. & L. Carter** from 1835-46; and with son **Charles Carter** as **R. & C. Carter** from 1847-48. He started a tool store that was continued by son **Edward Carter** and grandson **Richard Carter, Jr.** In 1860, in the industrial census, Richard Carter was listed as sawing and turning, producing 3000 "plains", and a large amount of moldings and pine boards with 10 hands. In 1864, **Richard Carter** retired. (see *American Marking Gauges*, by Milton H. Bacheller, Jr.). *

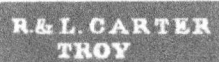

R. & C. CARTER
R. & C. Carter was a brief partnership from 1847-48 between **Richard Carter** and **Charles Carter**, his son, as planemakers at 11 Ferry St. Troy, NY. *

R. & L. CARTER
R. & L. Carter was a partnership between **Richard Carter** and brother **Leonard Carter**, at 11 Ferry St. Troy, NY, from 1835-46. **Charles Carter**, Richard's son, joined the firm, in 1843. **Leonard** boarded with **Richard**, in 1836-37. There is no record of **Leonard** after the partnership of **R. & L. Carter**. *

S. CARTER
Example: on a 9 1/4" beech complex molder, ca. 19c. **UR**

T. F. CARTER
Example on a 26" raze center toted joiner made of tropical wood, ca. Mid. 19c. **UR**

CARTER, DONALDSON & FUGATE
CARTER, DONALDSON & CO.
Carter, Donaldson & Fugate was a partnership between **Lewis R. Carter**, **James F. Donaldson** and **Thomas Fugate**, planemakers in Cincinnati, OH, in 1831. It was succeeded, in 1832, by **Lewis R. Carter** and **James F. Donaldson** as **Carter, Donaldson & Co. No imprints have been reported**.

CARTER'S TOOL STORE
The imprint was for **Edward Carter** alone or with his brother **Charles Carter** or stepbrother **Cyrus Carter**, when **Edward** added a tool store in Troy, NY, to the family's various enterprises in the 1860's. ****

WARD CARTER
Ward Carter was possibly a hardware dealer from Troy, NY. This name with **TROY N.Y.** has been reported on a 9 1/2" beech skewed rabbet with round chamfers, marked with a style number **157** on the heel, this is the **H. Chapin** style number for a skew rabbet. **A & B: UR**

S. CARUTHERS
Samuel Caruthers (b. Dec. 26, 1733 in England, d. 1780 in PA) is the earliest of the documented Philadelphia planemakers. He advertised in the *Penn Gazette*, printed by **Benjamin Franklin** as early as May 23, 1754-1765 and in the *Pennsylvania Chronicle* on March 6, 1767, when he indicated that his wares included: "double-iron planes of a late construction far exceeding any tooth planes or uprights what so ever for cross grained or curled stuff." In 1765, **Samuel Caruthers** indicated that he has: "practiced the art of plane making upwards of 20 years in this City," implying a starting date of 1745 for Philadelphia plane making. On Jan. 18, 1768, he advertised: "**Samuel Caruthers**, In Third Street, Continues to keep a general assortment of hardware, particularly adapted to carpenters and joiners, also smiths, coopers, shoemakers, &c. also there is, and is intended to be continued, the making of all sorts of carpenters and joiners planes, with the usual care and fidelity." Apprenticed to **Samuel Caruthers** were **Hezekias Niles** and **Benjamin Armitage Jr.**. **Samuel Caruthers** was elected to the Carpenter's Company of the City and County of Philadelphia, in 1771. The appearance of his planes reflected the style of mid 18c English planes, for Philadelphia followed the latest London fashions. He was the first to use the italicized print style (letters sloping to the right) in his imprint. This was subsequently used by other Philadelphia planemakers and carried to Providence, RI, by **I. Lindenberger**. Planes have been found with both flat and round chamfers. ****

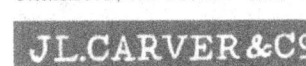

HIRAM CARVER
Hiram Carver of Edinburgh, VA, was issued Patent No. 7543, on Aug. 6, 1850 for a scraper used by cabinet-makers. **No imprint has been reported**.

JL. CARVER & Co.
Example: on a 9 3/8" beech size **18** hollow with shallow round chamfers, ca. 1830. **UR**

C. CARY
Example: on a 9 1/4" beech complex molder with heavy round chamfers, ca. 1820. **UR**

C. A. CARY & CO.
C. A. Cary & Co. was a hardware dealer in Rochester, NY. Example: on a smoothing plane made by the **New York Tool Co.**, and a smoother with a **Thistle Brand** iron (see **Auburn Tool Co.**), ca. 1860-90. **UR**

63

J. H. CARY

Jonathan Haskell Cary (b. 1802 in Bridgewater, MA, d. Mar. 28, 1875 at New Salem, MA) was the son of **William Holman Cary**. **Jonathan** was listed in New Salem, MA, from 1830-70, as a carpenter. He was also a maker of log calipers, as supported by the inventory of his workshop, and was also a gunsmith. His estate inventory also includes the following planes:

1 folloe plane	1 long joiner
2 short joiners	3 smoothing planes
2 lag planes	2 rabbet planes
1 pair of match planes	6 pairs of H & R
8 molding planes	3 small rabbets

Indicating he continued to use planes, but may not have continued to make them. Example: on a 9 1/2" beech skew rabbet with heavy round chamfers and a relieved wedge, indicating that this was probably made in the early period of his career, ca. 1820.   *****

W. H. CARY

William Holman Cary (b. May 12, 1779 in Bridgewater, MA, d. Jan. 27, 1859 at Houlton, ME) was the father of **Jonathan Haskell Cary**. In 1800, after his marriage to **Catherine** in New Salem, MA, he relocated to New Salem. In 1802, he was a housewright; and took up available land in Houlton, ME. This land was available to citizens of New Salem, MA, granted by the Commonwealth of Massachusetts, Maine then being part of MA. His son **Shepherd**, operated a store out of his father's house and went on to own extensive timber interests, in addition to owning a foundry, carding and grist mills. **William H. Cary Sr.** was associated with the operation of the various **Cary** mills and is unlikely to have made any planes in ME. In 1850, **William H. Cary, Jr.** was listed as a carpenter in Houlton, ME. Examples: on molding planes 9 7/16"-10" mostly of beech, one cherry, with flat and round chamfers, ca. 1800-20.   *****

E. W. CASE

E. W. Case was a Columbus, OH, planemaker and/ or hardware dealer. ****

H. CASE

H. Case was a tool manufacturer and planemaker active in Columbus, OH, in 1848. **No imprint has been reported.**

L. CASE

Lorenzo Case (b. 1821, d. 1887) made planes in Watertown, NY, under his own imprint from 1850-55, after having earlier made planes as an employee of **Benjamin F. Berry**, in the 1840's. The 1850 census lists **Lorenzo Case** as employing six men and producing carpenter's tools worth $3500. In 1855, **Samuel Adams** (b. 1838 in England), a toolmaker, was living with **Lorenzo**. In 1870, **Lorenzo** was listed as a carpenter and builder with his son **Richard Case,** as a carpenter, in Watertown, NY.   A*; B & C **

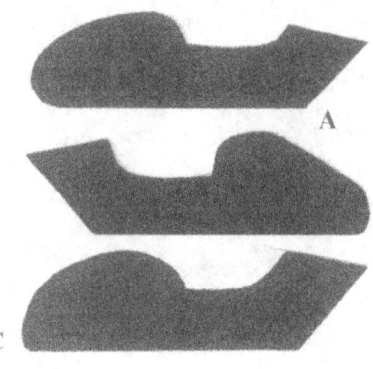

CASEY & CO.

George Casey (b. Mar. 6, 1807 in Dover, NY, d. Nov. 5, 1890 in Auburn, NY) moved to Auburn, in 1813, with his family, apprenticing to **Mr. Smock**, a builder. **George** became a builder in Auburn, from 1830-50's. He was also credited with inventing a machine for cutting the throats in planes. Apparently he made planes under this imprint in Auburn, NY, in 1857. He was in business with several sets of partners all of whom used prison labor: **Casey, Kitchel & Co.**, from 1847-58; **Casey, Clark & Co.**, from 1858-64; and the **Auburn Tool Co.**, from 1864 to the early 1880's.   FF

CASEY, CLARK & CO.

George Casey bought out his partners in **Casey, Kitchel & Co.** and with new partners **J. N. Starin, Nelson and Adejiah Fitch, Noah P. Clark,** and **Alonzo Beardsley**, manufactured under **Case, Clark & Co.** in Auburn, NY from 1858-64, when the firm, on Oct 8, 1864, was reorganized as a stock corporation into the **Auburn Tool Co.**, with **George Casey** as President. The 1860 census listed 65 hands employed with $45,000 worth of planes & plane irons produced. One example from the Shelburne Museum is on an 8 1/8" beech coffin smoother with an **Excelsior Works/ Auburn, NY**, iron and more than 20 different incuse imprints on the toe and heel, probably of bench hands, some marked twice.   FF

CASEY, KITCHEL & CO.

Casey, Kitchel & Co. was a partnership consisting of George Casey, Adam Miller, Joshua Douglas and Nelson Kitchel, that bought the Auburn prison labor contract from Z. J. McMaster & Co. in 1847 and made carpenter's and cabinetmaker's tools from 1847-56. Casey bought out the others and operated briefly in 1857 as Casey & Co. The 1850 census indicated that the firm employed 40 convicts, used a steam planning mill producing $22,000 worth of carpenters' and joiners' tools. Example: on an ebony plow with boxwood washers, nuts and arms, ivory tips, a brass depth stop and an integral handle.   A, B, B1 & C *

 C

M. CASHEL
Example: on a 9 1/2" beech combination tongue & groove plane with a relieved wedge and round chamfers, ca. 1805-20.   **UR**

N. CASS
Example: on a 9 1/4" beech tongue plane with a birch wedge and flat chamfers, ca. 1800.   **UR**

H. CASSEBEER
Herman Cassebeer was a hardware dealer in Rochester, NY, from 1884-94. He was part of **Cassebeer Reed & Co.** from 1878-84. This imprint has been reported on the heel of a quarter round made by **G. W. Denison & Co.**   ***

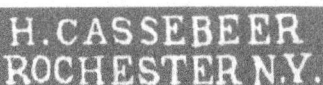

CASSEBEER REED & CO.
Cassebeer Reed & Co. was a New York City hardware firm consisting of **Herman Cassebeer**, **William A. Reed** and **Louis H. Auerbacher** operating from 1878-84 in the premises previously occupied by **Nathusius, Kugler & Morrison**. The firm was succeeded by **Reed & Auerbacher** from 1884-1910. Example: the B imprint has both **H. Cassebeer** and **Cassebeer Reed & Co.** on a 1 3/4" wide hollow made by **G. W. Denison & Co.**
A ***; B *****

D. CASSEL
This imprint is created with the **H. Cassel** imprint with the H overstruck with a D. Example: on an 11 1/4" beech square rabbet with flat chamfers, possibly from rural eastern, PA, ca. 1800-20   **UR**

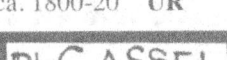 

H. CASSEL
Examples: on a 9 13/16" narrow double-reeding plane; a 10" complex molder; and a 10 1/4" large side bead, all beech with flat chamfers, possibly from rural eastern PA, ca. 1790.   ****

W. CASSIL
Examples: on a 9" round plane; and a jointer, both beech with flat chamfers from Beaver Co., PA, ca. 1820.   **UR**

I. CASSON
Example: on a 9 1/2" beech molder with round top wedge and round chamfers. ca. 1820. **No imprint is available**.

CATION
Example: an embossed imprint on a jack plane with offset tote and flat chamfers. ca. 1800. **No imprint is available**.

CATION
David W. Cation (b. 1802 in Litchfield Co., CT, d. before 1876 in NY) was a New York City planemaker from 1835-44. In 1834, he was a partner with **J. W. Gibbs** as **Gibbs & Cation**. In 1872, he was listed a toolmaker; and in 1874 as a planemaker. In 1876, **Eliza**, **David's** wife was listed as widow.   ***

A. CAUGHTER & CO.
This name was reported with a location imprint of **LOUISVILLE, KY**, on a small hollow. Possibly a hardware dealer. **No imprint is available**.

A. F. CAULKING
Example: on an 8 1/2" beech thumb-screw plow plane. The thumb screws are iron and the depth stop has a wooden shaft and a iron foot, ca. 19c.   **UR**

CAVANACH & MILLER
Cavanach & Miller was a hardware dealer from Natchez, MS. Example: on a 26" razee jointer with centered closed tote and an **Ohio Tool Co.** cast steel iron, ca. 1850.   *****

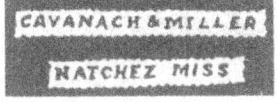

CAYUDUTTA FACTORY
Johnstown, NY, is on the Cayudutta Creek which empties into the Mohawk River at Fonda, NY. The imprint may be a trade name for one of the central NY state planemakers, ca. 19c.   A & B ***; B1 ****

A

B

B1

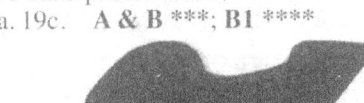

CAYUDUTTA WORKS

A trade name for **Wm. H. Livingston & Co.** Example: on an 11 1/2"x 1/2" beech tongue & groove pair, ca. 19c. ****

CAYUGA

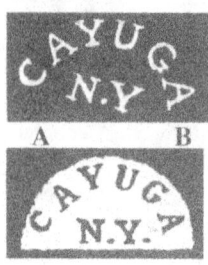

Probably a brand name used on various bench planes made by the **Auburn Tool Co.**, located in Cayuga Co., NY. Example: The A imprint is on a bench plane also imprinted **New York Tool Co.** A & B **

JOHN CECIL
John Cecil (b. Dec. 10, 1801) age 14, was apprenticed on May 29, 1846 to **William Vance** to be taught the trade of a planemaker. **No imprint has been reported**.

B. CHACE
Believed to be **Benjamin Chace** who was listed in the 1810 census for Portsmouth, RI. Examples: on a 12 5/8" single-iron fixed sash with offset open pegged tote, a **Weldon** round top iron and wedge, and flat chamfers; and a birch Yankee plow, with thumbscrews, a relieved wedge and round chamfers. Also reported is a **Jo, Fuller** molder, overstamped by **B. Chase**. Both the **Jo, Fuller** molder and the plow were found together in Westport, MA, near Providence, RI, ca. 1800-10. *****

R. CHAFFIN
Robert Chaffin is listed in Acton, MA, from 1750-91 and from 1790-1840. He stated in an ad that he was a joiner. Examples: on a coopers' planes; a birch howel with rams horn nuts; a croze; and a topping (sun) plane of birch. ca. 1790. UR

CHAMBERLIN

Example: on a jack plane. ca. 1830. (see **B: Chamberlin** and **W: Chamberlin**) UR

B: CHAMBERLIN
The **CHAMBERLIN** portion of the imprint is the same as that used by **W. Chamberlin** indicating a relationship. Example: on a 9 3/4" beech complex molder with heavy round chamfers, ca. 1805-20. UR

J. CHAMBERLIN.
This imprint has the location **BRANDON./ VT.** Examples: on a 2" wide beech skewed rabbet plane. The blade is marked **S. SANDERS**; and on a single-iron beech smoothing plane, ca. 19c. UR

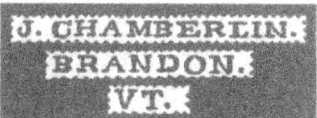

W: CHAMBERLIN
Possibly **William Chamberlin** (b. Oct. 23, 1754 in Petersham, Worcester Co., MA, d. Aug. 25, 1842 in Barnard, Windsor Co., VT) who was listed, in 1798, as a chairmaker in Boston, MA. This imprint uses the same **CHAMBERLIN** die as **B. Chamberlin** indicating a relationship. Examples: on a 9 1/2" beech narrow complex molder with heavy flat chamfers; and a 14" beech jack with offset tote round-top wedge and round chamfers, ca. 1800-20. UR

W. B. CHAMBERLIN
W. B. Chamberlin was probably a hardware dealer from Westfield, NJ, ca. 1845. Example: on a **H. Chapin/ Union Factory** dado plane with style number **138**. ****

CHAMBERLIN & WINANS
Chamberlin & Winans were hardware dealers in New Brighton, PA, no known date. Example: on a size 8 hollow made by the **Ohio Tool Co.**. ****

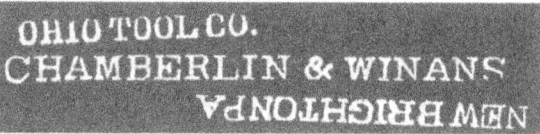

D. CHAMBERS
Examples: on a 9 3/4" beech molder with a double imprint on the toe, rosewood boxing, and round chamfers, found near Baltimore, MD. A second example with the straight border was found on a 13 3/4" beech wedge locked tongue groove pair with round chamfers and found in OH, ca. 1810-20. A & B: UR

A & B

Wm. CHAMBERS
Example: on a 9" beech wedge locked split sash with shallow round chamfers, ca. 19c. UR

E. P. CHANDLER
Example: on a 9 1/2" beech skew rabbet with slide-arm fence, wood thumbscrews and shallow round chamfers, ca. 1820. UR

P. F. CHANDLER
Example: on a 10" applewood cock bead, with the slanted letters, from Philadelphia, PA, ca. 1830-40. UR

C. CHANEY

Examples: on a 9 3/8" moving filletster with hand made brass hardware; a modified 9 1/2" narrow round with heavy round chamfers; a door-joint groove; a 9 1/2" skew rabbet; and a 10 1/4" plow with solid brass tombstone depth stop, and slide arms secured by a wood thumbscrew, shallow round chamfers, found in CT, all beech, ca. 1820-30. **UR**

JACOB CHANEY

Example: on a 9 1/4" beech gunstock plane with flat chamfers, ca. 1790. **UR**

FPC/ F. P. CHANNEL

Example: on a 9 1/2" beech quarter round with an **I. Sleeper** style wedge and flat chamfers, ca. 1795-1805. **UR**

E. CHAPIN

Eliphalet Chapin (b. Sep. 18, 1741 in Somers, MA, later part of CT, d. Jan. 9, 1807 at East Windsor, CT) a noted cabinetmaker of East Windsor, CT. He apprenticed as a cabinetmaker in Hartford or East Windsor from 1755-62. In 1767, he fled to Philadelphia, PA, to avoid a marriage after fathering a child and to obtain further training. He returned to East Windsor, in 1769. On April 25, 1771, he purchased 1/2 acre on Main St. in East Windsor (now the East Windsor Hill section of South Windsor). **Eliphalet Chapin** established a large cabinet shop using the latest Philadelphia "Rococo" style. **Julius Barnard** apprenticed with **Eliphalet Chapin** prior to 1792. On May 3, 1790, **Ebenezer Williams** advertised in *The Connecticut Courant and Weekly Intelligencer* that he "carries on the Windsor chairmaking business, at the shop of **Mr. Eliphalet Chapin** in E. Windsor." **Eliphalet Chapin** was active from 1771-1802. On Sep. 28, 1795, **Eliphalet Chapin** advertised in *The Connecticut Courant* that his property including the "Brick Dwelling Houfe, Cabinet-makers Shop, Barn, Wood Houfe etc. in Eaft-Windfur, 80 rods South of the Meeting houfe." was for sale as he "intends to remove into New-York State the beginning of next Summer, he defires all thofe that have accounts with him to bring them for fettlement." Examples: on a 10" rabbet; a 9 7/8" round; and a 9 11/16" complex molder, all birch with flat chamfers, ca. 1770-90. ****

H. CHAPIN/ UNION FACTORY

Hermon Chapin (b. Oct. 9, 1799 at Westmoreland, NH, d. Jan. 31, 1866 at Savannah, GA) was the younger brother of **Nathaniel Chapin**. He apprenticed on May 20, 1822 with **D. & M. Copeland** at Hartford after becoming experienced in timber and being well trained as a sawyer in the family business. On Dec. 17, 1825, he formed a partnership with **Daniel Copeland** in the plane making firm of **Copeland & Chapin**, which started operation in 1826, on the North branch of the Farmington River at Pine Meadows near New Hartford, CT. On Oct. 21, 1828, **Hermon Chapin** purchased **Daniel Copeland**'s interest and became the sole owner of the business, now called **Union Factory**. No Copeland & Chapin imprint has been reported, and it is supposed that the **D. COPELAND** imprint was used. The **Union Factory** was one of the major manufacturers of planes in New England. The company employed 40 shop hands and produced $30,000 worth of product, according to the 1850 census. The 1860 census showed 36 employees and production worth $33,000. (see *Wooden Planes in 19c America, Vol. II*, by Kenneth D. Roberts). This book contains an extensive history of the **Chapin** plane making enterprises, as well as describing the large number of plane types produced, including the **Rust-Chapin** adjustable patent plow plane.) **H. Chapin & Sons** the successor to **H. Chapin/ Union Factory** was formed, in 1860, in New Hartford, CT, by **Hermon Chapin** and his sons, **Edward Merrill Chapin** (b. Sep. 5, 1833 at New Hartford, d. Dec. 10, 1896 at New Hartford), **George Washington Chapin** (b. Feb. 22, 1837 at New Hartford, d. Aug. 10, 1884 at Cleveland, OH), and **Philip Eugene Chapin** (b. Dec. 1, 1838 at New Hartford, d. 1915, PA). No H. Chapin & Sons imprint has been reported. **Edward** and **George** assumed ownership under the name of **H. Chapin's Sons**, in 1865, and continued in New Hartford. In 1868, **George Chapin** sold his interest to **Edward Chapin** who continued the firm until his death, in 1897. **E. M. Chapin & Solon Rust** were jointly issued Patent No. 76,051, on Mar. 31, 1868. Offered for the first time in 1874 was the "Patent adjusting plow" handled plane available in:

A

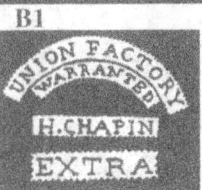

B

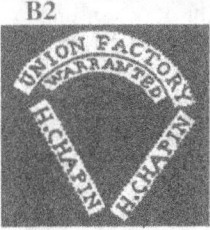

B1

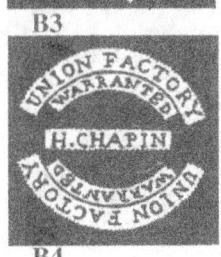

B2

No. 236   beech
No. 237   beech, boxed fence
No. 239 1/2 applewood, boxed fence
No. 240   boxwood
No. 240 1/2 rosewood, boxed fence
No. 241   ebony
No. 240 1/2 ebony, boxed fence

These were listed in **Chapin** catalogs from 1874-97 and **Sargent & Co.** catalogs in 1877. The 1870 census showed 28 employees producing 40,000 planes that sold for $45,000. Two water wheels produced 50 hp that ran three saws and other machinery. No H. Chapin's Son imprint has been reported. **H. Chapin's Son & Co.** was formed in 1897 upon the death of **Edward** by two of his sons, **Hermon Mills Chapin** (b. Sep. 17, 1866 at New Hartford, d. 1928 at New Hartford) and **Frank Mills Chapin** (b. June 28, 1869 at New Hartford, d. 1942 at New Hartford) and **Rufus E. Holmes**. In 1901, it was merged into the **Chapin-Stephens Co.** No H. Chapin's Son & Co. imprint has been reported. The C imprint is the ruler mark applied to a plane. The B1 imprint is with **EXTRA** found on bench planes with steel reinforcement rods down thru the handle and steel strikes on the top of the front. The B4 imprint has the date **1838**. The B5 imprint also has the 1874 catalog number **No 240 1/2** that describes a "handled plow, solid rosewood, boxed fence, best plate, polished, and 8 irons,

B3

B4

for $9.00". **A & B: FF; D ***;
B1, B2 & B3 ****;
B4, B5 & C *******

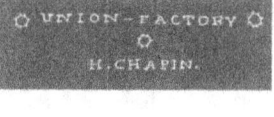

N. CHAPIN & CO./ EAGLE FACTORY
Nathaniel Chapin (b. Nov. 21, 1792 at Orange, MA, d. 1876) was the older brother of **Hermon Chapin**. He served in the War of 1812 and was commissioned a Captain of a company from Walpole, NH. After the war he was in the lumber business with his father and brothers. Upon the death of his father in 1833, **Nathaniel** sold his property at Walpole, NH, and relocated to CT. In 1835, he was employed by **H. Chapin** as a supervisor under a five-year contract that paid him $450 the first year and $500 per year thereafter. Some time after 1838, he organized and made planes under the **Eagle Factory** name in New Hartford, CT. He moved his factory to Westfield, MA, in 1847. He was listed, in 1849, in New England Mercantile Union directory as a plane manufacturer in Westfield, MA. He was listed in the 1850 industrial census as a planemaker in Westfield, employed six hands, used water power and produced 8000 bench and molding planes worth $7000. **A & B: FF; B1 & C ***; C1 ****; D *******

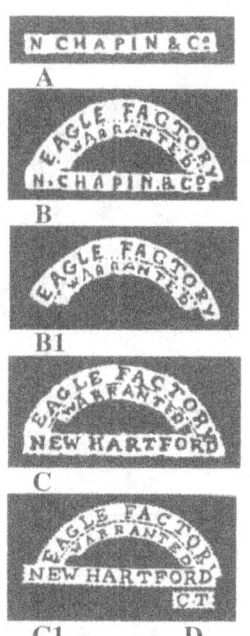

CHAPIN/ P. CHAPIN
Philip Chapin (b. Sept. 3, 1805 at Walpole, NH, d. after 1862 at New Hartford, CT) was among the most prolific of the Baltimore, MD, plane manufacturers. He was a brother of **Hermon Chapin** for whom he worked, probably as a supervisor, prior to 1830. He moved in 1830 to Baltimore and according to directories was in the following plane firms: **Ward & Chapin**, in 1831; **Chapin & Kendall**, in 1833; **Philip Chapin**, in 1835-36 at 36 Light ST., in 1842-43 at corner of Light & Balderston & 1845-55 at 44 Light ST.; and **Atkinson & Chapin**, in 1836. His advertisement in the 1853-54 *Matchett's Baltimore Directory* stated he operated a plane manufacturer and tool store carrying: "carpenter's, carver's, cabinet, coach and pattern maker's tools of Am. and Engl. manu. of best stamps and qual."

After 1856, **Philip Chapin** was listed as a turner and screw manufacturer and last noted in the Baltimore Directory, in 1860. He was succeeded in the late 1850's by **A. B. Seidenstricker & Co.** In 1860, **Philip Chapin** returned to New Hartford, CT as a house carpenter. In Baltimore, **Philip Chapin** continued a close relationship with his brother **Hermon Chapin** and bought a large quantity of planes from **H. Chapin**. (See **Wm. C. Ross, E. L. Matthews,** and **A. B. Seidenstricker & Co.**) **B: FF; A, B1, B2 & C ****

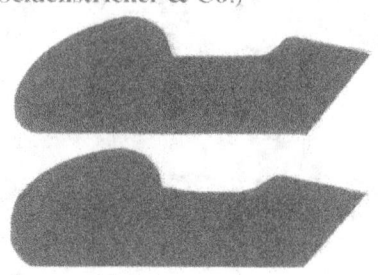

CHAPIN & KENDALL
Chapin & Kendall was a partnership of **Philip Chapin** and **Thomas Kendall,** that made planes at McCellan's Alley, in Baltimore, MD, in 1833. **A, A1 & B ****

CHAPIN-STEPHENS
Chapin-Stephens was the product of a merger in 1901 of **H. Chapin's Son & Co.** and **L. C. Stephens & Co.** at Pine Meadow, CT. The president of the firm was **Frank Mills Chapin**, son of **Edward Merrill Chapin** and grandson of **Hermon Chapin**. In 1929, the firm was dissolved. **Stanley** acquired the line of rules, but discontinued the line of wooden planes. (see **C. S. C.**) The imprint **SECOND** has also been reported on the heel of a 7/8" wide rabbet of second quality with saw marks and stain the only finish. The original A imprint die exists. **A: FF; B ******

O. R. CHAPLIN
Example: on a 9 1/2" beech narrow table hollow with 19c. chamfers, ca. 1850. **UR**

CHAPLIN'S PATENT
Orril R. Chaplin of Boston, MA, was issued patent No. 126,519, on May 7, 1872 for a wood bottom transitional plane sold by **Tower & Lyon** of New York City and listed in its catalog of March 1888. Example: on a 9" beech handled smoothing plane and other bench planes. (see *Patented Transitional & Metallic Planes in America, 1827-1927*, p. 161-63, by Roger K. Smith). **No imprint is available.**

I. CHAPMAN
Isaac Chapman (b. 1814 in NH) was listed in the 1850 census as a carpenter in Williston, VT. Examples: on a molder; and a 30" beech jointer with the location imprint of **WILLISTON, VT**, which is just east of Burlington. ***

J. CHAPMAN
Example: on a 9 5/8" beech hollow & round pair with heavy round chamfers, ca. 1820. **UR**

M. CHAPMAN
Example: on a 22 7/8" beech short jointer with pegged closed offset tote and wide flat chamfers, ca. 1790-1805. **UR**

A. CHAPPEL
Example: on a 7" beech coffin, compass smoother with a radius adjustment on the toe and slight round chamfers. With a double-iron by **Middlesex Mfg. Co./ Middletown, CT. USA/ Baldwin/ Warranted**, ca. 19c. **UR**

J. CHAPPELL
James Chappell was listed in the 1839 Pittsburgh, PA, directory as a planemaker at the corner of Ferry & Fourth, upstairs. Earlier, he was a partner in **A. Bright & J. Chappell** in 1836-37. Example: on a 9 1/2" fully-boxed side bead.
A, A1 & B ***

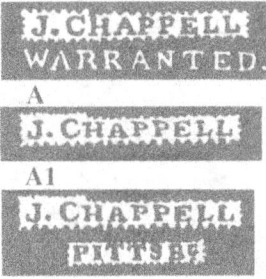

CHARLTON BROs
Example: on a 10 1/4" beech single-boxed complex molder. **UR**

C: CHASE
Examples: on a 9 13/16" beech molder; a 9 3/4" beech quarter round; and a 9 7/8" birch molder, all with flat chamfers and found in the Portland, ME, area. Also reported is a double-handled 14 1/2" match plane with metal skate and runner, ca. 1780. ***

E. CHASE
Possibly **Emery Chase** (b. 1737 in Newbury, MA, d. Aug. 19, 1788 in Andover) who was a housewright in Newburyport, MA. His inventory included a number of planes and carpenter tools. Examples: on a 10 1/2" birch coming & going, tongue & groove plane; and a 10" beech bead, both with flat chamfers and an **I. Sleeper** style wedge, ca. 1780-90. ***

F. A. CHASE
Example: on a size **7/8** match tongue & groove pair with totes, found on Cape Cod, ca. 1850. **UR**

G. CHASE/ G. CHASE & CO.
George Chase was a joiner and ship's carpenter active from 1841-46, in Portland, ME, who also made and sold planes. Examples: the B imprint is on a 13 3/8" sash plane with two irons; an ovolo; and a rabbet, all beech. The A imprint is on a 9 13/16" rabbet; and a 9 7/16" round, both beech.
A & B: **

A

B

J. CHASE
James Chase (b. Dec. 25, 1735 in Hudson, NH, d. 1812) of Gilmanton (later Gilford), NH, was a joiner and cabinetmaker who made and sold planes along with other woodworking tools, active from 1797-1812. Examples: on a complex molder; and a hollow, both 9 3/4" beech with an **I. Sleeper** style wedges and flat chamfers. The B imprint is from a 13 1/2" beech panel raiser with an offset pegged tote and flat chamfers, ca. 1790. ***

J. CHASE.
The location Cato is near Syracuse, NY. Example: on a nosing plane dated **1857**. **UR**

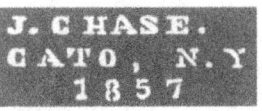

L. M. CHASE.
L. M. Chase with **MAKER** and the location imprint **N. CONWAY. N.H.** is on a 15 7/8" beech raze jack plane with a centered tote, ca. 19c. **UR**

S. CHASE
Possibly **Stephen Chase** (b. Jan. 22, 1742 in Lynn, MA, d. 1805) who was a housewright in Portsmouth, NH. He built the **Chase** house in 1762 and from 1799-1805 he was a farmer; or **Somerby Chase** (b. Mar. 2, 1746 in Newbury, MA, d. 1822 in Newbury, MA) a joiner and housewright of Newburyport, MA. Examples: on a 10" round & hollow pair; a 9 7/8" tongue

plane; a 9 3/4" bead; and an 8 1/2" Yankee plow, all beech with flat chamfers, and with **I. Sleeper** style wedges, ca. 1790. ***

S. E. CHASE
Sylvanneus Elliott Chase's (b. Jun. 3, 1830 in Fletcher, VT, d. Feb. 29, 1884 in Fletcher, VT), earliest dated plane is **1847**. He was listed as a cabinet and furniture producer and mechanic in the 1850's. He operated a sap bucket mfg. shop, in 1875. Examples: on a common smoother; a handled smoother; two jack planes; a joiner; and handled match tongue & groove with nicker and wedge pair, all beech, ca. mid-19c. ****

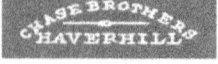

W. CHASE
Examples: on a 9 9/16" fixed sash; and a 9 3/8" single boxed complex molder, both beech with heavy round chamfers, possibly from New England, ca. 1805-15. **UR**

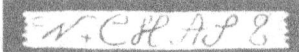 

CHASE BROTHERS
Example: on a slide-arm plow with thumbscrews and the additional location Haverhill, which is along the Merrimack River between MA and NH. *****

CHASE, SARGENT & SHATTUCK
John H. Chase (d. May 5, 1879), **Frederick W. Sargent** and **Horace B. Shattuck** traded as **Chase, Sargent & Shattuck**, active from 1866-79, as hardware dealers in Lowell, MA. Earlier **Buebank, Chase & Co. Hardware** was listed in the Lowell city directories, from 1851-58. **John H. Chase** died in 1879, and in 1880, the firm had split and Shattuck was the hardware man and **Chase, Sargent & Sons** operated as merchant tailors. Examples: on two bench planes; a 22" jointer; and a 9 1/4" coffin miter, both beech. ****

CHEBRINGTON BROTHERS
Probably a Boston, MA hardware dealers. Example: on an 8 1/2" smoother made by **Taber Plane Co.**, New Bedford, MA and patented Feb 28, 1865, ca. 1865. *****

CE. CHELOR/ CESAR CHELOR
Cesar Chelor (b. ca. 1720, d. 1784 at Wrentham, MA) is one of the most famous names in early New England planemaking. He was a black slave owned, perhaps as early as 1736, by **Francis Nicholson** who is the earliest documented American planemaker. **Cesar Chelor** quite possibly made many of the planes bearing the **F. NICHOLAS** imprint. **Chelor** was admitted as a member to the Congregational Church in Wrentham Center, on Sept. 20, 1741, and probably was at least 21 years old at that time. In **Francis Nicholson's** will, dated April 1, 1752, and recorded in Jan. 18, 1754, he freed **Chelor**, giving him his bedstead, bed and bedding, a variety of tools, his bench, ten acres of land and grazing and timber rights. **Chelor** married **Judith Russell**, on April 20, 1758, raised a family of nine children, and died intestate at Wrentham, in 1784. His estate inventory was valued at 77 pounds 2 shillings, including sundry tools and old lumber. **Jethro Jones** (see **I. Jones**), another black planemaker, may have had some association with **Chelor** during **Jones's** stay in Wrentham ca. 1765-69. **Sambo Freeman** possibly also worked for **Chelor** from 1758-61, and was recorded in Holliston, MA, in 1772. **Chelor's** imprints have two major variations. The A imprint consists of three separate die stamps, one for each line. The location imprints **LIVING IN** and **WRENTHAM** are the same as used by **Francis Nicholson** and son **John Nicholson**. The B imprint with the full **CESAR** is rare with only four examples having been reported. The B1 wedge with a flat back is local to the Wrentham area and is found on the later planes dating about 1770. **A, A1 & A2** **; **B** *****;

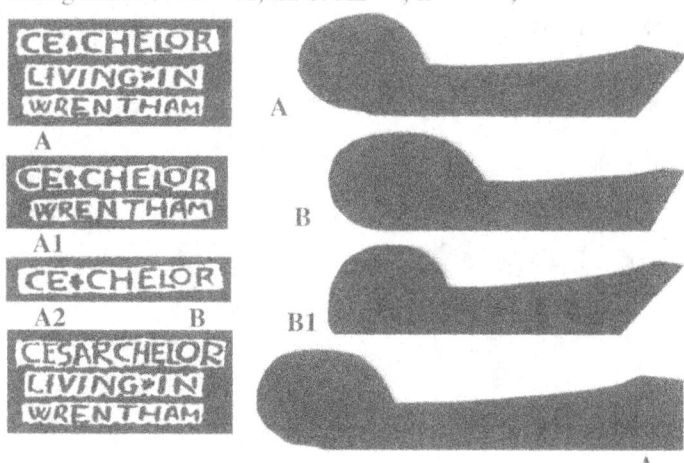

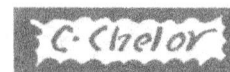

C. Chelor

Possibly a **COUNTERFEIT**, not to be confused with **Cesar Chelor**.

C. CHENEY
Examples: on a plow; dado; bead; and a ship rabbet, all 9 1/2" beech with round chamfers, ca. 1820. **UR**

C. C. CHENEY
Examples: on a 9 1/4" birch gunstock plane with flat chamfers, ca. 1790; and a 17"x 1 1/4" beech ship's rabbet with round chamfers, ca. 1820 **UR**

E. V. A. CHICHESTER
E. V. A. Chichester was listed as a planemaker in Norwalk, CT, active from 1856-65. **No imprint has been reported.**

A. CHICKS
Amos Chick (b. 1834 in Winterport, Waldo Co., ME) listed in 1856-57 Portland City Directory, age 22, as ship carpenter in Back Cove Village. Married **Emeline (Emily) Willcutt**, of Boston, MA, on Jan. 11, 1865, and was listed as carpenter. In

1870 in Cambridge, MA. Example: with **MAKER** on a 9 1/2" beech square rabbet with rosewood boxing, ca. 19c.   *****

GEORGE CHICK

George Chick (b. 1828 in Parsonsfield, ME, d. 1904 in Brooklyn, NY) listed as a ship joiner, carpenter. In 1849, **George Chick** of Portland married **Frances N. Davis** of Buxton, ME. In 1860 census, **George** was listed in Boston, MA. In the 1870 census for Kennebunk, ME, **George** was listed as a ship carpenter. In 1876 & 80 Bath, ME directories, **George** is listed as a ship Joiner. The 1888 Brooklyn, NY City Directory lists **George Chick** as carpenter. The 1892 New Utrecht, Kings Co., NY census lists **George Chick** as a builder. In 1898-1901, listed **George** as a carpenter in Brooklyn NY City. Examples: on an 8 1/2" rosewood smooth plane; a rosewood razee fore plane; a 17" lignum vitae shipwright's jack; and a 17 1/2" lignum vitae double-iron shipwright's rabbet, ca. 1850.

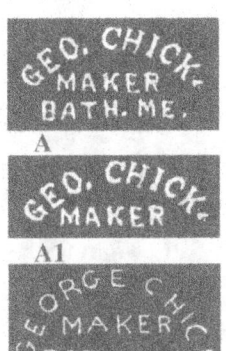

A, A1 & B *****

B Child

Benjamin Child from Woodstock, CT. Example: on a 24"x 2 3/4" birch jointer with a single iron, offset pegged tote, diamond strike knob and flat chamfers, ca. 1790-1800.   *****

I. CHILD

Examples: on a 9 7/16" beech wide round chamfers; and a 9 1/2" molder. **No imprint is available**.

J. E. CHILD/ J. EDWIN. CHILD

John Edwin Child (b. 1829 in RI, d. Jun. 2, 1911 in Providence, RI) was a Providence, RI, plane and edge tool maker, active from 1850-80, who also supplied plane bodies to, and did contract work for, the **Greenfield Tool Co.** He was listed in the 1850 census as a planemaker, living in his father's house along with planemaker **Isaac Battey**, age 33, who was married to **Child's** sister. **Child** probably worked for **Battey**. In 1879, **J. Edwin Child** was listed in the Providence directory as a planemaker at 46 Pine St.   A *; B & B1 **

CHILD, FARR & CO.

Alonzo Child and **Asa Farr** ran a hardware business in St. Louis, MO, from 1847-51, and succeeded by **Child, Pratt & Co.**   **

CHILD, PRATT & CO.

Child, Pratt & Co. was a St. Louis, MO, hardware business with **Alonzo Child**, **Elon G. Pratt** and **Asa Farr**, that was a successor to **Child, Farr & Co.** from 1852-1859, when it was succeeded by **Child, Pratt & Fox** from 1860-63 and then **Pratt & Fox** in 1863.   *

CHIPAWAY

These imprints of the **E. C. Simmons Hardware Co**. of St. Louis, MO, was used on its second-quality planes. The B imprint is on a 16 1/16" beech jack plane, marked on the top of the plane in front of the strike button, ca. 1900.

A & B ****

B. CHRISTIAN

Examples: the A imprint is on a 7 3/4" smoother; and a 20" jointer. The B imprint is on a group of 30 planes found in a tool chest with planemaker floats and chisels in the Springfield, MA area, ca. 1875.   A & A1 ****

A. CHURCH

Alonzo Church (b. Oct. 13, 1805 in MA, d. Jun. 27, 1871 in Amherst, MA) was the brother of **Horace Church**. He married **Hanna Hyde** on Mar. 7, 1833 in Amherst. **Alonzo** worked for **Kennedy & Co.** as a planemaker starting in 1837. He also appears in **Truman Nutting's** journal in 1842-43 for plane transactions and, in 1847, he purchased plane handles. **Alonzo Church** are listed in Boston, MA, in 1850, with **Alonzo** a machinist. He is listed, in 1860, back in Amherst as a mechanic. In 1870, he is listed in Amherst as a wagon maker. Examples: the A imprint is on a jack. The B imprint is on a 22" closed-tote jointer; and a smoother. The imprint of name and location **GRANBY** (CT) appears on a 28" jointer. No example of the Granby imprint is available.
(see **J. Church**)   A & A1 *****

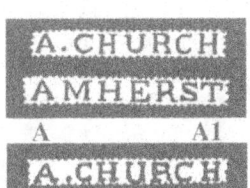

HORACE CHURCH

Horace Church (b. Oct. 29, 1803 in MA) was the brother of **Alonzo Church**. He was an Amherst, MA, planemaker. On Nov. 24, 1832, he married **Sarah S. Ewing** in Amherst, MA. In 1833, he acquired from **Truman Nutting** jack and smoother planes in exchange for making jointers. Land records show that on Apr. 5, 1836, **Horace Church** was in Hardin, OH. On May 4, 1837, he married Sarah's sister **Prudence Ewing** in Amherst. In 1840, **Horace** was back in Hardin, OH. In 1850, **Horace** returned to Amherst where he was listed as a jointer. In 1860, **Horace** was back in Hardin, OH, but listed as a druggist. **No imprint has been reported.**

I. CHURCH

I. Church with the added imprint **MAKER** and the location **NORWALK, CONN** with a Masonic symbol appear on a

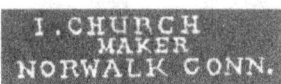

17"x 2 1/2" fruitwood, raze fore plane with a pegged tote and shallow round chamfers, ca. 19c. ****

J. CHURCH

Jonathan Church (b. Mar. 24, 1783 in CT, d. Jan 2, 1853 in Granby, CT), who appears in the 1810-50 Granby, CT, censuses. In the 1850 census, he was listed as a farmer, age 67. Examples: the A1 imprint is on two birch molders; a beech sash; and two rounds, all 9 1/2". The A imprint is on a 9 1/2" molder (see **Alonzo Church** and **Horace Church**), ca. 1820.
A *****; A1 ****

A

A1

CHURCH & CAULKINS

Appears to be a hardware dealer. The imprint is on the heel of a 5/8" ogee molder made by

L. & I. J. White in Buffalo, NY, ca. 19c. ****

JOSEPH CHURCHILL

Joseph Churchill (b. 1748, d. 1824) apprenticed on Oct. 31, 1765 to **Simeon Doggett** in Middleboro, MA. **Joseph Churchill** was listed as a house joiner & housewright. Example: on a hollow, ca. late 1800's. **UR**

CINCINNATI PLANE FACTORY

Jesse Walker advertised in the *Western Spy and Literary Cadet*: "Who makes planes of all kinds, and of the latest fashions, which he will sell lower than any other factory in the western country." **No imprint has been reported**.

W. H. H. C./ W. H. H. CLAFLIN

William H. H. Claflin (b. Jan. 9, 1815 in Brookfield, VT, d. May 1, 1895 in Northfield, VT) was listed as a carpenter and contractor/ builder in Northfield, VT, active from 1872-80. Most of the planes came from one lot which also included a **M. Read** and an **A. Fish** plane, possibly **Claflin's** own tool kit. One was dated **1865**, and would have been made at age 50. **A, B &C** ****

CLAGETT–JOHNSON & Co

Clagett–Johnson & Co. of Louisville, KY was probably a hardware dealer, ca. 19c. ****

J. R. CLANCY

J. R. Clancy probably was a hardware dealer in Syracuse, NY. Example: on a rabbet made by **Sargent & Co.** ****

J * CLAP

There are four generations of **Joshua Clap (Clapp)** from Walpole, MA. The eldest **Joshua Clap** (b. Apr. 9, 1671 in Dedham, MA, d. Mar. 30, 1728 in Walpole, MA). Walpole was separated from Dedham in 1724. **Joshua Clapp** (1671-1728) is too early for these planes. The next generation, **Capt. Joshua Clapp Jr.** (b. 1707 in Walpole, d. May 6, 1802 in Walpole, MA) is the right age to be the **Joshua** who took **Charles Dupee Sr.** as his ward in 1750. **Charles Dupee** was subsequently a housewright and planemaker in his own right. **Capt. Joshua Clapp Jr.** (1707-1802) is also too early for the planes. **Joshua Clap III** (b. Sep. 7, 1729 in Walpole, MA, d. 1790 in Scituate, MA) is believed to be the maker of these planes. It was this **Joshua Clap III** (1729-1790) who was a Patriot during the American Revolution. He was a Private in Capt. Sabin Man's Co. of Walpole Minutemen, Col. John Greaton's Regt., which marched on the alarm of April 19, 1775 to Lexington and Concord and serviced for 12 days. **Joshua Clapp Jr.** (1707-1802) was a Captain of the Walpole North Co., Col. Ephraim Wheelock's Regt., Commanded by Maj. Metcalf, that marched to Warwick, RI on the alarm of Dec. 8, 1776, and served for 24 days. **Joshua Clap** (b. Apr. 16, 1750 in Walpole, MA, d. 1804 in Walpole) could have also been the maker of these planes and was also a Patriot during the American Revolution. **Joshua Clap** (1750-1804.) served in Capt. Joshua Clap's Walpole North Co. during the march to Warwick, RI on the alarm of Dec. 8, 1776 and serviced 21 days (drafted for 3 weeks). Examples: on a 9" boxed small bead; a 9 1/2" hollow; a single boxed side bead; and a 17" skew ship rabbet, all birch with flat chamfers and an elongated relieved wedge, ca. 1770, are attributed to **Joshua Clap III** (1729-90). Two 9 3/8" birch plows with riveted guide plate, the fence is secured by wood thumb screws, a relieved wedge with a rounded finial (finial not shown) and heavy round chamfers, ca. 1790, is attributed to **Joshua Clap** (1750-1804).
****

U. CLAP

Believed to be **Uriah Clap (Clapp)** (b. Jul. 16, 1769, d. Aug. 16, 1852 in Gardner, MA) of the Oakham Dist. of Rutland, which was incorporated as a town in 1775. **Uriah Clap** was a cabinetmaker in Gardner, MA, active 1817-38. The **Clap** genealogy noted **Uriah Clap** as "a man of superior mechanical ability". **Jonathan Tower** (b. 1758, d. 1846) also made planes in Rutland, MA and his uncle married **Uriah Clap's** aunt. Another reference is from an original 1800 almanac that had been used by David Fisher of Royalston, MA, northwest of Oakham and Gardner. Notes in the margins indicate that Fisher was building a barn that year. One line identifies **Uriah Clap** as creditor for "642 feet boards at 13 shillings." **Uriah** was noted as living in Gardner, ca. 1820-40. Examples: on a 15 1/2" beech jack with heavy flat

A

A

chamfers; an 18" birch fore plane; a 24" birch joiner with flat chamfers; a smoother; and a 9 3/4" birch table hollow with small flat chamfers, all with the B imprint. Also reported is a birch smoother; a Yankee plow; and a 9 5/8" beech hollow with flat chamfers with the A imprint, ca. 1800. **A ***; B ******

B

B

CLARK
Example: on a 10" beech molder with flat chamfers. The wedge mortise is relieved, ca. 1790-1800. **UR**

D. CLARK
Possibly **Dudley Clark** (b. Nov. 9, 1788 in Candia Twp., Rockingham, NH, d. Aug., 7, 1867 in Winchester, MA) was a joiner and wheelwright. **Dudley** married **Hannah Clarkson** (1792-1860) on Nov. 1, 1820, in Sanbornton, NH. He was listed in Sanbornton, as late as 1860, as a farmer. He moved to Winchester, MA, after 1860. Examples: on a 9 7/16" thumbnail plane; a wide complex molder with heavy round chamfers; a 9 5/8" tongue plane; and a 15 7/8" skew fillister with slight offset tote found in NH, all beech, with shallow round chamfers, the molders with pointed finials, ca. 1800-30. *******

DAVID CLARK
David Clark was a planemaker in Cumberland, RI, which is adjacent to Wrentham, MA, the home of **F. Nicholson**, **I. Nicholson**, and **Cesar Chelor**. **David Clark** like **John Nicholson**, used an **IN CUMBERLAND** as a location imprint. Examples: on a 9 3/4" birch round with flat chamfers. *********

E. CLARK
Probably **Ebenezer Clark** (b. 1765 in Lebanon, CT, d. Oct. 4, 1801 in New York City) of Hartford, CT, who advertised in the **Courant** on Feb. 2, 1796: "Made, making, and will shortly be ready for market a universal assortment of joiners tools made in the neatest manner from English patterns." Also advertised on Aug. 3, 1795: "An excellent opportunity is there by offered to a few likely young boys, who wish to obtain the art of Architecture in house building by becoming apprentices to **Ebenezer Clark**." **Ebenezer Clark** appeared in the 1790 & 1800 census for Hartford. **Leonard Kennedy** was a listed creditor in **Clark's** petition to be declared insolvent on Mar. 28, 1798. **Clark's** main vocation was as a builder or housewright, often on speculation in New York City, in 1786-87, and Hartford, CT, 1791-99. It is believed that **L. Kennedy** leased land from **E. Clark** and **Kennedy** may have made the planes that **Clark** marked and advertised. Example: on a 9 3/8"x 1/2" beech round with flat chamfers, found with **L. Kennedy** planes. The wedge bears a resemblance to early **Leonard Kennedy** examples. ********

E. CLARK/ MILWAUKEE
Edwin Clark was a Milwaukee, WI, planemaker who appears in city directories from 1848-58, listed as a planemaker, a tool maker and plane manufacturer. **A1****; A ****

A

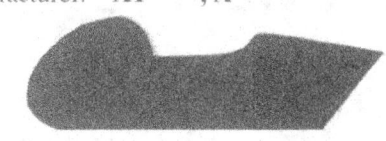
A1

E*CLARK/ MIDDLEBORO.
Elisha Clark of Middleboro, MA. (b. 1752, d. 1835 in Middleboro, MA) He married **Lucy Tinkham** (1757-1834), **Levi Tinkham's** first cousin, on Jan. 9, 1777 in Middleboro. **Elisha Clark** was a private "minute man" and responded to the alarm of April 19, 1775. He also served in Abisha Tinkham's Co. from 1778-1800. He was listed as Lt. Warden in 1787, and Captain in 1800. From 1802-08, **Elisha** was surveyor of lumber. **Levi Tinkham** is believed to have been apprenticed to **Elisha Clark**. In 1794, **Levi Bisbee** was apprenticed to **Elisha Clark** "to learn the art and mistery of cabinetmaker or shop joinery" In **Elisha Clark's** will of 1819, amended in 1828, and entered in probate in 1835, he was called "gentleman". He left "one half of all my cabinet and carpenter tools" to his son, **Elisha, Clark Jr.**, and the other half to his son **Abisha Y. Clark**. The A imprint is similar to those of **H. Wetherel** who made planes in nearby Norton, before 1790, and to those of **Levi Tinkham**. Examples: the A imprint is on a 9 3/4" birch molders with flat chamfers and 1 1/2" long shallow flutes. Some of his irons bear the imprint **N. Bennett**, a local blacksmith. ca. 1780. The B imprint has a later appearance and may have been made by **Elisha Clark Jr.** Examples: on a 9 1/2" beech molders with round wedge finial and heavy round chamfers, ca. 1790-1820.
A ****; B ***

ELI. CLARK
Example: on a 10 1/4" beech fixed sash with heavy flat chamfers, ca. 1790. **UR**

EZRA CLARK
Example: on a pair of 9 1/2" beech right & left side rabbets, ca. early 19c. **UR**

G. CLARK
Example: on a 9 3/4" maple complex molder with a low molded shoulder and flat chamfers. The **NWC** owner's initials carved in the side may be another **Clark** and may help in identifying **G. Clark**, ca. 1800. **UR**

G. G. CLARK

Example: on a 24 3/8" beech jointer with a slight offset, closed tote and round chamfers. With a Double **W. Butcher, Warranted, Cast Steel** iron, ca. 19c. **UR**

G. W. CLARK

Example: on a 21" rosewood raze jointer, ca. 1850. **UR**

HENRY CLARK
Henry Clark was listed as a planemaker and joiner in the 1847-54 Milwaukee, WI directories. **No imprint has been reported**.

HENRY H. CLARK
Henry Haston Clark (b. 1811 in PA) was listed in Mercer, PA, in 1850, as a wood turner; in 1860, a joiner; and in 1870, working at a planning mill. Examples: on a conventional smoothing plane with an **Auburn Tool Co.** double-iron; and a 12" smoother with an open tote, a strike button, and a round heel, ca. 1850. ****
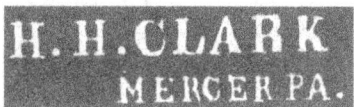

H. CLARK
Hiram Clark (b. Oct. 1820 in New Hartford south of Utica, d. Feb 3, 1906) and came to Utica, NY in Aug. 1841 and worked as a carpenter and joiner. In 1844, **Hiram** married **Susan C. Reed** (1824-1909) the sister of **Charles Reed**. In 1845-46, **Hiram Clark** was listed as a carpenter. In 1847-48, he was a planemaker, probably at **John Reed Jr.'s** plane factory. In May 1848, **Hiram Clark** moved to Rochester, NY and worked for **D. R. Barton** as a planemaker. In 1857, **Hiram** was granted a patent, witnessed by **D. R. Barton**, for an improved harvester. In Mar. 1861 & Apr. 1862, while still working for **D. R. Barton**, **Hiram** patented an ice skate and made them using the **D. R. Barton** imprint. In 1862, Hiram moved to Jordan, near Syracuse, NY. In Mar. 1866, **Hiram Clark** while working on his own in Jordan, was granted a fourth patent for an improved ice skate. In 1877, **Hiram Clark** was still manufacturing ice skates. Example: on a large hollow with a **W. Butcher** iron, ca. 1850. ****

I. CLARK
Example: on an 8" birch small hollow with flat chamfers that stop with a backward slope then a long tapered cut-out, ca. 1780. **UR**

I. CLARK
Examples: on a 9 1/2" single boxed complex molder; a wedge-locked plow with a brass plate on the skate, brass diamond washers on the arm rivets and a brass depth stop; and a similar moving fillister with a boxed edge, all beech with heavy round chamfers, ca. 1820. **UR**

J. CLARK

Example: on a 10" birch plow with wood screws stops and depth stop, a riveted skate and flat chamfers, ca. 1800. **UR**

J. CLARK
All three imprints are different from the British **J. Clark**. Examples: the A imprint is on a 9" cove with the iron set at a York or hardware pitch. The B imprint is on a 6" double boxed bead cluster; a 9 3/4" grooving plane; and a 10 1/4" dado with a wood depth stop. The C imprint is on a 9 1/2" medium hollow & round pair; and a 9 5/8" large hollow, all beech with round chamfers, ca. 1820. **UR**
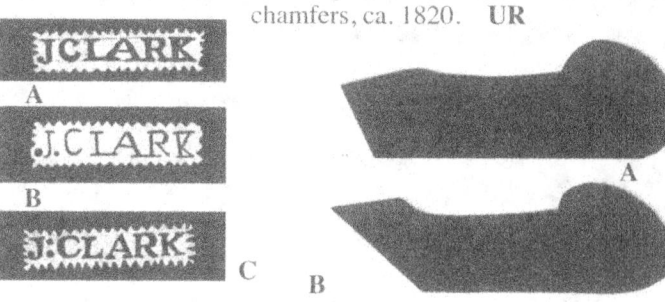

JOHN F. CLARK
John F. Clark (b. 1831 in MA) was listed in 1850, in Smithfield, RI as a planemaker boarding with and working for **Ezekiel Smith**. **No imprint has been reported**.

J. R. CLARK
Example: on a 9 1/2" beech skew rabbet with heavy round chamfers, ca. 1820. **UR**

IOSEPH CLARK
Joseph Colville Clark (d. 1799) was a cabinetmaker in Middletown, CT. He advertised in the *Middletown Gazette* on Apr. 28 & May 12, 1797 as **Joseph C. Clark Co.**, cabinet works, possibly a descendant. Examples: on three 9 15/16"-10" birch rounds with flat chamfers, one found in Middletown, CT, ca. 1750. *****
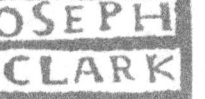

M. C/ M. CLARK
M. Clark with the location imprint of Calais, VT has been reported. A & B: **UR**
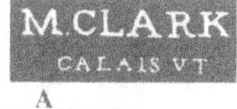

T. CLARK
Thomas Clark (Clarke) (b. 1797 in CT, d. prior to 1870 in Allegheny, PA) was a planemaker in Pittsburgh, PA working as a journeyman for **Swetman & Hughes**, in 1819. **Clark** is believed to be the **Thomas Clark**, "an apprentice boy about twenty years of age" that **Leonard Kennedy** advertised for in the Hartford, CT paper on Jan. 24, 1818, as having run away.

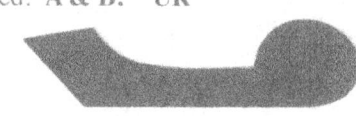

In 1826, **Clark** was listed as a planemaker on the east side of Penn St. below Irwin's Alley. In 1839, his shop was located on Fountain St. in the same block as that of **William Evans**. His last directory listing was in 1847. The 1850 census lists **Thomas Clark** as a "Plain Maker" living in the household of his son **Robert W. Clark**, 26, a coach blacksmith in Allegheny, PA. Examples: on a single boxed, toted complex molder. The B imprint has been reported from a smoother; and a square. (see **Planemakers of Western Pennsylvania and Environs**, by Charles W. Prine, Jr.) A ***; B *****

T. S. & CLARK
T. S. & Clark, probably a hardware dealer, with the location of NY, has been reported on a 21" fore plane, made by **Allen & Eldridge** of So. Williamstown, with a **Providence Tool Co.** double-iron, ca. 19c. ****

W. B. CLARK
An incuse imprint, with the date **1845** has been reported on a 16 3/16" jack plane with a **Spears & Jackson** iron. UR

W. P. CLARK
Example: on an 8 3/4" square beech miter plane, ca. 1850. UR

CLARK, HYDE & Co.
Clark, Hyde & Co. consisted of **Robert A. Clark** and **Simeon Hyde**, who was a successor to **Roosevelt Hyde & Clark**, a Charleston, SC hardware company listed in a 1855 city directory. Example: on a 9 1/2" x 1" beech grooving plane. *****

CLARK & WILLIAMS
Bill Clark and **Larry Williams** operated a contemporary planemaking firm from 1996-2010 in Eureka Springs, AR. The firm was joined in 2005 by **Don McConnell**, from OH. In 2010, the firm was reorganized into **Old Street Tool, Inc**. with **Don McConnell** and **Larry Williams**. Examples: on a 9 7/8" cocobolo skew rabbet, dated **1998**; and a hollow & round set, dated **1997**, all beech with heavy flat chamfers. Examples are in the historic trades at Williamsburg. **

CLARK & WISWALL
Clark & Wiswall was a New Hartford, CT plane manufacturer, active in 1856. They may have been involved with **H. Chapin/Union Factory** the giant of that small town. The 1852 map of New Hartford, CT, by Richard Clark, shows an "**I. CLARK, Wagon Works**". **No imprint has been reported**.

W. CLARY
Example: on a 9 1/2" beech hollow with a York pitch and flat chamfers, ca. 1800. UR

D. CLAY
Daniel Clay (b. Sep. 10, 1770 in New London, CT, d. Apr. 8, 1857 in New York, NY) was a cabinetmaker in Greenfield, MA from 1794-1829. In 1785, **Daniel Clay** was in Middletown, CT, and is believed to have been apprenticed in Windham, CT to either **Jabez Gilbert**, a Windsor chairmaker or **Orin Ormsby**, a joiner. He advertised in the *Greenfield* in Greenfield, MA on Mar. 12, 1794: "that he has taken the Shop, formerly the Printing Office, where he makes and fells all kinds of Cabinet, and Shop Joinery work...Cherry Boards, Pine Lumber, and moft kinds of Country Produce will be received in payment". **Daniel** married on Nov. 22, 1795, in Greenfield. In 1796, he bought property on Federal St. and built a house. From 1813-15, **Daniel Clay** was in a partnership with **Alexander Morgan**, conducting a retail business in general merchandise. In 1818, he was forced to sell his house to pay debts. **Daniel Clay** then entered a partnership with **D. Munger** and later **R. F. Field**. His shop burned in a fire of lower Federal St. and was rebuilt. His business partnerships were dissolved, in 1829. In 1832, **Daniel Clay** moved to New York City and became a druggist. Example: on a handled 14 5/8" x 2" birch hollow with round top iron & wedge and heavy flat chamfers. The **Clay** wedges have a pointed final typical of the Connecticut river valley, ca. 1795. A & B *****

CLEAN CUT
Dunham, Carrigan & Hayden of San Francisco, CA offered a line of wooden planes under this brand name in its 1914 catalog. **No imprint has been reported**.

A. CLEMENT
Example: on a 22" beech raze fore plane with a closed tote found in ME, ca. 1850 UR

H. CLES
Example: on a 11 3/4" beech nosing plane with a centered tote and flat chamfers, possibly from PA, ca. 1800. UR

H. H. CLEVELAND
H. H. Cleveland made wooden bench planes in Boston, MA, using **Leonard Bailey's** Jun. 22, 1858 & Aug. 31, 1858 adjustment and lever cap patents. A & B: UR

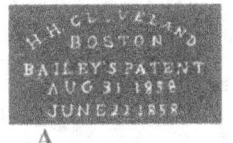

B

EC/ E. CLIFFORD
Ebenezer Clifford (b. Oct. 29, 1746 in Kensington, MA, d. Oct. 1821) was a prominent joiner, turner, cabinetmaker, master builder, architect in Kensington MA, from 1772-93; and Exeter, NH, from 1793-1808. In 1784, he was also a Justice of the Peace for Rockingham Co., MA. **Jeremiah Fellows**, a Kensington blacksmith, clockmaker, and tavern keeper noted in his day book the sale of quantities of plane irons and plow plane skates to **Clifford** from 1772-94. **Ebenezer Clifford** made clock cases for **Fellows**. **Ebenezer Clifford** served in the Revolutionary War as a Quarter Master Sergeant, until 1777. Examples: on a 13 5/8"x 4 1/2" birch crown molder with a heavily offset pegged tote and heavy flat chamfers (replaced wedge); a plow; a sash molder; a 13 1/2" wedge-arm adjustable fence panel plane with offset tote and a round topped skewed **Weldon** iron; a reed & follow; and a coping plane. The last two are 9 3/4" birch with flat chamfers, ca. 1770-80. The **EC** initial is on a 11 1/8" birch toted complex molder found with **Ebenezer Clifford** planes. ca. 1770. **A ****; B *****

E. C. CLIFFORD
Example: on a 9 1/2" beech skew rabbet with round chamfers on the top and flat chamfers on the ends, ca. 1800-10. **UR**

J. CLIFFTON
Example: on a 9 15/16" beech tongue plane with flat chamfer and carpenter names branded on the side. The imprint design and the wedge are similar to **W. Powel**, and is most likely from Philadelphia, PA, ca. 1780-1800. **UR**

J. CLINES
Example: on a 9 7/8" birch round with shallow flat chamfers, with a replaced wedge, (see **Glines**) ca. 1800-10. **UR**

HK/ H. CLOCK
Henry Clock (Klock) (b. Aug. 7, 1749 in Palatine, Albany, NY, d. Jun. 20, 1810 at Herkimer, NY) was of German decent. His Grandfather **Johann Henrich Klock** (signed his will **Henry**) (b. 1663 in Kassel, Hessen, Germany, d. 1760 in St. Johnsville, NY) arrived in New York, NY, in 1710, and was an Indian trader and early settler of the Mohawk River Valley. His Son **Johannes Heinrich Klock** (signed his will **Henry Clock**) (b. Oct. 30, 1711 in West Camp, Columbia, NY, d. 1801 in St. Johnsville, NY) was married in 1737 to **Anna Margaretha Fox** (1712-1800) in Fort Plain, Montgomery Co., NY. He built the stone Fort Klock, ca. 1750, as a fur trading post and fortification as a place of refuge during the French and Indian War, and later during the Revolutionary War. **Henry Clock** (1749-1810) fought in the American Revolution, as a Private, in Col. Jacob Kock's 2nd. Reg. of Tryon Co. NY, Militia. He married **Margaretha Wagner** (1755-1836) in 1777, in Little Falls, Herkimer, NY. He owned 2 farms in Little Falls. In 1796, he was the director of building of the octagonal church in Little Falls. His descendents moved to OH. Eight planes were found together in CO. Examples: all 10" beech with flat chamfers and a decoratively molded shoulder. Several of the irons are marked **G. BISHOP** (Sheffield, England, 1787). A wrought iron door latch is also marked with the HK initials and the date **1775**, ca. 1775-85. *****

N. H. CLOSSON
N. H. Closson was a Middletown, CT planemaker, active from 1849-58. **No imprint has been reported**.

G. M. CLOUGH
G. M. Clough, Warren, NH. Example: on a 23 5/8" beech jointer with a centered tote, ca. 19c. **UR**

M. CLOUGH
Examples: on a 9 1/2" fixed sash; and a 17 3/4" bench plane, both beech with flat chamfers, ca. 1800. ****

P. CLOUGH
Very similar in wedge and chamfer style to **M. Clough**. Examples: on two 9 1/2" complex molders; and a 10" molder, all beech with flat chamfers, ca. 1800. ****

J. L. CLUFF
J. L. Cluff imprinted with **MAKER**. Examples: on a fruitwood block plane found in the Skowhegan, ME area; a miter plane; and on a 22" raze ship fore plane, ca. 1850. ***

P. CLVM
P. CLVM or **P. CLUM**. Example: on a 9 7/8"beech skew rabbet with flat chamfers, ca. 1800-15. **UR**

I. CLYD
Example: on a 13 1/4" beech fielding plane with heavy flat chamfers and a single round top iron by **Newbold**, ca. 1800. **UR**

JAMES COATES
James W. Coates (b. Apr. 1817 in Greene Co., PA, d. after 1900) was listed on a Jun. 26, 1840 land deed in Wheeling VA. **James Coates** probably worked for **William Steele** of Wheeling, VA prior to 1846. **James Coates** was a Washington, PA (30 miles south of Pittsburgh), planemaker active, from 1846-59. In 1850, he was listed as a planemaker. On a 1855 map of Washington Co., PA, his "Plane Factory" is shown on Wheeling St., Washington. Some of his planes carry imprint dates; the earliest of those reported is **1846**. Although he owned the plane factory until May, 1861, he appears in the 1860 census as a house carpenter. In 1870, he was listed in Richhill Township, Green Co., as a farmer. From 1873-88, he was again in Washington and listed as a carpenter. Prior to 1897, he had moved to Lawrence Co., MO. The 1900 census for Aurora, Lawrence, Co., MO, lists **James Coates** as widowed, age 83.

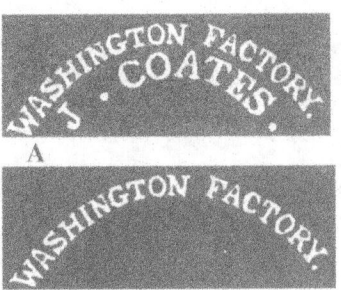

Examples: the A imprint on a 15" crown molder; a size 10 round, all beech; a 9 1/2" beech table plane has the C imprint. The D imprint is on a 15"x 3 1/2" beech, double boxed ogee molder with a open centered tote, also marked **W. STEELE & Co./ WHEELING**. **William Steele** was a plane maker in Wheeling from 1838-51. He also made a wedge arm match tongue & groove pair with the tongue iron split and held in place by a side set screw similar to the style of **E. W. Carpenter**. (see *Planemakers of Western Pennsylvania and Environs*, by Charles W. Prine, Jr.) B ***; A, A1, C ****; D *****

J. COB(B)
John Cobb's (Nov. 9, 1745 in Plymouth, MA. D. Jan. 23, 1822) father, **John P. Cobb** died when he was five years old. He was apprenticed, on Mar. 29, 1762, to **Simeon Doggett** of Middleboro, MA, by his step father and guardian **William Cushman**. "(to) Learn his said apprentice the art or trade of shop joyner & houseright; and also to learn his said apprentice to read and to write; and also to learn him to cypher as far as the rule of three; and also to procure & provide for his said apprentice sufficient meat, drink, apparel, washing & lodging both in sickness and health fitting for an apprentice." **John Cobb** married Mar. 21, 1767 to **Jael Tinkham**, daughter of **Levi Tinkham** in Middleborough, Plymouth Co., MA. **John** was a joiner and housewright. He was listed in **Tinkham**'s account book for the charge of 75 cents for "mending your old cart wheel/ 2 felloes & 2 spokes". Example: on an much used 8 3/4" large round with flat chamfers, ca. 1780. *****

N. COBB
Possibly **Nathaniel Cobb** of Plymouth, MA who was listed as a housewright, in 1737-38. Examples: the A imprint is on a 10" beech complex molder with heavy flat chamfers. ca. 1790. The B imprint is on an 8 1/8" beech plow with wood thumb screws, a brass plate on the skate & brass tips on the arms, and round chamfers, ca. 1810-30. **A & B: UR**

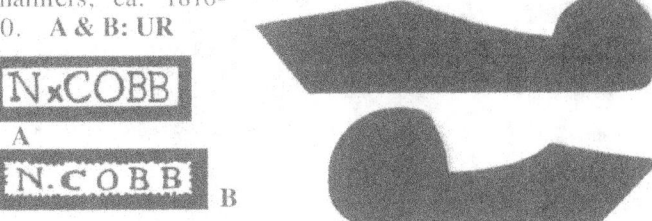

SAMUEL COBB
Samuel Cobb was listed as a planemaker in Cincinnati, OH, active in 1855. (see **Schaefer & Cobb**) No imprint has been reported.

W. COBB
Examples: on a shoulder or chamfer plane; and a complex molder, both 10" beech with a pointed wedge finial, and heavy flat chamfer, ca. 1790. **UR**

C. COBURN
Example: on a 9 1/2" beech astragal bead with a fixed fence, and heavy flat chamfers. This imprint was also found on an **I. Gregg** plane, ca. 1800. **UR**

JOHN A. COBURN
John A. Coburn of Maysville, KY is probably a hardware dealer. Example: on a 15" handled pump log plane with an Ohio Tool Co. iron, ca. 1850. ****

M COBURN
Examples: on a 9 1/2" birch medium round with flat chamfers; and a birch skew torus bead with iron or bone boxing and round chamfers, ca. 1800-10. **UR**

BC/ B. CODDINGTON
Benjamin Coddington (b. Aug. 5, 1815 in Warren, OH, d. Mar. 14, 1885 in Lafayette, Tippecanoe Co., IN) was a planemaker and saw filer, who was listed in 1850, as a planemaker. He was listed in 1850 as having a plane "manufactory" with only hand power, one hired male hand and producing 300 "plains" worth $700. **Benjamin** married **Sarah Ann Mead** (1820-1903) on Oct. 24, 1839, in Vermillion Co., IL. He worked in IL, from 1840-43, where his oldest two sons were born. **Benjamin Coddington** moved to Lafayette, in 1844, where his youngest son was born, in 1846. In the 1860, Lafayette census, he was

listed as a carpenter. In 1870, he was a saw filer. In 1880, a plane maker. He was still living in Lafayette, IN, in 1894. Examples: found in a tool chest were a number of B. Coddington planes including two panel raisers; and a dado with the **BC** imprint. Another round also with the same **BC** imprint was found in IN. **A & B** ****

J: CODER
Jacob Coder (b. Nov. 8, 1781 in Hilltop Twsp., Buck Co., PA, d. Mar. 18, 1854 in South Huntington Twsp., Westmoreland Co., PA) moved to South Huntingdon Twsp., about 1795, with his father and family. He married **Elizabeth Aspey** in 1807. In 1822, he bought 53 acres of land from his brother **Phillip Coder**. **Jacob Coder** added to his land until it totaled 148 acres with a stone house, log house, wagon shed and cabinet maker shop. **Jacob Coder** was working as late as 1853 until he received a wound to his wrist which, through neglect, became abscessed. Neurosis set in from blood poisoning. His death certificate lists his occupation as farmer and cabinetmaker. Examples: on a 9" cherry bead with interrupted boxing and shallow flat chamfers; a 9 3/8" cherry ogee with bevel molder with shallow flat chamfers; an applewood fillister with integral closed tote, slide arm with brass screw stops and a similar brass screw at the depth stop; a 12 3/4"x 2 1/2" beech bench plane; a 1 1/4" or size **5/4** stair nosing plane with centered tote and shallow flat chamfers; and a closed handled plow, applewood with iron screw arms and nuts and a fancy brass protective plate on the top of the handle, ca. 1810-30. *****

G. W. COFFIN
G. W. Coffin (**Coffen**) was reported to be a ship's carpenter living in Freeport, ME. There was a **George Washington Coffin** (b. Oct. 1, 1797 in Freeport, ME, d. Apr. 20, 1844 in Freeport) who was a tinsmith. Listed was his son, **George William Coffin** (b. Oct 2, 1835 in Freeport, Me, d. Jan. 3, 1919 in Freeport) no occupation given. Example: on a 16 1/2" beech razee crown molder with shallow round chamfers and a **Moulson Bros.** iron, ca. 1840. **UR**

Wm. COFFIN
Example: on an 8 3/4" skew fixed sash with heavy flat chamfers. An embossed **SC** carved on the side. The same owner's imprint and carved initials have been reported on a **C. Toby/ Hudson** plane. This may help in locating **Wm. Coffin**, ca. 1800. **UR**

DNL. COLBY
Examples: on a 10" birch boxed small bead; and a 9 3/4" beech boxed bead with a birch wedge, all with heavy flat chamfers, ca. 1790-1800. **UR**

L. T. COLBY.
Examples: on a 10" beech bead with heavy flat chamfers; and a 10" birch complex molder with medium flat chamfers, ca. 1790-1800. **UR**

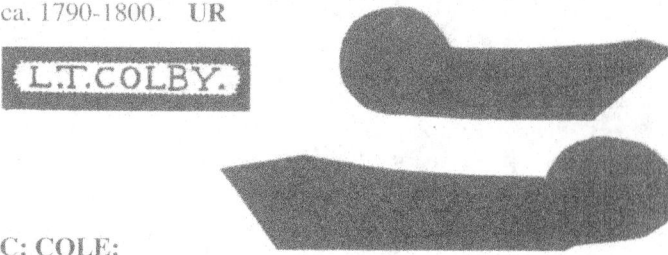

C: COLE:
Examples: on a birch plow; and a beech plow with a slide-arm fence, wood thumbscrews, a relieved wedge, an ivory depth stop, two ivory wear strips on the fence and flat chamfers, ca. 1790-1800. **UR**

J. COLE
Possibly **Jacob Cole** who was a Baltimore, MD cabinetmaker in 1794 and a Windsor chairmaker in 1796. He was listed in the Baltimore, MD tax records from 1796-1803, ca. 1800. **UR**

W. COLE
Possibly **William Cole** (b. 1795 in England, d. Jun. 10, 1877 in Cambridge, VT) who emigrated from England to Cambridge, VT, before 1830. He was listed in 1840 engaged in Manufactures and Trades; and from 1850-70 as a cabinetmaker. Example: on a 16 1/4" beech gutter plane with open tote and heavy round chamfers, ca. 1820. **UR**

WILLIAM A. COLE
William A. Cole of New York City was a planemaker who was issued Patent No. 5,620, on June 6, 1848, for a joiner's plane. Example: on an 8 3/8"x 2 1/2" beech circular plane with a flexible steel sole imprinted **A. B. HOYT/ PATENT'd 1848** (see *Patented Transitional & Metallic Planes in America, 1827-1927*, p. 131, by Roger K. Smith)
No imprint is available.

R. J. COLEMAN
Example: on a 9 7/8"x 1 3/8" beech straight rabbet with flat chamfers, ca. 1820. **UR**

S. O. COLEMAN
S. O. Colemann (b. ca. 1811 in KY) was a St. Louis, MO, hardware dealer. Example: on a **J. Donaldson**, St. Louis, MO plane. *****

J. COLHSON & BRO.
J. Colhson & Bro. is probably a hardware dealer. This imprint was reported on an **Ohio Tool Co.** plane with a **75** inventory number. **No imprint is available.**

IRA. A. COLLAMER
Example: on a 9 1/2" beech molding plane with small round chamfers, ca. 1820. **UR**

A. COLLER
Example: on a 9 1/2" fruitwood large hollow with heavy round chamfers, ca. 1820-30. **UR**

A. S. COLLINGS
Algerman S. Collings was listed in the Ravenna, OH directories as a planemaker and contemporary of **Collins**, active from 1838-50. **No imprint has been reported**.

COLLINS
Example: on a 9 3/4" beech cove plane with small 1/4" round chamfers, ca. 1810-20. **UR**

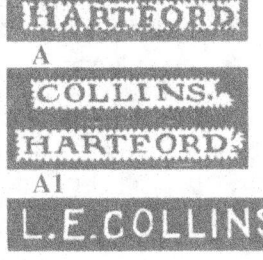

COLLINS/ HARTFORD
This was an imprint used by **Robert J. Collins, Jr.** as a planemaker in Hartford, CT, in 1806-07. (see **L. Kennedy**) Example: The A1 imprint is on a 9 1/2" beech double-boxed complex molder with **24** in ink on the wedge and the side of the plane, indicating that at least 24 planes were being made at once and the maker did not want to mix up the wedges after they were fitted to the plane. Also unique to the A1 imprint is the defects to the right. There is also an owner imprint of **L. E. COLLINS** on the heel of the plane.
A ***; A1 *****

COLLINS/ RAVENNA, COLLINS & CO./ RAVENNA
Fitch K. Collins (b. 1808 in NY) and probably **Robert J. Collins III** (b. 1804 in CT, d. Sep. 1860 in Clay, IA), both sons of **R. J. Collins Jr.** and nephews of **L. Kennedy**, made planes in Ravenna, Oh, where they were listed in the 1840-50 censuses. A broadside catalog sheet, dated Jul. 5, 1838, lists a full range of joiner's planes "Manufactured and sold wholesale and retail by **F. K. Collins**" at Ravenna, OH. A **; B ***

COLLINS/ UTICA
An imprint used by **Robert J. Collins III** (b. 1804 in CT, d. Sep. 1860, Clay, IA) a cousin to **Leonard Kennedy Jr.** (b. 1800 in CT). **Robert J. Collins** worked for **Leonard Kennedy Jr.** from 1828-29 in Utica, NY. He was in partnership with **Enos Robbins** as **Collins & Robbins**, from 1832-38. He made planes under this imprint at 81 Broadway, Utica, **L. Kennedy Jr.**'s former address. In 1834, **Robert J. Collins** was noted as an agent for **L. Kennedy Jr.** Example: on a plane marked **UTICA/ EXTRA** overstamped with **RAVENNA**. **

ALFRED COLLINS
Alfred Collins (b. 1809-14) was the son of **R. J. Collins JR.** and was listed as a planemaker in Utica, NY. In 1829, **Alfred Collins** was boarding with **R. J. Collins III** and working for **L. Kennedy**. **No imprint has been reported**.

DAVID COLLINS
An advertisement appeared in the Apr. 12, 1809 *Connecticut Courant* of Hartford, CT, stating: "**David Collins** has on hand a good assortment of molding tools, bench planes & etc. where he continues to manufacture all kinds of joiner tools." **David Collins** (b. Mar. 19, 1782 in Hartford, CT, d, Jan. 7 in Ravenna, Portage Co., OH), and his brother **Daniel Collins** (b. Jan. 27, 1785 in Hartford, CT, d. Jan. 19, 1855 in Ravenna, OH) and **Jonathan Collins** helped to build the Central Church in Hartford, CT. They carved the pulpit, pews with half doors, altar etc. In 1805, **Daniel Collins** was listed as a carpenter in Hartford, CT. In 1811, **David Collins** and **Daniel Collins** moved by ox team to Rootstown, near Ravenna, Portage Co., OH where they were known as wood carvers.
No imprint has been reported.

F. COLLINS
Possibly **Fitch K. Collins** (b. 1808 in NY) (see **Collins/ Ravenna**) Examples: on a 10 1/4" fruitwood complex molder; and a 10" beech complex molder, both with heavy flat chamfers, ca. 1790-1800. **UR**

J. J. COLLINS
Example: on a 9 1/2" beech skew rabbet, ca. 1850. **UR**

R. COLLINS
Examples: on a 10 3/16" oak molding plane with flat chamfers, ca. 1790-1800; and a beech wedge-lock plow with friction-fit wood depth stop and shallow round chamfers, ca. 1820-30. **UR**

RJC/ R. J. COLLINS
Probably **Robert Johnson Collins Sr.** (b. Jul. 2, 1752 in England, d. Apr. 26, 1837 in Roosterstown, near Ravenna, Portage Co., OH) was a planemaker in Hartford, CT. He was a British soldier who became a prisoner of war when captured on Long Island, NY. His molding planes are 9 5/8"-10" beech with flat chamfers, identical in style to **L. Kennedy's** earliest planes. Example: on a 9 5/8" beech complex molder with wide flat chamfer with this imprint and initials RJC. ****

R. J. COLLINS/ HARTFORD
R. J. COLLINS/ ROCHESTER
R. J. COLLINS/ RAVENNA
Robert Johnson Collins, Jr. (b. Feb. 8, 1780 in Hartford, CT, d. Nov. 2, 1835 in Ravenna, OH) was the son of **Robert Johnson Collins, Sr.** and father of **Fitch K. Collins** and **Robert J. Collins III**. **Robert J. Collins** married **Leonard Kennedy's** younger sister **Eunice**, in Nov. 1802. He may have learned plane making from **Leonard Kennedy** with whom he began a partnership in 1803 "to carry on the house carpentry and joiners business and manufacture joiners' tools." Imprints used by the partnership were **Kennedy & Collins** and **K&C**. The partnership continued until 1805, after which **Robert Johnson Collins** made planes under his own name (see **Collins/ Hartford**), from 1805-08. Between 1809-11, **Collins** moved to NY and used the **Collins/ Rochester** imprint, prior to moving to Ravenna, OH, in 1811. A, B & C ****

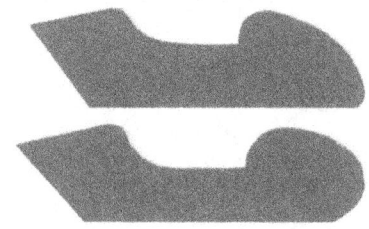

COLLINS & ROBBINS
A plane making partnership of **Enos Robbins** and **Robert J. Collins III**, that operated in Utica, NY, from 1828-30. The 1828 Utica Directory has **Robert J. Collins III**, living with **Leonard Kennedy**. **Enos Robbins** (b. 1806 in CT) was living with **Leonard Kennedy**, in 1829. The 1830 census lists **Robert J. Collins** in Utica, NY. **

COLLISON
Examples: the A imprint is on a 10" beech round; and 9 15/16" molder with flat chamfers. The B imprint is on a 10" medium round with round chamfers, a **Robert Moore** iron and the B wedge, ca. 1800-20. UR

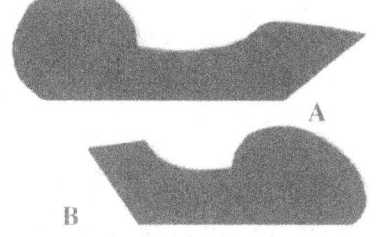

WM-K. COLLYER

Example: on a beech round. UR

C. COLMAN
C. Colman with the location Boston. Example: on a slide-arm plow with a **Joseph Smith** iron and a triple boxed raze open toted sash, both beech, ca. 1850. UR

P. COLMAN
P. Colman with a location Boston. No other information is available, ca. 1850. UR

A. COLTON
Arron Colton (b. 1758 in Longmeadow, MA, d. Jun. 3, 1840) was a cabinetmaker in Hartford, CT. He advertised from Aug. 1792 to Apr. 1, 1807 in the *Connecticut Courant* as a cabinetmaker and maker of washing machines. He last appeared as a paper mold maker in the Hartford directory in 1840. In 1792, he was instrumental in organizing the Society of Cabinetmakers of Hartford that met at his home. Example: on a 9 1/2" beech molder with small flat chamfers, ca. 1800. UR

A. J. COLTON
Alfred J. Colton (b. Oct. 1837, d. Dec. 5, 1902 in Philadelphia, PA) was the son of **David Colton** and a Philadelphia, PA, hardware dealer and planemaker, active from 1861-96. He worked with his father at the Callowhill shop, previously occupied by **Henry G. White**, from 1861-65. In 1865, the address was changed to 355 N. 4th. St. and again in 1883 changed to 338 N. 4th. St. He exhibited stair handrail planes, double-routers and carpenter's molding planes (for which he received an award) in the 1876 Centennial Exposition. An advertisement lists: "**Colton's** Celebrated Plane Manufactory, successor to **White's** and also to **D. Colton**." He indicates that the firm was established in 1812. The article must have run shortly after 1880. **No planes with his imprint have been reported** and it is believed that he used his father's imprints, both during his father's lifetime and until he ceased plane making about 1896. In 1900, **Alfred J. Colton** was listed as age 62, with the occupation of laborer.

D. COLTON
David Colton (b. Aug. 10, 1813 in Longmeadow, MA, d. Dec. 10, 1880) was the father of **Alfred J. Colton** and brother of **John Colton**. David Colton was a Philadelphia, PA, planemaker active from 1837-80. He worked with his brother intermittently during

A1

the early years and then his son, **A. J. Colton**. In 1854, he was listed at 327 Market St. In the 1860 Industrial census, **David Colton** was listed as a plane manufacturer, employing two and producing planes with an annual value of $2,500. The **D. COLTON** plane imprints, which consist of several separate dies provide the collector with a number of varieties, many of which have their origin in the **Israel White** dies. The H imprint suggests that the **Coltons** took over some of **Henry G. White's** stock in 1858. For biographical information (see *American Marking Gages*, by Milton H. Bacheller, Jr.)

F: FF; A, A1, A2, B, C, D, E, E1, G, H, I & J*

A2

B

C

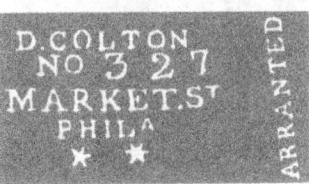
D

E

E1

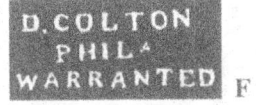
F

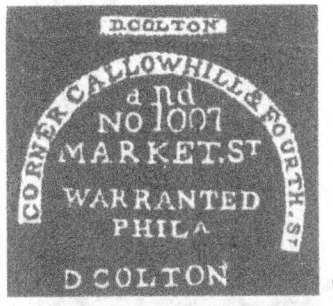
G

H

I

J

D. COLTON / J. COLTON

A

David Colton and **John Colton** imprints have appeared on the same plane. **David Colton** and **John Colton** were brothers and worked together at 379 Market St., Philadelphia, PA, from 1837-41 and at the corner of Callowhill and 4th. St., from 1858-60. They soon split up and **David Colton** was joined by his son, **Alfred J. Colton**. They took over **Henry G. White's** shop and used parts of the old **Israel White** imprint dies creating a vast variety of imprint design elements.

A, B, C, D & E **

B

C

D

D. COLTON/ B. SHENEMAN
David Colton and **Benjamin Sheneman** were in partnership as planemakers and hardware dealers in Philadelphia, PA, from 1846-52.
A, A1, A2, A3 & B *

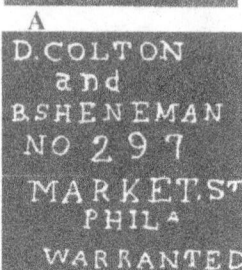 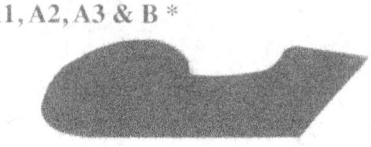

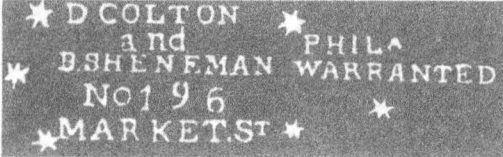

J. COLTON
John Colton (b. May 2, 1807 in Longmeadow, MA, d. Sep. 29, 1889) was a Philadelphia, PA, planemaker and brother of **David Colton**, with whom he sometimes worked in the early years from 1837-41 and 1858-60. Between 1842-57 and 1861-89 he worked under his own name. The 1850 Industrial census for Philadelphia, listed **John Colton** as a planemaker producing 2000 planes valued at $2000 and employing 3 hands. The 1860 Industrial census listed **John Colton** as a plane manufacturer employing two, producing planes with an annual value of $1800. An ebony handled square with a 12" blade, signed by **J. Nichols**, a Philadelphia square maker (1837-57) is also imprinted on the handle **J. COLTON/ 370 MARKET ST/ PHILa**. This imprint is different from any of those used on his planes.
A, A1, B, & B1 *;
C, D, E, F, G & G1 **; B/C ****

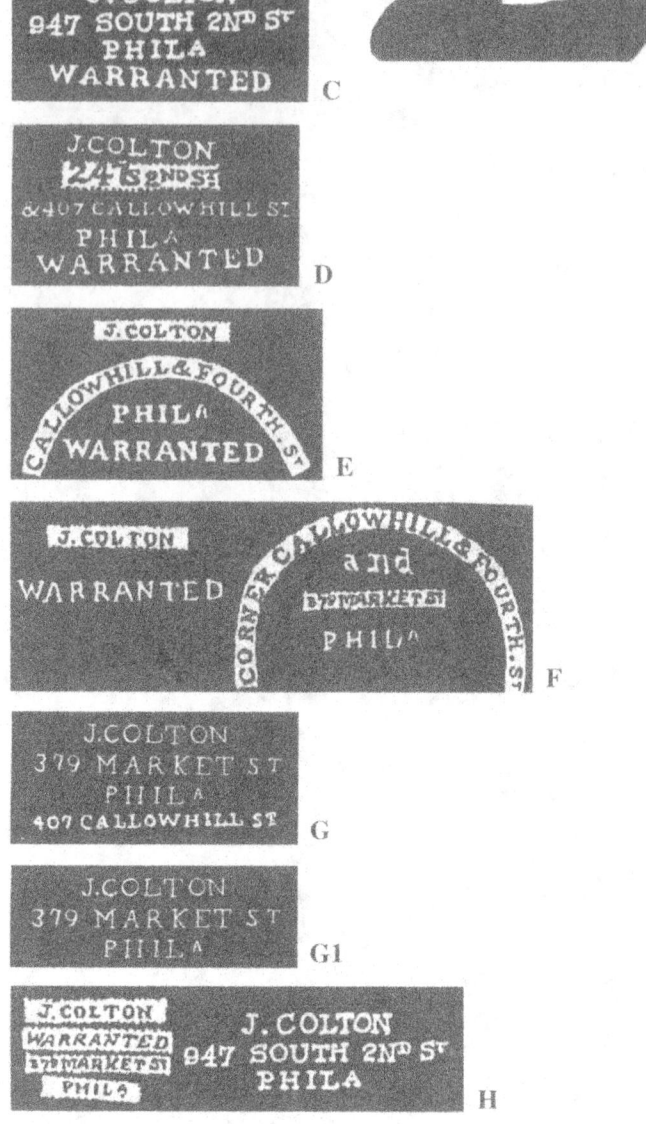

M. COLTON
Examples: on a 9 3/8" beech narrow fenced straight rabbet; and a wide rabbet, both with shallow round chamfers, ca. 1830. **UR**

COLUMBIA/ COLUMBIA TOOL CO.
The A imprint, ink imprinted on the side, are of Russian white beech, imported from Germany from 1920-25, and distributed by the **United Hardware & Tool Corp. of New York City**. The company's 1925 catalog, reprinted by the Mid-West Tool Collectors Association, lists six pages of various plane styles, including horn smoothing planes, jacks, joiners, T-rabbets, weather-stripping, and various molding planes. The B and C imprints appear to be American made and of earlier appearance.
A *; B & C ***

COLWELL & CO.
Colwell & Co. was a wholesale and retail dealer in "hardware and metals" in Cleveland, OH, active from 1860-68. After 1868, the name was changed to **Colwells, Lewis and Armstrong**. The planes probably were a private brand supplied by the **Ohio Tool Co**. ******

COLYER
Example: on a 9 5/8" beech quarter round with flat chamfers, ca. 1810. **UR**

S: COMINGS
Samuel Comings (b. Nov. 18, 1742 in Westford, MA, d. Jan. 16, 1826 in Cornish, NH) was a millwright and carpenter. In 1757, **Samuel** age 15, moved from Westford, MA to Dunstable, MA, with his family. In 1753, his father, also named **Samuel Comings**, (b. 1718 in Westford, MA) was one of a committee of three that built the Dunstable, MA meeting house. **Samuel**, the son, married, on Oct. 31, 1765, **Sarah Butterfield** (1745-1804) and lived in Westford, MA, where a son **Leonard**, was born on Dec. 5, 1769. **Samuel Comings** was living in Packersfield, NH, east of Keen, where another son **Eben**, was born on Jun. 24, 1779. The name of the town was changed to Nelson, NH, in 1814. **Samuel Comings** was living in Pelham, NH, north of Dunstable, MA, where a daughter, **Sophia**, was born, on Apr. 10, 1789. By 1790, **Samuel Comings** had moved to Cornish, NH, on the Vermont border, where he and his father carried on farming, ran a grist mill, a carding mill and a carpentry shop, all three of his sons worked in the family mills and carpentry shop. Examples: on a 10 3/4" beech fenced straight rabbet with the A wedge; and a 10 1/4" birch complex molder with the B wedge, both with flat chamfers and flutes, ca. 1760-80. *********

I. COMINS
Believed to be **Issachar Comings** (b. Aug. 28, 1782 in Charlton, MA, d. Dec. 4, 1861 in Charlton, MA). His estate inventory included among "carpenter tools", one lot of planes and one lot of molding planes. Early records list him as "a carpenter and finished workman" who had served earlier as an apprentice, from age 14-21, where he "learned his trade and receiving as pay his board and clothes and four weeks of schooling a year." **Issachar Comings** was the grandson of **Jacob Comings** (1700-1762) a housewright; the son of **Reuben Comings** (1737-) a farmer and tanner and the brother of **Barnabas Comings** (1771-1829) also a woodworker and whose probate inventory included 12 planes. Examples: on a 10" birch hollow with flat chamfers, a relieved wedge and similar in appearance to **Jo. Fuller** planes; and a 9" beech complex molder with rosewood boxing and round chamfers, indicating that he made planes over a period of time, ca. 1790-1810. *******

COMP. of ARTISTS.
Examples: on a small hollow; and a bead, both 9 1/2" beech. ca. 1850. (This imprint is not in W. L. Goodwan's *British Planemakers from 1700, 3rd. Edition*, but it is possibly British?) ********

J. CONANT
Probably **John Conant** (b. Feb. 2, 1773 in Ashburnham, MA, d. Jun. 30, 1856 in Brandon, VT) who was trained as a carpenter, joiner, and builder. In 1796, he came to Brandon, VT. He was a partner in an ore furnace and produced the Conant Cook Stove. With his sons **John A. Conant** and **Chauncy W. Conant**, they ran a store and gristmill from 1796-1841 as **John Conant & Sons**. In 1809, he was a representative to the State Legislature, serving 4 terms. Examples: the A imprint is on molders from 9 1/4"-9 7/8", of beech and birch with a relieved wedge and full round top and end chamfers. ca. 1820. The B imprint is from a 10 5/16" birch complex molder with wide shallow flat chamfers, ca. 1780-1800. **A ***; B *******

S. CONANT
Example: on a 9 1/2" beech skewed rabbet with flat chamfers, ca. 1800. **UR**

CECO
CONCRETE ENGINEERING COMPANY OMAHA
CECO made metal weather stripping. This imprint is on a **Sandusky Tool Co. SPECIAL** weather stripping plane with a metal adjustable fence attached by two metal thumb screws ********

J: CONEY
Example: on a 9 1/2" beech small astragal bead with a birch wedge and flat chamfers, ca. 1800. **UR**

JOHN P. CONGAR/ F. B. CONGAR
John P. Congar and **F. B. Congar** were edge tool and wooden plane makers listed in Newark, NJ, active from 1835-50. **No imprint has been reported.**

S. CONGDON
Example: on a yellow birch plow with wood screw locked square arms and depth stop. From southern New England, ca. 1790-1810. **UR**

L. G. CONKLIN
Luther G. Conklin (d. Jun. 2, 1872 in St. Louis, MO) was a St. Louis, MO, planemaker, active from 1840-50. **Luther G. Conklin** was listed as a planemaker in New York City in the 1831 American Advertising Directory. *******

JAs. CONNELL
Examples: on a 6" beech oar plane with round chamfers; a 9 3/8" beech molder with heavy flat chamfers; and a round, ca. 1800-20. **UR**

H. W. CONNER & Co.
Henry W. Conner (b. 1790, d. in Charleston, SC) was a planemaker from 1819-39, when the plane factory burned down putting him out of business. In later years, He was a hardware dealer and active in politics. He was a signer of the Ordinance of Succession that separated the United States and lead to the Civil War. In the 1860 Charleston, SC slave schedule, **H. W. Conner** is listed as owning 10 slaves. In 1865, **H. W. Conner & Co.** was listed as a broker. In 1867, he was a partner in **Conner & Wilson**, banking, collection & insurance agents. Example: on a 9 1/2" fruitwood single-boxed complex molder, ca. 1850. *********

M: CONNER
Example: on a 6 1/4" beech spar plane with chamfered wedge, a single round top iron and round chamfers, ca. 1810-20. **UR**

T. CONNER
T. Conner was a hardware dealer on P St., the City and date is unknown. Example on a **John Cuddy** plane, ca. 1810-40. **UR**

I. K. CONNOR
Example: on a 11 3/4" beech handled match plane, ca. 1840. **UR**

JOHN D. CONOVER
John D. Conover (b. 1803 in PA) was listed as a planemaker in Cincinnati, OH, from 1829-31. He was believed to have moved to Louisville, KY, after 1831, where he worked with **Thomas Fugate.** The 1840 census lists Conover in New Albany, IN, ca. 19c. ********

CONROY'S' CORNER
Conroy's Corner with location San Francisco probably was a hardware dealer. Example: on a **Greenfield Tool Co.** plane, ca. 19c. ********

CONWAY
Example: on a 6 1/2" beech smoothing plane with flat chamfers. The imprint is on the toe and heel, ca. 1800-10. **UR**

CONWAY TOOL Co.
On Apr. 15, 1850 the **Conway Tool Co.** was incorporated by **Alonzo Parker** (b. 1814 in Berkshire, MA, d. May 16, 1892 in Greenfield, MA); **Horace Hubbard** (b. Jan. 23, 1808, d. Oct. 22, 1851 in Conway, MA); **Daniel Rice 2nd**.; and "associates" at Burkeville (Conway), MA for the manufacture of carpenter's and joiner's tools. The **Conway Tool Co.** was the successor to **Parker, Hubbard & Co.** They employed 80 before the facility burned down, in July 1851. Within a month after the fire, the company was reincorporated as the **Greenfield Tool Co.** just north in Greenfield, MA. A, B, B1, & C *******

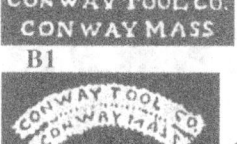
A

B

C

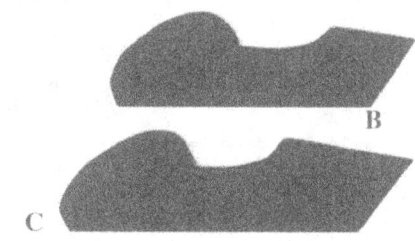
B

C

S. CONYERS
Example: on a 9 1/2" beech adjustable sash with wood slide arms & wood wedges and round chamfers, ca. 19c. **UR**

COOK
Examples: on a 9 3/8" hollow; and a side bead, both with flat chamfers, ca. 19c. **UR**

B. COOK
Examples: the A imprint is on an 8 1/8" beech center bead. The B imprint (struck twice) is on a 9 9/16" birch molder; and a skew rabbet, all with relieved wedges and flat chamfers, ca. 1800. **UR**

A
B

GEORGE COOK
George Cook (b. 1794 in Dover, DE) was listed as a planemaker in Philadelphia, PA, as early as 1810 and active in 1817. **No imprint has been reported**.

J. P. COOK
John P. Cook (b. 1824 in MI, d. May 17, 1898 in Detroit, MI) was a Detroit planemaker listed for a tool factory in 1850, and for a plane factory from 1852-63. He was listed as a machinist in 1871 & 75. **J. P. Cook & Son** was listed in 1877, but no trade cited. Example: the B imprint is on a size **6** hollow with **72** on the toe, an **Ohio Tool Co.** inventory number. **A & B *****

L+ COOK
Example: on a 9 1/2" beech grooving plane with a riveted skate, round top and flat end chamfers, ca. 1810. **UR**

S. COOK/ S. COOK & CO.
Solomon Cook (b. 1809 in NJ) was apprenticed in the East and was a plane maker, first listed in Cincinnati, OH. In 1829, he was reported boarding with, and a bench hand for, **John Conover**. Solomon Cook appears in the 1830 census for Marion Co., IN. From Jan. 9, 1835 to Jun. 4, 1836, **Solomon Cook** advertised in the *Indiana Journal of Indianapolis* which listed **S. Cook** as a planemaker, who shared a shop with **F. T. Luse**, a cabinetmaker. In 1840, he was in New Albany, Clinton Co., IN; before moving to Louisville, KY, where the city directories listed **Solomon Cook** as a planemaker, in 1843-44, at **Wm. W. Richards**; in 1844-45, at **Benchard's**; in 1845-46 at **Woodruff's** (**Alexander S. Woodruff**); and in 1848 as **Woodruff & McBride's**. He was listed in the 1850 census, as a planemaker in Clark Co., IN, where Jeffersonville is located next to New Albany and just across the Ohio River from Louisville, KY. In 1850, he married **Sarah** in Jeffersonville. In 1855, he was a partner in **S. Cook & J. Gilmer**. The **NEW ALBANY, IA** imprint is similar to the location imprint of **Charles Woodruff**. In 1859-60, he was listed as a planemaker in Memphis, TN, located at Washington between Main and Front Row. The 1860 census lists **Solomon Cook**, age 52, in Shelby Co., TN. In 1865-66, he was listed as a saw filer in Memphis, TN at 113 Poplar St. **A, B, C, D, D1 & E *****

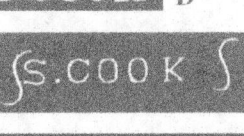
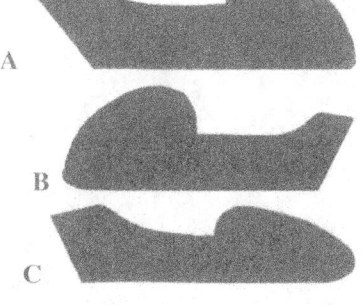

S. COOK & J. GILMER
S. Cook & J. Gilmer was a short lived partnership between **Solomon Cook** and **Joseph Gilmer**, in 1855. The **J. GILMER/NEW ALBANY** imprint is the same as the **J. GILMER** used earlier when in business for himself. ********

S. C. COOK
Samuel C. Cook (b. 1800 in New Brunswick, NJ, d. Jan. 26, 1858 in New Brunswick) was a prolific New Brunswick, NJ, planemaker from 1825-45. In the 1830 census, he was listed as a planemaker with four apprentices including **Benjamin Norton**. Samuel's planemaking operation was succeeded by **Ellsworth Danberry**. On Aug 7, 1841 and again on Mar. 14, 1849, **Samuel C. Cook** was appointed as Postmaster for New Brunswick, NJ. His will was probated Feb. 8, 1858. **B: FF; A ****

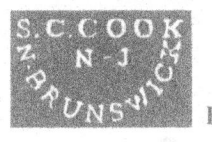
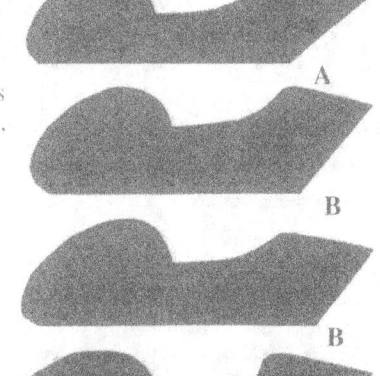

J. COOK & CO.
James Cook (b. 1798 in Morristown, NJ, d. Jul. 26, 1872 in Terre Haute, Vigo Co., IN) in 1847, moved to Terre Haute, IN where he operated a hardware store. In 1858, his son, **Louis M. Cook** (b. 1825 in NJ) became a partner and the business name was **J. Cook & Son**, at No. 1 Union Row, Main St.; in 1863, at 92 Wabash; from 1868-72, at 152 & 154 Main. After the death of **James Cook** in 1872, the name was changed to **L. M. Cook**; and in 1876, it was changed again to **L. M. Cook & Son** and continued until 1879. ********

I. COOKE
Example: on a 9 1/2" size **6** round with flat chamfers, ca. early 19c. **UR**

B. COOLEY
Examples: on a 9 1/8" bead size **2/4** on the heel with the A wedge; and a 9 1/4" complex molder marked **4**, both with flat chamfers, ca. 1800. **UK**

JC/ I. COOLEY
J. Cooley as the initial would suggest. Examples: on a bead; a triple bead; a 9 7/16" hollow; a 9 1/2" round; a complex molder; and a 9 9/16" thumb, all beech with flat chamfers, ca. 1800. **A & A1: UR**

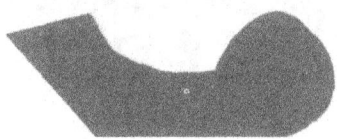

W. COOLEY
William Cooley (b. 1806 in Hartford, CT, d. Mar. 8, 1876 in Burlington, MA) was a Boston, MA planemaker and an edge tool maker from 1832-34; and produced planes under this imprint from 1834-49; except 1844 when he was part of **Cooley & Montgomery**. He was listed in the 1849 New England Mercantile Union directory as plane manufacturer at 10 R. R. Block, Lincoln St., Boston, MA. **B ***; A & C ****

COOLEY & MONTGOMERY
Cooley and Montgomery was a planemaking partnership of **William Colley** and **Joseph A. Montgomery** at 94 Blackstone St., Boston, MA that operated during 1844 only. ******

B. D. COOMBS
Example: on a 9 1/2" beech round, ca. 1850. **UR**

I. COOMBS
I. Coombs with the location imprint of **BANGER** (ME). Examples: on a 9 1/2" beech round; a side bead; and an applewood screw-arm plow with egg shaped ivory tips, segmented washers and elongated turned nuts. The A1 imprint is on a 9 1/2"x 1 7/8" skew rabbet with two nickers, ca. mid 19c. ********

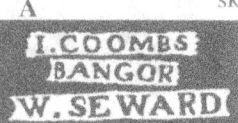

L. A. COOMBS
L. A. Coombs was a hardware dealer in Vinal Haven, ME. Example: on a 1 1/4" wide nosing plane made by the **Ohio Tool Co**. ********

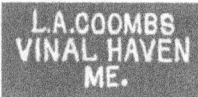

C. B. COOMES
Examples: on a 9 7/8"x 3/8" applewood astragal; and two complex molders, all with heavy flat chamfers, possibly from New England, ca. 1790-1800. **UR**

E. COONS
Example: on a 9 3/8" beech skew rabbet, ca. 1850 **UR**

COOPER
Examples: on a complex molder; a double boxed complex molder; a boxed bead with size **8/8** on the heel; a 14" grooving plane; a hollow; and a sash, all 9 1/2" beech with small round chamfers, ca. 1820. *******

E. L. COOPER
Ebenezer L. Cooper (1832 in NY, d. Jan. 9, 1890 in Kings, NY) was listed in the 1850 & 70 census as a sash maker. In the 1860 census, he was listed as a carpenter. He enlisted in the Civil War as a Private, serving from May 7, 1861 to Aug. 1, 1861 in Co. E, NY 11th. Infantry Regiment. From 1863-73, he was a NY City hardware merchant who also dealt in cooper's tools. **No imprint has been reported.**

J. COOPER
Joseph Cooper was a Cincinnati, OH, planemaker, active in 1839-40. Examples: on a 1/4" and a 3/4" wide beading planes, both are 9 1/2" beech with boxed soles, found in Marietta, OH. ********

R. COOPER
Example: on a 9 9/16"x 1/2" beech astragal bead with a decorative shoulder (beaded) and wide flat chamfers, possible from rural PA, ca. 1800. **UR**

WM. COOVER
Example: on a 22" beech fore plane with a closed offset tote, ca. 1830. **UR**

A. COPELAND
A. Copeland was a Columbus, OH, planemaker, whose working period is not known. Possibly **Alfred Copeland** (b. Apr. 17, 1801 in Sturbridge, MA, d. Nov. 9, 1858 in New Hartford, CT), with working dates between the demise of **M. & A. Copeland** in 1831 and **Alfred's** listing in the 1850 census, as a bedstead manufacturer in Chester, MA, with 16 hands making 3,000 beds worth $7500. ******

CHARLES COPELAND
Charles Copeland (b. 1817 in MA) was listed in the 1850 Amherst, MA census as a planemaker. **No imprint has been reported.**

D. COPELAND

Daniel Copeland (b. Jul. 6, 1794 in Sturbridge, MA, d. Mar 2, 1853 in Huntington, MA) was the brother of **Melvin Copeland** and **Alfred Copeland**. He probably apprenticed with **Leonard Kennedy Sr.** and was a partner in **D. & M. Copeland** with **Melvin Copeland**, in Hartford, CT, from 1820-25. In 1826, he joined **Hermon Chapin** in **Copeland & Chapin**, establishing what was to become the **Union Factory**. In 1828, **Hermon Chapin** bought out **Daniel Copeland**, after which he made planes under this imprint. After 1842, he moved to Huntington, MA, and worked with **Melvin** in **M. Copeland & Co.**
A & B: FF

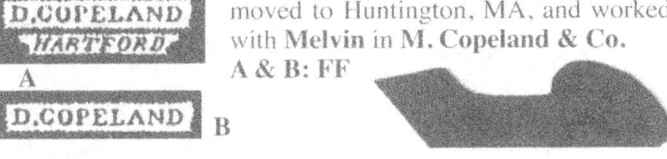

D. & M. COPELAND

D & M Copeland was a plane making partnership in Hartford, CT, with brothers **Daniel Copeland** and **Melvin Copeland** from 1822-25. *The Pocket Register For the City of Hartford, CT* of 1825, lists **D. & M. Copeland** as manufacturers of joinery tools at No. 7 Central Row, upstairs.
A & B *

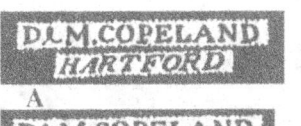

GEORGE COPELAND

George Copeland Sr. (b. 1795 in VT) and **George Copeland, Jr.** (b. 1823 in VT) operating a plane factory in the 1850 census for Columbus, OH. **No imprint has been reported**.

M. COPELAND/ M. COPELAND & CO.

Melvin Copeland (b. Mar. 12, 1797 in Sturbridge Village, Worcester Co., MA, d. Mar. 5, 1866) was the brother of **Daniel Copeland** and **Alfred Copeland**. He probably apprenticed with **Leonard Kennedy, Sr.** in Hartford, CT. Melvin worked in 1827 in Chester Village MA, west of Huntington. He was a partner with **Daniel Copeland** in **D. & M. Copeland** between 1831-42. **L. B. Bidwell** advertised on Dec. 17, 1842 in *The New England Weekly Review* that he "Purchased of **Melvin Copeland** his stock in trade" at 110 State St., Hartford, CT. In 1842, Melvin Copeland moved his firm to Huntington, MA, where he was joined by brothers **Daniel** and **Alfred Copeland**. He was listed in the 1849 New England Mercantile Union director as a plane manufacturer in Cummington, MA. He was listed in the 1850 Industrial census as employing 15 hands using water power planers, circular saws, lathes, and producing planes worth $12,000. Plane irons cost $3000 and beech & Turkish boxwood cost $3000. By 1855, the firm was succeeded by **Copeland & Co.** Example: on a screw-arm plow with style number **IOI** on the toe, the designation for the **Ohio Tool Co.** The C2 imprint is on a solid boxed bead with size **6/8** and an ink stamp on the side (**Xxxxx**) **M. COPELAND/ EDINBURG, IND.** in a scroll similar to the **Copeland & Co.** imprint. Edinburg, IN is between Indianapolis, IN and Louisville, KY, not far from Cincinnati, OH. There where Copeland's in Edinburg and possibly was a local hardware firm.
C, C1,D & E: FF; A, B, B1, C2 ****

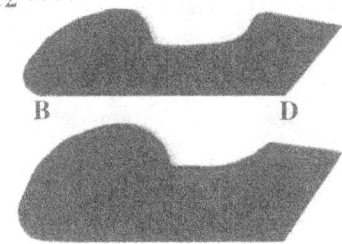

M. & A. COPELAND

M. & A. Copeland was a partnership of brothers **Melvin Copeland** and **Alfred Copeland**, who made planes in Hartford, CT, under this imprint from 1826-30 after dissolving the **D. & M. Copeland** partnership in 1826. **Daniel Copeland** became a partner with **Hermon Chapin** from 1826-28 as **Union Factory**. How **M. & A. Copeland** planes came to also carry the **UNION FACTORY/ WARRANTED** imprint is unclear.
A: FF; A1, B, C & D: ***

W. COPELAND

William Copeland (b. 1770 in CT) worked as a master carpenter/ shipbuilder on the North River in Plymouth Co., MA, from 1799-1832. Between 1815-32, he was known to have worked on 14 ships. In 1819, he was a partner in **Copeland, Ford & Co.** whose name was changed, in 1824, to **Wm. Copeland & Co.** In 1832, it was sold to **Th. Waterman** and **Jos. S. Bates**. Examples: on a 10" beech center bead with heavy flat chamfers and a **I. Sleeper** style wedge; an 8 7/8" beech round found in southeast MA, with the B relieved wedge and small round chamfers, ca. 1790-1820.   A & B ****

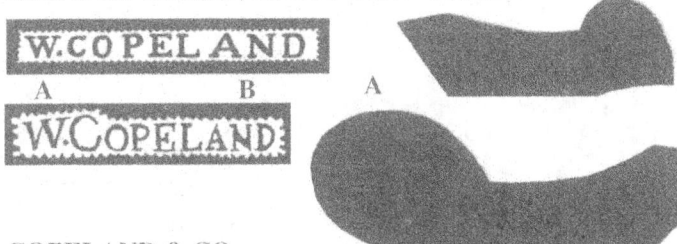

COPELAND & CO.

Copeland & Co. was a Huntington, MA plane making firm, from 1855-66 with **Melvin Copeland** and **Alford Copeland** that was the successor to **M. Copeland**. The MA census listed 15 hands producing $12,000 worth of product and the 1860 census listed 16 hands who produced $22,000 worth of bench planes. Example: imprint A1 on a plane with a bolt through the heel to adjust the iron, which is the **Thomas D. Worrall/ Multiform Molding Plane Co.** patent.
A: FF; A1 ****

COPELAND & CHAPIN
Copeland & Chapin was a partnership between **Daniel Copeland** and **Hermon Chapin** in Pine Meadow, CT, from 1826-28. On Oct. 21, 1828, **Hermon Chapin** purchased **Daniel Coleland's** interest and renamed the business **Union Factory**. **No imprint has been reported**.

S: COPP
Examples: on a 10" large astragal with a relieved A wedge; a 15 3/8" bench style tongue plane; and a 10" Yankee groove plank pair with offset tote and wedge lock short arms, an iron strike, no depth stop and the B wedge, all birch with flat chamfers and flutes, ca. 1780. *****

W. COPP
Example: on a 9 3/8" beech full round or nosing plane with flat chamfer on the right side and round chamfer on the left. The iron is marked **COPP** as the body but with out the initial, ca. early 19c. UR

T CORBISHLEY
Example: on a 9 1/2" beech small nosing plane with flat chamfers, ca. 1800. UR

JOHN CORELL
John Corell was listed as a planemaker located at Copak Falls, NY, active from 1850-72. Some of his planes bear dates. **No imprint is available**.

P. CORELL
P. Corell was listed as a planemaker located at Grove St., New York, NY, active from 1850-70. Some of the planes bear dates. **No imprint is available**.

ABR CORY
Possibly this represents **Abraham Corey**. Example: on a 13 1/8" panel plane with an adjustable bottom fence, a skew iron marked **Iohn Green**, an offset tote, wood depth stop and round chamfers, ca. 1810-20. UR

COREY, BROOKS & CO.
Corey, Brooks & Co. was a Boston, MA, Hardware dealer, active in 1875. Examples: two small coffin smoothing planes. ***

T. CORLISS/ A. P. C

Example: on a 14 3/4" fruitwood cornice plane with a birch wedge, pegged handle, and round chamfers. The **A.P.C** could represent a second generation Corliss, ca. 1820. UR

I. D. CORNELL
Example: on a closed toted cocobolo plow plane with boxwood fence, arms & nuts and wedge, ca. 19c. UR

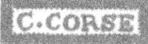

G+ CORSAN
Example: on a 10 1/4" birch grooving plane with riveted skate and round chamfers, ca. 1820-30. UR

C. CORSE
Example: on a skew rabbet, ca. 19c. UR

E. CORY
Examples: on a 9 3/8" beech bead; an 8 3/4" beech complex molder; a 13 11/16" beech sash with a **Newbould** iron; a 15 1/8" fruitwood gutter plane with closed tote and wedge, a rosewood strike and a **Weldon** iron, all with flat chamfers. ca. 1800-10. A & B: UR

J. CORY.
Example: on a 13 3/4" beech panel raiser with an adjustable bottom fence and round chamfers, ca. 1820. UR

S: CORY
Example: on a 10" beech square compass rabbet with heavy flat chamfers, a relieved wedge and a dovetailed depth stop, ca. 1790. UR

A. COSGROVE
Example: on a 9 1/4" beech center bead with round chamfers, ca. 19c. UR

J: COTTRELL
Examples: on a 10 1/4" birch double-iron fixed sash marked twice on the toe, with flat chamfers; and a bench plane, ca. 1780-90. UR

S. COUDEN

S. Couden's imprint appears on planes made by **James Burke** of Madison, IN and **Samuel Sloop** of Cincinnati, OH. He is reported to be an employee of both but may have been a dealer who added the imprint before resale. ***

J. COUGHTRY

Joseph Coughtry (b. 1824 in Albany, NY, d. 1897 in Albany) was a New York City planemaker, active from 1849-50. In 1850, he was listed as "hardware" in New York, NY. He returned to Albany, in 1851, and worked for others. He was listed in 1855, as plainmaker in Albany. He worked for himself from 1891-97 in Albany.
A, A1 & B **

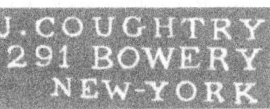

F. COUMBS

Example: on a 9 1/2" beech triple boxed, size **7/8**, Grecian ovolo with bead and round chamfers, ca. 19c. **UR**

J. COWEE.

The **Cowee** family were chair manufacturers in Gardner, MA. Example: on a 10 1/4"x 1 1/2" beech skew rabbet with round chamfers, ca. 1840-50. *****

COX

Cox was probably a hardware dealer in Philadelphia, PA. Example: on a handled raze smoother with a **D. R. Barton** iron, ca. 19c. ****

A. S. COX

Example: on a 9 1/2" beech molder with round chamfers, ca. 1820. **UR**

DANIEL COX

Daniel Cox was a journeyman for **E. W. Carpenter** in 1829 and was reported as a Baltimore, MD planemaker at 29 N. Exeter, active in 1840-41. **No imprint has been reported.**

W: COX

Possibly **William Cox** (b. 1744, d. 1826) who was listed as a cabinetmaker in Bristol, MA, in 1782. Example: on a 9 1/2" beech astragal with heavy round chamfers, ca. 1810. **UR**

RICHARD COXE

Richard Coxe (b. 1801 in AL) probably was a hardware dealer in Montgomery, AL. Example: on a molder by **A. & E. Baldwin**, ca. 1840. **UR**

D. COYE

Example: on a 9 3/8" beech hollow with shallow round chamfers, ca. 1830. **UR**

J. M. CRAE

Examples: on a complex single-boxed molder made by **C. Harwood**; and a single blade fixed sash, both 9 1/4" beech with round chamfers, ca. 1820. **UR**

JOHN ALTHAN CRAFT

John Althan Craft (b. Sep. 1, 1824 in Youngstown, OH, still living in 1906 in IN) He came to Hancock Co. IN, in 1836, at age 12, with his family. **John** apprenticed himself, at age 20, to **Peter Probasco** to learn the trade of a plane maker. **Peter Probasco** had moved from Cincinnati to a farm near Charlottesville, Hancock Co., IN and built a shop and engaged in plane making. During his apprenticeship, **John** received his board and lodging and extra pay of 1$ per day for help in the fields. In 1846, he walked to Cincinnati where he worked for **E. F. Seybold & Co.**, wholesale hardware merchants and manufacturers. **John** became ill and returned to Charlottesville. He was sent materials and made planes for Cincinnati as well as for his local market. **John** married **Eliza Ann Fries**, on July 26, 1849. He continued to make planes under his own name until 1857. **John Craft** fought in the Civil War from 1861-March 1864, in Co. A, 57th. Indiana Infantry, and rising to the rank of Captain. In 1864, **John** and his family moved into Charlottesville where he engaged in the dry goods business until 1881. From 1891-1904, he had an interest in a general store in Charlottesville under the name of **Craft & McGraw**. **No example of his imprint has been reported.**

A. CRAM

Examples: on a 9 5/16" beech wide round; a 15"x 5 1/2" beech crown molder; and a plane made by **I. COX** (John Cox, Birmingham, England 1770-1843). **UR**

L. CRAM & CO.

L. Cram & Co. is probably a hardware dealer. Examples: on a complex molder with the A1 imprint and a molding plane with the A imprint, found in ME, ca. 1840. **A & A1 ****

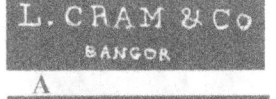

A CRANDAL

Example: on a 9 7/16" beech skew coping plane with round chamfers, ca. 1820. **UR**

D. O. CRANE
David Orville Crane (b. Oct. 10, 1804 in CT, d. 1858 in Monroe Co., NY which includes Rochester) was the brother of **Harvey Crane** and a cousin of **S. G. Crane**. He learned plane making from **Leonard Kennedy** in Hartford, CT. In 1828, **Crane** went to New Hartford, south of Utica, NY, probably working for **Leonard Kennedy Jr.** An advertisement by **Rowe & Woodruff** in the *Utica Intelligencer* of Jan. 27, 1829, offered a "selected assortment of Bench Planes, also moulding tools of almost every description by **L. Kennedy & Co.** and **D.O. Crane**. Persons wishing to purchase can have the privilege of selecting from either of the above named manufacturer's make." **David Crane** was recorded in Utica in the 1830 census. He is listed in the 1850 census in Seneca, NY as a dentist. From 1851-58, he was listed in Rochester, NY also as a dentist. **A **; B *******

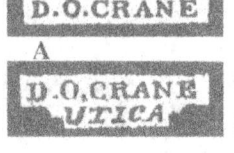

H. CRANE
Harvey Crane (b. 1805 in CT, d. after 1879) was the brother of **David Crane** and was listed in the 1840 census as living in East Hartford, CT, next door to **Peter Brooks**. By 1846, he was working in Springfield, MA. He was listed in the 1850 census as a planemaker. In 1860, he was listed as a toolmaker (mechanic) working for **T. W. Wason & Co.**, a manufacturer of railroad cars. **Harvey Crane** appeared again in an 1873 directory as a planemaker. **A & B ******

L. H. CRANE
L. H. Crane was listed as a cabinetmaker in Newark, NJ, active from 1830-36. Example: on a 9 9/16" yellow birch hollow. ********

R. S. CRANE
Example: on an 8 1/4" compass plane with an iron marked **K. ERICKSON** and round chamfers, ca. 1810-20. **UR**

S. CRANE
Example: on a crown molder with an open tote, the iron is marked **WEST, VA.**, ca. 1850. **UR**

S. G. CRANE
Samuel Gustin Crane (b. Jun. 12, 1809 in CT) was a first cousin of **D. O. Crane** and **Harvey Crane**. He came to Rochester, NY, about 1833. In 1849, he was working for **D. R. Barton**. The Rochester, NY city directories list him as a wood toolmaker, in 1849-50; a cooper's toolmaker, in 1851-52; and a planemaker, from 1853-58. On Jan. 19, 1858, he received a patent for a cooper's croze that was listed in the **D. R. Barton**'s 1865 catalog. He was a mechanic, in 1858; and a toolmaker, in 1861. He was a partner with **James Scott** in **Crane & Scott** from 1866-71. In 1875, he was a chairman at the **D. R. Barton Tool Co.** In 1879, he was a foreman at **D. R. Barton**. It is not clear when he made planes under his own imprint, but judging by the scarcity, his output was limited. *********

STEPHEN H. CRANE
Stephen H. Crane (b. 1810 in Scotland) appeared in the 1842-44 & 1847-48 NY City directories as a planemaker at 138 Sullivan St. In the 1850 census, **Stephen** was listed as a planemaker in Middletown, CT, working for the **Arrowmammett Works**. **No imprint has been reported**.

CRANE & SCOTT
Crane & Scott was a partnership of **Samuel G. Crane** and **James Scott**, who were listed in the 1866-67 Rochester, NY business directory as "tool" or "plane makers". Prior to this date they were in the shop of **D. R. Barton**. **No imprint has been reported**.

CRANE & WAY
Crane & Way was a partnership of **Harvey Crane** a planemaker in East Hartford, CT; and **William Way** who was a hardware dealer in Hartford, CT. Example: on a 22" beech jointer with a centered closed handle, ca. 1850. *********

JOHN CRANFORD
John Cranford was listed in Warren Co., OH under "Plane Mfgs.", in 1853-54. **No imprint has been reported**.

M. CRANNELL/ M. CRANNELL & CO.
Matthew Crannell, Jr. (b. ca. 1816 in NY, d. May 5, 1892) was part of **Bensen & Crannell**, from 1843-62, with **Nicholas Benson**. After **Bensen**'s death, **Matthew Crannell** made planes under the M. **Crannell** imprint, from 1863-78, at 108 State St.; and from 1878-92, at 208 Hudson St. The B imprint was used after 1870. He was listed in the 1850 census as a planemaker in Albany, NY. **J. Coughtry** was probably, at one time, an employee. Starting in 1851, **Matthew Carnnell** operated a mechanic's tool store in addition to his plane making business. **A, A1 & B: FF**

CRATHERN & CAVERHILL
Example: on a 16" jack plane, ca. mid 19c. **UR**

CREAGH/ J. CREAGH
John C. Creagh (b. England) was a Cincinnati, OH, planemaker who was part of **Creagh & Rickard**, in 1829 and **Creagh & Williams**, in 1831. From 1836-40, he made planes on his own. In 1836-37, **John Creagh** was listed as a plane and edge tool manufactory, Cincinnati. **John Creagh** ran a hardware

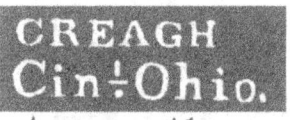

store from 1839-40. He was succeeded by **Lyon & McKinnell & Co**. The **J. CREAGH** imprint appears with other names as **J. W. Lyon, Lyon & McKinnell & CO., E.F. Seybold** and **W. Wintkle**. These are thought to be excess **J. Creagh** stock sold off while going out of business between 1840-42.
A, A1, B, B1, C, C1 & D **

J. CREAGH/ LYON McKINNELL & CO
John C. Creagh sold off stock between 1840-42 while going out of business. **Joseph W. Lyon** and **Henry McKinnell** were planemaker partners in **Lyon McKinnell & Co.** in Cincinnati, OH, from 1842-46. ***

J. CREAGH/ J. W. LYON
John C. Creagh sold off stock between 1840-42 while going out of business. **Joseph W. Lyon** was a Cincinnati, OH planemaker ***

CREAGH/ RICHARD
John C. Creagh and **Thomas J. Richard** were a plane and brush making partnership in Cincinnati, OH, at 231 Main St., in 1829. They also sold edge tools made by others. A & B ***

J. CREAGH/ E. F. SEYBOLD
These planes are thought to be excess stock that **J. C. Creagh** sold off while going out of business between 1840-42. **Emanuel F. Seymore** was a planemaker listed in Cincinnati, OH, 1836-44. ***

CREAGH & WILLIAMS
John C. Creagh and **David W. Williams** were hardware dealers in Cincinnati, OH, in 1831, at Main between 4th. and 5th.
A, A1, B & B1 **

J. CREAGH/ W. WINTKLE
John C. Creagh sold off stock while going out of business between 1840-42.
W. Wintkle was not listed as a plane maker in the Cincinnati, OH directories. ***

J. CREE

Example: on a 13 1/8"x 2 3/8" beech panel raiser with a birch tote and wedge. The tote is centered, flat chamfers, and found in south ME. UR

O. A. CREGER
Example: on a 14" applewood moving filletster with double adjustable fences, an open centered tote, and shallow round chamfers, possibly from PA, ca. 1830. UR

B. CREHORE
Believed to be **Benjamin Crehore** (b. 1765, d. Oct. 14, 1832 Milton MA) who had a cabinet shop in Milton, MA, in 1791. By 1797, he had become America's first pianoforte maker. Example: on a 10" birch complex moulder with a relieved wedge and flat chamfers, ca. 1790. ****

J. CREHORE
Jedidiah Crehore (b. Oct. 19, 1727, Milton, MA, d. Sep. 28, 1781, Wrentham, MA) or **John Crehore** (b. Nov. 8, 1736, Milton, MA, d. Feb. 1, 1808, Milton MA). The imprint is similar to that of **B. Crehore**. Examples: on a 10 5/16" cherry molder; a 1 1/2" wide cherry round; and a 13" birch panel raiser with a double pegged heavily offset tote that has "mouse ear" finial, all with flat chamfers and flutes. The panel iron is marked **S. Fox/ Late** and **Eadon Jessop & Fox**, ca. 1760-90. ****
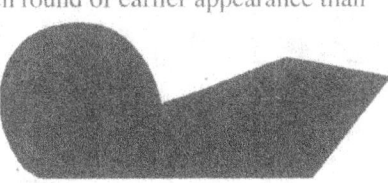

W. CRESSY
Example: on a 9 3/4" beech round of earlier appearance than **W: Cresy**, ca. 1780. UR
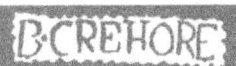

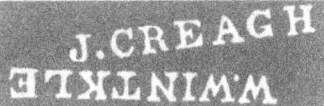

S. CRESWELL
Example: on a 10" birch full round or fluting plane with heavy flat chamfers, ca. 1800. **UR**

WC./ W: CRESY
Examples: on a 10" fixed sash; a 9 1/4" dust joint; and a round, all beech with flat chamfers. The dust joint plane also has **WC.** branded on the side, ca. 1790-1800. **UR**

H. H. CRIE & Co.
H. H. Crie & Co. was a hardware dealer in Rockland, ME with **H. H. Crie** and **R. Anson Crie**, from 1860-1914. Example: imprinted on the end and side of a crose made by **D. B. Titus**. **UR**

W.C/ W. CRILLEY
Example: on a 9 3/8" beech moving filletster with adjustable bottom fence, a brass side depth stop and nicker, with round chamfers, ca. 19c. **UR**

I. CRISP
Example: both imprints are on a 9" birch quarter round plane with round chamfers, ca. early 19c. **UR**

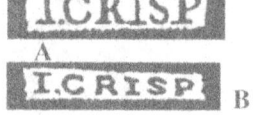

CRISTELKIN
Examples: on a 10 3/16" complex molder; a 10 1/16" halving plane; a 10" complex molder struck twice on the toe; and a 15" crown struck three times on the toe, all beech with heavy flat chamfers. One of the molders and the crown were found in Lebanon Co., PA, near Hershey, ca. 1790. ****

G. CROCKER
Example: on a 9 1/2" beech self-fenced rabbet imprinted on the toe and the heel, with a relieved wedge and flat chamfers, ca. 1800. **UR**

PETER CROCK
Peter Crock (b. 1802 in PA) was listed as a planemaker in Philadelphia, PA, active from 1837-45. The 1850 census listed **Peter Crock's** occupation as a planemaker.
No imprint has been reported.

J. CROHBIE
Examples: on a molder with lignum vitae boxing; a 9 3/8" tongue plane; and an 8 3/4"x 7/8" fluting plane, all beech with flat chamfers, ca. 1810-20. ****

S. CROMWELL
Example: on a 9 7/16" single-boxed beech molding plane with flat chamfers. The large incuse imprint was on the side of the plane, ca. 19c. **UR**

WM. CROOK & SON/ CROOK HARDWARE CO.
William Crook & Son was a hardware dealer who made planes and possibly rules and was located in Baltimore, MD, active from 1874-94. The 1878 Baltimore directory listed the firm located at 175-177 E. Baltimore. Example: The C imprint is black with white lettering paper label, 1 13/16" in diameter, on a **H. Chapin** size 8 hollow. The address on the paper label is 711 W. Baltimore St., date unknown.
A & B ***; C *****

CROSBY
Example: on a 9 1/2" birch narrow round with heavy flat chamfers, ca. 1800. **No imprint is available.**

J. CROSBY
Examples: on a 9 1/4" Yankee plow with wood depth stop and wood thumbscrews; and a 9" tongue & grove pair, all are beech with heavy flat chamfers, ca. 1790. **UR**

J: CROSBY
Example: on a 10" beech nosing plane with heavy flat chamfers that stop in a flat step and with long narrow flutes, possibly from southeastern New England, ca. 1780. **UR**

J. C./ I. CROSS
Example: on a 9 3/4" beech filletster with depth stop and a movable fence. **No imprint is available**.

R. CROSS
Example: on a 9" beech reeding plane boxed with rosewood. ca. 1820. **No imprint is available**.

H. CROUCHEN
Example: on a 9 1/4" beech astragal with flat chamfers, ca. 1810-20.   **UR**

A. CROUT
Example: on an 8 1/2" beech plow with wood screw-locked arms, wood depth stop also wood screw-lock, shallow round chamfers on the sides and no chamfers on the toe and heel, found near Burlington, VT, ca. early 19c.   **UR**

T. M. CROW
Example: on a 9 1/2" beech large hollow with heavy flat chamfers, possibly from PA, ca. 1800.   **UR**

W. CROW
Example: on a 9 1/2" beech large hollow with heavy flat chamfers, possibly from PA, ca. 1800.   **UR**

JOHN CRUGH
John Crugh (b. Nov. 14, 1799), on July 13, 1816, at age 17, was apprenticed to **William Vance** to be taught the plane making business. **No imprint has been reported**.

CRUM & SCHULTZ
John F. Crum (b. 1828) was listed as a merchant and **Frederick Schultz** (b. 1793) was a wagon maker who were possibly was a hardware partnership listed in the 1850 census for Winchester, VA. Example: on a handled plow plane with boxwood screws.   *****

W. CRUTCHFIELD
Examples: on a 9 7/16" beech adj. sash plane with two irons and wedges, wood thumb screws; and the B imprint on a **W. L. Epperson** round plane with the location **LOUISVILLE, KY.**, ca. 1850-70.   **A & B: UR**

JOHN CUDDY
Example: on a 9 7/16" beech moving filletster plane with wide round chamfers, wedged nicker, brass depth stop, no boxing and an **Oakes** iron, ca. 1810-40.   **UR**

W. CUDDY
William Cuddy was a planemaker in New York City, active from 1841-54. **Cuddy** also operated a tool store from 1850-54.   ****

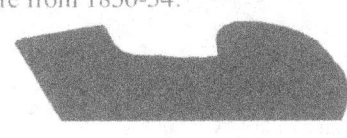

J. M. CULLY
J. M. Cully was listed as a planemaker in Pittsburgh, PA. **No imprint has been reported**.

C. CULP
Example: on a 10" birch bead plane with a beech wedge and heavy flat chamfers, probably from New England, ca. 1800.   **UR**

E* CULVER
Example: on a 25" beech joiner with a diamond strike, offset tote, and heavy flat chamfers, ca. 1800.   **UR**

S. CULVER
Samuel Culver (b. Dec. 15, 1798 in Shoreham, VT, d. Jul. 29, 1861) was listed in the 1830 census of Barnard, VT, no occupation given, but was not listed in the 1840 census. Examples: on a 9 1/16" grooving plane; and a sash, both beech with round chamfers. The mark after **BARNARD** is a three dot triangle, not a single dot, ca. 19c.   **A & A 1: ****

A. CUMINGS
Allen Cumings (**Cummings**) (b. 1813 in NY, d. 1875 in NY) was the son of **Allen Cummings, Sr.** (b. 1771) and brother of **Samuel Reed Cumings** (**Cummings**) (b. 1804). In 1837-38, Allen Cumings was listed in the Utica directory as a planemaker at 65 Broadway and believed to have worked for **R. J. Collins III** at 81 Broadway. **Allen Cumings** was listed as a Boston, MA, planemaker, appearing in the city directories in 1844-45, with **M. Reed & Co.**; from 1846-47 under the name **Read & Cumings** as a planemakers at 119 Commercial St.; and from 1848-54, he was listed under his own name. He was listed in 1849 in the New England

Mercantile Union directory as a plane manufacturer at Merrimack St., corner of Beacon St., Boston. He lived in East Boston during the 1840's but moved to nearby Chelsea, ca. 1850. He was listed in the 1850 census as a planemaker, in the same building as **George A. Benton**. The **Greenfield Tool Co.** ledger of 1854 showed the purchase of joiner, fore, and jack plane stock from **A. Cummings**, Boston. Several **A. Cummings** planes bear evidence of shaved **Greenfield Tool Co.** imprints underneath. The 1864 Chelsea directory lists **A. Cummings** as a traveling agent. Since **Allen Cumings** (**Cummings**) came from NY state, the imprints C, D & D1 probably represent his earlier work. Examples reported include a complete set of bench planes, ca. 1850. The C imprint is on a 25 7/8" beech joiner with round chamfers, ca. 1830. A, A1, B *; B1, C, D & D1 ****

O. CUMINGS
Example: on a 9 1/2" beech single boxed complex molder, ca. 1850. UR

S. CUMINGS/ S. R. CUMINGS/ S. R. CUMMINGS
Samuel Reed Cumings (**Cummings**) (b. 1804 in Barre, MA, d. Aug. 2, 1879 in Parke Ridge, Cook Co., IL) was the son of **Allen Cummings, Sr.** (b. 1771). **Samuel** married **Ester Reed** of Rehobeth, MA on May 15, 1794; and was the brother of **Allen Cummings Jr.** (b. 1813). It is believed that **Samuel Cumings** apprenticed in New York City to the planemaker **Enos Baldwin**. In 1828, **Samuel** left New York City and moved to Providence, RI. He is listed as a planemaker with his own shop, in the 1828 Providence directory. When **Samuel** was married on June 1, 1828, he was described as of New York City. In 1830-33, he was in a partnership with **Jonas R. Gale** as **Cumings & Gale**. **Jonas R. Gale** also apprenticed with **Enos Baldwin** in New York. The partnership ended when **Cumings** sold his half interest to **Gale** and moved to Attleboro, MA, where he worked from 1833-39, employing **Marcus Read**, **Joseph A. Montgomery** and **Moses P. Wilmarth**. **Cumings** established a steam powered manufactory outside of Attleboro on the road to Norton, MA. From 1842-44, **Cumings** made planes at Commercial St. in Boston, MA. By 1844, **Cumings** had become a house builder in East Boston. From 1847-50, he was living in Fairfield, Somerset Co., ME. In the 1849 New England Union Business director, he is listed as a "Door, Sash and Blind Manufacturer" in Fairfield. In 1852, **Cumings** was living in Winchester, Middlesex Co., MA, north of Boston. In 1856, he was working as a carpenter in Niles, Cook Co. IL. In 1864, **Cumings** returned to Chelsea, MA, working as a carpenter. In 1870, **Cumings** was listed in the Federal Census in Hyde Park, Norfolk Co., MA, as a Machinist. In 1872, **Samuel Cummings** (spelled with two m's) was working again as a planemaker listed in the Boston Business directory at 56 Albany St., Boston, MA. This address was a few doors from **P. A. Gladwin** who was working at 64 Albany St. The A imprint is on a 14 7/8" open toted skew rabbet. The C imprint is on a beech jack; a beech smoother; and a boxwood smoother. The D imprint, probably represents this last period of his work in 1872.
B *; A, C & D ****

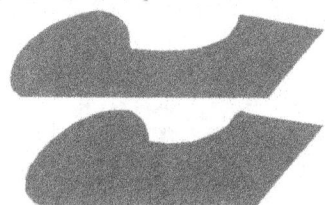

CUMINGS & GALE
Samuel R. Cumings and **Jonas R. Gale** were partners and planemakers at 62 then 77 Webossett St., Providence, RI, from 1830-33. In 1833, **Cumings** sold his half interest to **Gale**. Examples: The A imprint is on a 15 1/2"x 6 5/8" crown molder with a pull rod and centered tote. The B imprint is on a 11 7/8" tongue & grove combination plane with a closed tote, both beech. A & B **

J. CUMMING
John Cummings, a cabinetmaker of Maryville, Blount Co., TN, advertised in the *Religious and Literary Intelligencer* in which he offered his services as a cabinetmaker and wagonmaker and said he would make coffins as well as bench and molding planes. Example: on a 14 1/4" beech panel raiser with heavy round chamfers, ca. 1830. UR

CUNNINGHAM/ A. CUNNINGHAM
Andrew Cunningham was listed from 1846-52 as a edge tool finisher. In 1854, he was listed as a planemaker in Cincinnati, OH. In 1855, **Andrew** was part of **Seybold, Cunningham & Sprague**. He was listed as a edge tool maker and blacksmith. From 1856-70, he ran a tool factory. ca. 1850.
A & B ****

Rx CURRIE
Possibly **Robert Currie** who was a cabinetmaker in Hartford, CT. ca. 1768. Examples: on a 9 7/8" small shiplap plane; and a 9 7/8" medium hollow, both birch with flat chamfers, from New England, ca. 1780. ****

W. CURRIER
Example: on a 10 1/2" Yankee plow with square arms stopped with wood thumb screws, no depth stop and flat chamfers, found in ME, ca. 1800.   **UR**

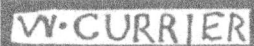

PETER CURTENIUS
Peter Curtenisu advertised in the 1767 New York *Mercury* announces that "he is intending to quit the iron-mongery business." There are many items listed including planes and plane irons. **No imprint has been reported**.

F. CURTIS
Frederick Curtis (b. 1793, d. Mar. 31, 1829 in Boston, MA) made planes in Boston, MA. He was listed in the Boston directory at 48 Court St. Example: The A imprint on a double-boxed complex molder.
A & A1 ***: B *****

F. H. CURTIS
Examples: on a 9 3/8" complex molder; and a 9 1/4" adjustable sash plane, both beech with round chamfers, ca. 1820.   **UR**

I. J. CURTIS
Examples: on a 10" pear complex molder; and a 9 1/2" boxed complex molder, both with heavy flat chamfers, ca. 1800.   **UR**

N. CURTIS
Nathaniel Curtis was a planemaker in Boston, MA, active from 1816-22. He was listed in the Boston directory at Henchman La. Examples: have been reported with round chamfers, ca. 1820.
A ***; B ****

P. CURTIS
Example: on a 9 7/8" beech fenced rabbet with narrow flat chamfers, ca. 1800.
No imprint is available.

P. G. L. CUSHING
Example: on a molder, ca. 1830.   **UR**

J. CUSHMAN
Examples: on a 9 1/2" beech size **6**; and a size **12** rounds, both with round chamfers, ca. 1820.   **UR**

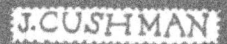

I. CUSTERD
Example: on a 10" beech panel raiser with offset tote and heavy flat chamfers, found near Philadelphia, PA, ca. 1790-1800.   **UR**

H. CUTLER
Examples: on a single-boxed bead and a double-boxed molder, both beech, ca. 1850.   **UR**

CUTLER & CO.
Example: on a beech wedge-arm plow with the location CLEVELAND, OHIO. This is probably a hardware dealer, ca. 1850.   ****

W. B. D
William B. Davis was a plane maker/ farmer from Jefferson, ME, ca. first half of 19c. A & B: UR

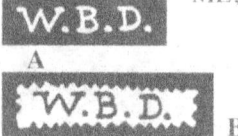

M. DABOLL
Example: on a 9 7/8" birch molder with flat chamfers that ends with a flat step then a long taper. UR

H. DAGGET
Henry Daggett was part of Daggett & Walker in Cincinnati, OH starting in 1820. Examples: The A imprint is on an 8 7/8" beech medium hollow with round chamfers. The A1 imprint is on a 9 5/16" beech sq. rabbit, ca. 1820.
A & B: ****

DAGGETT & WALKER
Henry Daggett and Jessey Walker advertised, on April 1, 1820, their partnership and the establishment of the "Cincinnati Plane Factory," a manufactory of carpenter's planes of all descriptions. Example: on a 9 3/8" beech size 11 round, ca. 1820. ****

Sx DAGGETT
Possibly Samuel Daggett (b. Jan. 3, 1731 in Attleboro, MA, d. Aug. 1806 in Schuylerville, NY) the son of Ebenezer Daggett (1690-1740) and married Abigail Kingsbury on Mar. 6, 1749 in Needham, MA. His son was Samuel Daggett Jr. (b. Feb. 25, 1755, in Needham, d. 1826); his fifth son, Ebenezer Daggett (b. May 16, 1762 in Needham), was a blacksmith. Samuel Daggett served as a Private in the American Revolution in Capt. Elihu Grifford's Co., for duty in RI. Examples: on a 7 1/2" fruitwood smoother with birch round-top wedge & iron, with a metal strike on the heel; and a 15"x 1 7/8" birch rabbit with 2 nickers and an open tote, both with flat chamfers, probably from New England, ca. 1760. ****

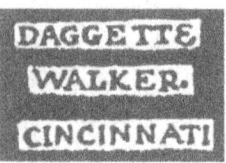

J. F. DAKE
Example: on a 20 1/4" beech joiner with closed off-set tote found at Mt. Vernon, VA. ca. 1820-30. UR

F. DALLICKER
The A imprint was used by both Frederick Dallicker, Sr. (b. Dec. 30, 1779 in Morris, NJ, d. Feb. 15, 1853 in Douglas, Montgomery Co, PA) and his son Frederick B. Dallicker, Jr. (b. 1799, d. Sep. 4, 1874 in Gilbertsville, Douglas Township), who were planemakers, from 1810-60. Frederick Dallicker, Sr. was the son of Frederick De la Cour (b. Feb. 2, 1738 of French Huguenot descent) who changed his name to Dallicker. The origin of the name is Talliker or candlemaker. He was a Minister in the Dutch Reform Church, in 1757; and served in Lebanon Borough, NJ, from 1768-82; before relocating to Goshenhoppen, PA, where he served until 1784. There is the possibility that Frederick (1779-1853) was apprenticed to P. Royer. Frederick married Catherina Royer Beiteman in Mar. 1798, shortly, after reaching 21. Frederick B. Dallicker was listed as a planemaker, in 1850. Examples: The wedge shape and chamfers vary, reflecting a long career. Planes are 9 1/2" beech with round to 19c style chamfers, ca. 1810-19c. The B imprint is the earliest and is on a 12 11/16" beech toted molding plane with heavy flat chamfers, with a round-top iron marked A. EBERTS. A*, B*****

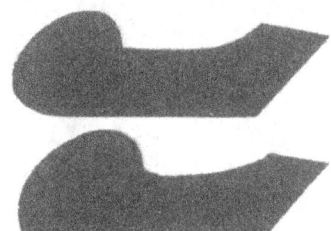

IOHN. DALMAN
Examples: from 9 1/2"-9 5/8" beech complex molders with shallow round to 19c style chamfers, found in central NY. The wedge is similar to that of the Oothoudts, ca. 1830. UR

SEM. DALPE'
Samuel Dalpe', dit Pariseau (b. Apr. 18, 1828 in Canada, d. Apr. 5, 1894) was of French Huguenot decent and was listed in the 1850 census in Worthington, Hampshire Co., MA, living with Benjamin F. Rhoads, age 25. From 1851-53, Samuel was at 11 Ferry St., Troy, NY, the site of E. & C. Carter's Plane Factory. His first child, Martha was born in Troy, in 1853. He returned to Canada, in 1855. His second child, Prictlle, was born in Quebec, on Dec. 20, 1855. Samuel founded the Canadian plane making industry at Roxton Pond, Province Quebec, which continued making wooden planes until 1930. In 1895, Mrs. Sem Dalpe. Esesse Nicol, and son William Dalpe were listed as tool manufacturer. In 1896, the company was sold to A. Monty.(see Troy Tool Co. and Orin Delpe')
No American imprint has been reported.

ISAAC DALTON
Isaac Dalton (d. Columbus, OH) was a planemaker in Columbus, OH; from 1867-70, at 356 s. High; in 1872, as a cabinetmaker; in 1874, as a carpenter; from 1875-77, as planemaker at 328 s. High. No imprint has been reported.

I. DALY
Example: on a 9 3/4" beech hollow with imprint struck twice on the toe, flat chamfers on toe & heel and round chamfers on top, ca. 1810. **UR**

P. DALY
Example: on a 9 1/4" beech round with flat chamfers, ca. early 19c. **UR**

E. DAMON
Believed to be **Ellis Damon** (b. Feb. 12, 1758 in Scituate, MA, d. Aug 26, 1805 in Hanover, Plymouth Co., MA) the son of **Zachariah Damon** (1723-71) a wheelwright. **Ellis Damon** is listed in the index of *MA Soldiers and Sailors serving in Revolutionary War*. Examples: on a 9 3/8" cherry nosing plane; and a 9 1/2" birch large hollow, both with flat chamfers, ca. 1780-1800. **UR**

J. DANA
Examples: on a 7 3/4" compass smoother with a single round-top iron and wedge, with tight round chamfers; and a 9 1/2" complex molder with flat chamfers, both beech, ca. 1800-10. **UR**

M. DANALD
Examples: on a 9 1/2" beech hollow & round with **H. H. NOBLE** branded on the side and a slightly relieved wedge, ca. 1820-30. **UR**

E. DANBERRY
Ellsworth Danberry (b. 1818 in New Brunswick, Middlesex Co., NJ, d. before 1885 in New Brunswick.) was a New Brunswick, NJ, planemaker who was probably associated with **S. C. Cook** and succeeded him, using the same location imprint. A plane has also been reported with its S. C. Cook mark overstruck by this imprint. **Ellsworth Danberry** was listed in the 1850 census as a planemaker in North Brunswick, Middlesex, NJ. By 1855, **Ellsworth** was listed as an express agent. He was last listed in 1863. ******

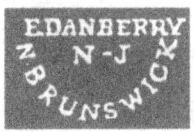 

J. M. DANE
Example: on a 10 1/16"x 1 1/2" beech hollow with shallow round chamfers, ca. 1830-40. **UR**

R. DANE
Example: on a 9 1/2" beech skew rabbet with an added side fence, ca. 1840. **UR**

A

B

W. DANIEL
Examples: on a 10" round; and a 9 3/4"x 1" skew rabbet, both birch with heavy flat chamfers, ca. 1790. **UR**

J. B. DANNER
J. B. Danner was listed as a planemaker in the 1854 & 59 Milwaukee city directories. In the 1857 & 58 directories, he was listed as a laborer but was not listed in 1860 & 61. In 1862, **Danner** was listed as a cabinetmaker.
No imprint has been reported.

DANT & RYAN
Dant & Ryan was a hardware firm in Alton, IL, with **Daniel Ryan** active from 1858-1910. Example: on a 9 1/2" hollow with a **72** style number and a **Sandusky Tool Co.** wedge. ********

G. DARLING & CO.
G. Darling & Co. was a hardware firm in Woonsocket, RI, founded by **Gilbert Darling**. In 1877, he was succeeded by his son, **Charles H. Darling**, who continued in business until after 1900. Example: on a **Gladwin & Appleton** 9 3/16" beech hollow with a size **21** number on the heel ********

H. DART
Examples: on a bead; and an astragal, both 9" beech with rosewood boxing, and relieved wedges, found in New England; and a 22 1/4" beech foreplane with a centered closed tote and heavy round chamfers, ca. 19c. **UR**

M. DAUB
Martin (Milton) Daub (b. Oct. 12, 1798 in Bethel Twp., Lancaster, PA, d. Jun. 10, 1883 in Lebanon, PA) appears in the 1850 census of Lebanon Co., PA, as a carpenter. In 1860, He was listed as farmer. Examples: the A imprint is on a 9" beech quarter round; a large bead with round

A   A

chamfers; a crown molder with an offset tote; and a panel raiser. The B imprint is on a 14" panel raiser, ca. 1825-35.

A & B: ****

DAUM & HELM
Probably **Daum & Helm** is a hardware dealer. Example: on a **D. R. Barton** 13 7/8" cooper's sun plane, found in Springfield, OH.   **UR**

G D/ G. D/ G: D/ G. DAVENPORT
Gideon Davenport (b. June 7, 1738 in Newport, RI, d. Sep. 6, 1810 in Newport) was the son of **Thomas Davenport** (b. 1681 in Dorchester, MA, d 1745 at 51, will probated Sept. 3, 1745) a cabinetmaker who moved to Newport, RI, ca. 1737; and grandson of **Jonathan Davenport** (b. 1659 in Dorchester, MA, d. 1729) a carpenter who ended up at Little Compton, MA, (Little Compton became part of RI in 1747) across the Narragansett Bay from Newport. In 1783, at age 45, **Gideon** was referred to as a blacksmith. This could be partly explained because the British occupied and destroyed much of the Town of Newport and its economy and tradesmen were in high demand. Examples: on a group of some 50 tools including twenty one 10" birch molders, two of which have the B relieved wedge similar to an early **Jo, Fuller**; two try planes; a smoother; a slide-arm beech Yankee plow with wood depth stop and thumbscrews; and a 10 3/4" beech panel raiser with a Wrentham style open offset tote, wood depth stop screw stopped from the off side, and a round-top chamfered wedge, all the molding planes have heavy flat chamfers, and appear to be ca. 1780. The A1 imprint, **GD** incuse initial group was used for narrow planes struck from the **G** and **D** of the full name stamp. The inclusion of an **F. Nicholson** molder with the incuse **GD** initials also assists in both dating and location. A number of the irons are signed **G. BISHOP, P. LAW,** or **GILLOT,** all listed in the 1774 & 87 directories for Sheffield, England. The try planes have an earlier look and may have been made by **Thomas Davenport**. Among the **G. Davenport** planes were two sash planes with **ED** embossed initials, made by **L. Little**. These probably represent an owner imprint of a later **Davenport** generation.   A, A1, B, C & D *****

W. DAVENPORT
William Davenport (b. Aug. 1, 1736 in Little Compton, Newport Co., RI, d. Dec. 31, 1807 in Little Compton) was a cabinetmaker and son of **Joseph Davenport**, and the nephew of **Thomas Davenport** (see **G. Davenport**). Two of **William's** account books have survived and show transactions in Milton, MA, from May 28, 1782 to Jan. 15, 1805. Example: on a 9 1/8" birch dado, probably from New England, ca. 1780-90.   *****

DAVEY & ALLEN
Davey & Allen was a Burlington, VT, hardware dealer. Example: on a paper label similar to that of **Davey & Doolittle**. It is not known which partnership came first. Example: on a **Copeland & Co.** moving fillister.   *****

FROM
DAVEY & ALLEN
DEALER IN
AGRICULTURAL IMPLEMENTS,
SEEDS, HARDWARE, SADDLERY,
MECHANIC'S TOOLS,
HOUSE TRIMMINGS, PAINT/ &C.
COLLEGE ST., BURLINGTON.

DAVEY & DOOLITTLE
Davey & Doolittle was a Burlington, VT, hardware dealer. Example: on a green paper label on a **Copeland & Co.** tongue plane in the tool collection of the Shelburne Museum, Burlington, VT.   *****   FROM
DAVEY & DOOLITTLE,
DEALER IN
AGRICULTURAL IMPLEMENTS,
SEEDS, HARDWARE, SADDLERY,
MECHANIC'S TOOLS,
HOUSE TRIMMINGS, PAINTS/ &C.
COLLEGE ST., BURLINGTON.

M DAVIDS
Example: on a 9 1/2"x 7/8" beech dado with a wood depth stop, a **Newbould** iron and heavy flat chamfers, ca. 1800.   **UR**

H. DAVIDSON
H. Davidson was probably a hardware dealer, location unknown. Examples: on a boxed side bead with style number **37** on the toe; a sash plane with **131 1/2**, which is the **Ohio Tool Co.** style number for a sash plane; and another sash plane with **No. 170** which is the **Sandusky Tool Co.** style number for a sash plane.   ***

I. DAVIDSON
Examples: on a 24" closed center toted foreplane with a single **James Cam** iron; a 9 3/4" skew rabbet; and a 9 1/2" dado, the molders with an **I. Sleeper** style wedge; all beech with flat chamfers, from New England, ca. 1790-1800.   ****

J. T. & R. G. DAVIDSON
This imprint along with a location imprint of **Mc LEAN** which is part of Groton, NY, represents a planemaking partnership with **Robert G. Davidson** (b. Mar. 1, 1827, d. Jan. 4, 1917 in McLean, NY) a Civil War veteran who was listed as a

foundryman in the 1850 census. His father, **John C. Davidson** (b. 1796 in NH) was a machinist. The **J. T.** of the imprint may represent a brother or some other relative. Examples: on a 22" foreplane; a 16" jack; and a skew rabbet with a **Humphreysville** iron, ca. 1850. ***

T. D. & CO.

Tyler Davidson & Co. was a Cincinnati, OH, hardware dealer, active from 1843-65. From 1836-42, the firm was called **Tyler Davidson**. From 1843-50, it was located at 126 Main bt. 3rd. & 4th.; from 1850-59, at 140-42 Main; from 1861-64 it was listed as importers and jobbers of hardware, cutlery and metals with **Tyler Davidson** (b. 1808, d. Jan. 5, 1866), **Henry Probasco** and **Caleb P. Marsh**. In 1865, the firm consisted of **Tyler Davidson**, **Henry Probasco** and **Wm. J. Lowry**. A & B **

S. DAVIE
Example: on a 9" washboard plane. **No imprint is available**.

C. J. DAVIES
Example: on a 9 3/8" beech nosing plane with flat chamfers, ca. 1810. UR

DAVIS
Examples: the A imprint is on a 10 1/8" molder; and a crown with offset tote, both beech with flat chamfers. The iron on the molder appears to be marked **DWARD**, ca. 1810. The B imprint is on a 12 1/8" x 6 1/4" birch crown molder with offset tote, heavy flat chamfers and heavy flutes, ca. 1780-90. UR

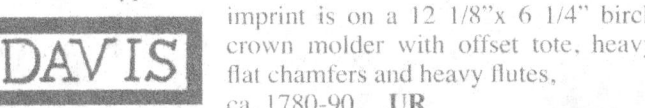

G. DAVIS
Example: on a 15 5/8" fixed sash with two irons & wedges and a closed tote, ca. 1850. UR

E. DAVIS
Example: A imprint is on a crown molder with small flat chamfers. The iron is marked **M. BISHOP**. The B imprint is on a 10" birch molder with relieved wedge similar to a **Jo. Fuller**, ca. 1800. A & B: UR

H. E. DAVIS
Example: on a 9 1/2" beech hollow, ca. 1850. UR

I. DAVIS
Example: marked twice on the toe of a 9 5/8" fruitwood large round with a molded shoulder and large, slightly rounded chamfers, ca. 1800-10. UR

J. DAVIS
Possibly **J. Davis**, listed as a planemaker in the 1837 classified Mercantile Directory for New York and Brooklyn, NY. Example: on a 9 1/2" beech complex molder with round chamfer, ca. 1820. UR

J. S. DAVIS
Example: on a 9 7/8" birch gutter plane, imprinted on toe and heel, with round chamfer; and a 10" birch smoother, ca. 1820. UR

MOSES H. DAVIS
Moses H. Davis was listed as a planemaker at 2 Cottage Pl., New York City, active from 1842-44. He was possibly a part of **Davis and King**. **No imprint has been reported**.

N. DAVIS
Example: on a 11 1/4" beech, toted double-bladed & wedged fixed sash with flat chamfers, ca. 1790-1800. UR

P. P. DAVIS
Example: on a 9 1/4" beech molder with 19c chamfers, ca. 1850. UR

W. DAVIS
Example: on a 9 3/8" beech complex molder with flat chamfers, ca. 1800-10. UR

Wm. B. DAVIS
William B. Davis (b. 1818 in District of Columbia, d. Mar. 10, 1875 in District of Columbia) was a planemaker from Washington, DC. **William's** daughter was born in D.C., in 1835. He was last listed in 1870, ca. 1850. ****

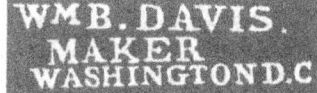 

W. S. DAVIS
William S. Davis (b. 1816 in MA, d. Sep. 1868 in Springfield, MA) was a journeyman planemaker with **H. Chapin** from 1837-40, and was in partnership with **John H. Lester** as **Davis & Lester** in Southampton, MA. In 1849, **William Davis** was listed in the New England Mercantile Union directory as a plane manufacturer, in Stockbridge, MA. From 1852-60, **William** was listed as a planemaker. Example: on a tongue plane that came with a **Davis & Lester** dado. Curtisville was located 4 miles southwest of Lenox, MA, ca. 1850. **A & B:** *****

DAVIS & KING
Possibly a partnership between **Moses H. Davis** and **Josiah King** in New York City, working dates are not known, but are probably before 1850. **

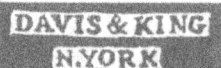

DAVIS, LAMB & CO.
Davis, Lamb & Co. was a hardware dealer in Petersburg, VA, who also made planes. **William Orgill** became a partner of **R. T. Lamb**, in 1846, and they moved to Memphis, TN, in 1847 as **R. T. Lamb & Co.** Example: on a beech small round with an iron by **W. Butcher**. This imprint preceded that move, ca. 1840's. ****

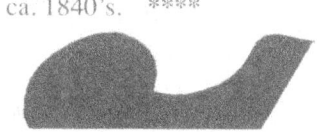

DAVIS & LESTER
Probably **William S. Davis** (b. 1816 in MA, d. Sep. 1868 in Springfield, MA) and **John H. Lester** (b. 1826 in MA, d. Aug. 5, 1884 in Orange, MA) who were listed as planemakers in Southampton, MA, in the 1850 census. In 1853, **John Lester** was producing small bench planes as a piece worker for the **Greenfield Tool Co.**; in 1860, **John** was listed as a planemaker in Chelsea, MA. ****

H. DAWES
Examples: on a 24" jointer; and a 9 1/4" beech molder with a relieved wedge, both with heavy flat chamfers, ca. 1810. **UR**

F. B. DAWLEY/ P. A. DAWLEY
F. B. Davis is the maker and **P. A. Davis** was a next generation user. Example: on a 9 1/2" birch complex molder with flat chamfers, ca. 1800. **UR**

A. DAY
Example: on a razee lignum vitae jack, imprinted on both toe and heel, with a rosewood wedge and a beech closed tote, ca. 1850. **UR**

D. DAY
Example: on a 9 1/4" birch halving molder with flat chamfers, ca. 1800. **UR**

G: DAY
Examples: on a skew rabbet; and a complex molder by **Collins of Hartford**, both 9 1/4" with flat chamfers. Also reported is a 16 1/2" applewood razee shipwright's jack with flat chamfers, found in ME. This imprint has also been reported on a **L. Kennedy** and on three **K & C** planes, ca. 1810. **UR**

I. DAY
At first believed to be **John Day**, who was apprenticed to Phillipson in London, 1756, and so recorded in W. L. Goodman's *British Planemakers, 2nd. ed.* It was noted, however, that the five sightings reported were all in the United States, and that two of the planes reported (a jack and a jointer), were made of birch and were therefore probably American in origin. Subsequently several planes were discovered double stamped **W. RAYMOND/ I. DAY**. Only one would probably have been the maker, in this case **W. Raymond**, and the other a merchant. The search for a merchant named **I. Day** revealed only one, **James Day** (b. before 1732, d. June 14, 1805) of Gloucester, MA, who was in business before 1762. The **I. Day** stamp appears also on a typical English keyed plow of the 1770-1780 period. The imprints below show the large (early) **W. RAYMOND**, with the large **I. DAY**, ca. 1785, and the smaller (later) **W. RAYMOND**, with the small **I. DAY**, ca. 1795. Examples: the A1 imprint are birch. The B1 imprint is on a 9 3/8" boxed side bead; and a 13 1/4"x 5 1/2" complex molder with an offset tote, both beech with flat chamfers and fluted. **A, A1, B & B1:** ****

I: DAY
Possibly a variation of **James Day** or a separate maker. Example: on a crown molder with wide flat chamfers, ca. 1800. **UR**

P. E. DAY
Example: on a 13 1/2" beech, single-iron fixed sash plane with an open tote, ca. 1830. **UR**

R. DAY
Examples: on a 10" tongue plane; and a 9 3/4" complex molder, both birch with flat chamfers, found in a tool chest with plane made by **S. Dean/ Dedham** and **S. Doggett/ Dedham**, ca. 1790-1800. **UR**

MILLER DAYTON
An 1808 source refers to the purchase of a plane from **Miller Dayton**. No imprint has been reported.

DEACON
Believed to be a Philadelphia, PA cabinetmaker. Example: on a 9 1/2"x 1" beech skewed rabbet plane with flat chamfers, ca. 1810. **UR**

B: DEAN
Believed to be **Benaiah Dean** (b. Mar. 7, 1754 in Raynham, MA, d. Feb. 8, 1831-32 in Taunton, MA) who served from 1775-76 as a Private in the Revolutionary War. By deeds in 1786 & 87, **Benaiah** was noted as a joiner in Raynham, MA. From 1804-10, he was listed as a carpenter. In 1814, he was a house carpenter in Raynham; in 1816, he was listed as a yeoman; in the 1830 census **Benaiah** he was listed in Taunton. The A1 wedge is on 9 7/8" molders with flat chamfers. The A2 & A3 wedges are on 9 3/4" molders with round chamfers and flutes. Examples: on a birch jack with offset pegged tote and flat chamfers; and a birch crown molder with flat chamfers. A group of 12 planes was found in an estate in Hanson, MA.
A ***, A1 *****

C. DEAN
Charles Dean was from MA. 13 planes were found together, nine H & R's and four complex molders; all 9 3/8" beech with flat chamfers. ca. 1800. The profiles are described on the heels in black ink and eleven are signed **C. DEAN** in ink on the toes, one is blank and one is signed **CHARLES DEAN FROM MASS.** Example: on an 8 7/8" beech plow with wood thumbscrews, wood depth stop, and a riveted skate with heavy round chamfers, ca. 1820. **UR**

C. P. DEAN
Charles Pinkney Dean (b. Mar. 5, 1813 in Berkley, MA, d. Sep. 15, 1892 in Muscogee, Columbus, Co., GA) was a creditor of the estate of **S. M. Burt,** who died in 1835, in Berkley, MA, near Taunton. **Charles Dean** married on Dec. 23, 1838 in Jones, GA. He was listed in the 1850 Muscogee census as a mechanic; in 1870, as a "farmer/ carpenter"; in 1880, he was listed as a farmer. Examples: on a 1/2" wide round; and a wide round, both 9 1/2" beech with shallow round chamfers, found in a lot containing a number of **Wm. Woodward** planes in Taunton, MA (see **B. Dean**), ca. 1830-40. ****

ELISHA DEAN
Examples: on a 9 3/4" birch Yankee plow with heavy flat chamfers; and a rabbet, ca. 1790. **UR**

J. DEAN
Examples: on a birch smoother; an 8 3/4"x 2 3/16" birch wide bench plane with slightly rounded sole and round chamfers; an 9 3/16" molder, marked with an incuse **1854**; and as an owner's imprint struck twice on the heel of an **I. Lindenberger** plane, ca. 1820-30. **UR**

J. DEAN
Example: include a tool chest, name die, ledger and billhead of **Joseph Dean, Contractor and Builder of Madison, Wisc,** ____, 189_.
No imprint is available.

R. DEAN
Possibly **Richard Dean**, a wood turner from Wilmington, DE. Example: on a 9" beech round with flat chamfers, found in the Philadelphia, PA area, ca. 1810. **UR**

S. D/ S. DEAN
The A and B imprints are possibly from **Samuel Dean** (b. Oct. 17, 1700 in Taunton, Bristol Co., MA, d. Mar. 30, 1775 in Norton, MA) who was a joiner and lived in Dedham, MA, between 1732-47, **Samuel** married **Rachel Dwight** (1705-1760 in Norton) on Apr. 20, 1732 in Dedham. Examples: the A and B imprints are from a 10" molder; two 9 3/4" square rabbet; a 9 5/8" hollow, all with relieved wedges; and a crown molder, all birch with heavy flat chamfers. ca. 1770. The C and D imprints, including the **S.D** initial group, are from a molder; and a 21" joiner, both beech with heavy round chamfers. ca. 1800-10. This may represent **Samuel Dean Jr.** (b. 1733 in Dedham, d. Aug. 30, 1814 in MA) or **Samuel Holmes Dean** (b. May. 7, 1767 in Norfolk Co., MA,

d. Jun 25, 1825 in Dedham) lived in South Dedham, MA. His estate included a number of carpenter's tools. **B & C *****; **A & D ******

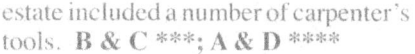
D

SETH DEAN
Example: on a 9 13/16" birch large hollow with shallow flat chamfers, ca. 1750-70. **UR**

S. DEANE
Example: on a 9" beech molding plane. **UR**

J D/ J. DEARBORN
Examples: the A imprint and initial group is on a 9 3/4" beech complex molder with heavy flat chamfers, ca. 1790. The A imprint alone is possibly from a second generation and is on a 9 1/4" single-boxed beech molder, a fixed sash with two irons and wedges, found in ME; and a 9 1/8" fruitwood slide-arm plow with thumbscrews, brass arm tips, brass depth stop and brass plate on the skate, and heavy round chamfers, ca. 1790-1830. **UR**

WARREN DEARBORN/ DEARBORN & SKINNER
A partnership of **Warren Dearborn** (b. Mar 1, 1802 in Grafton, NH, d. Feb. 3, 1863 in Sandwich, NH), a cabinetmaker and **Elijah Skinner** (b. 1786, d. 1871), a storekeeper and inventor in Sandwich, MA, who were known to make and sell planes (joiner and smoothing stock), from 1828-31. **Warren Dearborn** was active under his own name from 1832-62 also making wooden household tools, churns, washboards, tool handles, rules, saw handles, and squares as recorded in his account book.
No imprint has been reported.

J. DEARING
Examples: on an 8 7/8" Yankee plow with screw secured wood depth stop and riveted skate; a 9 3/8" square rabbet; a molder; and a 9 1/2" complex molder, all beech with flat chamfers; a later 9 1/2" beech molder with round chamfers on top and flat end chamfers; and a beech plow, ca. 1800-20. **UR**

NICOL: DEAS
Example: on a 6 3/4" birch molder with flat chamfers, ca. 1800. **UR**

J. DEERY
Example: on a 9 3/8" beech screw-arm split sash with two irons & wedges, struck three times on the toe, ca. 1840-50. **UR**

DeFOREST/ L. DeFOREST
Linson DeForest (b. 1822 in CT) made planes in Birmingham (Derby), CT, from 1850-57; in New York City, in 1857-58; and again in CT, in 1859-60. The 1850 census listed **DeForest** in Birmingham, employing six hands, making 8000 planes, selling for $6000. The 1860 census listed him as a planemaker and as part of **L. DeForest & Co.** **B & B1 ***; **A ****

L. DeFOREST & CO.
L. DeForest & Co. was a Birmingham (Darby), CT, plane making firm consisting of **Linson DeForest** and **Charles H. DeForest** (b. 1822 in CT). **Charles DeForest** appears in the 1860 census as a planemaker with the same age and birth location as **Linson DeForest**, possibly his twin. The firm's 1860 price list offered what must be the most extravagant plow plane ever commercially proposed: "**No. 494**, a handled ivory plow plane with solid gold nuts and washers, 22 carats fine, golden tips on arms and golden mounted - $1000."
No imprint is available.

SIMEON DeFOREST
Simeon DeForest was a planemaker in Birmingham (Derby), CT, from 1849-56. This name with the location **BIRMINGHAM** imprint has been reported. **No imprint is available**.

A. DELAND
Alvin Chauncey Deland (b. Jun. 9, 1801 in New Marlborogh, Berkshire Co., MA, d. 1871 in Ellicott, Chautaugua Co., NY), in 1806, moved with his family to Vernon, Oneida, NY. In 1816, he moved to Jamestown, Chautaugua, NY; purchased land in 1827; and was listed in 1850-70, as a farmer. Examples: the imprint with **MAKER** is on a beech double-iron smoother found in western NY.; and a 27" beech joiner with two eagle medallions, the name and location imprints, with a **W. Butcher** iron, ca. 19c. ********

ORIN DELPE'
Orin Delpe' (b. 1825) was listed in the 1850 census for Worthington, MA, as a planemaker. (see **Sem. Dalpe'**)
No imprint has been reported.

I D/ I. DELVE
Example: on a 9 3/8" beech sash ovolo with round chamfers, ca. 1820. **UR**

H. V. DEMING
Herbert Vilender Deming (b. July 3, 1830 in Watertown, NY, d. Oct. 5, 1903 in Port Lambton, Ontario) operated a wool mill in Essex, Ontario, Canada and a lumber business. He worked for the customs service at Windsor Port, next to Detroit, MI, in 1874. He probably marked and sold planes as part of the lumber business. **H. V. Deming** was listed in *Johnson's Detroit City Directory and Advertising Gazetteer of Michigan*, Detroit, 1861 as "**Deming, H. V.** plane maker, 133 Griswold, moving to Canada". Example: on a 9 1/2" beech size **10** hollow, ca. 1860. ****

I. DEMING
Joseph Deming was listed as a cabinetmaker in New Haven, CT ca. 1800. Example: on a 11 1/4" beech washboard or multiple reeding plane with flat chamfers, possibly PA, ca. 1800. **UR**

W. J. DEMOTT
W. J. Demott was a New York City hardware dealer. Examples: on a compass plane; and on a rabbet made by E. Danberry/ N. Brunswick N. J. (see **Demott & Devoys**) *****

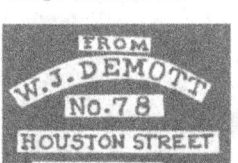

DEMOTT & DEVOYS
Demott & Devoys was a New York City hardware firm. This imprint is from several **Andruss** planes and a **J. W. Farr** plane (see **W. J. Demott**). ****

D. DEMPSY
Example: on a 9 1/4" beech round with heavy flat chamfers, ca. 1800. **UR**

A. DENEHOWER
Examples: on two 10 1/2" wedge locked plow plane with a riveted skate; and a 12 3/8" badger plane with a centered tote and single iron, all beech with heavy flat chamfers. One plow found in Lehigh Co. PA, believed to be from rural Eastern PA, ca. 1800-10. ****

C. DENISE
Example: on a 9 3/8" beech molder with size **3/8** on the heel and flat chamfers, ca. 1810. **UR**

D. DENISON
Daniel Denison, 2nd. (b. July 20, 1740 in Stonington, New London Co., CT, d. Mar. 17, 1818 in Norwich, Chenango Co., NY) a descendant of Capt. **George Denison**, a founder of Stonington, as are the **Denisons** of Saybrook/ Winthrop, CT. **John Wheeler Geer**, a New London, CT, cabinetmaker, was apprenticed to **Daniel Denison** until 1770. **Daniel Denison** was not only **Geer**'s master, but on May 28, 1771, he married **Geer**'s sister, **Martha Geer. Daniel Denison**'s sister, **Sarah Denison**, married **John Wheeler Geer** and his brother, **Elijah Denison**, married **John Wheeler Geer**'s other sister, **Mary Geer. Daniel Denison, Jr.** appears in the 1790 Federal census as living in North Stonington, New London Co., CT, where he lived until about 1800, when he moved to Pharsalia, Cheango Co., NY. Examples: all are 10" birch with relieved wedges, flat chamfers and flutes, ca. 1780. **A & B** ****

G. W. DENISON/ G. W. DENISON & CO.
A plane making partnership in Winthrop, CT, active from 1868-84, that consisted of **Gilbert Wright Denison** (b. 1835, d. 1897), **Gideon K. Hull** (b. 1828, d. 1900) and **Jedediah Harris** (b Feb. 6, 1838, d. Aug. 2, 1873). **Gilbert Wright Denison** was the son of **Elihu Wright** of Westbrook, CT, and was adopted in 1864, as son and legal heir of **Lester E. Denison**. In 1865, **Gilbert** married **Lester**'s niece **Sarah A. Denison**. **Gideon K. Hull** married **Eliza Denison Harris**, another niece of **Lester Denison**. In 1859, **Gideon** was listed as a "plane maker" with residence next to **John Denison. Jedediah Harris** was the nephew of **Lester Denison** and **John Denison**. There were no loose ends in this partnership, all were related by blood and or marriage. By a stroke of good fortune, the **G. W. Denison** account book from Mar. 1870-June 1884 is in the possession of the Deep River Historical Society and gives an intimate view of the core years of this partnership. Individual orders, payments received and wages paid were logged. The majority of planes sold were to hardware companies, though some were sold to planemakers, **John Gladding, P. A. Gladwin** and **Bodman & Hussey**. Plane irons were purchased from **Globe Mfg., Humphreysville Mfg.** and **Middletown Tool**. Beech was purchased from **H. L. Narramore,** a planemaker in Goshen and Cummington, MA. **Lester E. Denison** died in 1866 and left half of his estate to his son **Henry L. Denison** (who was employed by **G. W. Denison & Co.**) and the other half including the turning shop to his adopted son **Gilbert Wright Denison**. In 1868, **Gilbert** sold one third interest in the shop and land to **Gideon K. Hull** and **Jedediah Harris** for $750 each, thus forming **G. W. Denison & Co.**. In 1870, the firm grossed $8200 and employed between five and seven men, in addition to partners. The three partners took a profit of $300 each that year, plus their wages of 27 1/2 cents per hour. Prior to **Jedediah Harris**'s death in 1873, **Gilbert** and **Gideon** bought out **Jedediah**'s 1/3 interest for $1,600. In 1882, **Gilbert** deeded his shop to **Henry L. Denison** for which **Henry** received rent until 1884. By 1884, there were two employees in addition to the two partners, and sales were $2,000. **Henry**'s son **Lewis L. Denison** (b. Nov. 28, 1867) also worked

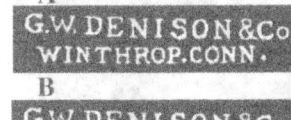

for the company from 1881-84. **Edgar W. Arnold** mostly manufactured the brass stops and plates for the fancy plows and other jointer planes.
A: FF; B, B1, C & D **

J. DENISON/ JOHN DENISON

John Denison (b. 1799, d. Aug. 25, 1876 in Winthrop, CT) was in business for himself at "**Denison's Tool Manufactory**," in the rear of his home in Saybrook, CT. from 1840-76. **John Denison** and his brother, **Lester Denison** earlier were partners in **J. & L. Denison** located on Cedar Swamp Rd. north of town. **John Denison** was listed in the 1850 census as a toolmaker with five employees, producing 1750 planes a year worth $3300.

In the 1860 census, the company claimed eight employees producing 12,000 planes worth $6000. Most of his planes carry only the name, without the **SAYBROOK**. It may be that the **SAYBROOK** location stamp ended up with the **Bulkleys** (see **C. & S. Bulkley**) and that most of the company overlap occurred early when the **JOHN DENISON** imprint was used. One example with **E. P. NUTTING/ SOUTH AMHERST/ MASS.**   D & E: FF; A, B & B1 *; C **

J. L. DENISON/ J. & L. DENISON

A partnership of **John Denison** and his brother **Lester E. Denison**, active from 1832-40. In 1836 **Jeremiah Gladding** became a 1/3 partner. After 1840 the original turning shop continued to produce planes by **Charles F. Buckley** and **Samuel S. Buckley.** (see **C. & S. Buckley**). **John Denison** continued to produce planes at the Winthrop four corners location from 1840-76. **Lester E. Denison** operated a turning shop on the main street west of the Winthrop center and produced an assortment of wood products including ship bungs, plane wedges, wood turnings and plane parts. The A imprint is the earliest and is typically double struck. The A wedge has an elongated finial. Examples: the A imprint is typically double struck; and on a beech smoother with the date **1847**. Another plane has been reported with the date **1842**.
B & B1 **; A & C *****

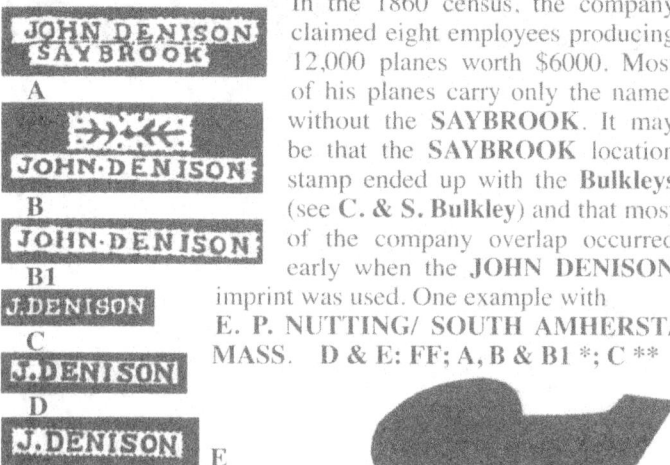

L. E. DENISON

Lester E. Denison (b. 1801, d. Oct. 6, 1866 in Winthrop, CT) was a partner with his brother **John Denison** as **J. & L. Denison** from 1832-40. He operated a turning shop on Main Street west of the Winthrop Center, as **L. E. Denison & Co.**, from 1840-66. In 1864, **Lester** adopted, as his son, **Gilbert W. Denison**, who in 1866 inherited the turning shop, that became the site of **G. W. Denison & Co. Lester's** estate included 3 lathes, 19 circular saws, 2 joiners, 2 jack planes, 6 smoothing planes and 25 molding planes, likely working tools. In addition, there was 124 "plough" (finished), 12 bodies, 17 plates, 12 handles, 27 stops and 40 fences. Lumber listed included beech, boxwood and rosewood. Example: on a 9 1/2"x 1 1/4" beech skew rabbet with **PATENT**. On Oct. 8, 1838, **L. E. Denison** of Saybrook, CT. was listed for Patent No. 001283; and No. 000972, on Aug. 12, 1839; both for corn shellers. He also held a Patent No 001835, on Oct. 22, 1840, for a burglar alarm; and possibly a patent on a reamer frame, but there is no record of a plane patent.   *****

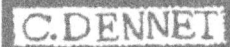

C. DENNET

Examples: on two slide-arm Yankee plows with wood depth stop and thumbscrews; and a 9 7/16" molding plane with lignum vitae boxing, all beech with flat chamfers, ca. 1800.   **UR**

DENNING & CAMBELL

Denning & Cambell were Chilicothe, OH, hardware dealers, active from 1843-56. ****

Wm. DENNIS

Possibly **William Dennis** of Newport, RI, who was listed in his will of 1826, as a cabinetmaker. Example: on a 7" birch toothing plane with a beveled wedge and round chamfers, ca. 1820.   **UR**

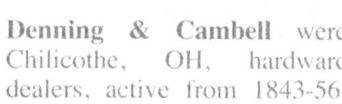

C. H. DENNISON

Charles H. Dennison (b. 1835) of Freeport, ME, was listed as a joiner in the 1860 census; and as a carpenter in the 1895 & 1901 Maine register, possibly a separate generations. Example: on a 9 1/2" beech spar plane with round chamfers, ca. 1850.   ****

I. DENNISON

Example: on a 9 9/16" cherry nosing plane with heavy flat chamfers and an **I. Sleeper** style beech wedge and an incuse owner imprint of **J. E. Dennison**. The **J. Dennison** imprint was found as an owner imprint on two **I. Sleeper** planes, probably from the Newburryport, MA area, ca. 1800.   **UR**

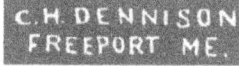

DENT & MULVANE
Dent & Mulvane were hardware dealers in New Comerstown, OH. Example: on a label on a joiner with style number **136** on the toe, ca. 19c. ****

```
        DENT & MULVANE,
          DEALERS IN
           HARDWARE,
          SASH, DOORS,
    GLASS, TABLE & POCKET CUTLERY.
     COR. OF SO. CANAL & BRIDGE STS.
         NEW COMERSTOWN, O.
```

DERBY PLANE CO. (see Birmingham Plane Co.)

R. DERBY
Example: on a slide-arm plow with wood thumbscrews and a wood & steel depth stop, ca. 1840. **UR**

G. DERCK
Examples: on a 13 5/8" wedge-lock match tongue plane with a diamond shaped wood start and an open tote; on a 9 1/4"x 1/4" single-boxed bead; and a size **1/8** round, all beech with heavy flat chamfers, found in the Mahontongo Valley, PA, ca. 1800. **UR**

D. DERR
Example: on a 7 3/8" beech round with the date **1851** and with shallow round chamfers. **UR**

DERRICKSON & FULLER
Derrickson & Fuller probably was a hardware dealer. Examples: on a **Ohio Tool Co.** style **116** skew rabbet, a pair of style **123** side rabbets, and several style **62** reverse ogees. ***

S. DESCHAUER
Stephen Deschauer was a Chicago, IL, hardware dealer, active from 1865-1907. He worked as a tinsmith from 1859-63. ***

E+ DETER
Example: on a 10" beech boxed side bead with round chamfers. An imprint of **J. Stam** of Lancaster, PA, has been reported on an E+Deter plane, ca. 1800. ****

M. DETER
Melchior Deter (Deeter) is one of the early Philadelphia, PA, planemakers who appeared in the city directories of 1797-1800 as a planemaker, but who may have worked earlier and as late as 1803. Examples: The A imprint is on a crown molder with an offset tote; and 9 3/4" molding planes. The B imprint is on a 9 7/8" narrow side bead, all beech with flat chamfers. **A ***; B *******

DE VALCOURT
Charles De Valcourt made planes at 107 Elm, New York City, from 1827-36. Imprinted on the heel was **SOLD/ 518/ GRAND ST**. Subsequently **De Valcourt** became a grocer. Examples: the A imprint is on a 9 1/4" size **2** round; and a size **12** hollow.

A, B, B1 & C **; D, D1 & E ***

DE VALCOURT & MORGAN
De Valcourt & Morgan were probably hardware dealers. Example: on a 9 5/16" size **14** hollow made by **E. Baldwin/ Warranted**. ****

W. DEW
Example: on a 9 1/2" beech skew rabbet with 19c. chamfers. **UR**

J. DEWALT
Examples: on a 10" hollow; a 9 3/8" hickory small round; and a 9 3/8" beech complex molder, all with flat chamfers. An owner mark **O: J. GEESAMAN** was reported on two of the examples, possibly from Reading area in Berks Co. PA. Sometimes the family would refer to **Old John Dewalt** or **Young John Dewalt** instead of Junior or Senior, ca. 1800. **UR**

DEWEES

Example: on a witchet that appears to be factory made and was found near Harrisburg, PA. **UR**

I. DEWEY

Example: on an 8 3/16" tiger beech molder with flat chamfers, ca. 1750-70. **UR**

JOHN. DEWEY.

Probably **John Dewey** (b. 1747, d. Jan. 17, 1807 in Suffield, CT), a cabinetmaker in Suffield. His account book is at the Kent Memorial Library, Suffield. Examples: on a 9 1/2" square rabbet; and a 9 3/8" molder, both beech with flat chamfers, one found in VT, ca. 1800. **UR**

DEWEY & BROWN

Henry S. Dewey and **Brown**, who also advertised as **Brown and Dewey**, from Bellows Falls, VT, advertised in 1856 as manufacturers of "bench tools, pianos and seraphine legs." Later **Henry** became part of **H. S. Dewey/ L. W. Newton**. ****

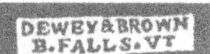

H. S. DEWEY/ L. W. NEWTON

Henry S. Dewey and **Levi W. Newton** were listed as planemakers in Bethel, VT, in 1857. **Henry S. Dewey** was issued Patent No. 16954, on Mar. 31, 1857, which was assigned to **H. S. Dewey** and **L. W. Newton**. The patent was for a machine for cutting the throats of carpenters' plane stocks and was apparently used in the several examples of their bench planes. ****

P: DEWIT

Example: on a 12 3/4" beech panel raiser with depth stop, single round top **Newbould** iron and flat chamfers, ca.1800-10. **UR**

J. A. DEXTER

Example: on a 9 1/2" fruitwood square rabbet with relieved wedge and tight small round chamfers, ca. 1805-15. **UR**

H. DIAMOND

Example: on a 9 1/8" beech complex molder with round chamfers, ca. 1820. **UR**

DIAMOND EDGE - see Shapleigh & Co.

WILLIAM DICKENSON/ DICKINSON

William Dickenson (b. 1817 in Worthington, MA) was listed as a planemaker in Worthington, MA, in 1850. In 1855, he was listed as a mechanic. **No imprint has been reported**.

DICKERMAN

Example: on a 7 1/2" coffin smoother. **UR**

D: DICKINSON

Example: on a 9 7/16"x 1 1/2" beech round with flat chamfers, found in Lehigh Co., PA. **UR**

E. P. DICKINSON

Edward P. Dickinson (b. 1848) was an Amherst, MA, planemaker, active from 1869-85. In 1870, he was listed as a machinist in Amherst, MA. In 1879, **Edward** took over his father's hammer, fork and edge tool manufacturing shop and smithy. ****

H. DICKINSON

Example: on a 7 7/8" beech rabbet with flat chamfers, found in Bucks Co., PA, ca. early 19c. **UR**

SAMUEL DICKSON

A Mar. 16, 1796, newspaper advertisement refers to **Samuel Dickson** (also possibly **Dixon**) as a cabinetmaker and planemaker residing in Frederick Town, MD, formerly of Wilmington, DE. His working period was from 1772-96. **No imprint has been reported**.

T. DICKSON

Example: on an 9 3/8" beech complex molder with heavy round chamfers. The plane is double-bladed and wedged, one in front of the other, both discarding to the right. The imprint is struck twice on the toe, possibly from rural PA, ca. 1810-20. **A & B UR**

J. DIEFFENBACHER

Example: on an 8 7/8" birch rabbet with small round chamfers, ca. 19c. **UR**

D= DIF

Example: on a 9 3/8" beech re-worked molder with flat chamfers, found on the Eastern Shore, MD, ca. early 19c. **UR**

M. P. DILL
Example: on a 10" beech skew rabbet with round chamfers, possibly from rural PA, ca. 1820. **UR**

P. DILL
Example: on a 13 1/2" beech moving fillester found in PA. Possibly from two generations, ca. 19c. **A & B: UR**

A (embossed)
B (incuse)

DILLWORTH BRANSON & CO.
Probably a Philadelphia, PA, hardware dealer. **Dillworth** may prove to be a first name rather than a second person. Examples: on **Conway Tool Co.** planes and a size **5/8** bead with **No. 123**, a **H. Chapin** inventory number, ca. 19c. ***

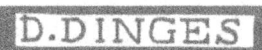

D. DINGES
Example: on a beech 1" wide rabbet plane, marked on the toe and heel, found in central PA. **UR**

H. DISSTON & SONS
Henry Disston & Sons was a well known Philadelphia, PA, sawmaker, from 1865-71, who apparently also handled other tools including wooden planes. Example: on a **Sandusky Tool Co.** triple-boxed reeding plane. **UR**

D DITLO
Example: on a 10 1/2" beech side bead with a **Newbould** iron, and heavy flat chamfers, possibly from PA, ca. 1800. **UR**

J. DIX
Examples: on a 9 3/4" hollow; and a 9 5/16" thumb plane, both birch with narrow flat chamfers, possibly from New England, ca. 1800. **UR**

C. W. DIXON
C. W. Dixon with the imprint **MAKER**. Examples: on a bench plane; an 8" smoother; and an 8 3/4" square miter plane, ca. 1850. **UR**

W. DIXON.
W. Dixon was a planemaker from Roxbury, MA. Example: on a single 21 5/8" razee rosewood bench plane with a closed beech handle, ca. 19c. **UR**

DOBS
Example: on a 9 1/2" beech complex molder with round chamfers, ca. 1820. **UR**

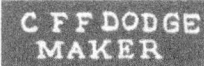

M. DODD
Example: on a 15 1/4" beech panel raiser with open beech centered tote and shallow round chamfers, ca. 19c. **UR**

C. F. F. DODGE
Example: on a 6" birdseye maple "T" coachmaker's rabbet with an iron sole and rosewood spacer, ca. 19c. ****

H. T. DODGE
Example: on a 9 3/16" skew rabbet, ca. 19c. **UR**

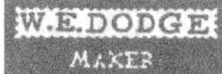

J. B. DODGE
J. B. Dodge with the imprint **MAKER**. Examples: on a short beech compass coffin smoother; and a ebony double pistol router, possibly from north coastal New England, ca. 19c. ****

W. E. DODGE
W. E. Dodge with the imprint **MAKER**. Example: on a 7" compass smoother, ca. 19c. ****

DODGE & WATRONS
Dodge & Watrons, with the location of **WAUKENGAN, ILL.**, was a hardware dealer. Example: on a size **18** round and with **180** on heel, the invoice number of **Auburn Tool Co.**, ca. 19c. ****

I+ DODS
Example: on a 10 5/8" fruitwood bead with heavy flat chamfers and small flutes, ca. 1780-90. **UR**

I. DOGGET
Believed to be Isaac Doggett (b. Jan. 11, 1758 in Dedham, MA, d. 1807), brother of **Samuel Doggett, Jr.** and son of **Samuel Doggett** (1727-94). Examples: on a 9 7/8" beech tongue with birch wedge and round chamfers, ca. 1780. *****

S: DOGGETT/ S DOGGETT/ DEDHAM
Believed to be **Samuel Doggett** (b. May 30, 1727 in Marshfield, MA, d. Mar. 6, 1794 in Dedham, MA) and/ or his son, **Samuel Doggett, Jr.** (b. Oct. 5, 1751 in Dedham, d. Nov. 19, 1831)

of Dedham, MA. **Samuel Doggett, Sr.** was a millwright in Dorchester as a young man before moving to Dedham in 1749, where he was a housewright, a toolmaker, and almost certainly a planemaker. Planes were made as early as 1747, and his estate inventory included, among many tools and supplies, a "Box of unfinished Tools and 37 pieces of Tool stuff." **Samuel Doggett, Jr.** was both a millwright, a housewright and also a planemaker. He served in the Dedham company of minutemen at Lexington & Concord, MA, in Apr. 1775. In 1818, he received a pension for his service. **Samuel Doggett, Jr.** was listed in 1818 as forming **John Doggett & Co.** at 28 Market St., Boston, with **Samuel S. Williams**. Examples: the A imprint is on planes that range in length from 9 3/8"-10 1/4", birch with heavy flat chamfers; and on a crown molder with a "mouse ear" tote are probably the earliest and precede his move to Dedham. The B imprint is probably the later, on planes with round chamfers. At least one B imprint is on a 10 1/4" birch small bead with flat chamfers and flutes, ca. 1775-1820. **B** ** **A** ****

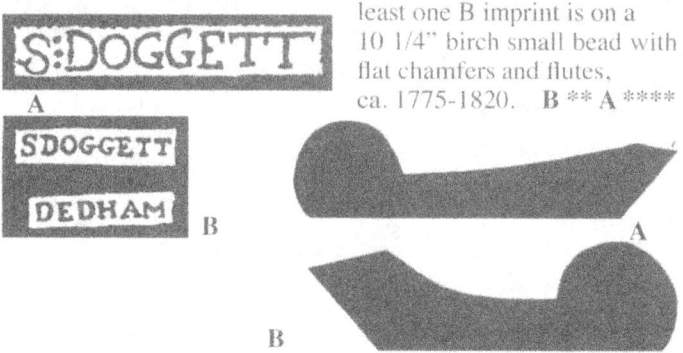

S + DOGGETT: IN/ MIDDLEBORO

Simeon Doggett (b. Jan. 4, 1738 in Marshfield, MA, d. May 6, 1823, in Middleboro, MA) was the son of **Thomas Doggett Jr.** (1706-88). **Simeon** moved as a child, age 4, to Middleboro with his family, where he spent his working years. He served at Crown Point in 1758 during the French & Indian Wars. On Feb. 28, 1760, **Simeon** married **Abagail Pratt** (1734-1813) in Middleboro, the daughter of a blacksmith. He was a constable and tax collector for Middleboro from 1771-73 and was listed as a joiner. **Simeon** was a Anglican and a loyalist during the American Revolution. His trials began soon after the battle at Lexington in, April 1775. Because he refused to take up arms against the British, **Simeon Doggett** was confined to his farm for over a year, from Jul. 1775 to Dec. 1776. He was forced to pay a ten pound fine for refusing to serve in the army. In Jun. 1777, **Simeon Doggett** stood trial for his beliefs. Found guilty, he was delivered to Boston for banishment. After eight weeks on board a prison ship, he was allowed to return home. An angry mob drove him out of Middleborough. **Simeon Doggett** wandered for more than a year, returning to his farm in early 1779. After the end of hostilities, **Simeon** regained his standing in the community. In 1796, he was on a committee to build the Town Hall. **Simeon Doggett** had five known indentured apprentices: **John Cobb** (1745-1822), on Mar. 29, 1762, for shop joiner; **Joseph Churchill** (1748-1824), on Oct. 31, 1765; **Moses Samson** (1751-81), on Dec. 12, 1769; **Jeremiah Samson** (1755-1830), on Apr. 16, 1772; and **Nathaniel Morton** (1769), on Jun. 20, 1783. Other possible apprentices were: **Ephraim Peirce** and **Walter Rickard**. Journeyman in **Simeon Doggett's** employment where: **John Allen, Jacob Miller, Caleb Norton** and **Jabel Soule**. **Simeon Doggett's** account book is in the Connecticut Historical Society. Examples: on a panel raiser; and a molder with a flat back wedge finial. Both of birch with flat chamfers, ca. 1770. *****

C. S. DOLE

Examples: on a moving filletster; and a 9 3/4" small round, both beech with shallow round chamfers. The round also has the incuse imprint **C. M. DOLE**, ca. 1830. **A & B: UR**

A (embossed), B (incuse)

E. DOLE

Two possible candidates: **Ebenezer Dole** (b. 1756, d. 1827) who worked as a cabinetmaker in Newburyport, MA, ca. 1809; and **Enoch Dole** (b. Mar. 21, 1756 in Essex Co., MA, d. May 29, 1827 in Newbury, MA) who was a cabinetmaker in Newbury. Examples: all 10 1/4" beech molding planes with wide flat chamfers and an **I. Sleeper** style wedge, ca. 1790. ****

L. DOLE

Example: on a 10 1/4" beech molder with an **I. Sleeper** style wedge, ca. 1790, Newburyport, MA. **No imprint is available**.

AUGUST DOLL

August Doll (b. 1849 in Germany, d. 1889 in Lena, IL) received Patent No. 334,943, on Jan. 26, 1886, for a wood bench plane with a cast iron throat insert. Example: on a 15 1/4"x 2 3/4" beech double-iron jack plane. (see *Patented Transitional & Metallic Planes in America 1827-1927*, p. 133, by Roger K. Smith) **No imprint has been reported**.

C+ DOLL

Examples: on a 10" complex molder; and a 10 1/4" thumbnail with interrupted boxing, both beech with flat chamfers, ca. 1790, possibly from rural PA. **UR**

W. F. DOMINICK/ W. F. DOMINICK & CO.

W. F. Dominick & Co. probably was a hardware dealer. He used his name only, from 1845-51 and added the **& CO.** from 1852-57. **A & B** ***

F D/ N D/ DOMINY

Planes were made by four generations of the **Dominy** family: **Nathaniel Dominy III** (b. Dec. 3, 1714, d. Mar. 30, 1778); **Nathaniel Dominy IV** (b. July 25, 1737, d. Oct. 23, 1812); **Nathaniel Dominy V** (b. Jan. 16, 1770, d. May 28, 1852); and **Felix Dominy** (b. Feb. 12, 1800, d. Dec. 20, 1868) were furniture and clockmakers of East Hampton, Long Island, NY. Many of the planes are dated, mostly from 1750-1815 and were made primarily for their own use. A number of the planes are in the Henry Francis du Pont Winterthur Museum as part of the restored **Dominy** workshop, and are described by Charles F. Hummel in his study of this family, *With Hammer in Hand*. There is an entry in the account book of **Nathaniel Dominy IV** listing "two plane stocks, finishing, May 1, 1786, 5 shilling 6 pence for **Nathan Conkling, Jr.**" Examples: on a smoother with the inscription in ink on the top, in front of the throat,

NATHANIEL DOMINY
Ye 3d JOYNER DECEMBER
Ye 25th AD 1763   (*****)

The A imprint is on a birch joiner's square. The B imprint, with the full name **Nathaniel Dominy**, is on a 33 1/2" beech jointer or try plane with a closed tote and is dated **1766**. The B, C incuse **ND**, and D embossed **ND** imprints are attributed to **Nathaniel Dominy IV** (1737-1812). The E embossed **DOMINY** imprint is attributed to **Nathaniel Dominy V** (1770-1852). The F incuse **FD** imprint is attributed to **Felix Dominy** (1800-68). The C, E and F dies are in the collection at the Henry Francis du Pont Winterthur Museum.
A, B, C, D, E and F *****

J. DONALDSON

James F. Donaldson was a planemaker in many partnerships: **Carter, Donaldson & Fugate** in 1831; **Donaldson/ L. R. Carter** from 1832-34; with **John H. Hall** in both Cincinnati and Troy from 1834-36; again with **Fugate**, ca. 1840; and again with **John H. Hall**, in St. Louis, MO, from 1842-54. All the imprints consist of individual name stamps and it is possible that they were working as individuals through most of the 1830's and interchanged stock as demand required. The E imprint has the **J. DONALDSON** with an **S. E. Farrand** imprint appearing on a 9 1/2" beech very complex molder. A, A1 & D *; B, C & F ***; E ****

J. DONALDSON/ L.R. CARTER

A partnership of **James F. Donaldson** and **Lewis R. Carter** located in Cincinnati, OH, from 1832-1834. Examples are possibly variants of the Cincinnati, OH, plane making partnership that sometimes appears as **Carter, Donaldson & Co.** (see **Carter, Donaldson & Fugate**)
A & A1 ***

J. DONALDSON/ J. CREAGH/ J. HALL

Examples appear with this name stamp combination and with a CINT. OHIO location imprint. It is believed that **J. Donaldson/ J. Hall** were plane making partners between 1834-36. **J. Creagh** purchased their plane stock before **Donaldson** went to Troy, OH.   ****

J. DONALDSON & T. FUGATE

A partnership of **James F. Donaldson** and **Thomas Fugate** in Cincinnati, OH, that was active in 1840.   ***

J. DONALDSON/ J. HALL

A partnership between **James F. Donaldson** and **John H. Hall** a plane making firm and hardware dealers. They were located in Cincinnati and Troy, OH, from 1834-36 and in St. Louis, MO, from 1842-54, although plane making may have ceased by 1847. (see **Hall & Lyon**; and **J. Donaldson/ J. Creagh/ J. H. Hall**)
A, C & D **; B & B1 ***

C. DONAT

Charles Donat (b. ca. 1809, d. July 3, 1842 in Poughkeepsie, NY) was a Poughkeepsie, NY, planemaker from 1830-42. Examples: on an 8" smoother;

and a nosing plane, both beech. **A & A1** ***

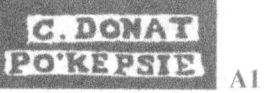 

T. DONOHO
Thomas Donahue was listed as a planemaker in the 1844-48 Philadelphia directories. He was working for **Israel White** and/or **Israel's widow Charlotte White**, from 1844-58, where he specialized in side beads. His incuse initials **T.D.** appear on a number of the **White** imprints. He worked for himself from 1846-54. **

O. DONOVAN
Example: on a 9 1/2" beech bead plane with heavy round chamfers, ca. early 19c. **UR**

JAMES DOOLETTLE
James Doolettle (b. 1833 in CT) was listed in the 1850 census as a plane maker in Wallingford, CT, living with **Joel Fenn**. **No imprint has been reported**.

J. DOREMUS
J. Doremus was the maker of regular and coach planes in Newark, NJ. Example: on a 9 3/8" beech tongue plane, ca. 1830. *****

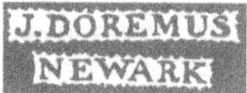

WILLIAM GEORGE DORRINGTON
William George Dorrington (b. 1762 in England) arrived in Philadelphia, PA, in 1773 and was apprenticed on Jan. 20, 1773, to **Robert Parrish**, a planemaker from Philadelphia, PA, for 8 years, 9 months and 7 days. He returned to England and was married, on October 9, 1783, at age 21, to **Sarah Porter** in Portsea, England. **No imprint has been reported.**

S. A. DORRISON
S. A. Dorrison was a hardware dealer in Clinton, MA. Example: on a toted tongue plane made by **A. Fish/Lowell**. ****

J. V. D/ J. V. DORROTY
Example: on a beech slide-arm plow with wood depth stop wood thumbscrews and heavy round chamfers, ca. 1820. **UR**

MARTEN DOSCHER
Marten Doscher (b. Oct. 28, 1852 in New York City) was a New York City hardware and tool dealer, active from 1879-94. **Marten Doscher** advertised in an 1887 issue of *Iron Age* listing himself as a commission hardware dealer at 88 Chambers St., New York, and offering:"**G. W. Bradley's** Edge Tools, Axes, Coopers' Tools, Cleavers, Bush Hooks, Draw Knives, Ship-Carpenters' Tools, &c. Also a full stock of Planes, Washita Stone &c." **Marten Doscher** was issued Patent No. 390,574, on Oct. 2, 1888. This patent appears on a 9 7/8" wood bottom smoothing plane with a razee back and an open tote. (see **Doscher Plane & Tool Co.**) In 1910, he was listed in "Real Estate". In 1930, **Marten Doscher** was retired and living at Mt. Vernon, Westchester, NY. The following hardware dealers imprints appear on his planes: **Hammacher Schlemmer & Co., Reed & Auerbacher**, and **Underhill, Clinch & Co.**
A: FF; B *****

DOSCHER PLANE & TOOL CO.
Doscher Plane & Tool CO. was a planemakeing firm in Saugatuck (now part of Westport), CT, active from 1886-1902. The company manufactured planes for **Martin Doscher** as well as for others. **FF**

T. DOTEN
Examples: on a double-boxed complex molder; and a crown molder with a cherry wedge and offset tote, both beech with flat chamfers, found in ME, ca. 1800. **UR**

J. DOTY Jr.
John Doty Jr. from CT moved to Lewistown, NY and worked for **Joseph Flint Saw Co.** in Rochester, NY. He became a Canadian inventor, patented wagon axles and R. R. car axles. He worked in Toronto with 300 employees. Example: on a 9 1/2" beech full round with round chamfers, ca. 1830-40. ****

DOUGLASS
Jeremiah Douglas and **John Douglas** were planemakers in New York City. They were listed in the 1796 directory only, but possibly produced earlier. Examples: on a complex molder with flat chamfers; a double-iron sash plane; and a full-boxed bead which provided the wedge, all 9 1/2" beech with round chamfers, ca. 1800-20. ****

A. DOW
Examples: on a fixed beech sash; and a 9" miter plane of beech with no chamfers, ca. 1810. **UR**

C. H. DOW.
Examples: on two boxwood smoothers, one single-iron and one double-iron, with the added incuse imprint MAKER, ca. 19c. **UR**

D. DOW.
Example: on a 14" beech tongue with a centered tote, and heavy round chamfers, ca. early 19c. **UR**

G. F. DOW
Examples: on a 9 3/4" birch hollow with flat chamfers; and a 10 3/4" beech rabbet with round chamfers and an **I. Sleeper** style wedge. ca. 1790-1820. **No imprint is available.**

I. DOW.
Example: on a 10" beech halving plane with a small stepped shoulder, an **I. Sleeper** style wedge, and flat chamfers.

J. DOW
Believed to be **James Dow** (b. Aug. 3, 1792 in Stoddard, Chester Co., NH, d. Jul. 2, 1876 in Littleton, Grafton Co., NH) a joiner and builder in Littleton, NH, active from 1812-76. He was the father-in-law of **David Page Sanborn** of Littleton, NH, and **Franklin J. Gouch** of Worcester, MA. Example: the A imprint is on a 9 7/16" beech bead with round chamfers. ca. 1820. The C imprint is on a 9 1/2" beech hollow with flat chamfers, ca. 1800-10.
A, B & C ****

W. N. DOW
Example: on an 8" coffin smoother, ca. 19c. **UR**

I. M. DOWELL
Example: on a complex molder. **UR**

G. DOWLING
G. Dowling with the location **EAST HAVEN CT** probably is a hardware dealer. Example: on a 10 1/8" compass hollow made by **W. H. Pond** of New Haven (CT) ***

I. DOWNING
Example: on a 9 5/16" birch molder with beech wedge and round chamfers, ca. 1820. **UR**

SAMUEL DOYEN
Samuel Doyen advertised, in 1867, in the Maine Business Directory as a "Manufacturer of coopers tools" in Bangor, ME, from 1867-75. **Matthew Moriarty** may have apprenticed to **Samuel Doyen** in 1867. **No imprint has been reported**.

M. DRAKE
Example: on a 16" jack plane with an open centered tote and a **W. Butcher** iron; and a smoother, ca. 1840. **UR**

W. DRAKE/ WD
Example on a 9 3/8" beech skew rabbet plane with heavy round chamfers, ca. 1820-30. **UR**

C. C. DRESSER
Caleb Cushman Dresser (b. ca. 1814 in Peru, MA, d. Mar. 25, 1880 in Goshen, MA) was a Goshen, planemaker, from 1854-56. He was one of the founders of the **Union Tool Co.**, which operated from 1852-54 and used both water and steam power in the manufacturing process. The B imprint is from a wide skew rabbet with the date **1856**. A **, B ****

G. W. DREW
Example: on a 9 1/4"x 1 3/4" beech round with a **SWINSCOW & MANUEL** iron, ca. 19c. **UR**

SAMUEL DREW
Example: on a 9" beech complex molder with round chamfers. This imprint was struck twice on the toe, both vertically and horizontally, ca. 1820. **UR**

WILLIAM H. DRIPS
William H. Drips (b. Jan. 14, 1835 in Westmoreland, d. Apr. 17, 1897 in Santa Ana, CA) on Apr. 20, 1861, enlisted as a Private in the Civil War, Co. D, 6th. Regiment, Ohio Infantry. From 1865-76, **Drips** was listed as a carpenter in Cincinnati, OH. **Drips** received a patent for a spill plane, on Aug. 26, 1873. In 1879, He was listed in CA. This imprint **PATD AUG 26, 73** has been reported on a 13 5/8" oak body bench plane with a walnut fence. (see *Patented Transitional & Metallic Planes in America, Vol. II*, p. 74, by Roger K. Smith)
No imprint is available.

SAM'L DRUCE
On Nov. 6, 1778, **Samuel Druce** (b. Aug. 5, 1767 in Wrentham, MA, d. Apr. 3, 1845, age 78, in Wrentham), "a child under 14 years of age," was adopted by **Josiah Blake**, a Wrentham carpenter. The 1810 census lists **Samuel** as a housewright. Examples: on several molding planes 10" birch or fruitwood with flat chamfers & flutes and relieved wedges. One example is also imprinted **I: GEORGE**, probably an owners imprint, ca. 1790. ****

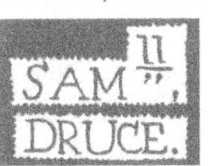

A. DRURY
Example: on a hollow; and a molder, both 9 3/4" with flat chamfers, ca. 1800. **UR**

IER H. DRWMMAND
Example: on a 9 7/8" beech boxed complex molder with a small ogee shoulder and heavy flat chamfers, ca. 1770. **UR**

S. DUBOIS
Example: on a 10 1/4" beech molder with flat chamfers, ca. 1790-1800. **UR**

DUCHARME FLETCHER & CO.
Ducharme Fletcher & Co. was a Detroit, MI, hardware firm, ca. 1855. In 1850-51, **Charles Ducharme** was in business with **Bartholmew** under the name **Ducharme & Bartholmew** hardware firm at 83 Woodward Ave. (see **Buhl, Ducharme & Co.**) Example: on a 16" jack plane. ********

R. DUCKWORTH
Examples: on a 16" gutter plane with an open tote; and a 15 3/4" jack plane with a double-iron, square wedge, centered tote, both beech with heavy round chamfers, ca. 1820-30. **UR**

P. DUDLEY
Example: on a 12" birch gutter plane with heavy flat chamfers and a pegged offset tote, ca. 1800. **UR**

CHRISTOPHER DUFFEY
Christopher Duffey (b. ca. 1810 in Ireland) was listed in the 1850 Federal census as a planemaker, living in New Albany, IN. During the Civil War, he served in the 105th Regiment, IL Infantry, as a Private. In 1866, he was listed in OH; and in 1870 again in New Albany. **No imprint has been reported.**

B. DUFFY
Example: on a 9 1/4" beech square rabbet with shallow round chamfers, ca. 1830-40. **UR**

PHI: DUFING
Examples: on a 9 3/4" large round; and a pair of handled 13 3/4" tongue & groove match planes, all beech with heavy round chamfers, found in Shupp's Grove, PA, ca. 1810-20. **UR**

JOHN DUKE
John Duke (b. 1828 in NY, d. before 1878 in Providence) was listed as a planemaker in Smithfield, Providence Co., RI, in the 1850 census, boarding with and working for **Ezekiel Smith** and listed as a planemaker. From 1857-61, **John Duke** was listed as a carpenter in the Providence directory. In 1878, **Mrs. John Duke widow** was listed. **No imprint has been reported.**

T. DUKE
Tristrim or **Tristran Duke** (d. before 1837 in Philadelphia, PA) was listed as a cabinet maker in the 1830 Philadelphia, PA City Directory. In 1833-35, he was a toolmaker in the 1833-35. On Jan. 10, 1835, in *The Pennsylvanian* Duke advertised "T. DUKE Manufacturer and Importer of all Kinds of Tools and Cabinet Maker's Trimmings." In 1837, **Widow Mary Duke** was listed at 138 s. 2nd., the same address as her Husband's in the earlier directories. In the same directory **William B. Glenn**, was listed as Tools & Hardware at the same address. (See **Glenn & Duke**) Examples: on an applewood screw-arm moving filletster with brass depth stop and boxed edge; a 9 1/2" adj. sash; and a 9 7/16" plow. ********

JAMES DUNAN
James Dunan was listed in the 1845 Philadelphia directory as a planemaker. **No imprint has been reported.**

DUNGAN
Examples: on a 13 3/4" panel raiser with an offset tote and a **Newbould** iron; a joiner with heavily chamfered wedge; a 9 1/2" complex molder with a **Weldon** iron; and a 9 1/2" tongue plane, all beech with heavy flat chamfers. The backwards **N** is different from the British **DUNGAN**, possibly from the mid-Atlantic, ca. 1790-1810. ********

L. DUNHAM
Example: on a 9 1/2"x 1/2" beech round with tight round chamfers. The iron is marked **HILDICK**, ca. early 19c. **UR**

DUNHAM, CARRIGAN & HAYDEN - see Clean Cut

DUNHAM & M'MASTER
S. C. DUNHAM/ T. J. M'MASTER
Samuel C. Dunham and **Truman J. M'Master** were in a partnership that made planes from 1821-25, using convict labor at Auburn State Prison, NY. **M'Master** made planes separately, but **Dunham** is not known to have done so. The A imprint is from a single die.
A ******; B & B1 *******

J. DUNLAP/ JOHN DUNLAP

John Dunlap (b. May 2, 1746 in Chester, Rockingham Co., NH, d. Jan. 12, 1792 Bedford, MA, buried in Billerica. MA) was a joiner/ cabinetmaker of Goffstown, NH, in 1769; and Bedford, NH, in 1777-92. **John Dunlap** was a Major in the American Revolution. A fore plane stock was noted as made and sold in his account book of 1782 (a copy is in the New Hampshire Historical Society). An indenture agreement between **William Huiston**, apprentice, and **Major (John) Dunlap**, dated Mar. 9, 1775, said in part: "...and at the end and expiration of the aforesaid time the aforesaid **John Dunlap** is to dismiss the said William from his service and help him to make the wooden part of a set of tools fit for the trade." Example: on a 13 3/8" beech toted sash plane with the B imprint, round top chamfers and square end chamfers, ca. 1780. **A & B. ******

JONAH DUNLAP

Jonah Dunlap (b. OH, d. 1880 in OH) was listed in the Shaffer's Advertising Directory of Cincinnati, OH of 1839-40 as a "plane-mkr." at **Seybold**'s in Cincinnati in 1839-40. **No imprint has been reported.**

SAMUEL DUNLAP

Samuel Dunlap (b. Feb. 17, 1752 in Chester. Rockingham Co., NH, d. Aug 2, 1830 in West Salisbury, Merrimack Co., NH) was a joiner/ cabinetmaker and the brother of **John Dunlap**. **Samuel Dunlap** was a Lieutenant in the American Revolution. **Samuel Dunlap** worked in Goffstown and Bedford, NH, from 1773-79, probably for his brother; in Henniker, NH, from 1779-97; and in Salisbury, NH, from 1797-1830. His account book (a copy of which is in the New Hampshire Historical Society) lists plane stocks made and sold from 1800-15. He also made washboards, cheese presses, rolling pins and various textile tools. It is reported that he marked his tools with an incuse **S.D. No imprint is available.**

DUNN & SPENCER

Dunn & Spencer was listed in the 1852 directory as a hardware dealer in Petersburg, VA. ********

CHARLES DUPEE

Charles Dupee, Sr., (b. 1734 in Boston, MA, d. Aug. 5, 1802 in Wrentham, MA) became the ward of **Joshua Clapp Jr.** of Walpole, MA, in 1750, at age 16. **Charles** became a housewright and most probably a planemaker, from 1755-65 in Walpole; and then Wrentham, from 1765-82. **Charles, Sr.** ran a tavern in Wrentham where, it is related, Captain Nathan Hale and his Company had breakfast on their way to relieve the siege of Boston, in 1775. **James Dupee, Charles'** oldest son, was awarded power of attorney for **Charles Dupee, Sr.**, in 1782. The earlier imprint A is on a jointer that has an iron imprinted **Dalloway** (Birmingham, England-1770). The later B imprint was probably used by **Charles, Sr.** during the later part of his working period. It may also have been used by **Charles Dupee, Jr.** (b. 1759 in Walpole, d. Feb. 19, 1803), his son. In 1765, **Charles Dunlap, Jr.** moved to Wrentham with his family. On Dec 8, 1776, **Charles Dupee Jr.**, a 17 year old fifer in Capt. Lemuel Kollock's Co., Col. Wheelock's Regiment answered the call to arms and marched from Wrentham to Warwick, RI. In 1777 & 80, he was listed as a Private. Examples: the B imprint is on a 7 3/8" birch compass-bottom smoother with flat chamfers and a carved throat like linen folds; and a 36"x 3 1/8" birch jointer, with the B imprint struck four times on the toe, round top wedge, centered tote, with a beaded edge chamfers and flutes. What makes this jointer special is an inscription engraved in a pewter inlay that reads: *********

> LIBER.
> I AM A GOOD AND WELL MADE PLAIN
> CHARLES DUPEE IS MY MASTERS NAME
> HE IS THE MAN THAT FORMED ME
> HIS FAITHFUL SERVANT I WILL BE
> FEB. 27, 1787

The plane has a large pewter initial C inlay engraved with **CHARLES** and a large pewter initial D inlay engraved with **DUPEE**. The wedge and mouth are both carved like linen folds. The B wedge is from a 10 3/8" birch large astragal with shallow flat chamfers. **A & B ******

J. DURELL.

Example: on a beech veneer slitter gauge plane with an open tote, ca. mid 19c. **UR**

D. DURGIN

Daniel Durgin (b. Mar. 26, 1792 in Durham, NH, d. Jan 13, 1847 Dover, Strafford Co., NH) was a house carpenter and occasional planemaker in Dover, NH, from 1824-47. Example: on a 7 7/8" beech smoother, ca. 1810. ********

J. Y. F. DURGIN

John Y. F. Durgin and location **DOVER, NH** is embossed on a leather inset. In 1843, he was listed as a house carpenter in Dover, NH. Examples: on a slide-arm plow with brass trim on the skate and arm tips; and a 12"x 3/8" birch fenced and

handled rabbet with round chamfers, ca. 1840.   ****

H. DURRIE
H. Durrie was a Fort Wayne, IN, hardware dealer who advertised, in 1855. He operated from 1851-1857. He was not in the 1858-59 directory. The IA was changed to IN, to represent Indiana. Examples: on planes made by the **Greenfield Tool Co.**   ****

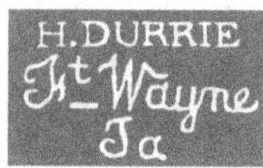

J. C. DURYEA
John C. Duryea (b. 1808 in NYC) operated a hardware store in Brooklyn, NY, from 1836-49. In 1850, he was listed as Manufacturer, and in 1855, as carpenter in NYC. Example: on a **J. J. Bowles/ E. Hartford** side rabbet.   ***

P. DURYEE
Peter Duryee ran a hardware store in New York City, from 1841-67. It became **Peter Duryee & Co.**, in 1867, with **Jacob A. Duryee** and **William H. Cowl** as partners. **No imprint with & Co. is available. A & A1 ***

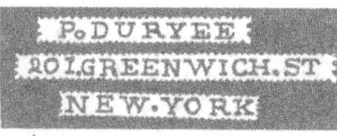
A

A1

DUSTIN
John Dustin (b. Jun. 17, 1785 in Hillsborough, NH, d. Feb. 11, 1844 in Francestown, Hillsborough Co., NH) inventory of estate listed: window sash finished and in preparation, 3 long and short jointers, 4 smoothing planes, plow chisel (plane), and 31 tools for molding, and other joiners tools with lumber in the shop, shed and barn indicating a shop in use at the time of his death, at age 69. Examples: on a match pair of crown molders of beech with flat chamfers and offset totes; a 7 1/2" beech smoother with round chamfers; a 10 1/8" molding plane with heavy flat chamfers; and a 10 3/8" large round with tight round chamfers, ca. 1800-30.   ****

WM. L. DUSTIN
William L. Dustin (b. 1825 in NH, d. Jun. 5, 1886 in Lawrence, MA) was listed in 1844 as a sash & blind maker in Lowell, MA. In 1853, he was a carpenter in Lowell. William L. Dustin was listed in the directories as a planemaker, from 1866-75; and a sashmaker from 1876-83, in Lawrence, MA.   **

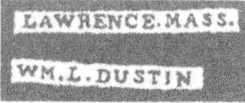

DUTTON
Possibly **Thomas Dutton** a carpenter and joiner working in Watertown, CT from 1795-97. Example: on a 9 3/8" birch cove plane with flat chamfers, ca. 1800.   *****

P D/ P. DUTY
Example: on a 9 7/8" rosewood skew rabbet with round chamfers, ca. 1820-30.   UR

THEODORE DUVAL (see HARTFORD PLANE CO.)

R: DYER
Rufus Dyer was a chairmaker and turner working in Providence, RI, in the 1790's. His account book is held by the RI Historical Society. Examples: on a 9 1/2" beech large round with heavy flat chamfers; a 30 5/8" jointer; a 9" coffin smoother; and a 13 7/8" panel raiser with an offset birch tote, all beech with heavy round chamfers. The jointer and panel raiser have round-top chamfered wedges and offset totes. The smoother also has a round-top chamfered wedge, ca. 1780-1820.   ***

S: DYR
Examples: on a 9 1/2" beech size 15 hollow; a size 13 round; and a gutter plane, all with heavy round chamfers; and as an owner imprint on a lignum-boxed reed & follow made by **I. Schauer**, from PA, ca. 1820.   UR

M. V. E.
Martin Van Buren Edgerton (b. Sep. 10, 1834 in VT, d. Feb. 18, 1930) was listed in 1860, age 26, as a laborer; in 1870, 80 & 1900, as Carpenter; in the 1882-83, Wallington, VT, *Gazetteer* listed **Martin** as a carpenter & joiner. In 1911, he was listed as "repair, job shop". He was also listed, in 1911, as contractor & builder. Example: on a pair of right and left fenced sash coping planes; a side hollow; and a fenced table round, all 9 5/8", birch with 19c chamfers. ****

E. S. MFG CO.
This imprint is similar to the **E. & S. MFG Co.** used by **Emerson & Stevens**, manufacturers of axes, sometime after 1902. They may have also made or marked wooden planes. Example: the B imprint on the toe of a size 4 round made by **Martin Doscher**. A & B: ****

EAGLE
Eagle probably is a brand name. Example: on a 7 3/4" smoothing plane with an **Auburn Tool Co.** double-iron (see **Eagle Tool Co.**), ca. 1850. ****

EAGLE FACTORY – (see N. Chapin & Co.)

EAGLE MNG. CO.
The location imprint of **WMS BURG MASS** (Williamsburg, MA) is identical to that used in the **H. J. James** B imprint, and the **H. Wells** B imprint and one tongue plane has both the **Wells** and **Eagle** marks together. This shared location die hints at a succession of businesses, a shared shop, or perhaps an outlet for second grade tools shared by **Wells** and **James** (see **James Mfg. Co.**), ca. 1850. A ***, B *****

EAGLE TOOL CO.
Examples: on two jack planes, one of which carries the **Auburn Tool Co.** inventory style **No. 13** for a jack and was found in Syracuse, NY. **Eagle Tool Co.** was believed to be used by **Auburn Tool Co.** as a brand name for marketing. (see **Eagle**), ca. 1850. ****

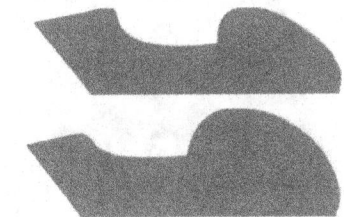

P. EALY
Example: on a 9 1/2" beech tongue plane with a birch wedge and flat chamfers, ca. 1800. UR

A. EARL/ A. R. EARL
Abel R. Earl (b. 1823 in VA, d. Mar. 3, 1894 in St. Louis, MO) was a St. Louis, MO, plane maker and hardware dealer, from 1850-69. He was listed in the 1850 census as a plane maker. In the 1866 city directory, he was listed in hardware & cutlery, retail; in 1867, he was in hardware, tools, etc. In 1870, he was listed as a provision dealer; from 1872-90, he was a physician; in 1893, he was listed as a carpenter.
A & B **, C & D ***

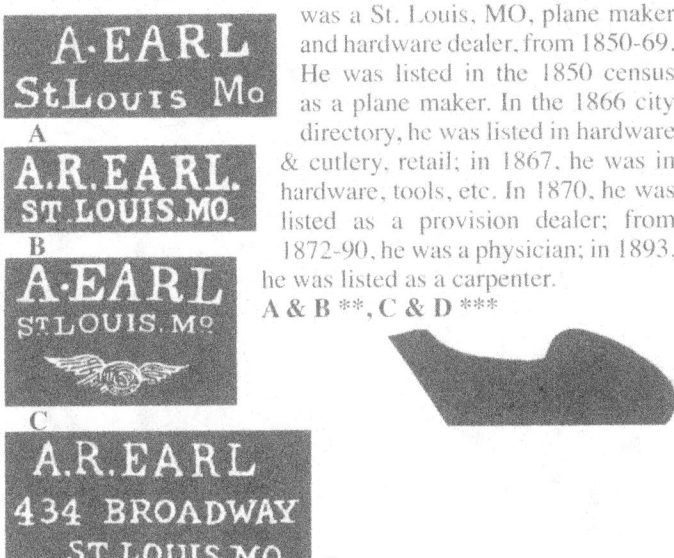

H. EARL
Examples: on an 8 1/2" sash coping plane with a 45 degree pitch and flat chamfers; and a 9 1/2" double-bladed fixed sash with round chamfers, both beech. The A wedge is from the earlier coping plane, the B wedge is from the later sash, ca. 1800-20. UR

I. EARLY
Example: on a 11 1/4" handled, beech, complex molder with heavy round chamfers, ca. early 19c. UR

EASTBURN/ R. EASTBURN
Robert Eastburn (b. Feb. 18, 1774 in Perth Amboy, NJ, d. Oct 21, 1854 in New Brunswick, NJ) was the father of **Joseph Eastburn** and made planes in New Brunswick, NJ, from 1802-26, possibly as early as 1795. He was probably New Jersey's earliest planemaker. In 1802, he advertised that: "...he carries on the plane making business and has on hand an assortment of fashionable molding planes and others of different kinds". During this period, he also operated a hardware and grocery store. An example has been reported on a **Stothert** of Bath, England (1785-1841), with the **EASTBURN** imprint, suggesting that he also marketed English planes. The 1820 census listed **Eastburn** as a planemaker employing two journeymen, **Collins Test** and **Robert Pumpton**. **Eastburn** as well as **Thomas Grant** used the crowned initials of owners. **Eastburn**, **Thomas Grant**, and **T. Napier**, all used the friction-fit arms for plow planes and plank-arm tongue & groove

planes. Some of the earlier **Eastburn** planes have flat chamfers, and the later are rounded, all are typically 9 1/2" and of beech.
A & C *, B ****

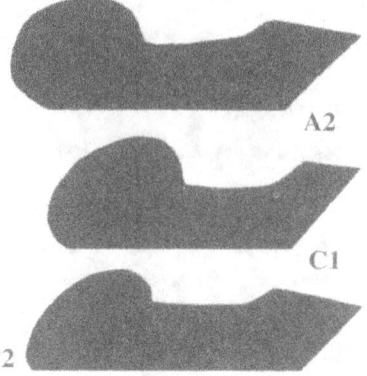

JOSEPH EASTBURN
Joseph Eastburn (b. 1812 in New Brunswick, NJ, d. Dec. 22, 1891 in New Brunswick) was the son of **Robert Eastburn** and appeared in the 1850 census; and the New Brunswick, NJ, city directory of 1868-74, as a planemaker. He was listed in the 1886 directory as a "kindling wood dealer". He probably worked for his father and then for others. **No imprint has been reported**.

D. EASTERBROOKS

D. Easterbrooks was probably a hardware dealer. Example: on a dado plane by **Young & M'Master**. UR

A. EASTERLY
Example: on a 30 1/8" jointer with round chamfers, ca. 1820. UR

EASTERLY & CO.
John M. Easterly (b. 1822 in NY, d. 1895 in Auburn, NY) operated as **J. M. Easterly & Co.** from 1867-68, taking over from the **Auburn Tool Co.**. He had a convict labor contract at Auburn Prison, NY, and made planes there in 1866-67. **Augustus Howland**, traded as **A. Howland & Co.**, succeeded **J. M. Easterly**, from 1869-74. **John M. Easterly** took over the convict labor contract from 1874-77. In 1870 & 80, **John M. Easterly** was listed as a "retired merchant". From 1884-94, **John M. Easterly** was in real state. The **EASTERLY & CO.** imprint was also used on plane irons. Example: on a single-boxed bead marked **No. 105**, the style number used in the 1869 **Auburn Tool Co.** price list, suggesting a continuation or relationship. **A, A1 & B ****

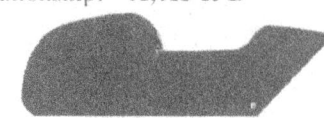

F. P. EASTMAN
Examples: on an 11 7/8" narrow shipbuilder's coffin smoother; a lignum vitae razee fore plane; two handled smoothers, one of lignum vitae; and an ebony-bodied handled plow plane, probably from New England, ca. 1860-70.
A ***, A1 ****

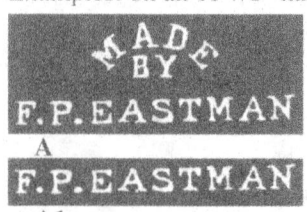

I. EASTMAN
Examples: on a 9 3/8" full-boxed side bead; and a 9 7/16" single-boxed, size **5/8,** side bead, both beech, ca. 1820. UR

S. P. EASTMAN
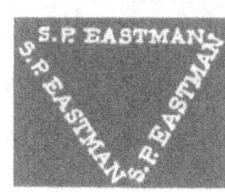
This imprint marked three times in a triangle on a jack plane found in Gardner, ME, ca. 1850. UR

EASTMAN/ T. W. EASTMAN
T. W. Eastman probably is a hardware dealer. The location **ROCK ISLAND** is probably Rock Island, Illinois.
T. W. Eastman was listed in Champaign, IL at 29 1/2 Main St., in 1923. Example: The A imprint is on a yellow birch plow with a riveted skate, a wood depth stop. The B imprint is on a beech thumb-screw locked, adjustable fenced rabbet. Both with round chamfers, ca. 1810-20. **A & B: UR**

EASTON
Example: on a 14" bench gutter plane with an offset tote, single-iron and heavy flat chamfers, ca. late 18c. UR

H. EATON
Example: on a 10" beech groove with riveted skate, snecked iron and flat chamfers, ca. 1800. UR

J. EATON
Examples: on a 9 1/4" molder; and a 9 3/8" complex molder with heavy round chamfers, both birch; and on a birch Yankee plow with **J. Fisher** as the maker and also struck twice by **J. EATON**. The plow was found in a house in Canton, MA, probably from New England, ca. 1780. ********

R. C. EATON
Example: on a 9 1/2" x 1/4" beech cove plane with almost no chamfers. The iron is by **W. M. Greaves & Son**, ca. 19c. UR

EAYRS & CO.

James Eayrs & Co. was probably a partnership of **John Eayrs** and **James Eayrs** of Nashua, NH, who ran a lumber mill, produced fine emery and made planes, ca. 1850. The **Eayrs & Co.** name was also used by **James Eayrs** and family; from 1870-81, as proprietors of the Pennichuck Drug Mill. Many of the planes found are rosewood smoothers, and others have rosewood boxing. **

J: EBERSOLE

Example: on a 9 1/2" round, found in Fredrick, MD, ca. 19c. UR

A. EBY

Example: on a 10" beech wedge locked fenced chamfer plane with flat chamfers, found in south eastern PA, ca. early 19c. UR

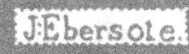

C. EBY

Example: on an applewood plow, found in Lancaster Co., PA. **No imprint is available.**

J. ECKER

Example: on a 14" beech grooving plane with hand forged riveted skate an open tote and heavy flat chamfers, possibly from rural PA, ca. 1790. UR

ECLIPSE TOOL CO.

The **Eclipse Tool Co.** was listed as a tool maker on Courtland St. in New York City, in 1901-02. Example: on a smoothing plane with an iron marked **Auburn Tool Co./ Thistle Brand, Auburn, N.Y.** ****

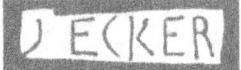

ECONOMY

Location imprint of the Shaker Community at **Old Economy** in Ambridge, Beaver Co., PA. One of three settlements established by the **Harmony Society** (1824-1906). Example: on a 10 1/16" apple bead and cove complex molder with spring, the blade is made from an old file. Two small beads run the length of the plane body, one on each side of the wedge. *****

B. EDDY

Examples: on a 9 9/16" double-boxed molder; and a 7 1/2" coffin smoother, both beech with the **Warranted**; on a 9 1/2" boxed complex molder; and a 9 3/8" astragal, both birch, all examples with shallow round chamfers, ca. 1800. UR

A1

G x EDDY

Examples: on a 9 7/8" beech hollow; and a 9 5/8" cherry Yankee plow with square arms, wood thumbscrews and depth stop and riveted skate, both with flat chamfers. One example has been reported from the Sturbridge Museum collection, possibly from New England, ca. 1790. UR

JAMES A. EDDY

James A. Eddy (b. Dec. 15, 1819 in Providence, RI, d. Jun. 28, 1886 in RI) was listed, in 1838, as working at **Joseph Belcher's** hardware establishment, at 11 Broad St. Providence, RI (see **Belcher Bros.**), presumable as a clerk. In the 1841 Providence directory, he was listed as working in hardware, at 5 Broad St, which was the address of **Battey & Eddy**, hardware and plane dealers from 1841-42. In 1860, he was listed as a laborer; in 1875, as a carpenter; in 1880, working for **Bronzer & Gilder**; in 1885, he was "retired". The planes reported imprints bear a very close resemblance to those of **Isaac S. Battey**. Both men used the same set of number stamps on the heel of the planes. Examples: on a moving fillister; a 9 1/2" beech round; and a 3" wide complex molder. ***

I. EDGAR

Example: on a 9 1/2" beech large round with shallow flat chamfers stopped with a horizontal line and a separate gouge. Branded on the side is an owner's incuse imprint **J. E. UNDERWOOD**, ca. early 19c. UR

EDGERTON

Orrin (Oren) Edgerton came from VT, to Utica, NY, in 1827. He was listed in the Utica directory for 1828-29 as a carpenter and joiner living at 59 Broadway and probably worked for **R. J. Collins,** from 1832-34. He moved to Rome, NY, in 1835 and was a planemaker in Buffalo, NY, from 1836-47. He was a part of **Edgerton, Reed & Co.,** ca. 1850. **Oren Edgerton** served in the Civil War and was listed as an officer in the NY militia, prior to Jan. 1858. A, A1 & B *

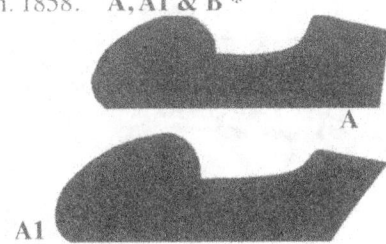

CF. EDGERTON

This name die along with 11 separate incuse number dies have been reported. It is not known what type of work he was engaged in, when or where. UR

H. S. EDGERTON
Example: with the location **GERMAN. N.Y.** and on a R. Carter/ Troy, NY, 1" wide beech skew rabbet. **H. S. Edgerton** is probably a hardware dealer in Germantown on the Hudson River about 55 miles south of Troy, NY. ****

EDGERTON, REED & CO.

Edgerton, Reed & Co. was a hardware dealer in Buffalo, NY. Example: on a sash plane (see **Edgerton**), ca. 1850. ****

A. EDSON
Example: on a 9" beech door plane with flat chamfers, ca. 1800. **UR**

B. EDSON
Believed to be **Bezaliel Edson** (b. 1781 in Enfield, NH), the son of known Shaker planemaker **Hosea Edson**. **Bezaliel Edson** was a member of the Shaker community at Harvard, MA, from Jan. 1792, at age 20, to Sep. 1, 1801, when he went to Marlborough, MA. Examples: on a 9 5/8" skew rabbet; and a 10 1/2" fenced skew rabbet with square-arms, wood thumbscrews and depth stop, both beech with heavy flat chamfers. The chamfers for the fenced rabbet stop on either side of the mortised depth stop, ca. 1800. *****

HOSEA EDSON
Hosea Edson (b. Feb. 4, 1753 in Bridgewater, Plymouth Co. MA, d. Aug. 5, 1829 at Harvard, MA) moved to Brookfield, Worcester Co., MA, before 1774. On Nov. 14, 1774, **Hosea** took the oath as a Minuteman from N. Brookfield and responded to the Lexington Alarm, on April 19, 1775. He was also at the battle of Bunker Hill. He married, moved to Enfield, NH, where he was a Housewright, and had three children, including his only son **Bezaliel Edson**. **Hosea** joined the Harvard Shakers on Mar. 26, 1791, followed by his son and two daughters. He returned to the "World", on Sept. 2, 1802, with tools and a tool chest, his children having already preceded him. In 1820, he was living in Pembroke, MA. **Hosea** returned to the Harvard Shakers prior to his death. Examples: on a 13 1/2" birch cornice plane with an offset pear wood tote, round-top wedge & iron; a 10 1/2" birch complex molder with applied fence and full round top (no chamfers); and a birch Yankee style plow with slide arms, wood thumb screws and depth stop with a full round top, ca. 1791-1802. *****

J. EDWARD
Example: on a 9 3/16" birch skew rabbet found in No. Windham, ME, ca. 1800. **UR**

B: A. EDWARDS
Benjamin Alvord Edwards (b. Jan. 23, 1757 in Hampshire CO., MA, d. 1828 in Northampton, MA), was a chairmaker and joiner in Northampton, working about 1800. **Edwards** and **Simeon Pomeroy** owned land together in Northampton. From Feb.-Dec., 1776, **Benjamin Edwards** served in the Revolutionary War as a Private in Capt. Chapin's Company, Col. Porter's Regiment, MA Line. In 1820, he was in Sodus, Ontario Co., NY, where he filed for his veteran's pension. His planes are birch and have a relieved wedge, ca. 1780. **A & B** ****

D. EDWARDS
Example: on a size **14** round with flat chamfers. **UR**

H. S. EDWARDS & BRO.
H. S. Edwards & Bro. was listed as a hardware dealer from Schenectady, NY, in 1889. Example: on a 9 1/2" beech hollow, ca. 1880. ****

W. EDWARDS
Example: on a 9 7/16"x 1/2" beech center bead with heavy round chamfers, ca. 1820. **UR**

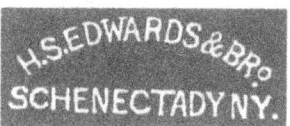

J. EGAN
Example: on a 9 1/2" beech complex molder with round chamfers, ca. 19c. **UR**

H. EHLEN
Herman Ehlen (Ehlan) was a carpenter, joiner and carver in Milwaukee, WI, from 1856-80. Example: on a plane like a cooper's joiner with side by side blades.
No imprint is available.

WM. A. ELA
This imprint has been reported. **UR**

S. ELAGG
Example: on a 9 1/2" beech narrow round. **UR**

ELDER & SON
Henry Lentz Elder (b. Dec. 25, 1819 in Philadelphia, PA, d. Nov. 30, 1897 in Alantic City, NJ) was listed as a merchant and probably hardware dealer in the 1842-53 city directories

 for Philadelphia, PA. Example: on a combination tongue & groove plane made by **A. Howland & Co.** ****

JAMES A. ELDRIDGE
James Alburtus Eldridge (b. ca. 1821 in Hancock, Berkshire Co., MA, d. Dec. 26, 1896 in Hancock, MA) was part of **Allen & Eldridge** of Williamstown, MA, ca. 1850; in 1850, he was a merchant. In the 1860 census, **James Eldridge** was listed as a planemaker in Pittsfield, MA, employing three hands, using water power and 20 hp of steam power to produce 6000 bench planes worth $2400, and other tools worth $1300. In the 1870 census, **James Eldridge** was again listed as a planemaker, but in Adams, MA; in 1880, he was listed as a farmer and surveyor. **No imprint has been reported**.

S. ELDRIDGE
Samuel Eldridge (b. ca. 1827) was listed as a planemaker in the 1850 census for Conway, MA. (see **Allen & Eldridge**)*****

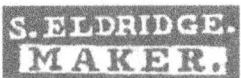 

ELEY & COOK
Eley & Cook was the manufacturer of a bench type fenced 12 1/2" beech complex molder with an open tote. The **PAT. AUG. 6. 67.** was for a carpenter's plane and assigned to **G. D. Spooner** of Rutland, VT and **L. N. Johnson** of Brandon, VT. *****

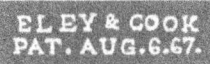

G. & S. ELFREY
George Elfrey (b. 1809 in PA, d. Apr. 27, 1873 in Philadelphia, PA) was listed as a planemaker in Philadelphia, PA, in the 1839-41 directories. He was also listed, as a planemaker, in the 1840 & 50 censuses. The **S** is possibly for **Samuel Elfrey**, who was listed in Philadelphia, in 1820, occupation unknown. ****

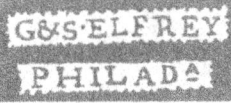

J. ELINE
Example: on a 9 3/8" unboxed sash molder, ca. 1800. **UR**

J. ELIS
Example: on a 9 1/2"x 1 1/2" beech skew rabbet with round top and flat end chamfers, ca. early 19c. **UR**

F. ELKINS RUNYON & BARTLETT
F. Elkins Runyon & Bartlett was probably a hardware dealers, located in Chicago, IL. Example: on a beech handled plow with applewood screw arms and nuts, imprinted **No. 97**, the **Ohio Tool Co.** style number for this type of plane, ca. 1850. **No imprint is available**.

C. ELLIOTT
Example: on a 9 3/8" beech, full boxed small side bead with shallow round chamfers, found in Findley, OH, ca. 1830. **UR**

H. ELLIOTT
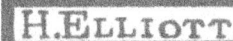 Example: on a 9 3/4" hollow with flat chamfers, ca. 1800. **UR**

J. G. ELLIOTT
Example: on a primitive 9" slide-arm fluting plane with iron screw-stopped arms and flat chamfers on toe and heel only, ca. 1850. **UR**

J. M. ELLIOTT
Example: on an 8" smoother, ca. 1850. **UR**

R. ELLIOTT
Possibly **Robert Elliott** who went into partnership with **William Vance** in Baltimore, in 1807. Examples: A imprint on a 9 1/2" beech very complex single-boxed molder with heavy round chamfers. The B imprint on a 7 3/8" beech plane with a saw blade for a cutter let in on the face of the plane with heavy flat chamfers; and a 5 7/8" beech coffin smoother with **1 1/2** on the heel and flat chamfers, ca. 1800-20. **A & B: UR**

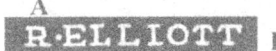

J. M. ELLIS & CO./ ELLIS & THRESHIE
J. M. Ellis & Co. was a partnership consisting of **Joseph M. Ellis** and **Charles Threshie** that was listed as a hardware dealer in the New Orleans, LA, directories, from 1851-56. In 1857, the name was changed to **Ellis & Threshie**. Examples: on a complex molder made by **A. & E. Baldwin** with the A imprint. The B imprint is on an **A. & E. Baldwin** round and an **Arrowmammett Works** size 16 round. **A & B *****

L. ELLIS
Example: on an 8" birch smoother with heavy round chamfers and a **Weldon** iron, ca. 1820. **UR**

M. ELLIS & CO.
M. Ellis & Co. placed an ad, on Sept. 16, 1806, in the *Pittsburgh Gazette*, announcing the opening of his "plain manufactory" at Second St., Pittsburgh, PA. Similar ads were placed in the *Kentucky Gazette and General* of Lexington, KY, on Oct. 9, 1806, and in *The Western Spy and Miami Gazette* of Cincinnati, OH, on Oct. 21, 1806. **No imprint has been reported**.

E. ELMES
Example: on a complex molder; and an 8" beech wedge-lock plow with heavy round chamfers. The depth stop is iron with a round top and held with a wood thumbscrew, ca. 1820. **UR**

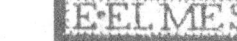

ELSWORTH & DUDLY
Elsworth & Dudly was listed in the Poughkeepsie, NY, directories as a hardware dealer, from 1870-84. Examples: on a

Sargent & Co. bead and a **H. Chapin** rabbet. ****

THO ELTON
Example: on a 10" grooving plane with screw applied fence and flat chamfers. **UR**

WILLIAM EMBODY
William Embody (b. Jul. 11, 1849 in Herkimer Co., NY, d. Apr. 26, 1906 in Aurelius, NY) was listed in the Auburn directory as a plane maker, from 1867-68. From 1875-77, he was listed as foreman of the Tool Shop in Auburn State Prison. After 1877, when **Auburn Tool Co.** left the prison, **William Embody** continued to be listed as a tool maker and plane maker. **No imprint has been reported**.

T. EMERSON
Examples: on an 8" beech smoother with a chamfered wedge and round chamfers, ca. 1820. **UR**

B. N. EMERY
Example: on a 9 1/2" beech gunstock plane with shallow round chamfers, ca. 1840. **UR**

N. EMERY
Possibly **Lt. Nathaniel Emery** (d. 1821) who was a cabinetmaker from the Newbury/ Newburyport area of MA. His estates inventory includes:

            joyner's chisles 0.3.10,
            joyner's plains and irons
                    & other tools 0.13.4
            karving apperril................ 2.15.0.

Examples: on a 9" beech plow with wood thumbscrews and depth stop; a 9 1/4" birch skew rabbet; and a gutter plane, all with an **I. Sleeper** style wedge and flat chamfers. Also on a 9 3/8" birch ovolo with med. flat chamfers and the B wedge, ca. 1800. ****
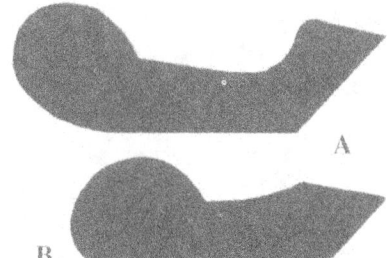

W + EMERY
Example: on a cherry bead with a birch wedge and flat chamfers, ca. 1780, possibly earlier. **UR**

EMERY WATERHOUSE & CO.
Emery Waterhouse & Co. was a hardware dealer in Portland, ME, that began business, ca. 1846, and is still in operation. From 1846-70, the firm's logo read **Emery+Waterhouse**. In 1871, it was changed to **Emery Waterhouse & Co.**; in 1894,

it was changed again to **Emery & Waterhouse Co.** Examples: on a handled match tongue & groove pair made by the **Taber Plane Co.** ***

EMPIRE TOOL CO.
Possibly one of the trade names and imprints used by **Auburn Tool Co.** to conceal its use of prison labor in marketing. In addition an **EMPIRE CO.** plane iron was found in a **Gerard**
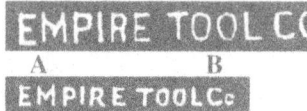
Tool Co. plane. **Gerard Tool Co.** is also believed to be a trade name used by **Auburn Tool Co.**   A & B *

WM. ENDERS
The imprint is believed to have been used on second quality planes and plane irons of the **Keen Kutter** brand of **E. C. Simmons Hardware Co.**, ca. 1905. **William Enders** was a clerk for **A. F. Shapleigh & Co.** in 1871; and became a salesman in 1875. He joined **Simmons Hardware Co. (Keen**

Kutter) as a salesman, in 1887, and eventually became a vice president of the company. The **William Enders Mfg. Co.** of Walden, NY, was still producing saws, as late as 1930. ****

ALBERT ENGLE
Albert Engle was listed in the 1845 Philadelphia directory as a planemaker. **No imprint has been reported**.

J. ENGLISH
Example: on a 12 3/8" beech wedge-lock slide-arm tongue

plane with a birch wedge, hickory fence and round chamfers, ca. 1810. **UR**

ENGLISH & MIX
English & Mix was a New Haven, CT, hardware dealer. Example: on a boxed side bead made

by **I. Hammond**, **J. & L. Denison** and **J. Denison**. ****

J. ENNIS & CO.
J. Ennis & Co. was probably a hardware dealer from
Columbus, OH. **UR**

ENSENORE WORKS
Ensenore Works was a brand of the **Owasco Tool Co.**,
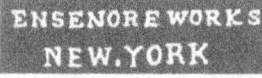
ca. 1875. The Owasco Tool Co. was in turn, a brand name of the **Auburn Tool Co.** The 1875 Russell & Ervin hardware catalog advertised the

Ensenore brand as an **Owasco Tool Co.** product. One example is also imprinted U. S. A. which implies it was made as late as 1893, after the Import Labeling Act of Congress. **A, A1 & A2** *

S. ENSIGN
Possibly **Seba Ensign Jr.** (b. Feb. 10, 1823 in NY, d. Feb. 10, 1886 in Mesopotamia, Trumbull Co., OH) or **Samuel Ensign** (b. 1817 in NY) who were possibly brothers and both listed as joiners & carpenters in Mesopotamia, in the 1850 census. **Seba** was listed, in 1870, in Wilton, Muscatin Co., IA, as a farmer. In 1880, **Seba** was back in Mesopotamia, as a house carpenter. **Samuel** was listed in 1860, as a carpenter in Trumbull, Farmington Co., OH. In 1870, **Samuel** was listed in Stark, Paris Co., OH, as "retired". Example: on an 8" beech smoother. ****

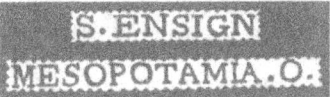

IA. EPPELE
Example: on a 9 1/2" beech molder with heavy flat chamfers, possible from rural PA, ca. 1810. **UR**

W. L. EPPERSON
William L. Epperson was listed as a planemaker in the Louisville, KY, in 1858-59, at Market between Jackson and Hancock; and again as a planemaker, in 1879 & 90. In the intervening years, his listings include carpenter, machinist, cabinetmaker, fishing rod maker and violin maker, he was a true renaissance man. Examples: premium quality plow planes using exotic woods, brass or silver fittings and inlay, and a 9 3/8" beech round with size **1** on the heel.
A & B ****

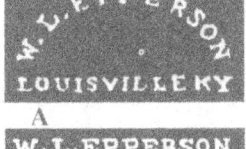

H ERHART
Examples: on a 11 1/2" beech skew ship's rabbet with heavy flat chamfers; a plane-like shave; and a 5 1/2" router with a body like a plane, round chamfers and the B wedge. ca. 1790. **UR**

H ERNST
Example: on a 12 3/4" applewood tongue plane with a birch tote and shallow flat chamfers that stop in a long taper at the front. The round top handforged iron is marked **I: FOGI**, from rural eastern PA, ca. 1800. **UR**

LOUIS ERNST
Louis Ernst (b. 1826 in Baden, Germany) and **Ferdinand Seifried** were partners in a Rochester, NY, hardware dealership, **Ernst & Seifried**, from 1856-68. From Sep. 13, 1862-Aug 15, 1863, **Louis Ernst** was commissioned an officer in Co. S, NY, 140th. Infantry Regiment. **Louis Ernst** was on his own as a hardware dealer and advertised as early as 1869. In 1885, The firm added **& Sons**. **Compliments of Louis Ernst & Sons** was found printed on a 1900 Morse Twist Drill & Machine Co. catalog. The **Louis Ernst** imprint was used some time between 1869-85. Examples: on planes made by **G. W. Denison, D. R. Barton, Sandusky Tool Co.** and **L. & I. J. White. A & A1** **

ESCOTT & SONS
Escott & Sons with Manufacturers and the location Louisville probably was a dealer. Example: on a 9 3/8" size **13** hollow plane made by **A. Copeland**, Columbus, Ohio, ca. 1830-50. ****

J. ESTON
Example: on a 10 1/4" cherry molder with flat chamfers, ca. 1800. **UR**

A: ETZLER
Probably **Andrew Etzler** (d. Feb. 8, 1813 in Heidelberg, York Co., PA) appeared in the Brunswick, Berks Co., PA tax list for 1789 & 98 with taxes for a shop. **Andrew Etzler** also appeared in the 1800 PA, septennial census in Brunswick Twp. then Berks Co. which is now Schuykill Co., PA, listed as a carpenter. Examples: on a 9 15/16" ovolo; a 9 5/8" molder; and a 10" coping plane, all beech with flat chamfers. The ovolo has a **NEWBOULD** iron, and provided wedge profile A. The 9 5/8" molder provided the B wedge profile and was found in a barn in Somerton, PA, north of Philadelphia with planes by **N. Schauer** and **Jn. Weaver**. The 10" coping plane, possibly modified, shows evidence of three wear strips and has **G. SNVDER** with the N reversed branded on the side, from rural PA, ca. 1800. ***

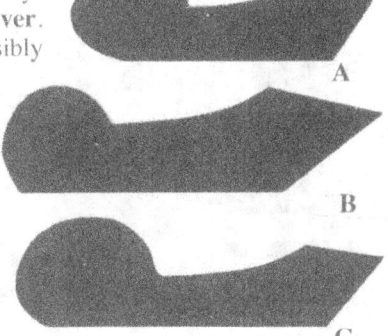

B. EVANS
Example: with the reverse **N**, on a 10" birch small ogee molding plane with a relieved wedge and flat chamfers & flutes. It appears in the **Jo. Fuller** style, ca. 1800. **UR**

C. EVANS
Examples: on a 9 1/2" single-boxed molder with flat chamfers, ca. 1800. **UR**

E. EVANS
Evan Evans (b. 1811 in New York City, d. 1885) was employed by, and boarded with, **John Reed** in Utica, NY, in 1829. He was part of **Benton, Evans & Co.** with **James S. Benton**, in Rochester, NY, from 1834-38. **Evan** was listed as a planemaker in Rochester, from 1834-41. He was a part of **E. & J. Evans**, after 1841, with **James Evans**, and was listed as a Rochester, NY, planemaker, in the 1850, 65, 75, & 80 census.
No imprint has been reported.

E. & J. EVANS
E. & J. Evans was a Rochester, NY, partnership, from 1841-85, between **Evan Evans** and **James Evans** (b. ca. 1806). The company was formerly **Benton, Evans & Co.**, from 1834-38.

Both **Evan Evans** and **James Evans** were listed as residing at the same address, 2 Franklin Sq.. Earlier in 1829, **Evan Evans** was employed by Utica planemaker **John Reed**.
A & A1 *, B & B1 **

H. EVANS
Example: on a 9 3/4" beech complex molder with heavy flat chamfers, ca. 1800. **UR**

I. EVANS
Examples: on a 10 3/4" closed handled tongue & groove pair; a 9 3/8" side bead; and a 9 1/2" astragal, all beech with shallow round chamfers. On a 9 7/16" beech special purpose plane with heavy round chamfers is imprinted **PATENT**, has two halves with adjustable wood side screws and cuts a small "V" groove & follow, both with steel skates, ca. 1810-20. A & A1 **UR**

S. EVANS
Example: on a 10 1/8" cherry complex molder with a birch wedge, large flat chamfers, dated **1778**. **UR**

T. EVANS
Examples: on a 11 7/8" crown molder with an open off-set tote, marked four times on the toe; two 10 1/4" molders with low decorative shoulders; and a 9 1/2" (possibly shot) small nosing plane, all birch with flat chamfers, ca. 1750-70. *****

W. EVANS
Example is on a 9 3/4" beech complex molder with heavy round chamfers, ca. 1820. **UR**

WILLIAM EVANS
William Evans with a location of Martinsburg, VA (now WV) (b. 1784, d. 1854 at age 70), Examples: on a 1 1/2" wide beech complex molder; a beech 9 1/2" hollow with size **16** and style number **No. 370** on the heel. This is the style number for a hollow in the 1872 **Greenfield Tool Co,** catalog. "to work a 2 in. circle", ca. before 1850. ****

EVANSVILLE TOOL STORE
The **Evansville Tool Store** was located in Waloner, OH. Example: on a 14" beech plank match tongue plane with wood bottom fence an wood side fence with screw arms, nuts and washers and round chamfers, ca. 19c. ****

W. EVENS
William Evens (b. Nov. 29, 1783 in England, d. Aug. 1, 1854 in Allegheny, PA) left England Apr. 8, 1804 as a ship's carpenter and arrived in Halifax, Nova Scotia, on July 13, 1804, where he tried the wheel wrighting business. He worked and traveled to Boston, Montreal, Kingston, Detroit, Philadelphia, and finally, in 1811, to Pittsburgh, PA. In the spring of 1812, he "engag'd to work for **Billy Scott** the planemaker on low wages for insight". In Nov. 1813, he announced the opening of his plane making business as being located on Market St. "Lately occupied by **Mr. Walter Lithgow**, deceased", and was listed in the city directory of 1815, as a planemaker, located two blocks from **W. Scott** and **Swetman & Hughes**. In an advertisement for the formation of a singing school placed in the *Pittsburgh Gazette*, on Oct. 10, 1817, he added "P.S. likewise the plane making business carried on as usual." He was located on Irwin St. between Allegheny River and Penn St. He was again listed in the 1819 & 26 directories at a different location on the same block as **Thomas Clark**. In 1831, he sold his property and offered for sale "mother planes and patterns" before moving across the Allegheny River to Allegheny Town, now part of Pittsburgh's north side. He had a dual career as a music teacher and planemaker; and in the 1837 directory, he listed himself as "plane manufacturer and teacher of music". In the 1839 directory, he was listed as "professor of music." In the 1850 & 52 directories, he was again listed as a planemaker, although

few planes were probably made after 1838. Examples: on a 9 1/2" beech molders with flat chamfers; a 14" panel raiser; and a wedge-lock sash plane. The mark between the **W** and **EVENS** is a small heart. (see **Wilson/ Pittsburgh**) (see *Planemakers of Western Pennsylvania and Environs* by Charles W. Paine, Jr.) **A & A1**: ******

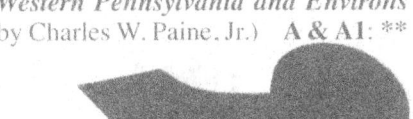

EVRARD
Example: on a 9 1/2"x 1" beech rabbet with flat chamfers, ca. 1800. **UR**

EXCELSIOR
Excelsior was used by **George Muller** of New York, NY who was issued Patent No. 55207, on May 29, 1866, for a throat mechanism in a bench plane. Example: on a 16 1/4"x 3" beech jack plane with a double-iron. ********

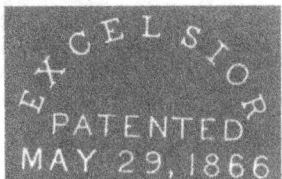

EXCELSIOR WORKS
The A imprint with **WARRANTED** and the B imprint with **AUBURN/ N.Y.**, have been found on the same 16" bench plane, and indicate another possible trade name for the **Auburn Tool Co.**, ca. 1850. **A & B *****

EXTRA QUALITY
Example: on a round; and a hollow, both with **72**; an 1 1/4" wide rabbet with **116**; an adjustable double-iron sash plane with **128**, all 9 1/2" beech with **Ohio Tool Co.** inventory numbers and there wedge profile, ca. 1860. **A & B ******

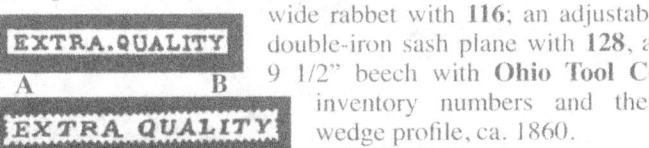

J. EYERS
This name **J. EYERS** with the location **WEST UNITY, O.** and **MAKER** appears on the heel of an open toted jack style rabbet plane. **No imprint is available**.

T∗ EYLES
Example: on a 9 1/2" gunstock plane with flat chamfers, ca. 1800. **UR**

C. EYMAN/ C. EYMANN
C. **Eyman** was a hardware dealer in Cincinnati, OH, from 1856-81. Examples: the A imprint is on an **H. & J. C. Taylor** round. The B imprint is on a hollow. **A & B *****

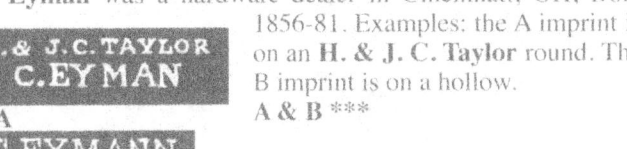

H. EYRE
The 1875-76 New York City directory lists a **Harry Eyre**, as "smith", at 135 Lewis and an Elizabeth Eyre, with occupations listed as "tools", from 1873-77; "hardware", in 1877-78; "saws", in 1878-79; and again "tools", in 1879-80, all at the same address. ********

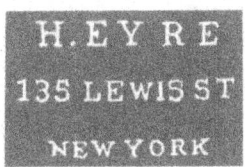

W. F. FAHNESTOCK
Walter Franklin Fahnestock (b. Sep. 13, 1815 in Harrisburg, PA, d. Dec. 18, 1892 in Harrisburg, PA) was a hardware merchant listed in the 1847-61 Pittsburgh, PA directories. In 1856-57, he was listed as **Fahnestock & Bro.** with **Samuel Fahnestock**, and **A. M. Fahnestock** as clerk. From 1847-50, they were at 184 Liberty St.; and from 1850-61, at 247 Liberty St, opposite the head of Wood St. In 1870, he was listed as "retired", in Harrisburg; and in 1880, no occupation. Example: on planes made by **H. Chapin/ Union Factory**, the **Ohio Tool Co.**, and **J. Coates/ Washington Factory**. ***

S. D. FAIRBANK
Samuel Dwight Fairbank (b. Dec. 4, 1835 in Georgia, VT) who moved in 1856 to IN; then Iowa and in 1860 in Cass, NE Territory. In 1866, he was listed in Elmo, MO; and in 1870-80 in Lincoln, Nodaway Co., Mo. In each state, he taught school and worked as a carpenter and a farmer. Examples: on a 9 1/2" beech, single-boxed, very complex molder with shallow flat chamfers; and a 12"x 3 1/2" and a 12"x 5" beech pair of crown molders with centered totes, applied fences with wrought-iron nails and found in CA, suggesting that he might have continued on to CA, ca. 19c. ****

T. FAIRBANK
Example: on a birch complex molder with flat chamfers. The iron is marked **H:P**. Another example is in the Old Sturbridge Village collection. **No imprint is available.**

LEONARD O. FAIRBANKS
Leonard O. Fairbanks (d. Feb. 9, 1865, Nashua, NH) was issued Patent No. 31,707, on Mar. 19, 1861, for a bench plane bevel, square and level attachment, that was made by **Geo. A. Rollins & Co.** of Nashua, NH, who manufactured stationary steam engines starting in 1853. Originally the firm was called **Rollins, Gilman & Co.**, but later it became **Rollins Engine Co.** and was still operating in 1890. (see *Patented Transitional & Metallic Planes in America, Vol. II*, p. 77, by Roger K. Smith) **No imprint has been reported.**

D. FAIRFIELD
Possibly **David Fairfield** (b. ca. 1775 in Gloucester, RI, d. Jan. 4, 1815 in Woodstock, CT) was married in 1797 to Hannah Thurber of Rehoboth, MA. Example: on a 12" beech panel raiser with centered tote, found on Nantucket, MA; and a 9 1/2" birch sash coping plane struck twice on the toe, both with heavy round chamfers, ca. 1815. **UR**

J. T. FALES
Example: on a massive 14 1/2" fruitwood skew rabbet with beech wedge and tote, double-nickers and round chamfers; and on a reverse ogee plan with the **CUMMING & GALE** imprint. Possibly **J. T. Fales** worked in the Providence, RI area, ca. 1830's. **A & A1 UR**

S. FALES
Examples: on a hollow; and a round, both 9 7/8" birch with round chamfers, and an ogee molded shoulder, ca. 1810-20. **UR**

ALEX FALL
Alexander Fall was listed in the 1865 Nashville, TN, directory as a hardware dealer, earlier in various partnerships: with **Fall & Cunningham**, from 1853-61; and with **Alexander Fall & John M. Gray** (b. 1841 in Georgia, d. Jan. 23, 1910 in Nashville, TN), from 1861-65. The 1860 directory listed **Fall & Cunningham**, wholesale dealers in hardware, guns and cutlery, 47 north side Public Sq. In 1867 & 1870, **Alex Fall** was listed under **J. T. Fall & Sons**. Example: a boxed side bead. ***

FALL & CUNNINGHAM
Fall & Cunningham was a Nashville, TN, hardware store partnership consisting of **Alexander Fall** and **G. W. Cunningham** (b. 1822 in TN) that appeared in the city directories, from 1853-61. In 1876, **Cunningham** was listed as a tanner, in 1880, as a farmer. Examples: on a number of planes made by the **Ohio Tool Co.** including a **55** filletster. ****

B. FARLEY
Benjamin Farley (b. Feb. 1, 1767 in Hollis, NH, d. Apr. 27, 1827) was a farmer and made cooper's tools. **Benjamin Farley**, the son, was listed in the 1849 New England business directory. Example: on a 4' cooper's joiner; cooper's planes; and a 10 7/8" birch skew rabbet with flat chamfers, ca. 1800 ****

L. W. FARLEY
Example: on a screw-arm 1/2" gouge howel with a 9" stock and 13" fence and a **L. Hardy** cast steel iron, ca. 19c. **UR**

FARLEY - CHRISTMAN & CO.
Farley-Christman & Co. was a Dubuque, IA, hardware dealer who operated in the early 1850's. Example: on a 9 1/2"x 5/8" beech boxed side bead. *******

I: FARNHAM
Example: on a 19 1/2" beech foreplane with centered closed tote and flat chamfers, ca. 1790. **UR**

J. W. FARR/ J. W. FARR & CO.
James W. Farr (b. 1811) made planes in New York City from 1832-36; in Brooklyn, in 1837-38; and again in New York City, from 1839-52. His indenture papers, dated Aug. 30, 1827 (he was 16 1/2 years of age), apprenticed him to **Enos Baldwin** for 4 years, 5 months and 13 days "to learn the art and mystery of a planemaker." He promised not to "absent himself day nor night from his master's service without his leave; nor haunt ale houses, taverns, dance houses, or play houses." He was paid $2 per week for the first 2 years, 5 months and 13 days and then $2.50 per week for the remaining 2 years. In 1843-44, he was listed in the New York City directory as a planemaker at 332 Third St. He did not add the **& CO.** to his name until, ca. 1850. The B1 imprint includes **PATENT**. A, C, D & D1 *****; B, E, F & G *******

S. E. FARRAND
Samuel E. Farrand (b. Dec. 26, 1789, d. Jul. 8, 1877 in Hanover, NJ) appeared in the 1835-36 Newark, NJ, directory as a planemaker at the same address as **George W. Andruss**. Also in that directory is a listing for **Farrand & Gould** for plane hardware at the same address. In 1837-38, he was listed as "machine maker" at 94 Market St.; in the 1840's, as a "machinist"; in 1849, as a "carriage dealer"; and in the 1850-70 census as a farmer, living in Parsippany, Hanover, Morris Co., NJ. His planes include a number of coach making types. *****

FARRAR & ALLIS
Farrar & Allis was a New York City hardware firm. Example: on a size **10** hollow found with a number of other New York City planes and on an **A. G. Moore** plane with the added date **1855**. ********

FARRINGTON & BURDITT
Farrington & Burditt was a Holyoke, MA, hardware dealer ca. 1850. Example: on a 9 1/2" beech round with **No. 180**, the style number of the **Auburn Tool Co.** for hollows and rounds. ********

L. J. FARWELL
Leonard James Farwell (b. Jan. 5, 1819 in Watertown, NY, d. Apr. 11, 1889 in Grant City, MO) was orphaned, at age 11, and apprenticed as a tinsmith. In 1838, having completed his apprenticeship, **Farwell** moved to Lockport, IL where he operated a small tinsmith shop and hardware store. On Jan. 5, 1840, at age 21, he sold the tinsmith shop and moved to Milwaukie, W.T. (old spelling of Milwaukee and W.T. for Wisconsin Territory) from 1840-51. He was a partner in **Cady & Farwell**, in 1841; **Clark & Shepardson**, in 1843; and then in **L. J. Farwell & Co.**, which became the largest wholesale and retail hardware company in Milwaukee. In 1846, **Farwell** traveled to the West Indies and upon his return, he purchased large land holdings in Madison, W.T. From 1847-49, he traveled to Europe, Asia, Africa and Great Britain. In 1848, while **Farwell** was abroad, Wisconsin became the 30th State in the Union. Upon **Farwell's** return, he sold his business in Milwaukee and began to develop the new state capital by laying out streets and erecting public buildings, making Madison a beautiful and prosperous city. **Farwell** owned the water power rights at the outlet of the Fourth Lake, where he erected a saw and grist mill, deepened the channel of the Catfish River between the Fourth and Third lakes, and drained the lowlands. He started a woolen factory, the first machine shop and foundry, built the gas works and city water system. In 1851, at age 32, **Farwell** was elected the second Governor of Wisconsin. In 1857, he suffered a heavy loss during the financial collapse. In 1863, **President Abraham Lincoln** appointed **Farwell** the Chief Examiner of "new inventions" at the U.S. Patent Office in Washington, D.C. On Apr. 14, 1865, **Farwell** was present in Ford's Theater when **President Lincoln** was assassinated by John Wilkes Boothe. In 1870, **Farwell** went into business in Chicago, only to be wiped out by the Great Chicago Fire of Oct. 8-10, 1871. In 1872, **Farwell** moved to Grant City, MO, and was in real estate and banking until his death. ********

JOHN FALKNER
Possibly **John Faulkner** (b. Mar. 7, 1785, d. Jun. 27, 1823), was listed as a cabinetmaker from Andover, MA, in 1810. Example: on a 10 5/8" skew rabbet. **No imprint is available**.

HENRY FAUST/ H. F. HARDWARE
Example: on a handled grooving plane with wedge-lock slide-arms and flat chamfers. **No imprint is available**.

T. FAVOR
Example: on a 9 3/8"x 3/8" beech boxed bead with flat chamfers, ca. 1800. **UR**

N. FAY
Example: on a 9 1/2" beech complex molder with shallow round chamfers, ca. 1830. **UR**

W. FEATHERSTONE
Example: on a 9 7/16"x 1/2" beech rabbet with flat chamfers, ca. 1800-10. **UR**

HUGH FEGAN
Hugh Fegan (b. ca. 1762, d. 1786 in Philadelphia, PA) was apprenticed, on Apr. 30, 1773, to **William Martin** a Philadelphia, PA planemaker. **No imprint has been reported**.

S. FEGELY
Example: on a 9 1/4" beech small bead with flat chamfers, ca. 1800. **UR**

D. M. FELCH
Example: on a 9 3/4" round with round chamfers, ca. 1820. **No imprint is available**.

S. FELCH
Possibilities: **Samuel Felch** (b. ca. 1720, d. Oct. 27, 1796), **Samuel Felch** (b. ca. 1748, d. Aug. 30, 1839), and **Samuel Felch** (b. May 15, 1778). They may be from three generations, all of Royalston, MA. **Isaac Metcalf** of Royalston, near the NH border, wrote in his account book, on Nov. 26, 1818, that **S. Felch** was to be paid 88 cents for every 100 feet of timber he scored (hewed). Examples: the A imprint is on a 10" thumbnail; and a 9 3/4" parallel-sided smoother with round top chamfered wedge and a **WELDON** round-top iron, both fruitwood with heavy flat chamfers, mostly on the side. Also reported is on a fruitwood marking gauge; as an owner's imprint on a **Ce. Chelor/ Living In/ Wrentham** crown; and a **F. Nicholson/ Living In/ Wrentham** crown, ca. 1775. The A1 imprint is on a 9 7/8" beech fixed-sash with flat chamfers, ca. 1790. The B imprint is on a 9 1/4" single-boxed complex molder; a 9 1/16" complex molder, both beech with flat chamfers; and a 9 7/16" beech full-boxed triple-reeding plane with round chamfers, ca. 1800-20. The C imprint is on a small round; and a two-iron & two wedge fixed sash, both 9 1/2" with small flat chamfers, ca. 1800. The D imprint is on a 9 1/2" beech molder with heavy flat chamfers, ca. 1790. **A, A1, B, C & D ****

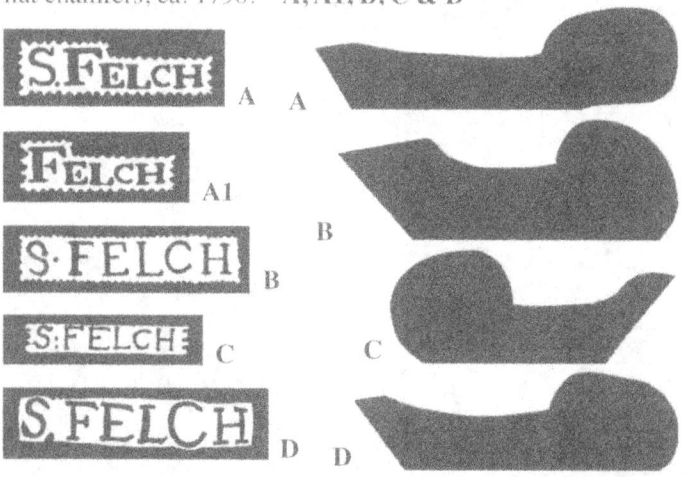

C. FELLOWS
Example: on a beech wood screw-lock plow plane with wood depth stop also wood screw locked, ca. early 19c. **UR**

C. H. FELLOWS & CO.
 Example: on a 7" smoother. **UR**

E. FELLOWS
Possibly **Ephriam Fellows** (b. Nov. 28, 1779, d. Feb. 4, 1842 in Ipswich, MA). His father also an **Ephriam Fellows** (b. Jan. 20, 1754 in Ipswich, d. Feb. 4, 1810 in Ipswich) and a son **Ephriam A. Fellows** (b. July 17, 1811 in Ipswich, d. Oct. 31, 1894 in Ipswich) who was listed at his wedding on Jul. 2, 1846, and the 1850 census, as a housewright. In 1865, He was listed as a carpenter. Examples: on a 10 3/8" tongue plane with an **I. Sleeper** style wedge; and a 14 1/2" panel raiser with a diamond ebony strike and a round top **Newbould** single-iron, both beech with flat chamfers, ca. 1790-1800. ****

I. FELLOWS
Example: on a 9 3/4" beech single-boxed bead with flat chamfers and a **I. Sleeper** style wedge, ca. 1800. **UR**

I. N. FELLOWS
Example: on a 9 1/4" beech skew rabbet struck twice on the toe with shallow slightly round chamfers, ca. 1830. **UR**

FELT & CO

Felt & Co. was probably a New York City hardware dealer. Example: on a 20" bench plane with the date **1874**. ****

FELTE. MER
This imprint is probably a non-professional attempt at a name stamp. Examples: on a 10" beech molder with flat chamfers; and a 13 1/4"x 3 3/4" beech crown molder with off set tote and flat chamfers from PA, ca. 1800. **UR**

JO. FELTHAM
Examples: on a 9 3/4" astragal with flat chamfers; and a 9 11/16" beech astragal with heavy round chamfers, ca. 1800-20. **UR**

JOEL FENN & CO.
Joel Fenn (b. Aug. 15, 1817, in New Haven Co., CT, d. Nov. 15, 1892 in Meriden, New Haven Co., CT) was a Wallingford, CT, planemaker, in 1849. He was listed in the Wallingford, CT, 1850 census as a planemaker with others in his household listed as planemakers: **Nathan Fenn**, probably his brother, (b. 1825 in CT); **William Wood** (b. 1824 in VT); **Merritt Tuttle** (b. 1832, in CT); **James Doolettle** (b. 1833 in CT). He was an agent for **Sawheag Works** in 1850; and a partner in **Gladwin & Fenn** from 1850-55. ******

NATHAN FENN
Nathan Fenn (b. 1825 in CT) was listed in the 1850 census as a plane maker in Wallingford, CT, living with **Joel Fenn**. **No imprint has been reported**.

I FENNER
Example: on a 11" birch square rabbet with narrow flat chamfers, ca. 1770-80. **UR**

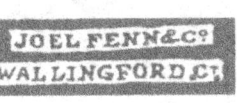

W. FENNO
Example: on a 13 1/2" birch skew rabbet with nickers, a pegged open tote, and round chamfers, ca. 1820. **UR**

M. FERRIN
Example: on a 9 1/2" beech hollow with flat chamfers, ca. 1800. **UR**

AARON FERRY
Aaron Ferry (b. Jul. 6, 1808 in Hampshire Co., MA, d. Feb. 15, 1897 in Brimfield, Portage Co., OH)) was a partner in **Burnham, Fox & Co.**; and worked in **Truman Nutting's** shop. **Aaron** began working for **Kennedy & Co.** in 1836. On May 9, 1837, **Aaron** married **Judith Nutting** a daughter of **Truman's** half brother **George Nutting**. In 1842, **Aaron** moved to Kent, OH. In the 1850-60 census for Franklin, Portage Co., OH, He was listed as a brick maker. **No imprint has been reported**.

L. FERRY
Examples: on a 7 7/8" cherry wedge-lock plow; a 9 1/4" birch complex molder with the A wedge; two 9 1/8" beech complex molders with the B wedge, all with flat chamfers, ca. 1790-1800. ********

ISAAC FIELD
Isaac Field (b. Oct. 26, 1781 in Cranston, RI, d. Aug. 6, 1860 in Providence, RI) of Providence, RI, listed his profession as a planemaker at his marriage, in 1804. **Isaac** was apprenticed to **Jo. Fuller** as early as 1796. In 1808, **Jo. Fuller** transferred land to toolmaker **Isaac Field**, witnessed by house carpenter **Wm. Field**, and toolmaker **James Snow III**. The **Jo. Fuller** E imprint planes are identical in body and wedge profile to a number of the birch **Isaac Field** planes. It is most likely that **Isaac Field** actually made the later **Jo. Fuller** planes. **Isaac Field** worked for **Jo. Fuller**, until his death in 1822, at which time he took over the shop; and stock and was listed in the 1824 RI directory as toolmaker at 138 Westminster St. The following advertisement appeared in *The Providence Directory* of Dec. 19, 1836: "**Isaac Field**; Toolmaker greatfull to his friends and the public for past patronage, respectfully gives notice that he continues to make all kinds of Carpenters' Tools; he also repairs Tools and whets Saws. Those in want of any thing in his line, are invited to call at No. 138 Westminster street, where the prices will always be found such as to give satisfaction." **Isaac Field** continued at that address until the directory listings of 1844-53, when he was at 64 Pine St. There is also an **Isaac Field** listed in the 1850 census, as a planemaker, in Providence, age 29, born in RI. This probably refers to his son **Isaac Field, Jr.** (b. 1821, d. Apr. 17, 1883), who may have used the same imprint. Examples: the B imprint is on two 10" birch, one single boxed, complex molders with a **Jo. Fuller** style relieved wedges, small tight round chamfers on top and flat chamfers with flutes on the ends. ca. late 1790's. The C imprint, with the ends of the name stamp filed down straight, appear on a 9 1/2" birch molders with round top and flat end chamfers. ca. 1820. The A & A1 imprints, with the ends of the stamp rounded, are on 9 1/2" beech molders with round top and flat end chamfers. The **PROVIDENCE** location imprint is the same as used by **Jo. Fuller**. A & A1*; C ****; B *****

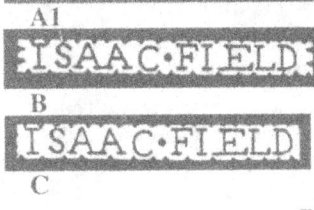

JOSEPH R. FIELD
Joseph R. Field (b. 1812 in Providence, RI, d. Dec. 5, 1878 in Fall River, MA) was the son of **Isaac Field** and was noted in a property transfer in Fall River, MA, in 1835; and lost $300 of personal property in the great Fall River Fire of 1843. He was listed as being "in commerce" in Fall River in the 1840 census; as a trader in the 1850 census; and as a grocer in the 1855-57 Fall River Directories. Examples: on a 9 1/2"x 2/8 beech bead with round chamfers; a molder; and on a 5" wide cornice plane, ca. 1840. ********

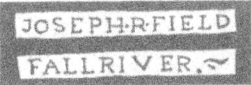

RICHd. M. FIELD
Richard Montgomery Field (b. July 8, 1775 in Providence, RI, d. Dec. 1, 1843 in Providence, RI) was the younger brother of **Joseph Field**, who was adopted by **Joseph Fuller, Sr.** and changed his name to **Joseph Fuller, Jr.**. Richard M. Field learned his tool making as an apprentice to **Joseph Fuller, Sr.** He was a partner in **Fuller & Field** with **Joseph Fuller, Jr.**, after 1798 when **Jo. Fuller, Sr.** and **Jo. Fuller Jr.** dissolved their partnership. **Arnold & Field** represents **Richard M. Field** in partnership with **Daniel Arnold**. The daughter of **Joseph Fuller, Jr.** was married to **Daniel Arnold's** younger brother, **Anthony B. Arnold**. A 1799 deed lists **Richard M. Field** as a toolmaker, while in an 1817 deed he was a merchant. Examples: four 10" birch round planes with **Jo. Fuller** style relieved wedges, flat chamfers and flutes, ca. 1800. ****

T. FIELD
Example: on a 9 3/8" beech, double-boxed, complex molder with flat chamfers, ca. 1810. **UR**

WILLIAM FIELD
William Field (b. 1777, d. 1844) witnessed the 1808 transfer of property between his brother **Isaac Field** and **Joseph Fuller**, at which time he was referred to as a house carpenter. Shortly after **Jo. Fuller's** death, in 1823-24, it is believed that **William Field** was working out of the 138 Westminster address with **Isaac Field**. Between 1840-43, he was into the manufacture of auger bits and plane irons in Pawtucket. **Field** held an April 15, 1840 auger patent. In 1848, he was an agent for **Providence Tool Co. No imprint has been reported**.

FIELD & HARDIE
Field & Hardie was believed to be a Philadelphia, PA, hardware dealer, ca. 1850. This partnership may have succeeded **Field & Langstroth**, ca. 1840. The **Field** is assumed to be **Charles J. Field** (b. Aug. 6, 1820, d. Apr. 3, 1899 in Philadelphia, PA) who succeeded this partnership, but is not known to have marked planes on his own. Examples: the A imprint is on planes made by **Sandusky Tool Co.** and **H. Chapin**. One example of the B imprint has a pencil date of **11/78** on the side. A **; B ***

FIELDING & BARTLETT
Fielding & Bartlett was a Lowell, MA, hardware dealer, listed in the city directories in 1866 & 68. ****

A. FILER
Example: on a 9 1/4" maple shiplap plane with flat chamfers, ca. 1800. **UR**

FILKINS, RUNYON & BARKER
Filkins, Runyon & Barker is believed to have been a Chicago, IL, hardware dealer, with a working dates unknown. ****

I. FILLIPS
The **I** may be a **K**. Example: on a 10 3/16" beech ogee complex molding plane with flat chamfers, ca. early 19c. **UR**

E. E. FILLMORE
E. Elisha Fillmore (b. May 23, 1812 in Clinton, NY, d. Jun. 17, 1897 in Zanesville, OH) was a hardware dealer in Zanesville, Muskingum Co., OH, from 1842-63. Earlier from 1835-42, Fillmore was a partner in **Patterson & Fillmore**. Examples: on planes made by **Ohio Tool Co.** **

L. FILLMORE
Lavius Fillmore (b. Oct. 5, 1767 in the West Farms Society of Norwich, CT, d. Aug. 13, 1850 in New Haven, Addison Co., VT) married **Philura Hartshorn** in Franklin, CT, on Sep. 8, 1791. They had 10 children, with their birth records, it is easy to track the families movements. The first 2 children were born in 1792 & 94, in Franklin, CT. The family moved to the Hanover Society in Lisbon, CT, about 1795, where the next 4 children were born in 1796, 98, 1801 & 03. The family again moved, prior to 1805, to Middlebury, VT, where the last 4 children were born, in 1805, 07, 10 & 11. **Lavius** was a cousin to the 13th. President, **Millard Fillmore**. Little is known about **Lavius's** training and career other than it began in Norwich, CT, in the late 1780's. **Lavius Fillmore** became a noted builder, architect and engineer, and most likely started his career as a journeyman carpenter/ joiner. **Lavius Fillmore** was only 24 when he was commissioned, in 1791, to design the Meetinghouse for the First Ecclesiastical Society in East Haddam, CT (known today as the First Church of Christ, Congregational). He returned, in 1801, to build the Norwichtown, CT, Congregational Church; followed by the Rocky Hill, CT, Congregational Church, in 1805; in 1805, **Fillmore** built the Bennington, VT, Congregational Church; in 1808, the Middlebury, VT, Congregational Church; and in 1805, the **Governor Galuska** (b. in Norwich, CT) house in Shaftsbury, VT. **Lavius Fillmore** was an important designer/ builder influenced by **Asher Benjamin**. These planes are unique, for they have a pointed finial and have a blacksmith-made irons with the embossed imprint **PECK**. Four examples were found together in Cranston, RI, with several planes from Norwich, CT, including two by **A. Hide**, one marked **IN NORWICH**. The imprint also appears on a **CE. Chelor** panel raiser plane. Four examples were found in RI, a small bead; three complex molders; and two others, a bead and a hollow, were found near

Dorset, VT, all 9 1/2" beech with the pointed finial and flat chamfers. ca. 1790. The B imprint is on a 9 1/2" beech hollow with wide round chamfers, ca. 1820. This example was found near Middlebury, VT. A & B ****

R, R, FINCH,
Examples: on a 9 1/2" solid-boxed beech side bead; a 9 5/8" beech round with a **Butcher** iron and its wedge and wedge opening are numbered and a cherry complex molder, ca. 1850. UR

FINGER
Example: on a horned toothing plane. UR

G. FINN
Example: on a 9 1/2" beech round, ca. 1830. UR

A. FISH
Ansel Fish (b. Jun. 28, 1804 in Falmouth, MA) was listed in the Lowell, MA city directories as a planemaker in most years between 1836-55, and in the 1850 census. One example also has an **S. A. FISH** imprint below the **LOWELL**. This is probably an owner's mark, possibly related to **Ansel**. The A1 wedge has a unique design, which was found on a group of ten planes. The name die is known to exist. Examples: reported are 9 1/2" beech, ca. 1850. *

A. O. FISH & CO.
A. O. Fish & Co. Manufacturer of Door & Window Screens, located 4 to 8 Elm St., Keen, NH on a red and gold paper label on a 7 3/4" oak deep fillet plane with the date **1909**, marked on the heel. **No imprint is available.**

J. FISH
J. Fish was apparently a New York City planemaker. Example: on a 9 3/8" beech round, ca. 1830.
A, B, B1 & C ****

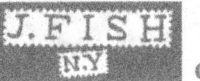

A. E. FISH & CO.
Example: A red paper label in the shape of a fish on an 8 7/8" crude oak weather stripping coping plane, probably included in a window or door screen kit, with the date **1909** on toe: ****

A. E. FISH & CO.
Manufacturers of
DOOR & WINDOW SCREENS
4th. & ELM St. KEENE, N.H.

J. & A. FISH
James P. Fish and **Alexander Fish** were planemakers listed in the Chicago, IL, directories of 1853-55, at 230 Lake. **James P. Fish** was listed as early as 1844 as a carpenter; in 1846-47 as a teamster. In 1856, **Alexander Fish** became a saloon keeper. Example: on a 9 1/2" beech size **18** hollow with an **Ohio Tool Co.** iron. A & B ***

S. A. FISH
Sally Anne Fishburn (b. Mar. 3, 1965) is a contemporary planemaker and Historic Trade Specialist in Washington, DC. UR

W. R. FISH
Embossed imprint with **Wm FISH** in incuse imprint on a beech round, ca. 19c. A & B: UR

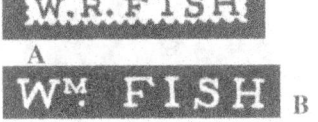

JOHN FISHAWK (FISHACK)
John Fishawk (b. Sept. 3, 1801, d. May 9, 1882) was apprenticed, age 16, on Feb. 18, 1818 to **William Vance** of Baltimore, MD, "to be taught the trade of a planemaker". **John Fishack** was listed in 1870, in Ringgold, Washington Co., MD, as a stone mason. In 1880, he was listed as a retired stone mason. **No imprint has been reported**.

I: F
I: (Fisher) Example: on a 9 1/2" birch thumb nail, the wedge is identical to **L. Fisher** and **C. Fisher** wedge profile, ca. early 19c. UR

FISHER
This name without initials could be of any of the VT **Fishers** listed below. Examples: on a 9 1/4" Yankee plow with wooden thumbscrews and depth stop; a 9" smoother with a **James Cam** iron and chamfered wedge;

and molders from 10"-10 3/16"; all birch with heavy flat chamfers. There is a 9 1/4" single-boxed complex molder with flat chamfers and the B wedge, ca. 1790-1810. **A & B** ****

C x F/ FISHER/ C. FISHER
Possibly **Charles Fisher** (b. Sep. 8, 1824, d. Nov. 19, 1904 in Woodstock, Windsor Co., VT) who was listed as a cabinetmaker in Windsor, Windsor Co., VT, in 1847, and in 1850. By 1860, **Charles Fisher** had moved to the nearby town of Woodstock, VT. In 1870, he was listed as a sash manufacturer. A number of **C. Fisher** planes have been found in Woodstock and Newfane, VT. One example has the initials CxF with the same imprint between the C and F as used by **L: Fisher** on his name and initial imprints, which were made by the same die maker. Examples: on a round; a thumbnail; and a small complex molder, all 10" birch with shallow flat chamfers, but may be later or from an earlier generation, ca. 1790. **A, B & C** ****

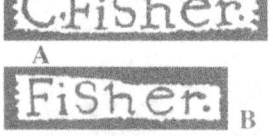

GEORGE FISHER
George Fisher (b. Jan. 9, 1820 in Springfield, Windsor Co., VT, d. Apr. 6, 1896 in Woodstock, Windsor Co., VT) was the son of **Jacob Fisher** and brother of **Isaac M. Fisher**. He learned cabinetmaking from his father. He worked in partnership with his brother as **I. M. & G. Fisher & Co.** from 1841-50. He was listed in 1850 & 60 as a cabinetmaker, in 1870 & 80 as a furniture dealer. **No imprint has been reported.**

I. M. FISHER
Isaac M. Fisher (b. 1816 in Claremont, NH, d. Jan. 30, 1900 in Woodstock, Windsor Co., VT) was the son of **Jacob Fisher** and came from Claremont, NH, to Woodstock, VT, as a small child. **Isaac** learned to be a cabinetmaker from his father, and was recorded in 1840 as engaged in Manufactures & Trades. **Isaac** was in partnership with his father as **Jacob Fisher & Co.**, until 1841, when **Isaac** went into a partnership with his brother **George Fisher** as **I. M. & G. Fisher & Co.**, from 1841-50. In 1860-80, **Isaac** was a cabinetmaker in Woodstock. Examples: a 9 9/16" beech hollow with flat chamfers, found in Pomfret, VT; and a 7 1/2" smoother with his and the **Fisher & Co.** imprints, ca. 1830. ****

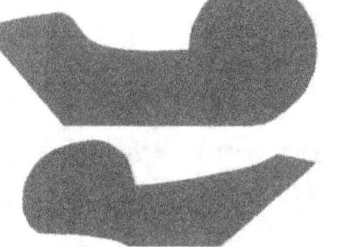

IOHN FISHER/ JOHN FISHER
Examples: the **IOHN FISHER** imprint with the S reversed and the HN conjoined, is on a 14 1/4" plank tongue plane with an off-set open tote and a diamond strike; the **IOHN FISHER** and the **JOHN FISHER** imprint, struck twice, is on a pair of 13 1/8"x 4 3/8" and 13 1/8"x 8 1/4" crown molders; and the **JOHN FISHER** is on a 10" beech wedge-lock strike plane with flat chamfers, ca. 1790. **A & B: UR**

J: F./ J: FISHER
Believed to be **Jacob Fisher** (b. Jun. 3, 1791 in Lancaster, Worcester Co., MA, d. Sep. 26, 1871 in Woodstock, Windsor Co., VT) a descendant of **Joshua Fisher** and a carpenter and blacksmith in Dedham, MA, in 1839. Jacob moved to Springfield, Windsor Co., VT, prior to 1820, where he was listed as engaged in manufacturing. About 1823, he moved to Woodstock as a cabinetmaker. **Jacob Fisher** was in two partnerships: **Fisher & McLaughlin** with **Jacob Fisher** and **Thomas McLaughlin** from 1823-36; and **Jacob Fisher & Co.** with **Jacob Fisher** and his son, **Isaac M. Fisher**, from 1836-41. **Jacob** was listed in Walton, VT, in 1842-43; and by 1860 as a cabinetmaker in Woodstock, VT. Examples: The initial group is on a 13" beech panel raiser with round-top wedge and iron, an offset tote and heavy flat chamfers. Molders include a halving plane; a hollowing plane; two beads; and a plow also marked **J. Eaton**, all 9 7/8-10 1/16" birch with a relieved wedge and heavy flat chamfers. Also reported is a birch wood clamp with wood screws, ca. 1790, but may be later or from an earlier generation. ****

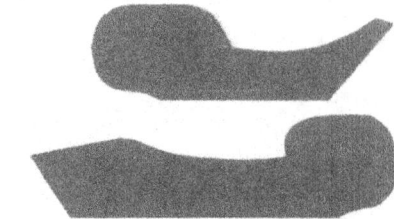

J: FISHER
Believed to be **Jonathan Fisher** (b. Mar. 12, 1798 in Blue Hill, Hancock Co., ME, d. Mar. 10, 1815 in Blue Hill) There is a house built by **Jonathan** as well as diaries and his tools. Examples: on a 9 3/4" birch Yankee plow with wedge-lock arms; a 29 1/4" joiner with a offset mouse ear tote, round-top iron, wedge missing, and heavy flat chamfers; a 15"x 3 1/2" cornice plane with an off-set tote, heavy flat chamfers, a single round-top iron and round-top wedge; and a 10 5/8" maple complex molder with the Roman numeral II stamped on the side of the (A) wedge and the side of the plane, both with 1/2" heavy flat chamfers, the latter found in Keene, NH, ca. 1780. ****

130

L x F/ L x FISHER

Examples: on a molder; and a coping plane, both 10" birch with heavy flat chamfers and flutes. Between the L and FISHER and also in the initial group, is the same mark as used in the CxF initial group of C. Fisher and which was probably made by the same die maker. The wedges are similar with rounding under the cutout, possibly from Woodstock, VT, ca. 1790. ****

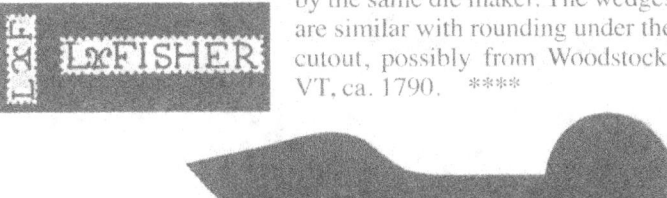

N. FISHER/ N. FISHER JU.

Probably a descendant of Joshua Fisher. Like the C. Fisher one example has a relieved B wedge. Examples: on three cornice planes with offset totes; a 10 1/2" molder; and a 9 7/8" hollow & round pair, all birch with heavy flat chamfers. Imprint B has a JU in a separate imprint marked after the N. FISHER, probably by the next generation. A & B ****

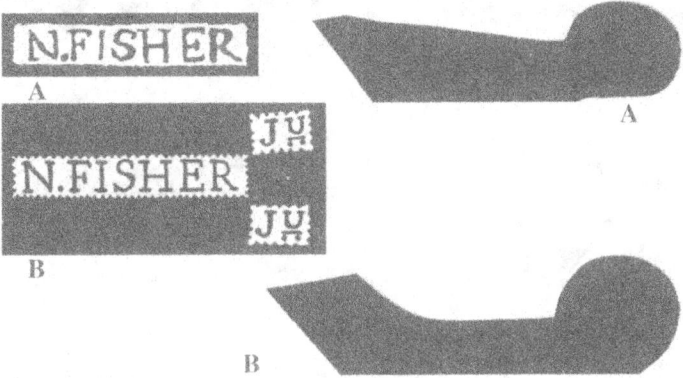

T. FISHER

Believed to be Thomas Fisher. The imprint is on the toe of a 9 3/8" beech tongue & groove pair, the grove wedge is hickory, with flat chamfers found at the Shaker Village of Pleasant Hill, near Lexington, KY. Branded on the side is
C. BANTY. Cornelius Banta (b. 1781 in Mercer Co., KY, d. 1816 at Pleasant Hill) from the Dutch colony of PA/ KY and joined the Pleasant Hill community, in 1806. Cornelius married Betsey Thomas. Her father Elisha Thomas founded the original Shaker settlement at Shawnee Run, in 1805. Cornelius worked in the joinery shop until 1815, ca. 1790. UR

FISHER & AGNEW

Fisher & Agnew with E. H. Fisher and John Agnew, appeared in the 1859-60 Columbia, SC, city directories, the earliest available, as a dealers in hardware and cutlery. John Agnew & Son with John Agnew Jr. was listed in the 1875-76 directories, the first after the Civil War, as a dealer in hardware and groceries. In 1879-80, John Agnew was listed as carriages, and buggies. A & A1 ****

FISHER & CO.

Fisher & Co. was possibly a partnership with Jacob Fisher and his son, Isaac M. Fisher, from 1836-41. Examples: on a 9" smoother; a 12" beech handled plow; a 9 3/4" birch molder; and a round, all with shallow round chamfers, ca. 1850. ****

ABM: FISK/ ABRAHAM x FISK

Abraham Fisk (b. 1762 in Providence, RI, d. Nov. 19, 1827 in Watertown, Jefferson Co., NY) served in the American Revolutionary War. In 1787, Abraham married Elizabeth (Betsy) Arnold in Providence, RI. In 1788, he moved to Whitesboro, Oneida Co., NY. Before 1802, he took up 500 acres south of Watertown, Jefferson Co., NY. Abraham Fish had three son's who served in the War of 1812. Examples: the A imprint is from a Yankee plow; a 10" rabbet; a 9 3/8" birch ogee; and several 9 7/8" beech molders, all with flat chamfers. The B imprint is on a Yankee plow; a 10" rabbet; and several 9 7/8" complex molders, all birch with flat chamfers and at least one of the molders has flutes. Several of the planes have been found in western NY and PA, ca. 1790. A & B ****

S. FISK

Possibly Samuel Fiske (b. 1769 in Waltham, MA, d. 1797) who was a cabinetmaker, had a shop in Salem, MA, ca. 1780's, and was in Boston by the 1790's; or Samuel Fisk (b. Mar. 23, 1727 in Rehoboth, MA). Examples: on a 30" jointer; a 10 3/16" birch Yankee plow with wood thumbscrews and wood depth stop, riveted skate, relieved wedge, round chamfers on top and flat chamfers on toe and heel; a 9 7/8" astragal with small round chamfers on top and flat chamfers on the ends plus flutes; and two panel raisers with off-set totes, one with an owner's imprint S. HILL, all birch, probably from southeastern New England, ca. 1.780. Stronger evidence of Samuel Fisk (1727), being the maker, is the fact that the plow and the astragal were found in the Wrentham/Norton, MA, area, and that the S. Hill is believed to be one of several Samuel Hill possibilities from Rehoboth, MA. The A wedge is from the plow, ca. 1760. The B wedge appears to be later, ca. 1780-90. ****

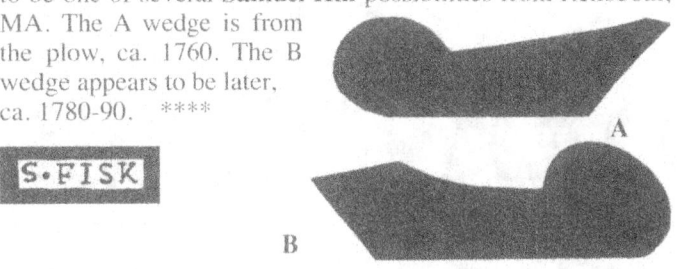

W. C. FISK

Example: on a 9 1/2" birch round, ca. 1840-50. UR

I: FITCH

Isaac Fitch (b. May 10, 1734, d. Sept. 25, 1791) of Lebanon CT, started as a country carpenter/ joiner or housewright; became a prominent cabinetmaker, architect and builder and was a major figure in the decorative arts. He was the grandson of **Rev. James Fitch**, founder of Norwich and Lebanon, CT. His father **Captain Nathaniel Fitch** was one of the first settlers of Lebanon. **Isaac Fitch** was a cousin of **Gov. Jonathan Trumbull** who wrote in 1784:

> "**Mr. Fitch** is the best Architect within the compass of my acquaintance... he is well acquainted with books of Architecture. His genius is extraordinary."

He was active from 1754-91, mostly at cabinetry and domestic architecture, with **Jonathan Trumbull** his major patron. **Isaac Fitch's** first classical Georgian house was for **Jonathan Deming** in Colchester in 1768-9 and the Colchester Meeting House in 1770-72. In 1777, **Isaac Fitch** renovated the **Gov. Jonathan Trumbull, Jr.** house in Lebanon, the **David Trumbull** house, in 1778-79, also in Lebanon. He is credited with the design and building of the Colchester, CT, Meeting House in 1770-72. The British attacked and burned New London and Groton, CT, on Sep. 6, 1781. In 1785, **Isaac Fitch** was commissioned to design and built the new New London court house which is still standing today. His estate inventory indicated an active shop and included 43 planes: jointers, fore, jack, smoothing and molding, and other cabinet and carpentry tools. The estate also included James Gibbs' *Book of Architecture*, 1728; Robert Morris' *Lectures on Architecture*, 1734, and a third unspecified book on architecture. His estate was insolvent. Examples: on a 20 1/2"x 2 1/2" fore plane with offset closed tote and diamond strike; and a 10" rabbit, both birch; and a large fruitwood round, all with heavy flat chamfers, ca. 1760. *****

W. FITCH

Examples, on a 9 15/16" birch molder; a 9 1/2" square rabbet, both with flat chamfers; and a 13" apple wood panel raiser with round chamfers, ca. 1790-1820. **UR**

A. FITTS.

Example: on a 9 1/2" beech skew rabbet with round chamfers, ca. 1830. **UR**

R. FITTS

Example: on a, heel shot, beech molder with heavy rounds chamfers. ca. 1800. **UR**

H. FLAGLER & CO.

Henry Flagler (b. 1802 in NY) was listed in the 1850 census as a merchant, living in Lockport, NY. Henry served, as a Private, in the Civil War, Co. C, 47th. Reg., NY Infantry. In 1875, **Henry Flagler** was listed as a tinsmith; and in 1883, as a polisher in Buffalo, NY. ****

J. FLAHERTY

J. Flaherty was listed as a planemaker from St. Joseph, MO. **No imprint is available**.

J. FLANDERS

Believed to be **John Flanders** (b. ca. 1787, d. Apr. 4, 1840) a Newburyport, MA, cabinetmaker. In the 1820-30's he was on the Pauper Records. Example: on a 9 5/8" beech bead with an **I. Sleeper** style wedge profile and flat chamfers. The plane was found in the **Little** family homestead in Newbury, MA, ca. 1800. **UR**

FLETCHER/ C. FLETCHER

Charles H. Fletcher (b. 1858 in NY) was the son of **John R. Fletcher**, and a New York City planemaker and hardware merchant at 307 West 7th, from 1875-83. This address was previously the address of **William J. C. Ward**. Example: on a 16" jack with a **W. Butcher** double-iron.   **A & B ****

JOHN R. FLETCHER

John R. Fletcher (b. Jan. 1826 in England, d. Nov. 16, 1905 in New York, NY) was listed, in 1850, as a carpenter and in 1860 as a mechanic in New York City. **John R. Fletcher** was the father of **Charles H. Fletcher** and was a partner in **Ward & Fletcher** from 1852-70. They made planes and other tools at 513 8th. Ave., New York City. From 1870-76, **Ward & Fletcher** was listed in Saddle River, NJ and listed as a plain and carpenter tool maker. **No imprint has been reported**.

JOSEPH FLETCHER

Example: on a 7 1/4" birch smoother with round chamfers and a round top iron marked **FISHER**, ca. 1800-10. **UR**

S. F. FLETCHER

Samuel F. Fletcher (b. 1819 in NC) moved to IN, before 1842. **Samuel** was a Richmond, IN, hardware dealer, at Main between Pearl and Marion, that succeeded **Fletcher & Benton,** in 1857. This imprint is from the heel of a 9 1/2"x 3/4" beech dado with an **Ohio Tool Co.** iron. ****

FLETCHER & BENTON

Samuel F. Fletcher (b. 1819 in NC) moved to IN before 1842; and **Thomas H. Benton** (b. 1803 in Elizabeth City, NC, d. 1871 in Richmond, IN) was a hardware and leather firm, from 1845-57. In 1857, they divided the stock. **Thomas Benton** was part of **T. Benton & Co.** and then **T. Benton & Son,** from 1857-71. **Samuel F. Fletcher** located at the west side of Main St., between Pearl and Marion as **S. F. Fletcher**, from 1857-65.

This imprint is from a screw-arm plow, ca. 1850. ****

H. W. FLEURY
Example: This imprint is on the heel of a **S. P. Francisco** round: ****

SOLD BY
H. W. FLEURY
CLEVD OH

E. FLINT
Ebenezer Flint (b. ca. 1800) was listed in the 1830 census in Castle, NY, 20 miles from Alexander, NY; and in the 1840 census for Alexander, NY, engaged in manufacturing and trades; active from 1836-42. Examples: on a wedge-arm plow; and a 9 3/8" beech complex molder, both found in central MI; a double-boxed side bead found near Alexander, NY; and a plank grooving plane. ****

JOHN FLYN
Example: on a 9 1/2" beech complex molder with heavy flat chamfers. ca. 1800. UR

E. E. FOBES
Example: on a 9 1/8" beech side bead with heavy round chamfers. ca. 1820. UR

S. FOBES
Example: on a 9 1/2" birch bead with flat chamfers and small flutes, ca. 1780. UR

I. FOGARTY
Example: on a 9 1/4" beech grooving plane with a turned up toe on the skate. **No imprint is available.**

C. S. FOGG
Example: on a 9 11/16" beech round with early 19c. style chamfers. UR

H. FOGG
Examples; on a group of eleven planes including a moving fillester (ca. 1850); two dados; seven molding planes; a sash coping; and a plow with the B wedge profile; a 29 3/4" joiner; and a 22 1/2" jointer with shallow round chamfers, a diamond strike; and three bead planes, all beech. One of the jointers was found in VT, and the beads in NH, one of which is also marked **T. B. Gove** suggesting a northern New England origin, ca. 1830-50. ****

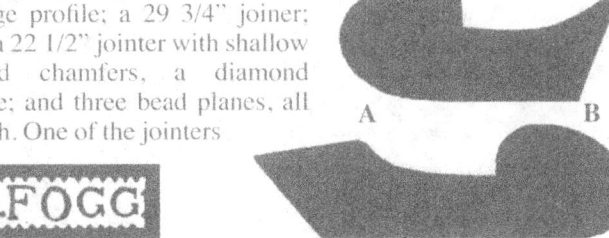

I F/ J. FOLEY
Possibly **John Foley**, a cabinetmaker from Baltimore, MD, active in 1799-1800. Examples: on a 9 5/8" beech narrow skew rabbet with small flat chamfers and the A wedge profile; a hollow; a round; a thumbnail; and a quarter round, all 9 1/4" with round chamfers and the B wedge profile. The quarter round also has the incuse initials IF. ca. 1800-20. UR

E. F. FOLGER & CO./ EDWARD F. FOLGER
Edward F. Folger (b. 1824 in NY, d. 1875 in Baltimore) was a hardware merchant in Buffalo, NY, from 1849-57. Listed as Chief Clerk N.Y.C.R.R in Albany, NY from 1861-64. From 1866-67, as Insurance Ag't. in Albany, NY. The full name imprint was reported on a handled tongue plane with a **Providence Tool Co.** iron. A, A1 & B ***

FOLLING/ FOLLINGS
The embossed marks show a transition from **FOLLINGS** with the S to **FOLLING**, then the die cut down removing most of the S. The incuse imprint, found on the side of at least two planes, was originally **FOLLINGS** then cut down to **FOLLING**. Examples: the A imprint is on a 15 5/8" skew rabbet with the B wedge and shallow round chamfers; a 13 3/8"; and a 13 1/2" toted complex molders; and two 10" complex molders, with the A wedge and flat chamfers. The B imprint appears on a 14 1/2"; and a 16" crown molders with heavy round chamfers, all examples, except one birch molder, are beech. Four of the planes were found in the Windham Co. area of CT, ca. 1800-20.
A, B, C & D ****

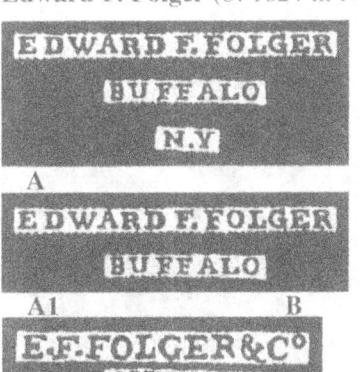
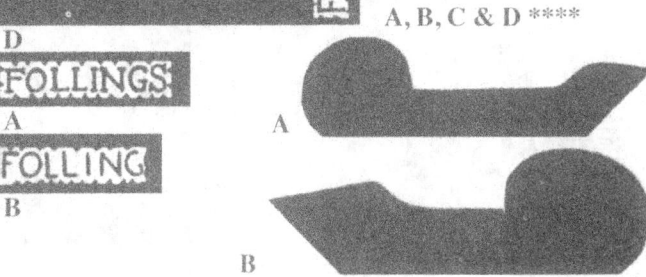

I. FOLSOM/ J. FOLSOM
Example: the A imprint is on a 11 5/8" beech square ship's rabbet with shallow round chamfers. The B imprint is on a full-boxed small bead made by **A. Smith/ Lowell**, probably as an owners imprint, ca. 1830 **UR**

S. N. FONDER
Example: on a tongue plane with the name **S. N. Fonder** plus the location **TERRA HAUTE**, (IN), ca. 19c.
No imprint is available.

H. FOOT
Possibly related to the **Homer Foot & Co.** who was listed as a hardware dealer in the **G. W. Denison & Co.** account book. Example: on a 16 3/4" birch bench plane with centered open tote and shallow round chamfers, ca. 1870-84. **UR**

R. FOOT
Possibly **Robert Foot** (d. Jul. 26, 1838 in Amesbury, Essex Co., MA) who was a housewright from Amesbury, MA. **Robert Foot** and **Susan Goodridge**, of Haverhill, MA, listed their marriage intentions, on Aug. 15, 1818, in Amesbury, MA and were married in Haverhill, on Dec. 6, 1818. Examples: on a 9 1/2" round; and large hollow; a 10 1/8" halving plane; and a grooving plane, all beech with an **I. Sleeper** style wedge and flat chamfers. ca. 1800. **UR**

J. FOOTE
Examples: on a 9 5/8" beech tongue with B wedge and the date **1870**; and a 10 1/2" beech plow with the A wedge, imprinted twice on toe, and the date **1860,** with an open maple tote. The rear arm is wedge-locked, the front arm has a wood thumbscrew, and a wood depth stop with calibrated brass sides. **UR**

A. FORBES
Example: on a 9 1/4" beech slide-arm plow with wood thumbscrews and a brass depth stop, ca. 1840. **UR**

G. FORBES
Examples: on a 10 1/8" complex molder; a 14 1/2" panel raiser with offset tote; a 9 1/4" round; and a 9 1/2" molder, all beech with flat chamfers, ca. 1810.
A & B: **UR**

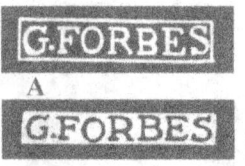

I: FORBUSH
Examples: on a panel raiser with open-centered tote and heavy round chamfers; and a 2" skew rabbet with an integral closed tote and shallow round chamfers, both 14" beech. The rabbet has the incuse owner's imprint **G. A. Forbush**, ca. 1820-30. **UR**

R. FORD
Example: on a 9 1/2" beech hollow, ca. 1850. **UR**

I. M. FORREST
Example: on a beech smoother with a **Dwight & French** iron. **UR**

J. FORRESTER
Example: on a 10 1/8" skew rabbet with round top and flat front chamfers. **UR**

M. FORSAITH
Example: on a double-blade and double-wedge beech fixed sash with flat chamfers, ca 1810-20. **UR**

A. FORSSKOL
Examples: on a left handed grooving plane with a screw applied skate; and a tongue plane, both 9 5/8" beech with flat chamfers, ca. 1800-15. **UR**

J. FORSYTH
Example: on a 9 1/2" beech single-boxed side bead with shallow round chamfers, ca. 1830. **UR**

R: FOSDICK
Richard Fosdick (b. Nov. 28, 1765 in New London, CT, d. Aug. 20, 1837 in Cincinnati, Hamilton Co., OH) was an active New London, CT, cabinetmaker from 1790-1815 and a primary exponent of Federal style. **Fosdick** advertised on Jul. 30, 1791 "wanted an apprentice to the CABINET-MAKING bufinefs; an active lad, about 14 or 15 years old." He again advertised in *Connecticut Gazette* of Jul. 31, 1794 & Jul 30, 1795 "that he was in need of an apprentice to the cabinet making business." He also placed an ad in *The Bee*, New London of Oct. 8, 1800 "that he was starting the chaise making business & repairer and continues the cabinet making business." **Fosdick** advertised in *True Republic*, Norwich of Jun. 26, 1805, "sale of lumber, continued making & repairing chaises, carried on his cabinet making business, and also had on hand an assortment of houfe and shop joiner's tools." He advertised on Apr. 16, 1806 and

again in *Connecticut Gazette* of Mar. 23 and Aug. 5, 1810: "For sale: two story dwelling house, two shops and lots including blacksmith shop, tools, stock in cabinet and carriage business." **Richard Fosdick** appeared in the 1800 & 10 census for New London, CT. In Sep. 1810, he sold his carpentry shop on Golden St. to **French & Jewett**, cabinetmakers, and relocated to Cincinnati, Hamilton Co., OH; but retained the blacksmith shop until 1815. Examples: the A imprint is on a 10 1/2" beech self-fenced square rabbet with heavy flat chamfers. The A1 imprint is on a 10 3/4" beech tongue plane with a birch wedge and heavy flat chamfers. The B imprint is on a 10 3/16" round; and a 10" tongue plane, both beech with flat chamfers, ca. 1790-1800.
A1 & B ****: A *****

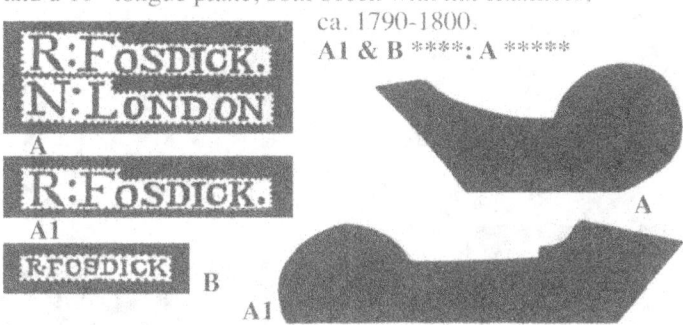

THO. FOSS
Believed to be **Thomas Foss** (b. 1728 in Greenland, Rockingham Co., NH) a carpenter and joiner in Portsmouth, NH. Example: on a 36" birch jointer with flat chamfers. ca. 1770. **UR**

A. FOSTER
Possibly **Abraham Foster** (bapt. Dec. 2, 1744 in Charlestown, MA) who was a cabinetmaker in Boston in 1780. In 1788, he was listed as a cabinetmaker in Charlestown, MA. Example: on a 12 1/2" birch razee tongue plane with a pegged centered fishtail tote in beech and flat chamfers, found in Westminster, MA, ca. 1790-1800. **UR**

D. FOSTER
Possibly **David Calvin Foster,** a cabinetmaker, active in Ipswich, MA, from 1831-46; and in Beverly, MA, in 1849. Example: on a 9 3/4" beech skew rabbet with a birch wedge, edge boxing, round chamfers on top and flat chamfers on the ends, ca. 1800-10. **UR**

FRANK A. FOSTER & CO.

Frank A. Foster & Co. with the added MAKER/ ASHLAND, PA is on a plane by a known planemaker, **I. White**, Philadelphia, PA. ****

G. P. FOSTER
G. P. Foster has been reported on a plane. On Feb. 2, 1875, a patent for a heel shave was given to **Fanny M. Foster** of Leicester, MA, on behalf of the deceased, **G. P. Foster**. **No imprint is available.**

I. FOSTER
Examples: on a 9 5/8" birch skew rabbet; and a beech round, both with flat chamfers, ca. 1800. **UR**

J. FOSTER
Possibly **Jesse Foster** who was a Boston, MA, turner and cabinetmaker, from 1795-1800. Examples: the A imprint with the straight border is on a 9 3/4" complex molder with flat chamfers mostly on the side. The B imprint with a serrated border is on a 9 1/2" miter plane with a **James Howarth** (Sheffield) iron. ca. 1800.
A & B: **UR**

J. FOSTER
Example: a jointer, ca. 1850. **UR**

J. FOSTER
Example: on a 9" sash filletster made by **A. C. Stevens**, ca. 1830. **UR**

J. L. FOSTER
John L. Foster (b. Dec. 10, 1830 in Bremen, Lincoln Co., ME, d. Dec. 24, 1878 in Boston, MA) was listed, in 1860, in Boston as a ship's joiner; in 1864, as a ship's carpenter; and at his death, in 1878, as a carpenter. Examples: on a 9 3/8" beech sash coping plane with boxing; a 21 5/8" jointer; and a jack, both rosewood and razee. ****

FOSTER & PORTER
Foster & Porter was probably a hardware dealer. Examples: on a **Sandusky Tool Co.** plane and an **Ohio Tool Co.** round with an inventory number **72**. ****

T. FOWLER
Thomas Fowler (b. Nov. 13, 1786 in Hopkinton, Hillsborough, NH, d. Jun. 29, 1819 in Salisbury, MA) was listed as a shipwright and a joiner in Salisbury, MA. Example: on a 9 1/4" beech plow with wedge locked arms and friction depth stop, screw applied skate, and early 19c chamfers. ca. 1820. **UR**

FOWLER BROS.
Fowler Brothers was a hardware dealer in Brooklyn, NY. Examples: on a bead; a dado; a 9 1/2"x 2" beech skew rabbet; and a filletster made by **Shiverick**, ca. 1860's. A & B ****

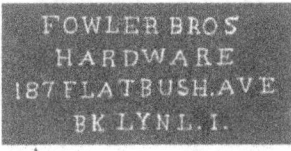

Ink on the side of filletster: B

FOWLER BROTHERS
HOUSE FURNISHING GOODS, MECHANICS TOOLS
187 FLATBUSH AVE. and 61 PACIFIC ST.
BROOKLYN, L. I.

A. & E. FOX
Examples: on a 9 1/2" beech hollow and round, ca. 1850. **UR**

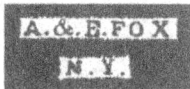

B. F. FOX
Benjamin Franklin Fox (b. Sept. 18, 1826 in Hamburg, Erie Co., NY, d. Apr. 23, 1904 in Springfield, IL) came to Springfield, IL, in 1852. He was a hardware dealer, from 1855-70; and possibly as late as 1874. Examples: on a side bead; and a moving filletster. ********

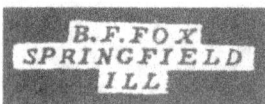

C. J. FOX
Examples: on a bead plane; and a round with **72** the **Sandusky Tool Co.** inventory number. ca. 1850. **UR**

G. FOX
George W. Fox (b. 1816 in England, d. Apr. 23, 1863 in Middletown, CT) is possibly related to **Luther Fox** of Amherst, MA. George was listed in the 1850 census as a planemaker in Middletown, CT, working for **Arrowmammett Works**. He has been suggested as the possible maker of planes with the name **G. FOX, AMHERST**. No imprint is available.

HIRAM FOX
Hiram E. Fox (b. Mar. 18, 1818 in Amherst, Hampshire Co., MA) was the son of **Luther Fox**. He made planes in Amherst, MA, prior to 1841. **Hiram** became a partner in **Burnham, Fox & Co.**, from 1842-44. He was probably the **Fox** of **Kellogg, Fox & Washburn**, in 1839; and **Kellogg & Fox** which was dissolved in 1840. No imprint has been reported.

IRVING FOX
Irving W. Fox (b. Dec. 1852 in NY) moved with his family to Rochester, MI, in 1855. By 1872, he was the proprietor of **Irving W. Fox Gun Shop**, at 15 East 6th. St., Rochester. On Aug. 10, 1873, he ran an add in the *Rochester Post*: "**Irving W. Fox** Gunsmith, model maker and repairer of Artists and Engineers instruments, fire arms, etc. New & experimental machinery made. Sign of the big gun, Broadway, Rochester, MN." In 1874, the *Rochester Post* recorded that he had an accident which left a thumb shorter. In 1878, he was part of the bed spring factory of **R. Grant** and enlarged his shop. In 1880, he was listed as a machinist, in Rochester. In 1890, he designed and manufactured the "Rochester Clipper Saw" used to cut cordwood. By 1902, he had shipped his 500th saw. In Jun. 1905, **Irving** sold his business to **Ellis & Edwards**. In Sep., he moved to Los Anglos, CA. From 1907-15, he was employed as a machinist. **UR**

L: FOX
Example: on a 10" beech small round with tight flat chamfers, ca. 1795-1805. **UR**

L. FOX/ LUTHER FOX
Luther Fox (b. ca. 1795, bapt. Jun. 21, 1801 in Amherst, Hampshire Co., MA, d. 1850 in Baltimore, MD) was an Amherst, MA, planemaker, from 1831-43. Between 1834-36, he was a partner with **Truman Nutting** in **Nutting & Fox**. **Luther Fox** was probably part of **Fox & Washburn** and **Fox, Nutting & Washburn**. George Burnham, Jr. worked for him as a journeyman. Soon thereafter, in 1843, **Luther Fox** sold out to **Burnham, Fox & Co.** Examples: the A imprint is from a compass smoother which also bears a faint **T. NUTTING** imprint. The B imprint is on a 7" beech smoother.
B *******; A *********

L. FOX & SON
L. Fox & Son with **Luther Fox** and his son, **Hiram Fox** was a partnership as planemakers in Amherst, MA. Example: on a beech plow with wood depth stop and thumbscrew-locked slide arms, ca. 1830's. ********

P. FOX
Example: on an applewood crown with an offset tote and flat chamfers, ca. 1780-95. **UR**

S. R. FOX
S. R. Fox was probably a hardware dealer in Madison, OH, halfway between Cleveland, OH, and Erie, PA. Example: on a molder by **L. & I. J. White/ Buffalo**. ********

FOX, NUTTING & WASHBURN
Fox, Nutting & Washburn was an Amherst, MA, planemaking partnership consisting of **Luther Fox**, **Truman Nutting** and **William Lyman Washburn**, that operated, ca. 1835. Example: on a bench jointer. *********

FOX & WASHBURN
Probably a partnership between **Luther Fox** and **William Lyman Washburn** who operated in 1835-36. They are reported to have bought planes and parts from **Nutting & Fox** and used their machinery. A bench plane has both the **Fox & Washburn** and the **W. L. Washburn** imprints. *******

JOHN FRACE
John Frace (b. Aug. 1842 in NJ, d. Feb. 14, 1902 in NJ) appeared in the 1860 census, as a carpenter in Newton, NJ. He served to the end of the Civil War, Co. B, 2nd. Reg. NJ Infantry from Apr. 16, 1861-Apr. 9, 1865. He received a pension on Jan 22, 1900. Examples: on a rosewood plow; and a grooving plane, ca. 1870. ********

JAMES FRAME
James Frame was listed in the New York Directory, for 1790, as a planemaker at 11 Bowery. **No imprint has been reported.**

ELIAS FRANCIS
Possibly **Elias Francis** of **Mockridge & Francis** of Newark, NJ, from 1835-68 who made planes, leather tools and marking gauges; and in 1837-38, a planemaker, at 145 Washington St., and across the street from **George W. Andruss**. In 1869-79, he was in real estate. **Elias Francis** was the superintendent of the **Newark Plane & Rule & Lever Co.**, for one year; and then back into real estate. Examples: on a beech size **16** hollow & round pair; and a size **18** round. ca. 1850. **A & A1** ****

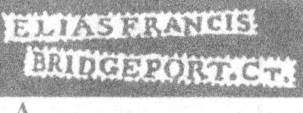

H. FRANCIS
Example: on a 16 13/16" birch jack plane with a 1 1/4" sq. strike button and a butcher iron, ca. 1800. **UR**

THOMAS J. FRANCIS
Thomas J. Francis was listed in 1848-49, in the Utica, NY directory as a planemaker, possibly employed by **John Reed**. **No imprint has been reported.**

P. S. FRANCISCO
P. S. Francisco (b. 1818 in NY) was listed in the 1850 census for Brooklyn, OH, next to Cleveland. Ohio City was incorporated in 1836, and became part of Cleveland, in 1854. Examples: the A imprint is on a 9 3/16" beech complex molder. The B imprint is on a 9 1/2" beech hollow; and a plow, ca. 1840. **A & B** ***

S. FRANKLIN/ FRANKLIN
Believed to be **Samuel Franklin**, a Cincinnati, OH, planemaker, active in 1831. Examples: The A imprint is on a 9 1/2" beech narrow hollow. The B imprint is on a 7 13/16" coffin smoothing plane, ca. 1840. ****

WILLIAM FRANKLIN
William Franklin was listed as a planemaker in the Cincinnati, OH, from 1842-44 & 58. Example: on a 9 1/4" beech molder, ca. 1850. **UR**

G. FRASER
Example: on a 9 5/8" beech narrow round with flat chamfers, ca. 1800. **UR**

J. FRAVER
Examples: on a 10 1/8" birch square rabbet; and a pump log plane, both with no chamfers, ca. 1790. **UR**

G. FREBURGER JR.
George Freburger Jr. was a Baltimore, MD, planemaker listed from 1849-51. Examples: a bead; a nosing plane; and a skew rabbet, ca. 1850. **A & B** ***

JF/ J. FREDENDALL
Example: on a 9 7/16" beech single-boxed side bead with size **1/8** on the heel and a **W. Butcher** iron, ca. 19c. **UR**

J. FREEMAN
Example: on a 10 1/4" beech Yankee plow plane with hickory screw-locked sq. arms and a birch wedge, steel depth stop held with a steel side screw, riveted skate, heavy round chamfers and found near Falls River MA/ RI line, ca. 1820. **UR**

J. FREESE
J. Freese was from Cairo, NY. Examples: on a massive 15" rabbet plane with a 2 1/2" blade and dated **1890**; and two marking gauges. ****

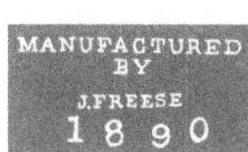

FRENCH
Believed to be **Bird French** from Chapinville a part of Salisbury, CT. **French** Married, Apr. 14, 1822 in Sheffield, Berkshire Co., MA. He was Listed in the 1830-40 census, in Salisbury, Litchfield Co., CT. Example: the A imprint on a 9 11/16" birch complex molder with heavy flat chamfers, mostly on the sides. The B imprint is on a 12" beech gutter plane with shallow round chamfers, possibly from two generations, ca. 1780-1820. **UR**

C. FRESE & CO.
C. Frese & Co. was an Indianapolis, IN, hardware dealer listed in the city directories, at 27 w. Washington St., in 1866 & 76 with **Charles Frese**. This firm superseded **Frese & Minter**, listed in 1865, at the same address. Earlier he was part of **Frese & Kropf** from 1863-65. ***

FRESE & KROPF
Charles Frese and **Gustav Kropf** were listed as **Frese & Kropf**, hardware dealers in Indianapolis, IN, at 11 W. Washington St., from 1863-65. (see **C. Frese & Co.**) Example: on an **Ohio Tool Co.** with invoice number **137**, full-boxed center bead. ****

REUBEN FRETZ MEDINA CO.
Reuben Fretz (b. Sept. 27, 1837 in Buck's Co., PA, d. Mar. 24, 1920 in Terre Haute, IN) was issued Patent No. 24,623, on July 5, 1859, for a "gauge plane" used to trim the edges of wagon wheels. He was a wagonmaker, in Montville, Medina Co., OH, from 1859-62. He served in the Civil War, from 1862-65; then removed to Clay City, IN, where he was a farmer and wagon maker. From 1890-95, he farmed in TN; and was also a detective for a NY firm. He made and sold planes until ca. 1900. The name **REUBEN FRETZ MEDINA CO. OHIO/ PATENTED JULY 5TH 1859** has been reported in ink on the top of a plane, but **no imprint is available**. (see *Patented Transitional & Metallic Planes in America Vol. II*, pp. 68-70, by Roger K. Smith)

CHAs. S. FRIES
Charles S. Fries made a prototype for **Z. J. M'Master**, in 1846, at Auburn, NY. The plane was never patented or commercially produced. The plane is a 9 1/8" unhandled ebony plow with a self-adjusting single center arm. (see *Patented Transitional & Metallic Planes in America, Vol. II*, p. 63, by Roger K. Smith) Example: on an **Ohio Tool Co.** fenced ogee molding plane, ca. mid 19c. ****

D. H. FRIES

This imprint has been reported. Working dated unknown. UR

A. FRINK
Example: on a 14" birch toted tongue plane, ca. early 19c. UR

JOHN FRISBIE
John Frisbie (b. Oct. 1851 in PA, d. Sep. 7, 1930 in Durell, Bradford Co., PA) incuse imprint with the location **RUMMERFIELD, PA**, and the date **1924**, is on an **Owasco Tool Co.**, New York moving fillister. UR

JOHN FROST
Examples: on a 9 1/2" beech coping plane; a 11 7/8" ship-lap with integral closed tote; and marked twice on the toe of a plow with a wood depth stop and wood thumb screws, ca. 1840-50. UR

JOHN A. FRY
John A. Fry was listed as a planemaker in Edinburg, VA in 1829, at Main bt. 6th. & 7th.; from 1839-50, at w. s. Plum bt. Ann & Mason; from 1851-64; at 467 Plum; from 1867-68; at 419 Plum. In 1872, Fry was listed as a pattern filer at **Crane & Breed & Co.**, and a maker of metallic burial cases, caskets, hearses, etc. **No imprint has been reported**.

E. W. FRYE
Example: on a 10 3/4" handled plow with square slide-arms, metal locking screws, brass & steel depth stop and round chamfers, ca. 1820. UR

T. FUGATE
Thomas Fugate (b. Dec. 10, 1801 in MD, d. Jul. 17, 1879 in Cincinnati, OH) was a Cincinnati, OH, and Louisville, KY, planemaker; working in Cincinnati under his own name from 1829-31 and intermittently, between 1839-70. In 1831, he was a partner in **Carter, Donaldson & Fugate**. In 1832, he was at E. Wall bt. Main & Water. As late as 1839, he was a partner in **T. Fugate & J. D. Conover**, Louisville, KY, planemakers. **Thomas Fugate** was the longest working plane maker in Cincinnati. In the 1850-51 directory, he was listed as a foreman at **G. Roseboom**. In 1870, he was listed as plane manufacturer. After 1872, he was listed as a maker of instruments or stereoscopes. A & B **

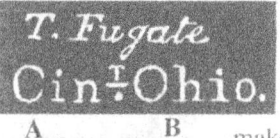

T. FUGATE/ J. D. CONOVER
Possibly a Louisville, KY, planemaking partnership of **John D. Conover** and **Thomas Fugate**. They were listed in the 1832 city directory, and may have continued until 1839, when **Thomas Fugate** returned to Cincinnati, OH.
A & B ***

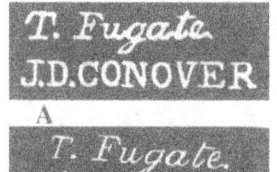
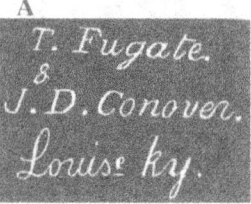

WILLIAM W. FULGHUM
William W. Fulghum (b. 1817 in NC, d. between 1860-65) moved to IA, before the Indiana designation was changed to IN, before 1841, when one of his children was born there. He was listed as a planemaker in Richmond, IN, in the 1860 census. **No imprint has been reported**.

A. FULLER
Example: on a 9 1/8" beech single-boxed complex molder with flat chamfers, ca. 1800. UR

C. FULLER
Charles Fuller (b. 1813, in Conway, NH, d. Nov. 7, 1887 in Boston, MA), was a Boston, MA, planemaker, from 1836-87. He was employed by others, until 1852, when he started his own business. He worked at Causeway St., from 1852-66; at Pine St., from 1867-72; and Waltham St., from 1873-87. The D imprint with the **GREEN STREET/ BOSTON** is very similar

to the **L. Gardner** imprint which was used between 1843-55. Apparently C. Fuller used it sometime after 1855. The 1860 MA Industrial census listed **Charles Fuller** employing two hands and producing 700 planes worth $1,700. A, B & C **; D *****

CHARLES H. FULLER
Charles H. Fuller (b. Aug. 8, 1843 in Lowell, MA, d. Feb. 17, 1871 in W. Gardiner, Kennebec Co., ME) worked as a planemaker for, and boarded with, **C. Fuller** ,from 1866-69; and may have made planes under his own name from 1870-71, at 64 Albany St., Boston, MA. **No imprint has been reported**.

D. FULLER
David Fuller (b. Jan. 19, 1795 in Ipswich, MA, d. 1871 in W. Gardiner, Kennebec Co., ME) was listed as a cabinetmaker in 1814; a joiner, in 1819; and in 1829, as a planemaker ,in W. Gardiner. In 1850, he was listed as a carpenter; in 1851, a joiner and architect. he was listed as a planemaker and carpenter in the Maine register of 1855-56. His personal papers indicate plane making during 1853-54. In 1860, he was listed as a farmer in W. Gardner. He probably learned plane making from his father, **William Fuller**, a joiner, cabinetmaker and architect. His son **Erastus Fuller**, sold his planes at his place of work in the Bath shipyards, prior to 1854, when he relocated to IL. Examples: The A2 imprint on a 9 1/2" beech side rabbet. The A1 imprint is on a 9 1/2" beech complex molder with a **Wm. Ash & Co.** iron, and dated **1851**.
A **; A1, A2, B & B1 ****

JAMES H. FULLER
Example: on a small smoother and a filletster, ca. 1850. **UR**

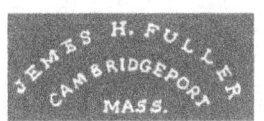

J. FULLER
Believed to be **Joseph (Field) Fuller, Jr.** (b. 1773 in Providence, RI, d. Aug. 8, 1845) who was the brother of **Richard M. Field**. He was born **Joseph Field** and changed his name after being adopted by **Joseph Fuller Sr.** He was part of **Fuller & Field** with **Richard M. Field** sometime after 1798. Example: The A imprint is on a 14"x5 1/4" birch crown molder with a centered tote, round top chamfers and flat toe and heel chamfers. This example probably represents work after the separation from **Jo, Fuller** in 1798 and before 1817 when he was listed as a blockmaker. The B imprint is on a birch jointer with a closed slighty offset tote, a single iron, and heavy round chamfers on top and flat chamfers on the ends, ca. 1800. *****

JO, FULLER
Joseph Fuller (b. May 3, 1746 in Lisbon, New London Co., CT, d. May 3, 1822) worked in Providence, RI, and was one of the most important and prolific of the early planemakers. An advertisement in the *Providence Gazette* of Dec., 26, 1772, announced "Joiners' Tools made and sold by **Joseph Fuller**". He was listed as a joiner, in 1773; and as a toolmaker, in 1808. He served as an officer during the American Revolution; and was a deacon of his church. He was a charter member of the Providence Association of Mechanics and Manufacturers, in 1789. He had no children of his own, but in Feb. 1791, he adopted **Joseph Field**, who then changed his name to **Joseph Fuller, Jr.** (b. 1773, d. Aug. 8, 1845). **Joseph, Fuller Jr.** was left a quarter share in **Joseph Fuller, Sr.**'s estate. Judging by the quantity and quality of his work, he probably was among the relatively few early planemakers who earned a significant part of his income from plane making. There was a notice in the *Providence Gazette* of Apr. 28, 1798, announcing that the partnership of **Joseph Fuller** and son **Joseph Fuller, Jr.** was "this day dissolved by mutual consent." It is possible that the partnership began about 1794 when **Joseph Fuller, Jr.** came of age. It is believed that **Isaac Field** apprenticed to **Joseph Fuller**, as early as 1796. It is also believed that brothers **George Snow** and **James Snow III**, were employees of **Joseph Fuller** and were listed as toolmakers, in a 1808 land transaction between **Joseph Fuller** and **Isaac Field**. Upon the death of **Joseph Fuller, Sr.**, in 1822, **Isaac Field** took over his shop and stock at 138 Westminster St. The **PROVIDENCE** location die was also used by **Isaac Field**. The evolution of plane making from the 18c to the 19c can be seen on the style changes **Joseph Fuller** made over his plane making career. During the early period, planes were 10" or longer with flat chamfers and decorative fluting on the toe and heel. Later, he adopted the standard 9 1/2" length, his chamfers became rounded, and the fluting disappeared. The wood used evolved from yellow birch to beech with a few maple examples. His wedge profiles became relieved and then rounded. His maker's imprints also changed. The B imprint is on a 10" birch grooving plane with relieved wedge, flat chamfers and flutes. The C, D, D1 & D2 imprints, used the same die for more than 25 years and deteriorated over time. He refilled the ends and re-engraved the individual letters; this explains the thickening of the walls of the imprinted letters. The arrow was not cleaned or re-engraved and weakened over time. The stronger the arrow the earlier the plane. Reported is a triple dot A imprint with the **IN/ PROVIDENCE** as used in the C imprint. The chronological order of use is A & B, then C & C1, then D, D1 & D2 and finally E & E1. **D, D1 & D2 *; A, C, E & E1 **; B *****

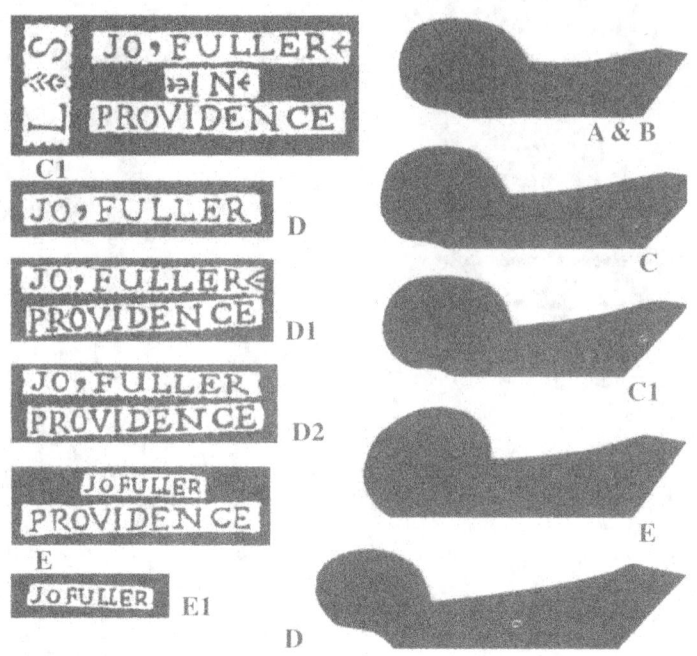

JOEL. FULLER
Joel Fuller (b. Dec. 13, 1796 in Sharon, MA, d. Apr. 28, 1877 in Fairmount, Onondago Co., NY) was listed in 1870, as a farmer. Example: on a 10 1/2" beech square rabbet found in RI, ca 1820. **UR**

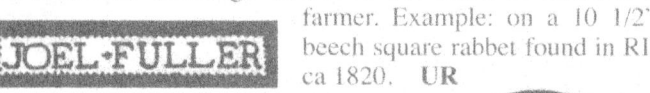

FULLER & FIELD
Fuller & Field was a partnership between **Joseph Fuller, Jr.**, the son of **John Field** and adopted by **Joseph Fuller, Sr.**, and **Richard Montgomery Field**, his brother, who were listed as toolmakers, in 1798, after the partnership between **Joseph Fuller, Jr.** and **Joseph Fuller, Sr.** was dissolved. The partnership lasted no longer than 1805. In 1817, **Joseph Fuller**, Jr. was a blockmaker and **Richard M. Field** a merchant, both cousins to **Isaac Field**. Examples: on 10" birch with relieved **Jo, Fuller** style wedges, flat chamfers and fluting. ***

THE FULTON
Example: on a smoother; and a 16" jack, both with **Sandusky Tool Co.** irons, ca. 1880. **UR**

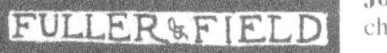

FULTON
Example: on a 20" transitional plane. The blade is marked: **FULTON TOOL CO. WARRANTED.** **UR**

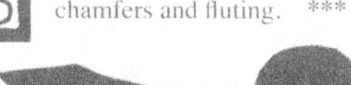

I F/ J. FUNK
Example: on a 10 1/4" hollow or nosing plane with flat chamfers, probably from PA, ca. 1800-20. **UR**

A. FURBER
Examples: on a 14" razee bench plane with a **Humphreysville** iron; a 9 7/8" beech molder; and a narrow 9 1/2" beech nosing plane with small round chamfers, ca. 1820. **A & B: UR**

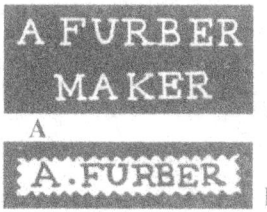

JEREMIAH FURBUSH
Jeremiah Furbush (b. Dec. 24, 1814 in Rome, ME, d. Mar. 19, 1889 in Waterville, Kennebec Co., ME), was listed in 1850, in Augusta, as a carpenter; in 1860, as a sash and door maker in Waterville, on the Kennebec River, ME; in 1870, as a door and blind manufacturer. The 1873 production was with water power, 30hp. with 30 employees. In the 1885-87 Waterville city directory, he was listed as a door, sash and "blind mnfr." at Mill and Cool St. Example: on a beech joiner with a centered tote, ca. 19c. ****

G. K. & E.
G. K. & E. probably represents a hardware dealer in BELLEVILLE, ILL. Examples: on a size **1/4** and **3/8** single-boxed side beads, both 9 1/2" with **Ohio Tool Co.** irons; and a molder with a **Hall Case & Co.** iron, ca. 1850. ****

S. W. G.
Example: on a 9 1/4" beech adj. fully boxed sash plane with wood screw arms with brass tips, found in OH, and dated **1846**. UR

I. GAFF
Believed to be **John Gass** (b. 1777 in PA) who married Apr. 9, 1799 in Salem Lutheran Church, Lebanon, PA. Two of their children were born in Lebanon in 1803 & 05. Their last child was born in 1820, in PA. Example: on a 10" beech skewed blade casing plane with flat chamfers, found in Lancaster Co., PA, ca. 1800. *****

A. A. GAGE
Example: on a 22" beech jointer with a centered tote and round chamfers, ca. 1820-30 UR

M. GAGE
Example: on a 9 3/16" beech ship-lap plane with flat chamfers, ca. 1800. UR

GAGE TOOL CO.
The **Gage Tool Co.** of Vineland, NJ, active from 1883-1919, was founded by **John Porcius Gage** (b. July 31, 1849 in Chicago, IL, d. Aug. 30, 1932 in Vineland, NJ). This company was also known as **Bridges, Gage & Co. David A. Bridges** (b. 1839 in VT) was listed in the 1880 census as a machinist in Vineland, NJ. In 1881-82, **Bridges** was listed as a cabinetmaker and patternmaker. He was issued Patent No. 271,569, on Jan. 30, 1883, and assigned 3/4 to **John Gage**. This patent was for a wood-body smoothing plane with a razee back and an adjustable metallic throat insert. Improvements had to do with the longitudinal adjustment of the cutter and cutter clamping device. **John P. Gage** was granted Patent No. 323,804, on Apr. 4, 1885. It was similar to **Bridges'** design but it made provision for a lateral adjustment lever. Patent No. 339,872, granted on Apr. 13, 1886, eliminated the lateral level and was the basic design under which all **Gage** planes were subsequently manufactured. These were classic transitional planes. The **Gage Tool Co.** was listed in the 1905-06 NJ Industrial Directory with five employees. On Apr. 17, 1917, Gage sold all interests in the **Gage Tool Co.** to **Philip J. Leavens** who in turn sold it to the **Stanley Rule & Level Co.**, in 1919. **Stanley-Gage** wood-bottom planes continued to be manufactured through 1934. (see *Patented Transitional & Metallic Planes in America 1827-1927*, p. 188-119, by Roger K. Smith) FF

S. J. GAGE
Sylvester J. Gage (b. 1822 in Addison Co., VT, d. Dec. 14, 1852 in Vergennes, VT) appeared as a carpenter and joiner in the 1849 New England directory from Vergennes, VT; and as a manufacturer of sash and window blinds in the 1850 Products of Industry for Vermont. Example: on a smoothing plane that has been reported with the name **S. J. GAGE/ VERGENNES**. No imprint is available.

C. C. GAINES & CO./ CHARLES C. GAINES
Charles C. Gaines (b. 1825 in New Orleans, LA, will prob. Oct. 16, 1863 in New Orleans) began business in New Orleans as a crockery and glassware merchant, becoming a hardware dealer in 1849. His partners included **William Heyl, Feret Jerdy**, and **L. A. Stone**. He was listed in his own name in 1849 only; and with **& CO.** in 1855. The store experienced a fire in 1862 that apparently terminated the business. Example: on 1/2" tongue & groove planes with style number **75**, made by the **Ohio Tool Co.** A, B & C ****

J. R. GALE
Jonas Russell Gale (b. Mar. 30, 1808 in Millbury, MA, d. 1891 in Denver, CO) "At the age of 18, he went to New York City, and there entered the plane factory of his cousin, **Enos Baldwin**, and became proficient in the manufacture of jointers' tools." **Gale** moved to Providence, RI in the spring of 1829, "having just turned 21 years old." **Jonas R. Gale** was a partner in **Cumings & Gale**, from 1830-33, at 77 Weybosset, Friendship, Providence, RI.; and He worked under his own name, from 1833-36. An advertisement of his "Plane Manufactory" in which he claimed "to make Planes and Tools of every description", appeared in the 1836 Providence directory. In Sep., 1836, **Jonas R. Gale**, age 28, sold his Providence planemaking business and moved to Alton, St. Clair Co., IL, a trading and transportation town on the Mississippi River, where he invested in a mill and other property. His business was taken over in Nov. 1836, by the short-lived firm of **Barrus & Bigelow**, who used the imprint **Bigelow & Barrus**. In 1836, **Gale** visited Tazewell Co, IL where he was shown a large tract of undeveloped prairie land, an area that **Gale** envisioned as a future farming community able to support its own town. He joined with the "land promoter and ardent American temperance advocate" Edward Delavan to form a land company that purchased the land in Tazewell Co, from the U.S. Government, divided it into 160 acre tracts and

sold the tracts at public auction in Providence on Nov. 24, 1836. While living in Alton, **Gale** was a supporter of the abolitionist **Elijah Lovejoy**. **Gale** suffered property loss through mob violence in the riot that resulted in Lovejoy's murder on Nov. 7, 1837. By 1838, **Gale** had relocated from Alton to his farm in Delavan. In 1850, 55 & 60, he was listed as a farmer; in 1870, a carpenter; and in 1880, a planemaker in Delavan, Tazewell Co., IL; in 1886 & 88, he was listed in Denver, CO. The A and B embossed imprints are believed to be from Providence, RI. The incuse C imprint is believed to be from Tazewell, IL.
A *; B **; C ****

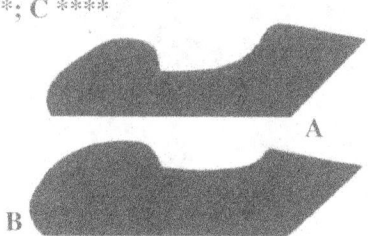

M GALE
Examples: on a 9 5/8" birch round; and a 10 13/16" birch rabbet, both primitive in appearance, ca. 1800. **UR**

P. GALLOWAY
Example: on a 9 3/4" beech molder with flat chamfers, ca. 1800. **UR**

J. GALLUP
A descendant of **John Gallup** (b. 1620, d. 1675), of New London CT, an Indian interpreter who was killed in the King Phillips' War. Examples: on an 8 3/4" birch Yankee plow with the imprint struck twice, square arms, wood thumbscrews and depth stop, a riveted skate, and flat chamfers; a 9 3/8" fruitwood complex molder with flat chamfers; and on a 12 3/4"x 3 3/4" fruitwood complex molder with offset birch tote, round top iron & wedge and heavy round chamfers, from New England, ca. 1790-1800, ****

GAMMAGE
Example: on a 9 7/16" beech tongue plane with a hickory wedge and heavy round chamfers, ca. 1820. **UR**

J: GAQUET
Example: on a 15" beech open offset toted multi-reed plane with boxwood diamond strike and shallow round chamfers. The same incuse imprint is on the plane and the iron, ca. 19c. **UR**

GARDNAR
Examples: on a 9 1/2" beech very small astragal bead; and a 9 1/2" triple boxed reed, both with small flat chamfers; and a 9 3/4" ovolo molder with round chamfers. ca. 1800-20. **UR**

A. B. GARDNER
Example: on a 9 1/2"x 1 1/2" beech right and left hand skew rabbet pair. **UR**

CHARLES GARDNER
Charles Gardner was a planemaker in Cornwall, CT, active in 1857-58. **No imprint has been reported.**

JOHN GARDNER
John Gardner was a planemaker in Boston, MA, from 1830-33; in 1834, he went into the hardware business at Liberty Square. **No imprint has been reported.**

L. GARDNER
Leavitt Gardner (b. Nov. 10, 1800 in Hingham, Plymouth Co., MA, d. Dec. 8, 1876 in Cambridge, MA) made planes in Boston, MA, from 1825-55, as a partner in **Gardner & Brazer**, in 1825 only; and as a partner in **Gardner & Murdock**, from 1825-42, at 4 Green St.; and under this imprint, from 1843-55. He was listed in the 1849 New England Mercantile Union Directory as a plane manufacturer at 4 Green St., Boston; in 1850, as a planemaker employing three hands and making planes worth $3,500; in 1855, as a planemaker in Boston; and in 1860, as Mechanic, retired. A boxed bead has been reported with an additional imprint **Patent April 9, 1851**, probably referring to its adjustable double-iron. **Leavitt Gardner** was possibly a partner in **Gardner & Appleton**. From 1855-70, he was listed as living at 49 Garden St., Boston, MA. The B imprint appears to be the **GARDNER & MURDOCK** stamp with the **MURDOCK** removed.
A: FF; B ****

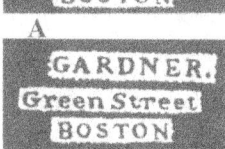

GARDNER & APPLETON
Gardner & Appleton was a Boston, MA, planemaking partnership comprised of **Leavitt Gardner** and **Thomas Appleton**. Working dates are unknown. **No imprint has been reported.**

GARDNER & BRAZER
Gardner & Brazer was a Boston, MA, planemaking partnership comprised of **Leavitt Gardner** and **Benjamin Brazer**, that operated in 1825 only. **Benjamin Brazer** also appeared in the Lowell, MA, directories 1832-35. **Gardner & Brazer** was succeeded by **Gardner & Murdock** at the same address, from 1825-41. ***

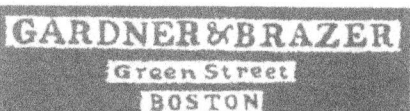

GARDNER & CO.

Example: on a cooper's beech croze, ca 19c. **UR**

GARDNER & MURDOCK

Gardner & Murdock was a Boston, MA, plane making partnership between **Leavitt Gardner** and **Amasa Murdock** that was active from 1825-41; and succeeded **Gardner & Brazer**. In 1841, the firm was listed in the Boston Almanac under "Plains" at 4 Green St. Example: the B imprint is on a double right & left compass bead router, fully-boxed. A: FF; A1 ***; B *****

GARDNER & SCHUTTE

D. Aloysius Schutte was a Chillicothe, OH, hardware dealer. Example: on an unhandled beech screw-arm plow with arms and nuts possibly of fruitwood and an **Ohio Tool Co**. iron. ****

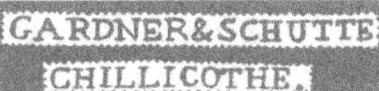

M. GARIS

Example: on an 11" beech skew rabbet with round chamfers, ca. 1820. **UR**

J. GARITY

Examples: on 4 rosewood and 2 lignum vitae bench planes, all from the ME coast, ca. 1850. **UR**

H+ GARLICK

Examples: on a 9 5/8" skew rabbet with a hickory wedge; and a 10 1/4" self fenced square rabbet, both birch with heavy flat chamfers, found in northern NH, ca. 1770-90. **UR**

WM. GARRELS & CO.

FROM WM. GARRELS & CO./ 720 CARONDELET AV./ ST. LOUIS was stenciled in ink on the side of a ca. 1850 plane. **No imprint is available.**

GARRETT & POLLARD

Garrett & Pollard is believed to have been a hardware firm from Montgomery, AL. Example: on the toe of a **Copeland & Co.** smoother. *****

DAYTON GARRISON

Dayton Garrison was listed as a Cincinnati, OH planemaker from 1836-37, boarding at Catharine Covert's. Also boarding at that location was **William McKimle**. **No imprint has been reported.**

D. N. GARRISON

David Nelson Garrison (b. 1818 in OH, d. Feb. 24, 1885 in Middletown, Butler Co., OH) was a Dayton, OH, planemaker and tool merchant, from 1850-54; who worked earlier as a planemaker for **Samuel Sloop** in Cincinnati, OH, in 1839-40. He was listed in the 1850 census as a tool merchant in Dayton, who operated a tool factory using water power, employing four hands and producing tools valued at $3330. **

D. N. GARRISON/ T. A. HEIM

David Nelson Garrison and **Thomas Andrew Heim** (b. Nov. 15, 1822, D. Jun. 4, 1859 in Hamilton, Butler Co., OH) were in a partnership in Dayton, OH, from 1849-50. Example: on a 9 1/2" beech table joint plane; and a size **6** hollow. (see **Heim & Smith**) ***

P. GARRISON

Examples: on a tongue & grove opposed beech combination plane with flat chamfers; and on a toted crown starter, ca. 1800. **UR**

I. GARVEY

I. Garvey was probably a hardware dealer from Owego, NY, west of Binghamton. Example: on the heel of a **D. R. Barton** Gothic bead. ****

E. GARY

Example: on a 9 1/8" beech complex molder with shallow flat chamfers, ca. early 19c. **UR**

J. GATES

Example: on a 9 5/8" beech astragal, with round chamfers, ca. 1810-20. **UR**

G. GAURD

Example: on a 9 1/2" beech complex molder, ca. 1850. **UR**

GAY
This imprint may have been modified from a die with either a full first name or an initial. Example: on a 9 3/8" beech coping plane with flat chamfers, ca. 1810. **UR**

M: GAY
Example: on a 9 5/8" (the heel has been shot) birch cove step with heavy flat chamfers, ca. 1790-1800. **UR**

T. GAZE
Example: on a 9 1/4" birch side rabbet with wide round chamfers and a **R. HILDICK** iron, ca. 1810. **UR**

D. S. & S. P. GEER
David S. Geer (b. Apr. 15, 1818 in Clyde, Wayne Co., NY, d. Sep. 29, 1885 in Syracuse, NY) and **Samuel P. Geer** (b. Dec. 20, 1821 in Oneida Co., NY, d. Feb. 25, 1867 in Syracuse, NY) were partners in a Syracuse, NY, hardware dealership from 1853-65. Previously they operated as **Geer Bros. Hardware & Locksmiths** from 1851-52, consisted of **David S. Geer, John R. Geer, John R. Geer, Jr.,** and **Samuel P. Geer**. ****

D. GEHRET
Examples: on a 2 1/4" wide maple complex molder with an iron marked **P. LAW**; a 24" jointer with offset tote and two 12"x 2 1/4" beech massive plows with wood thumbscrews, wood depth stop, screw applied skate and with shallow round chamfers, probably from eastern PA, ca. 1810-30. **A & A1 ******

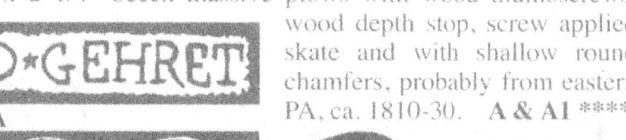

J: GEHRIG
Examples: on a 10" tongue plane with flat chamfers; a 9 1/2" round with flat chamfers; a 9 3/8"x 1 1/2" round with intermittent boxing with round chamfers; and a 9" torus bead, all beech and a distinctive wedge finial, probably from eastern PA, ca. 1800. ****

GENESEE TOOL CO.
Genesee Tool Co. may be one of the trade names used by the **Auburn Tool Co.** The Genesee River flows through Rochester,

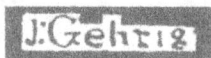
A

B C

NY, and Genesee Co. is nearby, both within 100 miles of **Auburn Tool Co.**; on a 16" jack plane that was found together with a "**Cayuga**" jack and an "**Ontario**" fore plane. **A & B *; C *****

I. C. GENN
Examples: on a sash found in Mahantongo Valley, 25 miles NE of Harrisburg, PA, on a 9 7/16" astragal; and a plow with a riveted skate, all beech with flat chamfers, ca. 1800. ****

D. GEORGE
Example: on a 9 1/2" beech double-iron sash coping plane, ca. 1830. **UR**

J. GEORGE
Example: on a 9 1/2" beech size **2** hollow, ca. 1850. **UR**

J. N. GEORGE
Examples: on a complex molder; a 2" wide skew rabbet with a relieved A wedge, both 9 1/4"; and a fixed sash with two wedges & irons, the B wedge, all beech with round chamfers, ca. 1820. ****

M' GEORGE
Example: on a 9 3/8" hollow with flat chamfers. **UR**

S. D. GEORGE
Examples: on a double-boxed molder; a handled, 3" wide molder with an applied fence, a birch wedge and pegged centered tote; a 13" skew toted rabbet; a fixed sash with two wedges & irons; and a 15 1/2" gutter plane, all beech with shallow round chamfers, possibly of eccentric provincial origin, ca. 1830. **A & B: ******

A

B

W: GEORGE
Example: on a beech size 1/4" side boxed bead, with small flat chamfers, ca. early 19c. **UR**

P. GEPHART
Examples: on a pair of wedge-lock match tongue & groove plank planes, ca. 1850. **UR**

GERARD TOOL CO.
The **Gerard Tool Co.** may have been a trade name used by the **Auburn Tool Co.**, as was the **Owasco Tool Co.** and the **Genesee Tool Co.**. **James Watson Gerard** (b. 1794, d. 1874) was a New Yorker who was responsible for the incorporation of the Society for Reformation of Juvenile Delinquents and who was the first to sponsor the wearing of uniforms by police, suggesting a possible Auburn Prison connection. Example: on a 6" beech smoothing plane with an **Empire Co.** iron. ******

C. GERE
Charles Geer (Gere) (b. July 19, 1776 in New London, CT, d. Feb. 5, 1842 in Hartland, VT.) was the brother of **Ebenezer Gere** and on Dec. 17, 1799, married **Sarah Denison**, daughter of **Col. George Denison** of Hartland, VT. The Susquehanna Co., PA, records show that **Charles Gere** was a carpenter, that he came to Brooklyn Twp. from Hartland, ca. 1804-07, and was active ca. 1830-40's. Example: on a 9 5/8" beech hollow with flat chamfers, ca. 1800. ********

C. M. GERE
Christopher Morgan Gere (b. Nov. 7, 1814 in New London, CT, d. June 15, 1892 in Montrose, PA) was the son of **Ebenezer Geer (Gere)** and came with his parents to Brooklyn Twp., Susquehanna County, PA, in 1821. At age 16, **Christopher Gere** entered his father's plane making shop and continued to work as a planemaker until He was elected sheriff in 1848 and moved to Montrose, PA. **A, B & B1 ****

E. GERE
Ebenezer Gere (Geer) (b. Feb. 8, 1779 in New London, CT, d. Dec. 2, 1845 in Brooklyn Twp, PA) lived in Groton and Preston, CT, and appears in the 1800's in Ulster Co., NY; and in 1821 in Brooklyn Twp., Susquehanna Co., PA. He was listed in the 1830 & 40 censuses, as being a planemaker. **Ebenezer Gere** was the brother of **Charles Gere** and the father of **Christopher Morgan Gere**. **Ebenezer Gere** is interred in a tiny cemetery in Brooklyn, PA, with **Justice Kent**, **Christopher Gere**, **Alford W. Mack**, and **John B. Mack**. Examples: the A imprint and A wedge is on 9 5/8"-9 3/4" beech molders with flat chamfers. The A1 imprint is on a 9 5/8" beech round. The B imprint is on 9 1/2"-9 5/8" beech molders with flat or round chamfers. Imprint A and A1 are believed to have been used in CT as most examples were found in southeastern New England, ca.1800-30.
B **; A ***; A1 & C ****

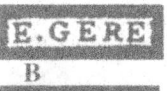

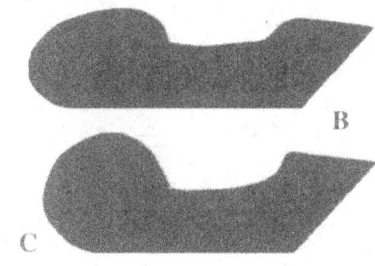

N. GERE
Attributed to **Nathan Gere (Geer)** (b. Apr. 30, 1781 in Preston, CT, d. April 7, 1868 in Preston, CT) the son of **John Wheeler Gere** (b. 1774, d. 1818) a cabinetmaker in Griswold and Preston, CT, and first cousin to **Ebenezer Gere** and **Charles Gere**. Examples: on an ogee molding plane with lignum vitae boxing; a round; and a door plane with a steel skate, all 9 3/8" beech with flat chamfers, ca. 1800. ********

GERE, ABBOTT & CO.; GEORGE GERE & CO.
Gere, Abbott & Co. was listed as a hardware merchant in the Columbus, OH, city directories of 1848-56. The **Gere** was **George Gere** (d. 1882 in Franklin, OH.) who later became the first president of the **Ohio Tool Co.** In 1864, he was listed as **GEORGE GERE & CO.** in Columbus, OH. In 1875, in addition to being listed as President of the **Ohio Tool Co.**, he was also listed as Pres. of **Ohio Furniture Co.** **Abbott** was **James Samuel Abbott** (b. Sep. 18, 1811 in Canton, Hartford Co., CT, d. Jan. 4, 1904 in Columbus, OH) who was listed as a tool merchant, as early as 1845-46; he continued in the hardware business by himself after the dissolution of **Gere, Abbott & Co.**; and later, in 1860-62, with his son, **H. J. Abbott** (b. 1838 in OH), continued as **J. S. Abbott & Son**, all were located in Columbus, OH. **A & B ****

JOSEPH GERRARD
Joseph Gerrard (b. ca. 1813, d. Nov. 24, 1880 in Maryville, Union Co., OH) at age 17, was apprenticed on Jan. 31, 1829 to **H. B. Miller** of Lebanon, OH. In 1840 & 50, He was listed in **Harmony, Clark Co.**, OH. In 1860 & 70, He was in Maryville as a store clerk. **No imprint has been reported**.

H. W. GETMAN
H. W. Getman is believed to have been a hardware merchant in Ilion, east of Utica, NY. In 1883-84, he was listed as a carpenter in Utica. In 1886; in Little Falls, NY, as **H. W. GETMAN & CO.** manufacturer of carriage wrenches. Example: on the toe of a size **8** round, made by **A. Howland & Co.**, NY. ********

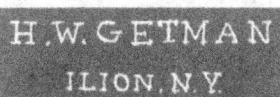

N. GIBB
Example: on a 9 3/8"x 3/8" beech round plane with flat chamfers. ca. 1800. **UR**

J. W. GIBBS
John W. Gibbs (b. 1801 in NY, d. May 22, 1879 in Providence, PA) was a New York City planemaker from 1829-33. He was part of **Gibbs & Cation** in 1834. In 1850, he was listed as a Minister of the Gospel in Findley, DE; in 1860, he was a Physician in N. Bergen, Hudson Co., NJ; in 1870, he was a Physician in Providence, Scranton Co., PA. The A imprint is from a wedge-arm beech plow with an appearance similar to that of **A & E Baldwin** suggesting a possible connection or an apprenticeship with **Enos Baldwin** before Enos' death in 1829. **A, A1 & B** **

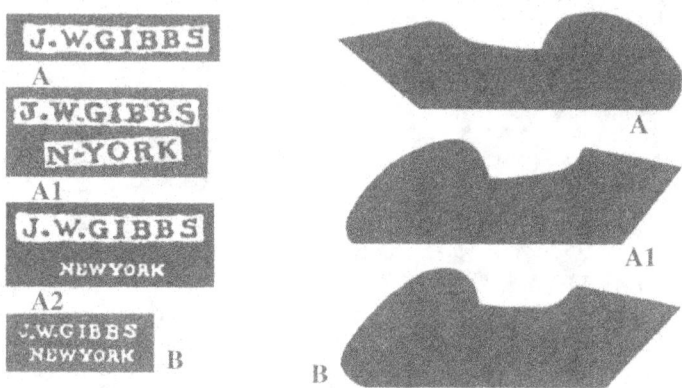

GIBBS & CATION
Gibbs & Cation was a partnership of **John W. Gibbs** and **David W. Cation** that made planes at 227 Grand, New York City in 1834. **A & A1** ***

J. GIBSON/ JOHN GIBSON
John Gibson (b. Nov. 8, 1796 in Ireland, d. Jul. 8, 1868 in Albany, NY) made planes in Albany, NY, under his own imprint from 1823-24, 1829-35, and 1839-52. He was a partner in **Rowell & Gibson** from 1824-28, and a partner in **J. & J. Gibson** from 1837-38. Sometime during this period he also must have worked in New York City, as evidenced by imprint E. John Gibson's advertisement in the 1842-43 Albany directory listed his establishment as a "Plane Factory, Plane & Board planning and sawing, and a Plaining Mill". In 1850-55, he was listed under plaining mill in Albany. Example: on a sash gauge. **A, B, C, C1, D & D1: FF; E, F & G** ***

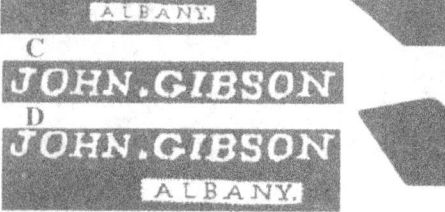

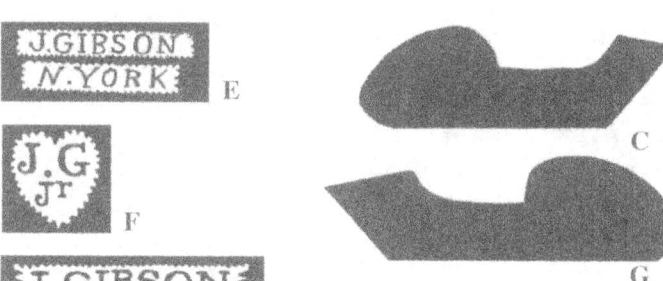

J+ GIBSON
This may be an early example of **John Gibson**, or may be a separate person. Example: This name, followed by what looks like a face, is from a 9 1/2" grooving plane; and an 8 1/2" wedge-lock plow with a riveted skate, wood thumbscrew-locked depth stop, both beech with round chamfers, ca. 1820. **A & A1: UR**

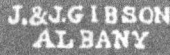

J. & J. GIBSON
J. & J. Gibson was an Albany, NY, plane making partnership, active in 1837-38, consisting of **John Gibson** and his brother **Joseph Gibson**. *

JOSEPH GIBSON
Joseph Gibson (b. ca. 1799 in Ireland, d. Aug. 17, 1870 in Kings, NY) was the brother of **John Gibson** and a partner in **J. & J. Gibson**, in 1837-38. **Joseph Gibson** immigrated on Aug. 1, 1826, from Londonderry, Ireland. He made planes under his own imprint in Albany, NY. from 1839-46. *

Z. GIBSON
Example: on a 9 5/8" beech grooving plane with a riveted skate and flat chamfers, ca. 1800. **UR**

GIDDINGS & MEEK
Giddings & Meek was a Hartford, CT, firm that may have been a planemaker but was probably a hardware dealer, ca. 1850. ****

G. GIFFING
Example: on a 10" beech tongue plane with flat chamfers, ca. early 19c. **UR**

A. GILBERT & SONS
A. Gilbert & Sons "Plane Manufactory" appears on an early map of Derby, CT. **A. Gilbert & Sons** consisted of **Ager Gilbert, Alfred L. Gilbert & William F. Gilbert** located on

Turnpike/ Milford Rd., Derby, CT. In 1860, **Ager Gilbert** (b. 1818 in CT) as a joiner. **No imprint has been reported**.

H. GILBERT
H. Gilbert was a Harrisburg, PA, hardware dealer who appeared as late as 1890 in the Harrisburg city directory. Example: on an **Israel White**, a **Kellogg & Co.** and a **Burnham & Bros.** plane.
A & B ****

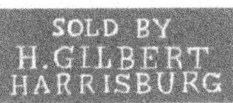
A

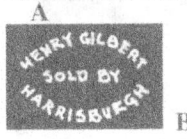
B

J. GILBERT
Probably **John Gilbert** who was listed in the 1840 New Haven, CT, directory as a joiner at the rear of 78 Crown St. A tool chest was found with 53 molding planes with this imprint and a **C. Morehouse** plane. Example: on a 9 7/16" beech small astragal bead with heavy round chamfers. ****

W. F. GILBERT
William F. Gilbert (b. Sep. 5, 1834 in CT, d. Dec. 16, 1917 in Shelton, CT) was the son of **Ager Gilbert** and was a Derby, CT planemaker. He was listed, in the 1850 census, as a planemaker, working for **L. DeForest** and **L. & C. H. DeForest**; and in the 1860 census, as a planemaker in Derby. In 1900, **William** was lister as "manf. of wood trusses"; In 1910, as occupation as "none". Example: on a 9 1/2" beech miter plane. ****

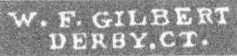

GILBERT, SWEET & LYON
Gilbert, Sweet & Lyon was a New York City hardware dealer that sold planes from 1887-89. The partners were **John A. Gilbert, Edwin S. Sweet** and **Henry M. Lyon**. It was succeeded by **Sickles, Sweet & Lyon**. ***

O. GILDER
Examples: on a 14 1/2" pair of beech tongue & groove toted plank planes; and a rabbet plane all with flat chamfers, ca. 1810. UR

T. GILES
Thomas Giles was a cabinetmaker in Salem, MA from 1759-62. Example: on a 10" skew rabbet with wide flat chamfers. UR

JOHN GILL
Example: on an 8" beech plow with solid bronze skate screwed from the off side, wood thumbscrews, and a double steel screw-adjusted full length depth stop, found in Winchester, NH, ca. 1800. UR

THOS GILL
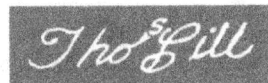
Example: on a 15" badger plane. UR

GILLESPIE
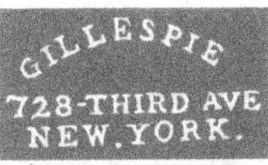
A

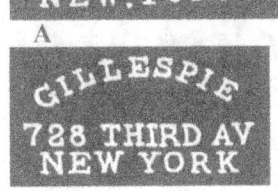
B

Benjamin Gillespie was probably a New York City hardware dealer. Example: on a **G. W. Denison & Co.** rabbet. The name **Benj. Gillespie** also appears in the **G. W. Denison & Co.** account book May 1882. A & B ****

A. GILLET
Examples: on an 8 3/4" beech plow with wood depth stop and thumbscrews; an ogee; a size 1/8" boxed bead; and a small astragal, all 10" beech with flat chamfers; a 9 9/16" round with round chamfers; and a 9 1/2" hollow with flat chamfers, both beech with an **I. Sleeper** style wedge. It appears that the planes were made over a period of time, ca. 1790-1810, possibly from Newbury/ Newburyport, MA. ***

F. GILLET
Example: on a 31" joiner with a closed-offset tote, diamond strike and flat chamfers, ca. early 19c.   UR

S. GILLIS
Samuel Gillis was listed from 1819-29 as a Lancaster City, PA joiner. He may have done piece work for **E. W. Carpenter**, from 1826-29. In 1830-32, **Gillis** was listed in Harrisburg, PA. Examples: on a group of 9 planes found together in eastern PA; three are by **E. W. Carpenter/ Baltimore**; four are by **E. W Carpenter/ Lancaster**; one is by **Kneass**; and one, a 10 3/8" bead with interrupted lignum vitae boxing. UR

A. H. GILMAN
Example: on a 28" beech jointer with slightly offset tote and round chamfers, found in NH; ca. 1800-10. UR

G. D. GILMAN
Example: on a 3 1/2" wide crown molder; and a mast plane of tropical wood; ca. 1825-50. **No imprint is available**.

I. D. GILMAN
Examples: on a 15"x 4 1/2" crown molder; and a 12" handled wide complex molder, ca. 1800. UR

J. GILMER

Joseph Gilmer (b. 1809 in NY) moved to IA (then used for Indiana) between 1836-40. He was listed as a planemaker in the New Albany, IN, city directories of 1848, 56, 59 & 60. He was also listed in the 1850 census as "Digging Gold Cal." with little success apparently for he was back making planes, in 1855. In 1869, 70 & 80, he returned to CA with his family, to Benicia, Soland Co., CA, as the "sup. of cement works". In 1885, he was listed in Alameda, CA. Examples: on two complex molders; and two jack planes. One of the molders is dated **1855**. **

ROBERT GILMORE

Robert Gilmore (b. ca. 1740 in MA, d. 1796 in Cambridge, Washington Co., NY) was a soldier in Sep. 1750, in the French and Indian War. He was in the service of King George III of England. For his service, he received a grant of land in Albany Co., NY. He married Dorothy Gray, on Nov. 8, 1754, in Pelham, north east of Amherst, MA. In 1761, **Gilmore** went to Cambridge, NY. He was an original proprietor of Cambridge when it was established in 1773. On Jan 11, 1774, **Robert Gilmore** sold his land in Pelham. Example: on a toted birch complex molder with round-top iron and shallow flat chamfers, found in the Springfield, MA area, ca. 1760. *****

J. GIVENS

J. Givens with the location **St. LOUIS/ MO** probably was a hardware dealer. Example: on a boxed beading plane, ca. mid. 19c. ****

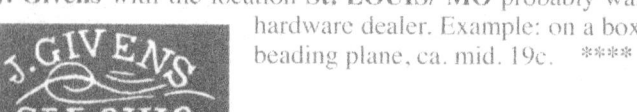

E. GLADDING

Possibly **Ezra Gladding** (b. 1798, d. Nov. 13, 1848 Saybrook, Middlesex Co., CT) who was listed in the Saybrook, CT, census for 1830 & 40. His church membership was "withdrawn" on Sep. 17, 1831. His estate, appraised by **Jeremiah Gladding**, included the contents of a full shop, which suggests that he was a cabinetmaker or joiner. Examples: are on 9 1/2"-9 5/8" beech with heavy round chamfers, ca. 1810-20. *****

J. GLADDING/ J. GLADDING, JR

There are several possibilities for the makers of these planes. **Jeremiah Gladding** (b. 1809) purchased a 1/3 interest in the **J. & L. Denison** plane business, in 1836. In 1847, when his daughter was born, he was called an architect, living in Saybrook, CT. In 1848, **Jeremiah** appraised the estate of **E. Gladding**. In 1860, **Jeremiah** was listed as a lumber merchant. Another possibility is **Josiah Gladding** (d. 1833) was living in Saybrook and listed in the 1810 & 20 censuses as a farmer and shipbuilder. Among his children were **Josiah Gladding** and **John Gladding** (b. 1795, d. 1847) who was a carpenter, house builder and joiner in Saybrook, CT. **John's** son, **John Gladding, Jr.** (b. 1819, d. 1896) was, listed in 1849, as a carpenter, living in Saybrook. In 1852 & 57, **John** was listed as a joiner. From 1870-72, the **G. W. Denison & Co.** account book recorded 10 occasions when **John Gladding** (who dropped the Jr. after his father's death in 1847) purchased planes, presumably for resale, with numerous duplicates. Examples: the B imprint, marked toe and heel, is on a sash plane; and an astragal bead, both 9 1/2" beech with round chamfers; and on a molder by **H. Wetherell/ Chatham**. The A imprint is on a 11 11/2" skew rabbet; and a 9 1/2"x 1" square rabbet, both beech with round chamfers, ca. 1835. **A &B:** *****

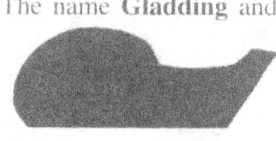

O. GLADDING

Examples: on two 9 1/2" beech single-boxed beads with heavy round chamfers; and a molder, with both this imprint and the **O. Gladwin** imprint, found in CT. The name **Gladding** and **Gladwin** were often interchangeable and by the early 1800's there was a trend to change from **Gladding** in favor of **Gladwin**, from Saybrook, CT, ca. 1830. *****

R. GLADDING

Possibly **Rufus Gladding**, recorded as marrying in Saybrook, CT, on Nov. 10, 1825. Examples: on a fixed sash; and a tongue plane, both 9 1/2" beech with heavy round chamfers, from Saybrook, CT, ca. 1830. *****

J. GLADWIN

There is no **J. Gladwin** in the Saybrook, CT, vital records but given the apparent flexibility of the use of **Gladwin** and **Gladding**, this imprint could represent one of the possible **J. Gladdings**. Example: on a 21 1/4" beech bench plane with a diamond strike, a centered-closed cherry tote, and round chamfers, possibly from Saybrook, CT, ca. 1830. *****

O GLADWIN

Example: on a 9 1/2" beech molder that has been altered to cut a "V". The chamfers are round and shallow. A second example with both **O. Gladding** and this imprint has been found in CT. With the interchanging of **Gladding** and **Gladwin** these imprints could have been by the same person, possibly from Saybrook, CT, ca. 1830. *****

P. A. GLADWIN/ P. A. GLADWIN & CO.

Porter A. Gladwin (b. ca. 1818 in Saybrook, CT, d. Feb. 4, 1887 in Somerville, MA) was first listed in the Saybrook, CT, vital records as **Porter A. Gladding** of Saybrook, marrying in Sept. 1839. It is not uncommon for the interchanging of the

Gladding and Gladwin surnames. He next appears on an April 20, 1840 patent, for a corn sheller with his residence listed as Chester, CT, which is the bordering town north of Saybrook. On April 6, 1843, **Porter A. Gladwin** sold land in Winthrop, the village in western Saybrook where **J. & L. Denison** was then working. There is circumstantial evidence suggesting that **P. A. Gladwin** learned plane making from **John Denison** and **Lester Denison**. **Porter A. Gladwin** was part of **Gladwin & Platts** with a **Platts**, possibly also from Saybrook, in Wallingford, CT, prior to 1850. From 1850 to 55, He and **Joel Fenn** were in partnership as **Gladwin & Fenn** in Wallingford. The **WALLINGFORD, CT.** location stamp was passed from **Gladwin & Platts** to **Gladwin & Fenn** then **Joel Fenn & Co.** and finally to **Sawheag Works**. The F imprint is believed to have been used in CT, and has been seen overstriking a Saybrook maker's imprint. **Porter A. Gladwin** was listed in Boston, MA, and nearby Chelsea directories, from 1857-58, 1868-73 & 1877-82, listed as a planemaker by himself, as a planemaker in partnership, as a match plane maker, and as an inventor. He was in partnership with **Thomas L. Appleton** as **Gladwin & Appleton** in Chelsea, from 1873-77. The **G. W. Denison & Co.** account book for 1871, records sales of numerous planes to **Porter A. Gladwin**, including many boxwood and rosewood screw-arm plow planes. He obviously found that he could buy less expensively than he could make these planes himself. He was an active inventor, with six patents, four of which concerned planes. The first, Patent No. 17541 was issued on June 9, 1857, imprint C, for an improved match plane that permitted, through the use of fences, the cutting of a tongue or a groove without having to reverse the direction of the plane. (see **R. Barnes**) The second, Patent No. 19359, was issued Feb. 16, 1858, for an eccentric level that would adjust the position of the iron. It also had a "T" shaped slot that would accommodate the detachable handle as patented by **Thomas Worrall** on Sept. 29, 1857. The third, Patent No. 185442, issued Dec. 19, 1876, imprint E, provided adjustable fences for his first patent, the match plane. His last, Patent No. 202105, issued April 9, 1878, was for a combination tool handle & plane and is found made of wood or metal. In 1865, **Porter** was listed in Boston as a mechanist; in 1870, as a plane maker; and in 1880, as a "plane mftg." in Chelsea, Suffolk Co., MA. From 1882-85, **Porter A. Gladwin** was probably an inventor only. He was listed for two other patents: one for augers and the other for a vise. Imprints B1 & A are alterations of the B imprint. A, A1 & D *; C **; B ***; B1, E & F ****

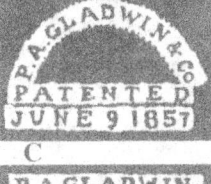

GLADWIN & APPLETON

Gladwin & Appleton was a partnership of **Porter A Gladwin** and **Thomas L. Appleton** that made planes in Chelsea, MA, from 1873-77. The C imprint is from a handled combination match "parallel" tongue & groove plane using the **P. A. Gladwin** patent.
A & B *; D **; C & C1 ***

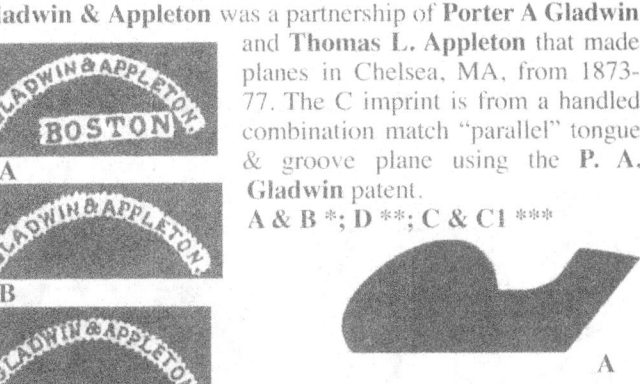

GLADWIN & FENN

Gladwin & Fenn was a plane making partnership of **Porter A. Gladwin** and **Joel Fenn**, in Wallingford, CT, from 1850-55. The **WALLINGFORD CT** location imprint was used previously by **Gladwin & Platts** and subsequently used by **Joel Fenn & Co.** and the **Sawheag Works**. **

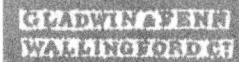

GLADWIN & PLATTS

Gladwin & Platts was a Wallingford, CT, planemaking partnership between **P. A. Gladwin** and an unknown **Platts**, active prior to 1850 and probably short lived. **Platts** was a common name in Saybrook, CT, where **Porter A. Gladwin** most likely got his start. The **WALLINGFORD CT** location die was subsequently used by **Gladwin & Fenn**. Example: on a plane made by **C. & S. Buckley** of Saybrook. **

G. W. GLAESCHER/ GLAESCHER & CO.

G. W. Glaescher was a Cincinnati, OH, hardware dealer from 1859-79, succeeded by **Glaescher & Co.** from 1879-89. Example: the A imprint is on the heel of a **Scioto Works** molder. The B imprint is on the heel of a **Sandusky Tool Co.** plane. One reported example has the **G. W. Glaescher** imprint overstruck by the **Glaescher & Co.** imprint.
A & B ****

A. L. GLEASON

Albert L. Gleason with the 1849-50 Utica City Directory mistakenly listing his middle initial as **S**. (b. Mar. 8, 1829 in NY,

d. May 28, 1907 in Watertown, NY) married **Charles Reed's** sister **Emily Reed** on Mat 29, 1850. Prior to 1850, He probably worked for **John Reed Jr.** **Albert** was listed as a toolmaker in 1850, in Pamelia, on the north side of the Black River opposite Watertown. In 1855, He was listed as a mechanic in Adams, Jefferson Co., NY. **Albert** was a planemaker in Watertown, NY, from 1859-75. In 1860, **Gleason** was listed as a partner in **Gleason & Wood** in Watertown; in 1880, a carpenter; and from 1900-07 as a mill wright.
A, B & B1 **

GLEASON & WOOD
Albert L. Gleason and **William W. Wood** were listed as manufacturers of joiner's tools in Watertown, NY in 1860. The firm existed no later than 1863.
A & A1 **

I. GLEIM
A group of over fifty planes was found at the auction for an undertaker named **Gleim** in Iowa. Also in the auction was a horse-drawn hearse built by **W. H. Gleim**, whose incuse imprint also appears on some of these planes. The undertaking business was combined with a furniture business. Most of the makers were **Auburn** and **Ohio Tool Co**, plus a **J. A. King**. Examples: with this imprint alone, on two 9 1/4" beech quarter rounds; and a complex molder; all with pointed finials and flat chamfers, ca. 1800, possibly from PA. ****

GLENN & DUKE
Glenn & Duke was a tool and hardware dealer consisting of **William B. Glenn** and **Mary Duke** listed in the Philadelphia, PA, city directories from 1837-40. In 1837, lists **Duke, Mary** widow of **Tristam Duke**, at 138 S. 2nd. The same 1837 directory lists **Glenn, William B.** tools and hardware, at 138 S. 2nd., the same address as **Mary Duke**. The *Philadelphia Circulating Business Directory* for 1838 contained the cards of the principal merchants, manufacturers and other business men of Philadelphia lists:

GLENN & DUKE'S
TOOL STORE,
138 SOUTH SECOND STREET
PHILADELPHIA

Glenn & Duke, tools & hardware, 138 S 2nd. was listed from 1839-40. After 1840, **William B. Glenn** was listed as a cabinetmaker and **Mary Duke** with no occupation. ****

J. GLINES
Examples: on a birch straight rabbet with offset tote and flat chamfers; and a 9 1/2" double-boxed bead with round chamfers. ca. 1810-15. (see J. Clines) UR

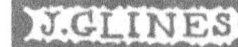

GLOBE MFG. CO.
In 1857, **Austin Baldwin**, sold the **Baldwin Tool Co.** of Middletown, CT, to the **Globe Mfg. Co.** of Rhodestown, CT, who made only plane irons. The **Globe Mfg. Co.** may have marked and sold leftover stock from the **Baldwin Tool Co.** The name **Globe Mfg. Co./ Rhodestown, CT** has been reported on a **Baldwin Tool Co.** plane. **No imprint is available.**

GLOCK & TALLMADGE
Glock & Tallmadge was a hardware dealer partnership in the Columbus, OH, directory in 1885-86. **Albert O. Glock** and **Darius Tallmadge** were the partners. The firm changed its name to **Glock & Tallmadge, Builders Hardware & Tool Depot**, in the 1890 directory. By 1895, it was changed to the **Tallmadge Hardware Co.**, and **Albert O. Glock** was listed with the **Columbus Brass Co.**
A & A1 ****

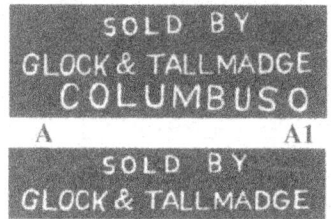

WINSLOW B. GLOVER
Winslow B. Glover (d. 1880, will probated Nov. 8, 1880, Boston, MA) married, on May 18, 1848, in Salem, Essex Co., MA. He was listed in 1850, as a carpenter in Salem. He was listed in the 1860-80 Boston Business directories, as a carpenter. He was issued Patent No. 108,586, on October 25, 1870, for a beech fore plane cap iron modification. The imprint **W. B. GLOVER/ PAT. APP'D FOR** appears on the toe of a 22" double-iron conventional jack plane made by **H. Wells**. The cap iron is marked **A. L. WHITING & CO./ WORCESTER, MASS**. (see *Patented Transitional & Metallic Planes in America- Vol. II*, p 83, by Roger K. Smith) **No imprint is available.**

B. GODARD
Examples: on a 9 3/4" fruitwood Yankee plow; and a 9 1/2" beech hollow, both with flat chamfers, ca. 1800. UR

J. GODSCHALL
Example: on a 9 1/2" beech skew rabbet with heavy round chamfers, possibly from eastern PA, ca. 1810-20. UR

GOTTFRIED GOEBBEL
Gottfried Goebbel (b. Germany) was a New York City planemaker, active from 1855-57. **Gottfried** made his

declaration on Oct. 9, 1854 in NY and was naturalized Sep. 25, 1860. He was listed in 1857 under tools in NY.
No imprint has been reported.

GOEDEKING & NEWHOFF
Henry Goedeking and **G. L. Newhoff** (**Neuhoff**) ran a dry goods store in Belleville, IL, in 1849, and succeeded by **Goedeking, Kircher & Eissenhardt**, also known as the **Belleville Hardware Store**. Example: on a 9 1/2" beech, single-boxed ogee molder, ca. 1850. ****

T. GOERING TOOL CO.
T. Goering Tool Co. is believed to be a hardware dealer from MA. Examples have been reported on planes made by others.
No imprint is available.

G. GOLD.
Example: on a 9 1/8" birch large hollow with an integral fence and flat chamfers, ca. 1790-1800. **UR**

ELI GOLDSMITH
Eli Goldsmith (b. 1828 in PA, d. Oct. 24, 1882 in Philadelphia, PA) may have been the son of **George Goldsmith** and was listed in 1850 and from 1856-80 in Philadelphia, PA, as a planemaker.
No imprint has been reported.

GEORGE GOLDSMITH
George Goldsmith (b. Jul. 19, 1782 in Middlesex, England, d. Feb. 7, 1864 in Philadelphia, PA) immigrated on May 1804. He was the brother of **Thomas Goldsmith**. He was listed in the 1845 directory and the Philadelphia, PA, 1850-60 census as a planemaker. His last listing appeared in 1864.
No imprint has been reported.

JOHN GOLDSMITH
John Goldsmith Sr., was listed in the 1856 Philadelphia, PA directory as a planemaker, at 44 Green, the same address as **William Goldsmith Sr. No imprint has been reported**.

JOHN S. GOLDSMITH
John S. Goldsmith was listed in 1853-58 Philadelphia, PA directories, as a Machinist, at 38 Laurel, the same address as **George Goldsmith**. About 10 years later, **John** was listed as a blacksmith, with his own shop, but still living at **George's** address. There were a lot of metal parts that needed machining in a wooden plane shop, plus all the grinding needed to fit the irons to the plane profiles. **No imprint has been reported.**

S. GOLDSMITH
S. Goldsmith was listed in the 1860 Philadelphia directory as a planemaker at the same address as **John Veit**.
No imprint has been reported.

STEPHEN GOLDSMITH
Stephen Goldsmith, no occupation listed, was listed in the 1876 Philadelphia directory, at the same address as **Eli Goldsmith**.
No imprint has been reported.

T. GOLDSMITH
Thomas Goldsmith (b. Nov., 1779 in Middlesex, England, d. Apr. 23, 1857 in Philadelphia, PA) was the brother of **George Goldsmith**. He was a prolific Philadelphia, PA, planemaker, from 1801-37. In 1837, there was also a listing for **Thos. & Son**, "plane manuf.", at 140 St. John. This was the last listing for **Thomas**, as a planemaker. In 1850 & 56, **Thomas Goldsmith**, age 77, was listed, as a farmer, in Collegeville, PA. Examples: **T. Goldsmith** planes have been reported overstruck by **R. A. Parrish**. Examples: the A imprint is on 9 3/4" beech planes with round chamfers. The earlier planes with the B imprint are 9 3/4" beech with flat chamfers. **B: FF; A ****

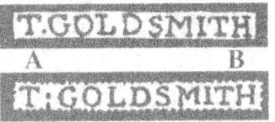 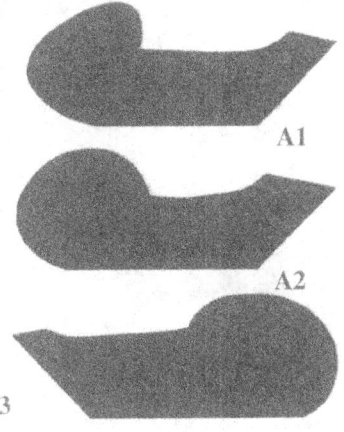

GOLDSMITH/ WM. GOLDSMITH
William Goldsmith (b. 1805, d. 1879, Philadelphia, PA) was the son of **Thomas Goldsmith**, and a Philadelphia, PA, planemaker, from 1837-68. The 1845 directory and the 1850 census listed **William Goldsmith**, as a planemaker. In 1856, **William Goldsmith** exhibited levels at the Franklin Institute Fair. In the 1857-58 city directories, he was listed as planemaker and spirit levels. His son, **Wm. Goldsmith Jr.** (b. 1832) was listed, in 1850, as a planemaker, living with his father. In the 1854 McElroy's directory, **William Goldsmith** placed an ad: "**William Goldsmith** Plane Manufacturer, Wholesale Planes and Retail, N. W. Corner of New Market and Green Sts. N. L. Philad'a." (N. L. refers to North Liberties) In 1856, **William Gouldsmith**, a planemaker, was listed with shop at New Market & Green, residence at 91 Green. **William Gouldsmith Sr.**, planemaker, was listed at 44 Green, Residence only. **William Goldsmith, Sr.** was succeeded by **John Veit**, in 1868. In 1872, he was again listed as planemaker, residence only, in 1870, as planemaker "retired"; in 1873-76, without occupation. The 1879 listing was as **Goldsmith, Cathrine, wd. of William**.
A, B, C & D *

 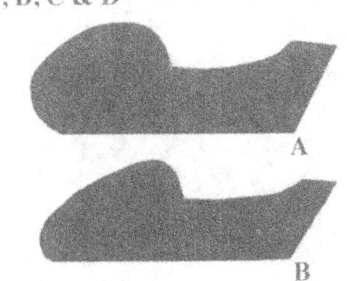

A. GOLDTHWAIT & CO.
A. Goldthwait & Co. was a hardware dealer in Salem, MA. Example: on a green/ blue label a **Greenfield Tool Co.** double-boxed 3/8" wide center bead that reads: ****

```
A. GOLDTHWAIT & CO.
FRONT STREET, SALEM, MASS.
DEALER IN
HARDWARE & CUTLORY
(     ) IN ESSEX COUNTY
```

P: GOOD
Examples: on an 8 3/4" wedge-arm plow; and a 10" astragal bead with a fence; a crown molder with an offset-tote and a around toped iron, all beech with wide flat chamfers. ca. 1790. **UR**

GOODALE
Example: on a 9 1/4"x 3" beech wide complex molder with size **1 1/2** marked on heel, an **I. Sleeper** style wedge and round chamfers, from northern New England, ca. 1790-1810. **UR**

J. W. GOODALE
John Willard Goodale (b. Apr. 14, 1834 in Amherst, MA, d. Nov. 13, 1905) was the son of **Orson Goodale**, a wagon maker, and **Mary B. Hills** and the granddaughter of **Samuel Hills**. He was listed, in the 1869 Amherst directory, as a mechanic; in 1873, as a planemaker; and in the 1879, as a toolmaker. The 1880 Federal census described his occupation as "Works at Plain Making". At some time between 1873-80, he worked for **William Kellogg**. By 1889, **John** was listed as employed as a box maker at the shop of **Levi E. Dickinson**. After 1897, **John** was retired. Examples: on a 15" razee jack plane, dated **1873**, with metal inserts in the sole ahead of the mouth; and a 28" jointer, both with a **Moulson Brothers** iron. The B imprint is on the toe and heel of a jack made by **S. Hills**, Springfield, MA, his grandfather. **John Willard Goodale** was issued a patent for an unrelated firearm mechanism. One smoother is imprinted by the Boston hardware firm of **Corey Brooks & Co.**. **William Goodale** applied decorative wooden inlays on the bodies & wedges of his planes.
A & B ****

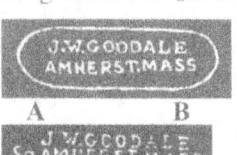

THE GOODALL CO.
Samuel I. Goodall Co. was a Philadelphia, PA, hardware firm, with **Samuel I. Goodall** (b. Jan. 1855, d. 1932 in Montgomery Co., PA) active from 1894-96, producing a line of wood-bottom planes, based on the **Bailey** patent. **Stanley** purchased the **Goodall** plane manufacturing business, in 1896. (see *Patented Transitional & Metallic Planes in America, Vol II*, p. 150-51, by Roger K. Smith) **UR**

GOODERICH, ANDREWS & CO.
The 1837 Detroit, MI, city directory listed **Gooderich, Andrews & Co.**, as a plane making company on Michigan Ave., making it probably the earliest of the Detroit planemakers. **No imprint has been reported**.

I. GOODFELLOW
Example: on a 9 1/2" beech size **1** hollow, ca. 19c. **UR**

M: GOODHU
Example: on a 13" beech jack style complex molder with offset open birch tote and flat chamfers, ca. 1800-10. **UR**

J. G. GOODHUE
Example: on a 9 3/8" beech wide round with shallow round chamfers, ca. 1810-20. **UR**

J. W. GOODHUE
Example: on a 7" lignum vitae smoothing plane made by **P. B. Rider/ Bangor**. **UR**

A. GOODRICH
Possibly **Ansel Goodrich** (b. 1773, d. 1803) who was in Northampton, MA, by 1795, and was listed as a chairmaker. Sandisfield, MA is on the CT border, west of Springfield, MA. Examples: on a size **1 1/8** round; a size **1** hollow; and a size **1/4** hollows, found with a **C. P. Woodruff/ Detroit** plane. *****

B. E. GOODWIN
Example: on a 10" beech skew rabbet with round chamfers, ca. 1820. **UR**

E. GOOLD
Possibly **Emerson Goold (Gould)** (b. 1750 in MA, d. July 10, 1794) was a trader from Marblehead, MA. Examples: 5 molders 9 1/2"-9 7/8" including a dust joint; a narrow panel raiser; a double-iron crown molder; and a handled complex molder, all beech with flat chamfers. The molders have an **I. Sleeper** style wedge, ca. 1780-1800. ****

WM. GOOLD
Example: on a 9 1/8" cherry, or possibly apple, single boxed complex molder; and a 9 3/8" maple skew rabbet with flat chamfers, ca. 1800. **UR**

Jn GORDON

John Gordon appeared in the 1808 Philadelphia, PA, directory as a planemaker. Judging by the variety and quantity of the planes that have survived, he was apparently active over a long period. Examples are 9 1/2" beech with heavy round chamfers, ca. 1820. **

EDWARD. GORE

Example: on a 9 1/2" beech single-boxed complex molder with flat chamfers. **UR**

GORHAM CO./ GORHAM MFG. CO.

The **Gorham Mfg. Co.** was a Providence, RI, hollow-ware, pitchers and teapots, manufactory, from 1820-1970. **Gorham** could have been a dealer or the planes may have been imprinted for its own use in the **Gorham** factory wood shop. Examples: the A imprint is on a boxed bead; and a complex molder. The B imprint is on the heel of a full-boxed size 1/8" bead with **69/4**, probably a date, all planes were made by **J. E. Child**. A & B: ****

ISAAC GOSLIN

Isaac Goslin (b. 1823, d. 1896) was listed as a planemaker in 1844 St. Louis, MO. **No imprint has been reported**.

J. W. GOSNELL

John W. Gosnell (b. 1821 in OH, d. Oct. 29, 1890 in Bosnorth, Carroll Co., MO) was a St. Louis, MO, planemaker listed in the 1847-48, 50 & 54 city directories. ***

J. W. GOSNELL/ W. HALL

John W. Gosnell and **William Hall** were partners in St. Louis, MO, as planemakers, hardware and tool dealers, 1849-52. ***

F. J. GOUCH

Franklin J. Gouch (b. 1817 in Northampton, Hampshire Co., MA, d. Jan. 20, 1881 in Poughkeepsie, Dutchass Co., NY) was the brother of **George Gouch**. **Franklin Gouch** was a planemaker in Worcester, MA, from 1847-68. **Gouch** was earlier part of **Sanborn & Gouch**, from 1845-48. On Nov. 30, 1846, **Franklin J. Gouch** married **Mary T. Dow**, the daughter of **James Dow**. **David P. Sanborn** was his brother-in-law. **Gouch** was listed in the 1849 New England Mercantile Union Directory, as a plane manufacturer in Litche's Mills, Worcester. In the 1850, 55 & 65 directories, he was listed as a plain maker in Worcester, MA. In 1870, **Gouch** was listed as a knife sharpener, in Poughkeepsie, NY. In 1877 & 79, he was listed as Foreman, Buckeye, Poughkeepsie, NY. **Gouch** was also known to have made levels. Example: a "V" groove molder with the A1 imprint and with **J. DOW**, his father-in-law.

A, A1 & A2 **; B *****

GOUCH & DEMOND

The 1850 census listed a **Daniel Demond** (b. Sep. 13, 1790 in MA, d. Apr. 17, 1857 in Springfield, MA) as a joiner in Springfield, MA. **George Gouch** (b. 1822 in Northampton, Hampshire Co., MA, d. May 24, 1874 in Springfield, Hampden Co., MA), was the brother of **Franklin J. Gouch** and was listed in the 1850, 60 & 70, as a carpenter, in Springfield, MA. Examples: on a crown molder; a miter; and a skew rabbet. ****

H. GOUDY

Example: on a 16" birch centered toted bench plane with a **W. BUTCHER** flat top iron, 19c. style chamfers and the location of **HARRISBURG**. **UR**

JAMES GOUGE

James Gouge was listed as a plane maker in Cincinnati, OH in 1839-40 at **Lyon & Co**. No imprint has been reported.

I G/ I x GOULD

Joseph Gould (b. Dec. 30, 1730 in Stoneham, MA., d. Aug. 5, 1810 in Reading, MA) apprenticed to the housewright, carpenter and planemaker **John Walton Jr.**, of Reading. He completed his apprenticeship, at the age of 21, on Dec. 30, 1751. He began recording his work in a day book, on Jan. 2, 1752, as a journeyman, now in the possession of the Society for the Preservation of New England Antiquities, Boston. **Gould** continued working for **John Walton Jr.** as he took on more and more independent work. Eventually his skills as a wheelwright set him apart. His wheelwright and carriage business led to boarding and renting horses, wagons and buggies. In 1770, Reading formed 4 militia companies including South Reading's First Parish Train Band under the command of Col. David Green, including **Joseph Gould**, age 45, listed as a joiner and wheelwright. South Reading responded to the alarm of April 19, 1775, arriving to engage the British south of Concord on the Lexington Rd. In 1786, **Joseph Gould**, age 56, was again called into service when the Reading Militia was activated to help put down the rioting and attack on the Springfield arsenal. On Dec. 1, 1789, **Joseph Gould** placed an ad that his wife, **Mary**, eloped and that he was no longer responsible for her debits. The **I x GOULD** imprint and the **IG** initial imprint are similar to that of **John Walton Sr. & I.W** initials. Examples: molders are 10"-10 1/16" birch with an **I x WALTON** style small rounded wedge finials, flat chamfers and long shallow flutes. The A1 imprint, with the initial group, is on a 11 3/4" birch jack with an offset tote, a round top wedge and iron and shallow flat chamfers. The

A2 imprint has been found alone. ca. 1750-80.
A ****; A1 & A2 *****

A2

GOULD & BROTHERS
Gould & Brothers probably is a hardware store. Example: in ink on the toe of two skew rabbets made by **D. R. Barton**. No imprint is available.

G. GOULDING
G. Goulding was probably a Watertown, NY, hardware dealer. Example: The A imprint is on a **J. Lord/ Watertown** plane and the larger B imprint is on a **B. F. Berry** plane.
A & B: ****

C. GOVE
Possibly **Charles C. Gove** (d. 1893) a carpenter whose shop burned in 1840, set on fire by varnish boiling over upon a hot stove. Example: on a 9" beech plow with one rosewood thumbscrew, a rosewood fence, flat chamfers, found in Kittery, ME, ca. 1840-50. **UR**

D. L. GOVE
Examples: on a razee beech ship jack found in Essex, Co., MA, ca. 1850. **UR**

J. GOVE
Example: on a 9 3/4" beech table round with a removable fence and an iron set at a York pitch, ca. 1850. **UR**

J. H. GOVE
John H. Gove (b. 1828 in NH, d. 1887) married, in 1856, in Hampton Falls, NH and was listed as being of Weare, NH. His daughter was b. in 1869, in Newburyport, Essex Co., MA. He was listed, in 1880, as a boat builder in Newburyport. Example: on an 8 1/4" maple compass smoothing plane, with 19c chamfers and a double **Buck Brothers** iron. The A embossed imprint GOVE, with out an initial, is similar to that of **L. Cove**, ca. mid 19c. **A & B: UR**

L. GOVE
Examples: on a 9 3/4" molder; a 9 7/8" and a 10 3/4" beech rabbet; a 12 1/2" and a 13 3/8" birch sash plane, with open pegged totes; and a 13 1/2" tongue plane, all with flat chamfers. The molders have an **I. Sleeper** style wedges, ca. 1800. ****

S. GOVE
Example: on a 9 1/4" beech large bead with flat chamfers, ca. 1810. **UR**

T. B. GOVE
Possibly **Timothy Blake Gove** (b. Aug. 23, 1781 in Hampton Falls, Rockingham Co., NH, d. Aug. 7, 1831 in Lowell, MA) who married on May 3, 1805, in Deerfield, Rockingham, NH. He was also listed in Deerfield, in 1810-20. **Timothy B. Gove** was reported in the 1830 Lowell, MA, census. Examples: on two beech slide-arm plow planes with thumbscrews; a 9 3/8"x 3/8" side bead; a 9 3/8"x 1/2" round; a 9 1/2" square rabbet; and a 9 7/16" complex molder. All beech with flat chamfers, ca. 1810. ***

W. A. GOVERN & CO.
The **WARRANTED** imprint is very similar to that used by the **Winsted Plane Co.** and identical to that of the **Phoenix Company/ Hitchcockville, CT**, and bears a striking resemblance to the fancy mark of **Copeland & Co.** Example: on a beech round, from western Connecticut River valley, ca. 1850. *****

I. GOWDREY
Example: on a 22" beech rabbet plane with centered closed tote, marked **13** on the front of the tote and on the wedge, a diamond hardwood strike, and round chamfers, ca. 1820-30. **UR**

ALEX P. GOWIE
Example: on a 9 1/2" beech moving filletster with a boxed edge and round chamfers, ca. 1810-30. **UR**

CHAs. GOWLAND
Example: on a double boxed 9 1/2" beech complex molding plane with double irons and wedges, ca. 19c. **UR**

J. GRAHAM
Example: on a 9 3/8" beech hollow with heavy flat chamfers, ca. 1800. **A & B: UR**

A

B

JA GRAMLNG
Believed to be **Johann Adam Gramling, Sr.** (b. 1757 in Berks Co., PA, d. 1841) who fought in the American Revolutionary War. He was located in Brecknock or Cumru Townships, Berks Co., just above Adamstown. Example: on a 9" reeding plane, ca. 1780. *****

JO. GRAMLING
Believed to be **Johann Adam Gramling, Jr.**, son of **Johann Adam Gramling, Sr.**, listed in the 1830 census. Example: the A imprint is on a screw-arm split sash plane. The B imprint is from 9" beech molders with round chamfers, ca. 1820.
B ***; A ****

THO: GRANT
There were several **Thomas Grants** in 18c New York City who were variously planemakers and merchants. The A imprint with the location **NEW: YORK** is believed to be the earlier and appears on planes that may have been made by **Thomas Grant, Jr.**, the joiner, and sold by his cousin **Thomas Grant**, the merchant and ironmonger (married 1755, d. 1802 in New Brunswick, NJ). An ad in the *New York Gazette and Weekly Mercury* on Jul. 1, 1776, shortly before the British occupied New York, reads: "**Thomas Grant.** Is removed from this City to Newark Mountains....". **Thomas Grant** returning to New York City prior to the British evacuation, in 1783. He was still in New York City as late as 1786, but by 1787 **Thomas Grant** was listed as a subscriber for a pew in the First Presbyterian Church of New Brunswick, NJ. Also a member of this church was **Robert Eastburn**. **Thomas Grant** appeared on the tax rolls for Middlesex Co. (New Brunswick), in 1785-93. The varying styles suggest that the planes may have been made by more than one person, and may include examples imported from England. Examples: on molding planes up to 10 1/4" beech with heavy flat chamfers, ca. crowned owner's initials, appear on many of the **Thomas Grant** planes, as well as on other American planes made by **Eastburn**, **W. Raymond** and **L. Little**, and on a few English planes made by **Cauldwell, Holbrook, I. Cogdell** and **Phillipson**. A characteristic common to **Grant**, **Eastburn**, and **J. Stiles** was to use friction fit, rather than wedge or thumbscrew lock arms, on some plow planes and fenced plank planes, ca. 1775-1800.
A1 **; A & B ***

 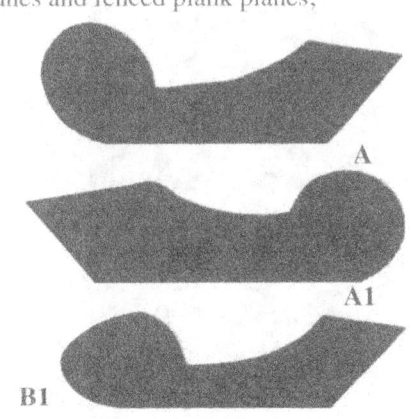

J. GRAVES
Example: on a 9 1/2" beech complex molder with flat chamfers, found in Newberryport, NH, ca. 1810. UR

W. GRAVES
Examples: on a 9 1/2" beech ogee molding plane with flat chamfers with spring and layout lines. The iron is marked with **C (heart) H**, with the A wedge, ca. 1790-1800. There is also a group of four, found together, branded **H. H. NOBLE** including a round; a hollow; and a rabbet. The B wedge is on an adj. fenced tongue plane with brass slides for screws to engage the fences; a boxwood strike diamond, offset open tote, and a single iron, all 9 1/2" beech with round chamfers, ca. 1820-30. UR

ARTHUR GRAY
Arthur Gray of Naples, ME, was issued Patent No. 65,562, on June 11, 1867, for a transitional jack plane with a heavy cast iron frog attached behind the throat with four wood screws. **PAT. JUNE 11, 1867** was cast into the lever cap. (see *Patented Transitional & Metallic Planes in America, vol. II*, p. 86, by Roger K. Smith) **No imprint has been reported.**

BENJAMIN GRAY
Benjamin Gray (b. ca. 1817 in Philadelphia, PA, d. Sep. 7, 1876 in Philadelphia) was listed in the 1845, 50 & 60 Philadelphia, PA directories as a planemaker. **No imprint has been reported.**

F. GRAY
Examples: on two crown molders, one 14 1/2"x 4 1/2"; a pair of 9 3/4" hollows; and a 12 5/8" halving plane with a closed integral handle, all beech with flat chamfers. ca. 1800. ****

H. GRAY
Example: on a 6 1/2" beech toothing plane with small flat chamfers. The round top iron is marked **NEWBOULD/ WARRANTED**, ca. 1800-10. UR

J. A. GRAY
Example: on a 10 1/4" cherry small quarter round with a molded shoulder and small shallow flat chamfers, ca. 1780-90. UR

JAMES C. GRAY
James Crum Gray (b. Mar. 24, 1830 in PA, d. Sep. 14, 1909 in OH) was listed as a Columbus, OH, planemaker, active from 1856-60. He was listed in the 1860 Columbus, OH directory, as a planemaker. **No imprint has been reported**.

P. GRAY
Examples: the A imprint with the wedge shown is on a 9 1/2" cherry square dado with flat chamfers and long flutes, ca. 1780. The B imprint is on a 9 3/4" beech hollow; and a 9 3/4" birch astragal, both with flat chamfers, ca. 1810. Appearance of the two planes is different and possibly made by two separate persons. **A & B: UR**

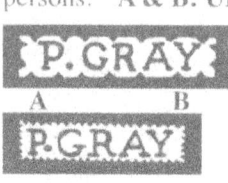 

S. GRAY
Examples: on a 26" beech joiner; a 22" rosewood joiner; and a 9 1/2" beech table round, ca. 1850. **UR**

W. GRAY
Possibly **William Gray** was a carpenter & joiner in Kent, Ct, from 1795-97. Example: on a 9 7/8" beech small ogee with flat chamfers, ca. 1810. **UR**

GRAY & DONALDSON
Gray & Donaldson was a Nashville, TN hardware dealer, in business after **Donaldson & Hall** of St. Louis and before **Gray & Kirkman** of Nashville, dating between 1854-67. Example on a 9 1/2" beech centered bead with an **AUBURN TOOL CO.** mark on the toe and the **No. 108** Auburn inventory number with the 5/16 size and this imprint on the heel. ****

GRAY & KIRKMAN

Gray & Kirkman was a hardware dealer partnership that was listed in the Nashville, TN, city directories from 1867-70. Examples: on planes made by the **Auburn Tool Co.** and the **Ohio Tool Co.** ****

E. H. GREEN
Example: on a 16" washboard plane. **No imprint is available**.

ELI. GREEN
Example: on a 10" applewood skew rabbet with a relieved wedge and heavy round chamfers, ca. 1800-15. **UR**

G. L. GREEN
Example: on a 10 1/4" beech skew rabbet with flat chamfers and an **I. Sleeper** style wedge, ca. 1780-1800. **UR**

J. GREEN
Jacob Green (b. Nov. 16, 1825, d. Feb. 4, 1913) made planes in New York City, from 1850-54. He was listed, in 1855, as a plane maker in NY, Ward 20; in 1860, as overseer in "mld. mill"; in 1870 as "moulding mill"; and in 1880, as wood molding manufacturer in NY, Ward 20. In 1900, he was listed as a decorator; and in 1910, occupation "none", both in Hudson, NJ. Example: The A imprint is from a **No. 14** round. **A & A1 ****

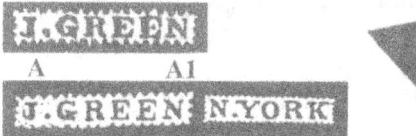 

M. GREEN
Example: on a 9 3/8" beech molder with a relieved wedge and flat chamfers, ca. 1790-1800. **UR**

GREENFIELD TOOL CO.
The **Greenfield Tool Co.** was a major wooden plane manufacturer in 19c America. It was the successor to the **Conway Tool Co.**, founded by **Alonzo Parker, Horace Hubbard** (see **Parker, Hubbard & Co.**) and **Daniel Rice II**. The **Conway Tool Co.** factory burned down in 1851 and was rebuilt in Greenfield, MA, as the **Greenfield Tool Co.**. Construction began in Aug. 1851, and the directors were **Daniel Rice II, Alonzo Parker** and **Simeon Phillips**. **Alonzo Parker** was appointed agent of the Company. Two planes are known to carry the name **S. Phillips Works**, Greenfield, Mass. The **Greenfield Tool Co.** also made an "Iron Plane Gauge", patented July 26, 1887, by **Edward B. Shepardson**, that was still being sold in 1905. In the 1850's, power was supplied by a steam engine and distributed to the shop machinery by a system of overhead shafts and leather belts. The factory was two story with 10,000 sq. ft. of space, employing 60-70 and producing 10,000-12,000 planes a month. The 1860 MA Industrial census showed the **Greenfield Tool Co.** using 60 hp of steam, employing 30 hands with a monthly payroll of $1560 and producing $40,000 worth of carpenters' tools/ year. In the 1870's, the company to decline, feeling the increased competition of metal planes. On Jan. 8, 1883, the company was declared insolvent with liabilities of $104,000. One **Greenfield** sash has a **Greenfield** paper lable. **A, B, C, D & E: FF**

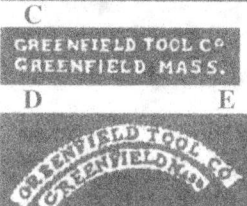 

GREER & LAING
Greer & Laing was a partnership of **Jacob R. Greer** (b. ca. 1822 in OH) (see **Ott & Greer**) and **Alexander Laing** (b. Jun. 25, 1824 in Rafford, Morayshire, Scotland, d. Feb. 25, 1907 in Wheeling, WV) (see **Anderson & Laing**). Laing immigrated in 1846. **Greer & Laing** operated a hardware company listed in the Wheeling, WV, city directories, starting in 1856, at 13 Monroe St., the former address of **Anderson & Laing**; and continuing in business until 1965. In 1870, **Alexander Laing** was a wholesale hardware in Wheeling; in 1900, as hardware "merch.", in Wheeling. Example: on a table plane with **138**, the **Ohio Tool Co.** style number for this plane. ***

C. GREGG
Example: on a 9 1/2" birch quarter round with flat chamfers, ca. 1810.   UR

D. T. GREGG.
Example: on a 22 5/8" birch jointer with a closed, centered tote and flat chamfers. A number of these planes were found in South Weare, NH. Also reported is a birch panel raiser with initials **DTG**, ca. 1800.   UR

I. GREGG
Examples: are 9 1/2"-9 9/16" beech with wide flat chamfers and include a dado; a tongue plane; a complex molder; a halving plane; and a large hollow, ca. 1800.   ****

J. GREGG
This imprint is made from the same die as **I. Gregg**, but with the **I** made into a **J**. This could represent a single maker working over a period of time or two generations. Examples: on a hollow; and a tongue plane, both 9 1/2" beech with round chamfers, ca. 1820 ****

J. H. GREGG
John H. Gregg of New Boston, NH, was declared insane on Dec. 18, 1883. An inventory taken at that time listed carpentry shop tools valued at $100, and a blacksmith shop at $50, together representing about one-half of his estate. Example: on a 23 1/4" beech jointer with a slightly offset birch handle and heavy flat chamfers, ca. 1800-20.   ****

M. GREGG
Mahlon Gregg appeared in the Rochester, NY, directories, from 1853-59, as a Millwright in wood and iron. An 1861 advertisement listed cooper's, shipwright's & carpenter's tools produced at the race, and sold at Sears's hardware store. The race was Brown's Race, which served as a power source, for most of the flour mills, and was the second location of **D. R. Barton**, purchased in 1853. In the 1864-65, directory the address for the factory was the flats, which is a lower area, below the 90 ft. second falls, below **D. R. Barton**, and the flour mills up along the race. In 1870's as an edge tool maker, in 1866 as **Gregg & Hamilton** listed as a short-lived partnership. An 1884 History of Rochester, NY, listed "**Mahlon Gregg & Son (J. N. Gregg)** Manufacturing cooper's tools on the flats, Foot of falls". They employed 15-20 hands.   ***

GREGG & HAMILTON
Gregg & Hamilton probably was a hardware dealer in Rochester, NY. Example: on a sun plane both the wood body and the iron, ca. 19c.   UR

GREGG & SON
Gregg & Son was a hardware dealer from Nashua, NH, in 1896, who offered doors, sash, blinds, window and door frames, brackets, moldings, mantle shelves, stair rails & balusters, and marbleized wood shelves. Example: on the heel of a complex molder made by **Addison Heald**.   ***

GREGORY/ G. W. GREGORY
G. W. Gregory (b. ca. 1820) was a Binghamton, NY, hardware dealer, ca. 1850. **A, B & C **

GREIER
Example: on a 9 7/8" complex molder; and a 9 1/2" beech molder, both with round chamfers, possibly from PA, ca. 1810-20.   UR

S. GRESWELL
Example: on a 10" hickory grooving plane with flat chamfers. ca. 1790-1810.   UR

JOSEPH GRIBBLE
Joseph Gribble (b. ca. 1833 in Cincinnati, OH, d. Sep. 25, 1888 in Cincinnati) was listed as a planemaker in the 1850 census, living in Brownville, Union Co., IN, in the home of a blacksmith. This was four houses away from **Benjamin Lape** for whom he may have worked. In the 1860 census, he was listed as a carpenter in Cincinnati. He served in the Civil War, enlisting on Jul. 20, 1862, as a Private in K Co., Ohio 83rd. Infantry Reg. He was discharged a Corp., on Jul. 24, 1865, at Galveston, TX. In 1866, he was again listed as a carpenter in Cincinnati; in 1880, he was listed as "works in planing mill"; in

1885-87 he was listed as "mech. hand".
No imprint has been reported.

W. GRIFFEN
Example: on a 9" beech large hollow with flat chamfers, ca. 1800. UR

E. GRIFFIN
Example: on a 9 5/8"x 1/4" beech single-iron double bead with narrow flat chamfers. ca. 1810. UR

GRIFFIN
 Griffin is believed to be a New York City hardware dealer. Example: on a rabbet; and a round. UR

GRIFFIN
Orlando Henry Griffin (b. Oct. 5, 1817 in NY, d. Aug. 4, 1894 in Ravenna, OH) married in Ravenna, on Jun 12, 1843, who was listed in the 1850-60 Ravenna, OH censuses, as a planemaker. At some time in his career, he worked with **Algernon S. Collins** at "carriage making". In an advertisement dated Nov. 1842, **O. H. Griffin** announced: "At the old stand of **F. K. Collins & Co.** will be kept constantly on hand or made to order every variety of plane. Good white beach (sic) timber taken in exchange for planes". (see **Collins/ Ravenna**) The 1850 census of industry listed **Orlando Henry Griffin** as employing two men and producing 800 planes worth $800. In 1870-80, he was listed as works in "hub factory". **

HENRY GRIFFIN
Henry Griffin (b. 1800, d. 1863 in Remsen, Oneida, NY) was listed in the 1830 census, in Newport, NY. **Henry** was listed in 1837-38, in the Utica, NY directory, as a planemaker boarding with **Allen Cummings** and probably working for **R. J. Collins**. In 1850, he was listed as a farmer in Remsen, NY.
No imprint has been reported.

J. A. GRIFFIN
J. A. Griffin with the location, **PORTLAND** (ME) and an owner's imprint **G. E. TABER** is on a 9 1/4" birch smoothing plane, in rectangular shape, with round chamfers, ca. 19c. ****

C. M. GRIFFITH
C. M. Griffith (b. ca. 1815 in PA, d. Aug. 1, 1858 in Evensville, IN) was listed in 1850, as a merchant, in Evansville, IN. Examples: on a 9 1/2" beech side bead with an **Ohio Tool Co.** iron; a 5/8 beech grooving plane; and a 27" beech joiner with a centered tote, and 19c. chamfers. ****

A x GRIMES
Example: on a 9 1/2" skew rabbet with flat chamfers, ca. 1800. UR

W. G. G./ W. G. GRIMES
W. G. Grimes was a New London, CT hardware dealer. Examples: on an 8 7/8" applewood smoother; a 27" beech joiner with a centered tote; and a 9 7/16" beech hollow made by **H. Chapin, Union Factory**. ****

D x G/ DANIEL GRIMM
Example: on a 9 1/2"x 3/8" beech side bead with heavy flat chamfers possibly from New England, ca. 1800-10. UR

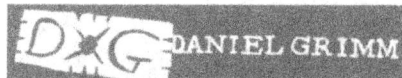

I. GRIMSON/ J. GRIMSON
Example: on a 22" beech fore plane with a centered tote, and a double-iron by **James Howarth**. ca. 19c. **A & B: UR**

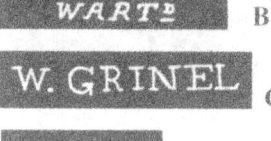

A&B

W. GRINEL /W. GRINELL
William Grinel (Grinell) (b. 1781, d. Oct. 11, 1841 in Philadelphia, PA) was a Philadelphia planemaker, from 1814-19. **Grinel** was also a partner in **White & Grinell** with **George White** and **Jacob White** in 1818. Examples: the D imprint is on a 13 1/8" beech wedge-lock slide-arm fenced plank grooving plane with heavy round chamfers, ca. 1820. This may represent a separate person. **A, B & C ***; B1 & D ****

PETER GRINNELL & SON
Peter Grinnell & Son of Providence, RI was a partnership with **Peter Grinnell** (b. Jun. 4, 1764 in Little Compton, Newport Co., RI, d. Sep. 13, 1836 in Providence, RI) and his son **William Taylor Grinnell** (b. Nov. 12, 1787, d. Nov. 9, 1835 in Providence, RI) and was listed as a "looking glass manuf. and hardware merchant", from May 1809-24, on Main St., Providence. They advertised, on Aug. 7, 1824, Joiners' tools of superior quality with irons fitted. This partnership was preceded by **Peter Grinnell**, who dealt in hardware and ship chandlery, from 1787-1809, and **William Taylor Grinnell** listed as "looking glass manuf. and hardware merchant, gilder & oramental painter" 1807-09. **No imprint has been reported.**

L. W. GRISWOLD

Example: on a 17" beech jack plane with a centered tote and a **W. Butcher** iron, ca. 1850.   **UR**

GRISWOLD & DICKINSON
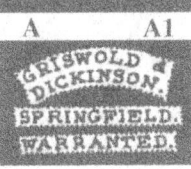
Griswold & Dickinson was a Springfield, MA, planemakeing partnership, ca. 1860. **A & A1 ******

GRISWOLD & WOODWORTH
Griswold & Woodworth was a Hartford, CT, plane making partnership, whose working dates are not known. Examples: on a size **18** round; and a 9 1/2" beech dado, ca. 1850.   ********

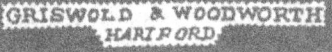

I: GRISWOULD
Example: on a 9 1/2" skew hollow with flat chamfers, ca. 1810.   **UR**

JOHN. GROS
Examples: on three 10 7/8" beech molders, found in Mansfield, OH, ca. 1830.   **UR**

A. GROSS
A. Gross was found on both the iron and the wood body of a D router. **No imprint is available**.

GROVES
Example: on a 9 1/2" beech dado with flat chamfers, ca. 19c.   **UR**

F. GRUS
Example: on a beech rabbet with heavy round chamfers, ca. 1820.   **UR**

R. C. GUENTHER
R. C. Guenther was a hardware dealer in Quincy, IL. Example: on the toe of a **Sandusky Tool Co.** size **9** round.   **UR**

J. GUINEE
J. Guinee is a hardware dealer from New York City. Example: on a howel.   **UR**

A. GUILD
Abner Guild (b. Aug. 17, 1772 in Dedham, Norfolk Co., MA, d. Jul 6, 1843 in Dedham) was listed as a partner with **Elisha Adams** as **Guild & Adam**, from 1796-98, at Federal St., Boston, MA. From 1800-25, **Guild** was listed, as a cabinetmaker under his own name, at 48 Orange St., Boston. **Abner Guild** was a Capt. in the Dedham Light Infantry in the War of 1812 and was promoted to a Col. Example: on a 10" beech round with tight round chamfers, ca. 1800-20.   ********

D. GUILD
Example: on a 9 1/2" beech skew rabbet with round chamfers, ca. 1820.   **UR**

P. GUILMET
Example: on a 9 11/16" fruitwood fixed sash; and a 10" birch door coping plane, imprinted twice on the toe, with shallow round chamfers, ca. 1810-20.   **UR**

L. GULLIVER
Example: on a birch smoother with a round toped iron and flat chamfers, ca. 1800.   **UR**

D. J. GUNDRUM
Example: on a 9 5/16"x 2 7/8" beech wide ogee with bevel molding plane, with spring and slight almost square chamfers, a **W. Butcher** iron and found in central PA, ca. 19c.   **UR**

GWYNNE & RICHARDSON
Gwynne & Richardson was a hardware dealer in New York City. Example: on a **Lamb & Brownell** skew rabbet, ca. 1870.   ********

D. H
Examples: 30 planes with flat chamfers have been found in the Auburn to Skowhegan section of Maine. The initialed imprint is similar to that used by **L. Sampson**, ca. 1790-1800. *****

H. & SON
This name probably represents a hardware dealer, ca. 1850.
No imprint is available.

H. C. & CO.
This initial imprint probably represents a hardware dealer located in Boston, MA. Example: the A imprint is on a narrow center bead. The B imprint is on a small hollow made by **A & E Baldwin**, ca. 1850. **A & B: ****

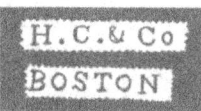
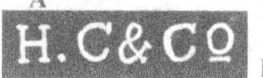

H. F. HDW.
This probably represents a hardware dealer, ca. 1850.
No imprint is available.

M. H.
Mark Haeminerle is a contemporary plane maker from Paramus, NJ. The **O8** is for 2008. Example: on a pocket plane 4"x 1 1/2" made from purple hart wood. **UR**

Hammacher Schlemmer & Co. were hardware merchants in New York City, active, ca. 1885-1900. ****

H. S. B. & Co.

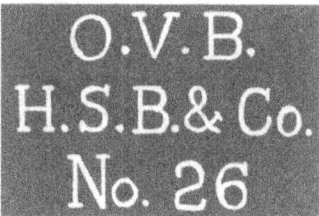

Hibbard, Spencer, Bartlett & Co. was a major hardware company in Chicago, IL, active, ca. 1883-1923. ****

D. HAAS
Example: on a 10" beech skew rabbet with heavy round chamfers found in southeastern PA, ca. 1820-30. **UR**

J: HAAS/ JOHN: HAAS
Johannes Haas (b. Apr. 28, 1814 in Schuylkill, PA, d. Jan. 15, 1856 in PA) of Upper Mahantongo Township, Schuylkill Co., PA, was a well-known cabinetmaker of decorated Mahantongo furniture, and also operated a smith and carpenter shop with his sons, **David Haas** and **Samuel Haas**. His account book, was kept in High German. He made many things besides furniture: rakes, wheelbarrows, straw benches, cabbage cutters, complete wagon wheels, handles for chisels and shovels, planes and harrows. Examples: the A imprint is on a 10 15/16" applewood wedge-lock plank match grooving plane with 5 1/2" arms, a riveted skate, a snecked iron and wide flat chamfers. The B imprint is on a 9 3/4" beech wedge-lock fenced rabbet, ca. 1835. **A & B *****

G: HAASZ
Examples: on a 9" tiger maple ogee molder found in northwestern PA; and a 13 1/4" beech gutter with iron strike and round chamfers found in Adams Co., PA. **UR**

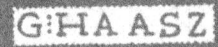

HACHENBERG
Examples: on a 3 1/8" wide cornice plane, with off-set tote, a round top iron, and iron strike button; and a molder, both beech, found in Union Co., PA, on the West side of the Susquehanna River, ca. 1810-20. **UR**

P. HACHENBERG
Johann Peter Hachenbergs worked in Lebanon Co., PA, and was an Ensign during the Revolutionary War. A son **Peter** and a grandson **Peter** are also candidates for this mark. The grandson is listed as a carpenter and joiner. Example: on a 10 1/8" beech, ogee molder, with flat chamfers, found on the east side of the Susquehanna River in Annville in Lebanon Co. **UR**

G. HACKET
Example: on a panel plane with off-set tote and flat chamfers, ca. Early 19c. **UR**

G. HADEN
Example: on a 7 1/4" beech compass smoother with a round top wedge and iron by **John Green**, and round chamfers, ca. Early 19c. **UR**

S. HADLY
Example: on a 10" beech molder with flat chamfers, ca. early 19c. **UR**

GEO I HAGAR
George Ingersoll Hagar (b. Oct. 17, 1835 in Sherburne, VT, d. Feb. 25, 1899 in Burlington, VT) was the originator of **Hagar Hardware**, located on Church St., Burlington, VT. In the 1863 directory the firm was listed as **M. I. & G. I. Hagar,** and in 1872 it was listed as **G. I. Hagar**, active from the 1870's-1970's. In the 1899 Burlington City Directory, **Lucia E. Widow of George** was listed and with a large add: Example: on a bead made by the **Taber Plane Co.   A & B *******

GEORGE I. HAGAR, HARDWARE
Mill supplies, Mechanics tools,
cutlery, oils, varnishes, brushes, etc.   (A)

B

H. HAIGHT & CO.
H. Haight & Co. was a hardware dealer in Rochester, NY, in 1845-46, then succeeded by **W. W. Bryan** at the same address. Examples: the A imprint is on a 9 1/2" match tongue & groove pair. The B imprint is on a 22" fore plane made by **Z. J. M'Master & Co.   A & B *****

A

B

A. HAIN
Example: on a 10" birch skew rabbet with heavy flat chamfers, ca. 1800.   UR

HAINES & SMITH
Haines & Smith was a hardware dealer listed in Portland, ME, active in 1869. Example: on a beech jointer, ca. 1850.   *********

HALB
Examples: on 9 15/16"-9 13/16" beech complex molders with flat chamfers, possibly from eastern PA, ca. 1800.   ***

HUDSON HALE
Hudson Hale (d. 1870) was listed in the 1849-50 New Haven, CT, directory as a planemaker. In 1952-54, he was listed as **H. & Co. No imprint has been reported**.

I. HALE
John Hale (b. Dec. 29, 1728 in West Springfield, MA, d. 1788) was a wood worker and housewright in Springfield and Longmeadow, MA. His estate inventory of 1788 included:

carpenter tools	3.12.4
joiners tools	1.13.3
Coopers & Masons tools	2.7.9

Example: on a 9 5/8" beech hollow with flat chamfers.   UR

JOSEPH HALE
Joseph White Hale (b. Feb. 3, 1816 in Glastonbury, CT, d. Jan. 6, 1895 in Newark, W. VA) was a partner in **Bidwell & Hale Co.**, planemakers in Newark, Wirt Co., VA. The **Bidwell** was **Leonard B. Bidwell** who had made planes in Hartford, CT, in the 1840's. **Joseph Hale** was listed in the 1850 industrial census as running a sawmill and grist mill. In the 1850 & 60 censuses, he was listed as farmer. In 1864, **Joseph Hale** was elected to the VA State legislature. **No imprint has been reported**.

L. F. HALE
Example: on a 28 3/4" jointer. **No imprint is available**.

W. HALE
Example: on a 10" birch grooving plane with wedge-locked Yankee-style fence and short arms, a decorative shoulder with relieved wedge, and round chamfers, possibly from southeastern New England, ca. 1790.   UR

W. HALE
Example: on a 9 1/2" beech double-boxed complex molder with heavy round chamfers, found in PA, ca. 1820.   UR

HALE & CO.

The EAIA, **Directory of American Toolmakers**, suggests that this may be **Henry Hale & Co.** from MA. Example: on a pair of match planes, and a screw-arm plow.   ***

A: HALL
Examples: on a 13 3/4"x 4 3/8" beech cornice plane with an offset tote, a hickory pull bar, and round top iron and wedge; a 14" panel raiser; and several 9 7/8"-10" beech molding planes with relieved wedges, all with flat chamfers. One example is on a **B. Dean** plane, probably from southern New England, ca. 1780-1800.   ***

B. HALL
Example: on a 9 15/16" molder with flat chamfers, ca. 1790.   UR

CALVIN HALL
Example: on a 30" birch jointer with flat chamfers, ca. 1800.   UR

E. B. HALL
Example: on a 9 1/2" (shot at the heel) birch rabbet marked twice on the toe, with an applewood D shaped wedge and flat chamfers, possibly from New England, ca. 1800.   UR

G. H. HALL
Example: on a 10 1/8" birch skew rabbet with flat chamfers mostly on the sides, and flutes, possibly from New England, ca. 1780-1800. **UR**

J. HALL
Possibly **John Hall**, a cabinetmaker, on Washington St., Boston, MA, in 1798-1800. Examples: on a rabbet; a violin maker's set; a 9 1/2" beech complex molder with flat chamfers; and a 9 1/2" beech plow with a friction depth stop, a screwed-on skate, hickory thumbscrews, birch wedge, found in Epsom, NH, ca. 1790-1800. ****

Jn HALL
Example: on an 8 1/4" birch compass smoother with heavy round chamfers. The body has minimal tapering at heel and toe. Single round top **Weldon** iron, ca. 1800. **UR**

J. HALL/ J. H. HALL/ J. DONALDSON
John Harcourt Hall (b. Jan. 8, 1801 in Bourbon Co., KY, d. ca. 1875 in St. Louis, MO) had two children born in 1830-34, in Warren Co., OH. Two children born in 1837-39, in Cincinnati, OH. **John H. Hall** was a partner in the firm of **J. Donaldson/ J. Hall** which was a planemaker and hardware dealer located in Cincinnati and Troy, OH, from 1834-36. In Mar. 1840, **John** was listed in Cincinnati; in May 1840, in St. Louis, MO. On Nov. 01, 1841, St. Louis newspapers announced a partnership with **James Donaldson** in a hardware business. The 1857 St. Louis Directory lists **John H. Hall & Co.**, at 96 North Main. The E imprint, listing **J. H. Hall** by himself, is on a 9 3/8" beech side bead plane; and a 9 3/8" beech fenced rabbet. The 1870 directory lists **John H. Hall** as "retired". **Mary Hall wife of John H. Hall** was listed as widow in 1880 census.
A, B, C & D *, E ****

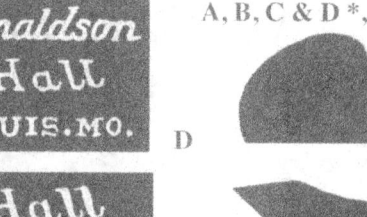

J. HALL/ J. H. HALL/ J. W. LYON
John H. Hall and **Joseph W. Lyon** had a plane making partnership in Cincinnati, OH, in 1839-40. A, A1 & B *

R. HALL
Richard Hall (b. Dec. 17, 1791 in Windham Co., VT, d. Dec. 23, 1875 in Athens, Cambridgeport, Windham Co., VT) was listed in 1870, in Athens, as a carpenter & joiner. Examples: on a 10 3/8" beech molder; a 9" birch complex molder; a 9 15/16" beech round, and a 14 5/8" beech ogee crown molder with a **Weldon** iron, all with flat chamfers, ca. 1780-1800. **UR**

R: HALL.
Example: on a 9 7/8" beech round with flat chamfers, ca 1800. ****

S. HALL
Two possibilities are **Simon Hall** a cabinetmaker active in backbay Boston, MA, from 1780-99; and in 1796, **Simon Hall** was a partner in **Hall & Bisbe**, on Washington St.. Another possibility is **Sewell Hall**, another cabinetmaker active in Boston, in 1796. Example: on a group of eight planes found in a kit including beads; a rabbet; and hollows & rounds. **S. Hall** is believed to have been a ships' carpenter.
No imprint is available.

S. H. HALL
Examples: on two sash planes; and a molder, ca. 1810.
No imprint is available.

W. HALL
Example: on a beech plow, ca. 1850. **UR**

W HALL
William Hall was listed as a planemaker in Cincinnati, OH, from 1842-44. **William Hall** then appeared in the St. Louis, MO, directories as a planemaker, in 1844 & 1865-66. Hall was also a partner in **J. W. Gosnell/ W. Hall**, from 1849-52; and **Hall & Hynson** from 1851-60. **

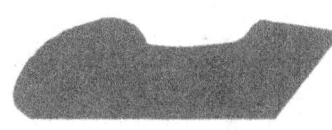

Z. B. HALL
Example: on a 9 1/2" beech shiplap plane with shallow round chamfers, ca. 1830. **UR**

HALL, CASE & CO.
Hall, Case & Co. was a Columbus, OH, plane making firm, active from 1847-52; which was dissolved after losing the contract for the use of convict labor at the Ohio Penitentiary to the newly formed **Ohio Tool Co.**. The principals included **John Smith Hall** (b. Apr. 9, 1807 in CT, d. Jun. 23, 1888, in Columbus, OH), **Harvey Case** (b. Dec. 29, 1793 in CT, d. Mar. 21, 1853 in Columbus, OH), **Joseph Armstrong Montgomery** (b. Nov. 25, 1812 in MA, d. 1895), and **James F. Ward** (b. ca. 1802 in NJ, d. Feb. 27, 1887 in Daton, Montgomery Co., OH). In the 1850 Products of Industry census, the company was listed as having 100 employees, using steam power, and producing 48,000 tools worth $75,000 for the year. In 1858, **Joseph A. Montgomery** was listed as "forman", **Ohio Tool Co.**, Columbus, OH. **James F. Ward** enlisted on Oct. 9, 1861, as an Infantry Private in the Civil War. In the 1860's-70's, Ward was a farmer in Douglas Co., Kansas. In 1880, **James F. Ward** was a retired carpenter living in the National Military Home, Daton, OH.   **A, B & C: FF**

HALL & HYNSON
William Hall and **Augustus R. Hynson** were partners as hardware dealers and planemakers, active from 1851-60, in St. Louis, MO. In 1867, **Hynson** was in a partnership as **Hynson & Coleman** with **Augustus R. Hynson** and **Rudolph E. Coleman**. In 1875-77, **Hynson & Co.**; and in 1895, **Hynson Hardware Co.**, in St Louis, MO.   **A, B & B1 ***

HALL STONE & CO
A partnership between **John S. Hall** and **A. P. Stone** (b. 1812 in MA, d. 1865 in Columbus, OH), active in 1845, that used convict labor at the Ohio Penitentiary. It was succeeded by **Hall, Case & Co.**. In 1858, **A. P. Stone** was Pres. of Columbus Woolen Manufacturing, Co. In 1860, He was Treasurer of the State of OH. In 1864, he was listed as a collector for the Int. Rev. Service.   ******

AM: HALLMAN
Examples: on a beech 7 5/16" coffin style smoothing plane with a **W. Butcher** iron and flat chamfers, found in Montgomery Co., (southeast) PA; and a 10 1/4" beech recessed quarter round found in Hatfield, Montgomery Co., PA, ca. early 19c.   **UR**

T. HAM
Believed to be **Timothy Ham** (b. ca. 1745 in Rockingham Co., NH, d. Jun. 5, 1824 in Portsmouth, NH) a joiner & cabinetmaker, carpenter and housewright in Portsmouth, NH, active from 1767-1818, or his son **Timothy Ham Jr. Timothy Ham Sr.**, was a Revolutionary War Patriot. He was one of 497 men of Portsmouth, NH, who signed The Association Test of 1776. Examples: on a beech gutter plane; a 12 3/4" birch molding plane with an offset pegged tote and flat chamfers, found in NH; a 9 7/8" astragal; and a 9 1/2" small round, with **0/8** on heel. Both beech with heavy flat chamfers. ca. 1790.   ********

W. HAM
Example: on a 9 1/2" birch molder with round chamfers, found with a **T. Ham** plane in NH.   **UR**

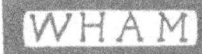

M. HAMILTON
Charles M. Hamilton (b. Aug. 6, 1810 in Grafton, NH, d. Apr. 2, 1882 in Greenbush, Sheboygan, WI) was listed in the 1849 New England Business directory, as a Mfg. of joiner's tools in Canaan, NH. In 1850 census, he was in Crawford, IL. He served in the Civil War in the Quarter Master Corp., 22nd. Regiment, Illinois 1st. Light Infantry. In the 1870-80's, he was listed as a physician in Sheboygan, WI.
No imprint has been reported.

HAMLER TOOLS
Paul Hamler is a contemporary tool maker from Blairsville, GA. who has made miniature and reproduction planes. Examples are dated, one **1999** and another **2008**.   **UR**

ROBERT HAMILTON
Robert Hamilton (b. Mar. 24, 1815, d. Aug. 19, 1907 in Delaware, OH), age 14, was apprenticed, on Oct. 8, 1828, to **H. B. Miller** of Lebanon, OH. In 1870 & 1900, he was listed as a carpenter in Delaware, Brown Co., OH.
No imprint has been reported.

HAMLIN
Examples: on a combination tongue & groove plane; and a double-boxed side bead, ca. 1850.   **UR**

HIRAM HAMLIN
Hiram Hamlin was listed as a planemaker, in 1832, in Utica, NY, boarding and working for **R. J. Collins**.
No imprint has been reported.

A. HAMMACHER/ A. HAMMACHER & CO.
Albert Hammacher immigrated from Hamberg Germany to New York City. He made his declaration, on April 16, 1866, and his oath, on Aug. 7, 1870. He was a New York City hardware merchant, active from 1864-84, as **A. Hammacher & Co.**, at 209 Bowery, hardware and upholstery goods, in 1885 by **Hammacher, Schlemmer & Co. A & B *

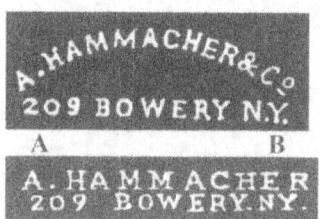

HAMMACHER SCHLEMMER & CO.
Albert Hammacher in partnership with **William Schlemmer** were hardware merchants in New York City, active from 1885-1900. **William Schlemmer** (b. Apr. 20, 1841 in Schwelm Germany, d. Dec. 23, 1916 in Manhattan, NY) worked for **A. Hammacher & Co.** from 1867-84 (except for 1871-72 when he had his own hardware store). In 1885, **Schlemmer** became a partner. The successor firm operating today in New York City. (see **H. S. & CO.**) A, B, C & D *

HAMMITT & BRO.
Hammitt & Bro. was a Wilmington, DE, hardware dealer active, ca. 1860. Example: on a **Phoenix Company plane**. ****

D. HAMMON
Example: on a 9 3/4" large round with an **I. Sleeper** style wedge and flat chamfers, ca. 1800. **UR**

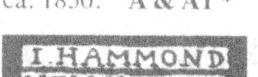

I. HAMMOND
Isaac Hammond was listed as a plane manufacturer at 19 Artisan in New Haven, CT, active from 1840-45, ca. 1850. **A & A1 *

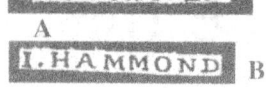

HENRY HAMMONTRY
Henry C. Hammontry (b. May, 1832, MD, d. Sep. 26, 1894 in Logansport, Case Co., IN) was listed, in 1850, as a plane maker living with **Pillip Chapin** in Baltimore, MD. In 1860, Hammontry was listed as a plane maker, living with **W. P. Webb** in Washington, DC. **Henry Hammontry** was a Private in the Civil War in Co. K, 88 Reg, IN, serving from Aug. 11, 1862 to May 26, 1865. In 1870, **Henry** was listed as a plane maker in Longsport, IN; in 1880, as "furniture manufactuary". **No imprint has been reported**.

HANCOCK
Examples: a plow with wood thumbscrew locking arms and wood depth stop, and four other molding planes, ca. 1800. **No imprint is available**.

D. HANCOCK
Example: on a 9 3/4" square rabbet plane with round chamfers. ca. 1830. **UR**

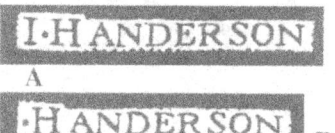

I. HANDERSON/ . HENDERSON
Examples: the A imprint is on a 9 1/2" beech round with round chamfers. The B imprint is after the die had been altered, and is on a dado; a rabbet; and hollows & rounds, all 9 1/2" beech with round chamfers. Five of these planes were found in a group in Lancaster Co., PA, ca. 1820. **UR**

J. P. HANDFORD
J. P. Handford was probably a hardware dealer. This imprint is on the lower part of the toe of a half dozen examples, ca. 1850. ****

HANEY & DEBOW
Haney & Debow was a Milwaukee, WI, hardware dealer active ca. 1850. Example: on a toothing plane made by **Casey & Co.** of Auburn, NY, with a **Providence Tool Co.** iron. ***

DAVID HANLEY
David Hanley (d. 1849 in Philadelphia, PA) was listed as a planemaker in New York City, active from 1827-37. He moved to PA; and was listed in the 1837, 41 & 45 Philadelphia, PA, directories. He worked for the **Whites** making two screw-arm plows and using the initial imprint **D.H.** on the **Israel White** planes. **No imprint is available**.

R. HANNAH
Possibly related to **W. Hannah**. Example: on a 9 1/2" beech double-boxed fixed sash with two blades & wedges and shallow round chamfers, ca. 1830. **UR**

W. HANNAH
Possibly related to **R. Hannah**. Example: on a 7 1/4" beech open front router plane, ca. mid 19c. **UR**

J. HANNAN
James H. Hannan (b. 1820, d. Jan. 18, 1894 in NY) manufactured planes in New York City, active from 1849-57. During 1856-57, he also operated a tool store. James served in the Civil War, from Aug. 19, 1863 to Nov. 10, 1964, in Co. B, NY 16th. Heavy Artillery Reg. In 1872 & 74, he was listed, as a pianomaker, in NY. He apparently made planes in Middletown (NY or CT). The A imprint has been reported over struck with **W. B. Belcher**/ New York, B imprint. The B imprint appears on a 3 1/4" beech miniature smoother with a metal sole. Miniature planes made and imprinted by a planemaker are quite rare. The C imprint is from a boxwood screw-arm plow.
A & B ***, C & D ****

HANNING & CO.
Examples: on a 9 1/2" beech hollow; and small dado, both with small flat chamfers, ca. 1810.   **UR**

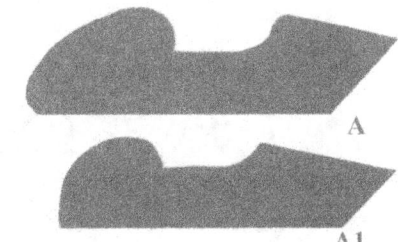

B. HANNIS
Benjamin Hannis (d. 1808 in Philadelphia, PA) was listed in the 1803-08 Philadelphia, PA city directories, as a planemaker. His widow was listed in the 1809 Philadelphia directory. He was possibly in the partnership of **Hannis & Abbott** in Philadelphia, PA, ca. 1810. No **Hannis & Abbott** imprint has been reported.   ****

M. HANSCOM
Example: on a 7 5/8" smoother with a **Humphreysville Mfg. Co.** iron, ca. 1850.   **UR**

L. W. HAPGOOD
Lyman W. Hapgood (b. Nov. 27, 1811 in Worcester, MA, d. Oct. 18, 1874 in Ashburnham, MA) was listed as a planemaker in the Lowell, MA, directories from 1835-37. In the 1850 census, **Lyman W. Hapgood** was a wheelwright in Athol, MA. In 1870, he was listed as a manufacturer in Athol. Examples: on a 9 1/2"x 5/8" beech double-reeding plane with guide, and a filletster.   **

D. HARBAUGH
Example: on a 9 1/2" beech complex molder with round chamfers, ca. 19c.   **UR**

I + HARDIE
Possibly **Joshua Hardy**, a chairmaker, on Orange St. in Boston, MA, listed from 1796-1800. Examples: are on 9 3/8"-9 1/2" birch molders including a hollow; a small round; and a shiplap rabbet, all with flat chamfers, ca. 1800.   ****

A. C. HARDON
A. C. Hardon was probably a hardware dealer. Example: on an **A. J. Kellogg**/ Amherst, MA, 8/8 nosing plane.   ****

HARDWARE. STORE
With the added location of **No. 73/ HOUSTON. ST./ NEW. YORK**. Example: on a beech screw-arm plow with boxwood threads, nuts and washers, ca. 19c.   ****

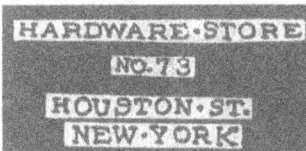

A. HARDY
Examples: on a jack plane; an 8 7/8" beech fixed sash with shallow round chamfers, found in VT; and a 10" beech complex molder with flat chamfers and an **I. Sleeper** style wedge, ca. 1810-30.   ****

C. W. HARDY
C. W. Hardy with the added **MAKER**. Example: on a 29 1/8" beech jointer with a centered tote, **W. Butcher** iron and round chamfers, ca. mid 19c.   ****

D. HARDY
Examples: on a 16" and a 30" beech bench planes, ca. 1850.   **UR**

E. B. HARFORD
Examples: on a group of several planes with 19c style chamfers. Goshen is about 60 miles northwest of New York City.   ****

C. HARIMAN
Examples: on 9 7/8"-10" beech molding planes with an **I. Sleeper** style wedge and flat chamfers. One example has all three imprints. Also reported is the A imprint on the end grain of a 16 1/2"x 27" fruitwood square, ca. 1800.   A & B ***; C *****

R HARIS
Example: on a 11" birch skew rabbet with heavy flat chamfers, ca. 1780-90. **UR**

A. HARMAN
Examples: The A imprint is on a 10" moving filletster. The B imprint is on a beech panel raiser with integral fence and no depth stop, possibly from PA, ca. late 18c.
A & B: UR

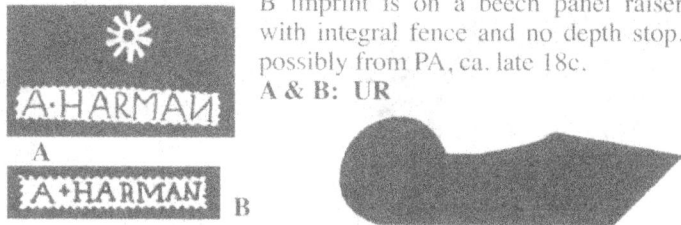

A. HARMON
Believed to be **Abner Harmon** (b. May 15, 1756 in Glarborough, Cumberland Co., ME, d. Jan 30, 1830 in Buxton, York Co., ME) received a land grant for service in the Revolutionary War. In 1810, **Harmon** was listed in the census for Scarborough, Cumberland Co., ME, adjacent to Buxton. In the 1820-30 censuses, **Abner Harmon** was listed in Buxton, York Co., ME. In 1836, his widow applied for a pension. Examples: on a 12 7/8" beech double-blade fixed sash with offset tote, and an 8 1/2" beech single-boxed center bead, ca. 1815. ****

B. HARMON
Believed to be **Benjamin Harmon** (b. Apr. 23, 1772 in Sanford, York Co., ME. d. 1842 in Alfred, York Co. ME) who was listed in the 1810 census for Scarborough, Cumberland Co., ME, adjacent to Buxton. In the 1820-30 censuses, **Benjamin Harmon** was listed in Buxton, York Co., ME. In 1844, **Benjamin** was listed as a wagon maker in Portland, ME. Example: on a 9 11/16" beech astragal with an **I. Sleeper** style wedge and flat chamfers. ca. 1790-1800. ****

D. HARMON
Dominicus Harmon (b Feb. 21, 1821 in Burham, ME, d. Sep. 2, 1888 in Caribou, ME) married **Roxanna McKenney**, on Aug. 6, 1841, in Limington, Me. He was deeded property, on May 2, 1845, in East Limington where he built a mill and carriage shop. He was listed in 1850, as a carpenter, in Limington. In 1860, Harmon was listed as a carriage maker, in Limington. In 1862, He moved north to Caribou, ME. **Harmon** was known as a Mill and House wright, mechanic, blacksmith and a wagon/ carriage maker. He was said to be a "genius with tools". Examples: The A imprint is on a 11 1/8" beech razee, double-iron fixed sash plane with an integral closed tote; and a smoothing plane with a double-iron and swivel mounted on a long hickory handle for a floor plane. The B imprint is on a 15 7/8"x 3 1/4" beech, open toted ogee with an applied fence, ca. 1850. **A & B: ****

I + HARMON Ir
Possibly: **Ismiel Harmon** (b 1791) who was in the 1820-30 censuses from Buxton, ME, and listed as a carpenter in Benton, ME, from 1820-50, or **John Harmon, Jr.** (b. 1775, d. Sep. 1, 1857 in Buxton, York Co., ME) who was also listed in the 1820 census from Buxton, York Co., ME. Example: on a 10" beech fixed sash with slightly rounded chamfers; and a 10 1/2" beech complex molder, with round chamfers, ca. 1800-10. ****

P. HARMON
The location imprint **BIDDEFORD** is believed to be Biddeford, ME. ****

HARMONY/ H. MONIE
The **Harmony Society** founded a community north of Pittsburgh, PA, in 1805. The central town was called **Harmony**. They created a new industrial-agrarian society whose members migrated from the Stuttgart area of Germany. In 1814, they moved to IN, before returning to western PA, in 1824. The A imprint is from a massive 15 1/2"x 8 1/4" with a 5" iron, crown molding plane, dated **1822,** and with an ogee chamfers and on a halving plane. The B imprint is believed to have been made prior to the 1814 move to IN, and represents an abbreviation of the original German spelling for the Harmony Society. It is on a 9 5/16" beech round with heavy round chamfers. Several planes are in the cabinet shop of old Economy, PA, near Pittsburgh. The C imprint is from a group of planes made by **David Schreiber** (b. Mar. 3, 1803, d. Apr. 26, 1883) and imprinted **D. S.** and with dates from 1844-52. (see *Planemakers of Western Pennsylvania and Environs* by Charles W. Prine, Jr.)
A, B & C *****

H. J. HARPEL
Henry J. Harpel was listed in the 1840-50 censuses as a carpenter, living in Douglas, Montgomery Co., PA. He was a neighbor of **Frederick Dallicker Jr.**. Examples: on a 13 3/4" tongue plane with an offset tote; a 9" beech unhandled screw-arm plow with a screwed skate; and a 9 1/2" beech double-boxed side-bead with rosewood, all with round chamfers. ca. 1825. ****

J. HARPEL
The **Harpel** family was strong in Montgomery Co., PA through the 1800's. Example: on a beech toted tongue plane. **UR**

T. P. HARPER
Examples: on a 15" birch straight large rabbet; and on a 10 5/8" wide round with a maple body and beech wedge, ballection molded shoulder and heavy round chamfers. The later incuse **J. R. HARPER** imprint is that of an owner possibly related, ca. 1820. **UR**

HARPER & HOUSMAN
John H. Harper (b. Mar. 8, 1825 in Glasgow, Scotland, d. Dec. 31, 1874 in Shippensburg, PA) and **Henry Housman** (b. 1833 in Germany) were hardware dealers in Denver, CO. **John Harper** arrived in NY, on May 30, 1833. The 1860 census lists **John H Harper** in Rock Island, IL. Henry became the mayor of Denver, in 1871-73. **Henry Housman** was listed as a peddler in Denver, in 1895. Example: on an 11 1/2" toted tongue match plane with a **Sandusky Tool Co.** style wedge and **77** on the toe, which corresponds to the **Ohio Tool Co.** inventory number. ****

HARPER & STEEL
John H. Harper and Alex E. Steel are believed to have been hardware dealers in Rock Island, IL, active from 1855-70. In 1867, there was also **Harper & Co.** also with a **W. W. Harper** and **J. R. McCalister**. Alex Steel worked for himself from 1871-76 and then as **Alex Steel & Son**, from 1877-85 with **Alex** and **George T. Steel**. An 1885 ad reads:

ALEX STEEL & SON
Dealers in Hardware, Est. 1855
1703 2nd. Ave.
Moline, Rock Island, IL

Example: on a 1 1/2" skew rabbet with **116** on the toe, which is the **Ohio Tool Co.** inventory number for a skew rabbet. ****

WM. HARREN
Example: Probably a retailer with the imprint on a **E. F. Seybold**, Cincinnati, OH plane. **UR**

C. E. HARRINGTON
C. E. Harrington was probably a hardware dealer or maker located in Lowell, MA, ca. 1850. Example: on a **G. W. Manning** plane. ****

B. HARRIS
Example: on a 10 3/8" applewood fixed sash with heavy flat chamfers from PA, ca. 1790-1810. **UR**

G. J. & B. HARRIS
G. J. & B. Harris is probably a hardware dealer. Example: on a molder made by **Isaac Field**. **UR**

HORACE HARRIS
Horace Harris of Gorham, NY, was issued Patent No. 13,575, on Sept. 18, 1855. This had a screw adjustment of the iron in relation to the cap. This cap was actually a case for the iron to travel in, but still required a wooden wedge to hold the cutter. Example: on a 22"x 3 1/8" beech double-iron jointer with **PATENTED NO. 4/ SEPTEMBER 18, 1855** imprinted on the toe. **No imprint is available.**

I. HARRIS
Example: on a 9 3/8" beech double-boxed complex molder with heavy round chamfers. The plane also bears the incuse imprint **J. T. HARRIS** as an owner's mark, ca. 1830. **UR**

J. HARRIS
Example: on a birch 2" wide skew rabbet with heavy shallow flat chamfers, found in Waterbury, CT, ca. 1770-80. **UR**

N. HARRIS & CO.
N. Harris & Co. was listed as a planemaker in Cincinnati, OH, active in 1856-57. The B imprint is from a wide panel raiser and a nosing plane, ca. 1850. **A & B ***

A   B

S. HARRIS
Example: on a 10" beech round with an **I. Sleeper** style wedge and flat chamfers, ca. 1800-10. **UR**

S. A. HARRIS
S. A. Harris is probably a hardware dealer. Hyde Park is located in north central VT, about 40 miles east of Burlington. Example: on a 28" jointer made by **H. L. James**, ca. 1850. ****

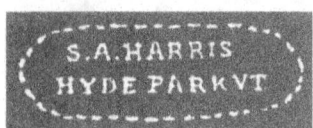

T. W. HARRIS
Thomas White Harris (b. Feb. 4, 1821 in Gloucester, ME., d. May 3, 1880 in Presque Isle, ME) was listed in 1844-47 Portland City Directory, as joiner; in 1850 census as a farmer, in New Gloucester, ME. In the 1856-57 Maine Business Directory, he was listed as a carpenter in New Gloucester. In the 1860 census, he was listed as a joiner in Gorham, ME. **Thomas W. Harris** served in the Civil War, 25th. Reg., ME Infantry for 9 months in 1862-63 as Captain. From 1874-76, he was listed as a carpenter and builder in Marysville, ME. This imprint has been reported on the ends of a 30" wooded level from Portland, ME. Example: on an adjustable sash plane, ca. 1850. ****

W. HARRIS
Possibly **Capt. William Harris, Jr.** (b. Dec. 12, 1742 in New London, CT, d. Mar. 9, 1809 in New London) who was listed as a chairmaker in New London, CT. He advertised in *The Connecticut Gazette*, from Nov. 14, 1788 thru Dec. 21, 1796. In 1798, he advertised for an apprentice. In Aug. 1803, **Harris** sold his shop. Examples: the B imprint with the heavily serrated border is on a 9 1/8" beech single-boxed complex molder with flat chamfers. The B1 imprint with the serration's filed off and a straight edge is on an early round (no length or type of wood listed), both have the same B relieved wedge, possibly from southeastern New England, ca. 1800. The A imprint is on a 9 7/8" quarter round; a 9 11/16" complex molder; and a 9 3/4" skew rabbet, all birch with flat chamfers, probably from New England, ca. 1790. A, B & B1 ****

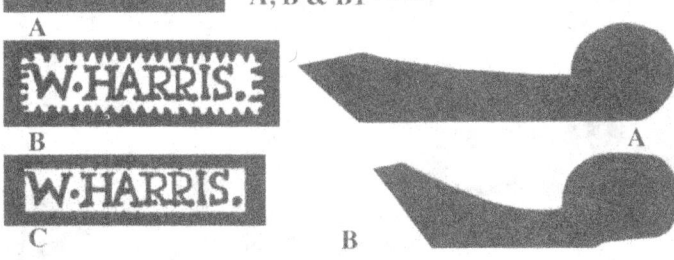

HARRIS & AMES
Harris & Ames is listed as a New London, CT, planemaker active in 1857-58. **No imprint has been reported**.

HARRIS & SHEPHERD
Isaac Harris (b. Nov. 18, 1814, d. Aug. 18, 1899 in Schenectady, NY) and **Alexander W. Shepard** (b. Mar. 1836 in NY, d. 1896) operated a hardware and cutlery business in Little Falls, NY, active from 1864-69. **Alexander W. Shepard** was listed in Little Falls as a hardware merchant. ***

J. HARRISON & CO.
John Harrison (b. ca. 1797 in NJ) appeared in the 1830-40 Zanesville, OH, censuses. He was listed as a planemaker in the 1856-57 and 1860-61 city directories. In the 1850 census, he was listed as employing one planemaker to whom he paid $40 per month, and producing $800 worth of planes. In 1870, he was listed as a plane maker in Dresden, Muskingum Co., OH. In 1880, he was listed as a plane maker in North Fork, Sweetwater, WY. Example: on a 14" beech wedge-arm tongue & groove match pair of planes; and a toothing plane with a **Buck Brothers/ Millbury, MA** iron. The B imprint includes the **W. Baum & Co.** a Cincinnati, OH planemaker, ca. 1850-52.
A**, B****

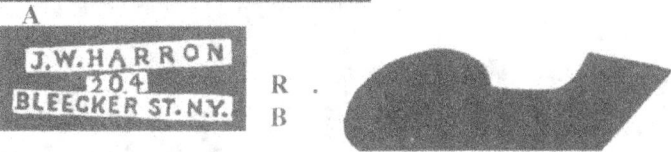

J. W. HARRON
John W. Harron (b. 1836, d. Jan. 18, 19117 in Manhattan, NY) was probably the son of **Robert Harron** and was listed as a planemaker in New York City, active from 1863-1917. A*, B**

HARRON
Robert Harron (b. 1810 in Ireland, D. Jan. 25, 1862 in NY) arrived in NY, on May 14, 1828, and was naturalized on Apr. 12, 1842, in NY. **Robert** was probably the father of **John W. Harron** and was listed, as a planemaker, in New York City, active from 1843-65. **Robert Harron** was listed in New York City directory, for 1843-44, at 182 Chrystie St. The 1850 census showed him having three employees and making 1200 planes worth $2100 annually. In 1857, he was listed as planes at 197 Bleecker St., NY. In 1859, he was listed as a tool store at the same address. Example: on a 3/8" left-hand dado has both the **R. HARRON** and the **J. W. HARRON** imprints.
A & A1: FF

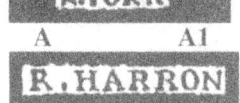

P. HARROP.
Example: on a 9 7/8"x 1/2" beech double-reeding plane imprinted toe and heel and with heavy flat chamfers. ca. 1800. UR

E. HART
Possibly **Ebeneezer Hart, Jr.** of Shelburne MA, who was a joiner and carpenter. Example: on a 9 1/2" applewood plow with wood thumbscrews, wood depth stop, beech fence & arms and flat chamfers, ca. 1780-1800. UR

H. L. HART
Holloway Long Hart (b. Oct. 4, 1804 in Shelburne, MA, d. June 12, 1870 in Deerfield, MA) listed in 1840-70 censuses in Greenfield, MA. Listed variously as cutlery, knife factory, tool

cutter or mechanic. Possibly he was a joiner or carpenter prior to his listing in 1840. **Holloway's** estate included a chest of joiner's tools valued at $7.00. Example: on a Yankee plow with a birch body and a fence of apple or pear, wood depth stop, wood thumbscrews and heavy round chamfers, ca. 1810-20. *****

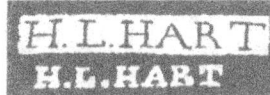

I: HART
Examples: on a 9 5/8" applewood Yankee plow with a beech fence and flat chamfers; and as an owner's imprint on a **D. Heis** 9 1/2" reed and follow plane, found north of Harrisburg, PA, ca. 1800. **UR**

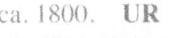

J. HART
Hart Hardware Co. was located in Louisville, KY. Example: on a 20 1/16" beech fore plane with **No. 21** on the heel, the inventory for the **Ohio Tool Co.** ****

J. HART
Possibly **Jonathan Hart** (b. Sep. 18, 1795, d. Apr. 21, 1886) a cabinemaker in Riverton, RI. Example: on a 15 7/8" beech jack with a birch centered tote and shallow round chamfers, ca. 1830. **UR**

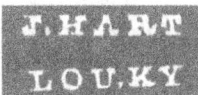

J. R. HART
Examples: on a 9" beech complex molder with flat chamfers; and on a 9" beech large bead with heavy round chamfers, ca. early 19c. **UR**

N. F. HART & CO.
N. F. Hart & Co. was listed as a planemaker from Meriden, CT, active in 1857-58. **No imprint has been reported**.

S: HART.
Possibly **Stephen Hart** a carpenter working in Torrington, CT, from 1795-98. Example: on a 21" beech jointer with a centered closed tote, a diamond strike and heavy round chamfers, ca. 1820. **UR**

HARTFORD PLANE CO.
Theodore Duval (b. in Canada) of Hartford, CT, was listed as a joiner from 1857-79. He was granted a Patent No. 97,177, on Nov. 23, 1869, for an adjustable dado plane to cut grooves of varying widths and depths. He signed his patent application with an **X**, his mark. This patent was a bridge in the development of a multi-purpose dado plane. In 1879, **Duval** was listed as a carpenter with a **Theodore Duval, Jr.** living with him. **Theodore Duval, Jr.** was listed as an engineer, in 1882-85. From 1880-91, **Theodore Duval Sr.** was listed, as a carpenter, in Hartford. From 1899-1900, he was a laborer, in Hartford. In 1901, he was listed with no occupation in E. Glastonbury, Hartford Co., CT.

Planes using this patent were made by the **Hartford Plane Co.** This imprint with **PAT. NOV. 1869** is from a 9 1/2"x 13/8" beech wood dado with a brass depth stop and **No. 1337** on the heel. *****

J. HARTMAN
Examples: on a 9 3/4" beech large bead with flat chamfers and intermittent boxing, possibly from PA, ca. 1810. **UR**

M. HARTMAN
Example: on a 14 1/2" handled tongue plane with heavy flat chamfers, possibly from PA, ca. 1800. **No imprint is available**.

J. & E. HARTNETT
J. & E. Hartnett is believed to be a Chicago, IL, hardware dealer. Example: on a 9 1/2" beech size **16** hollow with an **Ohio Tool Co.** iron. ****

J. HARTWELL
Examples: an 11 1/2" beech shiplap skew rabbet with a closed integral handle and double-gouge-stopped heavy flat chamfers. Molders are 9 1/4"-9 1/2" beech with flat, round, early 19c chamfers, ca. 1810-30. ****

P. HARTY+
Examples: on three 9 1/2" beech astragals; a boxed complex molder; and a 9 1/2" birch ogee, all with flat chamfers; a 9 1/4" round; and a 15" offset toted stair rail plane with an ebony diamond strike, marked three times on the toe, both with round chamfers, ca. 1800-30. ****

I: HARVEY
Possibly **Ira Harvey** (b. Nov. 22, 1772 in MA, d. Mar. 30, 1834 in Waterford, Caledonia Co., VT) who moved to Barnet, VT, from MA, before 1800. He was a cabinetmaker and engaged in agriculture. Ira was in partnership with his son **Darius Harvey** (b. Dec. 19, 1801 in Passumpsic, VT), until 1832, when the shop was sold. Example: on a 6 3/4" compass smoother with flat chamfers, ca. 1810. **UR**

J. HARVEY
Possibly **John Harvey**. Example: on a 10 1/4" birch shiplap plane with small flat chamfers. **JOHN** is carved in script on the side. The A1 imprint is reported on a 7" beech compass plane with heavy flat chamfers, ca. 1790. **UR**

A. HARWOOD
This elusive name is on a 9 3/4" beech bead; and a slide-arm plow, ca. 1790. **No imprint is available**.

C. HARWOOD/ C: HARWOOD
Clark Harwood (b. May 4, 1760 in Amherst, MA, d. Apr. 25, 1835 in Rutland, VT) moved with his family to Bennington, VT, in 1761 or 62. **Clark** married **Susanna Green**, on Aug. 29, 1785, in Bennington, VT. He moved to Rutland, VT, by 1790. **Clark** advertised in the *Farmer's Library* on Jul. 1, 1793 and May 6 & 20, 1794 in Rutland: "Joiner tools of all kinds, for ready pay, in cafh or wheat." The A imprint with serrations and the A1 imprint with the serrations filed off, are from the same die. Examples: the A imprint is on a 10" birch fixed sash, and the A1 is on a 10" birch round, both with relieved wedges and heavy flat chamfers; a 10" complex molder; and a 12 3/4" panel raiser. The B imprint, is on a 10" birch round. The C imprint is on 9 1/8" beech planes with heavy flat or round chamfers, ca. 1790-1820.
C.**, B ****, A & A1 *****

R: HARWOD
Example: on a 10" beech complex molder with heavy flat chamfers and an **I. Sleeper** style wedge; a 9 3/4" bead; and a 14" single-iron sash with an open slightly offset pegged tote, ebony strike, and a **Weldon** iron (Sheffield 1774-88), ca. 1790. **A & B: ****

R. HARWOOD
Examples: on a 9 3/4" beech bead; a 9 1/8" round; and a 9" beech slide-arm plow with heavy round chamfers, ca. 1820. ****

G. HASTINGS & CO.
G. Hastings & Co. is from Cleveland OH, ca. 1850. **A & B: ****

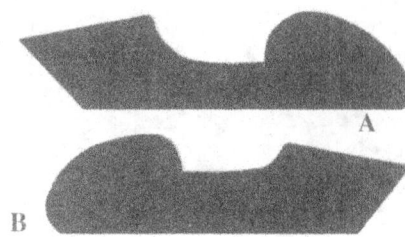

J. HASKINS
Example: on a side chamfer plane with round chamfers. **UR**

S. HASTINGS
Samuel Hastings (b. Mar. 9, 1816 in Amherst, Hampshire Co., MA, d. Nov. 16, 1885 in Amherst, MA) was listed in 1840, as living in Amherst and in "manufacturing". He was listed in 1850 & 70 as a toolmaker in Amherst. In 1880, he was listed as a farmer. Example: on a 22" bench plane; a smoother overstamped by a **J. Kellogg** B imprint.
A ***, A1 ****

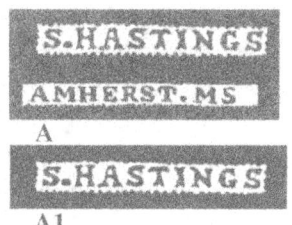

S. HASTINGS
S. Hastings was listed as a plane manufacturer in the 1853-54 Cleveland, OH business directory. (see **Kellogg & Hastings**) **No OH imprint has been reported**.

B. W. HATCH
Example: with an incuse **MAKER** imprint on a 7 7/8" lignum vitae double-iron smoothing plane, probably from coastal New England, ca. mid 19c. ****

E. HATCH
Believed to be **Edwin Hatch** (b. Oct. 16, 1807 in Glover, Orleans Co., VT, d. Aug. 18, 1882) of Craftsbury, VT, who was listed in the 1840 census, as in "manufacturing and trades"; in 1850, as a house joiner; in 1860, as a mechanic; in 1870, as a farmer; and in 1880, as a carpenter. Hatch was also noted as a chairmaker. Examples: on a fixed sash; a skew rabbet; a single boxed complex molder; and a grooving plane with a riveted skate, all 9 3/8"-9 1/2" beech with large shallow round chamfers, ca. 1830-40. ****

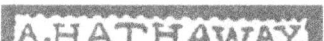

A. HATHAWAY
The molding planes are 9" birch with maple boxing. Examples: on a tongue & groove match pair; a double-iron sash; an astragal; a large hollow; a double-boxed complex molder; and a boxed bead, all with tight round chamfers, some with fluting. **A. Hathaway** planes are similar in detail to planes by **A. Barnard**, from New England, ca. 1800. ***

I. HATHAWAY

Example: on a 9 15/16" birch hollow with flat chamfers and a sheared relieved wedge; and a by-directional rabbet plane, from southeastern New England, ca. 1800. **A & B: UR**

N. HATHAWAY

Example: on a 13 1/2" beech handled tongue plane with round chamfers, ca. 1820. **UR**

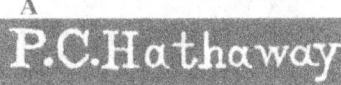

P. C. HATHAWAY

Believed to be **Patrick Clark Hathaway** (b. Apr. 9, 1842 in Warren Co., OH, d. June 27, 1872 in Lebanon, Warren Co., OH) who served during the Civil War, from Aug. 5, 1862 to Jun. 11, 1865, with the Ohio Volunteer Infantry, as a Private. **Hathaway** contacted TB and was discharged. This imprint is similar to others from Cincinnati of the same period. Examples: on a 9 7/16" beech skew rabbet, ca. mid 19c. The wedge style suggests possibly an earlier date. **A & A1 *****

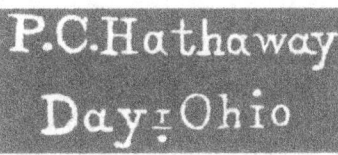
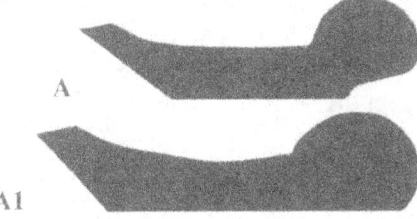

WM. HATHAWAY

Possibly **William Hathaway** (b. Dec. 24, 1793 in Freetown, MA, d. July 29, 1860, Falls River, Bristol Co., MA) who was listed as a ship's carpenter, in 1850 & 60. On June 4, 1822, **William** married in Fall River. Example: on a birch sun plane; a 12 1/2" beech double-iron fixed sash, dated 1814; and a 9 3/4" beech round, both with heavy round chamfers. ********

W. W. HATHAWAY

Possibly a **William W. Hathaway** (b. Mar. 12, 1845 in MA) who was a carpenter, in Tioga, PA, in 1880. He lived next door to his brother **Henry Hathaway** and their father, **George Hathaway**, a blacksmith (b. Dec. 31, 1810 in New Bedford, MA, d. Dec. 9, 1884 in Tioga, PA). Examples: on rounds, somewhat crudely made and found together, ca. 1860. ********

O. HATHEWAY

Example: on a 32" beech joiner. **UR**

T. HAUSE

Examples: on a beech wedge-arm plow with riveted skate, and friction-fit wood depth stop; and a 13" beech crown molder with an offset tote, and an iron signed **C. Smith**, both with round chamfers, found in eastern PA, ca. 1820. **UR**

HAUSWERTH

Example: on a 9 5/16" maple astragal; and a 10 7/16" rabbet with a full length depth stop, both with heavy flat chamfers and a beveled wedge, possibly from PA, ca. 1800. **UR**

D. HAVELY

Example: imprinted four times on the toe of a wide round, ca. 1850. **UR**

ALBERT S. HAVEN

Albert Sanger Haven (b. Jun. 21, 1829 in Suffock Co., MA, d. May 5, 1903 in Quincy, MA) was a Boston, MA, hardware dealer who appeared in the Boston city directories, from 1858-83. ******

T. HAVENS

Examples: The A imprint is on an 8" birch smoother with a round-top **Weldon** iron; and a 10 1/2" beech hollow, both with flat chamfers. The B imprint is on a 14 5/16" birch grooving plane also with flat chamfers. ca. 1800. **A & B: UR**

JOSEPH HAVILIN

Joseph Havilin was listed in the 1850 census for Newark, NJ, as a carpenter tool manufacturer, living with and working for **Philip Quigley**. **No imprint has been reported**.

C. HAWES

C. Hawes with the added location imprint **N.Y.** is from a grooving plane. **No imprint is available**.

G. H/ G. HAWES

Georage Hawes (b. Jan. 31, 1762 in Wrentham, MA, d. May 9, 1847 in Wrentham) was a Wrentham, MA, planemaker, active ca. 1790. Examples: are on 9 7/8"-10" birch molders with round chamfers, fluting and a relieved wedge or flat backed wedge.

A & A1 ****, B & C *****

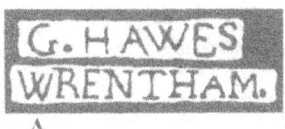

L H/ L. HAWES
Examples: on a 9 1/2" beech square rabbet with an added **LH** initial imprint; and 10"-9 3/4" beech complex molders, all with round chamfers, ca. 1810-20.   **UR**

S: HAWES
Example: on a 10" beech halving plane with flat chamfers, found in southern VT. ca. 1790-1810.   **UR**

HAWES. WENTE & CO.
Hawes. Went & Co. was a hardware store, from 1869-89, at 3 Pike St. in Covington, KY, consisting of **James Morrison Hawes** (b. Jan 7, 1824 in Lexington, KY, d. Nov. 22, 1889 in Covington., KY) and **Herman P. Wente** (b. Mar. 25, 1833 in Hanover, Germany, d. Sep. 27, 1915 in Cincinnati, OH). **James Morrison Hawes** was the son of **Richard Hawes**, the second and last Confederate Governor of KY. James received an appointment to the U.S. Military Academy, on Jul. 1, 1841 and graduated as a 2nd. Lieutenant of Dragoons. He served in the Mexican War and became an instructor at West Point. When the Civil War broke out in 1861, He was offered a post in the Union. He resigned his commission and became a captain in the Confederate Army. He served through the Civil War as a Confederate Officer rising to the rank of Brigadier General and cavalry commander of the Western Dept. of the Confederacy. He settled in Covington, in 1866. **Herman P. Wente**, his partner, immigrated from Germany in 1845. He was a lesser partner listed mostly as a clerk and hardware salesman, from 1870-90 in Cincinnati, OH. Examples: on a 9 1/2" size **3** hollow; and a size **9** round, both with inventory **No. 72**; a 9 1/2"x 1 1/2" skew rabbet with the inventory **No. 116**; a 9 1/2" drop leaf table plane; and a 16" jack plane with the inventory **No. 15**, all made by the **Ohio Tool Co.** *****

S. W. HAWKS
Example: on a 9 3/4" beech plow with square arms, wood thumb screws and flat chamfers, ca. early 19c.   **UR**

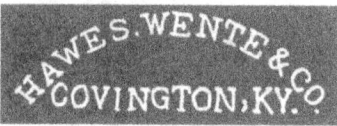

T. HAWKSLEY
Example: on a 9 5/16' Ovolo molding plane. ca. 1840.   **UR**

J. HAWLEY
Example: on a 13"x 1 1/8" beech skew rabbet with heavy round chamfers, possibly from PA, ca. 1810-20.   **UR**

HAXBY & BRENGLE
Haxby & Brengle is probably a hardware dealer. Example on a plow with the **Ohio Tool Co.** inventory **No. 96**.   **UR**

JAMES HAY
James Hay (b. 1813 in MD) was listed as a planemaker in Cincinnati, OH, active from 1842-44, at London, bt. Baymiller & Linn and could be related to **William Hay**. In 1860, James Hay was a iron molder in Cincinnati; in 1870, a carpenter at Wabash, Somerset, IN. **No imprint has been reported**.

WILLIAM HAY
William B. Hay (b. 1810 in MD, d. Feb. 11, 1884 in Kenton, KY) was listed as a planemaker in Cincinnati, OH, from 1836-46, at 8th. bt. Baymiller & Linn and could be related to **James Hay**. In 1860, **William Hay** was listed as a planemaker in Cincinnati; and in 1880, as a planemaker in Kenton, KY. **No imprint has been reported**.

HAYDEN
Joseph T. Hayden (b. Aug. 20, 1815, d. Jul 8, 1893) was a planemaker in Syracuse, NY, from 1849-51. Hayden was also part of **Hayden & Nolton**, listed as a tool and hardware store, ca. 1850. **W. H. Blye**'s April 10, 1849 patent was for a hinged plane fence, which Blye apparently licensed to Hayden.   **A & C *, B *****

E. T. HAYDEN
E. T. Hayden with the location imprint **Syracuse N.Y.** is the same as used by **Hayden** and **Hayden & Nolton**.   *******

I. HAYDEN
Examples: on a complex molder; and hollow, both 9 1/2"; and a 9 1/8" birch complex molder, all with shallow flat chamfers, ca. 1790 and possibly earlier. ****

L. F. HAYDEN
Example: on a rabbet plane with a closed integral tote, ca. 19c. **UR**

P. HAYDEN & CO.
Peter Hayden (b. Sep. 15, 1806, d. Apr. 6, 1888 in Columbus, OH) was a planemaker in Columbus, OH, who began to employ prison labor to produce carpenter, joiner and cabinet tools, in 1842. The firm continued until 1851, when it became the **Ohio Tool Co.**, with **Hayden** as director. In 1870, he was listed in industry; and in 1775, as **P. Hayden & Son**, Saddlery & Coach Hardware, Columbus, OH. A, B & B1 **

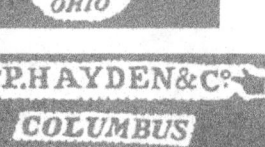 

T. HAYDEN
Thomas Hayden (b. Jan. 14, 1745 in Windsor, CT, d. Nov. 28, 1817 in Windsor, CT) was a housewright and architect in central CT. Lt. **Hayden** served in the Artisans Corps during the Revolution. **Asher Benjamin** worked under **Thomas Hayden**, in 1794, on the addition to the Burbank-Phelps-Hatheway house in Suffield, CT. Three of his sons became architects. At the time of his death, **Thomas Hayden's** estate contained "Joiners and Carp. Tools, valued at $67.81", a large amount for the period. He also owned numerous architecture books including "Practical Builder" probably William Pain's *The Practical House Carpenter* (London, 1789). Examples: on a 9 3/8" chestnut shiplap rabbet with shallow flat chamfers and a flat backed wedge; and a 9 1/2" birch hollow with flat chamfers and a relieved wedge, ca. 1790. *****

HAYDEN & NOLTON
Hayden & Nolton was a Syracuse, NY, partnership of **Joseph T. Hayden** and **Lyman Nolton** that operated as a tool and hardware store, ca. 1850, and probably sold planes made by the two partners. **Nolton** was also reported with a Salina, NY, location. The location imprint was the same used by **Hayden** and **E. T. Hayden**   A & B ***

F. HAYEK
Example: on a 6 5/8" beech toothing plane made by the **Doscher Plane & Tool Co.** and patented on March 6, 1877. **UR**

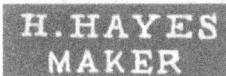

H. HAYES
An incuse imprint with **MAKER**. Example: on a 6 1/2"x1 1/16" beech coachmaker's rabbet, ca. 19c. ****

P. HAYES
Example: on a 25" beech jointer with a round-top wedge and iron, an offset pegged birch tote and round chamfers, ca. 1820. **UR**

J. HAYLES
The imprint **J. Hayles** appears on a 6 1/4" beech wedge-arm plow plane, found in a rulemaker's shop, that was used to cut grooves for sliding rules. It has a 3/16" wide wooden sole spline attached with small nails. **No imprint is available.**

J. L. HAYNES
Jonathan L. Haynes (b. 1817 in NJ) was listed as a planemaker in Newark, NJ, in 1850. Examples: The embossed A imprint is on a 9 1/2" beech moving fillister, ca. 1820-30. The incuse B imprint is on a plane that also bears the imprint of **J. Parker** and a location of **NEWARK, NJ**, ca. 1850. Possibly a partnership between **J. L. Haynes** and **Joseph Parker**.   A & B: ****

HAYWARD
Example: on a 10 3/8" birch square rabbet, with a molded low shoulder and heavy flat chamfers, possibly earlier, and probably from New England, ca. 1770. **UR**

A + HAYWARD
Abraham Hayward (b. 1750 in MA, d. Mar. 5, 1796 in Boston, MA) was a cabinetmaker, furniture maker and carriage maker, active from 1780-89, at Ann St.; and from 1789-96

at White Beard Alley in Boston, MA. During the American Revolution he was a fifer, and a Private. Examples: on molders from 9 3/8"-9 1/2" birch and beech, with flat and round chamfers. The A and B wedges are birch. The C wedge is beech and later, probably from New England, ca. 1790-1820. ***

S. HAYWARD
Example: on an 8 3/4" beech astragal bead with flat chamfers, ca. 1800. **UR**

HAYWARD REFFELL & CO
Hayward Reffell & Co. was probably a hardware dealer, active ca. 1890. It was also listed in *British Planemakers* with a location of Peterborough, although that may be in error.

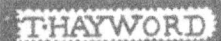

Example: on a **D. Kimberly & Sons** (Birmingham, England 1883-1901) 22" jointer. ****

HAYWOOD, CARTLEDGE & HONORE
Haywood, Cartledge & Honore was probably a hardware dealer, active ca. 1850. Examples: on bench planes made by the **Ohio Tool Co.**, and the **Auburn Tool Co.**. ****

T. HAYWORD
Example: on a 9 7/8" beech complex molder with heavy round chamfers, ca. 1810-20. **UR**

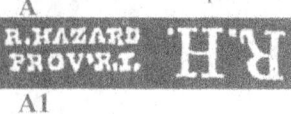

R. H./ HAZARD
William Robinson Hazard (b. Jan. 11, 1810 in RI, d. Sep. 26, 1873 in RI) made sight levels in Providence, RI, ca. 1840. He was listed, from 1853-65, as a mechanic in Kingstown, RI. In 1867, he was listed as a salesman in Providence, RI. In 1870, he was listed in N. Kingston with no occupation. Examples: on a 9 7/16" beech hollow with round chamfers. This imprint is from the same die he used to imprint his levels and marking gauges. ca. 1840. **A & A1:** ****

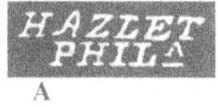

HAZLET
Hugh Hazlet (b. 1784, d. 1868 in Zanesville, OH) was listed as a planemaker in the 1817 Philadelphia, PA, directory. He worked at the same address as **Tho. Napier**. **A, A1 & B** ****

A. HEALD/ A. HEALD & CO./ ADDISON HEALD
Addison Heald (b. Feb. 25, 1817 in Nelson, NH, d. Jan. 30, 1895) was a prominent NH. planemaker, cabinetmaker, and Congregational minister. He trained as a cabinetmaker in Keene, NH, before entering the ministry and spending two years in Marion, OH, where he was involved in a school for escaped slaves. Shortly after 1852, he returned east to live with his father-in-law, also a minister, in Hudson, NH, living across the street from **William Warren**. He probably learned plane making from **Cyrus Warren** and/ or **William Warren**. In 1856, Addison Heald was working in Nashua, NH, as **A. Heald & Co.**, "Manufacturer of tools" and then as **Warren & Heald**, ca. 1860. He worked alone in Hudson, ca. 1868, and from 1868-73, in Milford, NH, where he set up a plane shop in the steam-powered furniture factory of his brother, **David Heald**. In 1873, he was joined by his son, **David**, as part of **A. Heald & Son** until his death in 1895. One example is a lignum vitae razee toted smoothing plane. **A & A1 **, B ****

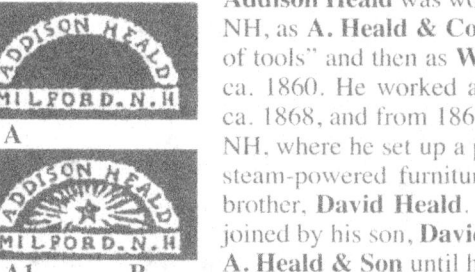

A. HEALD & SON
A. Heald & Son was a plane making partnership of **Addison Heald** (b. Feb. 25, 1817 in Nelson, NH, d. Jan. 30, 1895) and his son **Daniel Milton Heald** (b. Jan. 9, 1852 in Marion, OH, d. Oct. 30, 1929), in Milford, NH, active from 1873-1906. Addison possibly apprenticed as a planemaker under either **Cyrus Warren** or **William Warren**, in Hudson, NH, prior to 1857. **Addison Heald** started under his own name, ca. 1868, in Milford, NH. Son **David Milton Heald** joined the firm, in 1873. The firm continued under the same name after the death of **Addison Heald**, in 1895 until 1906. It was listed in 1907, in the Nashua, NH, Directory as a manufacturer of picture frames. It specialized in bench planes and cooper's tools. Some wedges utilized an unpatented screwing device at the top of the wedge on both wood & metal planes. This caused the toe of the wedge to press the plane iron against the plane bed and secure it. The device was unique to **Heald** planes and is thought to be a precursor of the plane iron cap patented by **Daniel Heald**, Patent No. 209969, issued on Nov. 19, 1878. This was a device that held the plane iron and permitted it to be adjusted for proper depth of cut by turning a screw. In addition to planes, **Daniel** made an iron shave based on his patent. (see *Patented Transitional & Metallic Planes in America – Vol. II*, p. 96-98, by Roger K. Smith) **

H HEALY
There are two possibilities from central Worcester Co., MA. The first is **Harmon Healy** (d. Jun. 30, 1802 in Beverly, Essex Co., MA), who married **Sally Pierce**, in Paxton, in 1792. **Harmon** was listed in 1794-96, in Leister, Worcester Co., MA, as a joiner

and a shop joiner. In **Hermon's** 1802 estate and 1804 inventory listed him, as a cabinetmaker, in Beverly, MA. The inventory was assessed by **William Raymond**. The second is **Hezekiah Healy** (b. Oct. 8, 1766, d. Dec. 1817) married **Rebecca Corbin**, on Nov. 14, 1798, and had a son **Hezekiah Healy Jr.** (b. 1809, d. 1821 by an accident). **Hezekiah** was listed in Dudley, MA, as a cabinet maker and as an ingenious mechanic who invented the "fly shuttle" used before the power loom became common. In 1804, he built a tavern called **Healy's Inn**. He was a Capt. of the local Militia Company. Deeds from 1802-16 listed **Hezekiah** as a "Gent" and once as a Yeoman. His probate inventory of 1818, listed jointer tools and wood refuse in the shop, 71 chairs, cherry and maple boards. Examples: the A imprint with the heavy serrated border is on a 10 1/8" birch complex molder with flat chamfers and fluting. The A1 imprint was made from the same die as the A imprint by filing off the serrations, and is on two 10" unhandled grooving planes, at Sturbridge Village, a 10 3/8" large hollow; and a 10 1/4" round, all birch with relieved wedges, flat chamfers and fluting, a 28" jointer has a swept tote similar to **U. Clap** and other Worcester Co. planemakers, ca. 1790. **A & A1 *******

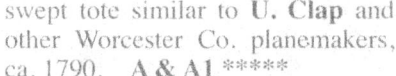
A

A1

E. HEARNE
Examples; on a 7 15/16" side bead; and a 7 15/16" complex molder, both beech with boxwood boxing, ca. 19c. **UR**

I: HEATH
Possibly **Joseph Heath** a cabinetmaker who worked in Tauton, MA, in 1801. This double imprint is from a 10 9/16" hollow with flat chamfers, ca. 1800. **A & B: UR**

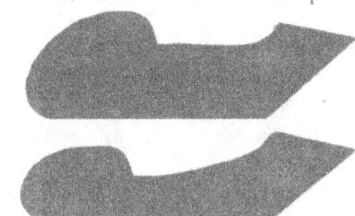

S. HEATH
Example: on a 13 3/8" beech specialty grooving plane with a centered cherry pegged open tote and flat chamfers. It cuts a series of parallel narrow shallow "V" grooves. The skate is adjusted by a hand forged thumbscrew on the side, ca. 1790. **UR**

HEATHER & WELLMAN
Heather & Wellman was a Cincinnati, OH, hardware dealer, from 1871-78. ********

C. HECKENDORN
This imprint with some creative edge filing is from a 9 1/2" beech shiplap rabbet with flat chamfers, from PA, ca. 1800. **UR**

HEGNY & BOLLERMANN
Probably **John L. Hegny** (b. ca. 1842 in Bremen, Germany, d. 1880 in NY) and **Bollermann**, a New York hardware dealer, This imprint has appeared on **G. W. Denison & Co.** and **Shiverick** planes, ca. 1870. *******

D. HEIM
Example: struck twice on the toe of a 9 3/4" beech round with narrow flat chamfers, probably from rural PA, ca. 1810-20. **UR**

T. A. HEIM
Thomas A. Heim (d. before 1880) was a partner of **David N. Garrison** (b. 1818 in OH, d. Feb. 24, 1885 in Middleton, Butler Co., OH) was listed in Dayton, OH, active in 1849-50. Heim also was a partner with **Charles J. Smith**, in 1851, as the **Hamilton Plane Factory** in Cincinnati, OH. *******

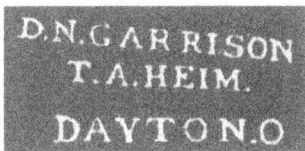

HEIM & SMITH
Thomas A. Heim and **Charles J. Smith** were hardware and edge tool dealers, at 280 Main St., Cincinnati, OH, active in 1849-50. (see **C. J. Smith & Co., J. & C. Smith**)
No imprint is available.

CH. HEINIKE
Ch. Heinike planes have been found in eastern PA, both with and without English planemaker imprints, raising the question whether he was both a dealer and a maker. The English makers include **Blizard** (1800-28), **I. Cox** (1770-1843), and **Wm. Moss** (1775-1843). Examples with only the **CH. HEINIKE** imprint include a molder with size **3/8** on the heel; a size **2** and **12** rounds, all 9 3/4" beech with heavy flat chamfers, ca. 1800. *******

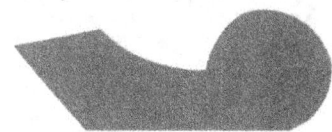

D. HEINSELMAN
Example: on a 10 1/2" birch complex molder with a cherry wedge and heavy flat chamfers, possibly connected to the **Heinselmans** of Manheim, PA. ca. 1790. **UR**

D. HEIS/ D. HEISS
Dietrich Heiss (also spelled **Heis**) (b. May 22, 1745, in Germany, d. Jul. 15, 1817 in Lancaster, PA) was a Lancaster, PA, joiner, carpenter and planemaker. He was the father of **John Heiss** and **Jacob Heiss**. He was first listed as paying taxes

in 1769, working in Lancaster as a "schreiner" which means joiner and carpenter. He worked in Philadelphia, PA, from 1782-85, returning to Lancaster where he worked until 1814. Examples: the A imprint is the earliest, and is on a 10" beech square shiplap rabbet with heavy flat chamfers. The B imprint is on 9 3/4" planes with flat chamfers, some with intermittent boxing; a 9 1/2" planes with round chamfers; and a later 9 1/2" applewood square shiplap rabbet with round chamfers, also imprinted **J. Stam** as an owner.
B **, A ****

IOHN HEIS
John Tobias Heiss (b. Aug. 20, 1769 in Lancaster, PA, d. May 7, 1849 in Philadelphia, PA) was the son of **D. Heiss**, and the older brother of **Jacob Heiss**. He was listed as a joiner, carpenter and painter in Lancaster, PA, from 1792-1825. Examples: on a toted cornice plane; a 13 1/2" applewood complex molder with an offset tote, round chamfers and an iron marked **A.T.** (blacksmith **Archibald Taylor**, Lancaster, PA, ca. 1812); a 9 3/8" beech small round with a **James Cam** iron and small flat chamfers, found in Lancaster Co.; and a 10" beech skew rabbet with heavy round chamfers, ca. 1810-20. ****

JACOB HEISS/ JACOP HEISS
Jacob Heiss (b. ca. 1780 in Lancaster, PA, d. June/ July 1841) was the son of **D. Heiss** and the brother of **John Heis**. He was listed as a Lancaster, PA, "plain maker", in 1807. He could have worked as early as 1803, the year Jacob first paid taxes, and continued as a planemaker, thru 1840, with the exception of 1819-25, when he was listed as a house carpenter. Examples: the A imprint is on 9 5/8" beech molders with round chamfers, some with intermittent lignum vitae boxing; and a 7 3/4" beech smoother with round chamfers. The A1 imprint preceded the A imprint, before the **JACOP** was corrected to **JACOB** and is from a 9 1/2" applewood molder with a skew-iron and round chamfers, ca. 1820-30.
A **, A1 *****

J. HEISSER
Jacob Heisser (b. 1824 in Bavaria, Germany, naturalized Sep. 23, 1840 in NY, d. 1877 in NY) was a hardware dealer in New York City, from 1851-77, with several listings for **J. Heisser & Son**. After **Jacob's** death, the business was continued by his son **William H. Heisser**, through 1888. The store was located at 481 8th. Ave., from 1851-70; and then at 511 8th. Ave., from 1870-77. **W. J. C. Ward** was operating at 513 8th. Ave., during part of this period. Example: 3 3/4"x 1 1/8" boxwood smoother with the iron marked **JACOB HEISSER, NEW YORK** in a circle with **CAST STEEL** in the center. ***

HEMING
Example: on a beech 9 7/16" skew moving fillister with brass inserts on a sliding bottom fence, wood dovetailed depth stop, and heavy round chamfers, found in southeastern PA, ca. 1810-20. **UR**

R. W. HENDRICKSON
Richard W. Hendrickson (b. Sep. 25, 1832 in NJ, d. Mar. 21, 1889 in Somerville, Somerset Co., NJ) made planes and ran a tool shop in New York City, from 1859-67, at 65 1/2 Bowery, an address he shared with **A. G. MOORE** during 1859-61. **Hendrickson** also made planes in Brooklyn, NY, from 1868-70.
A **, A1 & B ****

J. HEMINGWAY
J. Hemingway was an apprentice to **Samuel Noyes** of East Sudbury, MA. **No imprint has been reported**.

J. HEMINGS
Believed to be **John Heming(s)** (b. Apr. 24, 1776 at Monticello, Albemarle Co., VA, d. 1833 in VA) was a slave owned by **President Thomas Jefferson**, through his wife's inheritance. **John** was the youngest son of slave **Betty Hemings** and **Joseph Neilson**, a white house joiner hired by **Jefferson**, in the 1770's. In 1793, he learned joining as an apprentice to hired joiner **David Watson**. At age 17, **John Heming** was the principal assistant to **James Dinsmore** an Irish Joiner. **Hemings** crafted interior wood work at Monticello and Poplar Forest. He made furniture, was a wheelwright and made the wooden parts of a large Landau carriage, in 1814. **Jefferson's** sons by **Sally Hemings**: **Beverly**, **Madison** and **Eston Hemings** were apprenticed to **John Hemings** for training as fine carpenters. **Jefferson** freed **John Heming**, in his will in 1826, allowing him the tools from the joinery and the work of his two apprentice assistants, **Madison** and **Eston Heming**. **John Heming** made **Thomas Jefferson's** coffin. **John** continued to live at Monticello, after 1826, and worked for wages, until 1831. **John** was literate, leaving a dozen letters to **Jefferson** describing his progress at Poplar Forest. Examples: on a 9 9/16" beech belection molder with round top chamfers and square front and rear chamfers, size **2** on heel, and an iron by **Robert Moore**, ca. 1800; and on a 9 1/4" beech single-boxed ogee molding plane with wide round chamfers, ca. 1820-25. *****

P. HEMINGWAY
Example: on a 13 1/4" beech crown molder with an offset tote and flat chamfers, ca. 1790.

 UR

C O H/ CO. HENDRIK
Cornelius Hendrik with a Dutch name, appeared in the 1790 census, in Canajohairie, Montgomery Co., NY, located on the Mohawk River west of Albany. The 1800 census listed a **Cornelius Hendricks** in New York City; and the 1810 census listed two **Hendriks** in Ontario Co., south of Rochester, NY. Of help may be the owner imprint **JA**, branded on the side and **JOSEPH ADAMS** on the heel. The **HENDRIK** is from the same die as the **CO. HENDRIK**, possibly indicating several **Hendriks** at work and is from a wedge-arm Yankee plow with flat chamfers, a riveted skate and a wood friction-fit depth stop. Of interest is the constructed **COH** initial group, found alone and with the B imprint. Examples: are on 9 3/8"-10" beech molders, and a 13 3/4"x 3" molder with an offset tote, all beech with round chamfers on top and flat chamfers on the toe and heel, ca. 1800.
A ***, A1 & B ****

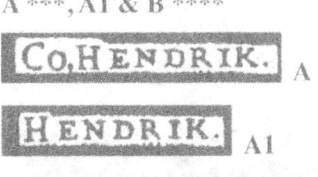

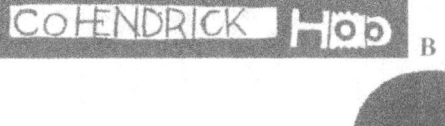

G. HENI
Example: on a 10" yellow birch double-flute plane with flat chamfers. Possibly from the PA or MD area, ca. 1800. **UR**

I: HENNY
Example: on a 9 1/2" beech complex molder with flat chamfers found in PA. ca. early 19c. **UR**

ANDREW HENRY
Andrew Henry was listed as a planemaker in New York City, active in 1835. **No imprint has been reported**.

H: HENRY
Example: on a 9" beech plow with wood depth stop, wood thumbscrew-locked arms and flat chamfers, possibly from PA, ca. 1800. ****

R. W. HENRY
With the location **CLEVELAND/ OHIO** on two rounds and one hollow, ca. 19c. ****

WM. HENRY JR.
William Henry Jr. (b. Jan. 1822 in Logan, Germany, d. Mar. 24, 1862 in Wooster, Wayne Co., OH) was a hardware dealer located in Wooster, OH, ca. 1850. He served in the Civil War as a Private in the 26th. Reg., Ohio Infantry from Jul. 8, 1861- Mar. 17, 1862, possibly wounded. Example: on a combination tongue & groove plane made by **Hall Case & Co.** of Columbus, OH. ****

H. HERBERT
Example: on a 15" beech jack with a centered tote, a diamond strike, double-iron by **W. Butcher** and round chamfers, dated **1827**; and a 9 1/2" beech boxed bead, dated **1832**, found in PA. **UR**

G. HERDER
Gustavus Herder (b. Feb. 10, 1810 in Germany, d. Mar. 16, 1884 in Cincinnati, OH) and arrived in Dec., 1832, in Baltimore, MD. He was a Cincinnati, OH, hardware dealer, active from 1839-66. In 1867, the store was listed under **Sittedding & Niehads Hardware**. **

FRANK HERITAGE
Frank Heritage was listed as a planemaker in Columbus, OH, active ca. 1850. In 1858, he was listed as artist and advertised Winchester's Daguerrean, Columbus, OH.
No imprint has been reported.

C H/ C HERMAN
The **CH** initials also have been found on planes marked **Herman. & Mohr,** from Muncy, PA. Examples: on a 10" beech molder; and a round, both with flat chamfers, ca. 1800. ****

JAMES HERMAN
James Herman was issued a restored Patent No. 9055x, for a modified ordinary tongue & groove plane, by inserting metal rollers to help the fence move more easily.
No imprint has been reported.

SAMUEL HERMAN
Samuel Herman was listed in the Cleveland, OH, directory, as a planemaker located, at 146 Superior St., active in 1845-46.
No imprint has been reported.

HERMAN & MOHR
Probably a partnership with **C. Herman** and **Nathaniel Mohr** (b. 1817 in PA, d. 1861 in Muncy, Lycoming Co., PA). **Nathaniel** was listed as a chair maker & other items related to

the trade and advertised in 1848 & 55 in Muncy, PA. Example: on a 9 1/2" beech bead; and a 13 3/4" open-tote ogee molder found in Bradford Co. PA, which is adjacent to Lycoming Co, ca. 1840-50. ***

I. HERNER

This imprint is on a medium round. **UR**

M. HERNER
Example: on a 9 3/4" beech large bead with heavy round chamfers, ca. 1830. **UR**

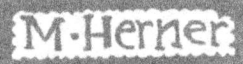

I. HERPES
Example: on a 10 1/2" beech skew rabbet with flat chamfers, ca. early 19c. **UR**

J. HERRICK
John Herrick (b. Dec. 27, 1793 in Topsfield, MA, d. Aug. 26, 1872 in Burlington, VT) was in Burlington, VT, prior to 1816; and appears in the 1842-44 city directory, as a planemaker. He was listed in the 1850 census, as a house joiner. He is believed to have been a partner in **Nichols & Herrick**, from 1816-36. In 1860, he was listed as a master carpenter, and in 1870, a house carpenter in Burlington, VT. Example: on a 9 9/16" beech fixed sash with round chamfers made by **Nichols & Herrick** with the A imprint below, ca. 1820. The A imprint is on a 9 5/16" beech bead with wide shallow round chamfers, ca. 1830. The smaller B imprint is on a double-iron sash; and a complex molder, both 9 1/2" beech, ca. 1840. **A & B ***

TOD HERRLI

Tod Herrli of Mississinewa Valley Planes is a contemporary maker of 18c. reproduction molding planes. Tod is from Marion, IN. **UR**

J. L. HERSEY
Joel L. Hersey (b. 1810 in MA, d. May 15, 1862 in Portland, ME) appeared in the Portland, ME, city directories as a joiner, from 1834-52. In 1860, he was listed as a grocer in Portland, ME. Several examples have been reported, all 9 1/2" beech. **A & A1 ***

S. C. HERSEY
Examples: on a single-boxed bead; and a tongue & groove pair found in ME, both 9 3/8" beech with round chamfers; and a 9 3/8" cove & bead complex molder, with heavy flat chamfers, ca. 1800-20. ****

I. HESS

I. Hess was carved in the side of a 9" beech plow with a riveted skate, iron depth stop with a heart shaped thumbscrew, wedge lock arms, the iron marked **G PETERS**; found near Rochester, NY. The toe also has a German double hawk/ eagle emblem. **UR**

W. J. HEUISLER
W. J. Heuisler is believed to be a Baltimore, MD, cabinetmaker, active from 1847-88. Examples: on a 9 3/8" astragal; and a 9 1/2" beech 4 round, ca. 1850. ****

A. HEWET
Example: on a 10" birch skew rabbet with heavy flat chamfers and flutes from New England, ca. 1790. **UR**

HIBBARD, SPENCER, BARTLETT & CO.
Hibbard, Spencer, Bartlett & Co. was a major Chicago, IL, hardware company that sold planes made by **Sandusky Tool Co.** under the brand name **A. C. Bartlett's Ohio Planes**. The company began in 1883, as a successor to **Hibbard, Spencer & Co.** with **William G. Hibbard** (b. 1826, d. Oct. 11, 1903 in Chicago, IL), president; **Franklin F. Spencer** (b. ca. 1818, d. Nov. 1, 1890 in Chicago, IL), vice president; and **Adolphus C. Bartlett** (b. 1830 in OH, d. 1919 in Cook Co., IL), secretary, and located at 22-23 Lake St., Chicago. In 1907, **Hibbard, Spencer, Bartlett & Co.** was located at State St. & Bridge with **A. C. Bartlett**, president; **Charles Conover**, vice president; and **Wm. Hubbard Jr.** as 2nd. vice president. From 1917-1923, at 303 State St, using the brand names **OUR VERY BEST**, **OVB**, **AJAX**, **BLACK DIAMOND**, **HIBBARD** and **HIBSPEBAR**. The **REV-O-NOC** imprint was used after 1900, when **Charles Conover** (**Revonoc** is **Conover** spelled backwards) became a company official. **(for imprint see H. S. B. & Co.)**

W. O. HICKOK
William Orville Hickok (b. Oct. 6, 1815 in Warsay, Wyoming Co., OH, d. May 25, 1891 in Harrisburg, Dauphin Co., PA) made bookbinding tools in Harrisburg, PA, in 1844. **William** was also listed as a coppersmith. His plant was called **THE EAGLE WORKS**, with electricity as motive power and light, and that name was used in some of his imprints as was **KEYSTONE**. In 1886, it became **W. O. Hickok Mfg. Co.**. In 1981, the company was being run by a fifth generation **William O. Hickok**. Example: from a bookbinding plane. ***

P. A. HICKMAN & BRO

P. A. Hickman & Bro was listed in 1871 as stove and hardware dealer. Example: on the toe of a coffin smoother made by the **Greenfield Tool Co.** ****

HICKORY

Hickory is a brand name used by **Kelly-How-Thompson Co.**, Duluth, MN, ca. late 19c-early 20c. **No imprint is available.**

A. G. HICKS

Andrew George Hicks (b. 1807 in MI, d. Oct. 12, 1866 in Cleveland, OH) was married Dec. 6, 1842 in Hamilton, Butler Co., OH. A daughter was born in Cleveland, on Sep. 2, 1848. **Andrew G. Hicks** was listed, in the 1850 census, as a planemaker, in Brooklyn, OH, on the outskirts of Cleveland. He was listed in the 1857 Cleveland City directory, as a planemaker, at 45 Root St., 1859-61, and 1864-65. He was also a noted knife maker. (See *American Marking Gauges*, by Milton H. Bacheller, Jr.) The B1 & C imprints are the A imprint with the stars filed off. A, B, B1, C & D ***

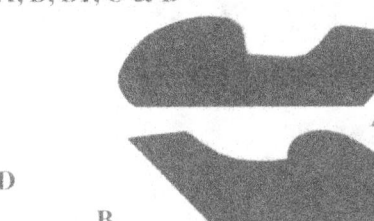

A: HIDE

Believed to be **Asa Hide** (**Hyde**) (b. July 21, 1741 in Norwich, CT, d. March 26, 1797 at Lisbon, CT), a descendant of one of the founders of Norwich, **William Hyde**. Asa married, on May 12, 1763, and resided in Norwich where the first 9 of his 12 children were born, between 1764-80. In 1780, he moved to Lisbon, where the last three children were born between 1783-88. **Asa Hide** was the father of **Joel Hyde**, **Asa Hyde**, and **Ezra Hyde**. He appears in the 1790 census, as residing in New London Co., CT, which includes Norwich and Lisbon. It should be noted that **Jo, Fuller** was born in Lisbon, CT, in 1746. Examples: the B imprint is on a plow plane; a rabbet; a round; and several molding planes, all 10"-10 5/8" birch with heavy flat chamfers. The A imprint is on a plow; and a complex molder, ca. 1770. A & B *****

H. HIES

Example: on a 13 1/4" beech crown molder with a pull bar and heavy flat chamfers, probably from PA, ca. 1790-1800. **UR**

THE HIGGIN MFG. Co

The Higgin Mfg. Co. was located in Newport, KY which is contiguous to Covington, KY and across the Ohio River from Cincinnati, OH, and sold planes made by others. Example: on a 7 5/16" beech fluting plane made by the **Sandusky Tool Co.**, and also marked **SPECIAL**, ca. 1875-95. ****

H. I. HIGGINS

H. I. Higgins was a hardware dealer in Chester, MA. Example: a match tongue & groove pair made by **Hills & Richards** of Norwich, MA. **UR**

B. HIGH

Example: on a 9 7/8" beech moving filletster with a bottom fence and heavy flat chamfers, ca. 1800-10. **UR**

J. HIGH

Examples: on a 9 1/2" tiger maple wedge-arm moving filletster with flat chamfers; a 9 1/2" beech, double-boxed with lignum vitae, size **6/8** on the heel and **6** on wedge from the same die, heavy round chamfers; and a beech jack plane with an iron marked **Robt. Sorby**, ca. 1800. **UR**

M. E. HIGLEY

Martin Ephraim Higley (b. June 24, 1824 in Port Byron, NY, d Mar. 17, 1885) was also a partner in **Higley & Hicks** with **Andrew G. Hicks**, of Ohio City. Ohio City was incorporated in 1836 and became a part of Cleveland, in 1854, indicating a working period, before 1854. The 1850 industrial census for Cleveland lists **M. E. Higley** as an edge tool maker producing 500 sets of planes valued at $1000, other articles at $1000 and employing 3. The 1850 census listed **Martin**, as a machinist living with his father-in-law, a shipwright. In 1856, **Martin E. Higley** was listed as having a plane factory in Cleveland; in 1859-75, he was listed as making truss hoops, board rules and cooper's tools. In 1875-79, **Martin** worked for **I. E. Canfield & Co.**; in 1879, **Higley** was in a partnership with **M. D. Norris**, as **Higley & Norris**, making truss hoops, cooper's tools and tool handles. (see *American Marking Gages*, by Milton H. Bacheller, Jr.) Imprint C was found on a sun plane. Imprint D on a complex molder with an **Ohio Tool Co.** iron., ca. mid 19c. A, B, C & D ****

HIGLEY & HICKS

Higley & Hicks was a partnership of **Martin Ephraim Higley** and **Andrew George Hicks**, both listed in 1850 census in Brooklyn, OH. **Higley & Hicks** made planes in the Ohio City, prior to 1854. Ohio City was incorporated in 1836 and became part of Cleveland, in 1854. Examples: a tongue & groove match pair with the A imprint on a grooving plane and the B imprint on the tongue plane, both 9 1/4" beech, ca. 19c. **A & B *****

A. HILL

Allen Hill (b. Jul. 26, 1804, in Foster, Providence, RI, d. Jul, 21, 1881 in Foster) was a woodworker, a shop joiner and a farmer in Foster, RI. His father, **Jonathan Hill** (1773-1853) was a wheelwright and housewright in Foster. **Allen Hill** was listed as Yeoman in the land deeds of 1835 & 56. In his 1881 will, **Allen** left his "Carpenters tools" to his son **Albert F. Hill** who was a builder in Warwick, RI. **Allen's** oldest son **William A. Hill** (b. ca. 1840) was married, in Foster, in 1863, and was listed as a joiner in West Hartford, CT. In 1878, William lived in Phoenix Village which became West Warwick, RI. From a tool chest, found in West Warwick, came four **Jo, Fuller** planes with the A imprint of **A. Hill** and the incuse imprint **W. A. Hill**. Examples: the B imprint is on a 21 7/8" birch jointer with a centered closed tote and round chamfers. The A & A1 imprints are on a group of **Jo, Fuller** planes and with both single and double imprints on the toe, of 10" apple molders, one a birch bead, all with relieved wedges and flat chamfers & flutes, some with the date **1828**; an apple plane makers measuring gauge with a wood thumbscrew and the A imprint on both ends; and a 17" skew birch rabbet with round chamfers on the top and flat chamfers on the toe and heel with flutes and a centered open tote, with the date **1829**. **A & C ******; **A1, A2, B & D *******

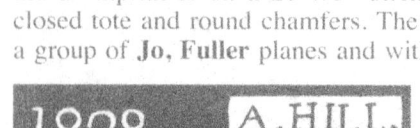

A. R. HILL

Alvan R. Hill is a contemporary planemaker from South Woodstock, CT who used this imprint on wooden planes he made during his restoration career, ca. 1970's. Example: on a 9 1/2" tiger maple molder with the iron also imprinted **A. R. Hill** and set at a York pitch of 50 degrees. *******

D x HILL

Examples: on a 9 7/8"x 1 1/2" birch square rabbet with a relieved wedge and flat chamfers and flutes; three rounds; two hollows; and a shiplap rabbet, possibly from New England, ca. 1790. **UR**

D. T. HILL

Example: on a 9 1/2" beech astragal bead with a birch wedge and heavy flat chamfers, ca. 1800-10. **UR**

E H/ E. HILL

Possibly **Ephram Hill**, a New Milford joiner, working in 1802. Example: on a 9 1/4" beech round with heavy round chamfers, ca. 1820. **UR**

F: HILL

Example: on a 9 1/4" beech with birch wedge, belection w/ bead boxed complex molder with flat chamfers, ca. 1800-10. **UR**

I + HILL

John Hill was a Portsmouth, NH, joiner, active from 1792-1803. Examples: a plane dated **1792,** and with the location **PORTSM NH** picked in, not imprinted, and a molder with size 8 on the heel. **No imprint is available.**

J. HILL

Examples: on a 9 3/8" hollow; and a 9 5/8" round, both beech with flat chamfers, ca. 1800. **UR**

JAMES. HILL

Two **James Hills** were listed in the 1810 census from Stoneham, MA. Examples: on 9 3/8"-9 9/16" single-boxed complex molders; and a 13 3/4" wedge-lock tongue plane with an offset double-pegged applewood tote, all beech with heavy round chamfers, ca. 1810-15. **A 1****; A *******

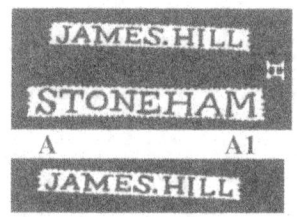

180

J. HILL/ JOHN HILL /JOHN HILL'S TOOL STORE

John H. Hill operated a tool store from 1813-18, at 60 Broadway in New York City. In 1819, there was a **John H. Hill**, merchant at Pearl St. and a **John Hill** (b. 1788 in Ireland), a hardware merchant at 203 Pearl St. In 1820, **John H. Hill** was located at 67 Beekman. **John Hill** remained at Pearl, until 1822; from 1823-25, he was listed at Water St.; from 1825-53, at 397 Broadway; and from 1853-60, at 390 Broadway. Imprints are on planes made by **Bensen & Crannell** and **Greenfield Tool Co.** A**, B, C, D & E ***

L. HILL

Example: on a 7 15/16" beech smoother with a double **W. M. Ash** iron and a fore plane, ca. 1840. **UR**

LEVI HILL

Example: on a 16" beech razee jack with an open tote round chamfers, and a double **Butcher** iron, ca. 1850. ****

N. HILL

Example: a double-iron rabbet, similar in appearance to **J. R. Tolman**, ca. 1850, possible from New England. **UR**

S. HILL

Possibly **Swinselle Hill** listed as a Springfield, MA, planemaker, whose working dates are unknown. Example: on a 10" birch skew rabbet, marked four times, with heavy round chamfers; and on a **J. Killam 4/8** boxed bead, probably from New England, ca. 1810-20. **UR**

S. HILL

The A imprint is on an **S. Fisk** plane, believed to be **Samuel Fisk** of Rehoboth, MA. There were several **Samuel Hills** in the Rehoboth records but the most likely is a **Samuel Hill** (b. Aug. 13, 1753). Examples: the A imprint alone is on a 9 7/8" birch medium round with flat chamfers that stop and with a long turnout. The B imprint is on a 9" birch hollow with round chamfers made by **E. Pierce** B imprint, believed to be **Ephram Pierce** of Middleboro, MA. The B imprint alone is on a 9 7/8" birch small hollow with flat chamfers and a relieved wedge, probably from southeastern New England, ca. 1770-90. **B: UR; A ****

HILLE. BRAND & WITTE

Hille. Brand & Witte was a hardware dealer in St. Louis, MO. Example: on a 5/8" side bead; and a complex molder, both 9 1/2" beech made by **Scioto Works**, found in St. Louis. ****

J. I. HILLER.

Example: on an 8 5/8" beech square rabbet with shallow round chamfers, ca. 1830. **UR**

A: HILLS

Examples: on two 10 1/4" beech molders; and a 10 7/8" birch thumbnail or quarter round, all with heavy flat chamfers mostly on the sides and a sloping molded shoulder, possibly from New England. ca. 1770-80. **UR**

H. HILLS

Hervey (Harvey) Hills (b. Oct. 16, 1806 in Granby, CT, d. Aug 25, 1881 in Granby and buried in Springfield, MA) married in Amherst on May 1, 1831. **Hervey Hills** was a manufacturer of joiner's planes "wholesale and retail" who worked in Springfield, MA, from 1845-51. He was listed in the 1849 New England Mercantile Union directory, as a plane manufacturer in Springfield. He was earlier part of **S. & H. Hills** of Amherst, from 1829-30, **Hills & Wolcott** of Amherst, in 1829; and possibly **Hills & Winship** of Springfield, in 1832. In the 1860 census, **Hervey** was listed as a mechanic in Davenport, IA. In 1880, he was in Davenport, no occupation given. Example: The B imprint is on a 7 7/8" beech plow with a 9 1/8" fence, round top arms, wood thumbscrews and depth stop. **A & A1: FF; B ****

J HILLS/ JOSHUA HILLS
Example: on a 9 5/8" beech complex molder, imprinted on the toe and heel, and the full name carved on the side, with an **I. Sleeper** style wedge profile and heavy flat chamfers, from New England, ca. 1800. **UR**

 A

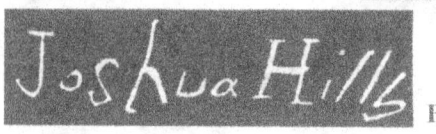 B

R. HILLS
Example: on a 9 1/2" birch hollow with round chamfers and a relieved wedge, ca. early 19c. **UR**

S. HILLS
Believed to be **Samuel Hills** (b. Sep. 26, 1805 in CT (probably Granby), d. Nov. 24, 1890 in Salt Lake City, UT), a planemaker of Amherst and Springfield, MA, who possibly worked alone after 1830. He married on Apr. 4, 1834, in Springfield, MA. His father **Samuel Hills Sr.** advertised, as a cabinetmaker, in Granby, CT in the *Connecticut Courant* of Aug. 15, 1804, as selling land and a cabinet shop. He was reported to be the grandfather of **J. W. Goodale** a planemaker of Amherst, MA. **Samuel Hills** was also a part of **S. & H. Hills** *

S. & H. HILLS
Samuel Hills and **Hervey Hills** were planemakers who succeeded **Hills & Wolcott** in Amherst, MA, in 1829 and continued until 1830. They also apparently operated in Springfield, MA, as indicated by imprint C.
B, C & D **, A ***

T. HILLS
Example: on a 10 1/4" birch complex molder with wide flat chamfers mostly on the side, possibly from New England, ca. 1790. **No imprint is available**.

HILLS & RICHARDS
Hills & Richards was a Norwich, MA, plane making partnership of **Samuel Hill** and/ or **Hervey Hill** and **Fredrick Richards** with unknown working dates. Norwich was part of Huntington, MA. **

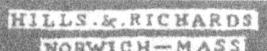

HILLS & WINSHIP
Hills & Winship was a Springfield, MA, plane making partnership, ca. 1832, that included **William Winship**, who earlier from 1826-32, had worked for **H. Chapin**, and possibly **Hervey Hills**. *

HILLS & WOLCOTT
Hills & Wolcott was a partnership of **Hervey Hills** and perhaps **Gideon Wolcott**, a CT planemaker who earlier, in 1828, had worked with **Leonard Kennedy**, in Utica, NY. **Hills & Wolcott** made planes for one year only, in 1829, in South Amherst, MA, and was succeeded by **S. & H. Hills**. **

CHARLES HILLYER
Charles Hillyer (b. Mar. 4, 1822 in Germany, d. Aug. 6, 1898 in Cincinnati, OH) was listed as a plane maker in Cincinnati, OH, in 1849-50, at n.s. 6th. bt. Lock & Corp. line; in 1850-52, at s.s. 8th. bt. Sycamore & Broadway. **Charles** served in the Civil War as a Private in Co. F, 58th. Infantry Reg. OH.
No imprint has been reported.

J. HILTON
Believed to be **John H. Hilton** (b. 1794 in ME) was a cabinetmaker in Kennebunk Landing, ME, active in 1823. Examples: on a 21 1/2" shoot board plane in beech, designed as an oversized jack rabbet turned on its side; a 24" joiner; a 10 1/4" beech split sash with screw arms, rosewood nuts with mother-of-pearl inset rings centered with silver buttons and shallow round chamfers; a 9 1/2" beech sash coping plane with a tote on the side and flat chamfers; and a level. The sash and coping planes were found on the coast of ME, ca. 1810-30.
****

WILL: HILTON
Example: on a 9 7/16" beech side-bead, dated **JUN 1738,** with flat chamfers. **UR**

J. W. HINCKLEY
Example: on a skew rabbet; and a narrow hollow, both 10" beech with shallow round chamfers, ca. 1830. **UR**

J. G. HINDERER
Example: on a 7/8" wide bead, ca. 19c. **UR**

J. HINDS
Example: on an 11" handled toothing plane with round top iron, a round strike, and heavy round chamfers, ca. early 19c. **UR**

G. C. HINES & CO.

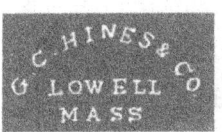

Example: on a handled razee smoother plane, ca. 1850. ****

D. HISTAND

Example: on an 8 1/4" fruitwood nosing plane with flat chamfers, possibly from PA, ca. 1800. **UR**

HISTER

Hister (Heister) was listed as a "forge man" in 1860, from south eastern PA, ca. 1860. **UR**

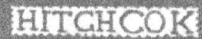

HITCHCOK

Example: on a 9 5/8" birch side rabbet that undercuts at about 10 degrees, with flat chamfers and a slightly relieved wedge profile, probably from New England, ca. 1780-1800. **UR**

I. HITCHCOK

Two possibly makers: **John Lee Hitchcock** (b. 1753 in CT, d. Mar. 29, 1813 in New Haven, CT) was the father of **Lambert Hitchcock** (b. June 28, 1795). **John Hitchcock** was a soldier in the American Revolution, serving in Apr. 1778, as a Private in the 1st. Reg., CT. Also a possibility is **Joel Hitchcock** (b. Nov. 19, 1779, d. 1813 in New Hartford, Litchfield Co., CT) who married on Dec. 27, 1803 in New Hartford and was listed as a cabinetmaker, in New Hartford, from 1804-29. Example: on a 9 13/16" birch halving plane with flat chamfers and a slightly relieved wedge profile. It was found 40 miles from Hitchcockville, now Riverton, CT, on the Farmington River, where **Lambert Hitchcock** made Hitchcock chairs, from 1818-46. Later the factory became the site of **A. A. Alford Plane Co.**, from 1849-53, ca. 1780-90. *****

HITCHCOCK & ARMSTRONG

A partnership of **Joel Hitchock** & **James D Armstrong**, in 1818. **No imprint has been reported**.

HITCHCOCK & KELLOGG

A partnership of **Joel Hitchcock** & **Warren Kellogg**, in 1804. **No imprint has been reported**.

HENRY HISER

Henry Hiser (b. Mar. 8, 1805 in PA, d. Jan. 16, 1866 in Columbus, Franklin Co., OH) was listed as a planemaker in the Wooster, Wayne Co., OH, directory, active from 1850-60. **No imprint has been reported**.

HLYFORD

Example: on a 9" birch bead, with shallow round chamfers, ca. 1820-30. **UR**

E. HOADLEY

Probably **Erastus W. Hoadley** (b. Aug. 10, 1781 in Branford, CT, d. May 23, 1831 in New Haven, CT) who came to New Haven, in 1809, and was a joiner. Examples: The A imprint is on a 9 7/16" tongue & groove pair; a applewood wedge-lock plow with a wood thumbscrew-locked depth stop and heavy round chamfers; and two planes also imprinted **D. Smith** found in ME-NH area. The B imprint is on a 9 1/2" beech fixed sash with a double iron & wedge and tight round chamfers; and a plow with brass screws, ca. 1820. A ****, B *****

P. HOBART

Peter Hobart (b. Nov. 19, 1806 in Suffolk Co., MA, d. Jul. 15, 1879 in Boston, MA) was listed in the 1850 Boston, MA census, as a carpenter; in 1860, as a master carpenter; and in 1870, as a carpenter. The B imprint is on an astragal made by **Hills & Winship**; and another plane made by **H.Hill**, both from Springfield, MA. This indicating that **P. Hobart** also sold planes made by others. Examples: The A imprint on a 9 7/8" birch large round with flat chamfers, found in the CT-RI area; and on a 9 15/16" birch wide hollow with flat chamfers that stop with a tipped down cut and a lamb's tongue, ca. 1730-50. A & B ****

J. HOBBS

Example: on a 9 1/2" Lignum vitae skew rabbet with a rosewood wedge; and a 9 7/16" birch ovolo, both with round chamfers, ca. 1820-30. A & A1: **UR**

S. HOBBS

Examples: on a 9 1/2" birch hollow with small round chamfers; and a 9 5/8" Yankee plow with a screwed on skate and with heavy round chamfers, ca. 1810. **UR**

R. & J. HOCKENHULL

Robert Hockenhull (b. Nov. 23, 1815 in Cheshire, England, d. Apr. 3, 1891 in Jacksonville, IL) and **John Hockenhull** (b. 1812 in England, d. Jacksonville, IL) were hardware dealers in Jacksonville, Morgan Co., IL, which is located about 30 miles west of Springfield. **Robert** served as a Private in the Spanish American War in the 1st. IL Cavalry and 5th. IL Infantry. Example: on a 16" beech jack, ca. 1850. ****

V. HODGE

Examples: The A imprint is on a 9 1/2"x 1" skew rabbet with size **8/8** on the heel; and a 9 1/8" double-iron sash, both beech with shallow round chamfers. The B imprint is on a

16 3/16" beech bench plane with an offset open tote, heavy round chamfers on top and flat chamfers on toe & heel, and a single iron, ca. 1830. **A & B: ******

S. HODGKIN
Example: on an 8" coffin shaped smoother, ca. 19c. **UR**

W. HODGSON
Examples: on 9 1/2" beech complex molding planes, ca. 19c. **A & B: UR**

C. R. HOLDEY
Example: on a 9" bead with heavy flat chamfers, ca. early 19c. **UR**. (Imprint not to scale)

R. HOE & CO.
Robert Hoe (b. Oct. 29, 1784 in Leichestershire, England, d. Jan. 4, 1833 Westchester, NY) was indentured to a joiner before coming to NY, in 1803, where he worked as a master carpenter. **Robert Hoe** was associated with **Peter Smith** and **Matthew Smith** in the business of carpentry and the manufacture of a hand printing press inventor by **Peter Smith**. On Jan. 10, 1805, **Robert** married **Rachel Smith** in North Salem, Westchester, NY. **Robert Hoe** was the father of **Richard March Hoe** (b. Sep. 12, 1812 in NY, d. Jun. 7, 1886 in Florence, Italy) and **Robert Hoe II** (Jul. 19, 1815 in NY, d. Sep. 13, 1884 in Terrytown, NY) and **Peter Smith Hoe** (b. Aug. 24, 1821 in NY, d. Aug. 28, 1902 in Upper Monclair, NJ). **Robert** became sole proprietor of **R. Hoe & Co.**, in 1823, retiring in 1832; and was succeeded by his son **Richard March Hoe**, and possibly his brothers **Robert Hoe II** and **Peter Hoe**, under the same name, **R. Hoe & Co.**, **Robert** was a skilled mechanic, constructing and introducing the original **Hoe** press and was an early user of steam power in his plant. The firm **R. Hoe & Co.** was a major producer of printing presses in New York, until 1909. **Robert** was a founder of the National Academy of Design and a patron of young artists. Examples: on a 9 1/2" beech side-handled steel-clad wood plane, possibly a printer's shoot plane, with an iron by **Mottram** (Sheffield 1800-33); and on a 1 1/2" round made by **G. W. Denison & Co.**. ********

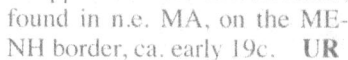

M. HOERNER
Example: on a 14" beech large nosing plane with a centered open tote, flat chamfers, a round topped iron and an iron strike, found in n.e. MA, on the ME-NH border, ca. early 19c. **UR**

R. HOEY
Robert Hoey made planes under his own name in New York City, active from 1834-36. Later **Hoey** was part of **Hoey & Taber** from 1836-40. *****

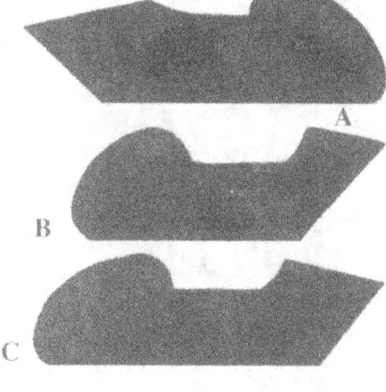

HOEY & TABER
Hoey & Taber was a partnership of **Robert Hoey** and probably **Wing H. Taber** that made planes, at 77 John St. in New York City, from 1836-40. Example: the B imprint and wedge is from a 9 7/16" beech single boxed, Grecian ovolo with fillet, and round chamfers, a size **3/4** imprinted on the heel, and a **W. Butcher** iron, ca. 19c. **A & B *****

W. HOFFMANN/ W. HOFFMANN/ MARLEY
William F. Hoffmann (b. Feb. 8, 1832 in Frankfort, Germany) and arrived in NY, on Jul. 23, 1853. **Hoffmann** made planes in New York City, from 1856-87, his beginning year coinciding with **Marley**'s last year. **Marley** was active from 1820-56, and his last address was 360 Broome St., which is where **Hoffmann** opened his business. Imprint B and C would seem to confirm that **Hoffmann** succeeded **Marley**. There may have been a short-term partnership. **William F. Hoffmann** served in the Civil War, as a Private, from Sep. 9, 1862-Jun. 2, 1863. **A *, B & B1 *****

HOGAN
Example: on a skew rabbet with heavy round chamfers, ca. 1830. **UR**

T. J. HOIT
Example: on a 9 7/8" beech skew rabbet with round chamfers, possibly PA, ca. 1810. **UR**

A. HOLBROOK
Example: on a 10" birch grooving plane with a riveted skate and heavy flat chamfers. The wedge slot is relieved, ca. 1800. UR

S. HOLCOMB
Examples: on a table hollow; a 9 3/8" unhandled grooving plane with the A wedge; and a 9 1/2" single-boxed snipe with the later B wedge, all beech with heavy round to shallow round chamfers, ca. 1820. ****

HOLCOMB & SLENTZ
Holcomb & Slentz probably was a hardware dealer in East Dayton, OH, whose dates are not known. Example: on a 9 1/2" beech complex molder; and a hollow & round, both with the Ohio Tool Co. style number 72., ca. 1850. ****

C. W. HOLDER & CO
Charles W. Holder was a Bloomington, IL, hardware dealer, listed from 1855-60's. In 1866, the name became McClun, Holder & Co.; then from 1872-91 Holder, Milner & Co. ****

C. W. HOLDEN
Charles W. Holden (b. Oct. 25, 1816 in CT, d. Jun. 7, 1875 in Norwich, New London Co., CT) was a Norwich, CT, planemaker, active from 1850-75, who was listed as a plane maker, in the 1850, 60 & 70 census. A & A1 *

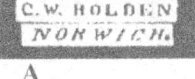
A

A1

N. HOLDEN
Example: on a 9 3/8" beech small round with flat chamfers, ca. 1810. UR

P. HOLDEN
Philbrook Holden (b. Aug. 15, 1816 in Northfield, Franklin Co., MA, d. Dec. 6, 1858 in Warwick, Franklin Co., MA) was listed as a carpenter, in 1850, in Greenfield, Franklin Co; and in 1855, as a carpenter, in Gill, Franklin Co., MA. Example: on a size 12 hollow marked by both J. J. Bowles/ E. Hartford and P. Brooks/ E. Hartford. UR

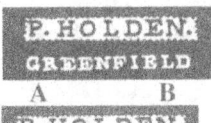
A   B

W. HOLDRIDGE
Example: on a 9 1/2" maple medium round with round chamfers, ca. 1810. UR

H HOLDSHIP
Example: on a 9 1/2" beech large cove with heavy round chamfers, ca. 1820. UR

A. HOLIDAY
Example: on a 9 3/8" beech size 10 hollow. UR

P. HOLL
Peter Holl Jr. (b. 1766, in PA, d. Aug. 24, 1816 in Strasburg, Lancaster Co., PA) was listed as a joiner and carpenter. His son also Peter Holl (b. 1806 in Strasburg, PA, d. 1837 in Strasburg) was also listed as a carpenter but would be to late for this plane. Example: on a 9 3/4" friction-arm fenced chamfering plane with flat chamfers, ca. 1800. UR

T. HOLLIDAY/ THOS HOLLIDAY & CO.
Thomas Holliday (b. 1821 in OH, d. 1880 in Cincinnati, OH) operated under the name Thomas Holliday & Co. as a Cincinnati, OH, hardware dealer, active ca. 1853-77. Thomas Holliday served in the Civil War, in Aug. 26, 1861, as a Private. In 1873-77, Thomas Holliday & Co. was listed with Thomas Holliday, Wm. R. Attee, and John G. Attee selling hardware, nails, tools Etc. n.e.c. 5th. & Central Ave. Examples: the B imprint is on hollow & round planes; and a fore plane. A & B **

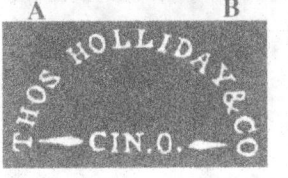

HOLLIDAY & SMITH
Holliday & Smith was a partnership with Thomas Holliday and John W. H. Smith, a Cincinnati, OH, hardware partnership operating, in 1880. Example: on a size 6 round made by the Ohio Tool Co. ***

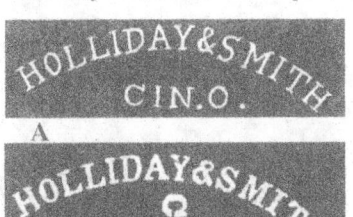
A

A1

A. HOLLISTER
Example: on a 9 1/4" beech boxed side rabbet; and a round. Both with shallow round chamfers, ca. 1830. **UR**

W. C. HOLMAN
Example: on a 9 1/2" beech dado plane with two nickers, large flat chamfers and layout lines. The iron is marked **Wm Ash & Co.**, ca. early 19c. **UR**

E. HOLMES
Example: on a 9 3/4" beech dado with shallow round chamfers and an **I & H Sorby** iron; a beech 10" rabbet, birch wedge, heavy round chamfers on top and flat chamfers on the ends. ca. 1820-30. **A, A1, & B: UR**

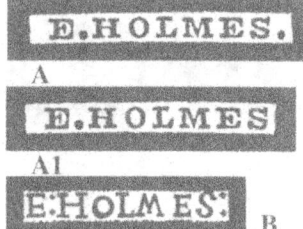

I. P. HOLMES
Example: on a 10" beech molder with flat chamfers, ca. 1810. *******

J. HOLMES
Three imprints have been reported which could be from the same or different person(s). Examples: the A imprint is on planes 9 3/8"-9 1/2" of birch or cherry with flat chamfers and long flutes, much like those of **E. Clark**, Middleboro. Several irons have the touch mark **SS**. The B imprint, marked toe and heel; on a 9" birch bead with flat chamfers. The C imprint is from two complex molders; and a tongue & groove pair, all 9 1/2" beech with heavy flat chamfers with several of the irons marked **I PARKER**; on an **I. COX** molder; and a size **4/8** boxed side bead, as an owner's imprint. The D imprint is on a 9 1/2" beech size **15** round with flat chamfers, ca. 1790-1800. **B, C, & D: UR; A *****

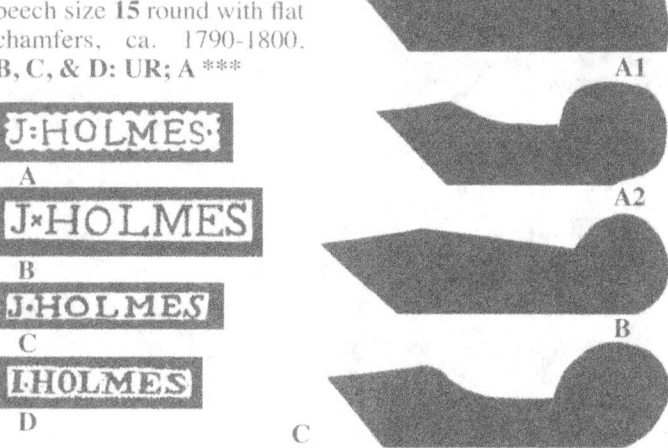

A. HOLT
This name has been reported from a fore plane. **A. HOLT** is surrounded by a border with two parallel lines on top, a zigzag or diamond border at the bottom and a stack of several very short parallel lines at each side. The letters of the mark slant slightly backwards to the left. **No imprint is available.**

D. B. HOLT
Example: the A imprint 15 1/8" panel raiser made by **David Bensen**; and a 9 1/2"x 2 1/2" beech skew rabbet, ca. 1850-60. **UR**

HENRY A. HOLT
Henry A. Holt (b. 1828 in Wilton, NH, d. Nov. 8, 1899 in Durand, Pepin Co., WI), received a Patent No. 122,609, on Jan. 9, 1872, for a carpenters plane. **No imprint has been reported.**

I. F. HOLT
Example: on a 21 1/2" beech bench plane with a diamond strike, slightly offset tote and with tight round chamfers, ca. 1820. **UR**

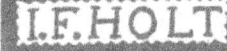

J. HOLT
There was a **John Holt** (b. Dec. 6, 1746 in New London, CT, d. Sep. 8, 1781 in Groton, CT), a New London, CT, cabinetmaker with "sundry joiners tools", who was killed in the massacre at Fort Griswold during the attack by the British led by **Gen. Benedict Arnold**. Although he is too early for this plane, the maker could be a descendant. Example: on a 9 1/2" beech, full-boxed reed & follow plane with flat chamfers. ca. 1810-20. **UR**

WM. HOLT
Example: on a 10" beech wedge-lock plow plane with a wood depth stop, a skate attached with screws, and heavy flat chamfers, ca. 1800. **UR**

WM. HOLTRUP
Example: on a 9 9/16" beech hollow with a **Robert Moore** iron (1750-70 - Birmingham, England) and flat chamfers, ca. 1785. **UR**

HOLYOAKE-LOWNES & CO.
Henry Lownes was a Memphis, TN, hardware dealer who succeeded **R. T. Lamb & Co.**, in 1847-48; **Lownes & Co.**, in 1849, **Holyoake (Holyoke) -Lownes & Co.**, from 1851-54; **Lownes, Beekman & Co.**, from 1854-57; and finally, upon Lownes' death, in 1857, the firm became **Orgill Bros & Co.**. Example: on a 14" panel raiser with an iron marked **Thames River Works**. ********

HOMER. BISHOP & CO.
(See under **Bishop**)

J. HOMPSHER

Example: on a 21 1/2"x 3 1/2" beech toted skew rabbet with nickers, added fence and round chamfers, ca. 1820. **UR**

R. HOOPER

Example: on a 7 5/8" birch smoother with round chamfers, and an iron marked **Nnay & Kinder**, ca. early 19c. **UR**

J. A. HOPKINS

James Allison Hopkins (b. May 22, 1844 in Oxford, Chenango Co., NY, d. Dec. 2, 1928 in Oxford) was in the hardware business and his obituary read, "always interested and gifted in a mechanical way." He could have been the maker or marked planes made by others. In 1910, **Hopkins** was listed as a carpenter in Oxford; in 1920, his occupation listed was "none". Example: on a 9 1/8" beech quarter round with size **5/16** on the heel, ca. 1870. ****

M. B. HOPKINS

Hopkins with a reverse S. Example: on a 9 3/8" miter plane., ca. 19c. **UR**

P. HOPKINS

Examples: on a 9 3/4" beech thumbnail molder with shallow flat chamfers; and a 9 1/2" birch round with heavy flat chamfers, both with relieved wedge profiles, possibly from New England, ca. 1790. **UR**

W. HOPKINS

Example: on a 9 1/4" birch large round with flame-birch wedge and shallow round chamfers, possibly from New England, ca. 1790-1820. **UR**

ZEB; HOPKINS

Zeb; Hopkins planes were found in a tool chest from a man who worked in Voluntown, New London, Co., CT. Examples: on a 10"x 1/2" hollow with and a 9 5/8"x 3/8" bead. Both birch with shallow flat chamfers ending in long flutes, ca. 1780-90. **UR**

WM. C. HOPPER PATENT

William C. Hopper (b. ca. 1825 in Elkins, VA, d. Oct. 26, 1894 in Elkins WV) came to Pittsburgh, PA, about 1845. He was issued Patent No. 12,234, on Jan. 16, 1855, that provided an iron mouth piece in the sole which could be adjusted closer to the mouth, in bench planes, as the stock was worn. Examples: the A imprint is on an 8 1/4" smoother. The B imprint reads:

WM. C. HOPPER'S
PATENT
1855

and is shown in *Patented Transitional & Metallic Planes in America, Vol. I*, p. 21, by Roger K. Smith. **Hopper** was listed in the 1850 census and in the Pittsburgh business directories of the 1850's & 60's as a cabinetmaker. In the 1867-68 directory, Hopper was part of **Myer, Hopper & Co.**, as a furniture dealer. In 1870, he was part of **Fulton & Hopper** as manufacturers of furniture; and from 1872-88, as a lumber merchant. In 1888, **Hopper** was listing for **W. C. Hopper & CO.**, hardwood lumber at Clark & Kilbuck Streets, Allegheny, PA. ****

A. HOR

Example: on an 8 1/8" fruitwood full-boxed complex molder with shallow round chamfers, ca. 1830. **UR**

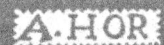

B. F. HORN/ BENJ. F. HORN

Benjamin Franklin Horn (d. May 23, 1911 in Fayette, IL) made wood, metal, and hybrid cooper's planes and tools in East St. Louis, IL. **Benjamin F. Horn** served in the Civil War, enlisting on Aug. 21, 1862 in Co. F, 120th. Regiment, IL Infantry. In 1889-90, **Horn** was listed as a barrel manufacturer in Belleville, IL. In 1891, he was a cooper, in Belleville. In 1906, the firm was **Benjamin F. Horn Cooperage CO.**, located at 100 Missouri Ave., East St. Louis, IL. **Benjamin** was President, **Benjamin F. Horn Jr.** was Vice. President & Treasurer, and **Chas W. Horn**. Examples: The C imprint is from a sun plane with inventory number **240**. A, B & C: ***

CH- HORN

Example: on an 11 1/4" beech molder with flat chamfers mostly on the side, found in eastern PA, ca. 1790. **UR**

E: HORNER

Example: on a 12 3/4" birch toted nosing plane with a round-top **NEWBOULD** iron and heavy round chamfers, ca. 1790-1820. **UR**

N. HORN IER
Example: on a narrow beech round with a hickory wedge and flat chamfers, ca. 1800. UR

HORNOR & SON
Joseph P. Horner (b. ca. 1805 in Philadelphia, PA, d. Mar. 24, 1885 in Philadelphia, PA) was a quaker and a hardware dealer at 47 Market St., Philadelphia, PA, the same address as **Hornor & Son**, and was listed as a customer of **H. Chapin**, in 1836. Examples: on a 14 1/2" beech panel raiser; and on planes made by **M. & A. Copeland/ Union Factory, H. Chapin/ Eagle Factory, N. Chapin/ Union Factory, Hills & Winship** and **Fox & Washburn**. A & A1 **

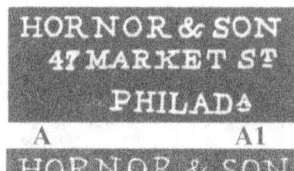

H HORTON
Example: on a 9 1/2"x 5/8" beech tongue plane with size **5/8** on the heel and heavy flat chamfers, ca. 1800. UR

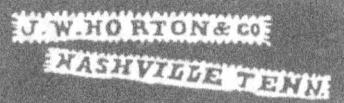

J. W. HORTON & CO.
J. W. Horton & Co. was a hardware dealer in Nashville, TN. Example: on a 9 1/2" beech skewed rabbet with number **166** the **Ohio Tool Co.** inventory number for a rabbet, ca. mid 19c. ****

R. A. HORTON
R. A. Horton was listed as a planemaker in Nashville, TN, in 1859. This name with the location **NASHVILLE TENN.** has been reported. **No imprint is available**.

HORTON & CRANE
Horton & Crane was a hardware dealer located in Buffalo, NY. Example: on a slide-arm plow with round chamfers; and on a bead made by **T. J. M'Master**, ca. 1820. A & A1 **

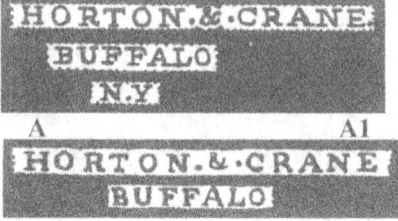

NS. HOSMER
There was a **Hosmer** family of cabinetmakers in Concord, MA. The large A imprint and the smaller B imprint are both on a 10 1/2" beech skew rabbet. The B imprint is on a 9 1/2" birch small round, both with heavy flat chamfers, and as an owner's imprint, on a plane by **L. Little**. The incuse **1860** date, which appears on one example, appears to have been added later and does not represent the age of the planes, ca. 1800. A & B: ****

S. HOTCHKIN
Example: on a molder; and a skew rabbet with a "wooden iron", both 9 1/2" beech, ca. 1840. UR

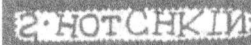

HOUGHTON
Example: on a 7 7/8" beech plow with wood thumbscrew-locked arms and flat chamfers, ca. 1800. UR

H. HOUGHTON
Example: on a 14 1/4"x 1 3/4" birch skew ship's rabbet with two nickers, a centered tote and no chamfers, ca. 1830. UR

J. HOULDEN
Example: on a 9 1/2" birch large astragal bead with round chamfers, ca. early 19c. UR

A. HOURT
Example: on a 10 5/8" birch Yankee plow with wedged arms, a friction-fit wood depth stop, a riveted skate; and a 9 3/4" beech molder, all with and small round chamfers, ca. early 19c. A & B: UR

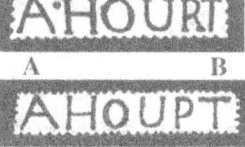

DANIEL HOUSTON
Daniel Houston (b. ca. 1824 in Ireland) was listed as making cooper's tools and planes in New York City, from 1846-57. **Houston** was naturalized on Oct. 16, 1855, in NY. **No imprint has been reported.**

I. HOUSTON
Several possibilities are: **James L. Huston (Houston)** who married in 1794, in Windham, CT; **John Houston** who married on Feb. 14, 1788; and was listed in the 1790 census for Voluntown, Windham Co., CT; and **Joseph Houston** (d. Apr. 4, 1788) who married on April 1, 1784, and was from Voluntown, New London Co., CT. Example: on a 10 1/2" birch skew round with heavy flat chamfers that stop with a long sweeping turnout, possibly from southeastern New England, ca. 1790. UR

G. T. HOVEY
George Theodore Hovey (b. July 23, 1837 at Manchester, NH, d. Jan. 20, 1914 in Marietta, Washington Co., OH), was the son of **John Hovey,** and was a builder and noted architect in Marietta, OH, from 1870's to 1900. Example: The incuse imprint is on a wooden brace. UR

I HOVEY

Joseph Hovey (b. Dec. 17, 1762 in Ipswich, Essex Co., MA, d. Oct. 9, 1825 in Londonderry, Rockingham Co., NH) was the father of **John Hovey**. **Joseph** moved to Londonderry, NH, in the early 1780's. This incuse imprint is made by individual letter stamps and with the tail of the **Y** carved. Examples: on a rabbet with a pegged offset tote, found in NH; a plow found in southern VT; a gutter plane found on the coast of ME; and a 13" crown molder with an offset pegged tote, found in Plaistow, NH, half way between Londonderry, NH, and Newburyport, MA, all birch with heavy flat chamfers, ca. 1790. **A & A1** *****

I H

John Hovey (b. Oct. 15, 1786 in Londonderry, Rockingham Co., NH, d. July 20, 1851 at Marietta, Washington Co., OH) was the son of **Joseph Hovey** and the father of **Milton Hovey** and **George Theodore Hovey**. In 1808, **John** was called to military duty. **John** was a house carpenter living in Londonderry, until 1839, when he emigrated to Marietta, OH. Example: on two double-iron & wedge **I. Sleeper** cornice planes. **John Sleeper** moved from Newburyport, MA, to Chester, NH, in 1814, where he died in 1834. **John Hovey's** first wife was from Chester, which is about 10 miles from Londonderry. The connection to **John Sleeper** is further strengthened by two receipts for payment dated May 28, 1823 and March 5, 1829, made out to **John Hovey** and signed by **John Sleeper** for the purchase of planes as well as for halving planes "fixed" or altered and irons ground. ****

M. HOVEY

Milton Hovey (b. Sept. 11, 1828 at Londonderry, NH, d. Apr. 1, 1861 at Marietta, OH) was the son of **John Hovey**, a carpenter and builder, listed in 1850-60, as a carpenter and noted for his fine carving and workmanship. He decorated the Unitarian Church in Marietta, OH. Example: on a **L. B. Bidwell** panel raiser. There are receipts of Aug. 24 & Sept. 20, 1860 to **M. & G. Hovey** for planes purchased from **Bidwell & Hale** of Newark, VA, across the Ohio River from Marietta. The panel raiser does not carry the **HARTFORD** imprint, which would indicate that **Leonard B. Bidwell** continued to use the same name imprint, after leaving Hartford, CT, in the late 1840's. **A & B:** ****

J. HOW

Examples: the A imprint is on a 9 1/2" birch round, with a beech wedge and small round chamfers, ca. 1810. The B imprint is on a 10" birch round; and a 9 7/16" birch coping plane, found with several **R. Bacon** planes, both with flat chamfer, possibly from southern New England, ca. 1800-10. **A, B & C:**

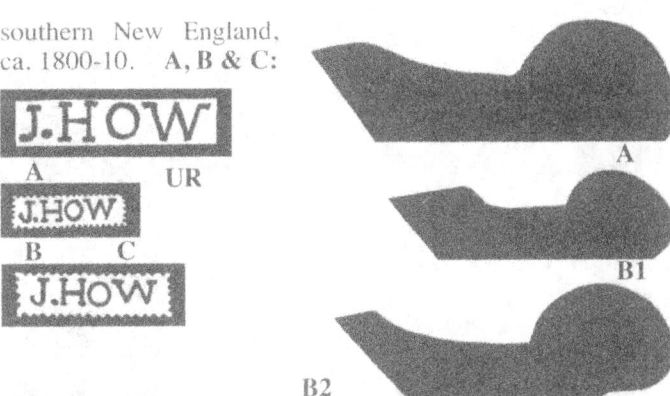

B. HOWARD

Possibly **Benjamin M. Howard** (b. Oct. 24, 1814, d. May 10, 1883 in Middlebury, Addison Co., VT) listed in 1850, as a cabinetmaker and chairmaker in Middlebury, VT. In 1860-70, he was listed as a farmer, in Canaan, Grafton, NH. Example: on a 7 1/4" beech compass smoother with shallow round chamfers and a **NEWBOULD** iron, ca. 1830. **UR**

W H/ W HOWARD

The **WH** initials are from individual letter dies with the **OWARD** carved. This imprint is from a beech plow with wedge lock arms, a large wood tombstone depth stop and flat chamfers. The initials alone are on a 9 3/8" beech fixed sash plane with round chamfers, both planes were found in the same toolbox from southern VT, ca. 1800-20. **UR**

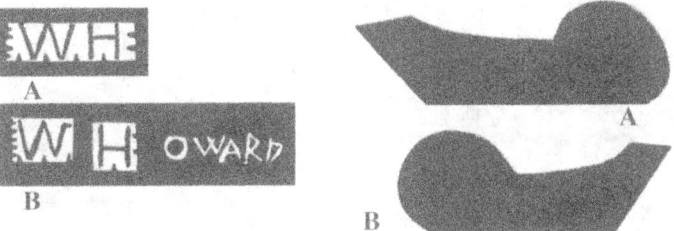

E. HOWARD & CO.

E. Howard & Co. with the location **BOSTON** is from a cooper's croze. This may be the same company with the same name listed in N. Bridgewater, MA; in 1849, the firm also made cooper's tools. **No imprint is available**.

HOWARD & PERRY

Examples: on a 9 3/8" beech skew rabbet with round chamfers, which was found with several CT planes, possibly raising a connection with **W. & E. Perry** of West Haven, CT. Also reported was a coffin compass smoother; a 9 3/8" large hollow; and a square rabbet, all beech with heavy round chamfers, ca. 1810-20. ****

B. S. HOWE

B. S. Howe was probably a hardware dealer. Example: on a boxed bead made by **J. A. McCellus** who we believe was located in central NY State. The Otsego location would tend to support that supposition, ca. 1850. ****

J. HOWE.

Possibly **James B. Howe** (d. Jul. 12, 1805 in Doolitester, MA) of Roxbury, MA, who was listed as a cabinetmaker in 1796-

1800. Examples: on a 9 3/4" & 9 1/2" beech complex molders, one with flat chamfers and one with round chamfers, both with decorative molded shoulders, ca. 1810. **UR**

N. HOWE
Example: on a 9 1/2" beech single-boxed (rosewood) large bead with heavy round chamfers, ca. 1820. **UR**

SETH C. HOWE
Seth C. Howe of South Chatham, MA, was issued Patent No. 37,694, on Feb. 17, 1864, for improvements in bench planes, and Patent No. 40,483, on Nov. 3, 1863, for an improvement in planes for bead molding, both provided means of holding and adjusting the cutters. **No example has been reported.**

W: HOWE
Examples: on a 9 1/2" birch hollow and round pair and a birch panel raiser, all with heavy round chamfers, ca. 1800-20. **UR**

D. HOWELL
Example: on a 9 1/2" beech dado with two wood depth stops, one in front and one behind the iron with a **5/8** size mark on the heel and heavy round chamfers, ca. 1810-20. **UR**

ALFRED HOWES
Alfred Howes (b. May 8, 1817 in Chatham, Barnstable Co., MA, d. Aug. 17, 1886 in MA) was listed in 1860 & 70 as a hardware dealer in Watertown, MA. Examples: on a jack plane; a 22" jointer with centered tote; and a 9 1/2" boxed bead. *****

I. HOWES
Example: on a 10" beech molder of Newburyport style. This same imprint is also on a **CE. Chelor** complex molder as an owner's imprint, ca. 1780. **No imprint is available.**

A. HOWLAND
Abraham Howland (b. Feb. 6, 1810 in Washington Co., NY, d. May 10, 1892 at Kelloggsville, NY) lived in Kelloggsville, eight miles south of Moravia, Cayuga Co., NY. He was listed in the 1850 census, as a cabinetmaker; in 1855, as a toolmaker; in 1865-68, as an undertaker and farmer; in 1880, as a cabinet maker in Niles, Cayuga, NY; in 1883, as a toolmaker; and in 1892, as "retired". He may have had some business relationship with **J. Sawyer**, as their planes have similar unique features and their **MORAVIA, N.Y.** location imprint are the same. Example: on a miter; 3 smoothers; 2 jacks; a jack rabbet; a double match plane; and two match pairs, all are beech, although maple has been reported, all are handled with the exception of the miter.

The jacks and the jack rabbet planes have closed totes. A smoother was reported with an iron marked **Auburn Tool Co.**, ca. 1840. A **. B ****

A. HOWLAND & CO.
Augustus Howland (b. 1811 in MA, d. 1873) was a bank president and, along with **Nelson Howard**, **C. P. Fitch**, **Edward Myderse**, and **Charles N. Tuttle**, under the name **A. Howland & Co.** held a contract for convict labor, used in making planes, at Auburn State Prison, from 1869-74. **Auburn Tool Co.** was part of a collective effort between **H. Chapin's Son**, **Greenfield Tool Co.** and **Sandusky Tool Co.** called the **Plane Maker's Association**, organized, ca. 1858, to fix prices. In 1866, the Auburn Tool Co. lost their prison labor contract, out bid by **J. M. Easterly & Co.**, which became **A. Howland & Co.**. In 1874, the **Auburn Tool Co.** resumed the use of prison labor. On Nov. 14, 1893, **Auburn Tool Co.** merged with the **Ohio Tool Co.** of Columbus, OH. While plane production continued in Aurbun, it was under the Ohio Tool Co's. name. Testimony of **A. Howland & Co.** before the NY State Commission on Prison Labor, in 1870, revealed that it employed 100 prisoners @ 73 1/2 cents per day; that the hardware trade did not consider prison-work quality equal to that on the outside; that most of its production was sold to wholesalers in the west, some to the southern states, Texas, and California; that the total commercial value of the year's production was about $80,000; and that each prisoner made only a part of a plane. The company made a plane patented by **J. Ceville Spencer** of Phelps, NY, Patent No. 138,591, on May 6, 1873. **Tuttle** was issued on Nov. 1, 1870, plane-iron cap patent. The A2 imprint is on a hollow with the **180** style number used by the **Auburn Tool Co.** for hollows and rounds.

A, A1 & A2: FF; A3, B1, C & C1 **; B & A3 ***

S. HOWLAND
Southworth Howland (b. Mar. 29, 1775 in Barnstable, MA, d. June 9, 1853) was the father of **Warren S. Howland** and was a house carpenter. **Southworth** was involved in building an elegant house in West Brookfield, MA, designed by the distinguished architect **Asher Benjamin**. In the 1846 Worcester, MA directory, he placed an ad for making artificial limbs saying that he was formerly of West Brookfield and had been making

artificial limbs for over 30 years. **Howland** stated that he was "prepared to do jobs of carpenter's work, setting glass, etc." Examples: on an 8 3/8" birch plow, found in western MA; a 9 5/8" beech complex molder; and an 11 15/16" birch hollow, all with flat chamfers, ca. 1800. ****

W. S. HOWLAND
Warren Shoe Howland (b. Aug. 31, 1798 in Conway, MA, d. Jul. 4, 1872 in Amherst, MA) was the son of **Southworth Howland**, and in 1846, he was listed as a carpenter in Worcester, living at the same address as his father. **Warren** was listed in the 1850 Amherst, MA census, as a joiner and a planemaker. In 1860 & 70, he was listed as a carpenter; and in 1865 a house builder, ca. mid 19c. ***

I. HOWLETT
Example: on a 9 1/2" beech small ogee complex molding plane with heavy round chamfers, ca. 19c. **UR**

M. HOXIE
Example: on a 9" beech shiplap rabbet with shallow round chamfers, ca. 1830. **UR**

I: HOYER
Example: on a 10" beech molder with narrow flat chamfers, ca. 1810. **UR**

A. B. HOYT
A. B. Hoyt was a New York City planemaker who manufactured a plane using **William A. Cole's** Patent No. 5,620, on June 6, 1848, for a wooden compass plane with a flexible steel sole. Example: on an 8 3/8" beech compass plane. (see *Patented Transitional & Metallic Planes in America, Vol. I*, p. 131, by Roger K. Smith) **UR**

D: C: HOYT
Example: on a 10 1/2" beech skew rabbet with a birch wedge, that may be an early replacement. The chamfers are round on top and shallow round on the ends, ca. 1830. **UR**

J. HOYT
Example: the A imprint is on a 7 3/4" beech slide-arm plow with brass tips and a 14 1/2" x 4 1/2" center toted cornice plane. The B imprint is on a compass smoother with flat chamfers, a round top iron and square top wedge; and as an owner's imprint on the nose of an **I. Sleeper** bead, ca. 1800. **A & B: UR**

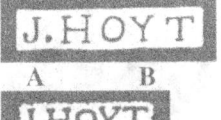

M. HOYT
Example: on a beech plow with an **I. Sleeper** style wedge. **UR**

C. HUBBARD
Example: on a 16" jack, with the date **1860**; and a wedge-arm sash filletster. **UR**

D. H/ D. HUBBARD
Daniel Hubbard (b Aug. 16, 1777 in Rutland, Worcester Co., MA, d. Apr. 11, 1866 in Royalston, Worcester, MA) was a housewright and carpenter, from 1810-34, in Royalston, MA, near the NH border. In 1827, **Hubbard** took **Luther Harrington** as an apprentice "to learn the carpenter trade". From 1850, **Hubbard** was listed as a farmer. The majority of the 20 or so examples reported are bench planes. One 30" joiner was signed on the back of the wedge in pencil, "Made by **D. Hubbard** Royalston Mass. 1834 for **C. Bacon**." Examples: on a 9 1/2" beech large round with flat chamfers; a 9 3/4" Yankee plow with wood depth stop, wood thumbscrews and a riveted skate; a 9 1/2" complex molder; a 24" joiner; and an 8" smoother, all beech with double-irons on the bench planes and shallow round chamfers, ca. 1830. The closed tote on some of the bench planes have a long sloped front. Influenced by **Jn. Tower** and **U. Clap**. **A & B: ***

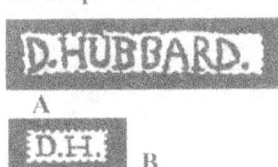

E. HUBBARD
Example: on a smoother with a steel sole; and a 23" beech fore plane, both with shallow round chamfers. The double-irons are by the **Providence Tool Co.**, Providence, RI, active from 1850-70. **UR**

F. HUBBARD
Example: on a 7" beech coffin smoother with the location **WORCESTER**, ca. 19c. ****

I. HUBBARD
This imprint has been reported. **UR**

B. HUBBEL
Example: on a 16" beech panel raiser with a centered tote, a skew blade, and shallow round chamfers. An incuse owner imprint of **A. B. HUBBELL** is later, ca. 1810-20. **UR**

ELI. HUBBEL

Example: on a screw-arm toted plow with a riveted skate, ca. 19c. **UR**

HUBBELL & LUNNAGAN

Benjamin Hubbell and **John S. Lunnagan** were listed as planemakers, at 292 Division St, New York City, in 1842-43. **Benjamin P. Hubbell** is believed to be the same person who was listed as a planemaker under his own name in the New York City directory, from 1852-54. The names are on separate dies. *******

A. HUBER

Examples: on a 10" beech molder found in eastern PA; a wedge-locked chamfering plane; and a handled cove, all with flat chamfers. The iron on the molder is marked **A. NEWCOM**. This imprint has also been reported on a screw box, ca. 1790, possible from eastern PA. ********

SH/ S. HUCHES

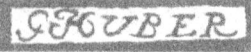
Example: on a 9 1/4" beech ovolo (quarter round) with wide flat chamfers, ca. 1780-1810. **UR**

G. HUBER

Example: on a 10" side bead with four lignum vitae boxing inserts and heavy flat chamfers, possible from eastern PA, ca. 1800. **UR**

J. H. HUEPEL & CO.

J. H. Huepel & Co. with **John H. Huepel** was a hardware and cutlery dealer in Cincinnati, OH. From 1868-73, he was listed as a clerk; from 1874-92 it was listed as **J. H. Huepel & Co**. Example: on an **Ohio Tool Co**. hollow, ca. 1890. ********

B. HUFF

Benjamin Huff was a Baltimore, MD, planemaker and sign painter, active from 1849-51. Example: on a 3 1/2" wide panel raiser. **A & A1 ****

FIDLE HUFF

Fidle Huff (b. Jul. 8, 1822 in Germany, d. Jan. 6, 1916 in Columbus, Franklin Co., OH) was listed as a planemaker in Columbus, OH, from 1856-57; in 1880, he was listed in Prairie, Franklin, OH. **No imprint has been reported**.

O. K. HUFF

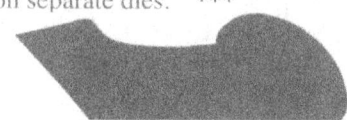
Example: on a 9 1/8" lignum vitae razee, toted smoother with a chamfered wedge, ca. 1840. **UR**

HUGHES

Possibly **William Plummer Hughes** (b. Feb. 22, 1794 in Baltimore, MD, d. Aug. 28, 1874, Cincinnati, Hamilton Co., OH) who was apprenticed on Nov. 6, 1809, at age 15, to the planemaker **William Vance** of Baltimore, MD, "to learn the trade of plane maker." **Hughes** enlisted in the War of 1812, on Aug. 19, 1814, from MD; and was discharged on Nov. 30, 1814. In 1815, **Hughes** was a part of the short-lived partnership of **Barkley & Hughes** which took over the plane making business of **Owings & Roy**, at 3 Light St. in Baltimore. Hughes moved to Pittsburgh, PA, and worked for **William Scott**, from 1815-18; and was part of **Swetman, Hughes & Co.**, from 1818-20. **William Hughes** was married on Jun. 10, 1819, in Pittsburgh, PA. **William P. Hughes** was listed in the census for Cincinnati, OH, in 1820. The directory of 1829-31 listed **Hughes** as a plane maker; in 1850, he was listed as "Grocer"; in 1860, as Exchange Officer; and in 1870, as Policy & Lottery Agent. **A & A1: *******

J. HUGHES

John Hughes (b. 1785) was listed as a carpenter, in the 1850 census, living in Wayne Twp., Wayne City, IN, both the **J. HUGHES** and **H. M. PARK** imprints are on a 12 1/4" handled plow plane, which may have been a partnership or a succession. Examples: with the **J. Hughes** name alone include a beech smoother; and a single-boxed bead with size **5/8** marked on the heel. The B & C imprints are on a 9 1/2" x 1 1/2" beech skew rabbet made by **J. W. Farr**. The New York imprints predated **John Hughes'** move to IN. **A **; A1, B & C ******

S. HUGHES

Examples: on two 9 3/4" beech molders with multiple boxing and heavy round chamfers, ca. 1790-1810. **UR**

C. HULBERT

Examples: on a 10 15/16" beech complex molder with the A wedge; and a 10" maple molder with the B wedge, both with heavy round chamfers, ca. 1820. **UR**

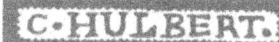

HULINGS
Americus Hulings (b. 1821 in OH) was a Cincinnati, OH planemaker, who was a partner in **Hulings & Kemper,** in 1842, with **Samuel Kemper**, and a planemaker and tool store operator, from 1843-44. **Kemper** married, Feb. 14, 1844, in Campbell, KY. He was listed in the 1848 Louisville, KY city directory, as a planemaker, at **Woodruff & McBride**; and in the 1850-60 Cincinnati censuses, as a planemaker. Some time during this period, **Hulings** was in a partnership with **William E. Levoy**, as **Hulings & Levoy**. Hulings enlisted on Oct. 16, 1862, as a Private from OH, and was mustered out on Feb. 10, 1864, Co. M, OH, 5th. Cavalry, Reg. ***

HULINGS. & KEMPER
Was a plane maker partnership in Cincinnati, OH. Example on a 9 3/8" beech round with size **12**. ca. 1842. **UR**

HULINGS & LEVOY
Americus Hulings and **William E. Levoy** were in a plane making partnership in Cincinnati, OH, dates unknown. **Hulings** was five years younger than Levoy. ****

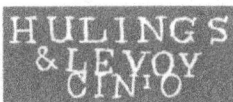

HULINGS. G. ROSEBOOM.
Was a plane making partnership in Cincinnati, OH, some time between 1850-60. Example: on a 13 3/4" beech gutter plane with a **Jacob Busch** single iron. ****

W. HULL
William Harris Hull (b. 1815 in Raynhan, Bristol Co., MA, d. Oct. 22, 1888 in Boston, MA) was a Boston, MA, planemaker, in 1847-48. **Hull** was part of **Hull & Montgomery** from 1845-46, both at 86 Blackstone, Boston, MA. ***

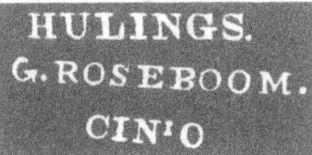

HULL & MONTGOMERY
William Hull and **Joseph A. Montgomery** were planemakers in a partnership in Boston, MA, from 1845-46. **A & B** ***

I H/ J. HUME
Example: on a 9 3/8" beech full-boxed center bead with flat chamfers, found in PA, ca. 1800-10. **UR**

R. HUMPHREY
Example: on a 8" beech compass smoothing plane with flat chamfers, ca. early 19c. **UR**

WM. HUMPHREYS
Example: on a 9 3/4" beech round with flat chamfers. ca. 1810. **UR**

D. H/ D. HUNKINS
David Hunkins (b. May 20, 1753 at Haverhill, Essex Co., MA, d. March 13, 1826 at Sanbornton, Strafford Co., NH) was a woodworker and son of **Robert Hunkins**, a bricklayer. He was married on Sep. 26, 1783, in Haverhill, MA. **David** moved from Haverhill (10 miles from Newburyport) to Sanbornton, in 1806. Examples: on a 12 3/8" tongue plane; a 13 1/4" panel raiser, both beech with a centered pegged tote and a diamond strike and heavy flat chamfers. Molders are 9 3/4"-9 7/8" beech with an **I. Sleeper** style wedge and heavy flat chamfers. Three also have embossed initials **D.H**, ca. 1790-1800. Two later planes, a 14 1/2" handled pump plane; and a skew rabbet with a flat backed wedge. Both beech with round chamfers, ca. 1820. ****

 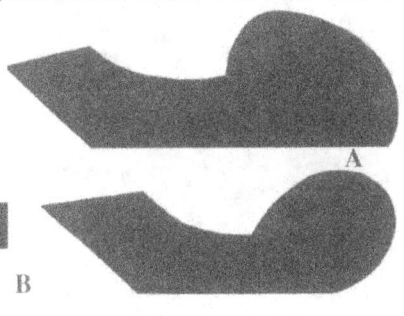

D-HUNT
Examples: on a 15 1/2" jack; and a 14 1/2" panel raiser, both with pegged heavily offset totes, a **NEWBOULD** round-top irons and flat-topped wedges; and four molding planes 10 5/8"-9 7/8", all beech with flat chamfers, and found in PA. This mark is different from that reported from England by Goodman, possibly from PA, ca. 1790. ***

D. A. HUNT
Example: on a 10 3/4" beech square rabbet, ca. 1810. **UR**

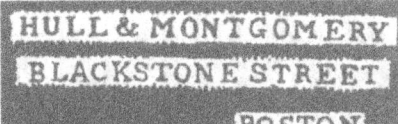 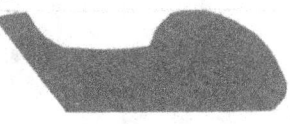

E HUNT
Example: on a 9 7/8" beech large round with flat chamfers, ca. 1800-10. **UR**

E. HUNT
Edwin Hunt (b. 1824 in NY) was a hardware dealer in Chicago, IL, active from 1848-63. He was listed as **Edwin Hunt** under Wholesale Cutlery, at 84 Lake, Chicago, IL.; and as **Edwin Hunt & Sons** in wholesale hardware, from 1864-1908. Example: on a 16" panel raiser with a **William Ash & Co.** iron and a match grooving plane with inventory number **22** on the toe. ****

HOSEA HUNT
Hosea P. Hunt (b. 1829 in Huntington, MA, d. Jul. 20, 1896 in New Salem, Franklin Co., MA) was married on Nov. 28, 1854 in Prescott, MA. **Hunt** was in the Huntington, MA, census of 1855-60, as a planemaker. **No imprint has been reported**.

J. HUNT
Example: on a 9 7/8" birch complex molder with small round chamfers, ca. 1810. UR

JOSEPH HUNT
Joseph Hunt (b. 1810 in NY) was listed in the New York City directory of 1835, as a planemaker, at 151 Elizabeth St. In 1870, **Hunt** was listed in 1870, as a carpenter, in Bethel, Sullivan Co., NY. **No imprint has been reported**.

LEWIS HUNT
Example: on a bead made by **Spear & Wood** with the location imprint **CHELSEA**; a dado made by **Gladwin & Appleton/Boston**; a plow with the imprint **HUNT/CARLESTON** has also been reported. Both Charlestown and Chelsea are part of the Boston area. ***

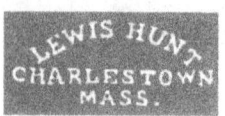

S. C. HUNT
Sheridan Cockey Hunt (b. 1817, d. May 30, 1871 in St. Louis, MO) was listed in 1864-65 & 1868-69 in St. Louis, MO, as a plane manufacturer. **Hunt** was also a hardware dealer from 1863-71; and part of **Hunt & Wiseman**, from 1850-60. **No imprint has been reported**.

W. HUNT
Example: on a 9 1/2" beech ogee complex molder with tight round chamfers, ca. early 19c. UR

W. J. HUNT
The location **RACINE** was probably Racine, WI. One was marked with **W.T.** which is probably for Wisconson Territory. Examples: on a 9 9/16" rabbet, and a bead, ca. 1850. A & B: ****

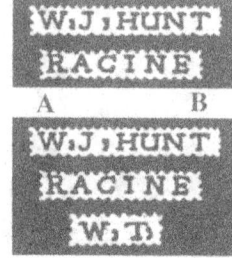

HUNT & WISEMAN
Sheridan C. Hunt and **James R. Wiseman** were manufacturers of planes and wholesale/ retail dealers in hardware and tools in St. Louis, MO, from 1850-60. FF

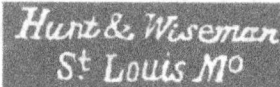

A. HUNTER
Example: on a 10" birch skew rabbet with flat chamfers, ca. 1800. UR

R + HUNTER
Example: on a 9 3/8" beech boxed bead with flat chamfers, ca. 1800. UR

W. HUNTER
William Hunter was listed as a planemaker in Utica, NY, in 1833, boarding with **John Reed**, and probably a bench hand. Example: on a 9 7/8" beech large round with flat chamfers, ca. 1810-20. UR

HUNTINGTON
Possibly **Sylvanus Converse Huntington** (b. 1800, d. 1893 in Oswego, NY) who was listed in the 1850 census, as a carpenter, in Oswego, Oswego Co. NY. A & A1 ****

A

A1

M. HUNTLEY
Examples: on a 12" toted fixed sash; and a 10 3/8" skew shiplap plane, both birch with flat chamfers, ca. 1790. UR

T. HURLBIRT
Example: on a 13" birch skew rabbet with three lignum vitae wear strips dovetailed into the sole and with heavy round chamfers, possibly from PA, ca. 1810. (this plane was illustrated in *American Woodworking Tools*, p. 130, by Paul B. Kebabian & Dudley Witney) UR

I: HURIBUT
Example: on a 9" birch thumbnail plane with flat chamfers, found in Port Jefferson, NY, ca. 1780. **UR**

JEREMIAH HURLBURT
Jeremiah Hurlburt was a Goshen, CT was a joiner. His 1776 estate inventory includes sets of joiner's and carpenter's tools. **No imprint has been reported.**

C. G. HURLEY
Clarence G. Hurley (b. 1933, living 2002 in Covington, IN) was a machine operator in 1950; and in 1957 a "pre. opr.", **Bryan Mfg. Co.**, Peru, IN. **Hurley** is a contemporary planemaker on a 9 1/2" beech rabbet, dated **1977**, in Covington, IN. **UR**

J. HUSSEY
John Hussey (b. 1844 in MA, d. Oct. 8, 1877 in Cunnington, Hampshire Co., MA) was a planemaker in New Bedford, MA; in 1870, working for **J. M. Taber**. In the 1870 census, **Hussey** was listed in New Bedford, Bristol Co., MA, as "works in plane factory". In 1871-72, **Hussey** was a part of **Bodman, Bearse & Hussey**, in Pawtucket, RI; and in 1872, a part of **Bodman & Hussey**. After 1873, **Hussey** was in Cunnington, MA, where he worked for himself. Examples: on a partial set of hollows & rounds, some also imprinted by **J. Lovell**. ****

L. H/ L. HUSSEY
Example: on a 9 1/2" beech single boxed complex molder, ca. 1850. **UR**

 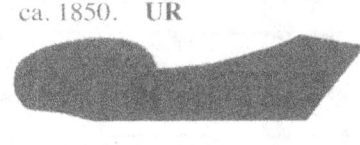

IOHN HUUN
Example: on a 9 1/2" beech chamfer plane with slide-arm wedge-stopped plow plane with heavy flat chamfers, possibly from rural PA, ca. 1820. **UR**

M x HUVER
Example: on a 14" handled grooving plane with heavy flat chamfers, probably from PA, ca. 1790-1800. **UR**

A. HYDE
Asa Hyde (b. Aug. 1783 at Lisbon, CT, d. Oct. 29, 1839 at Bennington, VT) was the 6th son and 10th child of **A. Hide**. In 1804-06, **Lavius Fillmore** designed and built the First Congregational Church of Bennington, VT. "A man named **Asa Hyde** was brought from CT to do the carving." **Asa** settled in Burlington where he was listed in the 1810 census; in 1820, he was listed, as "engaged in manufacturing"; in 1824, **Hide** advertised "Journeyman Cabinet Maker Wanted". In 1829, **Hasting & Kendrick** advertised as located in the shop on Main Street, formerly occupied by **Mr. Hyde**; in 1830, **A. Hyde** was listed as "resident". Examples: on a 9 5/8" skew rabbet with ebony edge boxing; and a 9 3/8" fixed sash, both with heavy round chamfers and a relieved wedge, ca. 1810. ****

C. R. HYDE
Example: on a 21 3/4" beech fore plane, razee style with a W. Butcher iron and a chip breaker, with round chamfers, ca. 1850. **UR**

D. HYDE
Believed to be **Daniel Hyde** (b. Mar. 1, 1756 at Lebanon, CT, d. Dec. 24, 1831 at Bainbridge, NY) who served in the Revolutionary War. In 1795, **Hyde** went from Lebanon to Middleburgh, NY; then Claverack, NY; and finally, in 1806, to Bainbridge, which is north of Binghamton and east of Ithaca. Examples: on a 10" beech door plane with flat chamfers that stop and with a long sweeping run-out; and a beech plow with flat chamfers and an **I. Sleeper** wedge, screw attached skate and a fence that extends beyond the toe, found in a tool box in Ithaca, NY, ca. 1790-1810. ****

E. HYDE
Possible **Ezra Hyde** (b. Jan. 21, 1776 in Norwich, CT, d. Jul. 6, 1845 in Norwich, CT) the 7th child of **A. Hide**. Examples: the A imprint is on a beech plow with the fence extending beyond the body, a wood depth stop & thumbscrews, and the skate is attached with screws. The B imprint is on a 9 1/2" maple skew rabbet, both with flat chamfers. ca. 1800. **A & B** ****

J: HYDE
Possibly **Joel Hyde** (b. Mar. 23, 1764 at Norwich, CT, d. Jan. 24, 1853 at Lisbon, CT) the eldest son of **A. Hide**. **Joel** served in the Revolutionary War and was a cabinetmaker and a farmer in Preston, CT. He advertised in the *Chelsea Courier* offering

cherry boards for sale, on Feb., 22 1804 and Jul. 31, 1805. In 1810, he moved to Lisbon, CT. Example: on a 9 1/2" (heel shot) birch skew rabbet with flat chamfers, ca. 1790. ****

HYNSON
Augustus R. Hynson (b. Jan. 1827 in MD, d. Dec. 1910 in St. Louis, MO) was a St. Louis, MO, hardware dealer and possible plane manufacturer, active from 1861-63. **Hynson** was earlier part of **Hall & Hynson**, from 1851-60; and later part of **Hynson & Coleman (Colemann)**, from 1864-73. On Nov. 17, 1885, **Augustus R. Hyson** received a patent for the invention of the "safe edge scoop", a coal shovel and scoop with a round edge and a corrugated deep bowl for hard and soft coal. It was advertised by **Hynson Hardware Co.**, located at 204 N. 6th. St., St. Louis, MO. Example: The A imprint is on a 10 1/4" rosewood plow with boxwood screw-arms, nuts, wedge and fence made by **J. Bracelin**, from Dayton, OH, ca. 1861-69. The B imprint, with **TENN**, is on a 15 7/8" jack plane probably made before moving to St. Louis. A & B: ****

HYNSON & GORMLY
Hynson & Gormly was located in Nashville, TN. Example: on a rosewood plow plane with a boxwood fence and arms, and on a 2 1/2" wide complex molder also stamped **E. F. Seybold**, who worked from 1836-44 in Cincinnati, OH. ****

HYNSON TOOL & SUPPLY CO.
Hynson Tool & Supply Co. was a St. Louis, MO, hardware dealer, active from 1899-1920, that handled cooper's tools. Example: on the toe of a **Sandusky Tool Co.** with the inventory number **240** applewood "leveler" sun plane. **

D. IODER
Example: on a beech molder; and a 10 1/16" filletster plane. Both with **NEWBOULD** irons and with heavy round chamfers, ca. 1810-20. ****

GEORGE INGHAM
George H. Ingham (b. May 1, 1826 in KY, d. Aug. 27, 1894 in Columbus, Franklin Co., OH) was listed as a planemaker in Columbus, OH, active in 1856-57 & 1875-1889; in Sandusky, Erie Co., as a planemaker, from 1870-72. **Ingham** was listed, as a carpenter, in 1893-94. **Ingham** served in the Civil War, as a Corporal, from Sep. 1861-64, in Co. H, 5th. Regiment, from Columbus, OH. **No imprint has been reported**.

ALBERT INGLES
Albert Ingles (Engles) was listed as a planemaker in Philadelphia, PA, in 1837. **No imprint has been reported**.

INGLIS/ A. INGLIS
Archibald Inglis (Ingliss or Englis) (b. 1810 in, Scotland, d. Oct. 1, 1887 in Delhi, NY) arrived in NY, on Jun. 15, 1842, and made planes in Delhi, NY, from 1850-80. Also reported is a paper label on a bead:

ARCHIBALD INGLIS
PLANE MANUFACTURE
DELHI, N. Y.

B **, A, B1, C & D ****

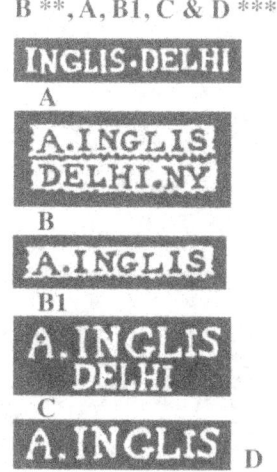

EI/ E. INGRAHAM
Edward (Ted) Ingraham (b. Jun. 15, 1947) is a contemporary planemaker, of 18c. style planes, from North Ferrisburg, VT. ****

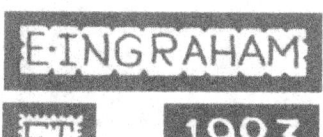

J. W. INGRAM
Example: on a 9 3/4" beech adjustable fenced chamfer plane, ca. 19c. **UR**

WM. P. IVES
William P. Ives was listed in the, 1850 census for New York. The Vermont cabinetmakers checklist includes a **Wm. Ives** (b. ca. 1803 in VT) who was listed, in the 1850 census, as a cabinetmaker, in Cambridge, VT. Examples: on a bead; and four 9 1/2" molders found together, all with dates on the heels. An astragal with the eagle mark is dated **1847**, two are dated **1856**, and one **1857**. ********

J. C. & CO
J. C. & Co. was probably a hardware dealer. Example: on a grooving plane made by **Reed/ Utica**. **UR**

J. L. & CO.
Example; on a 16" jack plane, ca. 19c. **UR**

J. H. W
Possibly related to **T. Waterman** of Waldoboro, ME. Example: on a 9 1/2" beech skew rabbet. The **WALDOBORO** location imprint is the same as used by **S. C. Soule**, ca. 1850. **UR**

J W M (see James W. Mason)

G. JACKMAN
Example: on a 9 9/16" beech quarter round with flat chamfers, ca. 19c. **UR**

E. B JACKSON
Eri B. Jackson (b. 1793, d. Aug. 27, 1828 in Newfane, Windham Co., VT) married on Jul. 10, 1817 in New Fane. Examples: the A imprint is on a 9 1/2" beech plow with a double ended fence, wood thumbscrews, a wood depth stop, riveted skate and heavy round chamfers. The A1 imprint is on a 9 1/8" beech double-boxed, complex molder with heavy round chamfers, found in Newfane, VT; and on a 10" apple dado plane with flat chamfers and a relieved wedge, ca. 1810-20. **A & A1: *******

EDWARD JACKSON
Examples: on a 9 15/16" beech hollow with narrow flat chamfers, ca. 1800. **UR**

J. JACKSON
Example: on a 9 3/8" beech large round with heavy flat chamfers, ca. 1810. **UR**

WM. JACKSON
Assumed to be **William Jackson**. Example: a dado and a crown, both with flat chamfers, ca. 1790. **No imprint is available**.

J. JACOB
Examples: on a 16 1/4" birch plank-match tongue plane; a 9" beech wide round; a 9" birch dado; an 8 7/8"x 3/4" birch bead; and an 8 7/8" birch shiplap, all with heavy round chamfers, ca. 1820. **UR**

S. f. IACOB (JACOB)
Example: on a 10" beech molder with flat chamfers and a **NEWBOULD** iron, found in York Co., PA, ca. early 19c. **UR**

A. JACOBS
Example: the A imprint is on a 9 15/16" grooving plane; and a 9 3/4" beech round with size **1 4/8** imprint on the heel, both with heavy round chamfers, ca. 1820. Imprint B is on a 9 7/8" beech grooving plane, ca. 19c. **UR**

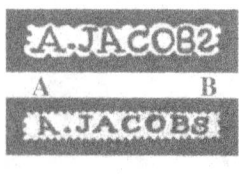

K. JACOBS
Kenneth W. Jacobs of Milwaukee, WI, was issued Patent No. 459,457, on Sept. 15, 1891, for a combination wood and metal cooper's croze imprinted K. JACOBS/ MILWAUKEE/ PAT.-91, cast into the iron holder for the cutter. The wood body has no imprint. In 1882, **Jacobs** was listed, as porter; in 1886-89, as clerk, in Milwaukee, WI; in 1912-15, as cooperage; in 1894, he working for **B. A. & Son**. In 1922, **K. W. Jacobs & Co.** with **Kenneth W. Jacobs** as President; **Roy M. Jacobs** as Vice President; **Kenneth L. Jacobs** as Sec.; and **Bjrleigh C. Jacobs** as Treas. **K. W. Jacobs Co.** was listed as cooperage & barrel manufacturers (1827-1923). **No imprint is available**.

JACUD & SHICK
Jacud & Shick from Strasburg, VA, were listed as planemakers. **No imprint has been reported**.

IACOB. IAISER (JACOB. JAISER)
Example: on a 9 5/16" molder; and a 10" beech ogee molder with **VIII** on both the plane stock and the wedge, both with heavy flat chamfers, from PA, ca. 1800. **UR**

G: JAMAIN
Gerrit Jamain (bapt. Aug. 14, 1728, at the Dutch Reform Church of New Amsterdam in New York City, d. between 1756-59) the son of **Joseph Royden Jamain** (b. ca. 1700) of French Huguenot descent and **Sarah Burger** (bapt. Oct. 22, 1706) who were married on May 22, 1725 at the Dutch Reform Church of New Amsterdam. **Gerrit Jamain**'s grandfather, **Gerret Burger** (will probated Jan. 26, 1726/27) was a housewright and his granduncle, **Hermanus Burger**, was a blacksmith. The first U.S. census of 1790, lists no Jamains in New York. This may represent the earliest New York planemaker. Example: on a 10 1/4"x 1 7/8" applewood complex molder with a relieved birch wedge and wide flat chamfers. It is unboxed with straight-up layout lines on the front and heel, ca. 1750-75. *********

C. B. JAMES & CO.
Charles B. James & Co. was a Detroit, MI, hardware dealer, ca. 1850-60. **Charles B. James** was listed, in 1862, working for **John James & Son**, as hardware. In 1872-75, he was listed under wholesale hardware; from 1877-1908 as manufacturers agent; in 1913, no occupancy was listed. The B imprint is on a size **18** hollow with inventory number **180** on the heel, an **Auburn Tool Co.** style number. A & B: *******

D. IAMES
Examples: on a 9 13/16" beech complex molder with interrupted boxing, heavy flat chamfers, found in PA; and on a wedge lock birch plow with a beech fence, wood depth stop and small round chamfers, ca. early 19c. **UR**

HENRY A. JAMES
Henry A. James (b. 1827 in England) was a planemaker in New York City, in 1851 only. **No imprint has been reported**.

H. L. JAMES
Example: on the toe and heel of a **DeForest**, Birmingham, CT tongue plane, and a double-boxed adjustable sash plane. There does not appear to be a connection with the **H. L. James** of MA, but he could have worked in NJ, before appearing as a merchant in MA, in 1850. A & B: ********

H. L. JAMES
Henry L. James (b 1819) was a plane manufacturer in Williamsburg, Hampshire Co., MA, active from 1855-70. **James** was listed in the 1850 census, as a merchant. The 1860 MA Industrial census listed him, as a tool manufacturer, employing 11 hands, utilizing water power and producing 5000 planes. In the 1870 census, **James** was listed as a manufacturer; and his

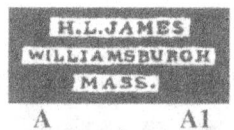

shop was burned out some time before 1879; in the 1880 census, he was a woolen manufacturer. The **WMS BURG/ MASS** location stamp on the B imprint also appears on an **Eagle Mfg. Co.** panel raiser, and together with an **H. Wells** B imprint, suggesting a relationship.
A, A1, B, B1 & B2; FF

JAMES MFG. CO.
James Manufacturing Co. represents a planemaker in Williamsburg, MA, ca. 1850. There is a possible connection with **H. L. James** also of Williamsburg at about the same time. A round plane has both the **H. Wells** A imprint and the **James MFG. Co.** imprint. ******

D. JARVIS
Examples: on a 9 1/2" beech, size **2** hollow and round pair, ca. 19c. **UR**

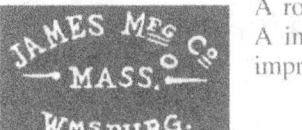

S. S. JARVIS & SON
S. S. Jarvis & Son with **Stephen S. Jarvis** (b. Oct. 24, 1812) and son **William H. Jarvis** was a hardware/ tool dealer that purchased planes from **G. W. Denison & Co.** In 1873-77, the firm was listed under hardware in Bridgeport, CT. In 1888, **Stephen S. Jarvis** was listed as manager, **William H. Jarvis** was listed as "removed to Philadelphia, PA". Examples: on a pair of **G. W. Denison & Co.** match planes with a portion of a **S. S. Jarvis & Son** paper label remaining. ********

G. JEFFERS
Example: on a 10 1/2" beech skew rabbet, with shaved sides and therefore no chamfers, ca. 1830. **A & B: UR**

I. JEFFERSON
Possibly **Isaac Jefferson** was an apprentice trained as a tin smith and blacksmith slave for **Thomas Jefferson** at Monticello, VA. **Isaac Jefferson** moved to Petersburg, VA, before **Thomas Jefferson**'s death. Example: on a 9 3/8" beech size **6** hollow with flat chamfers, ca. 1790-1810. **UR**

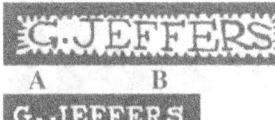

I. JENKINS
Example: on a 10" beech side bead with interrupted boxing and flat chamfers, found in Western PA, ca. 1800. **UR**

JOHN. JENNE
Example: on a 10" applewood fixed double-bladed sash with birch wedges and heavy round chamfers, and as an owner's mark on a **N. Taber** molder, ca. 1810. **UR**

C. E. JENNINGS & CO.
C. E. Jennings & Co. was a New York City manufacturer of a variety of tools, including bits, augers, drawknives, chisels, and saws, under its name, with an arrowhead trademark. There were no planes included on its 175 page, 1913 catalog, reprinted in 1985, by the **Mid-West Tool Collectors Assn**. Although the firm's beginnings was 1818, this was probably based on the date **L'Hommedieu** was established. **Charles A. Jennings** started the firm in 1878, and it continued to 1923. Example: on a smoother with the iron also marked **C. E. Jennings & Co.** *********

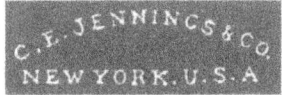

C. JENSEN
Conrad Jensen (b. 1843 in Denmark, d. 1880 in Middlesex Co., MA) took the oath of citizenship in Boston, MA on Mar. 27, 1873. **Jensen** was issued Patent No. 126707, on May 14, 1872, in which **Jensen** claimed that his plane combined, in a single tool, a tenon cutter, a dado, a filletster, and two rabbets of different widths. It used only two irons which didn't need to be changed in performing the various operations. Examples are known with both beech and rosewood bodies. **J. H. Lamb** was the probable manufacturer of the **Jensen** Patent. In 1905, **Conrad Jensen** was listed as a carver in Boston. ********

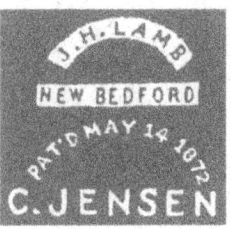

J. JEPSON
Examples: on a 13 7/8" beech panel plane with a centered tote, a strike button and shallow round chamfers, imprinted toe and heel, and with a **James Cam**, warranted, cast steel iron; and on a 9 1/2" beech molder, ca. 1820-30. **UR**

J: JEWET
James Jewet (b. 1718, d. 1792) was listed as a prominent Newburyport, MA, merchant. Example: on a 10 1/4" beech Yankee-style plow plane with an **I. Sleeper** style wedge, riveted skate, mortised arms, and flat chamfers, probably from Northern New England, ca. 1790. ********

E. JEWETT
Example on a 13"x 4 1/8" wide crown molder with an offset maple tote and heavy round chamfers on the top and flat on the ends, ca. 1800-20. **UR**

J. C. JEWETT
John Calvin Jewett (b. Aug. 7, 1800 in Cornish, ME, d. Oct. 22, 1883, in Machiasport, ME) was married on Oct. 31, 1822 in Machias, ME. Three children were born in Waterville, ME, from 1825-29. In the 1830 census, **Jewett** was listed in Waterville, ME; in 1840, he was in Norridgewock, in manufacture; and in 1850, in Machiasport, Washington Co., as a house carpenter; in 1860, as a farmer, in Newburgh, Penobscot, ME; in 1870, a joiner, in Machiasport; and in 1880, a carpenter. Example: on a plow; a jack; a sash; a side rabbet; a 9 7/16" hollow; and a 9 1/2"x 3/4" dado, all beech with round chamfers, ca. 1820.
A & A1 **

S. JEWETT
Example: on a 9 5/8" beech round with flat chamfers, ca. 1800. **UR**

T+ JEWETT
Example: on a birch 10" ogee molder with flat chamfers, ca. 1790. **UR**

C. L. JILLSON
C. L. Jillson was listed as a planemaker, in Utica, NY, in 1864-65, possibly working for **John Reed**.
No imprint has been reported.

G. JOHN
Possibly **G. John** a cabinetmaker from Chester Co., PA, active from 1760-80. Examples: on several 10" beech molding planes with heavy flat chamfers. ***

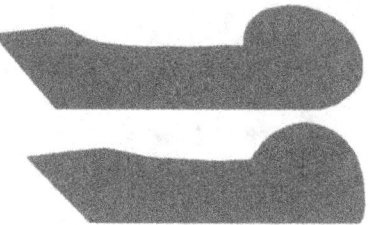

IOHNSON (JOHNSON)
Example: on a 10 3/4" fruitwood (cherry) plow with large flat chamfers, found in PA, ca. early 19c. **UR**

A. JOHNSON
Example: on an 8 1/2" applewood reed & follow with steel boxing, iron fence arms and thumb screws, with flat chamfers, ca. 19c. **UR**

A. JOHNSON

Example: on a 18" lignum vitae ship wrights razee jack with a beech handle and wedge and double-iron, possibly from coastal New England, ca. 1850-60. **UR**

C. JOHNSON
Examples: on a group of eight planes found together including a 9 9/16" beech molder with heavy flat chamfers. ****

D. D. JOHNSON
D. D. Johnson possibly a plane maker and/ or a hardware dealer in Vincennes, IN, ca. 1850. ****

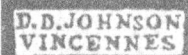

D. T. JOHNSON
Examples: on a 9 1/2" beech fenced rabbet, ca. 1850. **UR**

E. JOHNSON
Possibly **Edward Johnson** (b. Aug. 16, 1722 in Lynn, MA, d. Jan. 24, 1799 in Salem, MA) active until 1795; or son **Edmund Johnson** (b. 1744, d. Jul. 12, 1811 in Salem, MA) a Salem cabinetmaker, active from 1793-1811. Examples: on a 9 1/2" beech narrow molder; and a wide molder, both with flat chamfers, ca. 1790-1800. **UR**

G. JOHNSON
Example: on an 8" smoother with a "gutter" sole and an **Auburn Tool Co. Thistle Brand** iron. **UR**

J. JOHNSON
Example: on a 10" fruitwood plow with out a depth stop, screw locked sq. arms, a relieved wedge, and flat chamfers with flutes, ca. late 18c. **UR**

J. JOHNSON
Example: on a try plane with a **Auburn Tool Co. Thistle Brand** iron and on a 10" fruitwood plow, ca. 1870. ****

IAMES IOHNSON (JAMES JOHNSON)
Example: on a 9 1/2" beech body with birch wedge, medium hollow with size **16** on the heel, an **Aron Hildick** iron, and flat chamfers. Found with a large group of later Albany planes, ca. early 19c. **UR**

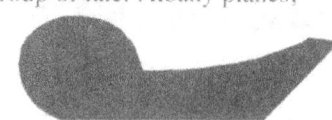

L. D. JOHNSON
L. D. Johnson from Hamilton, NY. Examples: on a 9 1/2" dado; and a 9 1/2" beech, single-boxed Grecian Ogee made by **J. Kellogg** of Amherst, MA. (1835-39). **UR**

S. JOHNSON
Believed to be **Stephen Johnson**, of Brookline, Windham Co., CT, who was listed in the 1790 census. Examples: on a 14" beech crown molder with a offset birch tote, round-top iron, birch wedge and heavy round chamfers; a side bead; and a skew rabbet. The last two are 9 1/2" beech with heavy round chamfers, possibly from New England, ca. 1820. ********

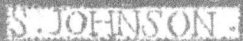

W. IOHNSON (JOHNSON)
Example: on a 9 1/4" birch square rabbet plane with flat chamfers, ca. 1800. **UR**

W. E. JOHNSON/ W. E. JOHNSON & CO.
William Erskine Johnson (b. Jul. 23, 1830 in S. Deerfield, MA, d. Mar. 21, 1895 in Pittsfield, MA) was listed in the 1850 census, as a planemaker, living with **Wm. Webb** in Pittsfield, MA. **Johnson** married, on May 20, 1853, in Goshen, MA. Johnson was listed in 1855, as a planemaker, in Goshen, employing six hands; and in the 1860, as a master planemaker in Pittsfield; in 1870-80, he was listed as a carpenter in Pittsfield.
A, A1 & B *******

G. IOLLY (JOLLY)
Example: on a 9 1/2" beech very complex molder with shallow round chamfers, ca. 1810. **UR**

R. JOLLY
R. Jolly struck twice on the toe of a 9 1/2" beech complex molder with round chamfers, ca. 1820.
No imprint is available.

A. JONES
Two possibilities **Asahel Jones** (b. Mar. 31, 1766, d. Nov. 22, 1822 in Hubbarton, VT) a cabinetmaker who moved from Raynham, MA to Castleton, Rutland Co., VT, in 1789; then to Hubbarton, VT, from 1800-22. The 1820 census lists **Asahel Jones** as engaged in manufacturers. Or **Asa Jones** (b. 1765, d. Apr. 21, 1841 in VT) of Bridgewater, Northampton Co., MA. **Asa Jones**, worked from 1790-1840, as a cabinetmaker, housewright, turner and chair maker. Example: on a 10 3/8" birch tongue with a relieved wedge and heavy flat chamfers, ca. 1790. **UR**

E: IONES (JONES)
The last name is probably **Jones**. Examples: on a 14 1/2" crown molder, struck twice on the toe, with birch offset tote; a 13" double iron & wedge sash, with a birch tote; a 9 3/8" complex molder; a plow with riveted skate; a 9 1/2" hollow; and a 9 1/2" double bead, found in ME, all beech with heavy flat chamfers with the exception of the crown which has round chamfers, ca. 1790-1810. ********

E x JONES
Example: on a 9 1/2" single-boxed beech large bead with flat chamfers, ca. 1810. **UR**

ELLIS JONES
Example: on a 9 1/4" beech rabbet, ca. 1850. **UR**

EVANS JONES
Evans Jones (b. Mar. 12, 1820 in Wales, d. Jun. 19, 1869 in Columbus, Franklin Co., OH) was listed as a planemaker, in Columbus, active in 1856-57. **Jones** enlisted, as a private, in the Civil War, from Aug. 5, 1862 to Oct. 2, 1863.
No imprint has been reported.

I + IONES (J + JONES)
Jethro Jones (b. ca. 1733, d. Jan. 12, 1828 at Blanford, MA) was an early black planemaker, active from 1764-67; and a contemporary of **Cesar Chelor** with whom he may have been associated. **Jones** appeared, in 1758-59, in Medway, MA, on a list of inhabitant soldiers in the French and Indian Wars. He then appears in Wrentham, MA, on poll tax lists for 1764-66. On May 2, 1767, he married **Juda King** in Wrentham. **Jones** then appears on the Holliston, MA, tax records of 1771. **Sambo Freeman** was also listed in Holliston, in 1772, another possible black planemaker. **Freeman** appears on the Medway 1758 tax list; and in Wrentham, from 1758-61. **Jones** served in the Continental Army, from May 1777 to Dec. 1783, enlisting from Leichester, MA, near Worcester. **Jones** was then 45 and listed his previous occupation, as toolmaker. He moved, in 1790, to Blanford (Blandford), MA, where he spent the remainder of his life. Examples: on molders are 9 7/8"-10 1/16" birch with flat chamfers. The relieved wedge is from a 9 7/8" birch round with flat chamfers and flutes and has the A1 imprint.
A & A1 ********, B *********

I + IONES (J. JONES)

Example: on a 9 1/2" beech adjustable fenced coping plane with heavy round chamfers, ca. 1830.
A & B: UR

I. IONES (J. JONES)

The last and possibly the first names begin with **J**. Examples: on a 13" handled sash; a 10" large bead; a 10" astragal; and a 9 1/2" (heel shot) molder, all birch with the A relieved wedge and wide flat chamfers and fluting. The B wedge is from a slightly later 9 1/2" beech molder with flat chamfers, ca. 1790-1800. ****

I- JONES

Example: on a 9 1/2" beech skew rabbet with heavy round chamfers, ca. 1820. **UR**

JONES/ I. JONES

Isaac Jones (b. Feb. 1839 in Wales, d. 1921) was an Albany, NY, planemaker, who was self-employed from 1891-95, and earlier from 1857-91 probably worked for others. One or both of the following imprints may have been his. Examples: the A imprint is on an 8" rosewood coffin smoother. The B imprint is on a 28 1/4" joiner, found in Oneonta, NY; a 16" beech jack, dated 1862, and a handled applewood smoother, ca. 1860. **A & B: ***

J. E. JONES

Example: on a slitting gauge; and the heel of a 9 1/2" (toe shot) beech hollow with wide shallow flat chamfers, ca. 1790. **UR**

J. F. JONES

John F. Jones was a Philadelphia, PA, planemaker, active from 1825-35. **No imprint has been reported**.

JONES/ J. T. JONES

John T. Jones (b. 1806, PA, d. Jul. 24, 1871, Philadelphia, PA) was a Philadelphia, PA, planemaker, active from 1831-46. **Jones** was listed in the 1870 Philadelphia, PA directory, as plane manufacturer. Examples: on a screw-arm sash plane with the B imprint and with brass plates set into the body where the knobs turn is stamped **PATENT**; and a label on the heel **5/14/36 PAT'D**. When the knobs are turned the body halves separate and there are no locking nuts. One 9 7/16" double rosewood-boxed astragal has been reported with a paper label: ****

JOHN T. JONES
MANUFACTURER OF WARRENTED
BENCH & MOULDING PLANES
OF EVERY DESCRIPTION

His imprint has also been reported on a Sheffield style brace.
A, A1, A2, A3, A4, B *;
C, C1, D & E **; E1, E2 ***

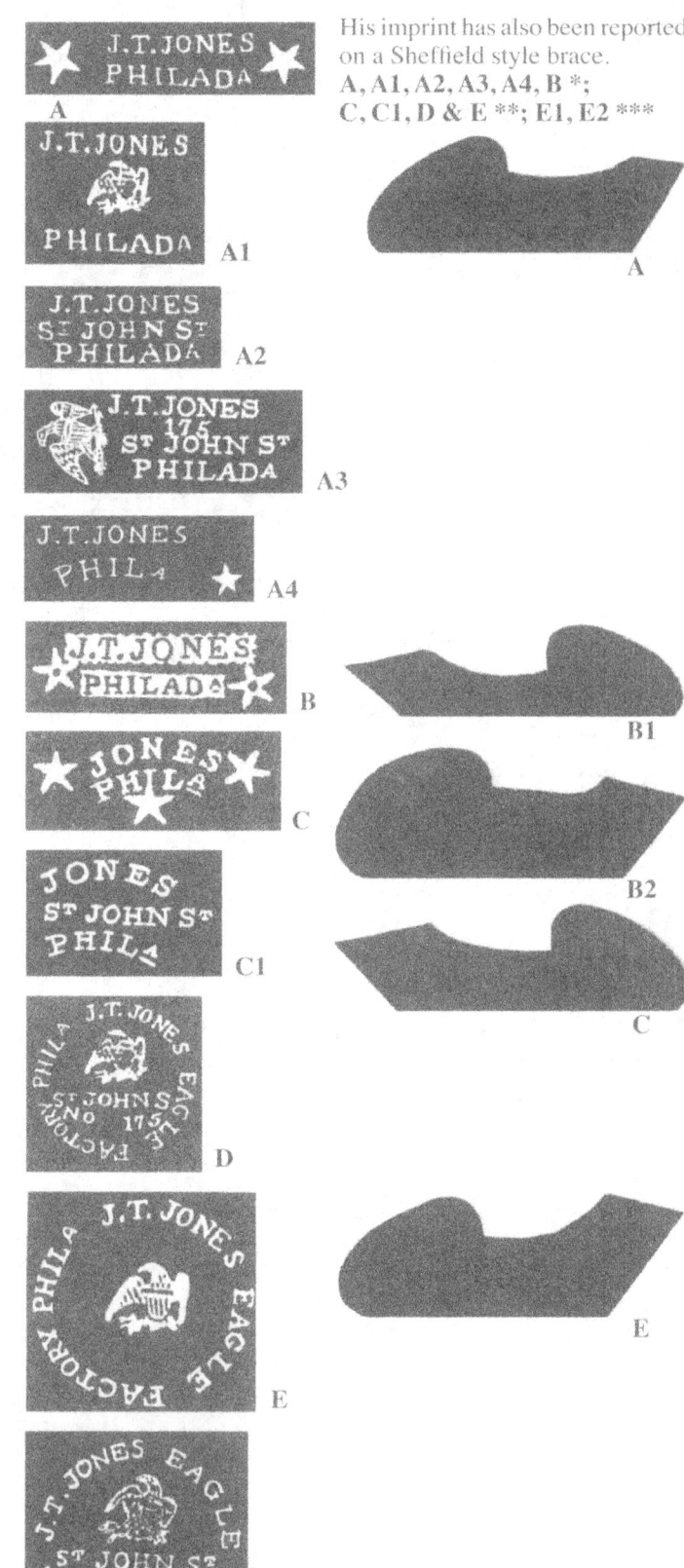

202

E2

JOSEPH JONES
Joseph Jones (b. 1830 in England) of Newark, NJ, active from 1866-76, was issued Patent No. 52,719, on Feb. 20, 1866, for a wooden shoot board plane. The prototype was made by **Mockridge & Francis** of Newark, NJ, and is 13 1/4"x 2 3/16" beech with a cherry base. A brass name tag **JONES PATENT FEB, 20TH, 1866** was attached and **NO. 1** was imprinted in four places. **Jones** was listed, in 1870, as a carpenter in S. Orange, NJ. **Joseph Jones** also had a patent for a metal plane and a scraping plane. **No imprint on the wood body**. (see *Patented Transitional & Metallic Planes in America, 1827-1927*, p. 146-47, by Roger K. Smith)

L. M. JONES
Example: on an 8 1/16" lignum vitae smoother; a 16 1/2" lignum vitae jack; and a cocobolo bench plane, found in Portland, ME, all with a imprint of **E. E. Bowden**, a shipwright. ca. 1850. ****

M. F. JONES
Example: on a 7 5/8" beech coffin smoother, ca. 1850. **UR**

R. JONES
Example: on a 7 5/8" beech smoother with heavy round chamfers and a double-iron; and a 9 1/16" beech tongue plane with a wood depth-stop secured by a wood thumbscrew from the offside. ca. 1820. **UR**

R. L. JONES
Possibly **Robert L. Jones** (b. 1819 in Nova Scotia) who was listed in the 1850 Boston, MA, census as a carpenter. Example: on a panel raiser. ca. 1830. **No imprint is available**.

S. JONES
Example: on a 9 1/2" beech grooving plane with a riveted skate and heavy round chamfers. ca. 1820. **UR**

S. E. JONES
Samuel E. Jones (b. Jan. 11, 1760 in Worcester, MA, d. Feb. 1835 in Whitehall, Washington Co., NY) placed this advertisement in *The Northern Sentinel and Lansingburgh Advertiser* on July 2, 1787: (Lansingburgh founded in 1771 and was incorporated into Troy, NY in 1902) "**Samuel E. Jones**, Joiner & Tool-Maker. Takes this method to inform the public, that he carries on his business at the corner of Queen St. opposite Mr. Thompson's tavern, where gentlemen may surply (sic) themselves with Joiners Tools of all sorts, of the best kinds, as cheap as those imported from Europe. Cash or Country Produce will be received in payment." **Samuel E. Jones** also advertised in the *Federal Herald* on Feb. 1, 1790. The **S. E. Jones** wedge style and imprint resemble that of **C. Allen** of Lansingburgh, who may have apprenticed or worked for Jones. One **S. E. Jones** plane is in the Farmers Museum at Cooperstown. Examples: on a 10" beech molders with heavy flat chamfers; and a 13 1/8" beech panel raiser with a round top. **Weldon** iron, and shallow flat chamfers. ca. 1790. ***

T. JONES
Examples: on a group of 14 planes found in Seabrook, NH, with the A imprint including nine single-sash coping planes of different varieties. All 9 1/2" beech; 13 with round chamfers and one with heavy flat chamfers; several with the B imprint are 9 1/2" birch with round chamfers and relieved wedges. ca. 1810. **UR**

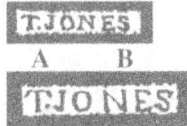

THOMAS WYNNE JONES
Thomas Wynne Jones (b. Oct. 30, 1822 in Limerick, Montgomery Co., PA, d. Jan. 14, 1888 in Limerick) Example: on an 8" smoother plane. ca. 19c. **UR**

WALTER F. JONES & CO.
Walter F. Jones (b. 1810 in OH). Examples: The A imprint on a side bead with the location **BURLINGTON, IOWA**. ca. 1860; and the B imprint on a 1" skew rabbet made by **Hall, Case & Co.** with the location **PITTSBURGH**. ****

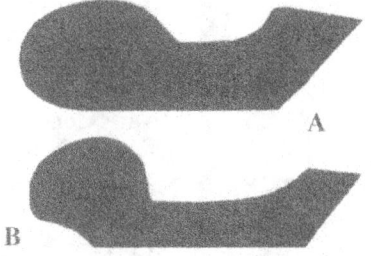

R. IONSON (JONSON)
R. Jonson was a planemaker from the lower VT/ NH section of the Connecticut River Valley where most examples of his planes have been found. He usually double stamped his name, one vertical the other horizontal when room was available. Examples: on molding planes 9 1/4"-10" beech, some boxed with lignum and at least one, a rounding plane, is of rosewood;

a plow plane has ebony inserts dovetailed in the arms to prevent wear from the thumbscrews. ca. 1800-1810. A & C **, B ****

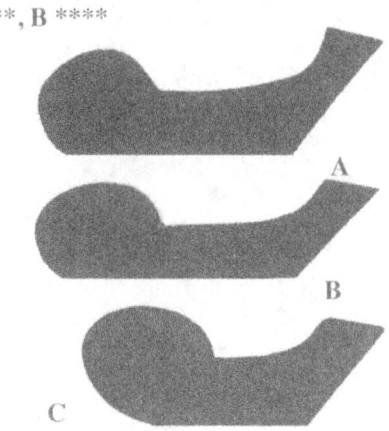

J. H. JORDAN
Example: on a 8 7/8" beech double right and left side bead with shallow round chamfers. ca. 1830-40. **UR**

J. T. JORDAN

Example: on a rosewood razee fore plane; and a jack. Both from CA. This could be from a maker of ship's joiners tools. ****

JORDAN HARDWARE CORP.
The **Jordan Hardware Corp.** was located in New York City. Example: on a **Joh. Weiss & Sohn** (Austria) horned smoothing plane with a **Chapin-Stephens** iron. The imprint appears on the top of the plane between the mouth and the horn. ***

: IOSEPH (JOSEPH)
This probably represents **JOSEPH**. Examples: on a 15 1/2" birch jack with an offset tote, a diamond strike, and round chamfers, ca. 1810. **UR**

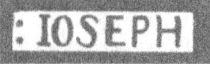

S. H. JOSL
Examples: on a 12 1/4" beech shipwright's miter plane with a **Moulson Bros.** iron and with round chamfers, ca. 1820. **UR**

R. JOYCE
Examples: on a 9 1/2" beech boxed bead with the location **PHILA**. **UR**

T. JUBB
Example: on a 9 1/2" beech coping plane with a York pitch, ca. 19c. **UR**

K & C (see Kennedy & Collins)

KACKLEY
Joseph Kackley (b. ca. 1779) of Kernstown, VA, was listed as a planemaker, and a friend of another planemaker, **Henry Kern**. **Henry's** brother, **Jacob Kern**, made irons for **Kackley**, the administrator of **Samuel Kern's** will. **Joseph** Married, Jan. 19, 1803, in Shenandoah Co., VA. Example: on a 13 1/2" beech gutter plane, with the iron marked **J: KERN**, a diamond start, offset tote and heavy flat chamfers, found in the Shenandoah Valley of VA, ca. 1800-10. ****

JOE KAINZ

Joe Kainz was probably a hardware dealer in Detroit, MI. Example: on a 15 3/8" European Jack. ****

C. KALTENBACH
C. Kaltenbach was probably a hardware dealer. Example: on a 28" joiner with a **D. R. Barton** iron. ****

H. A. KAMMERER
The name **H. A. Kammerer Inc.** of Mt. Vernon, NY appears incised on the nose of a 9 1/2" narrow round, possibly modified from a rabbet. Also incised on the side is: ****

NO. 10 PEERLESS
JORDAN
H. A. KAMMERER INC
MT. VERNON. N.Y.

Jordan Hardware Corp. of New York was the American agent for **Joh. Weiss & Sohn** of Vienna, Austria. **UR**

I. KAMP
Examples: on a 10 1/4" complex molder and; a 9 7/8" beech halving plane with round chamfers on the top and square end chamfers, possibly from PA. ca. 1800. ****

KANE MFG CO.
Kane MFG Co. with the location of Kane, PA. Example: on the nose of a **Sandusky Tool Co.** weather-stripping plane. ****

P. KANTZ
Example: on a 15" cherry toted plank-match grooving plane, with wedge lock arms, a snecked iron and flat chamfers. There are bone or ivory wear strip inserts on the sole. ca. 1800. **UR**

JOHN KARMIKLE
John Karmikle (b. Feb. 20, 1808) was apprenticed Mar. 11, 1820, at age 12, to **William Vance** to be taught "the trade of a planemaker." **No imprint has been reported**.

GEORGE KARRMANN (see Upson Nut Co.)

A. KASSON
Example: on a 16"x 4" cornice plane. **UR**

JACOB KATZ
Jacob Katz (b. Feb. 19, 1787, PA, d. Dec. 1, 1868 in PA) was listed as a planemaker in Philadelphia, PA, active in 1817. **No imprint has been reported**.

J. KATZ
Julius Katz (b. 1832 in Wurttemberg, Germany, d. Nov. 19, 1889 in Cincinnati, OH) was listed as a Cincinnati, OH, cabinetmaker, in 1868, 1870-72 & 1874; and a carpenter in 1869. On April 26, 1870, **Julius Katz** was issued Patent No. 102,406, for an improvement in "Plane-Stock". His improved facing device for the sole of a plane consisted of "strips of bone, ivory, or similar hard organic substance glued together in two pieces or slabs". Example: on a 6 1/4" 2 1/16" mahogany smoother with a lignum vitae sole. (see *Patented Transitional & Metallic Planes in America, Vol. II*, p. 75, by Roger K. Smith) **UR**

J. H. KAUFMAN
Example: on a match pair of screw-armed tongue & groove plank planes, probably from PA, ca. 19c. **UR**

I. M. KEAN
Example: on a 9 1/4"x 1 1/2" beech skew rabbet with heavy flat chamfers, ca. 1800. **UR**

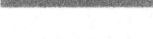

P. KEATING
Example: on a 12 1/4" beech match t. & g. plank pair with round chamfers, and a brass face on a steel skate, boxwood wear face on fence. ca. 1820-30. **UR**

J. KEEFER
Example: on a 9 3/8" size **4/8** single-boxed bead with a **W. Butcher** iron, ca. 1825. **UR**

H. B. KEEN
Examples: on a 9 1/2" molder; and a coping plane made by joining two plane bodies at right angles, both 9 1/2" beech, ca. 1850. **UR**

J C. KEEN
John C. Keen was listed as a planemaker in Philadelphia, PA, in 1799-1800; and as a carpenter from 1800-11. Example: on a 9 1/2" molder with flat chamfers and the imprint **I. POWEL** branded on the side. **UR**

N. KEEN
Nathaniel Keen (b. ca. 1813 in MA) was listed in 1880, in Marshfield, Plymouth, MA, as a carpenter and house wright. **UR**

R. KEEN
Reuben (Rubin) Keen (Kean) was listed as a planemaker in Philadelphia, PA, in 1814 & 17. FRANKFD is for Frankford, which was just outside of Philadelphia, and is now part of the city. **A & A1** ****

KEEN KUTTER
Edward Campbell Simmons (b. Dec. 24, 1839 in Fredrick, MD, d. Apr. 18, 1920 in St. Louis, MO) at age 17, was in the wholesale mercantile business. **Simmons** moved to St. Louis, MO, in 1846, with his family. In 1856, he apprenticed to **Child-Pratt & Co.** Upon completion of his three year commitment, he began working for **Wilson, Levering and Waters**. He raised from clerk to partner in what became **Waters, Simmons & Co.** In 1869, at age 30, **Simmons** obtained control of this **Co.** and reorganized it as **Simmon Hardware Co. Simmons** had a flare for promoting and selling his products by the use of slogans. In 1870, the new firm chose the **KEEN KUTTER** as the brand name of their line of high grade tools and cutlery. Other slogans were "The recollection of the quality remains long after the price is forgotten." and in 1881, "A jobber's first duty is to help his customers to prosper." **Simmons** introduced traveling salesmen into the business, employing more than any other enterprise in the country. In 1892, **Simmons** employed 200; and in 1916, employed 500. In 1874, **Simmons** employed profit

sharing, the first mercantile business in the country to do so.

In 1881, **Simmon Hardware Co.** issued their first comprehensive catalog and pioneered "same day service". St. Louis, MO was the headquarters with warehouses in New York City; Sioux Falls, IA; Minneapolis, MN; Atlanta, GA; Toledo, OH; and Philadelphia, PA. **Simmons** retired in 1887, turning over the Co. to three sons, **Wallace Simmons**, **Edward Simmons** & **George Simmons**. The firm went into bankruptcy in 1934 and sold out to **A. E. Shapleigh Co.** on July 1, 1940. **Shapleigh** continued to use the KEEN KUTTER trademark, until 1961. Example: the C imprint is from a 5 1/2"x 1 1/2" size 1 beech coffin smoother with black wood knobs. The A imprint is ca. 1900-05; the B imprint, ca. 1905-12; the B1 imprint, ca. after 1905-12; the C imprint, ca. 1895. **A, B & B1 *, C ******

C. KEENE
Example: on a 7 1/2" beech wedge-arm plow plane; two 9 7/16" fruitwood skew rabbets, one with a **VII** on the wedge and iron, both found in ME; and on a **S. Cumings** complex molder with shallow round chamfers, ca. 1830. **UR**

I. KEIM
Examples: on a 9 1/4" beech washboard plane with wide flat chamfers and a **NEWBOULD** iron; and two molders, one a side bead, both 9 3/8" beech with flat chamfers, probably from PA, ca. 1800. ********

S. J. KEIM
Example: on a 14 1/4" beech handled molder with a maple applied fence and heavy round chamfers, probably from PA, ca. 1820. **UR**

W. & J.H. KEIM/ WM & J.H KEIM & CO
Examples: on the toe of a **John Bell** crown molder. An **E. W. Carpenter** combination tongue & groove plane carries an ink imprint: A *********

```
        FROM
W. & J. H. KEIM'S HARDWARE
     NORTH 3rd. STREET
       READING PA.    (****)
```

 A imprint

D. P. KEINE
Example: on a 9 3/8"x 3/4" beech tongue & groove pair, the groove with a snecked iron, both with heavy round chamfers, ca. 1820-30. **UR**

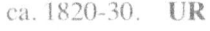

I. KEISER
Examples: on a molder modified to a Gothic bead; and a plow plane, both 10" beech with heavy flat chamfers, possibly from PA, ca. 1790. **UR**

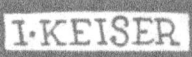

JACOB KEISER
Jacob Keiser with a date **1834** has been reported from a wedge-arm match plank grooving plane, possibly from PA. **No imprint is available.**

KELKER/ KELKER & BROTHER/ KELKER & SON
Luther R. Kelker was a partner in **Kelker & Brother** a hardware dealer in Harrisburg, PA, active from 1845-90. It was apparently the successor to **Oglesby & Pool** and in the 1840's was known as **Kelker & Co.**; by the 1850's, the name was **Kelker & Bro.** The **Kelker & Son**, was used sometime after 1860. An 1890 Harrisburg directory lists **Luther R. Kelker** as a dealer in hardware including "mechanics tools". Examples: on the heel of a boxwood plow; on an **Arrowmammett** coming & going tongue & groove plane and on a **Greenfield Tool Co.** boxwood smoother. ********

KELLER/ I. KELLER (J. KELLER)
John Keller was one of Baltimore's early planemakers, active from 1796-1808, at Sligh's Lane. The earlier A imprint is on a 10 1/8" hollow with heavy flat chamfers. A ********, B & C *******

VICTOR KELLER
Victor Keller (b. 1815 in Germany, d. 1885, in Allegheny, PA) as a hardware dealer from Allegheny, PA, the name for the north side of Pittsburgh before it was incorporated into the city. **Keller** was listed as a grocer, in 1840. On Mar 3, 1851, he was naturalized in PA. From 1856-65, **Keller** was listed as a hardware dealer, at 230 Ohio St. in Pittsburgh, PA; in 1874, a baker; and in 1878, as a liquor dealer. Examples: on planes made by **H. Chapin/ Union Factory**, the **Greenfield Tool Co.** and the **Ohio Tool Co.**. *******

GEO. W. KELLEY
Geo. W. Kelley was listed as a toolmaker and planemaker, in the 1854-57, in Milwaukee, WI, directories; in 1873, a machinist. **No imprint has been reported.**

C. F. KELLNER
Charles F. Kellner was listed in 1889, as a blacksmith; in 1890-91, as a carpenter, at 301 s. 6th. street, Philadelphia, PA. Example: on a side bead made by **H. Chapin**. **UR**

ARCHD KELLOCK
Example: on a 9 1/8" beech size **6** round found in PA, ca. 1850. **UR**

H. S. KELLOGG
Henry S. Kellogg (d. 1862) was in the hardware business in Cincinnati, OH, as **H. S. Kellogg**; **Wells & Ogden**, in 1839-40; and as **H. S. Kellogg & Ogden**, from 1842-44. **H. S. Kellogg** was listed in Cincinnati in 1846, in Cambridge City, IN, in 1846-47; and in Indianapolis, IN, from 1847-55. In 1855, the firm became **H. S. Kellogg & Son**, with **Charles H. Kellogg**, **Justin A. Kellogg** as a clerk, as a salesman, that continued until 1858. From 1860-61, **Henry S. Kellogg** was a salesman for **City Hardware**, at 12 w. Washington with **A. D. Wood** proprietor. Example: the B imprint is on a plane made by **J. Burke** of Madison, IN. **A & B** ***

KELLOGG/ J. KELLOGG
Believed to be the **Kellogg** in **Kellogg & Hastings** a partnership that made planes in Cleveland, OH, from 1846-48. **A & B** ***

J. KELLOGG
James William Kellogg (b. Jan. 13, 1792 in New Salem, MA, d. Mar. 23, 1868 in Amherst, MA) made planes, starting in 1835, at **Eli Dickinson**'s faucet shop, in the Nuttingville section of Amherst. **James Kellogg** was part of **Kellogg, Fox & Washburn**, in 1839, of **Kellogg & Fox**, from 1839-40; and of **J. Kellogg & Son**, from 1865-67; otherwise he worked alone. In 1839, **Kellogg** moved from S. Amherst to that part of Amherst on Belchertown Rd. that became known as Kelloggville, where he erected two factories, one wood and one brick. **James Kellogg** was listed in the 1849 New England Mercantile Union directory, as a plane manufacturer, from Amherst. One smoother made by **S. Hastings** is overstamped by **J. Kellogg** B imprint. His son **William Kellogg** continued to use this imprint after his father retired in 1867. During this same period from 1835-67, **William Kellogg** also operated a "mercantile store". The 1850 industrial census noted that **James Kellogg** employed 14 hands, used water power and produced $12,000 worth of tools.

James Kellogg was listed in the 1860 general census, as a merchant; in the 1860 Industrial census, as a manufacturer using 15,000 feet of beech, water power and eight hands to produce $8000 worth of tools. In 1886, the mill dam gave way and operations ceased. The A & C imprints are earlier than the B imprint. **B: FF; A, A1 **; C & C1 *****

J. D. KELLOGG
J. Dwight Kellogg (b. 1795) was a Northhampton, MA, planemaker, active in 1848. Kellogg was listed in the 1849 New England Mercantile Union directory, as a plane manufacturer, at South St., Northampton. The same eagle imprint was used by **H. Wells, Arnold & Crouch**, and **Peck & Crouch**, all of Northhampton. ****

J. KELLOGG & CO.
J. Kellogg & Co. was an Amherst, MA, planemaker, working dates are not known. This may be a successor company to **J. Kellogg & Son** after the retirement of **James Kellogg**, in 1867. This imprint is from a size 6/8 single-boxed bead, ca. 1860. **A & A1 ***

WILLIAM KELLOGG
William Kellogg (May, 28, 1820 in Amherst, MA, d. Mar. 17, 1897, Amherst, MA) was the son of **James Kellogg** who he joined in both the planemaking and mercantile businesses In 1867, **William Kellogg** bought his father out. In 1869, **William Kellogg** was listed as making planes from beech, boxwood and rosewood, fitted with irons bought from New Haven, CT, with daily output from 150-200 planes. **William Kellogg** continued to operate until 1886, when a flood carried away the power dam and damaged the plane factory. **No imprint has been reported** and it is presumed that he used the **J. KELLOGG/ AMHERST MS** imprint.

KELLOGG & CO.
Kellogg & Co. was the firm name of **Charles Augustus Kellogg** (b. Sep. 7, 1821 in NY, d. 1897 in Keokuk, Lee Co., IA) listed as a hardware dealer in the New Orleans, LA, city directory, in 1853-54. **Kellogg** became a hardware dealer in Keokuk, Lee Co., IA. ****

KELLOGG & FOX/ KELLOGG, FOX, & WASHBURN
Kellogg & Fox and **Kellogg, Fox & Washburn** were plane making partnerships consisting of **James Kellogg**, **Hiram Fox** and **W. L. Washburn** that operated in Amherst, MA, prior to 1839, when it was succeeded by **Kellogg & Fox** "for the merchandising and manufacturing of joiner's tools in Amherst". The partnership was dissolved in 1840.
No imprint has been reported.

KELLOGG & HASTINGS

A planemaking partnership of **J. Kellogg**/ Cleveland, OH, and Hastings that operated from 1846-48. The spelling "Cleaveland" became "Cleveland" in 1831. ****

S. KELLUM

Possibly the same person or related to **S. Killum**. The wedge profile is similar to that of **James Killam** and **Samuel Killum** of Glastonbury, CT, ca. 1850. ****

KELLY-HOW-THOMSON CO.

Kelly-How-Thomson Co. was a hardware dealer in Duluth, Minnesota from 1904-55. Example: on a 15" wood bottom transitional plane made by **Sargent & Co.**, ca. 1920. ****

A KELLY

Examples: on a square rabbet; and a rosewood boxed complex molder, both 9 1/2" beech, both with maple wedges as **A Kelly & CO**. ca. 1850. ****

A. KELLY & CO.

Abner Kelly (b. Jun. 21, 1782 in Ashfield, MA, d. Jul. 30, 1874, Ashfield), a planemaker, listed in the 1856 Ashfield, MA, directory. The 1854 ledger of the **Greenfield Tool Co.** shows purchases of "best plough plates, plough and fillester stops", from **A. Kelly**. In the 1860 industrial census, **A. Kelly & Co.**, employed two hands, using water power, and producing 3600 planes worth $1200. **

 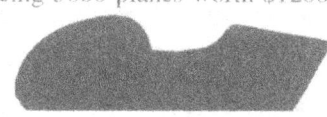

EDWARD P. KELLY

Edward P. Kelly (b. Jul. 27, 1800, d. Aug 25, 1873 in Baltimore, MD) was apprenticed on Mar. 25, 1807, at age 9, to **William Vance**, planemaker. **No imprint has been reported.**

W. KELLY

Example: on a 10" beech plow with sq. arms with heavy flat chamfers. **UR**

I. KELNAN

Example: on a 9 1/4" ogee molder with flat chamfers, ca. early 19c. **UR**

I. KEMBEL

Examples: on a large single-boxed bead; and a center bead, both 9 1/2" beech with flat chamfers, from PA, ca. 1800. ****

H. KEMP

Example: on a 10 3/4" beech molder with flat chamfers, ca. early 19c. **UR**

A + KEMPER

Examples: the A imprint is on a 9 1/2" molder; a 9 3/8" double reed; and a 9 7/16" nosing plane, all beech with wide flat chamfers. The B imprint is from a 24" jointer with wide flat chamfers, from PA, ca. 1800. ****

A B

GEORGE KEMPER

George Kemper was a Cincinnati, OH, planemaker, active from 1842-44. In 1880, **Kemper** was listed, as a blacksmith, in Cincinnati, OH; in 1892, at "mach. works". **George Kemper** was related to **Samuel Kemper** with res. Walnut Hills.
No imprint has been reported.

SAMUEL KEMPER

Samuel Kemper (b. Jan. 1, 1815 Hamilton Co., OH, d. Feb. 19, 1905 in Cincinnati, OH) was a Cincinnati, OH, planemaker, active in 1843-44. In 1842, **Kemper** was part of **Hulling & Kemper** with **Americus Hulling**. **Samuel Kemper** was related to **George Kemper** with res. Walnut Hills. In 1860, **Samuel Kemper** was listed, as a coach painter, in Cincinnati.
No imprint has been reported.

KENDALL

Thomas Kendall was a Baltimore, MD, planemaker, active from 1831-33 & 1835-42. **Kendall** was part of **Chapin & Kendall** with **Philip Chapin**, ca. 1833; and of **Kendall & McCubbin** from 1837-38. He married on Oct. 8, 1844, in Baltimore, MD. **A & A1** **

A A1
A2

A. KENDALL

Example: on a 15 1/2" beech double-boxed crown molder with a centered tote, ca. 1840-50. **UR**

G. KENDALL

Gilman Kendall (b. Sept. 22, 1827, d. Nov. 11, 1847 in Woburn, Dunstable, MA) was a Dunstable, MA, cabinetmaker. Example: on a 7 1/2" smoother with a **Moulson Bros.** iron, ca. 1850. **UR**

H. L. KENDALL

Henry Lee Kendall (b. 1824, d. May 7, 1873 in MD) was a Baltimore, MD, planemaker, active from 1849-60, and a hardware and home furnishings merchant. On June 8, 1858, he received Patent No. 20483, for an adjustable wedge that compensated for the wear on a bench plane's mouth opening. The patented B3 imprint **PATD. JUNE. 8. 1858** has been reported on a 22" fore plane. Henry was part of **Kendall & Schroeder** in 1858-59, with **Richard F. Schroeder**, and of **H. L. Kendall & Co.**, in 1860. No imprint with **& CO** has been reported although this name appears in a 1860 directory. In 1860, **Kendall** went into the steamed oyster business. It is not known when **Kendall** worked in Washington, DC.

A, B, B1 & B2 **, B3 & C *****

J. KENDALL

John Kendall (b. Jul. 21, 1810 in Northbridge, Worcester, MA, d. May 19, 1892 in New Lebanon, NY) was a son of **Thomas Kendall Jr.** (b. 1810 in MA) (no known relationship with the **Thomas Kendall** of MD) and succeeded his father as a thermometer maker in New Lebanon, NY, in 1835. One imprinted **J. KENDALL/ N. LEBANON N.Y.** Examples: on a 9 5/8" beech comp. rabbet with heavy flat chamfers; and on a 11 1/2" handled grooving plane made by **A. Fish**, Lowell, MA. **UR**

THOMAS KENDALL

Thomas Kendall was listed as a planemaker working on his own, from 1831, at 47 Pitt St.; in 1833, at cor. Ensor & Monument; in 1835-36, at 9 McClellan St.; in 1837-41, at Pine St. at S. Lexington; in 1842, at Pearl St. S. Lexington.
No imprint has been reported.

KENDALL & MacCUBBIN

Kendall & MacCubbin consisted of **Thomas K. Kendall** (b. 1815) and **Robert W. MacCubbin** were Baltimore, MD, planemakers, active from 1837-39.
No imprint has been reported.

KENDALL & RICHARDSON

Examples: An ink imprint on the side of a **N. Chapen/ Eagle Factory** sash coping; and on a double-bladed fixed sash with double boxing: ****

KENDALL & RICHARDSON
SHIP CHANDLERS
& HARDWARE DEALERS
Front St. Bath, ME

KENDALL & SCHROEDER

Kendall & Schroeder consisted of **Henry Lee Kendall** and **Richard F. Schoeder** made planes in Baltimore, MD, in 1858.
No imprint has been reported.

D. W. KENEDY

Example: on a 9 3/4" narrow beech hollow with a relieved wedge and wide flat chamfers.
ca. 1800. **UR**

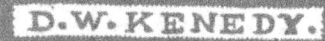

KENEWA TOOL CO.

Kenewa Tool Co. was a brand name used by **Sargent & Co.** of New Haven, CT. **

G. KENNEDY

Example: on a 15" beech fillester with adj. bottom fence and a closed center tote and heavy round chamfers, and a back pitch wood depth stop, found in VA, ca early 19c.

KENNEDY/ KENNEDY & CO./ L. KENNEDY

Leonard Canada Kennedy, Sr. (b. Mar. 3, 1767 in Windham, CT, baptized Oct. 1792 in Hartford, CT, d. Feb. 19, 1842) possibly was apprenticed with **Isaac Fitch** who lived in the next town of Lebanon, CT. **Leonard's** mother was a **Fitch**. **Kennedy** advertised himself as making all kinds of "joiner's molding tools" as early as Aug. 28, 1797, and may have supplied some of the planes that **Ebenezer Clark** of Hartford advertised, in Jan. 1796. In 1800, **Kennedy** advertised for journeymen, joiners, and apprentices, and was also selling lumber. By 1802, **Kennedy** was advertising all types of planes and also wooden screws and a few sets of "Scotch braces and bitts," suggesting the sale of imported tools. In 1802, **Kennedy** obtained a patent for, and advertised, a spring let into window sash to eliminate the use of sash weights. He also sold rights to this invention to carpenters. In 1803, **Kennedy** was an agent for **Daniel Pettiborn** of Philadelphia in licensing his welding process, patented on Dec. 22, 1802, for welding cast steel to iron for use in edge tools. From 1803-05, **Kennedy** was a partner with **Robert J. Collins Jr.** in Kennedy & Collins. The 1825 *Pocket Register for the City of Hartford* (CT) listed **L. Kennedy & Co.**, probably comprising **Leonard Kennedy, Sr.**

and **Leonard Kennedy, Jr.**, as manufacturers of joiners' tools. Primarily a planemaker, he also made looms, bookbinders' presses and fanning mills. A square, imprinted **Kennedy & Co.**, Hartford, appears to be English. Those who probably learned plane making from **Leonard Kennedy, Sr.** include: **Samuel Lewis Kennedy, Leonard Kennedy, Jr., Robert Collins III, Fitch K. Collins, D. O. Crane, Daniel Copeland, Melvin Copeland**, and **Consider Alford**. He continued until ca. 1830.

Samuel Lewis Kennedy (b. 1792, d. 1840) was the son of **Leonard Kennedy, Sr.** and brother of **Leonard Kennedy, Jr.** He probably worked at **Kennedy & Co.**, in Hartford, from 1813-17 and under the **Kennedy** name in New York City, from 1817-22. He may have succeeded **Consider Alford**, for he worked at **Alford's** old address. He was a partner in **Kennedy & White** in New York City, from 1822-40; and in **Kennedy, Barry & Way** in New York City; in 1840.

Leonard Kennedy, Jr. (b. 1800, d. 1879) was the son of **Leonard Kennedy, Sr.** and brother of **Samuel Lewis Kennedy**. **Leonard Kennedy, Jr.** worked in Hartford, CT, ca. 1821- 25; in Utica, NY, from 1825-32; in 1825, as part of **Kennedy & Lewis** selling tools and "joiners hardware". On Nov. 8, 1825, **Kennedy & Lewis** advertised in the *Utica Sentinel & Gazette* that they now have a "joiners' tool manufactory" on Genesse St. and also "wanted, white beech timber". In 1827, an ad for "joiners tool manufactory of moulding tools and bench planes" was for **L. Kennedy & Co.** In 1828, **L. Kennedy, Jr.** he moved to 81 Broadway and remained there until 1830, when he left Utica. He continued to operate as an absentee, at that address, with business partners **James S. Benton**, in 1833; **Robert L. Collins III**, in 1834; **John Brandish** in 1835, and selling the property in 1842. **L. Kennedy, Jr.** was in Rochester, NY, ca. 1833-38; and in Hartford, CT, from 1838-46. **Truman Nutting** of Amherst, MA, was shipping large orders of planes to **Kennedy & Co.** in the 1830's. He was part of **Kennedy & Way**, from 1838-43 and **Kennedy & Bragaw**, from 1844-46; He was in Milwaukee, WI, from 1847-50.

L. Kennedy, Jr. was listed as an insurance agent in Milwaukee, in the 1850 census, after which he returned to Hartford, CT, and other pursuits. An advertisement in the Utica city directory of 1828 stated that **L. Kennedy & Co.** "manufacture all kinds of moulding tools and bench planes" and "all tools manufactured by **L. Kennedy & Co.** Hartford, Conn., **Kennedy & White** New-York or **L. Kennedy & Co.** Utica, not proving good, will be repaired gratis." This indicated a business relationship among these firms, with **Leonard, Jr.** making planes in Utica, brother **Samuel Kennedy** in New York and perhaps father **Leonard Kennedy, Sr.** still making planes in Hartford. An ad in the *Rochester Daily Democrat* on Apr. 8, 1834 referred to **L. Kennedy, Jr.** selling a part of his business, the "joiner Tool Manufactory" to **J. S. Benton** and **E. Evans**. Examples: on a 9 3/8" beech complex molder with flat chamfers. Imprint H is on a square. Imprints G & G1 are the earliest.
A, B, C & E: FF; D & I *;
B1, C1, F, G, G1 & H
*****

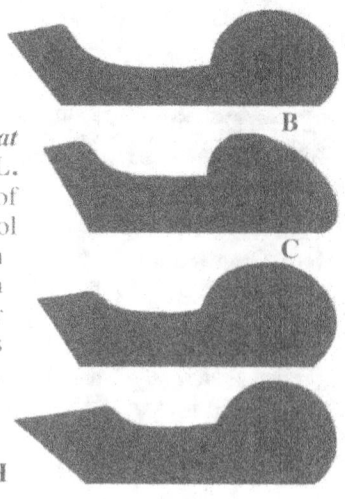

KENNEDY, BARRY & WAY
Samuel L. Kennedy, Samuel S. Barry, both planemakers and **William Way**, a hardware merchant, were partners in this New York City hardware store, in 1840. The firm became **Barry & Way** upon Kennedy's death in 1840. ***

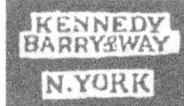

KENNEDY & BRAGAW
This was probably a partnership between **Leonard Kennedy, Jr.** and **Isaac Bragaw** who made planes in Hartford, CT, from 1844-46. This firm was succeeded by **Bragaw & Blake**.
No imprint has been reported.

K & C/ KENNEDY & COLLINS
A partnership of **Leonard Kennedy, Sr.** and **Robert J. Collins, Jr.** formed in Hartford, CT, on Apr. 4, 1803 to "Carry on the house Carpenter and Joiners business and manufacture Joiners Tools." The partnership was dissolved on Mar. 18, 1805, when Collins moved west and Kennedy carried on the business. Robert was married to **Eunice Kennedy**, Leonard's sister, making them brothers-in-laws. The B imprint is on a 9 1/2" beech size **6** hollow with heavy flat chamfers.
A, A1 & B ****

KENNEDY & WAY
Kennedy & Way is listed as having made planes in Hartford, CT, from 1838-43. **Samuel L. Kennedy** was working in NY, with a **William Way** in **Kennedy, Barry & Way**, until his death in 1840. **Leonard Kennedy, Jr.** had returned to Hartford from upstate NY, by this date and might be the **Kennedy**. **William Way** of New York City had relatives in Hartford, CT, and **George M. Way** married a daughter of **Leonard Kennedy**.
No imprint has been reported.

KENNEDY & WHITE
Samuel L. Kennedy and **Dyer White** (b. 1788 in CT, d. 1852) were in a plane making partnership, from 1822-40. Dyer was

the brother of **Charles White** and may have moved to OH, after the partnership was dissolved. *

JA. KENNER
Example: on the toe of a 14 1/2"x 3 3/4" crown molder with an offset tote and attached fence and flat chamfers, found in the Shenandoah Valley of VA. **UR**

L. KENNEY
Leonard Kenney (Kenny) was listed as a planemaker in Albany, NY, in 1818-19, and was a partner in **Rowell & Kenney**, from 1820-24. **A & B ***, B1 ****

I. KENT
Justice Kent (b. May 6, 1771 in MA, d. Dec. 22, 1858 in Brooklyn Twp. Susquehanna Co., PA) came to Windsor, Broome Co., NY, ca. 1795, where he lived until 1811 when he settled in Brooklyn Twp., farmed, built and operated a gristmill, and was a carpenter. **Kent** is interred in a tiny cemetery in Brooklyn with **Ebenezer Gere, Christopher Gere, Alford W. Mack,** and **John B. Mack**. Example: the A imprint is on a 10 1/2" birch plow with wood thumb screws, a relieved wedge, riveted skate, and arms mortised into the fence; and a 9 9/16" beech hollow with round chamfers, that provided the wedge. A hollow is in the collection of the Farmers Museum at Cooperstown, NY; and on a 28 1/2" beech joiner with a round wood strike, a round top wedge, off set tote and round chamfers, ca. 1800-20 ***

J + K/ J + KENT
Example: The A imprint is on an 8" birch, narrow nosing plane with a relieved wedge, flat chamfers, and flutes; a 14 3/4" birch tongue plane with pegged offset tote, round chamfers on top and flat on the ends; and a 10 1/2" birch Yankee plow with wood thumbscrews, a wood depth stop, riveted skate, snecked iron, and round chamfers. The B imprint is on a gutter plane, possibly from New England, ca. 1790-1820. A, A1 & B ****

N. KENT
Example: on a 15 1/2"x 5 1/2" crown molding plane. **UR**

KENTUCKY TOOL CO.
Kentucky Tool Co. with a location of **LOUISVILLE, KY.** was probably a hardware dealer. Example: on a 9 1/2" beech match groove plane with catalog number **75** on the heel, a

Ohio Tool Co. number, ca. 1840-50. ****

I. KER
The **I. KER/ I. N. KER** imprints could be the same person or a different generation, both imprints were found on a 6 3/4" birch smoother with round chamfers and a round top **Green** iron, ca. 1820. **A & B: UR**

WM. KER
Example: on a 10" beech molder with heavy flat chamfers, ca. 1800. **UR**

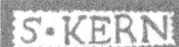

H. KERN
Henry Kern (b. Nov. 14, 1775 Frederick, Shenandoah, VA, d. Aug. 8, 1828 in Woodstock, Shenandoah, VA, was killed from falling off a horse) of Kernstown, VA, was the twin brother of **Samuel Kern** and the brother of **Nicholas Kern** and **Jacob Kern**. Some of his planes may have been partially made by **John T. Brown** and finished by **H. Kern**. Example: on a 35" beech jointer with an **W. Greaves & Son** iron, a diamond start, slight offset tote and heavy flat chamfers. *****

S. KERN
Samuel Kern (b. Nov. 14, 1775 Frederick, Shenandoah, VA, d. Jul. 6, 1857, Strasburg, Shenandoah, VA) of Kernstown, VA, was the twin brother of **Henry Kern** and the brother of **Nicholas Kern** and **Jacob Kern**. Jacob and Henry both worked as blacksmiths and made plane irons. **Samuel** was also an inventor and surveyor who had a July 31, 1846 patent, for a survey compass. **Samuel** was listed, in 1850, as a farmer. **Kern's** will was administrated by **Joseph Kackley**. Example: on an astragal; and a hollow, both 9 5/8"; and a 14 1/4" crown molder with an offset tote, a diamond start and a iron marked **N. Kern**, all beech with heavy flat chamfers that were found in the Shenandoah valley of VA, ca. 1800. *****

I* KERRIDGE
Example: on a beech complex molder with flat chamfers. **UR**

M. KEYSEY
Example: on a 10 1/2" beech hollow with heavy flat chamfers. The William Penn Memorial Museum at Harrisburg, PA, has five or six examples: the molders are 10" and the toted molders are 13 1/2", all with heavy flat chamfers, from PA, ca. 1800. **UR**

W. L. KIDDER
Example: on a 10 1/2" cherry ship-lap rabbet with a closed integral tote and heavy flat chamfers; and a 22" beech jointer with round chamfers, found in ME, ca. 1810-20, possibly from

 New England. ca. 1810-20. **UR**

KIEFFER & AUXER
Kieffer & Auxer was a Lancaster, PA, partnership of **William Kieffer** (Keifer) and **Samuel Auxer** that took over from **Sarah Carpenter**, from 1863-69. **Kieffer & Auxer** was listed, in the 1869-70 directory, as planemakers. **William Kieffer** (b. ca. 1822 in PA, d. Oct. 27, 1873 in Cincinnati, OH) married **Susanah Elizabeth Carpenter** and was a son-in-law of **E. W. Carpenter**. Kieffer was listed as a planemaker in the 1850-60 census, the 1857-59 & 1866-67 Lancaster directories. In 1870, **Kieffer** was listed as a cabinetmaker. **Samuel Jacob Auxer** (b. Sep. 17, 1834 in Elizabethtown, Lancaster Co., PA, d. Jan. 5, 1909 in Lancaster, PA) was also listed in the 1850 census as a carpenter; in the 1860-70 census, as a planemaker; in 1880, as book store; and in 1900, as a book seller. **Kieffer & Auxer** were succeeded by **Auxer & Remley** who operated for a short time in 1869-70. The planes with this imprint are similar in style and wedge profile to E. W. Carpenter. ******

KILBOURNE KUHNS & CO.
Kilbourne Kuhns & Co. was a hardware firm of **L. Kilbourne**, **W. J. Kuhns** and **John Joyce** that was listed in the 1856-59 Columbus, OH, directories. **Kilbourne Jones & Co.** was its successor and was listed, in 1894, with **Ida E. Jones** and  **J. Kilbourne Jones** as retail hardware that continued until 1902. *******

ELISHA/ KILBORN
Elisha Kilborn was a cabinetmaker in Wethersfield listed in account book on March 24, 1752. Example: on a 9 7/8" birch complex molder with heavy flat chamfers, ca. 1760-80. **UR**

S. KILBURN. NO.
Example: on a 9 1/2" birch hollow & round pair with relieved wedges and large shallow flat chamfers; and a 9 1/2" birch skew rabbet with heavy round chamfers on top and heavy flat chamfers on the toe and heel, ca. 1790-1810. ********

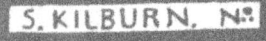

J. KILLAM
James Killam (b. Oct. 26, 1798 in Preston, New London Co., CT, d. May 24, 1878 in S. Glastonbury, Hartford Co., CT) was a Glastonbury, CT, planemaker, active from 1822-60. **James** was the son of **Lyman Killam** (1771-1831) who married **Lucinda** Geer, sister of **Ebenezer Geer** on June 12, 1795 in Groton, CT. In 1816, **Lyman, Lucinda** and **James** moved to Glastonbury, a shipbuilding town on the Connecticut River, by boat. That same year 1816, James purchased land in Glastonbury on the Rocky Hill Ferry Road. **James** built a carpentry shop which was destroyed during the Connecticut River flood of 1936. **James** married **Caroline Holden** on Apr. 4, 1821. His brother **Samuel Killum** (1804-) and his two sons **James Lyman Killam** (1824-1897) and **John Wilson Killam** (1829-1909) were all planemakers. He was listed in the 1850 census, as a planemaker with production estimated at $1,200. The family was involved in feldspar mining, the Glastonbury/ Rocky Hill Ferry operation and shop carpentry. Example: on a size **3/8** boxed bead with round chamfers also imprinted S. Hill, a planemaker from Springfield, MA. **A & B2 *; B, B1, B3 & C *****

A

B

B1

B2

B3

C

J. W. KILLAM
John Wilson Killam (b. Jun. 9, 1829 in Glastonbury, Hartford Co., CT, d. Aug. 1, 1909 in Glastonbury) was the son of **James Killam** and brother of **James Lyman Killam** and a plane maker in Glastonbury, CT. Example: on an 8 1/2" square rabbet with round chamfers and an incuse **4** on the wedge and body, ca. 1845-50. ********

JAMES LYMAN KILLAM
James Lyman Killam (b. Feb. 29, 1824 in Glastonbury, Hartford Co., CT, d. Dec. 22, 1897) was the son of **James Killam** and brother of **John Wilson Killam**. He was listed as a planemaker in Glastonbury, CT, from 1850-58. **No imprint has been reported.**

S. KILLUM
Samuel Killum (b. Feb. 24, 1804 in Preston, New London Co., CT) He was married in Glastonbury, CT. He was listed in 1850, in Durell, Bradford Co., PA, as a farmer; in 1860-80 in Asylum. Examples: on a sash; a size **3** hollow & round pair; and a size **4/8** boxed bead, all 9 1/2" beech with round chamfers, ca. 1835. **UR**

M: KIM
Example: on a 10" beech astragal with flat chamfers, found in Lancaster Co., PA, ca. 1800. **UR**

J. D. KIMBALL
John D. Kimball (b. Apr. 11, 1821 in Andover, MA, d. Apr. 20, 1897 in Boston, MA) was listed in the 1850 census as a cabinetmaker, living with **Samuel W. Abbott,** in Montpelier,

 VT. Example: on a plane made by **Burnham Fox & Co.** of Amherst, MA. **UR**

S. KIMBALL
Example: on a gutter plane and a panel raiser, both 13 7/8" beech with round chamfers, ca. 1820.
 **UR**

W. A. KIMBALL & CO.
W. A. Kimball & Co. was a Lawrence, MA, hardware dealer, active ca. 1875. **William Archer Kimball** (b. Jun. 25, 1846 in Webster, Worcester, MA, d. Apr. 15, 1918 in Edmond, Oklahoma.), in 1916, was in Hot Springs, SD, at the Battle Mountain Sanitarium. Example: on the heel of a **Gladwin & Appleton** size **12** round. ****
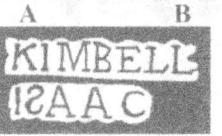

ISAAC KIMBELL
Examples: the A imprint is on a 9 7/16" birch molder with heavy flat chamfers mostly on the side and with flutes. The B imprint appears to be from the same die. Five examples were found together in NH and branded IK on the side, ca. 1790. **A & B: UR**

N. KIMBELL
Example: on a 23 5/8"x 3 1/4" fruitwood jointer with offset tote, diamond strike, a double-iron, and heavy round chamfers, ca. 1810-20. **UR**

KIMBERLY & ROWE
Kimberly & Rowe was a brief hardware partnership in New Haven, CT, in 1874. **Kimberly & Clark**, which operated from 1869-74, was preceded by **Smith & Kimberly**, succeeded by **James B. Rowe & Co.** and the **Rowe Hardware Co.** In 1879, **James B. Rowe** was listed as a salesman for the **Bassetts**. A printed tan label on a 1 3/4"x 1 1/16" reading: ****

MANUFACTURED FOR
KIMBERLY & ROWE
DEALERS IN
CARRIAGE AND GENERAL HARDWARE
JOINERS AND MECHANICS TOOLS
276 CHAPEL ST., NEW HAVEN, CONN.

This location was just up the street from **J. E. Bassett & Co.**, and was on a **W. H. Pond** bead. Example: This imprint is on a **H. Chapin** round. *****
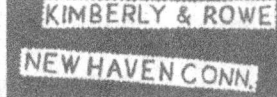

E. KIMPTON
Example: on a 2" wide skew rabbet, struck twice on the toe, and a tongue & groove pair, all 9 1/2" beech with heavy round chamfers, ca. 1820. **UR**

F. KINER
Example: on a 9 1/2" beech large hollow with flat chamfers, ca. 1800, found in Lancaster Co., PA. **UR**

B. KING
Example: on a 7 3/4" beech molder with relieved wedge and shallow round chamfers, ca. 1830. **UR**

B. KING
Benjamin R. King (b. May 23, 1777 in RI, d. Jun. 15, 1860, Mt. Pleasant, Wayne Co., PA) very likely came to Pittsburgh from Baltimore and was listed, in 1819, as working for **Swetman, Hughes & Co.** in Pittsburgh, PA. King was listed in the 1820 Cincinnati, OH census with both **James Swetman** and **William P. Hughes**. He was listed in the Cincinnati directories, as a planemaker, from 1825-44. At some time during this period he was part of **B. King & T. Fugate** and **B. King/ J. Walker** and possibly **King & Cunningham**. ***
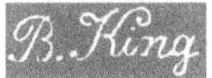

B. KING & T. FUGATE
B. King & T. Fugate was a partnership with **Benjamin R. King**. This imprint appears on several examples suggesting a partnership between these two Cincinnati, OH, planemakers, ca. before 1829. **A & A1 ***
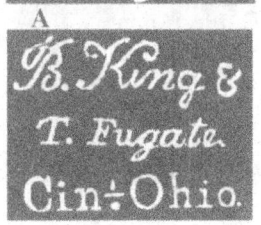

B. KING/ J. WALKER
Example: on a wedge-arm plank plane, suggesting a partnership between **Benjamin King** and **Jesse Walker**, both Cincinnati, OH, planemakers, ca. 1830. ***

C. W. KING
Example: on a beech smoother with a **D. R. Barton** iron. Nunda is located 40 miles south of Rochester, NY, ca. 1850.   **UR**

E. KING
With a location of **COLUMBUS** (probably Columbus, OH) Example: on a 9 1/2" beech size **7**, round, ca. 19c.   **UR**

E. R. KING
With **MAKER** and the location **E. BOSTON**. Example: on a 16" razee jack with a closed tote, ca. 19c.   *****

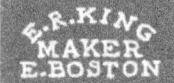

G. KING
Examples: on a 9 1/2" beech molder with heavy round chamfers, two pairs of hollow & rounds, and a toted match plank plane, found in Middlefield, OH, ca. 1820-30.   **UR**

H. & J.W. KING
H. & J.W. King is probably a New York City hardware dealer. Example: on an 8" block plane, dated **1856**, with a **Thistle Brand/ Auburn Tool Co.** iron and the number **48**, which is the **Arrowmammett Works** style number for a smoothing plane; and on a double center bead.   ****

JA: KING
Example: on an unhandled beech plow with birch arms. The screw-arms are huge, a full 7/8" in diam. and 2 3/4 threads per inch, the depth stop hardware is hand wrought iron, and the chamfers are round, ca. 1820. **No imprint is available.**

I x KING (J. KING)
One possibility is **Joseph King** of North Hampton, MA, a house joiner and cabinetmaker who advertised in the *Hampshire Gazette*, on Jan. 3, 1798. He wanted immediately: "a boy, 14, 15 or 16 years of age, as an apprentice to the house joiner and cabinet business, a steady active boy, will find the best encouragement, by applying to **Joseph King**." Another possibility is **John King** who came from CT, to Guilford, VT, ca. 1783, "bringing his set of joiners' tools on his back" as reported in the Brattleboro directory. There is also a **John King** (b. 1777, d. 1835) whose chest of joiners' tools is at the Suffield, CT Historical Society. Examples: the A imprint is on a birch ogee crown molder, with a round top wedge and struck twice on the toe; a 10 5/8" beech Yankee plow with wood thumbscrew, wood depth stop, riveted skate, and flat chamfers; a 9 7/8" beech skew rabbet with a relieved wedge; and a wide beech hollow. The B imprint, a modification of the A imprint, is on a 9 1/2" (heel shot) beech sash coping plane, ca. 1800.
A & B ****

I. KING
John King was listed as a planemaker in the Newark directories from 1835-37, at 29 Pine St.; and in 1837-38, at 23 Commerce St. This imprint is from a three arm, self regulating, beech toted plow plane. The handle has cast-iron supports and the bridge is cast metal with a metal nut in the middle, the front arm is inlayed with a steel strip, with a locking thumbscrew, and the arms have brass tips. This example is very similar in style to the three-arm plows manufactured by **Mockridge & Francis**. *****

J. A. KING
John A. King (d. 1849) was listed as a "colored" planemaker, in directories, from 1835-37, at 20 Academy St., Newark, NJ. At his death, **King** was insolvent and unable to pay his debts. His land was sold at a Sheriff's sale, in 1851, to **Abraham Mockridge**. His planes are similar in appearance to those by **Andruss and Searing**. Example: on a complex molder made by **J. Searing** was overstamped by the this imprint.   ***

J. K. KING
Example: on an 11" birch closed toted rabbet; a 9 5/16" beech skew rabbet; and a 9 1/2" beech side rabbet, all with round chamfers. The side rabbet also has the incuse imprint branded on the side and was found in ME with two planes by **S. King**, ca. 1820-30.   **UR**

J. KING/ JOSIAH. KING/ JOSIAH. N. KING
Josiah King was a prolific New York City planemaker who, together with his two sons, made planes under various names from 1835-1887. **Josiah King's** son was **Josiah Nicholson King** (b. Mar. 19, 1835 in NY, d. Jan. 10, 1884 in NY). In 1876, **Josiah N. King** was listed as "tools"; in 1877-80, "hardware"; in 1882-83 "planes", all at 373 Bowery, NY. Originally on Houston St., prior to 1849, when he moved to Grand and 4th. Ave; in 1851, he was at 383 Bowery; and then 373 Bowery, from 1858-87. In 1870, the business became **Josiah King & Son** with **Josiah N. King** and then **Josiah Kings Sons**, in 1886-87. The 1850 census reported the firm employing two men who produced 1880 planes

worth $1800. **Josiah King** was also a partner in **Davis & King**, probably prior to 1850.
A, B, C, D, E & E1: FF; F *

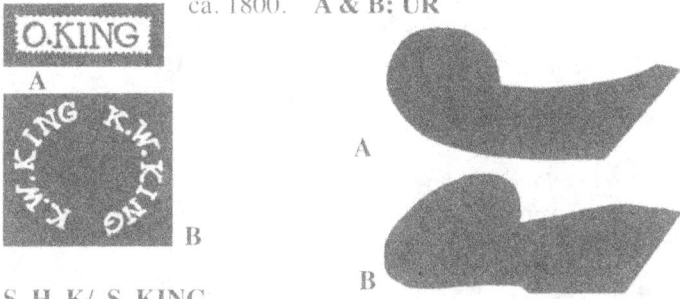

O. KING
Example: on a 9 1/2" maple round; and an 8 7/8" birch complex molder, both with an **I. Sleeper** wedge profile. The B owners imprint **K. W. KING** is on a 9 3/8" birch hollow with a relieved hickory wedge, both with flat chamfers, ca. 1800. **A & B: UR**

S. H. K/ S. KING
Examples: the molders are 9 1/4"-9 7/8" birch and beech, with flat and round chamfers, indicating a transitional planemaker; a 10" beech Yankee plow with wedge arm lock, wood depth stop, screw locked; and a 29" beech bench plane with single irons, center closed tote and 19c style chamfers. Two have been found with **J. K. King** planes from ME, suggesting a possible connection. The initial imprint has the same construction details, wedge profile and imprint design as the full name. It appears on a 9 1/2" beech skew-rabbet with heavy round chamfers, probably from New England, ca. 1780-1820. (**S. King** is not to be confused with **S. King** of Hull, England.) **A & B ***

S. KING
Example: on a 9 1/2" beech ogee molding plane, ca. 1840-50. **UR**

S. R. KING
Example: on an 8" **Tolman** style beech stair/ boat rail plane, ca. 1850-60. **UR**

T. KING
Possibly **Timothy King** (d. 1800) a Sharon, CT cabinetmaker. **King**'s estate inventory includes an extensive collection of cabinetmaker's tools in addition to furniture. Example: on a 10 1/2" beech skew rabbet with heavy round chamfers, ca. 1820. **UR**

THOS. KING
Examples: on a 9 7/16" bead; and a 9 1/2" complex molder, both birch with flat chamfers, ca. 1790-1800. ****

WM KING
William King (b. ca. 1810 in NY) was a New York City, cooper's tool maker, active from 1841-48. He was listed in 1840, as a machinist and from 1855-60, as an engineer, in NY. Example: on a cooper's howel plane. **UR**

KING & CUNINGHAM/ KING & CUNNINGHAM
Possibly a partnership of **B. King** and **Cunningham**. Although the **Cuningham** in the A & B imprint has one **N**, it is probably the same firm. The B imprint preceded the **CUNNINGHAM** imprint, which is apparently the same die with the "KING &" filed off. The **CUNNINGHAM** imprint still retains a portion of the &. The B imprint is from a cove, ca. 1850. **A, B & C ****

S. KINGMAN
Example: on a 13" beech plane that looks like a jack but does not have a tote, with shallow round chamfers. ca. 1830-40. **UR**

A. KINGSBURY
Possibly one of several **Amos Kingsbury** candidates from southeastern, MA. Examples: on a 13 1/8" open toted beech tongue with a birch wedge and heavy round chamfers; and a 9 3/8" boxed double-reed & follow with flat chamfers, ca. 1800-20. **UR**

A. P. K./ A. P. KINGSBURY
Amos P. Kingsbury (b. Oct. 6, 1804 in Spencer, MA, d. 1887 in Scriba, Oswego Co., NY) who married in 1833, in Kingston, MA. The initial group appears on the nose, with the brand name on the side, of a crudely made 10 1/4" beech skew rabbet with an applewood wedge and round chamfers. The initial group has

been reported on a **S. Doggett** plane, ca. 1820.   **UR**

L. KINGSBURY
Example: on a 9 1/2" beech hollow with a birch wedge and flat chamfers, ca. early 19c.   **UR**

IA: KINL
John Jacob Kuntzle (b. Feb. 28, 1779 in Myerstown, Heidleberg Township, Dauphin Co., PA, d. Oct. 26, 1830 in Lebanon Co., PA) was the son of **Rudolph Kinsle** and brother of **Gottlieb Kinsle**. Lebanon Co. was formed, in 1813, from areas of Dauphin and Lancaster Co's. Myerstown, Heidleberg Township became, Jackson Township. **John Jacob** used **Jacob**. Examples: on a 9 1/2" beech complex molder with flat chamfers, mostly on the side; and on a 10 1/8" beech skew rabbet with flat chamfers, both found in PA. The border is similar to that of **Rud Kinsle**, ca. 1800.   ****

J. KINNE
Examples: on an 8" beech coffin shaped smoother with a double-iron; and a round, possibly from western NY, ca. 1850.   **UR**

S. KINNE
Example: on a 8 1/2" beech smoother with round chamfers, ca. 1830.   **UR**

G. KINSLE
Gottlieb Kinzel (b. Sep. 13, 1776 in Myerstown, Heidleberg Township, Dauphin Co., PA, d. 1858 in PA) was the son of **Rudolph Kinsle** and the brother of **John Jacob Kuntzle**. Gottlieb was listed as a cabinetmaker and a coach maker. Examples: on a 9 1/2" beech hollow with heavy flat chamfers; and a 13"x 2 3/4" beech skew panel raiser with **MITCHILL** imprinted on the iron and round chamfers, both ca. 1800.   ****

RUD KINSLE
Rudolph Kinsel (b. Jan. 13, 1749 in PA, d. Sep. 13, 1836 in Myerstown) was the father of **John Jacob Kuntzle** and **Gottlieb Kinzel**. The variation in spelling is typical in 18c rural PA. **Rudolph** was listed as a carpenter and joiner, from 1787-1802. The 1798 direct tax listed **Rudolph** with **Gottlieb Kinsly** as a tenant with house and joiner shop. Examples: on a 6 7/8" beech thumbnail molder with a birch wedge; a 9 3/8" complex molder, both with flat chamfers; and a spinning wheel made in Myerstown, possibly from PA, ca. 1800.   ****

JOHN KINTZEL
Examples: the A imprint is on a 10" beech skew-rabbet, dated **1830**; and a 13" handled molder, dated **1831** with a slight offset tote and size **7/8** on the heel. The B imprint is on a 9 1/2" beech dado by **G. WHITE/ PHILADa**.   ****

A

B

IA. KINYAM (JA. KINYAM)
Example: on a 11" beech self-fenced molder with round chamfers, ca. 1800.   **UR**

W. KINYON
Example: on a 9 1/2" birch molder with shallow chamfers, ca. 1810.   **UR**

E. KIPPON
Example: on a bookbinder's plow, with an iron marked: ca. 1840.   A & B: **UR**

A

M. STANDISH
WARRANTED
NEW YORK.   (B)

J. KIRK
Example: on a 9 3/8" beech quarter round with flat chamfers, ca. 1800   **UR**

W. KIRK
Example: on a 9 1/4" beech complex molder with heavy round chamfers, ca. 1820.   **UR**

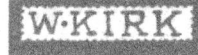

I. H. KIRKLAND
Example: on an 8 1/2" beech narrow round, ca. 19c. **UR**

S. KIRKLAND
Examples: on a 9 1/2" beech single-boxed small side bead; and on a 10 1/8" complex molder, both beech with narrow flat chamfers on top and narrow round chamfers on the ends, ca. 1810. ****

A. KIRKMAN & CO.
A. Kirkman & Co. probably was a New Orleans, LA, hardware dealer. Example: on a M'Master complex molder. ****

T. KIRKUP
Example: on a 9 1/2" beech bead mother plane with flat chamfers, ca. 1800. **UR**

OTTO KLEIST
Otto Kleist (b. 1836 in Prussia, d. Jul. 16, 1895 in Milwaukee, WI) arrived in the U.S., on Jun. 6, 1868. **Otto** was listed in Milwaukee, WI, directories from 1869-92, as a toolmaker, a carpenter, a builder and joiner. In 1884, he was listed as a planemaker; in 1874, a cooper for a brewing company. The imprint **OTTO KLEIST/ MIL WIS** has been reported from a cooper's howel. **No imprint is available**.

G. KLUGH
Example: on a 14" beech panel with double-adjustable fences and intermittent wear strips; and a 9 1/2" beech single-boxed molder with heavy round chamfers, possibly from PA, ca. 1820. **UR**

A. T. KNAPP
Example: on a beech moving filetster with boxwood arms and nuts/ washers, brass depth stop, dated **1854**, ca. 19c. **UR**

H. H. KNAPP
Henry H. Knapp (b. 1813 in MA, d. Jul. 4, 1899 in Byron, Genesee Co., NY) was listed in the 1850 Rochester, NY, census, as a planemaker. No Rochester, NY, imprint has been reported. In 1880, Knapp was listed as a plane maker in Byron, Genesee Co., NY. **A & A1 ****

IOHN KNAPP (JOHN KNAPP)
Example: on a 13" beech panel raiser with an offset tote, dovetail depth stop; and a 9 13/16" beech round, both with heavy flat chamfers, ca. 1790. ****

JACOB KNAUER
Example: on a 9 1/2" beech narrow chamfer plane with tight round chamfers found in Morgantown, near Knaurtown and Knaurs, PA, ca. 1820. **UR**

I. (possibly a J) KNAUS
This imprint has been reported. **UR**

J. E. K./ J. E. KNAUSS
J. E. Knauss probably was a hardware dealer in Waterloo, NY. Example: on a plane made by **Reed/ Utica**. **UR**

KNEASS/ Kneass & CO.
Michael Kneass (b. Apr. 20, 1784 in Lancaster, PA, no death date) and brother **Frederick Feltman Kneass** was a planemakeing partnership listed as **Kneass & Co.**, "plane manufac.", at 8 South 8th. St., Philadelphia, in 1818; On October 18, 1818, the following advertisement appeared: ****

> **KNEASS & Co's**
> **MANUFACTORY OF**
> **CARPENTERS PLANES,**
> **PHILADELPHIA,**
> **HAVE ON HAND,**
> **COMPLETE Setts of HOLLOWS and ROUNDS bench planes, double and single irons warranted.**
> **Moulding Planes of every description.**

The 1819-20, directories lists, **Kneass Michael**, planemaker; **Kneass, Fred F.** "plane &c. manuf."; and **Kneass & Co.** "plane and tool manuf." at 10 South 8th. St. Michael was listed in Philadelphia, as a planemaker, until 1833. **Frederick** was listed in 1828, as a saddler. The New York City directory of 1835, lists **Michael Kneass**, as a plane manufacturer, at 9 King St.; from 1836-40, as a carpenter. The 1850 census lists **Michael Kneass**, planemaker, at the Philadelphia Alms House, as a pauper. Example: the A imprint is on a 9 3/8" beech single-boxed bead. The B imprint is on a 9 1/2" beech round, both with heavy round chamfers, ca. 1820. **A *; B & B1 ****

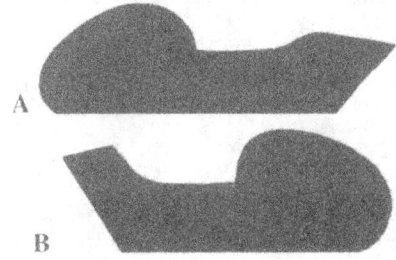

D. KNIFF
Example: on a 9 5/16" beech round with flat chamfers, ca. 1810.   **UR**

KNIGHT TOOLWORKS
Steven Knight is a contemporary tool maker in Portland, OR. Example: with model **50** on heel and dated **06/2003**.   **UR**

W KNIGHT
Possibly **William Knight** (b. 1798) who worked as a cabinetmaker, from 1820-56, in New Bedford, MA. From 1820-23, he was in a partnership with **George W. Baker** as **Baker & Knight**. Examples: on a birch hollow; a beech dado, both 9" with flat chamfers; and on a 10 1/16" birch bead, all with flat chamfers. ca. Early 19c.   **UR**

KNITE
Example: on a 9 1/2" beech boxed bead with heavy flat chamfer, ca. early 19c.   **UR**

KNOWLTON & STONE
Knowlton & Stone was a partnership of **William H. Knowlton** and **Charles H. Stone**, who were Keene, NH, hardware dealers, active from 1870-1900.   ********

I (J). KNOWLES
Example: on a 9"x 1" rabbet; and a 9 1/4" narrow coffin smoother, both beech, ca. 1850.   **UR**

S. KOBEL
Examples: on a 10 7/16" cherry complex molder; and a 9 1/2" beech bead, both with flat chamfers, probably from PA, ca. 1800.   ********

A. T. KOOMANOFF, NY
Example: on a 6 3/4" smoother, ca 19c.   **UR**

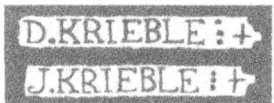

J. KOCH
Example: on a 10" beech medium round with heavy flat chamfers, ca. 1800.   **UR**

J KOONS
Example: on a fancy 10 5/8" beech handled shallow hollow, dated **18*29** with an offset tote, a bench type wedge, an octagonal strike and flat chamfer, possibly from Lehigh Co., PA, ca. 1800-10.   **UR**

P. KOUP
Example: on a 9 1/2" beech bead with heavy round chamfers found in PA, also marked with **J. B. KOUP** on the toe and heel, probably an owner's imprint, ca. 1820.   **UR**

E. F. KRAFT/ E. F. KRAFT & CO.
Emilius F. Kraft & Co. was a St. Louis, MO, planemaker and hardware dealer, active from 1853-60. Example: on a 9 3/8" beech combination tongue & groove plane with shallow round chamfers, ca. 1850.
A, B & B1 ******

J. KRAHOR
Example: on a 9 1/4" fruitwood, full-boxed double center-bead found near New Holland, PA, ca. 1830.   **UR**

I. KREBER/ J. KREVER
Examples: on a 9 7/8" beech molder with a York pitch; on a 13" toted applewood ogee molder; all with heavy flat chamfers, ca. 1800.   A, B & C: ********

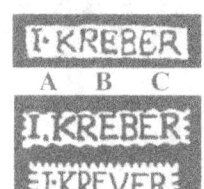

D. KRIEBLE/ J. KRIEBLE
The die was made by the same person, therefore, **D. Krieble** and **J. Krieble** were probably related. Example: on a 24 3/4" beech jointer with a off-set maple tote and flat chamfers, possibly from Lancaster, PA, ca. 1790-1800.   **UR**

CHARLES KROLL
Charles Kroll was listed in the 1857-58 directory, as a planemaker in Utica, NY. **No imprint has been reported.**

P. KROP
Example: on a 9 7/8" beech round with heavy flat chamfers, from PA, ca. 1800. **UR**

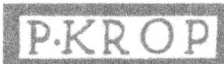

E. R. KRUMM
Emil R. Krumm was a hardware and cutlery dealer in New York City, active from 1869-96. Examples: on a rabbet made by **Greenfield Tool Co.**; and on a 22" beech fore plane by **Taber Plane Co.**. **A & B** *****

L. KRUSE/ L. KRUSE & CO.
Lewis Kruse was a Cincinnati, OH, hardware dealer, active from 1850-59; and was succeeded by **Kruse & Bahlmann Hdw. Co.**, active from 1859-1928. Example: on a double-boxed skew rabbet made by **H. Taylor**. **A, B, B1 & B2** ***

JOHN KUCKER
John Kucker was listed in the Philadelphia, PA, directory, as a planemaker. **No imprint has been reported**.

THE KUHLMANN HDWE CO.
The Kuhlmann Hardware Co. was a hardware dealer in Cincinnati, OH, active in 1889-1900. ***

B. KULP
Examples: on a 9 3/8" maple complex molder, dated **1879**; and on a 9 3/8" maple moving filletster, dated **1862**, both with early 19c chamfers and found in Kulpville, Montgomery Co., PA. *****

D. KUNS
D. Kuns, also spelled **Koons, Kuhns** or **Kuntz**, was listed in Lehigh Co. PA. Example: on a 36" jointer; a 14 1/2" beech adjustable screw-arm, open-toted, plank grooving plane; a 10" wedge-arm plow plane with flat chamfers; an 8" beech coming and going tongue & groove plane with tight round chamfers; and a 9 3/8" beech coping plane with round chamfers, ca. 1800-20, probably from Lehigh Co., PA. ****

CHARLES KURZON
Charles Kurzon was a high grade hardware/ quality tools, located at 97-103 E. Houston Street, New York. Example: on the side of a European beech tongue plane with a paper label of blue, orange on a gold background, ca. 19c. ****

219

L. G. & CO.
Examples: on a smoothing plane and a fore plane, each with an **Empire Tool Co.** iron; a 26" razee closed-toted jointer with an **Ohio Tool Co.** iron; a jack with a **Sandusky** iron; and on a 9 1/2" beech center bead. ***

L. I. & S. CO.
L. I. & S. Co. probably represents a hardware dealer. Example: on a round made by **Samuel Auxer/ Lancaster, PA**. ****

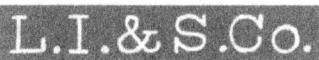

LABAYE N.Y.C/ MATANZAS
Example: on a 9 1/2"x 1/2" beech single-boxed side bead, ca. 1850. ****

JAMES LACEY
James Lacey was listed in the 1827 New York City directory as a planemaker. **No imprint has been reported**.

HENRY M. LADD
Henry M. Ladd was listed in the 1834 Utica, NY, directory, as a planemaker. In 1839-40, Ladd was also listed as boarding with and working for **John Reed**. **No imprint has been reported**.

I. LAHR/ J. LAHNR
The **I. LAHR** imprint is on a 13 1/2" center-toted jack with flat chamfers, struck twice on the toe; a 7 3/4" reverse compass smoother with flat chamfers, struck three times on the toe; and an 8" smoother, struck twice on the toe. The **J. LAHNR** imprint is on a coffin smoother, all beech. ca. 1800-20. A & B: ****

P. LAHR
Examples: on a 15 1/2" center-toted jack; and a 7 3/4" compass smoother, both beech with heavy round chamfers and struck twice on the toe, ca. 1810-20. ****

LAIRD
Examples: molding planes are 9 3/8"-9 7/16" beech with flat chamfers; and a bead with lignum vitae boxing. One example has the **LAIRD** imprint overstriking an **Eastburn** imprint. Planes have been reported with **Green** and **NEWBOULD** irons. Probably a planemaker from NY or NJ, ca. 1800. ***

D. LAISDELL
Examples: on a 26 3/8" beech jointer with a closed offset tote and round chamfers; a 10 9/16" beech dado with tight round chamfers on top and flat chamfers on the toe and heel; and as an owner's imprint on a Yankee plow made by **G. Hawes/ Wrentham**, ca. 1790-1810. UR

R. LAIDLAW & CO.
R. Laidlaw & Co. is probably a hardware dealer. Example: on a 9 7/16" beech reverse ogee & bevel sash plane with a **THOMAS IBBOTSON & CO** iron. ca. mid-19c. ****

G. LAKE
George Lake (b. Nov. 7, 1750 in Topsfield, Essex, MA, d. Apr. 16, 1816 in South Woodstock, Windsor Co., VT) was the son of **Daniel** and **Sara Lake**, who settled in Rindge, NH, in 1767; the brother of **Jonathan Lake** (1761-1846) and the father of **George Bixby Lake** (b. Jan. 17, 1779 in Woodstock, Windsor Co., VT, d. Dec. 2, 1811 in Woodstock, VT) and **John Lake** (1786-1854), both **George** and **Jonathan** served in the American Revolution and were given land grants, in 1780, in Chittenden Township, Rutland, VT. In 1800, **George** was in Woodstock, Windsor Co., VT. Examples: on a 9 1/2" bead; a 9 3/8" wide hollow; and a 9 3/8" complex molder, all beech with heavy flat chamfers and found in VT, ca. 1800. ****

J. LAKE
Jonathan Lake (b. Mar. 18, 1761, Topsfield, Essex Co., MA, d. May 20, 1846 in Springfield, Windsor Co., VT) was the son of **Daniel** and **Sara Lake**, and the brother of **George Lake**. They both served in the American Revolution and were given land grants, in 1780, in Chittenden Township, Rutland, VT. The 1800 census lists **Jonathan**, in Chester, Windsor Co., VT. Another possibility is **John Lake** (b. Jul. 16, 1786 in Woodstock, Windsor Co., VT, d. Dec. 18, 1854 in Woodstock, VT) was the son of **George Lake** (1750-1816) and entered military service, on Sep. 8, 1813. **John** was listed, in Woodstock, VT, in the 1820 census, engaged in manufacturing. The *Woodstock Observer* listed **John**, in 1829-49, as a cabinetmaker; and in 1850, as a carpenter. Examples: on three molders; a fixed sash; and a skewed dado, all 9 1/2" beech with heavy flat chamfers and found in Hartland, VT, halfway between Woodstock and Chester, VT, ca. 1800. ****

T. LAKE
Example: on a 2 1/2" wide beech, double-boxed complex molder, ca. early 19c. UR

J. LAKEMAN
Example: on a 9 5/8" beech bead with birch wedge and tight round chamfers, possibly from PA, ca. 1805-20. UR

H. LAKIN
Example: on a 9 1/2" birch hollow, ca. 1810.   **UR**

R. LAMACRAFT
Example: on a 9 3/8" beech triple-boxed reeding plane with round chamfers, ca. 1820.   **UR**

CHARLES H. LAMB
Charles H. Lamb was listed in the New Bedford, MA, directories, from 1869-72, as a planemaker.
No imprint has been reported.

J. LAMB
Possibly **James Lamb**, a cabinetmaker from Shoreham, VT. Examples: The A imprint is on a 11" birch molder with flat chamfers; and the B imprint is on a 9 1/2" beech with early 19c chamfers. Imprints may be from two separate generations or different persons, ca. 1795-1830.
A & B: ****

J. H. LAMB
James H. Lamb was a brother of **William G. Lamb** and a New Bedford, MA, planemaker, active from 1869-74. **James** was a part of **J. & W. Lamb**, in 1869; and may have been a part of **Lamb & Brownell**, in 1871; and the **Taber Plane Co.**. James made a "Linton's patent" seat-riser; and was a dealer in hardware and mechanic's tools. One plane, was marked with **C. Jensen**'s May 14, 1872 patent.   **A *, B ******

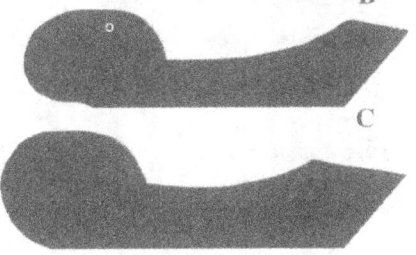

OB' LAMB

Example: on a 9 11/16" birch hollow with flat chamfers, ca. 1800.   **A & B: UR**

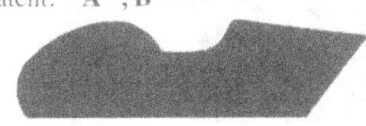

R. T. LAMB & CO.
R. T. Lamb & Co. was a Memphis, TN, hardware dealer, active from 1847-49. Upon **Lamb's** death in 1849, he was succeeded, in 1850, by Lownes & Co.   ********

W. G. LAMB

William G. Lamb was the brother of **James H. Lamb**, and a New Bedford, MA, planemaker, active from 1869-72. **William** was a part of **J. & W. Lamb**, in 1869; and may have been part of **Lamb & Brownell**, in 1871; and the **Taber Plane Co.**
A & B: ***

J. & W. LAMB
Presumably the brothers **James H. Lamb** and **William G. Lamb**, who were New Bedford, MA, planemakers, listed in the 1869 directory. **The Taber Plane Co.** succeeded this company, in 1866, and was in turn succeeded by the **New Bedford Tool Co.**, in 1873 (note the inconsistent dates). Example: on an 8" beech coffin smoother with a **Moulson** double-iron.   *******

LAMB & BROWNELL
Lamb & Brownell was a New Bedford, MA, planemakeing partnership, from, ca. 1869-73; and was listed in the 1871 directory. Possibly with **Charles H. Lamb, James H. Lamb** and/or **William G. Lamb**. Also reported on a rosewood handled screw-arm plow was a paper label: *****

MANUFACTURED BY
LAMB & BROWNELL
NEW BEDFORD, MASS.
EXPRESSLY FOR THE
RETAIL TRADE
N0.----

J. LAMBERT
Example: on a skew rabbet with round chamfers and with a T. HILDICK iron, ca. 19c.   **UR**

D. LAMES
Examples: on a 9 7/8" complex molder with B wedge; and a 10" large bead with intermittent boxing and the A wedge, both beech with heavy flat chamfers, ca. 1800.   **UR**

J. M. LAMPREY/ J. M. L.
Examples: on a 15 1/2" beech open-toted ogee complex molder with round chamfers; a beech square single-iron miter plan; and a toted pump plane with the added **J. M. L.** imprint, all with 19c chamfers, ca. 1820-40.   **UR**

T LAMSON
Examples: on a 9 3/16" birch molder, and a 9 5/16" beech molder, both with flat chamfers, probably from New England, ca. 1785-1805. ****

P. A. LANAUZE

Pierre Alexander Lanauze (b. Nov. 23, 1817 in France, d. Nov. 10, 1871 in New Orleans, LA) was a New Orleans hardware dealer, active from 1845-71. Example: the B imprint is on a 12" beech toted plank grooving plane. A & B ***

G. W. LANCASTER.
Example: on a 16"x 5 1/4" beech crown molder with a centered stubby open tote and round chamfers. ca. 1820. UR

R. A. LANCEY
Roswell Augustus Lancey (b. May 26, 1860 in Leominster, MA, d. 1948, in Townsend, MA) worked in Townsend, MA. Examples: on cooper's planes, ca. 1900. UR

S. LANDIS/ J. V. LANDIS
There are three possibilities: **Samuel Landis** (b. 1819) listed as a lumber merchant in Lower Swatara Township, Dauphin Co., PA; **Samuel Landis** (b. 1825) listed, as a carpenter, from Derry Township, Dauphin Co., PA; and **S. S. Landis** listed in Swatara Township, Dauphin Co., PA, as a pump maker and wood merchant. Example: on a black walnut screw-arm plow with a location **U. S. A.**, and the date **1879**. UR

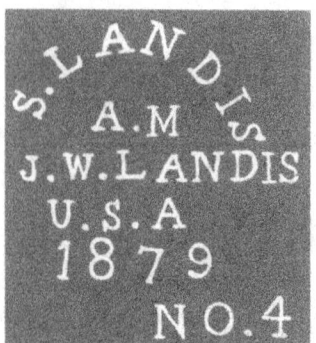

J. LANDON
Example: on a 15 3/4" open-toted birch skew ship's rabbet with nickers and heavy round chamfers, probably from New England, ca. 1810-20. UR

JOS. LANDSCHUTE
Jos. Landschute was probably a hardware dealer, even if marked **MAKER**. Example: on a round made by **Butler** from Philadelphia. In 1904, **Jos.** was listed in Pittsburgh, PA. ****

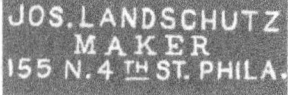

D: LANE
Examples: on a 10" wide round; and a 9 3/4" beech shiplap rabbet, both with an **I. Sleeper** style wedge and heavy flat chamfers, possibly from coastal MA or NH. ca. 1780-1800. ****

J. L/ I. LANE/ J. LANE
Possibly **Joshua Lane** (b. Fed. 9, 1748 in Stratham, Rockingham Co., NH, d. Oct. 28, 1813 in Stratham, NH) who was a cabinetmaker working in Poplin and Fremont, NH, from the late 1770's. Another possibility is **John Lane** (b. Jan. 30, 1758 in Chester, Rockingham Co., NH, d. Mar. 12, 1823 in Candia, Rockingham, NH) who was a cabinetmaker, from Candia, active from 1796-1800. Examples: the A imprint with multiple strikes on the toe of a 13" birch scrub plane with a pegged open tote slightly offset, wide shallow flat chamfers, and the **J. L** initial group imprinted on the heel; a 9 1/4" birch hollow; and a round. The large B imprint is from a slide-arm plow with wood thumbscrews; and a 9 3/4" dado, both beech with an **I. Sleeper** style wedge and flat chamfers; and on a 9 3/8" round with an incuse **J. J. LANE** with shallow round chamfers. The C imprint is on a 9 1/4" beech hollow with small flat chamfers. These imprints are probably from coastal MA or NH, ca. 1780-1810. A, B, C & D ****

J. W. LANE

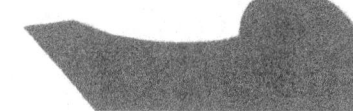

Example: the A and B imprints is on a 17" birch jack with a pegged off-set open tote and flat chamfers on the top and round on the ends. ca. early 19c. A & B: UR

W. L/ W. LANE

Example: on a 9 1/2" complex molder with both initials and imprint; and a 10" molder with imprint only, both birch with flat chamfers. ca. 1800. UR

E L/ E. W. LANG

Example: on a 22" beech fore plane with a centered tote, a single iron and shallow round chamfers, found in NH, ca. 1830. UR

J. B. LANG
J. B. Lang with location **BUFFALO** (NY). Example: on a 9 1/2" beech size **12** round, ca. 19c. ****

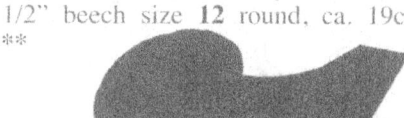

M. LANG

Michael Lang (b. Dec. 3, 1821 in Bavaria, Germany, d. Nov. 11, 1878 in Pittsburgh, PA) was listed as a joiner in 1853; and a toolmaker, hardware dealer, grocer, and planemaker, from 1853-76. In 1880, **Lang** was listed, as a cabinetmaker, in Pittsburgh, PA, at 63 Avery. Example: on a toted boxwood screw-arm plow. **

R. LANG/ ROBERT LANG

Robert Lang, Jr. was a Cincinnati, OH, planemaker and hardware store proprietor, active from 1842-51. The B imprint is from a size **5** round. A, A1 & B. **

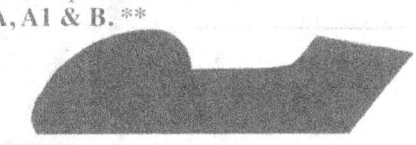

LANG & CO.

Lang & Co. was a Buffalo, NY, hardware dealer, active from 1858-71 with **Michael Lang** the proprietor. **

W. LANGBRIDGE

Example: on a casing molder with heavy flat chamfers, ca. 1800. ****

L & A LANGDON

L & A Langdon was a hardware dealer in Bel Mont, NY. Example: on a 1 1/2" rabbet made by **Greenfield Tool Co.**. ****

P.B. & C.C. LANGFORD

P. B. & C. C. Langford was a hardware dealer from Rome, NY. Examples: on a size **3/8** dado made by **Bensen & Cranwell** The imprint shown is on a 4" toted plane made by **Casey & Co.** ****

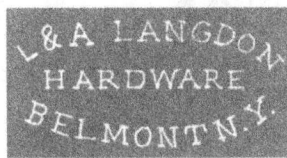

H. A. LANGHORST

H. A. Langhorst was a Cincinnati, OH, hardware dealer 1866-80. Example: on planes made by the **Sandusky Tool Co.** and **J. C. Taylor** **

L. LANPRON

Example: on a 9 1/2" beech very complex molder with tight flat chamfers, ca. 1800. **UR**

B. LAPE

Benjamin Lape (b. Mar. 28, 1820 in Hamilton Co., OH, d. Feb. 27, 1891 in Cincinnati, OH) was a Cincinnati, OH, planemaker, active from 1842-46; in 1846-47 Lape moved to Madison, IN, and was a partner in the plane making firm of **J. S. & B. Lape**. **Benjamin** was listed in the 1850 census, as a planemaker, in Brownsville, IN, living with his mother. In the 1850 census of Manufacturers, listed him as using $150 worth of wood and $50 for plane bits. His shop used only hand power, had one employee who was paid $20/ month and made planes worth $500 that year. In 1866-82, **Benjamin** built and operated the Queen City planing/ flooring mill and lumber yard at the corner of Central and Laurel Ave. Cincinnati, OH, with brother **Jacob S. Lape**. On Aug. 24, 1882, the Queen City Mill burned. In 1887, **Benjamin Lape**, retired, both Madison and Brownsville are within a 50 mile radius of Cincinnati, OH. Example: on a bridle plow with a depth stop marked by **John Wheatcroft**, Cincinnati, OH, active 1842-44. **

JACOB S. LAPE

Jacob S. Lape (b. ca. 1822 in OH, d. 1897 in Cincinnati, OH) was listed, as a planemaker, in the 1843-44 Cincinnati, OH, directory, as a sash maker, in 1846, and as a partner in the plane making firm of **J. S. & B. Lape** in Madison, IN, after 1846-7. In 1850, **Jacob** was listed, as a sash maker, in Cincinnati; in 1860, as a master builder. From 1866-82, **Jacob** was a partner in the Queen City Planing Mill with his brother **Benjamin Lape**. **No imprint has been reported.**

J. S. & B. LAPE

Jacob S. Lape and **Benjamin Lape** were partners in **J. S. & B. LAPE**, a plane making firm, in Madison, IN, after 1846-7. The location imprint **IA** is an abbreviation for Indiana, that was changed to IN, after 1846-50. ***

W. LARGES/ W. LARGE

Examples: on a 10 1/16" beech large hollow with heavy flat chamfers and a **Bishop** iron (**George Bishop** of Sheffield from 1774-86); and a 10 1/4" beech complex molder with flat chamfers, probably from Philadelphia, PA, ca. 1780-1800. A & A1: ****

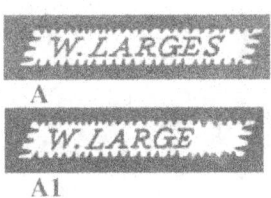
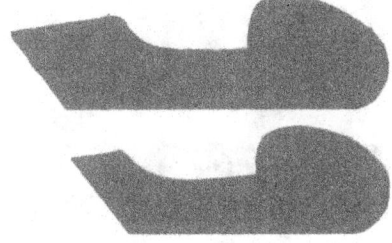

LARRABEE & NORTH

Larrabee & North was a Chicago, IL hardware firm listed as a wholesale dealer in the **G. W. Denison & Co.** account book.

 Example: on the heel of a 13 1/4" double-iron nosing plane made by the **Ohio Tool Co.**, ca. 1860-80. ****

G. R. LATHE
Example: on a 9 1/4" beech double-boxed complex molder with heavy round chamfers, ca. 1820. **UR**

AZEL J. LATHROP
Azel J. Lathrop (b. Nov. 30, 1813 in CT, d. Mar. 1880 in Utica, Oneida Co., NY) was listed as a planemaker in Utica, NY directory, in 1839-40, and probably a journeyman; in 1850, he was listed, as a carpenter; in 1860, a master builder; in 1870, an architect, all in Utica. **No imprint has been reported**.

J. LAUBACK
Jon D. Laubach (b. Apr. 28, 1946) is a contemporary planemaker working at Colonial Williamsburg, VA. He and **George D. Wilson** made 18c. reproduction planes used in the Williamsburg craft shops. **UR**

P. H. LAUFMAN
Philip H. Laufman (d. 1894 in Allegheny Co., PA) came to Pittsburgh, PA, in 1840, and was a part of **Huber & Laufman**, ca. 1850. Philip operated a hardware firm, at 78 Wood St. in Pittsburgh, PA, from 1852-59. From 1859-76 the firm became **P. H. Laufman & Bro.**, at 82 Wood St., with brother **Albert Laufman**. In 1872, it became **Rogers & Laufman**, a tin plate mill in Apollo, PA. In 1881, the firm became **Laufman & Co.** at 122 Sheffield Ave. Examples: on a screw-arm adjustable sash plane by **Casey, Clark & Co.**; on a moving filletster by **Arrowmammett Works**; and a rabbet by **L. DeForest**. ****

JN. LAURON
Example: on a 9 1/2"x 1" beech hollow with flat chamfers, ca. 19c. **UR**

J. LAUTNER/ J. LAUTNER & CO/ JOS. LAUTNER LAUTNER & SON/ LAUTNER HARDWARE CO.
Joseph Lautner (b. Jun. 17, 1836 in Germany, d. Jun. 1911 in Pittsburgh, PA) was a hardware dealer, from 1858-62; as **Joseph Lautner & Son**, from 1862-mid. 60's, in Pittsburgh, PA. In 1874-1913, **Joseph Lautner & Co.**, was at 214-18 Ohio St., Allegheny City, PA. "Wholesale and Retail Dealers in Hardware, Iron, Nails, Glass and Wagon Makers Supplies"; in 1896, **Lautner Hardware Co.**, whose proprietors were **Joseph Lautner** and **H. E. Lautner**. Allegheny City was incorporated into Pittsburgh in the early 1900's. Example: on an ebony, ivory-tipped center-wheel plow plane by **Sandusky Tool Co.**. A & C ***; B, D & E ****

LAW
Example: on a 9 1/2" birch Grecian ogee with heavy flat chamfers, ca. 1800. **UR**

THO: LAWDER
Example: on a 10" round beech molder with narrow tight flat chamfers. Number **7** on the heel, ca. 1800. **UR**

H. LAWRENCE
Possibly **Henry Lawrence** (b. Jul. 3, 1820 in Windham, VT) who was a partner in the firm of **Fisher, Kingman & Co.** In 1833, **Henry** was listed as a cabinetmaker in Woodstock, VT.; in 1835, a part of **Green & Lawrence** who made piano-fortes in Woodstock; in 1850, as a sawyer in Windsor, VT. Example: on a 9 1/4" molder. ca. 1820. **UR**

J. D. LAWRENCE
Possibly **J. Duncan Lawrence** (b. 1854 in NY). The location probably refers to Monticello, NY. Example: on a 22" bench plane with a centered handle. **UR**

P LAWRENCE
Example: on a 9" beech narrow round with round chamfers, ca. 1820. **UR**

T. LAWRENCE
Examples: on a 9 1/4" cove; and a 9 3/4" molder, both beech with round chamfers, ca. 1820. **UR**

J. LAWTON/ J. LAWTON & CO.
J. Lawton & Co. was a Cincinnati, OH, hardware dealer, active from 1849-52, at 312 Main bt. 7th & 8th. In 1866, Lawton was listed as clerk, in Cincinnati O. A & B ****

W+ LAWTON
Example: on a 10"x 1/4" beech round with narrow flat chamfers, ca. 1790. **UR**

I. LEACH
Example: on a 10 3/8" cherry skew rabbet with a birch relieved wedge and flat chamfers, ca. 1780-90. **UR**

J. B. LEAR
Examples: on a sash coping plane; a skew rabbet; and a moving filletster with a brass depth stop, all 9 1/2" beech, ca. 19c. **UR**

J. S. LEAMY
James S. Leamy (b. Mar. 16, 1945 is a contemporary plane maker, restorer and miniature plane maker located in E. Earl, PA. **A & B; UR**

C. W. LEATHERBEE
C. W. Leatherbee Lumber Co. Mill was a lumber co./ hardware dealer with no known location. Example: on a Ohio Tool Co. bead. **UR**

I + LEAVITT
Believed to be (**Capt.**) **John Wheeler Leavitt** (b. Jun. 20, 1724 in CT, d. Apr. 5, 1798 in Suffield, CT) who served in the French and Indian War from Suffield, CT. He was a 1st. Lt., in the 4th. Reg. under Col. Elihu Chauncey, 9th. Co. under Capt. Jonathan Pettibone. **John Leavitt** married, on Jun. 20, 1745, to **Abiah Kent**, in CT. **John Leavitt's** estate inventory included a chest of joiner's tools. Example: on a 10 1/8" birch round with heavy flat chamfers, found in central CT, ca. 1750-80. *********

J. LEAVITT
Probably **Jacob Leavitt** (d. 1759) who was listed as a joiner in Fairfield, CT. **Jacob** was admitted to the Church in Fairfield, on Jun. 1, 1740. **Jacob** was married to **Catee Gold**, on Oct. 18, 1742, in Fairfield, CT. His estate included an extensive inventory of tools. Examples: on a 9 15/16" tongue plane; a 9 13/16" cove; and a 9 7/8" ogee molder with the incuse **J. L** initials, all birch with relieved wedges and heavy flat chamfers, probably from southern New England, ca. 1740-50. *********

A   A1

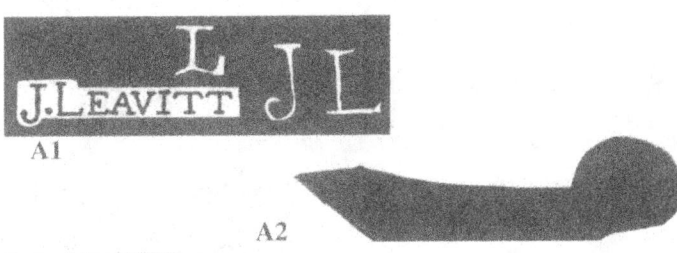
A1

A2

J. A. LEAVITT
Examples: on a 10 1/2" Yankee plow with a birch relieved wedge, wrought iron thumbscrews, wood depth stop and screw applied skate; a panel raiser; and a 9 9/16" beech hollow & round pair with relieved wedges, all beech with flat chamfers, ca. 1785-1800. ********

I. LEE
Examples: on a 10" roman ogee; a 9 3/4" beech complex molders; and an 10 7/8" rabbet, all with flat chamfers, ca. 1800. ********

JOHN LEE
John Lee, age 15, was apprenticed on Oct. 23, 1799 to **William Vance**, as a plane maker. **Lee** ran away in 1803, and was described as "5 ft. 6 in. with fair complexion, nock-kneed (sic), and when speaking fast stutters."
No imprint has been reported.

P. A. LEE
P. A. Lee, with the date of 1868. Example: on a 18" fore plane; on a beech closed centered tote with shallow round chamfers. The iron is marked **A. L. Whiting & Co.** **UR**

N. LEET
Example: on a 9 1/2" side bead; and a 9" molder, both beech with flat chamfers, ca. 1810. **UR**

J. LEFFINGWELL
John Leffingwell (b. May 1, 1755 in Norwich, New London County, CT) and **Joshua Leffingwell** (b. Dec. 26, 1762 in Norwich, CT, d. June 8, 1811 in Hartford, CT) were brothers, builders and architects in Hartford, CT. They were both listed in the 1790 census for Hartford. **Joshua** was also listed in the 1800 & 10 census. They were partners and credited with work on the CT State House, in 1796, the Hartford Bank and the Center Church. **Joshua's** diary and account book for the period, from 1805-08, is in the CT Historical Society, in Hartford. It notes that **Joshua** worked as a house carpenter; constructed houses, disassembled them and shipped them to Trinidad. He would then spend the winter reassembling them on that warm and sunny Caribbean Island. Examples: The A imprint with the location **HARTFORD** is on a beech panel raiser with an adjustable bottom fence, heavy flat chamfers. The B imprint is on a 9 1/2"x 1/4" beech quarter round with flat chamfers, ca. 1790-1800. **A & B *******

A

B

J. LEFFLER

The **Leffler** name is an early pioneer name in Perry Co., OH, where it was found. Example: on a 9 7/8" beech self-fenced bead, ca 19c. **UR**

E C LEIGHTON

Eden C. Leighton (b. 1817 in ME) was listed, in 1880, as a farmer. This name with Winthrop, ME was cast into the brass body of a brass and wood cooper's croze.
No imprint is on the wood fence.

J. T. LELAND

Example: on a 9" beech screw-arm plow, ca. 1840's. **UR**

F. LENDER

Frederick Beno Lender (b. Apr. 30, 1814 in Prussia, d. Feb. 17, 1895 in Cincinnati, OH) arrived in Baltimore, MD, in Aug. 1838. **Lender** was a Cincinnati, OH, planemaker, who worked for **S. Sloop**, in 1839-40 and was listed on his own, in 1862, as a planemaker. From 1862-64, **Lender** was listed in hardware; in 1870, as a retired merchant. The C imprint consists of the B imprint overstamping the **E. F. Seybold** imprint. Another C imprint has been reported overstamped by **Seybold & Spencer/ Cin. OH**. The D imprint is on a double **F. LENDER** imprint overstamping the B imprint of **Schaeffer & Cobb**.
A, A1, A2, B, C & D ******

JACOB LENING

Example: on a 9 3/4" beech small round with flat chamfers. **UR**

LENOX

Example: on a 9 1/2" beech round with heavy round chamfers, ca. 1820. **UR**

A. LEONARD

Example: on a 9 1/2" beech single-boxed complex molder with spring and round chamfers, ca. 19c. **UR**

B. LEONARD

Example: on a Yankee 13 1/4" wedge-arm plank grooving plane with an open tote, round chamfers on top and flat chamfers on the ends, ca. 1800. **UR**

E. LEONARD

The decoration at the end of the imprint is similar to that found on **Jo. Fuller** imprints. Examples: on a 9 1/8" boxed side bead; a skew rabbet; and an unboxed side bead. The last two 9" beech with a relieved wedge and heavy round chamfers, probably from MA. ca. 1820. ********

S. LEONARD

Example: on a 9" beech screw-arm "V" grooving plane imprinted on both the toe and heel, ca. 1850. **UR**

E. G. LEONARD & CO.

E. G. Leonard & Co. is possibly a Cincinnati, OH, planemaker, one example is overstruck by **Thos. Holliday**, a hardware dealer.
A & B: ********

G. W. LEONARD & SON

G. W. Leonard & Son probably was a hardware dealer. Example: on the heel of a 9 1/2" boxed molding plane by **F. Underwood/ C. B. Schaeffer** ********

FRD LEPENS
Examples: on a group of ten 9 1/8"-9 1/4" beech hollows & rounds with relieved wedges and flat chamfers, found in ME, all imprinted with an owner's mark **A. NASH** which may help in locating this maker, ca. 1800-10. **UR**

J. LERCH
Example: on a 13" wedge-lock slide-arm tongue plane with flat chamfers; and a 15 1/8" jack with round chamfers, both beech with offset totes, ca. 1800. **UR**

E. S. LEROY
E. S. Leroy probably was a hardware dealer from Oswego, NY. Example: on a wedge-arm plow, made by **Varvill & Son** of York, England (1829-40). ********

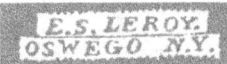

W. LESLIE & CO.
W. Leslie & Co. was a hardware dealer in Calcutta. Example: on a single-boxed side bead with shallow round chamfers, ca. 1850. **UR**

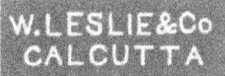

JOHN H. LESTER
John H. Lester (b. 1826 in MA, d. Aug. 5, 1884 in Orange, MA) is thought to have been the **Lester** of **Davis & Lester** of Southampton, MA, and **Lester & More** of Goshen, MA, in 1850. In 1853, **Lester** was at piece worker for the **Greenfield Tool Co.**, in Greenfield, MA. In 1860, he was listed as a planemaker in Chelsea, Suffolk, MA.
No imprint has been reported.

LESTER & MORE
Probably **John Lester** and **Abner C. More**. Example: on a 2" wide handled, skew-blade screw-arm fillester plane with boxwood nuts & washers, ca. 19c. **UR**

W. E. LEVOY
William E. Levoy (b. 1816 in Ireland, d. Mar. 1, 1887 in Cincinnati, OH) was listed in 1842, in Warren County, Deerfield Township, OH, which includes Mason, not far from Cincinnati, OH. The Cincinnati directories list **William Levy** (sic), in 1839-40 at s.s. Court bt. Walnut & Pine; and in 1846, at e.s. Jackson bt. 12th & 13th. In 1843-44, **W. Leovi** was listed as a planemaker, at Race north of Northern Row. In the 1860 census, **Wm. Levoy** is listed as a "plowmaker" probably a miss reading of "planemaker". **Levoy** was a partner with **Hulings & Levoy** in Cincinnati, OH, working date unknown. ********

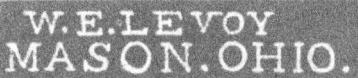

D. LEWIS
Examples: on a block plane with a **Mottram** single iron; and a narrow, unhandled tongue. The B imprint is on a group of four bench planes including two 7 1/2" smoothers, one with **1859** and the other with **1852**, found together in OH, with a plane marked **C. Pierce**, ca. 1850. **A & B ******

DB. LEWIS
Example: on a 9 7/16" birch skew-rabbet with heavy round chamfers. Also with the added imprint **MAKER**, and the date **1839-7-4**, on a 19 3/4" beech jointer plane with a centered closed tote and shallow round chamfers. **A & A1 *******

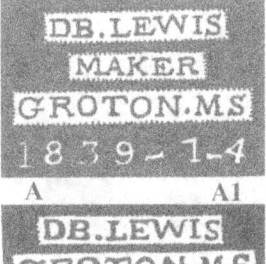

I. LEWIS
Not to be confused with the **I. LEWIS** imprint of **John Lewis** from Leeds, England. Examples: on a 9 1/2" single-boxed bead; and a 9" full-boxed center bead, both beech with flat chamfers, ca. 1810. **UR**

M: LEWIS
Possibly **Moses Lewis** (b. Feb. 12, 1775 in West Greenwich, Rhode Island, d. Feb. 3, 1839). **Moses's** father was **Daniel Lewis** (b. 1745, d. 1809 in Exeter, RI). Example: on a 10 1/4" birch round with flat chamfers; a 9 15/16" birch fixed sash plane with flat chamfers on the ends and round chamfers on the top; a 9 13/16 birch Yankee style plow with wood thumbscrew, riveted skate and tight round chamfers, found in an Exeter, RI, ca. 1780-1800. ********

S. LEWIS
Example: on a 9 9/16" beech cove and bead molding plane with heavy flat chamfers, ca. 1790-1800. **UR**

S. M. LEWIS
Possibly a relitive of **L. Kennedy Sr.** and a partner with **L. Kennedy Jr.** in **Kennedy & Lewis**, Utia, NY in 1825. Example: on a 9 1/2" beech astragal with flat chamfers. Probably **HARTFORD** refers to Hartford, CT, ca. 1800-10. *********

U. LEWIS
Example: on a 9 1/2" beech skew rabbet with round chamfers, ca. 1820. **UR**

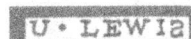

W. LEWIS.
Example: on a 10 3/8" birch skew-ogee molder, possibly modified from a rabbet, with heavy round chamfers, ca. 1800-20. **UR**

LEWIS. WILKES & CO.
Charles H. Lewis and William Wilkes were hardware dealers in Louisville, KY, active from 1848-56. *******

I. LIBBEE
Examples: on a 10" beech hollow; and a 10 1/16" birch molder, both with round chamfers, ca. 1800-20. **UR**

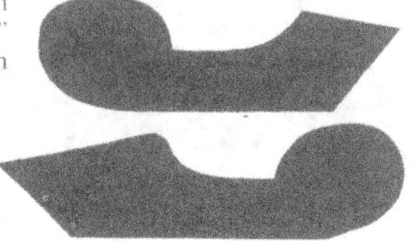

E. LIBBY
Libby is a common name in ME. Example: on a 10 1/2" beech skew rabbet with flat chamfers, possibly from ME, ca. 1790. **UR**

H: LIBHART
Examples: on a 9 1/2" beech molding plane and a wedge-lock plow plane, found in OH, and one or two other examples, found in PA, ca. 1810. ********

J. LIGHT
Example: on a beech wedge-lock plow. **UR**

G: LILLEV (LILLEY)
Example: on a coffin style "forkstaff" 7 1/2" beech with heavy flat chamfers, with a blade made from a file, and found in Lancaster County PA, ca. early 19c. **UR**

A. LINCOLN
Amos Lincoln (b. 1819, Boston, d. Jul. 17, 1870 in Boston) was listed, as a planemaker, in the 1841 Boston, MA, directory. Amos was married, on Apr. 2, 1849, to Mary A. Call in Boston. Amos Lincoln enlisted as a Private in the MA, 6th. Light Artillery Battery, on Jan. 20, 1862 and mustered out on Apr. 7, 1865, in Boston, MA. Example: on a 16 1/4" lignum vitae razee jack; and on a 9" molder, ca. 19c. ********

N. LINCOLN
Examples: on a 10" beech medium hollow with a hickory wedge and flat chamfers; and a 9 1/2" birch cove with round chamfers, ca. 1790-1810. **UR**

C. LIND
Example: on a 9" applewood wedge-lock plow with thumbstone wood depth stop & side iron screw and small round chamfers, ca. early 19c. **UR**

I LIND
Examples: on a 9 11/16" beech round with wide flat chamfers found in MD/ VA area; and a cornice plane with J. Sehner branded on the side, probably from eastern PA, ca. 1800. **UR**

LINDENBERGER
The work of one or more of John Lindenberger's sons, before or after their move from RI to OH, in 1817. John Lindenberger Jr. (b. 1796 in Providence, RI, d. 1874) was listed in the 1820 Kingston Twp., OH, census, engaged in manufacture. Christopher Lindenberger (b. 1798 in RI, d. May 7, 1864 in Delaware Co., OH) was not listed. An E imprinted in front of the LINDENBERGER, has been reported, which may represent Ebenezer Lindenberger. The B imprint with PITT refers to Pittsburgh, PA. One of the sons tested the market for planes in Pittsburgh, sometime between 1815-21, while on the way to his ultimate destination in OH. Example: The B imprint is from two 13" beech bench planes with open slightly offset totes and intermittent hardwood wear strips on the sole. The A imprint is from molders 9 3/8-9 1/2" beech with round chamfers, ca. 1820. **A ***, B *******

C. LINDENBERGER
Christopher Lindenberger (b. 1798 in RI), was the son of John Lindenberger, who most likely learned planemaking from his father and followed his brothers Ebenezer Lindenberger and John Lindenberger Jr., from RI to OH, arriving north of Columbus, some time after 1820. Christopher is listed in the 1850 OH census, as a planemaker, in Porter Twp. In Christoper's household are sons John Lindenberger, age 28, and Christopher Lindenberger, age 23, both planemakers, both born in OH. In the 1860, OH census, Christopher, age 62, is listed as a farmer. **A & B *****

I: LINDENBERGER

John Lindenberger (b. Mar. 6, 1754 in Baltimore, MD, d. Sept. 30, 1817 in RI) was the father of **John Lindenberger Jr.** and **Christopher Lindenberger**. John was trained as a cabinetmaker, probably by his father, **George Ernst Lindenberger** (b. ca. 1730 in Rotterdam, Netherlands, d. Jul. 26, 1796 in Baltimore, MD), a carpenter and joiner in Baltimore, MD. On Nov. 12, 1774, **George** was listed on the Committee of Observation for Baltimore Town, due to events leading up to the Revolutionary War. **John** possibly learned plane making from **Jacob Small**. **John** served in the American Revolutionary War and was present at the battles of Brandywine, Germantown, Trenton, and Princeton. He resigned from the army, on Feb. 3, 1779, and arrived in RI, before 1785. He settled in Providence, in 1786, having moved from Johnfton (Johnston), RI, about 6 miles west of Providence, where he was married and buried. In a 1786 land deed, **John** was listed, as a tool maker, from Johnston, RI. By 1787, **John** was advertising that "he was carrying on the planemaking business". In 1803, **John** advertised for an apprentice. **John** continued planemaking until he died, insolvent, in 1817. His estate inventory included:
- 962 molding plane irons.
- 1500 feet of beech and birch stuff.
- 1/2 "groce" sandpaper.
- 14 float files.
- 391 molding planes @ $.20.
- 59 bench planes @ $.50.
- 2 moving filletster @ $1.00.
- 3 plow planes @ $2.33.

Besides making planes **Lindenberger** was also a blacksmith, toolmaker, taught architecture, traded various goods and accepted country produce as payment. **John's** earlier planes were made of yellow birch and had flat chamfers. One example is a 10"x 1/8" birch rosewood boxed side bead similar in style to **Jo, Fuller**'s. Later examples were made of beech, cherry, and tended to have narrower flat or round chamfers. The italicized style imprint was brought from the Baltimore/ Philadelphia area. There were hands other than **John's** at work that added slight variations. Several planes similar to his have been reported with the **PROVIDENCE** imprint only.

A1: FF, A ***, A2 *****

JOHN LINDENBERGER

John A. Lindenberger (b. 1822 in OH, d. Sep. 11, 1867, Porter, Delaware, OH) was the son of **Christopher Lindenberger** (1798), and the grandson of **John Lindenberger** (1754), and the third generation of the **Lindenberger** planemakers. **John A.** was listed, in the 1850, OH census for Porter Twp., 20 miles north of Columbus, OH, as a planemaker, living with **Christopher Lindenberger**, his father and **Christopher Lindenberger, Jr.** his brother. In 1859, **John A.** operating a plane factory, in Kingston Center, OH. There is a Kingston, OH, located about 40 miles south of Columbus. In 1860, **John A.** was listed as a mechanic. **No imprint has been reported**.

LINDNER & CO.

It appears to be American and could be from AL, CT or MI. Example: on a bead, ca. 19c. **UR**

J. LINDSEY

Example: on a 12 3/4" beech off-set toted large gutter plane, with round chamfers on top and flat chamfers on the toe & heel, and a **James Cam** iron, ca. early 19c. **UR**

J. F. & G. M. LINDSEY

James F. Lindsey (b. 1829 in MA) and **George M. Lindsey** (b. 1826 in MA) were brothers and planemakers, in Huntington, MA, active from 1856-79. They were listed in the 1850 census, as mechanics, in Chester, MA; in 1870, as planemakers, in Huntington, MA; in 1880, **James** was listed, as a planemaker; and **George** as a deputy sheriff. The A1 imprint is on a 30" bench plane.

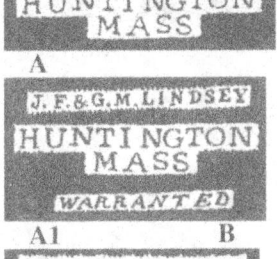

A1   B

B: FF, A *, A1 **

LH LINDSEY

Example: on a 9 1/2" beech filletster with nickers and a side brass depth stop, ca. 1830. **UR**

D. LINES

Daniel Lines (b. ca. 1765, d. Jan. 24, 1837 in New Milford, CT) was a joiner, working from 1790-1805. Examples: on a 12 1/2" handled beech grooving plane with riveted skate and flat chamfers, a 10 3/4" applewood double-bladed fixed sash with flat chamfers; and a 9 3/8" double-boxed small beech complex molder with shallow round chamfers, ca. 1800-20. ***

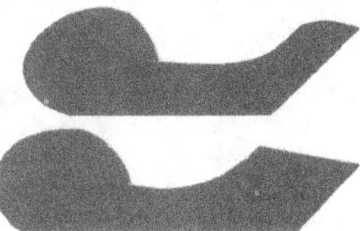

I. LINVILL

Example: on a 10 3/8" beech molder with flat chamfers. ca. 1800. **UR**

C. LITCHFIELD

Example: on a 10" birch small round with a relieved wedge and flat chamfers. The **C. LITCHFIELD.** imprint is the **F. C. LITCHFIELD.** imprint with the F removed, probably from southeastern New England, ca. 1790-1800. **UR**

F. C. LITCHFIELD
Example: on a 27 1/2" birch jointer with a centered closed tote and heavy flat shallow chamfers, ca. 1790. **UR**

LUTHER. LITCHFIELD
Example: on a 9 7/16"x 1/2" beech side-bead with ebony boxing, a relieved wedge and round chamfers, probably from southeastern New England, ca. 1790-1800. **UR**

L. M. LITEL
Example: on a 9 1/2" beech moving filletster with round chamfers, ca. 1820. **UR**

W. LITHGOW
Walter Lithgow (**Llithgow**) (d. Sept. 5, 1813) arrived Oct. 9, 1802 in Philadelphia, PA. **Walter** was among the earliest of the Pittsburgh, PA, planemakers, possibly as early as 1807. His name appeared in the 1810 census, and in Cramer's Pittsburgh Almanac of 1813, as a planemaker with a shop on Market St., taken over by **William Evens**. **Walter** served in the War of 1812 as a Captain and died in 1813, a few months after returning home. His estate included more than 200 "finished and unfinished" planes, "70 reverse planes for making tools", 22 floats, and a quantity of lumber. (see *Planemakers of Western Pennsylvania and Environs* by Charles W. Prine, Jr.) **A & A1 ******

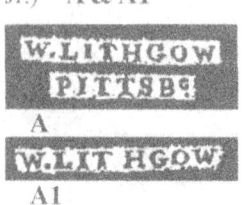

T. LITTELL/ T. ATKINSON
Thomas Littell (**Littel**) (b. Jan. 9, 1800 in Beaver, PA, d. Feb. 8, 1887 in Boise, ID) and **Thomas H. Atkinson** were partners in a plane factory, active from 1838-39, in Louisville, KY. **Thomas** was married on Apr. 27, 1837 in Jefferson, KY. In 1850, **Thomas** was listed in Stark, IL, as a farmer. *******

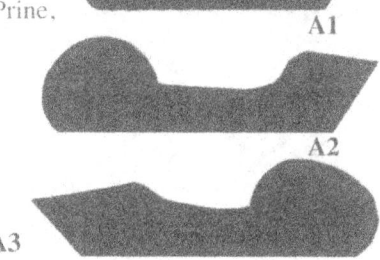

C.S. LITTLE/ C.S. LITTLE & CO.
Charles S. Little (b. 1814 in NY, d. Oct. 23, 1872, in NY) was a part of **Osborn & Little** a hardware dealer and continued the business after **Osborn**'s death, in 1846, as **C. S. Little**, until 1872. **Charles** was listed as a planemaker, in 1857, in New York City. He was succeeded, ca. 1872, by **Charles E. Little**, possibly a son.
A & C **, **B & B1 *****

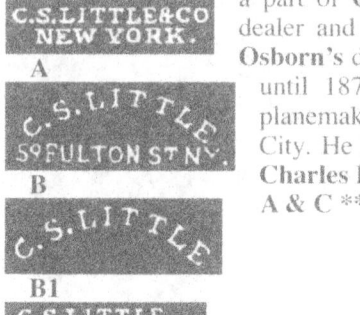

I. LITTLE
Possibly **John Little** (b. 1728, d. May, 9, 1799 in Newburyport, MA) was the father of **Levi Little** and **Noah Little**. Example: on a 9 1/2" beech complex molder with heavy flat chamfers (wedge missing), ca. 1780-90. ********

L. LITTLE
Levi Little (b. Nov. 12, 1770 in Newbury, MA, d. bet. Apr.-Jun. 1802 in Boston, MA) was the son of **John Little**, the brother of **Noah Little**, and a Boston, MA, housewright, tool dealer and planemaker. **Levi** was first listed in the Boston directory, in 1796, as a carpenter, at S. Bennet St.; then as a carpenter's tool maker, in 1798; and in 1800, at Orange Street. **Levi**'s house, occupied in 1798, included his workshop, was described as having two-stories, 936 sq. ft., 11 windows and valued at $900. At **Levi Little**'s death, his shop inventory indicated that he made planes as well as importing them:

- 2715 feet beech.
- 491 feet beech plank.
- 949 plain stocks.
- 518 plain stock jointures.
- crese plains.
- tools made.

There is an entry of 6 doz. planes $24.00, $4/ doz. at wholesale, $6/ doz. retail, $.50 each, or 3/2 each (3 shillings, 2 pence) "old money". In England, in 1796, hollows & rounds in the **Seaton Chest** sold at 3/0. In the 1790's, **L. Sampson** sold small planes from 3/2-3/6. Examples: molding planes are 9 1/2"-10" beech and birch with flat chamfers. Many A imprint planes have the **I. Sleeper** style wedge. Planes with the **I/ COX** imprint (**John Cox**, of Birmingham, England from 1770-1808) were imported for resale. Birch or beech planes with rosewood boxing were probably of his own manufacture. The C imprint has crowned owners initials similar to **Tho. Grant**, **Eastburn** and **H. Wetherel**.
C1 *, **A, B & C *****, **D & E *******

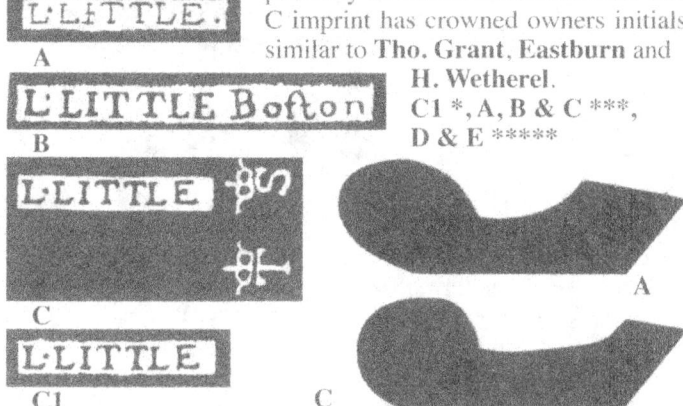

D E E

N. LITTLE
Noah Little (b. Sep. 27, 1772 in Newbury, MA, d. May 22, 1852 in Newbury, MA) was the son of **John Little** and brother of **Levi Little**. He was listed as a housewright, in 1800, and as a yeoman, when his estate was probated, in 1852. Examples: on planes from 9 7/8"-10 1/4" beech with **I. Sleeper** style wedges and flat chamfers, ca. 1800. *

W. H. LIVINGSTON/ W. H. LIVINGSTON & CO. WM. H. LIVINGSTON & CO.
This company was a hardware and cutlery importer and dealer in New York City, active 1840-66. **William H. Livingston** (b. ca. 1810 in NY) patented an ax-handle fastener, on Sept. 25, 1860.
A & A1 *, B & B1 **, A2 ****

A

A1

A2

B

B2

B1

C1

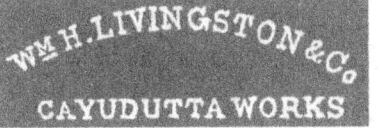

C

JOHN LLOYD JR.
John Lloyd Jr. was listed in Utica, NY, from 1848-52, as a planemaker working for **John Reed**.
No imprint has been reported.

B. LOCK
Examples: on several hollows & rounds; and a complex molder, all 9 1/2" beech with flat chamfers, most have **I. Sleeper** style wedges, found north of Boston, MA. One of the hollows has the B wedge, ca. 1780-1800. ****

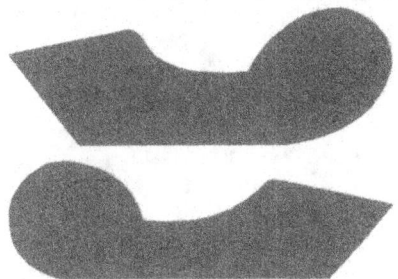

J. LOCK
The **Lock** family were woodworkers who lived in Bennington, NH, near Concord. Example: on a 14" tongue & groove pair. *****

LOCKPORT EDGE TOOL CO.
Lockport Edge Tool Co. operated between 1860-70. Boyd's 1865 Central NY Business Directory carried an ad by **Phineas Smith** as their sole agent. "Manufacturers of superior axes, hatches, hammers, picks, and every description of Cooper's Tools." **Smith** also offered planes in the body of the ad. Example: on a 12" double-iron jack made by **Excelsior Works**, Auburn, NY; and on an **Auburn Tool Co.** dado. ****

E. LOCKWOOD
Examples: on a 9 1/4" single-iron sash with flat chamfers; a 9 1/2" dado; and a 9 1/4" moving filletster, the last two with round chamfers, all beech, ca. 1800-20. ****

I. LOCKWOOD
Isaac Lockwood (b. ca. 1820 in NY) was listed as a planemaker in the Cincinnati, OH, directory for 1846, as an edge tool maker, from 1842-50, as a part of **Lockwood, Lyons & Smith**, in 1851-52, e.s. Broadway bt. 8th. & 9th.; and as a planemaker, in 1852. **No imprint is available**.

LOCKWOOD, LYONS & SMITH
Isaac Lockwood, **Charles J. Smith** and **Joseph W. Lyon** were the partners in this Cincinnati, OH. edge tool and planemaking firm, active from 1851-52, e.s. Broadway bt. 8th. & 9th.
No imprint has been reported.

G. R. LOGAN
Example: on a 9 13/16" birch hollow with relieved wedge and flat chamfers with flutes, ca. 1790-1800. UR

LOGAN & GREGG
Logan & Gregg was a Pittsburgh, PA, hardware company that succeeded **Logan, Wilson & Co.**, from 1857-67. It was succeeded by **Logan-Gregg & Co.** with **George B. Logan**, son of **John T. Logan, George Parke**, and **Joseph E. Johnson**, from 1867-96; and the firm was **Logan-Gregg Hardware Co.**, from 1896-1962. **Logan & Gregg** sold both wooden planes and wood-bottomed transitional planes under its own name and under the trade name **STERLING**, after 1912. ******

LOGAN & KENNEDY
Logan & Kennedy was a Pittsburgh, PA, hardware firm founded in 1831 by **John Thomas Logan** (b. Oct. 1, 1809 in MD, d. Apr. 16, 1871 in Pittsburgh, Allegheny Co., PA) and his cousin, **Robert T. Kennedy** (b. May 9, 1811 in PA, d. May 14, 1875, Pittsburgh, PA), both from Lancaster, PA. **Logan & Kennedy** advertised on Feb. 21, 1832 in the *Pittsburgh Gazette*: "new hardware store, No. 66 Wood Street, Pittsburgh" listing "a well selected assortment of **Union Factory** bench and moulding planes." It was succeeded, in 1848, by **Logan, Wilson & Co.**. Examples: on planes made by the **Union Factory**, **H. Chapin** and **W. Steele & Co.** A ***, B *****

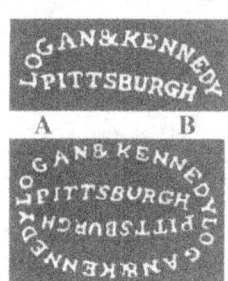

LOGAN, WILSON & CO.
Logan, Wilson & Co. was a Pittsburgh, PA, hardware dealer partnership of **John T. Logan, Philip Wilson** (b. ca. 1820 in PA, d. 1877 in Pittsburgh, PA), and **Edward Gregg** (b. 1815, d. 1890, Pittsburgh, PA), successor to **Logan & Kennedy** in 1848, located at 52 Wood St. It was succeeded by **Logan & Gregg**, from 1857-67. Example: on a **H. Chapin/Union Factory** grooving plane. ****

J. H. LOHR
J. H. Lohr was a Cincinnati, OH, hardware dealer, active from 1858-71. Example: on an **H. & J. C. Taylor** dado plane. ****

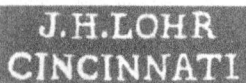

N. C. LOMBARD
N. C. Lombard with the location of **LOWELL** (MA). Example: on a 9 3/8" birch sq. rabbit with round chamfers, ca. 1810. **UR**

D. LONG
David Long was listed in 1820, for Wheatfield, Indiana Co., PA, living next door to **Mathias Long**. Examples: on a sash plane; and a bead with a **HILDICK** iron, both with lignum vitae boxing, heavy round chamfers, found in eastern PA, ca. 1820. A **, A1 ****

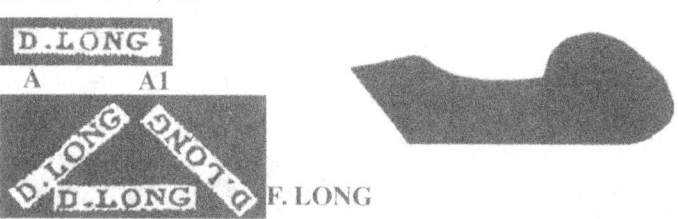

F. LONG

G :

LONG
Examples: the A imprint is on a 10" beech narrow hollow & round with small flat chamfers. The hollow has a **10** inked on the heel. The B imprint is from the same die with the border filed flat and is from a 10" filletster; a 9 1/2" triple lignum vitae-boxed molder; an 8" wedge-locked armed plow with a friction fit depth stop; and a 9 9/16" center bead, all beech with heavy round chamfers, possibly from eastern PA, ca. 1810-30. A, B & C **

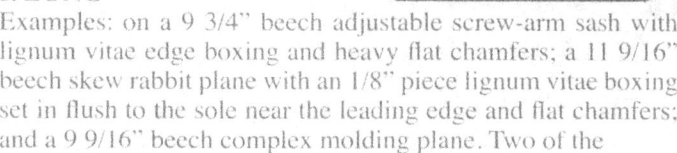

I. LONG
Examples: on a 9 3/4" beech adjustable screw-arm sash with lignum vitae edge boxing and heavy flat chamfers; a 11 9/16" beech skew rabbit plane with an 1/8" piece lignum vitae boxing set in flush to the sole near the leading edge and flat chamfers; and a 9 9/16" beech complex molding plane. Two of the **I. Long** plane irons are marked **WELDON**. The **I. Long** and **G. Long** planes have similar wedge profiles and have been found together in South East PA, ca. 1790-1800. ****

LONG/ I. LONG
Isaac Long (b. 1764, d. 1840), a Hopkinton, NH, joiner, active from 1797-1825, whose probate inventory included four sets of bench planes, 70 molding planes, 6 bench planes, 9 cornice molding tools, and 6 smoothing planes, among other tools. **Long** was connected to **Joshua Morse, Jr.** through the marriage of their children. An **I. Long** hollow & round with the B imprint, was overstamped by **J. MORSE** (incuse), suggesting that **Morse** may have succeeded **Long**. **Isaac Long** is not to be confused with the English planemaker, **I. LONG**, **Jeremiah Long**, active ca. 1770. Examples: the A imprint is from 9 1/2"-9 5/8" beech molders with flat chamfers. The A1 imprint is from the same die as the A imprint but with the **I** filed off and may have been used by a descendant. A & A1 *, B ****

M. LONG
Mathias Long (b. Mar., 1790 in PA, d. Oct. 3, 1857 in Reading, PA) was listed as a planemaker, in the 1850 census for Reading, PA. In the 1887-90 Reading census, **Mathias** was listed as a carpenter. In the 1820 census, **Mathias Long** and **David Long** were living next door to each other in Wheatfield, Indiana Co., PA. One example is on a plane by **Butler**. A & B1.*, B.**, B2 & B3 ***

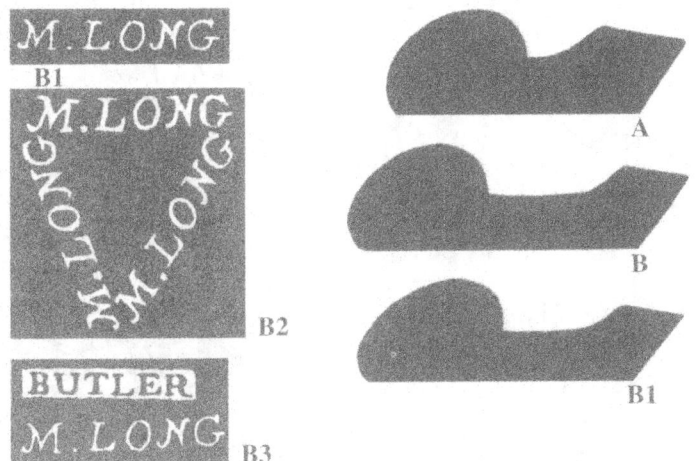

O. LONG

Example: the A imprint is on a 9 9/16" beech complex molder with flat chamfers, found in Salem, MA. The B imprint is on a plane by **T. J. M'Master/ Auburn/ NY**, as an owner's imprint, ca. 1800.

A & B; UR

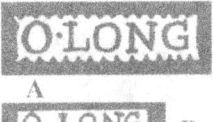

I. LONGLEY

Example: on a skew rabbet, and a narrow dado, both 9 1/2" beech with heavy round chamfers, ca. 1820. **UR**

D. LOOMIS

Believed to be **Daniel Loomis** (b. Oct. 29, 1798, d. Sep. 11, 1833 in Shaftsbury, Bennington Co., VT) who was listed from 1817-30 as a cabinetmaker located in Shaftsbury, VT, in 1820; and in Bennington, VT, in 1830. Example: on a 15 1/4" beech panel raiser with a diamond strike, offset tote, and round chamfers, ca. 1820. **UR**

J. T. LOOMIS

Joseph Talcott Loomis (b. Jan. 9, 1810 in Southwick, MA and bapt. Mar. 11, 1810 in Granby, CT, d. Apr. 7, 1874 in Hartford, CT) was listed in the 1850 census as a "plain maker," active from 1847-63. From 1866-74, **Loomis** was listed as clerk, in Hartford, CT. ******

A. LORD

Abraham Lord (b. Apr. 1, 1805 in Ipswich, MA, d. Mar 19, 1888 in Ipswich, MA) was listed, in 1855, as an Ipswich, MA, cabinetmaker. From 1870-80, **Abraham** was a farmer, in Ipswich. Example: on a pump plane. *********

C. LORD

Examples: on a 10 7/8" beech narrow dado with round chamfers and a molded shoulder; and on a 9 1/2" complex molder with flat chamfers, ca. 1800-20. **UR**

C. D. & O. H. LORD

C. D. & O. H. Lord was listed as a Norton, MA, planemaker, active in 1875. **No imprint has been reported**.

D: LORD

Possibly **Daniel Lord** (b. Oct 15, 1767, Essex Co., MA, d. Feb. 15, 1844 in Ipswich, MA) who was an Ipswich, MA, cabinetmaker, active in 1790. Example: as an owner's imprint on a rabbet made by **I. Sleeper**; and on a 9 3/4" bead; a 9 13/16" and 9 3/4" complex molders, all birch with heavy flat chamfers, ca. 1790. **UR**

J. LORD

Judah Lord (b. 1802 in VT, d. before 1880 in Watertown, NY) was a Watertown, NY, planemaker in Juellville, North Watertown, from 1832-34, when **Orange, Wood & Co.**, a sash & window shop, bought out **Judah Lord's** tool shop and continued making tools. **Judah Lord** also had a custom gun shop. He was listed in the 1850 census, as a machinist. In 1870, **Lord** was listed as "retired manufacturer". He was also part of **Lord & Ransom**, ca. 1850. **A *, B & B1 *****

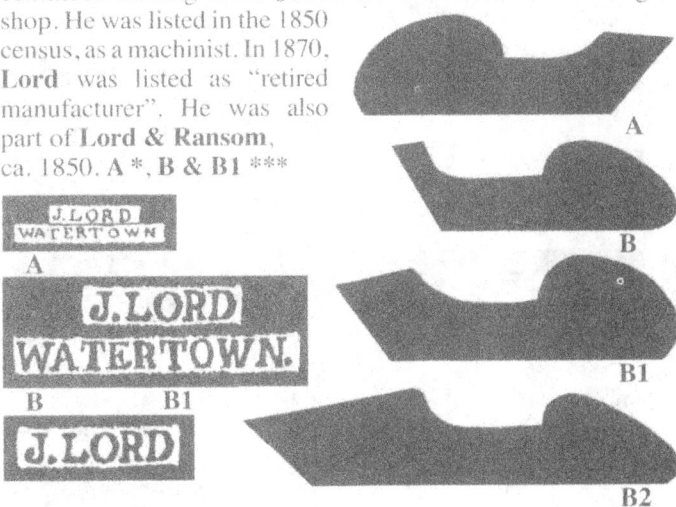

J. D. LORD

J. D. Lord is possibly an owner. The A1 imprint is on a molder by **S. Cumings** in Providence from 1828-33. Example: on a 15 13/16"x 2 15/16" beech shallow hollow with flat chamfers, ca. 1810.

A & A1; UR

M. L. LORD
Example: on a 9 1/2" beech medium round with a "wood blade", ca. 1850-60. **UR**

LORD & RANSOM
Lord & Ransom were listed in the 1850 census, as a planemaker, in Watertown, NY, with three employees and making tools and patterns worth $2000. The principals were **Judah Lord** and **John F. Ransom**. No imprint has been reported.

D. LORING
Examples: the A imprints are on 9 3/4"-10" birch molders with relieved wedges and heavy flat chamfers, ca. 1790. The B imprints are on 9 1/2" beech with round chamfers and probably represent a second generation, probably from New England, ca. 1820. *****

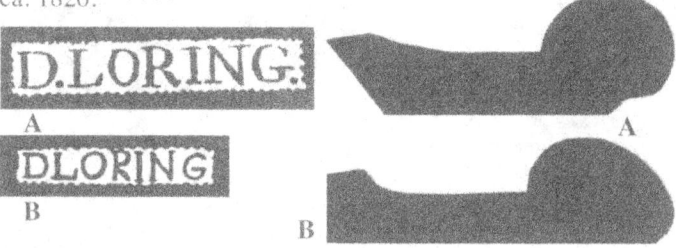

D. LOSE
Example: on a 15 3/8"x 3 3/8" beech fenced water pipe plane from Centre Hall, Centre Co., PA. Also as an owner imprint on a **John Bell**, Philadelphia plane. **UR**

E. LOSEY
Example: on a 9 1/2" beech molding plane with heavy round chamfers, ca. 1830. **UR**

A + LOTHROP
Examples: on a 9 1/2" birch large hollow with shallow round chamfers, ca. 1820-30. **UR**

E. R. LOTT
E. R. Lott was a hardware dealer located at 785 S. Halsted St., Chicago, IL. Example: on a beech miter-jack plane (approx 33 degree) razee style without a chip breaker and round chamfers made by and iron marked **Ohio Tool Co.**, ca. 1850-70. ****

C. LOUD
Caleb Loud, Jr. (b. Oct. 5, 1772 in Weymouth, MA, d. Jun. 11, 1839 Westhampton, Hampshire Co., MA) was orphaned, at age 10, when his father drowned. **Caleb** went to live with his uncle in Easthampton, MA, where he learned carpentry and joinery from **Ezekiel Baldwin**. After a short time working as a carpenter, in Boston and Weymouth, he returned to Easthampton, MA, in 1796. He was "a skillful mechanic, the first to introduce the square rule in framing buildings in place of the old scribe rule, or cut and try." He built churches, courthouses and other public buildings. **Loud's** second son, **Francis Loud** was a carpenter, builder and mechanic. His fourth son, **Caleb III Loud** was a carpenter, millwright and a builder of churches. Examples: on a 13 1/4" birch adj. fenced friction-fit rabbet with a nicker and open offset beech tote; a 9 3/4" birch large astragal bead with a relieved wedge; and a 9 1/4" complex molder with round chamfers, both with heavy flat chamfers, **C. LOUD** and **C. LOUD, Jr.** imprints, ca. 1790-1810. *****

C. LOUD JR.
Caleb Loud, Jr. or most likely **Caleb Loud III** (b. Jan. 24, 1809 in MA), son of **Caleb Loud, Jr.**, who lived in Westhampton, MA, and was a carpenter, millwright, and builder of churches, in Loudville, MA, which was named for him. Example: on a 9 3/16" beech ogee; and a 9 1/4" complex molder with round chamfers, with both the **C. LOUD** and **C. LOUD, Jr.** imprints, ca. 1830. *****

F. LOUD
Francis Loud (b. Sept. 20, 1803 in Easthampton, MA., d. Aug. 25, 1873 in MA, killed when he was thrown from a carriage), the second son of **Caleb Loud, Jr.**, who was a carpenter, builder and mechanic. The **Loud** family tool chest has recently come to auction including the embossed die stamps of **C. LOUD** and **F. LOUD**, one float and two mortise chisels. Examples: on a side rabbet; a single-boxed complex molder; a coping plane; a round; two astragals; and a bead, all 9 1/2" beech with shallow round chamfers. This imprint is on a slide-arm plow plane made by **D. Copeland**, ca. 1830. ****

G. L/ G LOUDON
Example: on a 15" birch shallow backing-out jack plane with a double **Butcher** round top iron, and an 8" beech coachmaker's compass bottom round. stamped twice on the toe, both with shallow round chamfers, ca. 1830. **UR**

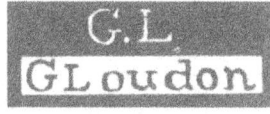

D. LOUGEE
Example: on a 9 3/8" birch coping plane with round chamfers, ca. 1820. **UR**

LOUISVILLE COOPERAGE
Possibly a hardware store/ dealer. Examples: on a 9 1/2" beech side bead; a screw-arm plow; and jack plane, ca. 19c. **UR**

J. LOVECRAFT
J. Lovecraft from Rochester manufactured on a 33" coopers jointer for **Stevens & Co.**, ca. 19c. ****

D: LOVEJOY

Daniel Lovejoy (b. 1827) was a Lowell, MA, planemaker, active from 1870-71, who was listed earlier in the 1850 census as a Lowell blacksmith. This imprint was probably from an earlier generation. Examples: on a 15 3/4"x 5 3/4" cornice plane found in a barn, in Storrs, CT; a 22" birch jointer; a 15 9/16" beech gutter plane; and a 9 1/2" beech large unboxed bead, all with heavy round chamfers; and on a 9 5/8" beech having plane with flat chamfers, ca. 1800-20. ****

H. LOVEJOY

Hubbard Lovejoy (b. July 10, 1807 in Wayne, ME, d. Oct 22, 1869 in Fitchburg, MA) was a house joiner, carpenter, builder and architect, active from 1830-68, in Wayne; and then Auburn, ME. Between 1848-50, together with **Wm. Burgess**, Lovejoy manufactured doors, sash and blinds. In 1862-63, **Lovejoy** was an Architect in Portland, ME; in 1864, he was an Architect and builder, in Lewiston; in 1868, an Architect in Lowell, MA. Example: on a 28" jointer; and a screw-arm plow, ca. 1840-50. ***

J. LOVELL

Jacob Lovell (b. 1829, d. Feb. 14, 1882 in Cummington, MA, from injuries sustained when he fell down a flight of stairs at his factory and a box of planes, he was carrying, fell on top of him) was listed, as a wood turner, in the Goshen, MA, 1850 census; as a merchant, in the Cummington, MA, in 1860; and as a planemaker, in Cummington, MA, in 1870 & 80. He was married to the sister of **Hiram Barrus** and there is a possible tie to **J. Hussey**, also of Cummington, MA. He first worked for the **Union Tool Co.**; and then for himself. In the diary entry from June 21, 1880, **Lovell** complained that he had no water power, "cannot run the shop... half the time."
A *** & B *****

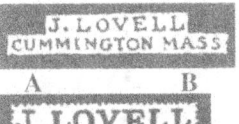
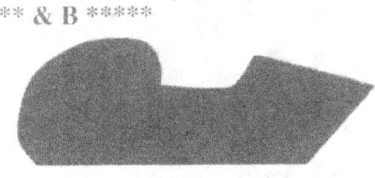

LOVELL & CO.

Lowell & Co. was a Boston, MA, hardware dealer whose working dates are unknown. ****

W. LOVLAND

Examples: the A imprint is on a 9 1/2" small lignum vitae boxed bead, found in upstate NY. The B imprint is on a 9 1/2" beech coping plane, both with shallow round chamfers, ca. 1830.
A & B ***

A. LOW

Asa Ward Low (b. 1791 in ME, d. 1831 in Warren, OH) made planes, furniture, bricks, and possibly dental work in Warren, OH, ca. 1820-31. In 1815, **Low** built a saw mill in Bloomfield. The 1820 census for Warren, OH, listed Low, as a cabinetmaker and manufacturer of bench and molding planes of every description, employing two men with total annual wages of $200, and the annual value of goods manufactured as $1000.
Example: on a 9 9/16" beech 3/8" round. **

E LOWELL

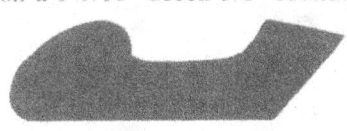

Example: on a 11 1/2" beech rabbet with a skewed iron and flat chamfers, ca. 1800. **UR**

R. LOWELL

Example: on a 9 1/2" beech curved rabbet plane, ca. 1850. **UR**

LOWELL PLANE & TOOL CO.

The **Lowell Plane & Tool Co.** made wooden bench planes with cast iron tops based on the May 27, 1856 and June 23, 1857 patents held by Thomas P. Worrall. (see **Multi-Form Molding Plane Co.**) The firm was active in Lowell, MA, from 1856-58.
A, A1, B & B1; **UR**

C. LOWER

Examples: on a 9 5/8" molder with four interrupted lignum vitae boxing strips; and a 9 3/4" quarter round, both with flat chamfers, ca. 1810. **UR**

LOWNES & CO.

Henry Lownes (d. 1857) operated a Memphis, TN, hardware Company. **Lownes** was an employee of, and successor to **R. T. Lamb & Co.**; in 1849, Holyoake-Lownes & Co.; in 1851, Lownes, Beckman & Co.; in 1854, Lownes, Orgill & Co.. It was succeeded upon Lowne's death, in 1857, by Orgill Bros. & Co. ***

LOWNER ORGILL & CO.

Lowner Orgill & Co. was the successor to **Lownes, Beckman & Co.**; after 1854 and upon **Lowne's** death, in 1857, by **Orgill Bros. & Co.** Example: on a size **6/8** beech side bead, ca. 19c. ****

SL. LOYD
Example: on a 9 1/4" beech large hollow with flat chamfers, ca. 1800. **UR**

E. & S. LUCE

Examples: on a smoother; and a 16" jack plane, ca. 1850. ****

JOHN S. LUNNAGAN
John S. Lunnagan was part of **Hubbell & Lunnagan** in 1842-43. **Lunnagan** was, a planemaker, at 23 Catherine St., New York City, from 1843-45, the same address as **Kennedy & White** earlier. The 1847-48 directory listed **Lunnagan**, at 48 Hamilton St.; in 1854-57, **Lunnagan** was again listed, as a planemaker, at 346 Third St. **Lunnagan** was listed as a Private in the Civil War in 1st. Reg. New York Marine Artillery, Co. G. **No imprint has been reported.**

J. LURS

Example: on a tongue plane with wide flat chamfers, possibly from PA, ca. 1800. **UR**

J. LURUE

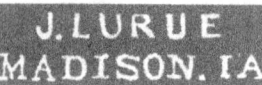

Example: on a plow, ca. 1850. **UR**

H. LUTTGEN
Herman H. Luttgen (b. 1838 in Germany, d. Sep. 1868 in Brooklyn, NY) was a hardware dealer at 194 Grove, in Jersey City, NJ, active from 1864-66. Examples: on a skew rabbet by **G. W. Dennison & Co.**; on a sash plane; and a hollow, the last two by **Shiverick**. *

I. LUXFORD
Example: on a 9 3/8" beech boxed complex molder with flat chamfers, ca. 1800. **UR**

H. LYFORD
Example: on a 9 1/8" complex molder, ca early 19c. **UR**

B. LYMAN
Benjamin Lyman (b. May 8, 1780, d. Nov. 26, 1858 in Manchester, CT) was a farmer and carriage maker. **Benjamin** married, in 1805, and settled at "the Green" in Manchester, half a mile west of his father's, on the Hartford and Providence Turnpike. **Benjamin** represented Manchester in the CT State Legislature. In the 1850 census, **Benjamin** and his youngest son **Charles**, age 16, were both listed as "waggan makers". Examples: on a 9 5/16" beech complex molder with heavy flat chamfers and a cherry or apple wedge; an 12 1/8" birch panel raiser with an apple or cherry open offset tote, **NEWBOLD** iron, diamond lignum vitae strike and flat chamfers; an 13 1/2" birch nosing or spar plane with open cherry or apple offset tote, a **NEWBOLD** iron, wood strike, round topped wedge and flat chamfers; on a 32"x 3" birch joiner with offset closed tote, round top wedge, iron strike, and small flat chamfers. The front of the throat and bottom of the wedge of the nosing plane and joiner are carved with "linen folds", ca. 1800-10. *****

D. LYMAN
Example: on a 10 1/8" beech Yankee plow with heavy flat chamfer, square arms held with wood screws and a iron rod depth stop, ca. 1790-1800. **UR**

H. B. LYMAN

Example: on an 8" beech coffin smoother plane, ca. 19th. ****

C+ LYNCH
Example: on a 10" beech complex molder with heavy flat chamfers and from PA, ca 1800.. **UR**

J. P. LYNE & SON
John. P. Lyne & Son was probably a hardware dealer in Carlisle, PA. Example: on a rosewood plow plane with ivory tips and nuts made by the **Greenfield Tool Co.**; a complex molder with an **Auburn Plane Co.** style wedge and **141** imprinted on the heel, the 1869 **Auburn** catalog inventory number; and on a 22"x 3 1/8" beech fore plane with **M. B. Tidey**'s patented iron throat insert.
B ***, A ****

G. LYON
Example: on a 10" beech complex molder with a birch shallow pitch long relieved wedge and tight round chamfers, ca. 1820. **UR**

J. W. LYON
Joseph William Lyon (b. Dec. 4, 1810, d. 1855 in OH) was listed as a Cincinnati, OH, planemaker, in the 1834 Cincinnati directory, active from 1834-53. **Lyon** was a partner in **J. H. Hall & J. W. Lyon**, in 1839-40; **Lyon, McKinnell & Co.**, from 1842-46; **Lyon & Smith**, from 1849-53; and in **Lockwood, Lyon & Smith**, from 1851-52. *

J. W. LYON/ J. H. HALL
A Cincinnati, OH, plane making partnership of **Joseph W. Lyon** and **John H. Hall**, active from 1839-40. *

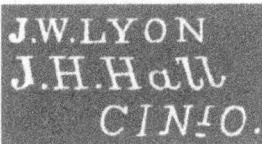

J. W. LYON/ McKINNEL
Joseph W. Lyon and **Henry McKinnell** and/or **William McKinnell**. This imprint is possibly a variant of the **Lyon McKinnell & Co.** imprint. Example: on a **J. Creagh** plane. **

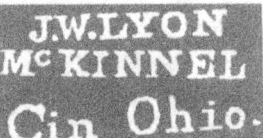

L. LYON/ L+L
Example: on a 10" beech hollow with flat chamfers, ca. 1790-1800. **UR**

W. LYON
Examples: on a complex molder; and a medium hollow, both 10" birch with relieved wedge and flat chamfers, probably from New England, ca. 1770-1800. **UR**

LYON & CO.
James Gouge was listed as being with **Lyon & Co.**, a Cincinnati, OH, planemaker, active from 1839-40. **Joseph Lyon**, the most obvious candidate, was part of **Hall & Lyon** in these years. **No imprint has been reported**.

LYON & KELLOGG
Lyon & Kellogg was probably a hardware dealer. Example: on the heel of a boxed skew rabbet made by the **Phoenix Factory/ W. Warner**. ****

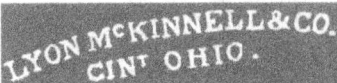

LYON, McKINNELL & CO.
Joseph W. Lyon and either **William McKinnell**, **Charles McKinnell** or **Henry McKinnell** were plane and edge tool manufacturers in Cincinnati, OH, active from 1842-46. They were successors to **John Creagh**, in 1842. **

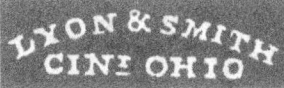

LYON & SMITH
Joseph W. Lyon and **John H. Smith** (b. Jan. 20, 1817 in NJ, d. Jul. 1, 1893 in Hamilton, Butler Co., OH) of Cincinnati, OH, made and sold planes, edge tools and hardware, from 1849-53. In 1850, they reported manufacturing 14,000 planes worth $12,000, edge tools worth $14,000, and employing 20 workers who were paid $6000. **

M & B
Probably a hardware dealer. Example: on a 5/16" single-boxed complex molder with a **No. 160** style number on the heel, made by the **Greenfield Tool Co.**, ca. 19c. **UR**

MCD
Mark C. Donovan is a contemporary planemaker from Portland, OR and apprenticed to **Leon Robbins**. Example: on a 4 1/2" laminated hardwood (walnut & jatoba) **Luthier's** smoothing plane, with a 5/8" **Starrett** tool steel blade, and a birdseye maple wedge. One example is dated **2004**. **UR**

M. P. & CO.
Example: on a plane made by **J. Kellogg**, Amherst, MA **UR**

R. MACCOMB
Example: on a 9 5/8" beech left-hand snipe bill plane with lignum vitae boxing, ca. 1850. **UR**

R. W. MACCUBBIN
Robert W. Maccubbin (b. Nov. 1, 1812, d. aft. 1900 in Baltimore, MD) was a Baltimore, MD, planemaker listed in 1840, from 1845-58 and 1865-77. **Robert** married on Jun. 7, 1835, in Baltimore, MD; was part of **Kendall & McCubbin** from 1837-39; from 1870-89, he was listed as Collector; from 1891-95, he was a Broker. **A & B** *

G. R. MACDONALD
Gordon R. MacDonald (b. ca. 1896 in Canada, arrived in US in 1912) was an Erie, PA, violin maker. Example: on an instrument maker's plane. **No imprint is available**.

MACEY & HAMILTON
Macey & Hamilton was a hardware dealer in Nashville, TN, from 1855-57. Example: on a beech side bead with **37** on the nose, an **Ohio Tool Co.** style number. ****

MACK
Example: on a 9 3/8" single-boxed beech bead with round chamfers, ca. 1840-50. **UR**

A. W. MACK
Alford W. Mack, the brother of **John Bouton Mack** (b. ca. 1811 in PA) was a planemaker in Brooklyn Twp., Susquehanna Co., PA, active ca. 1840. He is interred in a tiny Brooklyn cemetery with **John B. Mack, Justice Kent, Ebenezer Gere,** and **Christopher Gere**. Examples: on several 9 3/8" beech single-boxed complex molders up to 3 1/4" wide, two with the date **1838** with star bursts and shallow round chamfers. **A, A1 & A2 *****

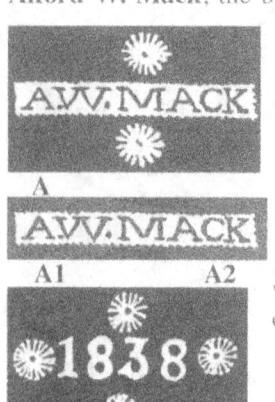

J. B. MACK
John Bouton Mack (b. ca. 1811 in PA) the brother of **A. W. Mack**, was a planemaker in Brooklyn Twp., Susquehanna Co., PA, active ca. 1836. **A & B ****

MACK & CO.
William R. Mack and **Royal L. Mack** joined **D. R. Barton Co.**, in Rochester, NY, in 1865, providing needed capital. In 1874, **David R. Barton** and his sons, **Charles Barton** and **Edward Barton**, left to organize a new firm, **D. R. Barton Tool Co.**. The **Macks** then changed the firm name to **Mack & Co.** but retained **D. R. Barton & Co.** as their trade name. The **D. R. Barton Tool Co.**, failed in 1879, and the **Macks** took it over as **Mack & Co.**; in 1882, as an edge tool manufacturer, consisted of **William W. Mack, Royal L. Mack, William R. Mack,** and **Amos P. Mack**, located at 120 Mill. In 1887, **Mack & Co.** was at 18 Brown's Race, ft. Platt. **Mack & Co.** was in business, until 1939, using the **D. R. Barton** trademark. **No planes have been reported with a Mack & Co. imprint** although cutlery and ice tools have been found with this imprint.

MACKEREL
Example: on a pair of 9 1/2" beech narrow hollow & round planes with birch wedges and a birch panel raiser, all with flat chamfers. The irons were marked **UTTERWORTH**. ca. 1800. **UR**

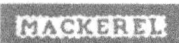

MACKRELL
Example: on a 13 1/2" birch sash, modified from a skew panel raiser, with offset tote, round top **GREEN** iron and heavy flat chamfers; and a 9 3/4" ogee molder, ca. 1800. **A & B: UR**

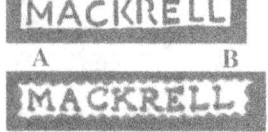

J. F. MACNEIL
John MacNeil (McNeil) (b. Aug. 1854 in NY, d. aft. 1915 and bef. 1938 in Poughkeepsie, NY) was listed in the 1880 census for Poughkeepsie, NY, as a toolmaker. Example: on a quarter round, dated **1881**; a cooper's chiv, dated **1878**; a molding plane, dated **1879**; a miter plane, dated **1880**; a table plane, dated **6-20 1883**; and a quarter round, dated **6-21 1883**. The last two dates included both the month and day. In 1900 & 15, **MacNeil** was listed as a machinist.
A, B & B1 ***

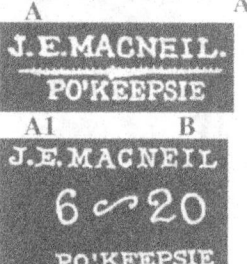
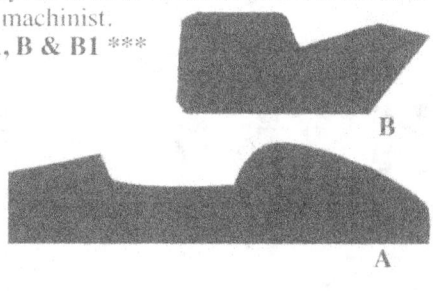

MACOMBER, BIGELOW & DOWSE
Macomber, Bigelow & Dowse was a Boston, MA, hardware dealer, listed in the 1874-83 city directories. The firm succeeded **Homer Bishop & Co.**; in 1874, was succeeded by **Bigelow & Dowse**, in 1884. Example: on an 8 3/16" coffin smoother with a single iron. ********

G. MACY
Example: on a 9 1/2" beech double-iron and wedge sash with round chamfers, ca. 1820. **UR**

J. G. MADDIN
Example: on a left-hand beech sun plane.
No imprint is available.

MADE IN USA
Example: on a 16" beech Razee Jack plane with a continental style wedge and line, with a **Buck Brothers** iron, no chamfers. Made for the European market, ca. 1920. ********

J. MAGOUN
Example: on a 9 1/2" birch ogee mother plane, a plane that cuts the opposite profile, with heavy round chamfers, ca. 1820. **UR**

S: MAGOUN
Stephen S. Magoun (Magoon) (d. 1836 in Boston, MA) was a builder of a church, in 1795, a joiner, and a planemaker in New Hampton, NH, from 1807-50. Example: on a 9" birch Yankee plow with wood thumbscrews and depth stop, riveted skate, snecked iron, and round chamfers, ca. 1820. **UR**

GEO G. MAHAN
George G. Mahan (b. Mar. 1, 1825 in MO, d. Feb. 4, 1875 in Memphis, TN, burier in Muscatine, IA) was listed in 1850 as a merchant in Marion, MO.; and as a hardware merchant, in 1856-60, in Muscatine, IA. Example: on a 1 1/2" skew rabbet with a **166** style number on the toe, which was made by the **Ohio Tool Co.** ***

J. MAIN
Possibly **James Main** (b. Mar. 29, 1789, d. 1839) a Baltimore, MD cabinetmaker, active from 1813-22. Example: on a 9 7/8" beech dado, possibly altered from a fenced rabbet, with heavy flat chamfers, ca. 1800. **UR**

J. H. MAKER
Example: on a 9 1/2" applewood coping plane, ca. 1840-50. **UR**

MAKERS
Example: on a 9 1/2" beech boxed side bead, ca. 1850. ****

F. S. MALCOLM
Frederick S. Malcolm (b. Dec. 1817 in Middlesex Co., CT, d. Feb. 9, 1902 in Brooklyn, NY) worked alone in New Haven, CT, ca. 1846. **Frederick** was married Jun. 3, 1846, in Glastonbury, CT. He was part of **Pond, Malcolm & Welles** of New Haven, CT, ca. 1850; and of **Shiverick & Malcolm,** in Brooklyn, NY, from 1853-65, during which time **Malcolm** lived in Manhattan, NY. From 1878-80, **Frederick** was employed in an organ shop in Meriden, CT; in 1900, as "retired", ca. 19c. **UR**

D. T. MALLETT
D. T. Mallett was a hardware dealers in New Haven, CT; in 1892, **D. T. Mallett & Co.** with **D. T. Mallett, Newton H., Cox,** and **James R. Lyon**; as wholesale and Retail Hardware and Sporting Goods, 776 Chapel & 795 Grand Av. In 1893, **D. T. Mallett** was listed as "rem" to NY. Example: on a brass disk attached to the heel of planes, including a **177** inventory number on a dado made by the **Auburn Tool Co.**, Auburn, NY. ****

S. S. MALLETT
Samuel S. Mallett, in 1902-03, was listed as President of The **Mallett Hardware Co., Inc.** at 861 Chapel St., New Haven, CT. In 1878, **Samuel** was listed with **Atwater & Mallett** in New Haven, CT.; in 1882-83, as cutlery and builder's hardware, at 280 Chapel; in 1884, at 776 Chapel, the same address as **D. T. Mallett**. Example: on an orange paper label, glued to the side of a **Union Factory** side bead that reads: ****

SOLD BY
S. S. MALLETT
HARDWARE
61 CHURCH STREET
NEW HAVEN, CONN.

L. MALOY
Examples: on a 9 1/2" birch molder with flat chamfers mostly on the top; and a 9 5/8" birch round with round chamfers, ca. 1800-20. **UR**

ASA. MAN
Asa Man (baptized Apr. 5, 1755) was one of the **Man** or **Mann** family, ca. 1780. **UR**

B MAN
Beriah Man (b. Jun. 20, 1708 Wrentham, MA, d. Mar. 31, 1750 in Wrentham, MA.) was married to **Kezha Wade** on Jan. 1, 1733, 1st. cousin of **Sarah Ware**, **F. Nicholson**'s 2nd. wife & Mary Wade, **F. Nicholson**'s 3rd. wife. Example: An embossed **B. MANN** owner's imprint has been found on a **F. Nicholson** Yankee plow and an embossed **B. MAN** owner's imprint has been found on an **I. Nicholson** Yankee plow. Example: on a 12" birch panel raiser with an extremely offset tote and heavy flat chamfers, from southeastern MA, ca. 1770. **UR**

D. MAN
Example: The A imprint is on a 9 1/2" birch coping plane with flat chamfers. The B imprint is on a 9 1/2" sq. rabbet with flat chamfers, ca. 1790-1800.
A & B; UR

A

B

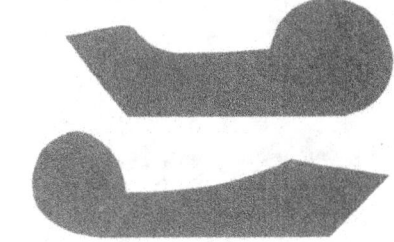

P. H. MANCHESTER
Pardon H. Manchester (b. 1818 in MA, d. Apr. 1858) was a Providence, RI, planemaker, active from 1841-58, who was listed in the 1850 census, as a planemaker. *

T. I. MANCHESTER
Example: on a 9 1/2" beech molder with dovetailed boxing on a side bead at Sturbridge Village. **No imprint is available.**

MANDER & DILLIN
James Mander (b. Feb. 1854 in England, d. Jan. 05, 1933 in Philadelphia PA) arrived in Philadelphia, in 1890; in 1910, **James** was a builder, in Philadelphia, PA. **Maurice R. Dillin** was listed from 1885-90, as a stairbuilder in Philadelphia, PA. **James Mander** and **Maurice R. Dillin** were also planemakers and issued Patented, No. 314338, on Mar. 24, 1885, and produced an improved chamfer plane. This English-style chamfer plane appears to have originated from **Mander**, a British citizen who

A
A1

assigned 1/3 interest to **Maurice R. Dillin**. An advertisement in *Carpentry & Building Magazine* of 1886 describes "the Excelsior adjustable chamfer plane" from **Mander & Mander**, at 2643 Germantown Rd. Philadelphia, probably a successor of **Mander & Dillin**. The A1 imprint appears on a chamfer plane imprinted **PAT AP'D FOR**, apparently made before the patent was granted and putting potential imitators on notice. **A ****; **A1 *****; **A2 ******

A2

MANHATTAN 28/ GOODENOUGH
Example: on a 9 1/2" cherry small rounding plane with round chamfers, ca. 1820. **UR**

D: MANN
Example: on a 10" birch medium hollow with large shallow flat chamfers, probably from New England, ca. 1770-80. **UR**

E. M/ E: MANN
Believed to be **Ebenezer Mann** (b. Feb. 19, 1787 in Natick, Middlesex, MA, d. Dec. 13, 1872 in Sherborn, MA) who was a housewright from Sherborn, and Natick, MA. In 1850 & 60, **Ebenezer** was listed as a carpenter; In 1870, at age 83, a farmer, in Sherborn. The initial group E.M is on a 11" beech Yankee plow with round chamfers, ca. 1820. An E: MANN owner's imprint is on a **Brown & Barnard** (Birmingham, English, 1800-03) jointer that was slightly charred when left on a hot stove or a fire in the Mann family carpenter shop. **A & B: UR**

A

B

MANN & COOKES
Mann & Cookes was a hardware dealer in Catskill, NY. Example on a complex molder made by **Bensen & M'Call**; a large hollow by **Kennedy & White**; and a match tongue & groove pair made by **Kennedy Barry & Way**, ca. 1840's. ********

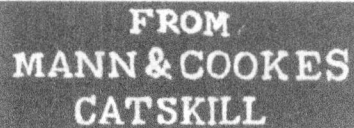

MANNEBACH/ MANNEBACH BROS./ J.MANNEBACH
The **Mannebach Brothers** consisted of **Charles J. Mannebach** and **Julius W. Mannebach** who were New York City planemakers, active from 1858-98. In 1891, the firm was called **Mannebach Brothers** and advertised miter planes as a specialty. One or more of the entities was located at 112 Stanton st. between 1880-98. **Charles Mannebach** was listed, as late as 1915, as a cabinetmaker. **Julius Mannebach** arrived in the US in 1850, and was naturalized on Aug. 20, 1853. **Julius** was listed in 1854, as a cabinetmaker and was variously listed as tools, toolmaker, planes, planemaker and industry; in 1918, as a notary. Example: on a 9 7/16"x 1 1/2" beech dado, European in appearance indicating that they were also importers and hardware dealers. **A, A1 & B ****

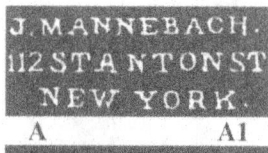
A A1

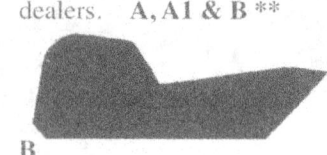
B

G. W. MANNING
George W. Manning (b. Oct. 16, 1853, d. Dec. 10, 1948 at Malden, MA) was a maker of cooper's tools in Hollis, NH. His original account book and a scrapbook exist. **George** started coopering ca. 1872, probably with **Addison Heald** or his son **Daniel Heald**; and on his own, from 1879-86. On Nov. 16, 1881, **Manning** was married to **Nellie Lovejoy**, daughter of **Augustus Lovejoy**, the blacksmith who provided his plane irons. In 1883, most of his work was related to wagon and furniture making and other woodwork. In 1885, **George** started the carving of Victorian oak furniture. In 1888, he moved to Malden, MA. Between Oct. 1895 and Apr. 1896, he worked by carving clock cases for **Henry S. Manning**. On Feb. 18, 1902, **George Manning** joined the United Brotherhood of Carpenters and Joiners of America. From 1898-1926, **George** worked for **L. L. Libby** for an hourly wage. Examples: on a 4 ft. cherry cooper's long joiner with double irons and wedges, and reversible for head and stave in one stock; a cherry cooper's topping plane with brass adjustment screws; and on a heel of a 9" mahogany coffin smoothing plane made by **C. E. Harrington**. *******

L. MANNING
Example: on a bench plane with an iron strike; a 12"x 2" skew rabbet with a wedged nicker and a pegged birch slightly offset tote; a 9" astragal, dated **1818** on the heel; and a 9 1/16" round, all beech with round chamfers, ca. 1800-20. ********

I: M
Deacon **John Mansfield** (b. Mar. 20, 1767 in Danvers, MA, d. Apr. 18, 1839 in Danvers) was a planemaker and farmer in Danvers, now Lynnfield, MA. The planes were found in a tool chest with fruitwood 10"molders with no spring; bench planes, a panel raising plane and a crown molder. The bench planes have round topped wedges and irons made by **SMITH, WELDON, GILLOT**. Also in the tool chest were planes by **I. Gould**, Reading, MA, **I Cox**, English, and **W. Raymond**, Bevery, MA, ca.1790. **UR**

J. MANROW
Example: on a beech size **5** grooving plane, ca. 1850. **UR**

J. MARANVILL

Example: on a massive 12" filletster with an adjustable fence with wood thumbscrews, wood depth stop, nicker and no tote, ca. 1850. **UR**

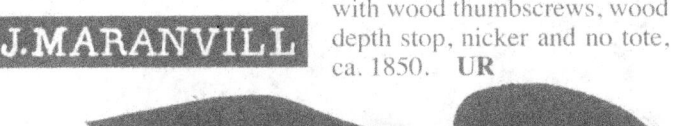

F. B. MARBLE

Francis Barnard Marble (b. Dec. 25, 1817 in Grand Isle Co., VT., d. Dec. 18, 1894 in Columbus, OH) was a manufacturer and dealer in joiner's and cooper's tools in Cleveland, OH, active from 1846-56. **Marble** was with **Marble & Vinall** from 1850-51; and with **Marble & Smith**, in 1856. A Patent, No. 46372, was issued on Feb. 14, 1865, to **F. B. Marble** of Columbus, OH, for a machine for dressing the throats in plane stocks. In 1870, **Francis** was listed as a Forman with the **Ohio Tool Co.** in Columbus, OH.

A, A1, A2, A3 & B **

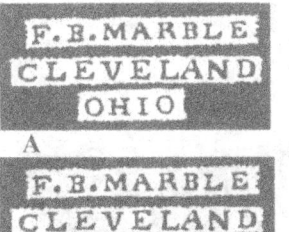

MARBLE & SMITH

Marble & Smith was a Cleveland, OH, plane making partnership of **Francis B. Marble** and **Smith**, listed in 1856. Example: the A1 imprint is on a 7/8" wide dado. A & A1 ***

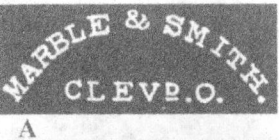

MARBLE & VINALL

Marble & Vinall was a Cleveland, OH, plane making partnership of **Francis B. Marble** and **John J. Vinall**, active from 1850-51. Example: on a beech slide-arm plow. The location die is similar to that used by **A. & W. Marsh** from 1837-38. ****

J. MARCY

Example: on a beech boxed bead, and a curly birch complex molder, both 9 1/2" with flat chamfers, ca. 1810. **UR**

J. MARDEN

Possibly **John A. Marden** (b. Apr. 7, 1823 in Palermo, ME, d. July 3, 1887 in Chicopee, MA) who was a joiner and millman in Bangor, ME, 1850 thru 1856. From 1860-72, he was in Veazie, ME, and worked as a house carpenter. **J. A. Marden** was issued Patent No. 125,823, on Apr. 16, 1872, for a marking gauge. In 1873, **John** moved to South Hadley Falls, MA, then Holyoke, MA, where he was a house carpenter and millwright, in 1880. (see *American Marking Gages*, by Milton H. Bacheller, Jr.) Example: on a 9 1/2"x 3/16" beech dado. **UR**

R MARES

Example: on an 11" birch skew rabbet with wide flat chamfers, ca. 1800. **UR**

MARKER HARDWARE CO.

Marker Hardware Co. with the location **239 MARKET ST/ NEWARK** has been reported as a purple ink stamp on the side of a 9 3/8" maple French style square rabbet. **No imprint is available.**

W. MARKEE

Example: on a 9" beech door joint plane with shallow round chamfers, ca. 1830. **UR**

MARLEY/ L. MARLEY

Luke Marley (b. 1791 in England, d. Feb. 12, 1856 in New York) was a New York City planemaker, active from 1820-56. **Marley** worked at 40 Elm St., from 1822-28; from 1843-44, at 54 Center St.; and by 1856, at 360 Broome St.; where he was succeeded by **William F. Hoffmann**.

A, A1, B, B1 & C **

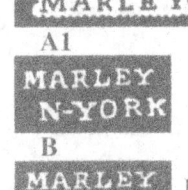
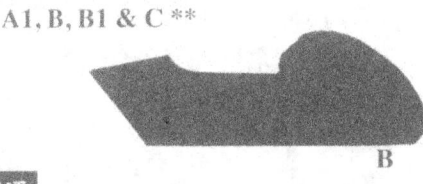
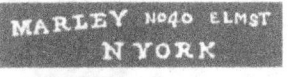

D. MARRINER

Example: on a 12" beech ship's rabbet with a double-iron by **Wm. Ash & Co.** The **B.K** probably refer to Brunswick, ME. The **Marriner's** established a sawmill & lumber yard in Brunswick which was operational into the 20c. ****

A. & W. MARSH

Archibald Marsh and **William Marsh** (b. 1809 in NY, d. Jun. 14, 1888, OH) were Cleveland, OH, planemakers, who appeared in the 1837-38 city directory as **A & W. Marsh**. **Archibald Marsh** worked for **H. Chapin**, as a planemaker, from 1831-35. **William Marsh** was working as a carpenter and joiner, in Cleveland, active from 1850-53. The location die **CLEVELAND/ OHIO** is similar to that used by **Marble & Vinall**, from 1850-51.   **A & A1 ****

M. MARSH/ M. MARSH & SON
Examples: on 9" beech molder with owner imprints of **J. E. Colegrove** and **I. Craig**. These same two owners appear on a **R. Hoey** plane; and a 9 7/16" boxed molding plane has been reported with an inverted **& SON** added, with the **&** to the left of the **M. MARSH** and the **SON** above, ca. 1850.   **A, B & C; UR**

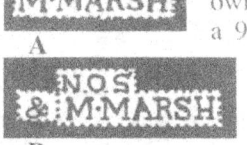

R: MARSH
Examples: on a 10" birch skew rabbet with heavy round chamfers, and a 9 3/4" birch medium hollow with fully rounded top and end chamfers and shallow flutes. This second example was found with an **I. Nicholson** and **I. Iones** planes, ca. 1790, possibly from southeastern New England.   *********

J. MARSHALL

Example: on a 9 3/8" beech shiplap rabbet with round chamfers, ca. 1820.   **UR**

PAUL MARSHALL
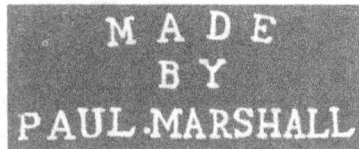
Example: on an 8" rosewood smoother, ca. 19c.   **UR**

MARSHALL & BROWN
Marshall & Brown was a Westfield, MA, planemaker, ca. 1840.   ********

MARSHALL WELLS HDWE. CO.
Marshall Wells Hdwe. Co. of Duluth, MN used the trade name **Zenith Tools** in their 1910 catalog including a fairly complete listing of hand tools. Planes include some transitional: unhandled smoothers 7, 8 & 9" long; handled smoothers 9 & 10" long; jacks, fores & jointers 15, 18, 20, 22, 24, 26, 28, & 30" long. One 8" smooth; and one 16" jack which are referred to as "common planes". Most planes offered by **ZENITH** were manufactured by **Sargent**. **Marshall Wells** ceased operation in US, ca. 1960. Example: on a transitional smoother; second quality tools were branded; **MARSWELLS HARTFORD, SUPERIOR** or **NORTHERN KING**.

O N M/ O. N. MARSTON
A progression of imprints from an incuse initial group to an embossed name and then an incuse name. Example: on a 9 1/2" beech complex molder, ca. 1840.   **UR**

M. MARTIEN
Listed in the Philadelphia, PA, directories were **Hibsam Martin** in 1799, 1800 & 1803 and **Mibsam Martien** in 1801 & 1807. **Hibsam** and **Mibsam** may be the same person as they occupied the same address as **William Martin**. **Martien Martin** was married Jan. 16, 1800 in Philadelphia, PA. Example: on a 9 1/4" small ogee with two short inserts of dark wood and flat chamfers.   **A & A1 ******

MARTIN
Examples: on 9 3/8"-9 1/2" beech molders with flat chamfers; and a plane that is side slipped, a characteristic of Philadelphia and Baltimore planemakers, similar in style to those of **W. Martin**. ca. 1810.   *******

D x MARTIN
This imprint is similar to that of **Mx Martin**. Example: on a 14" beech narrow crown molder with round chamfers; and a 9 5/8" beech adjustable sash. Both found in PA. ca. 1810-20   ********

D. A. MARTIN
Example: on a 10 1/8" bench style beech large hollow with a double iron with heavy round chamfers. found in southeastern PA. ca. early 19c.   **UR**

I. MARTIN
Examples: 17 planes were found in the Woodstock, VT area; a 12 1/2" cornice plane with an offset tote, round top iron and wedge, and an ebony diamond strike; a 30" birch jointer; a 9 1/2" birch hollow & round pair; a 9 5/8" solid lignum vitae complex molder and a birch sash plane. All with flat chamfers.

ca. 1780-1800. ****

J. MARTIN
Possibly **James Martin** (b. ca. 1780 in MD) a Baltimore, MD, cabinetmaker, active from 1799-1816. Examples: on a 13 3/4" beech narrow panel raiser with centered open tote and flat chamfers; a 9 3/8" molder; a complex molder boxed with lignum vitae and; a 9 1/2" beech round with round chamfers, ca. 1790-1800. ****

M x MARTIN
Examples: The A imprint is on a 9 5/8" beech wedge-arm plow; a 9 1/2" beech astragal with flat chamfers; and a 9 1/2" beech skew-rabbet with round chamfers, found in PA. The B imprint is on a 9 1/2" skew rabbet with flat chamfers, both ca. 1800-20. **A & B**; ****

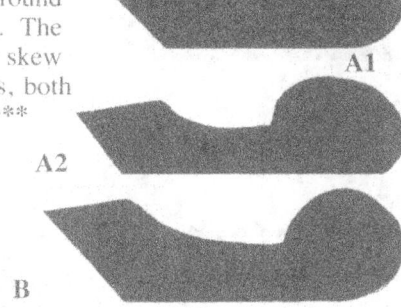

N. MARTIN
Examples: on a 10" beech fluting plane with tight flat chamfers, possibly from New England, ca. 1800. **UR**

N. M/ N. C. MARTIN.
N. C. Martin with the middle initial **C** or possibly **G** is on a beech slide-arm plow with wood thumbscrews, a wood depth stop, ca. 1840-50. **UR**

MARTIN/ W. MARTIN
William Martin was an early Philadelphia, PA, planemakers, active from 1773-1801. In 1773, **Martin** took as an apprentice, **Hugh Fegan** as an apprentice. It was **Martin** who bore the standard of the planemakers in the Fourth of July, Philadelphia Grand Procession of 1788. The banner included four planes, spring dividers, a square and a gauge. In 1785, **Martin** was at 3d bt. Arch & Race St.; from 1791-1801, at 16 Church Alley & No. 99 3d. St. Example: the B imprint on a 12 1/4"x 2" beech complex molder with an offset tote, round top **NEWBOULD** iron and interrupted lignum vitae boxing.
A *; **C & D ****; **B *****

MARTIN & COREY
A partnership of **Martin & Corey** consisting of **Howard R. Martin** (Jul., 1, 1820 in NY, d. Dec. 20, 1901 in NY). On Oct. 26, 1855, **Howard** was married in NY; and **William Edmund Corey** (b. Feb. 11, 1828 in NY, d. Sep. 28, 1875 in Pentwater. Oceana Co., MI) was a hardware store operators in New York City, active from 1857-65. Martin left in 1865 and **Corey** continued, first alone and then with **William H. Neve**. Example: on the heels of a **J. Denison** boxed bead; and a medium hollow. **

F. J. MARTZ & CO.
Frederick J. Martz (b. 1832 in Germany, d. Sep. 5, 1891 in Adrian, Lenawee Co., MI) was a Detroit, MI, hardware dealer. In 1886, **F. J. Martz & Co.** was listed with **Frank J. Martz** and **J. Anthony Marshall**. In the 1901, **F. J. Martz & Co.** was listed with **Frank J. Martz** & **Edward J. Maritz**, listing hardware, stoves, tinware, crockery, house furnishings goods, bicycle sundries, at 488-490 Gratiot Ave. Example: on the nose of a **Sandusky Tool Co.** 9 1/2"x 5/8" skew rabbet. ****

C. R. MASON & CO.
Charles R. Mason (b. ca. 1851, d. Boston, MA) was a Lawrence, MA, hardware dealer listed in the 1875 city directory. **A & B ***

E. MASON
Examples: on an 8" beech panel raiser with a round-top iron marker **HARRIS**, three dovetail lignum vitae wear inserts, a dovetail lignum vitae depth stop; and a 9 7/8" beech complex molder, both with flat chamfers, from PA, ca. 1790. **UR**

J W M/ J MASON
James W. Mason (b. 1822, in Rehoboth, MA) was listed in the 1850 census, as a blacksmith, living in Sterling, CT; in the 1869-70, as a planemaker in Saybrook, CT, and made planes in New York City from 1874-78. The **J. MASON** imprint is on a boxwood smoothing plane. Example: the initials **J. W. M.** are on an **I Hammond/ New Haven** plane. **UR**
No imprint of the full name is available.

S. MASON
Example: on a 9 5/8" complex molder with a relieved wedge and flat chamfers, ca. 1800. **UR**

J. W. MASSEY
James W. Massey (b. ca. 1779, d. Jul. 21, 1830 in Philadelphia, PA) was a Philadelphia, PA, planemaker, from 1808-30. He was part of **Stall & Massey**, ca. 1800. **A & A1 ****

SAMUEL MASSEY
Samuel Massey (b. ca. 1787, d. Mar. 26, 1834 in Paul's Run, Philadelphia Co., PA) was listed, as a plane manufacturer, in Paxton's 1818 Philadelphia, PA, directory. He operated a hardware store, in partnership with **Robert A. Parrish**, as **Parrish & Massey** from 1817-23 at 238 N. Third; and from 1823-32 at 16 South Third. **No imprint has been reported.**

L. MASSON
Example: on a 9 1/2" beech grooving plane with tight round chamfers, ca. early 19c. **UR**

EBENEZER MATHERS
Ebenezer Mathers of Morgantown, VA, was issued Patent No. 14363, on Mar. 4, 1856, for a bench plane. **No imprint has been reported**.

MATTESON & SULLY
Example: on a 14 1/2" pair of toted tongue & groove planes with **48** on the toe. ********

MATTHEWMAN & CO.
Matthewman & Co. probably was a hardware dealer in New Haven, CT. Examples: on two **Sandusky Tool Co.** planes, on an **Auburn Tool Co.** plane; and on the wedge of a 16" jack is a paper label: **A & B ******

A

```
           FROM
    MATTHEWMAN & CO.
       DEALERS IN
      FINE CUTLERY
    MECHANICS' TOOLS
    219 CHAPEL STREET
  CORNER UNION OPPOSITE
     RAILROAD STATION
    NEW HAVEN, CONN.   (B)
```

E. MATTHEWS
Example: on a 16" beech jack with centered tote, sq. strike and double-irons, found in central PA, ca. 19c. **UR**

E. L. MATTHEWS
Emerson L. Matthews (b. Nov. 17, 1830, d. Dec. 26, 1886 in Baltimore, MD) was a Baltimore, MD, planemaker, active ca. 1856-59. Examples: on several **P. Chapin** planes, suggesting a relationship. **A, A1 & B *****

J. W. MATTHEWS

Example: on a 9 1/2"x 7/8" beech single-boxed side bead made by **Miller & Probasco**. **UR**

J. MATTISON
Joseph Matteson (b. 1796, d. 1852) was a Chicago, IL, hardware dealer, from 1839-44. **Matteson** was part of **Gurnee & Matteson**, grocery & hardware, from 1845-52; and part of **Matteson & Calhoun**, in 1847; in 1848-51, as part of **Matteson, Calhoun & Co.**. From 1853-66, the listing was under **Mrs. Joseph Matteson**. ******

J. MAUD
Example: on an 8 15/16" beech sash plane with flat chamfers, ca. 1800. **UR**

MAURER
Example: on a 9 5/8" square rabbet with the sides shaved (no chamfers), an **I. Sleeper** style wedge, and a **James Cam** iron. **UR**

M+ MAY
Example: on a 13" birch panel raiser, stamped once on the toe and twice on the heel, with a Wrentham style mahogany offset tote, round-top cherry wedge & iron and flat chamfers. The bottom of the wedge and front of the shavings opening are both carved in linen fold, possibly from southeastern New England, ca. 1790. **UR**

G. MAYER
G. Mayer (b. in Germany, arrived in 1822) was a Lancaster, PA, hardware dealer. Example: on a match plane made by **J. Stamm**, and planes made by **John Bell** and **H. Chapin/ Union Factory**, ca. 1850. **A & A1 ****

J. MAYER
Johannes Mayer (b. Nov. 24, 1794, d. Dec. 23, 1883) was a documented furniture and toolmaker of the Mahantango Valley in PA, whose work is described and illustrated in *Decorated Furniture of the Mahantango Valley*, by Henry Reed. He was also listed as a carpenter, a joiner and a turner. A painted chest of drawers, by **Mayer**, sold at a Jan. 1989 auction for $203,500. Examples: on a crown molder; a 13 3/8" sash plane; a 14" panel raiser with offset tote; a 10 7/16" rabbet; a 9 1/2" bead; a 14" adj. wedge arm tongue plank plane; an 11" grooving plane with wedge arms, snecked iron and riveted skate; and a 14 1/2" jack with a offset tote, all beech with tight round chamfers, ca. 1820-30. *******

A MAYHEW
Examples: on a 10" complex molder; and a 9 1/4" small complex molder with a relieved wedge, both beech with tight round chamfers, ca. 1810. **UR**

A. W. MAYHEW
There were many early **Mayhews** on Martha's Vineyard in MA. Examples: the A imprint is on a 11" beech narrow bench plane with a centered tote; and a 10" beech small round, both with flat chamfers. The B imprint is on a skew rabbet; and a small round, both 9 1/2" beech with tight round chamfers, ca. 1800-20. ********

W. MAYHEW
Examples: on a 14" beech narrow panel raiser with offset tote, dovetail wooden depth stop and round chamfers; and molding planes 9 1/2" beech with flat and round chamfers, possibly from PA. ca. 1810-20. ********

B. MAYS
Example: on a 9 5/16" beech hollow, and a 9 1/8" dovetail plane, ca. 1840. **UR**

E B. MAYS
Examples: on a 9 5/8" beech hollow, ca. 1850. **No imprint is available**.

O. MAZANGE & CO.
Examples: on a 9 1/2" beech size **15** round with a **Providence Tool Co.** iron, ca. 1850. **UR**

D. MAZZAGLIA
Dana Mazzaglia was a contemporary planemaker and worked in the piano making industry. **Mazzaglia** lived in Haverhill, MA, from 1994-2004 and in Salem, NH, there after. His earliest imprint was a **DM** initial group with 1/4" characters. **No imprint is available**. The A imprint, with **MAZZAGLIA**, was used from 1992-94. A curved logo with **MAZZAGLIA TOOLS** was used, from 1995-97, and used mostly on piano making tools. The B imprint was used from 1997-2000. The B1 imprint with the **HAVERHILL** location imprint was used from 2000-02. From 2002-04, **MAKER** was added, as in the B2 imprint. The B3 imprint with the location **SALEM**, NH was used from 2004 thru at least 2007. The earliest planes were rock maple, the latter were beech. **A, B, B1, B2 & B3: UR**

D. McARTHUR
Examples: on a 13" matched pair of handled wedge-arm tongue & groove plane, found in OH; and on a 9 1/8" split-sash with double irons & wedges and with screw-arms & nuts and round chamfers, ca. 1825. ********

B. S. McAULEY
Example: on a 16 1/2" beech ogee complex molder with a centered tote and 19th. style chamfers; ca. 1850. **UR**

F. M'BEATH
Example: on a 9 1/2"x 1/2" beech hollow with **1/2** on the heel and round chamfers, ca. 1820-30. **UR**

A. McBRIDE
Alexander McBride (b. Nov. 1, 1811 in PA, d. Jul. 18, 1874 in Louisville, KY) was listed as an architect, from 1843-44; and a carpenter, from 1844-46. In 1844-45, **Alexander McBride** advertised:

ALEXANDER McBRIDE
MANUFACTURER of PLANES,
and DEALER in
HARDWARE & CUTLERY,
53 Third Street, Louisville, KY.

McBride was a partner in **Woodruff & McBride**, from 1848-49; as a planemaker, in 1851-52; and the sole proprietor in the hardware business, from 1851-66. **Alexander McBride** was listed as a planemaker or owner of a plane factory, in the 1867-8, 1872 & 73 directories.
A & A1 **; **B & B1 *****

A. McBRIDES SONS
Apparently **Alexander McBride**'s Louisville, KY, hardware business was successful enough to be carried on by the next generation, during the late 1860's or 70's. Example: on a side bead with a **Sandusky Tool Co.** with inventory number **47** on the toe. ********

MICHAEL McCAFERAY
Michael McCaffray (b. ca. 1816 in Ireland, d. Jan. 1847 in NYC) was listed as a planemaker, at 75 Mott St., New York City, active in 1843-44. **No imprint has been reported**.

THOMAS J. McCALL
Thomas McCall (b. Apr. 10, 1806 in PA, d. Nov. 28, 1850 in Albany, NY) was listed, in 1834-35, in the Albany, NY directories, as a planemaker. **McCall** was a partner in **Bensen & McCall**, in 1842; in 1850, a lumber inspector, in Albany. **No imprint has been reported**.

I. McCAMANT
Examples: on a wedge-lock skew rabbet with an adjustable fence and a friction-fit wood depth stop; a small astragal; a grooving plane; and a wedge-lock plow plane, all 9 1/2" beech with heavy flat chamfers, ca. 1800. ****

J. A. McCELLUS
John A. McCellus (b. ca. 1814) was listed, as making carpenter tools and planes, in Cooperstown, NY, in 1837. Example: on a 9 1/2" beech single-boxed side bead with size **5/8** on the heel with **B. S. Howe**, Otsego, N.Y. ***

R. McCLURE
Example: on a 9 1/2" beech bead with flat chamfers. **UR**

McCLURE/ Wm M. McCLURE
William M. McClure (b. ca. 1813, d. 1903) was a Philadelphia, PA hardware and tool dealer who entered six planes, made by **E. W. Carpenter**, in the Franklin Institute 1848-49 exhibits.
McClure was also a part of **Yarnall & McClure**, ca. 1840. Example: on a patented, No. 6226, smoother; and a plow plane made by **E. W. Carpenter** with this imprint on the heel. **A & B** ***

J. McCOBB
Examples: on a 9 1/2" round with shallow flat chamfers; and a 9 3/8" round with heavy round chamfers, both beech with medium rounds.
ca. 1820-30. **UR**

Mc COMBS & HAWKS
Mc Combs & Hawks, with the location **MEMPHIS, TENN** is probably a hardware dealer, ca. 19c. **No imprint is available**.

C. M'CORMICK
Example: on a 9 5/8" beech hollow with flat chamfers, ca. 1810. **UR**

W. B. McCORMICK
W. B. McCormick of Alton, O (OH) was a hardware dealer. Example: on a 10 1/4"x 1 7/8" maple spill plane, bench style, made by **H. W. Yates** of Detroit, MI, ca 1890. ****

P. McCUEN
P. McCuen was a maker of coopers tools in Brooklyn, NY, ca. 1850. ***

J. M'CULLY
James M. McCully (b. ca. 1799 in Ireland, d. Mar. 26, 1873 in an accident in Pittsburgh, PA) who was a wholesale grocer, carried hardware and building supplies, from 1827-73. **McCully** arrived in Allegheny Co., PA, in 1823. Example: on an all boxwood screw-arm plow; a complex molder; and a round, ca. 1850-60.
A, A1 & A2: ***

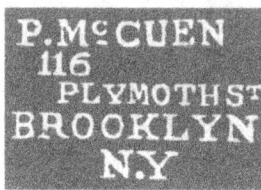

J. M. McCUNE & CO.
Jonas Mann McCune (b. Sep. 12, 1822 in VT, d. Mar. 4, 1907 Columbus, OH) was a planemaker and possible hardware dealer.
Example: on a hollow & round pair, with the added date **1887**; and a tongue plane with **75** on the toe, the **Ohio Tool Co.** inventory number for a tongue plane. The wedge is also similar to the **Ohio Tool Co.**, "D" shaped wedge. **A & A1** ***

WILLIAM McDANIEL/ WILLIAM McDANIELS
William McDaniel (b. 1796, NJ, d. ca. 1898) was listed in New York City, as a planemaker, active from 1825-27. A **William McDaniels**, possibly the same man, was listed as a planemaker in 1837, 1839-42, 1845-50 and intermittently through the 1850's in the Philadelphia, PA, directories. He worked for the **Whites'** making panel raisers with the initials **W. M. D.** **No imprint is available**.

McDONALD - FOSTER & PORTER
McDonald-Foster & Porter was a hardware dealer, active ca. 1840. Example: the A imprint is on a **D. R. Barton** complex molder with inventory number **61** on the toe; and a 9 1/2"x 1 1/2" wide single boxed complex molder by the **Ohio Tool Co.** with **141** on the toe. The A1 imprint

is on an **Ohio Tool Co.** round with inventory number **72** on the toe. **A & A1** ****

A1

J. McDOUGAL
Example: on a 9 1/2"x 1/8" bead, ca. 1850. **UR**

H. McDOWEL.
Example: on a 9 7/16" beech plank tongue plane with slide-arm fence, wood thumb screws and wide round chamfers, ca. 1810. **UR**

J. M'ELWEE
John M'Elwee was a frame, looking glass and hardware merchant in Philadelphia, PA, from 1791-1802. **M'Elwee** was listed as "painter & colourman", at 54 so. Front st., in 1791; "looking glass & colour merchant", at 75 so. Front st., in 1793-1802. Example: on a fruitwood complex molder with offset tote and flat chamfers, ca. 1800. ****

Wm. McFaden

Example: on an ogee molding plane, ca. 19c. **UR**

JAMES McGENNIS
James McGennis was listed as a planemaker in the Cincinnati, OH, in 1819, at 6th. bt. Plum & Western Row. **No imprint has been reported.**

Mc GIVERIN & CO.
Mc Giverin & Co. was probably a hardware dealer. Example: on the heel of a 6" smoother made by **D. R. Barton** of Rochester, NY. **UR**

A. M'GLINN/ A-McGLINN
Example: the A imprint is from the toe of a 9 1/2" beech complex molder with heavy round chamfers, and the B incuse imprint is on the side of the same planes. ca. 1820. **UR**

B A

A. O. McGREW
A. O. McGrew was a hardware dealer on Smithfield St., in 1850, Pittsburgh, PA. Example: on a sash plane; and a 5" crown molder or cornice plane, both made by **Hall, Case & Co.** of Columbus, OH, from 1847-52. In 1870, **A. O. McGrew & Co.** was under "liquors" in Pittsburgh, PA. ****

S. McIeHand

Example: on a 10 1/8" tongue & groove pair. **UR**

J. B. McINTOSH
Example: on a 16" open toted skew rabbet with a nicker and the location **ERIE, PA**, ca. 19c. ****

S. McINTIRE
Samuel McIntire (bapt. Jan. 16, 1757 in Salem, MA, d. Feb. 6, 1811 in Salem) was a housewright, apprenticed to his father; was called a carpenter/ joiner in the 1780's; an architect in the 1790's; and finally a sculptor/ carver, by 1800. **Samuel** married **Elizabeth**, daughter of **Samuel Field**, a local boat builder, on Aug. 31, 1778, in Salem. **Samuel's** family lived with his in-laws, from 1778-86, when he built his own one house and shop, at 31 Summer St. in Salem. His early career, as a carpenter/ joiner was shared with his brothers and billed as **Joseph McIntire & Brothers**, from 1779-86. He was a neo-classical architect and designed many prominent residents and public buildings. **Samuel McIntire** set the standard for a revival of national patriotism and American Federalist design in Salem. He would design the building on paper, hand it over to a housewright to be roughed out, then provide the carved ornaments, for the most important parts, such as the interior fireplace surrounds, staircases, built in case work, exterior entry and facade details. He also carved free standing furniture. The inventory of **Samuel McIntire's** estate included a writing table with two cases of drawing instruments and a box of paints (used as washes for his pen and ink drawings); 300 chisels, gouges, and two grindstones; 4 work benches; 46 "moulding"; and 20 large (bench) planes; Examples: on a 9 1/4" beech small ogee complex molding plane with heavy round chamfers, ca. 1790-1800. *****

JAMES McIVAINE
James McIvaine, age 17, was apprenticed, on Oct. 15, 1830, to **H. B. Miller** of Lebanon, OH. **No imprint has been reported**.

D. H. McKECHNIE
D. H. McKechnie probably was a hardware dealer. Example: on a coping plane made by the **Union Factory/ H. Chapin**. **UR**

McKEE
Example: on a 9 3/8" birch full-round or nosing plane with flat chamfers, ca. 1800. **UR**

JA. McKEE
Chester Court House was previously the county seat of Chester Co., SC. ****

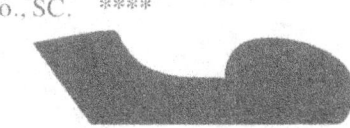

JNO. McKEE
John McKee, age 62, was listed, as a merchant, in Chester, SC in 1850. Example: on a beech plow plane, ca. 1850. ****

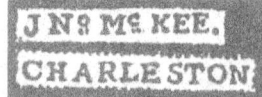

WILLIAM McKIMLE
William McKimle was listed, as a planemaker, in Cincinnati, OH, in 1836-37. **McKimle** boarded at Catharine Covert's with **Dayton Garrison**. **No Imprint has been reported**.

JAMES McKINNEL
James McKinnel, at age 10, was apprenticed, on Dec. 26, 1800, to **William Vance**, Planemaker. **No imprint has been reported**.

HENRY McKINNELL
Henry McKinnell was a Cincinnati, OH, planemaker and a part of **Lyon, McKinnell & Co.**, from 1842-46; **McKinnell & Co.**, from 1848-50; and **Charles B. Schaefer & Co.**, from 1850-52. **No imprint has been reported**.

McKINNELL & CO.
William McKinnell and **Henry McKinnell** of Cincinnati, OH, who were plane and edge tool Manufacturers, in 1848-50; succeeding **Lyon, McKinnell & Co.**, in 1850. Examples: the A imprint overstamping a **G. Roseboom** A imprint on a panel raiser. **A & A1: ***

McKINNEL & R. A. WARD
McKinnel & R. A. Ward was a partnership of **William McKinnel** and/or **Henry Mc Kinnell** and **R. C. Ward** in Cincinnati, OH. Example: on a 9 3/8" tongue plane, ca. 1840-50. ****

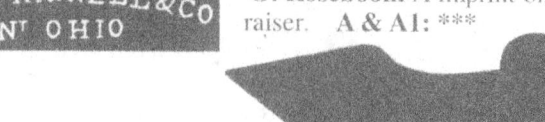

McKINNEY & ALLING
John McKinney and **Charles A. Alling** were hardware dealers in Madison, IN, active from 1857-65; who succeeded **Wells & Alling**, active from 1852-57; and were in turn succeeded by **Alling & Lodge**, in 1865. Example: on an **Ohio Tool Co.** plane. ****

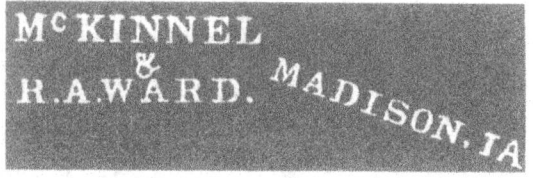

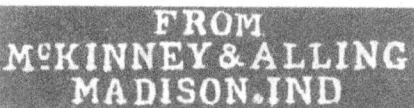

WM. R. McKINSTRY
Wm. R. McKinstry probably was a Lancaster, PA, hardware dealer. Example: on a bead made by **H. Chapin**. UR

S. McKNIGHT
Both imprints are on a 9 1/2" beech complex, double-iron & wedge molder, ca 19c. **A & B UR**

W. D. McLAUGHLIN
Example: on a 9 5/16"x 5/8" & 1/2" birch pairs of hollows & rounds; and a 3/4" round, all with heavy flat chamfers mostly on the side, ca. 1790-1800. UR

T. J. M'MASTER & CO.
Truman J. McMaster (b. Jul. 9, 1797 in Saratoga, NY, d. Sep. 24, 1880 in Auburn, NY) was a brother of **Zalmon J. Deluzon** (b. Oct. 17, 1807 in Saratoga, NY, d. 1859 in Auburn, NY) and **Alonzo Deluzon McMaster** (b. Feb. 22, 1812, d. Mar. 24, 1887 in Rochester, NY). **Truman** was part of **Dunham & McMaster** from 1821-25 with **Samuel C. Dunham**. Using convict labor, **Truman** made planes at Auburn prison, from 1823-1833, with **Nathaniel Garrow** and at Sing Sing Prison, from 1833-39. In 1839, **Truman** defaulted on his contract and it was taken up by **Young & McMaster**, with that **McMaster** being **Alonzo D. McMaster**. The 1833 contract for planemaking at Sing Sing Prison called for 30 convicts at 37 1/2 cents per day. Example: the H imprint stamp on the metal skate of a plane. **A, A1, G1 & G2: FF; B, B1, D & D1 *; C, C1, C2, E & G **; D2, D3, F & H ****

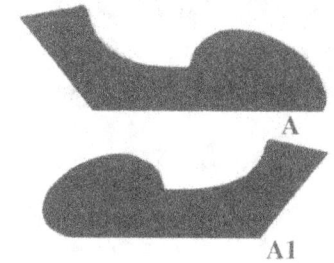

 C

 B1

 C1

 C2

 D

 D1

 D2

 D3

 E

F

G

G1

G2

H

 I

Z. J. M'MASTER & CO.

Zalmon J. McMaster (b. Oct. 17, 1807 in Saratoga, NY, d. Oct. 31, 1859 in Auburn, NY) was a brother of **Truman J. McMaster** (b. Jul. 9, 1797 in Saratoga, NY, d. Sep. 24, 1880 in Auburn, NY) and **Alonzo Deluzon McMaster** (b. Feb. 22, 1812, d. Mar. 24, 1887 in Rochester, NY). **Zalmon** was reported first as learning architecture and then as a house carpenter. In 1838, **Zalmon** worked in Auburn, NY as **Z. J. M'Master & C0.** with **Z. J. McMaster, Paul D. Cornell & Aurelius Wheeler**. **Zalmon** made planes with convict labor at Sing Sing Prison, from 1839-43, and at Auburn prison, in 1846-47, when the tool contract was sold to **Casey, Kitchell & Co.**. In 1847, **Z. J. McMaster's** contract at the Auburn Prison called for 21 convicts at 32 cents per day, 4 at 16 cents and one at 24 cents. In 1850, **Zalmon McMaster** was listed in Auburn as a plane manufacturer. **Zalmon** served in the Civil War entering as a First Lieutenant in the 5th. Reg. NY Calvary, K Co., and mustered out as a Captain. D: FF; E, E1, G *; A, B, C, F & F1 **; H, H1, I & J ***

A

B

C

D

E

E1

F

F1

G

H

 D

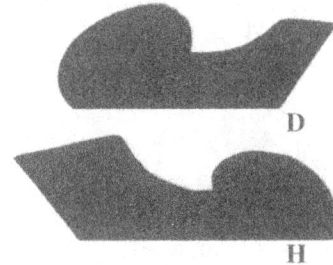 H

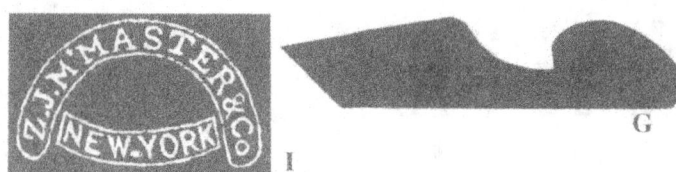

PATRICK McMENANY
Patrick McMenany (b. Jun. 1824 in Ireland) was listed, in the 1850 Newark, NJ census, as a carpenter tool manufacturer, working for and living with **P. Quigley**.
No imprint has been reported.

A. McMURTNE
Example: on a 10 1/4" fruitwood fixed sash with flat chamfers, ca. 1810. **UR**

McQUAID & CO.
James A. McQuaid (b. 1818 in Clearfield, Co., PA, d. 1880) came to Canton, IL, in 1844, where he was a gun maker, until he operated a hardware store, from 1855-63. In 1879, **McQuaid** was operating a grocery store. Example: on a panel raiser; a hollow with inventory number **72** on the toe; and a Grecian ogee with inventory number **61**, both **Ohio Tool Co.** style numbers. ****

A. McQUILLIN
Example: on a 9 3/4" beech hollow with flat chamfers, ca. 1800. **UR**

G. McREA
Example: on a 9 3/4" birch rabbet. **No imprint is available.**

A. MEAD
Example: on a 9 1/2" beech complex molder, ca. 1820-30. **UR**

J. MEAD
Possibly **John Mead** (b. Jul. 18, 1786 in Essex, MA, d. Feb. 21, 1824 in Salem, MA) who was a Salem, MA, cabinetmaker. Example: on a 9 5/8" beech plow with a relieved wedge, wood tombstone depth stop with shoulders, riveted skate, hickory thumbscrew locked arms, and round chamfers, possibly from New England, ca. 1820. **UR**

W. MEAD
On a razee jack, tiger strip maple body with burl tote, appears to be contemporary. **UR**

WM. M. MEAD
William M. Mead (b. 1818 in NY) was a hardware dealer in Westbury, NY. **Mead** appeared in the Civil War muster roll for Buttes, NY, in 1863. Example: on a **Bond & Sargent** plane. ****

MEAD SHELDEN & CO.
J. Mead and **Samuel Clark Shelden** (b. 1819, d. 1896) were partners of a wholesale hardware and cutlery company in Cincinnati, OH, in 1853. **Mead Shelden & Co.** predecessors were **Mead & Winsto**, from 1849-50; and **A. J. Mead & Co.**, from 1850-52. Example: on a 3/4" skew dado with a brass depth stop and a double nickers. **A & B** ****

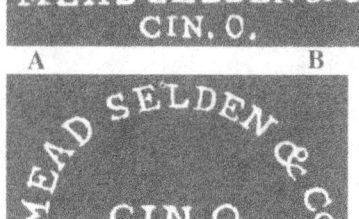

MECHANIC FALLS ME
Example: on an 8 5/8" spar plane with a **Moulson Brothers** iron, ca. 1850. **UR**

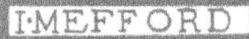

MECHANICS TOOL CO.
Examples: on a 16" jack with a **15** on the toe; and on an 8 1/4" smoother with a **3** on the toe; both with **Ohio Tool Co.** inventory number; and a 22" fore plane, all beech with **Ohio Tool Co.** irons, ca. 1890. ****

I. MEFFORD
Example: on a 10" ship-lap rabbet; a 10" round; and a 9 7/8" bead, all beech with flat chamfers, ca. 1800. ****

A. MEIR & CO./ A. MEIER & CO./ ADOLPHUS. MEIER & CO.
Adolphus Dietrich Meier (b. May 8, 1810 in Bremen, Germany, d. Aug. 20, 1888 in St. Louis, MO) left Bremen, on Oct. 20, 1836, and arrived in St. Louis, on Mar. 2, 1837. He was a successful businessman who ran a hardware business, in St. Louis, MO, from 1838-72. In 1860, **Adolphus Meier & Co.** consisted of **Adolphus Meier**, his eldest son & **John C. Rust**. A number of **P. Hayden** planes were overstruck, suggesting the purchase of **Hayden's** stock, ca. 1847. **A, B, C & D *; B1 ****

 C

 D

HERMAN H. MEIER
Herman H. Meier (b. Aug. 13, 1812 in Hanover, Germany, d. Nov. 28, 1880 in Emma, MO) was a St. Louis, MO, hardware firm, appearing in 1853, as "successor to **Thomas J. Meier**" (b. ca. 1815 in Bremen, Germany and arrived in MO in 1842), and continued until 1864. **Herman M. Meier** was a wagon maker, in 1850. Example: on a 9 7/16" carriage maker's round, ca. 19c. ****

JN. MEIKIEJOHN
Example: on a 9 3/8" beech steel soled rabbet with a York pitch iron & wedge, ca. 19c. UR

G. MEIGGS
Example: on a 9 9/16" beech hollow with shallow round chamfers, ca. 1830. UR

MEIGS' PATENT
P. Meigs, of Madison WI, was issued a restored Patent No. 6730X, on Feb. 9, 1831, for an adjustable cap iron on a wood bench planes. The cap iron is stamped **MEIGS' PATENT** in an enclosed double circle. **No imprint on the wood body.**

W. MELIUS/ WM
Example: on a 9 7/8" beech rabbet with relieved wedge and heavy flat chamfers, ca. 1780-90. UR

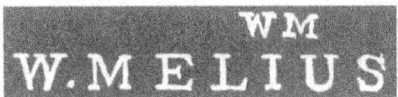 

I. MENNIE
Example: on a 9 1/2" beech side rabbet with flat chamfers, ca. 19c. UR

D. MERCER
Example: on a 9 1/4"x 2 3/8" rosewood boxed complex molder with round chamfers. Also with an incuse **HARRAR** imprinted, four times on the side, typical of PA planes, ca. 1820. UR

C. B. MERIHEW
Example: on a 15 1/2" beech cornice plane with a **W. Butcher** iron and flat chamfers, ca. 1800. UR

J. MERKER
Example: on a fully boxed 9 1/2" beech filletster with nicker and brass depth stop, ca. 1850-60. UR

I + MERRIAM
Example: on a 10 1/8" beech coping plane with flat chamfers, ca. 1790. UR

G. G. MERRICK
George Goupe Merrick (b. Jun. 16, 1814 in Thomaston, ME, d. Libertyville, Lake Co., IL) worked as a ship's joiner and planemaker, in Thomaston, ME, ca. 1840-60. After 1860, he moved to Libertyville, IL, where in 1870, Merrick was listed, as a wagon maker; and in 1880, as a wheelwright. Example: on a 7 1/2" smoother with a **James Howarth** double-iron. A, B & B1 ****

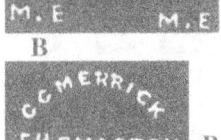
A
B
B1

A MERRIFIELD
Example: on a 7 1/2" beech compass smoother with a chamfered round-top wedge, and large shallow flat chamfers, ca. 1790. UR

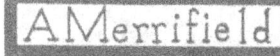

I. MERRILL
Jacob Merrill Jr. (b. Sep. 13, 1763 in Newburyport, MA, d. Apr. 18, 1841 in Plymouth, NH) was a Plymouth, NH, cabinetmaker, turner and carpenter, whose account books from 1784-1812, are in the NH Historical Society, indicate that he made smoothing planes, rabbets and fore planes, as well as other joiner's tools, farm and household tools and handles. Example: on a 10 1/4" rabbet; and a beech jack plane. ****

CHARLES H. MERRITT
Charles Henry Merritt (b. Mar. 22, 1827 in Scituate, MA, d. Sep. 9, 1894 in Norwell, MA) was a planemaker in S. Scituate, MA, from 1850-93. He was listed, in 1850 & 70, as a planemaker; in 1860, as a carpenter; and in 1880, as a plane manufacturer. He was a part of **Tolman & Merritt**, from 1864-93. **No imprint has been reported.**

J. MERRITT
James Merritt (b. Sep. 4, 1854 in Scituate, MA, d. 1940) was listed in the MA, business directory of 1878, as a Hanover, MA, planemaker. From 1870-78, he was in S. Scituate, MA, before moving to Hanover, MA. The location die **HANOVER/ MASS.** appears to be **T. J. Tolman**'s. S. Scituate is located on the coast and Hanover is located on the North River within 10 miles. *****

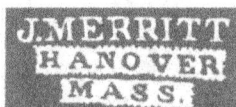

MERITT & CO./ MERRITT & CO.
Jacob Thorne Merritt (b. ca. 1810 in NY, d. ca. 1886 in Tuckahoe, NY) was a New York hardware dealer, chandler, and agent for **Z. J. McMaster** in the 1840's. The firm operated as **Jacob T. Merritt & Co.**, in 1841; and **Merritt & Co.**, from 1842-60; in 1848 & 50, as a plane-maker. **A, A1 & B** **

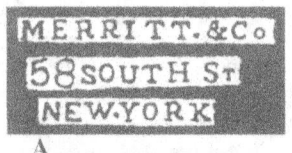

J. A. MERRY
Example: on a 6" smoother with a **Moulson Brothers**, warranted, cast steel iron, and a **Wm. Ash & Co.**, cast steel chip breaker, ca. 1850. **UR**

ABRAHAM MERSIER
Abraham Mersier (**Mesier**) advertised in the New York *Mercury*, the sale of recently imported items from Bristol and London. Included is an assortment of molding planes, long jack and smoothing planes. **No imprint has been reported.**

H. METCALF
Example: on a 9" beech triple bead, ca. 19c. **UR**

J. METCALF
Joseph Metcalf (b. Mar. 30, 1765 in Franklin, MA, d. Feb. 12, 1849 in Winthrop, ME) was apprenticed to his brother **Luther Metcalf**. He went to Hallowell, ME, by ox cart in 1789; then on to Winthrop, ME, where he was a cabinetmaker. **Joseph Metcalf**, apprenticed **Samuel Benjamin**, who became a furniture maker in Winthrop, and **Charles Robbins**. The shop that **Joseph** built, in 1789, together with lathe and hand tools was recently moved to the Fort Western Museum in ME. In 1800, **Joseph** was listed as a farmer and probably ended his plane making activities. Examples: on a 11" birch molders with heavy flat chamfers, found in ME, an early beech square; and a riveted birch adj. angle. ****

L: METCALF
Luther Metcalf (b. Sep. 7, 1756 in Franklin, MA, d. Jan. 27, 1838 in Medway, MA) was apprenticed to **Elisha May Richardson** (b. Aug. 4, 1730 in Methuen, MA, d. 1797 in MA) of West Wrentham, MA, beginning in 1770. The apprenticeship was interrupted by military duty during the Revolutionary War, during which he attained the rank of Major. He completed his training in 1778; and opened his own shop, making chairs and furniture. **Luther**'s brother **Joseph Metcalf** was probably apprenticed to him, in the 1780's. **Luther** advertised in *U. S. Chronicle* in Medway, Maf (MA), on Nov. 30, 1795: "ran-away, two indented apprentices, **Lemuel Ware**, age, 19; and **David Partridge**, age 20, **Luther Metcalf**, Cabinet Maker." On April 14, 1801, he advertised in the *Columbian Mercury*: "Wanted to Hire-A Journey man Windsor Chair Maker-also wanted one or two active Boys not exceeding 16 years of Age as apprentices to the Cabinet and Chairmaking Business. Inquire **Luther Metcalf**." In 1816, **Luther** made chairs and the communion table for the new Franklin, MA, meeting house. On Mar. 11, 1831, **Luther Metcalf** again advertised "Cabinet Furniture and Chairs", and signed the ad **Luther Metcalf & Son**, Medway. Examples: on a hollow, and a thumbnail, both 10" birch with a flat backed wedge and flat chamfers, found together in southern NH, with a **Ce. Chelor** thumbnail, an **I. Nicholson** thumbnail, a 10" birch complex molder, unfinished with the chamfer stops marked out but not cut; on a 10"x 1 1/4" birch straight rabbit with maple wedge and flat chamfers *****

CHRISTO METTER/
HENRY METTER/ THOMAS METTER
Christo Metter, **Henry Metter**, and **Thomas Metter** were listed as planemakers in the Columbus, OH, directory, in 1856-57, all at the same address. **No imprint(s) have been reported.**

JA. B. METZ
Jacob B. Metz (b. Sept. 8, 1826, d. Apr. 21, 1896) was a carpenter in Norriton, Montgomery Co., PA, and the son of **Nathaniel Metz** (b. Nov. 3, 1852). Example: on a 14" cherry screw-arm tongue plane with an owner imprint **N. METZ**. This imprint was also an owner imprint on an **E. W. Carpenter** screw-arm plow, ca. 1850. **A, A1 & B** ****

J + MEYER
Example: on a 9 5/8" beech coping plane with heavy round chamfers, probably from PA, one plane also imprinted with incuse **J. D. MYER** and **H. MYER**, ca. 1820. **UR**

MEYER & SCHULZE
August Meyer (b. ca. 1817 in St. Louis, MO, d. Apr. 27, 1865 in St. Louis) and **Charles E. Schulze** (b. ca. 1820 in Prussia) were St. Louis, MO, hardware merchants, active from 1857-59. **Schulze** continued as a hardware dealer after **Meyer**'s death in 1859. In 1867, the firm was listed as **Schulze Bros.** at 212 Vine, St. Louis, MO. **A & A1** **

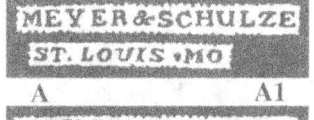

D. MICALIZZI
D. Micalizzi was a contemporary planemaker in Brooklyn, NY. Example on a 10" rosewood plane with a very fancy open toted plane. **UR**

D. MICALIZZI
B'KLYN
N.Y.

JOHN MICHAEL
John Michael (Michal) was listed in the 1849-53 Utica, NY directory, as a planemaker, working for **John Reed**.
No imprint has been reported.

G. MILES
Example: on a 9 1/8" beech square rabbet with shallow round chamfers, ca. 1830-40. **UR**

I: MILLAR
Example: on a 9 3/4" applewood nosing plane with heavy round chamfers, ca. 1810. **UR**

MILLER
Miller was probably a Providence, RI, hardware dealer. Example: on a jack; and a smoother with **Auburn Tool Co.** style numbers, ca. 1870. ******

A: MILLER
Examples: on a 9 13/16" beech complex molder with flat chamfers; and a round, both with the A wedge; a 10 1/2" applewood double-iron fixed sash with the B wedge profile, all with flat chamfers. ca. 1800. ********

A. MILLER
Examples: the A imprint is on a 16" panel raiser with the additional imprint of **Chas. Ashley/ Ogdensburg**, a hardware dealer, ca. 1860, possibly from upstate NY. The B imprint is from an 8" low angle miter plane with a single-iron; and a 16 1/4" bench plane, ca. 1850. **A & B *****

A. M/ A. MILLER (PHILADELPHIA)
Adam Miller (b. ca. 1811, d. ca. 1856) was a planemaker, in Philadelphia, PA, from 1839-50; and a journeyman who made bench planes for **Israel White** using the initials **A. M.**
No imprint is available.

A. R. & G. H. MILLER
Albion R. Miller (b. Jun 1832 in ME, d. Oct. 1, 1913 in Hennepin, MN) and **George H. Miller** (b. ca. 1830 in Ky, still living in IL in 1910) were listed in the Chicago, IL, 1865-66 directory as importers and jobbers of hard-ware and cutlery.

Albion R. Miller was listed in 1870, as a hardware dealer in Chicago, IL. In 1880, as a hardware dealer, in Hennepin, MN. *******

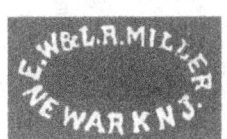

E. W. & L. R. MILLER
E. W. & L. R. Miller was a partnership with **Eliza W. Miller** (b. ca. 1820 in NJ, d. Feb. 10, 1876 in Jersey City, NJ) and **L. R. Miller**, probably a hardware dealer. Example: on an **Arrowmammett** plow plane. ********

F. M/ F. MILLER
Frederick Miller (b. 1817 in Hanover, Germany, d. Sep. 14, 1865 in Philadelphia, PA) was a planemaker, in Philadelphia, PA, from 1837-52. During part of this period **Miller** was a journeyman, for the **White** family, **Israel White, Charles White**, and **Henry G. White** using the initials **F. M.**. **Frederick Miller** enlisted in the Civil War as a Corporal, on Jul. 1, 1863, in the 45th. PA Militia and mustered out, on Jul. 7, 1863.
No imprint is available.

G: MILLER
Examples: on a 13"x 3 1/2" beech cornice plane with an offset tote, round-top iron and flat chamfers; a gutter plane with an offset tote; a 10" molder with the B wedge profile; and two 9 1/4" molders, all beech with heavy flat chamfers, from PA, ca. 1800. ********

H. MILLER/ HENRY MILLER
Henry Miller (b. ca. 1820 in Hanover, Germany, d. 1908) arrived in 1848 and was a St. Louis, MO, hardware merchant, from 1850-54 & 1860-65. **Miller** had previously clerked for **M. & N. H. Stout**. From 1857-1860, **Miller** was an agent for **W. W. Miller**; and during 1863, **Henry Miller** operated at **William W. Miller**'s address. Example: the B imprint is on a round with an **Ohio Tool Co.** iron. **A & B ****

H. B. MILLER
Henry B. Miller (b. ca. 1802 in OH, d. ca. 1860 in OH) of Lebanon, OH, located 20 miles northeast of Cincinnati, OH, was listed as a cabinetmaker, between 1828-31. He apprenticed:
Robert Hamilton, age 17, on Oct. 8, 1828, who he agreed to train, "in the trade".
Andrew McIvaine, age 17, on Jan. 31, 1829.
James Watson, Jr., age 17, on Oct. 15, 1830.
Joseph Gerrard, age 17, on May 25, 1831.
He was a partner with **Peter Probasco** in **Miller & Probasco** in Cincinnati, OH, in 1834. Example: on a 9 1/2" beech sash with round chamfers. The B imprint is on a 9 1/2" beech hollow with flat chamfers on the ends and round chamfers on the top. In 1850, **Henry B. Miller** was listed in

Cincinnati, OH, as a machinist, ca. 1830. **A & B** ***

Ix MILLER
Example: on a 9 1/2" beech sash coping plane with round chamfers, from PA, ca. 1820-30. **UR**

I. MILLER
I. Miller was possibly the same person as **Miller**, a hardware dealer of Providence, RI, active ca. 1870. Example: on a small smoother; and a cove plane, ca. 1850. **UR**

I. N. MILLER

Example: on a beech 5 5/16" child's match plane with a location of **McLEAN, N.Y.** and an inventory number **5**, ca. 19c. ****

J. MILLER
Examples: on a round plane with the location imprint **N. YORK**; a 9 1/4", size **5** hollow with the location imprint **75 CLAYTON** (possibly Clayton, NY); and a 9" beech bead, all with flat chamfers, ca. 1800. The wedge has Canadian influence. ****

J. MILLER
Centerberg is probably Centerberg, OH. Example: on a beech plow, found in OH, ca. 1840-50. ****

J. MILLER & BRO.
Examples: on two hollows, ca. 1850. **A & B** **

J. D. MILLER
J. D. Miller has been reported with the location imprint **BRIDGEPORT**; working dates are not known. **No imprint is available.**

JAMES MILLER
James Miller (b. Mar 1, 1815 in Ireland, d. Jan. 31, 1907 in Philadelphia, PA) arrived in Philadelphia, on Aug. 12, 1817. **James Miller** was listed, in the 1845 Philadelphia directory, as a planemaker. **No imprint has been reported.**

JOHN P. MILLER
John P. Miller (b. Jan. 12, 1809, d. Mar. 13, 1890 in Middletown) was listed as a planemaker, in Cincinnati, OH, in 1842, at the cor. 8th & Broadway. **No imprint has been reported.**

M. MILLER
M. Miller was a New York City, hardware dealer. Example: on a **Ohio Tool Co.** round and on a **Weiss & Sohn** (imported from Austria) rabbet. ***

PETER MILLER
Peter Miller (b. ca. 1816 in Germany, d. Dec. 27, 1877 in Cincinnati, OH) was listed as a planemaker, in Cincinnati, OH, in 1843-44. **No imprint has been reported.**

S. MILLER
Example: on a 14" beech single boxed complex molder with an offset tote, round top chamfers and flat toe and heel chamfers, ca. 1800-20. **UR**

W. W. MILLER
William Warden Miller (b. ca. 1819 in KY, d. Jul. 26, 1895 in Callaway Co., MO) was a St. Louis, MO, hardware merchant, active from 1857-60. **

MILLER & BOWERS
Miller & Bowers was a hardware dealer with a location of **CARLISLE** possibly north of Cincinnati, OH. Example: on the heel of a smoother made by **Auburn Tool Co.**, ca. 19c. ****

MILLER & PROBASCO
Probably a partnership of **Henry B. Miller** and **Peter Probasco** made planes in Cincinnati, OH, in 1834. **A & A1** ***

MILLIGAN
Thomas Milligan (b. ca. 1835 in Ireland) was listed in the 1868 Boston, MA, directory under hardware, at 210 Federal St. In the 1868 directory there is a **James Milligan**, listed as a carpenter, living at 16 Ontario. In an 1876 directory, **James Milligan** is listed under hardware, at 229 Federal, with a house at 18 Ontario. It is possible that **James** took over his father's business. Example: on an **Auburn Tool Co.** razee jack. ****

E. D. MILLIKEN
Example: on a hollow & round pair. One example has a Humphreyville Mfg. Co. iron made in Seymore, CT (1852-84), ca. 1850. ***

I. MILLS
Example: on a 9 1/2" beech molder with heavy flat chamfers, ca. 1810. UR

JAS. MILNE
Example: on a 9 1/2" beech molder with flat chamfers, ca. 1800. UR

GEORGE MILNOR
George Milnor (b. 1806, d. Sep. 1, 1854 in Philadelphia, PA) was listed, as a planemaker, in the 1837 Philadelphia, PA, directory. **No imprint has been reported**.

JAMES MILNOR
James Milnor (b. Mar 20, 1814, d. Aug 19, 1892 in Bucks Co., PA) was listed, as a planemaker, in the 1845 Philadelphia, PA, directory. In 1870, **James Milnor** was listed at a machine shop, in New Hope, Bucks Co., PA. **No imprint has been reported**.

D: MILSTED
Example: on an 8 3/4" birch small ogee molding plan with flat chamfers, ca. 19c. UR

J. MILTON
J. Milton with the location Lanesboro is on a 11" birch molder in the collection of the Shaker Museum, Chatham, ca. 1790. **No imprint is available**.

J. MILTON
Joseph Milton (b. July 22, 1789 in Henniker, NH, d. Sept. 22, 1864 in Canaan, NH), the father of **M. H. Milton**, was a cabinetmaker and planemaker, in Canaan, NH, from 1818-1850. Examples: on 9 1/2" beech molding planes with flat, round, and early 19c style chamfers. A, A1 & B: **

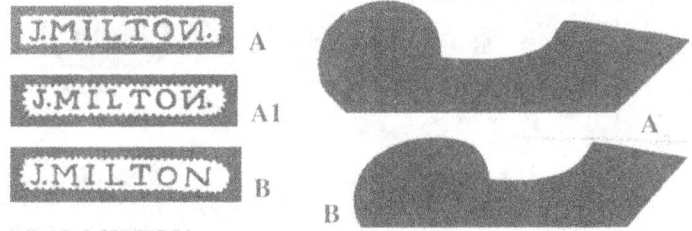

M. H. MILTON
Matthew Harvey Milton (b. Oct. 28, 1819 in Canaan, NH, d. Mar. 19, 1905 in Canaan) was the oldest son of **J. Milton**, a cabinetmaker and planemaker. **Matthew** specialized in joiners planes, in Canaan, NH, until 1854, when he became a merchant in Canaan and Lowell, MA. Examples exist bearing the imprint of both father and son, which may indicate that they worked together. On Jul. 11, 1861 and Dec. 15, 1866, **Matthew Harvey Milton**, was appointed Post Master of Canaan, Grafton Co., NH. In 1870, **Matthew Harvey Milton** was listed as Notary Public, in Canaan, NH. In 1881, he was listed as "country store" in Canaan, NH. ***

MILWAUKEE TRUE FIT
Example: on a 9 1/2" beech square rabbet with an adjustable metal fence and two wing nuts. ca. 1900. ****

E. MINER
Miner (**Minor**) is a common eastern CT name. Example: on a 9 3/8" beech modified "V" groove with flat chamfers, ca. 1800. UR

G. MINER
Example: an embossed imprint on the toe and incuse imprint on the heel of an 8 7/8" beech plow with wood thumbscrews, wood slopped depth stop, round top arms, riveted skate, and heavy round chamfers, ca. 1820. UR

JONA MINNICH
Example: on a 14"x 3 1/2" fruitwood panel raiser with two fences, probably from PA, ca. 1800. UR

P. MINOR
Peleg Minor (**Miner**) (b. Jan. 7, 1757 in Stonington, New London Co., CT, d. 1800) was an toolmaker and cabinetmaker, in Stonington, CT. A plane, double stamped, has been passed down with a highboy and is reported to be by the maker. **Peleg's** estate inventory showed a small quantity of woodworking tools, including 15 planes and "Carp. Tools", 3 chisels, augers, two old saws, a square, and a drawing knife. **No imprint is available**.

J. MINOT
James Minot advertised, in 1802, in the **Vermont Sentinel** for a journeyman/ cabinetmaker; and again, in 1803, for an apprentice to the coach and chaise making business, in Burlington, VT. Examples: molders are 9 1/4"-9 1/2" beech with both flat and round chamfers. One is marked on the heel with the incuse **10 CENTS**; and a 14 1/4" adjustable fenced tongue with the owner imprint **J. SAWIN**, a carpenter born in Windhall, VT, who in 1830, was in Londonderry, VT, ca. 1800-30. **

MISSOURI PREMIUM
Missouri Premium is a mystery imprint that is on a screw-arm plow made by **H. C. & T.** Haywood, Crow & Talbot, who worked in St. Louis in 1854-53, at 51 N. Main St.; a **G. H. Nichols** plane; and a **Scioto Works** plane, all ca. 1850.
A, A1 & A3 ****

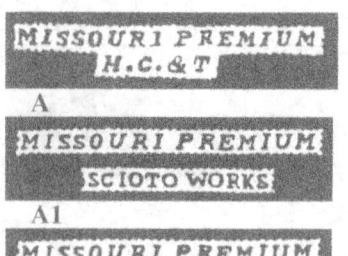

I. MITCHEL
Example: on a 9 1/2"x 1/4" bead, a double-boxed complex molder with size **3/8** on the heel, both beech with heavy round chamfers, ca. 1820. **UR**

E. MITCHELL
E. Mitchell probably was a hardware dealer. Example: on a size 4/8 match pair of tongue & groove planes made by **D. R. Barton & Co.** **UR**

H. E. MITCHELL
H. B. Mitchel was a saw and tool maker in Eastbourne, ca. 19c. ****

I. D. MITCHELL
Isaac D. Mitchell (b. Apr. 16, 1836 in IN, d. 1902, OH) was listed in the Dayton, OH, city directories, as a carpenter, in 1868, and a planemaker, from 1871-90 & 1898-1900. He also made cooper's tools, filed saws, and dealt in various craftsman tools. Example: on an 8 13/16" beech door check plane with a **W. Butcher** iron and breaker iron, ca. 19c. ****

J. MITCHELL
Example: on a 9 1/2" beech boxed side-bead plane with shallow round chamfers, ca. 1830. **UR**

R. MITCHELL
Examples: on a double coping plane; and a small nosing plane, both 9" beech. ****

W. A. MITCHELL & CO.
William A. Mitchell (b. May 14, 1818 in Ayrshire, Scotland, d. Mar. 5, 1885 in Philadelphia, PA) was part of **William A. Mitchell & CO.**, a hardware dealer, from 1846-52, at 148 N. 2nd, Philadelphia, PA. In 1853, **William A. Mitchell** was listed as a lumber merchant; in 1856, as "rolling mill"; and then as an iron manufacturer. In 1867, the listing was **Verree & Mitchell**, iron & steel manufacturers. Example: on the toe of a 22" fore plane made by **H. Chapin**. ****

JOHN T. MIX & CO.
John T. Mix & CO. was listed as a New Haven, CT, hardware dealer, ca. 1850. Mix was part of **English & Mix**. From 1849-54, John T Mix was listed, as a carpenter, in New Haven, CT; from 1855-71, as a joiner. Example: on a jack plane made by **W. H. Pond/ New Haven**.
No imprint is available.

N. MKELVEY
Example: on a wedge-locked armed plank grooving plane, probably from PA, ca. 1830. **UR**

A. MOCKRIDGE
Abraham Mockridge (b. 1802, d. Nov. 15, 1873 in Newark, NJ) was a partner with **David Bensen** in **Bensen & Mockridge**, in Albany, NY, in 1830-31. **Mockridge** left Albany for Newark, NJ, in 1833. He was listed in the Newark directories, in 1835-36 & 1840-41, as plane & coach tool maker, at 145 Washington St., across from 150 Washington St., the address of **George W. Andruss**. From 1835-68, he was a partner in **Mockridge & Francis** at the same address. **Abraham** was the father of **Oscar B. Mockridge** and from 1868-73 they were partners in Mockridge & Son. A & A1 *

EDWIN W. MOCKRIDGE
Edwin W. Mockridge (d. Sep. 14, 1923 in Newark, NJ) was listed as a planemaker in Newark, NJ, from 1850-1915, at 222 Plane. On Aug 29, 1861, **Edwin Mockridge** was listed as a Civil War Private in the 8th. Reg. from NJ. How **Edwin** relates to **Abraham Mockridge** or **Oscar B. Mockridge** is unknown.
No imprint has been reported.

MOCKRIDGE & FRANCIS
Abraham Mockridge (b. 1802, d. Nov. 15, 1873 in Newark, NJ) and **Elias Francis** (b. 1813 in NJ, d. May 30, 1892, in NJ) were partners in this Newark, NJ, plane making and hardware dealership, from 1835-68. Their planes are the most plentiful of any NJ planemaker. A three-arm adjustable plow plane with a metal center adjusting mechanism, both handled and unhandled, was apparently developed and sold by the firm. The firm was succeeded by **Mockridge & Son**, in 1868.
A, B & B1: FF

MOCKRIDGE & SON
Mockridge & Son was the successor to **Mockridge & Francis**, in 1868. It was headed by **Oscar B. Mockridge** (b. Jun. 10, 1844 in Newark, NJ) the son of **Abraham Mockridge**. The firm made planes and dealt in hardware and tools, at 235 Washington St., in Newark, NJ, from 1868-1902. **Oscar** continued to use this imprint after his father's death, in 1873. *

R. MOFFET
Example: on a 9 3/8" beech complex molder with heavy flat chamfers, ca. 1800. **UR**

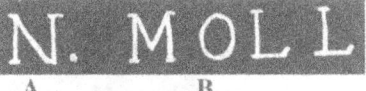

N. MOHR
Nathaniel Mohr (b. 1817 in PA, d. in 1861 in Muncy, PA) was listed as a "chair maker & other items related to the trade" and advertised in 1848 & 1855, in Muncy, PA. The imprint appears to be the same imprint as **HERMAN. &. MOHR./ MUNCY** with the "HERMA" and "&." removed, ca. 19c. ****

M. MOLINEUX
Example: on a 9 1/2" beech astragal with round chamfers, ca. 1820. **UR**

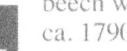

N. MOLL
Two imprints, the larger branded on the side the smaller with a date **1854**, on the toe of a gun stock plane, found in northern IN or southern MI area, ca. 19c. **A & B: UR**

N. P. MOLTON
Example: on a 12 1/8" nosing plane with an offset pegged tote; and a 13" (modified) panel raiser with a centered tote, both beech with flat chamfers, ca. 1790-1800. **UR**

H. MONG
Example: on three planes found together in OH; a 12 1/2" toted quarter round with the A wedge; a 9 3/8" full boxed bead; and a 9 1/2" single boxed bead, all beech with flat chamfers. ca. early 19c. ****

I. MONIOY
The last name is probably (**Monjoy**). Examples: molders are 9 3/8"-9 1/2" beech with narrow flat chamfers. The A wedge is on a 9 3/8" hollow. The B wedge is on a 9 3/8"x 1 3/8" beech rabbit with flat chamfers found in PA, ca. 1810. ****

O. MONNIG
Example: on a 9 9/16" beech round plane with shallow round chamfers, ca. 1840. **UR**

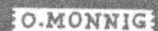

I. O. MONROE
Example: on a 9" beech coffin smoother, ca. 1850. **UR**

MONTGOMERY/ J. A. MONTGOMERY
Joseph A. Montgomery (b. Apr. 1, 1820 in Dorchester, MA, d. Mar. 3, 1899 at Sandusky, OH). In 1837, at age 17, he witnessed a land deed to **Samuel R. Cummings**, in Attleboro, to whom **Montgomery** probably apprenticed. **Montgomery** moved to Boston, MA, in 1843; and was part of **Cooley & Montgomery**, in 1844, at 94 Blackstone; a part of **Hull & Montgomery**, in 1845-46, at 86 Blackstone; and **Montgomery & Woodbridge**, in 1847, at 55 Blackstone. He was listed as a planemaker, in 1848 only. He was later part of **Hall, Case & Co.** in Columbus, OH, prior to 1852, when it was absorbed by the **Ohio Tool Co.**; He was foreman, from 1852-61; and a superintendent and manager of the **Sandusky Tool Co.**, starting in 1869. He received several patents for plane making machinery. A rosewood plow with ivory and silver made by the **Ohio Tool Co.**, was presented to foreman **J. A. Montgomery**, in 1857. Example: the B imprint is from two plows, one rosewood and the other boxwood, both with four ivory tips and found in New England. (see *Patented transitional & Metallic Planes in America, Vol. II*, p. 66, by Roger K. Smith) **A & A1** ***, **B** *****

ISAAC C. MONTGOMERY
Isaac C. Montgomery (b. Jan. 29, 1827 in Attleboro, MA, d. Jul. 2, 1894 in Sandusky, OH) was listed, as a planemaker, in the 1850 Smithfield, RI census, boarding with and working for **Ezekiel Smith**. In 1860, **Isaac** was listed, as a planemaker, in Indianapolis, IN; In 1870, a joiner, in Laramie, Wyoming Territory; in 1880, a toolmaker, in Sault Sainte Marie, MI. **No imprint has been reported**.

N. MONTGOMERY
Example: on a 9 3/4" beech bead with rosewood single-boxing and heavy flat chamfers, ca. 1790-1810. **UR**

W. H. MONTGOMERY
Example: on a 9 1/2" beech double-boxed bead, marked with size **8/8** on the heel, ca. 1850. **UR**

MONTGOMERY & WOODBRIDGE
Montgomery & Woodbridge was a partnership of **Joseph A. Montgomery** (b. Apr. 1, 1820 in Attleboro, MA, d. Mar. 4, 1899 in Sandusky, OH) and **Edwin C. Woodbridge** (b. 1821) of Boston, MA, who made planes in 1847. In 1850, **Joseph** was

listed as plane factory in Columbus, OH; In 1870, as working in "Tool Co.", in Sandusky, OH. in 1851, **Edwin** was listed under "planes", in Boston, MA. **A, B & B1** ***

W. MOODY
Example: on a 13 5/8" beech double-iron fixed sash with a centered tote and heavy flat chamfers, ca. 1810. **UR**

A. MOOER
Example: on a 9 3/8" birch skew rabbet with **VIII** imprinted on the iron and with round chamfers, ca. early 19c. **UR**

J. MOOHGY
Example: on a 9 5/8" beech fluting plane with flat chamfers found in Southeastern, PA, ca. early 19c. **UR**

MOON & LABY
Moon & Laby was listed as a Cincinnati, OH, "planemaker and coach tool manufacturer" in 1849-50, at n.s. 6th. bt. Broadway & Culvert. **

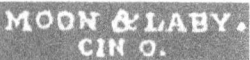

MOORE
William Moore was listed, as a hardware dealer, in New York City, from 1844-47. Example: on a plane made by **William Ward**. The C imprint is from a 9 7/16" beech single-boxed complex molder with round chamfers. This may be the same or two separate persons, ca. 1820. **A, B & C** **

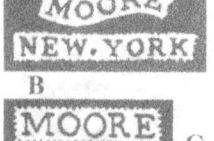

A. MOORE
Example: on a 10 1/4" beech molder. **UR**

A. G. MOORE/ A. G. MOORE & CO.
Albert G. Moore (b. Apr. 9, 1820, d. Sep. 2, 1898) was listed in the Newark, NJ, directories, from 1847-50's, as a planemaker. He was listed, as a New York City planemaker, from 1853-61, at 65 1/2 Bowery, the same address used by **J. W. Farr**, in 1852; and **R. W. Hendrickson**, between 1859-61. The two planemakers at the same address might account for the **& CO**. Example: on a plane, dated **1855**; and on a plane made by **J. Denison** which indicates that he may also have been a dealer. In 1855, **A. G. Moore** was listed, as a planemaker in NY; In 1860, as a tool maker, in NY; From 1865-70, as a planemaker, in Riverhead, NY; in 1880, as a carpenter, in Riverhead, NY. **A, A1, A2, A3 & B** *

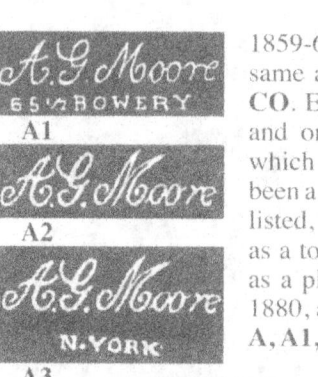

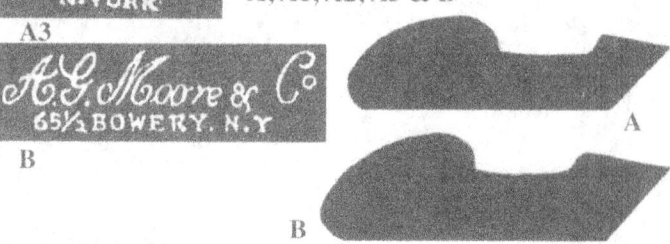

C. H. MOORE
C. H. Moore was probably a Cincinnati, OH, hardware dealer, with no known dates. Example: on a plane made by **C. Ashley** of Binghamton. ****

G. MOORE
Example: on a 9 3/8" beech round, ca. 1840. **UR**

JAMES MOORE & SON
James Moore & Son was a partnership of **James Moore** and his sons **Byron Moore** and **Ira B. Moore**, who were Concord, NH, hardware dealers, active from 1872-83. They advertised, as agents for joiner's tools. In 1850, **James Moore** was a carpenter, in Concord, NH. ****

P. MOORE
Examples: on a 9 3/8" beech round; and an 8 15/16" beech grooving plane with round chamfers, ca. 1820. **UR**

R: MOORE
Example: on a 9 15/16" birch round molder with heavy flat chamfers, ca. 1780-1800. **UR**

THEOPHILUS MOORE
Theophilus Moore was listed, as a planemaker, in Baltimore, MD, in 1819. An ad in the *American and Commercial Daily Advertiser* of Baltimore, MD, on May 15, 1819, read:

"**THEOPHILUS MOORE**, Plane maker, Respectfully informs the public that he has commenced his trade in Lexington, near North Street - where planes will be sold cheap and warranted equal to any made in America. His father carried on the business in England fifteen years, has been foreman in Philadelphia, New Jersey, New York and Baltimore, and will conduct the business for him. All orders by

him will be thankfully received and neatly executed. Planes made & repaired at New York premises."
To further confuse the issue, a **Theophilus Moore** was also listed as making planes in Liverpool, England, from 1823-67. **No imprint has been reported**.

T. MOORE/ THOS. MOORE
Thomas Moore was listed, as a planemaker, in Baltimore, MD, from 1814-16, 1823 & 1829-36 and possibly his son, **Thomas Moore** (b. 1822 in VA) who was listed, in the 1850 census, for Richmond, VA, as a cabinetmaker. A **Thomas Moore** made planes in Liverpool, England, and was listed as a planemaker in 1794 & 1807. Because of the similarity of the working dates, and the common Liverpool origin, it is felt that **Thomas Moore** and **Theophilus Moore** are closely related and possibly father and son. Example: the A imprint is on a 9 3/8" beech skew rabbet with wide round chamfers. The B imprint is from a 9 1/4" beech quarter round molder with round chamfers, ca. 1820. A & B: ****

W. MOORE
Example: on a 9 3/4" beech complex molder with flat chamfers. ca. early 19c. - UR

WILLIAM H. MOORE
William H. Moore (b. ca. 1810 in MD) was listed in the Baltimore, MD directory of 1835-36; in 1847-51, as a planemaker, at Lombard St; in 1860, as "furniture store" in Louisville, KY. **No imprint has been reported**.

MOORE & BRO.
Moore & Bro. was a hardware dealer. Example: on an **A. & E. Baldwin/ New York** plane, ca. 19c. UR

MOORE & CILLEY

Example: on a 14 1/2" beech jack with 19c chamfers, found in ME, ca. 1840-50. UR

I x MOORS
Examples: on a 9 5/8"x 1/2" beech dado with flat chamfers; a 12 5/16" beech tongue & groove pair with flat chamfers; a 13 1/8" panel raiser with a round top **James Cam** iron and wedge, and flat chamfers; a 12 1/4" beech gutter plane with double-pegged centered tote and 19c style chamfers; a 9 1/2" beech rabbet with 19c style chamfers; an 8" beech Yankee plow with wood thumbscrews, iron depth stop screw and flat chamfers; a 10" beech fixed sash with birch wedge and flat chamfers; and on a **W. Raymond** plane, probably as an owner imprint. The D

wedge was from a 9 1/2" beech quarter round with flat chamfers, from New England, ca. 1810-40. ****

R. MORATH
Example: on a 16 1/4"x 2 1/2" beech ogee with closed tote and round chamfers, ca. 1830. UR

A. C. MORE
Abner C. More (**Moore**) was a planemaker in Goshen, MA, from 1848-51. He sold his mill site and machinery to the newly formed **Union Tool Co.**, in 1851. Example: on a 9 7/16" beech size **12** round; and a bead. (see **Lester & More**) **

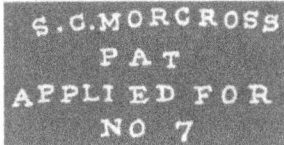

S. C. MORCROSS
Examples: on a 11 1/2" handled beech plow with brass depth stop, bronze arms, and a scissors mechanism held with thumbscrews to adjust the arms with **PAT. APPLIED FOR/ NO 7**. There is no record of this patent, ca. 1860-70. UR

C. MOREHOUSE
Charles P. Morehouse (b. ca. 1810, d. Mar. 6, 1897) was listed as a New Haven, CT, planemaker, from 1840-46; and as a joiner, from 1849-57. Examples: on a 9 1/2" beech boxed bead overprinted by a **W. H. Pond** imprint. **Pond** was a New Haven planemaker, from 1844-80, who used the same embossed **NEW HAVEN** die on his A imprint. Possibly **W. H. Pond** bought out **Morehouse**'s stock or **Morehouse** was a journeyman employee of **Pond**. ****

P MOREHOUSE & CO.
Examples: on a 9 1/2" beech full-boxed bead with size **5/8** on the heel; and a size **1/4** bead. ca. 1850. ****

E: MORGAN
Ebenezer Morgan (b. May 30, 1756 in Ledyard, CT, d. Mar. 23, 1831 in Groton, CT) was a Groton, CT, cabinetmaker. A plane with this **E: MORGAN** imprint is with the family. **Ebenezer's** widow **Oliver Morgan** received a Revolutionary War pension. **Ebenezer Morgan's** inventory included one chest of tools: $2.50. Examples: the A imprint is on a 10 1/8" birch hollow with birch wedge and heavy flat chamfers; a 9 3/4" birch skew thumbnail plane with small flat chamfers; a 9 3/4" beech bead with a steep pitched iron and round chamfers; and two 9 5/16" beech molders, one double-boxed, both with shallow round chamfers. The B imprint is on a 9 5/16" double-boxed bead, ca. 1790-1830. A & B ****

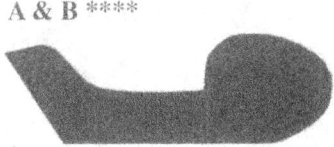

G. MORGAN
Example: on a 9 1/2" beech complex molder with shallow round chamfers. The B imprint was struck twice on a **B. King/ T. Fugate** 9 3/8" birch Gothic bead as an owner, ca. 1840.
A & B: UR

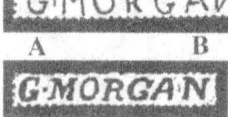

I. MORGAN
Possibly **John Morgan** (b. ca. Jul. 11, 1736 in Groton, CT, d. Nov. 8, 1799 at Groton, CT) whose inventory included "carpenter and joiners tools - 60." This name has been reported on a 9 1/4" molder. **No imprint is available**.

J. T. MORGAN
Examples: imprinted on both halves of a 9 3/4" beech double-coping plane, ca. 1850. **UR**

Z. MORGAN JR.
Examples: on a double-bladed fixed sash; a boxed bead with round chamfers; and two complex molders, one boxed, all 9 1/2" and beech, ca. 1840. ********

M. MORIARTY
Matthew Moriarty (d. 1911) arrived in Bangor, ME, in the 1860's as a sailor and apprenticed to **Samuel Doyen**, of Bangor, in 1867. **Moriarty** operated a cooperage for 40 years, retiring in 1906; listed, as a toolmaker, in the 1873 Maine directory, making cisterns and cooper's tools to order. On July 16, 1872, **Moriarty** was issued Patent No. 129419, for an adjustable howel. By 1880, he had 15 hands, paying mechanics $1.25/ day and laborers $1.00/ day; in 1887, he was still listed as a cistern builder; in 1895, he was listed as "water casks", both in Bangor, ME. ********

JULIUS MORISSE/ JULIUS MORISSE & CO.
Julius Morisse (b. ca. 1821 in St. Louis, d. Dec. 25, 1891 in St. Louis) clerked for **T. J. Meyer Hardware Co.** in 1847; in 1848, **Morisse** established his own hardware firm of **Julius Morisse & Co.** in St. Louis, MO; from 1849-91, it was simply **Julius Morisse**. The location die is identical in style to those of **Adolphus Meier** and **Child, Farr & Co.**
A, A1 & B *

F. L. MORONI
Francis L. Moroni (d. 1886 in Brockton, MA) was listed in Boston, in 1830; in 1872, **Moroni** was listed as a carpenter in Abington, MA; in 1874-76, as a carpenter, in Brockton, MA.
W. BRIDGEWATER is most likely West Bridgewater, MA, half way between Boston and Buzzard's Bay. Examples: on a pair of 9 3/4" right & left hand skew rabbet planes; a 9 9/16" beech side bead, with the date **1837**; a 9 1/2" hollow; an 8 1/2" fruitwood miter; moving fillester, with an apple body, bearing the date **1843**; and a 30 7/8" fruitwood joiner with a centered tote, dated **1848**. ********

A. MORRILL
Possibly **Adam Morrill** (d. Sep. 25, 1807 in Amesbury, MA) who was listed as a shipwright in Amesbury, MA. Examples: the A imprint is on an 11 1/8" rosewood miter plane. The A1 imprint is on a 10 13/16" rosewood miter.   **A & A1 ******

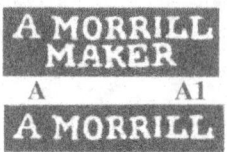

B. MORRILL
Benjamin Morrill (b. ca. 1789 in Newburyport/ Amesbury area, d. Oct. 14, 1862 in Bangor, ME) was a joiner and tool maker in Bangor, ME, from 1832-51. His father was a carriage maker. His two sons **Daniel Morrill** and **Benjamin H. Morrill** became wheelwrights and carriage makers. The Minutes of the Bangor Mechanics' Association, for Dec. 4, 1832, gave his occupation as "Plane Maker." **Morrill** was first listed in the Bangor city directory in 1834 as a toolmaker; in 1843 & 51 as a joiner; in 1850 as a carpenter; and in 1860 as a planemaker. He served in the ME State Legislature and was a captain in the state militia.   **A & A1: FF; B ****

C. G. MORRILL
Example: on a combination fruitwood tongue & groove plane cutting in the same direction, with components screwed together, and a handle similar to the **P. A. Gladwin**'s patent. **UR**

D. C. MORRILL
Example: on a 30" jointer, found in ME.   **UR**

E. C. MORRILL
Examples: on a 14 3/4" beech gutter plane with a cherry tote and wedge, a double-iron and shallow round chamfers; and a 28" joiner stamped **EM**, ca. 1830.   **UR**

S. MORRILL

Example: on a large round; and a birch jack with a pegged offset tote, ca. 1800. **A & B; UR**

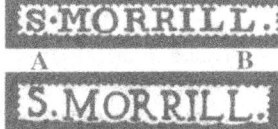

AARON MORRIS

Aaron Morris (ca. 1814 in NJ) was listed in the Newark, NJ, directory of 1837-38 as a "plane maker" at Market corner of High St.; in 1850, **Morris** was listed, as a carpenter, in Newark, NJ. **No imprint has been reported**.

E. MORRIS

Example: on a 9 1/2" hickory ogee complex molder with heavy flat chamfers, ca. 1800. **UR**

J. MORRIS

Example: on a 9 1/2" beech narrow filletster with flat chamfers, ca. 1810. **UR**

J. A. MORRIS

J. A. Morris (b. ca. 1842) was married on Sep. 21, 1905, in Bucksville, AR. Example: on a 9" coming & going plane, cuts an size **1/8** tongue and grove, with a bronze skate, with the date **1878** and **MAKER, BUCKSVILLE**, found in eastern PA. **UR**

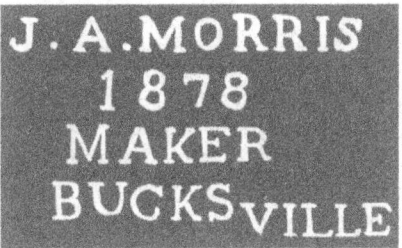

I. MORRISON

Possibly **James Morrison** a cabinetmaker of Pittsburgh, PA, who advertised in the *Pittsburgh Gazette* on March 25, 1803, for an apprentice who run away. Examples: on a complex molder, found in PA; a pair of handled match planes, found in the Erie, PA area; a 9 3/8" beech round with size **7/8** on the heel; and a side bead with size **3/8** on the heel, found in eastern PA, all with interrupted lignum vitae ware stripes in their soles and small round chamfers. An owner's brand **JNo. COGGINS** was branded into the side of the round, probably from PA, ca. 1800-20.
A & B **

J. MORRISON

Examples: on a 9 1/2" ogee; a 9 1/2" cove & bead; a 9 1/2" skew rabbet; and a 9 7/16" hollow, all beech with flat chamfers and with an **I. Sleeper** style wedge and probably from New England, ca. 1800. *****

J. MORRISON

John Morrison (b. ca. 1800 in NJ) advertised, as a planemaker, in the Chillicothe, OH, *Supporter and Scioto Gazette* during May & June 1826. In 1850, **Morrison** was listed as a tool maker in Vinton, OH. Examples: on a 14"x 4" panel raiser with full adjustable side and bottom stops, and a **James Cam** iron; a 22" jointer with an offset tote; a complex molder; a double-iron fixed sash; and a small tongue with the B wedge profile, all beech with round chamfers, ca. 1820. ****

A MORSE

Example: on a 9 9/16" birch rounding plane and a wedge-arm plow, both with heavy flat chamfers, ca. 1800. **UR**

A. H. MORSE

Example: on a 13 3/4" apple pump plane with offset pegged open tote, round top iron and wedge, and heavy flat chamfers, ca. 1800. **UR**

I. MORSE

Example: on a pair of 12" beech tongue & groove match planes with an integral closed tote and shallow round chamfers, found in NH, ca. 1830. This was too late for an early mark of **J. Morse, Jr.** but possibly his son **Joshua Morse** (b. July 5, 1804, d. 1833) who was also a carpenter. **UR**

J. MORSE JR

Joshua Morse, Jr. (b. Jan. 7, 1774 in Merrimack, NH, d. Mar. 14, 1826 in Hopkinton, NH) was a carpenter, joiner and toolmaker, in Hopkinton, NH, who advertised in 1816 & 19, that he made tools for joiners, cabinetmakers and coopers: "with stocks and irons for bench tools and molding tools of all descriptions, of the best quality, in the newest fashions, warranted good. He will take most kinds of Country Produce, Cash, or approved notes in payment. Orders by Post-Riders will be particularly attended to the same as if purchasers themselves were present." **Isaac Long** was connected to **Joshua Morse** through the marriage of their children. A hollow & round made by **I. Long** is overprinted by **J. Morse Jr.**, with the incuse B imprint, suggesting that **J. Morse** may have succeeded **I. Long** and acquired his stock.
A, B, C & D **; B1 ***

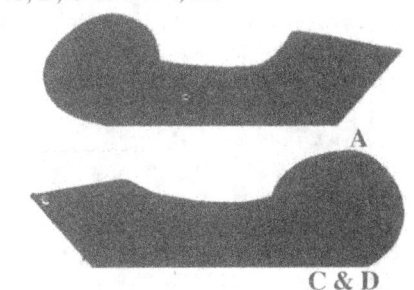

S. MORSE
Examples: on a 10 1/2" beech round with heavy flat chamfers; and a 10 1/4" quirk, ovolo & astragal, also imprinted **S. Chase**, ca. 1800. **UR**

A. S. MORSS
Anthony Smith Morss (b. Apr. 4, 1824 in Newburyport, MA) was a Boston, MA, hardware and chandlery dealer, from 1847-1900. Morss was first listed, in 1845-46, as a partner with **Curtis Haven** in **Haven & Morss Hardware**. Morss marked and sold carpenter's and cooper's tools. Example: on a **J. R. Tolman**. **A & B ****

C. W. MORSS
Charles W. Morss was a Boston, MA, hardware dealer from 1868-76. Morss was first listed, in 1866-67, as a partner with **John H. Burchsted,** in the hardware firm of **Morss & Burchsted**. In 1869-71, Morss was listed, as hardware, at 24 Union. ****

W. H. MORSS
Example: on a 9 1/2" beech with flat tight chamfers, ca. 1800-20. **UR**

E. MORTON
Examples: a 9 1/2" complex molder with flat chamfers and a 12" beech grooving plane with an integral closed tote and heavy round chamfers, ca. 1810-30. **UR**

E. S. MORTON
Example: on a 9 1/2" beech complex molder with shallow round chamfers, ca. 1840-50. **UR**

I: MORTON
Example: on a 9 1/2" birch complex molder with shallow wide flat chamfers, probably from New England, ca. 1800. **UR**

NATHANIEL MORTON
Nathaniel Morton (b. Feb. 20, 1769 in Middleboro) was apprenticed to **Simeon Doggett**, a planemaker, from Middleboro, MA, in 1783. Nathaniel was married, in 1791, and listed, as a joiner and housewright.
No imprint has been reported.

MORTON & COURTNEY
Morton & Courtney was a hardware store operational, from 1850-54, at 35 Hayne Street, Charleston, SC. The store was destroyed by fire, in 1854. The insurance claim was by **Courtney, Tennett & Co.** with **William Crocker Courtney** (b. Sep. 4, 1818 in Lexington, SC, d. Dec. 24, 1885 Charleston, SC) In 1850, **Courtney** was listed, as a merchant, in Charleston. In 1877, **W. C. Courtney & Co.** was in cotton factors at Boxce's whf., Charleston. In 1880, **Courtney** was listed as Bank of Charleston, President. Example: on a 9 1/2"x 2" wide molding plane, ca. 19c. ****

A. MORTON & CO.
This imprint with the additional location imprint **CLEVELAND**, probably Cleveland, OH, has been reported on several planes, ca. 1850. ****

QUIN MORTON/ Q. & W. L. MORTON
Quinn Morton (b. ca. 1829 in Charlotte, VA) and **W. L. Morton** were listed in the 1852 Virginia directory as Petersburg, VA, hardware merchants. Morton was also a part of **Van Lew & Morton**, ca. 1850. In 1872, **W. L. Morton** was listed, as insurance agent, in Petersburg. Example: on an 8" all boxwood plow. **A & B ****

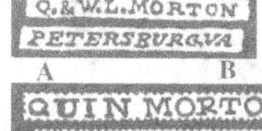

A. MOS
Example: struck twice on the toe of a squat unhandled plow with beech body and fence, hickory screw-arms, boxwood locking nuts, rosewood key locks, and a brass depth stop. The plane is constructed like an **E. W. Carpenter** improved-arms patent, with the arms threaded through the plane body, probably from Lancaster, PA, ca. 1840. **UR**

J. MOSELEY
James Moseley (Mosely) (b. 1811 in England) arrived from England, Oct. 9, 1832. James was listed, in the 1834, Utica, NY, directory, as a planemaker, possibly working for **R. J. Collins**. Moseley was listed, as a planemaker, in the 1850 census, living in Richmond, IN. He advertised his plane making in the Richmond *Jeffersonian* between 1846-51 as "selling at Cincinnati prices." How **James Moseley** may be related to the British **Moseley** toolmakers is unknown. ***

L. H. MOSELEY
Example: on a fruitwood 23" jointer with a centered closed tote and a **W. Butcher** iron, ca. 1830-40. **UR**

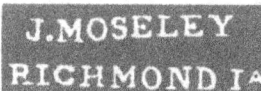

A. MOSES
Possibly **Artemus Moses** (b. June 23, 1773 in VT) was married on Jul. 26, 1809, in Middlebury, VT; in 1815, in Salisbury, VT, Moses was working, as a carpenter & joiner. Examples: on a 9 5/16" beech skew rabbet with round chamfers; and a 9 5/16" beech hollow with flat chamfers, found in Middlebury, VT, ca. 1820. ****

MOSES/ E. MOSES
Edward Moses (b. 1815 in CT, d. ca. 1894 in NY) made planes in E. Hartford, CT; Deposit, Hastings and Ashford, NY. In 1850, **Moses** was listed in Sanford, NY, as a planemaker. One

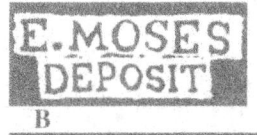 example of **E. Moses** is overstamping by **P. Brooks/ E. Hartford**. ca. 1850. **A, B, B1 & B2 **; C, C1, D & E *****

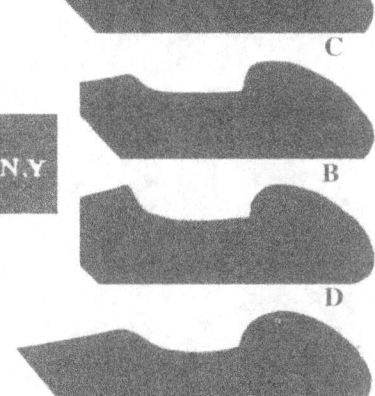

L. MOSES
Example: on a 9 3/8" birch coping plane, ca. 1800. **UR**

WILLIAM MOSEY
William Mosey was listed as a planemaker in Cincinnati, OH, in 1849-50. **No imprint has been reported.**

A. H. & W. V. MOSS
Augustus Hitchcock Moss (b. 1811 in NY, d. Dec. 6, 1888 in Sandusky, OH) and **William V. Moss** (b. 1821 in NY, d. Nov. 25, 1916 in OH) were listed in the 1850 census as merchants and probably hardware dealers in Portland, OH. Example: on a 9 1/2"x 3/4" bead with size **18** on the heel, found in the Cleveland, OH, area. ********

J: MOSSER

Example: on a 9 1/2" (shot at the heel) beech round with flat chamfers, ca. 1800. **UR**

I. MOTT
Example: on a 9 3/8" sash ovolo with round chamfers; and a 9 5/16" quarter round size **5/8** on the heel, both beech with birch wedges, ca. 1820. **UR**

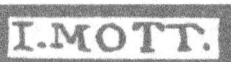

J. MOTT
Example: on a 13" beech fenced rabbit with an adj. bottom, offset open tote with flat chamfers and a diamond strike. ca. 1800. **UR**

MOUND CITY PLANE CO.
Mound City is the nickname for St. Louis, MO. This might be a brand name rather than a maker. Examples: on a 7 3/4" double-iron smoother with **3** on the toe; and a **13** bench plane. Both of which are **Sandusky Tool Co.** inventory numbers. A broad ax has been reported marked **MOUND CITY/ ST. LOUIS. MO.** ca. 1850. *******

S. MOXLEY
Possibly **Seth Moxley** (b. Mar. 21, 1759 in Groton Township, New London Co., CT, d. Oct. 1, 1802 in Tunbridge, Orange Co., VT) or more probably **Samuel Moxley**, who was a shipbuilder in New London, from 1802-23, according to *Mystic Built* by Bill Peterson. Examples: on a 12 1/2" birch mast plane or large hollow with a centered tote and heavy round chamfers; a 10" apple hollow with wide flat chamfers; a 10 1/2" apple ovolo molder also with flat chamfers; and a 6" fruitwood compass smoother, struck twice on the toe, with round chamfers, all found in southeastern CT, ca. 1800-20. ********

H. MOYER

Examples: on a 13 1/2" apple wedge-locked adjustable grooving plane with a centered open tote, screw-on skate, and heavy round chamfers, probably from PA, ca. 1820-30. **UR**

WM. MUIR & CO.
William Muir & Co. with **William Muir** (b. 1827 in England, d. Jul. 20, 1890 in Hartford, CT) made planes in Windsor Locks, CT, dates unknown. In 1870, **Muir** was an organ maker in Suffield, CT. **UR**

JOHN MUDIE
Example: on a 9 5/8" beech large round with flat chamfers with size **1 1/2** on heel, ca. 19c. **UR**

GEORGE MULLER
George Muller (**Mullear**) (b. ca. 1830 in Prussia, d. May 31, 1892 in NY) of New York, NY, was issued Patent No. 55,207, on May 29, 1866, for a transitional jack plane. Example: on a 16 1/4" beech jack with a double-iron marked **EXCELSIOR/ PATENTED/ MAY 29, 1866**. He also held Patent No. 50,378, issued Oct. 10, 1865, for similar mechanisms. (see *Patented Transitional & Metallic Planes in America, Vol. II*, p. 82, by Roger K. Smith) **No imprint is available.**

MULTI-FORM MOULDING PLANE CO.
Founded by **Thomas D. Worrall** (b. 1825-26 in England, d. 1902) in 1856, and operating, from 1856-58, in Boston, MA,

Charlestown was part of Boston. There is also speculation that **Porter A. Gladwin** had some interest in the company. The company manufactured planes with interchangeable soles, based on Patent No. 11635, granted Aug. 29, 1854. Other patents include No. 14979, granted May 27, 1856; No. 16309, granted Dec. 23, 1856; No. 17657 granted June 23, 1857; and No. 18312, granted Sept. 29 1857. The company made a wide range of plane types and sizes, including complex molding, though rare, plow planes, tongue & groove combinations, beads, etc. Planes were made of beech, boxwood and by special order rosewood. The company also made a few conventional planes. In 1858, **Thomas D. Worrall** was a part of **Lowell Plane & Tool Co.**, at 84 Broadway, Lowell, MA. Examples: on a beech screw-arm plow; a boxwood smoother; and a beech rabbet, using the B imprint. (see *Patented and Transitional & Metallic Planes in America, Vol. I*, p. 25-36, by Roger K. Smith).
A: FF; C, C1, B & D ***

G. MUNDORFF
Example: on a beading plane; a match plank grooving plane with 19c style chamfers; and a jack plane with the added location imprints **BERLIN** and **PA** which is in Western, PA, south of Johnstown near the MD border, ca. 1820-40.
A & A1 ***

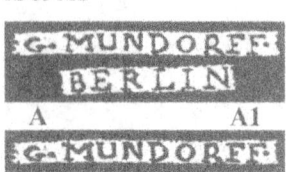

D. MUNRO
Examples: on a 9 7/16" beech complex molder with flat chamfers, ca. 1800. UR

Ix MUNRO
Example: on a 22 1/2" beech jointer with a decorative, closed heavily offset tote, heavy flat chamfers and the top pitched down forward and aft of the escapement. The 60% pitch of the iron is called "1/2 pitch" and is used by cabinetmakers for figured hardwoods. The plane exhibits Dutch influence and may have originated from the Hudson River Valley area where it was found, ca. 1800. UR

GEORGE MUNROE
George Munroe (b. 1828 in RI) was listed, as a planemaker, in Smithfield, RI, the 1850 census, boarding with and working for **Ezekiel Smith**. **No imprint has been reported**.

M. G. MUNSON
Example: on a 9 3/4" beech square rabbet, ca. 1850. UR

A. MURDOCK
Amasa Murdock Jr. (d. Apr. 6, 1843 in Boston, MA) made planes in Boston, MA, from 1825-50. In 1828, Murdock became a member of the MA Charitable Mechanics Assn., as a planemaker. He was part of **Gardner & Murdock**, active from 1825-42. Eden B. Foster, the administrator of the estate of the late **Amasa Murdock, Jr.**, planemaker, of Boston, ran an ad in the summer of 1843, announcing the auction of real estate. Examples: the A imprint is on a 10 1/16" beech center bead with the A wedge profile. The B imprint is from a 13 7/8" birch bench plane with an iron strike, an offset tote that is pegged with "mouse ear" top and a round-top wedge; and two 10" birch hollows with a relieved wedge slot, both with the B wedge profile and flat chamfers, ca. 1790-1810.
A ***; B *****

JN. MURDOCK
Example: on a 9 3/16" rabbet, ca. 1850. UR

I: MURIBUI
Example: on a 10" birch complex molder with heavy shallow flat chamfers, ca. 1780. UR

Js MURRAY
Example: on a 9 5/8" beech hollow with flat chamfers, ca. 19c. UR

W. D. MURRAY
W. D. Murray was probably a hardware dealer. Example: on a 9 1/2" moving filletster, and a rosewood plow with boxwood screw-arms and nuts, made by **J. Kellogg/ Amherst**, MA. UR

AARON MUSIC
Aaron Music was listed, as a planemaker, in the 1845 Philadelphia, PA, directory. **No imprint has been reported**.

C. MUZZY
Probably **Cephas Muzzy** (b. Sept. 29, 1785 in Spencer, MA, d. Dec. 11, 1861 in West Boylston, MA) who was a joiner and skilled woodworker, in West Boylston, MA. Examples: on several 9 1/2" beech hollows with skew blades and heavy round chamfers, ca. 1810-20.
A, B & C ****

M. MYER
Example: on a 7 1/2" beech wedge-lock plow plane with round chamfers, ca. 1820-30.   UR

JEREMIAH MYERS II
Jeremiah Myers II was listed under "Planes" in Boston, MA, in 1858 only. He was a maker of "planing, moulding, and matching machines, portable steam engines, etc". In 1870, **Myers** was listed as a sashmaker in Boston.
No imprint has been reported.

J. MYERS
John M. Myers (d. 1914 in Columbus, OH) was listed, as a planemaker, in Columbus OH, in 1856-57. In 1870, **Myers** was listed as "works at tool factory". Example: on a 7 1/4" beech plow plane with wedge arms.   UR

J. MYGATT
Jonathan Mygatt (b. Jul. 23, 1759, d. Sep. 18, 1822 in New Milford, CT) a New Milford, CT carpenter and Joiner working, from 1789-1803. Example: on a 9 7/8" applewood molder with flat chamfers, ca. 1800.   UR

N. E. TOOL WORKS
The **New England Tool Works** was located in Groton, CT, was a contemporary plane maker using exotic woods.   UR

J. NALL
Example: on a 9 1/4" double-boxed beech ovolo and bead with heavy round chamfers, ca. 1810-20.   UR

T. NAPIER/ THOs. NAPIER
Thomas Napier (b. Nov. 18, 1747 near Glasgow, Scotland, d. Nov. 19, 1812 in Philadelphia, PA) was apprenticed in Glasgow, became a journeyman toolmaker, in Edinburgh, and opened his own business, in 1773. In Sept. 1774, **Napier** intended to immigrate to New York, to escape the political unrest and depressed economic conditions in Scotland. The destination of the ship was changed to Philadelphia. He arrived in Philadelphia, in Nov. 1774, and set up a planemaking shop. Among his first orders, in Dec. 1774, was one from **James Stiles**, the New York planemaker and merchant, in the amount of one pound one shilling, "for making Sundry plans". Records of his activities during the Revolutionary War are non-existent, although he was a member of the Philadelphia militia. In 1785, **Napier** was again recorded, as having a shop in Philadelphia; in 1786, advertised that he carried, "all manner of carpenters, joiners, cabinet makers, chair makers, coach makers and coopers tools made in the best and neatest manner." Again in the *Pennsylvania Mercury*, for April 28, 1786, he advertised 57 different types of planes, "by **Thomas Napier**, a planemaker from Edinburgh" adding that he could make, "any kind of plane to drawing or pattern, to the greatest exactness, the charge according to the work in them." In 1794, **Napier** moved to Wilmington, DE, where he was engaged in coopering; returning to Philadelphia and plane making, in 1796. By 1797, he was also manufacturing and selling "**Napiers** Pills." His estate of approximately $500 was appraised by **William Grinel**. **Hugh Hazlet** the administrator of **Napier**'s wife's estate in 1820, and **George White** was the appraiser. **Thomas Napier** imprinted his name in both Scotland and America. The Scottish imprint **THO. NAPIER**, without the **S**, has been reported on a 9 3/4" beech molder with flat chamfers. The **T. NAPIER** B imprint is probably the later. One example of this imprint with the location imprint **PHILDA**, has been reported, and is designated the B1 imprint, but is not available. See *Thomas Napier - The Scottish Connection* by Alan G. Bates).   A **; B ***; A1 *****

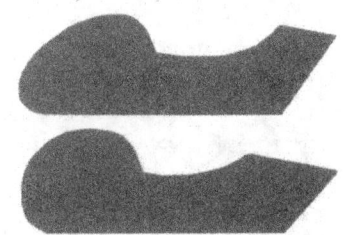

A. T. NAPPY
A. T. Nappy with a location of **PLYMOUTH**, MA and **WARRANTED** was reported on a 9 3/8" beech side round, ca. 19c. ****

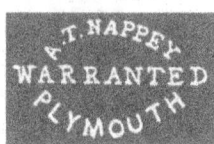

H. L. NARAMORE/ H. L. NARRAMORE
Henry Lyman Narramore (b. Jan. 19, 1836 in Goshen, Hampshire Co., MA, d. Nov. 05, 1898 in Sharon, Norfolk Co., MA) was listed, as a planemaker, in Cummington, MA, in 1859. **Narramore** made planes in Goshen, MA, from 1865-72. He was listed in the **G. W. Denison** account book, as supplying beech. **B & B1 *; A1 ****; A *******

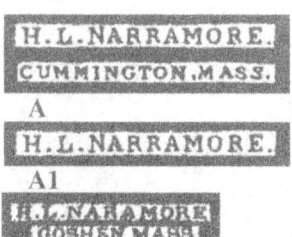

J. J. NASH
Examples: on a 9 1/2" beech complex molder, found in OH; a 9 3/8" beech round found near Lexington, KY, ca. 1850. ****

M. NASH
Examples: on two 9 1/4" beech complex molders with heavy round chamfers, found in the New Bedford/ Taunton, MA area, ca. 1820. **UR**

JOHN NASSON
Examples: on a panel raiser; a 12 9/16" beech sash plane; a 9 3/4" beech complex molder with very small flat chamfers and the A relieved wedge; a 10 1/4" beech complex molder with heavy round chamfers and B wedge; and a 11 1/2"x 1 3/4" skew rabbet with small round chamfers, ca. 1800-20. ****

NATHUSIUS, KUGLER & MORRISON
Oscar Albrecht Nathusius (b. Saxony, Germany, arrived in New York in Dec. 11, 1855) and **Charles E. A. Kugler** (d. probated Jul. 26, 1900 in NY) and **Robert Morrison** (b. ca. 1830 in Ireland) were partners in this New York City hardware firm, active from 1859-76. **Nathusius** was also part of **Nathusius & Kugler** and **Oscar A. Nathusius & Co.** either before or after this venture. Example: the A imprint is on a toothing plane made by **J. H. Lamb/ New Bedford**. The B imprint is on a 22" fore plane with an **Ohio Tool**

Co. double-iron. **A **; B *****

B

J. C. NAY
Example: on a 9 1/2" sash with double irons & wedges, ca. 19c. **UR**

GEO. W. NAYLOR
The **Geo. W. Naylor** imprint is similar to that of **John M. Naylor & Co.**. Example: on a 9 1/2"x 3/8" single-boxed bead made by **Owasco Tool Co.** **UR**

JOHN M. NAYLOR & CO.
John M. Naylor & Co. was probably a hardware dealer in Tiffin City, OH. **John M. Naylor** (b. 1817 in Adams Co. OH, d. Jan. 31, 1873 in Eugene, IN) was listed in the 1850 census as a merchant living in the village of Clinton, a suburb of Tiffin City. Examples: on planes made by **Casey & Co/ Auburn, N.Y.**, the **Sandusky Tool Co.**, and the **Auburn Tool Co.**, ca. 1870. ******

HENRY J. NAZRO.
Henry James Nazro (b. May 21, 1823 in Troy, NY, d. Sep. 21, 1905 in Boston, MA) was part of **Nazro & King** 1844-47, was a hardware dealer in Milwaukee, WI, in 1847, **Henry J. Nazro & Co.**, from 1848-59, consisting of **Henry J. Nazro** and **John G. Nazro**, a cousin. In 1860, **Henry J. Nazro** left the company and it was continued as **J. Nazro & Co.**, from 1860-80. **Henry Nazro** was part of **Hart & Nazro**, in Troy, NY, in 1840. In 1880, **Henry James Nazro** was listed, as Commissioner, "flour mkt." in Boston, MA. ******

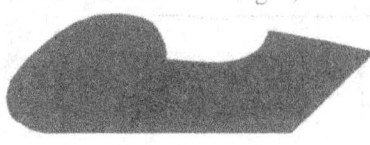

H. J. NAZRO & CO./ HENRY J. NAZRO & CO.
Henry J. Nazro & Co. was a Milwaukee, WI, hardware dealer, from 1848-59. This firm consisted of **Henry James Nazro** and **John G. Nazro** (b. 1826 in the West Indies, raised in Boston, MA, d. 1888 Milwaukee, WI), a cousin. It was succeeded by **J. Nazro & Co.** in 1860. **A *; B ****

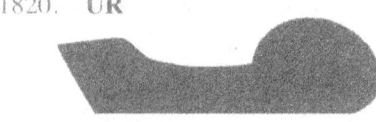

J. NAZRO & CO./ JOHN NAZRO & CO.
John G. Nazro (b. 1826 in the West Indies, raised in Boston, MA, d. 1888 in Milwaukee, WI) was a hardware dealer in Milwaukee, WI, from 1860-80, succeeding **H. J. Nazro & Co.**. He may have continued to use the **H. J. Nazro & Co.** imprint. Example: **J. NAZRO & CO./ MILWAUKIE** has been reported on a round. **No imprint is available**.

NAZRO & KING
Henry J. Nazro from MA, and **Henry Uriel King** (b. Sep. 1817 in CT, d. Oct. 11, 1877 in Philadelphia, PA), were hardware dealers in Milwaukee, WI, from 1844-47. Note at

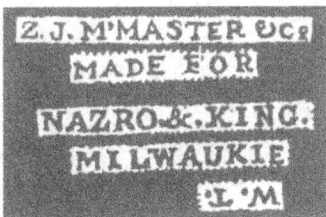
that time the location was spelled **MILWAUKIE** and **W.T.** for Western Territories. Examples: on **T. J. M'Master & Co.** and **Z. J. M'Master & Co.** planes. **

W. NEAL

Examples: on a 9 1/4" beech molder; and a 9 1/2"x 1/2" beech double-boxed bead made by **C. Warren/** Nashua, ca. 1850.
A, B & C: UR
B & C

S + NEALLY
Example: on a 10" beech dust-joint molder with flat chamfers, ca. 1800. UR

B. B. NEALS

Examples: on a 22" fore plane with the A imprint; and a coffin smoother with the A1 imprint, both with an **Auburn Tool Co./ Thistle Brand** iron. ****

A1

J. NEARY
Examples: on a 9 5/8" narrow round; a 9 3/8" single-boxed complex molder with the B wedge profile; and a 9 1/16" medium hollow, all beech with heavy round chamfers, ca. 1820-30. ****

SAMUEL NEEL
In 1875, **Samuel Neel** was listed as a planemaker in Columbus, OH. From 1880-88, as a carriage maker, working at **Booth's** carriage shop, Columbus. From 1890-93, **Neel** was listed as "body maker". **No imprint has been reported**.

S. NEEL
Samuel Neel (d. Aug. 27, 1859 Ohio, WV) was a hardware dealer in Wheeling, VA (now WV), from 1839-59. **Neel** was

listed in the 1839 Wheeling directory, as a dealer in hardware, cutlery and saddlery, 11 Monroe, St. ***

OTIS NEEREAMER
Otis Neereamer was listed as a planemaker in Columbus, OH, in 1856-57. **No imprint has been reported**.

PETER NEFF & SONS
Peter Neff (b. Aug. 28, 1822 in Ireland, d. Feb. 18, 1912 in Pultney, Belmont Co., OH) **& Sons** was a wholesale hardware

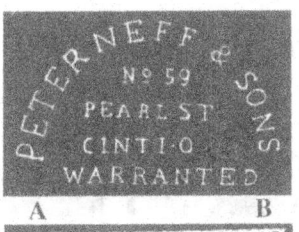
dealer in Cincinnati, OH, from 1849-65. Examples: the A imprint is on a skew moving filletster with **114** on the toe, the **Ohio Tool Co.** style number for a raising plane. The B imprint is on a 9 1/2"x 3/4" coming & going match plane. A & B **

THOs NEGUS & SONS
Thomas Negus & Sons was a hardware dealer and sold nautical

instruments in New York City. Example: on a bead with **123** marked on the heel which is a **H. Chapin**'s style number for a single bead. ***

NEALSON & HAYNER
Arba Nelson (b. 1806 in VT, d. probate Apr. 4, 1872 in Alton, Madison Co., IL) and **John E. Hayner** (d. probate Aug. 3, 1901 in Madison Co., IL) were partners in a hardware dealership in Alton, IL, from 1853-73. Alton is across the Mississippi River from St. Louis, MO. **Nelson** started the store, in 1836, and **Hayner**, his brother-in-law, worked for him starting in 1844 and was made a partner, in 1853. In 1874, **Mrs. Charlotte Nelson**, widow of **Arba** and **John E. Hayner** were in "maf." of lumber, lath, boxes, etc. for **A. H. Drury Co.** From 1862-79,
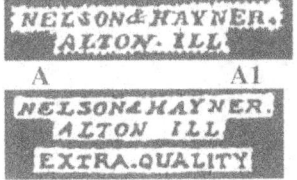
John E. Hayner was a trustee for Shurtleff College, in Alton, IL. From 1889-90, he was President of Alton Savings Bank and Treasurer of the Alton Building & Loan Association. A & A1 ***

S. NEVENS
Example: on a 11 3/8" birch pair of handled tongue & groove

planes with brass wear strips, ca. 1820. UR

NEW BEDFORD TOOL CO.
The **New Bedford Tool Co.** was listed in the New Bedford, MA, directories, from 1873-79, as a manufacturer of bench and molding planes, as well as a hardware and tool dealer. The company employed **W. G. Lamb** and his brother **J. H. Lamb** and is believed to be the successor to the **Taber Plane Co.** **No imprint has been reported**.

NEW HAVEN PLANE CO.
The **New Haven Plane Co.** was advertised at cor. St. John & Artizan Streets, New Haven Conn. "manufacture every description of planes and coach tools" with **John C. Page** and **M. A. Carrington**. Example: on a 16" beech jack with
N. H. Ct, ca. 1850. *****

NEWARK PLANE RULE & LEVEL CO.
Newark Plane Rue & Level Co. was listed in Newark, NJ, from 1878-86. In an advertisement in the 1879 city directory, **E. Francis**, late of **Mockridge & Francis**, was listed as superintendent of this company. They advertised: "full sets of

planes and all kinds of tools for carpenters, coopers, carriage and cabinetmakers furnished to order or made to draft. Level glasses reset, repairing and cutters made to order." *****

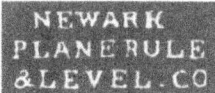 

A. H. NEWBOULD
Alexander H. Newbould (b. 1812 in NY, d. 1856 in Detroit, Wayne Co, MI) was a hardware dealer in Detroit, MI, from 1837-55, and was succeeded by **Buhl & Ducharme**. **Charles Ducharme** was a Clerk with **A. H. Newbould** in 1845-46.

 **A. H. NEWBOULD/ CHICAGO** has been reported but is unavailable. **

J. A. NEWBOULD
John A. Newbould (b. 1810 in NY, d. May 31, 1871 in Kings, NY) advertised as a Buffalo, NY, hardware dealer, in 1836. **John** married on Nov. 1, 1836 in Buffalo, NY. ***

J. A. & F. W. NEWBOULD
John A. Newbould and **Frederick W. Newbould** were partners as hardware dealers at 23 Main Street in Buffalo, NY, from 1861-69. In 1859, **Frederick** was listed as hardware, in NY. ***

NEWBURN
 **Edward M. Newburn** (b. 1811 in MD) was listed in the 1850 census for Henrico Co., Richmond VA, as a merchant probably a hardware dealer. Example: on a handled tongue plane. ****

BENJAMIN NEWBURY
Benjamin Newbury (b. 1765, d. Feb. 28, 1838 in Wethersfield, Hartford Co., CT) was listed, on May 4, 1790, as making and selling tools & planes, in the account book of **James Francis**, a house builder, in Wethersfield. **No imprint has been reported**.

A. NEWELL
Probably **Asa Newell** (b. ca. 1768 in Salem, MA, d. Jul. 8, 1845 in Charlton, Worcester Co., MA) **Asa** married on Oct. 24, 1790, in Charlton and was living in Charlton, from 1790-1820. Examples: the A imprint is on an ovolo with a double fillet and narrow flat chamfers; a size **7** hollow; a size **23** round; a 9 7/8" cherry ovolo; and a 13 1/4" applewood match tongue plane, struck twice on the toe, with a birch double-pegged off-set tote, a beech round top chamfered wedge, and wood thumb-screw locked birch fence, wood depth stop and flat chamfers. The B imprint is on a 9 1/4"x 3/4" rabbet found near Lanesboro, MA, ca. 1790-1810. **A & B** ***

A. NEWELL
Andrew Newell made planes in New York City, from 1886-92. Newell was a tool dealer from 1898-1905. **

E. NEWELL
Capt. **Ebenezer Newell** (b. 1747, d. May 2, 1808) of Lanesboro, MA, served in the American Revolution. His estate inventory, dated Oct. 5, 1810, included $25.50 of sundry joiner's tools, 20 "chisells", 20 files, 8 gouges, 5 handsaws and a lathe. Examples: his early molders are 10"-9 3/4" birch with flat chamfers. One example has fluting on the toe and heel similar to an early **Jo. Fuller** and heavy flat chamfers. The later examples are 9 1/2" beech with flat chamfers. At least one early example has a relieved wedge, ca. 1770-90. **A & A1** ****

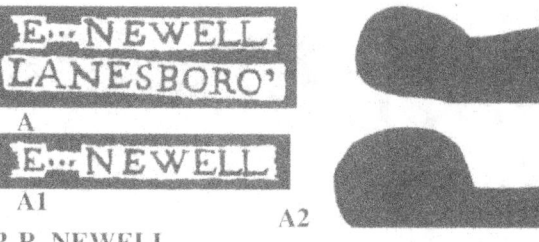

P. R. NEWELL
Example: on a 10" birch hollow with a beech wedge and heavy flat chamfers, ca. 1800. **UR**

S. NEWELL
Example: on a 10" astragal bead with round chamfers with a relived wedge, ca. 1820. **UR**

H. B. NEWHALL CO.
 Example: on a 16" jack with a double **Dwight French & Co.** iron, ca. 1850. ****

O. NEWHALL
 Example: on a molder with no chamfers, ca. 1850. **UR**

NEWHALL & STEBBINS
Newhall & Stebbins were probably hardware dealers, active ca. 1850. Example: on a **M. Copeland & Co.** molding plane. **UR**

A. N/ A. NEWTON
Probably **Asahel Newton** (b. Aug. 28, 1784 in Weathersfield, VT, d. Jan. 21, 1857 in Middlebury, VT) was listed in 1820 as in manufacturing, in Middlebury, VT; and in 1850, as a cabinetmaker. On Aug. 14, 1807, **Asahel** married **Thankful Heaton**. Example: on a 9 3/8" beech sash coping plane with heavy round chamfers; and a

9 1/2"x 1" beech molding plane with flat chamfers, ca. 1800-20. **UR**

 B

C NEWTON
Example: on an 8 1/4" birch boat-shaped smoother with a round-top wedge and a heavy flat chamfers; a 9 9/16"x 5/8" birch round; and a 14" cherry jack plane with an offset pegged tote and shallow flat chamfers, possibly from New England, ca. 1790-1810. ********

L. D. NEWTON
Example: on a 9 3/4" double-blade fixed sash with a bone ware strip; and two 9 1/2" beech molders, one with a skew blade; ca. 1830-40. ********

O. NEWTON
Example: on a 9 1/2"x 3" beech double-boxed Grecian ogee, and on a hollow by **H. Wells**, ca. 1850. **UR**

S. NEWTON
Example: on a 10 3/8" cherry nosing plane with heavy flat chamfers, ca. 1800. **UR**

W. NEWTON
Example: on a 10 1/4" birch sash with wide round chamfers and a relieved wedge, ca. 1790-1810. **UR**

L. W. NEWTON/ H. S. DEWEY
Levi W. Newton and **Henry S. Dewey** were partners in a plane making firm in Bethel, VT, from 1854-57. They were listed as manufacturers of planes in Atwater's 1857 Vermont Directory & Commercial Almanac. **Dewey** received Patent No. 16,954, on Mar. 31, 1857, for a machine to cut plane throats on carpenter's plane stocks. **Dewey** later became a millwright. In 1867, Newton was listed as a maker of washing machines. Example: on a 22" beech fore plane. ********

NEW YORK TOOL CO.
The **Auburn Tool Co.** used this brand name on planes, from 1864-93. **A, A1, A2, B, C & C1: FF**

NEW YORK WORKS
New York Works may be a brand name. Example: on an 8" smoother, ca. 1850. ********

H. NICE
Example: on a 9 1/2" beech tongue & groove pair, struck on the toe and heel, with round chamfers, ca. 1820. **UR**

MICHAEL NICE
Michael Nice was listed as a planemaker in Philadelphia, PA. No working dates were listed. **No imprint has been reported**.

B: NICHOLS
Example: on a birch jointer with an **I. Shaw** iron, ca. 1770. **No imprint is available**.

D. NICHOLAS
Example: on a wedge-arm plow plane with slightly rounded chamfers, ca. 1840. **UR**

G. M. NICHOLS
Example: on a 9 1/2" round, ca. 1850. (see **Missouri Premium/ H. C. & T.**) ********

H. F. NICHOLS
Example: an applewood fenced dado, ca. 1790. **UR**

J. NICHOLS
Examples: the A imprint is on a 27"x 2 3/4" beech narrow fore plane with an offset closed tote, a diamond strike and flat chamfers. The B imprint is on a 27"x 2 3/4" birch narrow fore plane with an offset tote and a diamond strike, ca. 1800-10. **A & B: UR**

J. B. NICHOLS
J. B. Nichols with **NY**. Examples: the imprint A is on a 15 1/2" beech shipwright's rabbet with an integral closed tote and a bottom adj. fence. the B imprint is on a 9 3/8" beech hollow with round chamfers, ca. 19c. ********

P. F. NICHOLS

Examples: the A imprint alone on a 10 7/8" coffin low-angle smoother with a strike button on the heel and a **Moulson Brothers** iron and heavy round chamfers; the A and B imprints on a 9 1/2" beech, full boxed, double bead also marked **M. Copeland/ Warranted**, ca. 1850. **A & B: UR**

W. NICHOLS

Possibly **Walter Nichols** (d. Oct. 1, 1832 in Warwick, Kent Co., RI) who married, on Oct. 5, 1775, in Newport, RI. **Nichols** was listed, as a cabinetmaker, in Newport, RI, starting in 1782-99. Examples: on a 10 1/4" beech shiplap plane with heavy flat chamfers; and a 9 1/2" beech quarter round with heavy round chamfers, ca. 1780-1820. **UR**

NICHOLS. BELLAMY & CO.

Nichols Bellamy & Co. was probably a hardware dealer. Examples: on a beech coffin smoother by **A. Heald & Son** and on a 1/2" dado by **Marten Doscher**. ********

NICHOLS & HERRICK

Nichols & Herrick was a partnership of **Samuel Nichols** (b. 1793 Chittenden Co., VT, d. Jan. 11, 1869 in Burlington, Chittenden Co., VT) and **John Herrick** (b. 1794 in Topsfield, MA, d. 1872) that may have started, before 1816-36. Example: on a 9 9/16" beech fixed sash with round chamfers and also imprinted **J. Herrick**, ca. 1820-30. ********

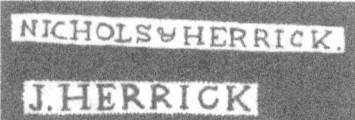

F. NICHOLSON

Francis Nicholson (b. 1683-4, d. Dec. 7, 1753 in Wrentham, MA) is believed to be the earliest documented American planemaker. **Francis** was the father of **John Nicholson** and the owner of the slave **Cesar Chelor**. The location of **Francis Nicholson**'s birth is unknown, he could have been born in England, but there is no record of his coming to America. There were however, **Nicholsons** who were joiners in Boston, MA, in the late 17c. **Francis** was in Boston, MA, by 1707 and until at least 1712. He married **Abigail Badger**, in Boston, on Mar. 10, 1707; and his son, **John** was born there on Mar. 4, 1712. **Francis** was listed as a joiner, in 1716, in Rehoboth, MA, when **Abigail** died. He married **Sarah Ware**, in 1727, and moved to Wrentham, in 1728. **Sarah** died, in 1729, and **Francis** married twice more, first to **Sarah**'s sister **Mary Ware**, in 1730; and then to **Hanna Gray**, in 1748. He was Town Clerk, in 1740; and became a deacon of the church in 1744. In his will of April 1, 1752, he refers to himself as a toolmaker; he left most of his tools to **John Nicholson** and some tools to **Cesar Chelor**, together with his freedom and some land. The C imprint was the first variation of the name die. Two examples exist, a crown molder and a 10 1/2"x 3/4" round, both birch with heavy flat chamfers. Neither has a location imprint and may have been made prior to his location in Wrentham, in 1728. The A imprint, a large **WRENTHAM** imprint with the **AM** joined, has been reported on two examples: on a 9 7/8"x 1" birch astragal; and a round. The B imprints are on molders 10 1/8"-9 3/4" birch with flat chamfers. The D imprint is cruder and probably is his earliest mark, from a 9 5/8" birch plow with wedge-locked arms, no depth stop and heavy flat chamfers. The earlier planes have small round finials and larger flat chamfers that end in a large lamb's tongue. The **LIVING IN** component of the B imprint appears to have been used later. Many planes with the B1 imprint have plenty of room for the extra line and show a consistency in the earlier features. Planes with the B imprint have the larger, "boxier" finial and smaller chamfers. The B2 imprint is on narrow planes of either style. The **WRENTHAM** die was used by **Cesar Chelor** and **John Nicholson**. **B, B1 & B2 ****; **A, C & D *******

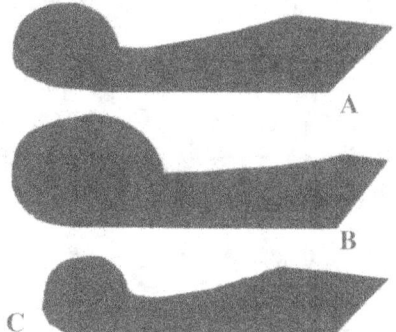

I. NICHOLSON

John Nicholson (b. Mar. 4, 1712 in Boston, MA, d. Oct. 8, 1807 in Union, ME) was the son of **Francis Nicholson**. **John** married **Mart Throop**, on Nov. 10, 1736, but she died in 1741 in Wrentham, MA. In 1739, **Francis** and **John**, age 27, both noted as joiners, bought land together. **John** remarried a **Mercy Ware** in 1742, a niece of **Francis**'s wife **Mary** and cousin-once-removed of **Sarah**. In 1746, **John** was living in Cumberland, RI, which may have resulted from a change in town and state boundary lines. In 1751, **John** was noted as a yeoman and joiner. Sometime between 1763-66, he moved back to Wrentham and was noted as a gentleman and probably no longer personally active in plane making. His second wife, **Mercy**, died in Wrentham, in 1785. By 1803, **John** and **Sarah**, had moved to Union, ME, where he died, on Oct. 8, 1807, at age 96. ME was a part of MA until 1820. The A imprints are on his earliest planes, made before 1739-40, while still working with his father and before acquiring land and moving some six miles away. The B & B1 imprints with

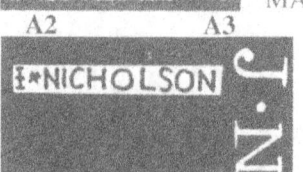

a new **IN** imprint were used, from 1739-47. The C imprint was used in Cumberland, RI, where he remained until 1763. He shared the same **WRENTHAM** die with **Cesar Chelor**. Examples: on a 13 7/8"x 3 1/2" birch crown molder with a round top wedge & iron, offset tote and heavy flat chamfers. **A, A1, A2, B, B1 & C **; A3 ******

G. NICOL
Example: on a pair of cornice planes with shallow flat chamfers. The irons are marked **A. JEWETT**, ca. 1790-1800. **UR**

H. NILES
Hezekiah Niles (b. 1742 in Philadelphia, PA, d. Oct. 8, 1791, "his death was occasioned by the falling of a large sign and sign-post, which struck him on the head, killed instantly as he came out of the doorway of his Market Street (carpentry) shop", in Wilmington, DE) was the son of a shipwright and father of **Samuel Niles**. He announced on May 3, 1764, the opening of his plane making shop in Church Alley, Philadelphia, PA, at the sign of the "Gilt Smoothing and Blue Long Planes," he also advertised for an apprentice and stated his intent to open a hardware shop shortly. Apparently **Niles** learned the plane making trade from **Samuel Caruthers**. On Mar. 14, 1765, **Hezekiah's** Penn Gazette ad stated that he moved his shop from the upper to the lower end of Church Alley ... at the Sign of the Gilt Long Plane and Handsaw. The previous shop, with the same sign, is used to be his ironmonger shop. **Hezekiah** married Jul. 16, 1766 in Wilmington, DE. In Oct. 1777, **Hezekiah** escaped Wilmington from the invading British Army, led by **Lord Cornwallis**. From 1767-91, he was listed as a carpenter in Market Street in Wilmington, DE. Inventory of **Hezikiah Niles** deceased, of Jul. 27, 1792, listed:
- sundry new plains part finished 11-11-3.
- sundry counter plains 10-0-0.
- sundry plain irons 0-12-6.
- two work benches with iron fasts 1-10-0.

Examples: on a 12 1/8" complex molder with an open offset tote; on a 9 7/8" hollow; a 9 7/8" bead; a 9 15/16" molder; a 9 5/8" round; a 9 5/8" complex molder; and a 10 1/8" halving plane. All beech with heavy flat chamfers. ca. 1760. ********

S. NILES
Samuel Niles (b. 1764-66 in Wilmington, DE, d. Jun. 28, 1796 in New Castle, DE, probated Sep. 27, 1796) was the son of **Nezekial Niles**. He advertised in the *Delaware Gazette* in 1791, that he carried on the plane making business. A local chronicle written in Wilmington in 1796 said: "**Samuel Niles** ... Carpenter and Cabinet Maker ... he also made Carpenter's Plains. **Samuel's** mother, **Mary Way Niles**, and his younger brother, **Hezekiah**, who was a printer and publisher, were executors of his estate. **Samuel Niles** inventory:
- quantity of split beech 7-10-0.
- lott of old planes and counters 10-0-0.
- lott of new planes 15-0-0.
- lott of plane irons 4-10-0.
- grindstone and 2 benches 1-10-0.

Hezekiah offered the business for sale and added that: "Carpenters, joiners &c. are respectfully informed that he has on hand a variety of plains which he will sell low for cash." ********

BARNABAS NILLS
Example: on a 9 5/8" birch ovolo molder with flat chamfers, ca. 1790. **UR**

J. R. NOBLE

Example: on a 9 1/2" bead with a **YOUNGSTOWN** location imprint, ca. 1850. ********

L. NOBLE
Example: on a 9 1/16" beech bead with a birch wedge and heavy round chamfers. ca. 1800. **UR**

TIMOTHY B. NOE
Timothy B. Noe (b. Feb. 18, 1811 in Essex, NJ, d. Feb. 9, 1861 in Essex, NJ) was listed as a plane maker, located at 162 Plane St., in the 1837 Newark, NJ, directory. This was the same address as **David Willis** possibly a residence.
No imprint has been reported.

H. R. NOLL. T
Example: an 8 3/4" bead plane with a **Newbould** iron and round chamfers, ca. 1820. **UR**

LYMAN NOLTON
Lyman Nolton (b. July 8, 1827 in Utica, NY, d. Nov. 13, 1916 in Adrian, MI) was listed as a planemaker in Salina, NY, in 1850. He may have been part of **Hayden & Nolton**.
No imprint has been reported.

S. N/ SAML. NORCROSS
There are two possible, one **Samuel Norcross** (b. 1777, d. Sep. 17, 1857 in Pemberton, Burlington Co., NJ) the other died in 1827, at age 67, both were Members of the Society of Friends or Quakers. Example: on a 14 3/8"x 4" beech crown molder with both the initial group and the imprint, an offset open tote, round top iron and heavy flat chamfers, found in upper NJ, ca. 1800. **UR**

W. NORCROSS
W. Norcross was a hardware dealer. Example: on a **Collins/Utica** reed molding plane also with, an incuse owners imprint **J. M. Cross**, ca. 1835. ********

B. NORMAN
Benjamin Norman (b. Mar. 1811 in Mercer Co, NJ, d. Mar. 3, 1902 in Pennington, Mercer Co., NJ), was one of the four apprentices to **Samuel C. Cook** enumerated in 1830. In 1840, **Norman** was employed in manufacturing and trades, in North Brunswick; In 1850, **Samuel** was in Trenton, NJ, with the occupation planemaker; he was listed in 1854-55 as a planemaker, but left that city and plane making in 1856. In 1860, he was living in Pennington, NJ, with an occupation of store and livery. Because his planes are so rare, it is possible that most of his North Brunswick work was for **S. C. Cook**. Example: on a cornice plane dated **1840**. A ***; B ****

A. NORMAND
A. Normand was listed in 1882-83, as carpenter/ builders, in Burlington, VT. Examples: on a size **1** hollow & round set; size **5/8 & 3/4** beads; a 12" double-iron ogee molding plane; and a set of five coachmaker (tailed) planes, ca. late 19c. ****

NORRIS. BRO./ NORRIS & BROTHER
Richard N. Norris Jr.; **George Washington Norris** (b. Mar.6, 1802 in Baltimore, d. Sep. 28, 1873 in Baltimore, MD) and **George S. Norris** were hardware dealers in Baltimore, MD, from 1840-58. A & B **

P. G. NORTHRUP
Example: on a 10" birch side-bead with round chamfers on top and flat chamfers on toe & heel, ca. 1810. UR

A. NORTON
Possibly **Alanson Chase Norton** (b. 1809, d. Jan. 18, 1870 in Bennington, VT) and listed in 1830-40, engaged in manufactures & trade and as a cabinetmaker and manufactory, in 1840-60, in Bennington, VT. Example: on a 9 5/8" beech halving plane, with heavy round chamfers and size **1/2** on heel, ca. 1820. UR

A. D. NORTON
Example: on a 9 3/4" beech Yankee plow, with wood thumbscrews, wood depth stop, round arms, a screwed/ riveted skate and shallow flat chamfers, ca. 1800. UR

M. NORTON
A number of **M. Nortons** were listed on Martha's Vineyard in the late 18c. Example: on a 9" birch round, with heavy flat chamfers, possibly from New England, ca. 1790. UR

N. NORTON
Nathan F. Norton (b. 1812 in PA) was a planemaker in Philadelphia, PA. He first appeared in the city directory of 1837. He was later listed in the Camden, NJ, section of the Philadelphia directories, from 1850-56; In 1865-68, he was a carpenter in Philadelphia. Earlier **Nathan** worked as a journeyman for the **Whites** and his initials **N. N** appear on some of the White's planes. Examples: The B imprint is on a 22" beech single-iron fore plane with slight offset tote. **

J. V. NOSTRAND
Example: on a 9 3/4" beech casemaker's double-male plane with a York pitch and flat chamfers, ca. 1810. UR

B. B. & W. R. NOYES
Benjamin B. Noyes (b. 1821 in RI) and **William R. Noyes Jr.** (b. 1823 in CT) were hardware dealers in Detroit, MI, from 1850-69. In 1846, it was listed as **William R. Noyes, Jr.**, hardware and cutlery. In 1870-76, **Benjamin B. Noyes** was listed as a fire insurance agent. Example: on a complex molding planes with **59**, an **Ohio Tool Co.** style number. A, A1 & B **

D. NOYES
Planes are similar to those of **S. Noyes**. Examples: on a 20" beech fore plane; a 22" fore plane; a 10 7/8" round; a 10" beech round; a 9 1/2" beech reeding plane; and a 9 3/8" applewood dado with the main wedge birch and the nicker wedge beech, all with heavy flat chamfers, ca. 1800. ***

E. O. NOYES
Example: on a 9 1/2"x 7/8" beech screw-stop dado made by **Gladwin & Appleton** and also has a **Southworth & Noyes** imprint. **E. O. Noyes**, as well as **Southworth & Noyes** of North Bridgewater, MA, were hardware dealers. Brockton and Bridgewater are near each other. ****

H. NOYES
Example: With an embossed imprint on a slide-arm plow plane with thumb-screws and brass insert wear plates on top of the arms, ca. 1850. **No imprint is available.**

P NOYES/ P. NOYES
Example: both imprints on a 9 5/8" beech skew-rabbet with flat chamfers, ca. 1810. UR

S. NOYES

Believed to be **Samuel Stone Noyes** (b. Feb. 12, 1785 in that part of Sudbury which became East Sudbury, in 1780, and Wayland, MA, in 1835, d. Sep. 16, 1832, in Sudbury) who was a successful cabinetmaker located near the causeway, active from 1810-32. **Noyes** was apprenticed to Wayland cabinetmaker **Michael Maynard** (b. 1771, d. 1807). He was in Charlestown, from 1807-10, where he worked with **Archelans Flint** (b. 1771, d. 1814). **Noyes** was in the War of 1812. He had one known apprentice, **J. Hemingway**. In 1824, he married his second wife, **Sarah Cook** (d. 1857) who carried on the business after his death, in 1832 (he had 5 daughters and no sons). His inventory of tools totaled $244, and all tools of the trade in the workshop $50. Examples: the A Imprint is on a 10 3/8" beech round with heavy flat chamfers, an **I. Sleeper** style wedge. The B Imprint is on a 14 1/2" toted sash plane; a 9 15/16" hollow; a 10 1/8" complex molder; and a 10 1/8" single lignum vitae boxed bead, all beech with heavy flat chamfers and an **I. Sleeper** style wedge, and on the heel of a 10" molding plane made by **E. Clifford**, probably from northern New England, ca. 1810. A ****; B **

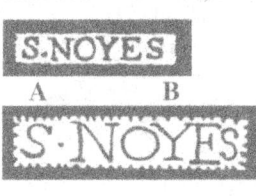

I. NUTTER

Believed to be **James Nutter** (b. 1775, d. Oct. 19, 1855 in Newington, Rockingham, NH) was apprenticed to **Elisha Whidden**. **Nutter** was a builder, architect and master joiner in Portsmouth, NH, active from 1804-09. Examples: on molders 9 1/2"-9 3/4" birch and beech with flat to heavy round chamfers and an **I. Sleeper** style wedge, from northern New England, ca. 1800-20. ***

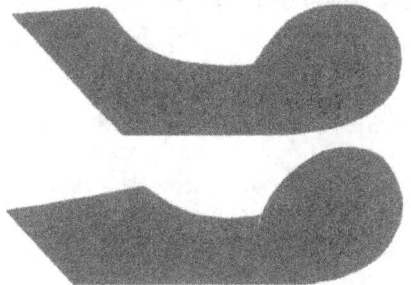

J. D. NUTTER

Example: on a 15" beech gutter plane with a centered tote and beveled wedge; and a 9 1/8" small match tongue, both with shallow round chamfers, ca. 1840. UR

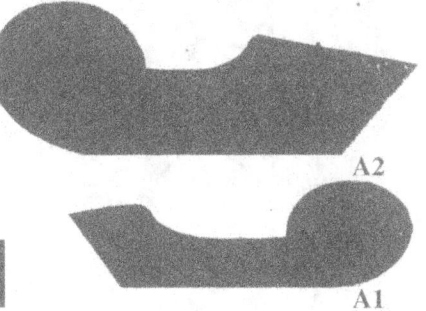

A. NUTTING

Possibly **Alonzo Nutting**, son of Trumon. Example: on a 9 1/2" beech round, ca. 1850. UR

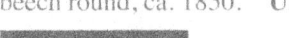

E. NUTTING

Ebenezer Nutting (b. Nov. 17, 1803 in Hampshire Co., MA, d. Apr. 30, 1886 Florence, Hampshire Co., MA) was a planemaker in an area of South Amherst, MA, known as "Nuttingville" and was active from 1830-65. **Ebenezer** was the elder brother of **Truman Nutting** and was listed in **Truman's** account book as having worked for **Kennedy & Co.**, on Dec. 5, 1836. **Ebenezer** lived in Greenwich, MA, east of Amherst, prior to 1834. By 1845, he was operating his own plane mill downstream from **Truman's** mill. **Ebenezer** was also an active Methodist preacher. He was listed, in 1830 40, in Leverett, MA, as a toolmaker. In 1850, he was listed for Amherst, MA, engaged in tool manufacturing. Living with **Ebenezer Nutting** was his son **E. P. Nutting** and three other planemakers. In 1837, $8000 worth of planes were manufactured with 10 employees; in 1845, he manufactured tools worth $14,975 utilizing 22 employees; in 1850, the industrial census showed him employing 11 male hands at $275/ mo. and two female employees at $24/ mo., utilizing water power to make 5,000 planes worth $4000 and 15,000 handles worth $3000; in 1855, he made tools valued at $18,000 with 20 hands; in 1865, he made tools valued at $3,000 with 3 hands. During his 35 year career, **Nutting** sold large amounts of lumber, lath, shingles, primarily bench type planes and a very large quantity of plane handles to other plane manufacturers or as a subcontractor. His account books listed 32 different recognized planemakers as customers. In 1870, **Ebenezer** was listed as a carpenter; and in 1880, he was a carpenter and joiner in Northampton, MA. Completed wooden planes with this imprint are quite rare. A & B ****

E. P. NUTTING

Edward Porter Nutting (b. May 31, 1828 in Hampshire, MA, d. Oct. 1863 in Amherst, MA) received a Civil War disability discharge, on Nov. 1, 1862, from Co. G, 27th. Regiment, MA Vols. **Porter**, was the oldest son of **Ebenezer Nutting** and made planes in South Amherst, MA, from 1852-57. In 1850, **Porter** was listed as a planemaker, living with his father. In 1851, **T. Nutting** bought planes from him. In 1855, **Porter** was listed as manufacturing $18,000 worth of tools; in 1856-57, he was in partnership with his father. Judging from the rarity of his imprint, a large portion of this production may represent subcontract work for his father. An **Ebenezer Nutting** broadside, of Jan. 1, 1856, listed **E. P. Nutting** as Agent. Example: Imprint B on a 16"x 2 3/4" beech double-iron jack with an open tote also imprinted with **H. H. READ/ WILINGTON, VT.** who was listed as working from 1854-59. A ***; B *****

H. P. NUTTING

Example: on a beech plow plane with the additional imprint of **C. WARREN./ NASHUA.** **Cyrus Warren** moved to Nashua, in 1857. ****

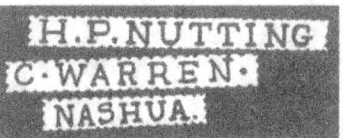

J. H. NUTTING

John Hastings Nutting (b. Feb. 1, 1818 in Hampshire, d. Sep. 25, 1897 in Springfield, MA) was the son of **Truman Nutting**'s half-brother **George**; and boarded with **Truman Nutting**, in 1834, when John was 16, presumably learning plane making. **John's** mother **Judith Hastings** was related to **Samuel Hastings**, a planemaker, in Amherst. Entries in **Truman Nutting**'s 1840-41 journal, indicated that he bought planes from, and sold planes to, **John Nutting**. **John** was credited for 37 days work at 77 cents per day. In April 1847, the journal reported that **John** sold **Truman** 669 smoothers. **John** remained in Amherst thru 1850; and was in Hadley, from 1853-57. *****

N. NUTTING/ OTISFIELD

Believed to be **Nathan Nutting** (b. Groton, MA, d. Apr. 9, 1847 in Otisfield, ME) who was married, on Aug. 24, 1784, in Groton, MA. **Nathan** moved from Groton, MA to Otisfield, ME, in 1795. There, he acquired and built up a 200 acre farm, and worked, as a carpentry. In 1850, a **Nathan Nutting**, possibly his son, was listed as operating a steam saw mill, in Otisfield, ME. Examples: on a large hollow; and a size 3/8 beech dado, both with flat chamfers, ca. 1800. ****

N. NUTTING

Nathan Nutting (b. 1804, d. 1867), possibly the son of **N. Nutting/ Otisfield**, was a journeyman carpenter, as early as 1833, and was listed in the 1855 & 1867 ME business directories, and as a mechanic, in the 1850 census. Example: on a 9 3/8" beech size 18 hollow with a **Greaves & Sons** iron. **A, B & C ***

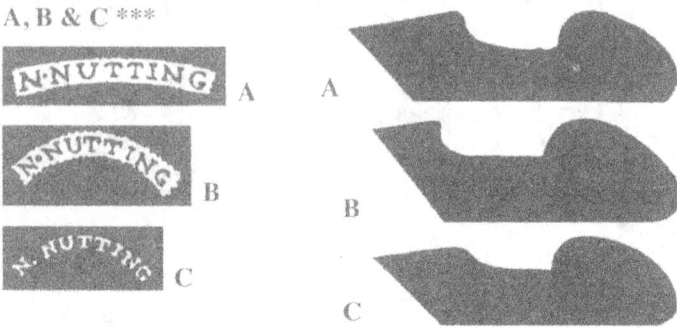

N. NUTTING & O. H. SMITH

N. Nutting could be any of several **Nuttings** descended from **John Nutting** of Groton, but not closely related to the Amherst **Nuttings**. An example of this combination of names has been reported with the added location imprint **NORTHAMPTON**.
No imprint is available.

T. NUTTING

Truman Nutting (b. Feb. 3, 1807 in Nuttingville/ South Amherst, MA, d. Sept. 23, 1891 in Cannon City, Rice Co., MN) was a planemaker, in Amherst, MA, from 1829-52. **Truman** was the brother of **Ebenezer Nutting** and operated a sawmill and shop, just upstream from **Ebenezer**. He also made plane parts, such as handles and stocks, for other plane manufacturers. **Nutting's** two volume account book, started Aug. 4, 1831, is in the Amherst Public Library along with the family genealogies. In the 1830's, **Truman** was shipping large orders of planes to **Kennedy & Co**. In 1836-37, **Truman Nutting** had boarders with him whom he described as working for **Kennedy & Co**. Nutting was part of **Nutting & Fox**, from 1834-36; and **Fox, Nutting & Washburn**, ca. 1835. He was listed in the 1839 New England Mercantile Union Directory as a plane manufacturer in South Amherst. His account books also record days starting in 1840, when his men (seven) began work for **Kennedy & Co**. He was listed in the 1850 census, as a tool manufacturer. His son-in-law **Wymann Hoyt**, age 21; and **Henry H. Nutting**, age 20, both planemakers, were listed as living with him; as were **Alonzo Nutting**, age 18; and **Frank Nutting**, age 16, who were described as toolmakers and sons. In the 1850 industrial census, **Truman** was listed as having 18 male hands, paid $468/mo. and 2 female employees, paid $24/mo.; utilizing water and steam power to produce 500,000 shingles worth $1000, 300,000 lath worth $1500, 200,000 ft. of lumber worth $200, and 90,000 plane handles worth $6600. The bulk of his production was sold whole sale or as a subcontractor. In 1852, **Nutting** left Amherst for Olean, NY, where he was a carpentry. In 1854, **Truman** moved on to MN, where he ran a hotel, farmed, and manufactured brooms. ****

NUTTING & FOX

A planemaking partnership consisting of **Truman Nutting** and **Luther Fox**, from June 19, 1834 to Sept. 14, 1836, in Amherst, MA. The partnership arranged for labor, apparently ran the mill and probably owned and sold the planes made. From Aug. 1835 thru Apr. 1836, **Fox & Washburn** used and paid for the machinery of **Nutting & Fox**.
No imprint has been reported.

JOSEPH NUZUM

Joseph Nuzum (b. 1822 in Marion Co., VA, d. Aug. 30, 1886 in Fairmont, Marion Co., WV) was listed in the 1850-60 census as a cabinetmaker, residing in Marion Co., VA. In 1863, Fairmont became part of WV. In 1870, **Joseph** was listed as a cabinetmaker, in Fairmont, WV. In 1880, he was listed as furniture manufacturer in Fairmont, WV. ***

A. NVBER

Example: on a 10" molder with flat chamfers, ca. 1800.
No imprint is available.

A. NYE

Example: on a 9 1/2" beech large round with flat chamfers; and on a 9 5/8" beech round with round chamfers, ca. 19c. **UR**

B. W. OAKLEY & SON
Benjamin W. Oakley (b. 1803 in NY, d. probate Jul. 14, 1873 in Fort Wayne, IN) was listed in 1850, as a tinner. In 1858, he was listed as a Fort Wayne, IN, hardware dealer, at 79 north side of Columbia St; in 1862, a wholesale and retail hardware dealer. By 1869, **Benjamin** had taken his son **Chauncey B. Oakley** into the firm as **B. W. Oakley & Son. Oakley** was also a part of **Oakley & French** in 1858. ***

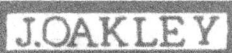

J. OAKLEY
Example: 10 7/8" beech large hollow with heavy flat chamfers, ca. 1800. UR

OAKLEY & FRENCH
Benjamin W. Oakley was in partnership with French as a Fort Wayne, IN, hardware dealer, between 1851-58. Example: on a plane with an iron marked **Ohio Tool Co.** ***

J. C. OAKS
Example: on a 9 3/4" birch pair of tongue & groove planes with relieved wedges and shallow round chamfers, ca. 1810. UR

O. OBEE
Example: on a 9 3/8" beech sash with round chamfers, ca. 1830. UR

B. B. OCKINGTON
B. B. Ockington was probably a hardware dealer. Example: on a **Jn. Tower** plane. UR

I. OCKS
Example: on a 9 1/2" beech torus bead with heavy round chamfers, ca. 1820. UR

CHARLES ODELL
Charles B. Odell (b. Oct. 26, 1839 in Essex Co., MA, d. Jun. 12, 1912 in Salem, Essex Co., MA) was listed as a Salem, MA, hardware dealer, from 1869-76. ***

ELI ODELL
Eli Odell (b. July 19, 1806 in IN, d. Dec. 3, 1878) was a toolmaker and planemaker, in Winterset, IA. **Odell** was granted Patent No. 41,317, on Jan. 19, 1864, for a device that closed the throat of a bench plane, to adjust for wear. He signed up for the Civil War, at age 54. Example: on a 12 3/4" plank match pair with applewood screw-arms. ****

J. OGDEN
Examples: three planes found together in Watervliet near Troy, NY, including a 10 1/2" birch plow-style skew iron chamfer plane with wedge-lock fence, marked three times on the toe and once on the fence end; a 10" beech small ogee complex molder; and a 10" birch molder that cuts a round bottom groove, all with heavy flat chamfers, ca. 1800. UR

OGONTZ/ OGONTZ TOOL CO.
Ogontz Tool Co. was a brand name used by the **Sandusky Tool Co.**, from 1885-1920, on tools distributed by **Hibbard, Spencer & Bartlett** and possibly others, and most often found on bench planes. **Ogontz** was a chief of the Ottawa who lived in Sandusky, OH, during the early 19c. Two planes were patented in Jan. 6, 1885, by **W. F. Achenbach** of Lebanon, PA. Example: on a **13** jack plane with the B imprint.
A, C & C1: FF; B **

OK/ OHIO KING
Ohio King was a trademark of the **Sandusky Tool Co.** Examples: on a 7 7/8" beech coffin smoother with style **03** stamped on the toe, used by the **Sandusky Tool Co.** for this plane with a double-iron. Also reported is an **Ohio King** imprint over an **Ogontz Tool Co.** imprint, a **Sandusky Tool Co.** brand mark, with **1876** and number **27**, the **Sandusky Tool Co.** inventory number for a double-iron jointer. The B imprint is believed to also represent **Ohio King**.
A & B ***; A1 *****

OHIO PLANES/ OHIO PLANE CO.
These imprints were used by the **Sandusky Tool Co.** on planes manufactured for **Hibbard, Spencer, Bartlett & Co.**, a large Chicago hardware firm from 1890-1920.
A, A1: FF; A2 **; B & C ****

OHIO TOOL CO.

Ohio Tool Co. was a major plane manufacturing company in the 19c & early 20c. There may have been some form of company, as early as 1823. It was incorporated in Columbus, OH, in 1851, by **Peter Hayden** and others, and had a tradition of periodically utilizing prison labor. The first president was **George Gere**, a hardware dealer. In 1851, the company was reported employing 200 hands, with carpenter's planes as the main line. By 1870's & 1880's, the ready acceptance of metal and transitional planes, and other competition, was increasingly felt. In 1887, the company employed only 70 hands (the use of prison labor having ceased in 1880); and in 1893, **Ohio Tool Co.** merged with the **Auburn Tool Co.**, with the **Ohio Tool Co.** the survivor. In 1913; the Ohio factory was destroyed by a flood. In 1914, manufacturing was re-established in a new plant in Charlestown, WV. Operations ceased altogether in 1920. The 1910 price list still offered an extensive line of wooden planes. The A1 imprint, is **Ohio Tool Co.** A imprint with **G. L. Bidwell** over imprint. The G imprint, with the U. S. A., occurred after the 1893 merger with the **Auburn Tool Co.** and was intended for marketing in Canada, partly in response to the shrinking U. S. market. A style number usually appears on the H imprint in the space under **OHIO TOOL CO.** The J imprint includes the **PATENTED/ AUG. 29, 1854 Multiform Moulding Plane Co.** a patent of **Thomas D. Worrall** and appears with the single notch in the body for a removable handle. The K imprint has the embossed **COLUMBUS/ OHIO** that was also possibly used by **Hall Stone & Co., P. Hayden & Co., Gere, Abbott & Co.,** and **Kilbourne Kuhns & Co.** The L imprint was used after 1893 and the merger with **Auburn Tool Co.** The **PAT. JUN. 11-95** appears on a 16" jack plane. **A thru D: FF; E thru F *; G thru J **; K ***; A, L & M ******

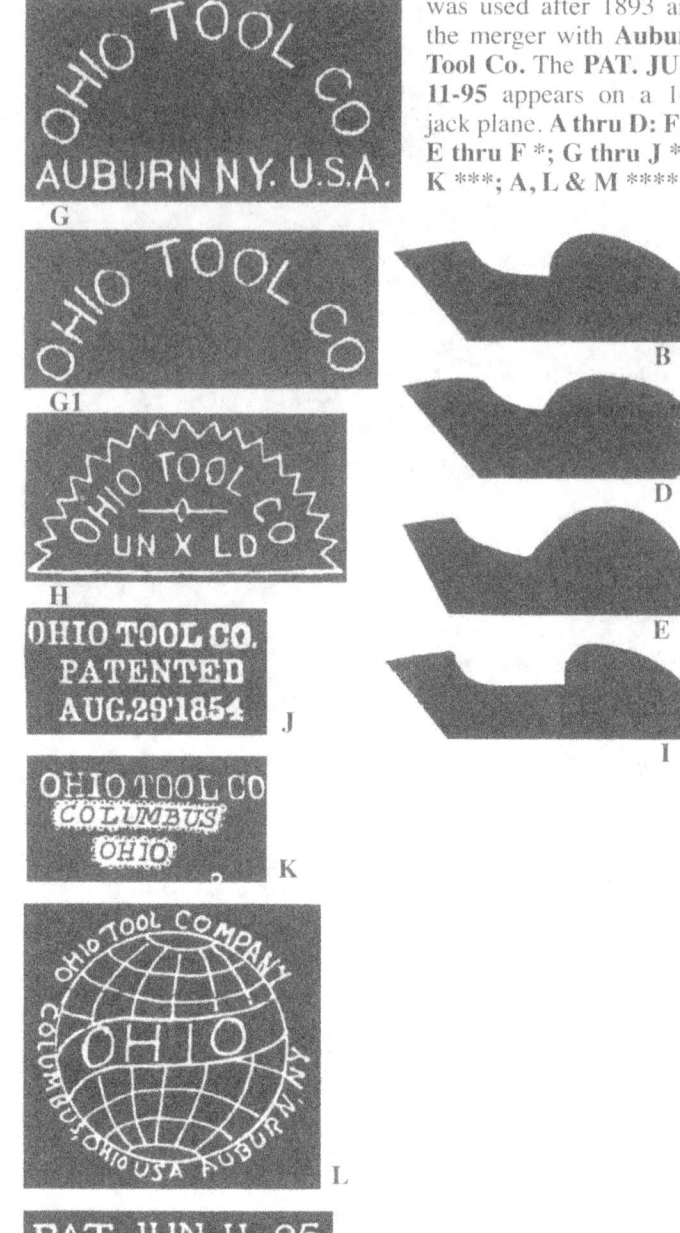

JAMES OLIVE
Example: on a 9 3/8" birch single-boxed Grecian ogee with round chamfers, ca. 1830. **UR**

JOHN OLIVER
Example: on a 9 3/4" beech molder with size **3** on the heel, and flat chamfers, ca. 1800. **UR**

OLNEY
Stephen Olney (b. Jan. 25, 1775, d. Aug. 7, 1854 in Scituate, RI) was the father of **S. H. Olney**. In 1810, **Stephen** was referred to as a housewright and in later years a farmer. He lived from 1810-22, in the village of Rockland, in the western part of

Scituate. (Rockland was flooded by the Scituate Reservoir in 1921) In 1828, he moved to a farm in North Scituate, where he remained until his death. In 1850, he was listed as a carpenter. His Oct. 7, 1854 probate inventory includes:

1 wood saw & horse at	$1.00.
3 axes at	$2.50.
1 lot carpenters tools & chest at	$4.00.

Examples: in the **Jo. Fuller** style including a 13 5/8" birch crown molder with offset tote, round top iron, and flat chamfers; a 10 1/8" ogee complex molder; on 10" & 9 3/4" skew rabbets; and a 10" wide hollow, all birch with flat chamfers and relieved wedges, ca. 1795-1800. *****

S. H. OLNEY
Steven Henry Olney (b. Sep. 28, 1814, d. 1894 in Scituate, RI) was the son of **Stephen Olney**. In 1850, he was listed as **Henry Olney**, a carpenter, living in Scituate, RI. (he probably used his middle name **Henry** to differentiate him from his father, **Stephen Olney**, who was still living) In 1860, he was listed as **Stephen H. Olney**, carpenter, living in Scituate, RI; in 1870, works in "cotton mill". Example: on a 23" beech bench plane with a closed tote, an iron marked **Groves & Sons**, the plane was dated **1842**, on the toe. *****

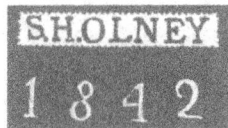

OMER PLANE CO.
Omer Plane Co., with the location imprint **NEW BEDFORD/ MASS.** has been reported. **No imprint is available**.

ONTARIO/ 2
There was a ferry called **Ontario II**, that was built in 1915 and ran between Coburg, Ontario and Rochester, NY, until 1951. Example: on a **D. R. Barton & Co.** jack and on an otherwise unmarked wide round and several other jack planes. ****

J. OOTHOUDT
J. Oothoudt is a Hudson Valley, NY, plane maker of Dutch origin. Examples: on molding planes 9 1/4"-9 1/2" beech with narrow rounded chamfers, a wedge with an extended narrow finial. Several are boxed and several have **W. Butcher** irons; a pair of 9 1/2" hollow & rounds are dated **1833**, on the toe; a group of 47 planes, 1 marked **W. Oothoudt**, including 8 as work in progress and 38 mother planes, found together in Collersville, NY, on the Susquehanna River, ca. 1830-40. **; dated 1833 *****

W. OOTHOUDT
W. Oothoudt is a Hudson Valley, NY, plane maker of Dutch origin. Examples: the A1 imprint is on a pair of beech handled tongue & groove plank planes, dated **1843**; one on a marked **J. Oothoudt** and found in Collersville, NY, on the Susquehanna River, ca. 1830-40. A **; A1 *****

JOHN: OPI
SOUTHWICK is probably Southwick, MA, located southeast of Springfield. Example: on a 9 3/4" birch skew rabbet with flat chamfers and flutes and of New England origin, ca. 1800. UR

ORANGE, WOODS & CO.
Orange, Woods & Co. was primarily a sash & window shop which bought out **Judah Lord**'s tool shop, in 1834, in Juellville, North Watertown, NY and continued making tools. **No imprint has been reported**.

ORDWAY
Possibly **Henry Ordway**, a cabinetmaker listed in Newburyport, MA, in 1848. More likely **Giles Ordway** (b. Oct. 4, 1777 in Haverhill, MA, d. May 31, 1847 in Concord, NH) who was listed as a carpenter and joiner. **Giles** moved to Bow, NH, ca. 1820; and then to Concord, NH. Example: on a beech plow; and a 9 9/16" beech square rabbet with tight round chamfers and an **I. Sleeper** style wedge, both imprints start at the edge of the plane as if initial(s) were intentionally being left off, probably from Newburyport, MA, ca. 1820. ***

ORGILL BROS. & CO.
Joseph Orgill arrived in NY, about 1830, from England and established an importing business. **William Orgill** (b. in England, d. May 22, 1895) followed and became a traveling salesman in NC, SC, VA, KY, and TN for his families import hardware line. **William** formed a partnership with **R. T. Lamb & Co.**. In 1847, the firm, with its entire inventory, was moved to Memphis, as **R. T. Lamb & Co.**. The firm advertised in the *Daily Enquirer* two weeks after opening, on Apr. 1, 1847, at 63 Front St. **R. T. Lamb** died in 1849, and his interest was bought by **Henry A. Lownes** (from VA) with the firm name becoming **Lownes & Co.**, at the corner of Front & Monroe, effective Jan. 1, 1850; in 1851, the **Holydark-Lownes & Co.** with **Thomas Holdark**; in 1854, the **Lownes, Beckman & Co.**; later in 1854, **Lownes, Orgill & Co.**. In 1850, **Edmund Orgill** (b. 1825 in England, d. Sep. 8, 1905) came to America and joined, his father, **Joseph Orgill** in New York, and moved to Memphis in 1857, upon his father's death. **Henry Lownes** died, in 1857, and the name was changed to **Orgill Bros. & Co.**, run by **William Orgill**, **Edmund Orgill** and **Joseph Orgill**, who remained living in NY. **Orgill Bros. & Co.** continued thru the Civil War retaining their English citizenship. A 1868 Memphis, TN listing for **Orgill Bros. & Co.** lists **William Orgill**, **Edmund Orgill**, **G. L. Denison** and **A. S. McNear** as importers of hardware, cutlery, nails and castings, at 312 Front. **William Orgill** retired in 1871, and returned to England, where he died on May 22, 1895. A 1905 Memphis,TN listing for **Orgill Bros. & Co.** lists **Edmund Orgill**, Pres.; **Frederick Orgill**, Vic-pres; **Wm. I. Moody**, 2nd. Vic-pres; **Joseph Orgill**, Treas.; **Nm. Orgill**, Sec. as wholesale hardware, stoves, saddlery and agricultural implements, at 28-32 Front St.. **Edmund** died while visiting England, on Sep. 8, 1905. **Edmund** was succeeded by his 3 sons **Fredrick Orgill**, **William Orgill** and **Joseph Orgill**, continued the company to today as one of the largest wholesale hardware companies in the U. S. Example: on a 9 1/2"x 3/4" beech skew rabbet plane with **116** on the toe, found in rural IN;

and a size **6** beech hollow with **72** on the toe, both inventory numbers for the **Ohio Tool Co.** ***

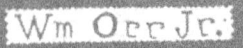

ORMSBY-BLAIR & CO.
Ormsby-Blair & Co. was a Louisville, KY, hardware merchant, located at 506 Main bet. 3rd. & 4th.. From 1855-56, the firm consisted of **Robert J. Ormsby** (b. ca. 1822 in Louisville, d. Feb. 20, 1879 in Louisville, KY) and **Henry Shreve Blair** (b. May 21, 1818, in Butler Co., d. Jan. 31, 1905 in Lilliopolis, Sangamon Co., IL). In 1851-52, **Robert J. Ormsby** was a wholesale & retail dealer of hardware, at 554 Main bet. 2nd. & 3rd; in 1858-59, it became **Colles Ormsby**, possibly a son, with **Robert J. Ormsby** listed as bookkeeper, at 332 W. Main. ***

ORMSBY & OWEN
Ormsby & Owen was a Louisville, KY, hardware dealer, ca. 1850. This probably predated **Robert J. Ormsby** who was listed on his own in 1851-52. ***

WM ORR JR.
The **Orr** family immigrated from Scotland and settled in Ryegate and Corinith, VT. There are two families with a **William Orr Jr.** The first was **John Orr** who came to Ryegate, in 1774. His son, **William Orr** (b. Aug. 11, 1790, in Ryegate). His grandson, **William Orr Jr.** (b. Nov. 10, 1807, in Ryegate). The second was **Robert Orr** who came to Ryegate, in 1774, and lived in Corinth. His son **William Orr** (b. July 5, 1785, in Corinth). His grandson **William Orr Jr.** (b. Jun. 6, 1813, in Corinth). Example: on a 9 1/8" beech molder; a 9 7/16" bead; a sash; and a sash coping planes, all found in VT, ca. 1850. ****

R. OSBON

Example: on a 9 1/2"x 1 1/2" beech complex molder with round chamfers, ca. 1820. **UR**

OSBORN
Examples: on a 9 3/8" birch and a 9 1/4" beech complex molders with heavy flat chamfers; and a 9 5/16" beech torus bead single-boxed with size **3/4** on the heel, found in PA, ca. 1800. **UR**

A. OSBORN
Example: on a 14 3/8" beech, open toted match plank grooving plane with flat chamfers. The fence is secured with hand made screws, ca. 1800. **UR**

A. J. OSBORN
Example: on a 9 3/4" beech rabbet with a birch fence, found in NH, ca. 1800. **UR**

C. A. OSBORN
Example: on an 8 1/2" beech plow plane with riveted arms and skate, and a wooden depth stop with wood screw, ca. 1800. **UR**

M. OSBORN
Example: on a 9 1/2" beech complex molder, ca. 1830-40. **UR**

OSBORN & ALEXANDER
A letterhead, dated June 20, 1890, lists **Osborn & Alexander** at the corner of Market & Fremont Sts./ 401 Market St., San Francisco, offering "hardware, mechanics tools, workshop and machines and appliances". Example: on a smoothing plane made by **Ohio Tool Co.**, ca. late 19c. ****

OSBORN BROTHERS
Osborn Brothers with the location **126 ARUNDEL STREET** and **PORTSMOUTH** (probably NH), probably a hardware dealer, ca. 19c. ****

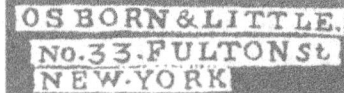

OSBORN & LITTLE.
Osborn & Little was a New York City plane making firm in 1846, consisting of **Charles Osborn** and **Charles S. Little**. After 1846, the firm was continued by **Little**, as a hardware dealer, under **C. S. Little & Co.. Osborn** may also have been part of **Osborn & Swan** before this partnership. ***

OSBORN & SWAN
Osborn & Swan was a New York City, hardware dealer and possibly a planemaker and was shown at the same address as **Osborn & Little**, in 1846. ****

A. OSGOOD/ AO

Example: on a 9 1/2" beech skew rabbet with flat chamfers, ca. 19c. A & B; **UR**

A   B

J. OSMAN
Example: on a 10" beech complex molder with flat chamfers, ca. early 19c. **UR**

H. OSTRANDER
Henry Ostrander (b. 1795, d. Nov. 17, 1879 in Clockville, Madison Co., NY) left Middleton, MA, as a youth in 1812, to Delhi, NY. In 1850-55 he was listed as farmer in Madison, Co., NY. Example: on a 9 1/2" beech square rabbet with round chamfers and a Wm. Ash iron, ca. 1820. **UR**

OSWEGO
The **Oswego** name only may have been a brand name. Example: on a 9 1/2"x 5/8" beech double-boxed side bead. **UR**

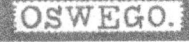

I: OTHEN
Example: on a 9 3/4" beech quadruple reeding plane with heavy flat chamfers, ca. 1800. **UR**

J. OTIS
Possibly **James Otis** (b. Jun. 6, 1767, d. Mar. 2, 1845 in Colchester, CT) who was a Colchester, CT, cabinetmaker, active from 1803-19. His estate included a chest of finishing planes, 7 bench planes, 19 old chisels, other small lots of tools and a glue pot. Example: on a 9 1/2" large beech bead, ca. 1850. **UR**

S. OTIS
Example: on a 9 5/8" beech hollow with flat chamfers, ca. 1810. **UR**

T. O
Possibly **Thomas Otois (Otis)** (b. 1823 in ME, d. ca. 1868, ME) worked as a sash maker or joiner in Old Town, north of Bangor, ME. Examples: on a number of planes from a tool chest including a fruitwood plow, a double-bladed fixed sash plane, and an applewood complex molders; and two coping planes, all 9 1/2" beech with shallow round chamfers. One example is on a plane made by **T. Waterman/ Waldoboro, ME**, as an owner's imprint, ca. 1840. **UR**

OTT
LOWELL is probably Lowell, MA. Example: on a 9 1/2" beech size **3/16** single-boxed bead, ca. 1850. ****

OTT & GREER
Ott & Greer was a hardware company that appeared only in the 1851 Wheeling directory. The partners were **Jacob Richard Greer** (b. Apr. 24, 1815, PA, d. Apr. 29, 1902 in Wheeling, WV) and **Samuel L. Ott** (b. 1793 in Woodstock, Shenandoah Co., VA, d. Aug. 22, 1868 in Wheeling, WV). By 1856, **Greer** was a part of **Greer & Laing**. **Samuel Ott** and **Morgan Ott** were part of **Ott & Boyd**. In 1864, **Samuel Ott, Son & Co.** was listed with **Samuel Ott, Morgan L. Ott & Wm. H. Hall** selling hardware, saddlery hardware, at n.w.c. Market and Monroe. In 1864, **Samuel Ott** was listed as President of the Wheeling Savings Institution. ****

OUELLET
Believed to be **Paul Ouellet** from East Freeport, ME. Example: a 9" beech skew rabbet with heavy round chamfers, of French Canadian influence, ca. 1820. **UR**

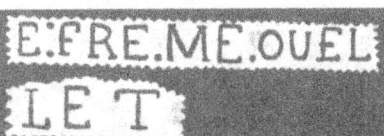

OWASCO TOOL CO.
The trade name **Owasco Tool Co** was used by the **Auburn Tool Co.**, from 1875-1893, and by the **Ohio Tool Co.** after its merger with the **Auburn Tool Co.**, in 1893. A, B & B1: FF; B2 **

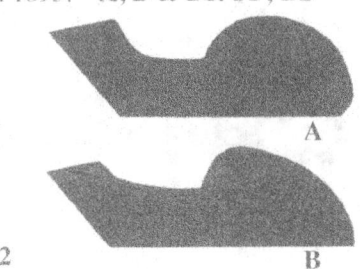

OWENS & BARKLEY/ O & B
Owens & Barkley probably was a hardware dealer. Example: on a 9 7/16" beech size **6** round plane with a **Ohio Tool Co.** inventory number **72**, found in OH, ca. 19c. ****

OWINGS & ROY
An advertisement for **Owings & Roy** appeared in Baltimore, MD, on Mar. 18, 1814, advertising a "New Plane Factory." On Feb. 14, 1815, **Barkley & Hughes** advertised that they were taking over the planemaking business of **Owings & Roy**. Example: on a 9 1/2" single-boxed side bead; and a round. ****

E. PACE

Example: on a 9 1/4" beech shiplap plane with tight flat chamfers, ca. 1810. **UR**

A. PACKARD
Example: on a 9 9/16" birch complex molder with flat chamfers, found near North Hampton, MA, ca. 1790. *********

WARREN PACKARD
Warren Packard (b. Jun. 1, 1828 in Trumbull Co., OH, d. Jul. 28, 1897 in Warren, Trumbull Co., OH) was a Warren, OH, hardware dealer from 1865-72, and was the father of the two sons who founded the **Packard Motor Car Co**. Example: on a style **96** beech screw-arm plow made by **Ohio Tool Co**. ********

G. PAGE
Example: on a 9 1/2" beech small round with flat chamfers, ca. 19c. **UR**

I. C. PAGE
Example: on a 9 7/16" x 7/8" beech boxed bead with round chamfers, ca. 1830. **UR**

J. PAGE
Example: on a 7 1/4" compass smoother; and a 9 1/2" beech crow's bill molder, both with heavy flat chamfers, ca. 1800. **A, B & C; UR**

J.. PAGE
John Page (b. ca. 1786 in Gilmanton, NH, d. Jul. 10, 1866 in Newburyport, MA) was listed as a cabinetmaker in Newburyport, MA, in 1850. Example: on a 9 1/2" birch dado with round top chamfers, flat toe and heel chamfers; and on a plane made by **I. Sleeper**, as an owner imprint. The wedge shown is from the dado nicker, the cutter wedge is sheared. This imprint is found on a hickory square with a riveted blade found in the Merrimack River area between MA and NH, ca. 1810-20. **UR**
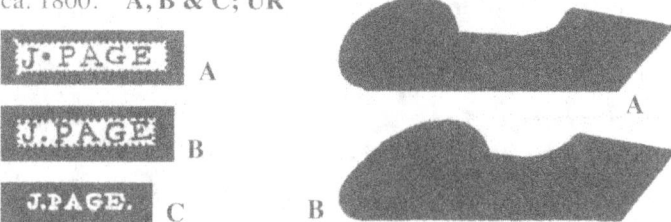

W. PAGE
Several **William Page**s were listed in Providence, RI, in the late 18c. Example: on a crown molder; a triple reeding plane; a 13 1/4" applewood panel raiser with heavy flat chamfers; a 10" maple large hollow with a birch B wedge and heavy flat chamfers; and a 9 3/4" beech small complex molder with a angled depth stop and a relieved A wedge, possibly from Providence, RI, ca. 1790. ********

I. PAINE
Example: on a 9 1/8" birch molder with flat chamfer found in Northern MA, ca. 1800. **UR**

I. W. PAINE
Examples: molders are 9 3/8"-9 1/2" beech with round chamfers. Six are from one group. One was as an owner's imprint on a planes made by **D. O. Crane** and **Collins/ Utica**, ca. 1850 **A & A1; UR**

PALM LEAF

Example: on a medallion attached to a **Ohio Tool Co.** plane, ca. 19c. ********

PALMER
Examples: on a 10 3/4" fenced door plane with a riveted skate; and a 10 1/4" astragal bead, both birch with a relieved wedge and heavy round chamfers, found together in central MA, probably from New England, ca. 1800. ********

A. PALMER
Possibly **Ashbel Palmer** (b. ca. 1819 in VT, d. Oct. 4, 1872 Panton, VT) who was listed as a furniture maker in N. Ferrisburg in 1849 and as a Furniture/ cabinetmaker, in 1850. Example: on a gutter plane. **UR**

A. C. PALMER.
Example: on a 10" beech large bead with flat chamfers, ca. 1800. **UR**

H. PALMER
Possibly **Henry Palmer** (b. ca. 1824 in NY) was listed in the 1850 census, as a cabinetmaker, in Westford, VT. Example: on a 9 1/2" beech skew rabbet. **UR**

S. PALMER
Possibly **Solomon Palmer** (b. Jun. 10, 1775 in New Milford, CT, d. 1818) was a joiner in Cornwall, CT, working ca. 1803. Example: on a 9 3/8" beech single-boxed side bead, and an open toted plank grooving plane, ca. 1840. **UR**

PALMER'S PATENT
Sidney W. Palmer (b. abt. 1830 in Cayuga Co., NY, d. Apr. 25, 1886) and **J. F. Palmer**, possibly brothers started manufacturing bench planes in Auburn, NY, in 1855. On Feb. 3, 1857, **J. F. Palmer** was issued Patent No. 16,569 and assigned the patent to **S. W. Palmer** of Detroit, MI. This patent provided longitudinal cutter adjustment. In 1863, **J. F. Palmer** sold his interest in the company to **Charles Conventry** who in 1871, sold it to **C. M. Palmer**. **S. W. Palmer** was listed, from 1867-83, as a washing machine and clothes dryer manufacturer. Example: on an 11 3/8" beech double-iron smoother with an integral handle and **PALMER'S PATENT/ FEB. 3, 1857** stamped on the toe. (see *Patented Transitional & Metallic Planes in America, vol. I*, p. 169, by Roger K. Smith) **UR**

T. PALMER
Probably **Theodore Palmer**, a planemaker in Poughkeepsie, NY, from 1866-68. In 1870, Theodore was listed as a sash & blind maker in Poughkeepsie, NY. Examples: on a pair of cherry handrail planes; a 16" closed-tote razee bench plane; and a 9 5/8" beech dado with a **Providence Tool Co.** cast steel iron, ca. 1850. ********

W. PARAMORE
Example: on a 9 1/2" beech, double-boxed, complex molder with heavy round chamfers and a location of **OHIO** and dated **1836**. **UR**

D. PARK
Example: on a 10" birch large hollow or nosing plane with eased edges and no consistent chamfer, ca. 1830. **UR**

EDWIN C. PARK
Edwin C. Park (b. Jun. 28, 1820 in PA, d. Jan. 1, 1906 in Wayne, Richmond Co., IN) was listed in the 1850 census, as a planemaker, in Richmond, IN. During the period from 1857-71, **Edwin** was variously described as a plow maker, a carpenter, and a woodworker. **No imprint is available.**

H. M. PARK
Harvey Park was listed as a planemaker, possibly a journeyman, in the 1836-37 Cincinnati, OH, directory; and is probably the same person who was listed in Richmond, IN, ca. 1840. **Harvey Park** and **John Hughes** may have been associated. **A & A1 *****

I. PARK
Example: on a 14" beech cornice plane with an applied fence and round chamfers; and a 9 13/16" triple-boxed reed & follow plane with heavy round chamfers. **UR**

W. PARK
Example: on a 9 3/8" beech combination tongue & groove plane with heavy flat chamfers, ca. 1800. **UR**

A. PARKER
Possibly **Avery Parker** (b. Dec. 10, 1738, Barnstable, MA, d. Nov. 21, 1794 in New Bedford, Bristol, MA) who was listed as a New Bedford, MA, carpenter. Example: the A imprint is on a 10" birch complex molder with flat chamfers and flutes, and a relieved wedge. The B imprint is on a birch bench plane, probably from southern New England, ca. 1790. **A & B: UR**

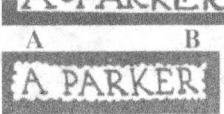

B. PARKER
Benjamin Parker (b. 1779 in Chesterfield, NH, d. Dec. 3, 1864 in Hingham, MA) made planes in Hingham, MA, in 1849. **Parker** was listed in the 1849 New England Mercantile Union directory as a plane manufacturer; and in the 1850 census, as a carpenter, in Hingham; in 1855, he was listed as a housewright in Hingham, Plymouth Co., MA. Example: on a double-iron fixed sash made by **L. Little**. **A & B: UR**

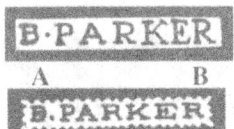

D. PARKER
Example: on a medium and a small hollow; and a wide round, all 10" beech with applied fences and flat chamfers, ca. 1810. **UR**

JOHN PARKER
John Parker was listed in the Utica, NY, 1834 directory as a planemaker, boarding with, and working for, **R. J. Collins**. **No imprint has been reported**.

J. PARKER
Joseph Parker was listed in the 1850 census, as a planemaker, in Newark, NJ. Example: on a 7 5/8" beech smoothing plane with a **Dwight & French** double-iron, ca. 1850. ****

N. PARKER
Possibly **Nahum Parker** (b. Feb. 22, 1789 in Stoddard, Cheshire, NH, d. Dec. 26, 1876 in Middlebury, VT) who moved before 1824, to Middlebury, VT. In the 1840 census, **Nahum** was recorded as engaged in manufactures and trades; from 1824-56, He was listed as Furniture Manufacturer in Middlebury. VT; from 1842-56, he was also listed, as a cabinetmaker. Example: on a 9 7/8" beech medium hollow with shallow round chamfers, ca. 1830-40. **UR**

Sx PARKER
Example: on a 12 7/8" birch mast plane with pegged tote, round top iron and shallow flat chamfers, ca. 1800. **UR**

S. C. PARKER
Stephen C. Parker was listed, in 1859, in Waitsfield, VT. In 1863-71, **Stephen** was listed in "mfg". One example on a **C. Warren**, Nashua on a 30" joiner as an owner imprint. Example: on a 9 3/4" beech dado with a boxwood depth stop and thumbscrews and shallow round chamfers, ca. 1830. **UR**

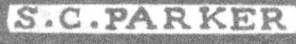

PARKER, HUBBARD & CO.
Alonzo Parker (b. 1807 in MA, d. 1892) and **Horace Hubbard** (b. 1808 in CT) were listed as tool manufacturers in Conway, MA, from 1842-49; and in April 1850, **Parker** and **Hubbard** founded the **Conway Tool Co.**. In 1830 & 1840, **Horace Hubbard** was shown living in East Hartford, CT. In the 1850 industrial census, the company was reported as employing 64 male hands at $2048/ mo. and 1 female at $12/ mo., using steam power, producing 130,000 molding tools worth $50,000 and 60,000 bench planes worth $25,000. After a fire destroyed the factory in July 1851, **Alonzo Parker** moved to Greenfield, MA, and started the **Greenfield Tool Co.**. The single die B imprint was from a 7 3/4" beech coffin smoothing plane.
A: ***; B ****

A

B

H. C. PARKES
Example: on a 9 3/8" beech single-boxed complex molder with size **5/8** on the heel and round chamfers, ca. 1820-30. ****

C. PARKHURST
Charles Parkhurst (b. ca. 1793 in NJ) appeared in the 1835-36 Newark, NJ, directory as a planemaker; and in the 1850 census as a turner. **Parkhurst** was also part of **Parkhurst & Coe**, which in the same 1835-36 directory, was listed as a toolmaker and planemaker. Examples: on a bead; a 9 3/8" beech skew rabbet with shallow round chamfers; and a pair of tongue & groove planes with size **6/8** on the heel, all 9 1/2" beech, ca. 1830. ****

D. PARKHURST
Example: on a 9 9/16" beech grooving plane with an inset metal skate and flat chamfers, ca. 1800. **UR**

J. PARKHURST
John D. Parkhurst (b. 1793 in NJ, d. abt 1853 in Essex, NJ) was listed in the 1850 census, as a carpenter, living in Springfield, Union Co., NJ. Example: on a tongue & groove pair.
A *****; A1 ***

A   A1

L. PARKHURST
L. Parkhurst with the added location imprint **HARTFORD** has been reported. **No imprint is available**.

PARKHURST & COE
Charles Parkhurst (b. ca. 1793 in Springfield, Union Co., NJ, d. 1862 in Newark, NJ) and **Joseph Davis Coe** (b. Mar. 28, 1800 in NJ, d. Aug. 9, 1874 in Newark, NJ) were listed in 1835-36, in the Newark, NJ, directory, as toolmakers and planemakers. **Charles** was listed in the 1837-38 directory, as a "turner and plane maker", at 55 Court St, both were listed in the 1850 census, as turners. **No imprint has been reported**.

T. PARKISON
Example: on a 10 7/8" beech square-rabbet with heavy flat chamfers, ca. 1790. **UR**

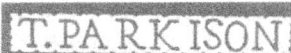

PARMELL
Example: on a 14 1/8" plank match tongue plane with an open tote, wood strike button and round chamfers, ca. 1820. **UR**

GEO. PARR
George Parr & Co., was listed as a maker of awls, saw sets, and other carpenters tools, in Buffalo, NY, in 1866. In 1861, George Parr (b. 1824 in England, Arrived in NY on Jun. 12, 1834) was listed as a Buffalo edge tool maker and may have been the **Parr** in **Parr & Parmelle**, who made edge tools in Buffalo, in 1865; in 1866, he was listed as **George Parr & Co.**. In Nov. 27 1866, **Parr** had a patent for a pocket knife. George was listed in 1862, as awl manufacturer, cor. Fifth & Court; in 1869, as edge tools, at 283 Court; in 1872, manf. mechanics' tools and light machinery, at 281-83 Court; in 1876, as "knives", at 281 in Court. Example: on a 4 3/4" beech coffin smoother, ca. 1850. ********

JOHN PARR
John Parr Jr. was listed as a hardware dealer at 546 8th. Ave., in the 1856 New York City directory. Example: on a 3 3/4" smoothing plane with the iron stamped in a circle **JOHN PARR-NEW YORK** with **CAST STEEL**. ********

A + PARRIS
Possibly **Alexander Parris** who was a joiner and builder in Portland, ME. Example: on a 10 7/16" complex molder; and a 10 1/16" complex molder with rosewood boxing, both birch with medium flat chamfers and the A wedge; and a 10 1/8" birch double-iron fixed sash with tight round chamfers and the B wedge, ca. 1800-20. ********

PARRISH/ R. PARRISH
Robert Parrish advertised plane making, in 1775, and continued in the trade, until after 1800. In 1807, a **Robert Parrish** was listed as gentleman, at 129 Vine. A record of early Philadelphia, PA, apprenticeships lists the apprenticing of one **William George Dorrington** to **Robert Parrish**, Philadelphia, on Jan. 20, 1773, for 8 years 9 months 7 days. **Parrish** was described as a "Wheat fan maker and Plain Maker". In 1751, in the *Pennsylvanian Gazette*, **Robert Parrish** was listed as a carpenter, and advertised for a runaway named **Benjamin Heathbourn**. On Aug. 23, 1775, in the *Pennsylvania Gazette*, (with a drawing of a bench plane), "Made and sold by **Robert Parrish**, at his houfe in third-ftreet, a few doors above Arch-ftreet, and nearly oppofite the Golden Swan Tavern, all forts of planes, fuitable for carpenters, joiners, cabinetmakers, coopers, &c. Which are allowed to be as compleat as any made in London." Again in 1776, **Robert Parrish** and a **John Nicholson** advertised in the *Pennsylvania Ledger* of Feb. 10, 1776, for the return of two runaway indentured servants, one a "gunstocker", the other a "plainmaker". Examples: the B imprint is on a chunky 14 5/8" panel raiser with an offset open tote, an adjustable fence, a wood dovetailed and canted depth stop, and the iron is marked **BROOKE**. The C imprint is on a 10" bead plane with large flat chamfers. **A, B & C *******

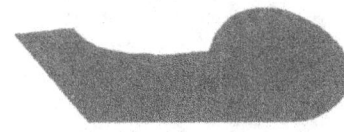

PARRISH/ R. A. PARRISH
Robert Austin Parrish (b. July 14, 1785 in Philadelphia, PA, d. Oct. 27, 1882 in Masonville, Burlington Co., NJ) was a Philadelphia, PA, planemaker, active from 1807-45. **Parrish** was listed, from 1807-15, at 40 St. John's & 217 N. Third; and in 1816-17, at 238 N. Third; **Parrish** was listed, from 1817-22, as part of **Parrish & Massey**, a hardware dealer at the same address; and was part of **Parrish & Barry**, planemakers, ca. 1820. **Parrish** was again listed at 238 N. Third St., from 1825-40, as a hardware merchant. After 1840, **Parrish** was listed as a gentleman in Lumberton, Burlington Co., NJ. Examples: on a marking gauge with the B imprint, on a **T. Goldsmith** plane overprinted **R. A. Parrish**; and a 9 1/2" small round with a tight round chamfers, ca. 1820. The D imprint is on a 9 1/2" beech round with round chamfers. **A & A1 *; B, B1, C & D ******

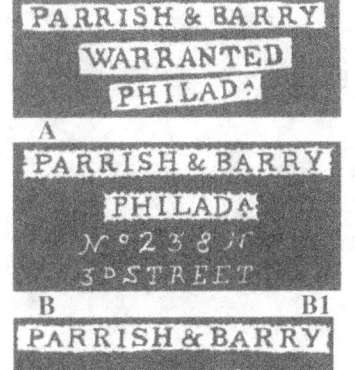

PARRISH & BARRY
A partnership between **Robert A. Parrish** and **Samuel Barry**, as planemakers in Philadelphia, PA, ca. 1820. The B imprint is on a single-boxed bead with size **6/8**. The B1 imprint is on a 9 1/4" ovolo & scotia with round chamfers. **A, B & B1 *****

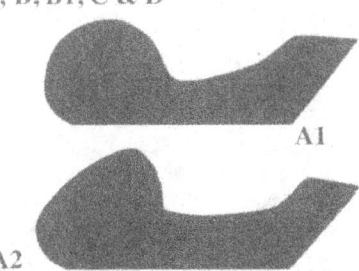

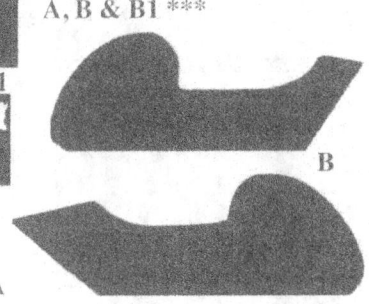

PARRISH & MASSEY
A partnership of **Robert A. Parrish** and **Samuel Massey**, who were listed in the Philadelphia, PA, directories from 1817-22,

as hardware dealers, at 238 No. 3rd. From 1818-19, they were listed as ironmongers. In 1823, **Robert A. Parrish** remained at that address and **Samuel Massey** was at 16 South Third. **No imprint has been reported**.

PARRY
John S. Parry (b. 1809 in Yates, Orleans, NY) made planes in New York City, in 1832; in Albany, NY, from 1833-37 & 1840-41; and in Brooklyn, NY, from 1842-54. He was also a partner in **Bensen & Parry**, from 1838-39. A, B & C **

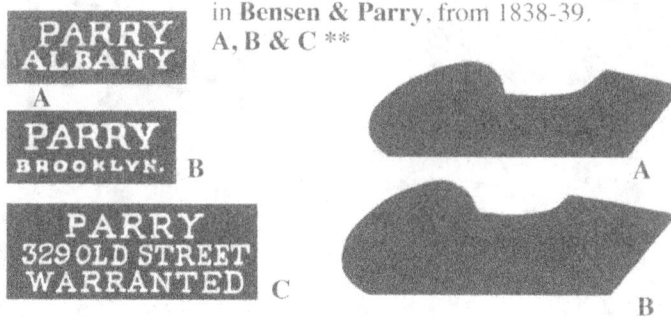

A PARSONS
Example: on a 31 1/2" beech jointer with heavy flat chamfers; and a 9 1/2" beech round with an iron set at a "York" pitch, and large round chamfers, found in ME, ca. 1810-20. UR

A. C. PARSONS
Amasa Chester Parsons (b. Nov. 1827 in Worthington, Hampshire Co., MA, d. Jul. 12, 1912, in Chesterfield, Hampshire Co., MA) made planes in Cummington, MA. Parsons was listed in the 1870 census, as a plane handle manufacturer; and in the 1880 census, as a planemaker. **No imprint has been reported**.

E. PARSONS/ J. M. BABBIT
Elisha Parsons (b. Nov. 4, 1807 in VA, d. Jun. 26, 1854 in KY) was listed as a planemaker, in the 1834 Cincinnati, OH. directory at 4th. bt. Elm & Plum; and **J. M. Babbit** was noted as a planemaker, in Mason, OH, from 1850-56. Example: on a molder. ****

S. B. PARSONS
Example: on an 8 7/8" beech Roman ogee molder with shallow round chamfers and the iron marked **A. D. Green**, ca. 1830. UR

PARTRIDGE
Example: on an 8 1/4" beech boxed filletster with wedge-locked armes, brass depth stop and arm ends, and round chamfers, ca. 1830. UR

I: PARTRIDGE
James Partridge (b. ca. 1714 in Plymouth, MA, d. Jan. 4, 1770 in Canaan, CT) married, Dec. 24, 1744, in Stonington, New London, Co., James was a shop and house joiner in Canaan, CT. **James Partridge** willed to his Sons **James Partridge** and **Stephen Partridge**, his shop and house joiner's tools. Example: on a 9 1/2" birch table round with a relieved wedge, small flat chamfers and flutes, from New England, ca. 1790. UR

O. PARTRIDGE
Possibly **Oliver Partridge** (d. 1838 in Medfield, Norfolk Co., MA) who on Jun. 14, 1794, listed his int. with marriage to **Cathy Knowten** in Medfield, MA. He was listed as a laborer at the time of his death. Examples: on a 9 7/16" narrow astragal with the A wedge; and a 10" complex molder with the B wedge, both beech with flat chamfers, ca. 1790. UR

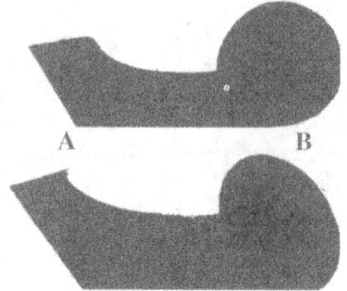

S. PARTRIDGE
Stephen Partridge (b. 1752 in Rutland District, Barre, MA, d 1790) was placed under the guardianship, in 1764, to **David Taft** (1736-69) of Mendon MA. **David Taft** died when **Stephen** was 17 years old. **Stephen** married **Jemima Taft**, 1st. cousin of **David Taft**, on Jan. 4, 1776, in Mendon, MA. **Stephen** was later described, in a Mendon deed, as a joiner. Examples: on a 10" Yankee plow with riveted skate, thumbscrews, a wood depth stop, and also imprinted by **E. TAFT**: a 10" hollow; and a 14" panel raiser, all birch with heavy flat chamfers. Partridge and Taft shared their location stamp. The flat back finial suggests a production period ca. 1780. A & B *****

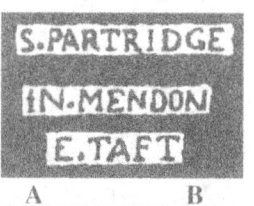

E. PASQUARELLI
Examples: on a 13 1/2" beech handled tongue match plane with shallow round chamfers and a plow, ca. 1830. ****

INO PASS
Example: on a 9 7/16" beech hollow with flat chamfers, found in Kingston, NY, ca. 1810. UR

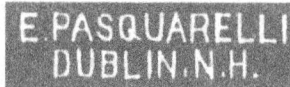

JOHN PASSCUE
John Paschal (Passcue) (b. Apr. 8, 1784 in Gironde, France, m. Jul. 25, 1811 in Philadelphia, d. Jul. 8, 1856 in Philadelphia, PA) was listed in the Philadelphia directories of 1797 & 99, as a

planemaker, and as **John Pascue**, in 1796. Example: on a 9 15/16" square rabbet with double nickers; a fixed sash; and a 9 1/2" ogee, all beech with heavy flat chamfers, ca. 1790   *****

PATENT APLIED FOR
Patent Aplied For is made up of three separate embossed dies. Example: on a 6" beech coffin smoother.   **UR**

J. O. PATT
Example: on a 9 1/2" double-iron side rabbet with round chamfers, ca. 1820.   **UR**

F. M. PATTEN
Example: on a 9 3/8" beech size **13** round with the imprint of hardware dealer **A. J. Wilkinson/ Boston**, ca. 1840.   **UR**

M. PATTEN
Possibly **Matthew Patten** (b. May 19, 1719, d. Aug. 27, 1795 in Bedford, NH) was a woodworker, joiner and toolmaker of Scotch-Irish background, in Bedford, NH, from 1754-88. **Patten** made handles including axe, saw and scythe; and planes, including smoothing, fore, rabbet, ogee, plows and cooper's jointers. **Patten** was also a farmer, logger, fisherman, land surveyor, justice of the peace, and judge of probate. His "day book" diaries, spanning thirty four years of work, weather, family and religious life, are located at the NH Historical Society. **Patten** took all sorts of woodworking jobs from making pails to building bridges, although his specialty was that of a joiner. Example: on a 16" double-slide fenced skew panel raiser, that is more typical of the mid-Atlantic region than NH, ca. 1800.   *****

H. A. PATTERSON & BROS.
H. A. Patterson & Bros. was a NY hardware dealer. Example: on a 21 1/2" bench plane made by **Mockridge & Francis**.   ****

PATTISON
Example: on a 9" birch quarter round with flat chamfers, ca. 1800.   **UR**

C PATTISON
Example: on a 10" applewood large bead with flat chamfers, ca. 1780.   **UR**

Tx PATTON
Example: on a 9 1/2" beech tounge plane with heavy round chamfers, ca 1820.   **UR**

I. PAUL
Example: on a 9 1/4"x 5/16" beech bead with flat chamfers, ca. 1800.   **UR**

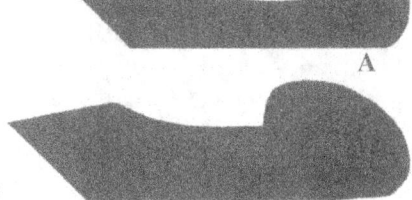

J. PAUL
Possibly **Josiah Paul** (b. Dec. 5, 1767 in England, d. Jul. 19, 1842 in Groton, Caledonia, VT) who was listed in the 1810-30 censuses, as a resident of Groton, VT; in 1820, his occupation was listed as agriculture. It was reported that he supplemented his farm work with the making of fine furniture and looms. Examples: on a 10" birch complex molder with tight round chamfers and the A wedge; a hollow; a round; a complex molder; and a center bead, all 9", three birch and one beech with heavy round chamfers, and the B relieved wedge, found in Starksboro, VT, ca. 1810-20.   ****

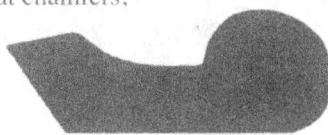

S. PAUL
Example: on a 9 3/8" beech round with round chamfers; and a 9 1/2" beech center bead with flat chamfers, ca. 1810-20.   ****

W. PAWLETT &. CO.
Possibly **William Pawlett** who was listed as a planemaker in Utica, NY, in the 1832 directory, boarding with, and working for, **R. J. Collins**. From 1911-15 **William Pawlett** was listed as machinist in Cleveland, OH. ca. 1850.   **A & A1 ****

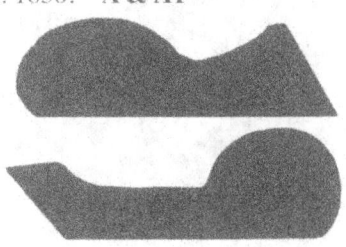

PE. RL
Examples: on a 9 7/8"x 3/8" beech astragal bead; and a 9 15/16" complex molder. Both with wide flat chamfers, found in Lancaster, PA, ca. 1800.   **UR**

J. A. PEABODY
Example: imprinted four times in a rectangle, on the toe of a molder, ca. 1850.   **UR**

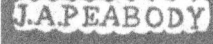

J. A. PEALE & CO.

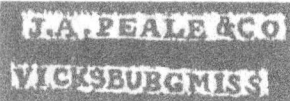

J. A. Peale & Co. probably was a hardware dealer in Vicksburg, MS. Example: on a Ohio Tool Co. plane, ca. 1885. ****

J. PEARCE

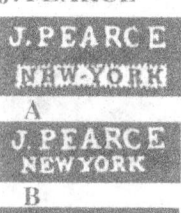

Examples: the imprint C is on a bench plane and is thought to represent the second line (non-warranted) of planes sold by the **Union Factory/ H. Chapin** to New York tool stores and wholesalers.
B, B1 & C1: FF; A *; C ****

J. W. PIRCE/ J. W. PEARCE

Jonathan W. Pearce (Pirce) (b. Aug. 15, 1815 in Wrentham, MA, d. Sept. 23, 1881) was living in Wrentham when his mother died in 1817, and his father in 1820. Orphaned, Jonathan was brought to Rehoboth, MA, by his uncle. In 1829, at age 14, he was apprenticed to **Ezekiel Smith**, as a planemaker. Jonathan complete his apprenticeship by 1835, at age 20, when he married Grace C. Peck, the daughter of **Otis Peck** of Rehoboth. **Otis Peck** was Ezekiel Smith's partner in the ownership of the Peck sawmill & gristmill, from 1827-36, located not far from Ezekiel Smith's plane making shop. **Jonathan W. Pearce**'s earliest planes were made in Rehoboth, from 1836-44. There is a **J. W. PIRCE** plow plane, dated **1840**. He worked in Fall River, MA, from 1845-53; and Providence, RI, from 1854-79. He was listed in the 1872 & 79 Providence directors as planemaker, at the rear of 287 High St. Examples: the B1 imprint is dated **1871**. The C imprint, dated **1853,** is on a beech plow with birdseye maple arms & fence, and nuts of ebony, and wedge of rosewood. A & A1 *; D & D1 **; B ****; B1 & C *****

T. PEARCE

Example: on a 9 1/8" beech dado with flat chamfers. UR

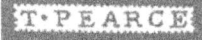

P. PEARL

Examples: on a pair of 9 1/2" beech hollow & rounds with shallow round chamfers, ca. 1830. UR

B. PEARSON

Possibly **Benjamin Pearson** (d. 1799) a joiner in Norton, MA. Example: on a 9 9/16" narrow fully-boxed bead; and a 9 1/2"x 1 3/8" wide skew rabbet with a **W. Butcher** iron, both 9 1/2" beech with heavy round chamfers, found separately in OH, ca. 1820. UR

E. PEARSON

Examples: on a skew rabbet; an astragal; a round; a bead and a complex molder. All 10" beech with flat chamfers, possibly from PA. ca. 1790. ****

C. F. PEASE.

Example: on a 9 1/16" beech hollow, ca. 1850. UR

E. B. PEASE & BRO

Edward B. Pease (b. ca. 1815 in Hudson, NY, d. Jan. 30, 1870 in Springfield, IL) and his brother **William W. Pease** (d. 1859 in Springfield, IL) were hardware dealers in Springfield, IL. Edward used his own name alone, from 1859; after William died, until his own death, in 1870. In 1860, **Mrs. Wm. Pearse** was in listed in Springfiels, IL with **John G. Pearse & Robert G. Pearse**, were both clerks, probably William's sons. Example: on a side bead. ***

J. S. PEASE

Example: on a plane with the location imprint **St. LOUIS, MO**, ca. 19c. ****

M. PEASLEE

Example: on a 10" beech skew rabbet with a birch wedge and flat chamfers, ca. 1800. UR

C. PEAVEY
Example: on a 9 1/2" beech small round with flat chamfers, ca. 19c.   **UR**

A Peck
Example: on a 9 1/2" beech small having plane with flat chamfers, ca. early 19c.   **UR**

E+PECK
Example: on a 9 3/8" birch hollow with flat chamfers, ca. 1800.   **UR**

H. M. PECK
Example: on a 10" birch wide round with flat chamfers, ca. 1800.   **UR**

I. PECK
Example: on a 9 3/8" beech molder with small round chamfers, ca. 1810.   **UR**

OTIS. PECK
The Rehoboth, MA, vital records list four **Otis Pecks** (b. 1750, 80, 85 & 1808). The most likely was **Otis Peck** (b. Mar. 23, 1785 in Rehoboth, d. Oct. 10, 1842 in Rehobeth). He either apprenticed to or worked for **Aaron Smith**. **Otis Peck's** uncle, **George W. Peck** (b. 1777) was appointed guardian of the four youngest children of **Aaron Smith** after **Smith's** death, in 1822. From 1827-37, **Otis Peck** and **Ezekiel Smith**, **Aaron Smith's** son, were partners in owning a 7/8 share of the **Peck** sawmill and gristmill, after **George W. Peck's** death. **Otis Peck** probably made planes, with his own imprint, after 1805, when he turned 20, to about 1815, when **Aaron Smith's** planes were switched from using birch to beech, shortened from 10" to 9 1/2", and the chamfers where changed from flat to round. Example: on a round; and a snipe bill plane, both 9 1/2" beech with small flat chamfers.   *****

PECK & CROUCH
Peck & Crouch was a Northampton, MA, plane making partnership consisting of **Francis Peck** and **Charles S. Crouch** (b. 1826 in MA) who worked together, ca. 1850. **Peck** was a principal in the **Conway Tool Co.**, from 1850-51. From 1853-54, they were both listed as working for the **Greenfield Tool Co.**. **Crouch** was also part of **Arnold & Crouch**, ca. 1855. The eagle die also appears on planes by **H. Wells** and **J. D. Kellogg**, also of Northampton, MA. Example: on a 9 1/2"x 1 5/8" beech skew rabbet also with an owner's incuse initials **W.P/ J.F.P**, ca. 1850.
A & B **

   A

C. H. PECKHAM
Example: on a 17 1/8" birch jointer with beech centered, closed tote and wedge, and flat chamfers, ca. 1810.   **UR**

P. MP./ P. M. PECKHAM
Perry Mumford Peckham (b. Aug. 14, 1789 in Middletown, RI, d. Aug. 20, 1880 in Fall River, MA) was a planemaker, in Fall River, MA, from 1850-60. At various times, **Peckham** was also listed as a cabinetmaker, a maker of deck plugs, wedges, ship's steering wheels, and was a saw filer. He appeared in Bristol, RI, in the 1820 census; in Troy, RI, in 1830; and in Fall River, MA, in 1840 & 1850, when he was listed as a planemaker. A group of 16 planes were marked by the same owner, an organ maker. 13 were imprinted with the B imprint and were 9 1/2", 2 were marked **L. Tinkhan** and one with the A imprint on a 10 1/4" molder with the A relieved wedge.   **B1 *; B **; A ******

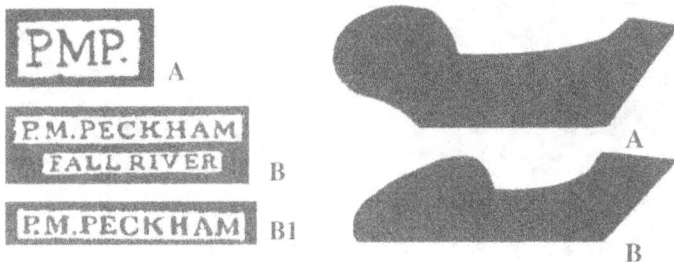

PEELER/ A PEELER
Believed to be **Alender (Allender, Allendis) Peeler** (b. 1774, d. Apr. 28, 1849 in Vernon, VT) of Vernon, VT. He was the father of **George Washington Peeler**. The **PEELER** in all imprints is from the same die. The A imprint with **PEELER** only is on a 14 1/2"x 2 1/4" birch panel raiser; and a 9 3/4" birch plow with oak thumb screws and wedge; a maple depth stop and arms mortised into the fence. The B imprint is on a birch jack; a 10 1/8" birch hollow; a 10 1/8" birch round with round chamfers, a double-iron and a relieved wedge; an 8 3/4" beech round; and a 9" birch smoother with round chamfers and the initial **A** repeated 15 times. ca. 1800-10.
A ***; B ****

G. W. PEELER
George Washington Peeler (b. Dec. 6, 1815 in Vernon, VT, d. Jul. 2, 1899 in Westminster, MA) was the son of **Alender Peeler**. **George** was listed, in 1850, as a carpenter, in Northfield, MA; in 1860, in Worcester, MA; in 1880, in Athol, Worcester, MA; then moved to Westminster, MA. This imprint has the same **PEELER** die as the **A PEELER** imprint and a separate **GW** initial die. Examples: on a bench plane with flat chamfers, a 9 1/4" beech quarter round molder with flat chamfers and a relieved wedge; and a 21" beech jointer with a closed tote and a wood start, ca. 1800.   ****

A. PEES

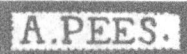
Example: on a 22" beech jointer with a offset tote and a double- iron, ca. 19c. **UR**

LEVI PEIRCE
Levi Peirce from Hollis, NH. Examples: on a 22" jointer; and a 16" jack plane with an open tote, a wood start, and a double **Buck Brothers** iron, ca. 1850. ********

H. W. PELL
H. W. Peel was a hardware dealer from Rome, NY, and of **Pell & Wright**; in 1883, as carriage (wholesale) in Rome; from 1887-89, as carriage, saddlery, and hardware, at 216-18 S. Washington, Rome, NY. Example: on an **Ohio Tool Co.** jack plane. ********

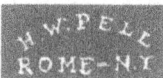

PELL & WRIGHT
Possibly **H. W. Pell** of Rome, NY, who was probably a hardware dealer. Examples: on a plow; a tongue plane; and a hollow imprinted **72** on the toe, in the distinctive **Sandusky** style numbers; and with a **Sandusky** style relieved wedge, ca. 1850. *******

C. PELTON
Example: on a birch skew rabbet; and a 7 7/8" birch smoother with round chamfers, both with the date **1831**. The single-iron in the smoother is marked **J. PRATT**. **UR**

F. PELTON
Examples: on a single blade sash plane and a table plane, ca. 19c. **UR**

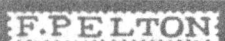

D. PENDELTON
Examples: on a 9 1/4"x 1/2" beech side bead plane with flat chamfers; a wedge lock plow with a wood depth stop; a groving plane with a rivited skate and round chamfers, ca. 1810-30. **UR**

E. W. PENNELL
Edward W. Pennell (b. 1814 in PA) was a Philadelphia, PA, planemaker from 1839-59. **Edward** was married on Apr. 23, 1838, in Philadelphia. **Pennell** was listed in 1850, as a planemaker. **George Gorbutt**, also a planemaker, was listed as living with **Edward**. **Edward Pennell** was also part of **Pennell & Miller** from 1848-54. In 1862, **Edward Pennell** was listed as a maker in Philadelphia. Example: on a 9 1/2" beech coping plane with the B1 imprint. **A, A1, B & B1 ****; **C ******

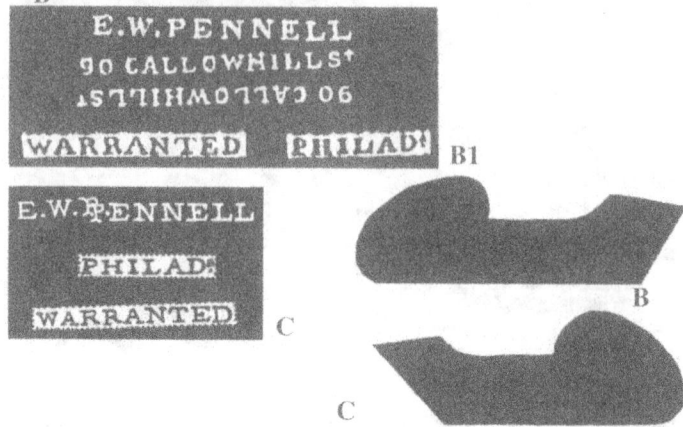

PENNELL & MILLER
Pennell & Miller was a planemaking partnership in Philadephia, PA with **Edward W. Pennell** and **Frederick Miller** (b. Apr. 18, 1810 in Philadelphia, PA, d. Mar. 1, 1892) in Philadelphia listed in 1848, 1850-52 & 1854. **A & B *****

V. PENSER
One example included the address of Arch Street which is probably from Philadelphia, PA. Example: on a 9 1/2" beech complex molder with flat chamfers. ********

D. PERCIVAL
Example: on a 15" beech double-iron crown molder with shallow round chamfers, ca. 1830. **UR**

A. W. PERKINS
Examples: the A imprint is on a 9" Yankee style plow with wood thumbscrews and wood depth stop; a 10" round; a 9 5/8" boxed complex molder; a 9 1/2" rabbet; and a 14" panel raiser with a centered tote, all beech with round chamfers, ca. 1820. The B imprint is on a 10" beech astragal bead with flat chamfers, ca. 1800. **A & B *****

C. PERKINS
Example: on a 9 1/2" birch single-boxed complex molder with round chamfers, ca. 1820. **UR**

DAVID PERKINS

 Example: on a 9 1/2" beech skew rabbet. **UR**

H. PERKINS/ H. PERKINS TOOL MAKER.
Hiram Perkins (b. Mar. 31, 1822 in Walden, VT, d. Jun. 8, 1872), was active from 1860-72. **Hiram** was married on Jan. 9, 1844, in Cabot, VT. He resided in Walden thru 1850; and in 1860, he was listed in Cabot, as a carriage maker. **Hiram Perkins** volunteered in 1862, for the War of Secession. On Oct. 4, 1862, he was a 2nd. Lt. in Co. H, VT, 13th. Infantry Reg. He was muster out on Jul. 21, 1863, at Bratteboro, VT. On Dec. 12, 1863, Perkins was promoted to a full 1st. Lt. He advertised in the *Cabot Advertiser*, on Jan. 1, 1869:

> "Tools! All Kinds of Carpenters and Joiners Tools made to order and for sale by **HIRAM PERKINS**. Also cash paid for Second Growth White Beech Butts."

In the 1870 census, he was listed as a farmer and toolmaker in Cabot, VT. When he died, in 1872, at age 50, he was listed as a carpenter. Examples: the A imprint is on a 30"x 3 1/8" beech jointer. The B imprint is on an 8 1/2" handled smoother. Also reported is a handled screw-arm plow; a sash plane; and a sash coping pair. **A & B ****

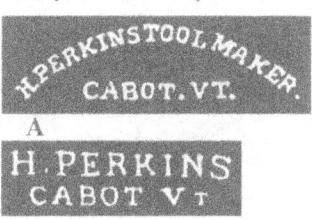 

H. PERKINS & CO.
H. Perkins & Co. probably was a hardware dealer. Examples: on an plow with boxwood screw-arms and nuts, with style number **243 1/2**, by **H. Chapin**; The B imprint is overstruck by a **H. Chapin/ Uniton Factory/ Warranted** on a closed toted rosewood screw-arm plow with boxwood arms, nuts and washers and marked with a **240** inventory number on the heel. **A & B: ****

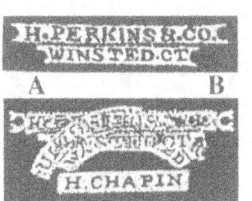

I + PERKINS + H
Possibly **John Perkins** (b. Dec. 17, 1723) was a chairmaker, shop at Battery & March St., Boston, from 1750-60. **John** was married on Mar. 13, 1745, in Boston, MA. He moved to Gorham MA (now Gorham, ME), by 1771. Example: on a 10" beech round with flat chamfers and number **VI** on the side of the wedge and plane body. **UR**

J. PERKINS/ .PERKINS.
Examples: on a 10" beech square miter plane, and a rounding plane; the B imprint with the J removed, on a double boxed side bead and on a 9 1/2" beech round with flat chamfers. ca. 1830. **A & B: UR**

L. W. PERKINS
Example: on two 9 15/16" beech medium rounds with shallow round chamfers, ca. 1830. **UR**

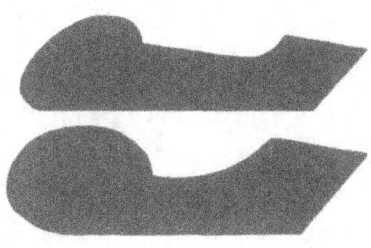

S. PERKINS
Possibly **Solomon Perkins** a joiner who worked in Bridgewater, MA, from 1737-43. Example: on a 10 1/2" birch complex molder with heavy flat chamfers, similar to **N. Potter** in style, ca. 1750-60 **UR**

W. PERRINE
Example: on a 14 1/2" beech toted plank grooving plane with shallow round chamfers, ca. 1830. **UR**

HENRY D. PERRY
Henry D. Perry (b. ca. 1807 in Wales) was listed in the Utica, NY, directories from 1837-41, working for **John Reed**. He was listed as a planemaker from 1843-47 & 1854-57. **No imprint has been reported**.

J. PERRY
James Perry (b. 1711, d. 1771) was listed as a chairmaker in Charlestown, MA, ca. 1736. There was also a **James Perry** who was listed as a Boston, MA, cabinetmaker, in 1809. Also listed in Boston was a **John Perry**, a housewright, in 1807-18. There may be more than one generation of **J. Perrys** involved in planemaking, who may or may not be related. Examples: the A imprint is on a crown molder with a heavily offset tote; a 10 1/4" Yankee plow with wood thumbscrew locked slide-arms and riveted skate; three 9 7/8"-10" molding planes; and a pair of 11 1/2" razee tongue & groove planes with fishtail open totes, all birch with heavy flat chamfers, ca. 1770. The B imprint is on a 9 1/2" beech filletster. Other B imprint examples are also marked **PATENT**, ca. 1810. **A & B ****

JOHN PERRY
John Perry was listed in the Utica, NY, directory in 1837-38, as a planemaker. **No imprint has been reported**.

JOSEPH PERRY
Joseph Perry (b. 1830) was listed as a planemaker in Smithfield, RI, in 1850, boarding and working for **Ezekiel Smith**.
No imprint has been reported.

J. B. PERRY & CO.
Examples: the A imprint is on a 9 1/4" beech ogee molding plane with an integral fence. The B imprint with **MAKER** is on a 10 3/4" maple moving filletster with no noticable chamfers, ca. 1830.   A & B:****

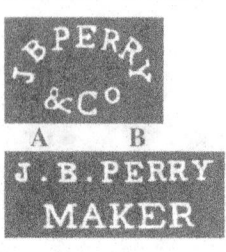
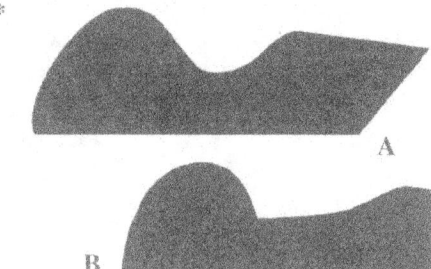

J. G. PERRY
Examples: The A imprint is on a 9 1/2" beech boxed large bead with large shallow round chamfers. The B imprint with the location **Nw. BEDFORD** (probably New Bedford, MA) is on a size 22 round by **P. Copeland**, B imprint, ca. 1830.   A & B: UR

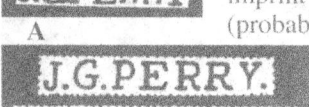

J. H. PERRY
John H. Perry (b. ca. 1829 in NY) was listed as a planemaker in New York City, from 1850-63. In 1880, **Perry** was listed as a ship's carpenter in Brooklyn, NY, ca. 19c.   ***

N. O. PERRY
Example: on a 11" beech match tongue plane with round chamfers, ca. 19c.   UR

W & E. PERRY
William Perry (b. 1791, d. 1856 in Woodbury, CT) and **E. Perry** were planemakers in West Haven, CT. Examples: on a complex molder; and a hollow with a size **8** on the heel, both 9 1/2" beech with flat chamfers, ca. 1805-15.   A, A1 ****; B *****

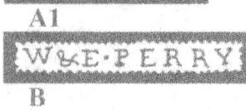

G. PETCH
Example: on a 9 1/8" x 1/2" beech single-boxed bead with shallow round chamfers and a later owner's **W. PETCH** incuse imprint, ca. 1830.   UR

K. PETER
Example: on a 13 1/2" applewood filletster with adj. side & bottom fences, and flat chamfers, found in OH, possibly from eastern PA, ca. 1800.   UR

PETERS & TRIMBLE
Norris Peters and **Joseph M. Trimble** were hardware merchants listed separately, in the 1857 Richmond, IN, directory. **Norris Peters** at Huntington House and **Joseph M. Trimble** at S. Front St. It appears that they were also in a partnership. Two complex molders are in the Wayne Co., IN Historical Museum.   ***

JOHN PETTINGELL
John Pettingell (b. abt. 1819 in MD, m. Dec. 11, 1862 in Lowell, MA, d. Jan. 27, 1899 in Amesbury, MA) was listed as a Lowell, MA, planemaker, in 1875 only; and was listed from 1844-78, as a carpenter. **Pettingell** supplied wood for plane stocks to other makers. There was also a **Walter Pattingell** (b. Aug. 8, 1812, in Salem, NH, d. Jan. 12, 1877 in Salem) listed in the 1850 census, as a carpenter, in Lowell, MA.
No imprint has been reported.

A. D. PETTINGILL
Example: on a 22" razee fore plane with a **W. Butcher** double-iron, ca. 1850.   UR

A. PHELPS
Example: on a 9 1/2" beech large hollow with heavy round chamfers, ca. 1820.   UR

C. PHELPS
Example: on a 16" beech jack with slight offset tote, and round top iron, ca.   UR

C. PHELPS. Jr.
Example: on a fore plane; on a 15 7/8" jack with a centered tote; and a smoother, all beech with heavy round chamfers, ca. 1820.   ****

D. PHELPS
Two examples found in the CT River Valley, one in VT and the other in MA. Examples: on a 10 7/16" cove; the other on a 9 13/16" fenced skew rabbet, both birch with flat chamfers, ca. 1800.   ****

E. PHELPS
Example: on a 9 1/2" beech hollow & round pair, ca. 1850.   UR

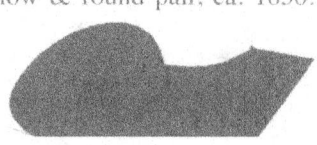

H. PHELPS
Example: on a 9 1/2" birch skew rabbet with a snecked iron and heavy flat chamfers, possibly from New England, ca. 1780. **UR**

J. PHELPS
E. Newell left 2/3 of his estate, in 1808, to **Joel Phelps**, providing **Phelps** would take care of his wife, Rhoda. **Phelps** moved to Worcester, and later back to Lanesboro, MA. In 1807, a **John Phelps** advertised that he was in the cabinet making business, in Danville, VT. **Phelps** also advertised for an apprentice. Examples: on a 9" beech molders with flat chamfers on the toe & heel and round chamfers on the top, and a medium round with size **7/8** on heel. ca. 1800. ********

R. PHELPS
Possibly **Russell Phelps**, a Charlton, MA, cabinetmaker from 1820-40, who worked for Southbridge, MA, cabinetmaker **Harvey Dresser**. Also listed, from 1865-73, was a **Russell Philips** (d. 1873 in Worcester, MA) as a pattern maker in Worcester, MA. Example: on a 9 1/2" beech double-lignum vitae boxed complex molder with flat chamfers, ca. 1810. **UR**

J. V. PHIEL
J. V. Phiea was an undertaker and cabinetmaker in Mercersburg, PA. Example: on a double-boxed size **1/4** beech bead, made by **Sargent Tool Co.** with the inventory number **624**. The imprint is ink: ca. 19c. *********

J. V. PHIEL
(drawing of a horse drawn hearse)
UNDERTAKER
and CABINETMAKER
MERCERSBURG, PA

PHILADA. WORKS
An abbreviation for "Philadelphia Works". Examples: on a 9 1/2"x 1/2" beech boxed side bead with **37** on the toe, the style number for the **Ohio Tool Co.** for a 1/2" boxed bead, and a toted beech plow plane, ca. 1850. ********

A PHILLIPS
Example: on a 9 1/4"x 1/2" beech single-boxed bead with heavy round chamfers, ca. 1820. **UR**

B. PHILLIPS
Benjamin Phillips was a Cincinnati, OH, planemaker, listed from 1836-52; from 1836-37, located at Elm bt. Canal & 12th; from 1839-42, at Charles St.; in 1843-44, Sycamore bt. 7th. & 8th.; in 1846, on ws. Pleasent bt. 14th. & 15th.; from 1850-52, at ws. Elm bt. Court & Canal. Example: on a 9 1/2" beech wide hollow & round pair. ********

I. PHILLIPS
Example: on a 16 1/4" single boxed beech large bead with flat chamfers, ca. 1800. **UR**

MILTON PHILLIPS
Milton Phillips was listed in Utica, NY, directories from 1832-34, as a planemaker working for **John Reed**.
No imprint has been reported.

N. PHILLIPS
Nathaniel Phillips was listed as a Boston, MA, planemaker, from 1807-23. **Phillips** was listed in the 1818 directory, at Pleasant St. Example: on a 9 1/2" boxed, beech complex molder with round chamfers. ******

P. PHILLIPS
Example: on a dado with flat chamfers, found in Lancaster Co., PA; and a 7 7/8" coffin smoother with heavy round chamfers, both beech, probably from PA, ca. 1800-20. ********

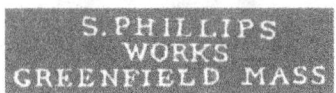

S. PHILLIPS WORKS
Simeon Phillips, Jr. (b. Feb. 22, 1815 in Greenfield, Franklin Co., MA, d. Jul. 5, 1904 in Greenfield) m. Apr. 27, 1846 in Greeenfield to **Loisa Carrier**. In Aug. 1851, **Simeon** was a founding director of the **Greenfield Tool Co.**. Examples: on a 20 7/8"x 3 1/8" beech fore plane with a **Dwight & French** double-iron; and a 16" toted gutter plane with a **Humphreysville** iron, ca. 1850. *********

T. PHILLIPS
T. Phillips was listed as a cabinetmaker from northeastern PA, from 1790-1815. Examples: on a 10 1/8" beech molder with flat chamfers; a 13 1/2" beech wedge-lock armed plank grooving plane with round chamfers; a 10" fixed sash with round chamfers; and a 10" birch shiplap plane with round chamfers, found in CT near MA, ca. 1800-20. ********

ZEPHANIAH PHILLIPS
Zephaniah Phillips (b. abt. 1837 in St. Clair, Toronto, Canada, d. Jan. 22, 1903 in Hillsborough, FL) was the son of **George Phillips**, a carpenter. On Feb. 27, 1862, **Zephaniah Phillips** from Shawneetown, a carriage maker, was mustered in, as a Private, into Co. F, 56th. IL Infantry. On Sep. 26, 1862, he was listed as "Deserted". On May 10, 1870, **Zephaniah Phillips** of Dixon, IL, was issued Patent No. 102,966. **PAT'D 1870** was cast on the throat piece only, on a 16" beech jack plane with a double-iron. The cutter was riveted to an adjustable fork, that became inefficient when the blade was worn down. In 1880, he was listed as a cabinetmaker in Wheeling, WV.
No imprint is available.

PHOENIX COMPANY

The **Phoenix Company** was founded by **Arba Alford** (b. Nov. 6, 1807 in Litchfield, CT, d. Jan. 9, 1881 in Barkhamsted, Litchfield) and brother-in-law **Alfred Alford** (b. Sep. 15, 1812 in Litchfield, CT, d. Aug. 28, 1892 in Barkhamsted, Litchfield), in 1853, as a reorganization of **A. & A. Alford & Co.**, which operated from 1849-53. The company was housed in **Lambert Hitchcock's** former chair factory, at Hitchcockville, CT. The plan was to make carpenter and furniture tools as well as chairs and furniture. In 1864, the company was sold to **L. C. Stephens & Co.** which was started by **Lorenzo Case Stephens** (b. 1809, d. 1871). He was succeeded by his son, **Deloss H. Stephens** (b. 1837, d 1919), who continued tool manufacturing, on the site until 1901, when the firm moved to Pine Meadows and became **Chapin Stephens Co.** In 1865, Hichcockville was renamed Riverton. CT. **FF**

PHOENIX FACTORY
(see **W. Warner** and **Warner & Driggs**)

J. PICKERING

John Pickering (b. 1739, d. 1811) Married on Feb. 14, 1813, in Salem, Essex Co., MA. or **John Pickering Jr.** (b. abt. 1787, d. 1822 Salem, Essex Co., MA) Examples: molders are 9 1/4"-9 1/2" beech with an **I. Sleeper** style wedge and narrow flat chamfers, probably from Newburyport, MA, ca. 1800. ****

JOHN PICKERING

John Pickering (Oct. 20, 1790 in Mendon, Worcester Co., MA, d. Jan. 22, 1865 in Nicholson, Wyoming Co., PA) was listed in the 1813-14 Philadelphia, PA, directory as a planemaker. In 1850, he was listed as a lumberman, in Nicholson.
No imprint has been reported.

T. & A. PICKERING

T. & A. Pickering was a Cincinnati, OH, hardware dealer, from 1866-1962. It succeeded **Joseph W. Wane & Co.** in which **T. Pickering** was a partner and **A. Pickering** was a Clerk. It was succeeded by **Pickering Hardware Co.** Example: the A1 imprint is on the heel of a **Scioto Works** coffin smoother, ca. 19c. ****

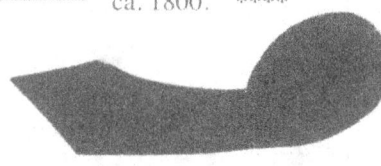

W. PICKERING

Example: on a 14"x 1 3/8" birch skew rabbet with an open tote and flat chamfers, ca. 1800. **UR**

C. PIERCE.

This embossed name with an incuse location **OHIO** is from a 11 1/2" low-angle smoother, found in OH, with a group of four **D. Lewis** bench planes, ca. 1850. **UR**

C. S. PIERCE

Example: on a 10 1/2" beech double-iron sash with shallow round chamfers, ca. 1830-40. **UR**

E. PIERCE

Two possibilities exist for the earlier A imprint: **Edward Pierce** (b. May 5, 1735 in Dorchester, Suffolk, MA, d. Feb. 22, 1818 in Dorchester), who was a Dorchester, MA, housewright, who built the residence for Col. Quincy in Wollaston, MA, in 1770; or **Ephram Pierce** (d. Abt. 1845, MA) of Middleboro, MA, who was apprenticed to **Simeon Doggett**, from May 1784 to Sept. 1789. Examples: on a 9 15/16" birch round; a birch tongue plane; a 9 13/16" beech complex molder; and a 7 1/2" cherry coffin smoother with round-top iron and chamfered wedge, all with large shallow flat chamfers, ca. 1770. The B imprint may represent a second generation, and is on 9"-9 1/4" birch (except one of cherry) molders with flat chamfers, ca. 1800.
A, B & B1 **

ERASTUS PIERCE

Erastus Pierce (b. 1830 in NJ, d. aft. 1920 in Worcester, Ostego, NY) was listed in the 1850 census, as a planemaker, in NJ. In 1860, he was listed as a toolmaker in New York, NY; in 1870, as a farmer, in Newtown, Queens, NY.
No imprint has been reported.

E. G. PIERCE JR

Elisha G. Pierce, Jr. (b. 1822) from Jamaica, VT, was listed in the 1850 census, as a carpenter; and as a carriage manufacturer, in 1861 & 64. In the *Walton's Vermont Register*, **Pierce** was listed as a "manufacturer of Carriages and Sleighs", from 1881-99. Example: on an 18" shipbuilder's dado; and a tongue & groove match plane on a single stock, similar to that of **P. A. Gladwin & Co.**, June 9, 1857 patent.
A & A1 **

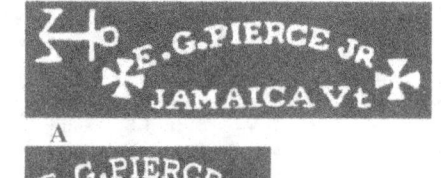

PIERCE/ S. V. PIERCE

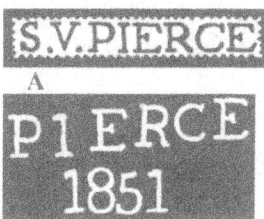

Examples: on 10 bench planes, 9 with closed totes, and a joiner with an open tote; and a marking gauge, dated **1851**; and 5 other tools.
A & B: UR

A. J. PIKE
Example: on a double-iron & wedge full-boxed small side bead, ca. 1840-50. **UR**

H. PIKE
Example: on a beech screw-arm handled plow with boxwood nuts, ca. 1850. **UR**

Ix PIKE
Probably **Jarvis Pike, Sr.**, active from 1726-33, or **Jarvis Pike, Jr.** (b. Apr. 25, 1709 in Roxbury, Suffolk Co., MA, d. bef. Aug. 7, 1750, MA) who married, on Nov. 29, 1735, in Dedham, MA, active from 1738-42, both were listed in Dedham. Possibly one of the earliest New England planemakers. Example: on a reworked dovetail plane. *****

J. PIKE
Probably **Joshua Pike** (b. Nov. 22, 1779 in Hampton Falls, Rockingham, ND, d. Nov. 18, 1872 in Hampton Falls) of Hampton Falls, NH, adjacent to the Exeter town line. Pike was listed as a carpenter and builder and said to be "a man of judgment and a good workman." Examples: molders are 9 5/8"-9 3/4" beech with wide flat chamfers; and on an **I. Sleeper** molder as an owner's imprint, ca. 1800. ****

NATHANIEL PILGRIM
Nathaniel Pilgrim was listed as a planemaker, in Baltimore Co., MD, from 1801-25. **Nathaniel** served in the War of 1812 as a Private in the 51th. Reg., MD Militia.
No imprint has been reported.

D. PILSBERY
Example: on a 7 3/4" beech smoother with flat chamfers, possibly from New England, ca. 1810. **UR**

M. PILSBURY
Example: on a 9 3/8" beech cove with heavy round chamfers, ca. 1820-30. **UR**

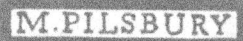

W. PILSBURY
Examples: on a 9 7/8" beech small astragal with small round chamfers, a **James Cam** iron and the A wedge; a 15 1/4" beech panel raiser with shallow round chamfers; and a 9 1/2" beech double-wedge single-boxed fixed sash with the B wedge, ca. 1830-40. **UR**

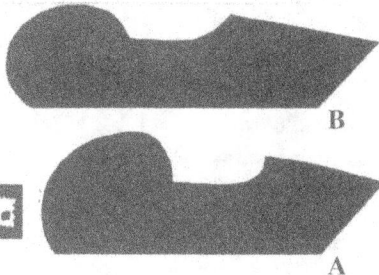

E. PINE
Example: on a 9 1/2" birch skew shiplap plane with relieved wedge and flat chamfers on top and round chamfers on toe and heel, probably from southeast New England, ca. 1800. **UR**

A. PION
Example: on a 9 3/8" beech complex molder with heavy flat chamfers, ca. 1810. **UR**

A. M. PIPER
Examples: the A imprint is on a 9 3/8" nosing plane. The B imprint is on a 9 7/16" beech narrow round, ca. 1830. ****

B. PIPER
B. Piper was listed, as a planemaker, in Newton, MA, in 1881.
No imprint has been reported.

R. PIPER
Believed to be **Rufus Piper** (b. Jan. 14, 1791 Temple, Hillsborough, NH, d. Mar. 4, 1874 Dublin, Cheshire, MA) a carpenter and planemaker, in Dublin, NH. He was listed in 1850 & 60, as a carpenter, in Dublin. Example: on a 9 1/2"x 1 1/2" skew rabbet.
A & B **

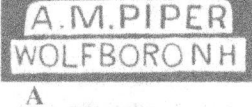

S. PIPER
Example: on a 15 3/8" skewed rabbet with an off-set handle, ca. early 19c. **UR**

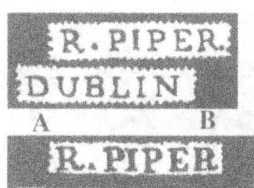

S. A. PIPER
Samuel A. Piper (b. 1836 in NH, d. Feb. 10, 1923 in Newton, MA) of Newton Upper falls, MA, was issued Patent No. 243,398, on June 28, 1881, for a plow plane with an adjustable fence. In 1880 & 1910, **Piper** was listed, as a carpenter, in Newton,

Middlesex Co., MA. Example: on an 11 3/4" rosewood plow plane with brass arms, a brass depth stop and a brass medallion inlet into the side of the fence inscribed: **A & B** ****
**S. A. PIPER
NEWTON UPPER FALLS, MASS.
PAT. JUNE 28/ 1881   (A)**

Example: on a 10"x 1 1/8" beech hollow made by **T. W. Piper**.

 B

S. B. PIPER
S. B. Piper was listed as a maker of household tools such as closepins, in 1856. Example: on a 9 1/4" beech molder with shallow flat chamfers, ca. 1810.   **UR**

S. F. PIPER
Example: on a 9 3/4" beech complex molder with flat chamfers, ca. 1810.   **UR**

T. P. PIPER
Example: on a 9 1/4" beech grooving plane with steel wear plates, ca. 1850.   ****

T. W. PIPER
Example: on a 10"x 1 1/8" beech hollow with shallow round chamfers, with the incuse imprint **S. A. PIPER** stamped twice on the toe and once on the heel, and the imprint **A. M. PIPER** struck once on the heel, ca. 1830.   **UR**

J. W. PIRCE (see J. W. Pearce)

D. PLAIN
Example: on a 9 5/8" birch center bead with flat chamfers, ca. 1800.   **UR**

I. PLANK
Believed to be **Jacob Plank** (b. Nov. 6, 1767, in Lancaster, PA, d. Jan. 10, 1851 in Wooster, OH) who in 1795, moved to Mifflin Co. Union Twp., nw of Harrisburg, PA. After 1821, he moved to Wayne Co., OH. His son, **Jacob Plank** (b. 1796, PA) was listed, in 1850, as a carpenter, in Wayne Co., OH. His grandson, **Jacob Plank** (b. 1821, in PA) was listed, in 1850, as a carpenter, in Wayne Co., OH. Examples: on a 9 9/16" full-boxed reed & follow, and a 9 7/16" beech ogee complex molder, both beech with flat chamfers found in the tri-county area of PA. (Berks/ Lancaster/ Montgomery), ca. 1800.   ****

HALSEY C. PLATT
Halsey C. Platt (b. 1836 in Saybrook, CT, d. 1918 in Saybrook Winthrop Cemetery, CT) was a planemaker, employed by **G. W. Denison & Co.**, prior to March 1873, at 20 cents per hour. He specialized in bench planes and was also paid by the piece: smoothers and horned smoothers at .30.
jacks at .31.
foreplanes at .38.
beechwood compass planes at .35.
boxwood compass planes at .45.
No imprint has been reported.

J. T. PLATT
John Taylor Platt (b. Abt. Jul. 8, 1820 in CT, d. Jan. 31, 1906 in Washington, Litchfield Co., CT) was listed as a planemaker, in New Haven, CT, in the 1850 census; and in Bridgeport, CT, in 1868 & 70 censuses. His daughter was born in PA, in 1856; In 1870, he was listed as a planemaker in Bridgeport, Fairfield Co., CT ***

M. PLATT.
Example: on a 9 1/2" beech skew rabbet with shallow round chamfers, ca. 1830.   **UR**

J. T. PLIMLEY & CO.
Example: on a 9 1/4" beech single-boxed complex molding plane, ca. 1850.   **UR**

N. PLUME
Example: on a 10" birch molder with flat chamfers, ca. 1800.   **UR**

C. M. PLUMER
Example: on an 11" beech tongue plane with a closed integral tote and round chamfers, ca. 1840-50.   **UR**

M. PLUMER
Example: on a 9 3/4" beech single-boxed complex molder with an **I. Sleeper** style wedge and flat chamfers, ca. 1800-10.   **UR**

S. PLUMER
Possibly **Samuel Plumer** (b. June 16, 1737 in Newbury, MA, d. Apr. 13, 1817) who was a carpenter. **Samuel** was said to be a large man. Examples: on a tongue plane; and a 9 11/16" beech molding plane with heavy flat chamfers and an **I. Sleeper** style wedge, probably from Newburyport, MA, ca. 1800.   **UR**

S. PLUMMER
Silas Plummer (b. Oct. 6, 1821, d. Mar. 12, 1882 in Durham, ME) was listed as a carpenter, in Lisbon Falls, ME, in 1850. In the 1870 Products of Industry census, **Silas Plummer** was listed as making $700 worth of plane stock and tool chests. Example: on a 28" beech jointer, ca. 19c. ****

J. POFFENBAUGH
J. Poffenbaugh was a contemporary planemaker who made replica planes, with dates of 1988-2001. **UR**

J. POH
Examples: on a 13 3/8" beech panel raiser with an offset tote and flat chamfers; and a 9 1/2" applewood complex molder with flat chamfers from PA, ca. 1810-20. **UR**

I. POLLARD
Example: on a 9 7/16" birch sash ovolo with round chamfers, ca. early 19c. **UR**

L. POLLARD
Possibly **Luke Pollard** (b. Feb. 19, 1774 in Harvard, Worcester Co., MA, d. Jan. 6, 1866 in Harvard). Several examples are owned by the Fruitland Museum of Harvard, MA. In 1850, **Luke Pollard** was listed as a carpenter in Harvard, MA. The B imprint is on a 10" fruitwood tongue plane with sloped shoulder and heavy flat chamfers. The A & C imprints are on 9 1/2" beech molders with flat chamfers and an **I. Sleeper** style wedges, ca. 1790-1810. **A, B & C** ***

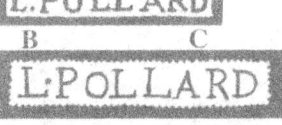
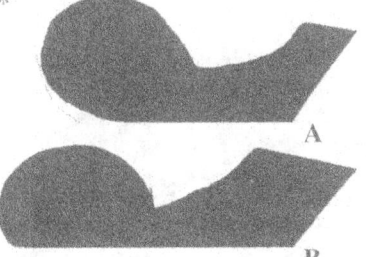

S. POMEROY
Simeon Pomeroy (b. Apr. 19, 1754 in Northampton, MA, d. 1842 in Windsor, VT) was a cabinetmaker, house joiner and plane maker, in Northampton, MA. **Simeon's** father **Capt. John Pomeroy** (b. ca. 1730, d. 1760, inventory with 21 molding planes, a cornish plane, 8 smoothers, and 6 jointers) was a cabinet maker. **Simeon** was six when his father died. **Simeon** was a militia Private (Fifer) from Northampton, who marched to the Lexington alarm, in 1775. **Clark Bridgman** was apprenticed to **Simeon Pomeroy**, as a joiner, in Apr. 3, 1786. **Simeon Pomeroy** married **Sarah**. An ad in the **Hampshire Gazette**, Northampton, MA, on Wed. May 10, 1797:

```
                    To Joiners
    The fubfcriber, maker and has on hand for
  fale, a variety of Joiners' Moulding Tools; fuch as
      Joiners,              Nofing,
      Fore & Smooth Planes,  Astragals,
      Rabbits,              Ovolos,
      Hollows & Rounds,     Ploughs,
      Quirk & plain O. Gee's, Match,
      Beads,                Halfing Planes,
      Quarter Rounds, Safh Planes,
                     Moving Gages,
    Of various fizes, and made of excellent beech
      timber- Workmen may be fupplied at a fhort
        notice. By Simeon Pomeroy.
```

An additional ad, by **Simeon Pomeroy**, on Dec. 26, 1797, notes his shops location "about a quarter of a mile north of the meeting house in Northampton" and advertises joiner and molding tools for sale. **Simeon's** son **Thomas Pomeroy** (d. 1843 with joiner tools in inventory) ran a newspaper in Northampton and briefly in Windsor, VT, in 1812; before going into partnership with **Lemuel Hedge**, as a bookseller. On May 20, 1816, **Pomroy & Hedge**, advertised books & stationary and cabinet furniture. In Nov. 1818, a fire destroyed the shop; in 1819 the partnership was dissolved. In Aug. 1832, **Simeon Pomroy** moved in with Thomas, in Windsor, VT. The 1840, Windsor, VT census listed Thomas as head of household and **Simeon**, age 86, with two involved in manufacturing. Examples: on an unmarked 10 1/8" birch skew rabbet with flat chamfers, an A relieved wedge, and an iron stamped **S. POMEROY**. This is believed to be **Seth Pomeroy**, in Northampton, MA, a blacksmith and toolmaker, active from 1806-12, who made numerous plane irons and metal plane parts for **Simeon Pomeroy**. Examples: on planes 10" birch & 9 1/2" beech, some with relieved wedges and with flat chamfers; and a 10 3/8" birch Yankee plow with a riveted skate, wedge locked arms, with added wood thumbscrews and flat chamfers, ca. 1780-1820. **A & A1** ***

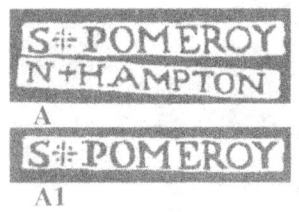
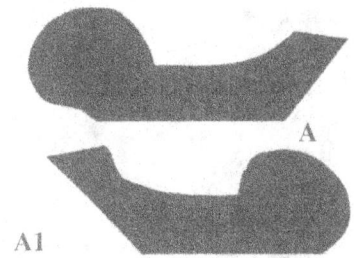

DAVID POND
David Pond (b. Apr. 11, 1832 in New Haven, CT, d. Jun. 3, 1901 in New Haven) was listed as a New Haven, CT, planemaker, from 1849-88. Listed in 1850-60, as a tool maker, living with **Wadsworth H. Pond** in New Haven; in 1868, David worked at 119 Railroad Ave., the same address as **Pond & Briggs**, which included **Wadsworth H. Pond** and **William A. Briggs**. In 1900, **David** was listed as an inmate at Springside Home, in New Haven, as a tool maker. **No imprint has been reported**.

J. POND
Example: on a 9 1/2" birch hollow with tight round chamfers, probably from New England, ca. 1820. **UR**

W. H. POND
Wadsworth H. Pond (d. Jan. 18, 1899 in New Haven, CT) was listed, as a tool manufacturer, in New Haven, CT, from 1844-90. He was part of **Pond & Welles**, ca. 1850; **Pond, Malcolm & Welles**, from 1846-53; and **Pond & Briggs** with **William A. Briggs**, from 1868-69.

The 1860 Industrial census listed six employees producing 18,780 planes worth $15,000. In 1870, **W. A. Briggs** advertised "planes of all kinds". An ad by **Pond** was placed in 1874. From 1871-80, **W. H. Pond** was listed as a planemaker, at 372 State St.; by 1890, he relocated to Boston, MA.
A, A1, A3, & B1 *; A2 & B ****

POND, MALCOLM & WELLES
Wadsworth H. Pond, **Frederick S. Malcom** (b. Dec. 1817 in CT, d. Feb. 9, 1902 in Kings, NY), and **Welles** had a plane making partnership, in New Haven, CT, from 1846-53. **Malcolm** was part of **Shiverick & Malcolm**, in NY, by 1853.
A & A1 **

POND & WELLES
A planemaking partnership of **Wadsworth H. Pond** and **Welles** in New Haven, CT, ca. 1850. **

G. POOR
Example: on a **J. C. Poor** plane, possibly a relation; and on **Auburn Tool Co.**, **J. R. Tolman** and **P. A. Gladwin** planes, ca. 19c.   UR

J. C. POOR
John Poor (baptized May 31, 1812 in MA, d. Feb. 26, 1903 in Newburyport, MA) was a cabinetmaker, in Newburyport, MA, active until 1891. He married **Nancy Titcomb** of Cumberland, ME, on Aug. 20, 1843. Example: on a 9 1/2" fruitwood skew rabbet; on a 9 3/4" birch small complex molder, struck twice on the toe; a beech handled grooving plane, all with flat chamfers; and a 9 1/2" beech round with 19c style chamfers, ca. 1800-30. ****

L. POOR
Example: on a slide-arm beech plow with wood thumbscrews, a brass depth stop and shallow round chamfers, ca. 1830.   UR

J. POORMAN
Example: on a 9 5/16" beech reverse ogee with heavy round chamfers and found in central PA, ca. early 19c.   UR

I. POPE
Example: on a 9 5/8" beech fenced grooving plane and an adjustable wood depth stop, ca. 19c.   UR

L. POPE
Example: the A imprint is on a 9 1/4" beech dado with narrow round chamfers on the top and flat chamfers on the toe and heel. The B imprint is on a 7 3/4" beech coffin smoother with 19c style chamfers, ca. 1830.   UR

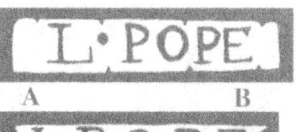

L. T. POPE/ LEMUEL T. POPE
Lemuel Thomas Pope was listed in the 1837-41 Boston, MA, directories, as a planemaker, at 81 Endicott St. He received Patent No. 639, on Mar. 17, 1838, for a machine for punching and shearing iron. Examples: the A imprint is on a 5/8" bead. The A1 imprint is on a full-boxed 9 1/2"x 1/2" double-bead with **Tolman** style double-irons; and a compass hollow. The B imprint is on a beech handled, curved scraper possible used for finishing of the 19c. chamfers on planes.   A **; A1 ***; B *****

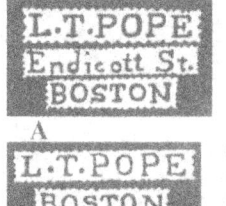

JOHN PORRITT
John Porritt (b. in England) is a contempory planemaker and restorationist from Spencertown, NY. Example: on a 18c. style, 10" birch molder with flat chamfers.   UR

J. PORTER
Possibly **John Porter** (b. 1773 in Hartford, CT, d. at age 29 in 1802 in Hartford) who was apprenticed, in 1793, to **Aaron Chapin**. He was a cabinetmaker, in Hartford, CT, from 1800-02. **Porter** advertised in the *Connecticut Courant* of Jul. 21, 1800, and other ads thru 1802. Examples: on a 9 3/16" birch dovetail plane, imprinted on toe and heel, with flat chamfers; a 12 1/4"x 2" complex molder with an offset tote; and a panel raiser, all found in eastern PA. Also reported is a quilting frame, found near Lancaster, PA. Although birch usually indicates a New England origin, examples made of birch are known from PA. The B wedge is on a 10" birch skew rabbet with round chamfers, ca. 1800.   ****

L. PORTER
Lemuel Porter (b. ca. 1775. He was abandoned by his father after the death of his mother and brother, d. ca. 1829, in Hudson, OH) was a clock and cabinetmaker, who worked in Watertown, CT, as early as 1795. **Porter** was listed, as a carpenter, in the 1816 tax rolls. He moved to Portage Co., OH, in 1818. He was involved with the designed and building of a church in the Western Reserve (OH). Example: the B imprint on a 9 1/8" fruitwood quirked ogee molder with flat chamfers, found in a tool chest from New Haven, CT; and a second example found in Portland, CT, ca. 1800. ****

S. PORTER
Example: on a 21 1/2" beech jointer with a centered tote and 19c. chamfers. **UR**

T. PORTER
Thomas Porter was listed as a planemaker, in Cummington, MA, from 1870-74. Example: on a **D. Copeland**, Hartford plane. **UR**

PORTER & SPERRY
Porter & Sperry were listed as planemakers, at 30 Lym ST., in the New Haven, CT, directory of 1860. **No imprint has been reported.**

S. PORTER & CO.
S. Porter & Co. was probably a hardware dealer in Worcester, MA. Example: on the heel of a 7" beech smoother made by **Union Factory/ H. Chapin**. ****

I. POSTLETHWAIT
Example: on a 10 1/16" beech molding plane with round chamfers, found in PA, ca. 1820-30. **UR**

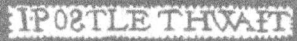

S. W. POST
This name with the added imprint **MAKER** is on a wood plane with a Masonic insignia. **No imprint is available.**

C. POTTER
Example: on a 9 1/2" beech double-boxed bevel with ogee bead & fillet molding plane with round chamfers, ca. 1820. **UR**

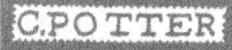

C. D. POTTER & CO.
Charles D. Potter's (b. before 1831) Mother was **Abigail Denison** from Saybrook (Winthrop) CT. The location of Delaware, OH, is north of Columbus, OH. Examples: on a pair of 14" handled tongue & groove plank planes with screw-arm fences. ***

N. POTTER
Three related possibilities: **Nathaniel Potter** (b. Apr. 14, 1663 in Lynn, MA) was a house carpenter and the son of **Robert and Ruth Potter**. **Nathaniel Potter** (b. 1693 in Lynn, d. 1768, and buried in Quaker Cemetery in Leicester, MA) was the son of **John Potter** (b. 1665 in Lynn, d. 1740 in Leicester, MA) and grandson of **Robert and Ruth Potter**, which makes **Nathaniel** (b. 1663) his uncle. **Nathaniel** (1693) like his father and grandfather was a house carpenter. **Nathaniel** (1693) married in Lynn, on Mar. 27, 1716, and his first four children, born in Lynn from 1717-29 and his last two born in Leicester, MA, including his son **Nathaniel Potter** (b. Apr. 11, 1732, d. 1792 and who had no tools listed in his estate inventory). By 1722, **Nathaniel** (1693) and his father John were living in Leicester, near Worcester, MA, where they were listed among the mechanics needed in the new town to fulfill the needs of the local farmers. In 1732, John and **Nathaniel** (1693) declared that they were Quakers (Friends). In 1739, **Nathaniel** (1693) was involved in building the Quaker meeting house. **Nathaniel** (1693) was the most likely maker and his estate inventory listed 3 fore planes, 3 long planes, three smoothing "plains", a plow plane, plus 69 other planes, 9 new "plains" and plane irons. Examples on a 10 7/16"x 1" skew rabbet; a 9 7/8"x 3/4" side bead; a 10 3/8" halving plane; a 10 1/8" Yankee plow with hickory thumbscrews but without a depth stop and a riveted skate; on a 12 3/4" adj. fenced panel raiser with a wood thumbscrew on the front arm only, the offset tote has a heavy pin that allows the tote to pivot and hold the rear arm, a riveted skate, round top iron and wedge; and a 3 5/8" wide crown molder with offset tote, round top iron and wedge, all birch with heavy flat chamfers. Examples are reported with crowned initials.
ca. 1720-50. ****

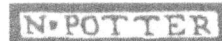

S. H. POTTER
Samuel H. Potter (b. 1809, d. Jan. 8, 1895 in Terre Haute, Vigo Co., IN) was a Terre Haute, IN, hardware dealer, from 1844-63. **Samuel** married, on Aug. 11, 1851, in Harrison, Vigo Co., IN. In the 1850 census, he was listed, as a merchant. He worked with **Lucius Ruce** as **S. H. Potter & Co.**, hardware & Cutlery, at 84 Main St., from 1844-58; and as **S. H. Potter**, hardware, from 1858-63; in 1868, he was listed as retired. Example: on a 3/4" full-boxed center bead with **37**, an **Ohio Tool Co.** style number. **A & A1** ***

POTTER & RITCHIE
Wm. W. Richey (Richey) and **Potter** were planemakers, in 1844-45, in Louisville, KY. ****

POTWINS
Anson Cloudin Potwin (b. Jul. 1, 1804 in Weathersfield, Windsor Co., VT, d. Jan. 15, 1888 in Chicago, Cook Co., IL) and **William Seymour Potwin** (b. Feb 21, 1838 in Terre Haute, Vigo Co., IN) were hardware dealers, in Terre Haute, IN, from 1858-64. They were successors to **Potwin & Bush** in 1858; and predecessor of **Potwin & Burnham**, ca. 1852; In 1857, **William** was enrolled in Williston Seminary, MA. In 1862, **William Potwins** enlisted, on Jul. 21, 1862 in Co. I, 76th. Infantry Reg., IN. He was mustered out, on Aug. 20, 1862, in Indianapolis, IN. In 1867, **Anson** was listed with **Frank Sturges & Co.**, Chicago, IL. **William** joines **Frank Sturges & Co.**, from 1867-74. From 1870-78, **Anson Potwin** was with **Potwin & Morgan** in Chicago, IL. In 1880-87, **Anson** was Pres. **Chicago Varnish Co.** **William** was with **Chicago Varnish**, from 1887-1900. ****

T. POULTNEY/ T. POULTNEY & SON
Thomas Poultney (b. Sep. 29, 1762 in Lancaster, PA, d. Dec. 25, 1828 in PA) was married on Apr. 16, 1790, in Philadelphia, PA. He was listed as an ironmonger, in Philadelphia, PA, in 1790. Example: the A imprint is on a 13 3/8" beech panel raiser with an offset tote, single round top iron marked **ROBERT MOORE**, wood depth stop, and round chamfers. The B imprint is on a plane made by **Mutter**, London, England (1766-99). A & B: ****

J. POWEL
Example: on a 9 3/8" birch V-grooving plane with round chamfers, ca. 1820-40. UR

W. POWEL
The records of the mayor of Philadelphia, PA, for the years 1770-74 include the record of one **Benjamin Thomton** apprenticed to **William Powell**, on Oct. 8, 1771, for 4 years, 6 months, and 12 days, for the sum of 21L-9 shillings. Thomas was to be taught plane making and given 5 quarters of school. Examples: on several molders just under 10"x 1/4" beech with flat chamfers. *****

POWELL
Powell was a Philadelphia, PA, hardware dealer. Examples: on two dado planes made by **H. Chapin/ Union Factory**, ca. 1850. **No imprint is available**.

POWELL & CHILD
Powell & Child was listed in 1856-57, as hardware, at s. s. of Second, e. of Brady St. Davenport, IA; with **William Powell** living at the business address; and **H. R. Child** of **Powell & Child** living at w. s. of Harrison, n. of Second. In 1858-59, listed **William Powell**, as laborer, and **Horace C. Child** in dry goods in IL. Example: on a rosewood handled adj. plow plane also imprinted **104**, the **Ohio Tool Co.** inventory number for a box or rosewood handled plow. ****

J. H. POWELL & CO.
J. H. Powell & Co. was in hardware, in Bloomville, New York. Example: on a pair of 9 1/2"x 7/8" match planes, made by **Auburn Tool Co.**. Printed in ink, on the side of each plane body: ****

I. POWER
Example: on a 9" birch complex molder with tight round chamfers, found north of Boston between Middleton and Danvers, MA, ca. 1800-20 UR

J. POWERS
J. Powers was believed to be a Shaker from the former Shaker community in New Lebanon, NY. Example: on an adjustable 9 1/2" beech special purpose grooving plane with an iron bar on a fixed wood fence, adjustable by two metal thumbscrews. No chamfers but the top 1" of both sides are sloped, ca. mid-19c. UR

C. PRATT
Example: on a 9 1/2" fixed sash; and a 9 1/4"x 3/4" single-boxed side bead, both beech with round chamfers; and a 30"x 3" birch wide jointer, found on the Eastern Shore of MD. ca. 1820. ****

F. C. PRATT
Example: on a match pair of tongue & groove planes, ca. 1800. UR

GEORGE PRATT
Examples: on two 9 5/8" beech complex molders, one with an applewood relieved wedge, both with shallow round chamfers and a hand carved imprint, probably from New England, ca. 1830. UR

H. PRATT
Possibly **Henry Pratt** (b. May 14, 1771 in Wrentham, MA, M. Feb. 10, 1795 in Winchester, Cheshire Co., NH, d. Aug. 28, 1841 in Winchester) who appeared in the 1790-1830 census, in nearby Sherburn, MA. An organ built by **Henry** is in the Meeting House in Sturbridge Village, MA. In 1820, his occupation was listed as farmer. Examples: on a 9 1/2" birch medium round with flat chamfers, a cherry complex molding plane that provided this wedge; and a beech Yankee plow with wood thumbscrews, a relieved wedge, and the location imprint **WRENTHAM**. ****

NATHAN PRATT
Nathan Pratt is probably a descendant of **H. Pratt**. This imprint is made up of two dies. The **PRATT.** is identical to the **H. PRATT.** die with the **H.** removed. Example: on a 9 5/8" beech hollow with a birch relieved wedge and round chamfers, probably from southeastern New England, ca. 1820. **UR**

S. PRATT
Example: on a 9 1/2" beech tongue plane with round chamfers, found in VT. **UR**

PRATT & CO/ S. F. PRATT/ S. F. PRATT & CO.
Pratt & Co was a large Buffalo, NY, hardware firm that operated from 1836-60. The 1850-70 census lists **Samuel Fletcher Pratt** (b. May 28, 1807 in Windham, VT, d. Apr. 28, 1872 in Buffalo, Erie Co., NY) as the hardware firm proprietor. Imprints have also been reported with **S. F. Pratt**; **S. F. Pratt & Co.**; and on an **Edgerton/ Buffalo** jointer. **A, B, B1 & C ***; **D, D1 & E ****

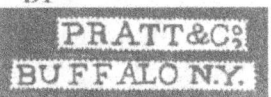

PRATT & FOX
Pratt & Fox was a St. Louis, MO, hardware dealer in 1863. It was the successor to **Child, Pratt & Fox**, active from 1860-63, which succeeded **Child, Pratt & Co.**, active from 1852-59. **Elon G. Pratt** was a partner in these companies.
No imprint has been reported.

PRATT & GIBSON
Pratt & Gibson, with the added location imprint **JACKSON, MICH**, has been reported on an 8 1/4" beech smoothing plane with 19c. chamfers. **No imprint is available**.

D. PRESBREY
Daniel Presbrey (b. Dec. 1, 1785, in Norton, MA, d. Jun 6, 1856 in Taunton, MA) was the son of **Simeon Presbrey**. Daniel was in Norton, MA, until 1815, then Taunton, MA, where he worked and lived for the remainder of his life. One group of 70 planes was reported including 13 by **D. Presbrey**, 1 by **S. Presbrey**, 8 by **Wm. Woodward**, and an assortment of other New England planes, from early to mid 19c. Examples: The large A imprint is on planes 9 1/2". The B imprint is on planes 9 3/8", both beech with round chamfers, ca. 1820.
A & B **

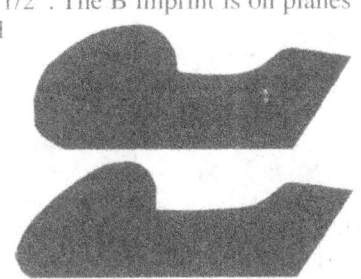

S x PRESBREY
Simeon Presbrey, Sr. (b. 1758 in Taunton, MA, d. 1840 in VT) was a carpenter and planemaker, who lived in Norton, MA, from 1781-1810. **Simeon Presbrey** moved, in 1820, to Coits Gore, Franklin Co., VT. Found, a group of 7 planes with the **C** imprint, both S's reverse, marked **JxP** and one **SP**. Simeon had 6 sons, the eldest **Simeon Presbrey, Jr.** (b. 1792, d. 1858) probably was the **SP**. Another plane from the same group, made by **H. Wetherel/ In Norton**, has a different **SP** imprint. **Simeon Presbrey, Sr.** or **Jr.** or both may have used the A and B imprints. One of two other sons **Josiah Presbrey** (b. 1784, d.1842) or **James Presbrey** (b. ca. 1788) may be the **JxP** imprint. The third son **Daniel Presbrey** (b. 1785, d.1856) was also a carpenter and planemaker, who lived first in Norton then in Taunton. Possibily **Simeon Presbrey, Sr.** learned plane making from **H. Wetherel** prior to his moving from Norton to Chatham, CT, before 1795. Examples: Most A and B imprints are from 9 3/8" beech planes with heavy flat to heavy round chamfers. The C imprint is on a 9 3/8" beech astragal with heavy flat chamfers, and with the owner incuse imprint **EP**. The E imprint is on a 9 3/8" beech fixed sash with round wide chamfers, ca. 1800-20.
A & B ***; C & E ****

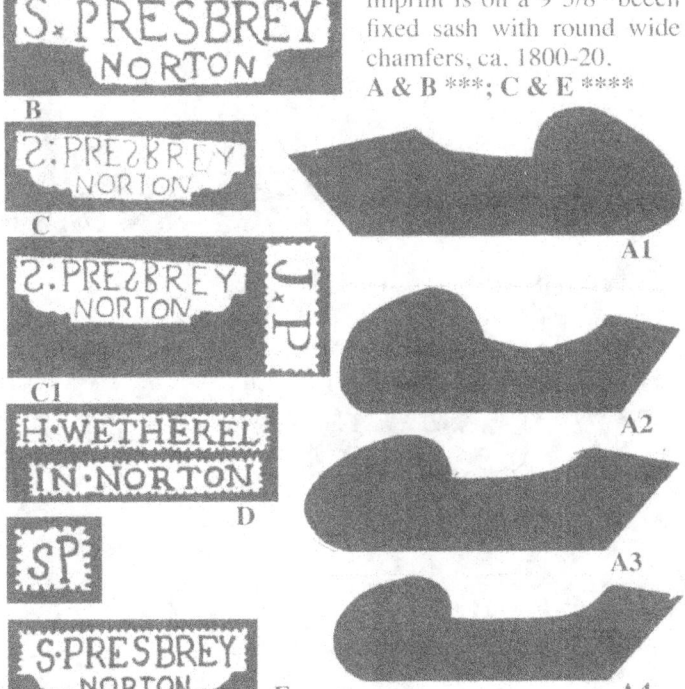

C. PRESCOTT
Charles Prescott (b. Oct. 27, 1805 in Middlesex Co., MA, d. Feb. 20, 1883 in Lowell, MA) married, on Apr. 10, 1831, in Lowell, MA. He was listed as a Lowell, MA, planemaker from 1832-55 & 1861-78; in the 1850, as a carpenter; and in the 1850 Industrial census as employing one hand and producing planes worth $600. ******

W PRESCOTT
Believed to be **William Partridge Prescott** (d. probate Dec. 8, 1820 in Merrimack, NH) who married, on Aug. 22, 1785, to **Deborah Welch**, in Sanbornton, NH, and listed as a "ploughmaker". Example: on a 24 1/8"x 2 13/16" beech skew rabbet with a closed birch centered handle, a sawtooth nicker, a dovetail wedge, and shallow flat chamfers with flutes, found in Sanbornton, NH, ca. 1790-1800. **UR**

A. A. PRESTON
Example: on a 9 9/16" triple-boxed adjustable double-bladed sash with wood threads and knobs; a single boxed complex molder; a size **14** round; and 9 1/2"x 3/8" & 8/16" single-boxed side beads, all 9 1/2" beech with shallow round chamfers, ca. 1830. ********

PRICE
Examples: on a 9 7/16" beech compex molder with flat chamfers, ca. 1800. **UR**

E. J. PRICE
E. J. Price was listed as a Columbus, OH, planemaker in 1856-57. Example: on a 9 1/2" beech reverse ogee molding plane with an **Ohio Tool Co.** iron, at 70 degree angle, ca. mid 19c. **UR**

GEO. E. PRICE
George Price (b. 1824 in VA) was a hardware dealer, listed in the 1850 census for Staunton, Augusta Co., VA, as a merchant. Example: on a **Greenfield Tool Co.** handrail plane. ********

W. B. PRICHARD
Examples: on a 21 3/4" and a 16" beech bench planes with heavy round chamfers, found together, ca. 1830. ********

PRIESTLEY & BEIN
Priestley & Bein was a New Orleans, LA, hardware firm, founded ca. 1841, by **John D. Bein** (d. probate Mar. 1, 1864 in Orleans, LA) and **William Priestley** (b. 1815 in LA, d. 1850 in Calaveras, CA). **William Priestley** was succeeded by his mother, **Margaret Foulke Priestley**, and **John Bein**'s brother-in-law, **Henry D. Richardson**. In 1860, the firm became **J. D. Bein & Sons**, and after the Civil War was absorbed by **Rice Brothers & Co.** ********

L B PRINDLE
Examples: on a pair of 9 3/4" beech rule-joint planes; and on a 10" birch molder, all with flat chamfers and with this imprint on the side of the planes, probably from PA, ca. 1810. **UR**

G. PROBASCO
Example: on a 14" wedge-arm tongue plank plane with a **James Cam** iron, ca. 1840. **UR**

P. PROBASCO
Peter Probasco (b. Oct. 23, 1799 in PA, d. 1865 in Charlottesville, Hancock Co., IN) was a planemaker, who appeared in the 1823-30 Philadelphia, PA, directories, at 125 N 2nd. He moved to Warren Co., OH, signing an apprentice agreement, on Feb. 10, 1829, in Lebanon, OH, "to teach the art, trade, mystery, and occupation of plane making" to **Charles Webber**, age 11, with the agreement to expire on Jan. 11, 1839. **Probasco** appeared, in the 1830 census, as living in Turtle Creek Twp., which was part of Lebanon. **Peter Probasco**, moved in 1831, to Cincinnati, OH, boarding with **J. D. Conover**. During 1834, **Probasco** was a partner in **Miller & Probasco**, plane makers, at Main b. 5th. and 6th. In 1839-40, he worked for **E. F. Seybold**, both in Cincinnati. In 1840, **Peter Probasco** moved to Hancock Co., IN, on a farm near Charlottesville & Indianapolis, some 75 miles northwest of Cincinnati. **Peter** built a shop and eastablished the business of plane making on his farm. **Peter P.** took on a young apprentice, **Craft** to "learn the trade of a plane maker" and **Craft** continued to work for **Peter Probasco**, until 1846, when he went to work for **E. F. Seybold & Co.** a wholesale hardware merchant and plane manufacturer. **A & A1 ****

PROCTER
Example: on a 9 1/2" beech large hollow, ca. 19c. **UR**

PROCTOR & BRO
Proctor & Bro was a hardware dealer. Examples: on a size **1** hollow; a size **5** hollow & round pair with an inventory number of **72** made by the **Ohio Tool Co.**; a size **9** hollow; and a molder with an inventory number **43 1/2**, ca. mid. 19c. **UR**

D. R. PROCTER
There are two possibilities, a **D. R. Procter** from Belfast, ME who was listed as a ship carver, ca. 1856; and a **D. R. Proctor**, also a ship carver, of Gloucester, MA. Example: on a 9 11/16" beech side bead with heavy round chamfers, found in Essex Co on the MA coast, ca. 1830. **UR**

J. PROCTOR
Example: on a 23" beech fore plane, ca. 1850. **UR**

PROUTY & CHEW
John S. Prouty was a hardware dealer in Geneva, NY, active in 1860, and financially backed by the **Chew** family. ********

J. S. PRUDEN & SONS
J. S. Pruden & Sons was a New York City, hardware dealer, with **Joseph S. Pruden** (d. probate Dec. 23, 1885 in NY). Example: on a **Shiverick** hollow; and a dado with **751 & 753 8th AV. NY**, a location that was not advertised by **Pruden** in the NYC directories. **J. S. Pruden** was listed at 727 8th Av., in 1865-68; and **J. S. Pruden & Sons** was listed at 861-863 8th Av., in 1869-84; with his son **William Edgar Pruden** and was listed under hardware, at 864 8th. Av., from 1884-1911. ******

E+ PVFFER
Elijah Puffer (b. Aug. 18, 1738 in Norton, Bristol Co., MA, d. Feb. 28, 1816 in Peterborough, Hillsborough Co., NH) lived in Norton, and later moved to Medway, MA. His mother, **Rebekah (Rebecca) Ware**, was the cousin of **Mercy Ware** who married **John Nicholson**, both were nieces of **Mary Ware** and related to **Sarah Ware**, **Francis Nicholson's** second and third wives. In 1764 Elijah, moved to Peterborough, NH. Example: on a 9 3/4" birch medium round with shallow flat chamfers and a Wrentham-style wedge. *********

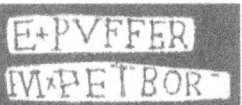

J. PUFFER
Possibly **Job Puffer** (b. Nov. 3, 1769 in Wrentham, Norfolk Co., MA, d. Jun. 4, 1836 in Monson, Hampton Co., MA), who was the nephew of **Elijah Puffer**. **Job** married on Dec. 8, 1787, in Medway, MA; by 1810, he was in Monson. Example: on a 9 1/2" beech skew rabbet with heavy round chamfers, found with the **E. Puffer** plane, ca. 1820. **UR**

J. W. PULIS
Example: on a 16" beech filletster with a closed offset tote, a hickory wedge, an adjustable bottom fence and no chamfers. **UR**

PULLMAN
Pullman with the added location **YORK, PA** has been reported. **No imprint is available.**

J. PURINTON
Examples: on a 9 1/2" fruitwood bead with bone boxing and pillowed shoulder chamfers; and on a 9 1/2" beech moving filletster with a metal depth stop, ca. 19c. **UR**

T. PURDY
Example: on a 9 7/16" boxed side bead with a **R. Hildick** iron; and a 9 1/2" unhandled grooving plane, both beech with flat chamfers, ca. 1800. **UR**

W. PURSE
Example: on a 9 7/8" beech complex molder with heavy flat chamfers, ca. 1800. **UR**

E. PUTNAM
Elisha Putnam (b. May 13, 1765 in Sutton, MA, d. Feb. 11, 1854 in Albany, NY) was a carpenter, builder, civil engineer, architect and contractor. **Putnam** came to Albany, about 1790. In Dec. 1792, he married **Hester Johnson**, in the Albany Dutch Church; in 1795-96, he built the First Presbyterian Church in Albany. In 1797, **Elisha** was in partnership with the architect **Philip Hooker** in the erecting of the North Dutch Reformed Church, in Albany. In 1801, he was a member of the Albany fire company; in 1803, as a carpenter, and a freeholder. He was a member and trustee of the Albany Mechanics Society. In 1813, he was listed, as a builder. **Elisha Putnam** was also known for his skills as a civil engineer, having laid the first pipes of hollowed wood, to supply Albany with water, was the Superintendant of the Albany Water Works, construction of one or more sections of the Erie Canal, and part of the Chesapeake and Ohio Canal. Elisha built the first nail mill in Troy, NY. Examples: on a 10 1/8" birch complex molder with heavy flat chamfers and an incuse date of **1805**; and a 9 7/8" beech moving filletster with heavy round chamfers. An example, as an owner imprint, is on a **C. Warren/ Nashua**, ca. 1805-20. **UR**

A

B

FR' PUTNAM
Example: on a 10" birch medium hollow with a relieved wedge and tight flat chamfers, ca. 1800. **UR**

P. PUTNAM
Example: on a 17" beech jack with a pegged birch centered tote, round top iron and shallow flat chamfers, ca. 1800. **UR**

J. E. QUACKENBUSH & SON
John E. Quackenbush (b. Sep. 1820, NY, d. Jul. 27, 1902 in Allenhurst, Monmouth Co., NJ) and **Abraham Quackenbush** (ca. 1824 in NJ) were listed as **J. E. Quackenbush**, hardware dealers, at 535 8th Av., New York City, from 1872-73. In 1873-74 the **& SON** was added; in 1847-72, **John** was listed under "umbrellas" and **Abraham** was a ship carpenter. in 1850-60 in NY   **A & B** **

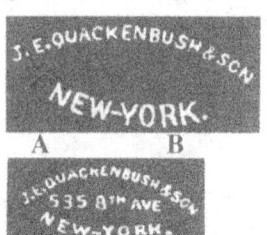

Q. T. & CO/ QUACKENBUSH TOWNSEND/ QUACKENBUSH TOWNSEND & CO.
Quackenbush Townsend Co. was a New York City hardware firm, that operated, from 1865-92. The partners were **Charles E. Quackenbush** (b. Nov. 15, 1835, d. Oct. 24, 1905 in Lee, MA) and **William H. Townsend** (b. 1836 in NY, d. 1896 in Brewster, Putnam Co., NY). In later years **Robert Townsend** (b. ca. 1848 in NY, d. Dec. 8, 1917 in Chicago, IL) joined the firm. In 1880, **Robert** was listed as hardware agent in Chicago, IL. Example: on a 16" bench plane with a **Sandusky Tool Co.** iron.
A, B & B1 **; **C** ****

QUEEN CITY TOOL CO.
Queen City Tool Co. was a Cincinnati, OH, hardware dealer. Working dates are not known.   ****

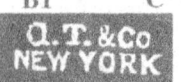

JNO. B. QUEGLES
John B. Quegles (b. Jun. 21, 1820, d. Jan. 10, 1903 in Natchez, MS) was a Natchez, MS, planemaker. In 1860-80, he was listed as "merchant", in Natchez, MS. Examples: on a boxed bead; and a square rabbet, both 9 1/2" with shallow round chamfers, ca. 1840.   ****

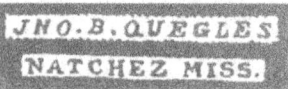

P. QUIGLEY
Philip Quigley (b. 1825 in Ireland, d. Feb. 6, 1871) came to America on May 23, 1837. He was listed in the Newark, NJ, directory of 1849-50, as a manufacturer of spirit levels and carpenter's tools, at 156 Quarry St. The 1850 census listed **Philip Quigley**, as a carpenter's tool maker, employing 12 hands, four of whom lived with him. His employees included **Joseph Havilin**, **Thomas Shepard**, **Patrick McMenamy** and **Joseph Bailey**. All listed as "carpenter tool manufacturer". In 1852, he left for San Francisco, and was listed in 1862, as a carpenter. From 1867-70, he manufactured spirit levels and carpenter's tools, at 914 Market St., prior to 1867; at 918 Market St. in 1867; and at 922 Market St., from 1868-70. In 1870, he was listed, as hardware, in San Francisco, CA. After **Phillips** death in 1871, his wife **Margaret Quigley** continued the business, until 1879. **James Quigley** was listed, in Newark directory under cutlery, at the address next to that of **Philip**, from 1856-57. Also **John Quigley** was listed nearby in Newark directories, from 1852-63, as a grocer and a carpenter's tool maker. No example of a **John Quigley** imprint has been reported.
A, B & C ****

P. QUIMBY
Example: on a 22" beech fore plane with a **Baldwin** double-iron, ca. 1850.   **UR**

H: QUINBY
Examples: on a 9 1/2" medium round; and a 9 5/8"x 1 1/4" complex molder, found in NH, both beech with tight flat chamfers, ca. 1810.   **UR**

A. M. QUINLAN
Example: on a 9 3/8" beech molder with flat chamfers, ca. 1800. **No imprint is available**.

L. R

Leon Robbins (d. 2007) of Bath, ME, was a 20th century planemaker who worked primarily in tropical woods. Imprint A is the earliest planes and used before **Robbins** founded the **Crown Plane Co.**. The B imprint was used prior to 1999, when Leon sold the **Crown Plane Co.**. The C imprint was used after 1999. Example: on a pair of 10 1/8" tiger maple table joint planes with the B imprint.
A, B & C: UR

D. I. RACK
Example: on a 9 5/8"x 1" skew rabbet with flat chamfers. ca. 1800. UR

G. RAFENSPERGER
Example: on a 9 3/8" applewood round with small flat chamfers, found in York Co., PA, ca. 1810-20. UR

RAMSAY
Example: on an 8" birch smoothing plane with flat chamfers, ca. 1790. UR

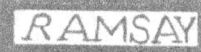

R. RANDAL
Examples: on a 10 1/16" large hollow; and two 11 1/4" complex molders, all imprinted on toe and heel, beech with decorative shoulders and heavy flat chamfers, probably from New England, ca. 1770. ****

B. RANDALL
Believed to be from a Freeport, ME, shipbuilding family. Examples: on two 10" beech molders with flat chamfers, found in ME, ca. 1790. **No imprint is available.**

S. RANDALL
Samuel Randall (b. Aug. 5, 1799 in Litchfield, CT, d. Oct. 26, 1860) made planes in Albany, NY, from 1826-41, although he appeared only in 1833-34. **Randall** was part of **Randall & Shepard** with **Daniel M. Shepard**, in 1826; **Randall & Bense**, from 1827-29; **Randall & Cook**, from 1835-40; and **Randall & Co.**, in 1840-41.
A *; B, C & C1 **

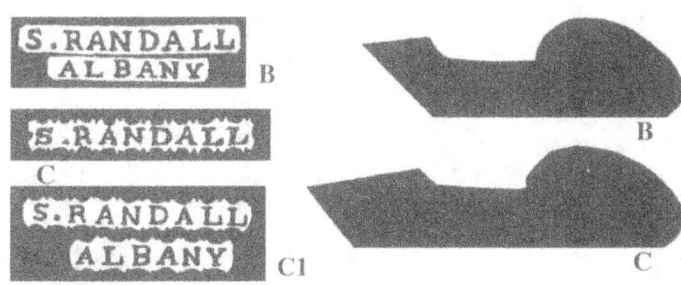

RANDALL & BENSEN
Randall & Bensen was a plane making partnership of **Samuel Randall** and **David Bensen**, in Albany, NY, active from 1827-29. **

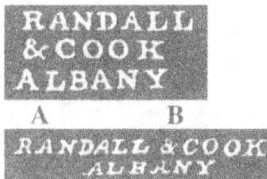

RANDALL & COOK
Randall & Cook was a plane making partnership of **Samuel Randall** and **Moses Cook** (b. 1813, d. Oct. 18, 1847 in Albany, NY), in Albany, NY, active from 1835-40. It was succeeded by **Randall & Co.**, in 1840-41, with the same partners. No example of the **Randall & Co.** imprint has been reported. B *; A **

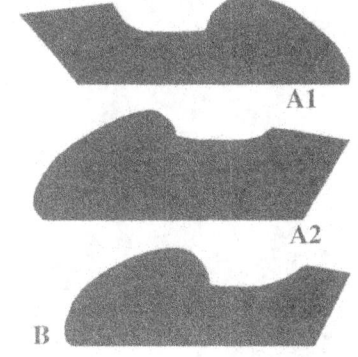

J. RANDELL
Examples: on a Yankee thumbscrew locked moving filletster with round top arms; a hollow & round pair; a narrow centered dado; and a medium hollow, all 10" beech with shallow flat chamfers, ca. 1800. ****

O. L. RANOLDS
O. L. Ranolds (Reynolds). Example: on a 28" beech jointer with a centered closed handle, ca. 1850-60. ****

J. F. RANSOM
John Ransom (b. 1820 in NY) was listed as a planemaker, in Watertown, NY. In 1840, **Ransom** was living next door to **Benjamin Berry**. The 1850 census listed **William Wood** (see **W. W. Wood & Co.** and **Wood & Smith**) living with **Ransom**. A plow plane, has been reported, imprinted with **CINCINNATI**. It is likely that **Ransom** spent some time between 1840-50 in OH, before returning to Watertown, in 1850. The 1850 industrial census listed **Lord & Ransom**, as planemakers in Watertown, with 3 employees making tools and patterns worth $2000. The 1855 Watertown business directory listed **Ransom**, as a sash manufacturer. In 1870, he was listed as a carpenter, in Watertown, NY. **

R RANSOM
Possibly **Richard Ransom** (b. May 13, 1740 in Lyme, New London, CT, d. Sep. 5, 1811 in Woodstock, Windsor Co., VT) advertised, in 1767, as a cabinetmaker, in Lyme, CT. He was later working in Woodstock, VT. Example: on a 9 1/4" beech complex molder with a flat back wedge, heavy flat chamfers and the iron with a York pitch, ca. 1790. **UR**

A. L. RAPLEE
A. L. Raplee with a location of Dundee, NY. Example: on a 9 5/8" x 7/8" beech dado with the iron imprinted, ca. 1850. **UR**

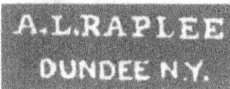 

J. E. RAWSON
Believed to be **Joseph Rawson** (b. Dec. 24, 1760, d. Jul. 19, 1835 in Providence, RI) who worked for his father's cabinetmaking firm, in Providence, RI, and was later active on his own, from 1790-1828. His son, **Joseph Rawson, Jr** (b. 1788, d. 1870) entered the family firm, as a cabinetmaker, from 1824-28, listed as **Joseph Ranson & Sons**. **Joseph Rawson Jr.** married on Dec. 10, 1785, in Providence, RI. From 1847-68, **Joseph Ranson Jr.**, was listed, as a cabinetmaker, in Providence, RI. Example: on a plow. **No imprint is available**.

RAY BROS
 Example: on a jack plane with a **Hancock Tool Co./ Extra Steel** iron. **UR**

T. B. RAYL & CO.
 **T. B. Rayl & Co.** was a major Detroit, MI, hardware firm founded by **Thomas B. Rayl** (b. Feb., 1838 in OH, d. Apr. 1908 in Detroit, Wayne Co., MI), in 1880. One of its later (ca. 1905) catalogs lists a small selection of wooden planes. **A & B; ******

B. RAYMOND
Benjamin Raymond (b. Aug. 13, 1793 in Beverly, Essex Co., MA, d. Jan. 04, 1879 in Beverly, MA), the son of **William Raymond** and half brother to **Ebenezer Berry**, who was a toolmaker, from 1836-46, in Beverly, MA. In 1836, **Benjamin** was designated "tool maker" in the bond for his father's estate. During the sale, he bought a large part of the tool trade articles, probably was continuing the business. At **Benjamin's** wedding, in Nov. 1846, he was listed as a "Tool maker". At **Benjamin's** death, he was a "mechanic". His estate included "lot of Old Iron and Tools in Shop." Example: on a size **4** hollow; size **5** round; and a 9 1/2" beech skew compass rabbet with a **Weldon** iron and shallow round chamfers. **A & B ******

B. RAYMOND
B. Raymond is a hardware dealer. An ad listed in the *Richmond Commercial Compiler* of Richmond, VA, for Jan. 13, 1819:
"**B. RAYMOND**, at the sign of the JOINER, H and Fifth Streets, Has on hand, and will constantly keep for sale, a complete assortment of PLANES, also screws, tools and machines of various kinds, made with neatness and dispatch:

Set of Bench "Plaines"	$2.75
do Bead	6.00
1/2 Set do Hollows and Rounds	10.00
Tongue and Grove Planes	2.75
Plows	4.00"

No imprint has been reported.

D: RAYMOND
Example: on a double sash plane with flat chamfers; and a 9 1/2" beech reed & follow with heavy flat chamfers, ca. 1800. **UR**

E+R/ E.R/ A.R/ ELIS RAYMOND
Examples: on a 9 15/16" complex molder; a shiplap square rabbet; a 9 7/8" complex molder; and an astragal bead, all birch with heavy flat chamfers and flutes, found on Cape Cod, MA. The embossed **E+R** appears to be the earliest mark and is the highest mark on the toe on all four examples. Three have the A relieved wedge and one the B wedge, ca. 1780. **UR**

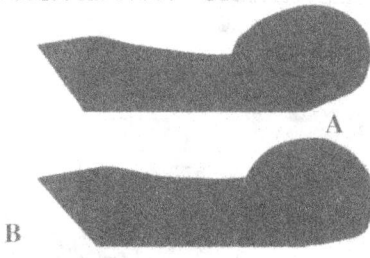

JAMES RAYMOND
Example: on a 7 1/2" beech smoother with heavy round chamfers, ca. 1820. **UR**

N. H. & C. H. RAYMOND
Nathan Hoyt Raymond (b. Oct. 10, 1791 in CT, probate May 2, 1874 in Cambridge City, Wayne Co., IN) and his son, **Charles Harvy Raymond** (b. 1818-20 in NYC, d. Oct. 30, 1886 in Washington, DC), were Cambridge City, IN first hardware dealers, from 1845-55. When **Edward Raymond**, another son, became a partner, in 1855, the name was changed to **C. H. & E. Raymond**; and then to **E. Raymond & Co.**; in 1867, it became **C. U. Raymond**; in 1850-60, **Nathan** was listed as a merchant; in 1870, **Nathan** was listed as retired merchant. In

1850-60, Charles was listed as a merchant; in 1870, as Minister of the gospel in Oxford, OH; in 1880, as "Preacher", in Richmond, Wayne, IN. ***

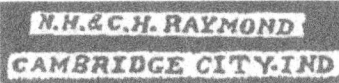

P. RAYMOND
Example: on a small full-boxed bead; and a round, both 9 1/2" beech with small round chamfers, ca. 1820   UR.

W. RAYMOND
William Raymond (b. Aug. 21, 1762, d. Feb. 22, 1836 in Beverly, MA) was the son of **Josiah Raymond**, a blacksmith. He was the father of **Benjamin Raymond** and step-father to **Ebenezer Berry**. In 1791, he is described as a "cabinet maker"; in 1799, as a "tool maker"; in 1810, as a "gentlemen." **William Raymond** was an active planemaker, in Beverly, MA, from 1791-1820. He died intestate with **Josiah Raymond**, mariner, as administrator, **Benjamin Raymond**, tool maker, and **William Raymond, Jr.**, machinist, as sureties. The estate appraisal was a detailed description of a well-equipped shop in operation. **Benjamin Raymond** bought a large part of the tool trade articles, at the estate auction, and continued in the business. One of the most dramatic of **William's** planes is a large cornice plane 16 3/4"x 9 1/8" wide with a 7 3/4" iron in the collection of the North Andover, MA, Historical Society.

The large imprint A is the earliest. The finials of the A & A1 wedges are larger than those of the later B wedges. The earlier planes are 9 5/8"- 9 7/8" beech with heavy flat chamfers. Some owner's initials on the A imprint are crowned. The **I. DAY** on the D & E imprints is believed to be **James Day** a Gloucester, MA, merchant. B: FF; A & C ***; D & E *****

Wm RAYMOND
Example: on a 9 7/16"x 3/16" beech center bead with no boxing and a **7** imprinted on the heel, found in ME.   UR

H. N. RAZE
H. N. Raze was a planemaker in Williamstown, MA, ca. 1860. **No imprint has been reported.**

DAVID READ
Example: on a 9 7/8" birch double-iron fixed sash with narrow flat chamfers and a relieved wedge, similar, in style, to **Jo Fuller**, ca. 1800.   UR

H. H. READ
Henry H. Read (b. Aug. 16, 1826, d. Nov. 14, 1860 in Wilmington, Windham Co., VT) was listed as a planemaker in Wilmington, VT, in 1854-59. Examples: on a 28"x 3 1/2" beech jointer; an 8" beech smoother; a 3" wide crown molder; and a 16" beech jack with a double-iron by **Spear & Jackson** and overstamped with the hardware dealer imprint of **E.P. Nutting** of South Amherst, MA.
A & B ****

M. READ
Marcus Read (b. Aug. 7, 1812 in Attleboro, MA, d. Feb. 16, 1897 in Taunton, MA) witnessed a land deed for **Samuel R. Cummings**, in Jan. 1837 & Aug. 1839; and probably learned plane making from him. **Read** was a planemaker, at 104 Commercial St., Boston, MA, from 1842-44; with **M. Read & Co.**, in 1845-46, at the same address; and as **Read & Cumings**, from 1846-47; in a partnership with **Allen Cumings**, at 119 Commercial St. From 1876-83, **Read** was listed, as a carpenter, in Taunton, MA; From 1885-96, as a farmer, in Taunton.
No example of the M. Read & Co. or Read & Cumings imprints have been reported.   *

F. REAGER
Probably **Frederick Reager** (b. Sept. 11, 1808, d. Nov. 2, 1888 in Aaronsburg, Centre Co., PA), who was a carpenter. He was first listed on the 1845 Center Co. tax list. From 1850-70, he was listed, as a carpenter, in Haines, Centre Co., PA; in 1880, as broom maker, in Aaronsburg. The estate inventory of his wife, **Rebecca**, who died, in 1892, included over 20 "plain" entries, with prices ranging from $.10-$1.10, and a box of "plain Pts."- $.30. Examples: the molding planes are 9 1/2" beech; a 12 1/2" beech center toted nosing plane, the iron with a York pitch; and a 16 1/2" beech jack, with a slightly off-set open tote, all with shallow round chamfers, ca. 1845.   ***

E. E. REAMS
Earl E. Reams was a paternmaker, in Battle Creek, MI, from 1910-1945. Example: on an iron die with this imprint.   UR

PHILIB: REBER
Examples: on a cornice plane with an offset tote and a round top iron; a 10 1/2" ogee complex molder; and a 10 1/4", 5x reeding plane, all beech with **Newbould** irons and flat chamfers. Also

on an 8 1/2" beech screwbox with 2 hickory wide adjusting screws, a ram's horn holding screw, probably from PA, ca. 1800. ****

V. RECHE

Example: on a 9 1/16" beech molder with heavy round chamfers, found in southeastern MA, ca. 1820.   UR

O. RECHT

O. Recht was a New York City hardware dealer. This name with the location **183 BOWERY N.Y.** has been reported on a **Sandusky Tool Co.** 3/8" side bead. ca. 19c. ****

C. R/ C. RECORD

Examples: the **C. R** initial group is on a 9" birch round; a 9 5/8" beech quarter round; and an 8 3/4" birch small cove. The quarter round and complex molders have an ogee molded shoulder, all with small flat chamfers and were found in ME. The **C. RECORD** examples: on a large hollow; and an astragal, both 9 3/8" beech with round chamfers, found together in ME. ca. 1790-1820. ****

REED

John Reed Jr. (b. ca. 1790 in Pembrokeshire, South Wales, d. July 24, 1868 in Utica, NY) came to Philadelphia, PA on Sep. 7, 1801, with his father **John Reed Sr.** (b. Apr. 19, 1740, d. Apr. 19, 1832 in Utica, NY). The family, including six sons **Henry Reed, James Reed, David Reed, John Reed Jr., Ebenezer Reed** and **William Reed**, traveled up the Mohawk River by flat boat to Little Falls, in 1801. In 1814, the family lived in Frankfort, Herkimer Co., near Utica, NY. **John Reed Jr.** was first listed in an ad in the *Columbian Gazette*, on Jun. 4, 1822, as producing joiner's tools. His first planes could have been made as early as 1820. By 1826, **John Reed Jr.** was making planes, at 46 Elizabeth St.; a planemaker, in 1828. In 1829, **Evan Evans** worked for **John Reed, Jr.** In 1835, **John Reed Jr**'s plane factory was expanded. From 1842-47, **John Reed, Jr.** was the director of, and from 1848-49, the manager of a professional group, the **Utica Mechanics Association**, formed in 1831 to promote the welfare of the "mechanical trades". The 1850 census listed **John Reed Jr.**, as a "plain maker" using 5 men and horsepower to produce 7200 planes that sold for $4500. The 1855 NY state census showed that he employed 3 men and one boy (probably **John Reed Jr., Edward Reed, Charles Reed** and apprentice **George Bartlet**, age 17, from England) to make 5000 planes that sold for $7000, using horse power for his shop. He paid a monthly wage of $40 (not including board) to his employees. The last listing for **John Reed Jr.** was in 1867. On Jan. 21, 1868, there was a fire in the two story plane factory.

William Reed, a brother of **John Reed Jr.**, was listed in 1832-33, as a planemaker, and living on Elizabeth St.

Charles Reed (b. ca. 1817 in Utica, NY, d. Feb. 15, 1890) was listed as a planemaker, in Utica, NY, boarding with, and working for **John Reed**, from 1837-38. **Charles Reed** was producing planes on his own, from 1841-44, on Cornelia St; from 1845-47, **Charles** worked for the U & S Railroad; from 1849-50, **Charles** returned to planemaking, opening a planemaking shop, at 30 Washington St., next door to his father, **David Reed**'s (b. 1788 in Wales, d. 1871, in Utica, NY) carpentry business. In 1852-53, **Charles** was listed as a sash maker; in 1854-55, as a planemaker. After this date, **Charles** worked for various rail roads and became a policeman. **Charles**' obituary notes that he was a police captain at his death in 1890.

Hiram Clark (b. Oct., 1820, d. Feb. 14, 1906) in 1844, married **Susan C. Reed** (b. Jun. 1824, d. Feb. 3, 1909), the sister of **Charles Reed**, and daughter of **David** and **Susan Reed**. **Hiram** moved to Utica, from New Hartford, a village to the south, in Aug. 1841, and worked as a carpenter and joiner. In 1847-48, **Hiram** was listed, as a planemaker. In May 1848, **Hiram** moved to Rochester, NY and began working, as a planemaker, for **David R. Barton**.

Edward Reed (b. Aug. 9, 1821 in Utica, NY, d. Jul. 23, 1899) was **John Reed Jr.**'s son. He working for his father, from 1840-Jan. 68. **Edward** rebuilt the plane factory in a smaller way, after the 1868 fire. Working with **Edward** was his son **Judson Reed** (b. Aug. 12, 1868 until his death at age 16, on Feb 3, 1885). **Edward** continued the planemaking business, until 1894, using the same A and A1 imprints. The house and shop, at 46 Elizabeth St., was sold in 1895. There has been a confusion as to the A and B imprints. In 1847, **John Reed Jr.** took out an ad in the *Utica Daily Gazette*: "I hereby caution all persons from selling or making Planes marked as mine, under the penalty of the law. My Planes are not hawked about, but sold in my Shop, wholesale and retail, and in the Hardware stores of **James Dana, Son & Co., T. H. & G. W. Wood**, and **Sayre & House**. Those Planes sold by **Foster & Co.**, marked (**Reed, Utica**), are spurious. **John Reed**." This refers to the B and B1 imprints.

A & A1: FF; B & B1 ****

G. W. REED

Example: on an 11" beech smoother with an applied closed handle and a **Buck Brothers** double-iron, ca. 1860.   UR

J. REED

Examples: on a 10" applewood dado; and an 8 1/2" beech molder, both with flat chamfers and a relieved wedge. The dado is also imprinted **E. JACKSON**. The B imprint is on a 9 3/4" beech full round with flat chamfers. This is a modification of the A imprint, ca. 1790.   **A & A1: UR**

JOB REED

Job Reed was listed from 1832-34, in the Utica, NY directories, as a planemaker, working **for R. J. Collins** plane factory. Example: on a 9 5/8" beech complex molder, ca. 19c.   UR

JOB REED

S. REED
Example: on a 10 1/8" beech round with tight flat chamfers, imprinted on the toe and heel with the location **PITTSh** on the heel only, ca. 1810. **UR**

W: REED
Examples: on a 1/2" bead; and two birch complex molders, all 9 5/8" with flat chamfers, found in ME, ca. 1800. **UR**

W. REED
Example: on a screw-arm unhandled beech plow plane with boxwood arms and nuts, ca. 1850. **UR**

W. REED
Possibly **William Reed** who was listed as a planemaker in Utica, NY, directory in 1832-33 and worked for **John Reed Jr.** Example: on a 9 1/2" beech side rabbet, ca. 1850. **UR**

REED & AUERBACHER
Reed & Auerbacher was a New York City hardware firm, active from 1884-1910. The partners were **William A. Reed** and **Louis H. Auerbacher**. The firm was the successor to **Cassebeer, Reed & Co.**. Examples: on planes made by **W. Hoffman, Marten Doscher**; and on a 7/8" dado made by **G. W. Denison & Co.**. Reed & Auerbacher has appeared as entries in the **G. W. Denison & Co.** account book. ******

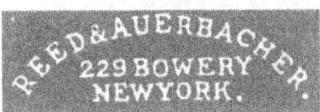

A. REEP
Examples: on a nosing plane; and a 3/4" round, both 9 15/16" beech with flat chamfers, ca. 1800. **UR**

E. REES
Example: on a 9 5/8" beech nosing plane with flat chamfers, ca. 1810. **UR**

SAMUEL J. REES
Samuel J. Rees (d. probate Mar. 1889 in Allegheny, PA) was married on Jun. 7, 1832, in Philadelphia, PA. he was listed as a planemaker, in Philadelphia, PA.. No date given. **No imprint has been reported.**

T. REES
Example: on a 9 3/8" beech hollow with round chamfers, ca. early 19c. **UR**

J. F. REESE
Example: on a 9 5/8" beech large round. **UR**

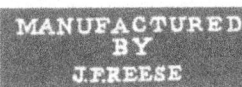

JNO. REEVES
Jno. Reeves was listed as a planemaker in Columbus, OH, in 1856-57. **No imprint has been reported**.

S. REEVES
Example: on a 9 5/16" beech cove molder with flat chamfers, ca. 1810. **UR**

M. REGER
Michael Reager (Rager or Reger) (b. before 1755, in 1800 census he was listed as being over 45) was recorded, in 1797, in a Meadville, PA grocery merchant's account book. Meadville is located in northwestern PA. In 1803-04, **Reager** bought "plane bits and plates" from a local blacksmith. He was listed in the 1800-10 census for Crawford Co.; and as a carpenter on the 1801 tax rolls. **Michael Rager** ran an ad in the *Crawford Weekly Messenger* of Meadville, PA, on June 20, 1810:
  "An Apprentice WANTED, to the Cabinet and Planemaking business; a lad of good character, and about 16 or 17 years of age, will meet with great encouragement by making application to   MICHAEL RAGER
  Meadville, June 13, 1810."

In Mar. 1812, **Rager** again advertised for an apprentice this time to the cabinet business. In 1813, a complaint was filed against **Michael Reager**, cabinetmaker, by an apprentice who said he had been "cruelly abused and ill treated". Example: on a 10 1/16" beech center bead with a 1" section of intermittent boxing on the sole, typical of early Philadelphia planemakers, and with flat chamfers, ca. 1790-1800. *********

H. REICHERT
Example: on a cooper's maple concave compass plane with a Sargent & Co. iron, ca. 1850. **UR**

REILY
Reily was a hardware dealer in Cape Girardeau, MO. Examples: on a screw-arm plow plane; and a size 5/8" double-boxed bead with **38** on the toe, the **Ohio Tool Co.** inventory number for this plane, ca. 1850. ********

P & J.C. REINHARD
P. & J. C. Reinhard was believed to be a hardware dealer. No location has been given. Example: on a table hollow plane made by the Ohio Tool Co.. ********

REINISNIDER & CO.
This label was reported on a plane: ****

REINISNIDER & CO.
DEALER IN
IRON BUILDER'S HARDWARE
LADDERS, OILS, PAINTS
GLASS & CLOTH GOODS.

RELIABLE
Reliable is believed to be a brand name used by the **Ohio Tool Co.**. Example: on a beech jack; and a smoother with number **3**, the **Ohio Tool Co.** inventory number for a double-iron smoother with a polished start (heel), ca. 1850. **

A. REMICK
Example: on a 11 1/8"x 7/8" beech match tongue plane with an integral closed tote, ca. 1840-50. **UR**

I REMLY
Example: on a 9 1/4" birch complex molder with heavy round chamfers, ca. 1820. **UR**

W. RENDELL
Example: on a 9 1/2" beech boxed complex molder with shallow round chamfers, ca. 1830. **UR**

E. R./ E. RENEHAN
Example: on a 9 1/4" beech complex molder with shallow round chamfers, ca. 1830-40. **UR**

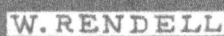

WM. RENFREW
William Renfrew was listed in an 1887 directory, as a manufacturer of sash, doors, and blinds for **E. & T. Fairbanks Co.**, St. Johnsbury, VT. Examples: at least 7 bench planes, including a 10" beech razee smoother with a closed tote; a double-iron and an adjustable throat opening with an ebony insert, ca. 1850. ****

A. REUTER & SONS
A. Reuter & Sons was a hardware dealer, from Baltimore, MD, with **Andrew Reuter** and sons **F. Lewis Reuter, Charles Reuter** and **Edward Reuter**. The firm was listed, in 1863, as hardware retail, builders and cabinet hardware, at 56 W. Baltimore; from 1872-78, at 246 Saratoga. Example: on the heel of a size 3/16" single-boxed bead, made by **D. R. Barton & Co.**. ****

P. REUTER
P. Reuter with a location imprint **LOUISVILLE. K.Y** is probably a hardware dealer. Example: on a size 1" bead with **38** on the toe; and a ogee with **80** on the toe, both inventory numbers used by the **Ohio Tool Co.**, ca. 1860-80. ****

S. REVE
Examples: on a 10 5/8" round with flat chamfers; a 9 3/8" straight rabbet with round chamfers; a 9 3/4" round with round chamfers; and a 9 7/8" table-joint pair with flat chamfers, all beech. The 2 rounds and the rabbet were found in a tool chest with **Ceaser Chelor** planes in Oswego, NY, ca. 1770-80. ****

RHSB & CO./ REVO-NOC
Rhsb & Co./ Revo-Noc is the brand name used by **Hubbard, Spencer, Bartlett & Co.**, an important Chicago, IL, hardware dealer, active from 1883-1960. The initials **Revonoc** is **Conover** spelled backwards. **Mr. Conover** was a vice-president of the company in 1907. Example: on a transitional type jointer. ***

A+T+REYNOLDS
Examples: on a size 3/8" bead with flat chamfers on the toe and heel and round chamfers on top; and a 3/16" bead with round chamfers, both 9 1/2" beech, ca. 1810-20. **UR**

E. REYNOLDS
Example: on a 9 7/16" birch complex molder with flat chamfers on the toe and heel and round chamfers on the top, ca. 1800. **UR**

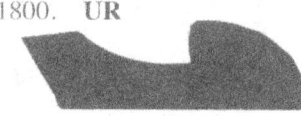

H. D. REYNOLDS
The **H. D. Reynolds** imprint has been reported. **UR**

Js REYNOLDS
Example: on a 9 3/8" beech size **16** round with heavy flat chamfers and the embossed owners imprint **S. Hill**, ca. 1800. **UR**

O. L. REYNOLDS
O. L. Reynolds with **MAKER** is on a 9 1/2" beech round, ca. 19c. ****

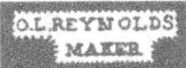

W. B. REYNOLDS
William B. Reynolds was reported in the *Franklin Institute Journals* Vol. XI (15), 1833, p. 94 #5 "For an improvement in the double-iron plane; **William B. Reynolds**, St. Clairsville, Belmont Co., OH, Patented July 7, 1832". Examples: on a beech adjustable sash, with the date **1835**; a 9 1/16" beech rabbet; and a bench plane with an open tote, a double-iron and metal wear strips, one at the toe and heel and, the third, before the iron, ca. 1830. ****

BENJAMIN F. RHOADES
Benjamin F. Rhoades (b. 1825 in MA) was listed as a planemaker, in the 1850 census for Worthington, MA. Also listed as living with him was **Sam Delpe**.
No imprint has been reported.

GIDEON W. RHOADES
Gideon W. Rhoades was listed in the 1850 industrial census, for Chesterfield, MA, as a manufacturer of plane handles, using steam power and six employees, to produce 55,000 for the year.
No imprint has been reported.

CHARLES W. RHOADS
Charles W. Rhoads (**Rhoades**) (b. Jun. 26, 1810, d. Nov. 1, 1873) is said to have made planes in Amherst, NH.
No imprint has been reported.

RHODES & KEYTE
Example: on a 14 1/4" beech ogee crown molder with a pull bar and centered tote, ca. 19c. **UR**

WILLIAM RICARD
William Richard was listed as a planemaker in Cincinnati, OH, in 1831, and boards at **E. Burn's**.
No imprint has been reported.

D. RICE
Examples: on a 9 1/2" beech square rabbet with shallow flat chamfers; and a 13 1/2" beech jack-style square rabbet with a centered open tote and round chamfers, both found on the coast of ME, ca. 1810-30. **UR**

I. RICE
Example: on a plow plane with wood thumb screws and a wood flat chamfers, ca. 1800. **UR**

J. RICE
Example: the A imprint is on a 9 1/2" beech round with flat chamfers. The B imprint is on a 14 3/4" beech gutter plane with a diamond strike, centered tote and heavy round chamfers. The Chemung Co. Historical Society in Elmira, NY, has a 1" rabbet, ca. 1810-30. **UR**

R. B. RICE
Royal Baxter Rice (b. Nov. 20, 1825 in MA, d. Nov. 3, 1907 in Northampton, Hampshire Co., MA) of Williamsburg, MA, who was granted Patent No. 98,108, on Dec. 21, 1869, for a spur cutter on a conventional plow plane skate. In 1870-80, **Royal B. Rice** was listed as a carpenter in Williamsburg, MA. Example: on a 9 5/8"x 1 1/8" beech hollow or "backing plane". It is believed that **Royal B. Rice** worked for the following four planemakers and added each of their imprints on this plane:
  J. KELLOGG - AMHERST, MS.
  H. WELLS of WMSBURG, MASS.
  GREENFIELD TOOL CO. - GREENFIELD, MASS.
  UNION TOOL CO. - GOSHEN, MASS.
(see *Patented Transitional & Metallic Planes in America - Vol. II*, p. 87, by Roger K. Smith)   A1 ***; A *****

T. RICE
Example: on a 21 3/4" beech foreplane with a double **James Howarth** iron and shallow rounded chamfers, ca. 1840. **UR**

W RICE
Example: on a birch smoother with round top wedge and iron, and heavy flat chamfers, ca. 1780-1800. **UR**

J. RICH
Example: on a 1" dado in the collection of the Chemung Co. Historical Society in Elmira, NY, ca. 1800.   **UR**

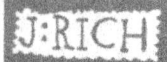

L. RICH
Examples: on a 9 3/8" beech molder with flat chamfers, found with planes of early Philadelphia makers; and a 9" beech plow with oak wedge-locked arms and oak round-top depth stop, found near Richlandtown, Bucks Co., PA, ca. 1810.   **UR**

WILLIAM RICH & CO.
William Rich & Co. was a hardware dealer, active in Amherst and Worcester, MA, ca. 1850.   ********

C. RICHARD
Examples: on a 9 1/2" beech single-boxed bead with size **3/8** on the toe; and a grooving plane, both with shallow round chamfers, ca. 1830.   **UR**

J. RICHARD
Example: on a 7 1/2" coffin smoother with shallow flat chamfers, ca. 1810.   **UR**

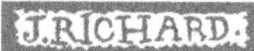

WALTER RICHARD
Walter Richard was apprenticed, as a planemaker, to **Simeon Doggett** of Middleboro, MA, from 1769-73.
No imprint has been reported.

RICHARDS
John Richards (b. ca. 1779 in Wales, d. Apr. 5, 1855 in Frankford, Philadelphia Co., PA) was a Philadelphia, PA, planemaker, who appeared in the 1809 city directory. Examples: on beech molders with flat chamfers on the toe and heel and round chamfers on the top.   **A & A1 ******

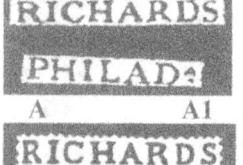

C. J. RICHARDS & CO.
Richmond is in NY. Example: the A imprint is on a 9 1/2" beech hollow. The B imprint is on an 8" coffin smoother, ca. 1850.   **A & B ******

F. RICHARDS & CO.
Frederick Richards (b. 1811 in CT) was a tool maker, in Springfield, MA, who advertised, in 1846, that he had on hand and manufactured all kinds of bench and molding planes. **Richards** also advertised repairs at short notice. He was a partner in **Hills & Richards**, date unknown. He appeared, in the 1847 directory, as a toolmaker; and in 1848, as a hardware dealer; in 1850, as a toolmaker, employed by **H. Chapin**.   *******

H. B. RICHARDS
Henry B. Richards (b. Jun. 23, 1810 in Philadelphia, d. Dec. 29, 1901) was a hardware dealer, in Lynchburgh, VA, from 1834-41, "at the Sign of the Golden Anvil." He took over the firm of **Theodorick Roberts & Co.**, on Feb. 13, 1834. By 1841 the name had changed from H. B. Richards to **Richards & Bassett**; in 1875, **Richards, Leftwich & Co.**.   *******

J. P. RICHARDS/ P. RICHARD
Example: the A imprint is on a rosewood screw-arm plow plane, ca. 1850.
A, A1, A2, & B: *******

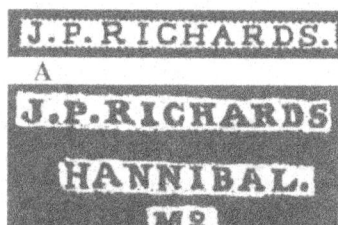

M. RICHARDS
This imprint has been reported.   **UR**

W. RICHARDS/ Wm RICHARDS
William Richards (d. 1895 in Cincinnati, OH) was listed as a planemaker, in Cincinnati, OH, in 1831-34. Example: the A imprint is on a dado. The B imprint is on a 9 1/2" beech table plane with size **7/8** on the heel, and wide round chamfers, ca. mid 19c.   **A & B: ******

W. S. RICHARDS
Example: an 8 1/2" lignum vitae low-angle shipwright smoother with a **Moulson Brothers** double-iron, ca. 1850, possibly from New England Coast.   **UR**

RICHARDS & FLEURY

Richards & Fleury was a New York City hardware dealer partnership of **Charles J. Richards** and **James A. Fleury** at 21 Pratt St., in 1852. In 1847-48, James A. Fleury was listed as "Agent" and Charles J. Richard as a hardware dealer, both at 21 Pratt St. **A, A1 & B ****

D. RICHARDSON

Example: on the side of a 9 1/2" beech round made by **J. W. Mersereau**. **UR**

R. J. RICHARDSON

Richard J. Richardson (b. 1828 in NY, d. 1908) was a hardware dealer in Janesville, WI, from 1846-65. In 1865, Richard Richardson and his brother, **Hamilton Richardson**, sold the hardware store and bought the **Doty Mfg. Co.**. Example: on the heel of a 13 3/4" handled razee molder with the **Ohio Tool Co.** inventory number **140** on the toe. ****

RICHARDSON BROS. & CO./ RICHARDSON BROS.

Richardson Bros. & Co. was probably a hardware store located in Waltham, MA. Example: The B imprint is on a beech screw-arm plow plane, struck twice on the toe, with boxwood arms, an integral closed handle, with a brass depth stop and trim, ca. 1860. **A & B: ****

A. RICHEY

Examples: on a round; and a single boxed bead, all 9 1/2" beech with narrow flat chamfers, ca. 1800. **UR**

W. W. RICHEY

William W. Richey was a plane manufacturer in Louisville, KY, in 1838-39. He was married on Mar. 1, 1837, in Warren Co., KY. Richey was part of **Potter & Richey**, from 1844-45. **Solomon Cook** was listed as working for a **William W. Richards**, in Louisville, KY, as a planemaker, in 1843-44. ***

A: RICHMOND

Example: on a 9 1/2" beech quarter round molder with heavy flat chamfers, ca. 1800. **UR**

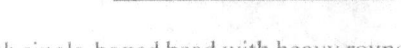

E. RICHMOND

Example: on a 9 1/2" birch single-boxed bead with heavy round chamfers, ca. 19c. **UR**

J. RICHMOND

Jacob Richmond (b. 1809 in Frederick Co., MD, d. Jan. 27, 1886 in Dayton, OH) was a planemaker, in Troy, NY, ca. 1836; and Dayton, OH, ca. 1841. Richmond was listed, in 1850, as a planemaker; and from 1860-80, as a carpenter, in Dayton. He was one who dated his planes with known examples from 1839-52. **A & B ***

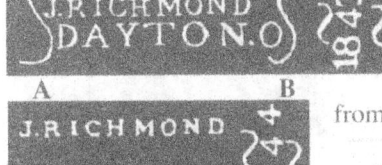

J. W. RICHMOND

Believed to be **Capt. John White Richmond** (b. May 18, 1799, in Bridgewater, MA, d. probate Oct. 9, 1866 in Knox Co., ME), or his son, **John W. Richmond** (b. 1828, d. probate Oct. 16, 1883 in Knox Co., ME), who were listed as **J. W. Richmond & Co.**, house builders, in the 1856-57 ME directory. In 1860, he was listed as a house joiner. Example: on a 13 3/8" handled tongue & groove pair; and a 9 3/8" beech complex molder with a relieved wedge and shallow round chamfers, found in ME, ca. 1810-30. ****

SAMUEL RICHMOND

Samuel Richmond (b. ca. 1802) was apprenticed on Feb. 6, 1816, to **Nathaniel Pilgrim**, a planemaker, of Baltimore Co., MD. In Jul. 17, 1836, Samuel Richmond enlisted in the U. S. Army with his occupation listed, as planemaker. In 1850, he was listed as carpenter, in Marion, FL.
No imprint has been reported.

SAMUEL H. RICHMOND

Samuel H. Richmond (b. Jun. 22, 1785, d. Feb. 18, 1826 in Cincinnati, Hamilton Co., OH) was listed in the Pittsburgh, PA 1819 directory, as a planemaker, at **Swetman & Hughes**. He also appeared as a "plainmaker", on an 1818 Pittsburgh tax list.
No imprint has been reported.

L. RICHTER

L. Richter was probably a hardware dealer, located at **76 EWEN ST**, possibly in New York City. Examples: on a skew rabbet; and a toothing plane, both made by **Sargent**. ****

T RICHARD/ RICKARD
Thomas J. Rickard was part of **Creagh & Rickard**, in 1829; and was listed in the Cincinnati, OH, directories, as a plane and edge tool maker, from 1831-32. He also worked in St. Louis, MO, dates unknown. The eagle and the starburst emblems on the St. Louis imprint is the same as that used by **H. Stout**, from 1836-38. The C imprint is overprinted on a **C. J. Smith**. **A & B ***, C ******

D. RIDER
Example: on a wedge-arm plow plane, ca. 1800. **No imprint is available.**

P. B. RIDER
Perry B. Rider (b. 1808 in Orrington, ME, d May 22, 1888 in Pembroke, NH) was a planemaker in Bangor, ME, from 1834-48, after which he moved to Boston, MA. Example: on a double-iron, boxed fixed sash with the date **1840**. **A & A1 ****

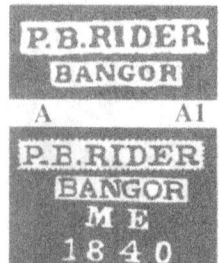

S. J. RIDER
Example: a 9 1/2"x 1 3/4" beech skew rabbet with shallow round chamfers. The name is imprinted twice and the location once, ca. 1830. **UR**

T. J. RIDER
Probably **Thomas Jefferson Rider** (b. Jul. 17, 1806, d. Feb. 27, Newmarket, NH) who was a joiner in Thomaston, ME, 65 miles south of Bangor, ME. **Rider** was also a guard at the state prison in Thomaston. In the 1861 business directory for ME, **Rider** was listed as a house and ship joiner, in Thomaston; in 1870, a joiner. Example: on a 9 3/4" beech complex molder with heavy round chamfers and the iron incised **BANGOR, ME**; a 22" beech fore plane with this imprint struck four times in the form of a square; and on a double-boxed center bead made by **M. Copeland & Co.**. **UR**

G. E. RIDLEY
Example: on a 9 1/2" beech square miter, ca. 1850. **UR**

J. RIDLON
Example: on a 9 1/2"x 1 3/4" beech skew rabbet. **UR**

WILLIAM RIEBLE
William Rieble was listed as a planemaker, from Philadelphia, PA. William married Dec. 6, 1835, in Philadelphia, PA. **No imprint has been reported**.

RIES & SCHUBES
Ries & Schubes with the added location imprint **NEW ORLEANS** has been reported on a 13"x 3 1/2" beech toted complex molder. **No imprint is available**.

A. M. RIFE
On an incuse imprint with the date **Oct. 17, 1879.** **UR**

D: RIFFAL
Example: on a 13 5/8" beech very complex molder with round top and flat end chamfers, possibly from PA, ca. 1800-10. **UR**

D. RIG
Example: on a 9 1/2" beech molder with flat chamfers, found in ME, ca. 1800. **UR**

J. H. RIGBY'S TOOL STORE
J. H. Rigbys Tool Store was a New York City tool dealer, whose imprint appears on a **J. Denison** plow plane; and on a **J. & L. Denison** plane, ca. 1850. **A & A1 ******

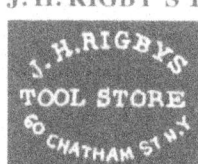

B. RING
Example: a molder with ebony boxing. **No imprint is available**.

E. C. RING
Ethan Crandall Ring (b. Sep. 7, 1812 in Chesterfield, Hampshire Co., MA, d. Sep. 18, 1898 in Melrose, MA) made planes in Worthington, MA, from 1843-55. Ringville was a

small village at the junction of two branches of the Little River, south of Worthington Center on the stage road to Huntington. He was listed as a planemaker, in the 1850 industrial census, employing five hands, using water power, and producing planes worth $4000. In Jul. 28, 1851, Ethan was appointed postmaster in Ringville, MA; in 1870-85, as a custom house officer in Melrose, Middlesex Co., MA.

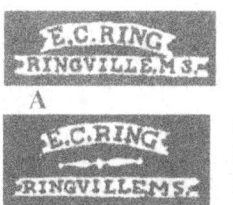

A, A1 & B *

E. & T. RING & CO.
Elkanah Ring (b. Oct. 2, 1809 in Chesterfield Hampshire Co., MA, d. Feb. 22, 1899 in Westfield, Hampden, MA) and **Thomas Ring** (b. May 22, 1812 in Chesterfield, Hampshire Co., MA, d. Aug 20, 1863 Worthington, Hampshire Co., MA), who were mill owners and manufacturers, in Worthington, MA, and made planes, from 1840-47. In 1840, **Elkanah Ring** and **Thomas Ring** were listed as having 17 people in their household working at manufacturing or a trade. **E. T. Ring & Co.** was listed, in the 1849 New England Mercantile Union directory, as a plane manufacturer, in Worthington. In 1858; the firm was relocated to Huntington, when the factory burned. In 1860, **Elkanah** was listed as a mechanic and manufacturer, in Huntington, MA. In 1855, **E. & T. Ring & Co.**, employed 8 hands and produced $4000 worth of product, including tools other than planes. *

R. RINGO
Example: on a 9 3/8" beech skewed rabbet with heavy round chamfers, ca. 1820. **UR**

J. RIPLEY
Joseph Ripley (b. May 9, 1819, d. Mar. 1, 1900 in Hingham, Plymouth Co., MA) who was a Hingham cabinetmaker, from 1846-80. In partnership with **Joseph Newhall** as **Ripley & Newhall**. Example: on a 8 3/8" beech plow with wood thumbscrew locked arms with a **W. Greaves & Sons** iron, brass plate and steel skate, and round chamfers, ca. 1830-50. **UR**

RIBKB
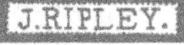
Example: on a 4 7/8" beech smoother with a York pitch, a single round top iron and tight round chamfers, ca. early 19c. **UR**

B. RISLEY
Example: on a 9 5/16" birch astragal, imprinted on the toe and heel and flat chamfers. **UR**

J. ROBB
Example: on an 8" birch sash coping plane with round chamfers, found with a **S. Robbe** plane, with a similar wedge, ca. 1820.
A & B: **UR**

S. ROBBE
Example: on an 8 3/4" beech dado with large shallow flat chamfers, found with a **J. Robb** plane, ca. 1810. **UR**

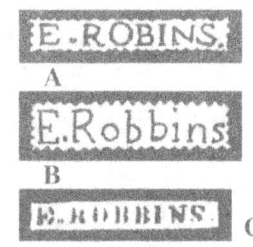

CHARLES ROBBINS
Charles Robbins was apprenticed to **Joseph Metcalf**, planemaker, ca. 1790. **No imprint has been reported.**

E. ROBINS/ E. ROBBINS
Enos Robbins (**Robins**) (b. 1806 in CT, d. Mar 13, 1858 in Middleville, NY) made planes in Utica, NY, as a partner in **Collins & Robbins** with **Robert J. Collins III**, from 1828-30. **Robbins** boarded with **L. Kennedy Jr.**, in Utica, in 1829. **Robbins** moved to New Hartford, south of Utica, in 1832; and to the village of Middleville in Newport, NY, in 1840-41. **Robbins** was listed as a planemaker, in the 1850 census; and a toolmaker, in the 1855 state census. Examples: the A imprint is on a complex molder, of early appearance with deep chamfers; and a 10" birch tongue plane with flat chamfers and a relieved wedge. The B imprint is on a 10"x 1/4" beech bead with an **I. Sleeper** style wedge and small flat chamfers; these planes may have been made by an earlier generation, ca. 1790-1800. **A, B & C ****

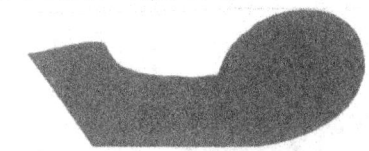

LEON ROBBINS (see L.R)

M. ROBBINS (see R. STEVENS)

R. C. ROBBINS
Rufus Coggwell Robbins (b. May 31, 1802 in Berkshire, MA, d. 1896 in Delatur, Macon Co., IL) was listed in the 1820 census, in Plymouth, MA; the 1830 census, in Duxbury, MA; and from 1830's-50's, as a carpenter, in Mendon, 10 miles south of Rochester, NY; in 1860, as a master carpenter, in Mendon, NY; in 1870-80, as a carpenter, in Decatur, IL. Examples: on a 9 1/2" miter plane; a nosing plane; and a 9 3/16" beech hollow, all with shallow rounded chamfers, mostly found near Rochester, NY, ca. 1850. ****

W. ROBENSON
Example: on a 10" beech round with small flat chamfers, ca. 1800. **UR**

ALVAN S. ROBERTS
Alvan S. Roberts (b. Jun. 12, 1820 in OH, d. Jun. 1, 1905 in Bellevue, Huron Co., OH) was listed as a planemaker, in Cincinnati, OH, in 1842; and is assumed to be the same person as **Alvine F. Roberts** listed in 1846. **No imprint has been reported**.

HUGH ROBERTS
Hugh Roberts was listed as a planemaker in the Utica, NY directories from 1832-34, boarding with and working for **John Reed**. **No imprint has been reported**.

HUGH ROBERTS, JR.
Hugh Roberts, Jr. was listed as a planemaker, in the Utica, NY directories from 1839-46, possibly also working for **John Reed**. **No imprint has been reported**.

J. ROBERTS
Possibly **John Roberts II** (b. May 1737 in Windsor, Hartford Co., CT d. 1781 in Hartford) was a cabinetmaker in Hartford. He advertised in *The Connecticut Courant and the Weekly Intelligencer* of Jun. 23, 1778, for journeymen cabinetmakers. In 1781, **Roberts** died insolvent, at age 44. His estate lists no cabinetmaking tools. His son **John Roberts III** (b. Mar. 28, 1780 in Windsor, Hartford Co., CT, d. Sep. 3, 1797 in Hartford) **John** drowned during his apprenticeship to Hartford joiner, and toolmaker **Leonard Kennedy**. Example: on a 10 3/16" skew bead, a removable fence, with the iron set at a York pitch. **No imprint is available**.

ROBERT ROBERTS
Robert Roberts (b. ca. 1807 in Wales) was listed as a planemaker, in Utica, NY directories, from 1832-41, boarding and working with **John Reed**. **No imprint has been reported**.

Wm. ROBERTS
Example: on an applied sole molding plane with PATd JUNE' 1 69 (1869). **UR**

T. ROBERTSON
Examples: the A imprint is on a match tongue plane with a size 3/4 on the heel and shallow round chamfers. The B imprint, on a 9 1/2" beech tongue plane with shallow round chamfers, includes the added location **RICHMOND**, probably Richmond, VA, ca. 1830-40. ****

W. ROBERTSON
Example: on a 9 1/2" beech double-iron fixed sash with shallow round chamfers, ca. 1830. **UR**

C. R./ C. ROBINS
Example: on a 9 3/8" beech complex molder with heavy round chamfers, ca. 1820. **UR**

G. ROBINSON
George Robinson (b. Feb. 17, 1799 in Fairfield, Herkimer Co., NY, d. Sep. 21, 1890 in North Russell, St. Lawrence Co., NY) was listed as a planemaker, in the 1829 Utica directory, boarding with and working for **L. Kennedy**. Example: on a wedge-arm plow plane, with the imprint of **Bewley**, a New York planemaker, in 1822-32; in 1850, as a carpenter, in Pierrepont; in 1860, as a carpenter and joiner, in Russell, NY. **G. Robinson** with an incuse location **N YORK**. **UR**

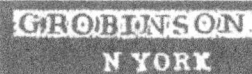

J. ROBINSON
Possibly **John Robinson** working (1770-74) as a joiner in Attleboro, MA. Examples: on a 9 5/8" combination tongue & groove match plane with a riveted skate and round chamfers; and a 9 1/8" beech dado with heavy round chamfers. One of the irons is marked **P. LAW** (English 1787-1833), ca. 1820. **UR**

J. C. ROBINSON
Example: on a 17" jack with an **Auburn Tool. Co.** iron, ca. 1850-60. **UR**

JOHN P. ROBINSON
John P. Robinson (b. ca. 1806 in Albany CO., NY, d. Mar. 11, 1891 in Allegheny Co., NY) of Matteawan, NY, was issued Patent No. 13,957, granted Dec. 18, 1855, for a wooden core box plane with a "V" shaped body. Example: on a 12 5/16" core box plane with a conventional open tote, molding-style wedge & iron, and an oval escapement in the top. ****

E. ROBURDS
Example: on a 10" Yankee plow with wood screws and depth stop; and on a 10" double wedge & iron fixed sash, both beech with flat chamfers, ca. 1790-1800. **UR**

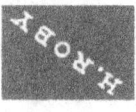

WM. ROBY
Example: on a 9 1/4" beech round with shallow round chamfers; and **H. Roby** as an owner's imprint. The **H. Roby** imprint has also been reported on a panel gauge and a marking gauge with 19c. characteristics, found in VT. **UR**

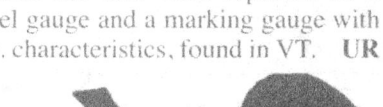

N. ROCKWELL
Example: on a 9 3/8" beech molder with a relieved wedge, small round chamfers on the top and flat chamfers on the ends, ca. 1800.   UR

D. ROE
Example: on a 9 1/2" beech hollow with flat chamfers.   UR

Ix ROGE
Example: on a slide-arm beech plow with red paint. Wedge stopped with wood thumb screws, wood depth stop, and flat chamfers, possibly PA, ca. early 19c.   UR

CHAS. ROGERS
Charles S. Rogers (b. Sep. 27, 1816 in Londonderry, Rockingham Co., NH, d. May 27, 1902 in St. Louis, MO) was a St. Louis, MO, hardware dealer from 1853-57. In 1857, the firm was listed as **Rogers, Anderson & Co.**. Rogers was a partner in the hardware firms of **Rogers & Field**, in 1844; in **Rogers, Shapleigh & Co.**, from 1843-47; and **Rogers & Barney**, from 1847-52; in 1860-70 as a steamboat Capt. in St. Louis; and in 1880, as president of a Packet Co.   ***

D. ROGERS
D. Rodgers apparently worked in both Lowell, MA & NY. ca. 1850.   A & B: ****

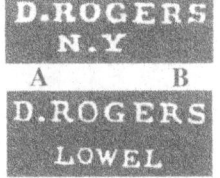

G. W. ROGERS
George W. Rogers (b. ca. 1818 in Curcenatus, NY, d. Dec. 11, 1907 in Chester, Eaton Co., MI) was a co-patentee of **M. B. Tidey's** double beveling plane, Patent No. 11,235, granted on July 4, 1854. His fellow patentee, **M. B. Tidey** made planes in Dundee, NY. George W. Rogers was listed, in the 1850, census, as a "plainmaker", living with **Marcus Spaulding**, age 17, also a planemaker, in Starkey, Yates Co., NY. In 1855, George W. Rogers was listed, as planemaker, in Starkey. Examples: on a 22" fore plane; and a 26" jointer.   ****

H. ROGERS SONS & CO.
H. Rogers Sons & Co. probably was a hardware dealer. No location is available. Examples: the A imprint on a 9 1/2"x 1/2" side bead; the B imprint is on a 9 3/8" beech grooving plane; and a 9 3/8" beech single-boxed side bead, both with heavy round chamfers, ca. 1830-50.
A, B & C: ****

JACOB ROGERS & CO.
Jacob Rogers & Co. was listed as a hardware dealer in Lowell, MA, in the city directories, from 1853-70. Examples: on an **Addison Heald** jointer, and on a **Warren & Heald** fore plane.
A **; B & C ***

N. ROGERS
Examples: on 9 1/2x 3/8" beech molders with round chamfers; and a 16 1/2" beech jointer plane with an offset tote and round chamfers, ca. 1820-40.   UR

R. H. ROGERS
Example: on a slide-arm beech plow with wood screws, located at the Fort Klock Historical Restoration, at St. Johnsville, on the Mohawk River, west of Albany, NY, ca. early 19c.   UR

W. ROGERS
Examples: on a 9 1/2" beech fixed sash; a 9 5/8" birch wide hollow; a 9 1/4"x 7/8" beech hollow; and a 9 3/8" beech hollow & round pair with **Newbould** irons, all with heavy flat chamfers, ca. 1800.   ****

ROGERS & FOWLER
Rogers & Fowler was a planemaker in Dayton, OH, from 1856-57.   ***

ROGERS, SHAPLEIGH & CO.
Rogers, Shapleigh & Co. was a hardware dealership in St. Louis, MO, from 1843-47. They supposedly were opened as a branch of **Rogers Bros. & Co.** of Philadelphia, PA. In 1847, it became **Shapleigh, Day & Co.**. **No imprint is available.**

ROGERS, TAYLOR & CO.
Rogers, Taylor & Co. consisting of **D. Rogers** and **Frederick Taylor** both of Lowell, MA. Example: on a 15 7/8" razee jack plane with a **Baldwin Tool Co.** double-iron.
****

I. ROGH
Example: on a 9 3/8" beech plow with wedges and thumbscrews and wood depth stop, stained red, riveted skate, and small flat chamfers, possibly from rural PA, ca. 1800.   UR

GEORG ROH
Example: on a 9 1/2" beech quarter round with flat chamfers, found in Lancaster, PA, ca. early 19c. **UR**

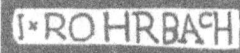 

I. ROHRBACK
Example: on a beech slide-arm plow with a riveted skate; and a 29" fruitwood jointer, struck twice on the toe with offset tote, **NEWBOLD** iron and flat chamfers, found in MD, south of York, PA, probably from PA, ca. 1800. **UR**

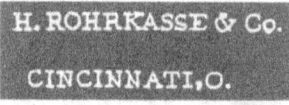

H. ROHRKASSE & CO.

H. Rohrkasse & Co. was a hardware dealer in Cincinnati, OH, from 1849-57. Example: the A1 imprint is on a size **6** round. **A & A1 *****

A. ROLAND & CO.
A. Roland & Co. was probably a hardware dealer. Example: on a hollow & round pair, ca. 19c. **No imprint is available**.

J. ROLF
Example: on an 8 3/8" beech plow with tight shallow round chamfers, iron thumbscrews, iron tombstone depth stop, and iron wear strips on the top of arms, found in Epsom, NH, ca. 1810-30. **UR**

D. G. ROLLINS
Example: on a 9 1/2" beech round with flat chamfers, ca. 1820-30. **UR**

R. ROLLING
Example: on a 9 9/16" beech reeding plane with rosewood boxing and flat chamfers, ca. 1800. **UR**

S. RONEY
Stephen Roney was a hardware dealer in Pekin, Tazewell Co., IL. Listed in 1870, as **S. Roney & Co.**, wholesale and retail dealers in hardware, nails, stoves, tinware, agricultural implements, seeds, coopers' carpenters' and blacksmiths' tools, at the n.w cor. Court and Second. Example: on a large round with **73** on the toe, the **Ohio Tool Co.** style number. *******

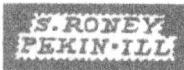

G. W. ROOKS

Example: on a chunky, square spar plane with a single **Moulson Bros.** iron, ca. 1840-50. **UR**

ROOSEVELT, HYDE & CLARK
Roosevelt, Hyde & Clark was a hardware dealer partnership in Charleston, SC, that consisted of **H. L. Roosevelt** (b. ca. 1813 in NY), **Simeon Hyde** (b. Oct. 24, 1810 in Groton, New London Co., CT, d. Jan. 21, 1886 in Charleston, SC), and **Robert A. Clark**. The firm was first listed in the 1849 city directory and again in 1852. There apparently were no directories between 1841-49. In 1855, the firm was listed as **Clark, Hyde & Co.**, consisting of **Robert A. Clark** and **Simeon Hyde**; in 1860, as **Hyde, Gregg & Day**. Earlier, and in 1840-41, there was a firm of **Harris, Roosevelt & Barker** at Hayes St. **A & A1 ******

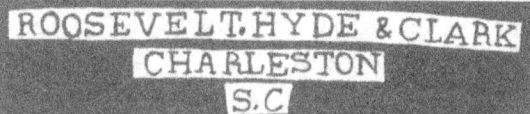

C. ROOT
Example: on a 9 3/8" birch narrow round with tight flat chamfers, ca. 1800. **UR**

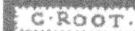 

E. ROOT

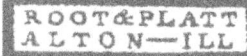

Example: on a modified beech molder with shallow large round chamfers, ca. 1820-30. **UR**

ROOT & PLATT
Augustine Kilbourn Root (b. Dec. 8, 1829 in Franklin, MA, d. July 13, 1906 Alton, IL) and **Anson B. Platt** (d. Sep. 19, 1872 in Alton, IL) were hardware dealers in Alton, IL, from 1858-72, at 3rd. between Belle and State. Root was later part of **Hayner & Co.**, until 1884; and was president of the **Alton Flour Roller Milling Co.**, from 1886-92. The hardware store was opened on Jan. 3, 1853, as **Platt & Ryan**. *******

G. ROPES
George Ropes (b. Nov. 29, 1800 in Orford, Grafton Co., NH, d. Aug. 29, 1869 St. Johnsbury, VT) who moved in 1825 up the Connecticut River to Newbury, VT. In 1839-40, he advertised in the NH *Democratic-Republican* for apprentices and promised "Cabinet Furniture of the latest fashion"; in 1840, he was engaged in manufacturer and trades in Newbury; in 1850 as a cabinetmaker, in Barnet; and in 1860, a journeyman cabinetmaker, in St. Johnsbury. Example: on a 10" birch small bead with tight round chamfers and an iron set at a York pitch, ca. 1800-20. **UR**

E. ROSE
Example: on a 10 1/4" beech fixed single-blade sash with heavy round chamfers, ca. 1810-20. **UR**

R. ROSE
Example: on a 10 3/16"x 1" birch hollow with shallow flat chamfers, ca. 1790. **UR**

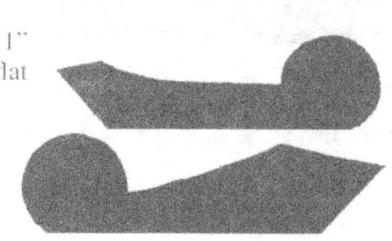

G. ROSEBOOM

Garret R. Roseboom (b. 1806 in IN) made planes in Cincinnati, OH, in 1839-40, for **E. F. Seybold**; and under his own name at various times, from 1842-61. In 1850, **Garret** was listed as a hardware merchant; from 1849-52, he was a part of **G. & W. H. Roseboom**; in 1853, **Roseboom & Roe,** with **Frank Roe** working, as a chairmaker; in 1853-54, as **Roseboom & Smith**; in 1853-54 as **Roseboom & Thomas**; and in 1855, as **Roseboom & Magill**. A & B *

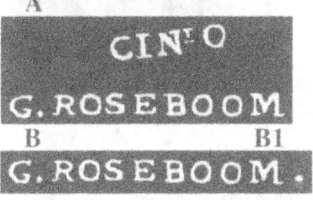
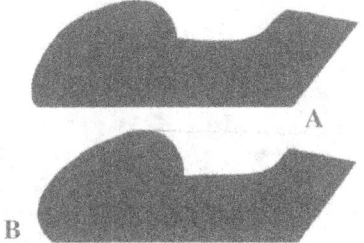

G. & W. H. ROSEBOOM

Garret R. Roseboom (b. 1806 in IN) and **William Henry Roseboom** (b. 1825 in IN, d. 1881, in Cincinnati, OH) made planes in Cincinnati, OH, from 1844-52; In 1850; the firm employed six hands and produced $4950 worth of planes. **William** was also listed, as a planemaker, in 1853, at 39 Chestnut, Cincinnati; in 1855-57 & 1859-60, at 29 Chestnut. **William** served in the Civil War from Jul. 8, 1861 until 1865, as a 1st. Sergeant. **

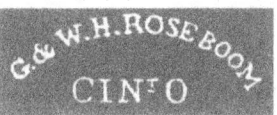

ROSEBOOM & MAGILL

Roseboom & Magill was a partnership consisting of **Garret R. Roseboom** and **Wesley Webster Magil** (b. Nov. 15, 1822 in St. Clarsville, Belmont Co., OH, d. Feb. 15, 1888 in Cincinnati, OH) who made planes in Cincinnati, in 1855. ***

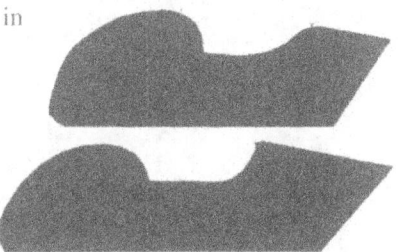

A. ROSS

Examples: on a 9 3/8" beech size **6** round & **10** hollow; a raising plane; and a 9 1/2"x 5/16" birch bead with small flat chamfers. The A imprint is from the bead. The B imprint is from a 9 7/8" beech adjustable sash, ca. 1800-30. UR

D. ROSS

Example: on a 10" tiger maple hollow. UR

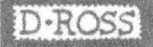

I x ROSS

Jonathon Ross was a cabinetmaker, in Salem, MA with a ledger entry of 1770-82. Examples on a 10" cherry sash ovolo with the A wedge; a 10" birch bead with size **6/8** on the heel, and the B wedge; a 10" rabbet with the B wedge, found with a **Jo. Fuller** molder; and an **E. Taft** Plow, found in RI; a 10 1/8" sash plane; and a round, ca. 1770-90. ****

JOSEPH L. ROSS

Joseph L. Ross (b. Mar. 4, 1822 in Essex Co., MA, d. Apr. 21, 1903 in Ipswich, Essex Co., MA) was a Boston, MA, cabinetmaker who was reported as having imprinted his stamp on planes, ca. 1842; In the 1850, **Ross** had 36 hands and made $50,000 in furniture. **No imprint is available**.

P. ROSS

Examples: on a 11" round bottom jack (altered) with a centered pegged tote; a 9 1/2" birch ovolo; and a 9 9/16" birch quarter round, all with heavy round chamfers, ca. 1805-20. ****

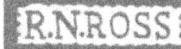

R. N. ROSS

Examples: on a side bead; and a side rabbet which provided the wedge, ca. 1830. UR

Wm C. ROSS

William C. Ross (b. 1817 in MD) was a Baltimore planemaker and maker of edge tools, from 1849-69. From 1862-66, **Ross** was listed at 44 Light St., the same address that **P. Chapin**, occupied, from 1845-55. An example of the **Wm C. Ross** imprint on a **P. Chapin** plane, bearing the B imprint has been reported. From 1867-69, **Ross** worked, at 37 Light St. He was succeeded at that address, from 1871-72, by **A. B. Seidenstricker & Co.**, who overstamped some **Wm C. Ross** planes and may have been a successor. A, A1, B & C *; D & E **

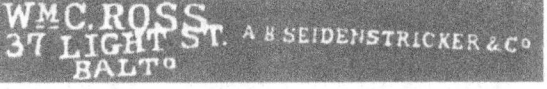

ROSS & WINN
Ross & Winn was a hardware dealer. Example: on a table hollow made by **Union Factory/ H. Chapin**. UR

J. ROUDENBUGH
Example: on a 9 1/2" beech quarter round, possibly from MA, ca. mid 19c. UR

H. ROUNDTREE
Example: on a **Mockridge & Francis** plane with a paper label, possibly from Yonkers, NY: ****

SOLD AT
H. ROUNDTREE'S
MECHANICS' TOOL STORE
NO. 60
CHATHAM STREET
(YONK)ERS NEW YORK

R. ROWE
Example: on a 9 1/2" beech bead with a **I. Sleeper** style wedge, ca. 1830-50. UR

C. S. ROWELL
Charles S. Rowell made planes under these imprints in Troy, NY, in 1832 only, having succeeded his father, **Simeon Rowell**. A & A1 ***

J. ROWELL
Example: on an 11 1/2"x 2" beech skew rabbet with heavy round chamfers, ca. 1800. UR

S. ROWELL
Simeon Rowell (b. Jun. 30, 1791, d. Feb. 24, 1884) father of **Charles S. Rowell**, was listed in 1814, as a carpenter in wood, furniture, and the carriage trade, in Albany, NY. In 1820, **Rowell** was listed, as plane & tool maker. **Simeon** made planes in Troy, NY, under his imprint, from 1828-32; in Albany, NY, from 1821-28, as part of **Rowell & Kenney** with **Leonard Kenney**, from 1821-24; and **Rowell & Gibson** with **John Gibson**, from 1824-28. Example: on a **S. Rowell/ Troy** imprint over an **Rowell & Gibson/ Albany** imprint. In 1832, **Sameon Rowell** was succeeded by his son **Charles S. Rowell**. **Simeon Rowell** operated a drug store, until 1855. A, A2 & B *; A1, C & D **

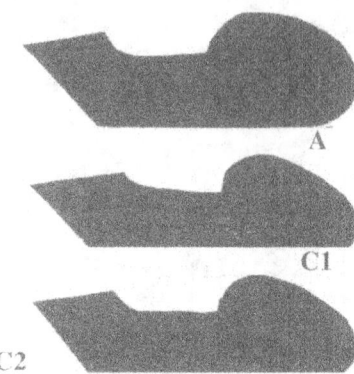

T. R./ T. ROWELL
Example: on a 9 1/2" beech dado, ca. 1850. UR

ROWELL & GIBSON
Rowell & Gibson consisted of **Simeon Rowell** and **John Gibson** made planes in Albany, NY, from 1824-28. A & A1 **

J. H. ROWLAND & CO.
James H. Rowland (b. Apr. 4, 1825, d. Apr. 28, 1895 in New Haven, CT) was listed in 1850, as a clerk in New Haven. In 1860, **Rowland** was listed, as a book keeper; in 1867, in foreign & domestic hardware, at 192 State St., south of Chapel St. Example: on a **W. H. Pond**, plane with a printed green label that reads: ****

BUY YOUR
HARDWARE & CUTLERY
OF
J. H. ROWLAND & CO.
192 STATE STREET
NEW HAVEN, CONN.

ROYAL
Example: on a 9 1/2"x 1 1/4" beech skew rabbet made by **D. R. Barton** of Rochester, NY. ****

P. ROYER
Example: on a 14"x 3 5/8" crown with an offset tote located at Sturbridge Village, MA; a 10" hollow; and a 10 1/16" quarter round, all beech with flat chamfers, ca. 1790. UR

GEO. A. RUBELMANN HDW. CO.
George A. Rubelmann (b. 1850, d. Jan. 18, 1912 in St. Louis, MO) was part of **Rubelmann & Co.**, in 1875; in 1876, was

under hardware and cutlery; from 1883-1909, as president of **Geo. A. Rubelmann Hardware Co.** in St. Louis, MO.

A & B **

A

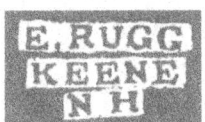
B

E. RUGG
Thought to be **Elias Rugg Jr.** (b. May 9, 1803 in Keene, NH, d. Mar. 5, 1882 in Keene, NH) who was listed, as a carpenter, pattern maker, and planemaker, in Keene, NH, from 1850-79. He was the son of **Elias Rugg** (b. 1774). In 1850, **Elias** was listed, as a carpenter; from 1860-70, as a pattern maker, in Keene, NH; in 1880, as wood mechanic, retired. Examples: on a 16" razee bench plane; and a 7 1/2" beech block plane, ca. 1850. ****

L. RUGG
Example: on a 9 1/2" beech double-wedge & iron sash plane with shallow round chamfers, ca. early 19c. **UR**

O. RUGG
Example: on a 9 1/4"x 5/8" birch molding plane, found in Claremont, NH, ca. early 19c. **UR**

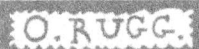 

GEORG RUI-M
Example: on a 9 1/2" molder with flat chamfers, possible from PA, ca. 1800. **UR**

T RULE
Example: marked three times on the toe and two times on the heel of a 9" beech complex molder with 3/8" flat chamfers, ca. early 19c. **UR**

J. RUMBAUGH
Example: on a 7 7/8" beech coffin smoother; and a 9 7/16"x 1 3/4" beech skew rabbet. In 1854, Ohio City merged into Cleveland, OH, ca. 1840. ****

JAMES RUMRELL
James Rumrell (b. ca. 1820 in Halifax, Nova Scotia, d. May 9, 1861 in West Roxbury, MA) made planes, at 32 Sudbury St., the same address as **James Stevens**, Boston, MA, from 1852-61. In an advertisement appearing in Adam's 1856 Boston Directory, he stated that he manufactured carpenter's planes, rules, tailor's squares, plumbs and levels, scales, bevels, T-squares &c with "particular attention paid to repairing".
No imprint has been reported.

E. RUMRY
Example: on a 9 1/2" birch small bead with relieved wedge and heavy flat chamfers, ca. 1790. **UR**

RUNYON & KING
Runyon & King was a hardware store in Springfield, OH, in 1852. **

J. A. RUSS
Example: marked on both halves of a single-boxed adjustable double-blade sash with brass diamond reinforcements at the adjustments, ca. 1850. **UR**

N. K. RUSS
Example: on a 14 1/4" skew rabbet with a closed tote and a nicker iron. **UR**

ASA RUSSELL
Examples: on a 9 1/2" beech complex molder; a 9 3/8"x 2" beech complex molder, both with heavy flat chamfers; and a beech jack with birch tote and heavy round chamfers, possibly from New England, ca. 1800-10. **UR**

G. E. RUSSELL
George E. Russell (b. 1831 in MA) was a hardware dealer, in Holyoke, MA. Example: on a **J. F & G. Lindsay** round, ca. 19c. ****

H. RUSSELL
Believed to be **Henry Hubbard Russell** (b. Mar. 8, 1810 in Weathersfield, VT), a resident of Cabot, VT, in 1830. He was listed in the 1840 census with two in his household, engaged in manufactures and trades; in 1849, listed as a furniture maker, in Cabot. Examples: on 9 1/2-9 5/8" molders; on three crown molders; and a screw-arm plow plane, ca. 1850. A, B, C & C1 ***

A

I. RUSSELL
Example: on a 9 3/8" complex molder, and a 9 1/2" single-boxed bead, both beech with flat chamfers, ca. 1800-10. **UR**

J. RUSSELL & CO.
J. Russell & Co. was a hardware dealer in Holyoke, MA, from 1870-1919. **Joseph J. Russell** (b. Sep. 1836 in Canada) was listed from 1860-65, as a mechanic, in Worcester co., MA. In 1870, he was listed in Holyoke, MA; in 1900, as a sawyer, in Worcester, MA. The label has been reported on a 18" jack rabbet made by **Lindsey** that reads: ****
J. RUSSELL & CO.
DEALERS IN HARDWARE
CUTLERY & MILL SUPPLIES
WORCESTER, MASS.

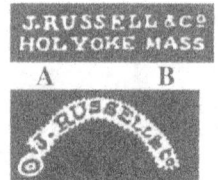

Example: the A imprint is on a **J. K. & G. M. Lindsey** quarter round. The B imprint is on a 5 1/2" coachmaker's round.
A & B ****

I: T RUSSELL
Example: on a 9 1/16" beech molder with a birch wedge and flat chamfers. Four examples have been found in VT, ca. 1800. **No imprint is available.**

T. RUSSELL.
Examples: on a 9 3/8" miter plane with a **William Ash & Co.** iron; and on a plow plane, ca. 1840. **UR**

T. H. RUSSELL
Titus H. Russell (b. between 1818-20, in VT, d. Ontario, Canada) was listed in 1850, as a millwright, in Windsor, VT; in 1860, as a millwright, in Northfield, Washington Co., VT; in 1870, as an engineer, in Lebanon, Grafton Co., MA. Examples: on a 14 3/16" beech transitional jack plane with a double-iron, a 5/16" applied rosewood sole and handle, and bronze frog; and a similar unhandled smoothing plane. The molder which supplies the wedge is also imprinted with the location **SHREWSBURY**. The planes were made sometime after 1867. (see *Patented Transitional & Metallic Planes in America - Vol. II*, p. 193, by Roger K. Smith). ****

V. RUSSELL
Examples: on a 9 11/2"x 5/8" astragal bead; and a complex molder, both 8 7/8" beech with round chamfers, possibly from New England, ca. 1830. **UR**

W. RUSSELL
Believed to be **William Russell** (b. Oct. 1, 1767 in Middlesex Co., CT, d. Sep. 1, 1838 in Middletown, Middlesex Co., CT) who was a cabinetmaker and chairmaker, in Middletown, from 1800-23. **William Russell** was also part of **Russell & Barnes**, (date unknown); **Plum & Russell**, from 1799-1800; and **Russell & Wilcox**, from 1800-01. Examples: on 9 3/8"-9 1/2" beech molders; one birch, two with boxing; and a grooving plane with a riveted skate, all with flat chamfers, ca. 1800. ****

J. A. RUST

Example: on a 9 3/8" birch complex molder with flat chamfers, ca. 1800. **UR**

Q RUST

Example: on a 9 3/8" birch hollow with small flat chamfers, ca. 1790. **UR**

ARTHUR E. RUST
Arthur E. Rust (b. 1863 in NY, d. Feb. 17, 1937 in Pine Meadow, CT) was the son of **Solon R. Rust** and a planemaker, serving his apprenticeship under his father at the **Chapin Factory**, in Pine Meadow. In 1880, **Arthur Rust** was a wood turner in New Hartford, Litchfield Co., CT; in 1900, as a mechanist, in New Hartford; in 1906, as removed to Terryville, Plainville, CT; in 1907, as a foreman with **JHS & Son** in Litchfield Co., CT. From 1930-36, he was a foreman with **ELNG Co.**, clock shop, in Plainville, Bristol Co., CT. **No imprint has been reported.**

SOLON RUST
Solon Ralzeman Rust (b. Sep. 7, 1832, d. 1908 in New Hartford, Litchfield Co., CT) of Pine Meadow, CT, apprenticed as a planemaker at the **H. Chapin Union Factory**, in Pine Meadow. In 1864, he supervised manufacture of plow planes. **E. M. Chapin** and **Solon Rust** were granted Patent No. 76,051, on Mar. 31, 1868, for the self-adjusting plow plane. Made in beech, applewood, boxwood, and rosewood, listed in **E. Chapin's** catalog, from 1875-97; and in the **Sargent & Co.** catalog, in 1877. Nine subsequent patents, relating to metallic planes, were granted to **Solon Rust** or jointly with his son, **Arthur E. Rust**. (see **Standard Rule Co.**) The A imprint, with hand stamped letters, is on a patented plow plane also imprinted with **UNION FACTORY/ H. CHAPIN**. The B imprint is on an applewood closed toted adj. plow with **6** on the bed of the throat. The B imprint was also found, struck 3 times in a triangle, on the toe of an unfinished plane body in **Solon Rust's** personal tool chest, found by **Ken Roberts**.
A & B ****

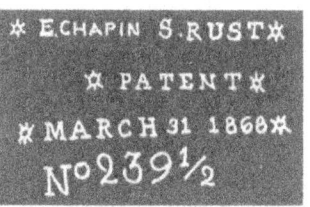

M. RUTH
Example: on a 10 1/2" beech round with an **I. Sleeper** style wedge with large flat chamfers mostly on the side, possible from Newburyport, MA, ca. 1790. **UR**

RYAN & BRO.
Daniel Ryan (b. 1819 from Ireland, d. Nov. 29, 1897) arrived in 1836, and was naturalized on Mar. 14, 1871. The firm was a hardware dealer, in Alton, IL, in 1858 only, succeeding **Platt & Ryan** who were active from 1853-58. It is believed he was part of **Dant & Ryan**, from 1858-1910. ***

R. S. RYON
Example: on three molders, ca. 1850. **UR**

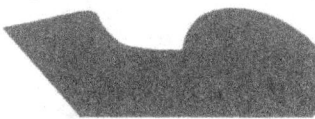

J. D. S/ OHIO

Example: on a 22 1/8" fore plane with a closed tote. The iron is marked: **EAGLE WORKS, WATERVILLE, NY**. The plane was found in WV. ********

L.S

Example: on a birch skew rabbet with flat chamfers and a relieved wedge, ca. 1800. **UR**

NS

Possibly **Rev. Nathan Stone** (b. Sep. 30, 1737 in Southborough, Worcester Co., MA, d. Apr. 26, 1804, Dennis, Barnstable Co., MA) or his son **Nathan Stone** (b. Jun. 10, 1766 in Yarmouth, Barnstable Co., MA, d. Dec. 28, 1839 in Dennis). Examples: on a 10"x 5/8" birch bead with flat chamfers, flutes and the relieved wedge, found in the **Nathan Stone** homestead, Dennis, MA; and a 9 1/2" beech quarter round molder with flat chamfers, ca. late 18c. **UR**

S. D. & F. CO.

Example: branded into the side of a 10" birch large round made by **JO (triple dot) Fuller**. **No imprint is available**.

S. H. A. & CO.

Example: on the heel of a plane made by **Taber Plane Co.**, in New Bedford, MA. **UR**

S. P. & A.

Example: on a block plane with an **Ohio Tool Co.** iron. **UR**

S. P. & CO.

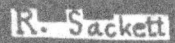

Example: on a block plane with an **Ohio Tool Co.** iron. **UR**

R. Sackett

Example: on a 9 1/2"x 1/4" birch round with flat chamfers and flutes, ca. early 19c. **UR**

E. SAFFORD

Elias Safford (b. Apr. 30, 1776 in Windsor, Berkshire Co., MA, d. Nov. 19, 1861 in Medina, Orleans Co., NY) appeared in the Albany, NY, directories, from 1813-21; and before as a toolmaker and planemaker. He was married to **Rebeca Shaw** on Jan. 5, 1801, in Sturbridge, Worcester Co., MA. The A1 imprint is the same die as the A imprint, but after the notch was filed over the **OR**. Example: the A imprint is on a short carriagemaker's "T" rabbet; and a 9 1/2" beech size **17** hollow with heavy round chamfers. The A1 imprint is on several 9 1/2" beech hollows & rounds with size numbers on the heels, and a round with the earlier **3/4** size, all with heavy round chamfers. **B & B1 *; A **; A1 *******

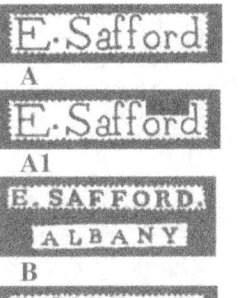

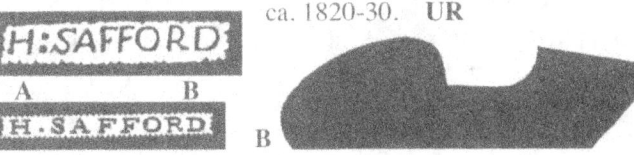

H. SAFFORD

Example: on a 9 3/8" beech round with round chamfers, ca. 1820-30. **UR**

N: SAFFORD

Example: on a 9 3/8" birch round with flat chamfers, ca. 1800. **UR**

P. SAFFORD

Example: on a 9 1/8"x 1/8" full boxed bead with a relieved wedge and flat chamfers, ca. 1800. **UR**

S. G. SAFFORD

Example: on a 9 7/16" beech table hollow with shallow round chamfers, ca. 1830-40. **UR**

I S/ I. SALLABANK

Example: on a 9 1/4" beech square rabbet with heavy round chamfers, ca. 1820. **UR**

B. SALMON

Example: on a 9 1/2" beech skew rabbet with round chamfers, found near Victor, NY, ca. 1820. **UR**

J K SALMON
Example: on a skew filletster; and a double-blade fixed sash, both 9 3/8" beech with heavy round chamfers, ca. 1820. **UR**

D. SALSBERY
Duty Salsbery (b. ca. 1766 in Smithfield, RI, d. Jan. 12, 1859 in Burrillville, RI) was a house carpenter, housewright, millwright and farmer. He and his son-in-law, **Thomas Slack**, erected and operated the first woolen mill at Pascoag, a village in Burrillville, RI. He lived in Glocester, RI, unit 1806, when the town boundary was changed and he became a resident of Burrillville. Examples: on a 9 3/4" birch ogee molder with flat chamfers; and an apple wood plow plane, both with the A wedge; a 10 1/8" birch complex molder, with the B relieved wedge and shallow flat chamfers; and a 13" birch panel raising plane with slightly round chamfers, ca. 1790-1810. *****

A. SAMPSON
Abel Sampson (b. Aug. 24, 1790 in Turner, ME, d. 1883 in Portland, ME) was a joiner, tool maker, and planemaker, in Portland, ME, from 1823-37. **Sampson** dictated an autobiography, in 1847, a copy of which is in the Bineky Rare Book Library at Yale University. In 1803-08, he was apprenticed to a house joiner. Several times between 1808-20 he went to sea and endured a seafaring life, being boarded and taken prisoner, forced to work on a slave ship, bringing Negroes from Africa to the U. S. He was captured and held prisoner by Africans, suffered smallpox, typhoid, and yellow fever. During the War of 1812, he was a privateer and involved in the capture of 23 ships. In 1814, he worked as a joiner, in New York City. In 1816, **Sampson** apprenticed to a planemaker in Bristol, England, for six months, at age 25. He was again in New York City, in 1817-18. On Dec. 7, 1818, **Abel** married **Sally (Sarah) Merrill**, in Portland, ME. He left the sea in June 1820. He was first listed in the Portland directories, as a toolmaker, from 1820-46. In 1823, he bought a house and shop that was burned in the great Portland fire of June 1825. In 1823, several men were in his employment, as were two apprentices. It is believed that **Joseph Bradford**, age 15 in 1823, may have been **Sampson's** apprentice. In 1846, **Sampson** relocated to Lawrence, MA, where he worked as a machinist. He is again listed in Portland, in 1850, as a machinist; in 1869, as a joiner; in 1870, as a retired joiner; in 1871, as a carpenter; in 1873, as a mechanic; and in 1874, as a furniture repairer. Examples: molders are 9 1/2" beech with round chamfers, ca. 1820. (see **Abel Sampson, Maine Privateer Turned Planemaker**, by Dale Butterworth and Bennett Blumenburg, *The Chronicle*, June 1992) **A & A1 ****

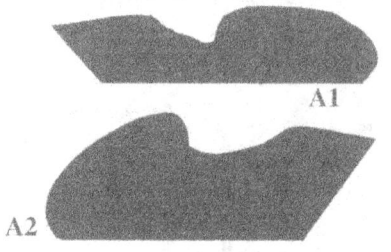

L. S/ L. SAMPSON
Luther Sampson (b. Mar. 25, 1760 in Duxbury, MA, d. Aug. 31, 1847 in Readfield, ME) was one of nine children, the son of **Paul Sampson**, a master house builder and the builder of several meeting houses in the Marshfield/ Duxbury area. The family relocated to Marshfield, MA, in 1764. **Luther** was a housewright and shop joiner, in Marshfield and Pembroke. **Luther**, and his father **Paul**, responded to the alarm of April 19, 1775, at Marshfield; no encounter occurred, as the Red Coats had withdrawn. On Jan. 10, 1776, **Luther**, not yet 16, enlisted as a Private in Capt. Thomas Turner's Militia Co., marching to alarms in Dorchester Heights, serving one month. On May 28, 1776, **Luther** again enlisted in Turner's Co. and fought in the battle of Long Island, NY, in Aug. 1776. In the winter of 1776-77, he was encamped at Trenton and Princeton, NJ. In Apr. 1777, **Luther**, under Capt. Amos Turner, marched to Tiverton, RI, serving 2 months, 6 days. He served from Sep. 28 to Oct. 31, 1777, on a secret expedition in RI. From July 1780 to Jan. 8, 1781, **Luther** served in the Continental Army at Camp Totoway in West Point, NY. Upon discharge, **Luther** received a pension and unspecified "land grant". This was common as the new Continental Government did not have the "cash" to pay its debts. On Aug. 28, 1783, **Luther** married **Abigail Ford**, in Pembroke, MA. Records list **Luther**, as a house wright. In 1785, Luther and his family moved to Duxbury, MA, purchasing the Blanie Philips homestead, listing his occupation as shop joiner. **Luther** built a 470 sq. ft. (16'x 29.5') shop with the date **1789** painted on a ceiling beam. The first floor rooms in the, ca. 1735, cape were finished in different high style Federal period architecture of the highest quality craftsmanship. It is believed that these rooms were used to show prospective clients the latest "federal period embellishments" and showcase his skills as a master shop joiner. In 1794, **Luther** suffered a severe back injury preventing him for continuing his trade. In 1795, **Luther** sold his house and shop business and returned to his father's farm in Marshfield. Three years later, in 1798, **Luther** claimed as his "government grant", a 200 acre parcel in Kents Hill in Readfield, ME. In 1821, **Sampson** founded the "Readfield Religious and Charitable Society", on 100 acres of his land. This became the Kents Hill School. The full name stamp **.SAMPSON** with the **L** removed is in the possession of a descendant in Readfield, ME. The initial imprint **LS** has a similar "arrowhead" touch marks as on **Jo, Fuller** planes. **Sampson** price-marked his planes behind the wedge slot, in shillings and pence before 1792 then in cents. Examples: a 9 1/2" **Jo, Fuller** plane has been reported with the **LS** imprint. **Luther Sampson's** planes are 10" birch with relieved wedges and heavy flat chamfers. Those with **LS** are the earliest with a 1/4" round mold cut in the shoulder on the right side; and a separate flute cut below the chamfer stop. The **L. SAMPSON** examples are ca. 1780-1800. **B ***; A *******

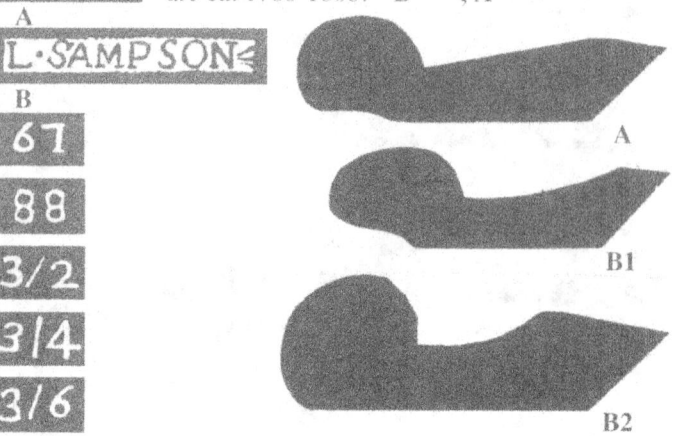

W. G. S./ W. G. SAMPSON

Example: on a 9 3/16" beech small unboxed bead with the imprint on toe and heel, and tight round chamfers, found in MA, ca. 1830. **UR**

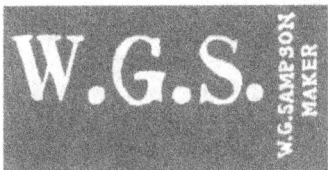

JER. SAMSON

Probably **Jeremiah Samson** (b. Dec. 15, 1755 in Plympton, MA, d. Sept. 23, 1830 at Kingston, MA) who spent most of his life working as a housewright, in Kingston, MA, from 1785-1830. **Jeremiah** called himself a housewright in his will. He was the brother of **Moses Sampson**. **Jeremiah** was apprenticed, in 1772, to **Simeon Doggett** of Middleboro, MA. On Feb. 5, 1793, **Jeremiah Samson**, of Kingston, MA, was appointed to a committee to build a new meeting house. Examples: several molding planes are 9 1/2" beech, some boxed, with flat chamfers and the B wedge. Other examples appear to be earlier, including a 10 1/16" cherry reeding plane with a relieved A wedge. The B imprint is on a 13" birch crown molder with an offset pegged tote, round top iron & wedge, and shallow flat chamfers.
A****; B*****

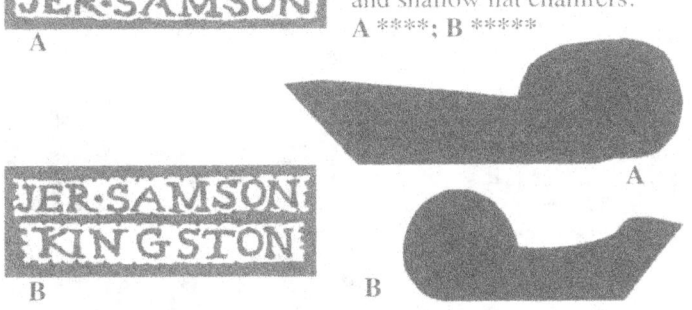

MOSES SAMSON

Moses Samson (b. May 30, 1751 in Plympton, MA, d. 1811) was the brother of **Jeremiah Samson**. Moses was apprenticed, on Dec. 12, 1769, to **Simeon Doggett** of Middleboro, MA. On Aug. 29, 1772, **Moses** married in Middleboro. **Moses** enlisted as a Private in Capt. Isaac Wood's, 2nd. Middleboro Co. of minute-men which marched in response to the alarm of April 19, 1775 to Marshfield, MA, serving, 3 days. **Moses** again enlisted as a Corporeal in Capt. Isaac Wood's Co., Col. Theophilus Cotton's Regt., on May 9, 1775, serving 3 months. **No imprint has been reported**.

S. SAMSON

Example: on a 7 1/8" coffin smoother with a single **James Cam** iron and heavy round chamfers, ca. 1820. **UR**

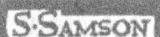

SAMPSON & HERSE

Sampson & Herse probably a hardware dealer, in Portland, ME, ca. 19c. **UR**

HY. SAN

Example: on a 12 7/8" beech wedge arm adj. fenced grooving plane with a riveted skate and flat chamfers, found in rural southeastern PA, ca. 1800. **UR**

SANBORN

Example: on a 10 1/2" birch square rabbet with a York pitch and small flat chamfers, ca. 1790. **UR**

D. P. SANBORN

David Page Sanborn (b. Feb. 8, 1810 in Belknap, Sanbornton, NH, d. March 1, 1871 in Littleton, Grafton, NH) married **Naomi Hughes Dow**, the daughter of **James Dow**, on Oct. 12, 1831; and **David** may have apprenticed under **James Dow**. **Sanborn** was listed, as a planemaker, in Littleton, NH, before 1840. He was a partner in **Sanborn & Gouch**, Worcester, MA, from 1845-48, with his brother in law **Franklin J. Gouch**. Based on the D imprint, he made planes, in Worcester under his own name; in ca. 1850, he returned to Littleton where he continued plane making, until 1871. The 1850 industrial census of Littleton listed **David P. Sanborn**, as a planemaker, with one employee, producing 220 planes worth $450. The 1860 industrial census listed **David P. Sanborn**, as a maker of planes, churns and other woodwork with two hands, producing 240 planes worth $340. The other hand may have been **Minot Weeks** (b. 1841, d. 1873) who married **David's** daughter **Ellen Josephine Sanborn**, on Oct. 23, 1866. By 1866, with his son, **Francis Davidson Sanborn** (b. 1834, d. 1880), he made planes as **D. P. & F. D. Sanborn**. By 1869, he was a part of **Sanborn & Weeks** with his son-in-law **Minot Weeks**. The 1870 industrial census listed **David P. Sanborn**, as a planemaker producing 250 planes worth $800. In the same 1870 census, **Sanborn & Weeks** was listed under products as making churns, washing machines and stair railings, but no planes. After **David P. Sanborn's** death in 1871 and **Minot Weeks'** death in 1873, **Francis D. Sanborn** continued to make all kinds of woodenware, including rules and tool handles, but no longer advertised planes. **David P. Sanborn** was one of a few American planemakers who made crown molders with two single irons. In a letter dated Sept. 5, 1866, he quoted prices on bench, fore, and other planes. (see *American Measuring Gauges*, by Milton H. Bacheller, Jr.) A1*; A, B, B1 & C **; A2, D & E ***

E. SANBORN

This imprint appears to be the same as **SANBORN** before the initial E was removed. Example: on a 9 15/16" birch ogee molder with flat chamfers and **E. Chase** is on the heel, ca. 1790. **UR**

J. A. J. F. SANBORN
J. A. J. F. Sanborn with **MAKER**. Example: on a 10 7/16" rabbet with the dated **1857**. UR

O. L. SANBORN
Example: on a 10 5/8" closed handle razee coffin smoother. UR

SANBORN & GOUCH
A partnership of **David P. Sanborn** and **Franklin J. Gouch**, brothers-in-law, who made planes in Worcester, MA, from 1845-48. In 1848, **David P. Sanborn** returned to Littleton, NH and **F. J. Gouch** remained in Worcester. Example: the B imprint is on a boxed filletster with boxwood screw-arms & rosewood nuts. **A & B *****

SANBORN & WEEKS
A partnership of **David Page Sanborn**, **Francis Davidson Sanborn** (b. Oct. 22, 1834 in Grafton, NH, d. 1880 in Bethlehem, Grafton, NH), his son, and **Minot Weeks** (d. Sep. 22, 1873 in Littleton, Grafton, NH), his son-in-law. In 1860, **Francis** was listed, as a house carpenter, in Littleton. In Sep. 19, 1862, **Francis** enlisted as Sergeant, Co. D, NH 13th. Infantry Reg., mustered out Jun. 21, 1865. **Sanborn & Weeks** made planes, log calipers, and board rules, in Littleton, NH, from 1869-73. They also made butter churns, washing machines, and patent models; in 1870, **Francis** was listed, as a wood turner, in Littleton; in 1880, as a farmer in Bethlehem, Grafton, NH. **No imprint has been reported.**

Jn SANDER
Example: on a 10" beech narrow round with round chamfers, ca. 1800-10. UR

H. M. SANDERS & CO.
H. M. Sanders & Co. was a hardware dealer in Boston, MA, from 1892-1973. *****

J. SANDERSON/ J. SANDERSON & CO./ J. E. SANDERSON
Jonathan E. Sanderson (**John**) (b. Mar. 23, 1815 in Franklin, MA, d. after 1870 Erie Co., NY) lived with **Truman Nutting**, in Amherst, MA, in 1844. According to James Smith's *Families of Amherst, 1728-1850*, **John Sanderson** was a "peddler for tools owned by **J. E. Sanderson**'s mills of South Worthington, in Dec. 1848." He was listed in 1850, as a toolmaker in Amherst. He moved to Concord, Erie Co., NY, in 1852, and made planes, from 1852-73. The 1855, Concord, Erie Co., NY census listed him as employing 2 men to produce "350 sets" of planes worth $2000 each year. In 1860-70, **John** was listed, as a planemaker, in Concord, Erie Co., NY. He reported his annual production at $800. In 1874, he became a partner in **Sanderson & Warren**, located possibly in the Buffalo, NY, area.
A & A1 *; B, C, D & D1 *****

R. SANDERSON
Example: on a 9 1/2" beech single-boxed complex molder with flat chamfers; and a 26 3/16" birch jointer with round chamfers, ca. 1800-20. UR

A. SANDI
Examples: on a 9 1/2" astragal; a complex molder; and a 32" joiner with an offset tote, all beech with flat chamfers, found in southeastern PA, ca. 1800-10. **A & A1: UR**

J. G. SANDKUHL.
John G. Sandkuhl (b. 1827 in Germany, d. Oct. 6, 1883) dealt in hardware and made planes in Poughkeepsie, NY, from 1850-83. The 1860 census listed one employee producing $675 worth of planes. From 1862-70, he was listed, as a planemaker, at 204 Main St, Poughkeepsie. In 1881, he advertised in the Poughkeepsie directory as a mechanic who made "Coopers tools, saws, files, molding irons, pattern making, models made for patents", established in 1850. In 1884, he was a "plane mfr." at 271 Main St., Poughkeepsie.
A, B, B1 & C **

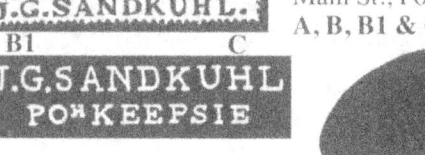
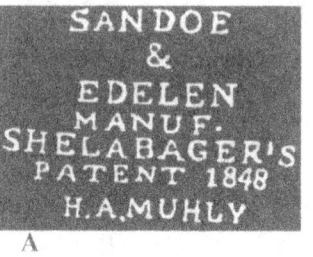

SANDOE & EDELEN
Sandoe & Edelen manufactured planes in Philadelphia, PA, including a beech smoothing plane, Patent No. 5486, on March 28, 1848, by **Benjamin F. Shelabarger** of Mifflintown, PA. This patent provided a cap iron made to close the plane's throat as the stock was worn. Examples were exhibited in the Franklin Institute Fairs of

 1849 & 50. **A & B** ****

B

JOHN. SANDS
Example: on a 10" complex molder with slight flat chamfers, probably from PA. ca. 1790-1800. **UR**

SANDUSKY TOOL CO.
The **Sandusky Tool Co.** located in Sandusky, OH, was organized in 1869 and continued making planes into the 1920's, under its label and private brands. It was one of the largest planemakers in this country, also producing plane irons for itself and others. The company issued printed catalogs and distributed its products throughout the country. After a series of unprofitable years and a destructive tornado, the company was essentially shut down in 1925. At the end **Sandusky Tool Co.** employed 100 workers and struggled unsuccessfully to market wooden planes, plane irons, wooden clamps, and hand hoes, all of which had been largely supplanted by newer, cheaper, or improved products. They were bought by the **American Fork & Hoe Co.**, in 1926. The B2 imprint however bears a **1928** date. While most of the imprints that were used are commonly found, certain types of **Sandusky** planes are extremely rare such as the self-regulating center wheel plow, ca. 1877, listed as No. 140, based on Patent No. 97,328, of Nov. 30, 1869, by **Harmon Vanbuskirk**, Vienna, MI. Other patented planes they made include one patented by **Cyrus Kinney**, Windsor, ON, ca. 1855; and two patented by Ellis H. Morris, Canton, OH, on Nov. 8, 1870 and Mar. 21, 1871.
A, A1, B, B1, C, E, F, G & H: **FF**; C1, E1 & I *; D & B2 ***

C1

C2

 H

I

E. SANFORD & CO.
E. Sanford Co. was a hardware dealer in Des Moines, IA, active from 1857-71. Ft. Demoin became Des Moines in 1857. ****

G. W. SANFORD
Example: a 9 1/2" black walnut plane, possibly a mother plane. ca. 19c. **UR**

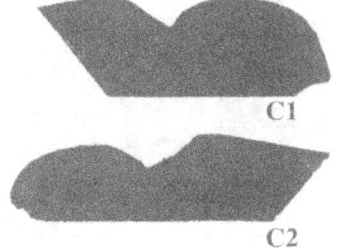

JOSEPH SANFORD JR
Joseph Sanford Jr. (b. Oct. 25, 1775, d. Oct. 13, 1841) was the son of **Joseph Sanford Sr.** a cabinetmaker. Examples: the A imprint is on the toe of a 24 1/2" applewood jointer with a centered tote and flat chamfers. Behind the wedge is the A1 imprint. Also reported on a marking gauge marked **WILLIAM BATTEY/ WICKFORD 1822** is: **UR**

JOSEPH SANFORD JUNR
MAKER NEWPORT R ISLAND

Another example is a 2 foot, 2 fold boxwood rule made by **Kutz** and imprinted: **UR**
JOSEPH SANFORD/ APRIL 1830

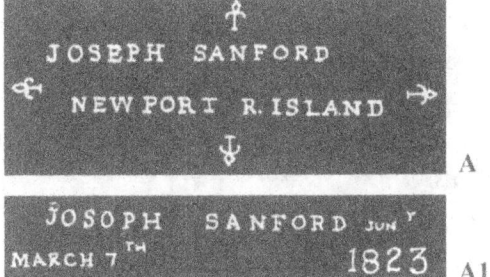

WC. SANFORD
Example: on a 9 3/4" beech double-iron and wedge sash with round chamfers, ca. early 19c. **UR**

L. SANFORDS
Levi Sanford of East Solon, NY, was issued Patent No. 3,838, on Nov. 26, 1844, providing a means of holding and adjusting the cutter with an adjusting screw that feeds into a cast steel bed plate rabbeted into the plane's throat. One example is also imprinted **N. WRIGHT/ KEENE** of whom nothing is presently known. The example shown in *Patented and Transitional Planes in America, Vol. 1*, p. 17, by Roger K. Smith, appears on a jointer imprinted **A. & E. Baldwin/ New York** that was active from 1830-41. **A. & E. Baldwin** may not have used the patent, the plane was probably modified later. **UR**

J. SANGER
Examples: on a smoothing plane, and on a bench plane made by **Gardner & Murdock**. UR

C. SAPP
Conrad Sapp (b. Dec. 1, 1812 in Portage Co., OH, d. Jul. 1903) was listed in 1850-60, as a carpenter, living in Ravenna, OH. A history of Portage Co., OH, mentions that he was apprenticed, as a planemaker, at age 21, and worked at the trade for 10 years. He may have trained under **Fitch Collins**. ***

G SARGEANT
Example: on a skew jack with an open tote and integral depth stop, ca. 1850. UR

D. SARGENT
Dana Sargent (b. Nov. 28, 1818 in Hudson, NH, d. Nov. 23, 1884 in Nashua, NH) may have learned plane making from **Cyrus Warren**. **Dana** married on Mar. 11, 1841, in Hudson, Hillsborough Co., NH. He worked, as a planemaker, in Nashua, NH, or nearby Hudson, ca. 1840; and then in Manchester, NH, where he was also in the hardware business as **Sargent & Cross**, during the 1840's. The company was a hardware and lumber dealer and made handspikes and serving mallets. He returned to Nashua, ca. 1860, where he became a merchant and later mayor of the city. In 1870-80, he was listed as lumber merchant in Nashua.

A, A1, A2, B & C ***

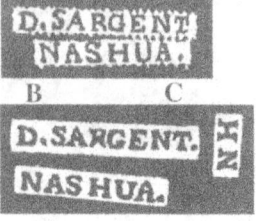
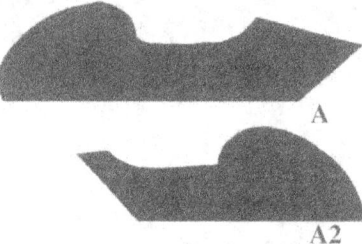

E + SARGENT
Example: on a ogee cornice plane with a 3" iron, and a 9 3/8" beech skew rabbet with flat chamfers, ca. 1800. UR

I. SARGENT
Example: on a 9 3/8" beech large hollow with an ash wedge and heavy flat chamfers, ca. 1810. UR

P. SARGENT
Philip Sargent (b. Oct. 24, 1790 in Bow, NH, d. 1858) made planes in Concord, NH. He was Married on Dec. 31, 1818, in Bow, NH. He came to Concord from Bow, before 1827, when he held the office as surveyor of timber. He was listed in the 1830 directory, as a house carpenter; in 1834, as a joiner; and between 1844-58, as a plane maker. He produced a number of coachmaker's planes, reflecting Concord's importance as a coach making center.

A **; B, B1 & B2 ***

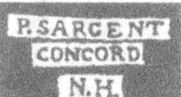
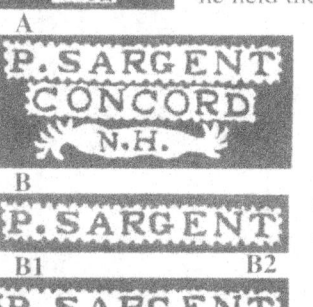

SARGENT & CO.
One of the oldest, and largest, hardware manufacturers and distributors in the country. **Sargent & Co.** was founded, in 1858, in New York, by the merger of three companies run by different **Sargent** brothers with **Joseph Bradford Sargent** as president. The family business started with **Joseph Denny Sargent** (b. Jan. 7, 1787 in Worcester, MA, d. May 24, 1849 in Leicester, Worcester Co.) who started **J. D. Sargent & Co.** who manufactured hand cards, used to straighten cotton & wool fibers prior to the spinning process in textile mills. **Joseph Denny Sargent** had four sons, **Joseph Bradford Sargent**, **Henry Sargent**, **George Sargent**, and **Edward Sargent**. **Joseph Bradford Sargent** (b. Dec. 14, 1822 in Leicester, MA, d. Jul. 15, 1907 in New Haven, CT) started as a factory worker at 16; worked in a dry goods business, in Boston, MA; became a partner with his brother **Harry Sargent** in a GA general store; and took over his father's business **J. D. Sargent & Co.**, in 1849. He became a sales agent for **Peck & Walter Co.** of New Britain, CT. In 1852, he took over management. In 1856, after the national business panic of 1857, he renamed the firm **J. B. Sargent & Co.** In 1864, **J. B. Sargent** relocated to New Haven, CT, in a state-of-the-art manufacturing plant with elevators, running water and flush toilets. In Oct. 1864, the business was incorporated as **Sargent & Co.** In 1871, **Sargent & Co.** became agent for **H. Chapin's Union Factory** line of rules and wooden planes. Later, they added a **Sandusky Tool Co.** line. First the **Sandusky** planes were all under the **Sandusky** imprint and later under the **Sargent** A & A1 imprints, which were derived from the **Sandusky** C imprint. In the Mar. 1877 catalog, **Sargent & Co.** listed **Leonard Bailey**'s Victor Planes. In the 1870's, **Sargent & Co.** occupied 16 acres of floor space, employing 1,700 workers earning 15 cents an hr. for 10 hr. per day and 6 days a week. In 1884, **Sargent & Co.** began manufacture of planes with 7 sizes of bench planes and 13 block planes. In 1894, **Sargent & Co.** added a line of wood bottom transitional planes using its patented lateral adjustment feature. In 1897, they used the **Page** patent lever cap. In 1906, **Shaw**'s patent frog adjustment. In 1907, after the death of **J. B. Sargent**, **George Sargent** took over as president of **Sargent & Co.** and started marketing with the slogan "Very Best Made", V-B-M, which was used from 1908-1918. In 1927, the brand name **HERCULES** was introduced, as a low price plane without polish, fit or finish and was used into the 1950's. **Sargent & Co.** manufactured planes for **Sears, Roebuck & Co.** under the **Craftsman** & **Dunlap** brands. By 1964, plane production ceased. In May 1967, **Sargent & Co.** was bought out by

Walter Kiddle & Co. and renamed **Sargent Manufacturing Co.**. **George Sargent** (b. Oct. 29, 1828 in Leicester, MA, d. 1917 in New Haven, CT) was a Harvard graduate, in 1853. In 1910, he was listed, as a hardware merchant, in NY. **Henry Sargent** (b. Nov. 7, 1821 in Leicester, Worcester Co., MA, d. Apr. 27, 1858 in Worcester, MA) was listed in 1850, as a physician, in Worcester. **Edward Sargent** (b. Mar 25, 1832 in Leicester, Worcester Co., MA, d. Jan 29, 1883 in Leicester, MA) was listed in 1880, as "hardware manuf.", in Leicester, MA. Examples: There is an example of a **Sandusky Tool Co.** tongue plane overstamped by **Sargent & Co.** The B imprint is on a 8 1/8" long beech transitional smoothing plane. The C imprint with **V-B-M (Very-Best-Made)** is on a 15" beech transitional jack plane. **A, B & C: FF; A1 ***

S: SATTERLE
Example: on a hollow struck twice on the toe; and a round, both 9 5/8" birch with heavy flat chamfers ending in a long lamb's tongue, ca. 1770-90. **A & B: ****

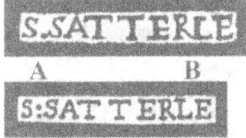

WM. R. SATTERLY
Example: on a 9 5/16" beech round with size **10** on the heel and small flat chamfers, ca. 1800. **UR**

JOHN SAUNDERSOD
John Saundersod was listed in the 1839-40 Cincinnati, OH, directory, as a planemaker. Possibly the same person as **John Sunsersond** listed in 1836-37. **No imprint has been reported**.

CHRISTIAN SAUNDERSOUS
Christian Saundersous was listed in the 1834 Cincinnati, OH, directory, as a planemaker. **No imprint has been reported**.

D. SAVAGE
Example: on a 9 5/16" beech door panel groove with shallow round chamfers, found in VT, ca. 1800-30. **UR**

SAVAGE & CARTER
Savage & Carter was listed as making carpenter tools and wood planes, in Middletown, CT, in 1849. Savage was also spelled **Sewage**. **No imprint has been reported**.

GEORGE SAVILLE
The Massachusetts Register and Business Directory of 1874 listed **George Saville** as a hardware dealer. Example: on a 16" beech razee jack made by **P. A. Gladwin & Co.** with a **Moulson Bros.** iron with a shield-shaped ink stamp on the top of toe reading: ****

GEORGE SAVILLE' HARDWARE DEALER
ELM STREET
GLOUCESTER
MASS.

SAWHEAG WORKS
Sawheag Works made planes and sold tools and hardware, in Wallingford, CT, in 1850. **Joel Fenn** was agent. The 1850 Industrial census showed 10 employees producing $15,000 worth of planes. Since the arrow, name, and location dies are separate, various combinations and placements are found, as shown in imprint A and A1. **A, A1 & A2 ***

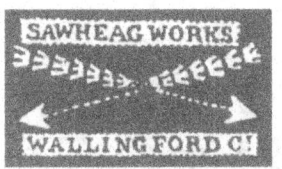
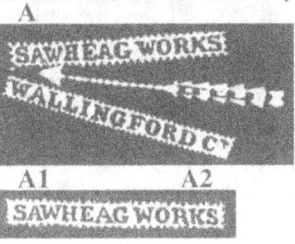
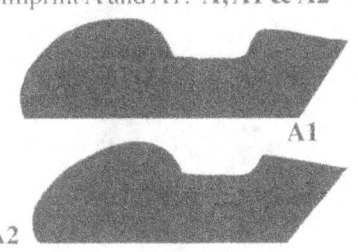

J. SAWIN
Jonathan Sawin (b. Mar. 30, 1802 in Windhall, Bennington Co., VT, d. May 17, 1871 in Westminster, Worcester, MA) Jonathan, in 1860-70, was a carpenter, in Westminster. Example: on a 9 3/8" applewood 1 1/4" complex molder with ivory boxing; a 7 5/8" birch compass smooth with round chamfers, and a beech jointer, ca. 1820. **UR**

JEREMIAH SAWSON
Jeremiah Sawson was apprenticed to **Simeon Doggett** of Middleboro, MA, on Apr. 16, 1772. Jeremiah was listed, as a joiner/ housewright, in Plympton, Kingston, MA. **No imprint has been reported**.

J. SAWYER
John Sawyer (b. Apr. 4, 1823 in Cayuga Co., NY, d. Aug. 22, 1894 in Moravia, NY) of Moravia, was granted Patent No. 60,265, on Dec. 4, 1866, for a miter plane, no example of which is known. The 1850 Cayuga Co. census listed him, as living in Sempronius (the next town east of Moravia), as a carpenter and joiner. The 1855 census lists him living in Moravia, and a mechanic. The 1865 census shows him, as a carpenter. He was noted in local histories as having been an excellent craftsman, carpenter, and builder, active in the 1850-60's, who built several structures in Moravia. Examples: on bench planes, one toted boxwood plow plane, two hollows, and a 9 1/2" ogee complex molder. **A & A1 ****

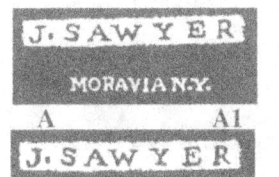

J. P. SAWYER
Example: on a 9 13/16" beech narrow nosing plane, found in ME; and a 9 3/4" beech molder with round chamfers, ca. 1820. **UR**

S. SAWYER
Example: on a wheelwright's jarvis with a double-iron marked **W. HOVEY** who was a plane iron maker in Boston, MA, from 1829-33. **No imprint is available.**

A. SAYLES
Ahab Sayles (b. Oct. 17, 1760 in Glocester, RI, d. Apr. 17, 1849 in Glocester) is the brother of **Esek Sayles** and **Elisha Sayles** and the son of **Israel Sayles** (b. 1726 in Smithfield, RI, d. 1801 in Glocester, RI) a prosperous farmer and "a man highly skilled in mechanical work". Each of the three brothers is described in Glocester and Burrillville, RI land records as house carpenters. Example: from a group of ten molding planes 9 3/4"–9 7/8" including hollows, rounds, side beads, and a quarter round, all birch with relieved wedges and flat chamfers located in the collection at Old Sturbridge Village. Two of the planes also bear the imprint **H. Wetherel/ In Norton**. Possibly **Ahab Sayles** had a working relationship with, or apprenticed to **Henry Wetherel** or was an owner's imprint, ca. 1780. **No imprint is available.**

E, SAYLES
Esek Sayles (b. 1753, d. Jul. 31, 1824 in Burrillville, RI) or **Elisha Sayles** (b. Jul. 15, 1757, d. Jul. 4, 1845) were brothers of **Ahab Sayles**. Each of the three brothers is described in Glocester and Burrillvile, RI land records, as house carpenters. Burrillvile was formed, in 1806, from part of Glocester. Example: on a 9 11/16" birch round with flat chamfers, ending in a long lamb's tongue, a relieved wedge, and similar in style to **H. Wetherel** planes, and found in the Village of Chepachet, Town of Gloucester, RI. (see **Duty Salsbery** also a carpenter in Burrillville, RI) ca. 1780 *****

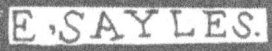

S. SAYRE
Examples: on a 9 7/8" beech complex molder struck twice on the toe with heavy round chamfers, a 9 3/4" dado with heavy round chamfers, and a 9 7/8" birch standing filletster, ca. 1820. **UR**

S. SAYRS.
Examples: on a double blade 9 1/2" beech molding plane with flat chamfers; and on a molder also marked **LAIRD**, ca. 1800. **UR**

E. F. SCAMMON
Example: on a 15 1/4" beech jack plane with double-iron, a centered tote, and heavy round chamfers, ca. 1810-20. **UR**

JA: SCH
Example: on a 9 7/8" molder; and a 10 3/4" bench style ogee molder with a slightly offset tote, both beech with heavy flat chamfers, possibly from PA, ca. 1800. **UR**

C. B. SCHAEFER & CO.
C. B. Schaefer & Co. consisted of **Charles B. Schaefer** (b. 1820 in Baltimore, MD, d. 1885 in Cincinnati, OH) and **Henry McKinnell** who made planes and edge tools and dealt in hardware in Cincinnati, OH, from 1850-52. It succeeded **McKinnell & Co.** and were succeeded by **Schaefer & Cobb**, in 1853-55. The store was located at 224 Main, and factory at w.s. of Lock bt. 5th. and 6th. **Charles** was also reported as part of **Underwood & Schaefer**, in 1854-57. In 1865, **Charles** was listed, as a salesman, in Cincinnati. **No imprint has been reported.**

SCHAEFER & COBB
Schaefer & Cobb manufactured planes, edge tools and dealt in hardware in Cincinnati, OH, from 1853-55. Located, in 1853, at 28 Pearl. In 1855, "tool manuf.", s.s. Lock bt. 5th. and 6th., Store at 224 Main. It consisted of **Charles B. Schaefer** and **Joseph E. Cobb** and succeeded **C. B. Schaefer & Co.** A, A1 & B *

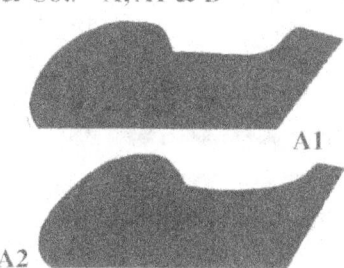

SCHANG & CO.
Schang & Co. probably was a Rochester, NY hardware dealer. Example: on a **D. R. Barton & Co.** size 12 hollow, ca. 1850 ****

I. SCHAUER
Probably **John Schauer** (also **Shower** in tax records) (b. 1776, d. 1834 at 58), who made planes in East Petersburg, PA, 5 miles NW of Lancaster, from 1820-43. In 1824, he sent **Oglesby & Pool**, a Harrisburg hardware dealers, who later became **Kelker & Co.**; then **Kelker & Bro.** a list of planes that he could provide:

sash gittics and ovlows @	$2.00
felisters @	1.37
screw arm plows with brass stops @	3.50
single iron foreplanes @	.80
dubble iron (foreplanes) @	1.20
beads and astragals	.45

He is believed to be related to **Joehanes Schauer** and **Nicklaus Schauer**. Examples: planes are 9 1/2" beech with both flat and round chamfers; on a 9 1/2" beech triple-lignum vitae boxed reed plane with tight round chamfers and also imprinted **S: Dyr**. ***

J. SCHAUER
Possibly **Joehanes Schauer** (b. 1800), a member of the Schauer family and related to **John Schauer** and **Nicklaus Schauer** who made planes in eastern PA. It is also possible that this incuse mark was made by **John Schauer** after 1840 when the use of **I** for **J** was becoming antiquated. ***

N. SCHAUER
Nicklaus Schauer (b. 1755, d. 1829) was an eastern PA, planemaker, ca. 1800. He was a member of the **Schauer** family and related to **John Schauer** and **Joehanes Schauer**. The **N. Shovar** and **N. Shoure** imprints are probably earlier imprints for **N. Schauer**, based on the stylistic similarities and probable location. Examples: on 9 5/8" beech molders with heavy flat chamfers; and a 14 1/8" x 4 3/4" beech crown molder with offset tote and heavy flat chamfers, ca. 1800. ***

E. SCHAUM
Elias Schaum (b. 1824 in Upper Tulpehocken, Berks Co., PA) Example: on a 10" fruitwood molder with shallow round chamfers, probably from PA, ca. 19c. **UR**

A. SCHIESLY
Examples: a pair of beech wedge-lock plank tongue & groove planes with flat chamfers (the tongue plane is 13", 1" longer than the groove), and a 9 1/2" complex molder with wide flat chamfers, possibly from eastern PA, ca. 1800. **UR**

P. A. SCHLAPP - AGT
Example: on a boxed hollow with an **Ohio Tool Co.** iron and **137** imprinted on the toe, the **Ohio Tool Co.** style number for a boxed table plane set. ****

F. E. SCHMIEDING & CO.
F. E. Schmieding & Co. was a retail and wholesale hardware dealer, in St. Louis, MO, from 1857-73. **Fredrick E. Schmieding** (b. Sep. 2, 1812 in Germany, d. Nov. 24, 1891 in St. Louis, MD) was also part of **Schmieding & Wulfing**, ca. 1850. **Schmieding & White** apparently coexisted with this company from 1867-73, with **F. Wiebusch** and **Fredrick A. Witte** principals of both companies. In 1866, **F. E. Schmieding & Co.** was listed with **Fredrick E. Schmieding, Frederick Wiebusch**, and **Frederick A Witte** dealers in American, English & German Hardware, at 161 Broadway, St. Louis, MO. **Fred Schmieding** had a hardware store, in his own name, from 1874-84. **A & A1** *

SCHMIEDING & WULFING
Schmieding & Wulfing, was a partnership of **Fredrick E. Schmieding** and **Wulfing**, as a hardware dealer, in St. Louis, MO, in 1850. Example: a beech grooving plane with size **3/4** on the heel. Appearance is ca. 1850. ***

H. SCHMITT
H. Schmitt is believed to have been a Newark, NJ, hardware dealer and/ or importer, ca. 1853. Example: on a **Joh. Weiss "Austria"** horned plane, two other horned planes, and a European fore plane. ***

JACOB. SCHMITT
Jacob Schmitt (b. ca. 1825, d. Aug. 1869) was a hardware dealer in Louisville, KY. Example: on a **72** hollow, the inventory number for the **Ohio Tool Co.** for hollows and rounds. ****

W. SCHMITT & CO.
W. Schmitt & Co. was a Newark, NJ hardware dealer in the 1850's. The imprint is similar to **H. Schmitt**. Example: is on the heel of a horned toothing plane with **AUSTRIA** on the toe and a Clamp insignia. ****

A: SCHNECKE
A: Schnecke probably is a hardware dealer. Example: on a 7 15/16" beech coffin smoothing plane. The plane has a **Sandusky Tool Co.** iron and **3** on the toe, the style number used by **Sandusky Tool Co.** for smoothing planes, ca. 19c. **UR**

F. W. SCHNEIDER
F. W. Schneider was a hardware dealer in New York City, ca. 1865. Examples: the A imprint is on the side of a plane made by **Sargent & Co.** and also on the wedge. The B imprint is on the wood portion of a transitional fore plane.
A, A1 & B ***

A. SCHNEIDER
A. Schneider is believed to have been a hardware dealer in Union Hill, NJ. Example: on the side of a handled plow, made by the **Sargent & Co./ USA/ 734** with a **Sandusky Tool Co.** style wedge, ca. 1880. ****

IA. SCHNEIDER
Example: on a wide beech hollow, a table joint plane with an iron by **G. Schorff**, and a birch chamfer plane with three crown imprints over the name, all 10" with heavy flat chamfers,

ca. 1800. ****

JACOB SCHOOL
Jacob School was listed as a planemaker, in Cincinnati, OH, in 1834, at Court bt. Race & Elm. **No imprint has been reported.**

M/ SCHOOLEY

Example: on a 9 1/2" beech small ogee molder with small flat chamfers, ca. 1800. **UR**

ROBERT SCHROEDER
Robert Schroeder was listed, as a planemaker, at 52 N. Eutaw St., Baltimore, MD, in 1860. **No imprint has been reported.**

D. SCHULTZ

D. Schultz with the location **MILWAUKEE** is on a 13 1/2" birch and hickory croze, ca. 19c. **UR**

W. SCHULTZ

Example: on a 9 5/8" complex molder with flat chamfers, possibly from PA, ca. 1800. **UR**

D. A. SCHUTTE
D. A. Schutte was a Chillicothe, OH, hardware dealer active from 1850-55. Chillicothe is 45 miles south of Columbus, OH. Example: the A1 imprint is on a hollow with an **Ohio Tool Co.** style number.
A & A1 **

N. SCHWERD
Example: on a 9 11/16"x 3/8" astragal, a 9 9/16" round with a **Newbould** iron, a panel raiser, and a plow, all beech with heavy flat chamfers, possibly from PA, ca. 1800. ****

SCHWING & McCARTY
Schwing & McCarty was a hardware company with an imprint on a **John Warren**, Louisville, 9 1/2" beech ogee and bead molder with flat chamfers on ends and wide round chamfers on top, ca. 19c. ****

SCIOTO WORKS
Scioto Works was a brand name used from 1893-1907 by the **Ohio Tool Co.** after its 1893 merger with the **Auburn Tool Co.**. It was believed to be used for a second-grade line of beech wood planes. It seems ironical that the phrase **EXTRA QUALITY**, as used on E imprint, be used to describe second-grade planes. The name may have originated from the fact that the **Ohio Tool Co.** was located near the Scioto River in Columbus, OH. The G imprint has in addition to **Scioto Works**, the imprint **MISSOURI PREMIUM**.
A & B: FF; C, C1 & C2 *;
E, F & G ****

I. SCOFIEM

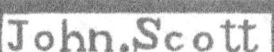

Example: on a 9 1/4" round. **UR**

C. SCOTT
Charles Scott (b. 1795 in Italy, d. Dec. 14, 1851 in Rochester, Plymouth Co., MA) was part of **Webb & Scott**, in Providence, RI, from 1816-22; and a cabinet maker and cabinet warehouse, from 1819-30, in Providence at 115 S. Main. An Ad placed in the *Providence Gazette*, on Aug. 28, 1822 reads "Useful and Ornamental Furniture, warranted for workmanship, style and stock to be equal to any that can be bought in Boston or New York." In 1850, **Charles Scott** was listed as a cabinet maker, in Rochester, Plymouth Co., MA. Example: on a 10 1/8" beech round with a relieved wedge, flat chamfers, found in western NY, ca. 1800-20. **UR**

JAMES SCOTT
James Scott (b. ca. 1836 in NY) was a planemaker; and a partner in **Crane & Scott** with **Samuel Gustin Crane**, in Rochester, NY, in 1866-67. He enlisted as a Private on Sep. 30, 1862 in Co. H, NY 13th. infantry Reg. He was mustered out on Oct. 2, 1862 at Rochester, NY. **No imprint has been reported.**

JOHN SCOTT
John Scott is possibly a planemaker and/or a tool dealer/ironmonger in the NY-NJ area. Example: on a 9 5/8" birch medium round, a 9 1/2" beech round, and a 7 1/2" applewood oar plane, all with flat chamfers. Also as an owner or dealer on a 10 1/8" beech complex molder with flat chamfers made by **Tho. Grant/ New York**, (1740-86), on a plane by **Eastburn**, (1802-26), and a **Loveage** plane (English 1735-51), ca. 1775-1815. ****

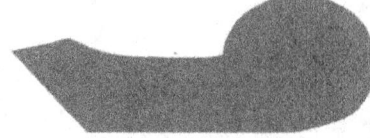

W. SCOTT
William Scott (b. ca. 1780-81 probably in Philadelphia, PA, d. May 27, 1857 in Allegheny, PA) was one of the earliest Pittsburgh, PA, planemakers probably learning plane making

in Philadelphia. He was identified as a planemaker as early as 1802 and in 1810 he was located on Front St. at the "sign of the hand saw and plane". He advertised on Feb. 16, 1810 in the *Pittsburgh Gazette*: "W. Scott carries on this plane making as usual. Orders will be thankfully received and duly attended to". By an Apr. 13, 1812 property purchase, he was listed, as a planemaker, in the 1813-26 city directories, located on Fourth Street between Wood & Market St. **James Swetman** and **William P. Hughes** worked for **Scott**, prior to 1818, when they went out on their own as **Swetman, Hughes & Co.**. In 1830, he moved from Pittsburgh City across the Allegheny River to "Allegheny Town", now known as Pittsburgh's North Side, where he was listed, in 1837, as "Plane Maker, AT."; giving rise to the B imprint. **William Evens** probably learned plane making from **William Scott**. In 1839, **W. Evens** was listed at the same address as **W. Scott**, in Allegheny. In 1843-50, **Scott** was listed clerk of the market in Allegheny. The earliest imprint C was reported from a wedge lock unhandled plow with riveted skate and a wood depth stop. Two molders with this imprint have interrupted lignum vitae wear strips. For more biographical information see *Planemakers of Western Pennsylvania and Environs*, by Charles W. Praine, Jr.
A **, B ***, C *****

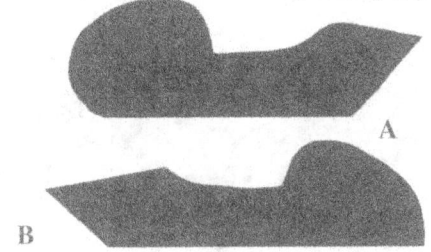

J. SCOVILL

John Scovill (b. Aug. 5, 1804 in Johnstown, Fulton Co., NY, d. Dec. 10, 1862 in Johnstown) was the son of **Lyman Scovill** and made planes in Johnstown, from 1827-30, when he joined the ministry. On Dec. 6, 1837, he was ordained as a Deacon at Trinity Church, New York City. On Oct. 16, 1838, he was ordained as a priest in the Protestant Episcopal Church at Greenville, NY. A ***

SCOVILL/ L. SCOVIL/ L. SCOVILL

Lyman Daniel Scovill (Scovil) (b. Mar. 5, 1781 in Granville, MA, d. July 25, 1840 at Johnstown, Fulton Co., NY) was the father of **J. Scovill**. He was a carpenter, builder, and planemaker in Johnstown. On Dec. 21, 1812, he was recorded as serving in the War of 1812 as a Private in Co. of Capt. Abraham Mattison, Reg. of Col. Daniel Davis. An 1837 statement of account, submitted by **Lyman Scovill** to **Lawrence Marcellus**, a carpenter, for planes made was signed as paid, on May 30, 1838, by **Scovill**, using two **L**'s in his signature. Also of interest is the fact that prices were still expressed in both English shillings and dollars:

1 Double Short Joiner	14/	$1.75
1 Double Smoothing Plain	9/	$1.13
1 Double Jack Plain	10/	$1.25
1 7/8 Ogee	14/	$1.75
1 1/2 Ogee	11/	$1.37

Even as late as 1838, the exchange rate of 12 1/2 was still the same as shown in the NY directory, of 1786. The C imprint may have been used by the father, son, or both.
A, A1 & C **; B ****

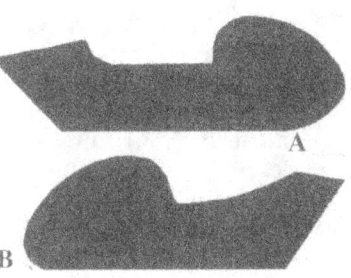

A. M. SEAMAN

Abram M. Seaman (b. ca. 1826 in RI, d. Jul. 25, 1892 in Ithaca, Tompkins Co., NY) was a carpenter and woodworker and made planes, in Ithaca, NY, from 1872-90. From 1850-70, he was listed, as a carpenter. In 1880, he was listed, as "plane mnfr.". By 1890, he was listed as **A. M. Seaman Novelty Works**, making billiard cues and wooden novelties. In 1892, he was again listed, as a plane maker, in Ithaca, NY. One smoother has both imprints. A & B **

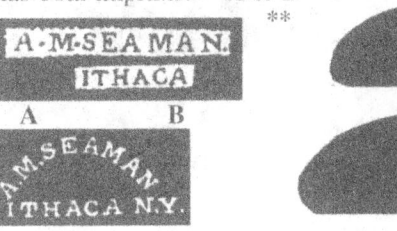

J. S/ J. SEARING

James Searing (b. Aug. 26, 1783 in Lyons, Somerset Co., NJ, d. Nov. 15, 1861 in Newark, Essex Co., NJ) was the father of **John D. Searing** (b. 1813 in Newark, NJ, d. Jan. 25, 1883 in Newark). They may have worked together and used the same imprint, in Newark, NJ, from 1821-49. **James** was one of the representatives of the planemakers, in the 1821 Fourth of July pageant, in Newark. The first city directory of 1835-36 lists only **John D. Searing**, as a planemaker. In the 1850 census **James** was listed, as a carpenter and **John D. Searing** was a sash and blindmaker. A & B *

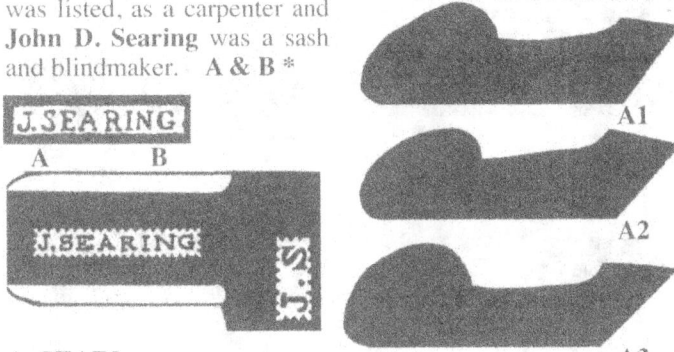

A. SEARL

Ashbel Searl (Searle) ran a hardware store in New York City, from 1849-53. During 1852-53, he occupied the premises just previously used by **Way & Sherman**. Example: on a 22" fore plane with a **Dwight & French** iron. ****

SEARS, ROEBUCK AND CO
MNFD FOR/ SEARS ROEBUCK & CO.

Sears, Roebuck & Co. was the largest retailing and mail order company in the country. It was founded by **Richard Warren Sears** (b. Dec. 7, 1863 in Stewartville, MN, d. Sep. 28, 1914 in Waukesha, WI) and **Alvah C. Roebuck** (b. Jan. 9, 1864 in Lafayette, IN, d. Jun. 18, 1948 in Evanston, IL). **Richard**'s father was a blacksmith and wagon maker. In 1880, **Richard Sears** was first employed as a telegraph operator in

North Branch, MN for the **Minnesota and St. Louis R. R**. In 1886, **Richard Sears** founded the **R. W. Sears Watch Co.** in Minneapolis, MN. In 1887, The **Co.** was moved to Chicago, IL and hired **Alvah Curtis Roebuck** as a watch repairman. In 1891, **Sears, Roebuck & Co.** was founded. In 1893, the first mail order catalog was issued and contained only watches. In 1897, **Sears** issued its first full mail order catalog. **Sears** sold wooden planes, made by others, from the late 1800's to around 1930. In 1908, **Sears** started selling mail order house kits. **Richard Sears** retired in 1908, at the age of 44, due to failing health. In 1925, **Sears** added retail stores. **Sears** was bought out, in 2005, by **K Mart**. **B: FF; A ****

W. K. SEAVER
Example: on a 10 1/4" beech skewed rabbet with flat chamfers on the toe and heel and rounder on top of body, ca. 1800. **UR**

S. SEAVEY
Example: on a 16" beech fore plane modified into a gutter plane with flat chamfers, made by **Sanborn** on the heel; a 9 1/2" beech astragal bead with flat chamfers; a 9 1/2" beech size **9** round with round chamfers; and a 14" plank match plane made by **Hills & Winship/ Springfield, MS** and style **9** on the heel, ca. 1820-35. **UR**

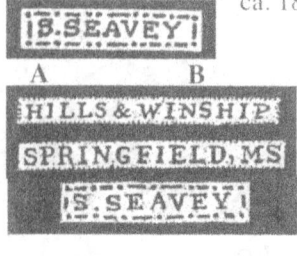

D. P. SECOME
D. P. Secome probably is a tool and hardware dealer, in Concord NH. Example: on a 15 3/4" beech complex molder with a closed cherry centered tote with flat chamfers, and a double-iron by **William Ash & Co.**, ca. 1830. **UR**

C. S. SEE
Cornelius Seamon See (b. May 26, 1806 in Terrytown, Westchester Co., NY, d. 1880) was a planemaker, in New York City, from 1829-46; and in Watertown, NY, dates unknown. Example: the A1 imprint with the misspelled **WARENTED** is on a 9 1/2" full-boxed bead. The A2 imprint is on a 9 1/8" center bead. The B1 imprint is on a graduated set of 5 single-boxed Grecian ovolos, and a double-boxed Grecian ovolo with bead. The C1 imprint is on two rounds, and a slide-arm plow. The C4 imprint is on a 9 1/2" boxed beech complex molder marked **7/8**. The D imprint is on a tiger maple skew hollow with a birch wedge. The E imprint is on an ogee molder. **A & B **; A1, A2, B1, C, C1, C2, C3, C4, D & D1 *****

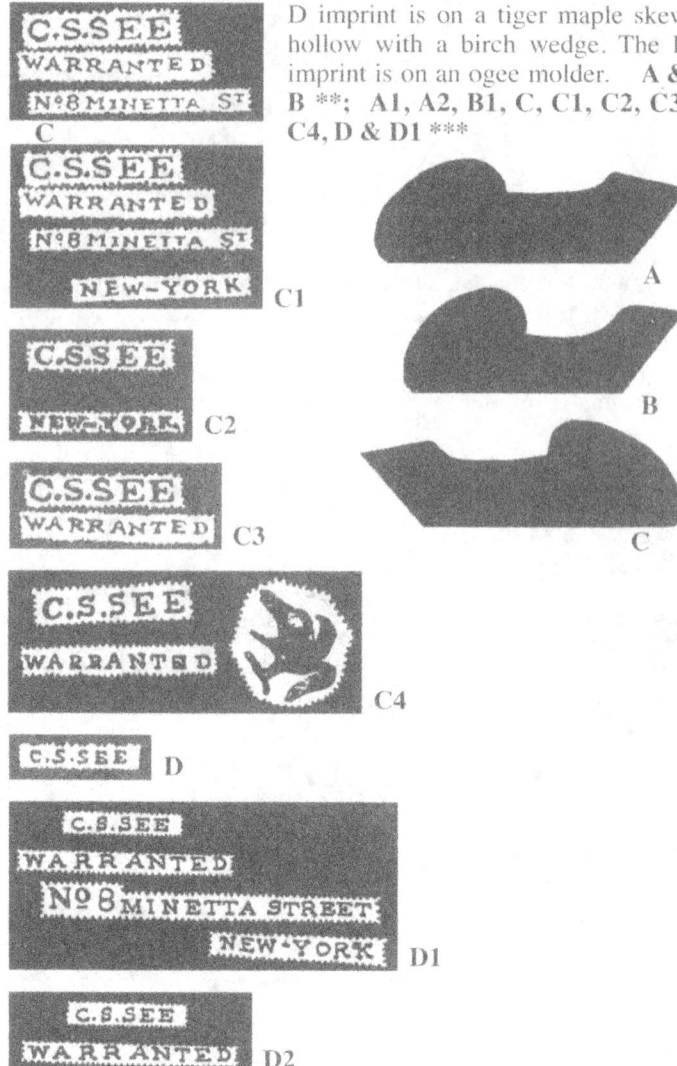

A. F. SEEBERGER
Anthony F. Seeberger (b. ca. 1830 in Prussia, Naturalization Apr. 30, 1879, d. Probate Sep. 25, 1901 in Cook Co., IL) In 1850, he was in Wooster, Wayne Co., OH. In 1856, **Anthony** was listed, as merchant, in Oskaloosa, Mahaska, IA. In 1870, the firm **Seeberger & Breakey** with **A. F. Seeberger** and **B. A. Breakey**, as hardware and tinner's stock, was located at 62 Lake, Chicago, IL. Example: on a 26" beech jointer with a closed tote and an octagonal strike, ca. 1850. ********

C. W. SEELY
Example: on an 8" beech slide-arm plow with a steel skate and bronze trim, and round chamfer, ca. 1830. **UR**

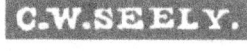

SEIBERT
Example: on a 10" beech complex molder with heavy flat chamfers, ca. 1790. **UR**

A. B. SEIDENSTRICKER
A. B. SEIDENSTRICKER & CO.

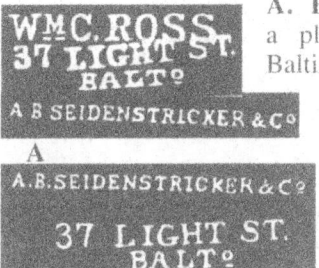

A. B. Seidenstricker & C0. was a planemaker and tool dealer in Baltimore, MD, from 1856-66; and described itself as the successor to **Philip Chapin**. **Albert B. Seidenstricker**, without the & CO. was used, from 1870-72, at Light St. It acquired the stock and assets of both **P. Chapin**, active from 1835-55, and **Wm. C. Ross**, active from 1849-69. Seidenstricker was part of **Young & Seidenstricker**, from 1868-69, with **George W. Young, Jr.**, it was succeeded by **Geo. W. Young Jr. & Co.**, in 1889-90.

A. B. Seidenstricker was listed as Clerk in Baltimore, MD. C **; A, A1, A2 & B ***

SELBY

Selby is believed to be a Boston, MA, hardware dealer. UR

A. B. SEMPLE & BRO.

A. B. Semple & Bro. was a hardware and cutlery dealer, in Louisville, KY, from 1848-56. The Semples of this company were **Alexander B. Semple**, **John Semple**, and **William W. Semple**. It succeeded **A. B. Semple & Co.**, active from 1838-46. In 1845-46, A. B. Semple & Co. was listed as importers and dealers of hardware and cutlery, mfg. of Smith Bellows and wrought iron, n.e. corner Main and Fifth. A. B. Semple & Co. were succeeded by **A. B. Semple & Sons**, in 1858-69. ***

G. SENER
Example: on a 10" molder with flat chamfers, and branded **J. Sehner** on the side, probably from PA, ca. 1810-20. UR

J. SENER/ JACOB SENER./ J. SEHNER
Believed to be **Jacob Sener** (christened Feb. 14, 1812 in Lancaster, PA) son of **Jacob Sener Sr.** (b. ca. 1780, d. Mar. 23, 1838 in OH). In 1834, **Jacob Sener Jr.** was married in Lancaster, PA. Examples: the A imprint is on a 14 1/2" molder with an offset tote; a 13 1/2" panel raiser with an offset tote and an adjustable fence on the sole; a 10" half round or thumbnail plane; and a large side bead, all beech with heavy round chamfers; and as an owners imprint on a side rabbet made by **Butler**, a Philadelphia, PA, planemaker (1819-35). The C imprint is typically branded on the side. This has also appeared as an owner's imprint on the side of a **I. Lind** cornice plane. The B imprint is on a plow, made by **I. Schauer**, marked on the toe and heel. **Schauer** worked in Petersburg, north of Lancaster, in 1824. In 1860, **Jacob Sener** was listed, as a carpenter, in East Hempfield, Lancaster, PA. A, B & C: ****

E. H. SENFT
E. H. Senft was a carpenter, listed in 1860 census, as living with **Philip Senft** (b. 1798), a farmer, in North Codorus, York Co., PA. Example: on a large walnut plow; and a screw-arm sash plane with arms and nuts of chestnut, wear strips of bone, and stamped with individual letters on toe and heel. Inside the halves, written in a nice hand, is: UR

MARCH 7 A.D. 1847
IN THE STATE OF M.D.
BY E. H. SENFT

L. SENTER
Possibly **Langdon Senter** who was listed in 1840, as living in Hudson, NH. Example: on a 30" beech jointer, ca. 1850. ****

I. SESSIONS
Example: on a 10" birch sash with wide flat chamfers, ca. 1790. UR

D. SEWALL
Example: on a 10 5/8" fruitwood skew sash filletster with wedge-lock arms and heavy flat chamfers, ca. 1780. UR

J. SEWALL
Example: on a 11 7/8" toted birch complex molder with heavy flat chamfers mostly on the sides, ca. 1780. UR

S. SEWALL
Maj. Samuel Sewall (b. Sep. 14, 1724 in York, ME, d. Jul. 23, 1815 in York, ME) who was a joiner, engineer/ bridge builder, architect, cabinetmaker, and carpenter, active from 1740-80's. His father, **Samuel Sewell Sr.**, was trained as a furniture maker in Boston, MA. Samuel built the First Parish Church, in York. He also built the Jonathan Sayward's house in York. Jonathan's diary entry of Nov. 10, 1761; "**Samuel Sewell** the joiner, 45 pounds old tenor toward work on my house". The moldings used in the house were identical in profile to moldings on a number of furniture pieces in the house. He made his own tools and templates. In 1761, he engineered and built the bridge over the York River, built with driven piles and a drawbridge. He served, at age 80, in the War of 1812, as a Major. Example: on

a wedge-locked slide-arm filletster of cherry with arms set into the fence with iron rivets. **No imprint is available**.

AUSTIN W. SEWARD
Austin W. Seward (Steward) (b. 1797 in VA, d. Oct. 27, 1872 Bloomington, Monroe Co., IN) was living in KY, in 1821 and moved to Bloomington, IN, between 1821-23. Bloomington was founded in 1816. The 1850 census listed **Seward** with the following business: Smithing Business, employed 6 hands and grossed $4000/ year; Threshing Machine Manufacturer, employed 3 hands and made 13 machines worth $1600; Plow Shop, employed 4 hands making 350 plows worth $3000; Foundry or Casting Business: employed 3 hands and grossed $4000. In 1850, 3 sons and 4 apprentices were living with him. He made edge tools and planes during his early working years, ca. 1820-30. He was also listed in 1850, as a blacksmith. After 1870, the firm was converted to a conventional hardware dealership and continued under this name, until 1985.
No imprint has been reported.

S. SEWARD
Example: on a 9 1/2" beech molder with round chamfers.
ca. 19c. **UR**

J. A. SEX & CO.
J. A. Sex & Co. probably was a hardware dealer in New York. Example: on a plane also imprinted **Chas. Ashley/ Ogdensburg**. **No imprint is available**.

E. F. SEYBOLD
Emanuel F. Seybold, originally from PA, was listed in the Cincinnati, OH, directories, as a planemaker, from 1836-44, at 219 Main. In the Western Address Directory of 1837, he was listed as a "Wholesale and Retail Plane Manufacturer and Tool Store, No.219, Main Street, Ciniccati." In 1849-52, he was listed as a hardware merchant, at 207 Main; though he was reported in the 1850 Products of Industry census, as employing 12 hands and manufacturing $12,000 worth of planes. The D imprint may have occurred from **Seybold** buying some of **Creagh**'s closing inventory. He was part of **Seybold & Smith** with **John H. Smith**, in 1846; and probably part of **Seybold & Spencer**, dates unknown. He was succeeded by his widow **Catharine Seybold**, from 1853-55. On an imprint that ties **E. F. Seybold** to **J. L. Wayne**: ****

> J. L. WAYNE & SON
> CINCINNATI, O.
> SUCCESSORS TO
> E. F. SEYBOLD
> CINCINNATI, O

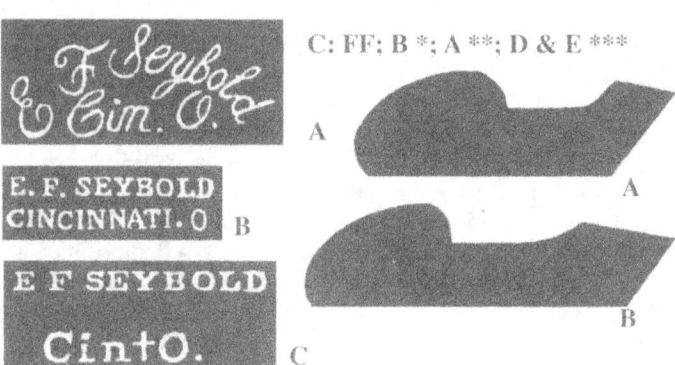

C: FF; B *; A **; D & E ***

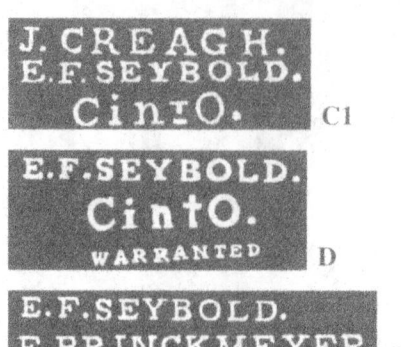

JOHN SEYBOLD
John Seybold was listed as a planemaker, in 1843-44. He was later listed, as a Clerk in **E. F. Seybold**'s hardware store from 1849-50. **No imprint has been reported.**

SEYBOLD, CUNNUNGHAM & SPRAGUE
Cathern Seybold, **Andrew Cunningham** and **Henry Sprague** formed an edge tool manufacturing partnership in Cincinnati, OH, listed in 1855, at 46th. e. 8th.
No imprint has been reported.

SEYBOLD & SPENCER
A partnership of **Emanuel F. Seybold** and **Spencer** in the hardware business, in Cincinnati, OH. Example: on a 14" beech screw-arm plank grooving plane. ****

EBENEZER SEYMOUR
There were several **Ebenezer Seymours** from the Farmington, CT, area including **Ebenezer Seymour** (bapt. Feb. 1, 1684 in Farmington, Hartford Co., CT, d. Sep. 17, 1733 in Farmington), the son of the founder **Richard Seymour** who built a fort. His estate inventory listed a number of tools including a "plow and irons". An **Ebenezer Seymour** of Farmington was arrested, in 1720, for making counterfeit bills. Another possibility is **Ebenezer Seymour** (b. May 16, 1729 in Norwalk, CT, d. Jun. 18, 1821 in Poundridge, NY). Lastly, **Ebenezer Seymour** (b. 1756, d. 1808 in Rome, NY) who was married, in 1777 in Farmington, CT, and was living in Herkimer, NY in 1790. His oldest son, **Archibald Seymour**, was a carpenter. Example: on the toe of an 11" birch Yankee plow with a riveted skate, 3/4" square arms, a wood depth stop, and heavy flat chamfers, ca. 1750, probably from New England. **UR**

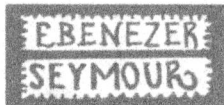

JOHN SEYMOUR
John Seymour was listed as a hardware dealer in Cincinnati, OH, in 1855. Example: on a **Ohio Tool Co.** size 7 round. ****

L. SEYMOUR
Luther Seymour was listed as a housewright and cabinetmaker in Farmington, CT, from 1762-1815. Example: on a 9 1/2" birch complex molder with fixed fence with round chamfers, and **7/8** on the heel, and a **Wm. Ash & Co.** iron, found in CT, ca. early 19c. **UR**

W. N. SEYMOUR & CO.
William N. Seymour & Co. with **William North Seymour** (b. Jul. 30, 1802 in Walton, Delaware Co., NY, d. Jun. 4, 1881 in Brooklyn, NY) was a New York City hardware dealer, from 1842-72. **W. N. Seymour & Co.**, active from 1828-72, and in the **G. W. Denison & Co.** account book as buying planes from 1870-72. Example: on a 9 1/2" **Greenfield Tool Co. 707** double-iron sash plane. **A & B** ****

I: SHADE
Example: on a 9" applewood complex molder with medium flat chamfers, found in eastern PA, ca. 1800. **UR**

L. SHADE
Example: on a 9" cherry complex molder with flat chamfers, ca. 1810. **UR**

H. SHAFER
Example: on a 9 1/2x 2" beech skewed rabbet with heavy round chamfers, found in southeastern PA, with early 19c. round chamfers. **UR**

J. N. SHALLENBERGER & CO.
J. N. Shallenberger & Co. was listed in 1862, as a hardware and cutlery dealer, at 101 Market in Pittsburgh, PA. Example: on a 15 7/8" jack plane with a centered tote, ca. 1850. ****

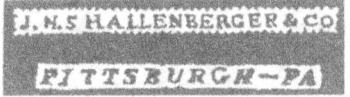

SHANNON & CO.
Shannon & Co. was possibly a hardware dealer partnership of both **J. B. Shannon**, at 1009 Market St. and **J. Jacob Shannon**, at 1707 Market St., Philadelphia, PA. Example: on a 3/16" **H. Chapin** center bead. ****

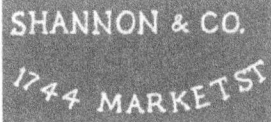

J. B. SHANNON
J. B. Shannon was a Philadelphia, PA, hardware dealer, located at 1009 Market St., active from 1870-73. **J. B. Shannon** may also have been a part of **Shannon & Co.**. Example: on a plane made and imprinted by **A. Kelly & Co.**. The B imprint with **MADE FOR** has been reported on a smoother made by **John Veit**. **A & B** ****

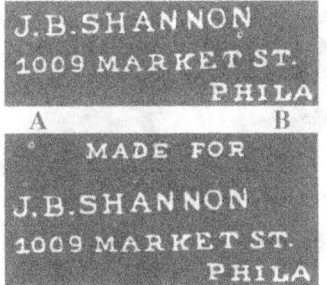

MADE FOR SHANNON/ J. JACOB SHANNON
J. Jacob Shannon (b. 1825) was a Philadelphia, PA, hardware dealer, located at 1707 Market St. He may have also been a part of **Shannon & Co.**. No specific dates of operation are known. Example: the A imprint is on a plane style **No. 133** made by **Union Factory/ H. Chapin**. The B imprint is on a 1/4" side bead made by **H. Chapin**. **A & B** ****

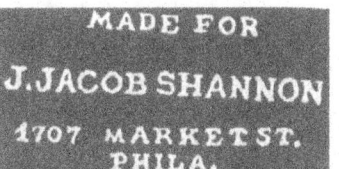

M. SHAPIRO & SON
M. Shapiro & Son was a New York City hardware dealer, active ca. 1870. Example: on a bead made by **Sargent & Co./ U. S.**, and **623** on the toe, the **H. Chapin** style number for a 1" side bead. ****

SHAPLEIGH, DAY & CO.
Shapleigh, Day & Co. was a St. Louis, MO, hardware firm organized by **Augustus Frederick Shapleigh** (b. Jan. 9, 1810 in Portsmouth, Rockingham Co., NH, d. Feb. 27, 1902 St. Louis, MO). As a youth, he clerked with a hardware firm in Portsmouth, NH. **Shapleigh** went to sea for 4 years. **Augustus** was a partner with **Rogers Brothers & Co.** in Philadelphia, PA. In 1843, he established a branch of the firm in St. Louis as **Rogers, Shapleigh & Co.** In 1847, **Shapleigh, Day & Co.** succeeded **Roger, Shapleigh & Co.**; **Shapleigh, Day & Co.** was then succeeded by **A. F. Shapleigh & Co.**, from 1863-80; **Shapleigh & Cantwell Hardware Co.**, from 1880-88; **A. F. Shapleigh Hardware Co.**, from 1888-1901. In 1901, **Saunders Norvell** bought a controlling interest and renamed the company **Norvell-Shapleigh Hardware Co.**; from 1901-13, then **Shapleigh Hardware Co.**. On Jul. 1, 1940, **Shapleigh Co.** purchased the **E. C. Simmons Co.** and the **Keen Kutter** line. The **D-E** or **Diamond Edge** trademark was adopted in 1864; and is still in use by the **Imperial Knife Co.** who purchased it in 1961, around the time **Shapleigh & Co.** went out of business. Planes with the **Diamond Edge** brand were manufactured by **Stanley**, **Sargent**, and **Ohio Tool Co.**. **A & B: FF; C** *

A. SHATTUCK
Example: on a 14 1/2x 5 3/4" beech crown with a centered tote with round chamfers and a pull-bar, ca. 19c. **UR**

I. E. SHATTUCK
Ira Edmund Shattuck (b. Apr. 21, 1848 in Burlington, VT, d. Apr. 6, 1875 in Chicago, IL, buried in Burlington) was a wholesale and retail hardware dealer in Burlington, VT, from 1872-74. Example: on a pair of 1" tongue & groove planes made by **A. Howland & Co.**, and a 3/8" center bead made by the **Green-field Tool Co.**. ****

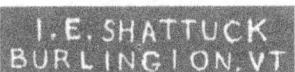

N. SHATTUCK
Example: on a 11 1/2" beech sun plane with heavy flat chamfers and 3 ivory diamond inlays; and a 10" birch complex molder with flat chamfers, made by **N. Ayer** with an **I. Sleeper** style wedge and an incuse **N. Shattuck** brand on the side. The B incuse imprint with **NS** is on a 9 3/8" birch straight rabbet with shallow flat chamfers, ca. 1800. **A & B: UR**

B SHAW
Two possibilities: **Benjamin Shaw** (b. Apr. 18, 1749 in Newport, RI, d. Sep. 1794 in Little Compton, RI) of Little Compton, Newport Co. who appeared in the 1774 & 90 RI censuses; or **Benjamin Shaw** (d. Sep. 4, 1831) who married on Sep. 28, 1823 to **Mary Ann Davenport** in Tiverton, RI. Examples: on a 9 3/8" beech quarter round, found in the southeastern MA/ RI area; a 9 1/8" beech slide-arm Yankee plow with wood depth stop and wood thumbscrews, and a 4/8 unboxed side bead, all with flat chamfers, ca. 1800. ****

JAS. SHAW
James Shaw (b. 1820 in PA, d. Nov. 28, 1895 in Cincinnati, OH) was listed, as a planemaker, in Cincinnati, OH, in 1839-40. **No imprint has been reported.**

N. SHAW
Example: on a 9 1/2" beech molder. **UR**

N. B. SHEARER
Example: on an all boxwood screw-arm plow plane, ca. mid 19c. **UR**

Z. SHELDON
Example: on a 9 5/8" birch skew fenced rabbet with wood thumbscrews, ca. 1800. **UR**

SHELTON & OSBORNE MFG. CO.
Shelton & Osborne MFG. CO. was a partnership of **Edward Nelson Shelton** (b. Sep. 4, 1812 in CT, d Sep. 16, 1894 in Derby, New Haven Co., CT) and **David Thompson Osborn** (b. 1820 CT, d. Jun. 6, 1904 in Derby, CT) in Birmingham CT. The town of Birmingham became a part of Derby, CT. **Edward Shelton** married **Mary Jane DeForest** (b. Feb. 26, 1819, d. Dec. 28, 1884 in Derby), the daughter of **Linson DeForest**. In 1880, **Edward** was listed as a manufacturer in Derby, CT. On Mar. 16, 1845, **David** married **Lucy J. Gillbert**, in Derby. In 1850, Lucy's father was **Truman Gillbert**, a joiner and living next to the **Osborn** family. In 1880, **David** was listed as a cabinetmaker in Derby. Examples: on a screw-armed, toted plow plane made of cocobolo with boxwood fence, and on three ebony body plows body, wedge, and fence, boxwood screw-arms and nuts, brass depth stops and fittings. One plow has ivory tips and another has ivory nuts, backing washers and tips. The ebony plow was accompanied by a set of 8 irons marked **J. DREW**, ca. 1850. **

BENJAMIN SHELABARGER
Benjamin F. Shelabarger of Mifflintown, PA, was issued Patent No. 5,486, on March 28, 1848, for a beech smoothing plane with a cap iron constructed that it would close up the throat as the wood stock was worn. (see *Patented Transitional & Metallic Planes in America 1827-1927*, p. 21, by Roger K. Smith) Example: on a chip breaker with the name **SHELABARGER**, dated **1848**, and **PATENT**. **A & B ****

B. SHENEMAN
Benjamin Sheneman (b. ca. 1816 in PA, d. before 1880 in Philadelphia, PA) was a prolific Philadelphia, PA, planemaker, from 1846-67. After working with **David Colton** as **D. Colton & B. Sheneman**, from 1846-52; **Benjamin Sheneman** worked alone, except for a period 1856-60, as **B. Sheneman & Bro.**, with a brother, **Thomas J. Sheneman**. Other Shenemans were **Edward Sheneman**, **Henry Sheneman** (b. 1830), **John Sheneman**, and **William Sheneman** who were recorded as Philadelphia planemakers, but none have recorded imprints.
A & B: FF; C & C1: *; D: *

B. SHENEMAN & BRO.

Benjamin Sheneman and Thomas J. Sheneman were in a partnership, as planemakers, at 297 Market Street, Philadelphia, PA, from 1856-60. The 1856 director listed this firm erroneously as B. Shuman & Bro..

A, A1 & B *

HENRY SHENEMAN

Henry Sheneman (b. ca. 1830 in PA) In 1850 was listed, as a planemaker, in Philadelphia, PA.
No imprint has been reported.

T. J. SHENEMAN

Thomas J. Sheneman (d. May 15, 1863 in Philadelphia, PA) was in a partnership as B. Sheneman & Bro. with his brother Benjamin Sheneman. He married on Feb. 6, 1855, in Philadelphia. In 1861, Thomas was listed, as a planemaker, at 733 Market ST., the address of B. Sheneman & Bro.. On Aug. 31, 1862, Thomas Sheneman listed as a Private in the Civil War, in the 2nd. Reg., Penn. Heavy Artillery (112th. Volunteers). Example: on a 12" beech slide arm plow with brass thumb screws, ca. mid 19c. *****

WILLIAM HENRY SHENEMAN

William Henry Sheneman (d. ca. 1900) was married Jan. 21, 1868, in Philadelphia, PA. In 1880-83, William was listed, as a planemaker, at 1224 Chestnut St., Philadelphia.
No imprint has been reported.

D. M. SHEPARD

Daniel M. Shepard (b. ca. 1799 in NH) was a planemaker, in Albany, NY, from 1827-28, under these imprints. He was in partnership as Randall & Shepard, in 1826. In 1855, Daniel was listed as a Clerk in Albany, NY. Example: on a 9 1/2" complex molder with a W. Butcher iron. A & A1 ***

S. SHEPARD/ S. SHEPARD & CO.

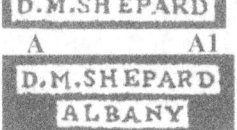

S. Shepard was possibly a Buffalo, NY, hardware dealer. Examples: the A imprint is on a 9 9/16" beech boxed bead; the A1 imprint is on a 12 round; and the B imprint is on a 22" & 16" fore planes, ca. 1850. (see J. Sanderson, who was possibly in a partnership)
A, A1, B & B1 **

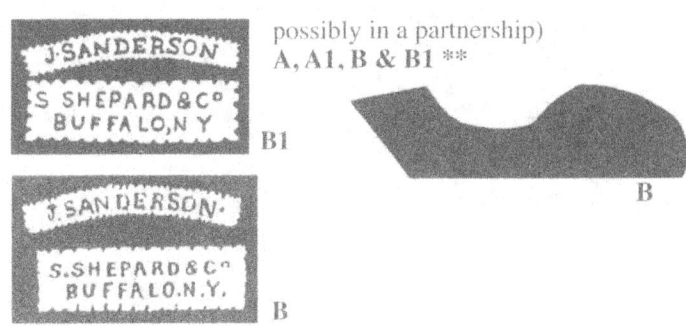

S. F. SHEPARD.

Example: on a 9 3/8" beech sash coping plane with flat chamfers.
ca. early 19c.   UR

T. SHEPARD

Possibly Thomas Shepard (b. 1833 in Ireland) and listed as a carpenter tool manufacturer, working for and living with P. Quigley, in Newark, NJ, in 1850. In 1863, Thomas was listed in Paterson, NJ. Examples: on a 16 1/2" fixed beech sash, triple boxed, with tote, centered bench type cutter and two side cutters; an adjustable sash; two dados; a filletster; and a pair of 14" tongue & groove planes, ca. 1850. ***

T. V. SHEPARD

Example: on a 9 7/8" birch square shiplap rabbet with flat chamfers and a relieved wedge, ca. 1790. UR

W. SHEPARDSON

Examples: on a 9 9/16" double-iron sash; a 9 3/8" halving plane; and a 9 3/8" small full round, all beech with heavy round chamfers, ca. 1830. ****

SHEPHERD & BUFFUM

Example: the A imprint is on a 9" miter plane. The B imprint is on a 9" beech coffin smoother with a wood strike button, and a Moulson Brothers iron.
A & B ****

L. SHERMAN'S

Example: a 9 1/2" full-boxed 1" rabbet with 8/8 on the heel.
ca. 1850. ****

SHERMAN BARNES
Sherman Barnes probably was a hardware dealer located in
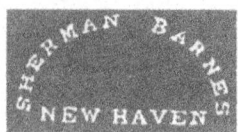
New Haven, CT. Examples: on a size **6** hollow, **2**, **4**, and **6** rounds made by **J. Killam** who was active from 1822-60, ca. mid. 19c. ********

SHERMAN BROS.
Byron Sherman (b. Jun. 3, 1824 in Herkimer, d. Feb. 27, 1899 in Morristown, NJ) and **Porter Sherman** were New York City hardware merchants, from 1853-73; at 19 Park Pl., in 1857; and at 267 Canal, in 1868. **Byron** was part of **Barry, Way & Sherman**, in 1847; and **Way & Sherman**, from 1849-52. ******

D. SHIELDS
Example: on a 28 1/2"joiner with a centered tote, strike button

on toe, a double-iron by **Robt Sorby/ Warranted**, ca. mid 19c. **UR**

H. SHILEY
Example: on a 14 3/4" mahogany reverse ogee cornice plane with an open tote. **UR**

INO SHILLINGLAS
Example: on a 9 1/2" beech nosing plane with flat chamfers, possibly from PA, ca. 1800. **UR**

R. D. SHIP
Richard Doniphan Ship (b. Oct. 14, 1779 in VA, d. Mar. 3, 1853 in Midway, Woodford Co., KY) was a joiner and builder in Woodford Co. KY. It was noted that he had Joiner's apprentices. Descendants have over 50 of his tools. In 1814, he built the John Regis Alexander house. His son **Richard D. Ship, Jr.** (b. Oct. 25, 1817 in Woodford Co., d. 1871 in KY) was also in the business. In 1850, he was listed as a merchant and also listed as a slave owner of about 21 slaves. In 1860, he was listed in Versailles, Woodford Co., Ky as a banker. Examples: a 9 3/4" x 1 1/2" rabbet with heavy flat chamfers, found in WV, a 9 5/8" x 1/2" ogee, a small round with round chamfers on top and flat chamfers on the toe and heel, found in KY, all beech. ca. 1800. *******

D. SHIVELY
Example: on a 9 3/8" beech molder, ca. 1840. **UR**

SHIVERICK/ D. SHIVERICK & CO.
David Shiverick (b. 1818 in MA) made planes in Brooklyn, NY, under these imprints; from 1865-67. From 1853-64, he was part of **Shiverick & Malcolm**. In 1870, **David Shiverick** was listed in Deep River (Saybrook) Middlesex Co., CT; in manufacturing. In 1875, he was listed as "manuf." of agricultural tools, in Brooklyn, NY. The B imprint resulted from the rework of the C imprint by removing the **D.** and the **& CO.**, however half of the & remains. **A: FF; B & C ****

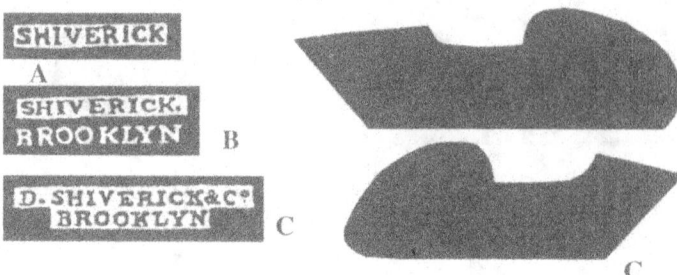

SHIVERICK & MALCOLM
David Shiverick and **Frederick S. Malcolm** dealt in tools and made planes in Brooklyn, NY, from 1853-64. **Frederick Malcolm** was listed, as a planemaker, in New Haven, CT, in 1846; and as part of **Pond, Malcolm & Welles** in New Haven, ca. 1850. The **134 GREENWICH AVE., N.Y.** location imprint referred to a Manhattan address believed to be a sales outlet, and was listed in the NYC directories, 1854-56. **Shiverick** lived and worked in Brooklyn; **Malcolm** worked in Brooklyn but lived in Manhattan. **A **; B & C *****

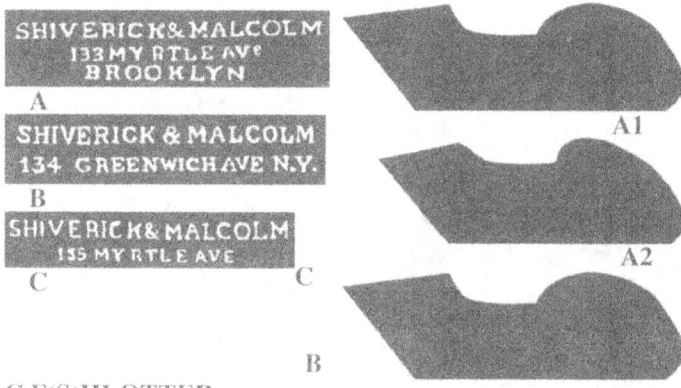

C F(S)HLOTTER
Example: on a 9 5/8" beech round with tight round chamfers, possibly from PA, ca. 1820. **UR**

I. SHORT/ I. S
John Short was listed, as a cabinetmaker, in Newburyport, MA, in 1736. Also possible is **Joseph Short** (b. June 30, 1771, d. Nov. 10, 1819) from the same family as **John Short**. He was also a Newburyport cabinetmaker, active from 1780-1825; and was a contemporary of **I. Sleeper**. Examples: Initial group was found on a 10" beech ogee complex molder; and a 9 7/8" beech halving plane, both with heavy flat chamfers, and an **I. Sleeper** style wedge; found in the **Little** family homestead in Newburyport. The **I. SHORT** imprint A is on a **I. Sleeper** round, ca. 1790. **A & B *******

N. SHOUAR
Possibly the early name variants of **Nicklaus Schauer** (b. 1755, d. 1829) an eastern PA planemaker. Examples: the A imprint is on a 9 1/2" beech complex molder with heavy flat chamfers. The B imprint is on a 9 7/8" beech single lignum vitae boxed bead with flat chamfers, ca. 1790-1800. **A & B** ****

J. SHOUT
Example: on a 10 1/2" beech fixed sash with heavy flat chamfers, ca. 1800. **UR**

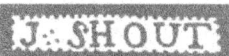

A. SHOVE
Abraham Shove (b. Aug. 22, 1780 in Bristol Co., MA, m. Sep. 22, 1803 in Swansea, Bristol Co., d. May 11, 1846 in Somerset, Bristol Co.) was a cabinetmaker and chairmaker, working from 1804-35. In May 1816, he was placed under guardianship for drunkenness, and then released in 1824. Examples: on a 24" jointer, an 8 3/16" fruitwood halving plane with a relieved wedge and flat chamfers; and a 6" applewood coach molder with flat chamfers, flutes and a relieved wedge, ca. 1790. ****

SHREVE, ANDERSON & THOMAS
Shreve, Anderson & Thomas was probably a hardware dealer located in Louisville, KY. Example: on a 14"x 4 3/8" beech plane with a fixed depth stop, open tote, nicker with a nicker wedge, an adjustable fence, and style number **114** on the toe suggesting it was made by the **Ohio Tool Co.**, Also reported is a plow made by the **Ohio Tool Co.** with style number **96 1/2**. ****

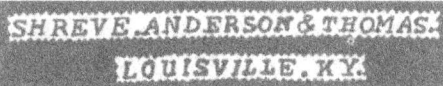

DANIEL SHRIEBER
Daniel Shrieber was a Harmonist at Old Economy Society, Ambridge, Beaver Co., PA. Examples: initials **D.S.** on two molding planes in the carpenter shop, dated **1844** and **1847**. No imprint is available.

G: SHULER
Example: on a 9 7/16"x 1/8" beech side bead with lignum vitae boxing and heavy round chamfers, found in southeastern, PA. The iron is marked **VIIII** and a **9** written in pencil on the wedge which may be production numbers. Also **R. SHULER** as a owner imprint below the maker imprint, ca. early 19c. **UR**

M. SHULER
Example: on a 9 1/2" birch moving filletster, possibly from PA, ca. 1800. **UR**

W. SHULTZ
Examples: on a 10" molder, and a 9 5/8" beech ogee molder with flat chamfers, found in Lehigh Co, PA, ca. 1800. **UR**

M. SHUTE
Example: on a 13 3/4" beech panel raiser with a cherry tote and wedge, a diamond strike, round chamfers on top and flat chamfers on the toe and heel; and a 9 11/16" birch complex molder with flat chamfers, ca. 1800-10. **UR**

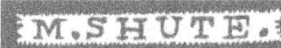

I D SHUTER
Example: on a 9 1/2" beech complex molder with flat chamfers, ca. early 19c. **UR**

SICKELS, SWEET & LYON
Robert Sickels, **Edwin S. Sweet** and **Henry M. Lyon** were partners in a New York City hardware firm, from 1890-97. Two of these partners, **Sweet** and **Lyon**, were part of **Gilbert, Sweet & Lyon**, from 1887-89. **

C. G. SIEWERS
Charles "Carl" Gottfried Siewers (Sievers, Siavers) (b. May 24, 1815 in the West Indies, d. Sep. 1882 in Covington, Newport, KY, buried in Cincinnati, OH) married **Anna Rebecca Carpenter** on Oct. 11, 1843, and became the son-in-law of **E. W. Carpenter**. He was listed, as a planemaker, in Cincinnati, OH, from 1839-40. He was also the **Siewers** of **Wheatcroft & Siewers**, edge tool makers, ca. 1840. **E. F. Seybold** acted as **Siewers'** agent. From 1842-66, he was listed as the maker of various carpenter's tools, saws, marking gauges, "sauares", and wood planes, at 93 e. 8th St. In 1867, he advertised as a "saw and cabinet tool factory", in Cincinnati, OH. In 1872, **Siewers & Co.** was listed in Newport, KY with **Albert C. Siewers** who was living with his father **Charles G. Siewers** and partner **John Schneider**. C. G. Siewers was listed, as a saw maker, until 1880. Example: the B imprint is on a 9 1/2" size **8** round with a **Butcher** iron. **A & B** ****

ADAM SIGLER
Adam Sigler with the date **No. 2. 1838** and an owner imprint **J. SIGLER** is on a 23" bench plane, found in IN, with a

W. Butcher iron, round chamfers and an applied wood sole (1/8" at the toe and 1/4" at the heel due to wear) held in place by 8 wood pegs of 1/4" diam. **UR**

R. I. SIKB
Examples: on a 9 1/2" birch bead; and a 10 1/8" beech rabbet, marked twice on the toe, both with heavy round chamfers, ca. 1820. **UR**

J. S/ JAMES SILCOCK

James Silcock (b. ca. 1796 in England, arrived in NY on Jun. 12, 1826, naturalized on Oct. 5, 1832) was a journeyman planemaker in Philadelphia, PA, who made the patented three arm plow planes for **Israel White** between 1834-39. **UR**

E. C. SIMMONS HARDWARE CO.
Edward Campbell Simmons (b. Dec. 24, 1839 in Fredrick Co., MD, d. Apr. 18, 1920 in St. Louis, MO) moved to St. Louis, MO, in 1846, with his family. At age 17, **Simmons** was in the wholesale mercantile business. In 1856, he apprenticed to **Child-Pratt & Co.**. Upon completion of his three year commitment, he began working for **Wilson, Levering & Waters**. He moved from a clerk to a partner which then became **Water, Simmons & Co.**. In 1869, at age 30, he obtained control of this **Co.** and reorganized it as **E. C. Simmon Hardware Co.**. **Simmons** had a flare for promoting and selling his products by the use of slogans such as "The recollection of the quality remains long after the price is forgotten." In 1870, the firm chose **Keen Kutter** as the brand name of their line of high grade tools and cutlery. In 1881, **Simmons** used the slogan "A jobber's first duty is to help his customers to prosper." **Simmons** introduced traveling salesmen into the business, employing more than any other enterprise in the country. In 1892, there were 200 salesmen; and by 1916 there were 500. In 1874, he started profit sharing, the first mercantile business in the country to do so. In 1881, they introduced their first comprehensive catalog and they pioneered "same day service". St Louis, MO was their headquarters, with warehouses in New York City; Siouse Falls, IA; Minneapolis, MN; Atlanta, GA; Toledo, OH; and Philadelphia, PA. **Edward Simmons** retired in 1887, and turned the company over to his 3 sons, **Wallace Simmon**, **Edward Simmons** and **George Simmons**. In 1934, the firm went into bankruptcy and was sold to **A. E. Shapleigh Co.** on July 1, 1940. **Shapleigh** continued to use the **Keen Kutter** trademark, until 1961.
No imprint has been reported.

H. SIMMONS

Example: on a 7" cherry smoother with round chamfers, ca. early 19c. **UR**

C. SIMONDS
C. Simonds has been reported as the maker of cooper's tools and cooper's planes in Antrim, NH. Example: on a cooper's howel, ca. 1800. **UR**

ARAD: SIMONS
Arad Simons (b. Aug. 27, 1754 in Windham, Tolland Co., CT, d. Nov. 19, 1836 in Lebanon, NH) was trained as a joiner, in Mansfield, CT. He married **Bridget Arnold**, on Feb. 15, 1775, in Mansfield. **Isaac Arnold** was apprenticed to **Arad Simons** while in Mansfield, from 1780-84. He came to Lebanon, NH, ca. 1785, at the end of the Revolutionary War, in which he served as a marine on the ship Oliver Cromwell. He was a joiner, carpenter, and planemaker, and made clock cases for **Jedediah Baldwin** between 1795-96. He appears in a number of land transactions, between 1795-1831, often described either as a gentlemen or a captain. Examples: His molding planes vary in length from 9 3/4"-10 3/16" beech and birch with **I. Sleeper** style wedges and flat chamfers. Also reported is a 13 7/8"x 4 1/8" birch crown molder with an offset pegged tote, a front pull stick, and heavy flat chamfers. ****

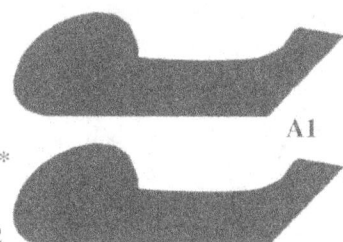

D. SIMPSON
Example: on a 9 3/8"x 3/8" beech round with flat chamfers, found in southeastern, PA, ca. early 19c. **UR**

J. SINNETT
Example: on a 9 1/2"x 1 3/4" fruitwood skew rabbet with two lignum vitae wear strips dovetailed into the sole and flat chamfers, probably from PA, ca. 1800. **UR**

C. J. SINTON & CO.
C. J. Sinton & Co. was a hardware firm in Richmond, VA, from 1850-88. **Charles J. Sinton** (b. ca. 1828 in VA, d. Jun. 30, 1902 in Richmond, VA) Example: on a plane made by **J. Kellogg**. ****

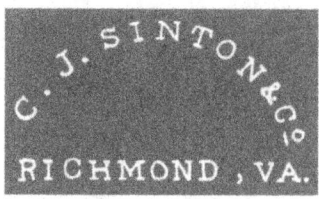

J. SIPE
Example: on a 9 1/2" beech full boxed 3/8" side bead, ca. mid 19c. **UR**

M. SIPPLE
Example: on a 9 1/8" beech skew small cove with flat chamfers, and a 14"x 3 1/16" beech panel raiser with heavy round chamfers, ca. 1810-20. **No imprint is available.**

SKIPPON

Skippon was listed as a maker of bookbinders' tools in New York City. This imprint appears on a bookbinding plow with an iron by **I. M. Carter**, Hyde Park, NY. ****

SLARK, DAY, STAUFFER & CO.

Slark, Day, Stauffer & Co. was a New Orleans, LA, hardware firm, from 1841-55, formed after **Augustus Whiting** withdrew from **Whiting & Slark** and his former partner **Robert Slark** (b. ca. 1795 in Sheffield, England, d. Mar. 3, 1868 in New Orleans, LA) formed a partnership with **James (Jas) Ingersall Day** (b. May 5, 1812 in New London, CT, d. Sep. 21, 1895 in New London, CT) and **Isaac Hull Stauffer** (b. May 1, 1813 in Lancaster Co., PA, d. Nov. 14, 1903 in New Orleans, LA). Their 1853-55 directory listing did not include the & Co.; and the 1856-66 listings were for **Slark, Stauffer & Co.** with **Robert Slark, Isaac H. Stauffer, Wm. A. Kent, J. K. Hoyt** and **Charles Macready** as importers and dealers in hardware, iron, tin plate, etc., located at 71 late 64 Canal, 11 to 23 Dorsier, and 52 to 56 Customhouse. From 1876-79, **Stauffer, Macready & Co.** with **Isaac H. Stauffer, Charles Macready** and **Benjamin F. Eshieman**. In 1897, **Stauffer, Eshleman & Co.** with **Isaac H. Stauffer, Benjamin F. Eshleman, Walter R. Stauffer** and **D. Perret**. Example: The B imprint has been reported from a plane with BY A. BALDWIN & CO.
A & B ****

J. M. SLATER

James Mathew Slater (b. 1812 in England, d. Mar. 3, 1884 in Detroit, MI) was a planemaker, in Detroit, MI, from 1845-60. He apparently lived in Michigan, as early as 1841. From 1845-46, he was a partner in **Slater & Byram** with **Ebenezer A. Byram**. An ad in 1845, listed this firm as the **Detroit Plane Factory**. He was listed in the 1850 census, as a planemaker. In 1861, he was listed in real estate. Examples: on a matched set of narrow number 2 hollow & round with the name on the hollow and the location on the round, probably because of the narrow width of the planes.
A & A1 **

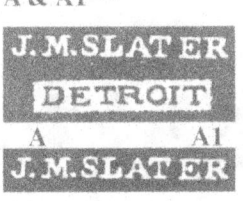

SLAUGHTER C & C

Slaughter, Carpenter & Co. was a Louisville, KY, hardware merchant, listed in the 1848, at 533 Main, between 2nd. & 3rd.; 1855-56 & 1858-59 city directories, with **James Burr Slaughter** (b. Jun. 9, 1815, m. Jun. 14, 1853 Louisville, KY, d. Jan. 29, 1895 in Jefferson Co.) as a partner. The firm was **James B. Slaughter**, from 1832-43; **James B. Slaughter & Bros.** with **George Clayton Slaughter** (b. 1823 in KY, d. bef. 1898), in 1844-45, at 533 Main; **Slaughter & Miles** with **Amos Duffield Miles** (b. Sep. 11, 1817 in Bucks Co. PA, d. Sep. 2, 1909 Brookline, MA, burial in Louisville, KY) in 1848-49 at 418 Main, bet. 6th. & 7th.; and **Slaughter, Honore & Carpenter**, in 1851-52, at 413 Main bet. 5th. & 6th. **

R. SLAYTON

Examples: a 23 1/2" birch jointer with a closed offset tote, round top wedge, and a 10 1/2" skew rabbet with round chamfers on top and flat chamfers on toe and heel. ca. 1810. **UR**

JS/ I. SLEEPER

John Sleeper (b. Aug. 2, 1754, d. June 27, 1834) was a cabinetmaker and planemaker, who was born and worked in Newburyport, MA. He was the youngest son of **Henry Sleeper**, a renowned Newburyport cabinetmaker, and brother of **Moses Sleeper**. **John**, who never married, was appointed guardian of his brother's children, in Newburyport, in 1792. In an 1813, Newburyport house transfer, to his sister **Mary**, he described himself, as a tool maker. In his will, dated Nov. 2, 1825, at Chester, he described himself, as a planemaker. In Benjamin Chase's *History of Chester*: "**Sleeper, John** was in the Battle of Bunker Hill; in the expedition under Montgomery, which went up through the woods to Quebec, suffering severely. Upon the death of Montgomery, he was taken prisoner, and lay in prison nine months. He went on a voyage as carpenter, in the frigate Boston, and several in privateers. He had quite a mechanical genius. I think that he once told me that he made the first joiners' moulding tools made in this country. He came to Chester with his brother-in-law **Nathl. Brown** in 1814." **John Sleeper** was one of the most prolific of the early planemakers, his molders were typically 10"-9 1/2" beech with heavy flat chamfers and a distinctive A wedge style. They frequently have irons signed by 18c Sheffield (England) makers and, on occasion, he used lignum vitae boxing. His early cornice planes have offset handles and two separate irons and wedges for convenience in honing and setting. His sash planes have separate ovolo and rabbet irons, which were sawed from a single iron and secured with a single flat wedge. His moving filletsters have a wooden depth stop held in a dovetailed slot instead of a purchased brass screw stop. Examples have been reported of what may be a later **I. Sleeper** plane style. They have tight round chamfers and the B wedge. Two of the three examples, a bead and a tongue, bear an owner imprint **D. Reed**. **Daniel Reed** came from Nashua, NH, and was a cabinetmaker in Newburyport, MA, in 1848. The imprint with the J S initials and B wedge is on a 9 1/2" beech hollow and round pair with flat chamfers.
A; FF, B *****

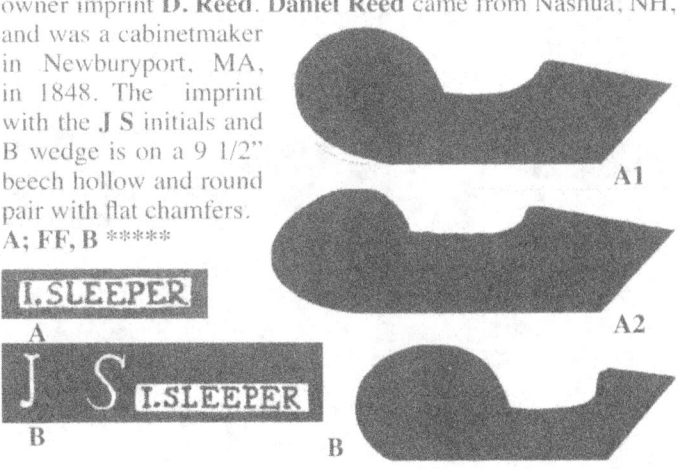

M. SLEEPER

Moses Sleeper (b. Sep. 28, 1752, in Newburyport, MA, d. 1792) was a cabinetmaker and planemaker, in Newburyport, MA. He was the son of **Henry Sleeper** and the older brother of **John Sleeper**. On May 1, 1775, **Moses** enlisted in the Co. of Capt. Ezra Lunt of Newburyport, Reg. of Col. Moses Little, until Sep. 10, 1775. **Moses** then enlisted in Capt. Samuel Ward's Co. in Cambridge, MA. He marched to Quebec under expedition commanded by Col. Arnold. **Moses** was taken prisoner at Quebec on Dec. 31, 1775 and continued as a prisoner at New Jersey until Sep. 27, 1776. Beginning in early 1777, **Moses Sleeper** was on Board the U. S. Ship Boston, Capt. McNeal, on its first exercise and served as a carpenter for one year. **John Sleeper** was made guardian of **Moses's** children, in 1792. His last known location was Newburyport, in 1789. His planes are 9 1/2" beech with flat chamfers and have the same characteristics as those of his brother.   ****

S. SLEEPER

Sherburn Sleeper (b. Feb. 23, 1800, in Corinth, VT, d. Jun. 13, 1862 in Berwick, York, ME) was listed as a planemaker in Dover, NH, in 1830. From 1830-60, he was listed in Somersworth, NH, as a machinist. Examples: on a 9 3/8" double-boxed molder with a paper label in front of the wedge slot:
A ***; Paper Lable *****

SHERBURN SLEEPER
MAKER
DOVER, N.H.

S. SLEEPR

Example: struck five times on the toe and twice more on the heel of a 11 3/4" beech single-iron toted sash plane with tight round chamfers, ca. 1820.   *****

D. SLOAT

Example: on a 9 1/2" beech hollow with shallow round chamfers and the iron set in a York pitch, ca. 1830.   UR

C. H. SLOCOMB

Cuthbert Harrison Slocomb (b. Aug. 16, 1831, d. Jan. 31, 1873 in New Orleans, LA) became a partner in this New Orleans hardware firm, in 1859, originally founded by his father, **Samuel B. Slocomb**, in 1821. In 1867, **Albert Baldwin** (b. Apr. 7, 1834 in Watertown, MA, d. Apr. 21, 1912 in Hancock Co., MS, Burial in New Orleans, LA) joined as a partner; and the firm was changed to **Slocomb, Baldwin & Co.**, at 74 Canal and 95 Common. An embossed name **C. H. SLOCOMB/ NEW ORLEANS** has been reported on a 28" jointer with a centered tote, ca. 1850. **No imprint is available.**

J. SLOCUM

Example: on a 10" birch cove with heavy flat chamfers, ca. 1800. **No imprint is available**.

S. SLOOP

Samuel Sloop (b. in PA) was listed as a plane maker in Cincinnati, OH, from 1829-40; in 1829, at Main bt. 9th. & Court; in 1831, cor. Abigail & Sycamore; in 1834, Elm bt. New Market & 9th.; from 1836-37, w.s. Main bt. 5th. & 6th.; from 1839-40 as a plane maker and dealer in edge tools, Main bt. 5th. & 6th. He advertised in the 1837 **Western Address Directory** as a "Wood Screw and Plane Manufacturer." In 1839-40, he was listed as an edge tool dealer.   *

G. SMALL

Possibly **George Small** (**Schmall**) of York, PA, who was the brother to **Jacob Small** and **Peter Small**. **George** built the steeple of the Old Courthouse, in York, in 1815. Example: on a 9 1/4" maple, wedge-lock, slide-arm adjustable sash with heavy round chamfers, both halves are marked on the toe, ca. 1820, probably from PA.   UR

I. SMALL

Example: on a 14" beech plank plane with an iron warestrip, single iron and open tote, ca. 1850.   UR

IACOB SMALL

Jacob Small (d. 1794) was a maker of carpenter planes, in Baltimore, MD. He advertised in the *Maryland Gazette*, on July 1790: "Wanted, immediately, a good journeyman Plane Maker". The ads continued into 1794, at which time he died. His estate contained new carpenter's tools and was administered by **Jacob Small Jr**. Another series of ads from 1790 outlined a dispute between **Jacob Small** and **Henry Kuhn** & **Jacob Kuhn** who were brothers of **Jacob Small's** wife. That dispute involved land in York Co., PA. This may or may not be the same **Jacob Small** (**Schmall**), who did carpentry work, in 1798-99, on the German Reformed Church in York, PA, along with **Peter Small** and **Henry Small**. Examples: on a 9 7/16" beech molder with heavy flat chamfers and the A wedge, and a 10 1/8" beech large astragal bead with heavy flat chamfers, a **Green iron**, and the B wedge, found in the Lancaster, PA area, which appear to be earlier, ca. 1790-1800.   *****

M: SMALL

Example: on a 9 7/16" beech special hollow with **8/6** on the heel with flat chamfers, ca. early 19c.   UR

P. SMALL

Peter Small (b. ca. 1770 in York Co., PA, d. ca. 1824 in York Co.) was a carpenter and housewright, in York, PA, from 1798-1815. He was the brother of **George Small** and **Jacob Small**. **Peter** built the following York, PA, structures: the German Reformed Church in 1798-99, the German Reformed Church steeple in 1799-80, and the German Lutheran Church Steeple in 1815. Examples: the A imprint is on molding planes 9 7/16"-9 11/16" beech with round chamfers, found in York, PA; a panel raiser with a round top **Newbould** iron; and a wedge-arm plow. The B imprint is branded on the side of a 9 1/2"x 1 1/8" beech round with tight round chamfers and a **Newbould** iron, ca. 1810.   **A ***; B ******

S. C. SMALL

Example: on an 8" beech smoother with a rounded sole, ca. 1850.   **UR**

T. SMALL

Examples: on a 9 3/8" beech molding plane with the A wedge, and a 9 1/4" beech tongue & groove pair with round chamfers and the B wedge, ca. 1820.   **UR**

A. S. SMART

Believed to be **Abial Stickney Smart** (b. Mar. 9, 1793 in Hopkinton, NH, d. Aug. 10, 1869 in Springfield, Windsor Co., VT) who emigrated to Springfield, before 1820, when he was recorded, as a cabinetmaker. In 1823, he advertised in the **Bellows Falls Intelligencer** for an apprentice to the cabinetmaker business in Springfield, VT. In 1840, he was "engaged in manufactures & trades", in 1850, as a carpenter; and in 1860, as a painter. Examples: on a massive 23 7/8"x 2" dado or shipbuilders jack; and a 22" jointer, both beech with a closed tote; and a compass soled smoother with a **Moulson Brothers** iron, ca. 1850.   **UR**

J x SMART

Example: on a 9 1/4" beech skew rabbet, imprinted on the toe and heel, and with heavy flat chamfers. ca. 1800.   **UR**

J S/ J. SMILEY/ JOHN SMILEY

John Smiley (b. Nov. 17, 1811 in Peterboro, Hillsborough, NH, d. Sep. 5, 1890 in Lowell, MA) was listed in the 1850 census, as a Lawrence, MA, carpenter. In 1870, he was listed, as a carpenter, in Lowell, MA. Various combination of the elements have been reported, all on bench planes, ca. 1850.

A, B, B1 & A/B ****

A. SMITH

Aaron Smith (b. Dec. 15, 1769 in Swansea, MA, d. Dec. 21, 1822 in Rehoboth, MA) was the son of **Ezekiel Smith** (b. 1747 in Swansea, MA, d. 1834 in Rehoboth, MA) a housewright. **Aaron** was the father of nine children, three of whom became planemakers: **Ezekiel Smith** (b. 1799, d. 1880); **Jarvis Brown Smith** (b. 1801, d. 1894) who in 1823, was referred to as a journeyman planemaker; and **Aaron Mason Smith** (b. 1805, d. 1834). **Aaron's** first record in Rehoboth, MA, was on a land transaction, in 1791, with his occupation given as housewright. In 1803, he was listed as a shop joiner; in 1806, as a toolmaker; and in 1816, as a planemaker. On April 10, 1820, **Aaron Smith** was admitted to the Providence Association of Mechanics and Manufacturers. He owned a blacksmith shop and was close to **Peck's** iron works, a possible source for plane irons. He was a prolific producer and apparently was active right up to his death. The estate inventory of Jan. 27, 1823 is fully described in *The Smith Family - Planemakers of Rehoboth*, in *The Mechanic's Workbench*, Vol. 8, Oct. 1979, by Don and Anne Wing. It is believed that **Aaron Smith** was apprenticed to **Joseph Fuller** or connected in some way. The A1 name and location imprints were both from the same dies as used for the A imprints. Examples: the A imprint is on a 10" birch cove & bead complex molder with the A relieved wedge (similar to the early **Jo, Fuller** planes), and flat chamfers with flutes, ca. 1790. The A1 & B imprints are on planes 9 1/2" birch with flat chamfers (no flutes) and the B wedge. Later planes, ca. 1800, were the standard 9 1/2" length, were beech with the non-relieved C wedge and flat chamfers, but without flutes.
B, B1 & C *; A1 & A2 **;
A & D *****

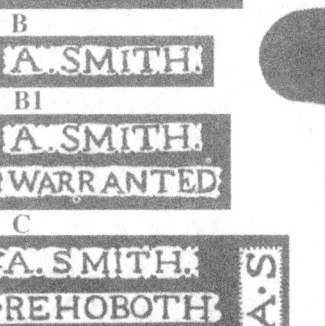

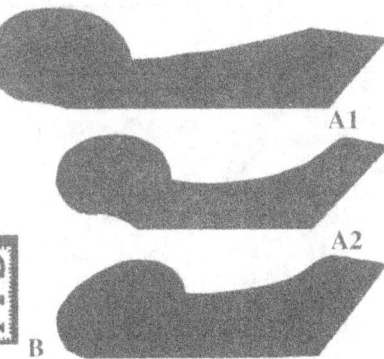

A. SMITH
Example: on a 9 1/2" beech double-iron sash with **Wm. Ash & Co.** and **W. Butcher** irons, and the incuse owner imprint **W. A. Smith**, ca. 1840.   **UR**

A: SMITH
Examples: on a 9" beech hollow with heavy flat chamfers; and a 9 3/4" beech fixed sash with heavy round chamfers, ca. 1790-1820.   **UR**

A + SMITH
Example: on a 10 1/4" beech medium hollow & round; and a 9 1/2" beech bead with interrupted boxing, all with flat chamfers, ca. 1800, probably from PA.   ********

A. SMITH
Example: on a 9 3/4"x 5/16" beech dado with flat chamfers, ca. 1800.   **UR**

A. SMITH
Examples: the A imprint is on a 1" hollow. The B imprint is on a 14 1/4"x 1 3/4" beech skew rabbet with large shallow flat chamfers. The C imprint with the initials **A.S** is on a 10 3/4" beech halving plane with flat chamfers, ca. 1830.

A, B, C & C1: **UR**

A SMITH/ LOWELL
Alpheus Smith of Lowell, MA, was a drygoods and hardware merchant, from 1832-37, at Town House, Merrimac St. Lowell. In the 1832 Lowell directory, he advertised that he made all kinds of carpenter's planes. In 1835 only, the firm was called **Smith & Burbank**, with **Alpheus Smith** and **Samuel Burbank** (d. 1868 in Lowell, MA). **Samuel Burbank** was listed from 1837-40, as hardware and clothing; and from 1859-64, as **Burbank, Chase & Co.**, Lowell. Example: the B imprint is on a moving filletster. Lowell is across the Merrimac River from NH.

A *; B ****

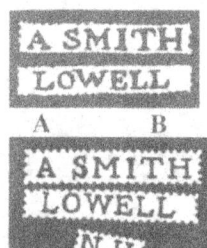

A. M. SMITH
Aaron Mason Smith (b. Sept. 8, 1805 in Bristol Co., MA, m. Dec. 11, 1831 in New Bedford, Bristol Co., MA, d. May 3, 1834, in New Bedford, age 29) was a son of **Aaron Smith**. He made planes in New Bedford, MA, from 1831-34. He was listed in a deed, in 1832, as a machinist.   A & A1 ******

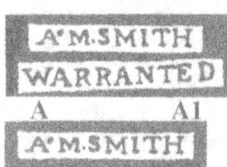

ARNOLD SMITH
Example: on a 9 15/16" applewood round with shallow flat chamfers, ca. 1750-75.   **UR**

B. SMITH
Example: on a birch slide-arm skew rabbet with wood thumbscrews and heavy round chamfers; ca. 1800-20.   **UR**

B + SMITH
Example: on a 9 3/8" fully boxed 3/16" bead made by **E. Smith**, ca. 1850.   **UR**

B. SMITH
Example: on a 9 5/8" birch large round with a relieved wedge and heavy flat chamfers; and a Yankee plow, ca. 1800.   **UR**

C. SMITH
Example: the A wedge is on a 9 1/2" beech hollow with flat chamfers. The B wedge is on a 9 1/4" beech dado with a wood depth stop, wood thumbscrew and round chamfers, ca. 1800-20.   ********

C. F. SMITH
Examples: the A imprint is on a screw-arm plow plane, imprinted twice on the toe, ca. 1850.   **UR**

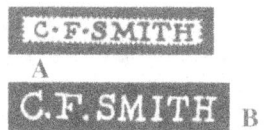

C. J. SMITH & CO.
Charles J. Smith (b. Nov. 22, 1823 in Baden, Germany, m. 1869 in Hamilton Co., OH, d. 1902 in Atchison, KA) was a Cincinnati, OH, hardware dealer, from 1853-58. In 1846, he was in partnership with **J. Kolp** and **E. F. Seybold** to manufacture edge tools in Cincinnati, OH. In 1949-50, he was part of **Heim & Smith**, at 280 Main St.; in 1851-56, he was part of **J. & C. Smith** with **John H. Smith**. An 1851 ad listed **J & C Smith**: "Planes, edge tools & tress hoops, and imports of hardware & cutlery, sales room at 260 Main St. bet. 5th. & 6th. Sts.". From 1860-69, **Charles** was listed as a hardware merchant in Atchison, KA. From 1880-

1900, he was committed to an asylum. Example: on a plane made by **Roseboom & Magill**, in 1855 only, and on a **T. Richards** plane. A & B **

B

C. S. SMITH
Examples: on a panel plane; a plank tongue plane; a slide-arm plow; and a smoothing plane. **UR**

CHARLES SMITH
Charles Smith (b. ca. 1828 in Bolton, d. Mar. 31, 1876 in Chester, MA) was listed in the 1860 MA Industrial census as making plane handles in Chester, MA.
No imprint has been reported.

D. SMITH
Believed to be **Daniel Smith** (d. 1815), a cabinetmaker in Newbury, MA. Examples: the molders are 9 1/4"-9 1/2" beech with flat chamfers and the A wedge with the **I. Sleeper** influence; two beech square rabbets, one 9 7/8" and the other 10 7/8"; and a 13 1/2" beech panel raiser with an ebony diamond strike and heavy flat chamfers. One example has the B incuse imprint on the heel of a 9 1/4" applewood halving plane with flat chamfers, ca. 1800, possibly from the Newburyport area.
B: UR; A ****

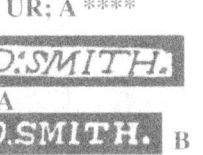
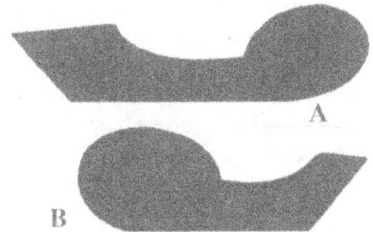

D. SMITH
Possible **David Smith** (bapt. Jul. 18, 1767 in Ipswich, MA) who was a cabinetmaker from Ipswich, MA, active ca. 1790. Example: on a 10 1/2" beech single-iron fixed sash with heavy flat chamfers, from New England. ca. 1790. **UR**

D: SMITH
Examples: a thumbnail with heavy flat chamfers and a relieved wedge similar to an early **Aaron Smith** or **Jo, Fuller**; and a quarter round with round chamfers and a non-relieved wedge (sheared), both are 9 3/4" beech, from southeastern New England. ca. 1800-20. ****

D SMITH
The **SMITH** imprint is from an A or B imprint of **E. SMITH** with an added **D** on a 12 3/8" large beech round with a cherry wedge. ca. mid 19c. **UR**

D. SMITH
Example: on a 9 5/8" beech complex molder with flat chamfers, ca. 1800. **UR**

E. SMITH
Ezekiel Smith II (b. June 18, 1799 in Rehoboth, MA, d. Sep. 10, 1880 in Worcester, MA) was the oldest son of **Aaron Smith**. He had an uncle, grandfather, and great grandfather also named **Ezekiel**; he was called **Ezekiel II**. Three of his sons, **Horace G. Smith**, **Ira E. Smith**, and **Edward H. Smith** were planemakers. He inherited his father's workshop in 1823 and worked as a planemaker in Rehoboth, MA, until 1849. **Ezekiel** apprenticed **N. L. Barrus** in ca. 1828. He was listed in the 1850 Smithfield, RI, census as a planemaker using water and hand power, employing 6 employees making 4000 planes worth $5,000. He was listed in Worcester, MA, directories during 1857-73 as a patternmaker, carpenter and planemaker. He turned the business over to his son who worked as **Edward H. Smith & Co.** in 1874. **Ezekiel Smith II** should not be confused with another **Ezekiel Smith** (d. 1808) who was the son of **Gideon Smith** of Hingham or his son **Ezekiel Joy Smith** (d. 1865), both of whom were carpenter/ woodworkers in Worcester.
Example: The E1 imprint with **MADE FOR** on a medium hollow.
A, B, B1, B2 & C: FF;
D, D1 & D2 **; E & E1 ***

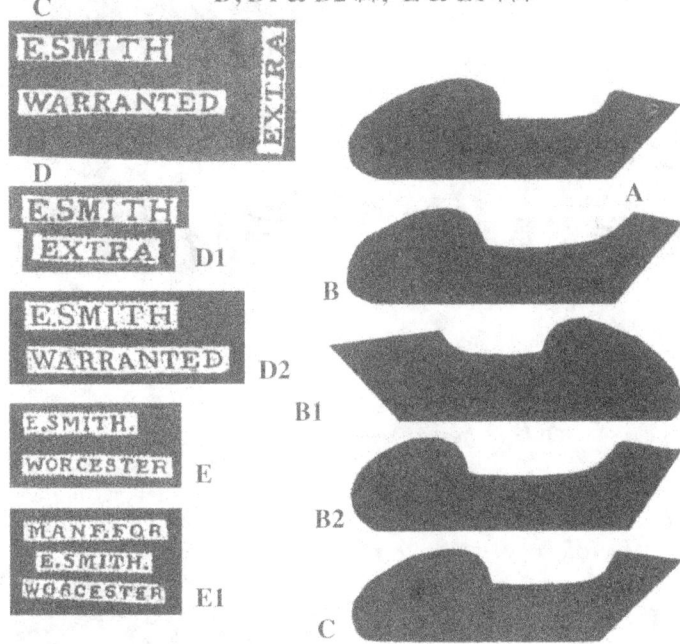

E. SMITH
A contemporary planemaker with the date **1984**, on a 9 1/2" beech table joint pair with 19c chamfers. **UR**

E. H. SMITH
Edward H. Smith (b. 1842 in Rehoboth, MA) was the son of **Ezekiel Smith**, brother of **Ira E. Smith** and **Horace G. Smith**. Edward was listed in the 1858 Providence, RI directory, as a planemaker, living with, and working for, his older brother **Horace**. In 1860, age 19, **Edward H. Smith** was listed, as a machinist, in Worcester, MA, living with his father **Ezekiel**, a planemaker. **Edward H. Smith** and **A. N. Learned** were

partners operating as **E. H. Smith & Co.**; and succeeded **Ezekiel Smith**, in Worcester, MA, in 1874 only. They advertised as manufacturers and retail dealers for carpenter's and joiner's planes. Examples: on a skew rabbet; a dado; and as an owner imprint on the heel of a style **42** match-handled 7/8" tongue plane made by **Copeland & Co.**. ****

ELI SMITH
Possibly **Eli Smith** (b. ca. Nov. 8, 1756, d. Mar. 29, 1824 in Litchfield, CT) a Litchfield, joiner. In 1788, he advertised for a runaway apprentice **Nathaniel Brown**. **Eli Smith** served as an Ensign in the Army in the Revolutionary War, in Col. Beebe's Reg., Capt. Potter's Co. Examples: mostly hollows & rounds; a single-boxed bead; and a very complex molder, all 9 1/2" beech (one birch), with flat chamfers (one with round chamfers), and relieved wedges. One has an **I. Parks** iron (Birmingham, England, ca. 1800), possibly from southeastern New England. ca. 1800. ****

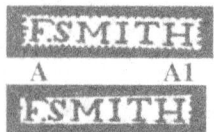

F. SMITH
Example: on an 8 7/16" beech square shiplap or fenced rabbet plane with shallow round chamfers, ca. 1830. **UR**

F. SMITH
Example: on a 5/8" bead. The B imprint is modified from the A imprint die, ca. 1850. **A & A1: UR**

F. C. SMITH
Frank C. Smith was listed as a carpenter, housewright and horse dealer in New Bedford, MA, from 1849-65. From 1871-78, he was listed as a planemaker, working at 14 Williams St. This is the address of the **New Bedford Tool Co.**. From 1879-80, he was still listed as a planemaker, but with out a business address. In 1885, **Frank C. Smith** was listed as a boat builder, at Weaver St., New Bedford. Example: on a **16** hollow, found with a group of New Bedford planes, ca. 1850. ****

G. SMITH
Possibly **Gilbert Smith** was a Canaan, CT & New Marlbough, MA, joiner. **Smith** worked in partnership with **Richard Smith**, from 1796-1811. He framed buildings, made window sashes, clapboards and furniture. Example: on a 9 1/2" beech very complex molder, with round chamfers, ca. 1820. **UR**

GEO. SMITH
Example: on a 9 1/2" beech **18** round with an **Ohio Tool Co.** iron, ca. 1850. **UR**

HENRY SMITH
Examples: on a 10" beech wedge-lock adjustable arm tongue & groove pair with large round chamfers on top, round heel chamfers and flat chamfers on the toe, ca. 1800. **UR**

HIRAM M. SMITH
Hiram M. Smith (b. 1827 in MA) was listed, as a planemaker, in 1850, in the Smithfield, RI census, boarding with and working for, **Ezekiel Smith**. **No imprint has been reported**.

HORACE G. SMITH
Horace Granville Smith (b. Jan. 3, 1825 in Rehoboth, MA, d. Apr. 26, 1906 in Boston, MA) was the son of **Ezekiel Smith** and brother of **Ira E. Smith** and **Edward H. Smith**. In 1853, **Horace G. Smith** leased a factory in North Providence, RI, for the "purpose of carrying on this business of making carpenter's planes." He was listed in the 1857-59 Providence directories, as a planemaker, at Eddy St. **No imprint has been reported**.

I. SMITH
Example: on a beech plow with wood depth stop and wood thumbscrews, ca. 1840. **UR**

I: SMITH
Possibly **Jonathan Smith** (b. Nov. 5, 1733 in New London, CT, d. 1776) who was listed, as a carpenter and cabinetmaker, in Groton, CT. His estate listed 26 planes and other cabinetmaker's tools. Examples: on a crown molder with offset tote and flat chamfers; a 10 9/16" birch slide-arm plow with wood thumbscrew, wood depth stop, the A relieved wedge and snecked iron; and a 10 3/4" beech astragal with large chamfers, mostly on the side, that end with a long taper; ca. 1790. ****

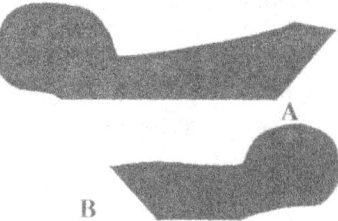

I. E. SMITH/ I. E. SMITH & CO
Ira E. Smith (b. 1830 in Rehoboth, MA, killed Oct. 29, 1857 in a building explosion in Providence, RI) was the son of **Ezekiel Smith** and the brother of **Horace G. Smith** and **Edward H. Smith**. Ira was listed in the 1850 Smithfield, RI census, as a planemaker, living with his father **Ezekiel Smith**. The *Pawtucket Gazette and Chronicle* lists an auction notice for the "late firm of **Ira E. Smith & Co.**, bench plane manufacturers." Ira was listed in the 1857 Providence directory, as a planemaker, at Eddy St., the same address as his brother, **Horace G. Smith**. Examples: the B imprint with **& CO** is on a 9 1/2"x 3/8" beech side bead with round chamfers, ca. 1850. **A, A1, B & B1 ****

Is SMITH

Example: on a 9 1/2"x 7/8" beech bead with heavy chamfers. **UR**

J x SMITH

Example: on a 9 1/2" skew rabbet; a 9 1/2" bead; a 14"x 3 15/16" crown molder, and a 13 3/4" panel raiser with an offset tote, all beech, ca. 1800. ********

J. SMITH

Example: on a smoothing plane with a **Dwight French** iron, ca. 1850. **UR**

J SMITH

Example: the A imprint is on a 9 5/8" beech quarter round with three intermittent lignum vitae wear strips and shallow flat chamfers; and a smoother struck twice on the toe and made by **G. White/ Philadelphia**. The B imprint, a damaged die, is on a 9 1/2" beech astragal plane with flat chamfers, from PA, ca. 1820. **A & A1: UR**

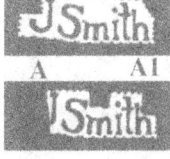

J. SMITH

Example: on a 9 5/8" beech small round, ca. 1850. **UR**

J. SMITH

Example: on a 16 1/2" beech panel raiser with open centered tote, nicker and wedge, wood adj. depth stop mounted on side and round chamfers, ca. 19c. **UR**

J: SMITH

Example: on a 10" beech ogee molder with heavy flat chamfers, ca. 1800. **UR**

J. B. SMITH

Jarvis Brown Smith (b. June 28, 1801 in Rehoboth, MA, d. Nov. 13, 1894 in Rehoboth) is one of the three plane making sons of **Aaron Smith**, was a wood turner, and farmer; and in a 1823 land deed, was referred to as a journeyman planemaker, in Rehoboth, MA. Besides planes, he made teapot handles for the silversmiths and pewterers of Taunton, MA. In 1850, he was listed, as a carpenter, in Rehoboth. In 1860, he was listed as a machinist. In 1880, he was listed, as a planemaker. Examples: the A imprint is on a 11 3/8" beech closed toted tongue plane with an integral fence and metal wear plates. The B imprint is on a 9 1/2" beech slide-arm plow with a wood depth stop, wood thumbscrews; and a 9 1/2" beech rabbet with round chamfers, found in a group of **A. Smith**, and **E. Smith** planes, reinforcing the belief that this is the imprint of **Jarvis Brown Smith**, both with round chamfers. The **WARRANTED** in the B imprint appears to be identical to that used by **E. Smith**'s B imprint and **A. Smith**'s C imprint, ca. 1820. **A & B *******

JOSEPH SMITH

Joseph Smith (b. ca. 1804 in Ireland, d. Sep. 1849 of fever in Utica, NY) was listed, as a planemaker, in a Utica, NY 1832 directory, boarding with, and working for, **R. J. Collins**. **No imprint has been reported**.

J. & C. SMITH

John H. Smith and **Charles J. Smith** were wholesale hardware and edge tool dealers in Cincinnati, OH, from 1851-52, at 218 Main. It was succeeded by **C. J. Smith & Co.**, from 1853-58. *******

J. H. SMITH

John H. Smith (b. Aug. 16, 1831 in Brown Co., OH, d. Jan. 11, 1881 in Charlotte, Eaton Co., MI, burial in Cincinnati, OH) was a Cincinnati, OH, hardware dealer, who was a partner in **Seybold & Smith**, in 1846; the J in **J. & C. Smith**, in 1851-52, and with **Lyon & Smith**, from 1849-53. Example: on a 7/8" Grecian ovolo with an **Ohio Tool Co. 63** style number. The B imprint is on a 9 1/2"x 1/2" boxed bead also imprinted **E. F. Seybold/ CinT. O.** **A & A1 ****; **B ******

J. W. SMITH

John W. Smith (b. May 26, 1808 in England, d. Feb. 12, 1896 in New Bedford) arrived in Boston, MA 1842-47. In 1850, he was listed in Wareham, Plymouth Co., MA. From 1856-89, he was listed, as a planemaker, in New Bedford, MA. In 1856, he was listed at 30 Elm St., the address of **John M. Taber** (d. in 1873 of "paralysis"). **John W. Smith** was still working at this address, until 1873-74, and then is recorded working at 14 William St. This is the same address listed for the **New Bedford Tool Co.**. From 1881-85, **John W. Smith** was listed, as a planemaker, at 119 N. Water St., around the corner from the William St. address. In 1888-96, he was listed, at 163 N. Water St., no occupation. Example: the A1 imprint is on a 13 3/4" beech skew panel plane with an open tote. The B imprint is on a live oak smoother. **A, A1 & B ****

L. SMITH

Examples: on a fenced rabbet with a high pitch iron; a cove; and an altered round, all 9 3/8" cherry with flat chamfer, possibly from New England. ca. 1800. ********

M. SMITH

Example: on a 9 5/8"x 1 3/4" beech rabbet with shallow round chamfers. **UR**

N. SMITH
Example: on a 9 3/8" beech bead with flat chamfers, ca. 1790. **UR**

NICHOLAS/ SMITH
Example: on a 9 1/2" small bead with heavy shallow flat chamfers, and on a **F. Nicholson** crown molder; and a halving plane, ca. 1750. **UR**

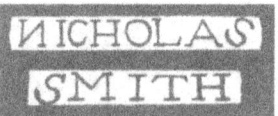

O. H. SMITH
O. H. Smith advertised on Mar. 18, listed as a general jobber, Lyman Block, Northampton (MA) included "PLANES". Examples: on a pair of handled tongue & groove planes, and a jointer with a decorative eagle stamp, similar to that of other Northampton makers. ca. 1850. **A & B *****

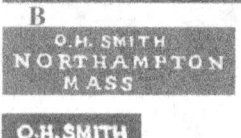

P. SMITH
Example: the A imprint on the toe and the B imprint branded on the side of a 9 7/8" beech Yankee plow, wedge-lock arms, with added wood thumbscrew in front and added iron heart-shaped thumbscrew in rear, riveted skate, wood depth stop, and small flat chamfers. ca. 1800. **A & B: UR**

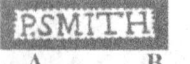

PHILIP SMITH
Philip Smith (b. 1827 in Darmstads, Germany) was listed in 1850, as a carpenter, in Columbus, OH. In 1856-57, **Philip** was listed, as a planemaker. In 1870, he was listed, as a carpenter/joiner. **No imprint has been reported.**

PHINEAS SMITH
Phineas Smith was a New York City, hardware dealer, from 1855-96. Examples: on a 6 3/4" coffin smoother made by **John Hill's Tool Store**; on a 14" jack with an open tote and a single unmarked iron. **UR**

R S/ R + SMITH
Example: on a 10 1/4" birch skew rabbet with flat chamfers, branded on the heel are the incuse initials **RS**, ca. 1780. **UR**

R. SMITH
Possibly **Richard Smith** (b. ca. 1782 in RI, d. Nov. 25, 1864 in North Kingston, RI) was married on Mar. 9, 1846 in N. Kingston. He was first listed in the 1810 census in North Kingston, Washington Co., RI. In 1850, he was listed as a carpenter; and in 1860; as a mechanic; in N. Kingston. Example: on two 7 1/2" smoothing planes, one beech and one apple with a iron strike button on the heel, and one found on Cape Cod. The B imprint is on a 24" birch joiner with an apple closed tote & wedge, and an iron strike button on the nose top, ca. 1815-30. **A & B: *****

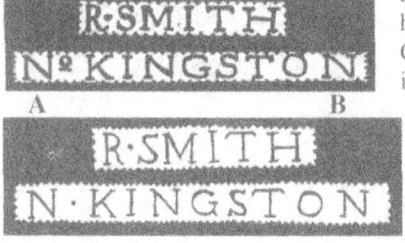

S. SMITH
Example: on a beech bead with lignum vitae boxing. While Natchez, MS, is a possibility, there is a Natchez as part of Zanesville, OH. *****

SAMUEL B. SMITH
Samuel B. Smith (b. ca. 1828, married Sep. 2, 1851 in New Haven, CT) Example: on a fully-boxed 1/4" bead by **J. Denison**, with a paper label: Paper label: *****

SAMUEL B. SMITH
WHOLESALE AND RETAIL DEALERS IN
HARDWARE, IRON AND STEEL
AXLES, SPRINGS, ANVILS, VISES, FILES, EMERY,
GLUE AND MECHANIC'S TOOLS OF ALL KINDS
148 CHAPEL STREET, NEW HAVEN, CONN.

SILAS F. SMITH
Silas F. Smith was listed, as a planemaker, in Philadelphia, PA, in 1837. **No imprint has been reported**.

W. SMITH
Possibly **William Smith** of Seekonk, Bristol Co., MA, a cabinetmaker, who worked ca. 1820. Examples: on a 21 7/16"x 3 1/8" beech jointer; and a 9 1/2" skew rabbet, both with round chamfers, and a large hollow, ca. 1820. **UR**

SMITH BIGELOW & CO.
Smith Bigelow was listed in the 1852 MA register, as a tool factory, located in Conway, MA. Example: one dated **1853**. **A & A1: *****

SMITH, COHU & CO.

Henry S. Smith and Thomas Smith were listed as cutlery dealers in New York City, from 1871-76 directories. Examples: on several bench planes. **

SMITH & GREEN

Example: on a **Ohio Tool & Co.** molding plane with an ink imprint within an broad ax outline that reads: ****

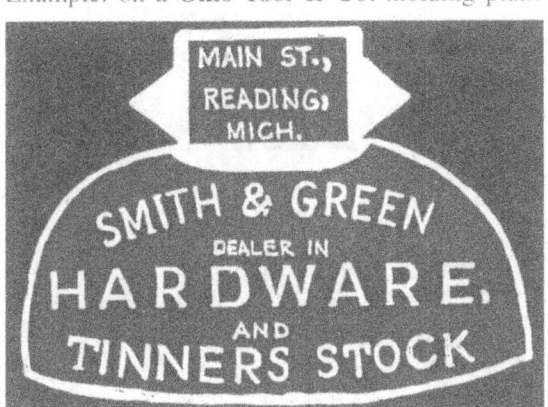

SMITH, LYON & FIELD

William Thomas Smith (b. 1852 in NY), **Judson A. Lyon**, and **Richard T. Field** were partners in a New York City hardware firm, active from 1884-95. Example: the B imprint is on a 7" smoother with a **Sargent & Co.** iron. A & A1 *; B *****

SMITH & ROBERTS

Smith & Roberts was a hardware dealer, in Richmond, VA, from 1850-55. ****

SMITH & STEWART

Smith & Stewart (Stuart) were hardware dealers in Springfield, MA, from 1873-75. Some planes bear the additional location imprint of **488 MAIN**. ***

SMITH, WINCHESTER & CO.

Smith, Winchester & Co. was probably a hardware dealer, located in South Windham, CT, working dates unknown. Example: on a **16** round made by **Greenfield Tool Co.** and with a **No. 367** on the heel. ****

I. SMYTH

Example: With **MAKER** and location **PHILA** on a 7 7/8" beech smoother with a W. Butcher iron. ca. 1825. ****

I. SNEVELY

Example: on a 9 13/16"x 1 1/4" square rabbet; a 9 11/16" cove, both beech with heavy round chamfers and **Newbould** irons; and a 9 1/2" beech cove & bead complex molder with heavy flat chamfers, probably from PA, ca. 1790-1810. ****

SNOW

Example: on a 9 1/8" maple molder with narrow flat chamfers, probably from New England, ca. 1800. **UR**

A. SNOW

Example: on a 9" complex molder with a relieved wedge, ca. 1800. **UR**

A. H. SNOW

Example: on a jack plane with a **Dwight French** iron. Billerica is just south of Lowell, MA, ca. 1850. ****

Dr. SNOW

Examples: on a 9 15/16" maple skew rabbet with flat chamfers; and on a 6 3/8"x 2 3/4"x 3" birch tap with hickory thumbscrews and heavy round chamfers, possibly from New England, ca. 1790-1820. **UR**

GEORGE SNOW

George Snow (m. on Mar. 7, 1822 in Providence, RI, d. prior to 1833) was the brother of **James Snow III**, and a toolmaker and journeyman working for **Joseph Fuller Sr.**. In 1822, **Joseph Fuller** (toolmaker) sold land to **George Snow** (toolmaker), witnessed by **Isaac Field**. In 1833, this same parcel was sold by **Sarah**, the widow of **George Snow** to **Joseph Fuller, Jr.**. **No imprint has been reported.**

H. SNOW

Example: on a 16 3/4" beech gutter plane with pegged tote, ca. 19c. **UR**

J. SNOW

James Snow III (b. 1782, d. 1873) was the brother of **George Snow**; and a toolmaker; and journeyman; working for **Joseph Fuller Sr.**. In 1808, **Joseph Fuller** (toolmaker) sold land to **James Snow III.** (toolmaker) witnessed by **Wm. Field & Isaac Field**. Example: on a 9" beech single-boxed complex molder with shallow flat chamfers, ca. 1810-20. A & B ****

L. SNOW
Example: on a 9 1/2" beech round with narrow flat chamfers, ca. 1800. **UR**

Z. SNOW
Example: on a 9 3/16" beech boxed snipe bill plane with shallow round chamfers, ca. 1830. **UR**

C. T. SNOWDEAL
Examples: the A imprint with the **THOMASTON, ME** is on a 9 3/8" spar plane with a double **William Ash & Co.** iron. The B imprint, is on a dado made by **Gladwin & Appleton/ Boston**, ca. 1850. ********

G. SNYDER
Example: on a 10" beech wedge arm plow plane with a upturned skate attached to the top of the front, 4 bone strips dovetailed into the fence, and heavy round chamfers. Stamped on the side is **I. H. SNYDER**. the plane was found in southeastern, PA. The imprint is incuse, slanted, and ca. early 19c. **UR**

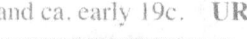

HENRY SNYDER
Henry Snyder (b. 1830 in Byron, Germany) was listed, as a planemaker, in Columbus, OH, in 1856-57. In 1870, listed as "works in foundry". In 1880, as turner, in Columbus, OH. Example: on a 10 1/2" beech filletser with short fence and round top chamfers and flat end chamfers, ca. 1820-30, found in OH. The Henry Snyder listed above is probably a descendant. **UR**

SODDING & RUSSELL
Sodding & Russell probably was a hardware dealer, in Towanda, PA. Example: on an **Auburn Tool Co.** bead. ********

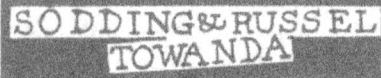

SOEDING BROTHERS
Casper Soeding (b. Nov. 9, 1825 in Schwelm, Germany, arrived in America in 1856) and Charles Soeding (b. 1828 in Germany, d. Mar. 11, 1888 in St. Louis, MO) were hardware dealers, in St. Louis, MO, from 1854-63. The firm became **Soeding & Brother**, in 1863-67; and **Casper Soeding** from 1870-83, at 2110 Franklin Ave. ********

J. SOLES
Example: on a 9 1/4" beech moving filletster with heavy flat chamfers, ca. 1820. **UR**

D. SOUDER
Example: on a 9 1/2" beech molder with narrow flat chamfers, possibly from PA, ca. 1810-20. **UR**

W. M. SOUDER
William M. Souder (b. ca. 1799 in PA, d. Dec. 27, 1868 in Philadelphia, PA) was a Philadelphia, PA, planemaker, from 1825-53. Souder was also part of **Souder & Summers**, in 1837. A hollow by **W. M. Souder** has been reported overstamped **A. Wallace/ Dundee**. **Alexander Wallace** made planes in Dundee, Scotland, from 1824-37, and in Montreal, Canada, from 1843-58. Also a **W. M. Souder** has been reported overstruck by **John Bell** who was active from 1829-51.
A & A2 *; **A1 & B *****

SOUDER & SUMMERS
Probably **William M. Souder** and **Martin Summers** who were listed, as a planemaker partnership, in the 1837 Philadelphia directory. Example: the A1 imprint is on a table hollow.
A & A1 ****

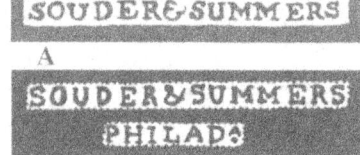

L. S/ L. S. SOULE
Believed to be **Lewis Starrett Soule** (b. Mar. 14, 1813 in Waldoboro, Lincoln Co., ME, d. Aug. 5, 1873 in Jefferson, Lincoln, ME, Burial in Waldoboro) of Waldoboro, ME, a joiner who made doors, sash, and blinds, from 1849-54; and who may have been a tool dealer. In 1850, he was listed as a tool manufacturer in Waldoboro, ME. Examples: on a 21 3/4" jointer; and a 1 1/2" grooving plane with steel skate and wear surface. The A imprint is on a **D. Copeland/ Hartford** plane.

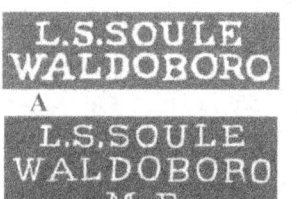

The A1 imprint is on an 8" coffin smoother. The B imprint is on a double-boxed, double-iron fixed sash made by **Union Factory/ H. Chapin**.
A, A1, B & B1 ***

R. M. SOULE/ RMS
Robert M. Soule (b. Oct. 30, 1921, d. Mar. 29, 2014 in West Haven, CT) was a contemporary planemaker using exotic woods of high quality. On Aug. 10, 1942, he enlisted in the U. S. Army as a Private. In 1947-48, he was listed as an "assembler"; and in 1951, as an "installer" in **WE Co.**. From 1953-1967 he was listed as a carpenter. In 1978, **Robert** was listed as the Superintendent of the Yale Art Gallery at the University of Yale, in New Haven, CT. **Soule's** custom made low-angle block plane was featured in *Fine Woodworking*, winter 2006-2007 special issue, Tools & Shops.
A & B ***

SOULE, WHITE & SPEAR
Soule, White & Spear was a plane making firm in Warren, OH, ca. 1845. The firm consisted of **Josiah Soule Sr.** (b. Jan. 13, 1794 in Plympton, MA, m. Mar. 2, 1817, d. Mar. 7, 1872), who arrived in OH, in 1817; was listed as a carpenter, later a house builder; and who received a pension for his service in the War of 1812; **Charles White** (b. Jun. 20, 1797 in CT, d. aft. 1858 in Warren, Trumbull Co., OH) who was listed in 1850, as a mechanic; and also served in the War of 1812; and **Edward Spear** (b. 1795 in PA, d. 1873 in Warren OH) a woodworker, who came from PA, in 1818. By 1850, **Edward Spear** owned a sash and blind shop. In 1870, **Edward Spear** was listed as a machinist, and a Justice of Peace. Example: on a 9 1/2" beech 1 1/2" complex molder. ***

T. SOUTHWORTH
Example: on a 9 13/16" beech molder with narrow flat chamfers, ca. 1800. **UR**

SOUTHWORTH & NOYES
The 1867 Plymouth Co., MA, directory carries an advertisement by **Southworth & Noyes** stating that they were dealers in "groceries, flour, and hardware", at 447 Main St., in North Bridge-water, MA, active from 1867-74. Possibly **Charles A. Southworth** (b. 1842 in CT) who was listed in 1880, as a soap dealer; and in 1910, as a box maker. Example: on a 9 1/2" beech dado with a **7/8** size on the heel and a brass/ steel depth stop. *****

S. SOWER
Example: on a 10" beech small round with tight flat chamfers, ca. 1800. **UR**

A. J. SPAFFORD
Almond J. Spafford (b. 1826 in Twinsburg, OH, d. Jun. 18, 1901 in Bedford, OH) may have been associated with **Vinall** in Cleveland, before setting up his own shop in Bedford, OH. Example: the B imprint is on the heel of a plane made by **J. J. Vinall** a Cleveland, OH, planemaker, from 1845-53. The A incuse imprint, with the date **1875**, is on a complex molder with a size number on the heel, **1866** on a single boxed complex molder, and **1891** on the toe of a skew rabbet. A & B ****

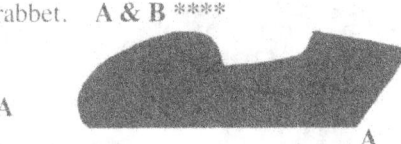

ALVIN SPALDING.
Example: on a 9 9/16" birch astragal with flat chamfers, ca. 1800. **UR**

MARCUS SPALDING
Marcus Spalding (b. 1833) was listed as a planemaker, in Starkey, NY, in 1850, age 17, and living with **George W. Roger**. **No imprint has been reported**.

W. H. SPALDING/ W. H. SPALDING & CO.
William Henry Spalding (**Spaulding**) (b. Jun. 17, 1822 in Groton, Tompkins Co., NY, d. Feb. 6, 1906 in Chicago, IL, buried Feb. 9, 1906 in Waverly, Tioga Co., NY) was the son of **Nathaniel Spaulding**. Imprint C indicates that **W. H. Spalding** made planes in McLean, Town of Groton, NY. Imprints A & B indicates that he made planes in Elmira, NY. The 1850 census reported **W. H. Spalding** employing two men. He does not appear in the first Elmira City Directory in 1857, as he had presumably moved to nearby Waverly. In 1880, he was listed as a carpenter, back in Elmira, NY.
A, B & C **

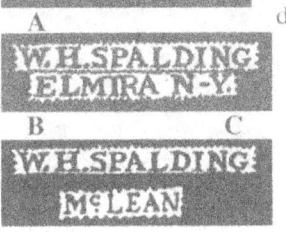

J. N. SPARRELL
James Newton (**Nuton**) **Sparrell** (b. May 5, 1798 in Scituate, MA, d. Mar. 1, 1859 in Scituate) was a cabinetmaker, in Norwell, Plymouth Co., MA, ca. 1820, who was reported as a planemaker. In 1855, he was listed as a house wright.
No imprint has been reported.

E. W. SPARROW

Ernest Willis Sparrow (b. Aug. 8, 1873, ME, d. Apr. 7, 1934 in Bremerton, Kitsap, WA) From 1910-30 he was listed as a ship carpenter at the Navy Yard in Bremerton, WA. Examples: on four bench planes: a jointer, a 9 1/18" smoother, a 16 1/8" razee jack with a closed tote, and a 22 3/8" razee fore plane with a closed tote, all made of Cuban or Honduras mahogany with maple totes and **Buck Brothers** double-irons (with the buck's head design), found on the Oregon coast, ca. 1880-1900. ****

J. SPAULDING

Example: on an 8 1/2" miter block plane with shallow round chamfers and a single-iron marked **PROVIDENCE/ EXTRA**. ca. 1850. **UR**

N. SPAULDING

Nathaniel Spaulding (b. Aug. 28, 1795 in NH, d. Dec. 13, 1871 in Newfield, Tompkins Co., NY), was the father of **William H. Spalding**. Nathaniel made planes, in the village of McLean, Town of Groton, Tompkin Co., NY, from 1824-50; and at the **Treman & Bros.** plane factory, at 11-13 South Cayuga St., Ithaca, NY, from 1860-70. The 1850 census listed **Nathaniel Spaulding** as employing three men and producing 2000 jointer planes, worth $1500.
A, A1 & B *

JOHN E. SPAYD

John E. Spayd (b. 1799 in Prussia, naturalized Oct. 13, 1846, d. Feb. 18, 1871 in Philadelphia, PA) married **Catherine Anna Bibighaus** in Aug., 1822, the sister of **Samuel H. Bibighaus** who was the brother-in-law and successor of **John Bell**. Spayd was listed, as a planemaker, in the 1831-33 Philadelphia directories; and in 1819, as a carpenter. He was part of **Spayd & Bell**, ca. 1830-40; and probably part of **Spayd & Wheeler**. In 1863, **John E. Spayd** was listed, as planemaker, at 613 Wood, Philadelphia.
A & A1 ****

SPAYD & BELL

John E. Spayd and John Bell were brothers-in-law and made planes in Philadelphia, PA, under this partnership sometime between 1830-40.
A & B: ****

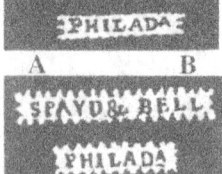

SPAYD & WHEELER

A partnership of **John E. Spayd** and an unknown **Wheeler**. Example: on a 22" fore plane with an offset tote and a single-iron. ****

EDWARD SPEAR

Edward Spear (b. 1795 in PA, d. 1873 in Warren, OH) who was a partner with **Charles White** and **Charles Soule** in **Soule, White & Spear**, in ca. 1840; and ca. 1845 in Warren, OH. In 1850, **Edward Spear** owned a sash and blind shop.
No imprint has been reported.

M. SPEAR

Example: on a 9 1/2" beech center bead, ca. 1840-50. **UR**

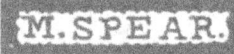

SPEAR & WOOD

Howard W. Spear was listed as a Chelsea, MA, planemaker, in 1874-76; and may have been in this partnership. Both Charlestown and Chelsea are part of the Boston environs. The **CHELSEA** imprint is the same die used by **Thomas Appleton** when he worked in Chelsea, MA. A bead plane has been reported with the B imprint and **LEWIS HUNT/ CHARLESTOWN MASS**.
A **; B1 ****; B *****

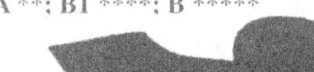

SPENCER

The firm of **E. & B. Spencer** of New Haven, CT, was listed as a planemaker, in 1831. The **B. Spencer** was probably **Benjamin Spencer** (b. Oct. 31, 1779, d. Mar. 6, 1857 in New Haven, CT) who lived in Saybrook, CT, from 1810-30, and was listed in the 1850 census, as a planemaker, in New Haven, CT. Patten's 1840 New Haven city directory, listed **Benjamin Spencer**, as a planemaker, at 27 Brewery, with his home at 25 Brewery. Some **Spencer** planes appear in the inventory of the **Duncan Phyfe tool chest** owned by the New York Historical Society. Examples: on a 9 5/8" beech double-iron fixed sash with flat chamfers, and a wedge-locked plow with heavy round chamfers, found in the New Haven, CT. **Spencer** also produced snipe bills and a pair of unusual graduated size, double wedge & iron molders. Another **Spencer** molder has four pieces of interrupted boxing, more common to PA, found with two **James Bradley** planes, one marked New Haven. Example: The B imprint is on a 9 1/2" beech complex molder, single boxed with staggered double irons & wedges, round chamfers, ca. 1810-50. A & B **

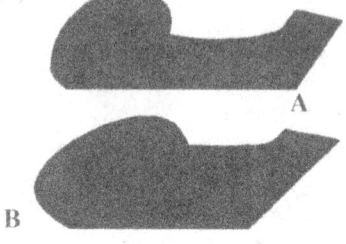

SPENCER/ F. G. SPENCER

Franklin G. Spencer operated a hardware store in New York City, from 1866-67, and was joined by **Oscar A. Spencer**, in 1869. They subsequently ran separate establishments from 1870-75. **Oscar** is listed only in the directories in 1878-84.
A, B & C ***

A. F. SPENCER

A. F. Spencer is a hardware dealer with a location imprint **WINSTED, CT** has been reported on a toted boxwood plow and a second plane with ebony body and fence, boxwood arms and nuts, and a fruitwood wedge. There is an incuse **240** under the tote which is a **H. Chapin** inventory number. ****

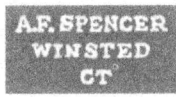 

J. CEVILLE SPENCER

J. Ceville Spencer of Phelps, NY, was granted Patent No. 138,591, on May 6, 1873. This patent date appears on the brass wheel of an 8 1/8" double-iron beech smoothing plane imprinted **A. Howland & Co./ NY**. (see *Patented Transitional & Metallic Planes in America 1827-1927*, p. 131, by Roger K. Smith) **No imprint is available.**

A x SPICER

Capt. Able Spicer (b. Mar. 29, 1736 in N. Groton, CT, d. May 3, 1784 in N. Groton) who was the brother of **Oliver Spicer** (1726-1804), uncle of **John Spicer** (1749-1826), and great uncle of **Able Chapman Spicer**. In 1758, he served in the French and Indian War at Crown Point. During the Revolutionary War, **Capt. Spicer** led Connecticut volunteers to Boston after the Battle of Lexington and fought in the battle of Bunker Hill and the siege of Boston. **Able Spicer** was reported as a cabinetmaker of Groton, CT. His inventory included 8 planes, 23 gouges and chisels, a turning wheel, glue pot & "phenearing saw." Also listed were 29 "plain chairs" and "one stamp". Examples: on 9 1/2"-9 5/8" birch molding planes with heavy flat chamfers that stop with a backward sloping stop and a long tapered turn out, and a wedge with a small round finial; on a 26 1/4"x 2 7/16" applewood joiner with flat chamfers, round top apple wedge and closed maple tote, ca. 1760-80. ****

A. C. SPICER

Able Chapman Spicer (b. July 29, 1796 in North Groton, d. Feb. 24, 1859 in Groton, CT). He drowned while oystering on the Thames River in Groton, CT. He is recognized as a cabinetmaker, carpenter, and mechanic, a term often used to refer to planemakers. On Sept. 1, 1836, he sold a building lot and carpenter's shop in Norwich. In March of that same year, he was in Plainfield, and later moved to Groton. His inventory included three tool boxes and contents, 17 molding planes, 54 chisels and other small tools, a lathe and its apparatus, a number of saws, and a glue pot. **Abel** also owned two "screw drivers," the earliest reference found to these tools previously called "turn screws." Examples: on a rosewood jointer with a closed offset tote; a rosewood rabbet; and a 9 1/2" beech double-boxed complex molder with shallow round chamfers that provided the B wedge, ca. 1830. A & A1 ***

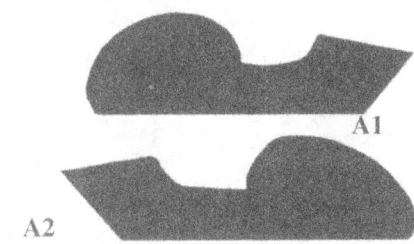

I + SPICER

There are two possibilities. **John Spicer** (b. April 20, 1749 in North Groton, d. Oct. 8, 1826 in North Groton) was a cabinetmaker, carpenter, and farmer. He served in the Revolutionary War, in 1775, in the company of his uncle, **Capt. Abel Spicer**, and took part in the Battle of Bunker Hill and the siege of Boston. He opened a store, in New London, CT, that sold coffins. He was blind the last years of his life and his estate included no tools. The more likely possibility is his cousin also **John Spicer** (b. 1770, d. 1856 in Ledyard) a cabinetmaker and carpenter in Ledyard, CT. The inventory of his estate included "a shop with 42 gouges and 66 planes and assorted other tools". Example: on a 9 7/8" beech skew rabbet with tight round chamfers, ca. 1820 ****

O: S/ O: SPICER

The most likely possibility for this imprint is **Capt. Oliver Spicer** (b. May 28, 1726 in North Groton, CT, d. Feb. 11, 1804 in North Groton) was the son of **John Spicer** (1698-1743) and **Mary Geer** (1701- ca. 1736), **Ebenezer Geer** sister; brother of **John Spicer** (b. 1724, d. 1769) and **Abel Spicer** (1736-1784) and father-in-law of **Abishai Woodward**. In 1754, 60 & 78, he was appointed Surveyor of Highways. In the 1775 Revolutionary War Roster, **Amos Park** (18) was listed as "prentice to **Lieut. O. Spicer**". From 1776-79, he served as a Captain in the Revolutionary War. He was a carpenter and joiner, and his 1804 inventory lists $20 worth of "Carpenter and Joiner tools." A less likely possibility is **Capt. Oliver Spicer** (b. Nov. 20, 1766 in North Groton, CT, d. Nov. 22, 1839 in Preston, CT). He was a carpenter, farmer, and was a Captain in the War of 1812. He died without sons. Examples: The initials are on a 9 15/16" molder with an **I. Sleeper** style wedge, and a 12 1/2" toted sash plane with a **Weldon** iron and flat chamfers. Molding planes are 9 1/4"-9 1/2" birch and fruitwood with flat chamfers that end with a backward sloping stop and a long tapered turn out, and a wedge with a small round finial. One exception is on a later plane with round chamfers, possibly the stamp being used by a succeeding generation, ca. 1760-80.
A & B ****

P. SPICER

Probably **Peter Spicer** (b. Dec. 7, 1795 in Preston, CT, d. June 24, 1873 in Westminster, CT). During the War of 1812, he was a Private. The 1820 census lists him, as a carpenter, living in Canterbury, CT. The **Spicer** Genealogy indicates that he was, a carpenter and wheelwright, in Canterbury, and an innkeeper in Westminster, CT. Example: on a 10" beech double-ebony boxed double-bead with round chamfers; and as an owner imprint on a molder, found in eastern CT, made by **Ebenezer Gere** (b. 1779) who was a Groton, CT, planemaker until **Ebenezer Gere** removed to NY about 1800. Also reported, as an owner imprint, on a match grooving plane made by **J. & L. Denison** of Saybrook, CT, ca. 1820. ****

P. E. SPICER
Example: on a 9 3/8" beech molder found with an **O. Spicer** plane, and a beech double-iron adjustable sash, that provided this wedge profile, ca. 1800. UR

S. SPICER
Believed to be **Silas Spicer** (b. Jan. 22, 1744/5 in North Groton, CT, d. in NY). He was a wheelwright, blacksmith and farmer. In the 1790 census, he was living next to **Oliver Spicer** (1726-1804), in North Groton; and bought land from the estate of **Able Spicer** (1736-1784). He adopted the Quaker faith, and in 1796, he moved to NY. Example: on a 9 7/8"x 7/8" birch ovolo with flat chamfers and a rounded wedge finial, in the collection of the Farmers Museum at Cooperstown, NY, ca. 1790.
No imprint is available.

I. SPILLER
Example: on a 28" beech jointer with round chamfers, ca. 1820. There is another **I. Spiller** plane but with a different imprint and flat chamfers, found in England and of 18c. appearance. UR

P + SPOONER
Examples: a 10" hollow, a birch Yankee style plow with square arms wood screw stopped, and a 9 3/4" birch 1 1/4" complex molder with flat chamfers, ca. 1790. UR

R. M. SPOONER
R. M. Spooner with the location imprint of **BOSTON** on an **E. Smith** 9 1/2" beech full boxed 1/2" double bead. Also present was the C imprint of **A. J. Wilkinson**, at 2 Wash St., Boston, as a hardware dealer. UR

H. SPRAGUE
Example: on a 9 1/2" beech hollow with heavy round chamfers and a relieved wedge, and a 7 1/8" beech toothing plane with a birch wedge, **James Cam** iron, shallow round chamfers, and the imprint marked four times in a box, probably from New England, ca. 1800-30. UR

M. SPRAGUE
Example: on a 9 7/8" birch Yankee plow with wood depth stop, wood thumbscrews, riveted skate, relieved wedge and flat chamfers, ca. 1775-1800. UR

N. SPRAGUE
Examples: on six 9 1/2" molders and a 10" plow with wood depth stop, wood screws stopped slide arms, all beech with round chamfers. The large wedge is from the plow, ca. 1810-20. UR

W. SPRAT/ W. SPRATS
William Sprats (Spratts) was born **William Pretcell** (b. ca. 1757 in Edinburgh, Scotland, d. 1810 in Carver Falls, VT), and trained as an architect in Edinburgh. He was pressed into the British Army and came to Canada with **General John Burgoyne's** force, in the spring of 1777. The British recaptured Fort Ticonderoga, in July 1777, and then struck Fort Edwards, on the Hudson River, north of Albany, NY, where **William** was taken prisoner. In 1779, **William Spratts** (in America, he used the Sir name of **Spratts**) was among a group of English prisoners who were jailed in Hartford, CT. Prisoners, with sought after skills, were "farmed out". **William Spratts** worked for **Justus Seelye** of Litchfield, CT. In 1781, he was offered repatriation to England but declined, and in April 1782, he was married to **Elizabeth Seelye**, the daughter of his employer. He was trained in the English Georgian tradition. In 1780, while still in Hartford, he designed and built the Barnabas Deane house. In the 1790's, he built houses for the Demings in Litchfield, Farmington and E. Haddam, CT, in the Federalist/ Palladian style. By 1797, **William Spratts** and his family had moved to Western MA. In 1800, his wife died, and he relocated north to Hampton, NY, near the VT border. In 1800-01, he designed and built a Town Hall and a Church in Georgia, VT. Examples: the A imprint is on a 10 1/4" birch skew rabbet with flat chamfers. The B imprint is on a 9 1/2" birch round; a 10 3/8" birch ovolo with flat chamfers; and a 10 1/8" birch complex molder, ca. 1790. A & B *****

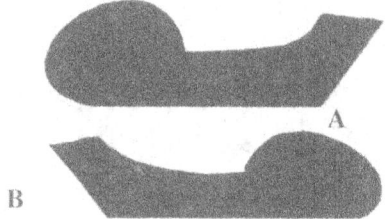

T x SPRING
Example: a 10 1/4" birch large round, and a 9 7/8" skew rabbet, both with heavy flat chamfers, ca. 1790. UR

J. SPRINGER
Example: on a 9 3/16" beech square rabbet, ca. 1815. **UR**

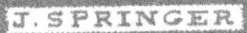

N. A. SPRINGER/ MAKER
Examples: on an 8 1/8" and a 9 1/16" rosewood coffin smoothers; a 24" and a 24 1/2" razee jointers of tropical wood, and a 17 15/16" lignum vitae razee jack, all found in Coos Bay, OR, ca. 1840. ****

I. SRORER
Example: on a 10"x 1 3/8" beech large full round with round chamfers, ca. 1820. **UR**

JOHN STAH/ JOHN STAHL
Possibly **John Stahl** (will proved Apr. 2, 1794) who was possibly **John Stall**'s father. Example: the A imprint is on a 10 1/8" beech complex molder with heavy flat chamfers, found in eastern PA. The B imprint is on a beech wide crown molder with a centered tote and a decorative carved wedge. The B imprint is from the same die as the A imprint before the die was cut in half and the **L** filed off, possibly from PA, ca. 1770. **A & B *****

P+STAHL/ STAHL
Example: on a 9 3/8" beech complex molder with flat chamfers, ca. 1800. **A & B: UR**

I. STALL/ J. STALL.
John Stall (d. 1801) was listed in the 1797-1801 Philadelphia directories, as a planemaker. The 1802 directory, listed his wife as a widow. He may have been a part of **Stall & Massey**, ca. 1800. Examples: the A2 imprint appears to have been from the same die as the A1 imprint but before the end was fled down removing the ".". The B imprint is on a 13 1/8"x 2 5/8" beech complex molder with an open offset tote and intermittent wear strips let into the sole. The imprint is similar to that of **W. Martin** of Philadelphia (1773-1801), ca. 1780. **A, A1 & A2 ***; B *****

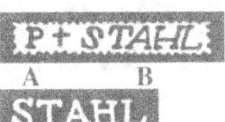

STALL & MASSEY
Believed to be **John Stall** and **James W. Massey**, as a planemaking partnership in Philadelphia, PA, ca. 1800. Example: on a wedge-arm plow; a molding plane; and overprinting on a molding plane made by **W. Brooks**. ****

J. STAM
Probably **Joseph Stam** (bapt. Sep. 4, 1778 in Berks Co., PA, d. Oct. 30, 1823 in Bernville, Berks Co.., PA) listed as a joiner and carpenter, in Manheim, Lancaster Co., PA, from 1807-46; and the father of **John Stamm**. Examples: on a group of six planes, including a 9 1/4" beech complex molder with flat chamfers; on a plane made by **E. W. Carpenter**, as an owner, and on a plane made by **E. Deter**, imprinted twice on the toe. ca. 1800-1810. ****

J. STAMFORD
Example: on a 9 3/8" beech halving plane with flat chamfers, ca. 19c. **UR**

J. STAMM
John Stamm (b. Nov. 29, 1808 in PA, d. June 1, 1877 in Mount Joy, Lancaster Co., PA), was the son of **Joseph Stam**. **John Stamm** was first listed in Cocalico Township, Lancaster Co., as a carpenter, in 1833; and as a cabinetmaker, in 1835-36. He made planes and marking gauges, from 1837-53, in Hinkletown, PA, or "Chickentown" in Pennsylvania Dutch, where he was a cabinetmaker, by trade, and an ordained preacher of the Church of God. In 1853, John moved to Donegal St., Mount Joy. The 1858 map of Mount Joy lists a "**John Stamm**, Planes & Gauges." He is known for making other products such as clamps, slaw boards, and onion slicers. The 1860 industrial census for Mount Joy, lists **John Stamm**, as a planemaker, with planes valued at $500 and other articles at $200. In 1870, he was listed, as a carpenter, maker of slaw cutters and washboards. He advertised in 1873, as the manufacture of patent medicine or vegetable bitters. Examples: the A imprint is on a marking gauge, made prior to 1853, while in Hinkletown. The "." at the end is not shown in the B imprint for Mount Joy and appear to have been filed off. The wedge outline was taken from a plane with no location imprint. The B imprint is on a jack plane with the same 1849 patented double-wedge found on **E. W. Carpenter** and **Samuel Auxer** bench planes.
A2, B & B1 **; A, A1 *

THE STANDARD RULE CO.
The Standard Rule Co. was established, in 1872, with **Andrew S. Upson**, as President. He employed 30 hands in Unionville, a village of Farmington, CT. In 1883, it added a line of wood

bottom transitional planes, manufactured under Patent Number 287,584, granted on Oct. 30, 1883, to **Solon R. Rust** and **Arthur E. Rust** of Unionville, CT. In 1888, the **Standard Rule Co.** merged with the **Upson Nut Company**. Example: on a 20" beech wood bottom double-iron razee. (see *Patented Transitional & Metallic Planes in America 1827-1927*, p. 201-05 by Roger K. Smith) **UR**

STANLEY RULE & LEVEL CO.
The **Stanley Rule & Level Co.** of New Britain, CT, made wood bottom planes with the **Bailey** Patent Number 67,398, granted on Aug. 6, 1867, and **Liberty Bell** type planes under Patent

No. 176,152, granted on April 18, 1876, to **Justus A. Traut** and **Henry Richards**. These planes were offered in the **Stanley** catalogs, through 1918. **J. A. Traut** of New Britain, also was granted Patent No. 645,220, on March 13, 1900, for a wood bottom plane with an adjustment mechanism. (see *Patented Transitional & Metallic planes in America 1827-1927*, p. 48-54 by Roger K. Smith) A, B, C, C1, D & E: **FF**

WM. STAPLE
Example: on a 9" beech wedge-lock plow with added wood thumbscrews, riveted skate, and tight round chamfers, ca. 1810. **UR**

F. B. STAPLES

Example: on a 16" beech jack with a double-iron made by the **Hancock Tool Co.**, ca. 1850. **UR**

L. R. STAPLES
Example: on a 9 1/2" beech edge-boxed moving filletster with a brass side depth stop and a nicker, ca. 1850. ****

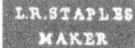

O. C. STAPLES
Example: on a 17 3/8" beech razee style crown molder with heavy round chamfers, ca. 19c. **UR**

S. B. S./ S. B. STAPLES
Samuel Brownin Staples (b. July 10, 1803 in Taunton, MA, d. Mar. 13, 1890 in Rochester, MA) who married, in 1824, in Taunton, MA. In 1855, he was listed as a wheel wright, in Darthmouth, Bristol Co., MA. From 1865-80, he was listed, as a wheel wright, in Rochester, Plymouth Co., MA. Example: the initial group and imprint is on a 9 1/2" skew rabbet with round chamfers; and imprinted alone on an 8" smoother, both beech, ca. 1820. **UR**

I. STAPLETON
Example: on an 8 15/16" beech complex molder with heavy round chamfers and the imprint struck twice on the toe, ca. 1820. **UR**

STARK, DAY, SHAUFFER & CO.
Stark, Day, Shauffer & Co. was a hardware dealer located in New Orleans, LA. Example: on a 18 hollow made by **A. & E. Baldwin** has the following imprinted: ***

MADE EXPRESSLY FOR
STARK, DAY, SHAUFFER & CO.
NEW ORLEANS.

L. G. STARKEY
Lewis G. Starkey (b. 1800 in NY) was listed as a wheelwright in Dearborn, MI, in 1820. Example: on a 9 1/4" beech single-boxed complex molder. Also reported is the name with the location **DEARBORN**, with no imprint available, ca. 1820. **UR**

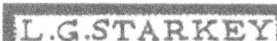

C. STARR
Examples: on a 9 1/2" beech Gothic bead with heavy round chamfers; and a 26" beech joiner with offset tote, diamond strike, round top wedge with a single iron, and round chamfers, ca. 1800-10. **UR**

G. STARR
G. Starr was probably a hardware dealer in Danbury, CT. Example: on a single-boxed complex molder made by **J. W. Gibbs/ N. York**. **UR**

J. STARR
James Starr (b. 1795 in PA, d. Jan. 12, 1872) was a carpenter, tool maker, planemaker, and inventor who came to New Lisbon (now Lisbon), OH, as early as 1823, based on the deed record for a lot purchased on 236 North Market Street and east High St.. He built a brick house, firing his own bricks and an attached workshop. "**John Star**" was listed as a "plainmaker", in the 1818 tax list of Pittsburgh, PA. This probably is the same person. The B imprint was reported from a plane found with several Pittsburgh planes. **James Starr** was listed as a plane and churn manufacturer, in the 1853-54 directory. Additionally he held Patent No. 3258, granted on Sept. 9, 1843, for an improved grain winnower, and was also a brickmaker, wood turner, wood worker, carpenter, bee keeper, and maker of cider presses. The cause of death, as shown on his death certificate, read simply "worn out". His estate inventory, dated 1872, included 49 reverse molding planes, 18 saws and rasps for planes. A number of the **J. Starr** planes are also imprinted with the owner name **T. STARR**. James Starr's builder brother. Example: the A imprint is on a clapboard gauge, with the date **1857**. The C imprint is on a boxed bead and on a 13 5/8" beech wedge-armed grooving plane.
A, A1 & A2 **; C & C1 ***; B ****

R. C. STARR
Probably **Reverend Robert C. Starr** (b. 1779 in Plymouth, MA, d. Dec. 11, 1862 in Thomaston, Knox Co., ME) who was a joiner in Thomaston, ME, before becoming a Baptist minister. Examples: on a birch match groove plane with heavy flat chamfers and a riveted skate; a 9 15/16" applewood coping plane with flat chamfers; and a beech round with flat chamfers, ca. 1800. ****

J. M. STAUFFER & SON
J. M. Stauffer & Son was a manufacturer & hardware dealer in Morristown, PA. Example: an ink imprint on the side of a large nosing plane with double iron and wedges. **No imprint is available**.

A. S/ A. STEAD
Examples: on a 10" birch molder; a 9 15/16"x 1/4" birch bead with flutes and a relieved wedge; a fixed sash with size **6/8** on the heel; a rabbet; at least two 10" birch Yankee style plow planes; and a 14 1/8" birch panel raiser with an offset tote, a round top chamfered wedge, flat chamfers and the added initial group **A. S.**, ca. 1790. ****

W. STEAD
Example: on a 9 1/2" beech fixed sash with shallow round chamfers, ca. 1830. **UR**

GEORGE STEADMAN
George Steadman (b. 1795 in VT, d. 1881 in Rome, NY) made planes as well as being a woodworker and cabinetmaker. In 1816, he took over the cabinet shop of **Sampson Warner** (b. 1783, d. 1821) in Chester, VT. In 1822, he moved to Jackson, NY; and by 1824, he was in Rome, NY. From 1839-41, **George** and his brother **Aaron Stedman** (b. 1800, d. 1879) established a furniture shop in Lee, NY. By 1844, **George** had returned to Rome. The 1850 industrial census reported **George W. Stedman** as a bedstead maker in Rome with 5 employees and an annual production of $3000. In the Boyd's Rome, NY directory of 1859-60, **George Steadman** was listed on Washington St., as a planemaker. In 1862, **George** joined the 81st. NY Regiment, was promoted to 1st. Lieutenant two months later, and was discharged for disability, in Beauford, NC, in 1864. The 1870 industrial census described his plane making business as having invested capital of $400, one employee, and an annual production of various types of planes with a value of $670. He was listed in 1873-74 & 78, as planemaker. In 1880, **George** was a resident of the Oneida Co., NY poorhouse and was listed as destitute, age 85. He is buried in a numbered grave in the Rome Cemetery. **No imprint has been reported**.

L. W. STEADMAN
Example: a 9 1/2" wedge-lock arm filletster. **UR**

STEBBINS
Example: on a 7 5/16"x 2 1/4" beech smoother with squared heel, round top wedge and single iron marked **WARD**, heavy round chamfers, ca. early 19c. **UR**

ALEX STEEL
Alex (Alexander) E. Steel (b. 1821, d. 1886) was a hardware dealer in Moline, Rock Island, IL, from 1871-76. He was part of **Harper & Steel**, from 1855-70. From 1877-85 it was **Alex Steel & Son** with son **George T. Steel**. The directory listing indicated it was established in 1855 and listed hardware, mechanics, building & garden tools, wagon and carriage stock, at 1703 2nd. Ave. Example: on a hollow also imprinted **72**, the **Ohio Tool Co.** catalog number for hollows & rounds. ****

A. P. STEEL
Examples: on a 7" beech toothing plane with the date **1867**; on four 7" beech hollows and rounds; and on a gear scale ruler. **UR**

J. STEEL
Example: a 10 1/4" beech skew rabbet with round chamfers. ca. 1820. **UR**

W. STEELE/ WM. STEELE/ W. STEELE & CO
William John Daily Fletcher Steele (b. 1814 in eastern PA, d. Aug. 10, 1879 and buried in Wheeling, WV) was "bound out" and learned plane making in Philadelphia, PA. He was a planemaker, in Wheeling, VA, now WV, from 1838-51. The 1839 directory for Wheeling lists "**William Steele & Co.** manufacturers of planes of every description, 199 Market Sq." He was associated with **James Coats** of Washington, PA, prior to 1846. Examples: the B imprint is on a 9 1/2" molding plane of different appearance from those with the A imprint. The C imprint is on a 14"x 4 3/4" beech panel raiser, with a **Butcher** iron, also imprinted by **Logan & Kennedy**, a Pittsburgh, PA, hardware dealer. The D imprint was used briefly when he worked at 211 Market St., just before he stopped making planes, in 1851. In 1852, **Steele** became an inventor and entrepreneur and advertised, on Oct. 30, 1852, as a mortise machine maker. He received Patent No. 12,449, on Feb. 27, 1855, for a tenon machine and on Oct. 19, 1858, he received Patent No. 21,856, for a barrel stave cutting machine. He advertised these machines, in 1859, as **Steele & Forsyth**, "Manufacturers of **Steele's** Patent Cooper's Machinery, Shingle Machines, Foot Tenoning & Mortising Machines, Wheeling Island, VA." In 1864, he was a partner in **Steele & Rider**, Shingle Manufacturers of Wheeling Island. In 1865, he moved to S. Stersville, WV, where he was listed, in the 1870 census, as a shinglemaker. Of interest is a screw-arm match tongue & groove plane with the tongue plane's iron split allowing for adjustment. (see **Planemakers of Western Pennsylvania and Environs**, by Charles W. Prine, Jr.) A**; C***; B, D & E****

W. STEERE
Example: a 10" birch split-sash with relieved wedges and small round chamfers. ca. 1800-20, probably from southeastern New England. **UR**

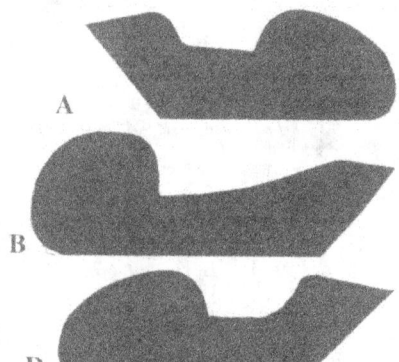

J. G. STEIGER
John Georg Steiger (**Sterger**) (b. May 6, 1832 in Switzerland, m. Feb. 6, 1862 in Crawford, OH, d. Jun. 17, 1912 in Bucyrus, OH) was a planemaker, in Cleveland, OH, from 1863-76. He received a patent, on April 3, 1866, for a combination spoke shave and box scraper. Example: on a 7" coffin toothing plane, and a cooper's three-arm croze. **A, B & C ****

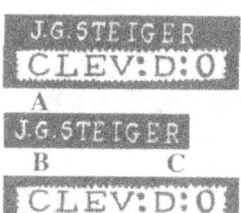

P. STEIN
Example: on a 10 1/16" beech complex molder with flat chamfers, ca 1800. **UR**

STEINMAN & CO.
Steinman & Co. was a Lancaster, PA, hardware company from 1744-1960, founded by **John Frederick Steinman**, stepson of Johann Christopher Heyne, a well known pewterer, and was sole agent for **E. W. Carpenter** for a period of time. Examples: on planes made by **E. W. Carpenter**, a style **124** screw-arm plow, and a style **47** boxed bead, both made by **Sandusky Tool Co.**. **A & B ***

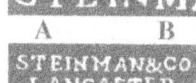

L. STEPHENSON
Levi Stephenson (**Stepenson**) (b. 1829 in MA, m. May 10, 1853 in Williamsburg, MA, d. 1900 in Johnstown, NY) was listed in the 1860 census for Johnstown, NY, as a planemaker. The *History of Johnstown, N. Y.* (1878) states, "In 1855 **Levi Stephenson** opened a manufactory of carpenters tools, the first of its kind in the county. In 1871, **Levi Stephenson** opened a lumber yard in Johnstown, NY." Example: the A1 imprint is on a 22" bench plane. **A & A1 ****

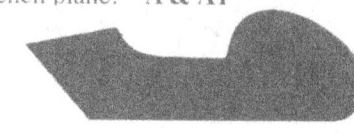

R + STERLIN
Example: on a 9 11/16" medium round; and 9 1/2" complex molder, both beech with flat chamfers, ca. 1800. **UR**

STERLING
Sterling was a trade name used by **Logan & Gregg**, a Pittsburgh, PA, hardware dealer, ca. 1912.
No imprint is available.

B. STERN & TOLLNER
B. Stern & Tollner was a hardware dealer in New York City, dates unknown. Example: the A imprint is on a toothing plane, and a hollow. The B imprint, with the location imprint **221 BOWERY**, is not available. This is the same location as for **C. Tollner** from 1851-61. **Tollner** was also part of **C. Tollner & Hammacher**, from 1862-63. **A ***

H. STETSON
Example: on a 9 3/8" birch molder with flat chamfers; a 28" beech joiner, centered tote, 3 1/4" double-iron, and heavy round chamfers, ca. 1800-20. **UR**

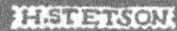

. STETSON/ IONAH. STETSON
Possibly one or both **Jonah Stetson** (b. July 1721 and bap. Feb. 25, 1722 in Scituate, Plymouth Co., MA, d. Dec. 1782 in Scituate) a housewright, and his son, **Jonah Stetson**, (b. Jul. 27, 1761 in Scituate, d. Apr. 2, 1825 in Scituate) a shipwright, who later worked in Charlestown, MA. **Jonah Stetson** (probably the Sr.) was a Private in the Scituate Militia, which marched to the alarm of Lexington & Concord at the start of the Revolutionary War. His probate inventory of 1785, includes saws, axes, adzes, joiners and other shop tools. Example: the A imprint is on a 9 3/8" birch molder with heavy flat chamfers, ca. 1770-80. The B imprint was from the same die but with the **IONAH** removed leaving the "." and on a 9 3/8" beech skew rabbet with heavy round chamfers; and a 7 3/8" birch narrow coffin block plane with shallow round chamfers, probably representing a later generation. ca. 1800-20. **B ****; A *******

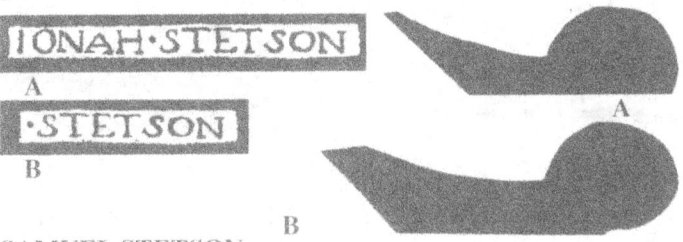

SAMUEL STETSON
Example: on a 14 1/2"x 4 1/4" crown molder with closed tote, ca. late 18c. **UR**

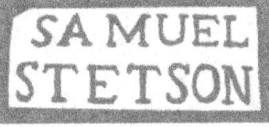

(Imprint not to scale)

STEVENS
There appears to be an initial above the name but it runs off the side of the plane and is unreadable. Example: on a 9 1/2" beech reed & follow plane with flat chamfers. Branded **T. WEAVER**, three times on the sides, possibly from PA. ca. 1800. ********

STEVENS/ A. C. STEVENS
A. C. Stevens was a planemaker, from Philadelphia, PA. Examples: the A imprint is on a 9 3/8" boxed complex molder; a 1/2" double match plane; a 9 7/16" 1 1/2" beech triple-boxed ovolo and bead. The B imprint is on an unhandled screw-arm sash filletster, ca. 1830. **A & B ******

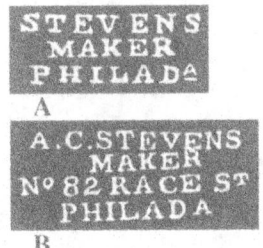
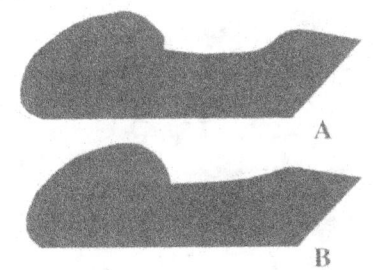

H. STEVENS
Example: on a slide-arm plow plane with thumbscrews and brass tips on the arms. **No imprint is available**.

H. R. STEVENS
H. R. Stevens was listed, as a planemaker, in the 1847-48 Providence directory, at 13 Orange St.
No imprint has been reported.

I x STEVENS
Example: on a 3" small square router with no chamfers, ca. 1800. **UR**

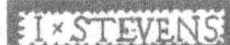

J. STEVENS
James Stevens (b. ca. 1799 in Rye, NH, d. Jan 17, 1872 in Boston, MA) relocated from New Castle, NH to Boston, MA, in 1816. **James** was a tool, plane, and rule maker at Court St. in Boston, MA, from 1821-22. He was listed in the 1849 New England Mercantile Union directory, as a plane manufacturer. He was at 5 Merrimack St., from 1823-50; at 94 Merrimack St., from 1851-58; and at 32 Sudbury St., the same address as **James Rumrell**, in 1859-60. **James Stevens** was listed in the 1861 Boston Almanac under "Planes", at 32 Sudbury St. Example: the A1 imprint is on a single-iron sash plane. The B imprint is on a double-iron and wedge sash plane.
A *; A2 **; A1 & B ***

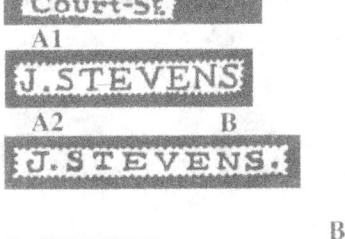
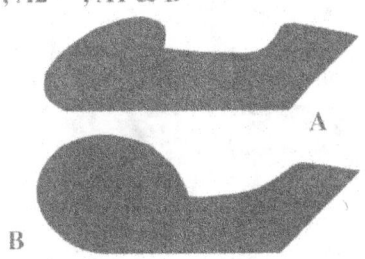

R. STEVENS
Richard Stevens (b. Dec. 25, 1772 in New Marlboro, Berkshire Co., MA, d. Apr. 8, 1852 in New Marlboro) married, in 1796, in Great Barrington, MA. Reported planes are also imprinted with **M. Robbins**, possibly **Marcus Robbins** (b. Sept. 15, 1770) in Pittsfield, Berkshire Co., MA. This imprint bears a striking resemblance to that of **E. Newell** of Lanesboro, with both the concave leading edge and the steps, top and bottom, after the initial. Examples: on a crown molder with a very offset tote; a 1/2" square rabbet; a 10 3/8" cove & bead molder, all birch with heavy flat chamfers, a relieved wedge, and found in western MA, ca. 1770-95. **A & B ******

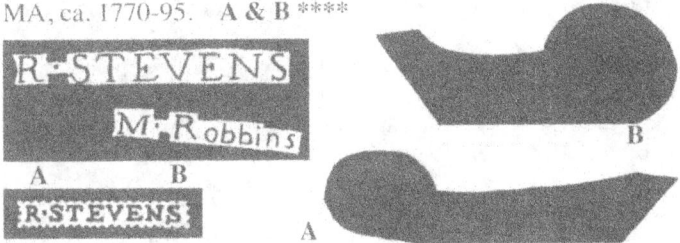

W. STEVENS
Example: on a 9 1/2" beech size **14** hollow with flat chamfers, ca. 1800. **UR**

STEVENS & CO.
Manufactured for **Stevens & Co.** by **J. Lovecraft** with a location of Rochester (NY). Examples: on a 33" coopers joiner, and a cooper's saw tooth croze, and a sun plane, ca. 19c. ****

L. STEVENSON
Example: on a 9 5/16" beech large round with heavy flat chamfers, ca. 1800. UR

AUSTIN STEWARD
Austin Steward of Bloomington, IN was listed as a blacksmith, gunsmith and planemaker who started business in 1823. **No example has been reported**.

J. C. STICKNEY
Example: on a 9 3/8" beech cove & bead molder with narrow dark boxing and flat chamfers; a beech hollow & round pair with heavy round chamfers; and a 14 1/2"x2 3/4" beech open-toted skew rabbet with shallow round chamfers, found in VT, ca. 1810-30. ****

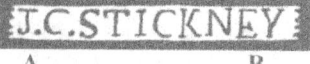

IA: STIESZ
Example: on a 9 7/8" beech bead with heavy round chamfers, possibly from mid Atlantic or PA. ca. 1790. UR

J. STILES
James Stiles (b. Oct. 24, 1743 in Berkshire, England, d. Oct. 16, 1830 in Kingston, NY) probably apprenticed in England and worked in New York City, as a carpenter, toolmaker, and planemaker, from 1768-75. There is a 1774 record of his having bought "sundry plans" from **Thomas Napier** for one pound, one shilling. He fought with the Colonists in the American Revolution and then settled in Kingston, NY, in 1783. **Stiles** was a lay preacher. **Stiles** married once, in 1768, in New York City; and twice more, in 1805 & 15, in Kingston. His son, James, was a Kingston silversmith and watchmaker. **James Stiles Sr.** turned his tools and shop over to his grandson, **J. J. Styles**, in 1823, although he apparently remained semi-active. In his will, of March 24, 1828, he used "**Styles**" instead of "**Stiles**." **J. Stiles** was one of the few American planemakers to date his planes. The A imprint is pre-revolutionary, ca. 1775. The earliest B imprint date is 1778. The D imprint has dates from 1812-30. The C imprint is on a 9 3/4" fruitwood tongue plane, and a 9 1/4" beech complex molder, both with heavy round chamfers, ca. 1820. His imprint has also been reported on a log rule. **A1 & D** *; **B** (post 1800) **; **A, B** (pre 1800) & **C** ****

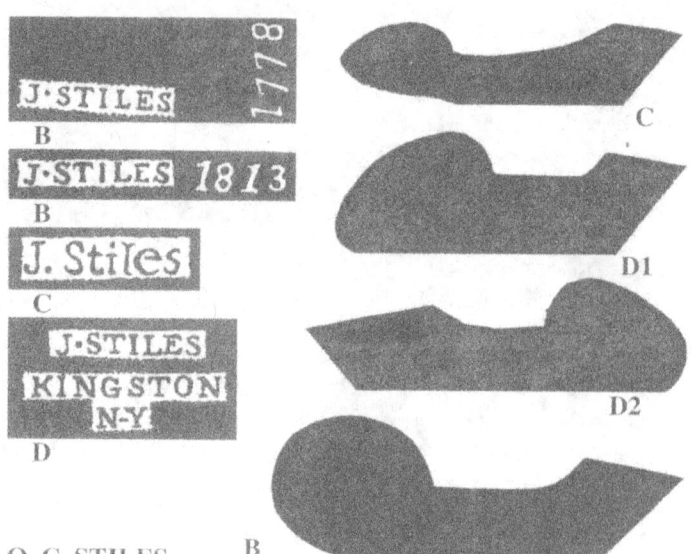

O. C. STILES
Believed to be **Orville C. Stiles** (b. Jan. 12, 1817, in Stratford, Fairfield Co., CT, d. July 30, 1862 in Fitchburg, Worcester Co., MA) who married, on May 1, 1842, in Gardner, MA. He resided, for a short time, in Fitzwilliam, NH; then Fitchburg where he was listed, from 1850-61, as a chair maker, working for **Davis & CO.**. Example: on a 10 3/16" narrow dado, ca. 1830. UR

S STILES A
Example: on a 12 7/8" beech panel raiser with an offset tote and shallow flat chamfers, struck three times on the toe; and a 9 7/8" birch adjustable fenced filletster with wood thumbscrews, no depth stop, flat chamfers with flutes, and a relieved wedge, probably from southern New England, ca. 1780. UR

JAS. STILL
Example: on a 9 3/4" beech dust joint molder with heavy flat chamfers, possibly from PA. ca. 1800. UR

H. G. STILLEY
Henry Gunn Stilley (b. Nov. 20, 1827 in DE, d. May 12, 1913 in Alameda, CA) was a carpenter, joiner, ship carpenter, ship joiner, and a part-time planemaker. He moved to Cincinnati, OH, in 1833-34; and was noted in the 1850 census; as "gone to California". His father, **James Stilley**, was listed, as a carpenter, in Cincinnati, from 1834-75. Henry returned briefly to Cincinnati, in 1860-61, before going back to CA. **Henry** was listed, from 1864-73, as a carpenter, in the San Francisco; from 1874-77, he was listed, as a carpenter, working for **D. A. MacDonald & CO.**; in 1878, **Stilley** was listed, as a carpenter, working for **Pease, Wetmore & Co.**, in San Francisco; from 1879-81, he was listed, as a carpenter working for himself. Henry moved to Oakland where he was listed, as a carpenter, from 1889-1906; From 1907-13, he was listed with no occupation. Most of his planes are bench planes and molders,

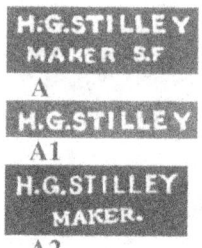

made of rosewood or other exotic woods. Examples: the A2 imprint is on a 9" low angle miter plane. The B1 imprint is on a 9 7/16"x 1 1/2" rabbet; and a 22"x 2 3/4" razee joiner with a **Buck Bros.** iron. The C imprint is on a 7 3/4" smoother, all rosewood.
A1 & A2 ***; A, B & B1 ****; C *****

J. STILLEY
Probably **James Stilley** (b. ca. 1800 in DE, d. May 24, 1875 in Cincinnati, OH) who was the father of **Henry Gunn Stilley** and **John Stilley** (b. Dec. 1830, d. Oct. 26, 1867 in Cincinnati) who was listed shoemaker, from 1839-44, in Cincinnati. **James Stilley** was listed, as a carpenter, in Cincinnati, OH, from 1834-75, ca. 1850. ****

Z. STILSON
Examples: on two 9 5/8" complex molders, one maple, the other single-boxed and beech, both with flat chamfers, ca. 1800. **UR**

A1

A2

A3

W. STILTON
Example: on a 10" beech astragal with heavy flat chamfers, ca. 1790. **UR**

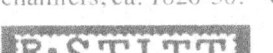

R. STITT
Example: on a 9 1/2" beech complex molder with heavy round chamfers, ca. 1820-30. **UR**

ROB' STODART
Example: an 8 1/8" beech wedge-arm plow with a riveted skate, wood depth stop and heavy flat chamfers, ca. 1820. **UR**

F. L. STODDARD
F. L. Stoddard probably was a hardware firm from Minneapolis, MN. no working dates are known. Example: on a 10 1/2" beech closed handled smoother, made by the **Ohio Tool Co.**. ****

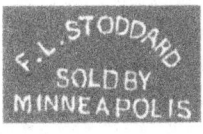

WILLIAM STODDARD
William Stoddard (b. 1821 in Lowell, MA) was listed in 1850, as a carpenter, in Lowell, MA. **William Stoddard** received Patent No. 17,645, on June 23, 1857, for a cam lever under the iron to secure it, thus eliminating a wedge but not providing an adjustment. This feature is on a bench plane made by **P. Sargent/Concord, NH**, with a **Wm. Ash & Co.** iron. **No imprint is on the wood body.** (see *Patented Transitional & Metallic Planes in America 1827-1927*, p. 19 by Roger K. Smith)

C. H. STONE
Examples: on the heel of a 10 1/2" beech Yankee style plow; and a cooper's shave with the added location imprint **OSWEGO, NY**, ca. 1840. ****

D. STONE
Examples: on a 9 3/4" hollow; and a 9 1/2" hollow, both birch with flat chamfers; and a 10 1/2" birch belection molder with heavy round chamfers, small separate flutes and a relieved wedge, ca. 1800-20. ****

E STONE
Possibly **Erwin Stone** (b. Aug. 7, 1818 in Litchfield, CT, d. bef. Apr. 11, 1873 in Los Angeles, CA) who was married on Sep. 7, 1843, in Litchfield Co., CT. In 1850, at age 31, he was listed, as a cabinetmaker, in Washington, CT. In 1860 & 67, **Erwin Stone** was listed, as a carpenter, in Los Angeles, CA. Example: on an 8 1/2" beech square box smoother, ca. 1840-50 **UR**

G. C. STONE
Gillman Stone (b. Aug. 20, 1805 in Farmington, CT, m. Nov. 3, 1829 in Providence, RI, d. Nov. 1, 1870 in Providence) was listed as a cabinetmaker in Providence, RI, in 1828. Example: on a 10" beech complex molder with tight round chamfers, ca. 1820-30. **UR**

H. D. STONE
Examples: on an 8" birch round; and a 9 3/4" beech skew rabbet with wide shallow chamfers, ca. 1830-40. **UR**

J. STONE
Example: on a 16 3/4" beech gutter plane with round top **Weldon** iron, and a birch jack, both with an offset open pegged tote and tight flat chamfers, ca. 1790-1800. **UR**

L. L. STONE & CO.
Example: a 9 3/8" beech 4/8" match tongue plane. ca. 1840. **UR**

NS
Possibly **Rev. Nathan Stone** (1764-1804) or his son **Nathan Stone** (1766-1839) (see **NS**)

S. STONE
Believed to be **Samuel Stone** (b. 1760 in Townsend, Middlesex Co., MA, m. Sep. 19, 1791 in Harvard, MA, d. Sep. 2, 1836 in Pittsfield, Monroe Co., NY) who was a cabinetmaker, in Boston MA, from 1794-1803. In 1794, he advertised in the *Massachusetts Gazette*. From 1792-96, he was a partner with **Giles Alexander**, on Ann St., Boston. In 1796, **Samuel** was listed at Pitts La.; in 1798, at Sunn Court St.; in 1800, at Ann St.; and in 1803, at Fish St. **Samuel Stone** was listed as a veteran of the American Revolutionary War. Examples: on a 10 3/8" birch Yankee plow with square-arms and wood thumbscrews, a wood depth stop, and riveted skate; a 14 3/4" beech jack with offset tote, and **James Cam** iron; a 10" birch rabbet; all with shallow flat chamfers, ca. 1790.   ****

S. STONE
Possibly **Silas Stone** (b. Oct. 17, 1818 in Dublin, Cheshire Co., NH, m. Mar. 19, 1856 in Brookfield, Orange Co., VT, d. Feb. 18, 1901 in Williamstown, Orange Co., VT) who, in 1860, was listed, as a carpenter, in Chelsea, Orange Co., VT. He moved to Williamstown, VT, in 1865, and built a wheelwright's shop on Staples Pond. He was listed, as a wheelwright and carriage maker, from 1872-80; as sleighs and wagons, from 1883-93; as shingles, in 1893; as carriage repairs, from 1894-98, at age 80. Examples: on a 9 9/16"x 1/2" and 3/4" beech hollow & round pairs, and additional rounds, all found in VT.   **UR**

H. STONER
Example: on a 9 5/8" beech skew rabbet with flat chamfers, ca. 1800.   **UR**

G. L. STORER
Examples: an 8" lignum vitae shipwright's smoother with a double-iron; a 9 1/2" beech square miter plane with a **Wm. Ash & Co.** iron; a spar plane; bench planes; a "V" compass groove plow; and a hollow & round pair, mostly with multiple name imprints and made of lignum vitae; typical of northern New England seacoast planemaking, ca. 1850.   ****

J. STORER
J. Storer was listed as a plane maker, in New Lisbond, OH, in 1815. **No imprint has been reported**.

J. P. STORER
Joshua P. Storer (d. bef. 1876 in Bath, ME) was a sparmaker and carpenter in Brunswick, ME, starting in 1854, and "made planes and stair rail manufr." at Androscoggin Bridge, from 1854-74.

A

B

B1

In 1860, he was reported producing 500 planes valued at $750, made of both lignum vitae and beech. From 1867-74, he was listed as a planemaker only.
A **; B & B1 ***

PERKINS STORRS
Perkins Storrs was listed, as a planemaker, in 1832-34, in Utica, NY directories. **No imprint has been reported**.

J. STORY
Possibly **John Story** was listed as a joiner in Winchester, CT. **John** with his family left Winchester, in 1825, to join the Shaker Community in Tyringham, MA. Example: on a 9 1/2" beech small hollow, ca. 1850.   **UR**

J. STOUGH
Example: on a 9 11/16" beech narrow dado with heavy round chamfers, found in KY, ca. 1820.   **UR**

M. STOUT
Moses Stout Jr. (b. Apr. 4, 1808 in NJ, d. Jan. 28 in 1881 in St. Louis, MO) made planes under his own name in St. Louis, MO, 1836-38, and with his brother as **M. & N. H. Stout**, from 1838-49. **Moses** moved to TN, in 1855, and was listed, as a hardware merchant, in the Memphis directory, in 1857.
A & B **

A
B

M. & N. H. STOUT
M. & N. H. Stout was a partnership of **Moses Stout Jr.** and brother **Nathaniel H. Stout** who made planes and cooper's tools, in St. Louis, MO, from 1838-49; and were hardware dealers, from 1847-54.   **

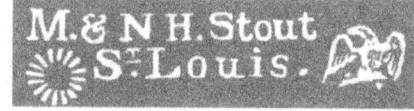

N. H. STOUT
Nathaniel Hixson Stout (b. 1806 in Cloverhill, Hunterdon Co., NJ, d. Oct. 5, 1867 in Memphis, Shelby Co., TE) was the brother of **Moses Stout Jr.** In 1836-38, he was part of **Stout & Richey**, in Louisville, KY. He joined his brother as part of

A

 M. & N. H. Stout, planemakers, in St. Louis, MO, from 1838-49, as part of N. H. Stout Bro. & Co.; by 1859-69, a hardware dealer. **A **; B *****

N. H. STOUT BRO. & CO.
A partnership of **Nathaniel H. Stout** and brother **Moses Stout Jr.** and **W. W. Richey**, who advertised in the 1859-60 Memphis, TN, city directories as dealers in Hardware, Cutlery, and Mechanics Tools.
N. H. Stout's brother **Isaac Stout**, was a salesman in the firm. *******

N. H. STOUT/ W. W. RICHEY
Nathaniel H. Stout and **W. W. Richey** were hardware merchants in Louisville, KY, from 1836-38, and were listed in the city directory as **Stout & Richey**. In 1837, they advertised as "Wholesale & Retail Plane Manufacturers and Tool Store." The C imprint is on a 9 7/16" beech match tongue plane. **A B & C: *****

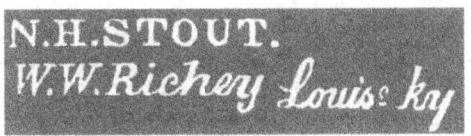

T. STOUT
Theodore Stout (b. 1824 in NJ) the brother of **Moses Stout Jr.** and **Nathaniel H. Stout**, was in 1836, in Louisville, KY. In 1842, he was listed as a journeyman planemaker, in St. Louis, MO. He was working for **M. & N. H. Stout**, in 1844; and in 1850, he was a planemaker, in New Albany, IN, where he remained until about 1855. *******

J. STOVER
Example: on a 9 11/16" beech bead with flat chamfers and A wedge, and a 9 1/2" beech large round with size **1 3/4** on the heel, heavy round chamfers, and B wedge, ca. 1800-20. ********

W. STRABER/ WM. STRAEBER
Believed to be **William Straber (Straeber)** (b. 1802, PA) was the son of **Peter Straber**. In 1830-50, he was listed as a carpenter, in York, PA. Examples: the A & B imprints are on a massive 14 3/4"x 6 5/8" beech ogee crown molder with a  wooden start, screwed on fence and wide flat chamfers, found in central PA, ca. 1800. **UR**

J. STRACHAN
James Strachan (d. Jan. 25, 1769 in New York City) was a New York City carver, gilder and cabinetmaker. The appearance of the plane is too late for this person, but may be a descendant. Example: on a 9 3/8" cove with shallow round chamfers, ca. 1830. **UR**

T. H. STRANGE
Thomas H. Strange (d. aft. 1888 in Providence, RI) was in North Providence in 1840. He advertised in the 1858-67 Providence directories, as a sash, blind, and door manufacturer, and the maker of "Mouldings of all sorts.", at 18 Smith c. Charles. The imprint with the added location imprint **PROV./ R.I.** is on a 1 1/8" hollow. **No imprint is available.**

JOHN STRATTON
John Stratton (d. 1811 in Bristol, MA) was listed in Fallriver, MA as a joiner and chairmaker. Example: on a 9 1/8" single rosewood boxed beech complex molder with wide flat chamfers and a slightly pointed finial, ca. 1800. **UR**

S. STRATTON
Examples: the A imprint is on a 9" beech molder with heavy round chamfers and this wedge. The B imprint is on a 9 3/8" birch center bead, the body with full round top and heavy round chamfers on toe and heel. The C imprint is on a 9 5/8" beech grooving plane with heavy round chamfers, ca. 1800-20. **UR**

STRAUB & SON/ JACOB STRAUB & SON
Jacob Straub (b. 1808 in Hesse-Darmstadt, Bavaria) was in partnership in **Straub & Son** with his son **Fred P. Straub**; and listed from 1863-68, as dealers in foreign and domestic hardware, cutlery, etc. at 74 Main St. Evansville, IN. From 1874-81, the firm became **Fred P. Straub & Co.** with **Fred P. Straub, J. Louis Straub** and **Henry E. Straub**, dealers in hardware & cutlery, tools etc. Examples: the A imprint is on an ogee by **Ohio Tool Co.**. The B imprint is on a triple-boxed split sash by **Scioto Works**. **A & B *****

G. G. STRAW
Example: on a 9 7/8" beech razee smoother with an open tote, double **Newbould/ Warranted** iron, ca. 1850. **UR**

P. STREBER
Possibly **Peter Streber** (b. Sep. 23, 1758 in York, PA, d. 1813 in York). who married, in 1782, in York. He was also listed in the 1810 census. His will was dated Sept. 23, 1813. Examples: on a 10" beech nosing plane with flat chamfers; a 15"x 7 1/4" and 13 1/2"x 3 7/8" beech crown molders, both with offset apple totes, diamond strikes, and heavy flat chamfers. The incuse owner imprint is from his son **Wm. Straber** (c. Dec. 26, 1797) listed in 1830, probably from PA. ca. 1800.   **UR**

C. A. STRELINGER & CO.
CHAS. A. STRELINGER & CO.
C. A. Strelinger & Co. was a large Detroit, MI, hardware and tool dealer begun by **Charles A. Strelinger**, and active from 1885-95. In 1880, he was listed as a Clerk for **T. B. Rayl & Co.**. The company's Woodworkers Tool Catalog has been reprinted (see Biography). Examples: on an ogee; and on a size 3/16" double-boxed molder, both made by the **Sandusky Tool Co.**; The C1 imprint is on a size 2/16" double-boxed center bead made by **T. B. Rayl & Co.**, with the **T. B. RAYL & CO.** mark obliterated with the **DETROIT** retained and **CHAS. A. STRELINGER & CO.** added.   **A , B & C ***; C1 *******

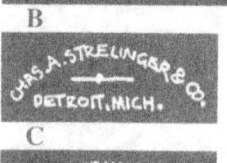

RICHARD A. STRIKER
Richard A. Striker with a location of **495 Greenwich St.** probably is a hardware dealer. Examples on two narrow round planes, both made by **E. Baldwin**.   ********

JOHN STROB
John Strob was listed as a planemaker, at 126 Lewis St., in the 1843-44 New York City directory. In 1850, he was listed, as a carpenter, in Eastchester, Westchester Co., NY
No imprint has been reported.

G. STRODE
George L. Strode (b. Mar. 1, 1824 in Fairfield Co., OH, d. Apr. 29, 1898 in Wichita, Sedgwick Co. KS) was the son of **John Strode**. **George** was married on Sep. 24, 1846, in Lancaster, OH. In 1850, he was listed, as a plain maker, in Greenfield Township, Fairfield Co., OH. In 1880, **George** was listed as a Jeweler in Anamosa, Jones, IA. Examples: on a 21 1/4" beech joiner with a **Butcher** iron also inscribed **WARRANTED** and a location of **DUMONTS VILLE/ OHIO**. Dumonts Ville, now Dumontville, north of Lancaster, OH. On a three-arm bridal center-screw beech plow plane, with rosewood arms and center knob, inlaid with rosewood where the arms go through the body, with ivory, ebony and brass inlays, ca. 19c.   **A & A1 ******

J. STRODE
John Strode (b. Jun. 30, 1795 Berkely Co., VA, now WV, d. Mar. 4, 1865 in Anamosa, Jones Co., IA) came to Fairfield Co, OH with his father, in 1804. In 1850, John was listed as a plane maker. In 1851, John sold his farm in Hocking Township and with the rest of the family, except his oldest son **George L. Strode**, to Fairview Jones Co., IA, where he was listed, as a farmer. **John** was also reported to be a furniture maker. Examples: on a 9 1/2" beech sash, table joint, side bead, center bead, and complex molding planes some boxes with single rosewood boxing, ca. 1840-50.   *******

H: STRONG
Examples: on a 10" beech square rabbet with flat chamfers and a relieved wedge; an applewood smoother; a 9 3/4" beech plow with a double-end fence, hickory thumbscrews, wood depth stop, riveted skate and flat chamfers; and a beech jack with offset tote, found in NH. ca. 1790-1800.   ********

STRONG H'DW'E CO
The **Strong H'dw'e Co** was first organized as **Strong Brothers Hardware Co.** of Burlington, VT, in 1852, and was incorporated in 1867. The **Strong Hardware Co.** name was adopted some time after 1867; and the company ceased business, in 1971. Example: on a **H. Chapin/ Union Factory** plane, a **New York Tool Co.** plane, and two **Auburn Tool Co.** planes.   ********

S. STUBBS
Samuel Stubbs (b. 1790 in GA, buried in the Quaker Friends Cemetery in West Elkton, Preble Co., OH) arrived in Preble Co., OH, on Jan. 6, 1810, listed as a mill mechanic, as late as 1860. The location **P. C. OHIO** probably represents Preble County, Ohio. Example: on a plank plane.   ******

J. STUCKEY
Example: on a 25 1/8"x 3 1/16" maple jointer with closed tote, double iron, early 19c.   **UR**

D. STUDLEY
Example: on a 9 1/8" skew rabbet with a slightly compass bottom and shallow flat chamfers, probably from PA, ca. 1790.   **UR**

J. STUMPF
J. Stumpf was a planemaker, in Berks Co., PA. Examples: on a 15" apple toted crown with a **James Cam** iron, flat chamfers and found in southeastern, PA; on a 13 1/8" beech panel raiser with an off-set tote, and a dove tailed wood depth stop, round top **James Cam/ Warranted** cast steel iron, a iron strike button and flat chamfers; and on a 10 1/2" beech complex molder, ca. early 19c.   ****

J. J. STYLES
James J. Styles (b. Mar. 6, 1800, d. Apr. 2, 1894) was a grandson of **J. Stiles** and inherited his grandfather's books, tools, stock of planes, and the use of his workshop. He made planes, in Kingston, NY, from 1820-76. The 1850 census reported $600 worth of planes produced. When stone cutting became a flourishing business in the area, he added stone rules. **Styles** also did clock repair, scissor and saw sharpening, at the corner of James and Pine St. He had a love of music and played the fife. **J. J. Stiles** was a volunteer fireman and avid fisherman. Unlike many planemakers, barely making a living, he was almost gentry. He was still active, at age 84, in 1883. **J. J. Styles**, like his grandfather, dated his bench planes. He stamped numbers in their throats, the number represented the month (top), the day (middle) and the last two digits of the year (bottom). His imprint is also reported from a lumber stick. One of his planes was also imprinted with the owner's imprint **J. R. STYLES**. A, A1 & B *

P. SUCKETT
Example: on a 9 1/2" birch round with flat chamfers, ca. 1800.   UR

FRED SUMLER
Fred Sumler was listed as a planemaker in Columbus, OH, in 1856-57. **No imprint has been reported.**

MARTIN SUMMERS
Martin Summers (buried Dec. 11, 1860 in Philadelphia, PA) was part of **Souder & Summers** with **William M. Souder**. They were listed, as planemakers, in the 1826-47 Philadelphia directories, and **Summers** was listed, as a planemaker, in the 1840 & 45 Philadelphia directories, at a different location from **Souder**. **No imprint has been reported.**

E. SUNDERLIN
Example: on a birch gutter plane with a vertical grain open off-set tote, round top iron and wedge, round strike button and tight round chamfers, ca. late 18c.   UR

JOHN SUNSERSOND
John Sunsersond was listed, as a planemaker, in the 1836-37 Cincinnati, OH, directory. Possibly the same person as **John Saundersod** reported in 1839-40.
No imprint has been reported.

SUPPLEE-BIDDLE
Supplee-Biddle was a hardware dealer, in Philadelphia, PA. Example: on a **Sandusky Tool Co.** beech plow plane with the inventory number **117**, a **W. Marples & Son** iron, and dated **1915**.   ****

B. SWAIN
Example: on a 9 3/8" beech square rabbet with an integral fence, flat chamfers and this unusual but original wedge. The imprint is similar to that of **R. Swain**. ca. 1810.   UR

R. SWAIN
Several examples are located at the Salisbury, NH, Historical Society. Example: two 9 1/2" beech complex molder, one 3/4" and the other 1 1/8" wide; and a 9 5/8" beech water pipe plane of 1 1/2" diam., all with heavy flat chamfers, ca. 1800.   ****

W. B. SWAIN
Examples: on a 10 3/8" dado; a 8 1/4" hollow; and a 9 3/4" dado, all beech with flat chamfers, ca. early 19c.   UR

WM. D. SWAIN
William D. Swain (b. ca. 1827 in MA) was listed in 1856, as a planemaker, in Rowe, MA. In 1852, he was a carriage builder. Example: on a 20" razee trying plane.   ***

E SWAN
Examples: on a 10" birch complex molder; and a hollow, both with flat chamfers and flutes; and on a mahogany panel marking gauge ca. 1790.   A & B: UR

FREDERICK A. SWAN & CO.
Example: on a 11" razee boxwood smoother with a closed handle, a double-iron and heavy round chamfers, found in ME, ca. 1830-40.   ****

SWANBERY
Swanberg with the imprint **MAKER**. Example: on a 9" rosewood shipwright's smoother with a **Sandusky Tool Co.** iron, ca. 19c.   UR

D. SWEET
Example: on a 13 1/2"x 6" beech crown molding plane with an applied fence, walnut centered tote, and heavy flat chamfers. With an owner imprint **V. Russell**, found in OH. ca. early 19c.   UR

D. D. SWEET & CO.
D. D. Sweet & Co. probably was a hardware dealer. Example: on a double-boxed center bead, made by **Gladwin & Appleton**, Boston.   UR

H. SWEET & CO.
The Rogerson's 1854 map of Rensselaer Co. lists **H. Sweet**'s shop in Stephentown, NY, on the Black River where there were a number of mills and water wheels. Stephentown is near the MA border and about 10 miles from Pittsfield, MA, where **M. Sweet** was located. Examples: on two fore planes and two smoothing planes, ca. 1850.   ****

M. SWEET
Moses Sweet (b. 1805 in MA, d. 1863 in Pittsfield, MA) was a planemaker, in Pittsfield, MA, from 1826-43. His shop was on the Onota Brook near the **Rufus Allen** iron forge. In 1840, **Moses** lived four houses from **J. Webb**. **Moses** was married on Jul. 28, 1845, in Pittsfield. In 1850, he was listed, as a carpenter.

Moses Sweet dated his planes. The earliest was **1826**. Examples: the C imprint is on a round; and a grooving plane, both 9 1/2" beech with round chamfers. The E imprint is on a small beech coffin smoother with a rounded sole. The D imprint is on a beech rabbet, ca. 1820-30.

A, B, B1 **; C & D ***; E & F ****

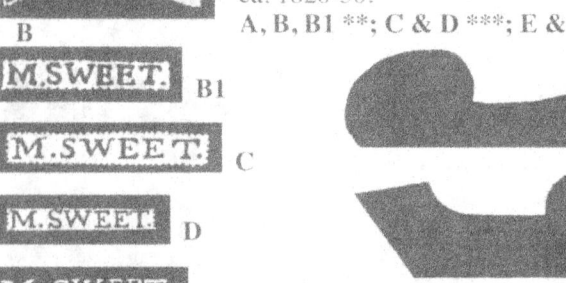

S. SWEET
Example: on a handled screw-arm plow made by **W. Webb**, from Pittsfield, MA. (see **M. Sweet**)   UR

SWETMAN
James Swetman's (b. Sept. 14, 1791 in Evercreech, Somerset, England, d. June 18, 1832 of cholera, in Montreal, Quebec, Canada) parents were Quakers. In 1809, his parents were found "of practise of things disgraceful to our religious Society" and were disowned from being a member of the Society. **James** registered as a British alien during the War of 1812 as "**James Sweetman**, age 21, 4 years in US, Baltimore, Planemaker". He worked for **W. Scott**, from 1816-18, as a journeyman. He was listed in the 1819 Pittsburgh, PA directory, as a planemaker; and was a partner in **Swetman & Hughes**, from 1818-20. He was listed in the 1820 Cincinnati, OH census. In 1825, he arrived on Amherst Island, Upper Canada with other Quakers. On May 22, 1825, he was married in Bath, Ontario, Canada. On Oct. 11, 1826, **James Swetman** advertised in the *Canadian Courier and Montreal Advertiser*, as a planemaker. One **J. SWETMAN/ BATH** imprint has been reported from an English auction. (see *Planemakers of Western Pennsylvania and Environs*, by Charles W. Prine, Jr.)   ****

SWETMAN/ HUGHES; SWETMAN/ HUGHES & CO.
Swetman & Hughes & Co. was a plane making firm from May 1818-20, consisting of **James Swetman** and **William P. Hughes**, who advertised its opening, on May 18, 1818, in Pittsburgh, PA. The firm was listed in the 1819 Pittsburgh, PA, directory. Among its employees listed in the directory was **Samuel H. Richardson**, **Thomas Clark**, and **Benjamin King**, who later became planemakers. On Jan. 17, 1820, **Swetman & Hughes** was dissolved by mutual consent as insolvent. **Swetman, Hughes & King** was listed in the 1820 Cincinnati, OH census. **Swetman** left for Montreal, Canada by 1825; **Hughes** was listed through 1831; and King was listed through 1844. Example: on a molder with an incuse **$125** on the heel, probably representing a $1.25 price.

A, B, C & D ****

L. SWIFT
Example: on a 10" birch molder with wide flat chamfers, ca. 1800.   UR

A. SWIGART
Examples: on a 9 3/4" apple table joint plane; and on a 7 1/2" apple coachmaker's bead found in southeastern, PA; and on a 10 3/8" beech reverse ogee molder with spring found in Lancaster Co., PA; all with flat chamfers, ca. 1800   UR

J. SYMONDS
Example: on a 34" beech joiner with a centered tote, single iron and flat chamfers, found in a barn in Ashburnhall, MA.   UR

T. D. & CO.
Tyler Davidson & Co was a hardware dealer in Cincinnati, OH, from 1843-65. From 1836-42, it was called **Tyler Davidson**.   A & B **

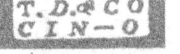

T. S. & CLARK
After an extensive review of the New York City directories, there is still no information as to who they were. Examples: the A1 imprint is on a 9 5/8" beech round with a **Humphreysville Mfg. Co.** iron. This was a CT plane iron manufacturer, ca. 1850.   A & A1 ***

EDWARD P. TABB/ E. P. TABB & CO.
Edward P. Tabb Jr. was a hardware dealer in Norfolk, VA, from 1851-76. In 1872-73, the firm also included **E. W. Moore, Pendleton Moore, William B. Tufts,** and **E. J. Griffith. E. P. TABB & CO.** was in the 1851-52 Norfolk directory. Also reported is **EDWARD TABB/ NORFOLK VA**, no imprint is available.   A & B ****

ALLEN TABER
Allen Taber (b. 1800 Fairhaven, Bristol Co., MA, d. May 3, 1882 in Augusta, Kennebec Co., ME) was the son of **Nicholas Taber** and the brother of **John Marshall Taber**. His father, in a will dated 1844, left him "all of my shop tools." **Allen Taber** came to Augusta, ME, from Fairhaven, MA, where he was listed in the 1830 & 40 censuses. In the 1850 census, he was cited as a farmer. In 1855, he bought a house in Augusta, having previously owned a farm some six miles from town. The 1870 & 80 censuses listed him, as a planemaker. His obituary in the *Kennebec Journal* of May 1882 said:

"He moved to Augusta (ME) in 1844 and cones-quently has been a resident of the city for some 30 years. He was very quiet, industrious man and highly esteemed by all those who had the pleasure of his acquaintance. Until enfeebled by ill health, he was a manufacturer of bench planes and all the carpenters far and near sought for **Taber's** planes."

No imprint has been reported.

J. TABER
Possibly **John Taber** (b. ca. 1700 in Bristol, MA, d. 1756, probated Nov. 18, 1756 in Tiverton, Newport, RI) worked in 1720's as a joiner and housewright. Examples: a 14" long crown molder with a 2 5/8" iron, an offset handle and a rounded wedge, a 2" wide single-boxed complex molder, and a narrow 1/4" halving plane. The latter two 9 1/2" beech with heavy flat chamfers and relieved wedge. Similar in style to **N. Taber** planes, possibly a relation. ca. 1790.   ****

J. M. TABER/ JOHN M. TABER
John Marshall Taber (b. Mar. 31, 1796, in Bristol, MA, d. Mar. 5, 1873 New Bedford, MA) was an active planemaker from 1820-72, in New Bedford, MA. He was the son of **Nicholas Taber**, whose business he took over ca. 1820, and the brother of **Allen Taber. J. M. Taber** was listed in the 1849 New England Mercantile Union directory, as a plane manufacturer, in New Bedford. The 1870 census listed seven men who worked in "**John M. Taber**'s plane factory": **Clarence Pearce**, 27 (sic. see **Clarence A. Bearse**); **John Hussey**, 26; **Arnold Townsend**, 20; **Charles H. Sherman**, 23; **John S. Southwick**, 26; **Henry E. Howard**, 19; and **Henry A. Bodman**, 38. (see **Bodman & Hussey, Bodman & Bearse,** and **Bodman, Bearse & Hussey**) Example: the C3 imprint is on a 13 1/2"x 2" razee skew rabbet with open tote and two nickers, ca. 19c.   A, B, C, C1, D & E: FF; C2 & C3 ****

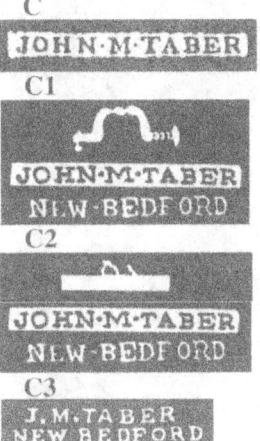
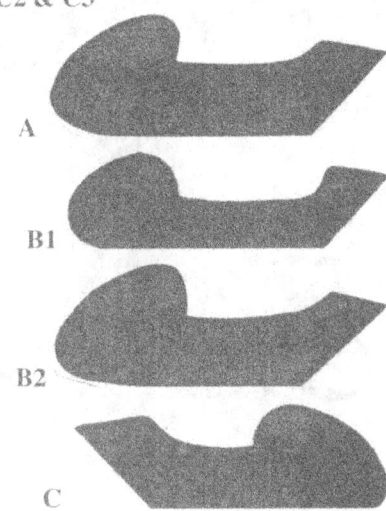

L. H. TABER
Leander H. Taber (b. ca. 1819 in Tiverton, Newport Co., RI) was listed in the New Bedford, MA, directories, from 1838-52, as a planemaker, in connection with **J. M. Taber**. The relationship is not known nor is the precise period in which he made planes under his own imprint. Example: the B imprint is on a 12 hollow, ca. 19c.   A & B **

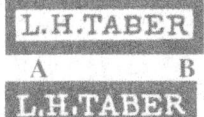

N. TABER
Nicholas Taber (b. Aug. 1761 in Fairhaven, Bristol Co., MA, d. Jan. 12, 1849 in Fairhaven) made planes in New Bedford and Fairhaven, MA, from 1785-1820. In **Nicholas Taber**'s will, dated 1844, he left his workshop to his son **John Marshall Taber** and all his shop tools to his son **Allen Taber**. Examples: One 10" birch ogee molder has shallow, flat chamfers, flutes, the A imprint and the A wedge. Almost all molders are 9 1/2" and beech. The A imprint with the C wedge can occur with either wide heavy flat or bold round chamfers. The A imprint with the B wedge has bold round chamfers. The B imprint is

later. A imprint is ca. 1785-1810. The B imprint is ca. 1810-20. **A & B ****

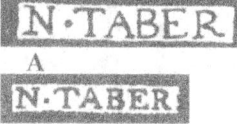

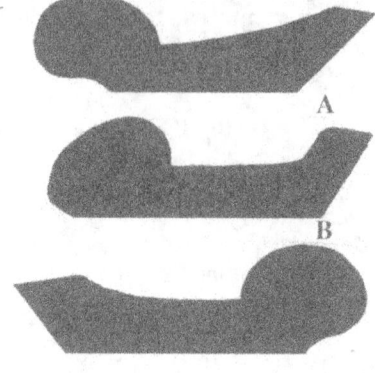

S. W. TABER
Example: on a 9 1/2" birch boxed side bead with a **Jo, Fuller** style relieved wedge and flat chamfers and flutes, ca. 1800. **UR**

V. TABER
Example: on a 7 7/16"x 5/16" beech side bead, found with a **J. M. Taber** and an **N. Taber** planes. **UR**

W. TABER
Possibly **Wing H. Taber** or more likely **William Taber** (b. Mar. 15, 1723 in Bristol Co., MA, d. Nov. 22, 1799 in New Bedford, Bristol.) the father of **Nicholas Taber**. Examples: on a 9 1/2" boxed bead with the iron set at a York pitch; a 9 3/8" hollow; and a plow, all beech with flat chamfers and a relieved wedge. Similar in style to **N. Taber** planes, possibly a relation, ca. 1800. ****

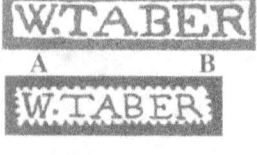

W. H. TABER/ WING H. TABER
Wing Howland Taber (b. Aug. 20, 1809 Fairhaven, Bristol CO., MA, d. Sonoma Co., CA) made planes, in Fairhaven, MA, in 1833. He probably apprenticed, as a planemaker, with **John Marshall Taber**, not a relative. From 1836-43, he was in New York City, possibly as partner with **Robert Hoey**, from 1836-40. **Taber** was listed in the 1843, New York City directory, as a planemaker. **Taber** was in Lowell, MA, from 1844-66, at 19 Market St.; and was listed in the 1849 New England Mercantile Union directory. as a plane manufacturer. He began experimenting with various methods of securing the irons by mechanical means. The 1860 MA Industrial census showed him having one employee and producing $800 worth of planes. He assigned to himself and **Thomas H. Abbott**, Patent No. 46,614, on Feb. 28, 1865, on a method of holding the iron in a bench plane by means of a metal frog. Planes using this patent were manufactured by the **Taber Plane Co.**, who purchased the rights to this patent in 1866. Earlier, **Wing H. Taber** and **John H. Currier** of Fairhaven, MA, received Patent No. 1224, on July 8, 1839, for a "new and useful machine for drilling iron, steel, brass, and the like substances.

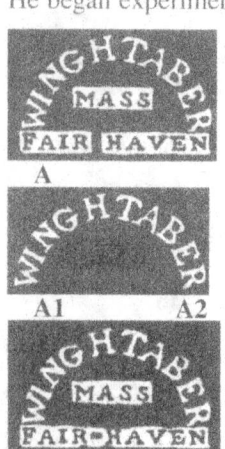

The nature of our invention consists in combining the power of the lever and screw so as to force forward the chuck and drill while it is turned by a crank." One of the witnesses to **Wing H. Taber**'s signature was **David Shiverick**. (see *Patented and Transitional Metallic Planes in America, Vol. I & II*, by Roger K. Smith). In 1880, **Wing H. Taber** was listed as retired mechanic in Petaluma, Sonoma Co., CA.
A *; C **; A1, B, D, E ***

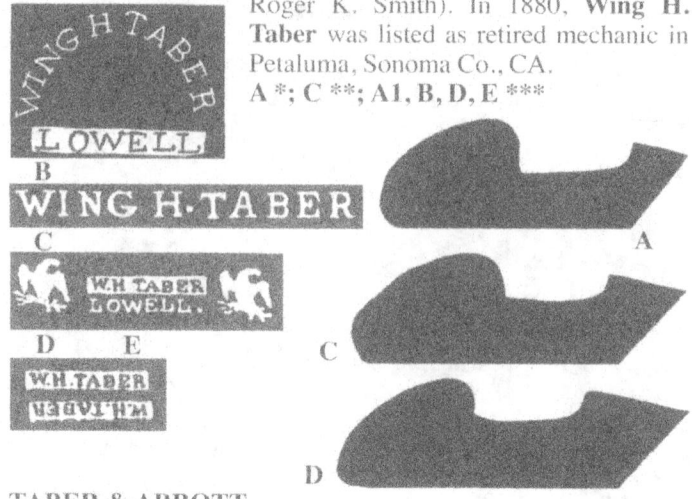

TABER & ABBOTT
Taber & Abbott was a planemaking firm, in Lowell, MA, from 1865-66. During this same time it was also joint owner of the **Providence Tool Co.**, in RI. This imprint appears on smoothing planes with varying types of cap screws that were made under Patent No. 46,614, dated Feb. 28, 1865, assigned to **Wing H. Taber** and **Thomas H. Abbott**. They sold the rights to that patent to the **Taber Plane Co.**, in 1866. ****

TABER PLANE CO.
The **Taber Plane Co.** made planes in New Bedford, MA, from 1866-72. In 1866, the company succeeded **J. & W. Lamb** and acquired the rights to the Feb. 28, 1865, patent of **Wing H. Taber** and **Thomas H. Abbott**. **William G. Lamb** and **James H. Lamb** were officers of the company. In 1872, it was succeeded by the **New Bedford Tool Co.**. Example: the C imprint is on a 5 7/8" beech **TOY** smoothing plane.
A: FF; B, B1 & C ***

E: TAFT
Enos Taft (b. Aug. 28, 1756 in Mendon, Worcester Co., D. Dec. 19, 1843 in Mendon) served in the American Revolutionary War, enlisting as a Private on Apr. 27, 1775 for 3 monts, 12 days in Capt. Andrew Peter's Co., Col. Joseph Road's Regt. **Enos Taft** first appeared in the Mendon land deeds as a carpenter in 1785, and then four more times as a joiner or housewright thru 1810. There were several other **E. Tafts** in the area in that period, but none were associated with woodworking. **E. TAFT** shared his location stamp with **S. PARTRIDGE** and cosigned a Yankee plow. **Partridge**'s wife was a cousin of **Enos**. This imprint with

IN: MENDON has been reported on a 12 7/8" tongue plane with a fish tail tote; and on a Yankee plow with square arms secured with wood screws and a wood depth stop, and a riveted skate, both birch with heavy flat chamfers, ca. 1780. *****

A. S. TANNER

Examples: on a 9 7/16"x 1" beech double-boxed side bead; and a 9 3/8" birch skew rabbet, both with flat chamfers; and a 9 1/2"x 1 1/8" birch skew rabbet with shallow round chamfers, ca. 1810-30. ****

R. M. TANNER

 Example: an 8 3/16" coffin smoothing plane with a single iron, ca. 1820. UR

TANNER & DAVENPORT

Richard W. Tanner (b. 1835 in England) of Albany, NY, was granted Patent No. 97,883, on Dec. 14, 1869 assigned to himself and Samuel J. Davenport. In 1875-1900, Richard was listed as a plane maker, in Albany, NY. Example: on a 6 7/8" beech veneer scraping plane with base and cross handle, single blade and brass thumbscrews. (see *Patented and Transitional Metallic Planes in America, Vol. II*, p. 80, by Roger K. Smith) UR

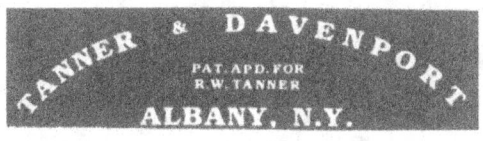

H. TAPPIN

Example: on a 9 1/2" beech single boxed complex molder with round chamfers, ca. 19c. UR

F. TARBOX

F. Tarbox made planes in Calais, ME, from 1871-80. **No imprint has been reported**.

I: TARNHAM

Example: on a 9 3/4" beech skew small complex molder with round chamfers, ca. early 19c. UR

TASKER

Example: on a 9 1/2" beech single boxed molder with flat chamfers, ca. 1800-10. UR

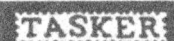

N. TASKER

Believed to be **Nathan Tasker** (b. ca. 1783 in Strafford, NH, d. Aug. 23, 1868 in Northwood, NH), a carpenter and joiner, from Northwood, NH. In 1810, in Barnstead, NH, in 1820, in Northwood. In 1850, he was listed, as a carpenter; and in 1860, as a cabinetmaker, in Northwood. NH. One example has an **N. Tasker** incuse owner's imprint on a 9 3/4" beech molding plane made by **I. Sleeper**. Examples: on a 9 7/8" beech dado; and a 10 9/16"x 7/8" beech rabbet, both with flat chamfers, an **I. Sleeper** style wedge, and a friction depth stop, ca. 1810. UR

W. TATE

William Tate (b. 1780's, d. 1833) was a Mifflinburg, PA, joiner. Mifflinburg was formerly named Youngmanstown, founded ca. 1730. He first appeared in the 1803 tax record. In 1806 he was listed as a joiner. In 1814 the tax records include a carpenter's shop. His inventory of Jan. 1834 includes:

5 Cornice planes	1.50
one set of Plough + Groove + Rabet	2.50
6 Table Planes + Sash Do	1.50
6 Bead + other Small Do	2.00
2 Sash Planes	1.25
4 Bead Do	1.00
1 Plough Do Moving	1.00
6 Planes of Different Kinds	1.25
11 Bench Planes	2.00
2 Mitre Boxes, 2 Metells & Plane Stock	.50

Amoung other Tools.

Examples: on a pair of plank-match planes; and a 9 13/16"x 1/2" beech single-boxed side bead with heavy round chamfers, ca. 1810-30. ****

FREDERICK TAYLOR

Frederick Taylor from Lowell, MA. Examples: on a lignum vitae fore plane; a rosewood scrub miter plane; and a 30" beech joiner with an iron stamped **GLOBE MFG CO.** with **BALDWIN** stamped below. **Globe Mfg. Co.** bought out **Baldwin** in 1875 and stamped their name above the **Baldwin** on the blades in stock, ca. 1850-75. ****

HARRISON P. TAYLOR

Harrison P. Taylor (b. Jun. 1840, d. before 1919) of Minerva, Columbiana Co., OH, received Patent No. 165,132, on June 29, 1875 and Patent No. 201,068, on March 5, 1878, for a bench plane beveling attachment; a 9" walnut fence with a steel plate for attaching it to the plane and for a bench plane. In 1880, he was listed as "patent right dealer" in Minerva. (see **Patented Transitional & Metallic Planes in America, Vol. II**, p. 76, by Roger K. Smith) **No imprint has been reported**.

H. TAYLOR

Hiram Taylor (b. 1807 in OH, d. Sep. 23, 1867 in Jefferson Co., OH) made planes in Cincinnati, OH, from 1839-40, as an employee of **E. F. Seybold**. He was listed, as a planemaker, in the city directories, of 1842-43; as a planemaker store, at Sycamore bt. 8th. & 9th., between 1844-46; as a partner in **H. & J. C. Taylor**, from 1850-61; as a planemaker, in 1857, at 49th. 8th.; as a "maker of edge tool" at 53 E. 8th., in 1862-63; for "agricultural implements", in 1865-66; as a plane maker, again in 1866-69, at 49 E. 8th.; and as a "maker of oil cups", in 1868. He was part of **Pelton & Taylor**, "maker of self oilers" at 47 E. 8th., from 1869-74. (see *Patented Transitional & Metallic Planes in America, Vol. II*, p. 116, by Roger K. Smith) ****

H. & J. C. TAYLOR
Hiram Taylor and John C. Taylor made and retailed planes in Cincinnati, OH, from 1850-67. The 1850 census showed them employing six hands and producing planes worth $2500. They held Patent No. 13,626, on Oct. 2, 1855, for a cast iron cooper's croze plane. They were listed separately after 1861, as H. Taylor and J. C. Taylor, both planemakers. Examples: the C imprint is on a cooper's cast-iron croze iron holder that read:
B & C **; A & A1 ***
H. & J. C. TAYLOR.
PAT'D. OCT. 2d, 1855 (C)

J. TAYLOR
Examples: The A imprint is on a 9 1/2"x 3/4" beech dado with flat chamfers, ca. 1800. The B imprint is on a 9 3/8" beech complex molder with relieved wedge and heavy round chamfers, ca. 1820. **A & B; UR**

J. TAYLOR/ J. C. TAYLOR
John C. Taylor (b. ca. 1810 in England, d. Feb. 1889 in Girton, Sandusky Co., OH) was listed as a planemaker, in the Cincinnati, OH, directories of 1842-44 & 1868-69. During the period 1850-61, he was a partner with Hiram Taylor in H. & J. C. Taylor. In 1863, he was a Clerk, at 54 W. Pearl. He worked for Hiram Taylor, from 1864-69. In 1870, John was listed as working for Carpint Ering in Cincinnati. In 1880, he was listed as fire insurance agent in Cincinnati.
A, B, C, D, E, E1 & E2 **

JAMES R. TAYLOR
James R. Taylor (b. ca. 1824) made a miter plane in New York City, in 1853. His address was the same as Joshua Terry who made an iron smoothing plane. **No imprint has been reported.**

L. TAYLOR
Example: on a 10 1/2" birch molder with flat chamfers, ca. 1800. **UR**

RICHARD TAYLOR
Richard Taylor (b. May 2, 1800) apprenticed, on July 26, 1815, to John M. Barkley to be taught the trade of planemaker. In 1870-80, he was listed, as a plane maker, in Baltimore, MD. **No imprint has been reported.**

S. TAYLOR
Possibly Solomon Taylor (b. ca. 1770, d. 1815) who in 1795, was a Hartford, CT housewright and a leading builder. His estate was valued at $10,924, which was very high for a tradesman, and included hundreds of joiners tools. Examples: on a 9 1/2" birch sash plane, and a 9 5/8" beech hollow with heavy flat chamfers, ca. 1790. **UR**

I. TEAL
John Teal (b. 1765 in Yorkshire, England, d. May 19, 1827 in Princeton, MA) made planes in Leeds before coming to the U.S. sometime before 1811. In 1811 he appeared on a deed as a carpenter's tool maker in Hubbardston, Worcester Co., MA. In the 1820 census he was listed as a planemaker in Princeton, also Worcester Co., with annual sales of $300. His probate inventory included 10 new planes and a box of plane irons. His estate was declared insolvent. *British Planemakers, 3rd edition*, shows the A & B imprints, used by Teal in England. Apparently he brought his die stamps to America and used them here, since they appear, one or the other, on all of the examples found in the U.S. Only the I. TEAL/ LEEDS English imprint offers a certainty of time and location. Examples: the A imprint is on an 8 1/4" wedge-lock plow, a 9 5/16" double iron complex molder, a 9 1/2" bead, and a 9 1/2" x 5/8" dado with wood depth stop; all beech with heavy round chamfers. The B imprint is on a 9 9/16" narrow beech round with tight round chamfers, and a 10" beech hollow with medium flat chamfers.
A & B ***; C ****

JOHN TEASMAN
John F. Teasman (b. 1794 in NJ) was listed in the 1835-37, Newark, NJ, directories, as a planemaker, "colored," and in the 1850-63, as a planemaker. In 1864, he was listed as "col'd engineer" in Newark, NJ. In 1869-70, as a laborer. In 1873-79, as a "col;d porter" in Newark. **No imprint has been reported.**

D. TENNEY
Possibly David Tenney (b. Nov. 10, 1786 in Temple, Hillsborough Co., NH, d. Feb. 14, 1814 in Brattleboro, VT). He advertised, in 1813, in *The Report* for an apprentice to the cabinet and sleigh making business, in Brattleboro, VT. In 1813, he sought a journeyman cabinetmaker. Example: the A imprint is on a slide-arm plow with heavy wood thumbscrews and with

the wedge shown, found in southern NH. The B imprint is on a pair of 10" handled tongue & groove planes with an **I. Sleeper** style wedge, from northern New England.
ca. 1800.   **UR**

A. TENNY
Example: on a 9 1/2" beech nosing plane with round chamfers on top and flat chamfers on the toe & heel. ca. 1810.   **UR**

A. THAYER

 Example: on a 9 1/2"x 1" beech bead with heavy flat chamfers. ca. 1800.   **UR**

BENONI THAYER
Benoni E. Thayer (b. 1814 in Amherst, MA, d. Oct. 8, 1854 in Amherst, MA) made planes for **T. Nutting** and **Nutting & Fox**, in 1834. In 1837, he was described as a grocer, but was again making planes, in 1842-44, as part of **Burnham, Fox & Co.**; In the 1850 census, he was listed as a journeyman mechanic. **No imprint has been reported**.

R. THAYER
Examples: on a 11 1/2" handled tongue plane, a 13" adjustable filletster with an offset "fish tail" open tote and iron strike; a Yankee plow; a 9 3/8" single-boxed complex molder; and a 9 7/16" cove, all birch with heavy flat chamfers similar in style to **J. Perry**, probably from New England. ca. 1790.   ****

E. THIESING
Ernest Thiesing (b. ca. 1810 in Germany) was a hardware dealer, at e.s. Main bt. 9th. & Court, in Cincinnati, OH, from 1839-46; and a partner in **Thiesing & Evans** with **Ernest Thiesing** and **Francis Evans**, a hardware and edge tools, at 367 Main bt. 9th. & Court, from 1849-51.   ****

THOMAS

 Example: on a 9 3/4" beech small bead with small flat chamfers, ca. 1800-10.   **UR**

A. THOMAS
Example: on an 8 7/8"x 3/8" beech round with heavy flat chamfers, found in Lititz, Lancaster Co., PA, ca. 1800.   **UR**

C. THOMAS
Example: on a 13 9/16"x 2 7/8" beech complex molder, with an offset tote and wide flat chamfers, ca. 1800.   **UR**

E. THOMAS
Elias Thomas (b. 1789, d. Mar. 6, 1853 in New York City) was listed as a carver, gilder, looking glass maker and merchant, from 1807-40. In 1807, he was located at 9 Elizabeth St; from 1809-18, at 214 Diane; from 1819-29, at 354 Pearl; from 1830-40, at 136 & 126 Canal. Example: on an 8 7/8" skew rabbet with heavy round chamfers, ca. 1830.   **UR**

J. THOMAS
The A die was filed to make the A1 die. Examples: the A imprint is on a 9 1/2" beech molder with the A wedge. The A1 imprint is on a 9 9/16" very complex molder; a 13 1/2" tongue plane with a centered open tote; and a 6 3/4" compass smoother, both have round top **Newbould** irons, all beech with heavy flat chamfers. The B imprint is on a 9 3/8" beech molder with heavy flat chamfers and the B wedge, ca. 1790.   ****

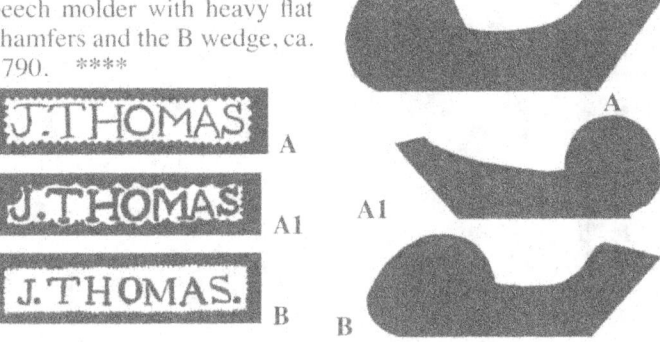

JOHN B. THOMAS
John B. Thomas (b. Jul. 15, 1821 in England, m. Feb. 1, 1853 in Ross Co., OH, d. Mar. 11, 1902 in Ross Co., OH) worked in Cincinnati, OH, received Patent No. 14,423, on March 11, 1856, using a glass face as the wear surface on a plane for durability and smoothness. **John Thomas** enlisted as a Private on Jul. 26, 1862, in the Civil War. **No imprint has been reported**.

T. THOMAS
Thomas Thomas was listed as a planemaker, in Baltimore, MD, in 1842, at 150 n. Paca St.. Examples: on a beech wedge-lock plow with brass depth stop and brass arm tips; and on a 9 5/16" beech fully-boxed ogee molder with spring; ca. 1850.   **UR**

W. THOMAS/ Wm. THOMAS
William Thomas (b. ca. 1806-13 in MD) was listed as a planemaker, in Baltimore, MD, from 1835-75. From 1835-36, he was located at Whitworth Row e. of Ross; from 1840-41, at George St. e. of Pine; from 1849-50, at 7 Chestnut al.; from 1853-58, at 140 Pine; from 1858-59, at 40 Pine; and from 1865-75, at 23 Lemmon. Example: the A imprint is on a 9 1/2" beech molder with heavy flat chamfers, ca. 1800-10. This is earlier than the reported dates for **William Thomas** and may represent an earlier generation. A bead bearing the name **Wm. THOMAS/ BALTIMORE** has been reported but is not available.
A, B, C & D: **UR**

I. THOMESON
Example: on a 9 1/2" beech astragal with flat chamfers, ca. 1810.   UR

ELIHU THOMPSON
Example: a 9 7/8" birch complex molder with shallow flat chamfers that stop with a backwards line and then a long turnout and a very slight relief to the wedge. ca. 1760, probably from New England.   UR

J. D. THOMPSON
Example: on a 13 5/8x 4 9/16" beech ogee complex molder with fence, a centered tote, little if any chamfer, style number **348** on the heel, and found in WV, ca. 1830.   UR

THOMPSON/ Wm. THOMPSON
Believed to be **William Thompson** (b. 1801 in Ireland, d. Dec. 19, 1868 in Jefferson, OH) of Steubenville, OH. The 1850 census and directory listed a **William Thompson**, as a carpenter, at Fifth and Adams. He was listed, as a carpenter, in the 1870 census and 1871 & 80 directories. There was another **William Thompson** (b. 1823) who came to Steubenville, in 1841, at age 18, to learn cabinet making. He moved to IA by wagon train, in 1854. Examples: on a single-boxed bead; a wide beech panel raiser with a **James Cam** iron, a 9 9/16" beech round, and wedge-arm plow that originally belonged to a Columbus, OH, cabinetmaker, **R. R. Ritchie** (b. 1843, d. 1938), ca. 1840-50.   A & A1 ****

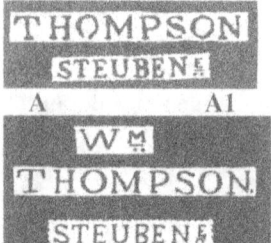

Wm. A. THOMPSON
William A. Thompson (b. in Scotland) operated a hardware store, in Buffalo, NY, 1839-46. William was listed in 1865, in Buffalo, Erie, NY. He was succeeded by his sons **Robert H. Thompson** and **Thomas M. Thomson** who worked as the **Thomas Bros.**, from 1847-59. Example: the B imprint with **PAT AP'L'D FOR** on a **18** beech round. The question is what was patented?   A & B ***

D THOMSON
Example: on a 9 9/16" and a 9 3/4" molder; and two 9 5/8" size **16** and **12** rounds, all beech with flat chamfers. One of the molding planes is also marked **JOHN STEWART**, possibly the maker, although the **D Thomson** imprint is in the proper position, ca. 1810.   UR

J. THOMSON
Examples: on a 9 3/4"x 1 3/4" birch round with heavy flat chamfers; and a 9 3/4" beech small bead with tight flat chamfers and a York pitch wedge, ca. 1800.   UR

THOMSON BROS
Robert H. Thomson (b. ca. 1822 in Scotland) and **Thomas M. Thomson** (b. ca. 1819 in Scotland) were the sons of **William A. Thomson** and succeeded their father in his hardware store in Buffalo, NY, from 1847-59. Example: on a **A & E Baldwin/ New York** plane.   ***

BENAMIN THOMTON
Benamin Thomton (**Benjamin Thomson**) was apprenticed to **William Powell** of Philadelphia, PA, on Oct. 8, 1771, "For 4 yrs., 6 mos., 12 days, to be taught plane making and given 5 quarters of school." **No imprint has been reported.**

W. THORBURN
Example: on a 9 3/8" beech complex molder wedge with shallow round chamfers, ca. 1820.   UR

T. THORN
Example: on a 9 1/2" beech skew dado with a brass depth stop and round chamfers, ca. 1830.   UR

I. THORNE
Example: on a 9 13/16" beech boxed reed & follow plane with round chamfers, ca. 1830.   UR

L. H. THORP
Example: on a 15" beech open-tote, panel raiser with adjustable fence on the sole and heavy round chamfers, ca. 1820.   UR

WILLIS THRALL & SON
Willis Thrall (b. ca. 1801 in CT, d. Jun. 20, 1884 in Hartford, CT) was the principal in **Willis Thrall & Son** a hardware dealer, in Hartford, CT, from 1860-95. In 1842, **Willis Thrall** was the successor to **S. A. Jones W & Co.**, in 1850, as a rule maker, in Hartford, CT; before expanding into the hardware business with his son **Edward Bissell Thrall** (b. Sep. 1834, d. 1909 in CT). In 1875, **Willis Thrall & Son** was listed as hardware, at located at 10 Central, Hartford, CT, with **Willis Thrall** and his son **Edward B. Thrall**. **Edward** was still listed thru 1907, as hardware, at 63 Church, Hartford. Example: on a 5/8" single boxed side bead made by **Union Factory/ H. Chapin** stamped in ink: A & B ****

FROM
WILLIS THRALL & SON
TOOLSTORE
NO. 76 CENTRAL ROW
HARTFORD, CONN   (B)

L. THWING
Example: on an 8" birch sash coping plane with a relieved wedge, flat chamfers and flutes, ca. 1790. **UR**

M. I. TIDAY
Example: on a 9 1/2" beech molder with large shallow round chamfers, ca. early 19c. **UR**

M. TIBBER
Example: on a 9 1/4" maple skew rabbet with a nicker, ca. 1850. **No imprint is available**.

A. TIBBETS CO.

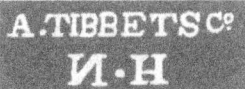

Example: on a skew rabbet with fence and nicker, ca. 1850. **UR**

M. B. TIDEY/ M. B. TIDEY & CO.
Marcus Baker Tidey (b. Jun. 26, 1829 in Niagara, Ontario, Canada of English and PA German descent, d. Apr. 1901 in Newark, NJ) learned plane making, in Dundee, NY, in 1849. It was here that he received his first patent for an improved hand groover, "a tool of great usefulness." The 1850 census listed **Tidey**, living in Starkey, Yates Co., NY, the same county as Penn Yan and Dundee, not far from Ithaca. He moved to Pen Yan, NY, where his models, tools, patents, and library, were destroyed by fire. He then moved to Ithaca, NY. **M. B. Tidey** is best known for his patented double-beveling plane, Patent No. 11,235, dated July 4, 1854, and issued to **M. B. Tidey**, **M. J. Wheeler**, **H. W. Pierce**, and **G. W. Rogers** in Dundee, NY. The C imprint with **& CO** was probably used on this plane. On March 10, 1857, **Tidey** was granted Patent No. 16,812, for a sawing machine table gauge. On Mar. 24, 1857, **Tidey**, in Ithaca, was also granted Patent No. 16,889, for his beech smoothing plane with an iron core which could be adjusted as the sole began to wear. He was also reported to have run the plane division of **Treman & Bros.**, an iron foundry in Ithaca. The 1870 Products of Industry census for NJ, listed **M. B. Tidey** as employing 10 men, building 75 machines and 20 dozen saw gauges in Newark, NJ. While in Newark, he was also part of the **Hedenberg Works**. In 1880, he was listed as "manf. wood working machinery" in Newark. In the last ten years, he was an invalid. His business was managed by his son. His mind remained sharp and he was constantly making plans for new devices. Tidey's imprinted non-patent planes are seldom found, suggesting that, although he used four different imprints, plane making was apparently not his major occupation. Examples: the C imprint is on a 9 1/2" beech round with a **23** size number on the heel, and a 26" beech jointer with a laminated strike button (rosewood, ebony & boxwood), 2 1/2"x 3" boxwood wear plates in the sole, and a double **Dwight & French & Co.** iron. **A, A1 & D ***; B & C ******

TIFFANY & CO.

Example: on a medium hollow made by **Greenfield Tool Co.**, ca. 19c. **UR**

J. TILBURN
J. Tilburn was listed as a planemaker, in the 1837 Philadelphia directory. **No imprint has been reported**.

R. M. TILBURN
Richard Mayer Tilburn was married in Newbury, MA, Nov. 29, 1806, and appeared there, in the 1810 census. In the 1820 New Jersey Federal Industrial census, he was listed, as a journeyman planemaker, in New Brunswick, NJ. **Richard H. Tilburn** (the "H" may be a misspelling of "M") was listed as a planemaker, in the 1837 Philadelphia city directory. Examples: earlier molding planes are 9 3/4" beech with heavy flat chamfers and an **I. Sleeper** style A wedge, representing his Newbury, MA work. The later planes are 9 1/2", beech with heavy round chamfers and a typical early 19c. B wedge representing his work in New Brunswick, NJ, and Philadelphia, PA. **A wedge ****; B wedge *****

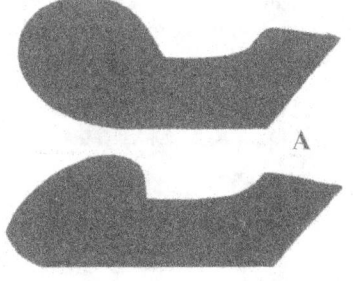

TILDEN
Possibly **John Tilden** (b. Nov. 6, 1758 in Norfolk Co., MA, m. 1795 in Bridgewater, d. Aug. 29, 1839 in Bridgewater, Plymouth Co., MA) was a cabinetmaker, in North Bridgewater, MA. Example: on a beech wedge-lock plow with heavy round chamfers, ca. 1800-20. **UR**

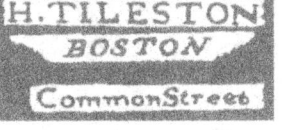

BENJAMIN L. TILESTON
Benjamin L. Tileston (b. ca. 1810 in MA, d. Nov. 30, 1869 in Boston, MA) was listed as a plane maker, in the Boston directory of 1841-42 & 55. **Benjamin** was the son of **Timothy Tileston**. **No imprint has been reported**.

H. TILESTON
Harvey Tileston (d. Sep. 28, 1844 in Boston, MA) was the brother of **Timothy Tileston, Jr**, and was listed as a planemaker, on Common St., Boston, MA, from 1801-25. He lived with his father, **Timothy Tileston**, a laborer and well digger. *******

T. TILESTON/ T. TILEFTON

Timothy Tileston, Jr.'s (b. ca. 1783 in Boston, MA, d. May 23, 1866 in Boston) first plane making, location was at 55 Orange St., Boston, MA, the same premises as **Levi Little**'s last listed address. **Tileston**'s name appears several times in the accounting of **Levi Little**'s estate, and it is probable that he worked for and took over after **Little**'s death, in 1802. **Timothy Tileston, Jr.**'s father, **Timothy Tileston** was a laborer and well digger, who lived on Pleasant Street. He had two other sons: **Harvey Tileston**, a planemaker, from 1801-25, who lived with his father; and **Charles Tilefton**, a hatter. **Timothy** dropped the **Jr.** after his father's death and his son, **Timothy. Tileston, Jr.**, a planemaker, was listed as residing at 16 Ash St., from 1834-40. This was property owned by **Timothy Tileston**, in 1824, and still owned by him at his death. Another son, **Benjamin L. Tileston** (b. 1811), was listed in the 1850 census, as a planemaker, who worked for, and resided with, his father, at 75 Front St., from 1840-57. No example of either of their imprints has been reported. **T. Tileston** was listed in the 1841 Boston Almanac under "planes", at 75 Front St.; and in the 1849 New England Mercantile Union directory, as a plane manufacturer, at 73 Harrison Ave., Boston. In the 1860 MA Industrial census, **Timothy**, age 77, was listed as a planemaker, with one employee and producing plane stock worth $700, indicating that his plane making had become rather inactive. His estate was appraised at $49,202.51, an unusually large amount for a planemaker. Of this only $389.25 was stock and tools.

Tileston's early planes are 9 1/2" beech with broad flat chamfers and round wedge finials. He used the same **Bofton** location imprint and boxed his planes with rosewood, as did **Levi Little**. The **Bofton** A & B imprints, date to 1802-08, when he worked at 55 and then 41 Orange Street. The D imprint is from the same die as C but with the edges filed to a zigzag. The E imprint was used starting in 1809. The F imprint was used until 1840. The F2 imprint used the same die as the F1 imprint, but prior to the filing a groove through the center of the die. The **Harrison Avenue** and with the **Boston** die filed on the G imprint was used, from 1841-66, when Front St.'s name was changed to Harrison Ave. The H imprint is on a 20 7/8" beech bench plane with flat chamfers and an offset closed birch handle. Birch components are not known on other **Tileston** planes. **Tileston** was the only one to use the **Front Street** imprint and he and **Little** were the only ones to use the **Bofton** imprint. Two planes have been reported with original **I. Sleeper** style wedges, possibly from a hired hand or left over Little stock. F & F1: FF; A, A1 & G **; D & F2 ***; C & E ****; B, H & H1 *****

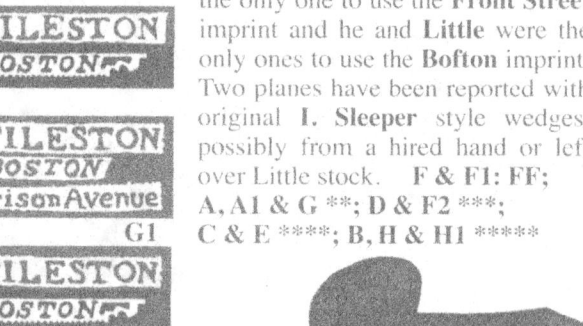

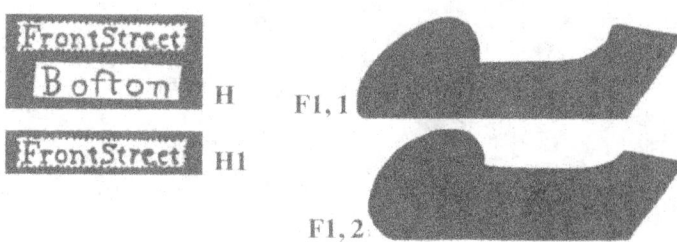

A. TILTON
Example: on a smoother. UR

J. TILTON
Believed to be **Jeremiah Tilton**. Examples: on an 8 3/4" plow with wood thumbscrews, wood depth stop, screw applied skate, and round chamfers, a beech panel gauge, and a 13 3/8" panel raiser with an ebony diamond strike and a centered tote, beech with shallow round chamfers, ca. 1820-30. ****

TINKHAM/ J. TINKHAM
Jesse Tinkham (b. Nov. 13, 1785 in Middleboro, MA, d. Feb. 17, 1868 in Athol, MA) was the brother of **Samuel Tinkham**, was a tool maker, as early as 1818; and was listed in the 1850 census, as a machinist, in Enfield, MA. In 1855, he was called a joiner. Enfield was one of four towns inundated when the Quabbin Reservoir was created in the 1930's to supply water to Metropolitan Boston. Examples: on a 7 3/8" smoother, with an iron set at 70 degrees, and a 9 1/8" beech round with shallow round chamfers. Also reported is a marking gauge, dated **1818**. The A1 imprint is on a 9 3/4" birch narrow round with round chamfers, ca. early 19c. (see *American Marking Gages*, p. 307, by Milton H. Bacheller, Jr.) A, A1 & B *****

L. TINKHAM
Levi Tinkham (b. Nov. 18, 1765 in Middleborough, Plymouth Co., MA, d. Sep. 17, 1857 in Middleborough) of Middleboro, MA, who was a cabinetmaker, carpenter/ joiner, turner, wheelwright, planemaker, mechanic in wood and a farmer. He was active in civil affairs and served as town treasurer, from 1822-27. **Levi**'s will, dated June. 24, 1854, included the following: "I give & bequeath to my grandson **Charles Carrol Tinkham** all my tools for cutting screws - also one half of my carpenters' joiners' & wheelwrights' tools... I give and bequeath to my grandson **Josiah Foster Tinkham** one half of my carpenters', joiners' & wheelwrights' tools... In the bequest of tools to the said **Charles** & **Josiah**, it is my meaning to give them only the tools which I have had in common use." The stipulation might imply a differentiation between working tools and a stock of unused tools. One **L. Tinkham** coffin smoother bears the owner initials **C. C. T.** on the heel. Examples: on a

9 1/2"-9 3/4" birch and beech, a bench plane with an offset tote, another with a centered tote. The C imprint is on a 9 13/16" birch astragal with shallow flat chamfers and flutes and a decorative **X** with dots as used by **E. Clark** also of Middleboro. The D imprint is on a beech molder with flat chamfers
A & B ****; A1, C & D *****

L. B. TINKHAM

Example: on a 1 1/8" round, ca. 1840. **UR**

L. N. TINKHAM

Example: on a 9 1/2" beech split sash with shallow round chamfers, ca. 19c. **A & B: UR**

S. TINKHAM
Samuel Tinkham (b. Feb. 18, 1798 in Middleboro, Plymouth Co., MA, d. Dec. 5, 1880 in Enfield, Hampshire Co., MA) was the brother of **Jesse Tinkham** and was in Enfield, MA, by 1823; and was listed in the 1850 census, as a cabinetmaker. In 1865 & 80, he was listed as a carpenter and a cabinetmaker. Examples: on a group of 11 planes 9"-91/2", including 7 molding, 2 beading planes, and a rabbet, an adjustable screw, double-iron sash plane, all beech, with relieved wedges and round chamfers, ca. 1820.
A & B ****

I. C. TITCOMB
Isaac Cummings Titcomb (b. Sep. 8, 1813 in Essex Co., MA, d. Aug. 15, 1859 in Newburyport, Essex Co. MA) who was a Newburyport, MA, cabinetmaker, ca. 1840. Isaac was the son of **Joseph Titcomb** and the brother of **Solomon Titcomb**. Examples: on a 14" crown molder, and a 16"x 6" beech double-throated crown. The **N.P** on the B imprint is believed to stand for Newburyport. **A ***, B *******

I. TITCOMB/ JOSEPH TITCOMB
Joseph Titcomb (b. May 16, 1770 in Newbury, Essex Co., MA, d. Oct. 6, 1850 in Newbury) was the father of **Isaac Cummings Titcomb** and **Solomon Titcomb**. He was described as a Newbury, MA joiner, in a 1805 surety, and as a toolmaker in his probate documents. His estate inventory included: "26 jointers, 12 fore planes, 2 ploughs (planes), three pairs of match plains, 42 crease tools (molding planes) and 20 plane irons". **Joseph**, **Solomon**, and possibly **Isaac** all used the same TITCOMB die for their last name with the front initial, **I** for **Joseph** or possibly **Isaac**, **S** for **Solomon** to individualize. Examples: molders are 9 1/2"-9 5/8" of beech with **I. Sleeper** style wedges and narrow flat or heavy round chamfers. One late 9 1/2" single rosewood boxed bead has shallow round chamfers with the A1 wedge. Another late 9 1/2"x 3/8" beech bead with one strip of rosewood boxing and one of boxwood has a A2 wedge. On the toe is **J. PAGE** which may refer to John Page (b. 1810), a Newburyport, MA, cabinetmaker. The C imprint is on a 9 15/16" beech skew rabbet with wide flat chamfers.
A **; B & C ****

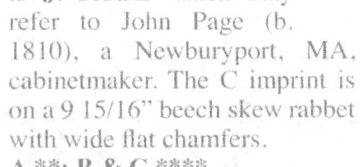
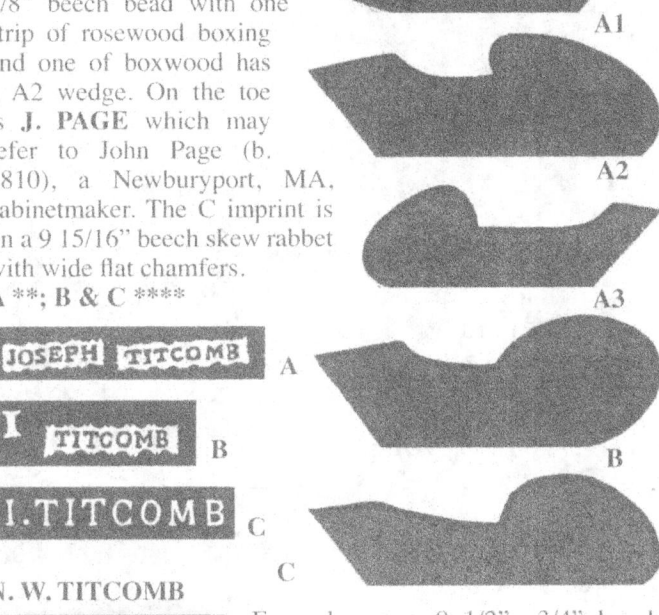

N. W. TITCOMB

Example: on a 9 1/2"x 3/4" beech single-boxed side bead with an **W. N. Starr & Co.** iron, and dated **1847**, with a "leaf logo". **UR**

S. TITCOMB
Solomon Titcomb (b. Dec. 5, 1803 in Newbury, MA, d. Apr. 6, 1887 in Newburyport, Essex Co., MA), the son of **Joseph Titcomb** and brother of **Isaac Cummings Titcomb**. Examples: on an astragal with flat chamfers, a very complex molder with slightly rounded chamfers, a 9 5/16"x 1/8" beech grooving plane with a rosewood skate and flat chamfers, a 9 1/2"x 1 3/8" beech molding plane with flat chamfers, and a 16" beech gutter plane with a pegged centered tote, a diamond strike and round chamfers. *****

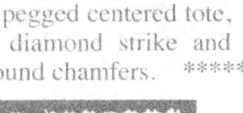

D. TITLOW

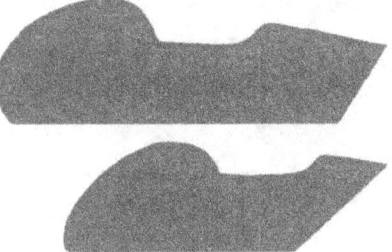

Example: on a birch complex molder. **UR**

D. B. TITUS
Daniel Butters Titus (b. Jan. 6, 1828 in Union, Knox Co., ME, d. Nov. 14, 1905 in Union) was in East Union, ME, from 1850-70, and noted as a mechanic; and in 1880, as a maker of mast and truss hoops and cooper's tools. In 1890, he was listed as a master hooper, in Union, ME. Example: on a cooper's croze has been reported bearing a paper label with a circular imprint that reads: **UR**

D. B. TITUS
MANUFACTURERS OF
MAST HOOPS, TRUSS
HOOPS AND CROZE
EAST UNION ME.

Also imprinted on the top edge was **H. H. Crie & Co.**, a hardware dealer in Rockland, ME. **No imprint is available.**

C. TOBEY.
Cornelius Tobey (bapt. Aug 14, 1768 in Darthmouth, MA, d. 1807 in Hudson, NY) was a builder, and active in Hudson, NY town affairs, from 1792-1807. He was the father of **John I. Tobey**. Example: The A & A1 imprints are on planes 10"-9 3/4" birch and beech with flat chamfers and relieved wedges. The B imprint is on planes 9 1/4"-9 1/2" of beech. Two example have the B imprint and a similar **S. TOBEY** imprint on a 9 1/4" beech round; and a complex molder, both with round chamfers, ca. 1800-20.   **B **;   A & A1 ***; C ******

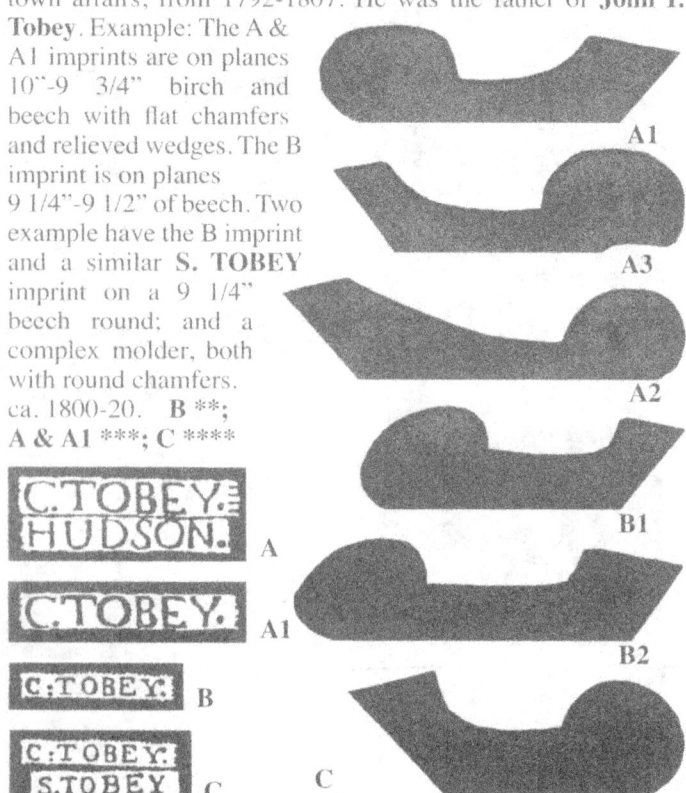

I. TOBEY
Example: on a 9 1/2" beech large hollow with a relieved wedge and heavy flat chamfers, ca. 1800.   **UR**

J. I. TOBEY
John I. Tobey (b. 1795, d. Oct. 11, 1867 in Hudson, Columbia Co., NY) was the son of **Cornelius Tobey** of Hudson, NY; and who was also an assistant alderman, in 1827-28. In 1835, he was listed, as a machinist, in New York, NY, ca. 1825.   **A & B *****

J. J. TOBEY & CO.
J. J. Tobey was listed in the 1868 Boston directory under hardware, at 1043 Washington St.; and in 1876, at 1291 Washington St. The **1060 Washington St./ BOSTON** imprint could have been before or after these listings.. ********

R. B. TOBIE
Example: on a 10 1/4" flame beech dust joint pair with a high pitch, applied fences, with hand made screws and small round chamfers, ca. early 19c.   **UR**

B. TODD
B. Todd was listed in Brunswick, ME. Example: on a 9 9/16"x 1 3/16" beech ogee molder with heavy round chamfers, ca. 1820.   **UR**

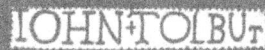

IOHN+ TOLBUT
John Tolbut (d. 1868 in Naugatuck, New Haven, CT) advertised in the **Connecticut Courant** on Dec. 30, 1799, as a cabinetmaker, in Farmington CT. He married on Oct. 11, 1811, in Canton, CT. Example: on a 9 5/16" beech large hollow with heavy round chamfers, ca. 1820-30.   **UR**

W. TOKELOVE
Example: on a 9 3/4" beech large half round with a shallow relieved wedge and heavy round chamfers, ca. 1820.   **UR**

C. TOLLNER
Charles Tollner (b. Jan. 1, 1823 in Germany, d. Jul. 15, 1897 in Pulaski, Oswego, NY) was naturalized Jun. 10, 1856 in New York City. **Charles** ran a hardware and tool store, in New York City, from 1851-61, at 209 Bowery ST. During 1862-63, he was in partnership with **Albert Hammacher** as **C. Tollner & Hammacher**. **Tollner** was part of **B. Stern & Tollner** at 221 Bowery, the same address as indicated on the B imprint. In 1880, **Charles Tollner** was listed as "boxes, wooden packing" employed by **Richard Dswego Co., NY**. The initial group **C. T. & Co.** may also be for **C. Tollner**. (see **A. Hammacher & Co.**)   **A, B & B1 ****

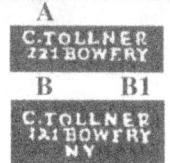

J. R. TOLMAN
Joseph Robinson Tolman (b. Feb. 10, 1787, d. Jun. 7, 1864 in Scituate, Plymouth Co., MA) was the father of **Thomas J. Tolman**. There is a listing of a **Joseph Tolman** in the 1818 Boston directory, as a ship joiner, on Ship Street. **Joseph** probably first made planes, in South Scituate, MA, in the 1820's. He is listed again in the Boston almanac, in 1841, under "planes", at 115 Commercial St. He was listed, in the 1849 New England Mercantile Union directory, as a plane manufacturer, in Hanover. In the 1860 MA Industrial census, he was listed as employing three hands and producing $3,000

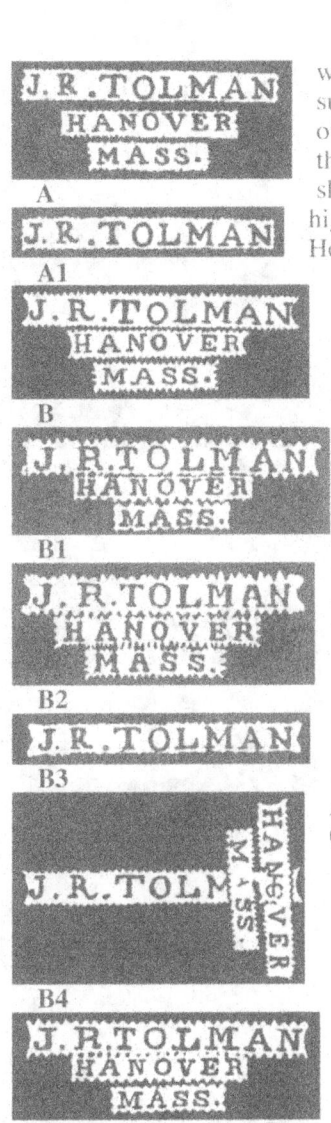

worth of planes. **J. R. Tolman** was succeeded by **Tolman & Merritt**, of Hanover, MA. He is notable for the large number of spar and other shipbuilder's planes, as well as the high quality of his workmanship. He tended to use double-irons in many of his planes. **Tolman** used at least three name dies creating four distinct imprints. He also employed at least three **HANOVER** dies and two **MASS.** dies. Obviously the combinations are almost endless. The A imprint is thought to be the earliest and is found on the conventional molders that are not ship planes. It was used to create the B imprint by modifying the ends. These imprints have a narrow **J** and a long leg **R**. The C & D imprints are similar but the C is the longest and the D is the shortest.
A, A1, B, B1, B2, B3, B4, C & D **

B

T-TOLMAN
Example: on a 25 3/4" beech joiner with a closed center tote, a double-iron by **Maw & Staley** and small round chamfers, ca. 19c. **UR**

T. J. TOLMAN
Thomas J. Tolman (b. Oct. 10, 1819 in S. Scituate, Plymouth Co., MA) was the son of **Joseph Robinson Tolman**, and a planemaker, in Hanover and South Scituate, MA, from 1850-64. In 1850, he was listed, as a planemaker, living with his father and **Charles H. Merritt**, age 23. **Tolman** received Patent No. 16,412, on Jan. 13, 1857, for a method for adjusting the mouth size of a plane. **Tolman** was later part of **Tolman & Merritt** with **Charles H. Merritt** in South Scituate, MA, from 1864-80. It is believed that **Merritt** continued the firm alone, from 1881-93. **T. J. Tolman**'s HANOVER and MASS. dies were used by **J. Merritt**, in 1878. Examples: on a 9 1/2" smoothing plane with an adjustable rosewood mouth, and a beech miter plane with an

A

adjustable boxwood mouth.
A **; B *****

B

TOLMAN & MERRITT
Tolman & Merritt was a partnership of **Thomas J. Tolman** and **Charles H. Merritt** located in Hanover, MA, from 1864-93. **Tolman & Werritt** listed on a list of prices of Ship Joiners and House Planes, noted that they were the successors to **Jos. R. Tolman**, Hanover, MA. **No imprint has been reported**.

I + TOMSON
Example: on a 9 3/8" beech skew rabbet with tight round chamfers, ca. 1830. **UR**

J. S. TONER
Example: on a 9 5/8" rabbet. **No imprint is available**.

R. TONGE
Example: on a 9 1/2" thumbnail molder with heavy flat chamfers, ca. 1800. **UR**

A. TOPPAN
Abner Toppan (b. Apr. 6, 1764 in Newburyport, Essex Co., MA, d. Dec. 31, 1836 in Newburyport) is a Newburyport, MA, cabinetmaker, ca. 1780-95. He is probably related to **Stephen Toppan**. **Abner Toppan** went to MD to sell clocks; and married **Elizabeth Stanford**, in Dorchester, MD, on Jan. 30, 1792. Examples: on a molder, and a 3/4" dado, both 10" beech with flat chamfers and an **I. Sleeper** style wedge, and on a plane made by **I. Sleeper** as an owner imprint. ****

E. C. TOPPAN
Probably **E. Clark Toppan**, a Newburyport, MA, ship joiner, listed in 1882-91, at 250 Merrimac, Newburyport. Examples: on an 8 1/2" rosewood narrow coffin smoother with a double-iron, a grooving plane, and a plow. ****

S. TOPPAN
Probably **Stephen Toppan** (b. Dec. 6, 1756 in Newbury, Essex Co., MA, d. Oct. 7, 1839 in Newbury), a housewright in Newburyport, MA. On Jan. 1, 1786, he married **Edma Little**, who was **Levi Little**'s aunt. He is listed in the **Little** genealogy as a carpenter. **Stephen Toppan** served in the Revolutionary War, as a Private, from Sep. 30, 1776 to Nov. 16, 1776, and as a Corporal, from Aug. 14, 1777 to Nov. 30, 1777. In the 1790's, he was known as a master builder; and known to have built several Federal mansions in Newburyport including Mrs. Tilton's, in 1796, and Mr. Sawyer's, in 1798. Toppan was also involved in furniture manufacturing. An 1830 ad in the Dover, NH, *Inquirer* offered cabinet furniture manufactured "in the latest and most improved patterns." The inventory of his estate included joiner's tools as the third largest item at $18.

Examples: on planes 10"-9 1/2" beech with flat chamfers, and an **I. Sleeper** style wedge, a panel raiser, a birch wedge-locked Yankee plow with riveted skate, square arms, and flat chamfers, and on a plane made by **I. Sleeper** as an owner's imprint. *****

TOPPING & BRO.
Erastus Doane Topping (b. Sep. 12,1817 in Chatham, Barnstable Co., MA, m. Jun. 27, 1851 in Alton, Madison Co., IL, d. Oct 8, 1862 in Alton) and **Marcus Hubbert Topping** (b. Jan. 1820 in Chatham, d. Nov. 1, 1906 in Jacksonville, Morgan Co., IL) established a Hardware & Iron Business, on March 23, 1849, in Alton. In 1858, **John Simeon Topping** (b. Sep. 12, 1826 in Chatham, d. Aug. 21, 1891 in Alton) joined the firm which became **Topping Bros.**, in hardware & cutlery, at 2nd. e. of State. In 1874, after **Erastus'** death, **Lucas Topping** (b. Feb. 2, 1822 in Chatham, m. Jan. 6, 1852 in St. Louis, MO, d. Jul. 2, 1903 in Wichita, Sedgwick Co., KS) also joined **Topping & Bros.**, On Jul. 25, 1884, **Topping & Bros.** was sold to **Wm. Siern**. In 1889, **Marcus H. Topping** was Pres. of IL Insurance Co., in Alton. In 1889, **John S. Topping**, was listed as commercial traveler, in Alton, IL. **A & A1** **

I. TORRANCE
Example: on a 9 7/8" beech round and flat chamfers. ca. 1810. **UR**

J. TORREY
Examples: on a complex molder and a skew rabbet, both 9 1/2" beech, ca. 19c. **UR**

S. T/ S. G. TORREY
Seth Green Torrey (b. Apr. 7, 1773 in Cummington, MA, d. Jun. 24, 1843 in Windsor, MA) was the son of **Luther Torrey** (b. Sep. 26, 1733 in Scituate, MA, d. Apr. 8, 1825 in Windsor). **Luther** was married, in 1751, in Killingly, CT, to **Dorothy Green**, daughter of **Seth Green**. **Luther** was a blacksmith. In 1799, **Seth Green Torrey** married **Leah Tower**, in Cummington. **Leah** died on Feb. 3, 1801, and in Nov. 1802, **Seth** married **Sabra Leonard** in Cummington. In 1805, **Seth** bought 45 acres in Windsor adj. to the Cummington line; and called himself a carpenter. In Jan.1819, the Cummington Selectmen noted that Mr. **Seth G. Torrey** was qualified to teach in the common schools. Thus **Seth** was a teacher, farmer and carpenter. Examples: on a group of 32 wooden planes, 4 with the A imprint with the full name and 1 with the B imprint. The A imprint is on a 25" birch jointer with a diamond strike, an offset tiger maple closed tote, a **Weldon** double-iron and flat chamfers, ca. 1790; a 28 13/16" birch joiner with a slight offset beech closed tote, a round strike and flat chamfers; a beech plow with a snecked iron, riveted arms and skate, a friction depth stop and wedge locked arms; and a beech fixed tongue. The B imprint is on a birch round. Of the 32 planes; 6 are bench planes; 1 plow; 3 smoothers; a 3 1/4" wide birch crown molder with a cherry highly offset cherry tote; a beech panel raiser with a slightly offset tote and **Newbould** iron; the 16 molders are 9"-9 1/2" beech, all with flat chamfers. With the exception of the 25" jointer, all are ca. 1800-05. **A & B** *****

C. TOUPIN
Example: on a wedged locked rosewood plow plane with boxwood arms and wedge. ca. **UR**

D. TOWER
Example: on a 9 3/8" beech round with med. flat chamfers. **UR**

Jn. TOWER
Jonathan Tower (b. Sep. 7, 1758 in Sudbury, Middlesex Co., MA, d. Apr. 20, 1846 in Rutland, MA) settled in Rutland, MA, north of Worcester, at the head waters of the Blackstone River; where he made carpenter's and cabinetmaker's tools. **Jonathan's** uncle married **Uriah Clap's** aunt, also of Rutland, MA. He had eccentric habits. He was very tender and considerate in treatment of his horse, keeping one until it was 30 years old. He would be seen trudging along the highway leading the horse by the bridle, instead of riding upon its back. He injured his foot with an adz early in his life, which limited his military duty, but he guarded prisoners after **Burgoyne's** surrender. The A1 imprint is from the same die as the A die, after the ends were filed. Examples: planes are 9" beech with heavy round chamfers. The earlier A imprint is on a 9 1/2" birch grooving plane with riveted skate and heavy flat chamfers, ca. 1780-1820. **A & A1** **

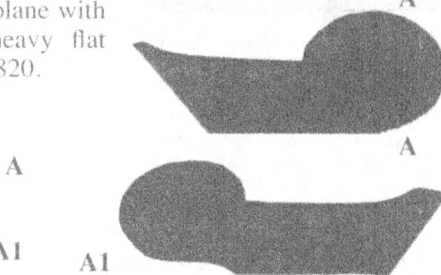

S. TOWER & CO.
S. Tower & Co. was listed in 1856, as a planemaker, in Chesterfield, MA. **No imprint has been reported**.

I. T/ I. TOWLE
Examples: on a 9 1/2" cove molder with heavy flat chamfers and a size **7/8** mark on the heel, ca. 1800. **UR**

E. C. TOWN.
Example: on a 13 7/8" skew beech panel raiser with an open wood pegged open tote and flat chamfers. The single iron is a **W. Greaves & Sons**. ca. 1800. **UR**

E. W. TOWNSEND
Example: on a 16" jack with a **Dwight French & Co.** iron. **UR**

JOHN TOWNSEND
Example: on a paper label on a size **5/8** dado made by **Sandusky**, that reads: ****

MADE EXPRESSLY
FOR
JOHN TOWNSEND.
ROME, N. Y.

N. TOWNSLEY
Believed to be **Nicanor Townsley** (b. Nov. 12, 1755 in Hampden, d. Oct. 26, 1830 in Walpole, Cheshire Co., NH) who arrived in Walpole, ca. 1785. He advertised, as a cabinetmaker, in Walpole, NH, from 1795-1807. He advertised that he seeks apprentices and lists furniture "in the newest fashion". He was a partner with **Asher Southard**, from 1803-07. In 1805, **Nicanor Townsley** was Secretary of the Walpole Mechanics Society. In 1805, the First New Hampshire Company of riflemen was empowered to meet at Walpole, as a militia, and included **Nicanor Townsley**. The inventory of his estate included 4 smoothing planes, 2 jointers, 2 jack planes, 2 rabbet "plains" and 36 molding tools. Example: on a 10 3/4" birch wedge-lock plow with shallow tight flat chamfers and an imprint struck twice on the toe. The wood depth stop is held in place with a wood wedge thru the plane body from side to side. The plane was found near Walpole, MA, ca. 1790. **UR**

TRACY
Example: on a 9 7/8" fruitwood thumbnail molder with large shallow flat chamfers with lamb tonges, ca. 1770-80. **UR**

R. TRACY
Example: on a 11 1/2" beech plow with iron arm screw stopped & wood depth stop, ca. 19c. **UR**

A. TREAT
Example: on a 9 3/8" beech molder with flat chamfers, ca. 1810. **UR**

B. TRELOAR
Example: on a 9 1/2" beech grooving plane with a iron skate secured with hand made screws, ca. 19c. **UR**

TREMAN & BROS./ TREMAN & BROTHERS
Treman & Brothers was a hardware firm in Ithaca, NY, consisting of **Leonard Treman** (b. Jun. 18, 1819 in Mecklenburg, Schuyler Co., NY, d. May 25, 1888 in Itaca, Tompkins Co., NY) and **Lafayette Lepine Treman** (b. Apr. 3, 1821 in Mecklenburg, d. Apr. 27, 1900 in Ithaca) that succeeded **Edward G. Pelton**, in 1844, as **L. & L. L. Treman**. **Leonard** had Clerked for **Edward G. Pelton**, from 1837-44. In 1849, a third brother, **Elias A. Treman** (b. Dec. 9, 1822 in Mecklenburg, d. Oct. 1, 1898 in Ithaca), joined the company, and the name changed to **Treman & Bros.**. The firm added an iron foundry and a plane factory, on the s.s. of South Cayuga St. An 1853 map lists "**Treman & Brothers**, Iron Works & Plane Factory." **Nathaniel Spaulding** was listed at 11- 13 S. Cayuga St., in the 1867 directory. **M. B. Tidey** ran their plane shop. In 1857, the firm became **Treman, King & Co.**, after **Leander Rutherford King** (b. Feb. 3, 1828 in Seneca, NY, d. Sep. 20, 1900 in Ithaca), a cousin, joined the firm, in 1851-52. The business continued until 1944. From 1864-88, **Leonard Treman** was President of New York State Electric & Gas Corp. Brothers **Lafayette Treman** and **Elias Treman** were officers and directors. Example: on an size **8/8** tongue plane both the A imprint and the **M. B. Tidey & Co.** C imprint. A & B **

A   B

I. TREYZ
Example: on a 9 1/2" beech full round with flat chamfers that stop with a long sloped turnout, ca. 1790-1800. **UR**

I. TRIPP
Example: on a 9 3/4" beech compass bottom center bead with heavy flat chamfers; and a 10 1/2" beech square rabbet with heavy round chamfers, ca. 1800-10. ****

J. S. TRIPP
Jonathan S. Tripp (b. 1783, d. Feb. 5, 1863 in Clove, NY, Dutchess Co., NY), lived in Union Vale, Duchess Co., NY, from 1830-50; listed in 1850 as a carpenter; in 1860, a farmer. Example: on a 9 1/2" moving filletster, with A wedge; a rabbet; a 9 1/4" narrow shiplap plane with B wedge; and a round, all beech with round chamfers, ca. 1830. ****

A   B

P + TRIPP
Philip Tripp (b. May 17, 1784 in Westport, MA, d. Feb. 29, 1868 in Freetown, Bristol Co., MA) was a Quaker, a Fall River mill carpenter and contractor. After 1835, he moved to Freetown, and engaged in farming. Examples: on 10 planes; two boxed beads; a double-boxed complex molder; and a moving filletster, all 9 1/2" beech with relieved wedges and flat chamfers, found in Beverly, MA. ****

PRESTON TROW

Preston Trow (b. 1810 in Hillsborough, d. Oct. 1, 1879 in Montpelier, Washington Co., VT) came to Montpelier, VT, in 1830. He was listed as a planemaker, in 1842-43, a joiner in 1850, and later as a carpenter and house builder. His name has been reported on a jointer. **No imprint is available.**

TROY TOOL CO.

The Troy Tool Co. was a hardware tool store, located in Troy, NY; and was supplied with planes by **Sam Dalpe**, who was working in Troy, in 1851; and then continued making planes, in Roxton Pond, Quebec. Examples: on a jack plane with an **Auburn Tool Co./ Thistle Brand** iron, and a 9 1/2" match grooving plane with a wedge of a Canadian style, ca. 1850. **UR**

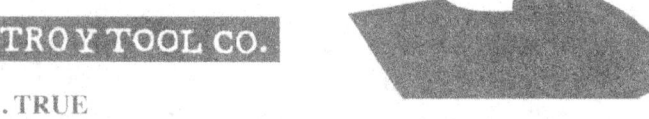

S. TRUE

Examples: on a plow with wood thumbscrews, wood depth stop, and a **James Cam** iron; a cove; a bead; and three molders, one single-boxed with rosewood, all with flat to round chamfers, ca. 1810-30. ****

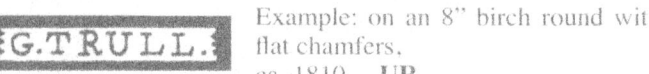

G. TRULL.

Example: on an 8" birch round with flat chamfers, ca. 1810. **UR**

I. TRUSSEL

Possibly **John Trussell** (b. Mar. 11, 1770 in NH, d. Sep. 13, 1851 in Hopkinton, Merrimack Co., NH) who was listed in 1810, in Hopkinton, NH. **Isaac Long** has very similar appearing planes, and was also in Hopkinton, NH, in 1810. Examples: all 9 1/2" beech with flat chamfers, ca. 1800. ****

WILLIAM TRYON

William Tryon (b. 1824 in Middlesex Co., CT, m. in Aug 12, 1841 in Westbrook, CT, d. after 1884 in Westbrook) was a journeyman planemaker of fancy screw-arm plow planes, in Saybrook, CT, ca. 1845-84. He first appeared in the **G. W. Denison & Co.** account book shortly after its beginning in 1870, probably having learned planemaking from and worked as a journeyman for **John Denison**. In 1884, at age 60, he was "filing bits". **No imprint has been reported.**

R: TUBBS

Example: on a 9 3/4" birch fixed sash with a relieved wedge slot and flat chamfers. **UR**

TUCKER & CO.

Tucker & Co. probably was a hardware dealer consisting of **Charles E. Tucker**, a partner in **Tucker & Appleton**, from 1868-71, or **Isaac F. Tucker**, who was listed under hardware, in the 1870 Boston directory, or perhaps both. Example: on a moving filletster, and a hollow & round pair. **A & A1 ****

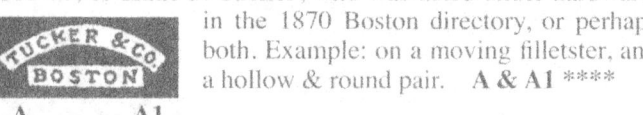

E. TUCKER

Possibly **Elisha Tucker** (b. 1784, d. 1827) was a "cabinetmaker, chair manuf., looking glass and framemaker", in Boston, MA, active from 1809-27. From 1809-23, at 40 & 17 Middle St.; and from 1825-27, at Williams Court. Example: on a 9 3/8"x 1" beech bead with shallow round chamfers, ca. 1820-30. **UR**

H. TUCKER

Example: on a 9 1/2" small astragal bead with a heavy round chamfers; a hollow; a round; and a moving filletster, ca. 1820. ****

S. W. & H. TUCKER

S. W. & H. Tucker was a hardware firm, in Keokuk, IA. Before coming to Keokuk, in 1852, **Samuel** was employed by **Simmons Hardware Co.** of St. Louis as a traveling salesman. The 1860 census for Keokuk, listed **Samuel Wood Tucker** (b. Sep. 21, 1820 in Cincinnati, Hamilton Co., OH, m. May 3, 1849 in St. Louis, MO, d. probate Feb. 17, 1905 in Keokuk, Lee Co., IA) and **Howard Tucker** (b. 1819, d. Mar. 24, 1893 in Keokuk) as hardware merchants, at 2nd. & Main. By 1870, both brothers had entered the insurance business. Example: on a 9 1/2" table plane pair with a **137** style number made by the **Ohio Tool Co.**. ****

TUCKER & APPLETON.

Tucker & Appleton was a hardware dealer, in Boston, MA, from 1868-71, consisting of **Thomas L. Appleton** and **Charles E. Tucker** (b. 1834 in MA). In 1860, **Charles** was listed as a turner, in Boston. **Charles E. Tucker** was issued a, July 26, 1870, patent and assigned half of its rights to a **T. A. Appleton**. Example: the A imprint is on a steel-sole compass plane, and a coffin miter. **A1 ****; A & A2 *****

A. TULLOCH

Alexander Tullock (b. in Scotland, d. probate Jan. 21, 1897 in Duanesburg, Schenectady, NY) was a planemaker, at 194 Grand St. New York City, NY, from 1821-30. Possibly **Tulloch** apprenticed and began making planes, in Scotland, before emigrating to New York. He was Naturalized, on Jul. 21, 1830, in NY; By 1840, he was listed in the Duanesburgh district of Schenectady, NY. From 1871-74, he was listed as "saw mills" in Duanesburgh. Examples: the A imprint is on 9 7/16" size **4** and **6** hollows;

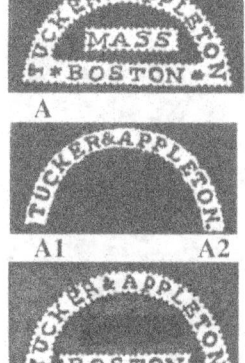

1/2" & 1" skew rabbets; a pair of snipe's bill planes; and a 2 1/4" Grecian ovolo complex molder. The A1 imprint is on a jointer, ca. 1830. **A & B ***; A1 ******

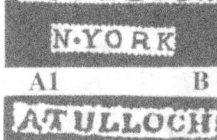

TULLOCH & BREWER
Example: on a full-boxed 3/16" astragal, found with other planes by NJ and New York City makers. The imprint is similar to that of **A. Tulloch**, as is the wedge. The chamfers are heavy round, ca. 1830. ********

F. TURNER

Example: on an 8 1/2" beech wedge-locked sash filletster. **UR**

ROBERT TURNER
Robert Turner was listed as a plane maker, in Cincinnati, OH. In 1839-40, **Robert** worked for **Lyon & Hall**.
No imprint has been reported.

W. TURNER
Examples: on a 9 7/16" beech moving filletster with round chamfers; and on a 7" beech toothing plane, ca. 1820. ********

WM. TURNER

Example: on a 9 3/4" beech quarter round with heavy flat chamfers, ca. 1790. **UR**

A. T./ A. D. TUTTLE
Alexander (Alexis) D. Tuttle (b. Sep. 28, 1839 in Rockingham, NH, d. Dec. 1, 1916 in Nottingham, Rockingham Co., NH) was listed in 1910, as a shoemaker, in Nottingham, NH. Imprinted on leather making tools was:
MANUFACTURED BY
A. D. TUTTLE
NOTTINGHAM
N.H.   (B)

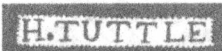

Example: on an 8 1/2" beech smoothing plane with a **Moulson Brothers** iron, ca. 19c. **A & B ******

H. TUTTLE
Examples: on a double-coping plane; and a tongue plane with round chamfers, both 9 1/2" beech; a 14" water pump plane with an offset tote; and two 9 3/8" beech complex molding planes found with a group of planes marked with an owner imprint from Cairo, Green Co. south of Albany, NY, ca. 1850. ********

MERRITT TUTTLE
Merritt Tuttle (b. Jan. 1832 in New Haven, CT, M. Dec. 3, 1851 in NY, d. 1891 in Englewood, Bergen Co., NJ) was listed in 1850, as a plane maker, in Wallingford, CT, living with **Joel Fenn**. In 1870, he was listed as a joiner, in Wallingford. In 1880, **Merritt Tuttle** was listed, as insurance.
No imprint has been reported.

TUTTLE, HIBBARD & CO.
Tuttle, Hibbard & Co. was a Chicago, IL, hardware and tin plate dealer, at 62 Lake, from 1856-65, with **Frederick Tuttle** (b. Oct. 26, 1808 in Oneida Co., NY, d. Nov. 10, 1890 in Chicago, IL) and **William G. Hibbard**. **Hibbard** was later part of **Hibbard, Spencer & Bartlett Co.** with **Franklin F. Spencer**. **Nelson Tuttle** (b. ca. 1816 in NY, d. Apr. 23, 1877 in Chicago, IL) and **George M. Gray** (b. 1818 in Sherburn, NY, d. Jun. 1, 1895 in Chicago, IL). In 1844, **Nelson** and **Frederick** were in a hardware firm of **N. & F. Tuttle** in Chicago, IL. ******

D. TYLER
Examples: on a 23" beech jointer with heavy round chamfers; a 9 1/8x 1/4" beech single-boxed side bead with heavy flat chamfers; a 10 1/2" birch having plane with a beech wedge and flat chamfers; and a 11" birch fork staff/ full round with a pegged centered tote, a micky mouse ear finial, and a double-round top, hand forged iron and flat chamfers, ca. 1800-20. ********

L. TYLER
Examples: on an 8 1/2"x 3/4" beech dado with heavy round chamfers; and a 13 1/4" beech wedge-lock narrow match tongue plane with heavy flat chamfers, both found in southern NH, ca. 1800-20. **UR**

P. TYLER
Putnam Tyler (b. Sept. 20, 1793 in Sterling, Worcester Co., MA, d. Aug. 7, 1888 in Marlow, Cheshire Co., NH) was listed in 1850, as a carpenter, in Milford, Hillsborough Co., NH. By 1870, **Putnam** was listed as a farmer, in Marlow. Examples: on a group of about twenty 9" beech molders; an 8 3/8" birch molder, a 15 7/8"x 5" wide cornice plane with a centered tote, and a Yankee style plow also imprinted **F. TYLER** on the heel, all with shallow round chamfers, found in Marlow, NH, ca. 1830. ********

J. W. TYZACK
Joseph William Tyzack (b. in England, d. Jan 18, 1858 in St. Louis, MO) was a hardware dealer. Example: on a size **6** round with **EXTRA. QUALITY** and **72** on the toe an **Ohio Tool Co.** inventory number. ca. 19c. ********

UNDERHILL, CLINCH & CO.
Underhill, Clinch & Co. was probably a hardware dealer. Examples: on a molding plane, and a smoother seen in the tool collection of the Huntington Historical Society, Huntington, Long Island, NY. ca. 1850. ***

F. UNDERWOOD
Frank Underwood (d. May 12, 1919 in Cincinnati, Hamilton Co., OH) was a planemaker, under his own name in Cincinnati, OH; he was a partner in F. Underwood/ C. B. Schaefer, from 1854-57. In 1866, Frank was listed in Cincinnati, as a carpenter, at 239 w. 3rd. Example: on a 9 1/2"x 1/4" beech single boxed center bead. ****

F. UNDERWOOD/ C. B. SCHAEFER
Frank Underwood and Charles B. Schaefer made planes together in Cincinnati, OH, from 1854-57.
A & B **

P. UNDERWOOD
Example: on a 9 1/8" beech complex molding with small round chamfers, ca. 1820. UR

UNION FACTORY
On Oct. 21, 1828, Hermon Chapin purchased Daniel Copeland's interest in Copeland & Chapin and became the sole owner of the business called Union Factory. The Union Factory was one of the major manufacturers of planes in New England. H. Chapin & Sons was the successor to H. Chapin/ Union Factory, in 1860. (see Wooden Planes in 19c America, Vol. II, by Kenneth D. Roberts) The A imprint is the typical imprint used for 32 years. The A1 imprint is on bench planes with a steel reinforcement rod down through the handle and a steel strike on the top of the toe, thus the EXTRA. The C imprint is the Chapin boxwood and ivory rule imprint applied to a plane. The D imprint is an overprint of UNION FACTORY/ WARRANTED over M & A COPELAND on a hollow plane.
A, A4, B: FF; A1, A2 ***;
A3, C & D *****

UNION MADE
This impressed imprint is a stylized version of the Carpenter's Union Logo. Hoquiam is located on the Olympic peninsula, where there was a large unionized shipbuilding and plywood industry. Example: on a 9 3/16" narrow rosewood ship round with a Sandusky iron, found in WA, ca. 1900.
No imprint is available.

UNION MANUFACTURING CO.
Union Manufacturing Co. of New Britain, CT, was active from 1900-20. John W. Carleton & George E. Trask of New Britain, CT, were issued Patent No. 746,285, on Dec. 8, 1903, for a lever-operated cutter adjustment. Carleton was issued Patent No. 746,286, on Dec. 8, 1903, for a plane iron fastening device. Examples: on a 7 7/8" wood bottom smoother plane with a double-iron, and a style No. 502; and a 20" wood bottom fore plane with a double-iron, and a style No. 539. Carleton & Trask were also issued a Patent No. 763,721, on June 28, 1904. Example: on a 9" Union wood-bottom smoothing plane with a handle overhang, a double-iron, and with the D imprint. (see Patented Transitional & Metallic Planes in America, 1827-1927, p. 256-260, by Roger F. Smith)
A, B, C & D **

UNION TOOL CO.
The Union Tool Co. made planes in Goshen, MA, from 1852-54, using a mill site and machinery bought from Abner C. More. Among those involved were Hiram Barrus, Caleb C. Dresser, and probably Oscar Washburn. It is believed that Jacob Lovell also worked for this company. Hiram Barrus was also part of H. Barrus & Co., from 1854-59. Caleb C. Dresser worked under his own name as C. C. Dresser, from 1854-56. The Union Tool Co. was one of the early users of both water and steam power in the manufacturing process. The company employed 20 hands and went bankrupt after two years. **

J. A. UPHAM
Probably **Jonathan Upham** (b. 1724 in Malden, Middlesex Co., MA, d. Mar. 30, 1802 in Sturbridge, Hampden Co., MA), who was a housewright, who built townhouses in Charlton and Brimfield, MA. In July 1759, he was paid for setting up the frame for the Charlton Meeting House. The district voted "to give **Jonathan Upham** 26l, 13s and 4p for setting up the frame of this building and to provide victuals and drink for the raising of the same". Examples: on a 13" birch "stubby" crown molder with an offset tote, a round-top wedge and wide flat chamfers, a 9 7/16" beech complex molder, and a 9 1/4" beech skew rabbet, both molders with flat chamfers, ca. 1760-70. **UR**

B. UPSON
Example: on a 9 1/2" hollow with flat chamfers; ca. 1800. **UR**

THE UPSON NUT CO.
In 1888, the **Union Nut Co.** and the **Standard Rule Co.** merged to form the **Upson Nut Co.**, with **Andrew S. Upson** as President. In **George Karrmann** (b. 1839 in CT, d. Jul. 7, 1928 in Coventry, Kent Co., CT) was listed from 1878-80, in Winsted, working for **Winsted Foundry & Machine Co.**, at Main op. Union. In 1880, **George** was listed in Winchester, CT, as a master Mechanic. In 1888, he was listed as a machinist, in Waterbury, Ct. In 1889, **George** was in Waterbury as removed to Unionville, CT. **George Karrmann** assigned Patent No. 410,710, issued on Sept. 10, 1889, to the **Upson Nut Co.** of Farmington, CT, with a lateral lever arrangement. In 1890, the company issued a catalog offering wood bottom planes of "**Bailey's Pattern**" in all the sizes manufactured by the **Stanley Rule & Level Company**. Example: on a 22 1/16" beech wood-bottom jointer plane with a double-iron. **UR**

W. UPTHEGROVE
W. **Upthegrove** was a hardware dealer, in MI, dates unknown. Example: on a molding plane made by **Reed' Utica**, ca. 1850. ****

AARON: UPTON
Examples: on a sash with a relieved wedge, and a "left hand skew small complex molder, both 9 1/2" beech with flat chambers, ca. 1800. **UR**

RALPH UTLEY
Ralph Utley (b. 1796 in Dalton, Berkshire Co., MA, d. Nov. 7, 1862 in Goshen, Hampshire Co., MA) was listed as a planemaker, in Goshen, MA, in 1845.
No imprint has been reported.

M. C. VAILE
Example: on a 9 7/8" beech dado, ca. 1880. **UR**

VAJEN NEW & CO.
Vajen & New was listed in 1880 with **Willis C. Vajen** and **George W. New** at 64 E. Washington, Indianapolis, IN. Example: on a dado plane made by the **Ohio Tool Co.**, ca. 1850. **UR**

J. H. VAJEN

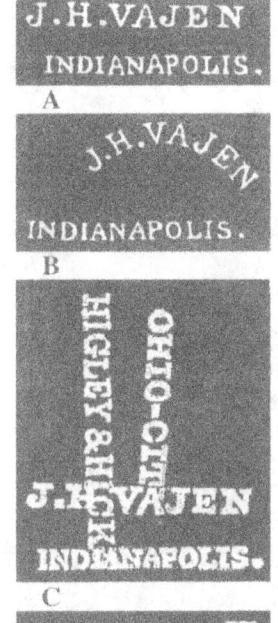

John Henry Vajen (**Johann Heinrich**) (b. 1828 in Hanover, Germany, d. May 28, 1917 in Indianapolis, Marion Co., IN) came to America, in 1836, and settled in Seymour, IN. In 1845, **John** went to Cincinnati; and was a Clerk in a Hardware store. In 1851, **Vajen** married **Alice Fugate**, in Cincinnati, probably related to **Thomas Fugate** of the same city. In 1851, he opened a hardware store in Indianapolis; and made planes, until about 1854. In 1861, **J. C. Fugate** became a partner in the hardware business. **Vajen** was also active in real estate, until 1876. In 1877, **J. H. Vajen & Co.** was listed, as wholesale & retail hardware & cutlery, at 64 E. Washington, Indianapolis. Example: on a plane made by **C. J. Smith & Co.** has been overprinted with this imprint. Example: The C and D imprint are on a 9 3/16" beech fenced tongue and grooving set also imprinted with **OHIO-CITY** and **HIGLEY & HICKS** with size 7/8 on the heels.
A, B, C & D: ****

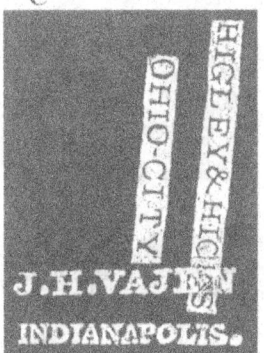

F. W. V. A.
Believed to be **F. W. van Allen**, a planemaker, in Delhi, NY. Example: on a 11 3/8" rabbet branded on the side with the date **1861** carved. His father, **Orran van Allen**, is also believed to have been a planemaker. **No imprint is available**.

VAN BAUN
Believed to be **William D. Van Baun** (buried Nov. 24, 1857 in Philadelphia, PA) who was listed as a planemaker, in the 1818 Philadelphia, PA, directory. He first appears listed as an "acknowledged Workman" in an Owings & Roy ad

placed in the *American and Commercial Daily Advertiser* of Baltimore, MD, on March 18, 1814. ****

W V/ VANCE/ W. VANCE

William Vance (b. May 1771 in England, m. Oct. 18, 1804 in Baltimore,MD) was one of the early planemakers of Baltimore, active from 1798-1833. In an 1816 ad he indicated "18 years experience", which would indicate a starting date of 1798. He was listed in 1799, as "plain maker", at 7 N. Charles St op. Union Bank, Baltimore. In 1806, he advertised the receipt of a complete assortment of edged tools, and that he: "manufactures all kinds of planes in the neatest manner and of the beast seasoned timber, which enables him to supply mechanics in the wood way in a superior manner. Moulding plane irons warranted". **Vance** was also reported as being in a partnership with **Robert Elliott**, in 1807. **Vance** has been recorded as taking on 12 apprentice planemakers including:
1. **John Lee**, age 15, in 1799, ran away in 1803.
2. **James McKinnell**, age 10, in 1800.
3. **Adam Deter**, age 11, in 1803.
4. **John M. Barkley**, age 13, in 1805.
5. **Edward Puteney Kelly**, age 9, in 1807.
6. **William P. Hughes**, age 15, in 1809.
7. **Joseph Burneston**, age 16, in 1811.
8. **William Dauk Allen**, age 12, in 1813.
9. **John Cecil**, age 14, in 1816.
10. **John Crugh**, age 16, in 1816.
11. **John Fishawk**, age 16, in 1818.
12. **John Karmikle**, age 12, in 1820.

John Barkley and **William Hughes** became planemakers as **Barkley & Hughes**. The WV initial group was found on 10 planes, 2 yellow birch and 8 beech with heavy flat chamfers, found with other **W. Vance** planes. This was possibly an early **W. Vance** imprint. The IK initial group was found on **W. Vance** planes, possibly **John Karmikle**. One example with **JOHN M. BARKLEY** overstamped a **W. VANCE** E imprint with the **BALTIMORE** as in the **W. Vance**, A1 imprint.
E *; C & D ***; A, A1, B & E1 ****

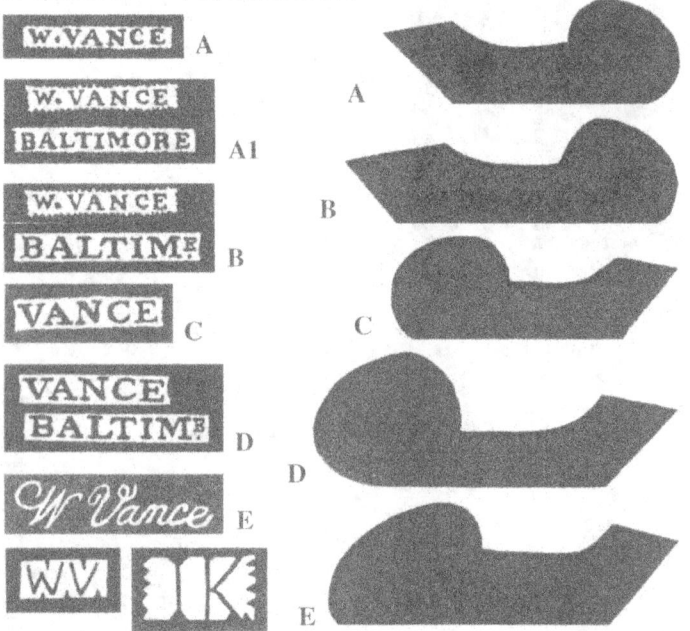

VANCE & MOORE
Example: on a 9 1/4" beech round (see **W. Vance**, **Theophilus Moore**, **Thomas Moore**, and **William H. Moore**) UR

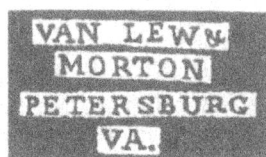

L. VAN FOSSEN
Two possibilities: **Levi Van Fossen** (b. Jan. 29, 1762 in Cumberland Co., PA, m. Dec. 27, 1787 in Milton, Northumberland Co., PA, d. Jun. 11, 1841 in Livonia, Livingston Co.,NY), a cabinetmaker, living in Dry Valley, Northumberland Co., PA., or **Leonard Van Fossen** (b. Jun. 21, 1748, d. Dec. 7, 1836 in Skippack, Montgomery Co., PA) a blacksmith, wheelwright and carpenter, who fought in the Revolutionary War as a Private and Sergeant; and lived in Evansburgh, Worcester Twp., PA. Examples: on a 12 7/8"x 2" complex molder with offset tote, a panel raiser with a diamond strike, and a 10 1/8"x 1 1/4" skew rabbet, all beech with heavy flat chamfers, probably from PA. ca. 1790. ****

VAN LEW & MORTON

Van Lew & Morton probably were hardware merchants in Petersburg, VA, ca. 1850. ****

VAN LEW & SMITH./ VAN LEW SMITH & CO.

Van Lew, Smith & Co. was a hardware firm in Richmond, VA, from 1845-46. Example: the B imprint is on a plane made by **Z. J. M'Master & Co./ Auburn**.
A, B, B1 & C ****

VAN VALKENBURGH & CO.
Van Valkenburgh & Co. probably was a hardware dealer located in New York. Example: on a 15 7/8" beech center-toted jack with a double-iron and 19c chamfers. ****

S. D. VANSANDS
S. D. Vansands was a planemaker, in Middletown, CT, in 1849. **No imprint has been reported.**

I. VANZANDT
Believed to be **Isaiah Vanzant** (d. 1850 in Sacramento, CA) of Georgetown, CT, Scott Co., KY. The 1820 census listed **Isaiah** engaged in agriculture and the agricultural implement business, possibly a dealer. **Isaiah Vanzant** was listed as a Private in Boswell's 10 Reg't., KY militia. Examples: on a 9 5/16" complex molder, a thumbscrew-lock plow; a wedge-lock plow; and a 22 1/4" beech jack plane with a **Butcher** iron, all with flat chamfers, ca. 1810. ****

C. L. VARNEY
C. L. Varney has been reported with the added location **HANOVER/ MASS**. **No imprint is available.**

T. VAUGHAN
Thomas Vaughan was a Chelsea (Boston), MA, plane manufacturer, who was listed in the 1874 directory. He received Patent No. 129,695, on July 23, 1872, for a beech smoothing plane with a cast steel sole and double-iron. He was listed as working at 171 Marginal, the same address as **Thomas Appleton** and **Porter A. Gladwin**. (see *Patented Transitional & Metallic Planes in America, 1827-1927*, p. 130, by Roger K. Smith) ****

JOHN VEIT
John Veit (b. ca. 1831 in Wurttemberg, Germany, d. Sep. 21, 1897 in Philadelphia, PA) arrived in America by 1856. **John** was a prolific planemaker, listed at 135 Green or NE Green & New Market or 601 New Market and Green c. New Market, Philadelphia, from 1857-93. **John Veit** was reported as succeeding **William Goldsmith**, about 1868. J. B. Shannon's 1873 catalog, lists "**Veit's** hand-made planes" and "**Veit's City** made warranted bench planes". In 1880 only, "**Veit John** (Belum & Veit) & planemaking B & V Basketmakers 601 New Market". **John Veit's** imprints have also appeared on a workbench, a wooden compass, a wooden shootboard plane, and various cooper's tools. **Charles Veit** (b. 1858 in Philadelphia, PA, d. Jan. 26, 26, 1908 in Philadelphia) was **John Veit's** middle son and appears as a planemaker, in 1880-1908 at 135 Green, the same address as his father, **John Veit**. **William Veit** (b. Jun. 1856 Philadelphia, PA, d. Aug. 21, 1923 in Philadelphia) was **John Veit's** oldest son and appears as a planemaker, in 1880-95, also at 135 Green, the same address. In 1900, **William** is listed as a house carpenter; from 1915-17, as a "peelmkr". (long handled wooden tools used by bakers to load and unload bread from ovens); and in 1920, as a machinist, in Philadelphia. **Henry Veit** (b. 1866 in Philadelphia, PA, d. Nov. 28, 1890 in Philadelphia) was **John Veit's** youngest son, and appears as a planemaker, in the 1885-90, also at 135 Green. There are no imprints know for **Charles, William and Henry** as they used their father's imprints. The B imprint is very large and found on workbenches and jointers. One has **COR NEW MARKET** precede by **NE**.
A: FF; B ***

J. H. VERBRYCK
John H. Verbryck (b. 1818 in OH, d. after 1902 in Delavan, Tazewell Co., IL) was listed as a planemaker, in Mason, OH, in 1853. In 1860, as a planemaker, in Deerfield, Warren CO., OH. **John H. Verbryck** served in the Civil War, enlisting Apr. 19, 1861, as a Private, in Co. F, OH 12th. Infantry Reg. and was mustered out on Aug. 18, 1861. In 1870, **John** was listed as a carpenter, in Boynton, Tazewell Co., IL; in 1880, as a stock horse keeper, in Delavan. **No imprint has been reported.**

VERMONT S. P./ VERMONT/ STATE/ PRISON
Imprints used on planes made in the **Vermont State Prison**. Examples: the A imprint is on a 12 5/8" skew rabbet with an open tote. The B imprint is on a beech jointer. ****

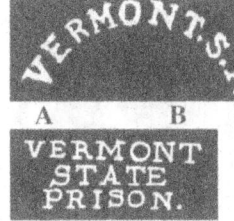

JAMES W. VINAL & CO.
Bogman & Vinal was succeeded by **James W. Vinal & Co.**, in 1882; and was a general hardware, builders materials, carpenters tools at wholesale & retail, at nos. 6, 7 & 8 Dock Sq., Boston, MA. **No imprint is available.**

O V/ O. VINAL
Example: on a 9 3/8" beech complex molder with flat chamfers, ca. 1800-10. **UR**

J. VINALL/ J. J. VINALL

John J. Vinall (b. May 6, 1818 in Manchester, England, d. Jan. 5, 1874 in Plymouth, Marshall Co., IN) arrived in America on Apr. 9, 1832, in New York. John was listed as a planemaker, in Cleveland, OH, from 1842-53. An ad of Aug. 18, 1842 states: "Dissolution, the copartnership heretofore existing under the firm of **MARBLE & VINALL** has been this day mutually dissolved. The business of the above firm will be settled by **JOHN J. VINALL**. The business of plane making will be carried out at the old stand, on Seneca Street, opposite the Commercial House, by **CUTLER & VINALL**". **John Vinall** advertised that he made cooper's tools, "did job work such as sawing, turning or anything that steam can be applied to," and sold wholesale and retail. A & B **

C. P. V./ C. P. VIRGIN

Charles P. Virgin (b. Jul. 4, 1824 in Concord, Merrimack Co., NH, d. May 6, 1910 in Everett, MA) was the son of **Simeon Virgin**. Charles worked as a carriage maker, at **J. Stephen Abbot & Abbot, Downing Co.**, Concord, NH, ca. 1853-1900. In 1900, **Charles** was listed under his own name as coach maker, Concord, Merrimack, Co., NH. Examples: the initial group is on a coach rabbet. The name imprint is on a 9 1/2" beech side bead with **177** on the heel, an inventory number from the **Greenfield Tool Co.**. UR

SIMEON VIRGIN

Simeon Virgin (b. Nov. 11, 1781 in Concord, Merrimack Co., NH, d. May 4, 1838 in Concord) was the father of **Charles P. Virgin**. **Simeon**'s grandfather **Ebenexer Virgin** (d. 1766) was one of the first settlers in Concord, NH, and was a cabinetmaker. **Simeon** was a joiner, carpenter and furniture maker, in Concord, from 1803-37. In 1825, **Simeon Virgin** was a partner in a saw mill erected on the Merrimack River and destroyed by fire, in 1837. **Simeon**'s account book is at the New Hampshire Historical Society. **Simeon** made handles, churns, cheese presses, wash boards, washing machines, and textile tools. He also is known to have made planes. Examples: on a smoothing plane; a plow; and a double-iron jointer.
No imprint has been reported.

C. L. VOLCKHAUSEN & CO.

Charles L. Volckhausen (b. 1837, d. Aug. 27, 1903 in Manhattan, NY). **C. L. Volckhausen & Co.** was a hardware firm listed, from 1878-1882, at 118 Wooster, New York. From 1886-88, at 38 W. 3rd. with **Charles L. Volckhausen** and **Henry Volckhausen**. In 1911, **C. L. Volckhausen & Co.** was listed as hardware, at 36 W. 3rd. with **Geo, V. Volckhausen**. In 1916, **C. L. Volckhausen & Co.** was listed as hardware, at 108 E. 12th. with **Wm. G. Killian** Pres. Examples: on a toothing plane; and a moving filletster made by **G. W. Denison & Co.** who made planes from 1868-84. ****

IRA: W

Example: on a 9 11/16" beech skew rabbet with round chamfers, ca. 1820. UR

E. F. WABAS

E. F. Wabas was a Belvidere, NJ, hardware dealer. Example: on a medium hollow made by **Ohio Tool Co.**, with style number **72** on the heel, and this ink imprint on the side: ****

E. F. WABAS
DEALER IN
CUTLERY TOOLS
BUILDERS HARDWARE
AGRICULTURAL INSTRUMENTS
FRONT SCREENS
BELVIDERE N.J.

J. WADDELL

Example: on a 10" slide-arm plow with wood thumbscrews, ca. 1850. UR

B. WADE

Example: on a 9 1/4" beech single-boxed astragal bead with flat chamfers, ca. 1810-20. UR

I. WADE

Examples: molders are 9 3/4"-10" with **I. Sleeper** style wedges and shallow flat chamfers. One example is on a plane made by **I. Sleeper**, as an owner imprint, probably from Newburyport, MA area. ca. 1800. ****

J. WAGENER

Example: on a 10" beech complex molder with heavy flat chamfers, ca. 1790. UR

J. WAGENHORST

Example: on a 13" beech wedge-arm tongue & groove match pair with open totes and a screw on skated, found in the Philadelphia, PA area, probably from PA, ca. 1830-40. UR

W. W/ W. WAIDE

Example: on a 10" fruitwood ogee molder, single boxed with heavy flat chamfers and a **NEWBOLD** iron. ca. 1800. UR

I. WAIN
Possibly **Jacob Wain** (b. 1766, d. 1814, buried May 12, 1814 in Harrisburg, PA) was a joiner working, in Lancaster, PA, until around 1792, then in Harrisburg, until 1814. Examples: molding planes are 9 3/4"-10" beech with flat chamfers, some with **Newbould** irons. The B1 imprint is on a 9 11/16" beech single boxed bead with small round chamfers and with the **I** removed from the die. ca. 1800-20. **A, B & B1** ****

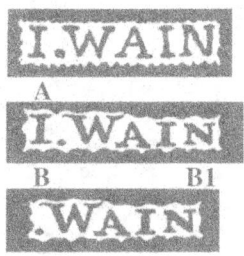

JOSEPH WAINWRIGHT
Joseph Wainwright was listed as a planemaker in New York City in 1827. **No imprint has been reported**.

WAIT/ J. WAIT. / J. WAIT. J
J. Wait Jr. was probably a descendant of **J. Wait** (b. 1651, d. 1700) of Charlestown, MA. Examples: The A imprints is on 9 1/2" beech molders with flat chamfers; there is an 8 3/4" beech plow with both the A & B imprints with wood thumbscrews and depth stop, screw applied skate, and heavy round chamfers. The C imprint is on a 10 1/4" beech rabbet with flat chamfers, ca. 1800-20. ****

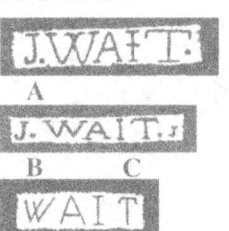
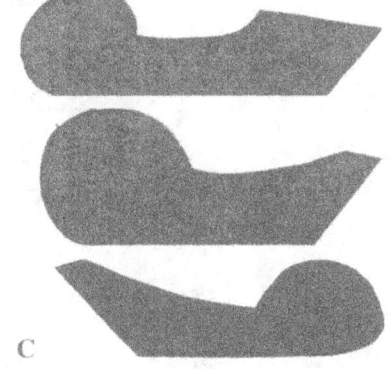

Z. WAITE
 Example: on a 10 1/4" birch Yankee plow with wood lock screws and flat chamfers, ca. 1800. **UR**

C. H. W.
Christopher Henry Wakefield (b. Sep. 3, 1838 in Montpelier, Washington Co., VT, m. May 28, 1864 in East Montpelier, d. Dec. 8, 1909 in Montpelier) was a carpenter, cabinetmaker, planemaker, and musical instrument maker. **Christopher** served in the Civil War in the fife and drum corps. He enlisted from East Montpelier, on Aug 29, 1862, as a musician, in Co. C, VT 13th. Infantry. His occupation was listed as carpenter. He was mustered out, on Jul. 21, 1863, at Brattleboro, VT. In 1880, **Christopher** was listed, as a carpenter, in Swanton, Franklin Co., VT; and in 1900, as a carpenter, in Montpelier. Example on three planes, one a 9 5/8"x 15/16" beech skew (left hand) rabbet, ca. 1860. **No imprint is available**.

E. WAL
Example: on a 9 7/8" birch molder with a beech wedge and flat chamfers, found in southwest OH, ca. 1800-10. **UR**

B. WALBMIEIER
 **B. Walbmieier** was probably a hardware dealer in Newark, NJ, with no known dates. Example: on a handled plane made by **Arrowmammett**. ****

S. WALDRON
Example: on a 9 1/2" beech astragal bead with flat chamfers, ca. 1810. **UR**

S. WALES
Examples: on a 10" molder with flat chamfers; a hollow & round; and a square rabbet, all 9 1/2" beech with shallow round chamfers, possibly from two generations, ca. 1790-1830. ****

D. WALKER/ D. WALKER/ J. H. HALL
 **David Walker** was a Cincinnati, OH, planemaker, in 1829, at 6th. between Main & Walnut; and in 1834, at 8th. between Vine & Race. He may have worked for **Esther Walker**, **Jesse Walker**'s widow, from 1829-31, at 204 Main Street. **David Walker** and **John H. Hall** were part of **Walker & Hall**, at Main between 6th. & 7th.; that succeeded **Esther Walker**, in 1831. The A2 imprint is on a boxwood screw-arm plow, with the date **1833**, and an owners imprint **C. C. WALKER**. **A & B** **; **A1** *****

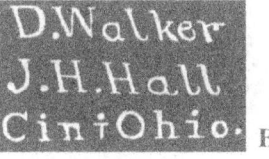

E. WALKER
Possibly **Ester Walker**, the Widow of **Jessey Walker** who was listed from 1829-31, at 204 Main Street, in Cincinnati, OH. In 1831, **Ester Walker** was listed as keeping a boarding house. Example: on a 22 3/8" beech fore plane with a closed tote and in the razee style, ca. mid 19c. *****

GUS WALKER
Gustavus Walker (b. May 7, 1830 in Manchester, Hillsborough Co., NH, d. May 5, 1902 in Providence, RI, buried in Concord, NH) was a hardware dealer, in Concord, NH, from 1855-83. He was succeeded by **Thomson & Hoague**. Example: on a 9" shipbuilder's type smoother, ca. 1870. ****

J. WALKER

Jesse Walker (will probated on Nov. 19, 1828 in Cincinnati, OH) was a Cincinnati, OH, planemaker, from 1800-29. Before 1806, he was part of **Daggett & Walker**, with **Samuel Daggett**. An ad, by **Daggett & Walker**, on Apr. 1, 1820, listed "Cincinnati Plane Factory". In 1825, he was also a part of **B. King/J. Walker** with **Benjamin King**. He was listed in the Cincinnati directory, as a planemaker, at 204 Main. In 1829, his widow, **Ester (Esther) Walker** was listed, as a plane manufacturer, and in 1831, as keeping a boarding house. It is possible that **David Walker** worked for her, from 1829-31, and then **Walker & Hall** succeeded her, in 1831. Examples: on a panel raiser, and a sash plane with the iron imprinted **J. WALKER**, see D imprint. The A imprint appears with and without an eagle. The C imprint is on four pairs of 9 7/16" beech hollows & rounds with flat chamfers and a size number on the heel. **A, A1, B, C & D** ***

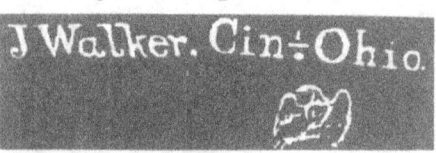
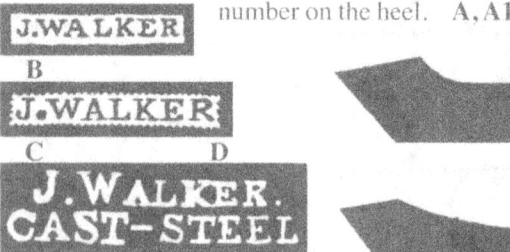

In. WALKER

Example: on a 9 3/4" beech single-boxed small bead with a birch wedge and flat chamfers, ca. 1800. **UR**

R. WALKER

Example: on a 9" beech size **18** round with round chamfers and a relieved wedge, found in ME. ca. 1820. **UR**

P. W. WALKER & CO.

There has also been a report of a **P. W. Walker** of Burton, OH, which could be a separate or the same firms. Examples: on a cooper's sun plane, tanner & currier's knives, and a cooper's jiggers were also reported. Example: on a sun plane, ca. 19c. ****

WALKER & HALL

Example: on an incuse arched imprint on a 12 3/8"x 2" beech "V" chamfer plane with a centered closed tote and flat chamfers, ca. 19c. **No imprint is available**.

A WALL

One of three 18c imprints on the toe of a 9 7/8" yellow birch skew rabbet with flat chamfers and a relieved wedge of **Jo. Fuller** style, ca. 1790. **UR**

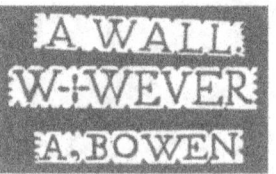

AB: WALLACE

Probably **Allen Briggs Wallace** (b. Mar. 16, 1820 in New Castle, Lawrence Co., PA, d. Mar. 24, 1912 in New Castle) who came to Pulaski, Lawrence Co., PA, north of Pittsburgh, in 1837-38; and was listed as a "flume stock maker". **Wallace** was listed as "plane-maker", in the 1850-51 Pennsylvania State Business directory. He was listed in the 1850 census, as a carpenter; and in 1860, as a master carpenter. From 1863-70, he operated a planing mill. In 1880, **Allen** was listed, as a carpenter, in New Bedford, Lawrence Co., PA. Examples: on two molders, one 2 3/16" wide with an old ink price **$1.25** on heel, the other 2 3/8" wide with **$1.35** on the heel; and a hollow & round pair, all 9 3/8" beech, ca. 1850. ****

G. E. WALLACE

Example: on a 9 3/8" beech complex molder, ca. mid 19c. **UR**

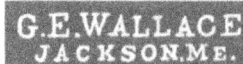

N. N. WALLACE

Example: on a 9 9/16" beech complex molder with a birch wedge and shallow round chamfers, possibly from northern NY, ca. 1850. **UR**

J. WALLER

Example: on a 9 7/8" beech ogee molding plane with flat chamfers, ca. early 19c. **UR**

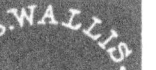

H. B. WALLIS

H. B. Wallis was probably a hardware dealer. Example: on a 3/8" dado made by **Gladwin & Appleton**. **UR**

P. WALP

Examples: on a beech panel raiser; and on a 10 1/16" beech round with flat chamfers, probably from rural PA, ca. early 19c. **UR**

H. WALT

Example: on a 9 3/8" beech moving filletster, ca. mid 19c. **UR**

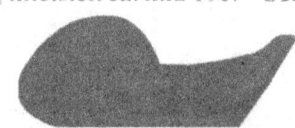

S. WALT
Example: on a 9" complex molder with flat chamfers, ca. 1810-20. **UR**

G. WALTER
Example: on a 10" beech complex molder with flat chamfers, ca. 1800. **UR**

B. WALTON
Benjamin Walton (b. before Oct. 14, 1750 in Reading, Middlesex Co., MA, d. Jun. 16, 1824 in Wakefield, Middlesex Co., MA) was a housewright, in the part of Reading, MA, which is now Wakefield. He was the son of **John Walton, Jr.** and the younger brother of **John Walton**. **Benjamin** was a Minuteman Private during the Lexington/ Concord alarm, of April 19, 1775; and served throughout the Revolutionary War. He became a Lieutenant in the War of 1812. An interesting item appears in the *Genealogical History of the Town of Reading*: "At the funeral of Timothy Bryant, "one of the bearers (**Benjamin Walton**) became intoxicated, and while carrying the body to the grave stumbled, fell, the coffin came to the ground, and burst open." **Benjamin** was in partnership with his older brother **John Walton**, as **I: B: Walton**, until 1771; the year his brother moved to Cambridge. His **B: WALTON** name die was made from the **I: B: WALTONS** die with the removal of the **I:** and the **S**. He used his father's **IN READING** location stamp. His planes are 10" or longer, of birch and apple wood, with flat chamfers. Example: on an 11 7/8" birch dado with a metal thumbscrew depth stop with a hole used for leverage. This feature was also used by **I. Walton**. ********

I: B: WALTONS
John Walton (b. Jun. 11, 1744 in Reading, MA, m. Jan. 16, 1770 in Waltham, Middlesex Co., MA, d. Nov. 23, 1823 in Cambridge, Middlesex Co., MA) and **Benjamin Walton**, his brother, were plane making partners, in Reading, MA; until **John** moved to Cambridge, MA, in 1771, to work as a housewright. Their father was **John Walton, Jr.** (1719-85). The **S** in Waltons was used to indicate a plurality. They used their father's **IN READING** location stamp. Their planes are 10" or longer of birch or apple wood with flat chamfers. The B imprint, with an incuse **IB**, on an **IxWALTON** 10" birch straight rabbet. A ****; B *****

I. W/ I x WALTON
John Walton, Jr. (b. Feb. 12, 1719 in Reading, MA, d. Apr. 14, 1785 in Reading, MA) was listed as a joiner and housewright, in Reading, MA. In 1754, he served as a lumber surveyor, a tax assessor, and on several parish committees. He fought in the French and Indian War, in 1762, with the rank of Lieutenant. On April 19, 1775, as a Captain, age 65, he led a company of Minutemen in response to the alarm of Lexington and Concord. **John Walton** died intestate, in 1785, and his son **Benjamin** was appointed administrator. His estate inventory, real and personal, came to 492 pounds sterling, of which lumber and joiner's and carpenter's tools were 34 pounds. The joiner's shop was additionally valued at 7 1/2 pounds. In **Benjamin**'s accounting of the estate, dated Nov. 6, 1786, an entry reads "to sundry tools sold out of the shop before the appraisal 3 pounds, 14 shillings, 4 pence." The sale of tools, or anything else, before an appraisal would not be permissible unless the items were normally for sale at the same price prior to the owner's decease, indicating that tools were being sold by the shop up to the time of his death. A plane has been reported, dated 1764 in ink, under an apparent owner's name. The monogrammed imprint **I.W** has been reported on several examples which are identical in style to those planes bearing the full name, and are believed to be his. **John**'s planes are 10" or longer of birch or apple wood with flat chamfers. His cornice planes have offset pegged totes, with round-top wedges and irons. The C imprint, with an incuse **IW**, is on an 11" birch wedge-arm moving fillester. An example of one of Walton's cornice planes is pictured in Kenneth Roberts' *Wooden Planes in 19th Century America*, p. 192.
A ***; B & C *****

D. O. WALTZ
Example: on a 9 3/16" beech stair-rail plane with a bench-style wedge, a single iron, shallow round chamfers, found in New Harbor, ME, ca. 1830. **UR**

J. WALTZ
Believed to be **Jacob Waltz** who was a planemaker, possibly from OH. Example: on a skew rabbet with double nickers and an open tote, ca. 1820. **UR**

A: WARBEN
Example: on a 10 3/4" beech skew rabbet with heavy flat chamfers, ca. 1800. **UR**

WARD
Example: on a 9 1/4" (possibly shot) birch complex molder, ca. 1800. **UR**

D. WARD
Examples: on an 8 7/8" beech quarter round with round chamfers; a rabbet; and a jack, ca. 1820. **UR**

F. WARD
A maker of cooper's adzes and wooden planes in Lockport, possibly NY, ca. 1840. **No imprint has been reported**.

GEORGE WARD
George Ward (b. 1840 in NJ) was listed as a planemaker, in 1856-59, in Zanesville, OH. He had the same address as **J. Harrison**, and may have worked for him. In 1860, **George** was listed in Cincinnati, Hamilton Co., OH, living with **William Fimday**, a planemaker. **No imprint has been reported.**

G. C. WARD
Believed to be **George C. Ward** who was involved in **Ward & Chapin**, in Baltimore, MD, about 1831. **Philip Chapin** of that firm was a brother of **Herman Chapin** and worked for **Herman**, in CT, prior to 1830. **G. C. Ward** agreed to work for the **Union Factory**, starting in April 1835, for six months at seven shillings per day and board. He was reported in Poughkeepsie, NY, in 1848-49. Examples: the C imprint is on a rosewood plow with boxwood arms & nuts. A ***; B ****; C *****

G. & H. J. WARD
George P. Ward (b. ca. 1844 in CT) and **Horace J. Ward** (b. Jun. 7, 1845 in Hartford Co., CT, d. May 25, 1926 in Winsted, Litchfield Co., CT) made planes, gauges, hand screws, bench screws, and levels in Riverton (New Hartford), CT, from 1870-73. In 1860, **George P. Ward** was listed in Hartland, Hartford Co.. **

J. G. WARD
Example: on a molder with the added location **NEW HARTFORD, CONN**. No imprint is available.

R. A. WARD
Robert Ward was listed, as a planemaker, in Cincinnati, OH, and Madison, IN, just down the river from Cincinnati. In 1836-37, **Robert** was listed in Cincinnati as working for **E. F. Seybold**. The A imprint also appears with the imprint **Lyon, McKinnell & Co.**, which possibly purchased remaining **Ward** stock, sometime between 1842-46. Example: the B imprint is on an ogee with bevel complex molder. A, A1 & B ***

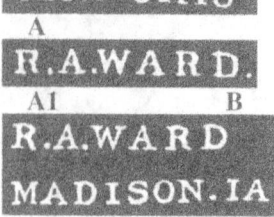
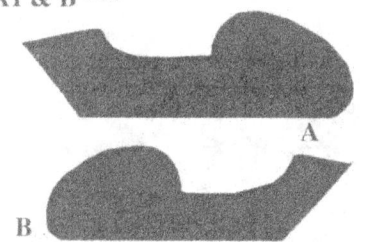

S WARD
Example: on a 7 13/16" beech wedge-lock plow with a riveted skate and flat chamfers, ca. 1800. **UR**

SL. WARD
Samuel Ward (b. Dec. 23, 1776 in Charlton, Worcester Co., MA, d. 1849 in PA) father, Jonas (b. 1743, d. 1811 at Charlton) built the Charlton Congregational Meeting House in 1798, and **Samuel** was listed in an 1801 Charlton deed as a carpenter. **Samuel Ward** married **Anna Baldwin** of Spencer in Jan. 1, 1804 and **Smith** of Sturbridge on Jan. 1, 1817 in Charlton. In 1831 Ward moved to central PA and was listed as a carpenter, cabinetmaker and conducted a little furniture store. Based on the style of Ward's 10" molders, he was much influenced by **R. BACON** of Spencer, Charlton and Sutton MA. Examples: molders are 9 1/2"-10 1/8" birch and beech with relieved wedges and flat or round chamfers, implying that they were made over a period of time. A grooving plane has a iron skate made from a hand-stamped rule, probably from southeastern New England, ca. 1790-1820. ***

S. P. WARD
Example: on a match tongue & groove pair, both with flat chamfers, ca. 1800. **UR**

W. WARD
Example: on a 9 1/2" beech nosing plane with a full round top chamfer and heavy toe & heel round chamfers, ca. 1820. **UR**

W. WARD/ WILLm WARD/ WILLIAM WARD
William Ward (b. Feb. 28, 1821 in Sheffield, England, d. May 16, 1890 in Orvil, Bergen Co., NJ) apprenticed in Sheffield and came to America on Sept. 27, 1845, settling in New York City. He was the father of **William J. C. Ward**. **William Ward** was listed in directories, as a tool maker, plane manufacturer, hardware dealer, carpenter tool maker, and bit brace manufacturer, from 1850-51; and from 1853-68, he was at 513 Eighth Ave. In 1862, he added 47 Chatham as his business location, possibly a tool store; which in 1865 was moved to 51 Chatham. In 1868-73, he was at 549 8th Ave.; and from 1873-74, at 307 W. 37th St. Between 1852-53, he was a partner in **Ward & Fletcher**. After 1873, he moved to Saddle River, NJ, where he established an edge tool factory, dam, and sawmill. In 1880, he was listed as a joiner tool

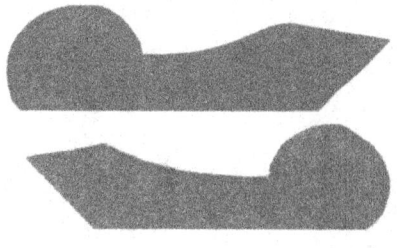

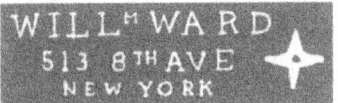

manufacturer in Washington, Bergen Co., NJ. Ward planes are not as numerous as his variety of name stamps and long working period that they would suggest. Among the examples that survive are some unusual types, including a three-arm plow quite similar to those made by **Mockridge & Francis**; and probably a precursor to the **Rust-Chapin** patent of 1868. Examples: on a screw-arm sash filletster, possibly reflecting his English background; as well as a handsome handled applewood moving filletster. The I imprint is on a 5" beech smoothing plane. The J imprint is on a 4 1/2" beech miniature smoothing plane.
A, B, B1, C, E, F, G & H **;
A1, D, I & J ***

W. J. C. WARD
William J. C. Ward (b. June 20, 1854 in NY, d. Sept. 6, 1891 in Orvil, Bergen Co. NJ) was the son of **William Ward**. **William J. C. Ward** was listed in the 1880 industrial census for Saddle River, NJ, "wks. in tool fac." living with his father, **William Ward**, an edge tool maker, with 3 hands. Also in the household was **Lawrence Cam** (b. 1850 in England). In 1885, **James W. Cam** was also listed in the Ward Household. ***

WARD & CHAPIN
George C. Ward and **Philip Chapin** made planes, at McCleman's AL., in Baltimore, MD, in 1831. **

WARD & FLETCHER
William Ward and **John R. Fletcher** (b. Jan. 1826 in England, d. Nov. 16, 1905 in NY City) who was the father of **Charles H. Fletcher** of **Charles Fletcher Hardware**. In 1850, **John R. Fletcher** was listed as a carpenter. In 1860, **John R. Fletcher** was listed as mechanic. **Ward & Fletcher** made planes and other tools, at 513 8th Ave., New York City, from 1852-70. From 1870-76, it was

listed in Saddle River, NJ. **Ward & Fletcher** was listed, as plain & carpenter tool maker, with 6 hands, producing 2000 plains, gauges, bevels, brace bits, and molder tools. Example: the D imprint is on a 9 1/2"-1 3/8" beech skew rabbet
A, A1, B & C ***; D ****

WARD - WELLER & CONE
Wade-Waller & Cone is a hardware dealer with the location imprint of Portsmouth, O (OH) on a round made by **Ohio Tool Co.** and the inventory number of **72**. ca. 19c. ****

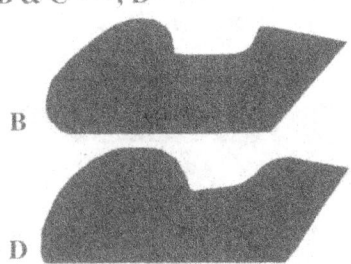

WARDE HUMPHREY & CO.
Warde, Humphrey & Co. was a hardware dealer consisting of **David Andrew Warde** (b. Feb. 1, 1828, in Henniker, Merrimack Co., NH, d. 1874), **Stillman Humphrey** (b. 1833 in Croydon, NH, d. Jan. 13, 1895 in Concord, NH), and **George P. Cleavers** (b. ca. 1840 in NH) located at 1 & 2 Exchange Block, 180 Main, Concord, NH, from 1860-69. They were succeeded by **Warde, Humphrey & Dodge** with **Howard A. Dodge**, from 1870-74. They were preceded by **Ward & Humphrey**; and **Warde & Walker**. Examples: on planes made by the **Greenfield Tool Co.**, **E. & T. Ring & Co.**, and **Lamb & Brownell**. ****

I. WARDILL
Example: on a 9 1/2" beech grooving plane with riveted skate & shallow round chamfers, ca. 1830. UR

WARDWELL & CO./ N. M. WARDWELL & CO.
N. M. Wardwell & Co. with **Newton Mann Wardwell** (b. 1821 in NY, d. 1911 in Adams, Jefferson Co., NY) was a Rome, NY, hardware store. In 1850, **Newton Wardwell** was listed as a merchant in Richland, Oswego, NY. In 1851, **N. M. Wardwell & Co.** was founded in Rome, Oneida Co., NY; and was still in business, in 1970, as **Wardwell Hardware Co.**. On Apr. 7, 1864, **Newton Wardwell** enlisted as a Captain in the Civil War; on Dec. 9, 1865, he was a Brevet Major and was mustered out on Dec. 13, 1865. Example: the A imprint is on a size **12** round made by **Bensen & Crannell**. A **WARDWELL & CO.** imprint on a bead made by **Casey, Clark**, active 1858-64, **is not available**. A ****

C. H. WARINER
Example: on a beech wedge-arm plow with added wood thumbscrews, ca. 1850. UR

Z. B. WARING

Example: on a 9 1/2" birch shiplap rabbet with round chamfers, ca. 1820. **UR**

WARING & STANTIAL
Daniel H. Waring (b. Nov. 1830 in NY, d. Jan. 5, 1916 in Manhattan, NY) and **John W. Stantial** (d. Nov. 23, 1924 in Basking Ridge, NJ) were New York City hardware dealers, at 1390 3rd. Ave., from 1875-91. From 1892-98, **John W. Stantial** was listed as "home furng.", at 1400 3rd. Ave. Example: on a 22" razee jointer. ***

J. WARNER
Example: on a 9 3/8" beech boxed moving filletster with a dovetail wood depth stop, a bottom adjustable fence, and heavy round chamfers, ca. 1820. **UR**

L. WARNER
Examples: on a skew rabbet, and a tongue & groove pair, both 9 1/2" beech with round chamfers and a relieved wedge, ca. 1820. ****

W. A. WARNER
William A. Warner (b. Nov. 1846 in NY) was a hardware dealer in New Haven, CT, ca. 1885. Example: on a **Thos. L. Appleton** rabbet plane with a green paper label reading: ****

W. A. WARNER
13 E. GRAND COR N. FRONT ST.
NEW HAVEN
HARDWARE

W. WARNER/ WM. WARNER
William Warner (b. Aug. 3, 1809 in Hartford Co., CT, d. 1898 in New Hartford, Litchfield Co., CT) made planes under this imprint, in New Hartford, from 1849-51. From 1831-35, he worked for **Hermon Chapin**, and was part of **Warner & Driggs**, from 1849-50. He was listed in the 1850 census for New Hartford, as a toolmaker, having five employees, and producing $2500 worth of planes annually. In 1880, he was listed as a farmer. **A & B** ***

WARNER & DRIGGS
William Warner and **Hiram Betal Driggs** (b. Feb. 11, 1824 in Litchfield Co., CT, d. Sep. 9, 1857 in St. Louis, MO. buried Sep. 19, 1857 in New Haven, CT) made planes in New Hartford, CT, from 1849-53. They were listed in a directory together as early as 1849, however. **Driggs** was listed in the 1850 census as working for **Hermon Chapin**. One example is overstruck on a **H. Chapen/ Union Factory Works**. **A** **; **A1** ***

A. WARREN
Example: on a 10 3/4" birch skew rabbet with heavy flat chamfers. ca. 1900. **UR**

C. WARREN
Example: on a wedge-lock birch plow with flat chamfers and a friction-fit wood depth stop, ca. 1800. **UR**

C. WARREN
Cyrus Warren (b. Jan. 29, 1804 in Hardwick, Worcester Co., MA, M. Jun. 6, 1826 in Nottingham, Rockingham Co., NH, d. Oct. 21, 1888 in Nashua, Hillsborough Co., NH) was a prolific NH planemaker who taught the art to his brother, **William Warren**, his son **George Henry Warren**, **Dana Sargent**, and **Addison Heald**. He was trained as a carpenter in Windsor, VT. He was trained in plane making in Lowell, MA, between 1829-37. In 1837, **Cyrus Warren** opened a plane making shop, in Hudson Hillsborough Co. NH, south of Nashua. His brother, **William Warren**, joined him in partnership, in 1853. The partnership was later dissolved, and **Cyrus** moved to nearby Nashua, NH, in 1857. He was the **Warren** in **Warren & Heald**, ca. 1860. **Cyrus** retired from plane making, in 1875. His planes marked NASHUA were actually made in Hudson. **B & C: FF; A** ****

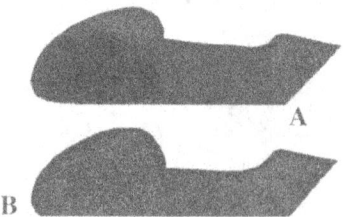

G. H. WARREN
George Henry Warren (b. 1829 in Nashua, Hillsborough Co., NH, d. May 12, 1900 in Nashua) was the son of **Cyrus Warren**; and a planemaker, in Hudson, NH, both alone and with his uncle, **William Warren**, from 1850-57, when he became a tailor. His planes marked NASHUA were actually made in nearby Hudson. **A & A1:** **

JOHN WARREN
John Warren was a Louisville, KY, planemaker, listed from 1832-48; in 1832, at 3rd. b. Main & Mkt., in 1838, at 10th b. Brook & Floyd. Example: on a 9 1/2" beech complex molder with flat chamfers on ends and round chamfers on top and also imprinted with **Schwing & McCarth**. **

W. WARREN
William Warren (b. 1818, d. May 9, 1861 in Hudson, Hillsborough Co., NH) was the brother of **Cyrus Warren**, and made planes in a partnership with his nephew, **George Henry Warren**, in Hudson, NH, from 1853-57. He was a member of the NH State Legislature, in 1852-53. He worked for, and probably was taught the art of plane making by, his brother

Cyrus Warren. In 1850, **William** was listed, as a mechanic, in Hudson; In 1860, as a plane manufacturer. Example: a **W. Warren** smoothing plane incorporating **Bailey**'s Aug. 31, 1858, patented lever plane iron cap. **William**'s planes marked **NASHUA** were actually made in Hudson. **A & B** **

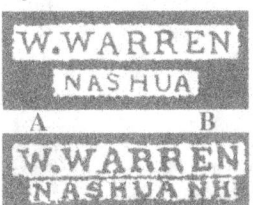

J. M. WARREN & CO.
Joseph Mabbett Warren (b. Jan. 28, 1813 in Albany, NY, m. Sep. 9, 1835 in Hartford, CT, d. Sep. 9, 1896 in Troy, NY) operated a hardware store in Troy, NY, from 1845-1962. In 1870, **Joseph** was listed under iron & hardware dealers in Troy; in 1880, as a hardware merchant, in Troy. Example: the B imprint is on a style **No. 121** plow plane made by the **Sandusky Tool Co. A & B** *

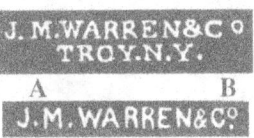

M. C. WARREN & CO.
Moses C. Warren (m. Sep. 14, 1842 in Boston, MA, d. probate May 9, 1887 in Brookline, Norfolk Co., MA). **Moses C. Warren & Co.** Hardware was listed, in the 1841 Boston, MA directory. Previously in 1838-40, **Moses Warren & Co.** was listed under Lumber. In 1842, it was listed as **Warren & Rogers** with **Daniel Rogers** (b. 1815 in NH) at 9 Dock Sq., Boston. In 1844, **M. C. Warren** was listed with **Whittemore**, under lumber. In 1846-47, **M. C. Warren** was listed with **G. E. Bogman** (see **Bogman & Vinal**). In 1877-85, **Moses C. Warren** was listed at 9 Dock Sq. In 1906, **Moses** was listed with **WH** and **CB**, as hardware, at 9 dock Sq. ****

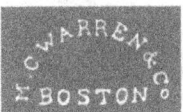

WARREN & HEALD
Warren & Heald was a plane making partnership of **Addison Heald** and possibly **Cyrus Warren**, ca. 1860.
A **; A1 **

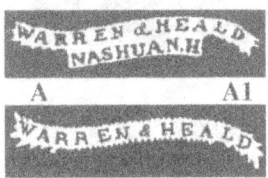

Px WASH
Example: on a 9 1/2" birch small round with a relieved wedge and flat chamfers, ca. 1800. **UR**

WASHBURN
Examples: on a 9 1/4" beech double-iron door plane with heavy flat chamfers; and a 9 1/2" beech molder with heavy round chamfers, ca. 1800-20. ****

E. WASHBURN
Example: on a 13 3/4" x 2 5/16" birch panel riser with an offset pegged tote and flat chamfers, ca. 1770. **UR**

I. WASHBURN
Isaac Washington (b. Feb. 1, 1755 in Middleboro, Plymouth Co., MA, m. May. 27, 1798 in Taunton, Bristol Co., MA, d. Nov. 21, 1832 in Taunton) of Taunton, who was listed 1800-32, as a chairmaker. **Isaac Washburn** served in the Revolutionary War from Taunton, as a Private, in Capt. Robert Crosman's Co. of Minutemen, Col. Nathaniel Leonard's Regt. which marched Apr. 20, 1775 in response to the alarm of Apr. 19, 1775 to Roxbury. Service 12 days and was discharged on Apr. 29, 1775. Example: on a 14 3/4" birch jack with an offset tote, a diamond strike, and shallow flat chamfers, from New England, ca. 1790. **UR**

O: WASHBURN
Oscar Fitzland Washburn (b. Nov. 27, 1825 in Goshen, Hampshire Co., MA, d, Jun. 7, 1912 in Goshen) made planes in Goshen, MA, ca. 1845. It is believed that he was a part of **Union Tool Co.** of Goshen, from 1852-54. Example: on a 9 1/2" grooving plane with the location imprint of Portland, ME, ca. 1840. **UR**

R. WASHBURN
Example: on a 12 3/8" beech double-iron fixed sash with a pegged tote and flat chamfers, ca. 1800. **UR**

T. WASHBURN
Example: on a 3/16" beech skew dado with a nicker held in plane with a wedge and flat chamfers, found in eastern PA. **UR**

W. L. WASHBURN
William Lyman Washburn (b. Mar. 1, 1810 in Williamsburg, Hampshire Co., MA, m. Oct. 3, 1836 in Amherst, d. Feb. 1892 in Belchertown, Hampshire Co., MA) made planes in Amherst, MA, from 1835-40. **Washburn** was also part of **Fox & Washburn** in 1835-36; **Fox, Nutting & Washburn**, in 1835; and **Kellogg, Fox & Washburn**, in 1839, all in Amherst. In 1848-51, Washburn was listed, as cabinetmaker, in Springfield, MA. Several examples have both the **Fox & Washburn** and the **W. L. Washburn** imprints. ****

W. T. WASHBURN
Examples: on a 9 1/2" maple side hollow with shallow round chamfers, and an adjustable sash plane, ca. 1840. **UR**

WASHINGTON FACTORY
James Coates of Washington, PA, used this trade name, ca. 1850. An 1855 map of Washington Co. shows his plane factory on Wheeling St. ***

I. WASSER
Examples: on a 12" jack; a 10" round; and a 9 3/4" molder, all beech with flat chamfers, probably from PA, ca. 1810. ****

BENJAMEN WATERMAN
Benjamin Waterman Jr. (b. Apr. 12, 1719, in that part of Providence that split off in 1754 to become Cranston, RI, d. Sep. 4, 1799 in Cranston) was listed as a house carpenter, in a deed in Providence, on May 31, 1750. On April 18, 1759, **Benjamin Waterman Jr.** is made a "freeman" of the Town of Johnston, RI. On Mar. 6, 1759, the Town of Johnston was incorporated including the Waterman land. After the death of his father in law in 1767, waterman became a prosperous "yeoman" in the Providence hamlet of Tripptown, 3 miles west of Providence harbor. In 1776, **Benjamin Waterman** bought a "Nigro women named Phillis" for "thirty pounds". In a 1792 deed, **Benjamin** is referred to as a housewright. **Benjamin Waterman**'s probate inventory, dated Nov. 23, 1799, lists "chest with old tools, in the garret". Examples: on a 9 3/4" double-reeding plane with molded shoulder and flutes, dated **1741**, with the A wedge, found in Glocester, RI; a 9 1/16" complex molder; and a 9 7/16" ogee molding plane with the B wedge, all birch with shallow flat chamfers and relieved wedges. ca. 1750. *****

J. WATERMAN & CO.
J. Waterman & Co. was a hardware firm listed in the city directory of New Orleans, LA, from 1843-52. This partnership included **Jedediah Waterman** (b. ca. 1814 in Orleans, LA, d. probate Jun. 14, 1873 in Orleans), his brother **Charles Marshall Waterman**, and their father, **Capt. Robert Waterman** (b. Dec. 12, 1781 in Nantucket Co., MA, d. Apr. 29, 1860 in New Orleans, Orleans Co., LA). **Robert Waterman** was the Captain of a packet ship. From 1853-60, the firm was known as **J. Waterman & Brother**. In 1856, **Charles Waterman** was a member of the Know Nothing Party and became the first merchant to be elected mayor of New Orleans. His election and term as mayor was marked by violence, which ended, in 1858, when he was impeached while armed mobs gathered in the city. In 1860, he disappeared after leaving his house and was believed to have committed suicide by drowning in the Mississippi River. His succession record notes that he was $20,000 in debt to the firm, at the time of his "apparent death." The firm lasted several more years under the name of **J. Waterman**, ending sometime during the Civil War or Reconstruction. ****

T. WATERMAN
Thomas Waterman (b. May 2, 1775 in Lincoln Co., ME, d. May 17, 1852 in Waldoboro, Lincoln Co., ME) was listed in the 1800-50 census as "head of family"; and in 1850 as a farmer, owning real estate valued at $1200. In 1809, **Waterman** was surveyor of lumber for Waldoboro, and was a selectman in 1819. His planes are 9 1/2" birch or beech with relieved wedges and flat chamfers to round chamfers, indicating work over a period of time, ca. 1790-1820. A & A1 ****

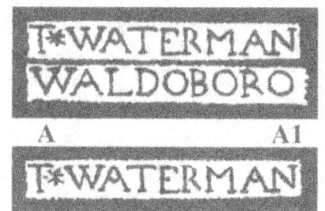

E. WATERS.
Possibly **Ebenezer Waters** (m. Dec. 4, 1771 in Boston, MA) or **Edward Waters**, both listed as cabinetmakers in Boston, MA, in 1789. Examples: on a 10" round with round chamfers; a 10" large round & hollow pair with flat chamfers; and a 9 3/4" skew rabbet, all birch with relieved wedges, from New England, ca. 1790-1820. ****

M: WATERS
Example: on a 10" birch wheelwright fellow plane with shallow flat chamfers, ca. 1790. **UR**

R. WATERS
Examples: on a reed & follow with the B wedge; two rounds; a hollow; a single-boxed bead; and a single-boxed complex molder, all 9 1/2" beech with round chamfers, ca. 1820. ****

JOSEPH WATKINS
Joseph Watkins (m. Sep. 1, 1762 in Philadelphia, PA, will probated Mar. 12, 1776) was listed, in 1745, as a joiner, in Philadelphia, PA. He placed ads in the *Pennsylvania Gazette*, on Feb. 10, 1757 and Dec. 12, 1758, in which he identifies himself, as making and selling carpenter's and joiner's planes. An ad in October 1757, lists "**Joseph Watkins**, in Philadelphia, Of whom may be had seasoned boards and scantlings of drivers kinds and sizes; and also Carpenters and Joiners Planes, of most sorts, made and sold by said Watkins". On April 17, 1776, an ad announced the settling the estate of **Joseph Watkins, Sr.**, late of Philadelphia, a carpenter. **No imprint has been reported.**

R. WATROUS
Riggs Watrous (b. ca. 1811 in Oneida Co., NY, d. bef. 1874 in Elmira, Chemunt Co., NY) was a hardware dealer, in Elmira, NY, 1843-60. His advertisement in the *Elmira Gazette* of Dec. 21, 1843, offered all types of hardware and "also connected with the above establishment, a plane factory." The connection was probably **William H. Spaulding**. In 1861, **Riggs Watrous** was listed, as a hardware merchant, in Elmira, NY with **Watrous & Cook**. ***

WATROUS & COOK
Watrous & Cook was a hardware partnership, in 1861, with **Riggs Watrous** and **Elisha H. Cook**, at 101-103 Water St., Elmira, NY. **No imprint has been reported**.

WATROUS & OSBORNE
John Lucian Watrous (b. Mar. 1, 1801 in Colchestor, New London Co., CT, d. 1862 in Auburn, Cayuga Co, NY) and **Joseph Osborne** (b. 1820 in England) ran a hardware store in Auburn, NY, ca. 1850. In the 1850 census, **John** was listed as a merchant. By 1857, both men were in other occupations.
A & A1 **

JAMES WATSON, JR.
James Watson, Jr., age 17, apprenticed, on Oct. 15, 1830, to **H. B. Miller** of Lebanon, OH. **No imprint has been reported.**

N: WATSON
Possibly **Nathaniel Watson** (b. 1777, d. May 4, 1859 in East Windsor, Hartford Co., CT) who was a cabinetmaker, in Farmington, Hartford Co., from 1800-21. Example: on an 8 7/8" cherry skew rabbet with an applied side nicker and shallow round chamfers, ca. 1820-30. UR

P. WATSON
These imprints could represent one or two separate planemakers. Examples: the A imprint is on a 9 1/4" plow with wood depth stop and thumbscrews; and a 9 1/4" round, both beech with flat chamfers. The B imprint is on a 9 1/4" complex molder; and a, 9 5/8" skew rabbet, both beech with flat chamfers. The C imprint is from a large beech round with heavy round chamfers, ca. 1790-1800.
A, B & C; ****

S. WATSON
Example: on a 9 7/16" beech round with heavy round chamfers, ca. 1820. UR

W. H. WATSON
W. H. Watson is believed to be a merchant from Greenville, SC. Example: on a 10 3/4" beech handled match grooving plane made by the **Auburn Tool Co.**, ca. 1864-93. UR

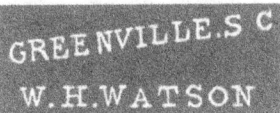

H. H. WATT

H. H. Watts, was a New York City hardware dealer, at 85 Av. D. Example: a bead, and on a boxed adjustable sash plane made by **J. W. Farr & Co.**, ca. 19c. ****

H. WATTS
Example: on a 9 5/16" beech quarter round with flat chamfers, ca. early 19c. UR

L. H. WATTS
Lewis H. Watts (m. Feb. 25, 1847 in New York City, d. Feb. 1901 in Brooklyn, NY) was a New York City, edge tool maker; and became a tool dealer, in the 1860's. A boxed bead has been reported with the imprint **FROM L. H. WATTS/ 85 AVE. D/ N.Y.** No imprint is available.

WILLIAM WAY
William Way of the Hartford, CT, operated a hardware store in New York City, in 1848, under this imprint. A **George M. Way** married a daughter of **L. Kennedy**. **William Way** was a partner in **Kennedy, Barry & Way**, in 1840; **Barry & Way**, from 1841-47; **Barry, Way & Sherman**, in 1847; **Way & Sherman**, from 1849-52; and **Way & Co.**, from 1853-59. **William Way** was listed in 1850-60, as an edge tool maker. In 1870, as "liquares" and in 1872 under "tobacco". From 1879-82, **William Way** was listed, as examiner, Hall of Records. In 1888, as Asst. Dep. Register, Hall of Records. In 1892, **William Way** was again listed, under tools, at 191 Lewis, NY. **

WAY & CO./ WILLIAM WAY & CO.
Way & Co. was a hardware firm operated by **William Way** in New York City, from 1853-59. It was the successor of **Way & Sherman**. Examples: the A imprint is on two 7/8" dados; and a filletster made by **Union/ Chapin**.
A & B ***

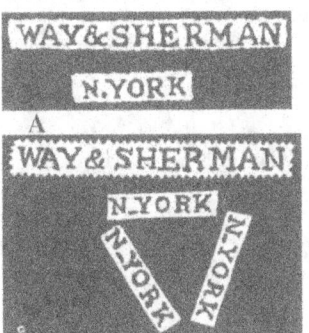

WAY & SHERMAN
William Way and **Byron Sherman** operated a hardware store in New York City, from 1849-52. It succeeded **Barry, Way & Sherman** and was succeeded in turn by **Way & Co.**. A **; A1 & B ****

J. L. WAYNE & SON
Jacob Lloyd Wayne (b. Jun. 8, 1832 in Clermont, OH, d. Feb. 2, 1915 in Cincinnati, OH) was a hardware dealers, at 124 Main in Cincinnati, OH, from 1857-77. **J. L. Wayne & Son** advertised that they were the successors to **E. F. Seybold**. They were succeeded by **Wayne Hardware Co.** with **J. L. Wayne, Jr.**, from 1878-1905, at 140-142 Main. **Jacobe L. Wayne** served in the Civil Was as a Lieutenant Colonel in Co. S. OH 139th. Inf. Reg., from May 20, 1864 and was mustered out on Aug. 26, 1864. **B **; A ******

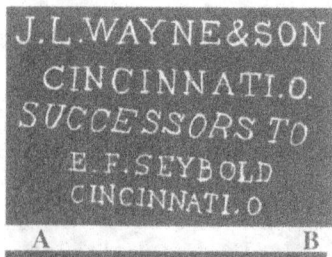

J. W. WAYNE & CO.
J. W. Wayne & Co. with **Joseph W. Wayne** (b. ca. 1825 in Rockingham, PA, m. Aug. 5, 1852 in Cincinnati, OH, d. bef. 1910 in Cincinnati) were hardware merchants at 196 Main Street, Cincinnati, OH, from 1846-50. Between 1850-65, it was called **Joseph W. Wayne & Co.**, with **T. Pickering** as a partner. In 1880, **Joseph W. Wayne** was listed as "ice chest manufacturer", in Cincinnati. Example: on an adjustable screw-arm sash plane made by **Schaefer & Cobb** of Cincinnati. ********

D. WEAVER
Examples: the A imprint is on a 14 1/2" beech panel raiser; and a 15" tongue plane with a mahogany tote and fence, both with an offset tote, diamond strike, and heavy flat chamfers. The B imprint is on a 7 3/4" maple shallow bead; and a 22" (reported birch, but may be mahogany) trying plane, both with heavy flat chamfers. The panel and the trying planes were found in central PA, probably from PA, ca. 1800. ********

GEO E. WEAVER
George Edwin Weaver (b. Jun. 20, 1848, m. Oct. 27, 1869, d. Jan 4, 1934 in Cranston, Providence, RI) was listed, in 1870, as Agt. Perkins Sheet Iron Co., Providence, RI. From 1879-80, as a planemaker, at 1039 & 1041 High St. Providence; in 1880, as hardware merchant; in 1900, as merchant, in Warwick, Kent Co., RI. In 1910-20, **George** was listed, as "merchant in paint oils" in Cranston, Providence. **No imprint has been reported**.

JN. WEAVER
Examples: with molders 9 1/2" beech with flat chamfers. Also reported is a 13 1/2" x 4" beech crown molder, struck three times on the toe, with an off-set tote and heavy flat chamfers; and a 9 1/2" beech single-boxed astragal with a mahogany fence that appears original, probably from PA. ca. 1800. ********

N. WEAVER
Example: on a 9 1/2" beech complex molder with flat chamfers, found in the Baltimore, MD area. **No imprint is available**.

B. WEBB
Example: on an 8" beech plow plane with cast iron arms and dated **1840**. UR

F. WEBB
Examples: on a 9 7/8" beech fixed sash; and a 9 3/8" beech round, both with flat chamfers, ca. 1800. UR

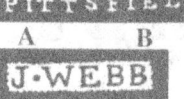

J. WEBB
John Webb (b. 1814 in England, d. Feb. 1, 1892 in Pittsfield, MA), was a brother of **William Webb**, and made planes in Pittsfield, MA, from 1837-49. Smith's *The History of Pittsfield Mass.* says: "The fulling mill was succeeded in 1816 by a Wooden Factory, forty feet by thirty feet in size. **John Webb** occupied most of the upper story for the manufacture of carpenter's planes from 1837 to Sept. 27, 1849, when the building was destroyed by fire." Field's *A History of the Town of Pittsfield*, 1844 relates: "The factory is now a plane and planing factory. Ten hands on average are employed." In 1840, **Webb** lived four houses from **M. Sweet**. The 1850 census listed **John Webb**, as a planemaker. The 1880 census, lists **John Webb**, at age 67, as a "plan mfg.", in Pittsfield, MA. **A & B *****

J. & W. WEBB
John Webb and brother **William Webb**, made planes separately in Pittsfield, MA, and then briefly together and in New York City under this imprint. *The Boston Daily Atlas* noted, on Tuesday, October 3, 1848, that the building in which the **Webbs** were located in Pittsfield, MA, was heavily damaged by fire. "**J. & W. Webb**, plane-makers, lost a considerable amount in tools, and in manufactured stock ready for market." **A, B & C *****

W. WEBB/ WEBB'S
William Webb (b. 1817 in England), a brother of **John Webb**, was listed in the 1850 census, as a planemaker, in Pittsfield, MA. He was part of **Webb & Baker**, in 1860, **Webb & Gamwell**, ca. 1850, and **J. & W. Webb** in New York City. In 1880, **William Webb** was listed, as a planemaker, in Fowlerville, Livingston Co., NY. Example: The B1 imprint is on a halving plane with a **Dwight French & Co.** iron. The C imprint is on a match set of beech side rabbets, ca. mid-19c. **A & B *****

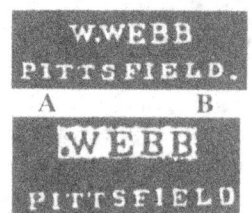

Wm. P. WEBB

William P. Webb (b. 1820 in MD) was listed as a planemaker, in the 1855 Washington, DC, directory. **Wm. P. Webb** probably came to DC from MD, ca. 1852. In the 1860 census, he was listed as a woodturner with **Henry Hammontry** (b. 1832 in MD), a planemaker, living with him. Example: on a 22" beech fore plane with the A imprint and **PATENDED/ Feb. 28, 1856**. There is no record of a patent under **Webb**'s name nor does the plane seem to incorporate any patent features.

A & A1 ***; B ****

WEBB & BAKER

Webb & Baker was a plane manufacturing partnership, consisting of **John Webb** and/ or **William Webb** and **Isaac Frederick Baker** (b. 1821 in Amherst, MA, d. Sep. 6, 1899 in Williamsburg, MA), that was listed in 1850, as a planemaker, in Pittsfield, MA. The 1860 MA Industrial census showed the firm employing six hands, using steam power, and producing $10,000 worth of planes. A complex molder with this imprint has a **1:12** imprinted on the heel, presumably a price. ***

WEBB & GAMWELL

Webb & Gamwell was a Pittsfield, MA, plane manufacturing partnership, probably consisting of **John Webb** and/ or **William Webb** and **Marcus Gamwell** (b. Nov. 17, 1827 in Hinsdale, MA), that was listed in the 1850 census. In 1855, **Marcus Gamwell** was listed, as a planemaker, in Huntington, Hampshire Co., MA. In 1860, **Gamwell** was listed as a mechanic, in Huntington. ***

WEBB'S

The location die **PITTSFIELD** is similar if not identical to that used by **J. Webb, J. & W. Webb** and **W. Webb**. ****

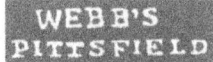

CHARLES WEBB

Charles Webb, age 11, was apprenticed, on Feb. 10, 1829, to **P. Probasco**, in Lebanon, OH "to learn the art, trade, mystery, and occupation of plane making."
No imprint has been reported.

S. WEBBER JR./ S. W. Jr.

Example: on a 15 3/4"x 4 1/4" birch body, beech offset tote beech wedge, crown molder with shallow flat chamfers, ca. 1780-90. UR

P. WEBER

Example: on a 10" beech quarter round with heavy flat chamfers, ca. early 19c. UR

P. WEBER & CO.

P. Weber & Co. made planes in Milwaukee, WI, dates unknown. Example: on a cooper's matching howel & croze. ****

J. WEBSTER

Possibly **John Webster** (b. Apr. 10, 1750 in Essex Co., MA, d. Nov. 13, 1807 in Salisbury, Essex Co.) who was a cabinetmaker, from Salisbury, MA. Examples: on an 8 7/8" beech square rabbet with large flat chamfers; a 9" slide arm, wedge stopped plow; and on a 9 3/8" beech quarter round with flat chamfers, found near Salisbury, ca. 1790. ****

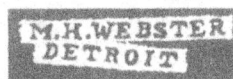

M. H. WEBSTER

Mathew Howard Webster (b. ca. 1815 in NY, d. May 30, 1893 in Detroit, Wayne Co., MI) was a hardware dealer, in Detroit, from 1837-58.
A **; B & B1 ***

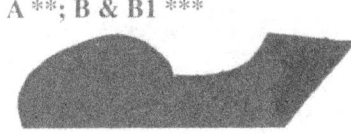

STEPHEN C. WEBSTER

Stephen C. Webster (b. Nov. 29, 1779 in Merrimack, d. Oct. 1850 in Salisbury, NH) was a joiner and carpenter, in Salisbury, active from 1804-43, who is known to have made and sold bench planes and other tools as listed in his account book.
No imprint has been reported.

J. WEED

Example: on a 9" beech table hollow with an **I. Sleeper** style wedge and flat chamfers, ca. 1810. UR

J. WEEDEN
Examples: the A imprint is on a 14 5/8" beech tongue & groove plank pair with open totes and heavy flat chamfers; and a beech single-boxed complex molder with flat chamfers. The B imprint is on 9 9/16" beech single boxed size **6/8** bead with heavy round chamfers, probably from NY or PA, ca. 1800-20.
A ***; B ****

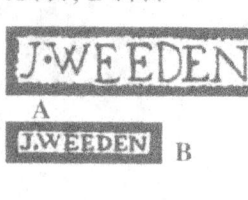 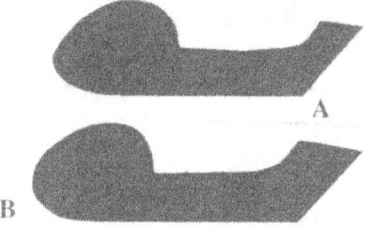

E. B. WEEKS
Example: on a 9 1/2" beech complex molder with heavy flat chamfers with an **I. Sleeper** style wedge, marked twice on the toe, ca. 1800. **UR**

JOs S. WEEKS/ J. S. W

Example: on a handled screw-arm rosewood plow with boxwood arms & wedge, ca. 19c. **UR**

N. C. WEEKS
Examples: The A imprint is on a 10 1/2" dado; a 9 7/8"x 3/8" birch halving plane with narrow flat chamfers; and a beech Yankee plow with a wood depth stop and thumbscrews, and flat chamfers. The A1 imprint is on a 9 1/2"x 1" birch rabbet with flat chamfers, from New England, ca.1810. **A & A1: ****

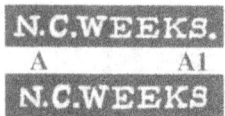 

THO. WEEKS
Thomas Weeks (b. Apr. 21, 1735 in Worcester, MA, m. Jul. 23, 1759 in Brookfield, Worcester Co., d. Apr. 20, 1817 in Goshen, Hampshire Co., MA) was in the French & Indian War, in 1760. In 1772, he moved to Greenwich, MA. On Apr. 20, 1775, in response to the alarm of Apr. 19, 1775, 2d. Lieutenant **Thomas Weeks** marched from Greenwich to Roxbury in command of a detachment of militia under Col. Elisha Brter's Regt.; served as Adjutant under Col. David Brewer's 9th. Regt.; engaged from Apr. 24, 1775 to Aug. 1, 1775; served as 1st. Lieutenant in Capt. Joseph Smith's Co., Col. Josiah Whitney's Regt., from Apr. 11, 1776 to Nov. 1, 1776, the Company raised for the defense of the town and harbor of Boston; served as Adjutant, Col. Thomas Marshall's 10th. Regt. Continental Army pay accounts from Jan. 1, 1777 to Aug. 1, 1777 when he resigned with the rank of Captain. Some time between 1778-9 he moved to Chesterfield "Gore" and was instrumental in obtaining its incorporation as the town of Goshen, in 1781. **Thomas** was the first Town Clerk, Surveyor of Land, and a school teacher. **Thomas Weeks** was a delegate to the State Constitutional Conventions of 1779-80. He was a cabinetmaker, turner and maker of spinning wheels. Examples: on a 10" dado with the A1 wedge; a 9 7/8" thumbnail molder with the A2 wedge, both birch with relieved wedges and shallow flat chamfers; and on a plane made by **F. Nicholson In Wrentham** as an owners imprint. The B imprint is on a 9 7/8" birch large hollow with a relieved wedge and flat chamfers, ca. 1750-80. **A & B *****

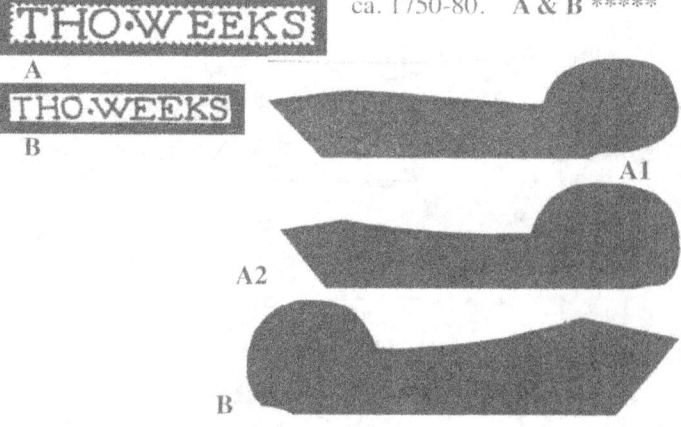

P. H. WEHRLEY
Example: on a 15"x 6 1/2" (5 1/2" iron) beech crown molder with a birch wedge, offset tote, applied fence, and flat chamfers, ca. 1780-1800. **UR**

R. WEIG
Example: on a 9 1/2" beech large round with flat chamfers, ca. 1800. **UR**

WELCH

Welch was a New York City hardware dealer, dates unknown. Example: on a **W. Cuddy/ N. York** plane, ca. 1850. ****

R. WELD
Example: on a 26" beech jointer with round chamfers, ca. 1820. **UR**

I. WELDY.
Example: on a 10" beech molder with heavy flat chamfers, ca. 1800. **UR**

WELLBORN
Believed to be a contemporary planemaker. Example: on a 15 1/8" jack with the location **THURSTON OREGON**. **UR**

A.W/ A. WELLES
A. Welles probably was a planemaker. Examples: the A imprint is on a 16" beech jack with a centered open tote and

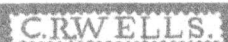 a single **Barry & Way** iron, found in ME. The A1 imprint with **WARRANTED** is on an unhandled screw-arm beech plow, ca. 1850. ****

C. R. WELLS
Chester Robbins Wells (b. Sept. 8, 1799 in Hartford, CT, d. Aug. 9, 1867) was the brother of **Elisha G. Wells** and first cousin of **Robert Wells**. It is quite likely that **Chester** apprenticed with the partnership of **Elisha** and **Robert**. The family moved to Trenton, NY, in 1800. On Dec. 16, 1820, the Presbyterian Society in Holland Patent had voted to erect a house of worship on the village square and among the subscribers listed was **Chester R. Wells** who pledged $50 in tools for joiners. **Chester** married Hanna LeMoyne DeAngelis in Nov. 1825. In 1828, **Chester** moved to New Haven, NY, near Oswego, where he spent the rest of his life, as planemaker and farmer. An account ledger has survived, listing many entries for plane making and repair between 1828-56. In 1863, his address was 13 First St. This imprint has also appeared with the imprint of **W. Woodward**. (see *A Planemaker's Account Ledger* by Patrick M. Kelley in the Bibliography.) **

C. S. WELLS
Charles S. Wells (d. bet. 1863-65 in Evansville, IN) was a hardware dealer in Evansville, IN, from 1857-63. In 1863, **C. S. Wells** was listed as hardware & cutler, at 13 N. 1st. b. Main and Sycamore in Evansville, IN. In 1865, **Wells, Kellogg & Co.** with **Hiram K. Wells**, **Charles H. Kellogg** & **Ed Boetticheri** was at the same address. **

E. WELLS
Example: on a very complex beech molder with two intermittent lignum vitae wear strips and flat chamfers, possibly from Philadelphia, ca. 1800. **UR**

E. A. WELLS
This appears to be a modification of an **E. G. Wells** imprint, however the imprint is larger. Example: on an 8 3/4" birch complex molder with round chamfers and a relieved wedge, probably from southeastern New England, ca. 1820. ****

E. G. WELLS
Elisha Griswold Wells (b. Mar. 5, 1788 in Hartford, CT, d. May 9, 1858 in Holland Patent, Oneida Co., NY) was the brother of **C. R. Wells** and first cousin of **R. Wells**. The family moved to Trenton, NY, near Oswego in 1800. He spent most of his life as a farmer and acquired some wealth as a land speculator. He was listed in Trenton in the 1820-40 census, in manufacturing. In 1850, he was listed in Oneida City, as a farmer. ***

E. G. & R. WELLS
E. G. & R. Wells was a planemaking partnership of **Elisha Griswold Wells** and **Robert Wells** who were first cousins. This partnership was formed after **Robert**'s 1815 arrival in Holland Patent, a village in the town of Trenton, Oneida Co., NY, north of Utica. **Elisha G. Wells** may have provided the facilities and possibly some capital while **Robert Wells** provided the know how. During the early years of this partnership, **Chester R. Wells** probably worked as a tool maker for the two older relatives who owned the business. According to land records, **Robert Wells** purchased 30 acres of land, in Nov. 1819. After this date, the partnership was dissolved and **Elisha G. Wells** and **Robert Wells** manufactured planes under their own imprints. In the 1840 census, both were listed in Trenton and in manufacturing. A & A1 ***

E. S. WELLS
Examples: on a 9 3/4" beech full round with the A wedge and flat chamfers that was found with an **O: Spicer** molder; and on a Yankee style beech plow with a relieved wedge, wood depth stop, thumbscrews, a riveted skate, the B wedge, and round chamfers, ca. 1790-1820. ****

G. F. WELLS
Example: on a 9 1/4" beech boxed bead with a skew iron and round chamfers. The **BOLTON** location could refer to Bolton, CT. On the heel is a **7** that probably refers to size 7/8". ca. 19c. **UR**

H. WELLS
Henry Wells (b. ca. 1817 in Williamsburg, Hampshire Co., MA, d. May 12, 1862 in Northampton, MA) was a planemaker, in both Northampton and Williamsburg (the towns are adjacent), from 1847-56. **Henry Wells**, as a minor, worked for **H. Chapin**, as an apprentice planemaker, from 1836-40. He was listed in the 1850 census, as a tool maker, with **C. Hendrick** living in his household; he was also listed as a tool maker. In the 1860 MA Industrial census he was listed as employing 12 hands and producing 31,000 planes (in Williamsburg). The eagle die that appears on some of the planes also appears on planes made by **J. D. Kellogg**, **Arnold & Crouch**, and **Peck & Crouch**, all of Northampton, MA. The **WMSBURG MASS** location die, of the B imprint, was used by **H. L. James** and the **Eagle Mfg. Co.**. A, B, B1: FF; C & C1 *****

JAMES H. WELLS
James Hancox Wells (b. Dec. 24, 1774 in Worcestershire, England, m. Oct. 4, 1803 in Middletown, Middlesex Co, CT, d. Oct. 25, 1857 in Hartford, CT) was a hardware dealer, in Hartford, from 1798-1820. Planes with **Wells'** imprint have been reported. Some of the planes that he advertised were made by **L. Kennedy**. **No imprint is available**.

R. WELLS
Robert Wells (b. Oct. 16 in Weathersfield, CT, 1792, d. Mar. 17, 1862 in Holland Patent, Oneida Co., NY) was a first cousin of **Elisha G. Wells** and **Charles R. Wells**. He moved to Holland Patent, a village in Trenton, Oneida Co., NY, north of Utica, in 1815. He was a partner in **E. G. & R. Wells** until shortly after he purchased 30 acres of land, in Nov. 1819; and produced planes under his own imprint. In the 1840 census, **Robert Wells** had two members of his household in manufacturing. In the 1855 & 60 NY censuses, his occupation was listed as planemaker.
A *; A1 & B ***

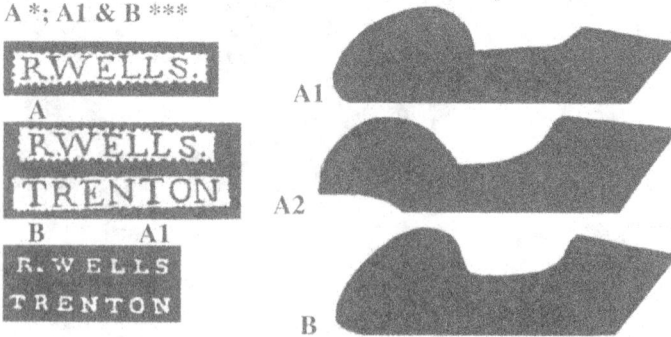

WELLS & ALLING
William W. Wells (b. Oct. 15, 1822 in IN, d. Jul. 24, 1885 in Paoli, Orange CO., IN) and **John A. Alling** (b. May 26, 1828 in Jefferson, IN, m. Jun. 8, 1865 in Wallingford, New Haven Co., CT, d. Apr. 3, 1900 in Chicago, Cook Co., IL) were listed as importers of hardware, Fitch's Blk. N. Side of Main Cross between Mulberry & West. in Madison, IN, from 1852-57. They were succeeded by **McKinney & Alling**, from 1857-65; and then by **Alling & Lodge**, after 1865. Examples: on a match pair of tongue & grooving planes with **5** on the toe. The wedge appears to be similar to that used by the **Sandusky Tool Co.**, ca. 1860. ****

WELLS & REED

Wells & Reed was a planemaking partnership with **Henry Wells**. Examples: on two beech jointers. *****

R. WELTON
Examples: on three molders, one a small quarter round and a gunstock round, both 10 3/16" with flat chamfers, ca 1800. ****

T. WENDELL
Example: on a 9 9/16" applewood hollow, ca. 1840-50. UR

J. WENTWORTH
J. Wentworth was a 19c. hardware dealer in Worcester, MA. Example: on a bead plane made by **T. Tileston**. ****

T. Y. WENTWORTH
Example: on an 8" beech boxed side bead, ca. 1850. UR

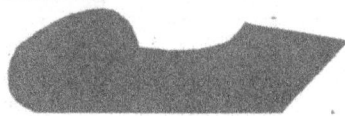

WENTWORTH/ WENTWORTH & BRAZER
The **Wentworth & Brazer** partnership was sometime between 1832-35 when **Benjamin Brazer** was listed in the Lowell, MA, directories, as a planemaker. **Brazer** went on to modify his die by removing the **&**. He used **BRAZER** with the **LOWELL** die, before 1835, and with the **BOSTON** die, after 1835. Examples: the A imprint is on a 19c. bead. The B imprint is on a 19c. dado with a brass depth stop. B ****; A *****

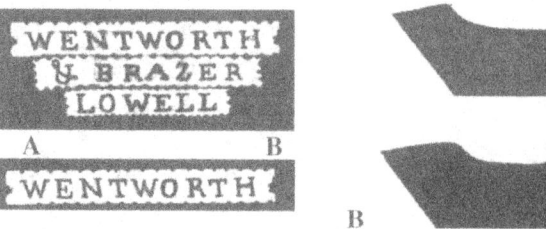

D WENTZ
Daniel Wentz (b. Feb. 11, 1794 in PA, d. Aug. 5, 1849 in Perry Co., PA) was the son of **Henry Wentz** and was a carpenter in Jackson Twp., Perry Co., PA. UR

H. WENTZ
Henry Wentz (b. Mar. 5, 1766 in Dover Twp., York Co., PA, d. Feb. 23, 1852 in Blain, Jackson Twp., Perry Co., PA) was the father of **Daniel Wentz** and was listed as a carpenter, joiner, and cabinetmaker. The spelling of **Wentz** was also recorded as **Wantz, Wintz, Winse, Wayentz**, and **Vance**. The German pronunciation of "W" sounds like "V" and therefore **Wentz** sounds like **Vance**. One branch of his family emigrated to Baltimore, MD, thus a possible distant relationship with **W. Vance**. **Henry** was listed in the 1800 census and a 1809 tax list in Dover, York Co.; in 1810-17, in Tyrone Twp. and Toboyne Twp., Cumberland Co., PA. In 1820, Tyrone Twp. & Toboyne Twp. combined to form Perry Co. and then Toboyne was divided to create Jackson Twp. **Henry** therefore probably stayed put, but the names of the towns and counties changed. Examples: The A imprint is on a reeding plane, found in Perry Co.; a fruitwood wedge-arm plow plane, found in York Co.; a pump log plane; a 10" complex molding plane with the A wedge; and a 13 1/2" grooving plane. The B imprint is on a

14 1/8" panel raiser with a fixed fence and a **M. Spealman** iron; and a 10" complex molder with flat chamfers and the B wedge.
A & B ****

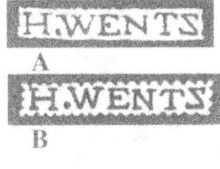
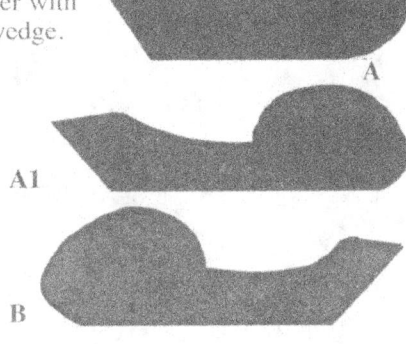

ANDREW WERLEY
Andrew Werley (b. Nov. 22, 1825 in Baden, Germany, m. Aug. 27, 1851 in Columbus, Franklin Co., OH, d. Jan. 26, 1908 in New Riegel, Seneca Co., OH) was listed as a planemaker in Columbus, OH, in 1856-57. In 1870, **Andrew** was listed as a dry goods merchant in New Riegel.
No imprint has been reported.

A. WERTMAN
Example: on a plane from PA, ca. 1800-10.
No imprint is available.

D. WEST
Example: on a 9" fruitwood plow, round top arms that are wedge locked, a riveted skate with a brass guard, a brass depth stop and round chamfers. ca. early 19c.   **UR**

I. WEST
Example: on a 9 1/2" beech size **6** hollow & round pair with small flat chamfers, ca. early 19c.   **UR**

J. R. WEST
Joseph R. West who was listed in Philadelphia, PA, from 1820-30. One example has a location imprint of **EASTON**, possibly Easton, PA. Examples: on a 9 5/8" beech complex molder with flat chamfers; and a 9 1/2" beech round with flat chamfers and the B wedge, ca. 1810.   ****

JOHN T. WEST
John T. West was listed as a planemaker in 1874, at 37 Commerce St., Baltimore, MD. **No imprint has been reported**.

J x WESTCOTT
Possibly **J. Westcott** who was listed in the 1790 census for Dighton, MA; he was listed in 1810, also from Dighton, as a carpenter. Examples: on a Yankee plow; a 14" birch crown molding plane with a offset tote and a round top iron & wedge; four additional molders, found in south-central CT; and 9 5/8" - 9 1/2" birch beads with round chamfers and relieved wedges, probably from southern New England, ca. 1810.   ****

G. WESTGATE
Example: on a 9 1/2" beech round with heavy flat chamfers. ca. 1810.   **UR**

H. WETHEREL
Henry Wetherel, Jr. (with one **L**) (b. ca. 1729, d. Jan. 28, 1797) was the father of **Henry Wetherell** (with two **LL**). In 1748, he was listed as a laborer. About 1743, he was possibly apprenticed to his uncle, **Isaac Wetherel**, a blacksmith in Norton, MA. On Sep. 27, 1760, **Henry** Married in Norton and was the father of **Henry Wetherell III**. **Henry** was a farmer, blacksmith, toolmaker, and a planemaker from 1750-95. His earlier planes are imprinted with the location **IN. NORTON**. In 1771, he was listed as having a house with shop adjoining. In 1772, 73 & 79 he was listed as a shop joiner. In 1776, he served in the Revolutionary War. In 1779, he moved to Chatham, CT (now East Hampton), on the Connecticut River, some 15 miles south of Hartford, and changed his location die to **CHATHAM**. On June 26, 1780, he took the Oath of Fidelity in Chatham. In his will, dated Dec. 20, 1793, **Henry, Jr.** left his blacksmith shop to his son **Henry III** and "all my trades in the different branches of it." His estate inventory was dated Dec. 24, 1797, and included a well-equipped multi-purpose shop which was set up for both blacksmithing and woodworking with one fore plane, two jointers, and 29 joiner tools. **Henry's** planes were 9 3/4" birch with flat chamfers.
B **; A ***; C *****

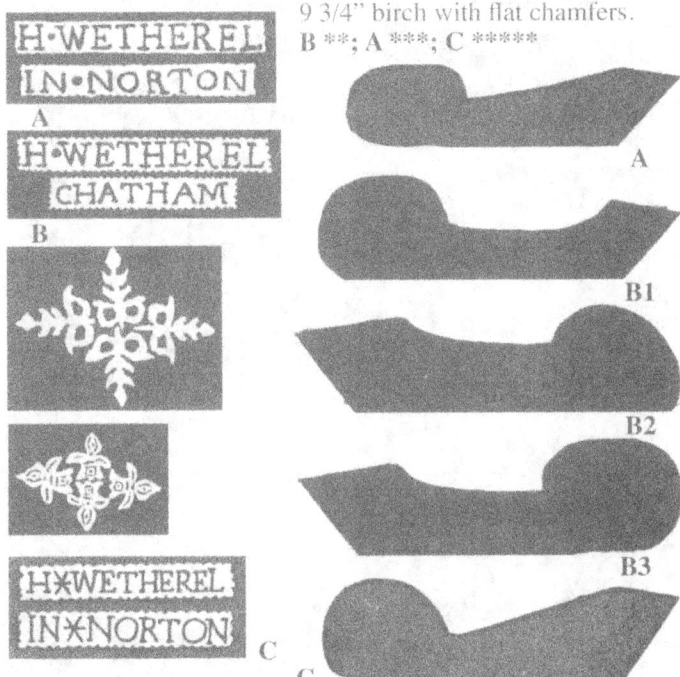

H. WETHERELL
Henry Wetherell III (with two **LL**) (b. Feb. 8, 1764 in Norton, MA, d. Nov. 20, 1840 in Chatham, CT) was the son of **Henry Wetherel, Jr.** (with one **L**) and inherited his father's blacksmith shop and stock of tools. His working dates are believed to be 1785-1830. **Wetherell** lived in Chatham, CT, until 1808, when he moved to adjoining Glastonbury, CT. In 1809, he returned to Chatham; from 1824-27, he lived in Middletown, CT; and by 1830, he was back in Chatham. He advertised on May 25,

1808, in the Hartford, CT, *Courant* :"Joiners Tools, all kinds of Joiners moulding tools made and kept constantly for sale by the subscriber, **Henry Wetherell**, Glastenbury". A similar ad was placed on May 10, 1809, but in Chatham. In his later years, he became a successful investor and left an estate valued at $24,000. He used a double or sometimes a single crown imprint, or fleur de lis. The earlier planes are 9 3/4" birch with flat chamfers. The later planes are 9 1/2" beech with round chamfers. Location dies exist for Chatham from 1785-1808, 1809-20, Glastonbury (Glastenbury), in 1809, and Middletown from 1824-27. Examples: on a plow plane with both the Glastonbury and Chatham imprints, and the date **1811**; and a Yankee plow with a Chatham imprint and a **1790** date. The A imprints are larger and earlier than the B imprints.

A1, B, B1 & B2: FF;
A, A2 & C ***;
D, E, F & G: *****

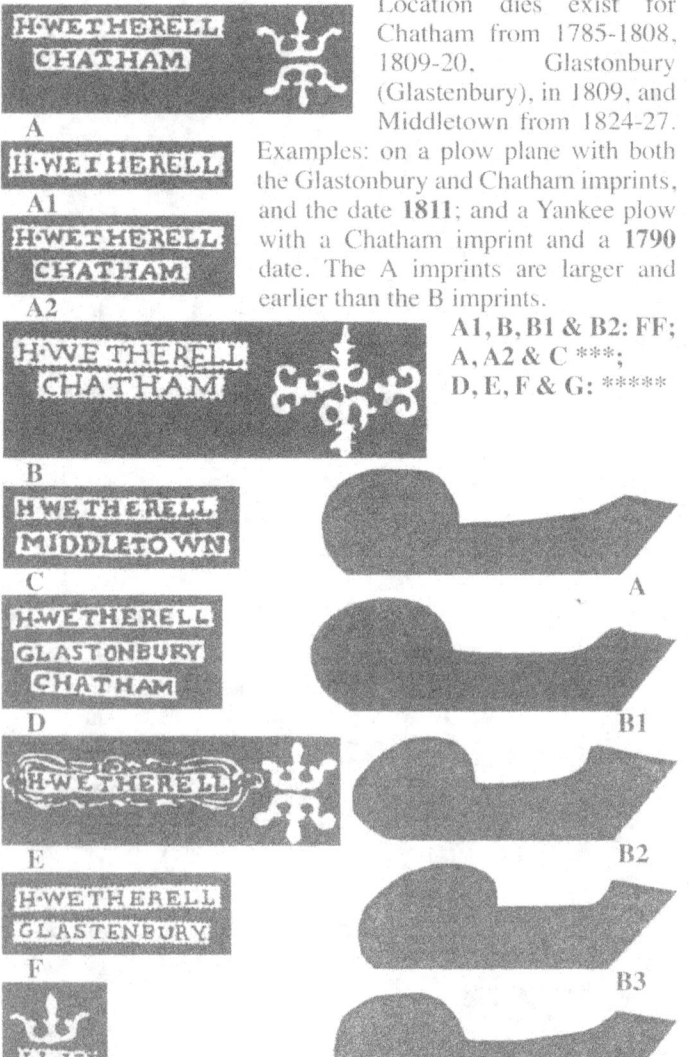

W + WEVER
One of three 18c imprints on the toe of a 9 7/8" yellow birch skew rabbet with flat chamfers and a relieved wedge of **Jo. Fuller** style, ca. 1790. **UR**

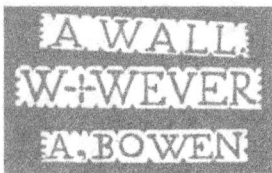

WHEATCROFT & SIEWERS
Wheatcroft & Siewers were Cincinnati, OH, planemakers and edge tool makers, from 1840-42. The partnership consisted of **John Wheatcroft** (d. probate Jul. 30, 1847 in Hamilton Co., OH) and **Charles Gothried Siewers**. Example: a pair of screw-arm plank match planes with open totes, ca. mid. 19c. **No imprint is available.**

A. WHEATON
Amos Wheaton Jr. (m. Nov. 9, 1794 in Philadelphia, PA, d. 1798 in Philadelphia) was an early Philadelphia, PA, planemakers. **Wheaton** was listed as a joiner, from 1769-72, in North Liberties, Philadelphia. He was listed, from 1773-91, as a joiner, at 386 N. 2nd. ST.; and from 1797-98, as a planemaker, at cor. 2nd. & Green Sts. **A & B ***

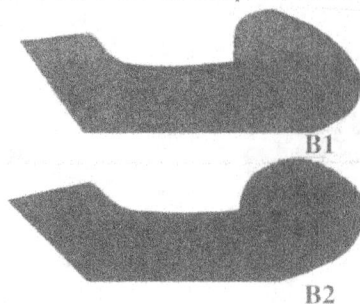

G. W. WHEELER
Example: on a slide-arm beech plow secured with wood screws and flat chamfers, ca. early 19c. **UR**

H. WHEELER
Example: on a plane with the incuse date of **9.11.1809**. **UR**

L. WHEELER
Example: on a 9" birch quarter round with flat chamfers, ca. 1790. **UR**

P. WHEELER
Examples: on a 14 5/8" gutter plane with a double-pegged tote; a 9 1/2" fenced skew rabbet, both birch with heavy flat chamfers; a birch tongue plane, found in ME, and two other examples, found in Fitchburg, MA, ca. 1790. ****

T. WHEEL(--)
Probably **T. WHEELER** has a heart between the **T** and the **W**. The last two letters are unreadable. Example: on 9 1/2"x 3/8" beech round with heavy round chamfers, found in southeastern, PA. Branded on the left side: **RALPH & GREGG**; stamped on left side: **H. J. BOCKIUS**; stamped on toe: **S. HUET**; branded on right side: **W. BOCKIUS**. There was a **William Bockius** (d. 1848) who entered into the Carpenters Co. of Philadelphia, in 1823, ca. early 19c. **UR**

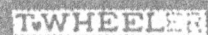

THOs WHEELER
Example: on a 10"x 1 3/8" beech skew rabbet with flat chamfers, ca. 1800. **UR**

W W./ W. A. WHEELER
Example: on four sets of 9 1/2" birch hollows & rounds with flat chamfers, ca. 1800-10. **UR**

JOHN WHELAN
John M. (Jack) Whelan (b. Sep. 12, 1921 in Lyndhurst, NJ, d. Aug. 10, 2014 in St. Petersburg, FL) was a contemporary planemaker from Murray Hill, Union Co., NJ. He received a B. degree in Mechanical Engineering; a M. degree in Chemistry; and a PHD degree in Organic Chemistry. **Jack** retired from Union Carbide Corp. in 1976. He was the Pres. of **CRAFTS of NJ** from 1990-96. **John Whelan** was the author of *The Wooden Plane, its history, form and function* and *Making Traditional Wooden Planes* as well as the column, *Plane Chatter* in The Chronicle. ****

W. WHIPS
Examples: The A imprint is on a 9 3/8" beech complex molder. The B imprint, with a location imprint of **LOUISVILLE** (KY) and added imprints of **T. LITTELL** and **T. ATKINSON**, possibly another partnership, is on a complex molder; a size **10** round; a size **7** hollow; a size **5/8 & 8/8** side beads, all with wide round chamfers, ca. 1840. **A & B;** ****

J. WHISTON
Examples: on a 10" complex molder; and a skew rabbet, both birch with a relieved wedge, flat chamfers and fluting; ca. 1790. ****

WHITAKER
Whitaker was probably a hardware dealer in Toledo, OH. Example: on a skew rabbet made by **Hall, Case & Co.** of Columbus, OH, ca. mid. 19c. ****

S. & J. H. WHITAKER
The 1850 census listed **Samuel Whitaker** (b. 1822 in OH, d. probate Oct. 5, 1864 in Clinton, OH) and **John H. Whitaker** (b. 1810 in OH, d. Jul. 7, 1870 in Toledo, Lucas Co., OH) as hardware merchants in Toledo, OH. In 1871, the firm was succeeded by **Whitaker, Phillips & Co.** importers and dealers in hardware, at 102 Summit St., Toledo, OH. Example: on an **Ohio Tool Co.** plane. ****

J. L. WHITCOMB
Examples: on a 9 5/8"x 1 1/2" rabbet; and a 9 5/8"x 1" rabbet, both beech with round chamfers, ca. 1820-30. **UR**

M. WHITCOMB
Examples: on a 9 3/4"x 1 1/2" fruitwood skew rabbet; an 8 1/4" beech smoother; and a 21" applewood bench plane with a centered open tote, all with heavy round chamfers, ca. 1820-30. ****

WHITE
Example: on a 10 3/16" beech quarter round with heavy flat chamfers. Found in southeastern PA, ca. early 19c. **UR**

A WHITE
Example: on a 12"x 2 3/8" chestnut wedge armed tongue plane with a small offset beech tote and heavy flat chamfers, ca. 1790. **UR**

B. WHITE
Example: on a 10" beech narrow round with flat chamfers, ca. 1780. **UR**

B. W./ B. WHITE
Example: a 12 1/4" beech ship's hollow with a birch centered tote and flat chamfers, ca. 1810. **UR**

CHARLES WHITE
Charles White (b. 1795 in CT, d. Jan. 4, 1866 in Warren, Trumbull Co., OH) arrived in Warren, OH, in 1817, and was listed first as a carpenter and later as a home builder. He was listed in the 1850 census, as a mechanic, in Warren. The 1850 census of industry listed **Charles White**, in tool and cabinetmaking, employing three hands, who made 1200 planes, cabinets worth $2000, and job work valued at $1000. He was probably the **White** in **Soule, White & Spear**, ca. 1840; and in **White & Spear**, ca. 1845. His older brother, **Dyer White** (b. 1788, d. 1852), was a partner in **Kennedy & White** and was listed living with **Charles White**, in 1850. **

CHARLOTTE WHITE

Charlotte White (b. Aug. 13, 1805 in PA, d. Aug. 18, 1887 in Delaware, PA) was the wife of **Israel White**, a well known Philadelphia, PA, planemaker. **Israel** died in 1839 and **Charlotte** took over the shop. The 1842 directory, lists her "**White, Charlotte** (late **Israel**), plane maker, 139 Callowhill." with a 1/2 page ad for the shop, "Plane Manufactory and General Tool Store." In 1843 & 44, **Charlotte** was listed as "**White, C.**, (late **Israel White**) n.e. cor. Old York road and Callowhill st.". Her last listing, in 1845, was after she remarried as "**Burnett Charlotte**, plane maker, 139 Callowhill." In 1846, her nephew, **Henry G. White** was listed with the shop at 139 Callowhill. In 1850, **Charlotte Burnett** was listed (without husband) living in the household of **Frederick W. Miller(s)**, planemaker, in Philadelphia. At her death, she was listed as **Charlotte White Burnett**. **No imprint, under her name, has been reported.**

G. W./ G. WHITE

George White (b. 1791 in PA, d. June 24, 1824 in Philadelphia, PA) was the son of **Jacob White**, brother of **Israel White**, and father of **Henry G. White**. He was part of **White & Grinnel**, from 1818-19, with his father and **William Grinnel**. He was operating a plane shop, in Philadelphia, PA, in 1824, when he died, at age 33. His widow, **Catherine**, succeeded him for a short time until her death on Nov. 27, 1825. She was listed as "**White, wid. C.**, planemaker", in the 1825 city directory. It is believed that his father, **Jacob White**, continued to run the business and used **George**'s mark until ca. 1831, when **Israel White** took over. The C imprint with the **I.W** initials probably represents **Israel White** as a journeyman working for his father from 1825-31. Other initials **T.D** stands for **Thomas Donoho**; and **N.N** stands for **Nathan Norton** have been reported. Examples: the B imprint, but with the name alone, and an incuse **G.W.** is on a 9 1/2" beech size 8/8 single-boxed bead made by **D. Copeland/ Hartford**. The A2 imprint with the incuse **PHILA** has the same die as used by **White & Grinnel** on a 9 1/2" beech double-rosewood boxed complex molder.

A & A1: FF; B *; B1 & A2 **; C *****

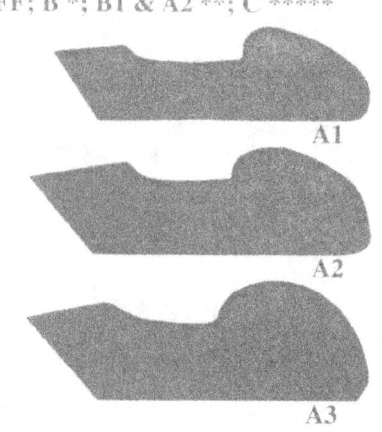

H. WHITE/ H. W. WHITE

Hiram W. White (b. Apr. 30, 1819 in NY, d. Dec. 1, 1903 in Yankton, SD) was a gunsmith and owned a hardware store, in Jackson, OH, from 1850-60. He was listed in 1870, as a gunsmith, in Dlnes, Richland Co., IL and in 1880, as a gunsmith in Yankton, Dakota Territory. On Nov. 2, 1889, the Dakota Territory was reduced in size, split and admitted to the Union as North and South Dakota. Example: on two rounds with **72** on the toe, the **Ohio Tool Co.** style number for hollows & rounds. A, B & C ***

H. G. W./ HENRY G. WHITE

Henry G. White (b. ca. 1798, d. 1860 in Philadelphia, PA) was the orphaned son of **George** and **Catherine White** and was raised by his aunt and uncle, **Israel** and **Charlotte White**. **Henry**, not their own son **Paul**, succeeded **Israel**'s widow **Charlotte**, and operated the White planemaking shop, at Callowhill, St., from 1846-58, when **David Colton** took over. **Henry G. White** used **Israel White**'s dies, substituting his own name. Example: the initial group is on a 9 3/8"x 1/2" beech round, found in Manheim, PA.

A: FF;
C, D, D1, E & F **;
B ***; C1 ****

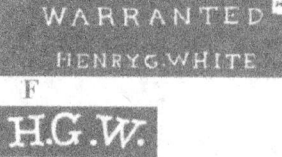
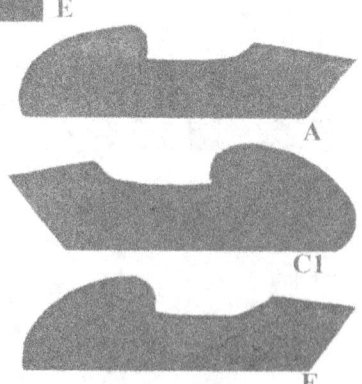

I. W/ I. WHITE/ ISRAEL WHITE

Israel White (b. 1804, d. April 12, 1839 In Philadelphia, PA) was the son of **Jacob White**, brother of **George White**, and uncle of **Henry G. White**. He probably worked as a journeyman under his father from 1825-31. He operated the **White** plane making shop and was listed as a planemaker, in Philadelphia, PA, from 1831-39. He probably did not imprint his own name until after his father's death, in 1833. The inventory at **Israel's** death listed "Finished Planes on hand- $2,106.91," which must have represented several thousand planes. His widow, **Charlotte**, continued running the shop, from 1839-45. In 1845, she was listed as a planemaker under her remarried name, **Charlotte Burnet**, at 139 Callowhill. **Henry G. White** took over the plane making shop, some time in 1845. **Israel White** made a wide variety of planes, some of exotic woods including a three arm plow. Patent No. 7951X, of Jan. 9, 1834. Of the eight surviving numbered examples No's. 26, 31, 138, 169 183 and 187 were made by Israel to the patent specifications. No's. 39, 160, and two by **Henry G. White**, had a bridge on the fence for the adjustment knob. Imprint D is for this model, with the No. 123 the inventory number. The initial **J. S** stands for **James Silcock**, the journeyman who made them. Some of these journeymen went on to become planemakers in their own right:
T.D (Thomas Donoho)
N.N (Nathan Norton)
E.W.P. (Edward W. Pennell)
Others were:
A.M. (Adam Miller)
D.H. (David Hanley)
W.M.D. (William McDaniel)
F.M. (Frederick Miller)
T.B. (Thomas Beckman)
J.S. (James Silcock)
W.F. (William Fennell)
S.L. (not known).

Israel also made a three-arm filletster that was reported in Vol. 18 (1834) p.109 of *The Franklin Journal*. The O imprinted planes were mother planes, possibly **Israel White's** shop tools.
C, H & I: FF;
B, B1, G & J *;
A, E, G1, K & M **;
A1, B2, F & I1, J1 ***;
D, F1, I2, L, N, O & O1 ****

A

A1

B

B1

B2

C

D

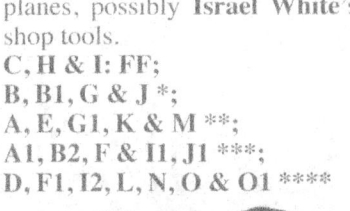
B

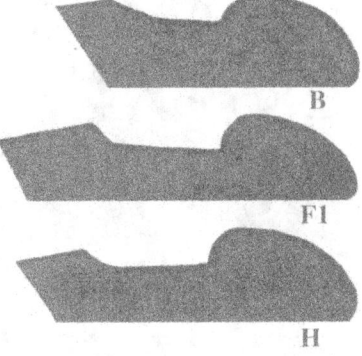
F1, H

E

F

F1

G, G1

H, I

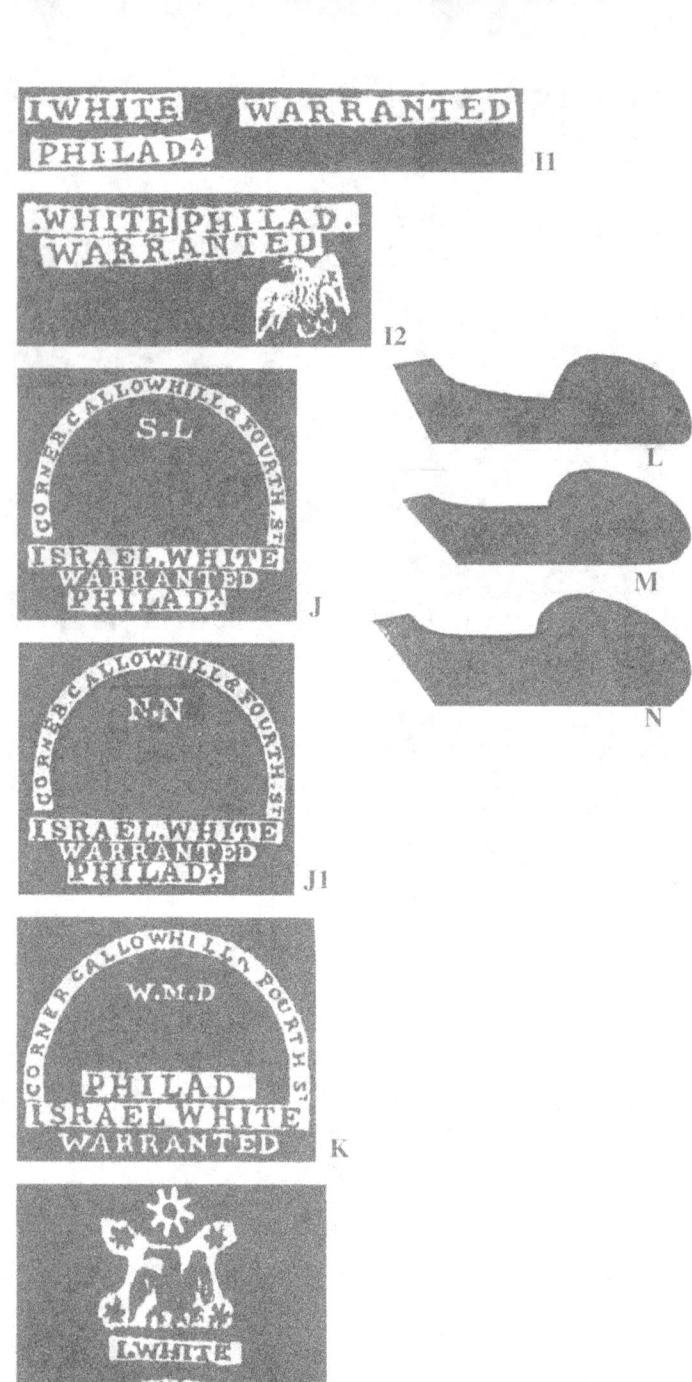

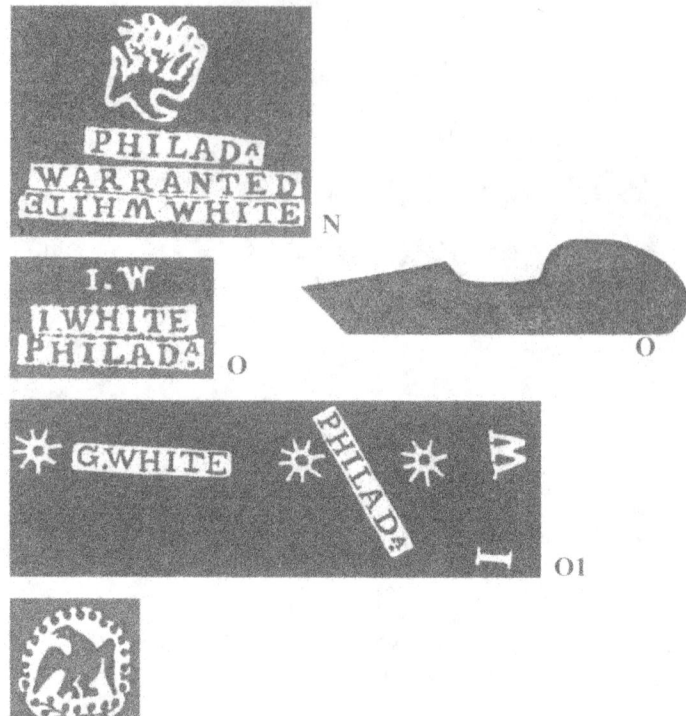

J. WHITE

Jacob White was listed as a planemaker, in Camden, NJ, from 1844-45, at the same address as his father, **Lemuel G. White**, an elocutionist who was the second son of **Jacob White**, the father of **Henry G. White** and **Israel White**. Later, **Jacob White** was listed at the same address as his cousin **Henry G. White**, and may have been working for him.

A, A1, B & C ****

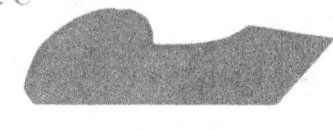

JACOB WHITE

Jacob White (b. 1760, d. July 8, 1833) was the father of **George White** and **Israel White**. He first appeared as a planemaker, in the Philadelphia, PA, directory in 1818 (when he was 58) working in the same location with his son, **George White** and **William Grinnel** as **White & Grinnel**. In 1823, he was listed as a planemaker; in 1825, a hardware merchant; in 1828 & 30 as a planemaker. He displayed his planes at the Franklin Institute fairs of 1830 & 31, and received an honorary mention. At his death, at age 73, he was operating 2 shops, one at Callowhill St. and a two story shop behind his home on Cedar St. His estate inventory listed 3000 finished planes and cut billets for over 9000 more. Also indicated were working places for 32 hands including "**Wheeler**'s bench place", "(James) **Silcock**'s bench place" and "**Israel White**'s bench place".

No imprint has been reported.

J. D. WHITE

J. D. White with the location imprint **WILLIAMSTOWN/ VT.** is on a 15 1/2" fore plane with a **Moulson** iron, ca. 19c. **UR**

JOHN K. WHITE

This medallion is on a 9 1/2" beech rabbet made by **John Bell** and also marked by **G. Mayer**, a hardware dealer in Lancaster, PA, ca. 1850. **UR**

L. & I. J. WHITE

Leonard White (b. Nov. 16, 1810 in Tolland, CT, d. Dec. 31, 1893 in Buffalo, Erie Co., NY) and **Ichabod Jewett White** (b. in CT, d. 1880) were brothers who made planes and edge tools, from 1837-44, in Monroe, MI; and then from 1844-1928, in Buffalo, NY. **L. & I. J. Whites** and **D. R. Barton** of Rochester, were the largest edge tool makers of their time in NY. **A, B, B1 & C *; D *****

N WHITE

Example: on a 9 1/2" beech small hollow with flat chamfers, ca. 1810. **UR**

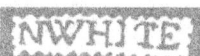

N. WHITE

Examples: on a grooving plane with a riveted skate and round chamfers; a 10" fruitwood rabbet; and a complex molder with flat chamfers, all 9 1/2", ca. 1800. ********

N. WHITE

Nathaniel White (b. Apr. 18, 1826 in Moravia, Cuyahoga Co., NY, d. 1916 in Edinboro, NY) was in Edinboro, in 1844; and opened a cabinetmaker's shop. He was a carpenter and built a number of homes. **Nathaniel** operated a sash mill, at Giles Run. He also bought tools and resold them. The A imprint with **MEADVILLE**, a town south of Erie, PA. Example: The B imprint with **EDENBORO/** (Edinboro) **ERIE. CO** is on a 9 1/2" beech complex molder, ca. 19c; and a 9 1/2" beech dado with 177 imprinted on the heel, an **Auburn Tool Co.** style number. **A & B ******

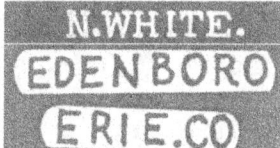

R. WHITE

Examples: the A imprint, with a centered period, is on a 10" birch complex molder with flat chamfers. The larger B imprint with a low period, is on a beech sash plane with a relieved wedge, ca. 1800. **UR**

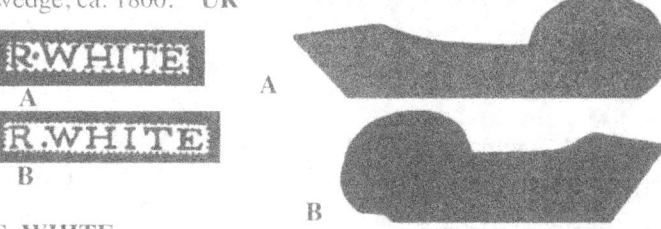

S. WHITE

Examples: on a 9 11/16" ogee complex molder with a relieved wedge; and a 9 1/16" bead, both birch with flat chamfers; a group of nineteen 10" planes including a mother plane, found in Waterbury, CT, with the B wedges, ca. 1790-1800. ********

T. W. WHITE

Possibly **Thomas White**, the son of **Henry G. White**. The imprint of **T. W. White** with the added location imprint of **PHILA.** is on a lignum vitae-boxed molding plane, but is not available. Example: on a 7 1/2" beech plow with brass arm end ferrules, brass depth stop, copper thumbscrews and shallow round chamfers, ca. 1840-50. **UR**

W: WHITE

Possibly **Walter White** (b. Jun. 13, 1765 in Hampden Co., MA, d. Jul. 14, 1819 in Longmeadow, Hampden Co., MA) who was listed as a cabinetmaker, from 1795-1819. Example: on a 9 7/16" birch astragal bead with flat chamfers, ca. 1800. **UR**

W. H. H. WHITE

William Henry Harrison White (b. Mar. 22, 1813 in NJ, d. Oct. 1859 in N. Brunswick, Middlesex Co., NJ) was listed in the 1830's as a planemaker; in 1850, as a carpenter, in New Brunswick, NJ. ********

WHITE & BATES

Possibly **Bates & White**, file makers in Yonkers, NY, about 1870-71. Example: on a pair of beech size 5/8" sash ovolos. **UR**

WHITE & CONANT

White & Conant was a Worcester, MA, hardware firm listed at 542 Main St., from 1880-93. Example: on a match tongue & groove pair

made by **J. F. & G. M. Lindsey**.
A ***; A1 ****

A1

WHITE & GRINNEL
White & Grinnel was a partnership of **George White**, **Jacob White**, and **William Grinnel** listed in the 1818 Philadelphia, PA, directory, as planemakers. A & A1 ****

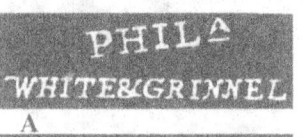
A

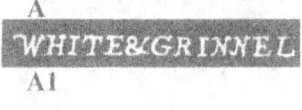
A1

WHITE & SPEAR
White & Spear was a plane making firm in Warren, OH, ca. 1840, consisting of **Charles White** and **Edward Spear** (b. 1795 in PA, d. probate Feb. 18, 1873 in Warren, Trumbull Co., OH) who was listed in the 1850 census, as a sash maker. **Edward Spear** was in Warren, in 1818, started a sash shop in 1848, and sold it in 1862. In 1872, **Edward Spear** was a Justice of Peace in Warren. **

WHITE RIVER WORKS
Possibly from the White River area of VT or the White River of IN that runs thru Indianapolis, IN. Example: on a 9 1/2" beech single-boxed narrow bead, ca. 1850. ****

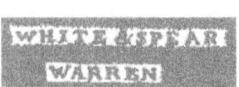

WHITE, VAN GLAHN & CO.
White, Van Glahn & Co. was a New York City hardware dealer, from 1816-1910, and was listed in 1889-90. Example: This imprint as an over-print on a center bead made by **Marten Doscher**. ****

D. J. WHITEMAN
Example: on a 9 3/8" beech skew rabbet with shallow round chamfers, ca. 1830-40. UR

L. WHITING
Examples: on a 10 3/16" birch Yankee plow with thumb-screws, wood depth stop, riveted skate and heavy flat chamfers. The square arms and the depth stop are marked in 1/8" intervals. A second example is on a 10 7/8" birch complex molder found in Prospect, ME. ****

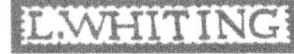

WHITING & SLARK
Whiting & Slark was a New Orleans, LA, hardware firm listed in the city directories from 1832-38, whose partners were **Augustus Whiting** (d. probate Mar. 12, 1873 in New Orleans) and **Robert Slark** (b. ca. 1798 in England, d. Mar. 3, 1868 in New Orleans). **Whiting** started the business in 1824; **Whiting & Slark** was succeeded by **Slark, Day, Shaffer & Co.**, from 1841-55. From 1866-67, the firm was **Slark, Stauffer & Co.**, importers & dealers in hardware, iron & tin plates, etc. ****

A

B

DANIEL D. WHITKER
Daniel D. Whitker (b. 1820 in NY) of Hudson, NY, received Patent No. 52,478, on Feb. 6, 1866, for a saw rabbet weather stripping plane. It had a 10 5/8" beech stock with a closed maple handle and an adjustable saw blade. In 1870, **Daniel** was listed as a carpenter, in NY. In 1889, he was a contractor, in Brooklyn, NY. (see *Patented Transitional & Metallic Planes in America, 1827-1927*, p. 136, by Roger K. Smith)
No imprint has been reported.

A. WHITTLESY

Example: on a 13 1/2" jack plane, ca. 1830-50. UR

J. WHITMAN
Example: a 9 3/8" beech fixed sash with double irons. ca. 1850. UR

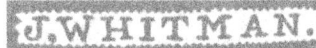

S. WHITMAN
Example: on a 9 1/4" beech astragal with size number **4/8** on the heel, and flat chamfers, ca. 1800. UR

W. WHITMAN
Example: on a 9 1/4"x 1/4" beech grooving plane with flat chamfers, ca. 1800. UR

WHITMAN & BURRELL
Whitman & Burrell was a hardware dealer in Little Falls, NY. Example: on a size 1/8" side bead made by the **Auburn Tool Co.**, marked on the heel. ****

A. WHITMARSH
Two possibilities **Abial Whitmarsh** (b. 1731, d. Mar. 16, 1816 in Dighton, Bristol Co., MA) of Dighton, MA, who was called a joiner and whose probate inventory and probate sale included many tools, including 40 planes. It could be **Asa Whitmarsh**

(b. Jul. 2, 1764 in Bridgewater, Plymouth Co., MA, d. Nov. 26, 1808 in Abington, Plymouth Co., MA) of East Bridgewater, MA, who was described as a housewright, in deeds from 1797-1805. Examples: the A imprint is on molding planes 9 7/8"-11" beech, some with rosewood boxing and heavy flat chamfers to heavy round chamfers; and a 14 3/8" beech double-iron fixed sash with an open tote and heavy flat chamfers, all found in southeastern MA. The B imprint is on a 9 1/2" birch astragal with flat chamfers, ca. 1800-1820. ****

A. C. WHITMARSH

A. C. Whitmarsh was a hardware dealer. Example: on a plow plane made by **G. W. Denison & Co.**, UR

WHITMORE & WOLFF

Whitmore & Wolff was a hardware dealer in Pittsburgh, PA, from 1836-53, with **Michael Whitmore** (b. 1815 in Licking, Clarion Co., PA, d. Jan. 4, 1897 in Clarion Co., PA) and **Christian H. Wolff** (b. Apr. 16, 1815 in Chambersburg, Franklin Co., PA, d. probated Sep. 18, 1885 in Allegheny Co., PA), located at the corner of Liberty and St. Clair Sts. It was succeeded by **Whitmore, Wolff & Co.**, from 1853-58; and then **Whitmore, Wolff, Duff & Co.**, from 1858-72. Example: on a 21" fore plane made by **Union Factory/ H. Chapin**. ***

WHITMORE, WOLFF, DUFF & CO.

Whitmore, Wolff, Duff & Co. was a Pittsburgh, PA, hardware company at 50 Wood, from 1858-72, whose principals were **Michael Whitmore**, **Christian H. Wolff**, and **George H. Duff** (b. Oct. 24, 1821 in Allegeny Co., PA). In 1871, **Whitmore, Wolff, Duff & Co.** was listed as "Importers and Dealers in Hardware". It succeeded **Whitmore, Wolff & Co.** and was succeeded by **Whitmore, Wolff, Lane & Co.**, at 149 Penn, from 1872-78, when **Thomas H. Lane** (b. Aug. 21, 1828 in Chambersburg, PA, d. Dec. 31, 1907 in Pittsburgh, Allegeny Co., PA) became a principal. No imprint has been reported. The company went thru several more name changes and continued until 1912. (see *Planemakers of Western Pennsylvania and Environs*, by Charles W. Prine, Jr.) **

MASON WHITNEY

Mason Whitney made cooper's sun planes exhibited at the Manchester Institute of Arts and Sciences in 1875.
No imprint has been reported.

O. WHITNEY
Examples: on two 8 1/2" coffin smoothers; a 9 1/2"x 2" miter plane; and a molder found in southern CT, all beech, ca. 19c. ****

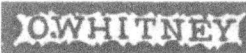

N. WHITTEN
Example: on a 9 1/2" beech large round, ca. 19c. UR

WHITTIER & SPEAR
Whittier & Spear was a plane making partnership in Chelsea (now part of Boston), MA, ca. 1874. **Howard W. Spear** was listed in Chelsea, as a planemaker, from 1874-78. The **CHELSEA** die used was also used by **Spear & Wood**; and then by **Thos. Appleton**, another Chelsea planemaker, starting in 1878. Examples: on several 16" jack planes.
A ***; A1 & A2 *****

A. W/ ARNOLD WICKES
Believed to be **Arnold Wickes** (b. Dec. 28, 1779 in Coventry, Kent Co., RI, d. Sep. 9, 1816 in Coventry) of Coventry, RI, southwest of Providence. The 1810 RI census lists **Arnold Wickes** as living in Coventry. The inventory of the personal estate of "**Arnold Wickes** late of Coventry, Deceased" lists carpentry, turning, and blacksmith tools. Included were "35 small moulding plains" and "two small moulding stocks without irons". Examples: the A1 imprint with **A. W** initials is on a birch 28" jointer. Molding planes are 10" birch with flat chamfers. His wedge finial is similar to that of **I. Lindenberger**, but without the chamfered wedge throat.
A & A1 ****

409

W. WICKLINE
W. Wickline is hand Carved. Example: on a 5" applewood wide crown molder with a centered tote, ca. 19c. **UR**

A. F. WIGHT
Example: on a 9 3/8" beech 1/2" hollow, ca. early 19c. **UR**

S. WIGHT
Example: on an 8 3/8" tiger maple plow with wood thumbscrews and depth stop, a riveted skate, a relieved wedge, and heavy flat chamfers and flutes, ca. 1790. **UR**

M WIGHT/ MAKER
Marvin Wight (b. Jul. 11, 1839 in Centerville, NY, d. Apr. 16, 1929 in Corry, Erie Co., PA) was a wood turner and pattern maker, in Corry. He served in the Civil War, married, and moved to MO. He returned to Corry, in 1870; before moving to Rockford, IL, in 1882. He again returned to Corry, in 1902. He was still working as a pattern maker, at the **Ajax Iron Work**, until a week before his death, at 90. It is likely that this imprint with the added **MAKER** and the location **CORRY. PA.** was made during the 1870-82 period. Examples: on a 11 3/4" large round with an integral handle; a spoke shave; and a router. (see *Planemakers of Western Pennsylvania and Environs*, by Charles W. Prine, Jr.) *********

E. WIGHTMAN
Examples: on a boxed double-bead plane; a 9 1/2" molder; and a 9 7/16" boxed complex molder, all beech. ********

IAMES WIGHTMAN
Example: on a 9 3/8" beech round with flat chamfers, ca. 1800. **UR**

I. WIHARD/ I.W
Example on an 8 1/8" birch single **Weldon** iron compass smoother with flat chamfers, ca. 1800. **UR**

JO: WILBUR/ J. WILBUR
Joshua Wilbur, Jr. (b. 1758 in Swansea, MA, d. 1836 in Exeter, NY) was a housewright in Newport, RI, from 1785-1803. His father, **Joshua Wilbur Sr.** of Swansea, was a loyalist during the American Revolution and was imprisoned "for refusing to take the oath of allegiance to the state." In 1774, at age 16, **Joshua** moved to Providence and was apprenticed to **David Burr**, as a house carpenter. In the 1777 Rhode Island Military Census, **Joshua Wilbur**'s name appears next to **David Burr**'s. In 1778 & 80, **Joshua** served 3 months of active duty in Col. Barton's Regiment of RI Militia during the American Revolution. **Joshua**, returned to Swansea, from 1784-85, where he married in 1784; and a 1786 land deed refers to him "of Swansea, House Carpenter." From 1785-1802, he was a housewright or carpenter builder and planemaker, in Newport. An advertisement in *Newport Mercury*, dated Dec. 10, 1799, indicates that a **William Langley** will sell "a general assortment of joiner's and carpenter's planes, made by **Joshua Wilbur**, late of this town, a constant supply of which he proposes to keep." In 1800, he built a Federal-style, three story house, at 51 Touro Street, Newport. In 1802, he returned to a farm in Swansea; and then in 1805, he made a permanent move to Exeter, Otsego Co., in central NY, near Cooperstown. Examples: the B imprint on a 9 1/2" beech sash plane with round chamfers, found in central NY; a filletster, found near Ithaca; and two bench planes found in upstate NY, all with 19c characteristics with the B1 wedge; and a 10" birch thumbnail plane with flat chamfers & fluting and the B relieved wedge, that is identical to that of **Jo, Fuller**; suggesting that while in Providence, from 1774-84, he may have learned plane making. Example: The A imprint is on a 4 3/4" wide birch crown molder; and a grooving plane. The C imprint with the initial W may be an early **Joshua Wilber** imprint. Little information exists as to the plane the imprint was from. B ***; A & C *****

C. H. WILCOX
Chauncy Wilcox (b. 1820, in NY, d. May 1876 in Toledo, Lucas Co., OH) was listed in 1850, as a planemaker, living in Kingsville, Ashtabula Co., OH. He was married on May 25, 1850, in Trumbull, OH. ********

E. WILCOX
Possibly **Edmund Wilcox** (b. May 25, 1793 in Gilsum, Cheshire Co., NH, d. Aug. 17, 1825 in Swanzey, Cheshire Co.) of Gilsum, NH, a town north of Keene. The *Gazetteer of Cheshire Co., NH 1736-1885* by Hamilton Child, states that **Edmund Wilcox** of Gilsum, was a "farmer and mechanic, manufacturing chairs and all kinds of tools." His probate inventory includes "8 Bench Plains" & "21 Crease Tools", molding planes. Examples: on a 10" beech Yankee plow with thumbscrew-locked square arms; and a 10 1/8" beech complex molder with heavy flat chamfers, from New England, ca. 1780-1800. ********

GEORGE SHELDON WILDER
George Sheldon Wilder (b. Mar. 1, 1828 in Shelburne, Franklin Co., MA, d. Jun. 5, 1900 in Hinsdale, Cheshire Co., NH) was listed in 1860, 65 & 75, as a planemaker, in Hinsdale, NH. He also worked with his uncle **Pliny Merrill**; and in **Merrill & Wilder**; **Wilder & Thompson**, and probably **Wilder & Hopkins**, making edge tools and carpenter's tools. **No imprint has been reported**.

J. WILDER
Possibly **Joshua Wilder** (b. Dec. 12, 1786, d. Oct. 4, 1850 in Hingham, Plymouth Co., MA) was apprenticed, ca. 1799, to **John Bailey** in Hingham, MA. **Joshua** worked as a journeyman cabinetmaker and clockcase maker, working from 1806-60. Examples: on a 9 1/2" thumb molding; a large side bead; a 9 7/16" tongue; and a 14 1/2" panel raiser, all birch with flat chamfers, ca. 1800; on a beech plow with wood screw locked, round top arms, riveted skate, and shallow round chamfers, probably from New England, ca. 1810-20. **A & B: ******

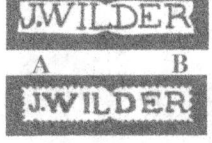 

L. WILDER
Example: on a beech plow with wood screw locked, round top arms, a riveted skate, and shallow round chamfers, ca. 1810-20. **UR**

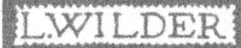

WILEY & FRICK
Wiley & Frick was a Jonesboro, IL, hardware dealer, no dates known. Example: on a wide bead made by the **Ohio Tool Co.**, ca. 1850. ********

I. WILKINS
Example: on a 9 3/8" spill plane with heavy flat chamfers, ca. early 19c. **UR**

A. J. WILKINSON/ A. J. WILKINSON & CO.
A. J. Wilkinson & Co. was a prominent Boston, MA, hardware company, active from 1842-1973. It started with **Andrew J. Wilkinson** (b. 1815 in Boston, Soffolk Co., MA, d. Sep. 27, 1881 in Boston) located at 18 Dock Sq., from 1842-45; in 1846, he moved to 2 Washington St.; in 1859, **William F. Haven** (b. Apr. 10, 1812, d. Feb. 13, 1882 in Northborough, Worcester Co., MA) became a partner in what became **A. J. Wilkinson & Co.**; in 1882, **Andrew J. Wilkinson & Co.**, with **W. H. Wilkinson**, hardware & tools, at 184 to 188 Washington. Example: the C imprint is the earliest, and has been found as an overstamp on a 1 1/4" nosing plane made by **A. Cumings**. Most wooden planes were made by **Addison Heald**. **A & B ***; **C ****

T. E. WILKS
Example: on a 9 5/16" beech Grecian ogee with heavy round chamfers, ca. 1830. **UR**

I. WILL
Examples: on a 9 1/2" table hollow with flat chamfers, found in central OH; a 12 1/4" open tote hollow; and a beech plane with the two eagles and heavy round chamfers, found in PA. ********

 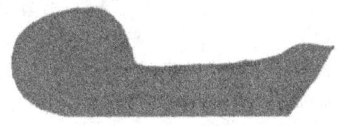

J. WILL
Example: on an 8" compass smoother with an **Ohio Tool Co.** iron, ca. 19c. **UR**

S. WILLARD Jr.
Simon Willard, Jr. (b. Jan. 13, 1795 in Roxbury, MA, d. Aug. 24, 1874 in Boston, MA) was the son of a noted clockmaker **Simon Willard** (1770-1854), who patented a banjo clock in 1802. **Simon Willard** worked at Washington Street in Roxbury. He retired in 1839. **Simon Willard, Jr.** was a student at the U. S. Military Academy, from 1813-15. In 1816, he resigned his army commission and was in the crockery-ware business until 1824. From 1824-26, he worked in his father's shop, then moved to Boston, at 9 Congress Street, until 1870. In 1850, his son **Zabdiel A. Willard** was admitted to the partnership and marked his clocks **Simon Willard & Son.**. In addition to a line of Banjo clocks, he made the astronomical clock now in the observatory of Harvard University. This for many years provided the standard time, for all New England railroads. Example: on a 9 1/2" beech complex molder, ca. mid-19c. *********

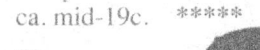
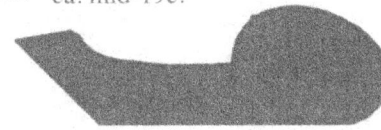

S. WILLCOX
Solomon Wilcox (b. Jun. 15, 1805, m. Mar. 27, 1825 in Foster, Providence Co., RI, d. Mar. 27, 1893 in Foster), in 1850, he was listed as a house carpenter; in 1860, he was listed as a carpenter, in Scituate, RI; in 1870, a farmer in Scituate. Examples: on a 9 15/16" x 1 1/8" tiger maple rabbet, marked twice on the toe with flat chamfers; a tiger maple bench plane with offset tote and flat chamfers; a 9 3/8" fruitwood double-iron fixed sash plane with round chamfers on top and square chamfers on toe and heel; a 9 9/16" birch complex molder with round chamfers; a 10 3/8" apple Yankee plow with wood thumbscrews, a wood depth stop, riveted skate and round chamfers; and on a 10" beech having plane with flat chamfers that stops in a slopping line and a long tapered turnout, ca. 1825-35. ********

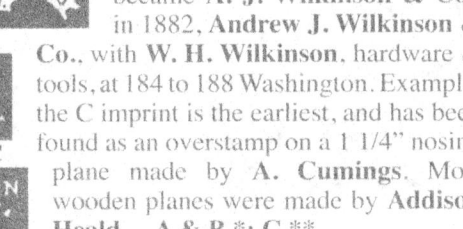
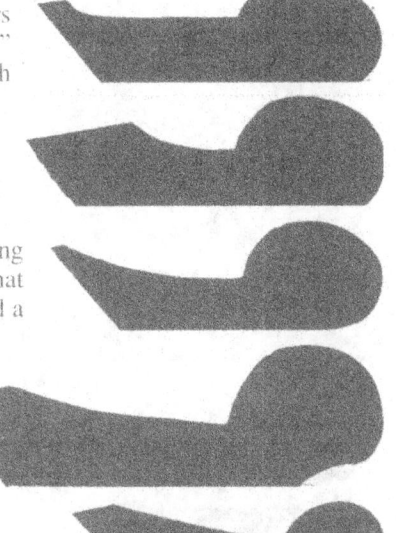

C. WILLE
Possibly **Calvin Willey** (b. Aug. 8, 1769 in East Haddam, Middlesex Co., CT, d. 1830 in New Haven, Addison Co., VT) who trained in Colchester, CT; and moved to Lenox, in western MA. Between 1800-30, he was a carpenter in New Haven, VT. Examples: on a 10" beech bead with heavy flat chamfers; and an 8 1/2" apple coping plane with round chamfers on top and flat chamfers on front and rear with flutes, ca. 1800-20. **UR**

ISAAC WILLEY
Examples: on a 15"x 2 1/2" handled crown molder with "Phila. Style Boxing"; a 9 1/2"x 2" birch smoother; a complex molder, and a beech side bead, ca. 1790. ****

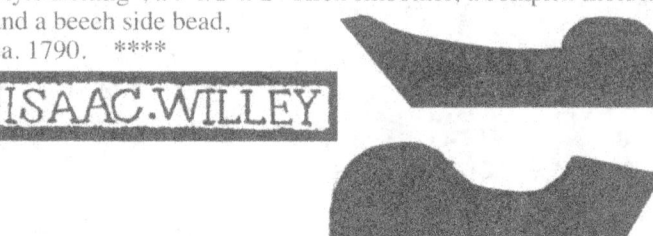

WILLIAMS
Example: on a 9 3/8" beech match tongue plane with narrow flat chamfers, ca. 1800. **UR**

G. WILLIAMS
George Williams (b. Jan. 1808 in NJ, d. Nov. 20, 1884 in Newark, Essex Co., NJ) was listed in Newark, NJ, from 1837-38, as an edge tool maker, at State near Broad St. From 1850-70, as an edge tool maker; in 1880, worked in tool shop. Examples: on 9 7/8" & 9 5/8" beech complex molders, both with flat chamfers, ca. 1810. This imprint may represent an earlier involvement in plane making. **UR**

STEPHEN WILLIAMS
Stephen Williams received Patent No. 43,360, on June 28, 1864, for a "universal plane". The plane features an 8 3/8", cast iron housing to hold a single cutter and wedge and eight vertical beech blocks secured by a brass U-shaped band with a tightening screw. Stamped on the left side is:

**WILLIAMS
UNIVERSAL- PLANE
PAT'D. JUNE 28, 1864**

(see *Patented Transitional & Metallic Planes in America- Vol II*, p. 75, by Roger K. Smith)

W. WILLIAMS
William Williams (d. 1848) made planes in New York City, from 1807-48, listed as plane manufacturer, at Elm c. Anthony; In 1810, a plane manufacturer, at 45 Magazine; in 1815-35, a plane manufacturer, at 528 Pearl; in 1839-48, a plane manufacturer, at 524 Pearl; in 1849-50, as "Late Planemaker". **B *; A & B1 ***

WILLIAM WILLIAMS
William Williams (b. ca. 1807, d. 1872 in Remsen, Oneida Co., NY) was listed in the Utica, NY, from 1845-67, as a planemaker; and in the 1845-47, as boarding with **John Ree**. From 1850-70, **Williams** was listed, as a carpenter, in Rome, Oneida Co. **No imprint has been reported**.

WILLIAMS RICH & CO.
Williams Rich & Co. was a hardware dealer, in Worcester, MA.

Example: on a **H. Wells** size **19** hollow. A similar imprint has been reported with the location **AMHERST MASS** but is not available. ****

A. WILLIAMSON
Example: on a 9 1/2" beech bead, ca. mid 19c. **UR**

WILLIAMSON/ D. WILLIAMSON
David Williamson (b. Jun. 6, 1808 in NJ, m. May 22, 1833 in Cincinnati, Hamilton Co., OH, d. Jan. 8, 1878 in Hamilton Co., OH) moved with his family, at age 6, to Colerain Township, Hamilton Co., OH. He was listed as an edge tool maker, at the corner of Gano & Miller, in Cincinnati, OH, in 1839-40. He apparently made or dealt in planes as well. In 1850, he was listed as a farmer. Example: the B imprint is on a 9 3/8" beech complex molder with round chamfers. **A & B ****

WILLIAMSON/ JOSEPH WILLIAMSON
Joseph Williamson advertised in the *Liberty Hall* newspaper dated: Cincinnati, Jul. 16, 1810, that "he still continues to made PLANES of every kind,at his f(s)t and in Water Street, near Squire Marhard's. Cabinet-Making carried on in the same shop." This ad appeared in 6 consecutive weekly issues. **Joseph Williamson** first appears in a petition, of Jul. 13, 1799, of citizens of Hamilton Co. Cincinnati is located in Hamilton Co., OH. The imprint **WILLIAMSON** with the location **CINCINNATI, has been reported but is not available**.

T. WILLINS
Example: on a 9 1/4" beech hollow with heavy round chamfers, ca. 1820-30. **UR**

DAVID WILLIS
David Willis (b. 1815, d. May 10, 1883 in Newark, NJ) was listed as a planemaker, in the 1837-38, at 162 Plane St., Newark, NJ. This was the same address as **Timothy B. Noe**, possibly a residence. **No imprint has been reported.**

WILLIS THRALL & SON/ WILLIS THRALL & SONS
Willis Thrall & Son was a tool store in Hartford, CT, and followed by **Willis Thrall & Sons, Tool Store** at No. 10 Central Row, Hartford, CT. Example: on a **Union Factory/ H. Chapin** single-boxed side bead, stamped in ink on the side: ****

FROM
WILLIS THRALL & SON
TOOLSTORE
NO. 76 CENTRAL ROW
HARTFORD, CONN.

I. WILLS

Example: on a 10" beech complex molder with flat chamfers, ca. 1800-10. **UR**

C. WILLSON
Possibly **Clark Willson** (b. Jun. 13, 1800 inn Alstead, Cheshire Co., NH, d. Dec. 13, 1840, Worcester, Worcester Co., MA) who

was listed in the 1830-40 census for Worcester, MA, but with no indication of an occupation. Example: on a 23" fore plane, ca. 1840-50. **UR**

W. WILLSON
Example: on a 9 1/2"x 2 1/4" complex molder with flat chamfers, ca. 1800. **UR**

M. P. WILMARTH
Moses Pratt Wilmarth (bapt. Oct. 22, 1820 in Attleboro, MA, m. Sep. 21, 1829 in Attleboro, d. 1864 in Attleboro) worked for **S. Cummings**; and witnessed a land sale in 1837, at age 17, in Attleboro, MA. He moved to and made planes in Central Falls, ca. 1840-44. Central Falls is located north of Providence, RI. He was listed as a machinist, in Attleboro, until 1865. Examples: on various hollow & round molding planes, ca. 1840. **A & A1 ****

(HEART) WILSON
Williams Wilson (b. Jul. 3, 1820, d. Dec. 15, 1889 in Allegheny Co., PA) was a planemaker, listed in the Pittsburgh, PA, directories, from 1847-63; and in the 1860 census. The owner imprint of **A. Easly** appears on a 2 3/4" cornice plane, **A. Easly** was a carpenter, with a shop in Allegheny, during the 1850-60's. The "Heart" imprint was also used by **William Evens**, one of the earliest Pittsburgh makers, from whom **Wilson** may have learned plane making. In the 1863-66 directories, he was listed as a carpenter; in 1870, he was listed as farmer, in Pittsburgh, Allegheny Co.   ****

A. WILSON
Example: on an applewood plow dated **1842**; a 1" wide ogee moulder, dated **1841**; a applewood razee joiner struck twice on the toe with a strike button and dated **1847**. **UR**

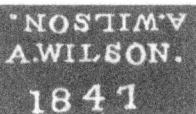

A: WILSON
Example: on a 16 1/2" beech panel raiser with open tote, a skewed **W. Butcher/ Sheffield** iron, and flat chamfers, ca. early 19c. **UR**

B. WILSON
Examples: on a 9 7/16"x 1/2" beech hollow; and a 9 3/8"x 2" beech size **15** round, both with flat chamfers, ca. 1800-10. **UR**

C. WILSON
Cyrus Wilson (b. Mar. 3, 1784 in Pelham, NH, m. Apr. 28, 1807 in Dracut, MA, d. Oct. 1824 in Dracut, prob. Nov. 9, 1824, Middlesex Co., MA) who was listed in the 1810-20 censuses, for Dracut, MA, 25 miles northwest of Boston. Example: on a 16"x 3 1/16" beech forkstaff plane with round chamfers; a gutter plane; and a 22" beech jointer, the jointer and forkstaff planes have **James Cam** irons, ca. 1820-40. ****

D. WILSON
Example: on a 9 7/8"x 2" beech skew rabbet with heavy round chamfers, ca. 1820. **UR**

GEO. D. WILSON, JON. D. LAUBACH/ G. WILSON/ G. WILSON & J. LAUBACK
George D. Wilson (b. Feb. 20, 1941) is a contemporary master tool maker, who organized the Machine Shop at Colonial Williamsburg, VA. He and **John D. Laybach** make the 18c. style hand tools that are used in the craft shops of Colonial Williamsburg. **George Wilson** started in 1970 and retired after 36 years. **A, B, C, D: UR**

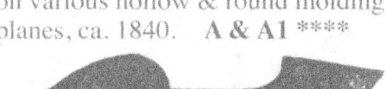

WILSON/ H. WILSON
Henry Wilson made planes in New York City from 1852-54, after having been a sawmaker. He was a tool dealer, from 1855-56. Example: the B imprint is on a size 7/8" dado, with a brass thumbscrew depth adjustment. **A, A1 & B ****

I. WILSON
Example: on a 9 1/2" beech table hollow with the iron set at a York pitch, a hickory wedge and flat chamfers; ca. 1810.   **UR**

J. WILSON
Example: on a 14 1/2" wedge-lock grooving plane with a snecked iron, found near Intercourse, PA; a 9 15/16" large hollow with a molded shoulder; a 9 3/4" beech wedge-lock fenced rabbet; and a smoother, all beech with heavy flat chamfers, later, from eastern PA, ca. 1800.   ****

J. WILSON
Example: on a 9 1/8" beech single-boxed complex molder with shallow round chamfers, ca. 1840.   **UR**

J. WILSON

Example: on a 26" beech jointer with a round strike and shallow round chamfers, ca. 1830.   ****

J. A. WILSON
Example: on a 9 3/8" beech size 14 hollow, ca. 1850.   **UR**

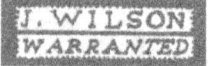

Jn WILSON
Jn Wilson in script in the makers slot with **W. WILSON** as an owners imprint. Example: on a pair of 9 3/8" match planes with round chamfers, ca. 19c.   **UR**

J.W/ WILSON/ JO. WILSON

The dot over the **I** in **WILSON** is a small heart. Example: on a 9 5/8" birch hollow with round chamfers. The **JO. WILSON** is branded on the side of the plane, ca. 19c.   **UR**

N: WILSON
Example: on a 10" cherry complex molder with heavy round chamfers, found in southern PA with a group of Baltimore planes, probably mid Atlantic, ca. 1820.   **UR**

R. WILSON
Example: on a 9 1/2" beech large hollow with flat chamfers, ca. 1800.   **UR**

WILLARD WILSON
Example: on a 14 1/8" x 2 3/8" birch jack with an offset open tote, an iron strike, single iron bed, iron and wedge missing, heavy round chamfers on the top and flat chamfers on the ends, ca. 1800.   **UR**

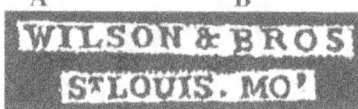

WILSON & BROS.
Wilson & Bros. was a St. Louis, MO. hardware firm, active from 1842-47, consisting of **William Knox Wilson** (b. Aug. 2, 1817 in MD, d. Oct. 4, 1892 in St. Louis, MO) and **Samuel Knox Wilson** (b. 1819 in Baltimore, MD, m. Apr. 27, 1843 in St. Louis, MO, d. 1869 in St. Louis). When **Lafayette N. Wilson** (b. 1830 in MD, m. Jan. 26, 1852 in St. Louis, MO) joined the firm in 1847, it became **Wilson Bros. & Co.** Sometime between 1859-60, it was changed again to **Wilson Brother & Co.**. in 1865, **William K. Wilson & Co.** was listed as hardware & cutlery, at 39 N. Main St., Louis; in 1867, at 220 N. Main St.   **A & B ****

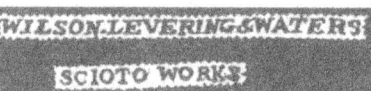

WILSON, LEVERING & WATERS
Wilson, Levering & Waters, also known as **Wilson, Levering & Waters Co.**, was a hardware dealer in St. Louis, MO, from 1859-69. One of the **Wilsons** of **Wilson Bros. & Co.** was probably involved. **E. C. Simmons** (b. 1829 in Frederick, MD, d. Apr. 18, 1920 in St. Louis, MO) reportedly worked for them until taking over the company, in 1869, as **E. C. Simmons Hdw. Co.**. The **SCIOTO WORKS** brand name was not used by **Ohio Tool Co.**, until ca. 1893. The connection with its use here is unknown. ****

J. WIMER
Examples: on a 10" beech nosing plane; and complex molder, both with flat chamfers, found in PA, ca. 1800.

B. WINCHESTER
Example: a 7 7/16" birch coffin smoother with a single iron, and a 9 7/16" birch narrow astragal, ca. 1800, probably from New England.   **UR**

J. WINCHESTER
Example: on a 14"x 3 1/4" beech open-toted cornice plane with heavy round chamfers, ca. 1820-30. **UR**

WINCHESTER
 **WINCHESTER** with **TRADE MARK** and **MADE IN U.S.A.** on the side of a Gothic bead. ca 19c. **UR**

WINCHESTER TOOL CO.
Example: on a 18 3/4" applewood skew rabbet with centered doubled pegged open tote, and small round chamfers, ca. 19c. **UR**

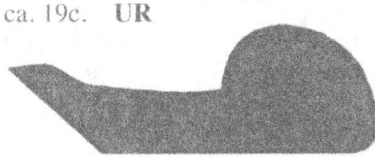

E + WING
Example: on a 9 1/2" birch complex molder with a relieved wedge and flat chamfers, possibly from New England, ca. 1800. **UR**

S W
Samuel Wing (b. Oct. 12, 1774 in Barnstable Co., MA, m. May 8, 1799 in Hembroke, Plymouth Co., MA, d. Feb. 24, 1854 in Sandwich, Barnstable Co.) was a furniture maker from Sandwich, MA, who was active, from 1797-1810. In the 1960's, Old Sturbridge Village acquired the surviving workshop of **Samuel Wing**. Examples: among the collection at Old Sturbridge village, all marked **SW**; on a 23" beech jointer with round chamfers, dated **1800**; a 22" beech fore plane with round chamfers; two spar planes with single-irons and flat chamfers; a smoothing plane with round chamfers and a double iron, dated **1806**; two 9 1/2" birch complex molder with flat chamfers, one dated **1798**, another dated **1799**; a 9 7/16"x 1/2" beech match pair with flat chamfers; a 16 1/2" beech jack with an offset birch tote and flat chamfers; a 29" beech jointer with a closed cherry tote, single **NEWBOLD** iron, flat chamfers, dated **1800**; and a 31" lignum vitae jointer with birch offset closed tote, and a bone strike button, dated **1797**. ****

S. WING
Example: on a 15" open-toted birch sash with slight flat chamfers, found on the CT/ MA border area, probably from Southern New England, ca. 1800. **UR**

Z. WING
Example: on a 10" beech bead with a relieved wedge and flat chamfers, ca. 1790-1800. **UR**

B. WINSLOW
Example: on a 9 5/8" birch molder with a beech relieved wedge and heavy flat chamfers, ca. 1790. **UR**

J. H. WINSLOW
James Hall Winslow (b. Oct. 5, 1817 in Noblesboro, Lincoln Co., ME) was a carpenter and probably also a planemaker, in Thomaston, Knox Co., ME, from 1842-65. He married in 1842. In 1840, he was listed in Noblesboro; and was listed in the 1850-70, working in Thomaston, as a carpenter and joiner.

 Examples: on an 18"x 3 1/2" beech crown with a **Dwight French & Co.** iron; and a spar plane. ****

N. WINSLOW
Example: on a 10" birch complex molder with heavy round chamfers possibly from New England, ca. 1820. **UR**

WINSTED PLANE CO./ WINSTED PLANE & L CO.
The **Winsted Plane Co.**'s certificate of incorporation, dated Dec. 23, 1837, states as the corporate purpose "to manufacture and deal in all kinds of joiners tools, sash blinds, doors, and all kinds of lumber". Winsted, CT, directories list the company as a maker of joiner's tools, from 1851-56. Examples: the A imprint is on a 16" & an 18" jack plane. The B imprint with the added **& L**, which stands for lever. **A *; B *****

W. WINTKLE
W. Wintkle was probably a planemaker, in Cincinnati, OH, active ca. 1840, but was not listed in the directories. Example: on a boxed bead with heavy round chamfers. **A & A1 *****

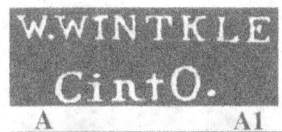
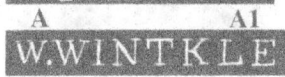

C. WIRE
Examples: on a 15 1/2" jack; and a 22 1/2" jointer, both with a **W. Butcher**, warranted cast steel irons. **UR**

J. WIRTS/ IOHN WIRT
Examples: The A imprint is on a 9 3/4" beech complex molder. The B imprint is on a 9 5/16" round with an owner imprint, **T. MENAICH**, branded on the side,

both beech with heavy flat chamfers, found in south eastern PA, ca. 1780-1800. **A & B: UR**

LUCIUS B. WISE

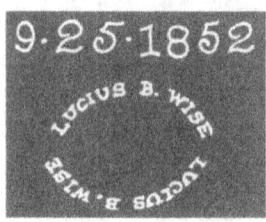

Example: on a 14 1/2" beech corner-boxed skew filletster with a centered tote, struck twice to form an oval with the incuse date **9. 25. 1852**, ca. 1850. **UR**

WISEMAN & ROSS

Wiseman and **William C. Ross** were planemakers, in Baltimore, MD, at 56 Light St., from 1842-43. **William C. Ross** (m. Nov. 25, 1847, Baltimore Co.) worked for himself from 1849-69. *******

D. WITWER

There was a **Daniel Witwer** and a **David Witwer** who were carpenters, in Lancaster, PA. Example: on a common (unhandled) 7 7/16" beech wood screw-arm plow plane, ca. mid-19c. **No imprint is available**.

E. WNTER

Example: on a beech plow plane with wood screw secured arms and depth stop, ca. 1820. **UR**

G. WOLCOTT

Gideon Wolcott Jr. (b. Jun. 30, 1805 in CT, m. Jun. 27, 1830, East Windsor, Hartford Co., CT, d. Mar. 31, 1867 in Clarkson, Monroe, NY) made planes on his own in New Haven, CT, in 1828. He moved to Utica, NY, where he made planes for and boarded with **L. Kennedy**, from 1828-29; and then for himself ca. 1832. He was listed as a planemaker, in the 1832 Utica, NY directory. *******

WOLFE DASH & FISHER

Examples: the A imprint is on a 9 11/16" tongue plane. The B imprint is on a beech smoothing plane with a **Baldwin** iron, ca. 1850. **A & B ******

WOLFE, GILLESPIE & CO.

Example: on a 21 3/4" beech jointer with the added location imprint **NEW YORK**, ca. 1850. **No imprint is available.**

B. WOLFF, JR

Bernard Wolff Jr. (b. Mar. 26, 1828, d. Apr. 22, 1901 in Pittsburgh, Allegheny Co., PA) was a hardware dealer in Pittsburgh, PA, from 1858-70. He succeeded **Wolff & Lane**, ca. 1850-58; and was succeeded by **Lane Brothers** with **Augustus H. Lane** (b. Apr. 1, 1838, d. Jan. 23, 1896 in Pittsburgh), and brother **Thomas H. Lane** (b. 1840 in PA), from 1870-78; then **Wolff & Lane**, from 1878-1906; and finally **Wolff-Lane Hardware Company**, from 1906-12. **A & B: *****

WOLFF & LANE

Wolff & Lane was a Pittsburgh, PA, hardware company, from 1850-58, at Liberty & St. Clair Sts.; with **Bernard Wolff Jr.** and **A. H. Lane**. From 1858-78, the name was changed to **B. Wolff, Jr. & Co.**. In 1878, the name was revived as **Wolff & Lane** with different family members involved; and used until 1906 when incorporated as **Wolff-Lane Hardware Company**, from 1906-12. *******

A W/ ADAM WOLFORD

Example: on a 11 1/2"x 3 5/8" birch crown molder with an offset tote, flat chamfers, and struck twice on toe, possibly from PA, ca. 1800. **UR**

S: J. WONNACOTT

Example: on a 13 1/4" birch jack with single round top iron, offset beech open tote and heavy round chamfers, ca. 19c. **UR**

WOOD

Example: on a 10" molder with flat chamfers, ca. early 19c. **UR**

A. D. WOOD

Augustus D. Wood (b. Dec. 3, 1824 in VT, d. Jan. 1, 1879, Indianapolis, IN) was a hardware merchant in Lafayette, IN, ca. 1850. From 1858-59, **Wood Hardware** was at 77 E. Washington St. Indianapolis. From 1860-61, **Henry S. Kellogg** worked as a salesman, in **A. D. Wood's City Hardware Store**. In 1861-62, **A. D. Wood** operated two hardware stores, one at 71 E. Washington St., at the sign of the big pad-lock. The other was at 12 W. Washington St. **A. D. Wood** served in the Civil War, enrolled Jul. 9, 1863, Co. G, 107 Reg., from Indianapolis, IN. By 1867, he was listed as a capitalist. In 1870, he was listed as a real-state agent in Indianapolis. Example: The A imprint is on a plow, ca. 1850. **A & B *****

BENJAMIN WOOD
Benjamin Wood was listed, as a planemaker, in Utica, NY 1828 directory, residing with **L. Kennedy**. He was listed in Cincinnati, OH, from 1831-34. **No imprint has been reported**.

I + WOOD
Example: on an 8 7/8" birch molder; and a 9" fruitwood narrow rabbet with a birch wedge, both with shallow flat chamfers, found in Jewett City, CT, ca. 1790. **UR**

I. WOOD
Examples: all 9 1/2" beech complex molding planes with **I. Sleeper** style wedges; and a boxed beading plane; both with flat chamfers, ca. early 19c. **UR**

J. WOOD
Examples: on a fruitwood shipbuilder's jack with a round wedge; a beech skew rabbet; a complex molder; a 9 1/2" birch tongue plane; and a birch jack plane with a diamond strike, all with heavy flat chamfers, ca. 1800-10. ********

J. WOOD

J. Wood was a Watertown, NY, planemaker, ca. 1850. Example: on a round. **A, A1, B & B1 ****

S. WOOD
Examples: The A imprint is on a 9 1/2" beech double-iron coping plane. The B imprint is on a 9 3/4" beech moving fillester, with iron depth stop on the side, nicker, a adjustable bottom fence, and a skew iron, ca. 1820. **A & B: UR**

WOOD/ T. J. WOOD/ WOOD'S TOOL STORE
Thomas J. Wood operated a tool store, at No. 7 Chambers St., New York City, from 1831-42, and at 62 Chatham St., from 1843-55. **A, B, B1, B2, B3 & C *****

WATSON WOOD
Watson Wood (b. 1833 in England, m. 1875 in Chelsea, MA) was listed as a planemaker, in Chelsea, from 1874 & 78; in 1884, as a brush maker, in Chelsea; in 1891-93, as a brush maker, in Malden, MA. **Mrs. Watson Wood** was a music teacher in Malden; in 1897, **Watson Wood** was listed as "musical instrument strings", at 51 N. Market, Boston, MA. From 1888-1900, **Watson Wood** was listed as a machinist, at 51 N. Market. **No imprint has been reported**.

W W/ WOOD
William Wood (b. Mar. 4, 1687 in Middlesex Co. MA, M. 1715 in MA, d. Jan. 2, 1733/4 in Concord, Middlesex Co.) was a carpenter in Concord. Examples: the **WW** initials were branded into the side of a 12" square rabbet. The **WOOD** imprint is on a 12" complex molder, made by the same hand, and found together, both beech with large shallow flat chamfers, ca. early 1700's. **A & B *******

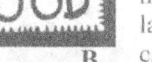

W/ W. WOOD
Examples: on a 10" beech complex molder with flat chamfers; and a 9 1/2"x 2 1/4" beech complex molder, ca. 1800. **UR**

W. WOOD
William Wood (b. 1824 in VT, d. Jul. 21, 1862 in Hartford, CT.) was listed in 1850 as a plane maker in Wallingford, CT, living with **Joel Fenn**. **No imprint has been reported**.

W. W. WOOD/ W. W. WOOD & CO.
William W. Wood (b. 1828 in Pamelia, Jefferson Co., NY, d. Dec. 12, 1875 in Watertown, Jefferson Co., NY) was listed as a planemaker, in the 1850 & 60 census, in the town of Pamelia, a few miles north of Watertown; as a joiner, in Watertown, NY, from 1855-59; and as a partner with **Albert L. Gleason** (b.

1829 in NY) with **Gleason & Wood**. In 1850, **Gleason** was listed as a toolmaker. In 1863-65, **Wood** formed a partnership with **Stewart Smith**, also a toolmaker and carpenter, as **Wood & Smith**. From 1865-70, he was listed as a tool manufacturer under the names **Wm. W. Wood**, **Wm. W. Wood & Co.**, and then **Wm. W. Wood & Bro.**.

A, B & C **

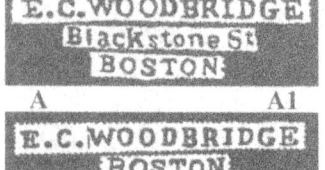
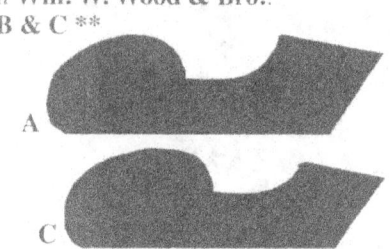

E. C. WOODBRIDGE
Edwin C. Woodbridge made planes, at 86 Blackstone, Boston, MA, in 1851-52. He was a part of **Montgomery & Woodbridge**, in 1847. The E. C. is a separate die, and the **WOODBRIDGE** was part of the **MONTGOMERY & WOODBRIDGE** die.

A & A1 **

CHARLES WOODBURY
Charles Woodbury (b Jan. 3, 1809 in Salem, Rockingham Co., NH, d. Jun. 20, 1891 in Hyde Park, Suffolk Co., MA) was listed as a machinist, in Boston, MA, in 1850, with one employee and making $1000 worth of planes. **No imprint has been reported**.

O. WOODCOCK
Example: on a plow with a fence and a steel depth stop, both secured by wood thumbscrews, a fancy toe on the skate, and heavy round chamfers. ca. 1820-30. **UR**

R. WOODFORD & CO.
Romeo Woodford (b. Jan. 3, 1820 in Owego, Tioga Co., NY, d. Jul. 8, 1856 in Owego) and Bissell Woodford (b. Oct. 23, 1816 in Owego, Tioga Co., NY, d. May 19, 1897 in Owego) were hardware dealers and tinsmiths, in Owego, NY, from 1839-55. In 1865, **Bissell** was listed as a farmer, in Owego. ***

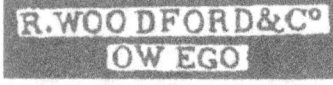

B. F. WOODMAN
Benjamin F. Woodman (b. Jul. 13, 1845 in Brentwood, NH, d. Feb. 15, 1928 in Brentwood, NH) was a carpenter and Joiner, in Fremont, Rockingham Co., NH, from 1872-82. Example: on a 12 1/4" beech miter plane with a steel sole. ****

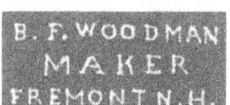

S. WOODMAN
S. Woodman with **S+W** on the side of the body and an owner imprint of **D MAN**. Example: on a 9 1/2" square rabbet with flat chamfers. ca. 1800. **UR**

W. WOODMAN
Example: on a 10 1/8" beech fenced rabbet with flat chamfers, ca. 1800. **No imprint is available**.

WOODRUFF
The **WOODRUFF** die appears to have been made from the **C. Woodruff** die, the location die **NEW ALBANY, Ia.**, with the low **a.** appears to have been used by **S. P. Woodruff**; and the **WARRANTED** die was used by **C. Woodruff**. ****

A. S. WOODRUFF
Alexander Sanders Woodruff (b. 1815 in Newark, Essex Co., NJ, d. Mar. 29, 1886 in Louisville, Jefferson Co., KY) was the son of **C. Woodruff**; and was a hardware dealer and plane manufacturer, at Pearl bt. Main & Market, in Louisville, KY, from 1844-46. From 1848-49, the company was **Woodruff & McBride**, at 53 3rd. bt. Main & Market; and in 1851-52, as **Woodruff & Evans**, edge tool manufacture, on west side of Floyd between Main & Washington. **Woodruff** learned the hardware business from **John Rust**. Before 1848, he had three plane making employees: **Richard Cox**, **Martin C. Winslow** and **Solomon Cook**. In 1848-48, **Alexander** was a partner in **Woodruff & McBride**. In 1851-52, the firm was **Woodruff & Evans**. In 1860 & 70, **Alexander** was listed as a Clerk with **M. Halbert & Co.**. In 1877, he was listed as a Bookkeeper for **W. L. Weller & Son**. In 1879-80, **Alexander** was listed as "Gov. (Goverment) Whisky Gauger at the U. S. Custom House". In 1886, he was Secretary, S. Baptist Theological Seminary, Louisville. Examples: The A imprint is on a 9 3/8"x 3/4" beech match tongue & groove pair with shallow round chamfers, ca. 1844-46. The B imprint is on a 9 1/2" beech match grooving plane. The B1 imprint is on a 9 9/16" beech size **7** round plane, both ca. 1850-60 **A, B & B1** ****

An advertisement reads:
ALEX S. WOODRUFF
Dealer in American and Foreigh
HARDWARE
and manufacturer of
PLANES of all Kinds.
east side Pearl between
Main and Market St

C. WOODRUFF
Charles Woodruff (b. ca. Sep. 2, 1790 in Elizabeth, Union Co., NJ, m. Sep. 4, 1828 in New Albany, Floyd Co., IN, d. Jan. 17, 1847 in New Albany) was the father of **Stephen P. Woodruff**

and **Alexander Sanders Woodruff**. **Charles** was one of five incorporators of New Albany, in 1817. He advertised as a planemaker, in New Albany, IN, in an Oct. 21, 1820 ad in *The Chronicle*: "If the general pressure of the times effects the merchants generally as it does the subscriber, they will find it to their advantage to use more planes, and his reduced prices will make it an object for them to give him a call". **C. Woodruff** appeared as a hardware dealer in 1856-57, on High between 1st. & 2nd., in the New Albany city directory. ***

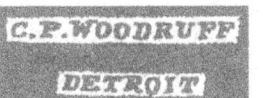

C. P. WOODRUFF
Charles Pierson Woodruff (b. Dec. 4, 1810 in Seneca Falls, Seneca Co., NY, d. Dec. 21, 1901 in Detroit, Wayne Co., MI) moved to Detroit, in 1845, and ran a hardware store, at 91 Woodward Ave.; in 1850 & 60, he was listed as a merchant; in 1870, as a land agent and involved in insurance. In 1900, his occupation was listed as capitalist. Example: on a 9 1/2"x 1 7/8" beech skew rabbet. ****

E. WOODRUFF
Examples: a 10 1/4"x 3/4" beech complex molder with tight round top chamfers and flat chamfers on the toe and heel; and a 11 3/4" birch crown molder struck twice, with an extreme offset tote and flat chamfers. ca. 1790-1800. **UR**

R. WOODRUFF
The **WOODRUFF** imprint is the same as in **C. Woodruff** with an incuse **R** added. Example: on a 9 3/8" beech combination lounge & groove plane (coming and going) with 2 irons & wedges. The plane is also overstamped with **McKINNELL & Co.** and a location **CINCINATTI**, ca. 19c. **A & A1**: ****

S. P. WOODRUFF
Stephen P. Woodruff (b. 1814 in NJ, d. Dec. 28, 1891 in Waveland, Montgomery Co., IN) was the son of **Charles Woodruff**. He was listed in 1850, as a carpenter, in New Albany, IN; in 1860, **he was listed** as a master carpenter, in Perry, Martin Co., IN; in 1870, as a carpenter, in Brown, Montgomery Co, IN; in 1880, as a carpenter, in Waveland, Montgomery Co. ***

T. WOODRUFF
T. Woodruff advertised in *Hartford (Conn.) Courant* of Nov. 22, 1831 and Nov. 15, 1886, that reeds:

T. WOODRUFF,
manufacturer and vender of
BENCH-PLANES

WOODRUFF & McBRIDE
Alexander S. Woodruff and **Alexander McBride** were hardware and plane manufacturers, in Louisville, KY, in 1848-49. Five planemakers have been identified as working for **Woodruff & McBride**, in 1848: **Americus Hulings**, **Solomon Cook**, **George Beale**, **James Bogert**, and **Martin C. Winslow**. In 1851-52, the firm was listed as **Woodruff & Evans**, edge tool manufacture. ***

J. WOODS
Examples: on 9 1/4"-9 1/2" beech molders with flat chamfers and **I. Sleeper** style wedges. Three planes are 10" beech, one with an **I. Sleeper** style wedge, one with a relieved wedge and one with a rounded wedge and round chamfers. One example also has a **L. M. WOODS** as an owner's incuse imprint, probably from Newburyport area, ca. 1800-20. **

J. WOODS
Example: on a beech screw-arm sash, ca. 1820-30. **UR**

WOODWARD
William Woodward (b. Mar. 12, 1785 in England, d. Oct. 10, 1868 in Medino Co., OH). Examples: with the location **LEBANON** (OH) on a 9 1/2" tonge plane with a iron fence; and on a 9 3/8" straight rabbet, both beech with heavy round chamfers, ca. 1810-20. **Wm. Woodward** advertised in the *Western Star on Apr. 27, 1819* that read:

APPRENTICES
Wanted,
Two or three boys from 15 to 17
years of age, who can come well recommended,
& are desirous of learning the
Plane making & house Carpenter
business, are wanted immediately by
the subscriber.
WM. WOODWARD.
Lebanon; April 23. (1819)

A. WOODWARD
Abishai Woodward (b. 1752 at Preston, CT, d. April 10, 1809 in New London, CT) was a joiner, housewright and Patriot in Preston, CT. He married March 20, 1774, **Mary Spicer**, daughter of **Capt. Oliver Spicer** (1726-1804). It is suggested that **Woodward** was also apprenticed to **Daniel Denison, 2nd.** (1740-1818) at about the same time as was **John Wheeler Geer** (b. 1752) ending in 1773-74. **Abishai Woodward** lived in Preston, from 1773-1787. **Abisha Woodward** served in the American Revolution, enlisting Sep. 8, 1776 in the 8th. CT Militia under Capt. James Morgan and was discharged Nov. 9, 1776. On March 31, 1787 he leased his Preston property and went to

New London, CT, as a builder, carpenter, and architect. **Abishai Woodward** advertised in the April 30, 1790 **Connecticut Gazette**: "wanted immediately, one or two journeymen house-joiners, to whom good pay will be made." **Woodward** built the Alms House, in 1800; the New London Lighthouse, in 1801; and possibly the Mason Hall. The inventory of his estate included "Joiners Shop," a building containing 122 planes, 38 chisels, assorted other tools, as well as 109 unfinished molding stocks, 16 new plane irons, 10 new chisels, and a steel stamp with his name. His inventory also included "Langley's Designs on Architecture" probably Batty Langley's, *City and Country Builder's and Workman's Treasury of Designs*, London, 1739; and "London's Act of Building". His estate was insolvent. Examples: the A imprint is on a 9 5/8"x 1" birch molder with heavy flat chamfers, found with **W. Woodward** planes. One imprint is on a plane by **T. DARBEY**, Thomas Darb(e)y of Birmingham (1767-85) as an owner's imprint. The B imprint is on a 9" maple complex molder with flat chamfers and the B1 wedge; and a 10 3/8" birch molder with small round chamfers and the B2 wedge, ca. 1770-90. The C imprint, with two reverse D's is on a 9 3/8" large birch round with wide flat chamfers that end with a tipped down line and a long lamb's tounge. The C is the earliest imprint and wedge, ca. 1750-60. **A & B ******; **C *******

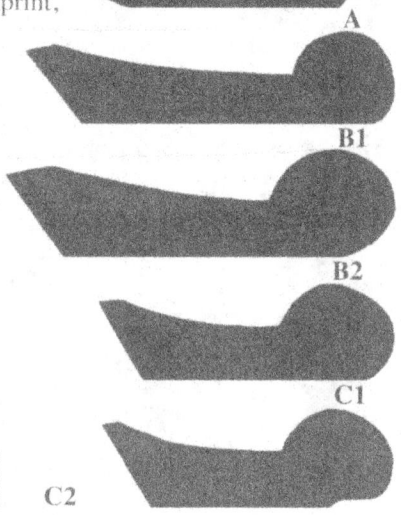

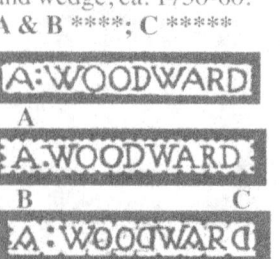

L. WOODWARD
Possibly **Luther Woodward** from Taunton, MAS who was a clock dealer & maker, in 1821. Example: on a 24" beech jointer with a birch tote and flat chamfers, ca. 1820. **UR**

W. WOODWARD
William W. Woodward was listed in the 1834 Utica, NY directory, as a planemaker. He was in New Haven, NY, in 1837-38, making planes for **C. R. Wells**. **UR**

Wm. WOODWARD
William Woodward (b. Mar. 14, 1782 in Taunton, Bristol Co., MA, d. Sep. 18, 1865 in Taunton) made planes in Taunton. He married **Betsy Dean**, in 1807, and last appeared in the 1850 census. He was variously listed as a house carpenter, mechanist, housewright and yeoman. The 1823 accounting of **Aaron Smith**'s estate shows "of William Woodward $5.31." An adjustable screw sash plane has been reported with the date 1839. Molding planes are 9 1/2" beech with 19c style chamfers. **A & A1 ****

JOSEPH WOODWELL/ JOSEPH WOODWELL & CO.
Joseph Woodwell (b. Jan. 25, 1807 in New York City, d. Aug. 28, 1899 in Pittsburgh, Allegheny Co., PA) went to Salem, MA, as a wood carver of scrollwork and figureheads for ships. In 1828, he moved briefly to Buffalo, NY, then moved to Pittsburgh, PA. **Joseph Woodwell** and his brother **James Albert Woodwell** (b. 1816 in NY, d. 1885 in Pittsburgh, Allegheny Co., PA) were partners in a cabinet shop and furniture store, from 1833-45. **Joseph Woodwell** started a hardware store in 1845-46 with **John Walker** (b. 1816 in Allegheny Co., PA, d. 1895). By 1847, it was listed under his own name as **Joseph Woodwell** located at Wood St. & Second Ave. By 1851, it became **Joseph Woodwell & Co.**, Pittsburgh's largest wholesale hardware establishment; remaining in business until 1954. By 1879, the company also included his two sons **William Knowho Woodwell** (b. Jun. 1831 in PA, d. probate Apr. 24, 1901 in Pittsburgh) and **Joseph Ryan Woodwell** (b. Sep. 7, 1843 in Pittsburgh, d. May 30, 1911 in Pittsburgh). **Woodwell & Co.** offered wooden planes as late as 1927. In the 1850's its trade sign was a four foot long jointer with **JOSEPH WOODWELL** on its side, that hung over the main entrance of the building. Examples: the A imprint with **& Co**, is after 1851, and is on an **Ohio Tool Co.** plane. The B imprint, is before 1851, and the founding of the **Ohio Tool Co.** **A ****; **B ******

A. WOODWORTH
Examples: on a 9 1/2"x 1/4" beech bead; and a birch jointer with an offset tote and flat chamfers, ca. 1800-20. **UR**

W. WOOLLETT

Example: on a beech-boxed sash plane, found in the Albany, NY, area. **UR**

I. WOOTTON
Example: on a 9 3/4" beech molder. **UR**

WORDEN, COLE & GIOR
Example: on a fruitwood cooper's head jointer with a birch wedge. **Eli Gior** (b. ca. 1825, d. 1888 in Grand Rapids, MI) was listed, in 1861, in Rochester, NY, as an edge tool maker at "Gregg's shop." **Mahlon Gregg** was an edge tool maker from 1861-65, who advertised cooper's tools. **Christopher Worden** was a blacksmith, in 1844, and as an edge tool maker for **D. R. Barton**, from 1855-59. **Eli Gior** was listed, in 1871, with **W. L. & T. J. White** in Buffalo, NY. In 1876, **Eli Gior** was listed as foreman with **G. R. Edge Tool Works**, Grand Rapids, MI. In 1885, he was listed as a "forger" with **E. A. Munson**, in Grand

Rapids. In 1887, **Gior** was listed as tool maker with **G. R. Edge Tool Works**. ****

WORDEN TOOL CO.
Worden Tool Co. was probably a hardware dealer located in Cleveland, OH. This name with the added location **CLEVELAND, O**. has been reported. **No imprint is available**.

THOMAS D. WORRALL
Thomas D. Worrall (b. 1818 in England, d. Sep. 14, 1889) was a Baptist minister who emigrated, in 1853, and settled in Mt. Holly, NJ. **Thomas Worrall**'s first patent No. 11,635, of Aug. 29, 1854, was for a plane with interchangeable soles. In 1855, he moved to Boston, MA. He was the founder of both the **Lowell Plane & Tool Co.** of Lowell, MA, and the **Multiform Moulding Plane Co.** of Boston, MA, from 1856-58. Bench planes manufactured by the **Lowell Plane & Tool Co.** have double-irons stamped **Multiform Moulding Plane Co.**, Boston. **Thomas Worrall**'s second Patent No. 14,979, of May 27, 1856, with a Boston address, specified the long bolt through the heel to clamp the iron. This patent showed the top metal plate with two brass thumbscrews for engaging the T-shaped slots in the interchangeable soles. **Thomas Worrall**'s third Patent No. 16,309, of Dec. 23, 1856, granted while in Lowell, provided a rack-and-pinion type cutter adjustment, a May 27, 1856 patent date, is stamped on all known planes. Licenses were granted to other wooden planemakers, **Copeland & Co.** of Huntington, MA, and **W. Warren** of Nashua, NH. **Thomas Worrall**'s fifth Patent No. 17,951, of Aug. 4, 1857, was for a vertical screw to lock the cutter. **Thomas Worrall**'s sixth Patent No. 18,312, of Sept. 29, 1857, was for a detachable handle. Both companies ceased operations, in 1858. From 1886-90, while in Lynn, MA, he was granted 11 patents for typewriting machines and printing presses. From 1887-89, he was listed as "physician." (see *Patented Transitional & Metallic Planes in America 1827-1927*, p. 25-33, by Roger K. Smith)
No imprint has been reported

D. WORTHINGTON
Examples: The A imprint is on a 9 3/16" beech ogee complex molder with heavy flat chamfers. The B imprint is on a 9 1/2" beech wedge-lock sash with heavy round chamfers, ca. 1800-20. **UR**

A

B

G. WORTHINGTON
Geo. Worthington & Co. with **George Worthington** (m. Nov. 15, 1840 in Cuyahoga Co., OH, d. Nov. 10, 1871 in Cleveland) was a hardware dealer in Cleveland, OH, founded in 1823, and still operating today. In 1853, it was listed as **Worthington & Co.**, a hardware dealers, at 1 Superior St., Cleveland. In 1870, **Geo. Worthington & Co.**, a wholesale hardware with **George Worthington**, **James Barnett** & **E. Binghall**, at 90-92 Water. In 1873, **Geo. Worthington & Co.** with **James Barnett**, **George Deming**, **Ralph Worthington**, **Alexander Gunn** and **George Worthington Jr.**, with "wholesale & retail hardware, iron, nails &c.", at 90-92 Water. Wooden planes were discontinued before 1880. **

WRIGHT
Example: on a 9 3/8" boxed beech side bead with birch wedge and flat chamfers, probably from New England, ca. 1810. **UR**

B. G. WRIGHT
Example: on a 9 3/4" beech square rabbet with flat chamfers, ca. 1800. **UR**

C. WRIGHT
Examples: on match plank tongue & grooving planes with adjustable fences, wood depth stop, riveted skate, and flat chamfers. **UR**

E. WRIGHT
Example: on 9 3/8" beech astragal plane with flat chamfers, ca. early 19c. **UR**

I. C. WRIGHT
Example: on a 10 5/8" birch plow with a relived wedge, wood depth stop and adjustment screws, a riveted skate, with shallow flat chamfers, ca. early 19c. **UR**

J. S. WRIGHT
Example reported with **J.S. Wright** and a location **CIN. O.**, ca. 19c. **UR**

L x I x WRIGHT
Possibly **Levi Jr. Wright** a joiner, in Plympton, MA, working ca. 1803. Examples: on a large apple cooper's howel with a chestnut fence, large wood screws, and a **James Cam** iron,

and a pair of birch molding planes. **UR**

N. WRIGHT
Examples: on 9 7/8" & 9 3/4" birch hollows, both with heavy flat chamfers, ca. 1800. **UR**

N. WRIGHT
Nothing is known of **N. Wright** of Keene, NH. Example: on a 26" jointer with a closed tote and double 2 3/4" iron. The

inscription **L. SANFORDS/ PATENT/ 1844** appears on the adjusting screw which feeds into the cast steel bed plate rebated into the planes throat. Patent No. 3838, on Nov. 26, 1844 was issued to **Levi Sanford** of East Solon, NY, for the purpose of holding and adjusting the cutter. **UR**

R. WRIGHT
Robert Wright (b. 1749 in England) who arrived in Philadelphia, PA, in 1774, and was one of the early Philadelphia, PA, planemakers. Philadelphia Taxpayers Records, in 1779, was listed as a toolmaker. He appeared in the 1793 city directories, at back 36 so. 3d. st.; and in 1794-97, at 5 Shepard's Alley, no. 3d. St., as a planemaker. Examples: on 10" beech molders with flat chamfers; and a 14" beech panel raiser with an offset tote and heavy flat chamfers, a wood depth stop dovetailed and forward pitched, an adjustable bottom fence, and a round top iron by **Iohn Green**. The larger B imprint is on a 10 1/16" beech complex molder with flat chamfers. Branded on the side is **T. SAVERY** and **WS** believed to be the initials of **William Savery** who was apprenticed to Philadelphia chairmaker **Solomon Fussell**, active ca. 1730-50. **A & B: *****

W. WRIGHT
Examples: on an 8 5/8" birch complex molder double-boxed with shallow round chamfers; and an 8 5/8" birch full round with the iron, set at a York pitch, and flat chamfers. Examples have interrupted boxing inset into the sole, ca. 1810-30. **UR**

A. WYCKOFF & CO.
A. Wyckoff & Co. with **Arcalous Wyckoff** (b. Apr. 10, 1816 in Warren Co., NJ, d. Jul. 6, 1898 in Elmira, Chiemung Co., NY) was a hardware dealer in Elmira. In 1850, he was listed as a chain pump maker, in Elmira. Examples: an 11" beech plow with carriage bolts to hold the slide arms and a double-pegged closed tote, found in Steuben Co., NY, and two or three complex molders, ca. 1890. ********

J. H. WYLIE JR & CO
J. H. Wylie Jr. & Co. with **James Henry Wylie Jr.** (b. Aug. 22, 1831 in Dunstable, Hillsborough Co., NH, d. Mar. 5, 1906 in Holyoke, Hampden Co., MA) was a Holyoke, MA, hardware dealer. In 1888, The firm was listed as **J. H. Wylie, Jr., & Co.**, dealers in "builder's and blacksmith's hardware, carpenters' tools, machinists tools and draughting tools", at No. 7 Dwight St., cor. of Main, Holyoke, Mass. Example: on the heel of a **J. F. & G. H. Lindsey** toothing plane. ********

R. WYMAN
Examples: on a 10 3/4" complex molder with heavy flat chamfers; and a 9 1/2" birch small hollow with beech wedge and round chamfers, ca. 1820. **UR**

W. WYMAN
Example: on a 1 1/4" rabbet plane. **UR.**

YARNALL & COOPER
Yarnall & Cooper was a hardware partnership in Philadelphia, PA, ca. 1840's. Example: on a molding plane made by  **B. Sheneman**, imprinted on toe and heel. ****

YARNALL & McCLURE
Yarnall & W. M. McClure was a Philadelphia, PA, hardware and tool dealer, listed in the 1840 Philadelphia directory. This firm advertised on May 27, 1841, in the *Public Ledger*, "**City Tool Store**, 347 Market Street, Philadelphia, **E. W. Carpenter**'s Lancaster Planes." Examples: on several **E. W. Carpenter** planes, including the patent plow. ***

F. W. YATES
F. W. Yates is reported to be a Buffalo, NY hardware dealer. Example: on a 9 1/2" beech complex molder, ca. mid-19c. **UR**

H. W. YATES
H. W. Yates was a Detroit, MI tool maker. Example: on a 10" beech manufactured spill plane sold in a cardboard box, one example is also imprinted with **W. B. McCormick**, Alton, O., a hardware dealer. **No imprint is available.**

G. YELDING
Example: on a 9 5/8" beech complex molder with flat chamfers, early 19c. **UR**

F. YEOMAN
Possibly **Francis Yeoman Sr.** (b. May 10, 1727 in Berwick-on-Tweed, Scotland, d. Mar. 15, 1819 in Delhi, NY) who was in NY, before Sep. 30, 1753, when his child was born, and served in the American Revolution for seven years, in the Albany Co. Militia, as Sargent in Houstion's Company, Lansing's Regiment. He was listed in 1800 & 10, in Delhi. He was described as a carpenter and skilled cabinetmaker. His son **Francis Yeoman Jr.** (b. Aug. 28, 1761) is another possibility. Examples: several 9 5/8" beech complex molders with flat chamfers; one was found in a mid-Hudson-Valley tool chest which also contained planes by **Tho. Grant**, **J. Stiles**, **C. Tobey**, and others, ca. 1790-1800. ****

I: YOH
I: YOH (possibly **Yohst**) on a 9 5/8x 1/8" apple match grooving plane with a riveted skate and flat chamfers found in Lancaster Co., PA, ca. early 19c. **UR**

C. YORK
Examples: on four 9" beech complex molders, one single-boxed; and another double-boxed, all with heavy round chamfers; and a 4" crown molder with a round top wedge and a pegged centered tote, ca. 1830. ****

J. C. YORK
Example: on a 9 1/2" beech double boxed complex molder with flat chamfers. ca. 19c. **UR**

L. YORK
Examples: a beech plow of **I. Sleeper** influence, and a 9 11/16" beech round with an **I. Sleeper** style wedge and heavy round chamfers, ca. 1830. ****

H. YOST
Herman (**Harman**) **Yost** (**Jost**) (b. Mar. 24, 1779 in Chester Co., PA, d. Sep. 18, 1864 in Lewisburg, Union Co., PA) was a carpenter, in Union Co., active from 1824-60. In 1820, he was listed in Catawissa, Columbia Co., PA. He lived in New Berlin from 1824-1834; when he moved to Lewisburg on 5th St. with a house and possibly a shop; owned by **Henry Noll** who may have also been a carpenter. In 1843, **Herman Yost** bought Lot 250 on the corner of 2nd. and St. Anthony Streets. By 1855, he was widowed, and sold 1/2 of the lot for $135, and the other 1/2 to **Mary Ann** and **William Reily** for $1. In 1860, **Herman** was listed as a carpenter living with the **Reilys**. In his will dated Nov. 26, 1856, **Herman Yost** is listed as a carpenter. The inventory of his estate of Oct. 13, 1864 lists:

39 small planes @ 30 cts.	-11.70
3 pair tongue & grove @ 2.5	- 7.50
10 fancy planes	-12.00
3 wood screw cutters @ 1.00	- 3.00
1 lot bitts	- 1.00
1 lot screw cutters	- 2.00
1 lot of planes	- 3.00

And carpenter tools such as, files, chisels, hammers, hand anvil, work bench and tool chest. Examples: The A imprint is on a 14 1/2" beech panel raiser with an adjustable fence and a **W. Butcher** iron. The A1 imprint is on a 9 1/2"x 5/8" hollow. The A2 imprint is on a 14 3/16" handled tongue plane with threaded arms, found in Lewisburg, ca. mid-19c. The B imprint is on a 12 3/4"x 3 1/4" beech toted crown molder with round chamfers, found SW of Lewisburg, PA, ca. 1820-30. **A, A1, A2 & B** ****

A. YOUNG

Example: a 9 1/4" beech side bead. UR

A. YOUNG

Example: on a 9 3/16" beech bead with flat chamfers, ca. 1800-10. UR

A. F. YOUNG

Alexander (Alex) F. Young (b. Dec. 1820 in Scotland, m. Jun. 7, 1847 in Stonington, New London Co., CT) was listed in 1850 & 60, as a cabinetmaker, in Stonington. In 1870, he was a pattern maker. In 1876, he was an upholsterer and undertaker on Front St., Mystic Bridge, New London Co. In 1880, he was again listed as a cabinet maker, in Stonington. Example: on a edge-boxed moving filletster made by **J. W. Farr**, N. York. ****

B. YOUNG

Example: on a 10 1/4" beech nosing plane with heavy flat chamfers, ca. early 19c. UR

CHARLES YOUNG

Charles Young (b. Jan. 1825 in OH, d. Feb. 27, 1907 in Southgate, Campbell Co., KY) was listed as a carpenter; and in 1846, as a gauge maker, in Cincinnati, OH. The 1850 directory lists his occupation, as planemaker. He was part of **Young & Holliday**, with **Thomas Holliday**, as tool manufacturers, from 1849-50. From 1857-61, he was listed, as jointer tools, tool manufacturer and toolmaker, at 91 Lock. From 1865, Young was listed at Walnut, Newport, KY, as toolmaker; from 1867-69 as woodturner and tool manufacturer. In 1872, this became the location of **C. G. Siewers**. (see **American Marking Gages**, by Milton H. Bacheller, Jr.) No imprint has been reported.

GEO. W. YOUNG JR. & CO.

George W. Young Jr. & Co. with **George W. Young Jr.** (b. 1843 in MD) made planes, at 90 W. Baltimore St., Baltimore, MD, in 1870. Young was also part of **Young & Seidenstricker**, with **Albert B. Seidenstricker**, were planemakers and hardware dealers, in 1868-69. **

J Y/ J. YOUNG

There are at least three candidates for this imprint: James Young a Manhattan, NY, cabinetmaker, active from 1801-20; his brother Joseph Young, a New York City cabinetmaker from 1821-25; and John Young, an 1811 cabinetmaker from Boston, MA, who was the partner to Thomas Emmons Jr. Examples: on a 9 7/8" beech complex molder with a **NEWBOLD** iron and small flat chamfers; and a 9 1/8" beech quarter round with round chamfers. ca. 1810-30. **A & B:** UR

A

A

B

B

J. B. YOUNG

Probably was a hardware dealer in Vernon, NY. Examples: on two 9 1/2" beech full-boxed size **1/4 & 1/2** side beads made by **Reed, Utica** with a **Wm. Ash & Co.** irons and round chamfers, ca. mid-19c. UR

L. YOUNG

Example: on a 9 1/2" beech size 1/4 bead with round chamfers, ca. 1820. UR

OTIS YOUNG

Example: on a 9 3/4" beech coffin shaped skew rabbet with shallow flat chamfers, ca. 1810. UR

T. V. YOUNG

Example: on a 9 1/2" birch skew rabbit with small flat chamfers, ca. early 19c. UR

W. YOUNG

Example: on a 9 3/8" beech astragal bead with size imprint **4/8** on the heel and round chamfers, ca. 1820-30. UR

YOUNG, BAGGS & CO.

John W. Young (b. 1824, d. Jun. 10, 1897 in Ohio, WV) of Wheeling, WV, was issued Patent No. 151,188, on May 19, 1874, for a glass faced cooper's croze. He assigned half its rights to **Andrew H. Baggs**, of Kirkwood, OH. No imprint has been reported.

YOUNG & M'MASTER

Young & M'Master was a plane making partnership of **Alonzo Deluzon McMaster** (b. Feb. 22, 1812 at Balston Spa, NY, d. Mar. 24, 1887) and **Jacob Young** (b. ca. 1796 in NY), who were respectively assistant superintendent and superintendent of **Truman McMaster**'s planemaking shop at Auburn Prison, NY, from 1829-38. In 1838, they succeeded to the convict-labor contract held by **T. J. McMaster**, and continued until 1843. Their five-year contract called for the employment of 30 to 40 convicts, at 37 1/2 cents per day per convict. In 1847-50, **Alonzo D.**

A

B   B1

A

McMaster was listed as a planemaker working for **D. R. Barton**, from 1850-53, as scale maker; and finally as a traveling hardware salesman. In 1855, **Jacob Young** was listed as a carpenter, in Auburn, Cayuga, NY. **A *; B, B1, B2 & C ****

YOUNG & SEIDENSTRICKER
George W. Young Jr. and **Albert B. Seidenstricker** were listed as planemakers and probably hardware dealers, at 90 W. Baltimore St., Baltimore, MD, in 1868-69.
No imprint has been reported.

P. YOUNGS
Examples: on a 9 1/2"x 1/2" tiger maple square rabbet; a 9 3/8" beech round; and a 9 3/8"x 3/8" beech skew rabbet, all with round chamfers, ca. 1810-30. ********

H Y/ H. YUILL
Examples: on two 9 1/2" beech fixed sash planes with double-irons, ca. 1850. **UR**

G. ZACHARIAS
Example: on a 7 1/2" beech coffin smoother, round top wedge and iron marked **James. Cam** with small flat chamfers, ca. 1780-90. **UR**

L. ZECKENDORF & CO.
L. Zeckendorf & Co. was a Tucson, AZ, hardware dealer established in 1854. In 1902 & 18, the listing read: "**L. Zeckendorf & Co.**, general merchandise and hardware, wholesale & retail", Tuson, Arizona with **Louis Zeckendorf** and **Albert Steinfeld**. Examples: on a dado; and a complex molder, with **Sandusky Tool Co.** inventory numbers on the toe. ********

C. ZELLER
Examples: on a 13"x 2 1/4" crown molder with an offset tote, iron strike button, found in the Lancaster Co. PA area; and a 9 1/2" large hollow, both beech with heavy flat chamfers, ca. 1790. ********

ZENITH
(see **Marshall - Wells Hdwe. Co.**)

J. ZIMMERMAN
John Zimmerman (b. 1802 in OH, m. Nov. 3, 1825 in Ross Co., OH) was listed in 1850, as a cabinetmake; and in 1860, as an undertaker; who also made wooden planes in Kingston, Ross Co., OH. He was listed, in the 1851 1856-57, Columbus, OH, directories, as a planemaker. Example: on a 13" panel raiser with an **Ohio Tool Co.** iron; a sash; a bead plane, and a plane with a **1839** date. **A & A1 ****

GLOSSARY

For a Much more detailed and complete view of planes and other tools, we suggest that the reader refer to John Whelan's *The Wooden Plane* and R. A. Salaman's *Dictionary of Woodworking Tools*. (see Bibliography)

ASTRAGAL: A molding comprised of a bead (approximately half-circle) set in some distance from the edge of the work, and the plane that makes such a molding.

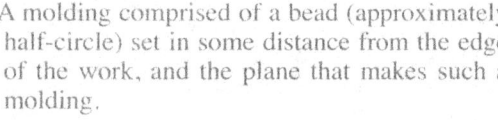

BACKING PLANE: Another name used for a mother plane or a counter plane. It has a sole that is opposite to the sole of the plane that is to be made. (see mother plane)

BADGER PLANE: (see Panel Plane) Similar to a jack plane but with a skewed cutting iron exposed at the right corner, used to cut or clean out a wide rabbet or panel.

BEAD or **BEADING PLANE**: A small convex, half-circle molding, either a center bead or a side bead, and the plane that makes it.

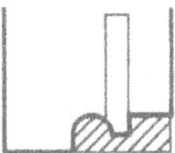 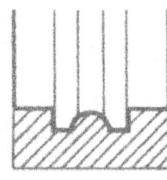

side bead (single boxed)   center bead (double boxed)

BED (of a plane): That surface on which the iron rests.

BENCH PLANE

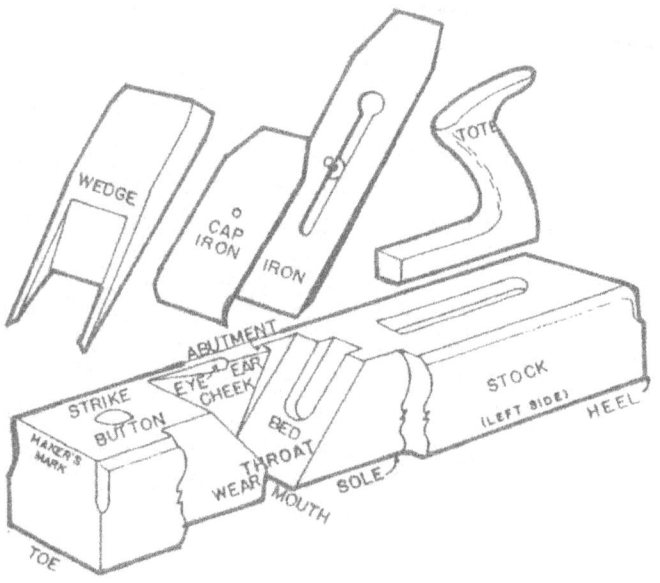

BENCH PLANES: A series of flat-soled planes with the throat opening at the top of the plane for the escape of shavings. They are used on the workbench to smooth the surfaces of boards. Ranging in size from the smallest to largest, they include:

- **SMOOTHING PLANE**: (or smoother) 6 1/2" to 10 1/2" long and used to do the final finishing or smoothing of the surface.

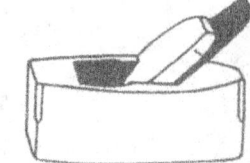

- **JACK PLANE**: 14" to 16" long and used for the rough work and rapid wood removal.

- **FORE PLANE**: 18" to 22" long and used to smooth off the work after using the jack plane.

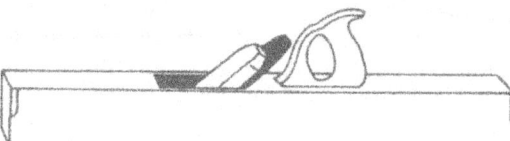

- **JOINTER PLANE**: 22" to 32" long, used to make the finishing passes on the long straight edges of the wood pieces preparatory to joining them. A plane of this type longer than 36" is usually called a floor plane.

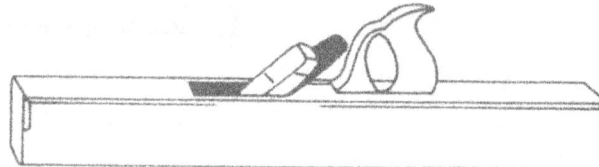

BEVEL: A section of a molding profile consisting of a sloping straight line.

BEVEL SQUARE: A straight stock with an adjustable blade for testing or setting out work at any angle.

BELECTION, BILECTION, or **BOLECTION MOLDING**: To rabbet a molding to fit over the edge of a frame work, such as a door.

BOXING: Inserts in the sole of a plane to resist wear, usually of boxwood, lignum, ebony or rosewood, intermittent boxing is where the boxing is where the boxing is not continuous but in short interrupted segments.

CABINETMAKER: Woodworkers in the building and allied trades.
- **CARPENTERS**: who work on the main structure, usually in the field.
- **JOINERS**: who make the stairs, doors, window sash and internal fittings.
- **CABINETMAKERS**: who specialize in the movable furniture.

CAP IRON: (see bench planes) A second iron in front of the plane iron to break the shavings and provide stability to reduce chatter.

CHAMFERS or CHAMFER STOPS: Important element of individual plane design used to give indications of approximate age and location of origin.

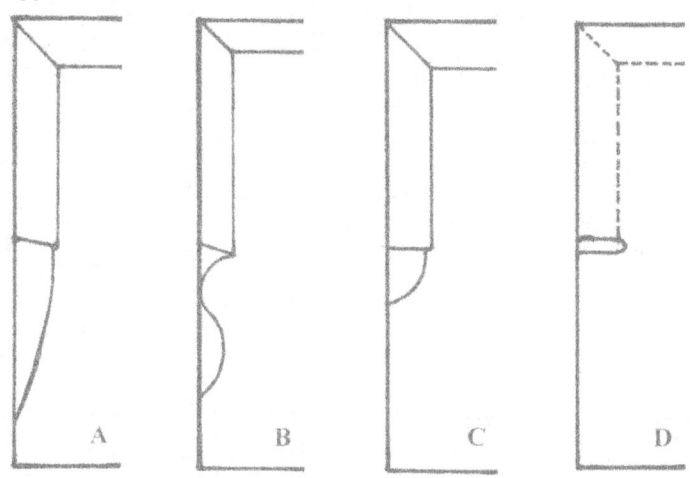

A. Flat chamfers that stop with a sloped line and a long tapered turnout. ca. 1750-80, New England.

B. Flat chamfers that stop with a sloped line and a lamb's tongue and separate flute. ca. 1780-1810, New England.

C. Flat or round chamfers that stop with a straight horizontal line and turnout. ca. 1760-1820.

D. Shallow round chamfers that stop with a gouge cut. ca. 1820-60.

CHAMFER PLANE: Flat or round surface made by planing off the right angle at the top and sides of a plane or other woodwork, and a plane to make such a flat surface.

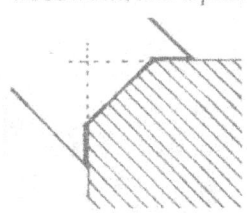

CHEEKS: (see bench planes) The side of the throat.

COFFIN SMOOTHING PLANE: A rectangular plane with sides curving inward towards the toe and heel.

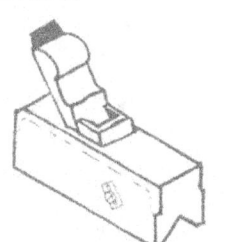

CLOSED TOTE: (see bench planes) Most commonly found on bench planes.

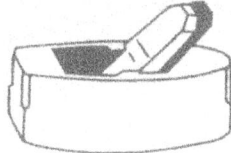

COMPASS or CIRCULAR PLANE: Similar to a smoother in appearance and use, except that the sole is convex and used on curved surfaces.

COMPLEX MOLDING PLANES: A plane that cuts compound curves, made up of subsegments, usually for decorative purposes.

COOPERS' PLANES: Planes used by a barrel maker, e.g. howel, croze, sun plane etc.

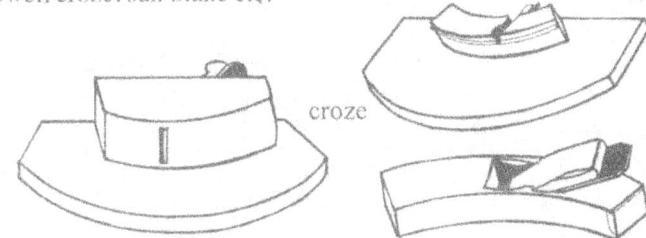

CORNICE PLANE: Planes used to make a wide complex molding, called a crown molder because the molding is often used at the top or crown between the wall and ceiling.

COPED JOINT or COPING PLANE: Used with sash planes and having a blade configured exactly the reverse of the sash plan's, since the sash molding had to fit into the coping cut.

COVE: A concave molding of one quarter of a circle.

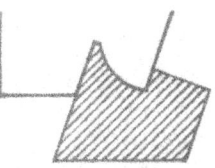

CROWN MOLDER: (see cornice plane)

CROWNED INITIALS: Imprints found on some early planes, consisting of a letter topped by a fleur-de-lis type crown, found frequently on planes of Thomas Grant, Robert Eastburn, and on a few other American and English planes. Believed to have been used by the seller of the planes, to imprint the buyer's initials.

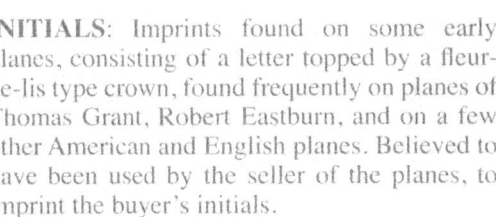

DADO PLANE: A plane made to cut a groove across the grain without tearing the wood. The iron is often skewed and is preceded by a vertical iron (nicker) that scores the edges of the cut.

DEPTH STOP: Device used on plow, dado, and grooving planes to limit the depth of the cut. Controlled by a screw.

DIRECTORY: A book published annually in many cities, listing the residents by address and occupation.

DOUBLE-IRON: (see bench planes) Refers to the use of a smaller cap iron placed in front of the cutting iron. Can also refer to a plane that uses two separate cutting irons.

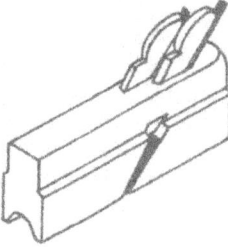

DRAW KNIFE: Consisting of a flat or curved blade with tangs at either end at right (or slightly larger) angles to the blade; the tangs fitted with wooden handles. Draw knives are used in place of planes to remove unwanted wood.

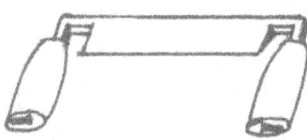

EARS: (see bench planes) The projections at the sides of the throat which retain the wedge and iron.

EDGE TOOL: Any tool with a sharpened blade. Can include planes, chisels, draw knives, axes, adzes, etc.

ESCAPEMENT: The exit port in the plane for shaving escape. Located on the side of molders or on the top of the bench planes.

FENCE: (see plow planes) An adjustable guide used on plow, filletster, grooving and tongue planes. It is held against one edge of the work piece and therefore controls the placing of the cut.

FILLET: A fillet is a small horizontal straight segment that usually serves to separate other elements of the profile or to terminate a profile.

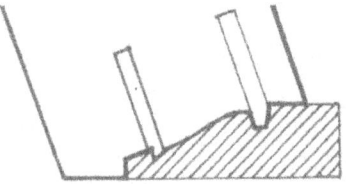

FILLETSTER (in England **FILLISTER**): A plane that does the same job as a rabbet and cuts a rectangular step on the edge of a piece of wood, except that the filletster has a fence and also has a small mouth like a molding plane and unlike the open, curved mouth of the rabbet.

FINAL: The rounded top part of a plane wedge.

FLOAT: A coarse rasp with parallel teeth, 4 or 5 to the inch, used by planemakers to form the throat of a plane.

FLUTING: Carved out curve below the chamfer stop and the bottom of the plane stock.

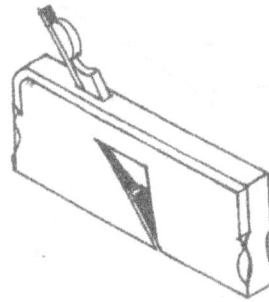

FLUTE MOLDING: A semi-circular concave molding, frequently repeated side by side and opposite of a reeding mold.

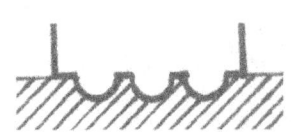

FORE PLANE (see Bench Planes)

FORKSTAFF PLANE: Similar to a square smoothing plane but with a half round hollow used for rounding handles.

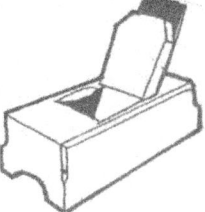

GROOVE or **GROOVING PLANE**: A plane used to make the groove into which the tongue fits when joining the edges two pieces of wood by this method. The groove and the tongue planes are called "match planes". The term grooving plane can also be used generally to refer to any plane that makers a groove, including groove planes, dado planes, and plow planes.

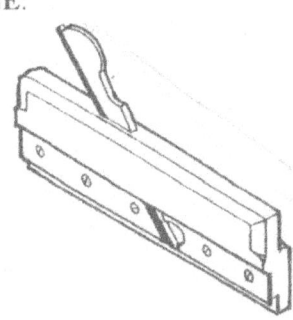

GUTTER PLANE: A jack-type plane, except with a convex, rounded bottom, used to hollow out wood to make gutters. Usually about 15"-16" long.

HALVING PLANE: This is a fixed filletster which cuts a rabbet as deep as it is wide, used for making half-lap joints.

HANGING HOLE: A hole through the heel of a plane through which a looped chord is placed to hang a plane for storage.

HOLLOW PLANE: A simple molding plane with a shallow concave sole. Together with its opposite, the round plane, it is the most common of the molding planes. It was sold in pairs available in 24 sizes, from 1/16" to 2" wide.

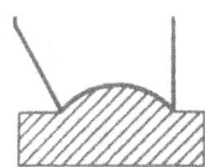

HOWEL: (see cooper's planes) Used to cut a shallow indentation (a howel) on the inside of the barrel at both ends. The croze (plane) was used to cut a sharp groove in the howel into which the top and bottom (heads) of the barrel were fitted.

IMPRINT: The planemaker's plane manufacturer's, hardware,or tool dealer's name and sometimes location or address were stamped usually onto the toe of a plane.

- **EMBOSSED IMPRINT**: An imprint where the background is struck into the end grain of the wood, leaving the raised letters. This may have either a straight, zigzag, or decorative border.

- **INCISED IMPRINT**: An imprint in which the name is cut, carved, branded, or engraved, into the plane side.

- **INCUSE IMPRINT**: An imprint in which the name is hammered, stamped, or pressed into the end grain of the wood, usually on the toe and usually without a border.

IRON: The cutting blade of bench or molding planes.

JACK PLANE: (see bench planes)

JOINER: A finishing carpenter.

JOINTER PLANE: (see bench planes)

KEY: (see plow plane) The wedge that secures the slide arms of a plow, tongue, or grooving plane.

LENGTH OF PLANE: In the 18th century the length varied, in New England from 9" to over 10", in mid-Atlantic states the length usually followed the standard, English 9 1/2". The length can be helpful in identifying origin and age.

LIGNUM: Lignum vitae (wood of life) is a very hard, extremely heavy, waxy wood, native to the Caribbean. The heartwood is dark brown in color and the sapwood is a light cream, creating a handsome contrast. Brought into seaports during the 19th century, it was often used on wear surfaces and the soles of planes for boxing. Occasionally the whole plane was lignum.

LINEN FOLD: A form of carving resembling draped linen.

MARKING GAUGE: Used for marking lines parallel to the edge of the wood. Consists of a fence that slides on a 9"-10" long stem and is fixed in place by a wedge or thumbscrew. The stem has a metal spur on one end that marks the wood as the fence is pushed along the edge of the wood. Layout lines found on planes are made by a marking gauge.

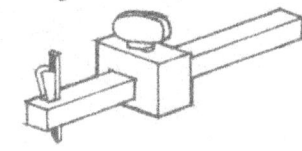

MAST PLANE: Used by shipwrights to smooth wood masts and spars. About the size of a smoothing plane, with a shallow concave sole.

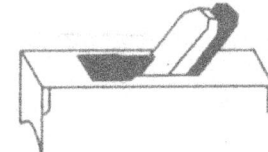

MATCH PLANES: Match tongue and groove planes in sets, sometimes both incorporated in the same plane. Used for creating a tongue and groove joint on the edge of boards or flooring.

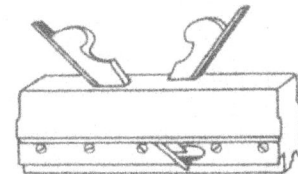

MITER PLANE: Like a smoothing plane except that the iron is usually set at a 35 degree rather than a 45 degree angle from the stock. Used to trim the end grain of wood.

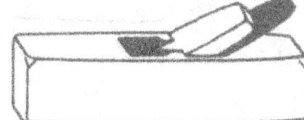

MOLDING PLANE or **MOLDER**: A wide variety of different planes used to make decorative wood surfaces.

MORTISING: Joining two pieces of wood by fitting a rectangular tenon on one piece into a rectangular hole or mortise in the other piece. Joints are usually pegged or pined. This procedure is used in attaching a tote to a bench plane.

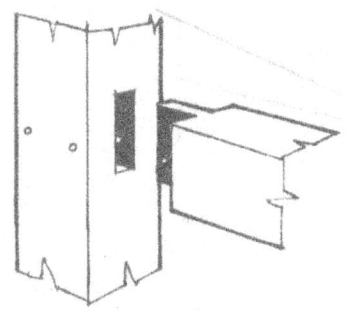

MOLDING PLANE

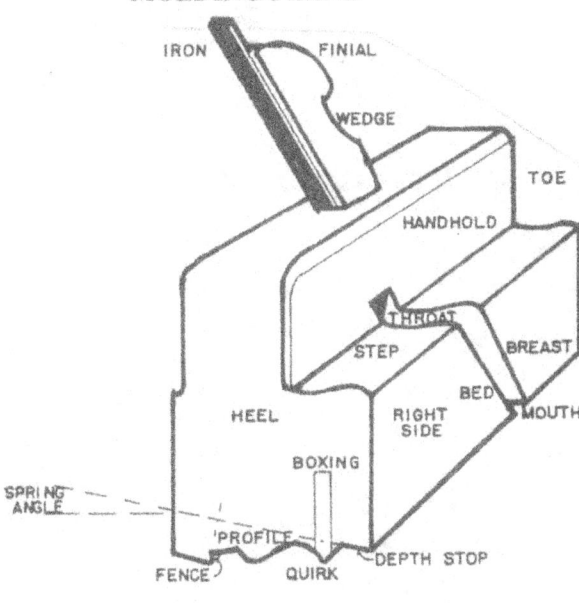

MOTHER PLANE: A reverse or mirror plane used to cut the profile on the sole of a molding plane. The mother plane is the configuration of the mold that the molding plane cuts.

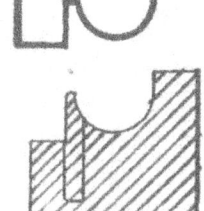

MOUTH: (see bench planes & molding plane) The slot in the sole of a plane through which the cutting edge was set.

NICKER: A secondary cutting blade usually to cut wood fibers at the edge(s) of the cut, on dado and filletster planes.

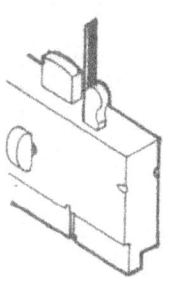

NOSING PLANE: A plane with large semi-circular molding profile, used to round the front edge of a stair tread.

OFFSET HANDLE: A term used to designate the placing of a plan's handle off to the right side of bench type planes.

OGEE: A molding plane that cuts an S-shaped curve; also the name of the curve that is cut.

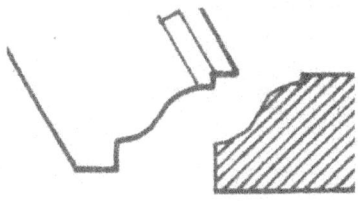

OVOLO: A molding plane that cuts a convex curve, round or elliptical; also the name of the curve that is cut.

PANEL RAISER or **RAISING PLANE**: A plane used to cut the wide beveled rabbet around the sides of a panel, so that the panel stands out in relief. A rather wide, flat-soled plane, with a skewed iron, and generally, a moving fence.

18th century or New England style panel raiser planes cut a sloped bevel, using an integral fence.

PITCH: The angle the face of the plane blade meets the work.

PLANK PLANES: Matched tongue and groove planes, about 14"-15" long, for use in planks of thickness 1 1/4" to 1 1/2". Compared with "board" match planes, which were used on boards 3/8" to 1" thick.

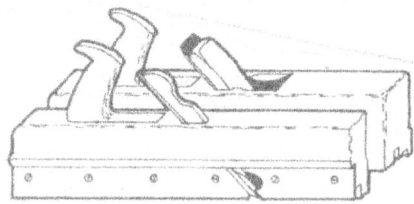

PLOW PLANE

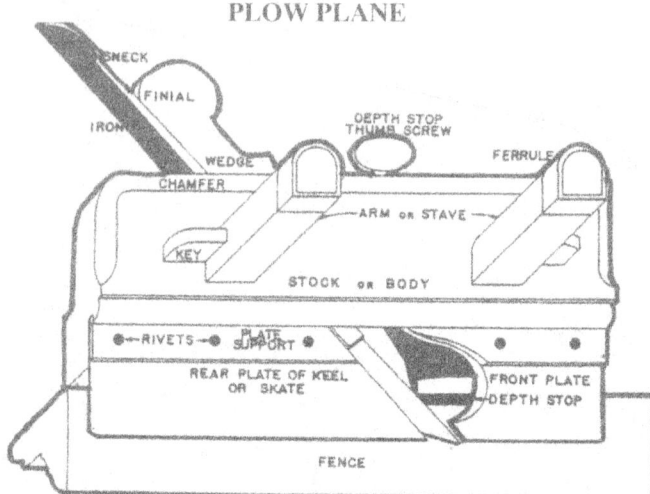

PLOW PLANE: A plane used to cut a groove parallel with the edge of the wood. Consists of two sections: the plane stock, usually 8" to 10" long, and a set of irons of varying widths; and the fence, whose attached arms fit through the stock and are fixed in place by wedges or by screw nuts. Usually the plow, like other grooving planes, is fitted with a depth stop.

Screw-arm plow (ca. 1850)   **Yankee plow** (ca. 1800)

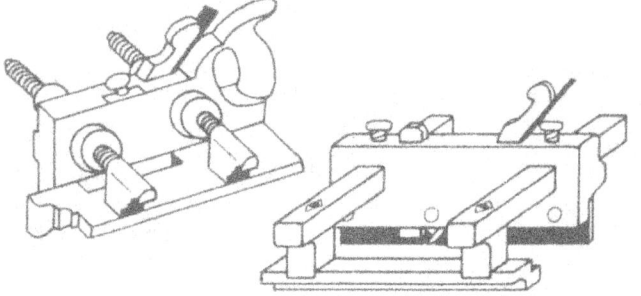

PULL HOLE: A horizontal hole through the front of a bench plane through which a rope or dowel is passed to be pulled by an assistant. Some planes have a cross bar attached to the top of the toe for the same purpose.

PUMP PLANE: A jack style plane with an astragal like shaped sole, making one half of a hollow pipe that was used with a chain pump.

QUARTER ROUND: A common convex molding consisting of one quarter of the arc of a circle; also the plane that makes such a molding.

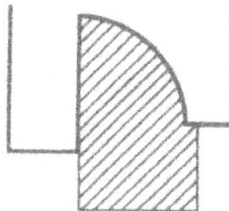

QUIRK: Generally a small angle or turning between one part of a molding and another.

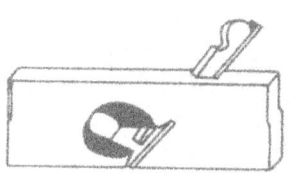

RABBET: (in England Rebate) A rectangle, or step, cut out along the edge of a piece of wood. Used for joining two pieces of wood, with rabbets cut in the edges of each. The rabbet plane has a flat sole, with either a straight or skewed iron, and is distinguished by a wide, curved mouth for shavings, often in a extremely graceful curve. (see filletster)

RAISING PLANE: (see panel raiser)

RAZEE: A plane on which the rear end of the stock is partially cut down so that the handle is seated lower than it ordinarily would be. The front end of the plane can also be razeed, though this is not so common.

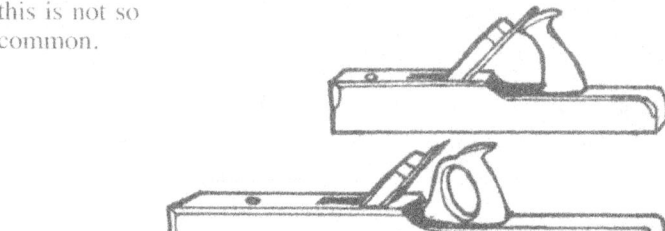

REEDING PLANE: Makes two or more convex beads, side by side or the opposite to a flute molding.

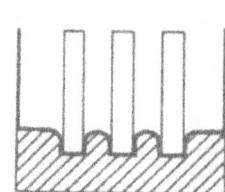

RELIEVED WEDGE: A wedge in which a small part of the finial, the back part, resting against the iron shank, is cut away, so that the wedge can be more easily removed. Typical of 18th century New England planemakers.

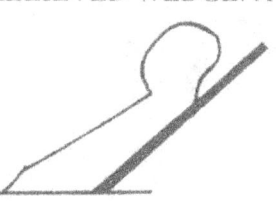

ROUND PLANE: A simple molding plane whose sole and iron are shallowly convex-shaped and therefore cut a concave molding. Together with its opposite, the hollow, it is the most common of the molding planes.

ROUNDING PLANE: Used to round ends of dowels, trenails, handles or any round taper on the end of the work.

ROUTER: Any plane or other tool that routs out waste from a groove or carved recess in wood. It has a single cutter, either in a plane or in a holder with handles on either side.

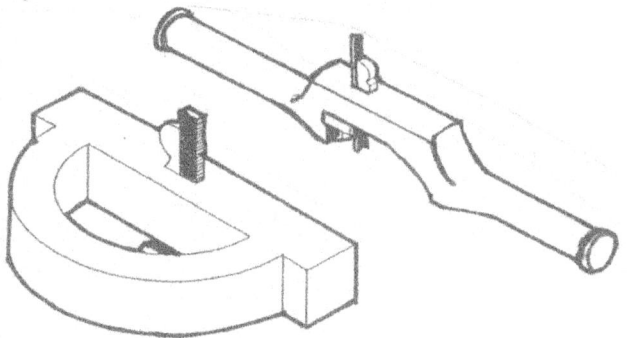

SASH PLANE: A combination rabbet and molding plane used in making window mullions. This is called a "stick and rabbet". The rabbet side cuts the groove for the glass to fit into, and the molding side cuts the decorative inside molding. Both cuts are made at the same time.

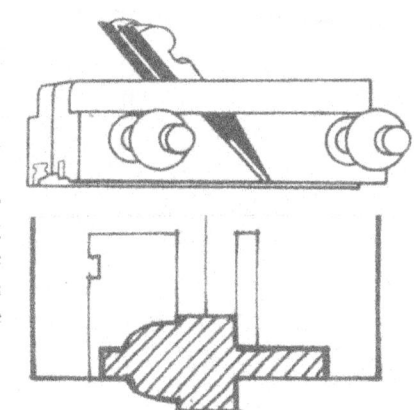

SCOTIA: An elliptical hollow, where a cove is circular in section.

SIDE BEAD: (see bead)

SIDE RABBET PLANES: A plane with the cutting edge on the side of the stock. Used to clean the side of a rabbet cut. Sold in right and left side pairs.

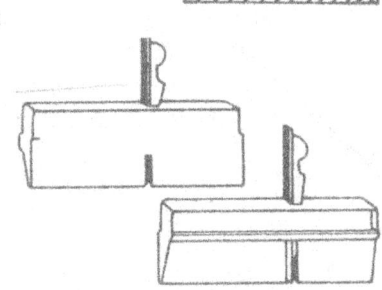

SKATE: (see plow plane) The metal plate found on grooving and plow planes that serves as a bed for the iron and a sole for the plane.

SKEW: Refers to a plane in which the iron is set at an angle to the length of the stock, rather than squarely at right angles.

SMOOTHING PLANE or **SMOOTHER**: (see bench planes)

SNECKED IRON: (see molding planes) A plane blade with a projection at its upper end, to assist in adjusting or resetting the iron.

SNIPE BILL PLANES: (also called side snipe) A plane used to clean up the cuts made by other molding planes. Sold as a right and left pair.

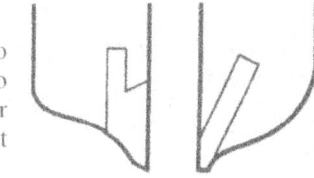

SPAR PLANE: (see mast plane)

SPILL PLANE: A plane used to make a curled shaving that was lit from the fire and then used to light a candle or pipe.

SPOKESHAVE: An iron with two tines set into a wood stock and drawn with both hands.

SPRING: (spring) A molding plane held at an angle to optimize the cut. (see molding plane)

STAVE: The wooden sections used to form the body of a barrel.

STOCK: (see bench, molding and plow planes) The main body of the plane, into which the iron is fitted.

STOP: (see depth stop) An adjustable portion of the plane used to limit depth or travel.

STRIKE BUTTON: (see bench planes) A metal or hardwood insert on the top of the toe of a bench plane, and sometimes on the heel of a smoother, which is struck to loosen the blade.

STUFF: An English term used to describe the wood that is being worked on.

SUN PLANE: (see cooper's planes) A jack size bench plane with the stock in a curve. Used to even up the top edge of the stave ends.

TABLE PLANES: Used in pairs for making a drop-leaf table; one cut the rounded edge of the table, the other cut the hollow edge of the leaf that fitted over it.

TENON: (see mortising) The square tongue that fits and is pegged into a mortise.

THROAT: (see bench planes) The opening at the top of the plane for the escape of shavings.

TOE: (see bench planes) The front end, lead, or foremost part of the plane.

TONGUE PLANE: A plane used to cut the tongue that fits into the groove, when joining the edges of two pieces of wood by this method. Together the tongue-making plane plus the groove-making plane are called match planes.

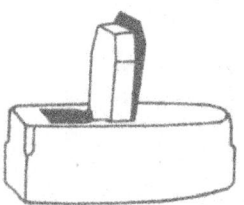

TOOTHING PLANE: Used to ridge the wood so that veneers can be glued to it. Similar to a smoothing plane, except that the iron is serrated and is set almost perpendicular to the stock. When used it functions as a toothed scraper.

TOPPING PLANE: (see cooper's planes) Another name for cooper's sun plane.

TORUS BEAD: A molding similar to an astragal, but usually of an elliptical shape and set off from the rest of the molding by a quirk and a fillet.

TOTE: (see bench planes) The handle on a plane. In a closed tote the wood completely encircles the finger opening; an open tote lacks the front enclosure.

TRYING PLANE: (see bench planes) Used for planing after roughing and before smoothing, to attain surfaces that are true and square to each other.

TURNING: Fixing the wood between two spindles on a lathe, then turning it while shaping it with gouges and chisels, etc.

WEAR PLATE: Located on the inside facing of a fence on a plow plane.

WEDGE: (see bench, molding and plow planes) Wood wedge that fits in front of the iron of a plane and holds it in place. Other movable parts of a plan may also be wedge or keyed, including fence arms and depth stops.

YANKEE PLOW PLANE: (see plow planes) 18th or early 19th century plow planes, usually made in New England. It is almost always oversize, 9 7/8" to 10", made of yellow birch or beech, with a plain unadorned fence the same length as the body of the plane, and square fence arms. The arms are fixed by wedges or wooden thumbscrews or both.

ZB: The zigzag border found around planemakers' imprints. The zb differentiates the imprint from those with no border or a straight-line border.

BIBLIOGRAPHY

We have listed below a number of books, pamphlets, catalogs and articles that we felt would be helpful to readers who might wish to delve more deeply into a particular subject. Many of them can be obtained through **The Astragal Press**, an imprint of Finney Company, 5995 149th. Street West, Suite 105, Apple Valley, Minnesota 55124-5711. www.astragalpress.com
We have divided the bibliography into three categories: General Background Information; Regional Studies of Planemaking and Planemakers; Articles on Planemakers, Dealers, and Tool Catalog Reprints. We will be referring to these sources in the following listings:

- **THE CHRONICLE** is the quarterly journal published by the Early American Industries Association, Inc. (EAIA) for members. Volumes 1-60 (1933-2007) in searchable Adobe PDF files 2009. Executive Director, John Verrill, P. O. Box 524, 402 South Main St., Hebron, MD 21830. www.EAIAinfo.org (available thru the Astragal Press)
- **PLANE TALK** was a quarterly journal published from 1976-86 as the Bulletin of the British-American Rhykenological Society then from 1987-91 by the Astragal Press that provided information of interest to plane collectors. No longer published but back issues are available from The Astragal Press.
- **THE MECHANICK'S WORKBENCH** was a catalog issued periodically by Anne and Donald Wing that provided articles of interest to collectors, Box 420, Marion, MA 02738.
- **THE CATALOG OF AMERICAN WOODEN PLANES** (CAWP) was a quarterly journal published from 1991-98 by Michael R. Humphrey that provided informative articles of interest to wooden plane collectors, Bacon Street Press, 368 Barne's Joy Rd., South Dartmouth, MA 02748.
- **SIGN OF THE JOINTER** (SOTJ) was a quarterly journal published 1999-2001 by Patrick Lasswell that offered articles of interest to wooden plane collectors, 6211 Elmgrove Rd., Spring, TX, 77389.

GENERAL BACKGROUND INFORMATION

- *ANCIENT CARPENTERS' TOOLS* by Henry C. Mercer 5th Edition, 1975, The Bucks County Historical Society. (Paperback 2000, available thru The Astragal Press)

- *THE WOODEN PLANE: Its History, Form, and Function* by John M. Whelan, 1993, The Astragal Press.

- *WOODEN PLANES In 19th Century America*, Vol. I, 1978, Vol. II, 1983, by Ken Roberts Publishing Co., Box 151, Fitzwilliam, NH 03447.

- *PATENTED TRANSITIONAL & METALLIC PLANES In America 1827-1927*, Vol. I, 1981, Vol. II, 1992, (P-TAMPIA) by Roger K. Smith, Box 177, Athol, MA, 01331.

- *DICTIONARY of WOODWORKING TOOLS, C. 1700-1970* by R. A. Salaman, 1975, Revised Edition 1990, The Taunton Press Inc.

- *DIRECTORY of AMERICAN TOOLMAKERS* by Robert E. Nelson, 1999, The Early American Industries Assoc. (Searchable CD-ROM 2007 available thru The Astragal Press)

- *BRITISH PLANEMAKERS from 1700* by W. L. Goodman, 3rd Edition Revised by Jane and Mark Rees 1993, The Astragal Press.

- *Guide to CANADIAN PLANE MAKERS & HARDWARE DEALERS*, 2nd Edition, by Robert Westley 1997, The MacLachlan Woodworking Museum, 2993 Highway 2, Kingston, Ontario, K7L 4V1.

- **TIES to BRITAIN and CANADA**, by Michael R. Humphrey, *The Catalog of American Wooden Planes*, December 1993.

- **CANADIAN CROSSINGS**, by Michael R. Humphrey, *The Catalog of American Wooden Planes*, March 1995.

- *The AMERICAN CABINETMAKER'S PLOW PLANE, Its Design and Improvement, 1700-1900*, by John A. Moody 1981. The Tool Box, 8219 Old Petersburg Rd., Evansville, IN, 47711.

- *TOOLS, Working Wood in Eighteenth-Century America*, by James M. Gaynor and Nancy L. Hagedorn 1993, The Colonial Williamsburg Foundation.

- *AMERICAN MARKING GAGES, Patented and Manufactured*, by Milton H. Bacheller, Jr. 2000, The Author, 185 South Street, Plainville, MA, 02762.

- *The CABINETMAKERS of AMERICA* by Ethel Hall Bjerkoe 1962, Schiffer Publishing Ltd., Box E, Exton, PA, 19341.

- *AMERICAN CABINETMAKERS, Marked American Furniture, 1640-1940* by William C. Ketchum, Jr. with The Museum of American Folk Art 1995, Crown Publishers, Inc.

- *COLLECTING ANTIQUE TOOLS* by Herbert P. Kean and Emil S. Pollak 1990, The Astragal Press.

- *PRICES REALIZED on RARE IMPRINTED AMERICAN WOODEN PLANES, 1979-1992* by Emil and Martyl Pollak 1993, The Astragal Press.

- *A PRICE GUIDE to ANTIQUE TOOLS*, Third Edition by Herbert P. Kean 2000, The Astragal Press.

- *EIGHTEENTH-CENTURY WOODWORKING TOOLS, Papers Presented at a Tool Symposium May 19-22, 1994*, The Colonial Williamsburg Foundation.

- *A FIELD GUIDE to the MAKERS of AMERICAN WOODEN PLANES* by Thomas L. Elliott 2003, The Astragal Press.

- *AMERICAN WOOD & METAL PLANES From the Collection of the D'Elia Antique Tool Museum* by Andrew D'Elia, 2010, The D'Elia Foundation, P. O. Box 164, Scotland, CT 06264.

- *APPRENTICES of CONNECTICUT 1637-1900* by Kathy A. Ritter, 1986, Ancestry Publishing, P. O. Box 476, Salt Lake City, UT 84110.

- *WOODEN PLOW PLANES, A Celebration of the Planemaker's Art* by Don ROSEBROOK and Dennis Fisher by the Author, 2003.

- *The CLASSIC PERIOD of AMERICAN TOOLMAKING, 1827-1930* by H. G. Brack, The Davistown Museum. (Paperback 2009, available thru The Astragal Press)

- **CHAMFER ENDS** by Michael R. Humphrey, *The Catalog of American Wooden Planes*, December 1994.

- **NUMBERS on WOODEN PLANES** by Michael R. Humphrey, *The Catalog of American Wooden Planes*, Part I September 1995; Part 2 December 1995.

- **STATISTICAL STUDY of some 19th CENTURY WOODEN MOLDING PLANES** by Peter S. Welcker, *The Chronicle*, December 1996.

- **EIGHTEENTH CENTURY DATED AMERICAN WOODEN PLANES**, by Patrick Lasswell, *The Chronicle*, Part I, September 2012; Part II, December 2013.

- **PLANES with MULTIPLE MARKS, and MULTIPLE USERS of the SAME STAMPS** by Michael R. Humphrey, *The Catalog of American Wooden Planes*, Part i, September 1998; Part 2, December 1998.

- **An INTRODUCTION to 18th CENTURY AMERICAN BENCH PLANES**, Part I, Summer 1999; Part II, Fall 1999; Part III, Winter 1999 by Patrick Lasswell, *The Sign of the Jointer*.

- **The PATTERNS in IMPRINTS** by Patrick Lasswell, *The Sign of the Jointer*, Fall 2000.

- **The MOTHER LODE** by Ted Ingraham, *The Chronicle*, June 2008.

- **An INTERESTING AMERICAN JOINTER PLANE** by Chris Bender, *The Chronicle*, June 2015.

- **EIGHTEENTH CENTURY DOCUMENTS: Survivors From Daily Life and Times of Early AMERICAN PLANEMAKERS** by Patrick Lasswell, *The Chronicle*, March 2015.

- **The Life of A CONVICT at AUBURN PRISON** by Chris Bender, *The Chronicle*, June 2016.

REGIONAL STUDIES OF PLANEMAKING AND PLANEMAKERS

- *DIRECTORY of BALTIMORE PLANE and EDGE TOOL MAKERS, 1796 TO 1900* by Richard E. Hay 1981, the Author, 1809 Midlothian Ct., Vienna, VA 22180.

- **A CHECKLIST of BOSTON PLANEMAKERS** by William B. Hilton, *The Chronicle*, June 1974.

- *FURNITURE and its MAKERS of CHESTER CO., PENNSYLVANIA* by Margaret Schiffer 1966, Schiffer Publishing Ltd., Box E, Exton, PA, 19341.

- *CINCINNATI PLANE, EDGETOOL MAKERS and DEALERS*, 2nd. Edition by Gil and Mary Gandenberger, the author, 5171 Willnet Dr., Cincinnati, OH, 45235.

- **PLANEMAKING in the Valley of the CONNECTICUT RIVER & HILLS of WESTERN MASSACHUSETTS** by Elliott Sayward and William Streeter, *The Chronicle*, July 1975.

- **The GREAT RIVER, ART & SOCIETY of the CONNECTICUT VALLEY, 1635-1820** by William Newell Hosley 1985, Hartford, CT; Wadsworth Athenaeum.

- *WOODEN PLANES at The Farmers' Museum* by David L. Parke, Jr. 1981, The Farmers' Museum, Cooperstown, NY.

- **TIES; Around GREENFIELD, MASS.**, *The Catalog of American Wooden Planes*, December, 1993.

- **INDIANA PLANE MAKERS** by Warren E. Roberts, *Midwestern Folklore Journal of the Hoosier Folklore Society*, Spring 1992.

- **Four PLANEMAKERS and APRIL 19, 1775 LEXINGTON and CONCORD, MASSACHUSETTS** by Patrick Lasswell, *The Catalog of American Wooden Planes*, September 1997.

- *To Please any Tast, LITCHFIELD COUNTY FURNITURE & FURNITURE MAKERS, 1780-1830* by Edward S. Cook, Jr., Ann Y. Smith, and Derin Bray 2008, The Litchfield Historical Society, CT.

- **DOWN EAST (MAINE) PLANEMAKERS** by Larry Brundage, *Plane Talk*, Vol. VII, No.1, Page 20, The Bulleten of The British-American Rhykenological Society, 1982.

- **The PLANES of MAINE** by Larry Brundage, *The Chronicle*, June 1984.

- *HARBOR & HOME FURNITURE of SOUTHEASTERN MASSACHUSETTS, 1710-1850* by Brock Jobe, Gary R. Sullivan & Jack O.Brien, University Press of New England, Hanover, 2009.

- **CHRONOLOGY of 18th CENTURY PLANEMAKERS in SOUTHEASTERN NEW ENGLAND** by Anne and Donald Wing, *The Mechanick's Workbench*, Autumn/ Winter 1984.

- **TRACKING ELEMENTS of STYLE (SOUTHEASTERN NEW ENGLAND) NICHOLSON to FULLER; CHAMFER ENDS and WEDGE FINIAL RELIEFS** by Michael R. Humphrey, *The Catalog of American Wooden Planes*, September 1993.

- **17th CENTURY NEW ENGLAND WOODEN PLANES: An Opertunity For Study** by Ted Ingraham, *The Catalog of American Wooden Planes*, March 1998.

- *INSTRUMENTS of CHANGE: NEW HAMPSHIRE HAND TOOLS and THEIR MAKERS, 1800-1900* by James and Donna-Belle Garvin, New Hampshire Historical Society, 30 Park St., Concord, NH 03301.

- *EARLY TOOLS of NEW JERSEY and the MEN Who Made Them* by Alexander Farnham 1985, 78 Tumble Falls Rd., Stockton, NJ, 08559.

- *SEARCH FOR EARLY NEW JERSEY TOOLMAKERS* by Alexander Farnham 1992, (address as above).

- *NEW LONDON COUNTY (CONNECTICUT) FURNITURE, 1640-1840,* The Lyman Allyn Museum 1974, New London, CT.

- *NEW LONDON COUNTY (CONNECTICUT) PLANEMAKERS of the 18th and EARLY 19th Centuries* by Thomas Elliott, *The Catalog of American Wooden Planes*, June 1997.

- *PLANES in CENTRAL NEW YORK* by Seth W. Burchard, *The Chronicle*, December 1975.

- *TIES; in NEW YORK CITY*, *The Catalog of American Wooden Planes*, December 1993.

- *PLANEMAKERS & Other EDGE TOOL ENTERPRISES in NEW YORK STATE in the NINETEENTH CENTURY* by Kenneth and Jane Roberts 1971, Ken Roberts Publishing Co., New York State Historical Assoc., Early American Industries Assoc.

- *CRAFTSMEN & ARTISTS of NORWICH (CONNECTICUT)* by The Society of the Founders of Norwich, Connecticut, Inc. 1965, The Pequot Press, Inc.

- *PLANEMAKERS of WESTERN PENNSYLVANIA and ENVIRONS* by Charles W. Prine, Jr. 2000, Historical Society of Western Pennsylvania, available thru the Astragal Press.

- *MADE in PHILADa* by Carl Bopp, *The Chronicle*, December, 2003; March 2004; September, 2004; December 2005.

- *EARLY PHILADELPHIA, and A LESSON on the HUNT*, *The Catalog of American Wooden Planes*, June 1996.

- *WHO'S WHO of PITTSBURGH (PA) HARDWARE COMPANY MARKS* by Charles W. Prine, Jr., *The Chronicle*, December 1996.

- *PORTSMOUTH FURNITURE, MASTERWORKS From the NEW HAMPSHIRE SEA COAST* by Brock Jobe 1993, Society For The Preservation of New England Antiquities.

- *PLANEMAKERS of 18th CENTURY PROVIDENCE, RHODE ISLAND* by Anne and Donald Wing, *The Mechanick's Workbench*, July 1978.

- *ROCHESTER, NEW YORK, A 19th CENTURY EDGE TOOL CENTER* by Frank Kosmerl, *The Cronicle*, Part I, December 1994; Part II, March 1995; Part III, July 1996; Part IV/ D. R. Barton, March 1997; Part V, March 2000.

- *PLANEMAKERS of SAYBROOK/ WINTHROP, CONNECTICUT*: Part 1, **John** and **Lester Denison/ Charles** and **Samuel Bulkey**; Part 2, **Porter A. Gladwin** and other **Gladwins** and **Gladdings**; Part 3, **G. W. Denison & Co.**; Part 4, Hardware Cos. derived from the G. W. Denison & Co. Account Book, by Thomas Elliott and Michael R. Humphrey, *The Catalog of American Wooden Planes*, June 1996 thru March 1997.

- *WOODWORKING TOOLS at Shelburne Museum*, Shelburne, Vermont by Frank H. Wildung 1957, The Shelburne Museum.

- *PLANEMAKERS of the 18c. SHENANDOAH VALLEY* by Lee Richmond and Hampton Williams, *The Chronicle*, December 1992.

- *DATING of ST. LOUIS PLANES* by George E. Murphy M. D., *The Chronicle*, Part I, June 1980; Part II, September 1980.

- *SHAVINGS From the PAST*: The Wooden Plane Collections of the Chemung County Historical Society and the DeWitt Historical Society of Tompkins County, NY, available thru the Early American Industries Assoc.

- *PLANEMAKERS in UTICA, NY, CITY DIRECTORIES: 1817-1867* by Patrick M. Kelly, *The Chronicle*, June 2000.

- *VERMONT CABINETMAKERS & CHAIRMAKERS BEFORE 1855, A Checklist* by Charles A. Robinson 1994, Shelburne Museum.

- *77 WEYBOSSET STREET (PROVIDENCE, RI)* by Barry Weaver, *The Catalog of American Wooden Planes*, September 1992.

ARTICLES ON PLANEMAKERS, DEALERS, AND TOOL CATALOG REPRINTS

- **THOMAS AIKMAN** by Kenneth K. Hopfel, *Plane Talk*, Vol. XIV, No. 3, 1990.

- **AUBURN TOOL CO.**: 1869 Price List and Catalog, reprinted by The Astragal Press.

- **RICHARD BACON** by Patrick Lasswell, *The Chronicle*, September 2014.

- **JONATHAN BALLOU** by Anne and Donald Wing, *Plane Talk*, Vol. XV, No. 2, 1991.

- **THE BARNES FAMILY, Orange Mass.** by Roger K. Smith, *Plane Talk*, The Bulleten of The British-American Rhykenological Society, Vol. III, Issue 4, Page 14, Spring 1978.

- **D. R. BARTON**: 1873 Catalog, reprinted by The Astragal Press.

- **D. R. BARTON IMPRINTS on PLANES** by Robert D. Graham Jr., *The Chronicle*, September, 1973.

- **ROCHESTER, NY; A 19th CENTURY EDGE TOOL CITY, Part V: DAVID R. BARTON** by Frank Kosmerl, *The Chronicle*, March 2000.

- **J. F. BAUDER: TWO LANCASTER COUNTY PLANEMAKERS** by Richard Peiffer, *The Chronicle*, June 1984.

- **J. F. BAUDER**, *Plane Talk*, Vol. XII, No. 3, 1988.

- **ASHER BENJAMIN** by Thomas Elliott, *The Chronical*, March 2013.

- **BIDWELL & HALE, NEWARK, VA.**, *The Catalog of American Wooden Planes*, June 1992.

- **LEONARD BENTON BIDWELL, NEWARK, WEST VIRGINIA, PLANEMAKER** by Peter Welcker, *The Chronicle*, June 2000.

- **E. BRIGGS** by John S. Kebabian, *Plane Talk*, Vol. II, No. No. 1, Page 2, Sprint 1977.

- **E. BRIGGS TOTED ROUND** by Patrick Lasswell, *The Sign of the Jointer*, Fall 2000.

- **JONATHAN BROOKS** by Thomas Elliott, *The Chronicle*, March 2008, June & September 2008.

- **S. M. BURT- Turner, Wheelwright, & Planemaker?** by Richard T. DeAvila, *The Chronicle*, June 1989.

- **LETTERS From E. W. CARPENTER, Lancaster (PA)** by John Tannehill and William Warner, *The Chronicle*, March 1994.

- **E. W. CARPENTER at Home** by Eugene Klinger, *The Chronicle*, June 1994.

- **SAMUEL CARUTHERS** by Patrick M. Lasswell, *The Chronicle*, December 1997.

- **ELIAS CARTER, ARCHITECT, of WORCESTER, MASS.**, by Mrs. Harriette M. Forbes, in the Bulletin of the Society for the Preservation of New England Antiquities, Vol. XI, No. 2, Oct. 1920.

- **THE CHAPIN-STEPHENS CO.**: 1914 Catalog, available thru the Astragal Press.

- **H. CHAPIN 1859**: Price List, available thru the Astragal Press.

- **H. CHAPIN'S SON**: 1890 Price List and Illustrated Catalog, available thru the Astragal Press.

- **CESAR CHELOR**: A Study of the Planes made by Francis and John Nicholson and Cesar Chelor by Emil and Martyl Pollak, *The Chronicle*, June 1985.

- **CESAR CHELOR and the World He Lived in** by Richard T. DeAvila, *The Chronicle*, Part I, June 1993; Part II, December 1993; The Smithsonian Institution, Anacostia Museum, 1999.

- **More on CESAR CHELOR** by Michael R. Humphrey, *The Chronicle*, September 2013.

- **JOSHUA CLAPP (CLAP) & CHARLES DUPEE** by Thomas Elliott, *The Chronicle*, March 2014.

- **DAVID CLARK IN CUMBERLAND** by David V. Englund, *The Chronicle*, December 1999.

- **LEVI BISBEE and ELISHE CLARK** by Patrick Lasswell, *The Chronicle*, December 2015.

- **T. CLARK, PLANEMAKER'S RUNAWAY APPRENTICE, Found 175 Years Later** by Charles W. Prine, Jr., *The Chronicle*, December 1994.

- **HENRY CLOUGH'S TOOL CHEST** by Patrick M. Lasswell, *The Sign of the Joiner*, Vol. I, No. 3, Winter 1999.

- **JAMES COATES, of WASHINGTON, PENNSYLVANIA, Made Unusual Planes in His Small Town** by Charles W. Prine, Jr., *The Chronicle*, June 1997.

- **D. O. CRANE Scattered Facts Hint at a Full Life** by Michael R. Humphrey, *The Catalog of American Wooden Planes*, No. 2, March 1992.

- **BENJAMIN CHEHORE Inventor and Stringed Instrument Maker** by Karl H. West, Jr., *The Chronicle*, September 1994.

- **G. DAVENPORT** by Thomas Elliott, *The Catalog of American Wooden Planes*, December 2015.

- **DAVIS & KING/ NEW YORK PIANO MAKERS MITRE PLANE** by Michael R. Humphrey, *The Chronicle*, June 2014.

- **THE STORY of BENAIAH DEAN** by Milton Bacheller, *The Chronicle*, June 1994.

- **G. W. DENISON & CO.** by Robert H. Carlson, *The Chronicle*, December 1973.

- **The PLANEMAKERS of SAYBROOK/ WINTHROP, CONNECTICUT G. W. DENISON & CO.**, Part 3; and **HARDWARE COs. From the G. W. DENISON & CO. ACCOUNT BOOK**, Part 4 by Thomas Elliott and Michael R. Humphrey, *The Catalog of American Wooden Planes*, December 1996 and March 1997.

- **The PLANEMAKERS of SAYBROOK/ WINTHROP, CONNECTICUT, JOHN and LESTER DENISON**, Part I, by Thomas Elliott and Michael R. Humphrey, *The Catalog of American Wooden Planes*, June 1996.

- **The DEWEY & NEWTON BENCH PLANE** by Paul B. Kebabian, *Plane Talk*, Vol. XIV, No. 3, Page 274, Fall 1990.

- **S. DOGGETT: The DOGGETTS of DEDHAM** by Richard T. DeAvila, *Plane Talk*, Vol. V, No. 1, Page 7, 1980.

- **SIMEON DOGGETT, MIDDLEBORO, MA, LOYALIST PLANEMAKER** by Anne and Donald Wing, *The Chronicle*, September 1995.

- *WITH HAMMER IN HAND, The DOMINY Craftsmen of East Hampton, New York* by Charles F. Hummel 1968, The Henry Francis du Pont Winterthur Museum, University Press of Virginia.

- **DOMINY PLANES** by Thomas Elliott, *The Chronicle*, June 2004.

- **CHARLES DUPEE'S JOINTER** by Patrick Lasswell, *The Sign of the Jointer*, Summer 2000.

- **ROBERT EASTBURN** by Emil and Martyl Pollak, *The Chronicle*, June 1982.

- **HOSEA EDSON** by Roger K. Smith, *The Chronicle*, December 1979.

- **B. A. EDWARDS** by John S. Kebabian, *The Chronicle*, March 1976.

- **WILLIAM EVENS- RENAISSANCE MAN, PLANEMAKER, and PROFESSOR of MUSIC** by Charles W. Prine, Jr., *The Chronicle*, September 1995.

- **An Early, Rare W. EVENS SASH PLANE** by Brian T. Hope, *The Chronicle*, December 1997.

- **ISAAC FIELD: PLANEMAKER 1781-1860** by Robert Bills, *The Catalog of American Wooden Planes*, December 1997.

- **LAVIUS FILLMORE & THOMAS HAYDEN** by Thomas Elliott, *The Chronicle*, March 2012.

- **S. FISH** by Richard T. DeAvila, *Plane Talk*, Vol. IX, No. 1, Page 6, 1984.

- *ISAAC FITCH of Lebanon Connecticut, Master Joiner 1734-1791* by William L. Warren 1978, The Antiquarian and Landmarks Society Inc. of Connecticut, 394 Main St., Hartford, CT.

- **ISAAC FITCH** by Thomas Elliott, *The Chronicle*, September 2010.

- **DAVID FULLER: Rural Planemaker of West Gardiner, Maine** by Dale J. Butterworth and Bennett Blumenberg, *The Chronicle*, Part I, September 1991; Part II, December 1991.

- **JOSEPH FULLER of Providence: An Update** by Anne and Donald Wing, *Plane Talk*, Vol. XV, No. 3, 1991.

- **JO FULLER BENCH PLANES** by Patrick Lasswell, *The Chronicle*, September 2016.

- **CARPENTER'S INVENTORY, NORTH PROVIDENCE, RHODE ISLAND 1796 (proformed by Joseph Fuller)** by Rick Slaney, *The Sign of the Jointer*, Winter 2001.

- **PORTER A. GLADWIN** by William B. Hilton, *The Chronicle*, March 1975.

- **PORTER A. GLADWIN and other GLADWINS and GLADDINGS, The Planemakers of Saybrook/ Winthrop, Connecticut**, Part 2, by Thomas Elliott and Michael R. Humphrey, *The Catalog of American Wooden Planes*, September 1996.

- **JOSEPH GOULD** by Thomas Elliott, *The Chronicle*, March 2009.

- *IN PLAIN SIGHT, Discovering the Furniture of NATHANIEL GOULD* by Kemble Widmer & Joyce King, 2014, Peabody Essex Museum, Salem, Mass.

- **THOMAS GRANT - Ironmonger** by Daniel M. Semel 1978, published by the Early American Industries Assoc.

- **GREENFIELD TOOL CO.** by Anne and Donald Wing, *The Mechanick's Workbench*, August 1980.

- **GREENFIELD TOOL CO.**: 1872 Catalog, reprinted by The Astragal Press.

- **HAMMACHER SCHLEMMER: The Country's Largest Tool Store at the Turn of the Century** by James Aber, *The Chronicle*, September 1971.

- **HAMMACHER SCHLEMMER & CO.**: 1896 Catalog, reprinted by the Early American Industries Assoc. and the Mid-West Tool Collectors Assoc.

- **The HARMONISTS Founded an Early Religious Industrial - Agrarian Society and made their own tools** by Charles W. Prine, Jr., *The Chronicle*, December 1998.

- **H. L. HART another Connecticut Valley Planemakers?** by Trevor Robinson, *The Chronicle*, December 1996.

- **The HEALDS** by William B. Hilton, *The Chronicle*, April 1974.

- **The Planemakers HEISS** by Alan G. Bates, *The Chronicle*, September 1978.

- **SIGN IN PLEASE (AARON SMITH, JOHN SLEEPER, and JOHN HOVEY)** *The Catalog of American Wooden Planes*, September 1992.

- **THREE GENERATIONS of HOVEY CRAFTSMEN** by Thomas Elliott, *The Chronicle*, September 2000.

- **PLANEMAKERS J. SAWYER and A. HOWLAND** by Bruce E. Bradley, *The Catalog of American Wooden Planes*, March 1993.

- **GERRIT JAMAIN** by Thomas Elliott, *The Chronicle*, March 2016 & December 2016.

- **The JETHRO JONES - CESAR CHELOR CONNECTION** by Richard T. DeAvila, *The Chronicle*, December 1989.

- **The H. L. KENDALL Patent** *Plane Talk*, Vol. XIV, No. 2, 1990.

- **The KENNEDYS: Planemaking in Early Hartford** by Anne and Donald Wing, *Plane Talk*, Vol. XIV, No. 4, 1990.

- **I. KING Jack Plane** by Patrick Lasswell, *The Sign of the Jointer*, Vol. 2, No. 4, Winter 2001.

- **HENRY and SAMUEL KERN, Planemakers of the 18c Shenendoah Valley** by Lee Richmond and Hampton Williams, *The Chronicle*, December 1992.

- **LINDENBERGERS,** *The Mechanick's Workbench*, Winter 1983, Winter 1984.

- **JOHN LINDENBERGER** by Anne and Donald Wing, *Plane Talk*, Vol. XIII, No. 1989.

- **Did LINDENBERGER'S Son Make Planes in Pittsburgh?** by Charles W. Prine, Jr., *The Chronicle*, December 1997.

- **WALTER LITHGOW, Planemaker** by Cherles W. Prine, Jr., *The Chronicle*, March 1995.

- **ASA LOW** by Larry Brundage, *Plane Talk*, Vol. XII, No. 1, 1989.

- **ASA LOW, A follow-up** by Larry Brundage, *Plane Talk*, Vol. XIV, No. 2, 1990.

- **GEORGE W. MANNING - Cooper's Toolmaker** by Roger K. Smith, *Plane Talk*, Vol. XI, No. 2, 1987.

- **DEACON JOHN MANSFIELD** Patrick Lasswell, *The Chronicle*, September 2009, March & September 2011.

- **I. N. MILLER** by Patrick M Kelly, *The Chronicle*, June 2004.

- **LUTHER and JOSEPH METCALF: Two Cabinetmaker/ Planemakers of New England** by Bennett Blumenberg and Dale J. Butterworth, *The Chronicle*, June 1991.

- **SAMUEL McINTIRE and DANIEL BANCROFT** by Thomas Elliott, *The Chronicle*, March 2017.

- **MATTHEW MORIATY - Cooper and Tool Maker** by Larry Brundage, *Plane Talk*, Vol. XI, No. 3, 1987.

- **A. S. MORSS** *The Catalog of American Wooden Planes*, March 1992.

- *THOMAS NAPIER: The Scottish Connection* by Alan G. Bates 1986, Published by The Early American Industries Assoc. Inc. and The Mid-West Tool Collectors Assoc.

- *THOMAS NAPIER* by Joseph T. Stakes, *The Chronicle*, March 1977.

- **The NICHOLSON Family** by Anne and Donald Wing, *The Mechanick's Workbench*, Autumn 1981.

- **The NICHOLSON Family: Joiners and Tool Makers** by Anne and Donald Wing, *The Chronicle*, June 1983.

- **FRANCIS and JOHN NICHOLSON: A Study of Planes Made by FRANCIS and JOHN NICHOLSON and Cesar Chelor** by Emil and Martyl Pollak, *The Chronicle*, June 1985.

- **NICHOLSON'S MOTHER** by Michael R. Humphrey, *The Catalog of American Wooden Planes*, December 1992.

- **One Dot, More or Less (F. NICHOLSON)** *The Catalog of American Wooden Planes*, September 1994.

- **An Early, Rare Mark of FRANCIS NICHOLSON** by Bennett Blumenberg, *The Chronicle*, September 1995.

- **A Study of Two FRANCIS NICHOLSON Planes** by David V. Englund, *The Chronicle*, March 1997.

- **FRANCIS NICHOLSON - Living in Wrentham** by David V. England, *The Chronicle*, March 2000.

- **FRANCIS, JOHN and CESAR: A Different View of Their Planes** by Ted Ingraham, *The Chronicle*, March 2001.

- **FRANCIS NICHOLSON, Up-date** by Ted Ingraham, *The Chronicle*, September 2005.

- **The Life and Times of TRUMAN NUTTING** by Michael R. Humphrey, *Plane Talk*, Vol. XIII, No. 2, 1989.

- **OHIO TOOL CO.**: Catalog #23, reprinted by Roger K. Smith.

- **NATHANIEL POTTER: Could He Be our Earliest Planemaker?** by Robert Wheller, *The Chronicle*, March 1993.

- **Who's on First (N. POTTER)**, *The Catalog of American Wooden Planes*, March 1996.

- **The PRESBREY Family** by Richard T. DeAvila, *Plane Talk*, Vol. V, No. 2, Page 4, 1880.

- **JOHN F. RANSOM** by Larry Brundage, *Plane Talk*, Vol. XV, No. 1, 1991.

- **RAYL'S**: Catalog #21 (ca. 1905), reprinted by Roger K. Smith.

- **WILLIAM RAYMOND** by Herman Freedman, *The Chronicle*, March 1981.

- **The REED Family Planemakers: JOHN Jr., WILLIAM, EDWARD & CHARLES, and in-laws HIRAM CLARK & ALBERT L. GLEASON** by Patrick M. Kelly & Louise A. Dean-Kelly, *The Chronicle*, March 2009.

- **ENOS ROBBINS and Other Early Utica Area Planemakers** by Patrick M. Kelly, *The Chronicle*, June 1999.

- **MICHAEL REGER (REAGER) (RAGER)** by Thomas Elliott, *The Chronicle*, December 2014.

- **Notes on some Yankees: SAMSON, SAMPON (SHURTLEFFE) and STETSON** by Michael R. Humphrey, *Plane Talk*, Vol. XV, No. 2, 1994.

- ABEL SAMPSON: Maine Privateer Turned Planemaker by Dale Butterworth and Bennett Blumenberg, *The Chronicle*, June 1992.

- LAZARUS SAMPSON by Tom Whalen, *The Chronicle*, September 2016.

- D. R. SANBORN Badger Plane, *The Sign of the Jointer*, Fall 2000.

- SANDUSKY by Thomas N. Tully, *The Chronicle*, Septemper 1977.

- SANDUSKY TOOL CO.: 1877 Catalog, reprinted by The Astragal Press.

- SANDUSKY TOOL CO.: 1925 Catalog, reprinted by The Astragal Press.

- The Sandusky Tool Co. Story by W. G. Schwer, *The Chronicle*, September 1993.

- Planemaker J. SAWYER and A. HOWLAND by Bruce E. Bradley, *The Catalog of American Wooden Planes*, March 1993.

- SCHAUER: Two Lancaster County Planemakers by Richard Peiffer, *The Chronicle*, June 1984.

- WILLIAM SCOTT Faced Hard Times as one of First "Western" Planemakeers by Charles W. Prine, Jr., *The Chronicle*, September 1997.

- JOHN SLEEPER by Herman Freedman with Anne and Donald Wing, *The Mechanick's Workbench*, Summer 1983.

- Sign in Please (AARON SMITH, JOHN SLEEPER, and JOHN HOVEY), *The Catalog of American Wooden Planes*, September 1992.

- AARON SMITH of Rehoboth by Anne & Donald Wing, *Plane Talk*, Vol. XV, No. 4, 1991.

- The Smith Family - Planemakers of Rehoboth by Anne and Donald Wing, *The Mechanick's Workbench*, October 1979.

- WILLIAM SPRATTS by Thomas Elliott, *The Chronicle*, March 2010.

- JAMES STARR by Richard F. S. Starr, *The Chronicle*, December 1980.

- WILLIAM STEELE, Wheeling Planemaker, Inventer and Entrepreneur by Charles W. Prine, Jr., *The Chronicle*, September 1994.

- H. G. STILLEY by Kendall Bassett, *Plane Talk*, Vol.II, No. 2, Page 11, Summer 1977.

- PETER STREBER'S Crown Molder by Patrick Lasswee, *The Sign of the Jointer*, Spring 2000.

- The Life and Times of JAMES & J. J. STYLES, *Plane Talk*, Vol. XII, No. 1, 1988.

- JAMES SWETMAN Planemaker by Charles W. Prine, Jr., *The Chronicle*, March 1999.

- JOHN TEAL, "D'ye ken John Teal? Carpenter Tool Maker, Leeds, England - Princeton, Massachusetts" by Larry Brundage, *The Chronicle*, September 1988.

- MARCUS B. TIDEY by Larry Brundage, *Plane Talk*, Vol. XIV, No. 3, 1990.

- LEVI TINKHAM by Richard DeAvila, *Plane Talk*, Vol. VII, No. 2, Page 14, 1982.

- LEVI TINKHAM by William A. Steere, *The Chronicle*, December 2011, December 2012.

- J. R. TOLMAN by Larry Brundage, *The Chronicle*, December 1976.

- SETH GREEN TORREY by Mike Humphrey, *The Chronicle*, December 2009 & December 2010.

- TREMAN & Bros. by Seth Burchard, *Plane Talk*, Vol. XIV, No. 2, 1990.

- BENJAMIN WATERMAN by Michael R. Humphrey, *The Catalog of American Wooden Planes*, June 1994.

- The WELLS Family Planemakers by Patrick M. Kelly, *The Chronicle*, March 1991, September 2006.

- CHESTER R. WELLS - A Planemaker's Account Ledger Patrick M. Kelly, *The Chronicle*, Part I, March 1992; Part II, June 1992; Part III, September 1992.

- HENRY WETHEREL by Anne and Donald Wing, *Plane Talk*, Vol. I, No. 4, Page 3, December 1976.

- The WETHEREL (L) S, Father & Son by Anne and Donald Wing, *Plane Talk*, Vol. XIV, No. 1, 1990.

- The WHITE Family of Philadelphia by Carl E. Bopp, *Plane Talk*, Vol. XI, No. 3, 1987.

- A. WHITMARSH, *The Catalog of American Wooden Planes*, March 1992.

- JO. WILBER by Richard Slaney, *The Sign of the Jointer*, Vol. 2, No. 1, Spring 2000.

- JO. WILBER (JOSHUA) by Richard Slaney, *The Chronicle*, March 2003.

- BENJAMIN WRIGHT/ BW by Thomas Elliott, *The Catalog of American Wooden Planes*, June 1992.

www.ingramcontent.com/pod-product-compliance
Lightning Source LLC
Chambersburg PA
CBHW081717100526
44591CB00016B/2408